Whitaker's Scottish Almanack
2002

LONDON
THE STATIONERY OFFICE

© The Stationery Office Ltd
51 Nine Elms Lane, London SW8 5DR

ISBN 0 11 702275 6

A CIP catalogue record for this book is available in the British Library

Editorial Staff
Publisher: Tim Probart
Consulting Editor: Magnus Linklater
Editor: Vanessa White
Contributing Editor: Mandy Macdonald
Development Editor: Inna Ward
Editorial Staff: Tom Brundle, Debbie Paola, Chris Sadowski, Sharon Taylor, Tara West

Contributors
Prof. Peter McGregor, Department of Economics, University of Strathclyde (Economy); Alan Boyd, McGrigor Donald (Government in Scotland); Diana Clayton (Education); Robson McLean, ws (Legal Notes); Gordon Taylor (Astronomical Data)

Text and Jacket designed by Compendium
Jacket Photographs ©PA Photos Ltd, Superstock Ltd, Allsport.
Maps by Oxford Cartographers
Typeset by The Stationery Office Limited, Parliamentary Press, London.
Printed and Bound in Great Britain by The Stationery Office Limited, Parliamentary Press, London.

Published by The Stationery Office Limited
and available from:

The Stationery Office
(mail, telephone and fax orders only)
PO Box 29, Norwich NR3 1GN
General enquiries/Telephone orders 0870 600 5522
Fax orders 0870 600 5533
www.thestationeryoffice.com

The Stationery Office Bookshops
123 Kingsway, London WC2B 6PQ
020 7242 6393 Fax 020 7242 6394
68–69 Bull Street, Birmingham B4 6AD
0121 236 9696 Fax 0121 236 9699
33 Wine Street, Bristol BS1 2BQ
0117 926 4306 Fax 0117 929 4515
9–21 Princess Street, Manchester M60 8AS
0161 834 7201 Fax 0161 833 0634
16 Arthur Street, Belfast BT1 4GD
028 9023 8451 Fax 028 9023 5401
The Stationery Office Oriel Bookshop
18–19, High Street, Cardiff CF1 2BZ
029 2039 5548 Fax 029 2038 4347
71 Lothian Road, Edinburgh EH3 9AZ
0870 606 5566 Fax 0870 606 5588

FOREWORD

by Magnus Linklater

The General Election of June 2001 provided the first test of voting opinion in Scotland since the introduction of devolution and the creation of the Scottish Parliament. Some commentators had suggested that rumbling criticism of the Labour-Liberal Democrat coalition and a general disappointment with the performance of the parliament itself would result in gains for the Scottish National Party, and presage a move towards eventual independence. In the event no evidence emerged to support this view, and the pattern of results north of the Border was not significantly different to that in England and Wales. Labour held onto all its seats, the SNP made no gains, and the only change was one in Galloway and Upper Nithsdale, where the Conservatives unexpectedly won back a Nationalist-held seat. On a significantly low turnout, the best achievement was that of the Liberal Democrats who greatly increased their share of the vote, particularly in the Edinburgh area. The general verdict, however, was that since this was a Westminster election, it did not provide a true measurement of opinion about Scotland's own political system. That would have to wait until 2003 and the next Holyrood election.

Scottish views about the parliament and its effect on national life over the first two years of its existence were measured in a detailed survey of public opinion in June, following the second anniversary of the Parliament. It suggested a measure of disillusion about the relative impact made by the new body compared to that of Westminster. The new parliament had not, it appeared, lived up to expectations, and it seemed that many people felt the major political decisions were still being taken in London. But that was not the whole story. The survey showed no evidence of any decline in support for the principle of devolution, and most of those polled wanted the parliament to have more power rather than less. The issue of "fiscal independence" — the notion that the Scottish Parliament should raise its own taxes rather than simply accepting the block grant assigned to it by Westminster — surfaced for the first time during the election, and will certainly continue to be a major debating issue. Meanwhile, whatever the public perception, there was no doubting the parliament's work-rate. In a speech marking its first two years, the Presiding Officer, Sir David Steel, noted that in that time it had scrutinised 30 bills, passed 24, and handled 16,000 written questions. It also continued to attract outside interest, being addressed by several world leaders, including the President of South Africa, Thabo Mbeki.

The tragic death in October 2000 of Donald Dewar, Scotland's First Minister, often described affectionately as the "Father of the Nation", cast a dark cloud over the life of the nation. Not only had he been instrumental in delivering the promise of devolution, he had, as a civilised and cultivated human being, imparted a sense of dignity to the new office that he had helped create. His deep knowledge of Scottish history, his love of the arts, and his wry sense of humour had helped cement a feeling of pride in the new democratic experiment that he launched. His funeral service in Glasgow Cathedral was the scene of a mass outpouring of grief, but also provided the occasion for a celebration of a distinguished and dedicated life. He was succeeded by his deputy Henry McLeish, MSP for Fife Central, who pledged his administration to carrying forward the work that Donald Dewar had begun. His early period in office was marked by heavy criticism from the media, which suggested that he lacked the stature and intellect of his predecessor. Labour ministers in London, sheltering behind the shield of anonymity, mocked as pretentious his claim that his cabinet should be referred to as a "government" rather than an "executive" and he was accused of promising reforms which had not been properly costed. However, the impact made by Mr McLeish in his first term of office has been considerable. Two of his measures, the awarding of improved pay and conditions for teachers, and a commitment to provide free health care for the elderly, have opened the gap between Scotland and England, and the growing confidence of his ministerial team suggests that this trend is likely to continue. The term "government" is now regularly used without noticeable embarrassment.

The Scottish Nationalist leader, Alex Salmond, stepped down, after a decade in which he had raised the profile of his party and helped steer Scotland towards major constitutional change. He was succeeded by John Swinney, MSP for North Tayside, who made it clear that his goal was to link independence to the key social issues of health, education and social services. He spoke of "completing the powers of the Scottish Parliament" rather than making independence itself the only goal of the SNP. As leader of the principal opposition party, he kept up pressure on the Executive over a range of issues, including the aftermath of a major fiasco at the Scottish Qualifications Authority which resulted in hundreds of pupils receiving wrong exam results, and the new parliament building at Holyrood, whose costs were revealed to have risen from an initial £40 million estimate to £190 million; the building is scheduled to be ready for occupation in 2003.

Against a background of continuing economic growth, the Executive produced a major appraisal of the Scottish economy, the 'Framework for Economic Development in Scotland', intended as the starting point for continuing review of priorities for policies in Scotland. Although GDP per head is still some 5% lower than the average level for the rest of the UK, it is higher than for either Wales or Northern Ireland, the other constituent parts of the UK. A titanic battle between the two major Scottish banks — the Bank of Scotland and the Royal Bank of Scotland — for control of the London-based National Westminster Bank, resulted in victory for the Royal, increasing its global status and making it the world's seventh largest bank. Elsewhere, the decline in the international market for electronics, led to the closure of the Motorola plant at Livingston, and significant job losses elsewhere. The textile industry in the Borders continued to suffer, and tourism and farming were hard hit by the outbreak of foot and mouth disease. On the Clyde, job losses were also recorded, despite a major defence contract to build six new Type 45 destroyers for the Royal Navy. However, Edinburgh remained a buoyant financial centre, and, with 70,000 people employed directly and indirectly in the electronics sector, a growing telecommunications industry, and a robust oil and gas sector, the country's overall performance, particularly in exports of computer equipment, food and whisky, remained encouraging. Exporting directly underpins more than 112,000 jobs in Scotland.

It would be a mistake to suggest that life in post-devolution Scotland is dominated by news about politics or the economy. More headlines by far were generated when the superstar Madonna decided to hold her wedding to film producer Guy Ritchie at Skibo Castle in Sutherland, and to christen her child at Dornoch Cathedral. Meanwhile, the imminent arrival of Prince William as a student at St Andrews University dominated the gossip columns. The Princess Royal's long-held interest in Scottish affairs was marked when the Queen awarded her the Order of the Thistle, Scotland's highest honour, at a ceremony in St Giles' Cathedral. It was also a year marked by the departure of some familiar and much-loved Scottish figures. Jimmy Shand, probably the most famous band-leader of his time, and Jimmy Logan, the actor, were mourned by fans throughout Scotland. But it was the death of Cardinal Thomas Winning, head of the Roman Catholic Church in Scotland that led to the greatest outpouring of national grief. A man of strong and often controversial views, he had not hesitated to speak up in defending traditional values and family life. When he died, it was not only Catholics who mourned his passing. Clearly, whatever the political mood of the nation, there is still a strong need in Scotland for moral leadership.

Magnus Linklater

PREFACE

By Vanessa White, Editor, Whitaker's Almanack

Welcome to the third edition of Whitaker's Scottish Almanack.

From its inception in 1999, the concept of Whitaker's Scottish Almanack was to provide a reference book which would mirror the long established appeal of Whitaker's Almanack, a title which has been widely used and loved for over 130 years. Initially, Whitaker's Scottish Almanack contained simply the Scottish elements of the original Almanack but the second and now the third edition have evolved to become what we hope is a reference tool specifically written to encapsulate the many key facets which make Scotland truly distinctive and unique. To this end we have engaged the assistance of a number of Scots, all experts in their fields, who we hope offer the insider's view and authenticity that a reference book on Scotland demands.

Readers can explore how Scotland is governed, starting with a review of the year in the Scottish Parliament. This section provides a clear and comprehensive guide to the structures, functions, roles and people who regulate Scotland. This of course spans the areas of devolved, local, central and european government. The Public Service Scotland section offers detailed overviews of the many elements which make up the public sector including education, health, the fire service, the police service, transport systems and social services. For those with an interest in the fine detail of Scottish Law, the Legal Scotland section offers comprehensive notes, also listing the legal structures and officials operating within the legal system. A review of the Scottish economy complete with statistical analysis is provided in the Business Scotland section, along with information on banking, currencies, the voluntary sector and much more. Whitaker's Scottish Almanack then goes on to describe the elements which make up Scotland's Media community; there is also a detailed section to examine the diversity of Religion in Scotland. Two sections which arguably give the true flavour of Scotland are those which examine its culture and environment. Within these sections, the essence of Scotland's cultural roots can be discovered in as wide a range of areas as the clans, the history of the monarchy, music, poetry, the climate, the evolution of the landscape and language, and profiles of famous Scottish artists, writers and sportsmen and women.

As a sister publication of Whitaker's Almanack we endeavour to make Whitaker's Scottish Almanack a snapshot of the past year and an essential reference work for the year to come. We have incorporated to this end the new *Events of the Year* section. This is a chronological profile of the significant news stories which have made an impact on Scotland, ranging from the tragic death of one of Scotland's most respected politicians Donald Dewer to the controversy surrounding the incorrect distribution of exam results by the Scottish Qualifications Authority.

I hope that readers will enjoy discovering all that Whitaker's Scottish Almanack has to offer as an accessible and comprehensive reference tool. May I also take this opportunity to thank the editorial team for their hard work and all those who have contributed to the compilation of this book. As with all the publications in the Whitaker's series we would be most grateful to receive your feedback. Please write with your comments to:

Editor
The Stationery Office Ltd
51 Nine Elms Lane
London
SW8 5DR
Tel: 020-7873 8442
Fax: 020-7873 8723
Email: whitakers.almanack@theso.co.uk
Web: www.whitakers-almanack.co.uk
www.clicktso.co.uk
www.thestationeryoffice.com

KEY DATES IN 2002

STATUTORY PUBLIC HOLIDAYS

New Year	1, 2 January
Good Friday	29 March
Early May	6 May
Golden Jubilee	3 June
Spring	4 June
Summer	5 August
Christmas	25, *26 December

LOCAL AND FAIR HOLIDAYS

In most parts of Scotland there are local and fair holidays; dates vary according to the locality. Dates can usually be obtained from the local authority; the only central source is Glasgow Chamber of Commerce (tel: 0141-204 2121) which publishes each January a diary of holiday dates for the year.

LAW TERMS

The terms of the Court of Session for the legal year 2001–2002 are:

Winter	25 September to 21 December 2001
Spring	8 January to 22 March 2002
Summer	23 April to 12 July 2002

TERM DAYS

Candlemas	28 February
Whitsunday	28 May
Lammas	28 August
Martinmas	28 November
Removal Terms	28 May, 28 November

CHRISTIAN

Epiphany	6 January
Ash Wednesday	13 February
Maundy Thursday	28 March
Good Friday	29 March
Easter Day (western churches)	31 March
Easter Day (Eastern Orthodox)	5 May
Ascension Day	9 May
Pentecost (Whit Sunday)	19 May
Trinity Sunday	26 May
Corpus Christi	30 May
All Saints' Day	1 November
Advent Sunday	1 December
Christmas Day	25 December

HINDU

Makara Sankranti	14 January
Vasant Panchami (Sarasvati-puja)	17 February
Mahashivaratri	12 March
Holi	28 March
Chaitra (Hindu new year)	13 April
Ramanavami	21 April
Raksha-bandhan	22 August
Janmashtami	30 August
Ganesh Chaturthi, first day	10 September
Ganesh festival, last day	20 September
Durga-puja	7 October
Navaratri festival, first day	7 October
Sarasvati-puja	12 October
Dasara	15 October
Diwali, first day	2 November
Diwali, last day	6 November

JEWISH

Purim	26 February
Passover, first day	28 March
Feast of Weeks, first day	17 May
Jewish new year (AM 5762)	7 September
Yom Kippur (Day of Atonement)	16 September
Feast of Tabernacles, first day	21 September
Chanucah, first day	30 November

MUSLIM

Muslim new year (AH 1421)	15 March
Ramadan, first day	6 November

SIKH

Birthday of Guru Gobind Singh Ji	5 January
Baisakhi Mela (Sikh new year)	13 April
Martyrdom of Guru Arjan Dev Ji	16 June
Birthday of Guru Nanak Dev Ji	11 November
Martyrdom of Guru Tegh Bahadur Ji	24 November

Burns Night	25 January
Chinese year of the Horse	12 February
Commonwealth Day	11 March
Europe Day	9 May
Remembrance Sunday	10 November
St Andrew's Day	30 November
Hogmanay	31 December

CONTENTS

GOVERNED

SCOTLAND

INTRODUCTION TO SCOTTISH GOVERNMENT
SCOTTISH EXECUTIVE
SCOTTISH PARLIAMENT
UK PARLIAMENT ELECTIONS AND MEMBERS
OTHER GOVERNMENT DEPARTMENTS
AND PUBLIC OFFICES
THE EUROPEAN PARLIAMENT
LOCAL GOVERNMENT
DEFENCE

THE GOVERNMENT OF SCOTLAND

The Scottish Parliament has now been in existence for over two years. In May 1999 the people of Scotland elected the first Parliament to sit in Scotland since the Act of Union 1707 and the newly elected Members of the Scottish Parliament (MSPs) met for the first time shortly thereafter. The Scottish Parliament was officially opened by the Queen on 1 July 1999, from which date devolution became effective, the Scottish Parliament and Scottish Administration assuming their full powers under the Scotland Act 1998.

PRE-DEVOLUTION GOVERNMENT

Scotland's parliament and administration developed in medieval times and were firmly established by 1603, when James VI of Scotland acceded to the English throne following the death of Elizabeth I of England. Despite the union of the crowns, the independence of the two countries' parliamentary systems was unaffected until 1707, when the Act of Union unified the two parliaments and transferred the government of Scotland to Westminster.

From the late 19th century the office of Secretary of State for Scotland (formerly the Secretary for Scotland) increased in importance, and became a Cabinet post in 1926. Over that period the Scottish Office also grew in size and importance. It provided the government departments in Scotland for education, health, local government, housing, economic development, agriculture and fisheries, home affairs, and law and order. Although required to operate within overall levels of funding set down by Westminster, the Scottish Office under the Secretary of State for Scotland and the Scottish Office ministers enjoyed a freedom of operation and flexibility of budget far greater than the departments of state in Whitehall. The 'Scottish Block' comprised a total allocation of money to Scotland with the Secretary of State being able to set his own spending priorities within the overall budget.

Movement Towards Devolution

However, the concept of Scottish home rule did not die with the Union. Following the general election in October 1974, which saw the Scottish National Party return 11 MPs to Westminster, the Scottish home rule movement gained fresh momentum. Legislation was put in place to establish a Scottish assembly (the Scotland Act 1978) but the required qualified majority did not materialise at the referendum held in March 1979. During the 1980s, support for a measure of home rule continued and a Scottish Constitutional Convention was established in 1989. The Convention, which included representatives from many political parties and other bodies representative of Scottish public life, produced a blueprint for a Scottish Parliament. The Labour government returned at the general election in May 1997 promised constitutional reform as one of its legislative priorities and an early referendum on the establishment of a Scottish Parliament.

The new Labour government published a White Paper, *Scotland's Parliament*, in July 1997. This document set out in detail the Government's proposals to devolve to a Scottish Parliament the power to legislate in respect of all matters not specifically reserved to Westminster. It further proposed limited tax-raising powers, a single-chamber Parliament with powerful committees, and also considered the Scottish Parliament's relationship with Westminster and the European Union. It proposed a measure of proportional representation for the first time in a British parliamentary election.

In a referendum on 11 September 1997, almost 75 per cent of those voting agreed 'that there should be a Scottish Parliament'. On the question that 'the Scottish Parliament should have tax-varying powers', almost two-thirds voted for the proposition. The Scotland Bill was introduced to the House of Commons on 17 December 1997. The Bill completed its Commons stages on 20 May 1998 after 32 days of debate and was subjected to 17 days of line-by-line scrutiny in the House of Lords before receiving royal assent on 19 November 1998. The Government itself tabled 670 amendments to the Bill.

In November 1997, the Government announced the establishment of an all-party Consultative Steering Group to take forward consideration of how the Scottish Parliament might operate in practice and to develop proposals for rules of procedure and standing orders; the Group reported to the Secretary of State in January 1999. The report enshrined four main principles: sharing the power; accountability; accessibility and participation; and equal opportunities. It proposed a modern, accessible and participative Parliament which would operate in a different manner from Westminster.

POST-DEVOLUTION GOVERNMENT

The Scottish Parliament is a subordinate legislature and can only legislate in respect of matters devolved to it. Westminster is sovereign and could, in theory, repeal the Scotland Act and do away with the Scottish Parliament, although all political parties are working to ensure that the Parliament works effectively. The role of the monarch is unchanged and Acts of the Scottish Parliament require royal assent before becoming law.

Devolved powers

The Scottish Parliament is empowered to pass primary legislation (known as Acts of the Scottish Parliament) and Scottish Ministers can also make secondary legislation in respect of devolved matters. The principal devolved matters are: health, education, local government, social work and housing, planning, economic development, tourism, some aspects of transport, most aspects of criminal and civil law, the criminal justice and prosecution system, police and fire services, environment, natural and built heritage, agriculture and fisheries, food standards, forestry, sport, and the arts. The Scottish Parliament is also responsible for implementing European Community legislation in respect of matters devolved to it (*see* below). It is an absolute requirement that all laws of the Scottish Parliament, whether in the form of primary or secondary legislation, and all actions of the Scottish Executive must comply with the European Convention on Human Rights, which has been given effect by the Human Rights Act, as well as being consistent with EU law.

Reserved powers

Despite the extent of devolved powers, a substantial range of matters are reserved to Westminster, including the constitution, foreign affairs, defence, the civil service, financial and economic matters, transport regulation, social security, employment and equal opportunities. If the Scottish Parliament attempts to legislate in respect of these reserved areas, the Secretary of State and the law officers may challenge in the courts the right of the Parliament to make a law. Such challenges will ultimately be dealt with by the Judicial Committee of the Privy Council, which has assumed a new role as Scotland's principal constitutional court and will be the final arbiter in disputes between Westminster and Edinburgh regarding legislative competence.

THE SCOTTISH EXECUTIVE

The Scottish Executive is the government in Scotland in respect of all devolved matters. The Scottish Executive comprises the First Minister, the law officers (the Lord Advocate and the Solicitor-General for Scotland) and other ministers appointed by the First Minister. The members of the Scottish Executive are referred to collectively as the Scottish Ministers. The Scottish Ministers assumed their full powers on 1 July 1999, the day on which powers and duties were transferred to them and other functions relating to devolved matters which were previously exercised by the then UK Ministers in Scotland. The transfer of powers was achieved by a series of Statutory Instruments.

The Lord Advocate and Solicitor-General for Scotland are entitled to participate, but not vote, in the proceedings of the Parliament even if they are not MSPs. In addition to being the senior law officer in Scotland, the Lord Advocate continues to be the independent head of the systems of criminal prosecution and investigation of deaths in Scotland and this independence is entrenched in the Scotland Act 1998.

The Secretary of State for Scotland continues to be appointed as a member of the UK Government and is not a member of the Scottish Executive. The Scotland Act recognizes that the UK Government will continue to need advice on Scots law, whether relating to reserved or devolved matters. To that end, a new law officer post in the UK Government, the Advocate-General for Scotland, was created; the first holder of this post is Lynda Clark, QC the first ever female law officer.

The Scottish Ministers are supported by staff who were initially drawn from the staff of the former Scottish Office and its agencies. On 1 July 1999 the departments of the Scottish Office transferred to the Scottish Executive. This name reflects the fact that the departments of the Scottish Office now work to the First Minister and his ministerial team. The structure of the Scottish Executive now reflects Scottish ministerial portfolios (for details, *see* Scottish Executive section).

All officials of the Executive hold office under the Crown on terms and conditions of service determined in accordance with the provisions of the Civil Service Management Code and remain members of the Home Civil Service. Established arrangements for interchange with other government departments also remain in place.

THE LEGISLATURE

The Scottish Parliament is a single-chamber legislature with 129 members. Of these, 73 represent constituencies and are elected on a first-past-the-post system. These constituencies are the same as for elections to Westminster with the exception of Orkney and Shetland, which comprise separate constituencies in the Scottish Parliament. In addition, 56 regional members (seven members for each of the eight former Scottish constituencies in the European Parliament) are elected on a proportional basis; this is intended to ensure that the overall composition of the Scottish Parliament reflects closely the total number of votes cast for each of the political parties. Each elector casts two votes, one for a constituency member and one for the party of their choice.

The Scottish Parliament has a fixed term of four years; governments cannot hold ad hoc general elections. Elections will normally be held on the first Thursday in May, although there is a limited measure of flexibility should this date prove unsuitable. Extraordinary general elections can be held in exceptional circumstances, such as failure of the Parliament to nominate a First Minister within 28 days or if the Parliament itself resolves that it should be dissolved with the support of at least two-thirds of the members.

The Parliament is responsible for agreeing its own methods of operation;. and has adopted its own standing orders in place of the transitional standing orders made by Westminster before the transfer of devolved functions.

The Legislative Process

There are three stages to the legislative process: pre-parliamentary procedure, parliamentary procedure, and procedure leading up to royal assent.

Under the pre-parliamentary procedure, before a Bill may be introduced to the Parliament, a member of the Scottish Executive must make a written statement to the effect that the Bill is within the legislative competence of the Scottish Parliament. Furthermore, the Presiding Officer must also certify that the provisions of the Bill would be within the legislative competence of the Parliament.

All Bills on introduction must be accompanied by a Financial Memorandum setting out the best estimates of the administrative, compliance and other costs to which the provisions of the Bill give rise, best estimates of time-scales over which such costs are expected to arise, and an indication of the margins of uncertainty in such estimates. Furthermore, government Bills must be accompanied by explanatory notes summarising the provisions of the Bill, and a Policy Memorandum which sets out the policy objectives of the Bill, what alternative ways of meeting these objectives were considered, a summary of any consultation undertaken on the objectives of the Bill, and an assessment of the effects of the Bill on equal opportunities, human rights, island communities, local government, sustainable development and any other matter which the Scottish Ministers consider relevant.

The parliamentary procedure has three stages: a general debate on the principle of the Bill with an opportunity to vote (analogous to the second reading debate in the House of Commons); detailed consideration of the Bill with the opportunity to move amendments (analogous to the Committee stage); and a final stage at which the Bill can be passed or rejected (analogous to the third reading).

After a Bill completes its parliamentary procedure, the Presiding Officer submits it for royal assent. There is an in-built delay of four weeks before royal assent is granted to allow one of the law officers or the Secretary of State to challenge the competency of the Parliament to pass the Act.

Committees

As the Scottish Parliament is a single chamber, there is no body such as the House of Lords to undertake detailed scrutiny of legislation. Instead, the Scottish Parliament has powerful all-purpose committees to undertake substantial pre-legislative scrutiny. These committees combine the role of Westminster standing and select committees and:

- consider and report on policy and administration of the Scottish Administration
- have the power to conduct enquiries
- scrutinise primary, secondary and proposed EU legislation
- initiate legislation
- scrutinise financial proposals of the Scottish Executive (including taxation, estimates, appropriation and audit)
- scrutinise procedures relating to the Parliament and its members.

Ministers are required to inform committees of the Government's legislative intentions in its area, including discussions about which relevant bodies should be involved in the pre-legislative consultation process. In practice, the Committees have operated with considerable success and have taken evidence from interested bodies and individuals on a wide range of matters. Scottish

Ministers have also been required to account to the Committees for matters within their portfolios. Most Committee business is undertaken in public.

Management of Parliament

The management of the business of the Parliament is undertaken by the Parliamentary Bureau (for members, *see* page 14). This meets in private and its main functions are:

* to prepare the programme of business of the Parliament
* to timetable the daily order of business for the plenary session
* to timetable the progress of legislation in committees
* to propose the remit, membership, duration and budget of parliamentary committees

The Parliamentary Bureau gives priority on certain days to business of the committees, to business chosen by political parties which are not represented in the Scottish Executive, and to private members' business.

The management of the business of Parliament as a corporate entity is the responsibility of the Scottish Parliamentary Corporate Body (for members, *see* page 14). This has legal powers to hold property, make contracts and handle money and also to bring or defend legal proceedings by or against the Scottish Parliament. It also employs staff engaged in the running of the Parliament who are not civil servants.

BUDGET AND RUNNING COSTS

The budget of the Parliament for 2001-2002 is £19.8 billion and the UK Government has agreed to the continuing application of the Barnett Formula to allow for uprating of the Parliament's budget in line with increases for corresponding matters for the rest of the UK. In addition, the Parliament has limited powers to vary the basic rate of income tax by a maximum of 3 pence. The only other financial powers held by the Scottish Parliament relate to the manner in which local authorities raise revenue, presently by way of council tax and business rates.

The Scottish Parliament will be permanently housed in a custom-built building under construction at Holyrood, Edinburgh. The project has been beset by problems and completion is not now expected until December 2002. The cost has risen from an original estimate of £40 million to around £230 million although in April 2000 the Scottish Parliament agreed that the cost should be capped at £195 million. It is generally accepted that this will be exceeded. Until the new Parliament building is completed, the Scottish Parliament is occupying the Church of Scotland General Assembly buildings at The Mound, Edinburgh.

The total running costs of the Parliament for 2001-2002 as set out in the Budget (Scotland) Act 2001 including salaries and allowances for MSPs, staff costs, accommodation costs and payments in respect of the Scottish Parliamentary Commissioner for Administration, are estimated at around £95 million.

Salaries and allowances

The initial salaries of MSPs were set at Westminster (for current salaries, *see* page 14), but in future the setting of salaries will be a matter for the Scottish Parliament. Enhanced salaries are payable to the Scottish Ministers and there is a system of allowances to cover MSPs' expenses in carrying out constituency and parliamentary work.

THE JUDICIARY

The role of the judiciary is specifically acknowledged in the Scotland Act and there are detailed proposals for the appointment and removal of judges. Judges are likely to be increasingly involved in matters of political significance, including legal challenges to legislation made by the Scottish Parliament and issues arising out of the European Convention on Human Rights.

Because of their increasing involvement in matters of political sensitivity, the procedures for removing judges have been made more rigorous. Judges can only be removed from office by the Queen on the recommendation of the First Minister following a resolution of the Parliament. Parliament may only pass such a motion following a written report by an independent tribunal concluding that the person in question is unfit for office by reason of inability, neglect of duty or misbehaviour.

RELATIONSHIP WITH THE UK GOVERNMENT

The devolution settlement has resulted in changes to the UK constitutional framework. The role of the Secretary of State for Scotland is diminished to the extent that he or she will only represent Scotland's interests with regard to reserved matters; there is no guarantee that the Secretary of State will continue to have a place in the Cabinet.

A system of concordats has been put in place to ensure that the business of government in Scotland and at the UK level is conducted smoothly. The concordats are non-statutory bilateral agreements between the Scottish Executive and the UK Government which cover a range of administrative procedures relating to devolution. They are intended to ensure that good working relationships and communications continue between the Scottish administration and UK government departments. They set out the principles on which working relationships will be based rather than prescribe the details of what those relationships should be. Concordats are intended to ensure that consultation takes place in relation to proposals for legislative and executive action, including advance notification.

There are likely to be further changes in future, for example, the number of Scottish MPs at Westminster is expected to be reduced following the next review of electoral areas carried out by the Boundary Commission for Scotland. As the legislation stands, this would also have the consequence of reducing the number of MSPs. Exact numbers will only be known after the Boundary Commission completes its work, but estimates suggest that the number of MSPs could drop from 129 to around 110. This possible reduction in numbers is already causing concern in view of the extent of the workload of Committees of the Scottish Parliament in particular and the UK Government has indicated that it will keep this matter under review.

RELATIONSHIP WITH THE EUROPEAN UNION

Relations with the EU remain a reserved matter. While the Scottish Parliament has the responsibility of scrutinising European legislation affecting Scotland, and the Scottish Executive the responsibility for applying that legislation in Scotland, it is the UK Government that represents Scottish interests in the Council of Ministers; this includes areas such as farming and fishing, where Scottish Office ministers may previously have led UK delegations. The Government has indicated that Scottish Ministers might be able to participate, on behalf of the UK, in EU meetings. It has indicated that it sees UK and Scottish Ministers agreeing a common line prior to negotiating with other EU member states.

One of the concerns expressed about the proposed relationship between the Scottish Executive and the EU institutions is accountability. Scottish Ministers are not members of the UK Parliament and are therefore not accountable to Westminster. As Scotland is not a member state of the EU, the responsibility for ensuring compliance with EU legislation rests with the UK Government. There is potential for conflict between the Scottish Parliament and Westminster with regard to the implementation of European legislation. In that event, the proposed concordats between the Scottish Parliament and Westminster will be tested.

Any financial penalties imposed by the EU for non-observance of an EU measure, even in respect of devolved matters, will be met by the UK. Where the fault is due to the failure of the Scottish Executive to implement EU legislation in respect of devolved matters, the financial consequences will be met out of the Scottish Block.

LEGISLATIVE PROGRAMME

As at the beginning of July 2001 the Parliament had passed the following legislation:

- Mental Health (Public Safety and Appeals) (Scotland) Act 1999

- Public Finance and Accountability (Scotland) Act 2000

- Abolition of Feudal Tenure etc (Scotland) Act 2000

- Adults with Incapacity (Scotland) Act 2000

- Census (Amendment) (Scotland) Act 2000

- Budget (Scotland) Act 2000

- Standards in Scotland's Schools etc Act 2000

- Ethical Standards in Public Life etc (Scotland) Act 2000

- Education and Training (Scotland) Act 2000

- Bail, Judicial Appointments etc (Scotland) Act 2000

- National Parks (Scotland) Act 2000

- Regulation of Investigatory Powers (Scotland) Act 2000

- Sea Fisheries (Shellfish) Amendment (Scotland) Act 2000

- Abolition of Poindings and Warrant Sales Act 2001

- Transport (Scotland) Act 2001

- Salmon Conservation (Scotland) Act 2001

- Budget (Scotland) Act 2001

- Leasehold Casualties (Scotland) Act 2001

- Eduction (Graduate Endowment and Student Support) (Scotland) Act 2001

- Convention Rights (Compliance) (Scotland) Act 2001

- Regulation of Care (Scotland) Act 2001

8 Governed Scotland

At that date the Parliament also had a total of 8 Bills in Progress. These comprise a combination of Executive and Members Bills (the Scottish equivalent of a private members bill) as follows:

- Housing (Scotland) Bill
- International Criminal Court (Scotland) Bill
- Mortgage Rights (Scotland) Bill
- Police and Fire Services (Finance) (Scotland) Bill
- Protection from Abuse (Scotland) Bill
- Protection of Wild Mammals (Scotland) Bill
- Scottish Local Authorities (Tendering) Bill
- Sexual Offences (Procedures and Evidence) (Scotland) Bill.

Up to date information on the progress of all Bills can be found on the Scottish Parliament website at www.scottish.parliament.uk.

THE SCOTTISH EXECUTIVE

The Scottish Executive is the government of Scotland in respect of all devolved matters. The Scottish Executive consists of the First Minister, the law officers (the Lord Advocate and the Solicitor-General for Scotland), and the other Scottish Ministers appointed by the First Minister. The First Minister is also able to appoint junior ministers to assist the Scottish Ministers.

The Secretary of State for Scotland continues to be appointed as a member of the UK Government and is not a member of the Scottish Executive.

Certain UK Ministers continue to have a degree of responsibility for reserved matters.

THE SCOTTISH MINISTERS

First Minister: The Rt. Hon. Henry McLeish, MSP (Lab.)

Deputy First Minister and Minister for Justice: Jim Wallace, QC, MSP (LD)

Minister of Education, Europe and External Affairs: Jack McConnell, MSP (Lab.)

Minister for Finance: Angus MacKay, MSP (Lab.)

Minister for Health and Community Care: Susan Deacon, MSP (Lab.)

Minister for Transport and Planning: Sarah Boyack, MSP (Lab.)

Minister for Enterprise and Lifelong Learning: Wendy Alexander, MSP (Lab.)

Minister for Environment and Rural Development: Ross Finnie, MSP (LD)

Minister for Social Justice: Jackie Baillie, MSP (Lab.)

Minister for Parliament: Tom McCabe, MSP (Lab.)

Lord Advocate: Colin Boyd, QC (Lab.)

JUNIOR MINISTERS

COMMUNITIES

Deputy Minister for Finance and Local Government: Peter Peacock, MSP (Lab.)

EDUCATION AND CHILDREN

Deputy Minister for Sport, The Arts and Culture: Allan Wilson, MSP (Lab.)

Deputy Minister for Education, Europe and External Affairs: Nicol Stephen, MSP (LD)

ENTERPRISE AND LIFELONG LEARNING

Deputy Minister for Enterprise and Lifelong Learning: Nicol Stephen, MSP (LD)

Deputy Minister Enterprise and Lifelong Learning and Gaelic: Alasdair Morrison, MSP (Lab.)

HEALTH AND COMMUNITY CARE

Deputy Minister for Health and Community Care: Malcolm Chrisholm, MSP (Lab.)

JUSTICE

Deputy Minister for Social Justice: Margaret Curran, MSP (Lab.)

PARLIAMENT

Deputy Minister for Parliament: Euan Robson, MSP (LD)

RURAL AFFAIRS

Deputy Minister for Environment and Rural Development: Rhonda Brankin, MSP (Lab.)

LORD ADVOCATE

Solicitor-General for Scotland: Neil Davidson, QC

DEPARTMENTS OF THE SCOTTISH EXECUTIVE

St Andrew's House, Regent Road, Edinburgh EH1 3DG (Tel: 0131-556 8400; enquiry line: 08457-741 741 Fax: 0131-244 8240
E-mail: ceu@scotland.gov.uk;
scottish.ministers@scotland.gov.uk
Web: www.scotland.gov.uk)

The Scottish Executive Ministers are supported by staff largely drawn from the staff of the Scottish Office, as constituted before devolution, and its agencies. On 1 July 1999 the departments of the Scottish Office transferred to the Scottish Executive and now work to the First Minister and his ministerial team. All officials of the Executive hold office under the Crown on terms and conditions of service determined in accordance with the provisions of the Civil Service Management Code and remain members of the Home Civil Service.

On 1 July 1999 the Scottish Office changed its name to the Scottish Executive and its departments were renamed; some reassignment of responsibilities also took place.

Scottish Executive Development Department — social inclusion, housing, local government, transport, planning and building control, European structural funds
Scottish Executive Education Department — pre-school, primary and secondary education, childcare, social work and legal provisions for young people (including justice), development of the arts, cultural and built heritage, sports and recreation, Gaelic, broadcasting and architectural policy
Scottish Executive Enterprise and Lifelong Learning Department — further and higher education, lifelong learning, and business and industry functions of Education and Industry Department, the New Deal
Scottish Executive Health Department — Health Department, community care functions of the Social Work Services Group
Scottish Executive Justice Department — police, fire, emergency planning, courts group, civil law, criminal justice, parole and legal aid, criminal justice social work
Scottish Executive Environment and Rural Affairs Department — Agriculture, Environment and Fisheries Department
Scottish Executive Finance and Central Services Department — replaces Finance Division

Scottish Executive Corporate Services — central support functions, including human resources, equal opportunities, the Modernising Government agenda
Scottish Executive Secretariat — parliamentary liaison, co-ordination of relations with UK Government, support to Scottish Ministers

Further information can be obtained from the contact points at the main Scottish Executive offices at St Andrew's House.

The following includes details of the departments of the Scottish Executive; details of the executive agencies of the Scottish Executive departments can be found in the Other Government Departments and Public Bodies section.

SCOTTISH EXECUTIVE CORPORATE SERVICES

16 Waterloo Place, Edinburgh EH1 3DN
(Tel: 0131-556 8400)

Principal Establishment Officer: Angus Robson
Head of Personnel: Ingrid Clayden

DIRECTORATE OF ADMINISTRATIVE SERVICES
Saughton House, Broomhouse Drive, Edinburgh EH11 3XD (Tel: 0131-556 8400)
Director of Administrative Services: Jim Meldrum
Chief Estates Officer: J. A. Andrew
Director of Information Technology: Paul Gray
Chief Quantity Surveyor: A. J. Wyllie
Director of Procurement and Commercial Services: N. Bowd

DIRECTORATE OF CORPORATE DEVELOPMENT
Director: Ian Walford

SCOTTISH EXECUTIVE FINANCE

Victoria Quay, Edinburgh EH6 6QQ
(Tel: 0131-556 8400)

Principal Finance Officer: Dr P. S. Collings
Assistant Directors of Finance: G. F. Dickson; J. G. Henderson; D. N. G Reid; A. Stobart
Head of Audit Unit: W. T. Tait
Head of Accountancy Services Unit: I. M. Smith

SCOTTISH EXECUTIVE SECRETARIAT

St Andrew's House, Regent Road, Edinburgh
EH1 3DG (Tel: 0131-556 8400)
Head of Executive Secretariat: Robert Gordon,
CB
Constitution and Parliamentary Secretariat:
Michael Lugton
Head of Cabinet Secretariat Division: Ms
Bridget Campbell
Legal Adviser: J. L. Jamieson, CBE
Chief Economic Adviser: Dr A. W. Goudie
Legal Secretary to the Lord Advocate: P. J.
Layden

EXTERNAL RELATIONS DIVISION
Head of Division: Mrs B. Doig

BRUSSELS OFFICE
Head of Office: G. Calder

MEDIA AND COMMUNCATIONS GROUP
For the Scottish Executive and certain UK services
in Scotland
Head of New Media and Prescutation: Roger
Williams
Head of News: O. D. Kelly
Chief Publicity Officer: S. Sutherland

SOLICITOR'S OFFICE
Solicitor: R. M. Henderson
Deputy Solicitor: J. S. G. Maclean

SCOTTISH EXECUTIVE DEVELOPMENT DEPARTMENT

Victoria Quay, Edinburgh EH6 6QQ
(Tel: 0131-556 8400)
Secretary: vacant
Group Heads: M. Batho; D. J. Belfall; S. B.
Martin; D. Middleton
Division Heads: S. Adams; J. Breslin; P.
Cornish; L. Evans; R. A. Grant; D.Hart; G.
Higgins; J. Howison; C. Imrie; N. MacKenzie;
L. Manson; M. McGinn; W. J. R. McQueen;
Mrs D. Mellon; A. Rennie; L. Rosborough; C.
Smith; Y. Strachani; B. Tait
Senior Economic Adviser: N. Jackson

Professional Staff
Chief Planner: J. MacKinnon

Inquiry Reporters
2 Greenside Lane, Edinburgh EH1 3AG
(Tel: 0131-244 5649)
Chief Reporter: R. M. Hickman
Deputy Chief Reporter: J. M. McCulloch

SCOTTISH EXECUTIVE EDUCATION DEPARTMENT

Victoria Quay, Edinburgh EH6 6QQ
(Tel: 0131-556 8400)
Secretary: J. Elvidge
Under-Secretaries: Mr M. Ewart; Ms I. Low;
Mrs G. Stewart
Assistant Secretaries: A. Brown; Mrs E.
Emberson; Mrs J. Fraser; J. Gilmour; R. N.
Irvine; G. McHugh; Mrs R. Menlowe; Ms S.
Smith
Chief Statistician: R. C. Wishart
Chief Architect: J. E. Gibbons, Ph.D, FSA Scot.
**Chief Inspector of Social Work Services for
Scotland:** A. Skinner
Assistant Chief Inspectors: Ms V.A. Cox; Ms S.
Perrott; I. Robertson

HM Inspectors of Schools
Senior Chief Inspector: D. A. Osler
Depute Senior Chief Inspector: G. H. C.
Donaldson
Chief Inspectors: P. Banks; J. Boyes; W. C.
Calder; F. Crawford; Miss K. M. Fairweather;
A. S. McGlynn; H. M. Stalker
There are 86 Grade 6 Inspectors

SCOTTISH EXECUTIVE ENTERPRISE AND LIFELONG LEARNING DEPARTMENT

Meridian Court, 5 Cadogan Street, Glasgow G2
6AT (Tel: 0141-248 2855)
Secretary: E. W. Frizzell

ECONOMIC DEVELOPMENT, ADVICE AND EMPLOYMENT ISSUES
Meridian Court, 5 Cadogan Street, Glasgow G2
6AT (Tel: 0141-248 2855)
Under-Secretary: M. B. Foulis
Assistant Secretaries: A. K. Macleod; Dr J. Rigg;
D. Wilson

LIFELONG LEARNING GROUP
Europa Building, 450 Argyle Street, Glasgow G2
8LG (Tel: 0141-248 2855)
Under-Secretary: E. J. Weeple
Assistant Secretaries: K. Doran; L. M. A.
Hunter; C. M. Reeves; D. Stephen

ENTERPRISE AND INDUSTRIAL AFFAIRS
Meridian Court, 5 Cadogan Street, Glasgow G2
6AT (Tel: 0141-248 2855)
Under-Secretary: S. F. Hampson
Industrial Adviser: D. Blair
Assistant Secretaries: J. A. Brown; I. J. C.
Howie; W. Malone; D. A Stewart; J. Morgan

LOCATE IN SCOTLAND
120 Bothwell Street, Glasgow G2 7JP
(Tel: 0141-248 2700)
Director: D. Macdonald

SCOTTISH TRADE INTERNATIONAL
120 Bothwell Street, Glasgow G2 7JP
(Tel: 0141-248 2700)
Director: L. Brown

EXECUTIVE AGENCY

Student Awards Agency for Scotland

SCOTTISH EXECUTIVE HEALTH DEPARTMENT

St Andrew's House, Regent Road, Edinburgh
EH1 3DG (Tel: 0131-556 8400)

NATIONAL HEALTH SERVICE IN SCOTLAND MANAGEMENT EXECUTIVE
Chief Executive: T. Jones
Director of Planning and Performance Management: Dr K. J. Woods
Director of Primary Care: Mrs A. Robson
Director of Finance: J. Aldridge
Director of Human Resources: M. Batler
Director of Nursing: Miss A. Jarvie
Head of Community Care: T. Teale
Chief Medical Officer: Dr M. Armstrong
Director of Trusts: P. Wilson
Head of Information Services, NHS: C. B. Knox
Head of Estates: H. R. McCallum
Chief Pharmacist: W. Scott
Chief Scientist: Prof. G. R. D. Catto
Chief Dental Officer: T. R. Watkins

PUBLIC HEALTH POLICY UNIT
Head of Unit and Chief Medical Officer: Prof. Sir David Carter, FRCSE, FRCSGlas., FRCPE
Deputy Chief Medical Officer: Dr A. Fraser
Head of Group: Mrs N. Munro
Assistant Secretary: J. T. Brown
Principal Medical Officers: Dr J. B. Louden (part-time); Dr A. Macdonald (part-time); Dr R. Skinner; Dr E. Sowler

Senior Medical Officers: Dr A. Anderson; Dr E. Bashford; Dr K. G. Brotherston; Dr D. Campbell; Dr J. Cumming; Dr B. Davis; Dr D. J. Ewing; Dr D. Findlay; Dr G. R. Foster; Dr A. Keel; Dr P. Madden; Dr H. Whyte; Dr D. Will

STATE HOSPITAL
Carstairs Junction, Lanark ML11 8RP
(Tel: 01555-840293; Fax: 01555-840024
E-mail: info@tsh.org.uk)

The State Hospital provides high security mental health services to patients from Scotland and Northern Ireland.
Chairman: D. N. James
General Manager: R. Manson

COMMON SERVICES AGENCY
Trinity Park House, South Trinity Road, Edinburgh EH5 3SE (Tel: 0131-552 6255)
Chairman: G. R. Scaife, CB
General Manager: Dr F. Gibb

SCOTTISH EXECUTIVE JUSTICE DEPARTMENT

Saughton House, Broomhouse Drive, Edinburgh
EH11 3XD (Tel: 0131-556 8400)
Secretary: J. Gallagher
Under-Secretaries: C. Baxter; N. G. Campbell; Mrs V. Macniven
Assistant Secretaries: P. Beaton; Mrs M. H. Brannan; D. Carmichael; Mrs E. Carmichael; D. Henderson; R. S. T. MacEwen; A. MacIntosh; A. Quinn; J. Rowell; I. Snedden; D. Stewart

HM INSPECTORATE OF CONSTABULARY
2 Greenside Lane, Edinburgh EH1 3AH
(Tel: 0131-244 5614)
HM Chief Inspector of Constabulary: W. Taylor, QPM

SCOTTISH POLICE COLLEGE
Tulliallan Castle, Kincardine, Alloa FK10 4BE
(Tel: 01259-732000)
Commandant: D. Garbutt

HM INSPECTORATE OF FIRE SERVICES
Saughton House, Broomhouse Drive, Edinburgh
EH11 3XD (Tel: 0131-244 2342)
HM Chief Inspector of Fire Services: D. Davis, QFSM

SCOTTISH FIRE SERVICE TRAINING SCHOOL
Main Street, Gullane, East Lothian EH31 2HG
(Tel: 01620-842236)
Acting Commandant: C. McGarva

HM CHIEF INSPECTOR OF PRISONS FOR SCOTLAND
Saughton House, Broomhouse Drive, Edinburgh
EH11 3XD (Tel: 0131-244 8481; Fax: 0131-244 8446)
HM Chief Inspector of Prisons:
  C. Fairweather, OBE

OFFICE OF THE SCOTTISH PARLIAMENTARY COUNSEL
Victoria Quay, Edinburgh EH6 6QQ
(Tel: 0131-556 8400)
First Scottish Parliamentary Counsel: J. C.
  McCluskie, CB, QC
Scottish Parliamentary Counsel: G. M. Clark;
  C. A. M. Wilson
Depute Scottish Parliamentary Counsel: J. D.
  Harkness; Miss M. Mackenzie
Assistant Scottish Parliamentary Counsel: A.
  C. Gordon

PRIVATE LEGISLATION OFFICE
50 Frederick Street, Edinburgh EH2 1EN
(Tel: 0131-226 6499)
Senior Counsel: G. S. Douglas, QC
Junior Counsel: N. M. P. Morrison

EXECUTIVE AGENCIES

National Archives of Scotland

Registers of Scotland

Scottish Court Service

Scottish Prison Service

SCOTTISH EXECUTIVE RURAL AFFAIRS DEPARTMENT
Pentland House, 47 Robb's Loan, Edinburgh
EH14 1TY (Tel: 0131-556 8400)
Head of Department: J. S. Graham
Group Heads: D. J. Crawley (Food and
  Agriculture); Dr P. Brady (Fisheries); S. F.
Hampson (Environment); A. J. Rushworth
(Agricultural and Biological Research);
A. J. Robertson (Chief Agricultural Officer)
Division/unit Heads: Dr J. R. Wildgoose; I. R.
Anderson; D. R. Dickson; Ms J. Polley; D. J.
Greig; W. M. Ferguson (Food and Agriculture
Group); A. G. Dickson; Ms J. Dalgleish; Ms B.
Campbell; P. Wright; M. Neilson; A. J.
Cameron; Dr J. Miles (Environment Group)
Division Heads: D. Feeley; G. M. D. Thomson
(Fisheries Group)
Assistant Chief Agricultural Officers: W. A.
Aitken; J. Henderson; A. Robb
Chief Agricultural Economist: vacant

EXECUTIVE AGENCIES

Fisheries Research Services

Scottish Agricultural Science Agency

Scottish Fisheries Protection Agency

GENERAL REGISTER OFFICE FOR SCOTLAND
New Register House, Edinburgh EH1 3YT
(Tel: 0131-334 0380; Fax: 0131-314 4400
E-mail: records@gro-scotland.gov.uk
Web: www.gro-scotland.gov.uk)

The General Register Office for Scotland is part
of the devolved Scottish Administration. It is the
office of the Registrar-General for Scotland, who
has responsibility for civil registration and the
taking of censuses in Scotland and has in his
custody the statutory registers of births, deaths,
still births, adoptions, marriages and divorces; the
old parish registers (recording births, deaths and
marriages, etc., before civil registration began in
1855); and records of censuses of the population in
Scotland. (*See* also Legal Notes)
  Hours of public access: Monday – Friday
09:00-16:30
Registrar General: J. N. Randall
Deputy Registrar General: B. V. Philp
Census Manager: D. A. Orr
Heads of Branch: D. B. L. Brownlee; P. M. Parr;
  F. D. Garvie; G. Compton; G. W. L. Jackson;
  F. G. Thomas

THE SCOTTISH PARLIAMENT

Edinburgh Assembly Hall, Edinburgh EH99 1SP
(Tel: 0131-348 5000 (switchboard);
0845-278 1999 (general enquiries);
E-mail: sp.info@scottish.parliament.uk (public information);
sp.media@scottish.parliament.uk (media enquiries);
education.service@scottish.parliament.uk (schools and colleges);
chamber.office@scottish.parliament.uk (business in the debating chamber);
committee.office@scottish.parliament.uk (business in committees);
petitions@scottish.parliament.uk (petitions)
presiding.officer@scottish.parliament.uk (office of the Presiding Officer);
webmaster@scottish.parliament.uk
Web: www.scottish.parliament.uk)

Elected: 6 May 1999; turnout was 59 per cent of the electorate
First session: 12 May 1999
Official opening: 1 July 1999 at Edinburgh Assembly Hall
Budget: £16 billion
Devolved responsibilities: education, health, law, environment, economic development, local government, housing, police, fire services, planning, financial assistance to industry, tourism, some transport, heritage and the arts, sport, agriculture, forestry, fisheries, food standards
Powers: can introduce primary legislation; can raise or lower income tax by up to three pence in the pound
Number of members: 129

STATE OF THE PARTIES
as at 11 May 2001

	Constituency MSPs	Regional MSPs	Total
Labour	52	3	55
SNP	7	28	35
Conservative	1	18	19
Liberal Democrats	12	4*	16*
Green	0	1	1
Socialist	0	1	1
Independent	1	0	1
Presiding Officer	0	1	1
Total	73	56	129

Excludes the Presiding Officer, who has no party allegiance while in post

SALARIES
from 1 April 2001

MSPs and officers are paid by the Scottish Parliamentary Corporate Body; ministers are paid out of the Scottish Consolidated Fund.

First Minister	£68,159*
Ministers	£35,358*
Lord Advocate	£44,849
Solicitor-General for Scotland	£32,429
Junior Ministers	£18,342*
MSPs	£41,255†
Presiding Officer	£34,327*
Deputy Presiding Officers	£17,807*

*In addition to salary as an MSP
† Reduced by two-thirds (to £13,364) if the member is already an MP or an MEP

OFFICERS
The Presiding Officer, The Rt. Hon. Sir David Steel, KBE, MSP, QC
Deputy Presiding Officers, George Reid, MSP (SNP); Patricia Ferguson, MSP (Lab.)

THE PARLIAMENTARY BUREAU
The Presiding Officer, Tom McCabe, MSP (Lab.)
Tricia Warwick, MSP (SNP)
The Rt. Hon. Lord James Douglas Hamilton, MSP, QC (C.)
Euan Robson, MSP (LD)

SCOTTISH PARLIAMENTARY CORPORATE BODY
The Presiding Officer, Robert Brown, MSP (LD)
Des McNulty, MSP (Lab.)
Andrew Welsh, MSP (SNP)
John Young, MSP (C.)

THE COMMITTEES
The committees of the Scottish Parliament are:

MANDATORY COMMITTEES

PROCEDURES
Convenor, Murray Tosh, MSP
Committee Clerk: John Patterson

STANDARDS
Convenor: Mike Rumbles, MSP
Committee Clerk: Sam Jones

FINANCE
Convenor: Mike Watson, MSP
Committee Clerk: Callum Thompson

AUDIT
Convenor: Andrew Welsh, MP, MSP (SNP)
Committee Clerk: Callum Thompson

EUROPEAN
Convenor: Hugh Henry, MSP (Lab.)
Committee Clerk: Stephen Imrie

EQUAL OPPORTUNITIES
Convenor: Kate Maclean, MSP (Lab.)
Committee Clerk: Lee Bridges

PUBLIC PETITIONS
Convenor: John McAllion, MP, MSP (Lab.)
Committee Clerk: Steve Farrell

SUBORDINATE LEGISLATION
Convenor: Kenny MacAskill, MSP (SNP)
Committee Clerk: Alasdair Rankin

SUBJECT COMMITTEES
JUSTICE 1: **Convenor:** Alasdair Morgan MSP,
  (SNP). **Committee Clerk:** Lynn Tullis
JUSTICE 2: **Convenor:** Pauline McNeill, MSP
  (Lab.) **Committee Clerk:** Lynn Tullis

EDUCATION, CULTURE AND SPORT
Convenor: Karen Gillon, MSP (Lab.)
Committee Clerk: Martin Verity

SOCIAL JUSTICE
Convenor: Johann Lamont, MSP (Lab.)
Committee Clerk: Lee Bridges

**ENTERPRISE AND LIFELONG
LEARNING**
Convenor: Alex Neil, MSP (SNP)
Committee Clerk: Simon Watkins

HEALTH AND COMMUNITY CARE
Convenor: Margaret Smith, MSP (LD)
Committee Clerk: Jennifer Stuart

**TRANSPORT AND THE
ENVIRONMENT**
Convenor: Andy Kerr, MSP (Lab.)
Committee Clerk: Shelagh McKinlay

RURAL DEVELOPMENT
Convenor: Alex Johnstone, MSP (C.)
Committee Clerk: Richard Davies

LOCAL GOVERNMENT
Convenor: Patricia Godman, MSP (Lab.)
Committee Clerk: Eugene Windsor

SCOTTISH PARLIAMENT CONSTITUENCIES AND REGIONS

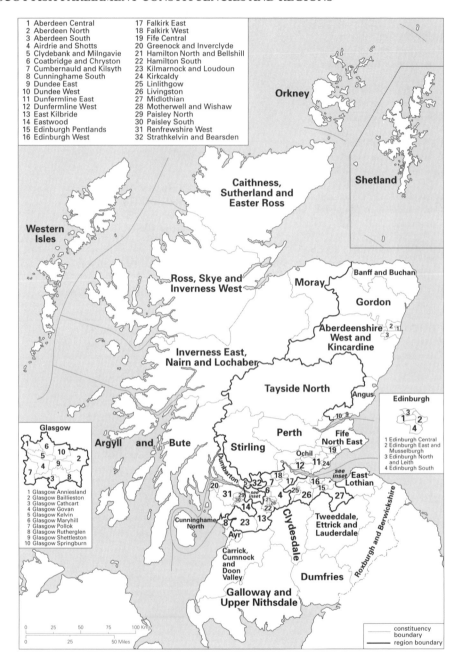

1 Aberdeen Central	17 Falkirk East
2 Aberdeen North	18 Falkirk West
3 Aberdeen South	19 Fife Central
4 Airdrie and Shotts	20 Greenock and Inverclyde
5 Clydebank and Milngavie	21 Hamilton North and Bellshill
6 Coatbridge and Chryston	22 Hamilton South
7 Cumbernauld and Kilsyth	23 Kilmarnock and Loudoun
8 Cunninghame South	24 Kirkcaldy
9 Dundee East	25 Linlithgow
10 Dundee West	26 Livingston
11 Dunfermline East	27 Midlothian
12 Dunfermline West	28 Motherwell and Wishaw
13 East Kilbride	29 Paisley North
14 Eastwood	30 Paisley South
15 Edinburgh Pentlands	31 Renfrewshire West
16 Edinburgh West	32 Strathkelvin and Bearsden

Orkney

Caithness, Sutherland and Easter Ross

Shetland

Western Isles

Ross, Skye and Inverness West

Moray

Banff and Buchan

Gordon

Aberdeenshire West and Kincardine

Inverness East, Nairn and Lochaber

Tayside North

Angus

Edinburgh

1 Edinburgh Central
2 Edinburgh East and Musselburgh
3 Edinburgh North and Leith
4 Edinburgh South

Perth

Fife North East

Glasgow

1 Glasgow Anniesland
2 Glasgow Baillieston
3 Glasgow Cathcart
4 Glasgow Govan
5 Glasgow Kelvin
6 Glasgow Maryhill
7 Glasgow Pollok
8 Glasgow Rutherglen
9 Glasgow Shettleston
10 Glasgow Springburn

Argyll and Bute

Stirling

Ochil

East Lothian

Cunninghame North

Ayr

Tweeddale, Ettrick and Lauderdale

Carrick, Cumnock and Doon Valley

Clydesdale

Dumfries

Roxburgh and Berwickshire

Galloway and Upper Nithsdale

0 25 50 75 100 Kms
0 25 50 Miles

constituency boundary
region boundary

on 6 May 1999

CONSTITUENCIES

Aberdeen Central
(Scotland North East region)
E. 52,715 T. 50.26%
L. Macdonald, Lab. 10,305
R. Lochhead, SNP 7,609
Ms E. Anderson, LD 4,403
T. Mason, C. 3,655
A. Cumbers, SSP 523
Lab. majority 2,696

Aberdeen North
(Scotland North East region)
E. 54,553 T. 51.00%
Ms E. Thomson, Lab. 10,340
B. Adam, SNP 9,942
J. Donaldson, LD 4,767
I. Haughie, C. 2,772
Lab. majority 398

Aberdeen South
(Scotland North East region)
E. 60,579 T. 57.26%
N. Stephen, LD 11,300
M. Elrick, Lab. 9,540
Ms N. Milne, C. 6,993
Ms I. McGugan, SNP 6,651
S. Sutherland, SWP 206
LD majority 1,760

Aberdeenshire West and Kincardine
(Scotland North East region)
E. 60,702 T. 58.87%
M. Rumbles, LD 12,83
B. Wallace, C. 10,549
Ms M. Watt, SNP 7,699
G. Guthrie, Lab. 4,650
LD majority 2,289

Airdrie and Shotts
(Scotland Central region)
E. 58,481 T. 56.79%
Ms K. Whitefield, Lab. 18,338
G. Paterson, SNP 9,353
P. Ross-Taylor, C. 3,177
D. Miller, LD 2,345
Lab. majority 8,985

Angus
(Scotland North East region)
E. 59,891 T. 57.66%
A. Welsh, SNP 16,055
R. Harris, C. 7,154
I. McFatridge, Lab. 6,914
R. Speirs, LD 4,413
SNP majority 8,901

Argyll and Bute
(Highlands and Islands region)
E. 49,609 T. 64.86%
G. Lyon, LD 11,226
D. Hamilton, SNP 9,169
H. Raven, Lab. 6,470
D. Petrie, C. 5,312
LD majority 2,057

Ayr
(Scotland South region)
E. 56,338 T. 66.48%
I. Welsh, Lab. 14,263
P. Gallie, C. 14,238
R. Mullin, SNP 7,291
Ms E. Morris, LD 1,662
Lab. majority 25
(by-election *see* page 25)

Banff and Buchan
(Scotland North East region)
E. 57,639 T. 55.06%
A. Salmond, SNP 16,695
D. Davidson, C. 5,403
M. Mackie, LD 5,315
Ms M. Harris, Lab. 4,321
SNP majority 11,292
(by-election *see* page 25)

Caithness, Sutherland and Easter Ross
(Highlands and Islands region)
E. 41,581 T. 62.60%
J. Stone, LD 10,691
J. Hendry, Lab. 6,300
Ms J. Urquhart, SNP 6,035
R. Jenkins, C. 2,167
J. Campbell, Ind. 554
E. Stewart, Ind. 282
LD majority 4,391

Carrick, Cumnock and Doon Valley
(Scotland South region)
E. 65,580 T. 62.66%
Ms C. Jamieson, Lab. Co-op. 19,667
A. Ingram, SNP 10,864
J. Scott, C. 8,123
D, Hannay, LD 2,441
Lab. Co-op. majority 8,803

Clydebank and Milngavie
(Scotland West region)
E. 52,461 T. 63.55%
D. McNulty, Lab. 15,105
J. Yuill, SNP 10,395
R. Ackland, LD 4,149
Ms D. Luckhurst, C. 3,688
Lab. majority 4,710

Clydesdale
(Scotland South region)
E. 64,262 T. 60.61%
Ms K. Turnbull, Lab. 16,755
Ms A. Winning, SNP 12,875
C. Cormack, C. 5,814
Ms S. Grieve, LD 3,503
Lab. majority 3,880

Coatbridge and Chryston
(Scotland Central region)
E. 52,178 T. 57.87%
Ms E. Smith, Lab. 17,923
P. Kearney, SNP 7,519
G. Lind, C. 2,867
Ms J. Hook, LD 1,889
Lab. majority 10,404

Cumbernauld and Kilsyth
(Scotland Central region)
E. 49,395 T. 61.97%
Ms C. Craigie, Lab. 15,182
A. Wilson, SNP 10,923
H. O'Donnell, LD 2,029
R. Slack, C. 1,362
K. McEwan, SSP 1,116
Lab. majority 4,259

Cunninghame North
(Scotland West region)
E. 55,867 T. 59.95%
A. Wilson, Lab. 14,369
Ms K. Ullrich, SNP 9,573
M. Johnston, C. 6,649
C. Irving, LD 2,900
Lab. majority 4,796

Cunninghame South
(Scotland South region)
E. 50,443 T. 56.06%
Ms I. Oldfather, Lab. 14,936
M. Russell, SNP 8,395
M. Tosh, C. 3,229
S. Ritchie, LD 1,717
Lab. majority 6,541

Dumbarton
(Scotland West region)
E. 56,090 T. 61.86%
Ms J. Baillie, Lab. 15,181
L. Quinan, SNP 10,423
D. Reece, C. 5,060
P. Coleshill, LD 4,035
Lab. majority 4,758

Dumfries
(Scotland South region)
E. 63,162 T. 60.93%
Ms E. Murray, Lab. 14,101
D. Mundell, C. 10,447
S.Norris, SNP 7,625
N. Wallace, LD 6,309
Lab. majority 3,654

Dundee East
(Scotland North East region)
E. 57,222 T. 55.33%
J. McAllion, Lab. 13,703
Ms S. Robison, SNP 10,849
I. Mitchell, C. 4,428
R. Lawrie, LD 2,153
H. Duke, SSP 530
Lab. majority 2,854

Dundee West
(Scotland North East region)
E. 55,725 T. 52.19%
Ms K. MacLean, Lab. 10,925
C. Cashley, SNP 10,804
G. Buchan, C. 3,345
Ms E. Dick, LD 2,998
J. McFarlane, SSP 1,010
Lab. majority 121

Dunfermline East
(Scotland Mid and Fife region)
E. 52,087 T. 56.94%
Ms H. Eadie, Lab. Co-op. 16,576
D. McCarthy, SNP 7,877
Ms C. Ruxton, C. 2,931
F. Lawson, LD 2,275
Lab. Co-op. majority 8,699

Dunfermline West
(Scotland Mid and Fife region)
E. 53,112 T. 57.75%
S. Barrie, Lab. 13,560
D. Chapman, SNP 8,539
Ms E. Harris, LD 5,591
J. Mackie, C. 2,981
Lab. majority 5,021

East Kilbride
(Scotland Central region)
E. 66,111 T. 62.49%
A. Kerr, Lab. 19,987
Ms L. Fabiani, SNP 13,488
C. Stevenson, C. 4,465
E. Hawthorn, LD 3,373
Lab. majority 6,499

East Lothian
(Scotland South region)
E. 58,579 T. 64.16%
J. Home Robertson, Lab. 19,220
C. Miller, SNP 8,274
Ms C. Richard, C. 5,941
Ms J. Hayman, LD 4,147
Lab. majority 10,946

Eastwood
(Scotland West region)
E. 67,248 T. 67.51%
K. Macintosh, Lab. 16,970
J. Young, C. 14,845
Ms R. Findlay, SNP 8,760
Ms A. McCurley, LD 4,472
M. Tayan, Ind. 349
Lab. majority 2,125

Edinburgh Central
(Lothians region)
E. 65,945 T. 56.73%
Ms S. Boyack, Lab. 14,224
I. McKee, SNP 9,598
A. Myles, LD6,187
Ms J. Low, C. 6,018
K. Williamson, SSP 830
B. Allingham, Ind. Dem. 364
W. Wallace, Braveheart 191
Lab. majority 4,626

**Edinburgh East and
Musselburgh**
(Lothians region)
E. 60,167 T. 61.48%
Ms S. Deacon, Lab. 17,086
K. MacAskill, SNP 10,372
J. Balfour, C. 4,600
Ms M. Thomas, LD 4,100
D. White, SSP 697
M. Heavey, Ind. You 134
Lab. majority 6,714

Edinburgh North and Leith
(Lothians region)
E. 62,976 T. 58.19%
M. Chisholm, Lab. 17,203
Ms A. Dana, SNP 9,467

J. Sempill, C. 5,030
S. Tombs, LD 4,039
R. Brown, SSP 907
Lab. majority 7,736

Edinburgh Pentlands
(Lothians region)
E. 60,029 T. 65.97%
I. Gray, Lab. 14,343
D. McLetchie, C. 11,458
S. Gibb, SNP 8,770
I. Gibson, LD 5,029
Lab. majority 2,885

Edinburgh South
(Lothians region)
E. 64,100 T. 62.61%
A. MacKay, Lab. 14,869
Ms M. MacDonald, SNP 9,445
M. Pringle, LD 8,961
I. Whyte, C. 6,378
W. Black, SWP 482
Lab. majority 5,424

Edinburgh West
(Lothians region)
E. 61,747 T. 67.34%
Ms M. Smith, LD 15,161
Lord J. Douglas-Hamilton, C. 10,578
Ms C. Fox, Lab. 8,860
G. Sutherland, SNP 6,984
LD majority 4,583

Falkirk East
(Scotland Central region)
E. 57,345 T. 61.40%
Ms C. Peattie, Lab. 15,721
K. Brown, SNP 11,582
A. Orr, C. 3,399
G. McDonald, LD 2,509
R. Stead, Soc. Lab. 1,643
V. MacGrain, SFPP 358
Lab. majority 4,139

Falkirk West
(Scotland Central region)
E. 53,404 T. 63.04%
D. Canavan, Falkirk W. 18,511
R. Martin, Lab. 6,319
M. Matheson, SNP 5,986
G. Miller, C. 1,897
A. Smith, LD 954
Falkirk W. majority 12,192

Fife Central
(Scotland Mid and Fife region)
E. 58,850 T. 55.82%

H. McLeish, Lab. 18,828
Ms P. Marwick, SNP 10,153
Ms J. A. Liston, LD 1,953
K. Harding, C. 1,918
Lab. majority 8,675

Fife North East
(Scotland Mid and Fife region)
E. 60,886 T. 59.03%
I. Smith, LD 13,590
E. Brocklebank, C. 8,526
C. Welsh, SNP 6,373
C. Milne, Lab. 5,175
D. Macgregor, Ind. 1,540
R. Beveridge, Ind. 737
LD majority 5,064

Galloway and Upper Nithsdale
(Scotland South region)
E. 53,057 T. 66.56%
A. Morgan, SNP 13,873
A. Fergusson, C. 10,672
J. Stevens, Lab. 7,209
Ms J. Mitchell, LD 3,562
SNP majority 3,201

Glasgow Anniesland
(Glasgow region)
E. 54,378 T. 52.37%
D. Dewar, Lab. 16,749
K. Stewart, SNP 5,756
W. Aitken, C. 3,032
I. Brown, LD 1,804
Ms A. Lynch, SSP 1,000
E. Boyd, Soc. Lab. 139
Lab. majority 10,993
(by-election *see* page 25)

Glasgow Baillieston
(Glasgow region)
E. 49,068 T. 48.32%
Ms M. Curran, Lab. 11,289
Ms D. Elder, SNP 8,217
J. McVicar, SSP 1,864
Ms K. Pickering, C. 1,526
Ms J. Fryer, LD 813
Lab. majority 3,072

Glasgow Cathcart
(Glasgow region)
E. 51,338 T. 52.55%
M. Watson, Lab. 12,966
Ms M. Whitehead, SNP 7,592
Ms M. Leishman, C. 3,311
C. Dick, LD 2,187
R. Slorach, SWP 920
Lab. majority 5,374

Glasgow Govan
(Glasgow region)
E. 53,257 T. 49.52%
G. Jackson, Lab. 11,421
Ms N. Sturgeon, SNP 9,665
Ms T. Ahmed-Sheikh, C. 2,343
M. Aslam Khan, LD 1,479
C. McCarthy, SSP 1,275
J. Foster, Comm. Brit. 190
Lab. majority 1,756

Glasgow Kelvin
(Glasgow region)
E. 61,207 T. 46.34%
Ms P. McNeill, Lab. 12,711
Ms S. White, SNP 8,303
Ms M. Craig, LD 3,720
A. Rasul, C. 2,253
Ms H. Ritchie, SSP 1,375
Lab. majority 4,408

Glasgow Maryhill
(Glasgow region)
E. 56,469 T. 40.75%
Ms P. Ferguson, Lab. 11,455
W. Wilson, SNP 7,129
Ms C. Hamblen, LD 1,793
G. Scott, SSP 1,439
M. Fry, C. 1,194
Lab. majority 4,326

Glasgow Pollock
(Glasgow region)
E. 47,970 T. 54.37%
J. Lamont, Lab. Co-op. 11,405
K. Gibson, SNP 6,763
T. Sheridan, SSP 5,611
R. O'Brien, C. 1,370
J. King, LD 931
Lab. Co-op. majority 4,642

Glasgow Rutherglen
(Glasgow region)
E. 51,012 T. 56.89%
Ms J. Hughes, Lab. 13,442
T. Chalmers, SNP 6,155
R. Brown, LD 5,798
I. Stewart, C. 2,315
W. Bonnar, SSP 832
J. Nisbet, Soc. Lab. 481
Lab. majority 7,287

Glasgow Shettleston
(Glasgow region)
E. 50,592 T. 40.58%
F. McAveety, Lab. Co-op. 11,078
J. Byrne, SNP 5,611

Ms R. Kane, SSP 1,640
C. Bain, C. 1,260
L. Clarke, LD 943
Lab. Co-op. majority 5,467

Glasgow Springburn
(Glasgow region)
E. 55,670 T. 43.77%
P. Martin, Lab. 14,268
J. Brady, SNP 6,375
M. Roxburgh, C. 1,293
M. Dunnigan, LD 1,288
J. Friel, SSP 1,141
Lab. majority 7,893

Gordon
(Scotland North East region)
E. 59,497 T. 56.51%
Ms N. Radcliffe, LD 12,353
A. Stronach, SNP 8,158
A. Johnstone, C. 6,602
Ms G. Carlin-Kulwicki, Lab. 3,950
H. Watt, Ind. 2,559
LD majority 4,195

Greenock and Inverclyde
(Scotland West region)
E. 48,584 T. 58.95%
D. McNeil, Lab. 11,817
R. Finnie, LD 7,504
I. Hamilton, SNP 6,762
R. Wilkinson, C. 1,699
D. Landels, SSP 857
Lab. majority 4,313

Hamilton North and Bellshill
(Scotland Central region)
E. 53,992 T. 57.82%
M. McMahon, Lab. 15,227
Ms K. McAlorum, SNP 9,621
S. Thomson, C. 3,199
Ms J. Struthers, LD 2,105
Ms K. McGavigan, Soc. Lab. 1,064
Lab. majority 5,606

Hamilton South
(Scotland Central region)
E. 46,765 T. 55.43%
T. McCabe, Lab. 14,098
A. Ardrey, SNP 6,922
Ms M. Mitchell, C. 2,918
J. Oswald, LD 1,982
Lab. majority 7,176

Inverness East, Nairn and Lochaber
(Highlands and Islands region)
E. 66,285 T. 63.10%
F. Ewing, SNP 13,825
Ms J. Aitken, Lab. 13,384
D. Fraser, LD 8,508
Ms M. Scanlon, C. 6,107
SNP majority 441

Kilmarnock and Loudoun
(Scotland Central region)
E. 61,454 T. 64.03%
Ms M. Jamieson, Lab. 17,345
A. Neil, SNP 14,585
L. McIntosh, C. 4,589
J. Stewart, LD 2,830
Lab. majority 2,760

Kirkcaldy
(Scotland Mid and Fife region)
E. 51,640 T. 54.88%
Ms M. Livingstone, Lab. Co-op. 13,645
S. Hosie, SNP 9,170
M. Scott-Hayward, C. 2,907
J. Mainland, LD 2,620
Lab. Co-op. majority 4,475

Linlithgow
(Lothians region)
E. 54,262 T. 62.26%
Ms M. Mulligan, Lab. 15,247
S. Stevenson, SNP 12,319
G. Lindhurst, C. 3,158
J. Barrett, LD 2,643
Ms I. Ovenstone, Ind. 415
Lab. majority 2,928

Livingston
(Lothians region)
E. 62,060 T. 58.93%
B. Muldoon, Lab. 17,313
G. McCarra, SNP 13,409
D. Younger, C. 3,014
M. Oliver, LD 2,834
Lab. majority 3,904

Midlothian
(Lothians region)
E. 48,374 T. 61.51%
Ms R. Brankin, Lab. Co-op 14,467
A. Robertson, SNP 8,942
J. Elder, LD 3,184
G. Turnbull, C. 2,544
D. Pryde, Ind. 618
Lab. Co-op. majority 5,525

Moray
(Highlands and Islands region)
E. 58,388 T. 57.50%
Mrs M. Ewing, SNP 13,027
A. Farquharson, Lab. 8,898
A. Findlay, C. 8,595
Ms P. Kenton, LD 3,056
SNP majority 4,129

Motherwell and Wishaw
(Scotland Central region)
E. 52,613 T. 57.71%
J. McConnell, Lab. 13,955
J. McGuigan, SNP 8,879
W. Gibson, C. 3,694
J. Milligan, Soc. Lab. 1,941
R. Spillane, LD 1,895
Lab. majority 5,076

Ochil
(Scotland Mid and Fife region)
E. 57,083 T. 64.58%
R. Simpson, Lab. 15,385
G. Reid, SNP 14,082
N. Johnston, C. 4,151
Earl of Mar and Kellie, LD 3,249
Lab. majority 1,303

Orkney
(Highlands and Islands region)
E. 15,658 T. 56.95%
J. Wallace, LD 6,010
C. Zawadzki, C. 1,391
J. Mowat, SNP 917
A. Macleod, Lab. 600
LD majority 4,619

Paisley North
(Scotland West region)
E. 49,020 T. 56.61%
Ms W. Alexander, Lab. 13,492
I. Mackay, SNP 8,876
P. Ramsay, C. 2,242
Ms T. Mayberry, LD 2,133
Ms F. Macdonald, SSP 1,007
Lab. majority 4,616

Paisley South
(Scotland West region)
E. 53,637 T. 57.15%
H. Henry, Lab. 13,899
W. Martin, SNP 9,404
S. Callison, LD 2,974
Ms S. Laidlaw, C. 2,433
P. Mack, Ind. 1,273
Ms J. Forrest, SWP 673
Lab. majority 4,495

Perth
(Scotland Mid and Fife region)
E. 61,034 T. 61.27%
Ms R. Cunningham, SNP 13,570
I. Stevenson, C. 11,543
Ms J. Richards, Lab. 8,725
C. Brodie, LD 3,558
SNP majority 2,027

Renfrewshire West
(Scotland West Region)
E. 52,452 T. 64.89%
Ms P. Godman, Lab. 12,708
C. Campbell, SNP 9,815
Ms A. Goldie, C. 7,243
N. Ascherson, LD 2,659
A. McGraw, Ind. 1,136
P. Clark, SWP 476
Lab. majority 2,893

Ross, Skye and Inverness West
(Highlands and Islands region)
E. 55,845 T. 63.42%
J. Farquhar-Munro, LD 11,652
D. Munro, Lab. 10,113
J. Mather, SNP
7,997
J. Scott, C. 3,351
D. Briggs, Ind. 2,302
LD majority 1,539

Roxburgh and Berwickshire
(Scotland South region)
E. 47,639 T. 58.52%
E. Robson, LD 11,320
A. Hutton, C. 7,735
S. Crawford, SNP 4,719
Ms S. McLeod, Lab. 4,102
LD majority 3,585

Shetland
(Highlands and Islands region)
E. 16,978 T. 58.77%
T. Scott, LD 5,435
J. Wills, Lab. 2,241
W. Ross, SNP 1,430

G. Robinson, C. 872
LD majority 3,194

Stirling
(Scotland Mid and Fife region)
E. 52,904 T. 67.68%
Ms S. Jackson, Lab. 13,533
Ms A. Ewing, SNP 9,552
B. Monteith, C. 9,158
I. Macfarlane, LD 3,407
S. Kilgour, Ind. 155
Lab. majority 3,981

Strathkelvin and Bearsden
(Scotland West region)
E. 63,111 T. 67.17%
S. Galbraith, Lab. 21,505
Ms F. McLeod, SNP 9,384
C. Ferguson, C. 6,934
Ms A. Howarth, LD 4,144
Ms M. Richards, Anti-Drug 423
Lab. majority 12,121
(by-election *see* page 25)

Tayside North
(Scotland Mid and Fife region)
E. 61,795 T. 61.58%
J. Swinney, SNP 16,786
M. Fraser, C. 12,594
Ms M. Dingwall, Lab. 5,727
P. Regent, LD 2,948
SNP majority 4,192

Tweeddale, Ettrick and Lauderdale
(Scotland South region)
E. 51,577 T. 65.37%
I. Jenkins, LD 12,078
Ms C. Creech, SNP 7,600
G. McGregor, Lab. 7,546
J. Campbell, C. 6,491
LD majority 4,478

Western Isles
(Highlands and Islands region)
E. 22,412 T. 62.26%
A. Morrison, Lab. 7,248
A. Nicholson, SNP 5,155
J. MacGrigor, C. 1,095
J. Horne, LD 456
Lab. majority 2,093

REGIONS

Glasgow
E. 531,956 T. 48.19%

Lab.	112,588	(43.92%)
SNP	65,360	(25.50%)
C.	20,239	(7.90%)
SSP	18,581	(7.25%)
LD	18,473	(7.21%)
Green	10,159	(3.96%)
Soc. Lab.	4,391	(1.71%)
ProLife	2,357	(0.92%)
SUP	2,283	(0.89%)
Comm. Brit.	521	(0.20%)
Humanist	447	(0.17%)
NLP	419	(0.16%)
SPGB	309	(0.12%)
Choice	221	(0.09%)

Lab. majority 47,228
(May 1997, Lab. maj. 166,061)

Additional Members
W. Aitken, C.
R. Brown, LD
Ms D. Elder, SNP
Ms S. White, SNP
Ms N. Sturgeon, SNP
K. Gibson, SNP
T. Sheridan, SSP

Highlands and Islands
E. 326,553 T. 61.76%

SNP55,	933	(27.73%)
Lab.	51,371	(25.47%)
LD	43,226	(21.43%)
C.	30,122	(14.94%)
Green	7,560	(3.75%)
Ind. Noble	3,522	(1.75%)
Soc. Lab.	2,808	(1.39%)
Highlands	2,607	(1.29%)
SSP	1,770	(0.88%)
Mission	1,151	(0.57%)
Int. Ind.	712	(0.35%)
NLP	536	(0.27%)
Ind. R.	354	(0.18%)

SNP majority 4,562
(May 1997, LD maj. 1,388)

Additional Members
J. MacGrigor, C.
Mrs M. Scanlon, C.
Ms M. MacMillan, Lab.
P. Peacock, Lab.
Ms R. Grant, Lab.
Mrs W. Ewing, SNP
D. Hamilton, SNP

Lothians

E. 539,656 T. 61.25%

Lab.	99,908 (30.23%)
SNP	85,085 (25.74%)
C.	52,067 (15.75%)
LD	47,565 (14.39%)
Green	22,848 (6.91%)
Soc. Lab.	10,895 (3.30%)
SSP	5,237 (1.58%)
Lib.	2,056 (0.62%)
Witchery	1,184 (0.36%)
ProLife	898 (0.27%)
Rights	806 (0.24%)
NLP	564 (0.17%)
Braveheart	557 (0.17%)
SPGB	388 (0.12%)
Ind. Voice	256 (0.08%)
Ind. Ind.	145 (0.04%)
Anti-Corr.	54 (0.02%)

Lab. majority 14,823
(May 1997, Lab. maj. 101,991)

Additional Members

Rt. Hon. Lord James Douglas Hamilton, C.
D. McLetchie, C.
Rt. Hon. Sir David Steel, LD
K. MacAskill, SNP
Ms M. MacDonald, SNP
Ms F. Hyslop, SNP
R. Harper, Green

Scotland Central

E. 551,733 T. 59.90%

Lab.	129,822 (39.28%)
SNP	91,802 (27.78%)
C.	30,243 (9.15%)
Falkirk W.	27,700 (8.38%)
LD	20,505 (6.20%)
Soc. Lab.	10,956 (3.32%)
Green	5,926 (1.79%)
SSP	5,739 (1.74%)
SUP	2,886 (0.87%)
ProLife	2,567 (0.78%)
SFPP	1,373 (0.42%)
NLP	719 (0.22%)
Ind. Prog.	248 (0.08%)

Lab. majority 38,020
(May 1997, Lab. maj. 143,376)

Additional Members

Mrs L. McIntosh, C.
D. Gorrie, LD
A. Neil, SNP
M. Matheson, SNP
Ms L. Fabiani, SNP
A. Wilson, SNP
G. Paterson, SNP

Scotland Mid and Fife

E. 509,387 T. 60.01%

Lab.	101,964 (33.36%)
SNP	87,659 (28.68%)
C.	56,719 (18.56%)
LD	38,896 (12.73%)
Green	11,821 (3.87%)
Soc. Lab.	4,266 (1.40%)
SSP	3,044 (1.00%)
ProLife	735 (0.24%)
NLP	558 (0.18%)

Lab. majority 14,305
(May 1997, Lab. maj. 54,087)

Additional Members

*N. Johnston, C.
B. Monteith, C.
K. Harding, C.
K. Raffan, LD
B. Crawford, SNP
G. Reid, SNP
Ms P. Marwick, SNP
*N. Johnston resigned on 10 August 2001. He was replaced by Murdo Fraser.

Scotland North East

E. 518,521 T. 55.05%

SNP	92,329 (32.35%)
Lab.	72,666 (25.46%)
C.	52,149 (18.27%)
LD	49,843 (17.46%)
Green	8,067 (2.83%)
Soc. Lab.	3,557 (1.25%)
SSP	3,016 (1.06%)
Ind. Watt.	2,303 (0.81%)
Ind. SB	770 (0.27%)
NLP	746 (0.26%)

SNP majority 19,663
(May 1997, Lab. maj. 17,518)

Additional Members

D. Davidson, C.
A. Johnstone, C.
B. Wallace, C.
R. Lochhead, SNP
Ms S. Robison, SNP
B. Adam, SNP
Ms I. McGugan, SNP

Scotland South

E. 510,634 T. 62.35%

Lab.	98,836 (31.04%)
SNP	80,059 (25.15%)
C.	68,904 (21.64%)
LD	38,157 (11.99%)
Soc. Lab.	13,887 (4.36%)
Green	9,468 (2.97%)
Lib.	3,478 (1.09%)
SSP	3,304 (1.04%)
UK Ind.	1,502 (0.47%)
NLP	775 (0.24%)

Lab. majority 18,777
(May 1997, Lab. maj. 79,585)

Additional Members

P. Gallie, C.
D. Mundell, C.
M. Tosh, C.
A. Fergusson, C.
M. Russell, SNP
A. Ingram, SNP
Ms C. Creech, SNP

Scotland West

E. 498,466 T. 62.27%

Lab.	119,663 (38.55%)
SNP	80,417 (25.91%)
C.	48,666 (15.68%)
LD	34,095 (10.98%)
Green	8,175 (2.63%)
SSP	5,944 (1.91%)
Soc. Lab.	4,472 (1.44%)
ProLife	3,227 (1.04%)
Individual	2,761 (0.89%)
SUP	1,840 (0.59%)
NLP	589 (0.19%)
Ind. Water	565 (0.18%)

Lab. majority 39,246
(May 1997, Lab. maj. 115,995)

Additional Members

Miss A. Goldie, C.
J. Young, C.
R. Finnie, LD
L. Quinan, SNP
Ms F. McLeod, SNP
Ms K. Ullrich, SNP
C. Campbell, SNP

BY ELECTIONS

Ayr

(16 March 2000)
T. 57.0%

J. Scott, C. 12,580
SNP, 9,236
Lab., 7,054
SNP, 1,345
LD, 800
Green, 460
Ind., 186
UK Ind., 113
ProLife, 111
Ind, 15
Majority, 3,344

Glasgow Anniesland

(23 November 2000)
T. 20,221

Bill Butler, Lab., 9,838
Tom Chalmers, SNP, 4,462
Kate Pickering, Scottish Conservative and Unionist, 2,148
R. Kane, Scottish Socialist Party, 1,429
Judith Fryer, LD, 1,384
Alasdair Whitelaw, Green, 662
Murdo Ritchie, Lab., 298
Majority, 5,376

Banff and Buchan

(7 June 2001)
T. 30,838

Stewart Stevenson, SNP, 15,386
Ted Brocklebank C., 6,819
Megan Harris, Lab., 4,597
Canon Kenyon Wright, LD, 3,231
Peter Anderson, SSP, 682
Majority, 8,567

Strathkelvin and Bearsden

(7 June 2001)
T. 41,734

Brian Fitzpatrick, Lab., 15,401
Jean M. Turner, Ind., 7,275
John Morrison, LD, 7,147
Janet E. Law, SNP, 6,457
Charles Ferguson, C., 5,037
Majority, 8,126

MEMBERS OF THE SCOTTISH PARLIAMENT

Adam, Brian, SNP, Scotland North East region

Aitken, William, C., Glasgow region

Alexander, Ms Wendy, Lab., Paisley North, maj. 4,616

Baillie, Ms Jackie, Lab., Dumbarton, maj. 4,758

Barrie, Scott, Lab., Dunfermline West, maj. 5,021

Boyack, Ms Sarah, Lab., Edinburgh Central, maj. 4,626

Brankin, Ms Rhona, Lab. Co-op., Midlothian, maj. 5,525

Brown, Robert, LD, Glasgow region

*Butler, Bill, Lab. Glasgow Anniesland, maj. 5,376

Campbell, Colin, SNP, Scotland West region

Canavan, Dennis A., Lab., Falkirk West, maj. 12,192

Chisholm, Malcolm G. R., Lab., Edinburgh North and Leith, maj. 7,736

Craigie, Ms Cathy, Lab., Cumbernauld and Kilsyth, maj. 4,259

Crawford, Bruce, SNP, Scotland Mid and Fife region

Cunningham, Ms Roseanna, SNP, Perth, maj. 2,027

Curran, Ms Margaret, Lab., Glasgow Baillieston, maj. 3,072

Davidson, David, C., Scotland North East region

Deacon, Ms Susan, Lab., Edinburgh East and Musselburgh, maj. 6,714

Douglas Hamilton, Rt. Hon. Lord James (The Lord Selkirk of Douglas), QC, C., Lothians region

Eadie, Ms Helen, Lab. Co-op., Dunfermline East, maj. 8,699

Elder, Ms Dorothy, SNP, Glasgow region

Ewing, Fergus, SNP, Inverness East, Nairn and Lochaber, maj. 441

Ewing, Mrs Margaret A., SNP, Moray, maj. 4,129

Ewing, Dr Winnifred, SNP, Highlands and Islands region

Fabiani, Ms Linda, SNP, Scotland Central region

Farquhar-Munro, John, LD, Ross, Skye and Inverness West, maj. 1,539

Ferguson, Ms Patricia, Lab., Glasgow Maryhill, maj. 4,326

Fergusson, Alex, C., Scotland South region

Finnie, Ross, LD, Scotland West region

*Fitzpatrick, Brian, Lab., Strathkelvin and Bearsden, maj. 8,126

Fraser, Murdo, C., Scotland Mid and Fife region

Gallie, Phil, C., Scotland South region

Gibson, Kenneth, SNP, Glasgow region

Gillon (elected as Turnbull), Ms Karen, Lab., Clydesdale, maj. 3,880

Godman, Ms Patricia, Lab., Renfrewshire West, maj. 2,893

Goldie, Miss Annabel, C., Scotland West region

Gorrie, Donald C. E., OBE, LD, Scotland Central region

Grahame (elected as Creech), Ms Christine, SNP, Scotland South region

Grant, Ms Rhoda, Lab., Highlands and Islands region

Gray, Iain, Lab., Edinburgh Pentlands, maj. 2,885

Hamilton, Duncan, SNP, Highlands and Islands region

Harding, Keith, C., Scotland Mid and Fife region

Harper, Robin, Green, Lothians region

Henry, Hugh, Lab., Paisley South, maj. 4,495

Home Robertson, John D., Lab., East Lothian, maj. 10,946

Hughes, Ms Janis, Lab., Glasgow Rutherglen, maj. 7,287

Hyslop, Ms Fiona, SNP, Lothians region

Ingram, Adam, SNP, Scotland South region

Jackson, Gordon, Lab., Glasgow Govan, maj. 1,756

Jackson, Dr Sylvia, Lab., Stirling, maj. 3,981

Jamieson, Ms Cathy, Lab. Co-op., Carrick, Cumnock and Doon Valley, maj. 8,803

Jamieson, Ms Margaret, Lab., Kilmarnock and Loudoun, maj. 2,760

Jenkins, Ian, LD, Tweeddale, Ettrick and Lauderdale, maj. 4,478

Johnstone, Alex, C., Scotland North East region

Kerr, Andy, Lab., East Kilbride, maj. 6,499

Lamont, Johann, Lab. Co-op., Glasgow Pollock, maj. 4,642

Livingstone, Ms Marilyn, Lab. Co-op., Kirkcaldy, maj. 4,475

Lochhead, Richard, SNP, Scotland North East region

Lyon, George, LD, Argyll and Bute, maj. 2,057

McAllion, John, Lab., Dundee East, maj. 2,854

MacAskill, Kenny, SNP, Lothians region

McAveety, Frank, Lab. Co-op., Glasgow Shettleston, maj. 5,467

McCabe, Tom, Lab., Hamilton South, maj. 7,176

McConnell, Jack, Lab., Motherwell and Wishaw, maj. 5,076

Macdonald, Lewis, Lab., Aberdeen Central, maj. 2,696

MacDonald, Ms Margo, SNP, Lothians region

MacGrigor, Jamie, C., Highlands and Islands region

McGugan, Ms Irene, SNP, Scotland North East region

Macintosh, Ken, Lab., Eastwood, maj. 2,125

McIntosh, Mrs Lindsay, C., Scotland Central region

Mackay, Angus, Lab., Edinburgh South, maj. 5,424

Maclean, Ms Kate, Lab., Dundee West, maj. 121

McLeish, Henry B., Lab., Fife Central, maj. 8,675

McLeod, Ms Fiona, SNP, Scotland West region

McLetchie, David, C., Lothians region

McMahon, Michael, Lab., Hamilton North and Bellshill, maj. 5,606

Macmillan, Ms Maureen, Lab., Highlands and Islands region

McNeil, Duncan, Lab., Greenock and Inverclyde, maj. 4,313

McNeill, Ms Pauline, Lab., Glasgow Kelvin, maj. 4,408

McNulty, Des, Lab., Clydebank and Milngavie, maj. 4,710

Martin, Paul, Lab., Glasgow Springburn, maj. 7,893

Marwick, Ms Tricia, SNP, Scotland Mid and Fife region

Matheson, Michael, SNP, Scotland Central region

Monteith, Brian, C., Scotland Mid and Fife region

Morgan, Alasdair N., SNP, Galloway and Upper Nithsdale, maj. 3,201

Morrison, Alasdair, Lab., Western Isles, maj. 2,093

Muldoon, Bristow, Lab., Livingston, maj. 3,904

Mulligan, Ms Mary, Lab., Linlithgow, maj. 2,928

Mundell, David, C., Scotland South region

Murray, Ms Elaine, Lab., Dumfries, maj. 3,654

Neil, Alex, SNP, Scotland Central region

Oldfather, Ms Irene, Lab., Cunninghame South, maj. 6,541

Paterson, Gil, SNP, Scotland Central region

Peacock, Peter, Lab., Highlands and Islands region

Peattie, Ms Cathy, Lab., Falkirk East, maj. 4,139

Quinan, Lloyd, SNP, Scotland West region

Radcliffe, Ms Nora, LD, Gordon, maj. 4,195

Raffan, Keith, LD, Scotland Mid and Fife region

Reid, George, SNP, Scotland Mid and Fife region

Robison, Ms Shona, SNP, Scotland North East region

Robson, Euan, LD, Roxburgh and Berwickshire, maj. 3,585

Rumbles, Mike, LD, Aberdeenshire West and Kincardine, maj. 2,289

Russell, Michael, SNP, Scotland South region

Scanlon, Mrs Mary, C., Highlands and Islands region

*Scott, John, C., Ayr, maj. 3,344

Scott, Tavish, LD, Shetland, maj. 3,194

Sheridan, Tommy, SSP, Glasgow region

Simpson, Richard, Lab., Ochil, maj. 1,303

Smith, Ms Elaine, Lab., Coatbridge and Chryston, maj. 10,404

Smith, Iain, LD, Fife North East, maj. 5,064

Smith, Ms Margaret, LD, Edinburgh West, maj. 4,583

Steel, Rt. Hon. Sir David (The Lord Steel of Aikwood), KBE, QC, LD, Lothians region

Stephen, Nicol, LD, Aberdeen South, maj. 1,760

*Stevenson, Stuart, SNP, Banff and Buchan, maj. 8,567

Stone, Jamie, LD, Caithness, Sutherland and Easter Ross, maj. 4,391

Sturgeon, Ms Nicola, SNP, Glasgow region

Swinney, John R., SNP, Tayside North, maj. 4,192

Thomson, Ms Elaine, Lab., Aberdeen North, maj. 398

Tosh, Murray, C., Scotland South region

Ullrich, Ms Kay, SNP, Scotland West region

Wallace, Ben, C., Scotland North East region

Wallace, James R., LD, Orkney, maj. 4,619

Watson, Mike (The Lord Watson of Invergowrie), Lab., Glasgow Cathcart, maj. 5,374

Welsh, Andrew P., SNP, Angus, maj. 8,901

White, Ms Sandra, SNP, Glasgow region

Whitefield, Ms Karen, Lab., Airdrie and Shotts, maj. 8,985

Wilson, Allan, Lab., Cunninghame North, maj. 4,796

Wilson, Andrew, SNP, Scotland Central region

Young, John, OBE, C., Scotland West region

* elected in by-elections, *see* above for results

Abbreviations of Party Names

Anti-Corr.	Anti-Corruption, Mobile Home Scandal, Roads
Anti-Drug	Independent Anti-Drug Party
AS	Anti-sleaze
C.	Conservative
Ch. U.	Christian Nationalist
BNP	British National Party
Comm.	Brit.Communist Party of Britain
D. Nat.	Democratic Nationalist
Falkirk W.	MP for Falkirk West
Green	Green Party
Highlands	Highlands and Islands Alliance
Ind.	Independent
Ind. Dem.	Independent Democrat
Ind. Ind.	Independent Independent
Ind. Prog.	Independent Progressive
Ind. R.	Independent Robertson
Ind. SB	Independent Sleaze-Buster

Ind. Voice	Independent Voice for Scottish Parliament
Ind. Water	Independent Labour Keep Scottish Water Public
Ind. Watt.	Independent Watt
Individual	Independent Individual
Ind. You	Independent of London: Independent for You
Lab.	Labour
Lab. Co-op.	Labour Co-operative
LD	Liberal Democrat
Mission	Scottish People's Mission
NLP	Natural Law Party
ProLife	ProLife Alliance
Ref.	Referendum Party
SCU	Scottish Conservative Unofficial
SFPP	Scottish Families and Pensioners Party
SLI	Scottish Labour Independent
SLU	Scottish Labour Unofficial
Soc. Lab.	Socialist Labour Party
SPGB	Socialist Party of Great Britain
SSA	Scottish Socialist Alliance
SNP	Scottish National Party
SSP	Scottish Socialist Party
SUP	Scottish Unionist Party
SWP	Socialist Workers Party
UK Ind.	UK Independence Party
Witchery	Witchery Tour Party
WRP	Workers' Revolutionary Party

SCOTTISH CONSTITUENCIES IN THE UK PARLIAMENT

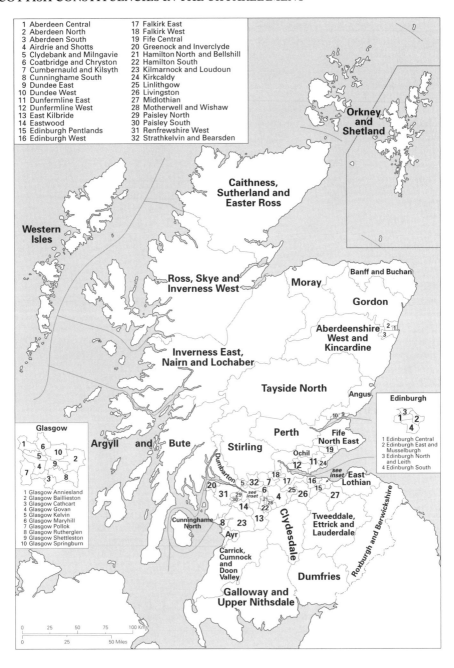

1 Aberdeen Central	17 Falkirk East
2 Aberdeen North	18 Falkirk West
3 Aberdeen South	19 Fife Central
4 Airdrie and Shotts	20 Greenock and Inverclyde
5 Clydebank and Milngavie	21 Hamilton North and Bellshill
6 Coatbridge and Chryston	22 Hamilton South
7 Cumbernauld and Kilsyth	23 Kilmarnock and Loudoun
8 Cunninghame South	24 Kirkcaldy
9 Dundee East	25 Linlithgow
10 Dundee West	26 Livingston
11 Dunfermline East	27 Midlothian
12 Dunfermline West	28 Motherwell and Wishaw
13 East Kilbride	29 Paisley North
14 Eastwood	30 Paisley South
15 Edinburgh Pentlands	31 Renfrewshire West
16 Edinburgh West	32 Strathkelvin and Bearsden

Orkney and Shetland

Caithness, Sutherland and Easter Ross

Western Isles

Ross, Skye and Inverness West

Moray

Banff and Buchan

Gordon

Aberdeenshire West and Kincardine

Inverness East, Nairn and Lochaber

Tayside North

Angus

Edinburgh
1 Edinburgh Central
2 Edinburgh East and Musselburgh
3 Edinburgh North and Leith
4 Edinburgh South

Perth

Fife North East

Stirling

Ochil

Glasgow
1 Glasgow Anniesland
2 Glasgow Baillieston
3 Glasgow Cathcart
4 Glasgow Govan
5 Glasgow Kelvin
6 Glasgow Maryhill
7 Glasgow Pollok
8 Glasgow Rutherglen
9 Glasgow Shettleston
10 Glasgow Springburn

Argyll and Bute

East Lothian

Tweeddale, Ettrick and Lauderdale

Cunninghame North

Ayr

Clydesdale

Carrick, Cumnock and Doon Valley

Dumfries

Galloway and Upper Nithsdale

Roxburgh and Berwickshire

Dumbarton

0 25 50 75 100 Kms

0 25 50 Miles

as at 7 June 2001

SCOTTISH CONSTITUENCIES
*MP in Previous Parliament

Aberdeen Central
Electorate 50,098
Turnout 26,429 (52.75%) **Lab. hold**
*Frank Doran (Lab.) 12,025**
Wayne Gault (SNP) 5,379
Ms Eleanor Anderson (LD) 4,547
Stewart Whyte (C.) 3,761
Andy Cumbers (SSP) 717
Lab. maj 6,646 (25.15%)
4.24% swing Lab. to SNP
1997: Lab. maj 10,801 (30.32%)

Aberdeen North
Electorate 52,746
Turnout 30,357 (57.55%) **Lab. hold**
*Malcolm Savidge (Lab.) 13,157**
Dr Alasdair Allan (SNP) 8,708
Jim Donaldson (LD) 4,991
Richard Cowling (C.) 3,047
Ms Shona Forman (SSP) 454
Lab. maj 4,449 (14.66%)
5.70% swing Lab. to SNP
1997: Lab. maj 10,010 (26.06%)

Aberdeen South
Electorate 58,907
Turnout 36,890 (62.62%) **Lab. hold**
*Ms Anne Begg (Lab.) 14,696**
Ian Yuill (LD) 10,308
Moray Macdonald (C.) 7,098
Ian Angus (SNP) 4,293
David Watt (SSP) 495
Lab. maj 4,388 (11.89%)
2.13% swing LD to Lab.
1997: Lab. maj 3,365 (7.64%)

**Aberdeenshire West &
Kincardine**
Electorate 61,180
Turnout 37,914 (61.97%) **LD hold**
*Sir Robert Smith (LD) 16,507**
Tom Kerr (C.) 11,686
Kevin Hutchens (Lab.) 4,669
John Green (SNP) 4,634
Alan Manley (SSP) 418
LD maj 4,821 (12.72%)
3.28% swing C. to LD
1997: LD maj 2,662 (6.16%)

Airdrie & Shotts
Electorate 58,349
Turnout 31,736 (54.39%) **Lab. hold**
*Rt. Hon. H. Liddell (Lab.) 18,478**
Ms Alison Lindsay (SNP) 6,138
John Love (LD) 2,376
Gordon McIntosh (C.) 1,960
Ms Mary Dempsey (Scot U) 1,439
Kenny McGuigan (SSP) 1,171
Chris Herriot (Soc Lab) 174
Lab. maj 12,340 (38.88%)
0.73% swing SNP to Lab.
1997: Lab. maj 15,412 (37.42%)

Angus
Electorate 59,004
Turnout 35,013 (59.34%) **SNP hold**
Michael Weir (SNP) 12,347
Marcus Booth (C.) 8,736
Ian McFatridge (Lab.) 8,183
Peter Nield (LD) 5,015
Bruce Wallace (SSP) 732
SNP maj 3,611 (10.31%)
6.67% swing SNP to C.
1997: SNP maj 10,189 (23.66%)

Argyll & Bute
Electorate 49,175
Turnout 30,957 (62.95%) **LD hold**
Alan Reid (LD) 9,245
Hugh Raven (Lab.) 7,592
David Petrie (C.) 6,436
Ms Agnes Samuel (SNP) 6,433
Des Divers (SSP) 1,251
LD maj 1,653 (5.34%)
9.60% swing LD to Lab.
1997: LD maj 6,081 (17.03%)

Ayr
Electorate 55,630
Turnout 38,560 (69.32%) **Lab. hold**
*Ms Sandra Osborne (Lab.) 16,801**
Phil Gallie (C.) 14,256
Jim Mather (SNP) 4,621
Stuart Ritchie (LD) 2,089
James Stewart (SSP) 692
Joseph Smith (UK Ind.) 101
Lab. maj 2,545 (6.60%)
4.01% swing Lab. to C.
1997: Lab. maj 6,543 (14.62%)

Banff & Buchan
Electorate 56,496
Turnout 30,806 (54.53%) **SNP hold**
*Alex Salmond (SNP) 16,710**
Alexander Wallace (C.) 6,207
Edward Harris (Lab.) 4,363

Douglas Herbison (LD) 2,769
Ms Alice Rowan (SSP) 447
Eric Davidson (UK Ind.) 310
SNP maj 10,503 (34.09%)
1.06% swing C. to SNP
1997: SNP maj 12,845 (31.97%)

Caithness, Sutherland & Easter Ross
Electorate 41,225
Turnout 24,867 (60.32%) **LD hold**
Viscount John Thurso (LD) 9,041
Michael Meighan (Lab.) 6,297
John Macadam (SNP) 5,273
Robert Rowantree (C.) 3,513
Ms Karn Mabon (SSP) 544
Gordon Campbell (Ind.) 199
LD maj 2,744 (11.03%)
1.64% swing Lab. to LD
1997: LD maj 2,259 (7.75%)

Carrick, Cumnock & Doon Valley
Electorate 64,919
Turnout 40,107 (61.78%) **Lab Co-op hold**
*George Foulkes (Lab Co-op) 22,174
Gordon Miller (C.) 7,318
Tom Wilson (SNP) 6,258
Ms Amy Rogers (LD) 2,932
Ms Amanda McFarlane (SSP) 1,058
James McDaid (Soc Lab) 367
Lab Co-op maj 14,856 (37.04%)
2.90% swing Lab Co-op to C.
1997: Lab. maj 21,062 (42.84%)

Clydebank & Milngavie
Electorate 52,534
Turnout 32,491 (61.85%) **Lab. hold**
*Tony Worthington (Lab.) 17,249
Jim Yuill (SNP) 6,525
Rod Ackland (LD) 3,909
Dr Catherine Pickering (C.) 3,514
Ms Dawn Brennan (SSP) 1,294
Lab. maj 10,724 (33.01%)
0.54% swing Lab. to SNP
1997: Lab. maj 13,320 (34.08%)

Clydesdale
Electorate 64,423
Turnout 38,222 (59.33%) **Lab. hold**
*Jimmy Hood (Lab.) 17,822
Jim Wright (SNP) 10,028
Kevin Newton (C.) 5,034
Ms Moira Craig (LD) 4,111
Paul Cockshott (SSP) 974
Donald MacKay (UK Ind.) 253
Lab. maj 7,794 (20.39%)
5.01% swing Lab. to SNP
1997: Lab. maj 13,809 (30.41%)

Coatbridge & Chryston
Electorate 52,178
Turnout 30,311 (58.09%) **Lab. hold**
*Rt. Hon. T. Clarke (Lab.) 19,807
Peter Kearney (SNP) 4,493
Alistair Tough (LD) 2,293
Patrick Ross-Taylor (C.) 2,171
Ms Lynne Sheridan (SSP) 1,547
Lab. maj 15,314 (50.52%)
0.39% swing Lab. to SNP
1997: Lab. maj 19,295 (51.30%)

Cumbernauld & Kilsyth
Electorate 49,739
Turnout 29,699 (59.71%) **Lab. hold**
*Ms Rosemary McKenna (Lab.) 16,144
David McGlashan (SNP) 8,624
John O'Donnell (LD) 1,934
Ms Alison Ross (C.) 1,460
Kenny McEwan (SSP) 1,287
Thomas Taylor (Scot Ref) 250
Lab. maj 7,520 (25.32%)
2.78% swing Lab. to SNP
1997: Lab. maj 11,128 (30.89%)

Cunninghame North
Electorate 54,993
Turnout 33,816 (61.49%) **Lab. hold**
*Brian Wilson (Lab.) 15,571
Campbell Martin (SNP) 7,173
Richard Wilkinson (C.) 6,666
Ross Chmiel (LD) 3,060
Sean Scott (SSP) 964
Ms Louise McDaid (Soc Lab) 382
Lab. maj 8,398 (24.83%)
3.51% swing Lab. to SNP
1997: Lab. maj 11,039 (26.84%)

Cunninghame South
Electorate 49,982
Turnout 28,009 (56.04%) **Lab. hold**
*Brian Donohoe (Lab.) 16,424
Bill Kidd (SNP) 5,194
Mrs Pam Paterson (C.) 2,682
John Boyd (LD) 2,094
Ms Rosemary Byrne (SSP) 1,233
Bobby Cochrane (Soc Lab) 382
Lab. maj 11,230 (40.09%)
0.93% swing Lab. to SNP
1997: Lab. maj 14,869 (41.95%)

Dumbarton
Electorate 56,267
Turnout 33,994 (60.42%) **Lab Co-op hold**
*John McFall (Lab Co-op) 16,151
Iain Robertson (SNP) 6,576
Eric Thompson (LD) 5,265

Peter Ramsay (C.) 4,648
Les Robertson (SSP) 1,354
Lab Co-op maj 9,575 (28.17%)
0.89% swing SNP to Lab. Co-op
1997: Lab. maj 10,883 (26.38%)

Dumfries
Electorate 62,931
Turnout 42,586 (67.67%) **Lab. hold**
*Russell Brown (Lab.) 20,830**
John Charteris (C.) 11,996
John Ross Scott (LD) 4,955
Gerry Fisher (SNP) 4,103
John Dennis (SSP) 702
Lab. maj 8,834 (20.74%)
0.64% swing C. to Lab.
1997: Lab. maj 9,643 (19.47%)

Dundee East
Electorate 56,535
Turnout 32,358 (57.24%) **Lab. hold**
Iain Luke (Lab.) 14,635
Stewart Hosie (SNP) 10,160
Alan Donnelly (C.) 3,900
Raymond Lawrie (LD) 2,784
Harvey Duke (SSP) 879
Lab. maj 4,475 (13.83%)
5.38% swing Lab. to SNP
1997: Lab. maj 9,961 (24.58%)

Dundee West
Electorate 53,760
Turnout 29,242 (54.39%) **Lab. hold**
*Ernie Ross (Lab.) 14,787
Gordon Archer (SNP) 7,987
Ian Hail (C.) 2,656
Ms Elizabeth Dick (LD) 2,620
Jim McFarlane (SSP) 1,192
Lab. maj 6,800 (23.25%)
3.65% swing Lab. to SNP
1997: Lab. maj 11,859 (30.56%)

Dunfermline East
Electorate 52,811
Turnout 30,086 (56.97%) **Lab. hold**
*Rt. Hon. G. Brown (Lab.) 19,487
John Mellon (SNP) 4,424
Stuart Randall (C.) 2,838
John Mainland (LD) 2,281
Andy Jackson (SSP) 770
Tom Dunsmore (UK Ind.) 286
Lab. maj 15,063 (50.07%)
0.60% swing Lab. to SNP
1997: Lab. maj 18,751 (51.26%)

Dunfermline West
Electorate 54,293
Turnout 30,975 (57.05%) **Lab. hold**
*Ms Rachel Squire (Lab.) 16,370
Brian Goodall (SNP) 5,390
Russell McPhate (LD) 4,832
James Mackie (C.) 3,166
Ms Kate Stewart (SSP) 746
Alastair Harper (UK Ind.) 471
Lab. maj 10,980 (35.45%)
0.77% swing SNP to Lab.
1997: Lab. maj 12,354 (33.91%)

East Kilbride
Electorate 66,572
Turnout 41,690 (62.62%) **Lab. hold**
*Rt. Hon. A. Ingram (Lab.) 22,205
Archie Buchanan (SNP) 9,450
Ewan Hawthorn (LD) 4,278
Mrs Margaret McCulloch (C.) 4,238
David Stevenson (SSP) 1,519
Lab. maj 12,755 (30.59%)
2.52% swing Lab. to SNP
1997: Lab. maj 17,384 (35.63%)

East Lothian
Electorate 58,987
Turnout 36,871 (62.51%) **Lab. hold**
Mrs Anne Picking (Lab.) 17,407
Hamish Mair (C.) 6,577
Ms Judy Hayman (LD) 6,506
Ms Hilary Brown (SNP) 5,381
Derrick White (SSP) 624
Jake Herriot (Soc Lab) 376
Lab. maj 10,830 (29.37%)
1.68% swing Lab. to C.
1997: Lab. maj 14,221 (32.74%)

Eastwood
Electorate 68,378
Turnout 48,368 (70.74%) **Lab. hold**
*Jim Murphy (Lab.) 23,036
Raymond Robertson (C.) 13,895
Allan Steele (LD) 6,239
Stewart Maxwell (SNP) 4,137
Peter Murray (SSP) 814
Dr Manar Tayan (Ind.) 247
Lab. maj 9,141 (18.90%)
6.35% swing C. to Lab.
1997: Lab. maj 3,236 (6.19%)

Edinburgh Central
Electorate 66,089
Turnout 34,390 (52.04%) **Lab. hold**
*Rt. Hon. A. Darling (Lab.) 14,495
Andrew Myles (LD) 6,353
Alastair Orr (C.) 5,643

Dr Ian McKee (SNP) 4,832
Graeme Farmer (Green) 1,809
Kevin Williamson (SSP) 1,258
Lab. maj 8,142 (23.68%)
5.15% swing Lab. to LD
1997: Lab. maj 11,070 (25.90%)

Edinburgh East & Musselburgh
Electorate 59,241
Turnout 34,454 (58.16%) **Lab. hold**
*Rt. Hon. Dr G. Strang (Lab.) 18,124
Rob Munn (SNP) 5,956
Gary Peacock (LD) 4,981
Peter Finnie (C.) 3,906
Derek Durkin (SSP) 1,487
Lab. maj 12,168 (35.32%)
0.41% swing SNP to Lab.
1997: Lab. maj 14,530 (34.50%)

Edinburgh North & Leith
Electorate 62,475
Turnout 33,234 (53.20%) **Lab. hold**
Mark Lazarowicz (Lab.) 15,271
Sebastian Tombs (LD) 6,454
Ms Kaukab Stewart (SNP) 5,290
Iain Mitchell (C.) 4,626
Ms Catriona Grant (SSP) 1,334
Don Jacobsen (Soc Lab) 259
Lab. maj 8,817 (26.53%)
3.67% swing Lab. to LD
1997: Lab. maj 10,978 (26.81%)

Edinburgh Pentlands
Electorate 59,841
Turnout 38,932 (65.06%) **Lab. hold**
*Dr Lynda Clark (Lab.) 15,797
Sir Malcolm Rifkind (C.) 14,055
David Walker (LD) 4,210
Stewart Gibb (SNP) 4,210
James Mearns (SSP) 555
William McMurdo (UK Ind.) 105
Lab. maj 1,742 (4.47%)
3.08% swing Lab. to C.
1997: Lab. maj 4,862 (10.63%)

Edinburgh South
Electorate 64,012
Turnout 37,166 (58.06%) **Lab. hold**
*Nigel Griffiths (Lab.) 15,671
Ms Marilyne MacLaren (LD) 10,172
Geoffrey Buchan (C.) 6,172
Ms Heather Williams (SNP) 3,683
Colin Fox (SSP) 933
Ms Linda Hendry (LCA) 535
Lab. maj 5,499 (14.80%)
7.19% swing Lab. to LD
1997: Lab. maj 11,452 (25.54%)

Edinburgh West
Electorate 61,895
Turnout 39,478 (63.78%) **LD hold**
John Barrett (LD) 16,719
Ms Elspeth Alexandra (Lab.) 9,130
Iain Whyte (C.) 8,894
Alyn Smith (SNP) 4,047
Bill Scott (SSP) 688
LD maj 7,589 (19.22%)
2.59% swing LD to Lab.
1997: LD maj 7,253 (15.22%)

Falkirk East
Electorate 57,633
Turnout 33,702 (58.48%) **Lab. hold**
*Michael Connarty (Lab.) 18,536
Ms Isabel Hutton (SNP) 7,824
Bill Stevenson (C.) 3,252
Ms Karen Utting (LD) 2,992
Tony Weir (SSP) 725
Raymond Stead (Soc Lab) 373
Lab. maj 10,712 (31.78%)
0.20% swing Lab. to SNP
1997: Lab. maj 13,385 (32.18%)

Falkirk West
Electorate 53,583
Turnout 30,891 (57.65%) **Lab. hold**
*Eric Joyce (Lab.) 16,022
David Kerr (SNP) 7,490
Simon Murray (C.) 2,321
Hugh O'Donnell (LD) 2,203
William Buchanan (Ind B) 1,464
Ms Mhairi McAlpine (SSP) 707
Hugh Lynch (Ind.) 490
Ronnie Forbes (Soc Lab) 194
Lab. maj 8,532 (27.62%)
4.15% swing Lab. to SNP
2000 Dec by-election: Lab. maj 705 (3.61%)
1997: Lab. maj 13,783 (35.92%)

Fife Central
Electorate 59,597
Turnout 32,512 (54.55%) **Lab. hold**
John MacDougall (Lab.) 18,310
David Alexander (SNP) 8,235
Ms Elizabeth Riches (LD) 2,775
Jeremy Balfour (C.) 2,351
Ms Morag Balfour (SSP) 841
Lab. maj 10,075 (30.99%)
1.33% swing Lab. to SNP
1997: Lab. maj 13,713 (33.64%)

Fife North East
Electorate 61,900
Turnout 34,692 (56.05%) **LD hold**
*Rt. Hon. M. Campbell (LD) 17,926

Mike Scott-Hayward (C.) 8,190
Ms Claire Brennan (Lab.) 3,950
Ms Kris Murray-Browne (SNP) 3,596
Keith White (SSP) 610
Mrs Leslie Von Goetz (LCA) 420
LD maj 9,736 (28.06%)
1.66% swing C. to LD
1997: LD maj 10,356 (24.75%)

Galloway & Upper Nithsdale
Electorate 52,756
Turnout 35,914 (68.08%) **Con gain**
Peter Duncan (C.) 12,222
Malcolm Fleming (SNP) 12,148
Thomas Sloan (Lab.) 7,258
Neil Wallace (LD) 3,698
Andy Harvey (SSP) 588
C. maj 74 (0.21%)
6.80% swing SNP to C.
1997: SNP maj 5,624 (13.39%)

Glasgow Anniesland
Electorate 53,290
Turnout 26,722 (50.14%) **Lab. hold**
*****John Robertson (Lab.) 15,102**
Grant Thoms (SNP) 4,048
Christopher McGinty (LD) 3,244
Stewart Connell (C.) 2,651
Charlie McCarthy (SSP) 1,486
Ms Katherine McGavigan (Soc Lab) 191
Lab. maj 11,054 (41.37%)
1.68% swing Lab. to SNP
2000 Nov by-election: Lab. maj 6,337 (31.35%)
1997: Lab. maj 15,154 (44.73%)

Glasgow Baillieston
Electorate 49,268
Turnout 23,261 (47.21%) **Lab. hold**
*****Jimmy Wray (Lab.) 14,200**
Lachlan McNeill (SNP) 4,361
David Comrie (C.) 1,580
Jim McVicar (SSP) 1,569
Charles Dundas (LD) 1,551
Lab. maj 9,839 (42.30%)
2.15% swing Lab. to SNP
1997: Lab. maj 14,840 (46.59%)

Glasgow Cathcart
Electorate 52,094
Turnout 27,386 (52.57%) **Lab. hold**
Tom Harris (Lab.) 14,902
Mrs Josephine Docherty (SNP) 4,086
Richard Cook (C.) 3,662
Tom Henery (LD) 3,006
Ronnie Stevenson (SSP) 1,730
Lab. maj 10,816 (39.49%)
1.80% swing SNP to Lab.
1997: Lab. maj 12,245 (35.90%)

Glasgow Govan
Electorate 54,068
Turnout 25,284 (46.76%) **Lab. hold**
*****Mohammad Sarwar (Lab.) 12,464**
Ms Karen Neary (SNP) 6,064
Bob Stewart (LD) 2,815
Mark Menzies (C.) 2,167
Willie McGartland (SSP) 1,531
John Foster (Comm) 174
Badar Mirza (Ind.) 69
Lab. maj 6,400 (25.31%)
8.14% swing SNP to Lab.
1997: Lab. maj 2,914 (9.04%)

Glasgow Kelvin
Electorate 61,534
Turnout 26,802 (43.56%) **Lab. hold**
*****George Galloway (Lab.) 12,014**
Ms Tamsin Mayberry (LD) 4,754
Frank Rankin (SNP) 4,513
Miss Davina Rankin (C.) 2,388
Ms Heather Ritchie (SSP) 1,847
Tim Shand (Green) 1,286
Lab. maj 7,260 (27.09%)
4.85% swing Lab. to LD
1997: Lab. maj 9,665 (29.60%)

Glasgow Maryhill
Electorate 55,431
Turnout 22,231 (40.11%) **Lab. hold**
Ms Ann McKechin (Lab.) 13,420
Alex Dingwall (SNP) 3,532
Stuart Callison (LD) 2,372
Gordon Scott (SSP) 1,745
Gawain Towler (C.) 1,162
Lab. maj 9,888 (44.48%)
1.76% swing Lab. to SNP
1997: Lab. maj 14,264 (47.99%)

Glasgow Pollok
Electorate 49,201
Turnout 25,277 (51.37%) **Lab Co-op hold**
*****Ian Davidson (Lab Co-op) 15,497**
David Ritchie (SNP) 4,229
Keith Baldassara (SSP) 2,522
Ms Isabel Nelson (LD) 1,612
Rory O'Brien (C.) 1,417
Lab Co-op maj 11,268 (44.58%)
1.27% swing SNP to Lab. Co-op
1997: Lab. maj 13,791 (42.04%)

Glasgow Rutherglen
Electorate 51,855
Turnout 29,213 (56.34%) **Lab Co-op hold**
*****Tommy McAvoy (Lab. Co-op) 16,760**
Ms Anne McLaughlin (SNP) 4,135

David Jackson (LD) 3,689
Malcolm Macaskill (C.) 3,301
Bill Bonnar (SSP) 1,328
Lab Co-op maj 12,625 (43.22%)
0.48% swing SNP to Lab. Co-op
1997: Lab. maj 15,007 (42.25%)

Glasgow Shettleston
Electorate 51,557
Turnout 20,465 (39.69%) **Lab. hold**
*****David Marshall (Lab.) 13,235**
Jim Byrne (SNP) 3,417
Ms Rosie Kane (SSP) 1,396
Lewis Hutton (LD) 1,105
Campbell Murdoch (C.) 1,082
Murdo Ritchie (Soc Lab) 230
Lab. maj 9,818 (47.97%)
5.60% swing Lab. to SNP
1997: Lab. maj 15,868 (59.18%)

Glasgow Springburn
Electorate 55,192
Turnout 24,104 (43.67%) **Speaker hold**
*****Rt. Hon. M. Martin (Speaker) 16,053**
Sandy Bain (SNP) 4,675
Ms Carolyn Leckie (SSP) 1,879
Daniel Houston (Scot U) 1,289
Richard Silvester (Ind.) 20
Speaker maj 11,378 (47.20%)
1997: Lab. maj 17,326 (54.87%)

Gordon
Electorate 59,996
Turnout 35,001 (58.34%) **LD hold**
*****Malcolm Bruce (LD) 15,928**
Mrs Nanette Milne (C.) 8,049
Mrs Rhona Kemp (SNP) 5,760
Ellis Thorpe (Lab.) 4,730
John Sangster (SSP) 534
LD maj 7,879 (22.51%)
2.97% swing C. to LD
1997: LD maj 6,997 (16.57%)

Greenock & Inverclyde
Electorate 47,884
Turnout 28,419 (59.35%) **Lab. hold**
David Cairns (Lab.) 14,929
Chic Brodie (LD) 5,039
Andrew Murie (SNP) 4,248
Alistair Haw (C.) 3,000
Davey Landels (SSP) 1,203
Lab. maj 9,890 (34.80%)
3.77% swing Lab. to LD
1997: Lab. maj 13,040 (37.59%)

Hamilton North & Bellshill
Electorate 53,539
Turnout 30,404 (56.79%) **Lab. hold**
*****Rt. Hon. Dr J. Reid (Lab.) 18,786**
Chris Stephens (SNP) 5,225
Bill Frain Bell (C.) 2,649
Keith Legg (LD) 2,360
Ms Shareen Blackall (SSP) 1,189
Steve Mayes (Soc Lab) 195
Lab. maj 13,561 (44.60%)
0.16% swing Lab. to SNP
1997: Lab. maj 17,067 (44.92%)

Hamilton South
Electorate 46,665
Turnout 26,750 (57.32%) **Lab. hold**
*****Bill Tynan (Lab.) 15,965**
John Wilson (SNP) 5,190
John Oswald (LD) 2,381
Neil Richardson (C.) 1,876
Ms Gena Mitchell (SSP) 1,187
Ms Janice Murdoch (UK Ind.) 151
Lab. maj 10,775 (40.28%)
3.85% swing Lab. to SNP
1999 Sep by-election: Lab. maj 556 (2.86%)
1997: Lab. maj 15,878 (47.98%)

Inverness East, Nairn & Lochaber
Electorate 67,139
Turnout 42,461 (63.24%) **Lab. hold**
*****David Stewart (Lab.) 15,605**
Angus MacNeil (SNP) 10,889
Ms Patsy Kenton (LD) 9,420
Richard Jenkins (C.) 5,653
Steve Arnott (SSP) 894
Lab. maj 4,716 (11.11%)
3.10% swing SNP to Lab.
1997: Lab. maj 2,339 (4.90%)

Kilmarnock & Loudoun
Electorate 61,049
Turnout 37,665 (61.70%) **Lab. hold**
*****Des Browne (Lab.) 19,926**
John Brady (SNP) 9,592
Donald Reece (C.) 3,943
John Stewart (LD) 3,177
Jason Muir (SSP) 1,027
Lab. maj 10,334 (27.44%)
6.07% swing SNP to Lab.
1997: Lab. maj 7,256 (15.30%)

Kirkcaldy
Electorate 51,559
Turnout 28,157 (54.61%) **Lab Co-op hold**
*****Dr Lewis Moonie (Lab Co-op) 15,227**
Ms Shirley-Anne Somerville (SNP) 6,264
Scott Campbell (C.) 3,013

Andrew Weston (LD) 2,849
Dougie Kinnear (SSP) 804
Lab Co-op maj 8,963 (31.83%)
0.60% swing SNP to Lab. Co-op
1997: Lab. maj 10,710 (30.63%)

Linlithgow
Electorate 54,599
Turnout 31,655 (57.98%) **Lab. hold**
Tam Dalyell (Lab.) 17,207
Jim Sibbald (SNP) 8,078
Gordon Lindhurst (C.) 2,836
Martin Oliver (LD) 2,628
Eddie Cornoch (SSP) 695
Ms Helen Cronin (R & R Loony) 211
Lab. maj 9,129 (28.84%)
0.75% swing SNP to Lab.
1997: Lab. maj 10,838 (27.33%)

Livingston
Electorate 64,850
Turnout 36,033 (55.56%) **Lab. hold**
Rt. Hon. R. Cook (Lab.) 19,108
Graham Sutherland (SNP) 8,492
Gordon Mackenzie (LD) 3,969
Ian Mowat (C.) 2,995
Ms Wendy Milne (SSP) 1,110
Robert Kingdon (UK Ind.) 359
Lab. maj 10,616 (29.46%)
1.02% swing SNP to Lab.
1997: Lab. maj 11,747 (27.43%)

Midlothian
Electorate 48,625
Turnout 28,724 (59.07%) **Lab. hold**
David Hamilton (Lab.) 15,145
Ian Goldie (SNP) 6,131
Ms Jacqueline Bell (LD) 3,686
Robin Traquair (C.) 2,748
Bob Goupillot (SSP) 837
Terence Holden (ProLife 177
Lab. maj 9,014 (31.38%)
1.69% swing SNP to Lab.
1997: Lab. maj 9,870 (28.00%)

Moray
Electorate 58,008
Turnout 33,223 (57.27%) **SNP hold**
Angus Robertson (SNP) 10,076
Mrs Catriona Munro (Lab.) 8,332
Frank Spencer-Nairn (C.) 7,677
Ms Linda Gorn (LD) 5,224
Ms Norma Anderson (SSP) 821
Bill Jappy (Ind.) 802
Nigel Kenyon (UK Ind.) 291
SNP maj 1,744 (5.25%)
8.25% swing SNP to Lab.
1997: SNP maj 5,566 (14.00%)

Motherwell & Wishaw
Electorate 52,418
Turnout 29,673 (56.61%) **Lab. hold**
Frank Roy (Lab.) 16,681
Jim McGuigan (SNP) 5,725
Mark Nolan (C.) 3,155
Iain Brown (LD) 2,791
Stephen Smellie (SSP) 1,260
Ms Claire Watt (Soc Lab) 61
Lab. maj 10,956 (36.92%)
1.00% swing SNP to Lab.
1997: Lab. maj 12,791 (34.93%)

Ochil
Electorate 57,554
Turnout 35,303 (61.34%) **Lab. hold**
Martin O'Neill (Lab.) 16,004
Keith Brown (SNP) 10,655
Alasdair Campbell (C.) 4,235
Paul Edie (LD) 3,253
Ms Pauline Thompson (SSP) 751
Flash Gordon Approaching (Loony) 405
Lab. maj 5,349 (15.15%)
2.26% swing SNP to Lab.
1997: Lab. maj 4,652 (10.63%)

Orkney & Shetland
Electorate 31,909
Turnout 16,733 (52.44%) **LD hold**
Alistair Carmichael (LD) 6,919
Robert Mochrie (Lab.) 3,444
John Firth (C.) 3,121
John Mowat (SNP) 2,473
Peter Andrews (SSP) 776
LD maj 3,475 (20.77%)
6.48% swing LD to Lab.
1997: LD maj 6,968 (33.72%)

Paisley North
Electorate 47,994
Turnout 27,153 (56.58%) **Lab. hold**
Ms Irene Adams (Lab.) 15,058
George Adam (SNP) 5,737
Ms Jane Hook (LD) 2,709
Craig Stevenson (C.) 2,404
Jim Halfpenny (SSP) 982
Robert Graham (ProLife) 263
Lab. maj 9,321 (34.33%)
1.61% swing Lab. to SNP
1997: Lab. maj 12,814 (37.54%)

Paisley South
Electorate 53,351
Turnout 30,536 (57.24%) **Lab. hold**
Douglas Alexander (Lab.) 17,830
Brian Lawson (SNP) 5,920
Brian O'Malley (LD) 3,178

Andrew Cossar (C.) 2,301
Ms Frances Curran (SSP) 835
Ms Patricia Graham (ProLife) 346
Terence O'Donnell (Ind.) 126
Lab. maj 11,910 (39.00%)
2.44% swing SNP to Lab.
1997 Nov by-election: Lab. maj 2,731 (11.65%)
1997: Lab. maj 12,750 (34.13%)

Perth
Electorate 61,497
Turnout 37,816 (61.49%) **SNP hold**
Ms Annabelle Ewing (SNP) 11,237
Miss Elizabeth Smith (C.) 11,189
Ms Marion Dingwall (Lab.) 9,638
Ms Vicki Harris (LD) 4,853
Frank Byrne (SSP) 899
SNP maj 48 (0.13%)
3.46% swing SNP to C.
1997: SNP maj 3,141 (7.05%)

Renfrewshire West
Electorate 52,889
Turnout 33,497 (63.33%) **Lab gain**
James Sheridan (Lab.) 15,720
Ms Carol Puthucheary (SNP) 7,145
David Sharpe (C.) 5,522
Ms Clare Hamblen (LD) 4,185
Ms Arlene Nunnery (SSP) 925
Lab. maj 8,575 (25.60%)
2.77% swing SNP to Lab.
1997: Lab. maj 7,979 (20.05%)

Ross, Skye & Inverness West
Electorate 56,522
Turnout 34,812 (61.59%) **LD hold**
*Rt. Hon. C. Kennedy (LD) 18,832
Donald Crichton (Lab.) 5,880
Ms Jean Urquhart (SNP) 4,901
Angus Laing (C.) 3,096
Dr Eleanor Scott (Green) 699
Stuart Topp (SSP) 683
Philip Anderson (UK Ind.) 456
James Crawford (Country) 265
LD maj 12,952 (37.21%)
13.57% swing Lab. to LD
1997: LD maj 4,019 (10.06%)

Roxburgh & Berwickshire
Electorate 47,059
Turnout 28,797 (61.19%) **LD hold**
*Archy Kirkwood (LD) 14,044
George Turnbull (C.) 6,533
Ms Catherine Maxwell-Stuart (Lab.) 4,498
Roderick Campbell (SNP) 2,806
Ms Amanda Millar (SSP) 463
Peter Neilson (UK Ind.) 453

LD maj 7,511 (26.08%)
1.73% swing C. to LD
1997: LD maj 7,906 (22.63%)

Stirling
Electorate 53,097
Turnout 35,930 (67.67%) **Lab. hold**
*Ms Anne McGuire (Lab.) 15,175
Geoff Mawdsley (C.) 8,901
Ms Fiona Macaulay (SNP) 5,877
Clive Freeman (LD) 4,208
Dr Clarke Mullen (SSP) 1,012
Mark Ruskell (Green) 757
Lab. maj 6,274 (17.46%)
1.27% swing C. to Lab.
1997: Lab. maj 6,411 (14.93%)

Strathkelvin & Bearsden
Electorate 62,729
Turnout 41,486 (66.14%) **Lab. hold**
John Lyons (Lab.) 19,250
Gordon Macdonald (LD) 7,533
Calum Smith (SNP) 6,675
Murray Roxburgh (C.) 6,635
Willie Telfer (SSP) 1,393
Lab. maj 11,717 (28.24%)
7.44% swing Lab. to LD
1997: Lab. maj 16,292 (32.77%)

Tayside North
Electorate 61,645
Turnout 38,517 (62.48%) **SNP hold**
Peter Wishart (SNP) 15,441
Murdo Fraser (C.) 12,158
Thomas Docherty (Lab.) 5,715
Ms Julia Robertson (LD) 4,363
Ms Rosie Adams (SSP) 620
Ms Tina MacDonald (Ind.) 220
SNP maj 3,283 (8.52%)
0.30% swing SNP to C.
1997: SNP maj 4,160 (9.13%)

Tweeddale, Ettrick & Lauderdale
Electorate 51,966
Turnout 33,217 (63.92%) **LD hold**
*Michael Moore (LD) 14,035
Keith Geddes (Lab.) 8,878
Andrew Brocklehurst (C.) 5,118
Richard Thomson (SNP) 4,108
Norman Lockhart (SSP) 695
John Hein (Lib) 383
LD maj 5,157 (15.53%)
5.86% swing Lab. to LD
1997: LD maj 1,489 (3.81%)

Western Isles
Electorate 21,807
Turnout 13,159 (60.34%) **Lab. hold**
*Calum MacDonald (Lab.) 5,924
Alasdair Nicholson (SNP) 4,850
Douglas Taylor (C.) 1,250
John Horne (LD) 849
Ms Joanne Telfer (SSP) 286
Lab. maj 1,074 (8.16%)
7.02% swing Lab. to SNP
1997: Lab. maj 3,576 (22.20%)

The UK Parliament

MEMBERS FOR SCOTTISH SEATS

*Member of last Parliament

*Adams, Irene; JP, (b. 1947), Lab., Paisley North, maj. 9,321

*Alexander, Douglas, (b. 1967), Lab., Paisley South, maj. 11,910

Barrett, John, (b. 1954), LD, Edinburgh West, maj. 7,589

*Begg, Anne, (b. 1955), Lab., Aberdeen South, maj. 4,388

*Brown, Rt. Hon. Gordon, (b. 1951), Lab., Dunfermline East, maj. 15,063

*Brown, Russell, (b. 1951), Lab., Dumfries, maj. 8,834

*Browne, Des, (b. 1952), Lab., Kilmarnock and Loudoun, maj. 10,334

*Bruce, Malcolm, (b. 1944), LD, Gordon, maj. 7,879

Cairns, David, (b. 1966), Lab., Greenock and Inverclyde, maj. 9,890

*Campbell, Rt. Hon. Menzies; CBE, QC, (b.1941), LD, Fife North East, maj. 9,736

Carmichael, Alistair, (b.1965), LD, Orkney and Shetland, maj. 3,475

*Clark, Lynda; QC, (b. 1949), Lab., Edinburgh Pentlands, maj. 1,742

*Clarke, Rt. Hon. Tom; CBE, JP, (b. 1941), Lab., Coatbridge and Chryston, maj. 15,314

*Connarty, Michael, (b. 1947), Lab., Falkirk East, maj. 10,712

*Cook, Rt. Hon. Robin, (b. 1946), Lab., Livingston, maj. 10,616

*Dalyell, Tam, (b. 1932), Lab., Linlithgow, maj. 9,129

*Darling, Rt. Hon. Alistair, (b. 1953), Lab., Edinburgh Central, maj. 8,142

*Davidson, Ian, (b. 1950), Lab./Co-operative, Glasgow Pollok, maj. 11,268

*Donohoe, Brian, (b. 1948), Lab., Cunninghame South, maj. 11,230

*Doran, Frank, (b.1949), Lab., Aberdeen Central, maj. 6,646

Duncan, Peter, (b. 1965), C., Galloway and Upper Nithsdale, maj, 74

Ewing, Annabelle, (b. 1960), SNP, Perth, maj. 48

*Foulkes, George, (b. 1942), Lab./Co-operative, Carrick, Cumnock and Doon Valley, maj. 14,856

*Galloway, George, (b. 1954), Lab., Glasgow Kelvin, maj. 7,260

*Griffiths, Nigel, (b. 1955), Lab., Edinburgh South, maj. 5,499

Hamilton, David, (b. 1950), Lab., Midlothian, maj. 9,014

Harris, Tom, (b. 1964), Lab., Glasgow Cathcart, maj. 10,816

*Hood, Jimmy, (b. 1948), Lab., Clydesdale, maj. 7,794

*Ingram, Rt. Hon. Adam; JP, (b. 1947), Lab., East Kilbride, maj. 12,755

Joyce, Eric, (b. 1960), Lab., Falkirk West, maj. 8,532

*Kennedy, Rt. Hon. Charles, (b. 1959), LD, Ross, Skye and Inverness West, maj. 12,952

*Kirkwood, Archy, (b. 1946), LD, Roxburgh and Berwickshire, maj. 7,511

Lazarowicz, Mark, (b. 1953), Lab., Edinburgh North and Leith, maj. 8,817

*Liddell, Rt. Hon. Helen, (b. 1950), Lab., Airdrie and Shotts, Maj. 12,340

Luke, Iain, (b. 1951), Lab., Dundee East, maj. 4,475

Lyons, John, (b. 1950), Lab., Strathkelvin and Bearsden, maj. 11,717

*MacDonald, Calum, (b. 1956), Lab., Western Isles, maj. 1,074

MacDougall, John, (b. 1947), Lab., Fife Central, maj. 10,075

*Marshall, David, (b. 1941), Lab., Glasgow Shettleston, maj. 9,818

*Martin, Rt. Hon. Michael J, (b. 1945), Speaker, Glasgow Springburn, maj. 11,378

*McAvoy, Thomas, (b. 1943), Lab./Co-operative, Glasgow Rutherglen, maj. 12,625

*McFall, John, (b. 1944), Lab./Co-operative, Dumbarton, maj. 9,575

*McGuire, Anne, (b. 1949), Lab., Stirling, maj. 6,274

McKechin, Ann, (b. 1961), Lab., Glasgow Maryhill, maj. 9,888

*McKenna, Rosemary; CBE, (b. 1941), Lab., Cumbernauld and Kilsyth, maj. 7,520

*Moonie, Dr Lewis, (b. 1947), Lab./Co-operative, Kirkcaldy, maj. 8,963

*Moore, Michael, (b. 1965), LD, Tweeddale, Ettrick and Lauderdale, maj. 5,157

*Murphy, Jim, (b. 1967), Lab., Eastwood, maj. 9,141

*O'Neill, Martin, (b. 1945), Lab., Ochil, maj. 5,349

*Osborne, Sandra, (b. 1956), Lab., Ayr, maj. 2,545

Picking, Anne, (b. 1958), Lab., East Lothian, maj. 10,830

Reid, Alan, (b. 1954), LD, Argyll and Bute, maj. 1,653

*Reid, Rt. Hon. Dr John, (b. 1947), Lab., Hamilton North and Bellshill, maj. 13,561

Robertson, Angus, (b. 1969), SNP, Moray, maj. 1,744

Robertson, John, (b. 1952), Lab., Glasgow Anniesland, maj. 11,054

*Ross, Ernie, (b. 1942), Lab., Dundee West, maj. 6,800

*Roy, Frank, (b. 1958), Lab., Motherwell and Wishaw, maj. 10,956

*Salmond, Alex, (b. 1954), SNP, Banff and Buchan, maj. 10,503

*Sarwar, Mohammed, (b. 1952), Lab., Glasgow Govan, maj. 6,400

*Savidge, Malcolm; JP, (b. 1946), Lab., Aberdeen North, maj. 4,449

Sheridan, Jim, (b. 1952), Lab., Renfrewshire West, maj. 8,575

*Smith, Sir Robert, Bt. (b. 1958), LD, Aberdeenshire West and Kincardine, maj. 4,821

*Squire, Rachel, (b. 1954), Lab., Dunfermline West, maj. 10,980

*Stewart, David, (b. 1956), Lab., Inverness East, Nairn and Lochaber, maj. 4,716

*Strang, Rt. Hon. Dr Gavin, (b. 1943), Lab., Edinburgh East and Musselburgh, maj. 12,168

Thurso, John, Viscount (b. 1953), LD, Caithness, Sutherland and Easter Ross, maj. 2,744

Tynan, Bill, (b. 1940), Lab., Hamilton South, maj. 10,775

Weir, Michael, (b. 1957), SNP, Angus, maj. 3,611

*Wilson, Brian, (b. 1948), Lab., Cunninghame North, maj. 8,398

Wishart, Peter, (b. 1962), SNP, Tayside North, maj. 3,283

*Worthington, Tony, (b. 1941), Lab., Clydebank and Milngavie, maj. 10,724

*Wray, James, (b. 1938), Lab., Glasgow Baillieston, maj. 9,839

OTHER GOVERNMENT DEPARTMENTS AND PUBLIC OFFICES

This section details executive agencies of the Scottish Executive, regulatory bodies, tribunals and other statutory independent organisations and non-governmental public bodies. UK Civil Service departments and public bodies are included where their remit continues to extend to Scotland.

ADJUDICATOR'S OFFICE

Haymarket House, 28 Haymarket, London SW1Y 4SP (Tel: 020-7930 2292; Fax: 020-7930 2298; E-mail: adjudicators@gtnet.gov.uk Web: www.open.gov.uk/adjolt/acctemo1.htm)

The Adjudicator's Office investigates complaints about the way the Inland Revenue (including the Valuation Office Agency) and Customs and Excise have handled an individual's affairs.
The Adjudicator: Dame Barbara Mills, DBE, QC
Head of Office: C. Gordon

ADVISORY COMMITTEE ON SITES OF SPECIAL SCIENTIFIC INTEREST

c/o Scottish Natural Heritage, 2 Anderson Place, Edinburgh EH6 5NP (Tel: 0131-446 2436; Fax: 0131-446 2405)

The Committee advises Scottish Natural Heritage in cases where there are sustained scientific objections to the notification of Sites of Special Scientific Interest.
Chairman: Prof. W. Ritchie
Secretary: D. Howell

ADVISORY, CONCILIATION AND ARBITRATION SERVICE

Regional Office: Franborough House, 123—157 Bothwell Street, Glasgow G2 7JR (Tel: 0141-204 2677; Fax: 0141-221 4697; Web: www.acas.org.uk)

The Advisory, Conciliation and Arbitration Service (ACAS) promotes the improvement of industrial relations in general, provides facilities for conciliation, mediation and arbitration as means of avoiding and resolving industrial disputes, and provides advisory and information services on industrial relations matters to employers, employees and their representatives.
Director, Scotland: F. Blair

ANCIENT MONUMENTS BOARD FOR SCOTLAND

Longmore House, Salisbury Place, Edinburgh EH9 1SH (Tel: 0131-668 8764; Fax: 0131-668 8765)

The Ancient Monuments Board for Scotland advises the Scottish Ministers, under the Ancient Monuments and Archaeological Areas Act 1979, providing protection for monuments of national importance.
Chairman: Prof. Michael Lynch, MA, Ph.D., FRSE, FSA Scot FRHistS
Members: Dr Colleen Batey, PhD, FSA Scot, MIFA; Michael Baughan; Dr Jeanne Cannizzo, Ph.D.; Ms Jill Harden, FSA, FSA Scot.; John C. Higgitt, FSA, FSA Scot.; Cllr Jean McFadden, CBE; Roger J. Mercer, FRSE, FSA, FSA Scot., MA; Prof. Christopher D. Morris, FRSE, FSA, FSA Scot., FRSA; Dr Scott Peake, Ph.D.; Allan Saville, FSA, FSA Scot, MIFA; Cllr Eoin F. Scott, FSA Scot, JP; Dr Carol Swanson, Ph.D., FSA Scot, MA; Malcolm J. Taylor, TD, FRICS; Miss Lisbeth M. Thoms, FSA Scot.; Andrew Wright, FRSA, FSA Scot.
Secretary: Ronald A. J. Dalziel
Assessor: Dr David J. Breeze, Ph.D., FRSE, FSA, FSA Scot., FRSA, FSA Scot

THE APPEALS SERVICE

Whittington House, 19—30 Alfred Place, London WC1E 7LW (Tel: 020-7712 2600)

The Service is responsible for the functioning of tribunals hearing appeals concerning child support assessments, social security benefits and vaccine damage payments. Judicial authority for the service rests with the President, while administrative responsibility is exercised by the Appeals Service Agency, which is an executive agency of the Department for Work and Pensions.
President: His Hon. Judge Michael Harris
Chief Executive, Appeals Service Agency: N. Ward
Regional Chairman for Scotland: K. Kirkwood
Operation Director for Scotland: B. Craig

AUDIT SCOTLAND

110 George Street, Edinburgh EH2 4LH (Tel: 0131-477 1234; Fax: 0131-477 4567)

Audit Scotland was set up on 1 April 2000. It provides audit and other services to the Accounts Commission and the Auditor General. Its principal work is the external audit of the Scottish Executive, local authorities, NHS bodies and

further education colleges to ensure the proper, efficient and effective use of public funds. Audit Scotland carries out financial and regularity audits to ensure that public sector bodies adhere to the highest standards of financial management and governance and performance audits to ensure that these bodies achieve the best possible value for money. All of Audit Scotland's work concerning the 32 local authorities, fire and police boards is carried out for the Accounts Commission while its other work is undertaken for the Auditor General.
Auditor General: Robert W. Black
Controller of Audit: Ronnie Hinds
Secretary: William F. Magee

THE BANK OF ENGLAND

Threadneedle Street, London EC2R 8AH
(Tel: 020-7601 4444; Fax 020-7601 4771;
Web: www.bankofengland.co.uk)

The Bank of England is the banker of the UK Government and manages the note issue. Since 1997 its Monetary Policy Committee has had responsibility for setting short-term interest rates to meet the Government's inflation target. As the central reserve bank of the country, the Bank keeps the accounts of British banks, who maintain with it a proportion of their cash resources, and of most overseas central banks.
Governor: The Rt. Hon. E. A. J. George, GBE
Monetary Policy Committee: The Governor; the Deputy Governors; Mr D. Clementi; M. King; C. Allsopp; K. Barker; C. Bean; Prof. S. Nickell; I. Plenderleith; J. Vickers; Dr S. Wadhwani
Chief Cashier and Deputy Director, Banking and Market Services: Ms M. V. Lowther

Scotland Agency

19 St Vincent Place, Glasgow G1 2DT
(Tel: 0141-221797)
Scotland Agent: Ms J. Bulloch
Deputy Agent: Ms C. Brown

BENEFITS AGENCY

Quarry House, Quarry Hill, Leeds LS2 7UA
(Tel: 0113-232 4000)

The Agency is an executive agency of the Department of Work and Pensions. It administers claims for and payments of social security benefits.
Chief Executive: Ms A. Cleveland
Directors: Charlie Mackinnon (Field Operations, Scotland and North); Tony Edge (Field Operations, South); Peter Ward (Performance Management); Phil Bartlett (Business Management)

MEDICAL POLICY
Principal Medical Officers: Dr M. Aylward; Dr P. Dewis; Dr P. Sawney; Dr A. Braidwood; Dr P. Stidolph; Dr R. Thomas; Dr M. Allerton; Dr S. Reed; Dr P. Wright; Dr M. Henderson

BOUNDARY COMMISSION FOR SCOTLAND

3 Drumsheugh Gardens, Edinburgh EH3 7QJ
(Tel: 0131-538 7200; Fax: 0131-538 7240)

The Commission is required by law to keep the parliamentary constituencies in Scotland under review. The latest review was completed in 1995 and its proposals took effect at the 1997 general election. The next review is due to be completed between 2002 and 2006.
Chairman (ex officio): The Speaker of the House of Commons
Deputy Chairman: The Hon. Lady Cosgrove
Secretary: R. Smith

BRITISH BROADCASTING CORPORATION

Broadcasting House, Portland Place, London W1A 1AA (Tel: 020-7580 4468; Fax: 020-7637 1630)

The BBC is the UK's public broadcasting organisation. It is financed by revenue from receiving licences for the home services and by grant-in-aid from Parliament for the World Service (radio). For services, *see* Media section.

BBC SCOTLAND

BBC Broadcasting House, Queen Margaret Drive, Glasgow G12 8DG (Tel: 0141-339 8844)
National Governor for Scotland: N. Drummond
Director, National and Regional Broadcasting: M. Thompson
Controller, BBC Scotland: J. McCormick

BRITISH WATERWAYS

Willow Grange, Church Road, Watford, Herts WD17 4QA (Tel: 01923-226422; Fax: 01923-201400; E-mail: info@canalshq.demon.co.uk Web: www.britishwaterways.co.uk)

British Waterways conserves and manages over 2,000 miles/3,250 km of canals and rivers in Great Britain. Its responsibilities include maintaining the waterways and structures on and around them; looking after wildlife and the waterway environment; and ensuring that canals and rivers are safe and enjoyable places to visit.

Chairman (part-time): G. Greener
Chief Executive: D. Fletcher

Scottish Office

Canal House, Applecross Street, Glasgow G4 9SP (Tel: 0141-354 7501; Fax: 0141-331 1688)

BUILDING STANDARDS ADVISORY COMMITTEE

Scottish Executive Building Standards Division, 2-H Victoria Quay, Edinburgh EH6 6QQ (Tel: 0131-244 7440; Fax: 0131-244 7454)

The Committee advises the Scottish Ministers on questions relating to their functions under Part II of the Building (Scotland) Act 1959.

Chairman: Dr S. Thorburn
Secretary: J. Carter

CENTRAL ADVISORY COMMITTEE ON JUSTICES OF THE PEACE (SCOTLAND)

Spur W1(E), Saughton House, Broomhouse Drive, Edinburgh EH11 3XD (Tel: 0131-244 2691; Fax: 0131-244 2623)

The Committee advises and makes recommendations as to problems arising in relation to the appointment and distribution of justices of the peace and the work of JPs in general and of the district court in particular.

Chairman: The Rt. Hon. Lord Cullen
Secretary: R. Oliver

CERTIFICATION OFFICE FOR TRADE UNIONS AND EMPLOYERS' ASSOCIATIONS

180 Borough High Street, London SE1 1LW (Tel: 020-7210 3734/5; Fax: 020-7210 3612)

The Certification Office is an independent statutory authority responsible for receiving and scrutinising annual returns from trade unions and employers' associations; for investigating allegations of financial irregularities in the affairs of a trade union or employers' association; for dealing with complaints concerning trade union elections; for ensuring observance of statutory requirements governing political funds and trade union mergers; and for certifying the independence of trade unions.

Certification Officer: D. Cockburn

Scottish Office

58 Frederick Street, Edinburgh EH2 1LN (Tel: 0131-226 3224; Fax: 0131-200 1300)
Assistant Certification Officer for Scotland: J. L. J. Craig

CHILD SUPPORT AGENCY

DSS Long Benton, Benton Park Road, Newcastle upon Tyne NE98 1YX (Tel: 0191-213 5000)

The Agency is an agency of the Department of Work and Pensions. It is responsible for implementing the 1991 and 1995 Child Support Acts and for the assessment and collection (or arrangement of direct payment) of child support maintenance. From June 1999 the Chief Executive took over the responsibilities of the Chief Child Support Officer when that office was abolished.

Chief Executive: Ms F. Boardman
Directors: M. Davison; M. Di Ciacca; V. Gaskell; P. Hedley; M. Isaac; J. Lutton

CMPS (Centre for Management and Policy Studies)

Civil Service College Directorate, Suite 19, 1 St Colme Street, Edinburgh EH3 6AA
(Tel: 0131-220 8267; Fax: 0131-220 8367)
199 Cathedral Street, Glasgow G4 0QU
(Tel: 0141-553 6021; Fax: 0141-553 6171)

The College provides training in management and professional skills for the public and private sectors.

COMMISSION FOR RACIAL EQUALITY, SCOTLAND

Hanover House, 45–51 Hanover Street, Edinburgh EH2 2PJ (Tel: 0131-240 2600; Fax 0131-240 2601)

The Commission was established in 1977, under the Race Relations Act 1976, to work towards the elimination of discrimination and to promote equality of opportunity and good relations between different racial groups. It is funded by the Home Office.
Head of CRE, Scotland: Dharmendra Kanani

COMMISSIONER FOR LOCAL ADMINISTRATION IN SCOTLAND

23 Walker Street, Edinburgh EH3 7HX (Tel: 0131-225 5300; Fax: 0131-225 9495)

The Local Commissioner for Scotland is the local government ombudsman for Scotland, responsible for investigating complaints from members of the public against local authorities and certain other authorities. The Commissioner is appointed by the Crown on the recommendation of the First Minister.
Local Commissioner: Ian F. Smith

COMPANIES HOUSE (SCOTLAND)

37 Castle Terrace, Edinburgh EH1 2EB (Tel: 0131-535 5800; Fax: 0131-535 5820; Web: www.companieshouse.gov.uk)

Companies House is an executive agency of the Department of Trade and Industry. It incorporates companies, registers company documents and provides company information.
Registrar for Scotland: J. Henderson

Edinburgh Search Room (Tel: 0870-333 3636; Fax: 0131-535 5820)
Glasgow Satellite Office, 7 West George Street, Glasgow G2 1BQ (Tel: 0141-221 5513)

CONSIGNIA ADVISORY BOARD FOR SCOTLAND

102 West Port, Edinburgh EH3 9HS (Tel: 0131-228 7300; Fax: 0131-228 7218; Web: www.ukpo.com)

Under new legislation which came into force last year (The Postal Services Act) the Post Office became a plc on 26th March 2001, with all shares held by the Government. The Post Office used this opportunity to effect a rebranding at corporate level, and changed its name to Consignia plc, largely better to reflect its current and proposed trading status in a global market. The Scottish Post Office Board was renamed the Consignia Advisory Board for Scotland. The familiar brands of Royal Mail, Parcelforce and Post Office remain. The legislation also established a regulator, the Postal Services Commission, which, among other things, has a duty to ensure the provision of a UK-wide universal postal service at an affordable and uniform tariff.

The Consignia Advisory Board for Scotland represents Consignia in Scotland especially to the Scottish Parliament and opinion former groups.
Secretary to the Board: Martin Cummins

COPYRIGHT TRIBUNAL

Harmsworth House, 13–15 Bouverie Street, London EC4Y 8DP (Tel: 020-7596 6510; Fax: 020-7596 6526)

The Copyright Tribunal resolves disputes over copyright licences, principally where there is collective licencing.
The chairman and two deputy chairmen are appointed by the Lord Chancellor. Up to eight ordinary members are appointed by the Secretary of State for Trade and Industry.
Chairman: C. P. Tootal
Secretary: Miss J. E. M. Durdin

COURT OF THE LORD LYON

HM New Register House, Edinburgh EH1 3YT (Tel: 0131-556 7255; Fax: 0131-557 2148)

The Court of the Lord Lyon is the Scottish Court of Chivalry (including the genealogical jurisdiction of the Ri-Sennachie of Scotland's Celtic Kings). The Lord Lyon King of Arms has jurisdiction, subject to appeal to the Court of Session and the House of Lords, in questions of heraldry and the right to bear arms. The Court also administers the Scottish Public Register of All Arms and Bearings and the Public Register of All Genealogies. Pedigrees are established by decrees of Lyon Court and by letters patent. As Royal Commissioner in Armory, the Lord Lyon grants patents of arms (which constitute the grantee and heirs noble in the Noblesse of Scotland) to 'virtuous and well-deserving' Scots and to petitioners (personal or corporate) in the Queen's overseas realms of Scottish connection, and issues birthbrieves.
Lord Lyon King of Arms: Robin O. Blair, LVO, WS

HERALDS
Albany: J. A. Spens, MVO, RD, WS
Rothesay: Sir Crispin Agnew of Lochnaw, Bt., QC
Ross: C. J. Burnett, FSA Scot.

HERALD EXTRAORDINARY
Orkney: Sir Malcolm Innes of Edingight, KCVO, WS

PURSUIVANTS
Unicorn: Alastair Campbell of Airds, FSA Scot.
Carrick: Mrs C. G. W. Roads, MVO, FSA Scot.

PURSUIVANT EXTRAORDINARY
Linlithgow: J.C.G George
Lyon Clerk and Keeper of Records: Mrs C. G. W. Roads, MVO, FSA Scot.
Procurator-Fiscal: D.I.K. MacLeod, WS
Herald Painter: Mrs J. Phillips
Macer: A. M. Clark

CRIMINAL INJURIES COMPENSATION AUTHORITY

Tay House, 300 Bath Street, Glasgow G2 4LN
(Tel: 0141-331 2726; Fax: 0141-331 2287)

All applications for compensation for personal injury arising from crimes of violence in Scotland are dealt with by the Authority and are assessed under a tariff-based scheme which took effect on 1 April 1996. Any applications received before 1 April 1996 and still outstanding at 31 March 2000, when the Criminal Injuries Compensation Board (the Authority's predecessor) was formally wound up, have been transferred for resolution by the legally qualified members of the Criminal Injuries Appeal Panel (CICAP).
Chief Executive of the Criminal Injuries Compensation Authority: H. Webber
Chairman of the Criminal Injuries Compensation Appeals Panel: M. Lewer, QC
Secretary to the Panel: Miss V. Jenson

CROFTERS COMMISSION

4–6 Castle Wynd, Inverness IV2 3EQ
(Tel: 01463-663450; Fax: 01463-711820;
E-mail: crofters–commission@cali.co.uk)

The Crofters Commission is a non-departmental public body established in 1955. It advises the Scottish Ministers on all matters relating to crofting, and works with other organisations and with communities to develop and promote thriving crofting communities and simplify legislation. It administers the Crofting Counties Agricultural Grants Scheme, Croft Entrant Scheme, and livestock improvement schemes.
Chairman: I. MacAskill
Chief Executive: S. Rankin

THE CROWN ESTATE

Scottish Estate, 10 Charlotte Square, Edinburgh EH2 4DR (Tel: 0131-226 7241; Fax: 0131-220 1366; Web: www.crownestate.co.uk)

The Crown Estate manages property held 'in the right of the Crown'. In Scotland this includes commercial property, agricultural land, half of the foreshore and almost all the seabed to the twelve-mile territorial limit. The Crown Estate Commissioners manage the Estate under the provisions of the Crown Estate Act of 1961. The entire net surplus is paid to the Treasury.
Head of Scottish Estates: M. J. P. Cunliffe

CUSTOMS AND EXCISE, HM

44 York Place, Edinburgh EH1 3JW
(Tel: 0131-469 7300; Fax: 0131-469 7340
Web: www.hmce.gov.uk and www.open.gov.uk/customs/c&ehome.htm)

HM Customs and Excise is responsible for collecting and administering customs and excise duties and VAT, and advises the Chancellor of the Exchequer on any matters connected with them. The Department is also responsible for preventing and detecting the evasion of revenue laws and for enforcing a range of prohibitions and restrictions on the importation of certain classes of goods. In addition, the Department undertakes certain agency work on behalf of other departments, including the compilation of UK overseas trade statistics from customs import and export documents.
Head of Business Services for Scotland: I. Mackay

DATA PROTECTION TRIBUNAL

c/o The Home Office, Queen Anne's Gate, London SW1H 9AT (Tel 020-7273 3755)

The Data Protection Tribunal determines appeals against decisions of the Data Protection Commissioner. The chairman and deputy chairman are appointed by the Lord Chancellor and must be legally qualified. Lay members are appointed by the Home Secretary to represent the interests of data users or data subjects.

A tribunal consists of a legally-qualified chairman sitting with equal numbers of the lay members appointed to represent the interests of data users and data subjects.

Chairman: J. A. C. Spokes, QC
Secretary: R. Hartley

DEER COMMISSION FOR SCOTLAND

Knowsley, 82 Fairfield Road, Inverness IV3 5LH (Tel: 01463-231751; Fax: 01463-712931; E-mail: deercom@aol.com: Web: www.dcs.gov.uk)

The Deer Commission for Scotland has the general functions of furthering the conservation, control and sustainable management of deer in Scotland. It has the statutory duty, with powers, to prevent damage to agriculture, forestry and the habitat by deer. It is funded by the Scottish Executive.

Chairman (part-time): A. Raven
Members, G. Campbell; R. Callander; D. Irwin-Houston, R. Cooke; R. Dennis; J. Duncan-Millar; Dr J. Milne; Sir M. Strangsteel Bt; J. MacKintosh; Dr P. Ratcliffe
Director: N. Reiter
Technical Director: vacant

DRIVER AND VEHICLE LICENSING AGENCY

Longview Road, Morriston, Swansea SA6 7JL (Tel: 0870-240 0009 (drivers); 0870-240 0010 (vehicles))

The Agency is an executive agency of the Department of Transport, Local Government & the Regions (DTLR). It is responsible for the issuing of driving licences, the registration and licensing of vehicles in Great Britain, and the collection and enforcement of vehicle excise duty in the UK. The Agency also offers for sale attractive registration marks through the sale of Marks scheme.

Chief Executive: Clive Bennett

Edinburgh Vehicle Registration Office

Saughton House, Broomhouse Drive, Edinburgh EH11 3XE (Tel: 0131-455 7919; Fax: 0131-443 2478)
Scottish Area Manager: D. Drury

DRIVING STANDARDS AGENCY

Stanley House, Talbot Street, Nottingham NG1 5GU (Tel: 0115-901 2500; Web: www.driving-tests.co.uk)

The Agency is responsible for carrying out theory and practical driving tests for car drivers, motorcyclists, bus and lorry drivers and for maintaining the registers of Approved Driving Instructors and Large Goods Vehicle Instructors, as well as supervising Compulsory Basic Training (CBT) for learner motorcyclists. There are five area offices, which manage over 430 practical test centres across Britain.

EMPLOYMENT APPEAL TRIBUNAL

Divisional Office, 52 Melville Street, Edinburgh EH3 7HF (Tel: 0131-225 3963)

The Employment Appeal Tribunal hears appeals on a question of law arising from any decision of an employment tribunal. A tribunal consists of a high court judge and two lay members, one from each side of industry.

Scottish Chairman: The Hon. Lord Johnston
Deputy Registrar: P. B. H McCaig

THE EMPLOYMENT SERVICE

Argyll House, 3 Lady Lawson Street, Edinburgh EH3 9SD (Tel: 0131-221 4000; Fax: 0131-221 4004; Web: www.employmentservice.gov.uk)

The Employment Service is an executive agency of the Department for Work and Pensions. Its aims are to help people without jobs to find work and employers to fill their vacancies.

Director for Scotland: A. R. Brown, CBE

EMPLOYMENT TRIBUNALS

Central Office (Scotland), Eagle Building, 215 Bothwell Street, Glasgow G2 7TS (Tel: 0141-204 0730)

Employment tribunals deal with matters of employment law, redundancy, dismissal, contract disputes, sexual, racial and disability discrimination, and related areas of dispute which may arise in the workplace. A central registration unit records all applications and maintains a public register.

Chairmen are appointed by the Lord President of the Court of Session and lay members by the Secretary of State for Trade and Industry.

President: C. Milne

EQUAL OPPORTUNITIES COMMISSION

St Stephens House, 279 Bath Street, Glasgow, G2 4JL (Tel: 0141-248 5833; Fax: 0141-248 5834; E-mail: scotland@eoc.org.uk; Web: www.eoc.org.uk)

The Commission works towards the elimination of discrimination on the grounds of sex or marital status and to promote equality of opportunity between men and women generally. It is responsible to the Department for Work and Pensions.

EXTRA PARLIAMENTARY PANEL

The Scotland Office, Dover House, Whitehall, London SW1A 2AU (Tel: 020-7270 6758; Fax: 020-7270 6812)

The Panel hears evidence for and against draft provisional orders in private legislation procedure at an inquiry, and makes recommendations as to whether an order should proceed, be amended or be refused. This is a reserved function and the secretariat for the panel is based at the Scotland Office.

FISHERIES COMMITTEE (ELECTRICITY)

Pentland House, Robb's Loan, Edinburgh EH14 1TY; (Tel: 0131-244 6229)

The Committee advises and assists the Scottish Ministers and any person engaging in, or proposing to engage in, the generation of hydro-electric power on any question relating to the effect of hydro-electric works on fisheries or stocks of fish.
Chairman: R. McGillivray
Secretary: Miss J. Dunn

Fisheries Research Services, Marine Laboratory
PO Box 101, Victoria Road, Aberdeen AB11 9DB (Tel: 01224-876544; Fax: 01224-295511)

The Agency provides scientific information and advice on marine and freshwater fisheries, aquaculture and the protection of the aquatic environment and its wildlife.
Director: Dr A. D. Hawkins, FRSE
Deputy Director: Dr R. M. Stagg

Freshwater Fisheries Laboratory
Faskally, Pitlochry, Perthshire PH6 5LB (Tel: 01796-472060)
Senior Principal Scientific Officers: Dr R. M. Cook; Dr M. Beveridge; Dr A. E. Ellis; Dr M.R. Heath; Dr C. Moffat
Inspector of Salmon and Freshwater Fisheries for Scotland: D. A. Dunkley

FORESTRY COMMISSION

The Forestry Commission is the Government Department responsible for forestry policy in Great Britain. It reports directly to forestry Ministries to whom it is responsible for advice on forestry policy and for the implementation of that policy. Through its agency, Forest Enterprise, it manages nearly 1 million hectares of public forests throughout Great Britain. The Secretary of State for the Environment, Food and Rural Affairs has responsibility for forestry in England, Scottish Ministers have responsibility for forestry in Scotland, and the National Assembly for Wales has responsibility for forestry in Wales. For matters affecting forestry in Britain as a whole, all three have equal responsibility but the Secretary of State for the Environment, Food and Rural Affairs takes the lead.

The Commission's principal objectives are to protect Britain's forests and woodlands; expand Britain's forest area; enhance the economic value of the forest resources; conserve and improve the biodiversity, landscape and cultural heritage of forests and woodlands; develop opportunities for woodland recreation; and increase public understanding of and community participation in forestry.
Chairman (part-time): Sir Peter Hutchison, Bt., CBE
Director-General: D. J. Bills
Secretary to the Commissioners: F. Strang

FORESTRY COMMISSION NATIONAL OFFICE FOR SCOTLAND

231 Corstorphine Road, Edinburgh EH12 7AT (Tel: 0131-334 0303; Fax: 0131-334 1903; Email: enquiries@forestry.gsi.gov.uk Web: www.forestry.gov.uk)

FOREST ENTERPRISE

231 Corstorphine Road, Edinburgh EH12 7AT (Tel: 0131-334 0303)

Forest Enterprise, a trading body operating as an executive agency of the Commission, manages its forestry estate on a multi-use basis.
Chief Executive: Dr B. McIntosh

Forest Enterprise Scotland
North: 21 Church Street, Inverness IV1 1EL (Tel: 01463-232811; Fax: 01463-243846)
South: 55–57 Moffat Road, Dumfries DG1, 1NP. (Tel: 01387-2724400; Fax: 01387-251491)

FOREST RESEARCH

Alice Holt Lodge, Wrecclesham, Farnham, Surrey GU10 4LU (Tel: 01420-22255)

Forest Research provides research, development and advice to the forestry industry in support of the development and implementation of forestry policy.
Chief Executive: J. Dewar

Northern Research Station
Roslin, Midlothian EH25 9SY (Tel: 0131-445 2176)

HEALTH AND SAFETY EXECUTIVE

Scotland Office, Belford House, 59 Belford Road, Edinburgh EH4 3UE (Tel: 0131-247 2000; Fax: 0131-247 2121)

The Health and Safety Executive enforces health and safety law in the majority of industrial premises. The Executive advises the Health and Safety Commission in its major task of laying down safety standards through regulations and practical guidance for many industrial processes. The Executive is also the licensing authority for nuclear installations and the reporting officer on the severity of nuclear incidents in Great Britain.

HM INSPECTORATE OF MINES
Daniel House, Trinity Road, Bootle L20 7HE (Tel: 0151-951 4000; Fax: 0151-951 3758)
HM Chief Inspector of Mines: D. Mitchell

NUCLEAR SAFETY DIRECTORATE
Rose Court, 2 Southwark Bridge, London SE1 9HS (Tel: 020-7717 6000; Fax: 020-7717 6717)
HM Chief Inspector of Nuclear Installations: Dr L. G. Williams

RAILWAY INSPECTORATE
Rose Court, 2 Southwark Bridge, London SE1 9HS (Tel: 020-7717 6000; Fax: 020-7717 6717)
HM Chief Inspecting Officer of Railways: V. Coleman

HEALTH APPOINTMENTS ADVISORY COMMITTEE

Room 181, St Andrews House, Edinburgh EH1 3DG (Tel: 0131-244 2579)

The Committee advises on non-executive appointments to health boards, NHS Trusts and health non-departmental public bodies.
Chairman: vacant
Secretary: Mrs E. Gray

HERITAGE LOTTERY FUND (SCOTLAND)

28 Thistle Street, Edinburgh EH2 1EN (Tel: 0131-225 9450; Fax: 0131-225 9454; Web: www.hlf.org.uk)

The Heritage Lottery Fund is the designated distributor of the heritage share of proceeds from the National Lottery. The Scottish office receives and assesses all applications for projects based in Scotland. A Committee for Scotland makes decisions on grant requests up to £1 million; the main board of trustees in London is responsible for decisions on larger applications, with input from the Committee for Scotland.
Chairman, Committee for Scotland: Sir Angus Grossart, CBE
Manager, Scotland: Colin McLean

HIGHLANDS AND ISLANDS ENTERPRISE

Bridge House, 20 Bridge Street, Inverness IV1 1QR (Tel: 01463-234171; Fax: 01463-244469; E-mail: hie.general@hient.co.uk; Web: www.hie.co.uk)

Highlands and Islands Enterprise (HIE) was set up under the Enterprise and New Towns (Scotland) Act 1991. Its role is to design, direct and deliver enterprise development, training, environmental and social projects and services. HIE is made up of a strategic core body and ten local enterprise companies to which many of its individual functions are delegated.
Chairman: Dr J. Hunter
Chief Executive: S Cumming

HILL FARMING ADVISORY COMMITTEE FOR SCOTLAND

c/o Room 347, Pentland House, Robb's Loan, Edinburgh EH14 1TW (Tel: 0131-244 6422; Fax: 0131-244 6950)

The Committee advises the First Minister on the exercise of his powers under the Hill Farming Act.
Chairman: Mr D. Crawley
Secretary: Miss A. McLure

HISTORIC BUILDINGS COUNCIL FOR SCOTLAND

Longmore House, Salisbury Place, Edinburgh EH9 1SH (Tel: 0131-668 8810; Fax: 0131-668 8788; Web: www.historic-scotland.gov.uk)

The Historic Buildings Council for Scotland is the advisory body to the Scottish Ministers on matters related to buildings of special architectural or historical interest; in particular to proposals for awards by them of grants for the repair of buildings of outstanding architectural or historical interest or those lying within outstanding conservation areas.
Chairman: Sir Raymond Johnstone, CBE
Members: Cllr. R. Cairns; Cllr. P. Chalmers; Bishop M Conti; Ms L. Davidson; Mrs A. Dundas-Bekker; Very Revd. G. Forbes; Dr J. Frew; D. Gauci; M. Hopton; E. Jamieson; Mrs P. Robertson; Ms F. Sinclair
Secretary: Mrs S. Williamson

HISTORIC SCOTLAND

Longmore House, Salisbury Place, Edinburgh EH9 1SH (Tel: 0131-668 8600; Fax: 0131-668 8699; Web: www.historic-scotland.gov.uk)

Historic Scotland is an executive agency of the Scottish Executive Education Department. The agency's role is to protect Scotland's historic monuments, buildings and lands, and to promote public understanding and enjoyment of them.
Chief Executive: G. N. Munro
Directors: F. J. Lawrie; I. Maxwell; B. Naylor; B. O'Neil; L. Wilson
Chief Inspector of Ancient Monuments: Dr D. J. Breeze
Chief Inspector, Historic Buildings: R. Emerson, FSA, FSA Scot.

IMMIGRATION APPELLATE AUTHORITIES

Taylor House, 88 Rosebery Avenue, London EC1R 4QU (Tel: 020-7862 4200)

The Immigration Appellate Authorities' powers are now derived from the Immigration and Asylum Act of 1999. The Immigration Adjudicators hear appeals concerning the need for, and refusal of, leave to enter or remain in the UK, refusals to grant asylum, decisions to make deportation orders and directions to remove persons subject to immigration control from the UK.

The Immigration Appeal Tribunal provides a second appellate level for those dissatisfied with an Adjudicator's decision. Leave to appeal needs to be obtained.

An adjudicator sits alone. The tribunal sits in divisions of three, normally a legally qualified member and two lay members.

Immigration Appeal Tribunal
President: The Hon. Mr Justice Collins
Deputy President: C. M. G. Ockleton
Immigration Adjudicators
Chief Adjudicator: His Hon. Judge Hodge OBE,
Deputy Chief Adjudicator: J. Latter

INDEPENDENT REVIEW SERVICE FOR THE SOCIAL FUND

4th Floor, Centre City Podium, 5 Hill Street, Birmingham B5 4UB (Tel: 0121-606 2100; Fax: 0121-606 2180)

The Social Fund Commissioner is appointed by the Secretary of State for Work and Pensions. The Commissioner appoints Social Fund Inspectors, who provide an independent review of decisions made by Social Fund Officers in the Benefits Agency of the Department of Work and Pensions.
Social Fund Commissioner: Sir Richard Tilt

INDEPENDENT TELEVISION COMMISSION (SCOTLAND)

123 Blythswood Street, Glasgow G2 2AN (Tel: 0141-226 4436; Fax: 0141-226 4682; Web: www.itc.org.uk)

The Independent Television Commission is responsible for licensing and regulating all commercially funded television services broadcasts from the UK. Members are appointed by the Secretary of State for Culture, Media and Sport.
Head of ITC (Scotland): Alan Stewart

INLAND REVENUE (SCOTLAND)

The Board of Inland Revenue administers and collects direct taxes and advises the Chancellor of the Exchequer on policy questions involving them. The Department's Valuation Office is an executive agency responsible for valuing property for tax purposes.

Inland Revenue (Scotland)
Clarendon House, 114–116 George Street, Edinburgh EH2 4LH (Tel: 0131-473 4000)
Director: I. S. Gerrie

Capital Taxes Office (Scotland)
Meldrum House, 15 Drumsheugh Gardens, Edinburgh, EH3 7UQ (Tel: 0131-777 4000)
Registrar: Mrs J. Templeton

Edinburgh Stamp Office
Spur X, Grayfield House, 5 Bankhead Avenue, Edinburgh EH11 4BF (Tel: 0131-442 3161)

Financial Intermediaries and Claims Office (Scotland)
Meldrum House, 15 Drumsheugh Gardens, Edinbrugh, EH3 7UQ (Tel: 0131-777 4000)
Assistant Director: Mr. R. Willoughby

Solicitor's Office (Scotland)
Clarendon House, 114–116 George Street, Edinburgh EH2 4LH (Tel: 0131-473 4053; Fax: 0131-473 4143)
Solicitor: I. K. Laing

Valuation Office Agency
50 Frederick Street, Edinburgh EH2 1NG (Tel: 0131-465 0700; Fax: 0131-465 0799)
Chief Valuer, Scotland: A. Ainslie

INTERVENTION BOARD

PO Box 69, Reading RG1 3YD
(Tel: 0118-958 3626; Fax: 0118-953 1370)

The Intervention Board is an executive agency of the four agriculture ministries in the UK; in Scotland it is an agency of the Scottish Executive Rural Affairs Department. It is responsible for the implementation of European Union regulations covering the market support arrangements of the Common Agricultural Policy. Members are appointed by and are responsible to the four agriculture ministers.
Chief Executive: J. McNeill

Regional Verification Office
Room E1/5, Saughton House, Broomhouse Drive, Edinburgh EH11 3XA (Tel: 0131-244 8382; Fax: 0131-244 8117)
Regional Verification Officer: P. R. Drummond

JUDICIAL COMMITTEE OF THE PRIVY COUNCIL

Downing Street, London SW1A 2AJ
(Tel: 020-7270 0483)

Following devolution, the Judicial Committee of the Privy Council assumes a new role as Scotland's principal constitutional court and will be the final arbiter in disputes raising issues as to the legal competence of things done or proposed by The Scottish Parliament or Executive.

The members of the Judicial Committee include the Lord Chancellor, the Lords of Appeal in Ordinary, other Privy Counsellors who hold or have held high judicial office and certain judges from the Commonwealth.
Registrar of the Privy Council: J. A. C. Watherston
Chief Clerk: F. G. Hart

JUSTICES OF THE PEACE ADVISORY COMMITTEES

c/o Spur W1(E), Saughton House, Broomhouse Drive, Edinburgh EH11 3XD
(Tel: 0131-244 2222; Fax: 0131-244 2623)

The committees, of which there are 32, keep under review the strength of the Commissions of the Peace in Scotland and advise on the appointment of new justices of the peace. Each committee has its own chairman and secretary. The Scottish Executive provides central advice to the committees.

LANDS TRIBUNAL FOR SCOTLAND

1 Grosvenor Crescent, Edinburgh EH12 5ER
(Tel: 0131-225 7996)

The Lands Tribunal for Scotland determines a broad range of questions relating to the valuation of land, including rating appeals, the discharge or variation of title conditions, questions of disputed compensation following compulsory purchase etc. and relating to tenants' rights to buy. The president is appointed by the Lord President of the Court of Session.
President: The Hon. Lord McGhie, QC
Members: J. Devine; A. R. MacLeary
Member (part-time): J.N. Wright, QC
Clerk: N. M. Tainsh

LOCAL GOVERNMENT BOUNDARY COMMISSION FOR SCOTLAND

3 Drumsheugh Gardens, Edinburgh EH3 7QJ; (Tel: 0131-538 7510; Fax: 0131-538 7511)

The Commission keeps under review the boundaries of local government administrative and electoral areas.
Chairman: J. L. Majoriebanks
Secretary: R. Smith

LORD ADVOCATE'S OFFICE

Crown Office, 25 Chambers Street, Edinburgh EH1 1LA (Tel: 0131-226 2626; Fax: 0131-226 6910)
Lord Advocate: The Rt. Hon. Colin Boyd, QC
Private Secretary: J. Gibbons
Solicitor-General for Scotland: Neil F. Davidson, QC
Private Secretary: J. Gibbons
Legal Secretary to the Law Officers: P. J. Layden, TD

MARITIME AND COASTGUARD AGENCY

Spring Place, 105 Commercial Road, Southampton SO15 1EG (Tel: 023-8032 9100)

The Agency is an executive agency of the Department of the Environment, Transport and the Regions, formed in 1998 by the merger of the Coastguard Agency and the Marine Safety Agency. Its role is to develop, promote and enforce high standards of marine safety; to minimise loss of life amongst seafarers and coastal users and to respond to maritime emergencies 24 hours a day.
Chief Executive: M. Storey

HM COASTGUARD

North and East Scotland Search and Rescue District

Aberdeen Maritime Rescue Co-ordination Centre, HM Coastguard
Marine House, Blaikies Quay, Aberdeen, AB11 5PB (Tel: 01224 592334; Fax: 01224 575920)
HM Regional Inspector: R. Crowther

West of Scotland and Northern Ireland Search and Rescue Region

Clyde Maritime Rescue Co-ordination Centre
HM Coastguard, Navy Buildings,Greenock PA16 (Tel: 01475-784621; Fax: 01475-724006)
Regional Inspector: B. Cunningham

MENTAL WELFARE COMMISSION FOR SCOTLAND

K Floor, Argyle House, 3 Lady Lawson Street, Edinburgh EH3 9SH (Tel: 0131-222 6111)

The Commission protects the mentally disordered by the investigation of irregularities and by visiting patients in hospitals and in the community, and reports as appropriate to the relevant authorities.
Chairman: I. J. Miller, OBE
Vice-Chairman: Mrs N. Bennie
Commissioners (part-time): Mrs F. Cotter; W. Gent; Dr P. Jauhar; Dr S. Jiwa; T. Keenan; Dr E. McCall-Smith; Revd Canon J. Morrow; M. D. Murray; Dr L. Pollock; A. Robb; Mrs M. Ross; Dr M. Whoriskey
Director: Dr J. A. T. Dyer

NATIONAL ARCHIVES OF SCOTLAND

HM General Register House, Edinburgh EH1 3YY (Tel: 0131-535 1314; Fax: 0131-535 1360; E-mail: enquiries@nas.gov.uk)

The history of the National Archives of Scotland can be traced back to the 13th century. The National Archives of Scotland (formerly the Scottish Record Office) is an executive agency of the Scottish Executive Secretariat. It keeps the administrative records of pre-Union Scotland, the registers of central and local courts of law, the public registers of property rights and legal documents, and many collections of local and church records and private archives. Certain groups of records, mainly the modern records of government departments in Scotland, the Scottish railway records, the plans collection, and private archives of an industrial or commercial nature, are preserved in the branch repository at the West Register House in Charlotte Square. The National Register of Archives (Scotland) is based in the West Register House.

The search rooms in both buildings are open Monday–Friday, 9–4.45. A permanent exhibition at the West Register House and changing exhibitions at the General Register House are open to the public on weekdays, 10-4.
Keeper of the Records of Scotland: G.P. Mackenzie
Deputy Keeper: Dr P. D. Anderson

NATIONAL AUDIT OFFICE

22 Melville Street, Edinburgh EH3 7NS (Tel: 0131-244 2739; Fax: 0131-244 2721; E-mail: edin.nao@gtnet.gov.uk Web: www.open.gov.uk/nao.home.htm)

The National Audit Office provides independent information, advice and assurance to Parliament and the public about all aspects of the financial operations of government departments and many other bodies receiving public funds. It does this by examining and certifying the accounts of these organisations and by regularly publishing reports to Parliament on the results of its value-for-money investigations of the economy, efficiency and effectiveness with which public resources have been used. The National Audit Office is also the auditor by agreement of the accounts of certain international and other organisations. In addition, the Office authorises the issue of public funds to government departments.

Director, Value-for-Money Audit: A. Roberts
Director, Financial Audit: R. Frith

NATIONAL GALLERIES OF SCOTLAND

73 Belford Road, Edinburgh EH4 3DS
(Tel: 0131-624 6200; Fax: 0131-343 3250;
E-mail: pressinfo@natgalscot.ac.uk
Web: www.natgalscot.ac.uk)

The National Galleries of Scotland comprise the National Gallery of Scotland, the Scottish National Portrait Gallery, the Scottish National Gallery of Modern Art and the Dean Gallery. There are also outstations at Paxton House, Berwickshire, and Duff House, Banffshire. Total government grant-in-aid for 2000-2001 was £8.839 million.

Chairman: Brian Ivory, CBE
Trustees: Ms V. Atkinson; J. H. Blair; G. Gemmell, CBE; Lord Gordon of Strathblane, CBE; A. Leitch; Prof. C. Lodder; Dr I. McKenzie Smith, OBE; Dr M. Shea; G. Weaver; Prof. I. Whyte
Director: T. Clifford
Keeper of Conservation: M. Gallagher
Head of Press and Information: Ms Catriona Black
Head of Education: M. Cassin
Registrar: Miss A. Buddle
Secretary: Ms S. Edwards
Buildings: R. Galbraith
Director, National Gallery of Scotland: M. Clarke
Director, Scottish National Portrait Gallery: J. Holloway
Curator of Photography: Miss S. F. Stevenson
Director, Scottish National Gallery of Modern Art and of Dean Gallery: R. Calvocoressi

NATIONAL HEALTH SERVICE TRIBUNAL (SCOTLAND)

66 Queen Street, Edinburgh EH2 4NE
(Tel: 0131-226 4771)

The tribunal considers representations that the continued inclusion of a doctor, dentist, optometrist or pharmacist on a health board's list would be prejudicial to the efficiency of the service concerned. The tribunal sits when required and is composed of a chairman, one lay member, and one practitioner member drawn from a representative professional panel. The chairman is appointed by the Lord President of the Court of Session, and the lay member and the members of the professional panel are appointed by the First Minister.

Chairman: M. G. Thomson, QC
Lay member: J. D. M. Robertson
Clerk: W. Bryden, SSC

NATIONAL LIBRARY OF SCOTLAND

George IV Bridge, Edinburgh EH1 1EW
(Tel: 0131-226 4531; Fax: 0131-622 4803;
E-mail: enquiries@nls.uk; Web: www.nls.uk)

The Library, which was founded as the Advocates' Library in 1682, became the National Library of Scotland in 1925. It is funded through the Scottish Executive. It contains about seven million printed and new media items, 1.6 million maps, 25,000 periodicals and annual titles and 120,000 volumes of manuscripts. It has an unrivalled Scottish collection.

The Reading Room is for reference and research which cannot conveniently be pursued elsewhere. Admission is by ticket issued to an approved applicant.

Opening hours
Reading Room, weekdays, 9.30–8.30 (Wednesday, 10–8.30); Saturday 9.30–1
Map Library, weekdays, 9.30–5 (Wednesday, 10–5); Saturday 9.30–1
Exhibition, Monday–Saturday 10–5; Sunday 2–5
Scottish Science Library, weekdays, 9.30–5 (Wednesday, 10–8.30)

Chairman of the Trustees: Prof. Michael Anderson, OBE, FBA, FRSA
Librarian and Secretary to the Trustees: I. D. McGowan
Secretary of the Library: M. C. Graham
Director of General Collections: C. Newton
Director of Special Collections: M. C. T. Simpson, Ph.D.

Director of Public Services: A. M. Marchbank, Ph.D.

Director, Information and Communications Technology: R. F. Guy

NATIONAL LOTTERY CHARITIES BOARD, *now* COMMUNITY FUND

Norloch House, 36 King's Stables Road, Edinburgh EH1 2EJ
(Tel: 0131-221 7100; Fax: 0131-221 7120; Web: www.community-fund.org.uk)

The Board is one of six independent bodies set up to distribute funds from the Lottery. It aims to help meet the needs of those at greatest disadvantage in society and to improve the quality of life in the community by supporting projects run by charitable, benevolent and philanthropic organisations. Grants can be for up to three years; the smallest award is £500 and the average award is around £120,000.
Director for Scotland: Adrienne Kelbie

NATIONAL MUSEUMS OF SCOTLAND

Chambers Street, Edinburgh EH1 1JF
(Tel: 0131-225 7534; Fax: 0131-220 4819; E-mail: feedback@nms.ac.uk
Web: www.nms.ac.uk)

The National Museums of Scotland comprise the Royal Museum of Scotland, the National War Museum of Scotland, the Museum of Scottish Country Life, Shambellie House Museum of Costume and the Museum of Scotland. Total funding from the Scottish Executive for 2000-2001 was £17million.

Board of Trustees
Chairman: R. Smith, FSA Scot.
Members: Prof. T. Devine; Dr L. Glasser, MBE, FRSE; S. G. Gordon, CBE; G. Johnston, OBE, TD; Ms C. Macaulay; Mrs N. Mahal; N. McIntosh, CBE; Prof. A. Manning, OBE; Prof. J. Murray; Sir William Purves, CBE, DSO; Dr A. Ritchie, OBE; The Countess of Rosebery; I. Smith; Lord Wilson of Tillyorn, GCMG

Officers
Director: M. Jones, FSA, FSA Scot., FRSA
Depute Director and Keeper of History and Applied Art: Miss D. Idiens, FRSA, FSA Scot.
Development Director: C. McCallum
Keeper of Archaeology, D. V. Clarke, Ph.D.d, FSA, FSA Scot.

Keeper of Geology and Zoology: M. Shaw, D. Phil.

Keeper of Social and Technological History: G. Sprott

Head of Public Affairs: Ms M. Bryden

Head of Technical Services: S. R. Elson, FSA Scot.

NORTHERN LIGHTHOUSE BOARD

84 George Street, Edinburgh EH2 3DA
(Tel: 0131-473 3100; Fax: 0131-220 2093; E-mail: nlb@dial.pipex.com)

The Lighthouse Board is the general lighthouse authority for Scotland and the Isle of Man. The present board owes its origin to an Act of Parliament passed in 1786. At present the Commissioners operate under the Merchant Shipping Act 1894 and are 19 in number.

The Commissioners control 83 major automatic lighthouses, 117 minor lights and many lighted and unlighted buoys. They have a fleet of two motor vessels.

Commissioners
The Lord Advocate
The Solicitor-General for Scotland
The Lord Provosts of Edinburgh, Glasgow and Aberdeen
The Provost of Inverness
The Convener of Argyll and Bute Council
The Sheriffs-Principal of North Strathclyde, Tayside, Central and Fife, Grampian, Highlands and Islands, South Strathclyde, Dumfries and Galloway, Lothians and Borders, and Glasgow and Strathkelvin
Capt. D. M. Cowell
Adm. Sir Michael Livesay, KCB
The Lord Maclay
P. Mackay, CB
Capt. Kenneth MacLeod
Chief Executive: Capt. J. B. Taylor, RN
Director of Finance: D. Gorman
Director of Engineering: M. Waddell
Director of Operations and Navigational Requirements: P. J. Christmas

OFFICE OF THE ACCOUNTANT IN BANKRUPTCY

George House, 126 George Street, Edinburgh EH2 4HH (Tel: 0131-473 4600 Helpline 0845-7626171; Fax: 0131-473 4737)

The office is responsible for administering the process of personal bankruptcy (sequestration) and recording corporate insolvencies in Scotland.
Accountant in Bankruptcy: S. Woodhouse

INFORMATION COMMISSIONER'S OFFICE

Wycliffe House, Water Lane, Wilmslow, Cheshire SK9 5AF (Tel: 01625-545745; Fax: 01625-524510)

The Data Protection Act 1998 sets rules for processing personal information and applies to some paper records as well as those held on computers. It is the Commissioner's duty to compile and maintain the register of data controllers and provide facilities for members of the public to examine the register; promote observance of the data protection principles; and disseminate information to the public about the Act and her function under the Act. The Commissioner also has the power to produce codes of practice. The Commissioner reports annually to parliament on the performance of her functions under the Act and has obligations to assess the breaches of the Act. The information commissioner is also responsible for freedom of information.

Commissioner: Mrs E. France

OFFICE OF GAS AND ELECTRICITY MARKETS (SCOTLAND)

Regent Court, 70 West Regent Street, Glasgow G2 2QZ (Tel: 0141-331 2678; Fax: 0141-331 2777)

The Office of Gas and Electricity Markets (Ofgem) is the independent regulatory body for the gas and electricity supply industries following the merger of the Office of Gas Supply and the Office of Electricity Regulation in 1999. Its functions are to promote competition and to protect customers' interests in relation to prices, security of supply and quality of services.

Chairman and Chief Executive: C. McCarthy
Managing Director for Scotland: C. Coulthard

OFFICE OF THE SOCIAL SECURITY AND CHILD SUPPORT COMMISSIONERS

23 Melville Street, Edinburgh EH3 7PW (Tel: 0131-225 2201; Fax: 0131-220 6782)

The Social Security Commissioners are the final statutory authority to decide appeals relating to entitlement to social security, including housing and council tax and benefits. The Child Support Commissioners are the final statutory authority to decide appeals relating to child support. Appeals may be made in relation to both matters only on a point of law.

Chief Social Security Commissioner and Chief Child Support Commissioner (London): His Hon. Judge Machin, QC
Commissioners (Edinburgh): W. M. Walker, QC; D. J. May, QC; Mrs L. T Parker
Legal Officers: C. F. Smith; Miss L. Hansford
Secretary (Edinburgh): Ms S. M. Niven

OFFICE OF TELECOMMUNICATIONS

50 Ludgate Hill, London EC4M 7JJ (Tel: 020-7634 8700; Fax: 020-7 634 8943)

The Office of Telecommunications (Oftel) is responsible for supervising telecommunications activities and broadcast transmission in the UK. Its principal functions are to ensure that holders of telecommunications licences comply with their licence conditions; to maintain and promote effective competition in telecommunications; and to promote the interests of purchasers and other users of telecommunication services and apparatus in respect of prices, quality and variety.

The Director-General has powers to deal with anti-competitive practices and monopolies. He also has a duty to consider all reasonable complaints and representations about telecommunication apparatus and services.

Director-General: D. Edmonds

PARLIAMENTARY COMMISSIONER FOR ADMINISTRATION AND HEALTH SERVICE COMMISSIONER

The Parliamentary Commissioner for Administration (the Parliamentary Ombudsman) is independent of Government and is an officer of Parliament. He is responsible for investigating complaints referred to him by MPs from members of the public who claim to have sustained injustice in consequence of maladministration by or on behalf of UK government departments and certain non-departmental public bodies. The Parliamentary Commissioner also investigates complaints, referred by MPs, about wrongful refusal of access to official information.

The Health Service Commissioner (the Health Service Ombudsman) for Scotland is responsible for investigating complaints against National Health Service authorities and trusts that are not dealt with by those authorities to the satisfaction of the complainant. The Ombudsman's jurisdiction now covers complaints about family doctors, dentists, pharmacists and opticians, and complaints about actions resulting from clinical judgment. The Health Service Ombudsman is also responsible for investigating complaints that information has been wrongly refused under the Code of Practice on Openness in the National Health Service 1995. The office is presently held by the Parliamentary Commissioner (*see also* Scottish Parliamentary Commissioner for Administration).

Parliamentary Commissioner's Office
Millbank Tower, Millbank, London SW1P 4QP
(Tel: 0845-015 4033; Fax: 020-7217 4000;
Web: www.ombudsman.org.uk)
Parliamentary Commissioner and Health Service Commissioner: M. S. Buckley
Deputy Parliamentary Commissioner:
A. Watson
Directors of Investigations: Ms C Corrigan; G. Monk; D. Reynold's

Health Service Commissioners' Office
Millbank Tower, Millbank, London SW1P 4QP
(Tel: 0845-015 4033; Fax: 020-7217 4000)
28 Thistle Street, Edinburgh EH2 1EN
(Tel: 0845-601 0456; Fax: 0131-226 4447
Web: www.ombudsman.org.uk)
Health Service Commissioner: M. S. Buckley
Deputy Health Service Commissioner: Ms H. Scott
Director of Investigations for Scotland: N. J. Jordan

PAROLE BOARD FOR SCOTLAND

Saughton House, Broomhouse Drive, Edinburgh EH11 3XD (Tel: 0131-244 8755; Fax: 0131-244 6974)

The Board is an independent body which directs and advises Scottish Ministers on the release of prisoners on licence, and related matters.
Chairman: D. J. J. McManus
Vice-Chairmen: H. Hyslop
Secretary: H. P. Boyle

PATENT OFFICE

Cardiff Road, Newport NP10 8QQ (Tel: 08459-500505 (enquiries); 01633-811010 (search and advisory service); Fax: 01633-814444;
E-mail: enquiries@patent.gov.uk
Web: www.patent.gov.uk)

The Patent Office is an executive agency of the Department of Trade and Industry. The duties of the Patent Office are to administer the Patent Acts, the Registered Designs Act and the Trade Marks Act, and to deal with questions relating to the Copyright, Designs and Patents Act 1988. It aims to stimulate the innovation and competitiveness of industry. The Search and Advisory Service carries out commercial searches through patent information.

There are two Patents Information Network (PIN) centres in Scotland (which are not connected to the Patent Office itself) where patent searches can be conducted:

Business and Technical Department
Central Library, Rosemount Viaduct, Aberdeen AB25 1GW; (Tel: 01224-652500)

Business Users' Service
Mitchell Library, North Street, Glasgow G3 7DN; (Tel: 0141-287 2905)

PENSIONS APPEAL TRIBUNALS FOR SCOTLAND

20 Walker Street, Edinburgh EH3 7HS
(Tel: 0131-220 1404)

The Pensions Appeal Tribunals are responsible for hearing appeals from ex-servicemen or women and widows who have had their claims for a war pension rejected by the Secretary of State for Social Security. The Entitlement Appeal Tribunals hear appeals in cases where the Secretary of State has refused to grant a war pension. The Assessment Appeal Tribunals hear appeals against the Secretary of State's assessment of the degree of disablement caused by an accepted condition. The tribunal members are appointed by the President of the Court of Session
President: C. N. McEachran, QC

POST-QUALIFICATION EDUCATION BOARD FOR HEALTH SERVICE PHARMACISTS IN SCOTLAND

c/o Scottish Centre for Post-Qualification Pharmaceutical Education, Room 163, SIBS Todd Wing, 27 Taylor Street, University of Strathclyde, Glasgow G4 0NR (Tel: 0141-548 4273; Fax: 0141-553 4102;
E-mail: scppe@strath.ac.uk)

The Board advises on the post-qualification educational requirements of all registered pharmacists working in the NHS in Scotland.
Chairman: Dr G. Jefferson
Secretary: Ms R. M. Parr

REGISTERS OF SCOTLAND

Meadowbank House, 153 London Road, Edinburgh EH8 7AU (Tel: 0845 6070161; Fax: 0131-479 3688; E-mail: keeper@ros.gov.uk Web: www.ros.gov.uk)

Registers of Scotland is the executive agency responsible for framing and maintaining records relating to property and further legal documents in Scotland. Information from these public registers can be obtained through personal visits, by post, fax or via e-mail.

The agency holds 15 registers; two property registers (General Register of Sasines and Land Register of Scotland), which form the chief security in Scotland of the rights of land and other heritable (or real) property; and the remaining 13 grouped under the collective name of the Chancery and Judicial Registers (Register of Deeds in the Books of Council and Session; Register of Protests; Register of Judgments; Register of Service of Heirs; Register of the Great Seal; Register of the Quarter Seal; Register of the Prince's Seal; Register of Crown Grants; Register of Sheriffs' Commissions; Register of the Cachet Seal; Register of Inhibitions and Adjudications; Register of Entails; Register of Hornings).

Keeper of the Registers: A. W. Ramage
Deputy Keeper: A. G. Rennie
Managing Director: F. Manson

REGISTRY OF FRIENDLY SOCIETIES (SCOTLAND)

58 Frederick Street, Edinburgh EH2 1NB (Tel: 0131-226 3224)

The Registry of Friendly Societies is a non-ministerial government department comprising the Central Office of the Registry of Friendly Societies, together with the Assistant Registrar of Friendly Societies for Scotland. The Central Office of the Registry of Friendly Societies provides a public registry for mutual organisations registered under the Building Societies Act 1986, Friendly Societies Acts 1974 and 1992, and the Industrial and Provident Societies Act 1965.

The Registry will be subsumed into the Financial Services Authority at a date to be fixed following the enactment of the Financial Services and Markets Bill.

Assistant Registrar for Scotland: J. L. J. Craig, WS

ROYAL BOTANIC GARDEN EDINBURGH

20a Inverleith Row, Edinburgh EH3 5LR (Tel: 0131-552 7171; Fax: 0131-248 2901; E-mail: press@rbge.org.uk; Web: www.rbge.org.uk)

The Royal Botanic Garden Edinburgh (RBGE) originated as the Physic Garden, established in 1670 beside the Palace of Holyroodhouse. The Garden moved to its present 28-hectare site at Inverleith, Edinburgh, in 1821. There are also three other Gardens: Benmore Botanic Garden near Dunoon, Argyll; Logan Botanic Garden, near Stranraer, Wigtownshire; and Dawyck Botanic Garden, near Stobo, Peeblesshire. Since 1986, RBGE has been administered by a board of trustees established under the National Heritage (Scotland) Act 1985. It receives an annual grant from the Scottish Executive Rural Affairs Department.

RBGE is an international centre for scientific research on plant diversity and for horticulture education and conservation. It has an extensive library and a herbarium with over two million dried plant specimens.

Public opening hours
Edinburgh site – daily (except Christmas Day and New Year's Day) November–January 9.30–4; February and October 9.30–5; March and September 9.30–6; April–August 9.30–7; Admission free. Donations are encouraged at the Glassware Experience. Guided tours are available. Specialist gardens – 1 March–31 October 9.30–6; admission charge

Chairman of the Board of Trustees: Dr P. Nicholson
Regius Keeper: Prof. S. Blackmore

ROYAL COMMISSION ON THE ANCIENT AND HISTORICAL MONUMENTS OF SCOTLAND

John Sinclair House, 16 Bernard Terrace, Edinburgh EH8 9NX (Tel: 0131-662 1456; Fax: 0131-662 1477; E-mail: postmaster@rcahms.gov.uk Web: www.rcahms.gov.uk)

The Royal Commission was established in 1908 and is appointed to provide for the survey and recording of ancient and historical monuments connected with the culture, civilisation and conditions of life of people in Scotland from the earliest times. It is funded by the Scottish Executive.

The Commission compiles and maintains the National Monuments Record of Scotland as the national record of the archaeological and historical environment. The National Monuments Record is open for reference Monday–Friday 9.30–4.30.
Chairman: Mrs K. Dalyell, FRSAS
Commissioners: Prof. J. M Coles, Ph.D., FBA, FSA; Dr B. Crawford, FSA, FSA Scot; Dr A. Macdonald, FSA Scot; Dr M. Mackay, Ph.D., FSA Scot; Prof C. Morris, FSA, FRSE, FSA Scot; Dr J. Murray, FSA Scot; Dr S. Nenadic; Prof R. Paxton, FICE; Miss A. Riches, FSA, FSA Scot; J. Simpson, FSA Scot
Secretary: R. J. Mercer, FSA, FRSE

ROYAL FINE ART COMMISSION FOR SCOTLAND

Bakehouse Close, 146 Canongate, Edinburgh EH8 8DD (Tel: 0131-556 6699; Fax: 0131-556 6633; E-mail: plan@RoyfinartforSco.gov.uk)

The Commission was established in 1927 and advises ministers and local authorities on the visual impact and quality of design of construction projects. It is an independent body and gives its opinions impartially.
Chairman: The Rt. Hon. the Lord Cameron of Lochbroom, PC, FRSE
Commissioners: Ms J. Malvenan; R. G. Maund; M. Murray; D. Page; B. Rae; Prof. R. Russell; M. Turnbull; A. Wright
Secretary: C. Prosser

SCOTLAND OFFICE

Dover House, Whitehall, London, SW1A 2AU (Tel: 020-7270 3000; Fax: 020-7270 6730)

The Scotland Office supports the Secretary of State for Scotland, who represents Scottish interests in the Cabinet on matters reserved to the UK Parliament and the Advocate General (a UK Law Officer and adviser to the UK Government on Scottish Law).
Secretary of State for Scotland: The Rt. Hon. Helen Liddell, MP
Private Secretary: Ms J. Colquhoun
Minister of State: George Foulkes, MP
Private Secretary: Ms F. Hesling
Advocate-General for Scotland: Dr Lynda Clark, QC, MP
Head of Office: I. Gordon

SCOTTISH ADVISORY COMMITTEE ON DRUG MISUSE

Substance Misuse Division, Department of Health, St Andrews House, Edinburgh EH1 3DG (Tel: 0131-244 2496; Fax: 0131-244 2689)

The Committee advises and reports on policy, priorities and strategic planning in relation to drug misuse in Scotland.
Chairman: The Deputy Minister for Justice
Secretary: Mrs M. Robertson

SCOTTISH ADVISORY COMMITTEE ON THE MEDICAL WORKFORCE

Room 6W:15, St Andrews House, Edinburgh EH1 3DG (Tel: 0131-244 2486)

The Committee advises on all matters relating to medical workforce planning in Scotland, other than matters concerning terms and conditions of service. (The Committee's status as a non-departmental public body is under review).
Chairman: Dr D. Ewing
Secretary: Mr S. Miller

SCOTTISH AGRICULTURAL SCIENCE AGENCY

East Craig, Edinburgh EH12 8NJ (Tel: 0131-244 8890; Fax: 0131-244 8940)

The Agency is an executive agency of the Scottish Executive Rural Affairs Department. It provides scientific information and advice on agricultural and horticultural crops and the environment, and has various statutory and regulatory functions.
Director: Dr R. K. M. Hay
Deputy Director: S. R. Cooper
Dr K. J. O'Donnell

SCOTTISH AGRICULTURAL WAGES BOARD

Pentland House, 47 Robb's Loan, Edinburgh EH14 1TY (Tel: 0131-244 6392)

The Board fixes minimum wage rates, holiday entitlements and other conditions for agricultural workers in Scotland.
Chairman: Mrs C. Davis, CBE
Secretary: Miss F. Anderson

SCOTTISH ARTS COUNCIL

12 Manor Place, Edinburgh EH3 7DD
(Tel: 0131-226 6051; Fax: 0131-225 9833;
E-mail: administrator@scottisharts.org.uk
Web: www.sac.org.uk)

The Scottish Arts Council (SAC) aims to create a dynamic arts environment which enhances the quality of life for the people of Scotland. It achieves this by providing leadership; developing new ideas and initiatives; working in partnerships; promoting the arts and artists; providing information and advice; investing in the arts for the people of Scotland. SAC is one of the main channels of public funding for the arts in Scotland and receives funding from two main sources: revenue funding from the Scottish Executive (£34.8m) and Lottery funding through the Department of Culture, Media and Sport (£20m).
Chairman: Magnus Linklater
Members: Sam Ainsley; Elizabeth Cameron; Richard Chester; Jim Faulds; Bill English; Dale Idiens; Maud Marshall; Ann Matheson; Robin Presswood; John Scott Moncrieff; Bill Speirs
Director: Tessa Jackson

SCOTTISH CHARITIES OFFICE

25 Chambers Street, Edinburgh EH1 1LA
(Tel: 0131-226 2626; Fax: 0131-226 6912)

The Scottish Charities Office is responsible for the supervision and regulation of charities in Scotland with the aim of enhancing the integrity and effectiveness of charities.
Director: B. M. Logan

SCOTTISH CHILDREN'S REPORTER ADMINISTRATION

Ochil House, Springkerse Business Park, Stirling FK7 7XE (Tel: 01786-459 500; Fax: 01786-495 533)

The Scottish Children's Reporter Administration supports the Principal Reporter in his statutory functions in relation to children who may be in need of care or supervision and provides suitable accommodation and facilities for children's hearings.
Chairman: Ms Sally Kuenssberg

SCOTTISH COMMITTEE OF THE COUNCIL ON TRIBUNALS

44 Palmerston Place, Edinburgh EH12 5BJ
(Tel: 0131-220 1236; Fax: 0131-225 4271;
E-mail: sccot@gtnet.gov.uk)

The Council on Tribunals is an independent body that advises on and keeps under review the constitution and working of administrative tribunals, and considers and reports on administrative procedures relating to statutory inquiries. Some 70 tribunals are currently under the Council's supervision. It is consulted by and advises government departments on a wide range of subjects relating to adjudicative procedures. The Scottish Committee of the Council generally considers Scottish tribunals and matters relating only to Scotland.
Chairman: R. J. Elliot, DKS
Members: The Parliamentary Commissioner for Administration (ex officio); Mrs P. Y. Berry, MBE; Mrs B. Bruce; I. J. Irvine; D. Graham; Mrs M. Wood
Secretary: Mrs E. M. MacRae

SCOTTISH CRIMINAL CASES REVIEW COMMISSION

5th Floor, Portland House, 17 Renfield Street, Glasgow G2 5AH (Tel: 0141-270 7030; Fax: 0141-270 7040; E-mail: info@sccrc.co.uk)

The Commission is a non-departmental public body which was established on 1 April 1999. It considers alleged miscarriages of justice in Scotland and refers cases meeting the relevant criteria to the High Court for determination. Members are appointed by Her Majesty The Queen on the recommendation of the Scottish Ministers; staff are appointed by the Commission.
Chairperson: (£372.00 per day) Prof. S. McLean
Members: (£217.00 per day) A. Bonnington; Prof. P. Duff; Very Revd G. Forbes; A. Gallen; Sir G. Gordon, CBE, QC; W. Taylor, QC
Chief Executive: C. A. Kelly

SCOTTISH ENTERPRISE

120 Bothwell Street, Glasgow G2 7JP
(Tel 0141-248 2700; Fax 0141-221 3217;
E-mail: scotent.co.uk; Web: www.scotent.co.uk)

Scottish Enterprise was established in 1991 and its purpose is to create jobs and prosperity for the people of Scotland. It is funded largely by the Scottish Executive and is responsible to the Scottish Minister for Enterprise and Lifelong Learning. Working in partnership with the private and public sectors, Scottish Enterprise aims to further the development of Scotland's economy, to enhance the skills of the Scottish workforce and to promote Scotland's international competitiveness. Through Locate in Scotland, Scottish Enterprise is concerned with attracting firms to Scotland, and through Scottish Trade International helps Scottish companies to compete in world export markets. Scottish Enterprise has a network of 13 local enterprise companies that deliver economic development services at local level.

Chairman: Sir Ian Wood, CBE
Chief Executive: C. Beveridge, CBE

SCOTTISH ENVIRONMENT PROTECTION AGENCY

Erskine Court, The Castle Business Park, Stirling FK9 4TR (Tel: 01786-457700; Fax: 01786-446885; E-mail: publicaffairs@sepa.org.uk Web: www.sepa.org.uk)

The Scottish Environment Protection Agency is Scotland's environmental regulator, responsible for preventing and controlling pollution to land, air and water. Its main aim is to provide an efficient and integrated environmental protection system for Scotland which will improve the environment and contribute to the Government's goal of sustainable development. It has area offices in East Kilbride, Edinburgh and Dingwall, and 18 offices throughout Scotland. It receives funding from the Scottish Executive.

The Board
Chairman: K. Collins
Members: Mrs D. Hutton; Prof. B. D. Clark; Prof. S. Clark; S. Dagg; F. Edwards; B. Furness; Mr D. Hallett; Ms P. Henton; B. Howatson; N. Kienssberg; C. McChord

The Executive
Chief Executive: Ms P. Henton
Director of Finance and Corporate Support: J. Ford
Director of Operations: W. Halcrow
Director of Public Affairs and Corporate Services: J. M. Beveridge
Director of Strategic Planning: Dr. C. Gemmell

SCOTTISH FISHERIES PROTECTION AGENCY

Pentland House, 47 Robb's Loan, Edinburgh EH14 1TY (Tel: 0131-556 8400; Fax: 0131-244 6086)

The Agency is an executive agency of the Scottish Executive Rural Affairs Department. It enforces fisheries law and regulations in Scottish waters and ports.
Chief Executive, Capt. P. Du Vivier, RN

Director of Corporate Strategy and Resources, J. B. Roddin
Director of Operations: R. J. Walker
Marine Superintendent: Capt. W. A. Brown

SCOTTISH HOSPITAL ENDOWMENTS RESEARCH TRUST

Princes Exchange, 1 Earl Grey Street, Edinburgh, EH3 9EE (Tel: 0131-659 8800; Fax: 0131-228 8118; Web: www.shert.com/www.shert.org.uk)

The Trust holds endowments, donations and bequests and makes grants from these funds to improve health standards by funding research into the cause, diagnosis, treatment and prevention of all forms of illness and genetic disorders and into the advancement of medical technology. It also engages in fundraising activities.
Chairman: Prof. Roland Jung, FRCP
Secretary: Turcan Connell

SCOTTISH INDUSTRIAL DEVELOPMENT ADVISORY BOARD

Meridian Court, 5 Cadogan Street, Glasgow G2 6AT (Tel: 0141-242 5674)

The Board advises the Scottish Ministers on the exercise of their powers under Section 7 of the Industrial Development Act 1982.
Chairman: Ian Good, CBE
Secretary: Peter Ford

SCOTTISH LAW COMMISSION

140 Causewayside, Edinburgh EH9 1PR (Tel: 0131-668 2131; Fax: 0131-662 4900; E-mail: info@scotlawcom.gov.uk)

The Commission keeps the law in Scotland under review and makes proposals for its development and reform. It is responsible to the Scottish Ministers through the Scottish Executive Justice Department.
Chairman (part-time): The Hon. Lord Gill
Commissioners (full-time): Prof. G. Maher; Prof. K. G. C. Reid; Prof. J. Thomson; (part-time) P. S. Hodge, QC
Secretary: Miss J. McLeod

SCOTTISH LEGAL AID BOARD

44 Drumsheugh Gardens, Edinburgh EH3 7SW (Tel: 0131-226 7061; Fax: 0131-220 4878; E-mail: general@slab.org.uk Web: www.scotlegalaid.gov.uk and www.slab.org.uk)

The Scottish Legal Aid Board was set up under the Legal Aid (Scotland) Act 1986. It is responsible for ensuring that advice and assistance and representation are available in accordance with the Act. The Board is a non-departmental public body whose members are appointed by the First Minister.

Chairman: Mrs J. Couper
Members: B. C. Adair; Mrs K. Blair; W. Gallagher; A. Jessop; N. Kuenssberg; D. O'Carroll; Mrs Y. Osman; Prof. J. P. Percy; Ms M. Scanlan; M. C. Thomson, QC; A. F. Wylie, QC
Chief Executive: L. Montgomery

SCOTTISH LEGAL SERVICES OMBUDSMAN

17 Waterloo Place, Edinburgh, EH1 3DL (Tel: 0131-244 3055; Fax: 0131-244 3056; E-mail: complaints@scot-legal-ombud.org.uk Web: www.scot-legal-ombud.org.uk)

The Office of the Scottish Legal Services Ombudsman examines the way in which the Law Society of Scotland, the Faculty of Advocates and the Scottish Conveyancing and Executry Services Board have handled the investigation of complaints against legal practitioners who are members of these bodies.

SCOTTISH MEDICAL PRACTICES COMMITTEE

Scottish Health Service Centre, Crewe Road South, Edinburgh EH4 2LF (Tel: 0131-623 2532)

The Committee ensures that there is an adequate number of GPs providing general medical services in Scotland.

Chairman: Dr G. McIntosh, MBE
Secretary: Mrs K. McGeary

SCOTTISH NATURAL HERITAGE

12 Hope Terrace, Edinburgh EH9 2AS (Tel: 0131-447 4784; Fax: 0131-446 2277; Web: www.snh.org.uk)

Scottish Natural Heritage was established in 1992 under the Natural Heritage (Scotland) Act 1991. It provides advice on nature conservation to all those whose activities affect wildlife, landforms and features of geological interest in Scotland, and seeks to develop and improve facilities for the enjoyment and understanding of the Scottish countryside. It is funded by the Scottish Executive.

Chairman: Dr J. Markland, CBE
Chief Executive: Prof. R. Crofts, CBE
Chief Scientific Adviser: Prof. M. B. Usher, OBE
Directors of Strategy and Operations: J. Thomson (West); Dr. I. Jardine (East); Dr. J. Watson (North)
Director of Corporate Services: Mr I. Edgeler

SCOTTISH OCEANIC AREA CONTROL CENTRE

Atlantic House, Sherwood Road, Prestwick KA9 2NR (Tel: 01292-479800; Fax: 01292-692733)

National Air Traffic Services (NATS) provides safety by ensuring aircraft flying in UK airspace, and over the eastern part of the North Atlantic, are safely separated. Safety is NATS' first and foremost priority but it also aims to provide the service in an efficient and expeditious way.

The two centres situated in Atlantic House, Prestwick are: the Scottish Area Control Centre (ScACC) which handles aircraft over Scotland and the adjacent sea areas, and

The Oceanic Area Control Centre (OACC) which handles aircraft flying over the Atlantic.

SCOTTISH PARLIAMENTARY COMMISSIONER FOR ADMINISTRATION

28 Thistle Street, Edinburgh EH2 1EN (Tel: 0845-601 0456; Fax: 0131-226 4447 Web: www.ombudsman.org.uk)

The Scottish Parliamentary Commissioner for Administration (the Scottish Commissioner) is responsible for investigating complaints referred to him by Members of the Scottish Parliament on behalf of members of the public who have suffered an injustice through maladministration by the Scottish Executive, the Parliamentary Corporation and a wide range of public bodies involved in devolved Scottish affairs. The Scottish Commissioner also investigates complaints, referred by MSPs, about wrongful refusal of access to official information.

Scottish Parliamentary Commissioner: M. S. Buckley
Head of Scottish Office: G. Keil

SCOTTISH PRISONS COMPLAINTS COMMISSION

Government Buildings, Broomhouse Drive, Edinburgh EH11 3XD (Tel: 0131-244 8423; Fax: 0131-244 8430)

The Commission was established in 1994. It is an independent body to which prisoners in Scottish prisons can make application in relation to any matter where they have failed to obtain satisfaction from the Prison Service's internal grievance procedures. Clinical judgments made by medical officers, matters which are the subject of legal proceedings and matters relating to sentence, conviction and parole decision-making are excluded from the Commission's jurisdiction. The Commissioner is appointed by the First Minister.
Commissioner: Joan N. Aitken

SCOTTISH PUBLIC PENSIONS AGENCY

St Margaret's House, 151 London Road, Edinburgh EH8 7TG (Tel: 0131-556 8400; Fax: 0131-244 3334)

The Agency is an executive agency of the Scottish Executive Education Department. It is responsible for the pension arrangements of some 300,000 people, mainly NHS and teaching services employees and pensioners.
Chief Executive: R. Garden
Directors: G. Mowat (Policy); M. MacDermott (Human Resources/ Teachers Scheme Manager); J. Nelson (IT and Finance); G. Taylor (NHS Scheme Manager)

SCOTTISH RECORDS ADVISORY COUNCIL

HM General Register House, Edinburgh EH1 3YY (Tel: 0131-535 1314; Fax: 0131-535 1360; E-mail: alison.rosie@nas.gov.uk)

The Council was established under the Public Records (Scotland) Act 1937. Its members are appointed by the First Minister and it may submit proposals or make representations to the First Minister, the Lord Justice-General or the Lord President of the Court of Session on questions relating to the public records of Scotland.
Chairman: Prof. A. Crowther
Secretary: Dr A. Rosie

SCOTTISH SCREEN

249 West George Street, Glasgow G2 4QE (Tel: 0141-302 1700; Fax: 0141-302 1711; E-mail: info@scottishscreen.com; Web: www.scottishscreen.com)

Scottish Screen is responsible to the Scottish Parliament for developing all aspects of screen industry and culture in Scotland through script and company development, short film production, distribution of Lottery film production finance, training, education, exhibition funding, the Film Commission locations support and the Scottish Screen Archive.
Chairman: J. Lee
Chief Executive: J. Archer

SCOTTISH SOLICITORS' DISCIPLINE TRIBUNAL

22 Rutland Square, Edinburgh EH1 2BB (Tel: 0131-229 5860)

The Scottish Solicitors' Discipline Tribunal is an independent statutory body with a panel of 18 members, ten of whom are solicitors; members are appointed by the Lord President of the Court of Session. Its principal function is to consider complaints of misconduct against solicitors in Scotland.
Chairman: J. W. Laughland
Clerk: J. M. Barton, WS

SCOTTISH TOURIST BOARD

23 Ravelston Terrace, Edinburgh EH4 3EU (Tel: 0131-332 2433; Fax: 0131-343 1513)
Thistle House, Beechwood Park North, Inverness IV2 3ED (Tel: 01463-716996; Fax: 01463-717233; Web: www.visitscotland.com)

The Scottish Tourist Board is responsible for developing and marketing the tourist industry in Scotland. The Board's main objectives are to promote holidays and to encourage the provision and improvement of tourist amenities.
Chief Executive: P. McKinlay, CBE (interim chief executive)

SCOTTISH VALUATION AND RATING COUNCIL

c/o LGF&P, Area 3-J, Victoria Quay, Edinburgh EH6 6QQ (Tel: 0131-244 7003; Fax: 0131-244 7058)

The Council advises on any matter pertaining to valuation and rating, including evaluation of representations and recommendations made to the First Minister, the identification of issues requiring consideration, and advice in the preparation of legislation.

Chairman: Prof. G. Milne
Secretary: H. Tristram

SEA FISH INDUSTRY AUTHORITY

18 Logie Mill, Logie Green Road, Edinburgh EH7 4HG (Tel: 0131-558 3331; Fax: 0131-558 1442; E-mail: seafish@seafish.co.uk)

Established under the Fisheries Act 1981, the Authority is required to promote the efficiency of the sea fish industry. It carries out research relating to the industry and gives advice on related matters. It provides training, promotes the marketing, consumption and export of sea fish and sea fish products. It is responsible to the Ministry of Agriculture, Fisheries and Food.
Chairman: E. Davey
Chief Executive: A. C. Fairbairn

SECRETARY OF COMMISSIONS FOR SCOTLAND

Spur W1 (E), Saughton House, Broomhouse Drive, Edinburgh EH11 3XD (Tel: 0131-244 2691; Fax: 0131-244 2623)

The Secretary of Commissions deals with the appointment of justices of the peace and of general commissioners of income tax, and with lord lieutenancy business.
Secretary of Commissions for Scotland: Mr A. Oliver

SPECIAL COMMISSIONERS OF INCOME TAX

15–19 Bedford Avenue, London WC1B 3AS (Tel: 020-7631 4242)

The Special Commissioners are an independent body appointed by the Lord Chancellor in conjunction with the Lord Advocate to hear complex appeals against decisions of the Board of Inland Revenue and its officials. In addition to the Presiding Special Commissioner there are two part-time special commissioners; all are legally qualified.
Presiding Special Commissioner: His Hon. Stephen Oliver, QC
Clerk: R. P. Lester

SPORTSCOTLAND

Caledonia House, South Gyle, Edinburgh EH12 9DQ (Tel: 0131-317 7200; Fax: 0131-317 7202)

Sportscotland is responsible for the development of sport and physical recreation in Scotland. It aims to increase participation in sport among young people and to provide the highest level of coaching and support for aspiring top performers. It advises the Scottish Parliament on sports matters, and it administers the Lottery Sports Fund in Scotland.
Chairman: A. Dempster
Chief Executive: F. A. L. Alstead, CBE

STUDENT AWARDS AGENCY FOR SCOTLAND

Gyleview House, 3 Redheughs Rigg, Edinburgh EH12 9HH (Tel: 0131-476 8212; Fax: 0131-244 5887)

The Agency is an executive agency of the Scottish Executive Enterprise and Lifelong Learning Department. It awards grants to Scottish students undertaking full-time or sandwich courses.
Chief Executive: K. MacRae

TRAFFIC COMMISSIONER (SCOTLAND)

Argyle House, J Floor, 3 Lady Lawson Street, Edinburgh EH3 9SE (Tel: 0131-529 8500; Fax: 0131-529 8501)

The Traffic Commissioners are responsible for licensing operators of heavy goods and public service vehicles. They also have responsibility for appeals relating to the licensing of operators and for disciplinary cases involving the conduct of drivers of these vehicles. Each Traffic Commissioner constitutes a tribunal for the purposes of the Tribunals and Inquiries Act 1971.
Scottish Traffic Commissioner: M. W. Betts, CBE

TRANSPORT TRIBUNAL

48–49 Chancery Lane, London WC2A 1JR (Tel: 020-7947 7493)

The Transport Tribunal hears appeals against decisions of Traffic Commissioners on passenger or goods vehicle operator licensing applications. The tribunal consists of a legally-qualified president, two legal chairmen, and five lay members. The president and legal members are

appointed by the Lord Chancellor and the lay members by the Secretary of State for the Transport, Local Government and the Regions.
President (part-time): H. B. H. Carlisle, QC
Legal member (part-time): His Hon. Judge Brodrick; J. Beech
Lay members: L. Milliken; P. Rogers; Ms P. Steel; D. Yeomans
Secretary: P. J. Fisher

UK PASSPORT SERVICE

Regional Office, 3 Northgate, 96 Milton Street, Cowcaddens, Glasgow G4 0BT (Tel: 0990-210410)
Central telephone number: 0870-521 0410
Central Fax number: 020-7271 8581
Web site: www.ukpa.gov.uk

The UK Passport Service is an executive agency of the Home Office. It is responsible for the issue of British passports. The passport offices are generally open Monday–Friday, 8.30–6.00 Saturday 9.00–3.00, but there are some regional variations. The majority of telephone calls are now handled by a call centre, but where it is essential that customers speak directly to a particular regional office calls are transferred. The call centre operates 24 hours a day.
Head of Glasgow Regional Office: R. D. Wilson

VALUATION APPEAL PANELS

c/o Convention of Scottish Local Authorities, Rosebery House, Haymarket Terrace, Edinburgh EH12 5XZ (Tel: 0131-474 9200; Fax: 0131-474 9292)

The valuation panels and valuation appeal panels drawn from them hear and determine council tax and non-domestic rating appeals. Members of the local valuation panels are appointed by the Sheriff Principal for the area and are required to live or

work in the area covered by the panel. A central secretariat service to the valuation appeal panels is provided by COSLA.
COSLA contact: Mrs B. Campbell

VAT AND DUTIES TRIBUNALS

44 Palmerston Place, Edinburgh EH12 5BJ (Tel: 0131-226 3551)

VAT and Duties Tribunals are administered by the First Minister in Scotland. They are independent, and decide disputes between taxpayers and Customs and Excise. Chairmen in Scotland are appointed by the Lord President of the Court of Session.
President: His Hon. Stephen Oliver, QC
Vice-President: Scotland, T. G. Coutts, QC
Registrar: R. P. Lester

WAR PENSIONS AGENCY

Norcross, Blackpool, Lancs FY5 3WP (Tel: 0800-169 2277)

The Agency is an executive agency of the Department for Work and Pensions. It administers the payment of war disablement and war widows' pensions and provides welfare services and support to war disablement pensioners, war widows and their dependants and carers.
Chief Executive: A. Burnham (acting)

THE EUROPEAN PARLIAMENT

European Parliament elections take place at five-yearly intervals; the first direct elections to the Parliament were held in 1979. In mainland Britain MEPs were elected in all constituencies on a first-past-the-post basis until the elections of 10 June 1999, when a 'closed-list' regional system of proportional representation was used for the first time. Scotland constitutes a region.

Parties submitted a list of candidates for each region in their own order of preference. Voters voted for a party or an independent candidate, and the first seat in each region was allocated to the party or candidate with the highest number of votes. The rest of the seats in each region were then allocated broadly in proportion to each party's share of the vote. The Scotland region returned eight members.

British subjects and citizens of the Irish Republic are eligible for election to the European Parliament provided they are 21 or over and not subject to disqualification. Since 1994, nationals of member states of the European Union have had the right to vote in elections to the European Parliament in the UK as long as they are entered on the electoral register.

MEPs currently receive a salary from the parliaments or governments of their respective member states, set at the level of the national parliamentary salary and subject to national taxation rules (the salary of British MEPs is £48,371). A proposal that all MEPs should be paid the same rate of salary out of the EU budget, and subject to the EC tax rate, was under negotiation between the European Parliament and the Council of Ministers at the time of going to press.

SCOTLAND REGION

at election on 10 June 1999

E.3,979,845 T.24.83%

Lab.	283,490	(28.68%)
SNP	268,528	(27.17%)
C.	195,296	(19.76%)
LD	96,971	(9.81%)
Green	57,142	(5.78%)
SSP	39,720	(4.02%)
Pro Euro C.	17,781	(1.80%)
UK Ind.	12,549	(1.27%)
Soc. Lab.	9,385	(0.95%)
BNP	3,729	(0.38%)
NLP	2,087	(0.21%)
Lower Tax	1,632	(0.17%)

Lab. majority 14,962

(June 1994, Lab. maj. 148,718)

SCOTTISH MEMBERS

Attwooll, Ms Elspeth (b. 1943), LD, Scotland
*Hudghton, Ian (b. 1951), SNP, Scotland
MacCormick, Prof. D. Neil, FBA (b. 1941), SNP, Scotland
*Martin, David W. (b. 1954), Lab., Scotland
*Miller, William (b. 1954), Lab., Scotland
Purvis, John R., CBE (b. 1938), C., Scotland
Stevenson, Struan (b. 1948), C., Scotland
Stihler, Ms Catherine D. (b. 1973), Lab., Scotland

* Member of the last European Parliament

EU INFORMATION

Relations with the European Union (EU) remain reserved to the UK government after devolution. However, since EU policies and legislation affect many of the matters for which the Scottish Parliament and Executive are responsible, both the Parliament and the Executive are involved in scrutinising EU proposals to ensure that Scotland's interests are taken into consideration.

Where national legislation is required to fulfil the UK's obligation to implement EC legislation, the Scottish Parliament and Executive may choose to use legislation in relation to devolved matters in Scotland. The Scottish Ministers will be actively involved in decision-making on EU matters.

The Scottish Executive has its own office in Brussels to help represent Scotland's interests and complement the work of the UK Permanent Representative to the EU (UKRep). The office may also gather information on behalf of the Scottish Executive and Parliament and acts as a base for visits to Brussels by Scottish Ministers and officials of the Scottish Executive.

SCOTTISH EXECUTIVE EU OFFICE

Scotland House, 6 Rond Point Schuman, B-1040 Brussels, Belgium (Tel: 00-322-282 8330; Fax: 00-322-282 8345)

INFORMATION SOURCES

Information about the EU is available from a variety of sources at different levels. The European Commission is developing a decentralised information network which aims to meet both general and specialised needs. The following are available in Scotland:

EUROPEAN COMMISSION REPRESENTATION IN SCOTLAND

9 Alva Street, Edinburgh EH2 4PH
(Tel: 0131-225 2058; Fax: 0131-226 4105;
Web: www.europa.eu.int)

EUROPEAN PARLIAMENT INFORMATION OFFICE

Hollywood Road, Edinburgh (from December 2001) Web: www.europarl.org.uk

EUROPEAN INFORMATION CENTRES

The centres provide information on Europe relevant to business (particularly small and medium-sized businesses), such as company law, relevant European legislation, taxation, public contracts, opportunities and funding. They can also offer an advisory service, for which a charge may be made.

GLASGOW
Franborough House, 123 Bothwell Street, Glasgow G2 7JP (Tel: 0141-221 0999; Fax 0141-221 6539; E-mail: euroinfocentre@scotent.co.uk; Web: www.euro-info.org/centres/glasgow)

INVERNESS
20 Bridge Street, Inverness IV1 1QR
(Tel: 01463-702560; Fax: 01463-715600;
 E-mail: eic@sprite.co.uk)

EUROPEAN DOCUMENTATION CENTRES

Based in university libraries, the documentation centres hold reference collections of major official documents of the EU institutions, and other publications.

UNIVERSITY OF ABERDEEN

The Taylor Library EDC, Dunbar Street, Aberdeen AB24 3JB (Tel: 01224-273334; Fax: 01224-273819; E-mail: e.a.mackie@abdn.ac.uk Web: www.abdn.ac.uk/diss/infoserv/sites/taylor)
European and Business Information Officer:
Ms L. Mackie

UNIVERSITY OF DUNDEE

The Law Library, Scrymgeour Building, Park Place , Dundee DD1 4HN (Tel: 01382-344102; Fax: 01382-344102;
E-mail: a.duncan@dundee.ac.uk;
Web: www.dundee.ac.uk/edu)

Senior Library Assistant: Ms A. Duncan

UNIVERSITY OF EDINBURGH

Law and Europa Library, Old College, South Bridge, Edinburgh EH8 9YL
(Tel: 0131-650 2043; Fax: 0131-650 6343;
E-mail: europa.library@ed.ac.uk;
Web: www.lib.ed.ac.uk/lib/sites/law.shtml)
Law and European Documentation Librarian:
K. Taylor

UNIVERSITY OF GLASGOW

The Library, Hillhead Street, Glasgow G12 8QE
(Tel: 0141-330 6722; Fax: 0141-330 4952;
E-mail: gxlr30@gla.ac.uk;
Web: www.lib.gla.ac.uk/Depts/MOPS/EU/index.html)
Director of Library Services: A. Wale

EUROPEAN REFERENCE CENTRE

The reference centre keep less comprehensive collections of publications.
The Library, Stirling University, Stirling FK9 4LA (Tel: 01786-467231; Fax: 01786-466866; E-mail: d.j.gardiner@stir.ac.uk;
Web: www.stir.ac.uk/infoserv)
Director of Information Services: Dr P. Kemp

CARREFOUR CENTRES

The Carrefour centres are based in rural areas. They provide information on EU policy concerning rural areas and rural issues, and promote awareness of rural development.

HIGHLANDS AND ISLANDS RURAL CARREFOUR CENTRE

Business Information Source, 20 Bridge Street, Inverness IV1 1QR
(Tel: 01463-715400; Fax: 01463-715600;
E-mail: bis.enquiries@bis.uk.com)

PUBLIC INFORMATION RELAY

These are information points at a number of public libraries where general reference documents about the EU are held and free information leaflets are available. At present there are public information relay points at about 34 local public libraries in Scotland, at least one in each local authority area.

EUROPEAN RESOURCE CENTRES

The resource centres hold printed and electronic information on Europe for schools, and stocks of free publications on European affairs, the EU institutions, and the countries of the EU.

EURODESK SCOTLAND

Community Learning Scotland, Rosebery House, 9 Haymarket Terrace, Edinburgh EH12 5EZ, (Tel: 0131-313 2488; Fax: 0131-313 6800; E-mail: UK001@cls.dircon.co.uk; Web: www.ercscotland.eurodesk.org)

CITIZENS FIRST

Citizens First is a free telephone service providing public information on various aspects of European citizenship. Callers can order free guides and factsheets on living, working and travelling in the EU, study and training in another EU country; equal opportunities, the single market, and other subjects. The materials are published in all EU languages, including Gaelic.
(Freephone: 0800-581591
Web: europa.eu.int/citizens)

POLITICAL PARTIES

Financial support for opposition parties has been set at £5,000 per MSP until 31 March 2000 in a draft SI laid at Westminster. The Scottish Parliament has no statutory power to overturn this level, although some MSPs are pressing for it to be reviewed by the Neill Committee as opposition parties at Westminster get £10,000 per MP. From 1 April 2000, the Scottish Parliament has set the level of financial support.

Although there are Liberal Democrat MSPs in the Executive, the party is deemed an opposition party because its members make up less than 20 per cent of the total number of ministers (four out of 22).

SCOTTISH CONSERVATIVE AND UNIONIST CENTRAL OFFICE

Suite 1/1, 14 Links Place, Leith, Edinburgh EH6 7EZ (Tel 0131-247 6890; Fax: 0131-247 6891; E-mail: centraloffice@Scottish.torys.org.uk; Web: www.scottish.toys.org.uk)
Chairman: Raymond Robertson
Deputy Chairman: W. Walker
Hon. Treasurer: D. Mitchell, CBE
Director: Simon Turner

SCOTTISH GREEN PARTY

14 Albany Street, Edinburgh EH1 3QB
(Tel 0131-478 7896; Fax: 0131-478 7896;
E-mail: info@scottishgreens.org.uk;
Web: www.scottishgreens.org.uk)
Principal Speakers: Ms E. Scott Robin Harper, MSP
Executive Convener: C. Hoffmann
Treasurer: I. Baxter

SCOTTISH LABOUR PARTY

John Smith House, 145 West Regent Street, Glasgow, G2 4RE (Tel 0141-572 6900;
Fax: 0141-572 2566;
E-mail: scotland@new.labour.org.uk;
Web: www.scottishlabour.org.uk)
First Minister in Scotland: H. McLeish, MSP
Chair: John Lambie
Vice-chair: Anne McLean
Treasurer: Susan Morton
General Secretary: Lesley Quinn

SCOTTISH LIBERAL DEMOCRATS

4 Clifton Terrace, Edinburgh EH12 5DR
(Tel 0131-337 2314; Fax: 0131-337 3566;
E-mail: scotlibdem@cix.co.uk;
Web: www.scotlibdems.org.uk)
Party President: Malcolm Bruce, MP
Party Leader: Jim Wallace, MSP
Convener: I. Yuill
Treasurer: D. R. Sullivan
Chief Executive: Kilvert Croft

SCOTTISH NATIONAL PARTY

107 McDonald Road, Edinburgh, EH7 4NW
(Tel 0131-525 8900; Fax: 0131-525 8901;
E-mail: snp.hq@snp.org;
Web: www.snp.org)
Parliamentary Party Leader: John Swinney, MSP
Chief Whip: Bruce Crawford, MSP
Senior Vice-Convener: Roseanne Cunningham
National Treasurer: Jim Mather
National Secretary: Stewart Hosie

SCOTTISH SOCIALIST PARTY

73 Robertson Street, Glasgow G2 8QD
(Tel: 0141-221 7714; Fax: 0141-221 7715;
Web: www.scotsocialistparty.org)
Convener: T. Sheridan
Treasurer: K. Baldasara
National Secretary: A. Green

UK INDEPENDENCE PARTY

268 Bath Street, Glasgow G2 4JR
(Tel: 0141-332 2214; Fax: 0141-353 6900)
Organiser: A. D. McConnachie

LOCAL GOVERNMENT

The Local Government etc. (Scotland) Act 1994 abolished the two-tier structure of nine regional and 53 district councils which had existed since 1975 and replaced it, from 1 April 1996, with a single-tier structure consisting of 29 unitary authorities on the mainland; the three islands councils remain. Each unitary authority has inherited all the functions of the regional and district councils, except water and sewerage (now provided by public bodies whose members are appointed by the Scottish Ministers) and reporters panels (now a national agency).

On taking office, the Scottish Parliament assumed responsibility for legislation on local government.

REVIEW OF LOCAL GOVERNMENT

The Commission on Local Government (the McIntosh Commission), reported to the First Minister in June 1999. Subsequently the Scottish Executive established the Renewing Local Democracy working group to consider how to make council membership more attractive, make councils more representative of their communities and advise on appropriate numbers of members for each council. It also considered possible alternative electoral systems and remuneration of councillors.

As recommended in the *McIntosh Report*, the Scottish executive has also set up the Leadership Advisory Panel. All Scottish local authorities are conducting reviews of their policy development and decision-making structures, working closely with the Panel. The Panel will assess each council's proposals for openness, transparency and accessibility.

ELECTIONS

The unitary authorities consist of directly elected councillors. Elections take place every three years, normally on the first Thursday in May. The 1999 local government elections were held on 6 May, simultaneously with the elections for the Scottish Parliament. Discussions are under way to change Local Government elections to every four years concurrent with Scottish Parliament elections.

Generally, all British subjects and citizens of the Republic of Ireland who are 18 years or over and resident on the qualifying date in the area for which the election is being held, are entitled to vote at them. A register of electors is prepared and published annually by local electoral registration officers. Candidates, who are subject to various statutory qualifications and disqualifications

designed to ensure that they are suitable persons to hold office, must be nominated by electors for the electoral area concerned. The electoral roll that came into effect in 16 February 2000 showed 4,009,424 people registered to vote.

The Local Government Boundary Commission for Scotland is responsible for carrying out periodic reviews of electoral arrangements and making proposals to the Scottish Ministers for any changes found necessary.

INTERNAL ORGANISATION AND FUNCTIONS

The council as a whole is the final decision-making body within any authority. Councils are free to a great extent to make their own internal organisational arrangements. Normally, questions of policy are settled by the full council, while the administration of the various services is the responsibility of committees of councillors. Day-to-day decisions are delegated to the council's officers, who act within the policies laid down by the councillors.

The functions of the councils and islands councils are: education; social work; strategic planning; the provision of infrastructure such as roads; consumer protection; flood prevention; coast protection; valuation and rating; the police and fire services; emergency planning; electoral registration; public transport; registration of births, deaths and marriages; housing; leisure and recreation; development control and building control; environmental health; licensing; allotments; public conveniences; and the administration of district courts.

The chairman of a local council in Scotland may be known as a convenor; a provost is the equivalent of a mayor. The chairman of the council in the cities of Aberdeen, Dundee, Edinburgh and Glasgow are Lord Provosts.

LORD-LIEUTENANTS

The Lord-Lieutenant of a county is the permanent local representative of the Crown in that county. They are appointed by the Sovereign on the recommendation of the Prime Minister. The retirement age is 75.

The office of Lord-Lieutenant dates from 1557, and its holder was originally responsible for the maintenance of order and for local defence in the county. The duties of the post include attending on royalty during official visits to the county, performing certain duties in connection with armed forces of the Crown (and in particular the reserve forces), and making presentations of honours and awards on behalf of the Crown.

Lord-Lieutenants

Title	Name
Aberdeenshire	A. D. M. Farquharson, OBE
Angus	Mrs Georgiana L. Osborne
Argyll and Bute	vacant
Ayrshire and Arran	Maj. R. Y. Henderson, TD
Banffshire	J. A. S. McPherson, CBE
Berwickshire	Maj. Alexander Trotter
Caithness	Maj. G. T. Dunnett, TD
Clackmannan	Mrs S. G. Cruickshank
Dumfries	Capt. R. C. Cunningham-Jardine
Dunbartonshire	Brig. D. D. G. Hardie, TD
East Lothian	W. Garth Morrison, CBE
Eilean Siar/ Western Isles	Alexander Matheson
Fife	Mrs C. M. Dean
Inverness	The Lord Gray of Contin
Kincardineshire	J. D. B. Smart
Lanarkshire	Gilbert K. Cox, MBE
Midlothian	Capt. G. W. Burnet, LVO
Moray	Air Vice-Marshal G. A. Chesworth, CB, OBE, DFC
Nairn	Ewen J. Brodie of Lethen
Orkney	G. R. Marwick
Perth and Kinross	Sir David Montgomery, Bt.
Renfrewshire	C. H. Parker, OBE
Ross and Cromarty	Capt. R. W. K. Stirling of Fairburn, TD
Roxburgh, Ettrick and Lauderdale	Dr June Paterson-Brown, CBE
Shetland	J. H. Scott
Stirling and Falkirk	Lt.-Col. J. Stirling of Garden, CBE, TD, FRICS
Sutherland	Maj.-Gen. D. Houston, CBE
The Stewartry of Kirkcudbright	Lt.-Gen. Sir Norman Arthur, KCB
Tweeddale	Capt. David Younger
West Lothian	vacant
Wigtown	Maj. E. S. Orr Ewing

The Lord Provosts of the four city districts of Aberdeen, Dundee, Edinburgh and Glasgow are Lord-Lieutenants for those districts *ex officio*.

COMMUNITY COUNCILS

Unlike the parish councils and community councils in England and Wales, Scottish community councils are not local authorities. Their purpose as defined in statute is to ascertain and express the views of the communities which they represent, and to take in the interests of their communities such action as appears to be expedient or practicable. Over 1,000 community councils have been established under schemes drawn up by district and islands councils in Scotland.

Since 1996 community councils have had an enhanced role, becoming statutory consultees on local planning issues and on the decentralisation schemes which the new councils have to draw up for delivery of services.

FINANCE

Local government is financed from four sources: the council tax, non-domestic rates, government grants, and income from fees and charges for services.

COUNCIL TAX

Under the Local Government Finance Act 1992, from 1 April 1993 the council tax replaced the community charge, which had been introduced in April 1989 in place of domestic rates. The council tax is a local tax levied by each local council. Liability for the council tax bill usually falls on the owner-occupier or tenant of a dwelling which is their sole or main residence.

Each island council and unitary authority sets its own rate of council tax. The tax relates to the value of the dwelling. Each dwelling is placed in one of eight valuation bands, ranging from A to H, based on the property's estimated market value as at 1 April 1991.

The valuation bands and ranges of values in Scotland are:

A	Up to £27,000
B	£27,001—£35,000
C	£35,001—£45,000
D	£45,001—£58,000
E	£58,001—£80,000
F	£80,001—£106,000
G	£106,001—£212,000
H	Over £212,000

The council tax within a local area varies between the different bands according to proportions laid down by law. The charge attributable to each band as a proportion of the Band D charge set by the council is approximately:

A	67%
B	78%
C	89%
D	100%
E	122%
F	144%
G	167%
H	200%

The Band D rate for each council is given in the individual local council entries. There may be variations from the given figure within each district council area because of different community precepts being levied.

NON-DOMESTIC RATES

Non-domestic (business) rates are collected by the billing authorities, which in Scotland are the local authorities. Rates are levied in accordance with the Local Government (Scotland) Act 1975. From 1995—6, the Secretary of State for Scotland prescribed a single non-domestic rates poundage to apply throughout the country at the same level as the uniform business rate (UBR) in England. The UBR for 1998—9 was 48p for property up to a rateable value of £10,000 and 48.9p for property over a rateable value of £10,000. Rate income is pooled and redistributed to local authorities on a per capita basis.

Rateable values for the current rating lists came into force on 1 April 1995. They are derived from the rental value of property as at 1 April 1993 and determined on certain statutory assumptions by Regional Assessors. New property which is added to the list, and significant changes to existing property, necessitate amendments to the rateable value on the same basis. Valuation rolls remain in force until the next general revaluation. Such revaluations take place every five years. New ratings lists came into force on 1 April 2000, based on rental levels as at 1 April 1998.

Certain types of property, such as places of public religious worship and agricultural land and buildings, are exempt from rates. Charities, other non-profit-making organisations, sole village shops and post offices, and certain other businesses may receive full or partial relief. Empty property is liable to pay rates at 50 per cent, except for certain specified classes which are entirely exempt.

In 2000–01, total receipts were £1,498 million (provisional) from non-domestic rates and £1,160 million from the council tax. The amount of council tax budgeted to be collected in 2001–02 is £1,302 million.

GOVERNMENT GRANTS

In addition to specific grants in support of revenue expenditure on particular services, central government pays revenue support grant to local authorities. This grant is paid to each local authority so that if each authority budgeted at the level of its standard spending assessment, all authorities in the same class can set broadly the same council tax.

EXPENDITURE

Local authority current budgeted expenditure, supported by aggregate external finance (AEF), for 2000–1 was:

Service	£000s
Education	2,997,406
Arts and Libraries	121,652
Social Work Services	1,223,442
Law, Order and Protective Services	950,668
Roads and Transport	352,681
Other Environmental Services	720,495
Tourism	8,778
Housing	4,222
Sheltered Employment	9,679
Administration of Housing Benefit	34,988
Consumer Protection	17,006
TOTAL	6,441,017

COMPLAINTS

Commissioners for Local Administration are responsible for investigating complaints from members of the public who claim to have suffered injustice as a consequence of maladministration in local government or in certain local bodies.

Complaints are made to the relevant local authority in the first instance and are referred to the Commissioners if the complainant is not satisfied.

LOCAL AUTHORITY AREAS

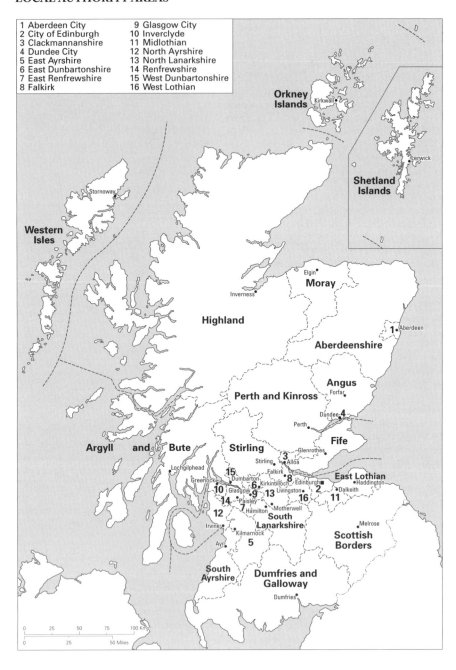

1 Aberdeen City	9 Glasgow City
2 City of Edinburgh	10 Inverclyde
3 Clackmannanshire	11 Midlothian
4 Dundee City	12 North Ayrshire
5 East Ayrshire	13 North Lanarkshire
6 East Dunbartonshire	14 Renfrewshire
7 East Renfrewshire	15 West Dunbartonshire
8 Falkirk	16 West Lothian

Orkney Islands
Kirkwall

Shetland Islands
Lerwick

Western Isles
Stornoway

Elgin
Moray
Inverness

Highland

Aberdeen
Aberdeenshire

Angus
Forfar

Perth and Kinross

Dundee
Fife

Perth

Argyll and Bute
Lochgilphead

Stirling
Glenrothes
Stirling Alloa
Falkirk
Greenock
Dumbarton
Kirkintilloch Edinburgh
East Lothian
Haddington
Glasgow Livingston Dalkeith
Paisley
Hamilton
Motherwell
South Lanarkshire
Irvine
Melrose
Kilmarnock
Scottish Borders
Ayr

South Ayrshire
Dumfries and Galloway
Dumfries

0   25   50   75   100 Km
0   25   50 Miles

COUNCIL DIRECTORY

Note: In Members of the Council **(LP)**=*Lord Provost,* **(P)** = *Provost and* **(C)** = Convenor.

ABERDEEN CITY COUNCIL

Town House, Broad Street, Aberdeen AB10 1FY
(Tel: 01224-522000; Fax: 01224-627213;
Web: www.aberdeencity.gov.uk)

Area: 184.47 sq. km
Population (1998 estimate): 213,070
population density (2000): 1,691 persons per sq. km
projected population in 2006 (1999-based): 208,714
number of households (1998): 96,661

Council tax (average Band D per two-person household), for 2001–02: £934.00
Notified net non-domestic rate income (1999–2000): £107,932,600

Education (pupils on register, 2000–01):
primary: 15,000
secondary: 10,981
special: 376
entitled to free meals: 13.5%

MEMBERS OF THE COUNCIL

Adam, George	(Lab.)
Allan, Yvonne	(Lab.)
Anderson, Janetta	(LD)
Cassie, Scott	(LD)
Clark, Ronald	(LD)
Clyne, David	(Lab.)
Cormack, Irene	(LD)
Dean, Katherine	(LD)
Dempsey, John	(C.)
Falconer, David	(LD)
Gordon, Stewart	(C.)
Graham, Gordon	(Lab.)
Graham, Marjorie	(C.)
Harris, Edward	(Lab.)
Hutcheon, Raymond	(LD)
Irons, Maureen	(Lab.)
Ironside, Leonard	(Lab.)
Jaffrey, Muriel	(SNP)
Lamond, James	(Lab.)
Lamond, June	(Lab.)
Leslie, Gordon	(LD)
MacDonald, Pamela	(LD)
MacLean, Allan	(Lab.)
Maitland, David	(Lab.)
McIntosh, Allan	(Lab.)
Milne, Alan	(C.)
Milne, Ramsay	(Lab.)
Pirie, Charles	(Lab.)
Porter, John	(C.)
Reynolds, John	(LD)
Rutherford, Brian	(Lab.)
Shirron, Karen	(SNP)
Smith, Margaret **(LP)**	(Lab.)
Stephenson, John	(LD)
Stewart, Kevin	(SNP)
Stewart, Marianne	(Lab.)
Thomaneck, Jurgen	(Lab.)
Traynor, William	(Lab.)
Urquhart, George	(Lab.)
Webster, Ronald	(Lab.)
Wisley, Jillian	(C.)
Wyness, James	(Lab.)
Yuill, Ian	(LD)

Total: 43 (Lab.22; LD.12; C.6; SNP.3)

CHIEF OFFICERS

Chief Executive: D. Paterson
Director of Contracting Services: D. Gordon
Director of Education: J. Stodter
Director of Finance and Information Technology: G. Edwards
Director of Housing: M. Scott
Director of Legal and Corporate Services: C. Langley
Director of Personnel: Richard Parker
Director of Planning and Strategic Development: P. Cockhead
Director of Environment and Property: D Murdoch
Director of Social Work and Community Development: J. Tomlinson
Local Agenda 21 contact: G. Robertson

SCOTTISH AND UK PARLIAMENTARY CONSTITUENCIES

Aberdeen Central; Aberdeen North; Aberdeen South

ABERDEENSHIRE COUNCIL

Woodhill House, Westburn Road, Aberdeen AB16 5GB, (Tel: 01467-620981; Fax: 01224-665444; Web: www.aberdeenshire.gov.uk)

Area: 6,318 sq. km
Population (1999 estimate): 227,440
population density (1998): 36 persons per sq. km
projected population in 2006 (1999-based): 227,267
number of households (1998): 90,000

Council tax (average Band D per two-person household), for 2001–02: £855.00
Notified net non-domestic rate income (1999–2000): £48,487,191

Education (pupils on register, 2000–01):
primary: 20,916
secondary: 15,328
special: 335
entitled to free meals: 6.4%

MEMBERS OF THE COUNCIL

Anderson, James	(LD)
Anderson, William	(LD)
Argyle, Peter	(LD)
Barnes, George	(SNP)
Benzie, Kenneth	(SNP)
Bisset, Alan **(C)**	(C.)
Bisset, Heather	(LD)
Bisset, Raymond	(LD)
Buchan, Alexander	(SNP)
Burnett, Mitchell	(SNP)
Cameron, Alan	(SNP)
Cameron, Douglas	(C.)
Carmichael, Kathryn	(LD)
Cormack, Harald	(Ind.)
Coull, Samuel	(LD)
Cowie, Norman]	(Ind.)
Cox, John	(SNP)
Davidson, James	(SNP)
Duguid, Douglas	(SNP)
Ewing, Doreen	(C.)
Findlay, Audrey	(LD)
Findlay, Walter	(LD)
Ford, Martin	(SNP)
Fowler, Helen	(Ind.)
Frain, Ian	(Ind.)
Howatson, William	(LD)
Humphrey, James	(C.)
Johnston, Paul	(LD)
Leitch, Alister	(LD)
Lonchay, Sheena	(LD)
Loveday, John	(LD)
Luffman, Bruce	(C.)
Lumsden, Gerald	(C.)
MacLeod, Alice	(SNP)
Mair, Stuart	(Ind.)
Mair, Sydney	(SNP)
Makin, Norma	(Ind.)
McGregor, John	(LD)
McHugh, Denis	(SNP)
McInnes, Alison	(LD)
McKee, Jeanette	(SNP)
McLean, John	(Ind.)
McRae, Margaret	(SNP)
Millar, Colin	(LD)

Morrison, John	(LD)
Nash, Mairi	(LD)
Nelson, Carl	(C.)
Norrie, Alisan	(Ind.)
Pratt, Stuart	(SNP)
Raeburn, Michael]	(LD)
Robertson, Elizabeth	(LD)
Saluja, Gurudeo	(LD)
Sheridan, James	(LD)
Smith, David	(LD)
Storr, Debra	(LD)
Strachan, Agnes	(SNP)
Strathdee, Joanna	(SNP)
Stroud, Richard	(LD)
Swapp, George	(Ind.)
Tait, Ian	(SNP)
Taylor, Sandra	(SNP)
Tennant, Stanley	(SNP)
Thomson, Norma	(SNP)
Topping, Brian	(SNP)
Towers, James	(SNP)
Tunstall, Anne	(LD)
Wallace, Alexander	(C.)
Watson, Jenny	(Ind.)

Total: 68 (LD.27; SNP.23; Ind.10; C.8)

CHIEF OFFICERS

Chief Executive: A. G. Campbell
Director of Education and Recreation: H. Vernal
Director of Finance: C. Armstrong
Director of Law and Administration: N. McDowall
Director of Personnel and Information Technology: P. Hay
Director of Planning and Environmental Services: E. Melrose
Director of Social Work and Housing: Mrs M. Wells
Director of Transportation and Infrastructure: I. Gabriel
Local Agenda 21 Officer: Ms D. Burroughs

SCOTTISH AND UK PARLIAMENTARY CONSTITUENCIES

Aberdeenshire West and Kincardine; Banff and Buchan; Gordon

ANGUS COUNCIL

The Cross, Forfar, Angus DD8 1BX (Tel: 01307-461460; Fax: 01307-461874;
Web: www.angus.gov.uk)

Area: 2,181 sq. km
Population (1998 estimate): 110,070
population density (1998): 50 persons per sq. km
projected population in 2006 (1996-based): 110,130
number of households (1996): 46,200
Council tax (average Band D per two-person household), for 2001–02: £821.00
Notified net non-domestic rate income (1999–2000): £21,069,069
Education (pupils on register, 2000–01):
primary: 9,315
secondary: 7,208
entitled to free meals: 10.1%

MEMBERS OF THE COUNCIL

Angus, Ian	(SNP)
Crowe, Bill	(SNP)
Duncan, Frances **(P)**	(SNP)
Ellis, Frank	(SNP)
Gibb, Jack	(SNP)
Gray, Alistair	(SNP)
Henderson, John	(SNP)
King, Alex	(SNP)
Leslie, Stephen	(SNP)
Lumgair, David	(C.)
Mackintosh, Ian	(C.)
McGlynn, Stewart	(SNP)
Melville, Ruth	(Ind.)
Middleton, Bill	(SNP)
Middleton, Glennis	(SNP)
Milne, Brian	(SNP)
Mowatt, Joy	(SNP)
Murphy, Peter	(Lab.)
Murray, Rob	(SNP)
Myles, Robert	(Ind.)
Nield, Peter	(LD)
Norrie, George	(Ind.)
Oswald, Helen	(SNP)
Ritchie, Kitty	(SNP)
Robertson, Bill	(SNP)
Selfridge, David	(SNP)
Spiers, Richard	(LD)
Welsh, Sheena	(SNP)
West, Sandy	(SNP)

Total: 29 (SNP.21; Ind.3; C.2; LD.2; Lab.1)

CHIEF OFFICERS

Chief Executive: A. B. Watson
Director of Contract Services: M. Graham
Acting Director of Cultural Services: N. Atkinson
Director of Education: J. Anderson
Director of Environmental and Consumer Protection: S. Heggie
Director of Finance: D. Sawers

Director of Housing: R. Ashton
Director of Information Technology: A. Greenhill
Director of Law and Administration: Ms C. Coull
Director of Personnel: Ms J. Torbet
Director of Planning and Transport: A. Anderson
Director of Property Services: M. Lunny
Director of Recreation Services: J. Zimny
Director of Roads: R. McLellan
Director of Social Work: W. Robertson
Local Agenda 21 Officer: Ms P. Coutts

SCOTTISH AND UK PARLIAMENTARY CONSTITUENCIES

Angus; Tayside North

ARGYLL AND BUTE COUNCIL

Kilmory, Lochgilphead, Argyll PA31 8RT
(Tel: 01546-602127; Fax: 01546-604138;
Web: www.argyll-bute.gov.uk)

Area: 6,930 sq. km
Population (1998 estimate): 89,980
population density (1998): 13 persons per sq. km
projected population in 2006 (1996-based): 89,461
number of households (1996): 37,700
Council tax (average Band D per two-person household), for 2001–02: £984.00
Notified non-domestic rate income (1999–2000): £23,747,965
Education (pupils on register, 2000–01):
primary: 7,616
secondary: 5,590
special: 57
entitled to free meals: 14.0%

MEMBERS OF THE COUNCIL

Banks, Robin	(NA)
Blair, Alasdair	(Ind.)
Cameron, Campbell	(SNP)
Chennell, Brian	(NA)
Coleshill, Paul	(LD)
Currie, Douglas **(C)**	(Ind.)
Currie, Robin	(LD)
Findlay, John	(NA)
Freeman, George	(NA)
Gillies, Ian	(NA)
vacant	
Hay, Alison	(LD)
Kinloch, Ronnie	(NA)
Latimer , Stanley	(NA)
MaCallum, Archie	(C.)

MacAskill, Allan	(NA)
MacDougall, Alistair	(NA)
MacIntyre, Duncan	(NA)
Macintyre, Robert	(SNP)
MacKinnon, Dugie	(NA)
MacMillan, Donnie	(NA)
Marshall, Bruce	(C.)
McIntosh, Donald	(SNP)
McKinven, Gordon	(NA)
McKinley, Alistair	(NA)
McQueen, James	(NA)
Morton, Ellen	(LD)
Petrie, William	(NA)
Robertson, Bruce	(NA)
Scoullar, Len	(Ind.)
Stewart, Moyra	(LD)
Stirling, John	(C.)
Strong, Isobel	(SNP)
Thompson, Eric	(LD)
Walsh, Dick	(NA)
Webster, David	(NA)
Wilson, Sheila	(C.)

Total: 36 (NA (Non-Aligned) 19; LD 6; SNP 4; C. 4; Ind. 3)

CHIEF OFFICERS

Chief Executive: J. A. McLellan
Director of Corporate and Legal Services: N. Stewart
Director of Development and Environment Services: G. Harper
Director of Education: A. Morton
Director of Finance: S. MacGregor
Director of Housing and Social Work: D. Hendry
Infrastructures Services Manager: Gerry Wilson
Application Support Manager: Gavin Boyd
Local Agenda 21 Officer: vacant
Scottish and UK Parliamentary Constituencies: Argyll and Bute; Dumbarton

CITY OF EDINBURGH COUNCIL

Wellington Court, 10 Waterloo Place, Edinburgh EH1 3EG (Tel: 0131-200 2000; Fax: 0131-529 7477; Web: www.edinburgh.gov.uk)

Area: 26,113 hectares
Population (1998 estimate): 450,180
population density (1998): 1,716 persons per sq. km
projected population in 2006 (1996-based): 455,608
number of households (1996): 198,200
Council tax (average Band D per two-person household), for 2001–02: £960.00
Notified net non-domestic rate income (1999–2000): £208,251,305

Education (pupils on register, 2000–01):
primary: 29,073
secondary: 19,814
special: 991
entitled to free meals: 22.9%

MEMBERS OF THE COUNCIL

Aitken, Ewan	(Lab.)
Anderson, Donald	(Lab.)
Aldridge, Robert	(LD)
Attridge, Philip	(Lab.)
Barrett, John	(LD)
Berry, Ian	(C.)
Burns, Andrew	(Lab.)
Cairns, Robert	(Lab.)
Cameron, Lesley	(Lab)
Cardownie, Stephen	(Lab.)
Child, Maureen	(Lab.)
Cunningham, Bill	(Lab.)
Dawe, Jenny	(LD)
Edie, Paul	(LD)
Fallon, Edward	(Lab.)
Fitzpatrick, William	(Lab.)
Forrest, Moyra	(LD)
Fraser, Hugh	(C.)
Gilchrist, James	(C.)
Gilmore, Sheila	(Lab.)
Grubb, George	(LD)
Guest, David	(C.)
Harrold, Kenneth	(Lab)
Henderson, Ricky	(Lab.)
Hinds, Lesley	(Lab.)
Houston, Brian	(Lab.)
Hunter, George	(C.)
Jackson, Allan	(C.)
Kennedy, Sheila	(Lab.)
Kerr, Douglas	(Lab.)
Lazarowicz, Mark	(Lab.)
Longstaff, John	(LD)
Lowrie, James	(LD)
MacKenzie, James	(C.)
Mackintosh, Fred	(LD)
Maclaren, Marilyne	(LD)
Maginnis, Elizabeth	(Lab.)
Marshall, Lawrence	(Lab.)
Meek, Brian	(C.)
Milligan, Eric **(LP)**	(Lab.)
Morton, Marion	(Lab.)
Munn, Robert	(SNP)
O'Donnell, Jack	(Lab.)
Paisley, Alastair	(C.)
Perry, Ian	(Lab.)
Ponton, Tom	(C.)
Pringle, Michael	(LD)
Russell, Frank	(Lab.)
Scobbie, Andrew	(Lab.)

Sleigh, Daphne	(C.)
Thomas, Kingsley	(Lab.)
Tritton, Susan	(LD)
Walls, James	(C.)
Wardlaw, Elizabeth	(LD)
Weddell, Brian	(Lab.)
Williamson, Paul	(Lab.)
Wilson, Donald	(Lab.)
Whyte, Iain	(C.)

Total: 58 (Lab 31; C. 13; LD 13; SNP 1)

CHIEF OFFICERS

Chief Executive: T. N. Aitchison
Director of City Development: A. Holmes
Director of Corporate Services: D. Hume
Director of Education: R. Jobson
Director of Environmental and Consumer Services: M. Drewry
Director of Finance and Information Technology: D. McGougan
Director of Housing: M. Turley
Director of Recreation: H. Coutts
Director of Social Work: L. McEwan
Local Agenda 21 Officer: D. Hume

SCOTTISH AND UK PARLIAMENTARY CONSTITUENCIES

Edinburgh Central; Edinburgh East and Musselburgh; Edinburgh North and Leith; Edinburgh Pentlands; Edinburgh South; Edinburgh West

CLACKMANNANSHIRE COUNCIL

Greenfield, Alloa, Clackmannanshire FK10 2AD (Tel: 01259-450000; Fax: 01259-452230)

Area: 157 sq. km
Population (1999 estimate): 49,000
population density (1998): 310 persons per sq. km
projected population in 2006 (1998-based): 48,183
number of households (1997): 20,200

Council tax (average Band D per two-person household), for 2001–02: £951,00
Notified net non-domestic rate income (1999–2000): £11,539,780
Education (pupils on register, 2000–01):
primary: 4,361
secondary: 3,068
special: 57
entitled to free meals: 21.3%

MEMBERS OF THE COUNCIL

Alexander, William	(SNP)
Balsillie, Donald	(SNP)
Brown, Keith	(SNP)
Calder, Billy	(Lab.)
Campbell, Alastair	(C.)
Douglas, William	(SNP)
Elder, Robert	(Lab.)
Forbes, Charles	(SNP)
Holden, Craig	(SNP)
Lindsay, Alison	(SNP)
McAdam, Walter (P)	(SNP)
Murphy, Tina	(SNP)
Paterson, Margaret	(Lab.)
Ross, Joanne	(Lab.)
Scobbie, Alex	(Lab.)
Stewart, Derek	(Lab.)
Wallace, William	(SNP)
Watson, Jim	(Lab.)

Total: 18 (SNP.10; Lab.7; C.1)

CHIEF OFFICERS

Acting Chief Executive: Keir Bloomer
Executive Director of Corporate Services: R. Dunbar
Executive Director of Development Services: G. Dallas
Executive Director of Education and Community Services: K. Bloomer
Executive Director of Environmental and Contract Services: W. Cunningham
Executive Director of Housing and Social Services: Ms B. Dickie
Head of Housing and Advice Services: C. J. Thirkettle
Head of Information Technology: Ms A. Easton
Head of Administration and Legal Services: Mrs J. McGuire
Head of Personnel: B. Hutchison
Local Agenda 21 contact: A. Shaw

SCOTTISH AND UK PARLIAMENTARY CONSTITUENCY

Ochil

DUMFRIES AND GALLOWAY COUNCIL

Council Offices, English Street, Dumfries DG1 2DD (Tel: 01387-260000; Fax: 01387-260034; Web: www.dumgal.gov.uk)

Area: 6,439 sq. km
Population (1999 estimate): 146,800
population density (1998): 23 persons per sq. km

projected population in 2006 (1998-based): 145,311

number of households (1998): 63,000

Council tax (average Band D per two-person household), for 2001–02: £857.00

Notified net non-domestic rate income (1999–2000): £33,402,835

Education (pupils on register, 2000–01):
primary: 12,504
secondary: 9,756
special: 33
entitled to free meals: 11.5%

MEMBERS OF THE COUNCIL

Agnew, John	(Ind.)
Bell, Helen	(Ind.)
Bell-Irving, Andrew	(C.)
Callender, Ian	(Ind.)
Cameron, Ken	(Ind.)
Campbell, Andrew	(Ind.)
Conchie, Brian	(Lab.)
Davidson, Kathleen	(SNP)
Dempster, Jim	(Lab.)
Dinwoodie, John	(LD)
Forster, Grahame	(Lab.)
Forteath, John	(Lab.)
Geddes, Alistair	(SNP)
Gilbey, Anthony	(C.)
Gilroy, Patsy	(C.)
Gordon, Beth	(Ind.)
Higgins, Robert	(SNP)
Holmes, Thomas	(Ind.)
Hyslop, Ivor	(C.)
Little, Billy	(SNP)
Lockhart, William	(Ind.)
Maitland, Jane	(Ind.)
Male, Denis	(LD)
Marshall, Sean	(Lab.)
McAughtrie, Thomas	(Lab.)
McBurnie, George	(Lab.)
McDowall, Sandra	(LD)
McKay, Neil	(C.)
McKie, David	(Lab.)
McQueen, Marjory	(C.)
Mitchell, Joan	(LD)
Murray, Fred	(SNP)
Nimmo, Bill	(Ind.)
Paterson, Wilma	(Lab.)
Pennie, Ian	(Ind.)
Prentice, George	(Ind.)
Purdie, Jock	(Ind.)
Ramage, John	(LD)
Saunders, Bert	(Lab.)
Scobie, Willie	(Lab.)

Sloan, Tommy	(Lab.)
Sword, David	(Lab.)
Thomson, Michael	(Ind.)
Turner, Tony	(LD)
Urquhart, Donald	(Ind.)
Vaughan, Lavinia	(C.)
Wright, Allan	(C.)

Total: 47 (Ind.15; Lab.13; C.8; LD.6; SNP.5)

CHIEF OFFICERS

Chief Executive: P. N. Jones
Director of Community Resources: L. Jardine
Director of Commercial Services: R. Blackburn
Acting Director of Education: F. Sanderson
Director of Environment and Infrastructure: Dr R. Guy
Director of Environmental Health: D. A. Grant
Director of Finance and Corporate Services: J. Cowie
Director of Housing Services: Ms Y. MacQuarrie
Director of Information Services: Dr J. Pearson
Director of Legal Services: B. Kearney
Head of Personnel Services: D. Archibald
Director of Social Services: K. Makin

SCOTTISH AND UK PARLIAMENT CONSTITUENCIES

Dumfries; Galloway and Upper Nithsdale

DUNDEE CITY COUNCIL

21 City Square, Dundee DD1 3BY
(Tel: 01382-434000; Fax: 01382-434666;
Web: www.dundeecity.gov.uk)

Area: 65 sq. km
Population (1998 estimate): 146,690
population density (1998): 2,252 persons per sq. km
projected population in 2006 (1996-based): 141,965
number of households (1996): 67,500

Council tax (average Band D per two-person household), for 2001–02: £1,046
Notified net non-domestic rate income (1999–2000): £43,670,230
Education (pupils on register, 2000–01):
primary: 11,420
secondary: 8,882
special: 160
entitled to free meals: 27%

MEMBERS OF THE COUNCIL

Barrie, Jim	(SNP)
Beattie, David	(SNP)
Beattie, Richard	(SNP)
Borthwick, Ian	(Ind.)
Bowes, David	(SNP)
Corrigan, John	(SNP)
Dawson, Andrew	(SNP)
de Gernie, George	(Lab.)
Farquhar, Charles	(Lab.)
Fitzpatrick, Joe	(SNP)
Fordyce, Elizabeth	(SNP)
Glen, Neil	(Lab.)
Grant, Fiona	(Lab.)
Guild, Ken	(SNP)
Letford, John	(Lab.)
Luke, Iain	(Lab.)
Mackie, Bruce	(C.)
Petrie, Allan	(SNP)
Powrie, Neil	(C.)
Presswood, Robin	(Lab.)
Regan, George	(Lab.)
Rolfe, Mervyn	(Lab.)
Sawers, Willie	(SNP)
Scott, Derek	(C.)
Shimi, Jill	(Lab.)
Sturrock, Julie	(Lab.)
Wallace, Rod	(C.)
Ward, Betty	(Lab.)
Wright, Helen **(P)**	(Lab.)

Total: 29 (Lab.13; SNP.11; C.4; Ind.1)

CHIEF OFFICERS

Chief Executive: A. Stephen
Director of Arts and Heritage: S. Grimmond
Director of Contract Services: R. Jackson
Director of Corporate Planning: C. Ward
Director of Economic Development: D. Grimmond
Director of Education: Ms A. Wilson
Director of Environmental and Consumer Protection: R. Gabriel
Director of Finance: D. Dorward
Director of Housing: Mrs E. Zwirlein
Director of Information Technology: vacant
Director of Leisure and Parks: A. Stuart
Director of Neighbourhood Resources: F. Patrick
Director of Personnel and Management Services: J. Petrie
Director of Planning and Transportation: M. Galloway
Director of Public Relations: L. Roy
Director of Social Work: Ms J. Roberts
Director of Support Services: Ms P. McIlquham
Local Agenda 21 Officer: Ms A. Anderson

SCOTTISH AND UK PARLIAMENTARY CONSTITUENCIES

Dundee East; Dundee West

EAST AYRSHIRE COUNCIL

Council Headquarters, London Road, Kilmarnock, Ayrshire KA3 7BU (Tel: 01563-576000; Fax: 01563-576500; Web: www.east-ayrshire.gov.uk).

Area: 1,252 sq. km
Population (1998 estimate): 121,300
population density (1998): 97 persons per sq. km
projected population in 2006 (1996-based): 115,597
number of households (1996): 50,100

Council tax (average Band D per two-person household), for 2001–02: £922.00
Notified net non-domestic rate income (1999–2000): £23,412,662
Education (pupils on register, 2000–01):
primary: 10,832
secondary: 8,028
special: 162
entitled to free meals: 21.9%

MEMBERS OF THE COUNCIL

Boyd, James **(P)**	(Lab.)
Carmichael, James	(Lab.)
Campbell, Alan	(SNP)
Coffey, Daniel	(SNP)
Coffey, William	(SNP)
Darnborough, Jane	(Lab.)
Dinwoodie, Elaine	(Lab.)
Farrell, Thomas	(Lab.)
Fauld, Julie	(SNP)
Hall, Kathleen	(SNP)
Hay, Ann	(SNP)
Jackson, Eric	(Lab.)
James, Raymond	(Lab.)
Kelly, James	(Lab.)
Knapp, John	(Lab.)
Linton, Iain	(SNP)
Macrae, David	(Lab.)
McDill, Robert	(SNP)
McIntyre, Andrew	(Lab.)
McLean, Lillian	(SNP)
McLean, Finlay	(SNP)
McNeil, Brian	(SNP)
Menzies, William	(Lab.)
Reeves, Brian	(Lab.)
Reid, Douglas	(SNP)
Ross, Eric	(Lab.)
Smith, George	(Lab.)

Taylor, Robert	(Lab.)
Walsh, Alexander	(Lab.)
Weir, John	(SNP)
Wilson, Henry	(SNP)
Young, Stephanie	(C.)

Total: 32 (Lab.17; SNP.14; C.1)

CHIEF OFFICERS

Chief Executive: D. Montgomery
Director of Community Services: W. Stafford
Director of Education and Social Services: J. Mulgrew
Director of Finance: A. McPhee
Director of Housing and Technical Services: J. Lavery
Head of Information Technology: M. Roulston
Head of Legal and Administration/Solicitor to the Council: B. Haughan
Head of Personnel: G. Hough
Head of Planning: A. Neish
Head of Protective Services: J. Crawford
Local Agenda 21 Officer: M. Buchanan

SCOTTISH AND UK PARLIAMENTARY CONSTITUENCIES

Carrick, Cumnock and Doon Valley; Kilmarnock and Loudoun

EAST DUNBARTONSHIRE COUNCIL

Tom Johnston House, Civic Way, Kirkintilloch, Glasgow G66 4TJ (Tel: 0141-578 8000; Fax: 0141-777 8576).

Area: 172 sq. km
Population (1998 estimate): 109,570
population density (1998): 638 persons per sq. km
projected population in 2006 (1996-based): 109,761
number of households (1996): 40,006

Council tax (average Band D per two-person household), for 2001–02: £872.00
Notified net non-domestic rate income (1999–2000): £16,025,013
Education (pupils on register, 2000–01):
primary: 10,396
secondary: 8,859
special: 176
entitled to free meals: 9.5%

MEMBERS OF THE COUNCIL

Baillie, Stephen	(Lab.)
Brown, Alan	(C.)

Cameron, Anne	(Lab.)
Dempsey, John	(Lab.)
Divers, Barry	(Lab.)
Duncan, Robert	(LD)
Geekie, Rhondda	(Lab.)
Gotts, Eric	(LD)
Hannah, Alex	(Lab.)
Hendry, Billy	(C.)
Jarvis, Anne	(C.)
Kennedy, Charles	(Lab.)
McGaughrin, Edward	(Lab.)
McInnes, Cathy	(LD)
McSkimming, Robert (P)	(LD)
Moody, Keith	(LD)
Moody, Vaughan	(LD)
Morrison, John	(LD)
O'Donnell, Michael	(Lab.)
Risk, Fiona	(LD)
Smith, Tom	(Lab.)
Southcott, Julia	(LD)
Steel, Pat	(LD)
Walker, Una	(Lab.)

Total: 24 (Lab.11; LD.10; C.3)

CHIEF OFFICERS

Chief Executive: Dr V. Nash
Assistant Chief Executive: V. Watts
Head of Protection Services: Hugh Sheridon
Head of Finance: K. Mitchell
Head of Human Resources: Ms A. Macpherson
Head of Partnership Planning: Alan Sim
Strategic Director of Commercial: J. Mundell
Strategic Director of Community: Sue Brule
Strategic Director of Development and Environmental: G. Thom

SCOTTISH AND UK PARLIAMENTARY CONSTITUENCIES

Clydebank and Milngavie; Coatbridge and Chryston; Strathkelvin and Bearsden

EAST LOTHIAN COUNCIL

John Muir House, Court Street, Haddington, East Lothian EH41 3HA (Tel: 01620-827827; Fax: 01620-827888
Web: www.eastlothian.gov.uk).

Area: 678 sq. km
Population (1998 estimate): 89,570
population density (1998): 132 persons per sq. km
projected population in 2006 (1996-based): 91,649
number of households (1996): 36,300

Council tax (average Band D per two-person household), for 2001–02: £909.45

Notified net non-domestic rate income (1999–2000): £26,795,274

Education (pupils on register, 2000–01):
primary: 8,078
secondary: 5,238
entitled to free meals: 14.6%

MEMBERS OF THE COUNCIL

Berry, David	(SNP)
Broun-Lindsay, Ludovic	(C.)
Costello, David	(Lab.)
Crawford, Frances	(C.)
Ferguson, Tom	(Lab.)
Ford, Peter	(C.)
Grant, Donald	(Lab.)
Hampshire, Norman	(Lab.)
Ingle, Charles	(Lab.)
Innes, Willie	(Lab.)
Jarvie, Kevin	(Lab.)
Kinnear, Diana	(C.)
Knox, Roger	(SNP)
Lawrie, Tom	(Lab.)
McCarthy, Ann	(Lab.)
McNeil, John	(Lab.)
Meikle, Gilbert	(C.)
Murray, Norman	(Lab.)
O'Brien, Pat **(P)**	(Lab.)
O'Donnell, Patrick	(Lab.)
Ross, John	(Lab.)
Shepherd, Bishop	(Lab.)
Talac, Maureen	(Lab.)

Total: 23 (Lab.16; C.5; SNP.2)

CHIEF OFFICERS

Chief Executive: J. Lindsay
Chief Environmental Services Officer: D. Evans
Council Solicitor: K MacConnachie
Directoras of Education and Community Services: A. Blackie
Director of Environment and Technical Services: R. Hannah
Director of Finance: A. McCrorie
Director of Social Work and Housing: B. Walker
Head of Community Services: T. Shearer
Head of Environment: P. Collins
Head of Information Technology: R. Dowie

Head of Personnel: G. Britain
Local Agenda 21 Officer: Ms L. Wason

SCOTTISH AND UK PARLIAMENTARY CONSTITUENCY

East Lothian

EAST RENFREWSHIRE COUNCIL

Council Offices, Eastwood Park, Rouken Glen Road, Giffnock G46 6UG (Tel: 0141-577 3000; Fax: 0141-620 0884; Web: www.eastrenfrewshire.gov.uk).

Area: 173 sq. km
Population (1998 estimate): 89,790
population density (1998): 509 persons per sq. km
projected population in 2006 (1996-based): 90,854
number of households (1996): 33,100

Council tax (average Band D per two-person household), for 2001–02: £859.00
Notified net non-domestic rate income (1999–2000): £11,159,987
Education (pupils on register, 2000–01):
primary: 8,755
secondary: 7,284
special: 44
entitled to free meals: 10.1%

MEMBERS OF THE COUNCIL

Collins, Daniel	(Lab.)
Cunningham, Elizabeth	(Lab.)
Drysdale, Iain	(C.)
Fletcher, James	(Lab.)
Forbes, Ian	(Lab.)
Garscadden, Roy	(Lab.)
Gilbert, Charlie	(C.)
Grant, Barbara	(C.)
Haniford, L	(C.)
Hutchison, Ian	(C.)
Lafferty, Alan	(Lab.)
McGee, Frank	(C.)
Montague, Mary	(Lab.)
Napier, George	(LD)
Pearce, Ian	(R)
Phillips, Edward	(Lab.)
Rosin, Leslie	(C.)
Shaw, James	(C.)
Steele, Allan **(P)**	(LD)
Taylor, Owen	(Lab.)

Total: 20 (Lab.9; C.8; LD.2; R.1)

CHIEF OFFICERS

Chief Executive: P. Daniels
Assistant Chief Executive: Mrs C. Innes
Deputy Chief Executive: C. Dalrymple
Director of Central Services: J. Hawkins
Director of Commercial Operations: R. A. Russell
Director of Community and Leisure: Mrs A. Saunders
Director of Education: Mrs E. Currie
Director of Environment: A. Cahill
Director of Finance: D. Dippie
Director of Social Work: G. Hunter
Local Agenda 21 Officer: M. Valenti

SCOTTISH AND UK PARLIAMENTARY CONSTITUENCY

Eastwood

COMHAIRLE EILEAN SIAR/ WESTERN ISLES COUNCIL

Council Offices, Sandwick Road, Stornoway, Isle of Lewis HS1 2BW (Tel: 01851-703773; Fax: 01851-705349; Web: www.cne-siar.gov.uk).

Area: 3,134 sq. km
Population (1998 estimate): 27,560
population density (1998): 9 persons per sq. km
projected population in 2006 (1996-based): 27,554
number of households (1996): 11,600

Council tax (average Band D per two-person household), for 2001–2002: £765,00
Notified net non-domestic rate income (1999–2000): £4,817,703
Education (pupils on register, 2000–01):
primary: 2,288
secondary: 1,928
entitled to free meals: 11.8%

MEMBERS OF THE COUNCIL

Blaney, David	(Ind.)
Bremner, Mary	(Ind.)
Campbell, Angus	(Ind.)
Campbell, Archibald	(Lab.)
Graham, Angus	(Ind.)
Graham, Malcolm	(Ind.)
Lonie, George	(Lab.)
Macarthur, James	(Ind.)
Macdonald, Alexander (C)	(Ind.)
Macdonald, Donald	(Ind.)
Macdonald, Norman A.	(Lab.)
Macdonald, Norman L.	(Ind.)

Mackay, Donald	(Ind.)
Mackenzie, Katie	(Ind.)
Mackinnon, Ronald	(Ind.)
Maclean, Donald	(Ind.)
Maclean, Philip	(SNP)
Macleod, Ian	(Ind.)
Macleod, Malcolm	(Lab.)
Macleod, Norman	(Ind.)
Macleod, Murdo	(Ind.)
Macrae, Alasdair	(Ind.)
Macsween, Doanld	(Ind.)
Manford, Donald	(SNP)
Morrison, Finlay	(Ind.)
Morrison, Iain	(Ind.)
Morrison, Roderick	(Ind.)
Munro, Morag	(Ind.)
Murray, Roderick	(Lab.)
Nicholson, Donald	(Ind.)
Nicolson, Angus	(SNP)

Total: 31 (Ind. 23; Lab. 5; SNP 3)

CHIEF OFFICERS

Chief Executive: B. Howat
Director of Corporate Services: D. O'Loan
Director of Education: M. Macleod
Director for Sustainable Communities: M. Gold
Director of Finance: R. Bennie
Director of Housing: A. Lamont
Director of Social Services: M. Smith
Director of Technical Services: M. Murray
Local Agenda 21 Officer: D. McKim

SCOTTISH AND UK PARLIAMENTARY CONSTITUENCY

Western Isles

FALKIRK COUNCIL

Municipal Buildings, West Bridge Street, Falkirk FK1 5RS (Tel: 01324-506070; Fax: 01324-506071).

Area: 299 sq. km
Population (1998 estimate): 144,110
population density (1998): 482 persons per sq. km
projected population in 2006 (1996-based): 142,109
number of households (1996): 59,100

Council tax (average Band D per two-person household), for 2001–02: £813.00
Notified net non-domestic rate income (1999–2000): £46,440,358

Education (pupils on register, 2000–01):
primary: 12,454
secondary: 8,508
special: 309
entitled to free meals: 19.2%

MEMBERS OF THE COUNCIL

Alexander, David	(SNP)
Anderson, William	(Lab.)
Bryson, David	(SNP)
Buchanan, William	(NA)
Coleman, Thomas	(SNP)
Connolly, John	(Lab.)
Constable, Harry	(SNP)
Constable, John	(SNP)
Eaglesham, Elizabeth	(SNP)
Forsyth, David	(SNP)
Fowler, Alexander	(Lab.)
Goldie, Dennis	(Lab.)
Goldie, Gerald	(Lab.)
Gow, Linda	(Lab.)
Graham, Andrew	(SNP)
Gray, Alan	(Lab.)
Jenkinson, John	(Lab.)
Johnston, James (LP)	(Ind.)
Kenna, Lynda	(SNP)
Martin, Craig	(Lab.)
Martin, Thomas	(Lab.)
McCafferty, Patrick	(Ind.)
Miller, Ian	(Lab.)
Nicol, Malcolm	(C.)
O'Dea, Thomas	(NA)
Patrick, John	(C.)
Pollock, Mary	(Lab.)
Short, James	(Lab.)
Spears, Robert	(NA)
Spiers, David	(Lab.)
Williamson, Diane	(SNP)
Wilson, James	(NA)

Total: 32 (Lab.14; SNP.10; NA (Non-aligned) 4; Ind. 2; C. 2)

CHIEF OFFICERS

Chief Executive: Ms M. Pitcaithly
Director of Community and Environmental Services: S. Dunlop
Director of Contract Services: vacant
Director of Corporate Services: S. Ritchie
Director of Education: Dr G. Young
Director of Finance: A. Jannetta
Director of Housing: I. Walker
Director of Law and Administration: Ms E. S. Morton
Director of Social Work Services: Ms C. Wilkinson
Director of Strategic Services: G. Peart

Local Agenda 21 contact: D. Gorman

SCOTTISH AND UK PARLIAMENTARY CONSTITUENCIES

Falkirk East; Falkirk West

FIFE COUNCIL

Fife House, North Street, Glenrothes, Fife KY7 5LT (Tel: 01592-414141; Fax: 01592-414142 Web: www.fife.gov.uk).

Area: 1,323 sq. km
Population (1999 estimate): 349,200
population density (1999): 270 persons per sq. km
projected population in 2006 (1998-based): 349,387
number of households (2000): 155,999

Council tax (average Band D per two-person household), for 2001–02: £891
Notified net non-domestic rate income (1999–2000): £91,226,077
Education (pupils on register 2000–01):
primary: 29,765
secondary: 23,197
special: 233
entitled to free meals: 16.7%

MEMBERS OF THE COUNCIL

Aitken, William	(Lab.)
Alexander, David	(SNP)
Allan, George	(Lab.)
Arbuckle, Andrew	(LD)
Arnott, David	(Lab.)
Ballantyne, Fraser	(Lab.)
Beveridge, Isabella	(Lab.)
Blyth, Henry	(Lab.)
Bradie, Jack	(LD)
Brand, William	(Lab.)
Brennan, James	(Lab.)
Brown, Andrew	(Lab.)
Cameron, John	(Lab.)
Clark, Susan	(LD)
Clarke, William	(O)
Connelly, Irene	(Lab.)
Connelly, James	(Lab.)
Cook, James	(SNP)
Coyne, Michael	(Lab.)
Dair, Thomas	(Lab.)
Doig, Margot	(Lab.)
Douglas, Peter	(LD)
Dow, Allan	(LD)
Duff, Gordon	(Lab.)
Eadie, Robert	(Lab.)

Edward Drew	(Lab.)
Farmer, John	(Lab.)
Garrett, Anthony	(LD)
Grant, Fiona	(SNP)
Grant, Peter	(SNP)
Gunn, Theresa	(Lab.)
Gunstone, Eleanor	(LD)
Harris, Elizabeth	(LD)
Hill, Sheila	(LD)
Hunter-Blair, Jane	(LD)
Kay, William	(Lab.)
Keddie, Andrew	(Lab.)
Kenney, Alan	(Lab.)
Latto, Catherine	(Lab.)
Law, Helen	(Lab.)
Leslie, George	(SNP)
Liston, Jane Ann	(LD)
Logan, Margaret	(Lab.)
Lothian, David	(LD)
McCallum, Angela	(Lab.)
MacDougall, John **(C)**	(Lab.)
McFee, Edith	(LD)
McGarry, Alice	(SNP)
McGovern, Anne	(Lab.)
Martin, Anthony	(LD)
Maxwell, Alexander	(O)
May, Christine	(Lab.)
Melville, Frances	(LD)
Morrison, Kay	(Lab.)
O'Sullivan, Bill	(Lab.)
Paterson, Andrew	(Lab.)
Patey, Alfred	(SNP)
Randall, Stuart	(C.)
Riches, Elizabeth	(LD)
Rodger, Andrew	(Ind.)
Rougvie, David	(Lab.)
Rumney, Robert	(Lab.)
Sawers, Alexander	(Lab.)
Scott-Hayward, Michael	(C.)
Simpson, James	(LD)
Simpson, John	(Lab.)
Smith, Agnes	(Lab.)
Stocks, Barbara	(Lab.)
Taylor, Margaret	(LD)
Taylor, Robert	(Lab.)
Thacker, Bryan	(SNP)
Thomson, Alexander	(Lab.)
Tolson, James	(LD)
Torrance, David	(SNP)
Toye, Anne	(LD)
Watters, Ann	(LD)
Woods, Michael	(SNP)
Young, Robert	(Lab.)

Total: 78 (Lab.42; LD.21; SNP.10; C.2; O.2; Ind.1)

CHIEF OFFICERS

Chief Executive: D. Sinclair
Head of Community Services: D. Somerville
Head of Corporate Procurement: J. McHugh
Head of Education: A. McKay
Head of Environmental Health: J. Stark
Head of Finance: P. Ritchie
Head of Housing: A. Davidson
Head of Information Technology: E. Brewster
Head of Law and Administration: S. Allan
Head of Personnel: M. Burnell
Head of Planning: D. Rae
Head of Social Work: M. Sawyer
Local Agenda 21 Co-ordinator: Ms S. Keast

SCOTTISH AND UK PARLIAMENTARY CONSTITUENCIES

Dunfermline East; Dunfermline West; Fife Central; Fife North East; Kirkcaldy

GLASGOW CITY COUNCIL

City Chambers, George Square, Glasgow G2 1DU (Tel: 0141-287 2000; Fax: 0141-287 5666; Web: www.glasgow.gov.uk).

Area: 177 sq. km
Population (1999 estimate): 611,440
population density (1999): 3,454 persons per sq. km
projected population in 2009 (1999-based): 595,510
number of households (1999): 275,100

Council tax (average Band D per two-person household), for 2001–02: £1,120.00
Notified net non-domestic rate income (1999–2000): £239,192,865
Education (pupils on register, 2000–01):
primary: 45,500
secondary: 29,886
special: 2,239
entitled to free meals: 42.3%

MEMBERS OF THE COUNCIL

Baird, Susan	(Lab.)
Beckett, Mary	(Lab.)
Burns, Kenneth	(Lab.)
Butler, William	(Lab.)
Butt, Shaukat	(Lab.)
Cameron, Elizabeth	(Lab.)
Chalmers, Patricia	(Lab.)
Coleman, James	(Lab.)
Colleran, Aileen	(Lab.)
Davey, Ronald	(Lab.)

Devine, Christine	(Lab.)
Dingwall, Tommy	(Lab.)
Dodds, Josephine	(Lab.)
Dornan, Stephen	(Lab.)
Fitzgerald, Eamon	(Lab.)
Flanagan, John	(Lab.)
Gaughan, Deirdre	(Lab.)
Gibson, Iris	(SNP)
Glass, Alexander	(Lab.)
Gordon, Charles	(Lab.)
Gould, Robert	(Lab.)
Graham, Archie	(Lab.)
Graham, Irene	(Lab.)
Gray, John	(Lab.)
Gray, Robert	(Lab.)
Green, Malcolm	(Lab.)
Hurcombe, Ellen	(Lab.)
Kelly, Christopher	(Lab.)
Kernaghan, Michael	(Lab.)
Lee, Martin	(Lab.)
Leonard, Gerald	(Lab.)
Lynch, John	(Lab.)
Lyon, Catherine	(C.)
McCafferty, Charles	(Lab.)
McCafferty, Margaret	(Lab.)
McCann, Gaille	(Lab.)
McCarron, James	(Lab.)
McDougall, Elaine	(Lab.)
McFadden, Jean	(Lab.)
McKenzie, John	(Lab.)
McLean, Malcolm	(Lab.)
McMaster, Catherine	(Lab.)
McNally, James	(Lab.)
McNicol, Colin	(Lab.)
MacBean, Robert	(Lab.)
Macdiarmid, Gordon	(Lab.)
Mackechnie, James	(Lab.)
MacLellan, Walter	(Lab.)
Macrae, Hugh	(Lab.)
Maan, Bashir	(Lab.)
Macey, Jean	(Lab.)
Malik, Hanzala	(Lab.)
Marshall, Robert	(Lab.)
Mason, Christopher	(LD)
Mason, John	(SNP)
Matheson, Gordon	(Lab.)
Mosson, Alex **(LP)**	(Lab.)
Moynes, John	(Lab.)
Mutter, James	(Lab.)
O'Neill, Marjorie	(Lab.)
O' Rourke, William	(Lab.)
Purcell, Steven	(Lab.)
Quinn, Ronald	(Lab.)
Redmond, George	(Lab.)
Renton, Catriona	(Lab.)
Roberton, Craig	(Lab.)
Ryan, George	(Lab.)

Sheridan, Tommy	(Soc.)
Shoaib, Muhammad	(Lab.)
Simpson, Ruth	(Lab.)
Sinclair, Margaret	(Lab.)
Smith, Elaine	(Lab.)
Stevenson, David	(Lab.)
Stewart, Alan	(Lab.)
Stewart, Allan	(Lab.)
Timoney, Bill	(Lab.)
Watson, Alistair	(Lab.)
Watson, Allan	(Lab.)
Winter, Robert	(Lab.)

Total: 79 (Lab.74; SNP.2; C.1; LD.1; Soc.1

CHIEF OFFICERS

Chief Executive: J. Andrews
Acting Director of Building Services: S. Fallis
Director of Cultural and Leisure Services: Ms B. McConnell
Director of Development and Regeneration Services: R. McConnell
Director of Direct and Care Services: F. Chambers
Director of Education Services: K. Corsar
Director of Financial Services: G. Black
Director of Housing Services: D. Comley
Director of Land Services: A. Young
Director of Personnel and Administration: H. Burke
Director of Environmental Protection Services: B. Kelly
Director of Social Work Services: R. O'Connor
Local Agenda 21 Officer: S. Gillon

SCOTTISH AND UK PARLIAMENTARY CONSTITUENCIES

Glasgow Anniesland; Glasgow Baillieston; Glasgow Cathcart; Glasgow Govan; Glasgow Kelvin; Glasgow Maryhill; Glasgow Pollok; Glasgow Rutherglen; Glasgow Shettleston; Glasgow Springburn

HIGHLAND COUNCIL

Glenurquhart Road, Inverness IV3 5NX
(Tel: 01463-702000; Fax: 01463-702111;
Web: www.highland.gov.uk).

Area: 25,784 sq. km
Population (1998 estimate): 208,300
population density (1998): 8 persons per sq. km
projected population in 2006 (1996-based): 214,031
number of households (1996): 85,800

Council tax (average Band D per two-person household), for 2001–02: £889.00
Notified net non-domestic rate income (1999–2000): £56,675,597
Education (pupils on register, 2000–01):
primary: 18,762
secondary: 14,655
special: 171
entitled to free meals: 14.6%

MEMBERS OF THE COUNCIL

Allan, Duncan	(Ind.)
Alston, David	(Ind.)
Anderson, Andrew	(SNP)
Balfour, Roderick	(Ind.)
Beaton, Allan	(Ind.)
Black, Stuart	(LD)
Briggs, Douglas	(Ind.)
Bruce, George	(Ind.)
Cairns, Peter	(SNP)
Campbell, Isabelle	(LD)
Clark, Neil	(Ind.)
Cole, John	(LD)
Corbett, Peter	(Ind.)
Coutts, Garry	(Ind.)
Cumming, Christina	(Lab.)
Davidson, Margaret	(Ind.)
Dick, Angus	(LD)
Downie, Morris	(Ind.)
Dunlop, Basil	(Ind.)
Durham, Richard	(Ind.)
Finlayson, Michael	(Ind.)
Finlayson, Rita	(Ind.)
Flear, David	(LD)
Foxley, Michael	(LD)
Fraser, David	(Ind.)
Fulton, William	(Ind.)
Goodman, Clive	(Lab.)
Gordon, Angus	(Ind.)
Green, David	(Ind.)
Green, John	(Ind.)
Gray, Jimmy	(Lab.)
Home, Janet	(Ind.)
Jardine, Barbara	(LD)
Keith, Francis	(Ind.)
King, Charles	(Ind.)
Lyon, Ron	(Ind.)
MacDonald, Alistair	(LD)
MacDonald, Eilidh	(Lab.)
MacDonald, Liz	(SNP)
Macdonald, Olwyn	(Ind.)
Macintyre, Roy	(Ind.)
MacKenzie, Sandy	(SNP)
Mackinnon, Ewen	(Ind.)
MacLachlan, William	(Ind.)
MacLennan, Margaret	(Ind.)
MacRae, Ella	(Ind.)
Magee, Alison	(Ind.)
Matheson, John	(Ind.)
Matheson, Kathleen	(Ind.)
McCreath, Gillian	(SNP)
Millar, Andrew	(Ind.)
Moncrieff, Gavin	(SNP)
Mowat, James	(Ind.)
Munro, David	(Lab.)
Murphy, Brian	(Lab.)
Norrie, Donald	(Ind.)
Oag, James	(Ind.)
Park, Alexander	(Ind.)
Paterson, Andrew	(Ind.)
Paterson, James	(Ind.)
Paterson, Margaret	(SNP)
Philip, David	(Ind.)
Rhind, Alasdair	(Ind.)
Rosie, John	(Lab.)
Ross, William	(Ind.)
Salmon, Bernard	(LD)
Saxon, Roger	(Lab.)
Severn, Robert	(SNP)
Shiels, Jack	(Ind.)
Slack, Andrew	(Ind.)
Sliman, Sheena	(Ind.)
Smith, Graeme	(LD)
Smith, William **(P)**	(Ind.)
Steven, Deirdre	(Lab.)
Sutherland, Angus	(Ind.)
Thomson, James	(Lab.)
Waters, Falconer	(Ind.)
Wilkerson, Lou	(Lab.)
Wilson, Carolyn	(Ind.)
Wynd, Robert	(SNP)

Total: 80 (Ind.50; Lab.11; LD.10; SNP.9)

CHIEF OFFICERS

Chief Executive: A. D. McCourt
Director of Commercial Operations: C. Mackenzie
Director of Corporate Services: A. Dodds
Director of Culture and Leisure: A. Jones
Director of Education: B. Robertson
Director of Finance: A. Geddes
Director of Housing: G. Fisher
Director of Information Systems: R. Metcalfe
Director of Planning and Development: J. Rennilson
Director of Property and Architectural Services: Dr A. Coutts
Director of Protective Services: D. Thompson
Acting Director of Roads and Transport: P. Shimin
Director of Social Services: H. Dempster
Local Agenda 21 contact: A. Dorin

SCOTTISH AND UK PARLIAMENTARY CONSTITUENCIES

Caithness, Sutherland and Easter Ross; Inverness East, Nairn and Lochaber; Ross, Skye and Inverness West

INVERCLYDE COUNCIL

Municipal Buildings, Clyde Square, Greenock, Renfrewshire PA15 1LY (Tel: 01475-717171; Fax: 01475-712010).

Area: 162 sq. km
Population (1998 estimate): 85,400
population density (1998): 528 persons per sq. km
projected population in 2006 (1996-based): 77,840
number of households (1996): 38,000

Council tax (average Band D per two-person household), for 2001–02: £1012.00
Notified net non-domestic rate income (1999–2000): £19,011,706
Education (pupils on register, 2000–01):
primary: 7,378
secondary: 5,774
special: 147
entitled to free meals: 24.6%

MEMBERS OF THE COUNCIL

Blair, Alan	(LD)
Calvert, Alex	(C.)
Campbell, Robert	(LD)
Hunter, Jim	(LD)
Jackson, Robert	(Lab.)
McCabe, Stephen	(Lab.)
McCormick, Patrick	(Lab.)
McGhee, Alex	(Lab.)
McGraw, Allan	(LD)
Mitchell, Jim	(LD)
Moody, John	(LD)
Morrison, Daniel	(Lab.)
Morrison, Margaret	(Lab.)
Nimmo, Sandy	(LD)
O'Rourke, Jim	(Lab.)
Rebecchi, Ciano	(LD)
Roach, David **(P)**	(Lab.)
Robertson, Allan	(Lab)
Robertson, Yvonne	(Lab.)
White, George	(LD)
Total: 20 (Lab. 10; LD. 9; C.1;)	

CHIEF OFFICERS

Chief Executive: R. Cleary
Deputy Chief Executive/Director of Economic Development Services: G. Malone
Director of Community and Protective Services: N. Graham
Director of Education Services: B. McLeary
Director of Information Services: M. Russell
Director of Legal and Support Services: E. Paterson
Director of Resource Services: M. McCrossan
Director of Social Work and Housing Services: T. Keenan
Local Agenda 21 Officer: D. Hall

SCOTTISH AND UK PARLIAMENTARY CONSTITUENCIES

Greenock and Inverclyde; West Renfrewshire

MIDLOTHIAN COUNCIL

Midlothian House, 40-46 Buccleuch Street, Dalkeith, Midlothian EH22 1DJ (Tel: 0131-270 7500; Fax: 0131-271 3050; Web: www.midlothian.gov.uk).

Area: 355 sq. km
Population (1999 estimate): 81,680
population density (1998): 230 persons per sq. km
projected population in 2006 (1998-based): 82,305
number of households (1999): 31,800

Council tax (average Band D per two-person household), for 2001–02: £1001.00
Notified net non-domestic rate income (1999–2000): £14,551,079
Education (pupils on register, 2000–01):
primary: 7,265
secondary: 5,574
special: 189
entitled to free meals: 18.3%

MEMBERS OF THE COUNCIL

Aitchinson, Jackie	(Lab.)
Anderson, Maureen	(Lab.)
Boyes, Peter	(Lab.)
Campbell, Sam **(P)**	(Lab.)
Dunsmuir, James	(Lab.)
Fletcher, David	(LD)
Hamilton, David	(Lab.)
Harkness, Sandy	(Lab.)
Imrie, Russell	(Lab.)
Marr, Graham	(Lab.)

Martin, Maira	(Lab.)	Flynn, Wilma	(Ind.)
Milligan, Derek	(Lab.)	Gorn, Linda	(LD)
Molloy, Danny	(Lab.)	Hamilton, Jeff	(Ind.)
Montgomery, Adam	(Lab.)	Hogg, John	(Ind.)
Pottinger, Bryan	(Lab.)	Howe, Tom	(SNP)
Purcell, George	(Lab.)	Jappy, Bill	(Ind.)
Russell, Margot	(Lab.)	Keith, Sandy	(Lab.)
Small, Richard	(Lab.)	Leslie, John	(Lab.)

Total 18 (Lab. 17 LD. 1)

Longmore, Sinclair (Ind.)
McIntosh, Rex (Ind.)

CHIEF OFFICERS

Paul, Pearl (SNP)
Sim, Ronnie (Lab.)

Chief Executive: T. Muir
Director of Community Services: G. Marwick
Director of Contract Services: B. Page
Director of Corporate Services: I. Jackson
Director of Education: D. MacKay
Director of Social Services: S. Adams
Director of Strategic Services: J. Allan
Local Agenda 21 Officer: Michelle Carroll

Shaw, Jennifer (Ind.)
Shepherd, Ronald (Ind.)
Towns, George (LD)
Urquhart, Alasdair (Ind.)
Watt, Percy (Ind.)
Wilson, Bob (Ind.)
Young, Iain (C.)

Total: 26 (Ind.15; Lab.6; LD.2; SNP.2; C.1)

SCOTTISH AND UK PARLIAMENTARY CONSTITUENCIES

CHIEF OFFICERS

Midlothian; Tweeddale, Ettrick and Lauderdale

Chief Executive: A. Keddie
Deputy Chief Executive: Ms K Williams
Director of Community Services: M. Martin
Director of Educational Services: D. Duncan
Chief Financial Officer: M. Palmer
Director of Environmental Services: R. Stewart
Local Agenda 21 Officer: G. Templeton

MORAY COUNCIL

Council Office, High Street, Elgin, Morayshire IV30 1BX (Tel: 01343-543451; Fax: 01343-540183; Web: www.moray.org).

SCOTTISH AND UK PARLIAMENTARY CONSTITUENCIES

Gordon; Moray

Area: 2,238 sq. km
Population (2000 estimate): 85,000
population density (2000): 38 persons per sq. km
projected population in 2006 (1998-based): 5,871
number of households (1998): 35,500

NORTH AYRSHIRE COUNCIL

Cunninghame House, Irvine, Ayrshire KA12 8EE. (Tel: 01294-324100; Fax: 01294-324144).

Council tax (average Band D per two-person household), for 2001–02: £825.00
Notified net non-domestic rate income (1999–2000): £20,021,799
Education (pupils on register, 2000–01):
primary: 7,810
secondary: 5,730
special: 317
entitled to free meals: 10.2%

Area: 884 sq. km
Population: 138,850
population density (1998): 158 persons per sq. km
projected population in 2008 (1998-based): 139,621
number of households (1999): 58,900

MEMBERS OF THE COUNCIL

Council tax (average Band D), for 2001–02: £877
Notified net non-domestic rate income (1999–2000): £39,015,488
Education (pupils on register, 2000–01):
primary: 12,212
secondary: 9,183

Aldridge, Eddie **(C)**	(Ind.)
Bisset, Alastair	(Ind.)
Burgess, Alan	(Lab.)
Coutts, Eddie	(Ind.)
Drivers, John	(Lab.)
Ettles, Muriel	(Lab.)
Fleming, Alistair	(Ind.)

special: 184
entitled to free meals: 25.7%

MEMBERS OF THE COUNCIL

Barr, Tom	(Lab.)
Bell, John	(Lab.)
Browne, Jacqueline	(Lab.)
Carson, Jack	(Lab.)
Clarkson, Gordon	(Lab.)
Clarkson, Ian	(Lab.)
Dewar, Stewart	(Lab.)
Donn, John	(Lab.)
Drew, Duncan	(Lab.)
Gallagher, David	(Lab.)
Gooding, Samuel	(Lab.)
Gorman, Jane	(Lab.)
Gray, Elliot	(Lab.)
Hill, Alan	(SNP)
Jennings, James	(Lab.)
Marshall, Elisabethe	(C.)
McDougall, Margaret	(Lab.)
McLardy, Elizabeth	(Ind.)
McNamara, Peter	(Lab.)
Moffat, John	(Lab.)
Munn, David	(Lab.)
Munn, Margaret	(Lab.)
Munro, Alan	(Lab.)
O' Neill, David	(Lab.)
Rae, Robert	(SNP)
Reid, John	(Lab.)
Reilly, Robert	(Lab.)
Sillars, John	(Lab.)
Taylor, Samuel **(C)**	(Lab.)
Wilkinson, Richard	(C.)

Total: 30 (Lab. 25; C. 2; SNP 2; Ind.1)

CHIEF OFFICERS

Chief Executive: B. Devine
Assistant Chief Executive, Development and Promotion: B. MacDonald
Assistant Chief Executive, Finance: A. Herbert
Assistant Chief Executive, Information Technology: J. Barrett
Assistant Chief Executive, Legal and Regulatory: I. Mackay
Assistant Chief Executive, Personnel: J. M. MacFarlane
Corporate Director, Educational Services: J. Travers
Corporate Director, Property Services: T. Orr
Corporate Director, Social Services: Ms Bernadette Docherty
Local Agenda 21 Officer: Alastair Osborne

SCOTTISH AND UK PARLIAMENTARY CONSTITUENCIES

Cunninghame North; Cunninghame South

NORTH LANARKSHIRE COUNCIL

PO Box 14, Civic Centre, Motherwell, Lanarkshire ML1 1TW (Tel: 01698-302222; Fax: 01698-275125; Web: www.northlan.gov.uk).

Area: 474 sq. km
Population (1998 estimate): 326,720
population density (1998): 690 persons per sq. km
projected population in 2006 (1996-based): 317,922
number of households (1996): 128,500

Council tax (average Band D per two-person household), for 2001–02: £907.00
Notified net non-domestic rate income (1999–2000): £68,667,996
Education (pupils on register, 2000–01):
primary: 29,015
secondary: 22,708
special: 817
entitled to free meals: 25.4%

MEMBERS OF THE COUNCIL

Barrie, Tom	(Lab.)
Brady, Brian	(Lab.)
Brooks, James	(Lab.)
Burns, Andrew	(Lab.)
Cameron, Campbell	(SNP)
Carmichael, William	(SNP)
Cassidy, John	(Lab.)
Cefferty, Charles	(Ind.)
Chadha, Bob	(Lab.)
Clark, Anthony	(Lab.)
Connelly, Patrick	(Lab.)
Cox, Sandra	(SNP)
Coyle, James	(Lab.)
Curley, Thomas	(Lab.)
Curran, Harry	(Lab.)
Devine, George	(Lab.)
Donnelly, Patrick	(Lab.)
Glavin, Faye	(SNP)
Gordon, John	(Lab.)
Gorman, Joe	(Lab.)
Gormill, Frank	(Lab.)
Grant, Stephen	(Lab.)
Gray, Charles	(Lab.)
Griffin, Francis	(Lab.)

Hebenton, Charles	(Lab.)
Hogg, William	(Lab.)
Holloway, Ernest	(Lab.)
Horner, William	(SNP)
Irvine, Elizabeth	(SNP)
Jones, Jean	(Lab.)
Lefferty, John	(Lab.)
Logue, James	(Lab.)
Love, Sam	(Lab.)
Lunny, Thomas	(Lab.)
Lyle, Richard	(SNP)
Maginnis, Thomas	(Lab.)
Martin, James	(Lab.)
Martin, William	(Lab.)
Mathison, Vincent	(Lab.)
McCabe, James	(Lab.)
McCallum, Neil	(SNP)
McCulloch, Barry **(P)**	(Lab.)
McElroy, Gerald	(Lab.)
McGee, John	(Lab.)
McGuigan, Harry	(Lab.)
McGuigan, James	(Lab.)
McKendrick, David	(Ind.)
McKeown, Kevin	(Lab.)
McKinlay, James	(Lab.)
McLaughlin, Gerard	(Lab.)
Moran, John	(Lab.)
Morgan, Thomas	(Lab.)
Morris, Donna	(Lab.)
Murray, Gordon	(SNP)
Murray, Margaret	(SNP)
Nolan, Thomas	(Lab.)
Pentland, John	(Lab.)
Robertson, James	(Lab.)
Ross, Michael	(Lab.)
Saunders, David	(Lab.)
Scott, Bernard	(Lab.)
Selfridge, Thomas	(Lab.)
Shaw, Joseph	(Lab.)
Shields, Bill	(Lab.)
Smith, James	(Lab.)
Stocks, David	(SNP)
Sullivan, Peter	(Lab.)
Valentine, Alan	(SNP)
Wallace, Brian	(Lab.)
Wilson, William	(Lab.)

Total: 70 (Lab.56; SNP.12; Ind.2)

CHIEF OFFICERS

Chief Executive: A. Cowe
Director of Administration: J. O'Hagan
Director of Community Services: P. Jukes
Director of Education: M. O'Neill
Director of Finance: R. Hinds
Director of Housing and Property Services: G. Whitefield

Director of Planning and Environment: D. Porch
Director of Social Work: J. Dickie
General Manager of Contracting Services: R. Ellerby
Local Agenda 21 Officer: A. Hendry

SCOTTISH AND UK PARLIAMENTARY CONSTITUENCIES

Airdrie and Shotts; Coatbridge and Chryston; Cumbernauld and Kilsyth; Hamilton North and Bellshill; Motherwell and Wishaw.

ORKNEY ISLANDS COUNCIL

Council Offices, School Place, Kirkwall, Orkney KW15 1NY (Tel: 01856-873535; Fax: 01856-874615).

Area: 992 sq. km
Population (2000 estimate): 19,810
population density (1998): 20 persons per sq. km
projected population in 2010 (2000-based): 19,181
number of households (1998): 8,200

Council tax (average Band D per two-person household), for 2001–02: £754,00
Notified net non-domestic rate income (1999–2000): £6,401,710
Education (pupils on register, 2000–01):
primary: 1,775
secondary: 1,360
special: 20
entitled to free meals: 8.2%

MEMBERS OF THE COUNCIL

Annal, C. A.	(Ind.)
Annal, J,	(Ind.)
Brown, J. F.	(Ind.)
Cormack, R.	(Ind.)
Drever, M. J.	(Ind.)
Foubister, J.	(Ind.)
Groundwater, F. J.	(Ind.)
Hagan, T. S.	(Ind.)
Halcro-Johnson, H. **(C)**	(Ind.)
Hamilton, J. M.	(Ind.)
Johnson, A. K.	(Ind.)
McLeod, R. R.	(Ind.)
Moodie, J.	(Ind.)
Murray, B. M.	(Ind.)
Petrie, M. A.	(Ind.)
Sclater, R. C.	(Ind.)
Scott, E. F.	(Ind.)
Scott, S. T.	(Ind.)
Sinclair, J.	(Ind.)

Sutherland, K. A.   (Ind.)
Taylor, B. A.   (Ind.)
Total: 21 (Ind. 21)

CHIEF OFFICERS

Chief Executive: A. Buchan
Chief Administrative Officer: M. Burr
Chief Environmental Services Officer: D. Tonge
Chief Legal Officer: D. Fairnie
Chief Trading Standards Officer: I. Watt
Director of Community Social Services: H. Garland
Director of Development and Planning: J. Baster
Director of Education and Recreational Services: W. L. Manson
Director of Finance and Housing: D. A. Robertson
Director of Technical Services: J. Panton
Personnel Officer: B. Evans

SCOTTISH PARLIAMENT CONSTITUENCY

Orkney

UK PARLIAMENT CONSTITUENCY

Orkney and Shetland

PERTH AND KINROSS COUNCIL

2 High Street, Perth PH1 5PH (Tel: 01738-475000; Fax: 01738-475710;
Email: enquiries@pkc.gov.uk;
Web: www.pkc.gov.uk).

Area: 5,311 sq. km
Population (1998 estimate): 134,030
population density (1999): 25 persons per sq. km
projected population in 2006 (1996-based): 136,454
number of households (2000): 61,792

Council tax (average Band D per two-person household), for 2001–02: £875.00
Notified net non-domestic rate income (1999–2000): £36,645,415
Education (pupils on register, 2000–01):
primary: 10,698
secondary: 7,732
special: 59
entitled to free meals: 8.0%

MEMBERS OF THE COUNCIL

Anderson, Hugh   (C.)
Baird, Kathleen   (C.)
Barnacle, Michael   (LD)
Barr, Alistair   (SNP)
Bushby, Sandy   (C.)
Caddell, Lorraine   (LD)
Cook, Michael   (SNP)
Crabbie, Colin   (C.)
Crawford, Bruce   (SNP)
Culliven, John   (SNP)
Doig, James   (Ind.)
Dow, David   (C.)
Ellis, Bob   (SNP)
Flynn, John   (Lab.)
Gilles, Callum   (Lab.)
Grant, Alan   (SNP)
Howie, Eleanor   (SNP)
Hulbert, John   (SNP)
Hunter, Gordon   (SNP)
Hunter, Iain   (SNP)
Jack, Alan   (C.)
Kelly, Jack   (Lab.)
Lennie, Margo   (Lab.)
Livingstone, Chris   (LD)
Lloyd, John   (Ind.)
Lumsden, Bob   (SNP)
Lyall, Ken   (SNP)
Mair, John   (C.)
McDonald, Helen   (C.)
McEwen, Joan   (Lab.)
Miller, Ian   (SNP)
Mulheron, Peter   (SNP)
O'Malley, Mike **(P)**   (Lab.)
Robertson, William   (LD)
Scott, Bob   (LD)
Scott, Dave   (SNP)
Stewart, Alexander   (C.)
Stewart, Heather   (C.)
Telfer, Alan   (SNP)
Wilson, William   (LD)
Young, Colin   (C.)
Total: 41 (SNP.16; C.11; LD.6; Lab.6; Ind.2)

CHIEF OFFICERS

Chief Executive: H. Robertson
Director of Education and Children's Services: B. Frew
Director of Environment: J. Milne
Director of Finance: A. R. McArthur
Director of Housing and Property Services: D. Roberts
Director of Human Resources: G. Farquhar
Director of Information Systems and Technology: A. J. Nairn

Director of Planning and Development Services: D. Munro
Director of Roads, Transport and Architectural Services: J. Irons
General Manager: I. Manson

SCOTTISH AND UK PARLIAMENTARY CONSTITUENCIES

Angus; Ochil; Perth; Tayside North

RENFREWSHIRE COUNCIL

Council Headquarters, North Building, Cotton Street, Paisley PA1 1BU (Tel: 0141-842 5000; Fax: 0141-840 3335; Web: www.renfrewshire.gov.uk).

Area: 261 sq. km
Population (1999 estimate): 178,340
population density (1998): 680 persons per sq. km
projected population in 2006 (1996-based): 175,632
number of households (1996): 75,100

Council tax (average Band D per two-person household), for 2001–02: £896.00
Notified net non-domestic rate income (1999–2000): £49,120,733
Education (pupils on register, 2000–01):
primary: 15,093
secondary: 11,969
special: 387
entitled to free meals: 24.9%

MEMBERS OF THE COUNCIL

Adams, Barbara	(Lab.)
Anderson, Marion	(SNP)
Burns, Ronnie	(Lab.)
Cameron, Lorraine	(SNP)
Cowan, Michele	(Lab.)
Glen, Roy	(Lab.)
Goldie, Jean	(Lab.)
Green, Jackie	(Lab.)
Hall, Ann	(Lab.)
Harkins, Jim	(Lab.)
Hogg, Iain	(Lab.)
Jackson, Nancy	(C.)
Kelly, Terry	(Lab.)
Kenny, John	(Lab.)
Lawson, Brian	(SNP)
Lawson, Celia	(SNP)
Macgregor, Nan	(LD)
Mackay, Derek	(SNP)
Macmillan, Mark	(Lab.)
Manser, Richard	(Lab.)
Martin, Bill	(SNP)
McCartin Eileen	(LD)
McDowell, John (P)	(Lab.)
McFee, Bruce	(SNP)
McGerty, Bob	(Lab.)
McGuinness, William	(SNP)
McGurk, Marie	(LD)
McMillan, Iain	(Lab.)
McNally, Robert	(Lab.)
Mitchell, Jim	(SNP)
Murrin, Alex	(Lab.)
Mylet, David	(SNP)
Nicolson, Iain	(SNP)
Nimmo, Alastair	(SNP)
Noon, Allan	(SNP)
Oldrey, Brian	(Lab.)
Pathucheary, Carol	(SNP)
Sheridan, James	(Lab.)
Vassie, Richard	(SNP)
Williams, Tommy	(Lab.)

Total: 40 (Lab. 21; SNP. 15; LD. 3; C. 1)

CHIEF OFFICERS

Chief Executive: T. Scholes
Director of Corporate Services: Ms M. Quinn
Director of Education and Leisure Services: Ms S. Rae
Director of Environmental Services: B. Forteath
Director of Finance and Information Technology: W. Hughes
Director of Housing and Property Services: M. Bailey
Director of Planning and Transport: I. Snodgrass
Director of Social Work: D. Crawford
Head of Legal Services: D. Sillars
Head of Personnel Services: Ms C. Proudfoot
Local Agenda 21 Officer: Ms J. Brooke

SCOTTISH AND UK PARLIAMENTARY CONSTITUENCIES

Paisley North; Paisley South; Renfrewshire West

SCOTTISH BORDERS COUNCIL

Council Headquarters, Newtown St Boswells, Melrose, Roxburghshire TD6 0SA
(Tel: 01835-824000; Fax: 01835-825001; Web: www.scotborders.gov.uk)

Area: 4,734 sq. km
Population (1998 estimate): 106,400
population density (1999): 22 persons per sq. km

projected population in 2006 (1998-based): 106,914
number of households (1998): 45,700

Council tax (average Band D per two-person household), for 2001–02: £785.00
Notified net non-domestic rate income (1999–2000): £18,811,036
Education (pupils on register, 2000–01): primary: 9,030
secondary: 6,691
entitled to free meals: 8.6%

MEMBERS OF THE COUNCIL

Angus, Oliver	(LD)
Borthwick, Anne	(LD)
Brockie, Bryan	(Lab.)
Dumble, Thomas	(Ind.)
Elliot, John	(Ind.)
Evans, Geoffrey	(LD)
Forrest, W. Logan	(Ind.)
Hardie, William	(Ind.)
Henderson, Thomas	(Ind.)
Hewat, Alastair	(Ind.)
Home Robertson, Catherine	(Ind.)
Jack, Robert	(LD)
Jones, David	(LD)
Lamb, William	(LD)
Law, John	(Ind.)
Lindores, David	(LD)
Meikle, John	(Ind.)
Mitchell, John	(SNP)
Nairn, James	(LD)
Nicol, Alexander	(LD)
Parker, David	(SNP)
Paterson, David	(Ind)
Pender, Norman	(LD)
Renton, Christopher	(SNP)
Rutherford, Robert	(LD)
Scott, James	(LD)
Scott, John	(LD)
Smith, Patricia	(LD)
Smith, William	(Ind.)
Suckling, David	(Ind.)
Tulley, Andrew (C)	(Ind.)
Waddell, Ian	(Ind.)
Wight, J. Hugh	(C.)
Younger, Anne	(Ind.)

Total: 34 (LD.14; Ind.15; SNP.3; Lab.1; C. 1)

CHIEF OFFICERS

Chief Executive: A. M. Croall
Director of Education: J. Christie
Director of Corporate Services: J. Campbell
Director of Housing: H. Blacklaws
Director of Leisure and Recreation: I. Yates

Director of Planning: P. Gregory
Director of Protective Services: W. Lillico
Director of Social Services: C. Johnson
Director of Technical Services: I. Brown
Head of Information Technology: Ms G. Hanham
Head of Personnel: D. Hunter
Head of Public Relations: J. Askew
Local Agenda 21 Officer: Mr. S. Hunt

SCOTTISH AND UK PARLIAMENTARY CONSTITUENCIES

Roxburgh and Berwickshire; Tweeddale, Ettrick and Lauderdale

SHETLAND ISLANDS COUNCIL

Town Hall, Hillhead, Lerwick, Shetland ZE1 0HB (Tel: 01595-693535; Fax: 01595-744509; Web: www.shetland.gov.uk).

Area: 1,438 sq. km
Population (1998 estimate): 22,910
population density (1998): 16 persons per sq. km
projected population in 2006 (1996-based): 22,383
number of households (2000–01): 9,929

Council tax (average Band D per two-person household), for 2001–02: £747.00
Notified net non-domestic rate income (1999–2000): £12,967,924
Education (pupils on register, 2000–01): primary: 2,120
secondary: 1,641
special: 24

MEMBERS OF THE COUNCIL

Anderson, Robert	(LD)
Angus, Leslie	(LD)
Begg, Christine	(LD)
Black, Robert	(Ind.)
Cluness, Alexander	(LD)
Colligan, Mary	(Ind.)
Eunson, Cecil	(Ind.)
Goodlad, Charles	(Ind.)
Grains, Florence	(Ind.)
Hawkins, Iris	(Ind.)
Hutchison, Loretta	(Ind.)
Irvine, James	(Ind.)
Malcolmson, Peter	(LD)
Manson, William	(Ind.)
Mitchell, Gordon	(Ind.)
Nicolson, John	(LD)

Ratter, William	(Ind.)
Ritch, James	(LD)
Robertson, Frank	(LD)
Stove, Thomas	(Ind.)
Stove, William (C)	(Ind.)
Tate, William	(Ind.)

Total: 22 (Ind.14; LD.8)

CHIEF OFFICERS

Chief Executive: M. Goodlad
Director of Community Services: J. Watt
Director of Corporate Services: A. Matthews
Director of Infrastructure Services: G. Spall
Local Agenda 21 Officer: A. Hamilton
Manager of Information/Communications Technology: J. Smith

SCOTTISH PARLIAMENTARY CONSTITUENCY

Shetland

UK PARLIAMENTARY CONSTITUENCY

Orkney and Shetland

SOUTH AYRSHIRE COUNCIL

County Buildings, Wellington Square, Ayr KA7 1DR (Tel: 01292-612000; Fax: 01292-612143; Web: www.south-ayrshire.gov.uk).

Area: 1,202 sq. km
Population (1998 estimate): 113,000
population density (1998): 95 persons per sq. km
projected population in 2006 (1996-based): 113,577
number of households (2000): 49,475

Council tax (average Band D per two-person household), for 2001–02: £874.00
Notified net non-domestic rate income (1999–2000): £29,390,735
Education (pupils on register, 2000–01):
primary: 9,102
secondary: 7,748
special: 83
entitled to free meals: 16.5%

MEMBERS OF THE COUNCIL

Baillie, John	(Lab.)
Bowie, Sadie	(Lab.)
Cairns, Alexander	(Lab.)
Campell, Brenda	(Ind.)
Campell, Douglas	(Lab.)
Campell, Robert	(Ind.)
Convery, Peter	(C.)

Cree, John	(Lab.)
Davies, Agnes	(Lab.)
Duncan, David	(Lab.)
Fitzsimmons, Ian	(C.)
Foulkes, Elizabeth (P)	(Lab.)
Hill, Andrew	(Lab.)
Hunter, Hugh	(C.)
Kerr, Alistair	(C.)
Kilpatrick, Mary	(C.)
Macdonald, Gibson	(C.)
McIntosh, Bill	(C.)
McKenzie, Gordon	(Lab.)
McNally, Bill	(C.)
McNicol, Lorraine	(Lab.)
Miller, Rita	(Lab.)
Murray, Alan	(Lab.)
Paterson, Pam	(C.)
Reid, Robin	(C.)
Sloan, Winifred	(C.)
Stewart, Ian	(Lab.)
Toner, Margaret	(C.)
Torrance, Paul	(Lab.)
Young, Cherry	(C.)

Total: 30 (Lab. 15; C. 13; Ind. 2)

CHIEF OFFICERS

Chief Executive: G. W. F. Thorley
Director of Community Services: Ms E. Noad
Director of Commercial Operations: R. Sheed
Director of Education: M. McCab
Director of Finance: T. Cairns
Director of Strategic Services: A. Harkness
Director of Support Services: J. G. Peterkin
Head of Housing: P. Whyte
Head of Information Technology: Ms I. Gillespie
Head of Legal Services: D. Russell
Head of Personnel: A. Stewart
Head of Social Services: Ms J. Thompson
Local Agenda 21 Officer: K. Gibb

SCOTTISH AND UK PARLIAMENTARY CONSTITUENCIES

Ayr; Carrick, Cumnock and Doon Valley

SOUTH LANARKSHIRE COUNCIL

Council Offices, Almada Street, Hamilton, Lanarkshire ML3 0AA (Tel: 01698-454904; Fax: 01698-454949; Web: www.southlanarkshire.gov.uk).

Area: 1,771 sq. km
Population (1998 estimate): 307,350
population density (1998): 173 persons per sq. km
projected population in 2006 (1996-based): 303,554
number of households (1996): 122,300

Council tax (average Band D per two-person household), for 2001–02: £924,00
Notified net non-domestic rate income (1999–2000): £74,688,174
Education (pupils on register, 2000–01):
primary: 26,337
secondary: 20,323
special: 653
entitled to free meals: 21.1%

MEMBERS OF THE COUNCIL

Addison, Lindsay	(SNP)
Ahmad, Mushtaq	(Lab.)
Buchanan, Archie	(SNP)
Burns, Jackie	(Lab.)
Caldwell, May	(Lab.)
Carlin, Anthony	(Lab.)
Clearie, Pamela	(Lab. & Co-op)
Clearie, Russell	(Lab. & Co-op)
Convery, Gerry	(Lab.)
Craw, Lorraine	(Lab.)
Crawford, Stewart	(Lab.)
Daisley, James	(Lab.)
Dick, Alan (P)	(Lab.)
Docherty, Gerald	(Lab.)
Docherty, James	(Lab.)
Duffy, Margaret	(Lab.)
Dunsmuir, Hugh	(Lab.)
Falconer, Alan	(Lab.)
Ferguson, Robert	(Lab.)
Forrest, Beith	(C.)
Gauld, Bev	(SNP)
Handibode, Elizabeth	(Lab.)
Handibode, James	(Lab.)
Hughes, Carol	(Lab.)
Keirs, David	(Lab. & Co-op)
Logan, Eileen	(Lab.)
Lowe, Joseph	(Lab.)
Maggs, Anne	(SNP)
Malloy, James	(Lab.)
McAlpine, T.	(SNP)
McAvoy, Edward	(Lab.)
McCaig, William	(Lab.)
McCann, Michael	(Lab.)
McDonald, Dugald	(Lab.)
McDonald, H.	(C.)
McGlynn, Michael	(Lab.)
McGuinness, John	(Lab.)
McGuire, Alex	(Lab.)
McInnes, Alexander	(Lab.)
McKenna, Brian	(Lab.)
McKenna, Dennis	(Lab.)
McKenna, Patrick	(Lab.)
McKeown, Jean	(Lab.)
McLachlan, David	(Lab.)
McNab, William	(Lab.)
McNeil, Mary	(Lab.)
Mitchell, Alice Marie	(Lab.)
Morgan, Patrick	(Lab.)
Murray, Robertson	(SNP)
Ormiston, John	(Lab.)
Roberts, Ian	(Lab.)
Rooney, Robert	(Lab.)
Ross, Gretel	(LD)
Ross, William	(Lab.)
Scott, Graham	(Lab.)
Shearer, D.	(SNP)
Smith, Mary	(Lab. & Co-op)
Smith, May	(Lab.)
Smith, Rita	(Lab.)
Thompson, Christopher	(Lab.)
Walls, Joseph	(Lab.)
Wardhaugh, James	(SNP)
Watson, D.	(SNP)
Watters, Patrick	(Lab.)
Winning, Ann	(SNP)

Total: 65 (Lab.48; SNP.10; Lab. & Co-op 4; C.2; LD.1)

CHIEF OFFICERS

Chief Executive: vacant
Executive Director of Community Resources: Ms G. Pain
Executive Director of Corporate Resources: A. Cuthbertson
Executive Director of Education Resources: Ms M. Allan
Executive Director of Enterprise Resources: M. Docherty
Executive Director of Finance and Information Technology Resources: W. Kirk
Executive Director of Housing and Technical Resources: S. Gilchrist
Executive Director of Social Work: S. Cameron
Head of Enforcement: R. Howe
Head of Information Technology: Ms K. Brown
Head of Legal Services: Ms S. Dickinson
Local Agenda 21 Officer: K. Boag

SCOTTISH AND UK PARLIAMENTARY CONSTITUENCIES

Clydesdale; East Kilbride; Glasgow Rutherglen; Hamilton North and Bellshill; Hamilton South

STIRLING COUNCIL

Viewforth, Stirling FK8 2ET (Tel: 01786-443322; Fax: 01786-443078; Web: www.stirling.gov.uk).

Area: 2,196 sq. km
Population (1998 estimate): 84,700
population density (1998): 38 persons per sq. km
projected population in 2006 (1996-based): 86,120
number of households (1996): 33,100

Council tax (average Band D per two-person household), for 2001–02: £954,00
Notified net non-domestic rate income (1999–2000): £26,968,347
Education (pupils on register, 2000–01):
primary: 6,989
secondary: 5,742
special: 63
entitled to free meals: 17%

MEMBERS OF THE COUNCIL

Beaton, Alastair	(C.)
Brisley, Margaret	(Lab.)
Brookes, Tommy (P)	(Lab.)
Coll, Tom	(Lab.)
Dickson, Ann	(C.)
Finch, Tony	(C.)
Greenhill, Pat	(C.)
Harding, Keith	(C.)
Hazel, Tom	(Lab.)
Hendry, John	(Lab.)
Holliday, John	(C.)
Kelly, Pat	(Lab.)
Love, Susan	(SNP)
McChord, Corrie	(Lab.)
O'Brien, Colin	(Lab.)
Organ, Catherine	(C.)
Paterson, John	(Lab.)
Power, Gerard	(C.)
Reid, Alastair	(C.)
Scott, Helen	(C.)
Strang, Ann	(Lab.)
Thomson, Gillie	(Lab.)

Total: 22 (Lab.11; C.10; SNP; 1)

CHIEF OFFICERS

Chief Executive: K. Yates
Director of Civic Services: R. Jack
Director of Community Services: Ms H. Munro
Director of Education Services: G. Jeyes
Director of Environmental Services: D. Martin
Director of Finance and Information Services: W. Dickson
Director of Housing and Social Services: vacant
Director of Technical and Commercial Services: A. Nicholls
Head of Personnel: Ms J. Jones
Local Agenda 21 Officer: A. Speedie

SCOTTISH AND UK PARLIAMENTARY CONSTITUENCIES

Ochil; Stirling

WEST DUNBARTONSHIRE COUNCIL

Garshake Road, Dumbarton G82 3PU (Tel: 01389-737000; Fax: 01389-737070; Web: www.west-dunbarton.gov.uk).

Area: 17,792 hectares
Population: 93,977
population density: 538 persons per sq. km
projected population in 2006 (1996-based): 90,596
number of households (1999): 42,500

Council tax (average Band D per two-person household), for 2001–02: £1,024
Notified net non-domestic rate income (1999-2000): £23,199,411
Education (pupils on register, 2000–01):
primary: 8,381
secondary: 6,883
special: 136
entitled to free meals: 29.9%

MEMBERS OF THE COUNCIL

Bollan, James	(SSP)
Calvert, Geoffrey	(Lab.)
Campbell, Mary	(Ind.)
Collins, Mary	(Ind.)
Devine, Anthony	(Lab.)
Flynn, James	(Lab.)
Macdonald, Alistair (P)	(Lab.)
McCafferty, Daniel	(Ind.)
McCallum, James	(Lab.)
McColl, Linda	(Lab.)
McColl, Ronald	(SNP)
McCutcheon, John	(SNP)
McDonald, Duncan	(Lab.)

McDonald, John	(SNP)
McElhill, James	(SNP)
McGregor, Margaret	(SNP)
McLaughlin, Craig	(SNP)
O'Sullivan, Connie	(Lab.)
Robertson, Iain	(SNP)
Syme, John	(Ind.)
Trainer, John	(Lab.)
White, Andrew	(Lab.)

Total: 22 (Lab.10; SNP.7; Ind. 4; SSP. 1)

CHIEF OFFICERS

Chief Executive: T. Huntingford
Director of Commercial and Technical Services: David McMillan
Director of Economic, Planning and Environmental Services: Dan Henderson
Director of Education and Cultural Services: I. McMurdo
Director of Corporate Services: E. Walker
Director of Social Work and Housing: Alexis Jay
Head of Corporate Policy and Public Relations: Ms M. Cullen
Head of Information Services: Ms A. Clements
Manager of Personnel and Training: G. McInerney
Local Agenda 21 Officer: T. Moan

SCOTTISH AND UK PARLIAMENTARY CONSTITUENCIES

Clydebank and Milngavie; Dumbarton

WEST LOTHIAN COUNCIL

West Lothian House, Almondvale Boulevard, Livingston, West Lothian EH54 6QG
(Tel: 01506-775 000; Fax: 01506-775 099; www.wlonline.org.uk).

Area: 425 sq. km
Population (1998 estimate): 153,090
population density (1998): 360 persons per sq. km
projected population in 2006 (1996-based): 160,620
number of households (1996): 60,300
Council tax (average Band B per two-person household), for 2001–02: £919.00
Notified net non-domestic rate income (1999–00): £44,261,659
Education (pupils on register, 2000–01):
primary: 14,984
secondary: 10,436
special: 197
entitled to free meals: 17.3%

MEMBERS OF THE COUNCIL

Anderson, Frank	(SNP)
Bartholomew, Carol	(Lab.)
Constance, Angela	(SNP)
Davidson, Alexander	(Lab.)
Day, Martin	(SNP)
Dickson, Jim	(SNP)
Dunn, Willie	(Lab.)
Ferrie, Bruce	(Lab.)
Fitzpatrick, Lawrence	(Lab.)
Gamble, Bert	(Lab.)
Gordon, Audrey	(SNP)
Johnston, Peter	(SNP)
Kerr, Tom	(C.)
King, Dave	(Lab.)
Lee, Robert	(Lab.)
Logue, Danny	(Lab.)
Mackie, Allister	(Lab.)
Maclean, Duncan	(Ind.)
Malcolm, Eddie	(SNP)
McGinty, John	(Lab.)
McGrouther, David	(Lab.)
Miller, Andrew	(SNP)
Graeme, Morrice	(Lab.)
Muldoon, Cathy	(Lab.)
Mutch, Wendy	(Lab.)
Owens, Hugh	(Lab.)
Russell, William	(Lab.)
Sibbald, Jim	(SNP)
Smart, Heather	(Lab.)
Smith, Tam	(SNP)
Swan, Jim	(Lab.)
Thomas, Joe (P)	(Lab.)

Total: 32 (Lab. 20; SNP. 10; C.1; Ind 1)

CHIEF OFFICERS

Chief Executive: A. M. Linkston
Corporate Manager, Community Services: D. Kelly
Corporate Manager, Education Services: R. Stewart
Corporate Manager, Strategic Services: J. Dickson
Corporate Manager, Environmental Services: B. Dixon
Head, Housing Services: J. Ritchie
Head, Social Work: G. Blair
Local Agenda 21 Officer: Ms C. Braithwaite
Manager, Administration and Legal: G. Blair

Manager, Development and Building Control:
R. Hartland
**Manager, Environmental Health and Trading
Standards:** A. Campbell
Manager, Finance: A. Logan
Manager, Human Resources: J. Nowak
Manager, Information Technology: Ms S. Aird

SCOTTISH AND UK PARLIAMENTARY CONSTITUENCIES

Linlithgow; Livingston

DEFENCE

Defence is one of the powers reserved to Westminster and the Scottish Parliament has no jurisdiction over it. However, there are a number of important armed forces installations in Scotland. In particular, all the UK's nuclear weaponry is held at the Clyde naval base.
The following gives details of the main commands and forces in Scotland.

SCOTTISH COMMANDS

Flag Officer Scotland, Northern England and Northern Ireland

HM Naval Base Clyde, Helensburgh, Dunbartonshire G84 8HL (Tel: 01436-674321).

Flag Officer Scotland, Northern England and Northern Ireland: Rear-Adm. A. M. Gregory, OBE

Army HQ Scotland, Annandale Block, Craigiehall, South Queensferry, West Lothian EH30 9TN (Tel: 0131-336 1761).

General Officer Commanding 2nd Division: Maj.-Gen. R. D. S. Gordon, CBE

HQ 51 Highland Brigade, Highland House, 7 St Leonard's Bank, Perth PH2 8EB

HQ 52 Lowland Brigade, Edinburgh Castle, Edinburgh EH1 2YT

Air Officer Scotland and Northern Ireland

RAF Leuchars, St Andrews, Fife KY16 0JX (Tel: 01334-839471).
Air Officer Scotland and Northern Ireland: Air Cdre J. H. Haines, OBE

NAVAL BASE

HM Naval Base Clyde

Helensburgh, Dunbartonshire G84 8HL (Tel: 01436-674321).

THE ARMY

Royal Armoured Corps

The Royal Scots Dragoon Guards (Carabiniers and Greys)
Home HQ, The Castle, Edinburgh EH1 2YT; (Tel: 0131-310 5100).
Colonel-in-Chief: HM The Queen

INFANTRY

Scots Guards

Regimental HQ, Wellington Barracks, Birdcage Walk, London SW1E 6HQ (Tel: 020-7414 3324).
Colonel-in-Chief: HM The Queen

Scottish Division

Divisional Offices, The Castle, Edinburgh EH1 2YT (Tel: 0131-310 5001).
HQ Infantry, Imber Road, Warminster, Wilts BA12 0DJ (Tel: 01985-222674).
Training Centre, Infantry Training Centre, Vimy Barracks, Catterick, N. Yorks DL9 4HH
Colonel Commandant: Maj.-Gen. Ash Irwin, CBE
Divisional Lieutenant-Colonel: Lt.-Col. R. M. Riddell

The Royal Scots (The Royal Regiment)

Regimental HQ, The Castle, Edinburgh EH1 2YT (Tel: 0131-310 5014).
Colonel-in-Chief: HRH The Princess Royal, KG, GCVO

The Royal Highland Fusiliers (Princess Margaret's own Glasgow and Ayrshire Regiment)

Regimental HQ, 518 Sauchiehall Street, Glasgow G2 3LW (Tel: 0141-332 0961/5639).
Colonel-in-Chief: HRH The Princess Margaret, Countess of Snowdon, CI, GCVO

The King's own Scottish Borderers

Regimental HQ, The Barracks, Berwick-on-Tweed TD15 1DG (Tel: 01289-307426).
Colonel-in-Chief: HRH Princess Alice, Duchess of Gloucester, GCB, CI, GCVO, GBE

The Black Watch (Royal Highland Regiment)

Regimental HQ, Balhousie Castle, Perth PH1 5HR (Tel: 01738-621281; 0131-310 8530).
Colonel-in-Chief: HM Queen Elizabeth the Queen Mother

The Highlanders (Seaforth, Gordons and Camerons)

Regimental HQ, Cameron Barracks, Inverness IV2 3XD (Tel: 01463-224380).
Outstation, Viewfield Road, Aberdeen AB15 7XH (Tel: 01224-318174).
Colonel-in-Chief: HRH The Prince Philip, Duke of Edinburgh, KG, KT, OM, GBE

The Argyll and Sutherland Highlanders (Princess Louise's)
Regimental HQ, The Castle, Stirling FK8 1EH (Tel: 01786-475165).
Colonel-in-Chief: HM The Queen

Army Personnel Centre
Kentigern House, 65 Brown Street, Glasgow G2 8EX (Tel: 0141-248 7890).
Chief Executive: Maj.-Gen. Ash Irwin, CBE

MAIN RAF BASES

RAF Kinloss
Kinloss, Forres, Moray IV36 3UH (Tel: 01309-672161)

RAF Leuchars
St Andrews, Fife KY16 0JX (Tel: 01334-839471)

RAF Lossiemouth
Lossiemouth, Moray IV31 6SD (Tel: 01343-812121)

RESERVE FORCES

Royal Navy Reserves
There are two Royal Naval Reserve units in Scotland, with a total of 395 members at April 2000.

HMS Dalriada
Navy Buildings, Eldon Street, Greenock PA16 7SL (Tel: 01475-724481)

HMS Scotia
c/o HMS Caledonia, Hilton Road, Rosyth, Fife KY11 2XT (Tel: 01383-425794)

Territorial Army
The post-Strategic Defence Review establishment of the Territorial Army in Scotland, including the Officers' Training Corps, is 4,794, with effect from 1 July 2001.

There are TA/reservist centres in Aberdeen, Arbroath, Cumbernauld, Cupar, Dumbarton, Dundee, Dunfermline, Dunoon, Elgin, Forfar, Glenrothes, Grangemouth, Invergowrie, Inverness, Keith, Kirkcaldy, Kirkwall, Lerwick, Leuchars, Perth, Peterhead, St Andrews, Stirling, Stornoway and Wick (Highlands), and Ayr, Bathgate, Dumfries, East Kilbride, Edinburgh, Galashiels, Glasgow, Irvine, Livingston, Hamilton, Motherwell and Paisley (Lowlands).

Highlands Reserve Forces and Cadets Association

Seathwood, 365 Perth Road, Dundee DD2 1LX (Tel: 01382-668283)
Secretary: Col. J. R. Hensman, OBE

Lowlands Reserve Forces and Cadets Association

Lowland House, 60 Avenuepark Street, Glasgow G20 8LW (Tel: 0141-945 4951)
Secretary: Col. R. S. B. Watson, OBE

Royal Auxiliary Air Force (RAuxAF)

There are three units of the RAuxAF in Scotland, with a total of about 280 members at April 2001.

603 (City of Edinburgh) Maritime HQ Squadron
25 Learmonth Terrace, Edinburgh EH4 1NZ (Tel: 0131-332 2333)

NO. 2622 (Highland) Squadron, RAuxAF Regiment
RAF Lossiemouth, Moray IV31 6SD (Tel: 01343-812121)

Air Transportable Surgical Squadron, RAuxAF
RAF Leuchars, St Andrews, Fife KY16 0JY (Tel: 01334-839471)

PUBLIC SERVICES

SCOTLAND

EDUCATION
THE ENERGY INDUSTRIES
THE FIRE SERVICE
HEALTH
AMBULANCE SERVICE
POLICE SERVICE
PRISON SERVICE
SOCIAL SERVICES
TRANSPORT

— PUBLIC SERVICES SCOTLAND —

EDUCATION

Overall responsibility for all aspects of education in Scotland lies with Scottish Ministers acting through the Scottish Executive Education Department and the Enterprise and Lifelong Learning Department (formerly the Scottish Office Education and Industry Department).

The main concerns of the Scottish Executive Education Department are the formulation of policy for pre-school, primary and secondary education, its administration and the maintenance of consistency in educational standards in schools. It is responsible for the broad allocation of resources for school education, the rate and distribution of educational building and the supply, training and superannuation of teachers. The Enterprise and Lifelong Learning Department is concerned with post-16 education, qualifications and student support.

EXPENDITURE

Expenditure on education by central government, in real terms, was £1,496.6 million in 2000–1, with a planned expenditure of £1,672.0 million for 2001–2.

The major elements of central government expenditure are: grant-aided special schools; curriculum development; special educational needs; school buildings; community learning; initial teacher education and professional development; research; support for higher and further education in universities and colleges (through the funding councils); and student awards and bursaries (through the Student Awards Agency for Scotland).

Significant expenditure is incurred by local authorities, which make their own expenditure decisions according to their local situations and needs. Local authority net expenditure on education (provisional) for 2000–1 was £2,752.4 million; planned net expenditure for 2001–2 is £2,952.8 million.

LOCAL EDUCATION ADMINISTRATION

The education service at present is a national service in which the provision of most school education is locally administered.

The statutory responsibility for delivering school education locally in Scotland rests with the education authorities and the schools under their management. The education authorities are responsible for the construction of buildings, the employment of teachers and other staff, and the provision of equipment and materials. Devolved School Management is in place for all primary, secondary and special schools, which means that they make their own decisions on at least 83 per cent of school-level expenditure.

Education authorities are required to establish school boards consisting of parents and teachers as well as co-opted members. Boards have a duty to promote contact between parents, the school and the community and are inolved, among other things, in the appointment of senior staff.

THE INSPECTORATE

HM Inspectorate of Education (HMIE) has a duty to promote improvements in standards, quality and attainment in Scottish education through independent evaluation. HM Inspectors (HMI) inspect or review and report on education in pre-school centres, nursery, primary, secondary and special schools, further education institutions (under contract to the Scottish Further Education Funding Council), initial teacher education and community learning. HMIs work in teams alongside lay members and associate assessors, who are practising teachers seconded for the inspection. In April 2001 HMIE became an executive agency of the Scottish Executive. In 2000—1 there were 87 HMIs and five Chief Inspectors in Scotland.

The inspection of higher education is the responsibility of inspectors appointed by the Scottish Higher Education Funding Council.

SCHOOLS AND PUPILS

Schooling is compulsory for all children between five and 16 years of age. Provision is being increased for children under five and many pupils remain at school after the minimum leaving age. No fees are charged in any publicly maintained school in Scotland.

Throughout the United Kingdom, parents have a right of choice of school for their children, within certain limits, and to appeal if dissatisfied. The policy, known as more open enrolment, requires schools to admit children up to the limit of their capacity if there is a demand for places, and to publish their criteria for selection if they are over-subscribed, in which case parents have a right of appeal.

The 'Parents' Charter', available free from education departments, is a booklet which tells parents about the education system. Schools are now required to make available information about themselves — their public examination results, truancy rates and destination of leavers — through the school handbook. Corporal punishment is no longer legal in publicly maintained schools in the United Kingdom.

The number of schools by sector in 1999–2000 was:

Publicly maintained schools	5,048
Pre-school centres/nursery	2,171
Primary	2,293
Secondary	389
Special	195
Independent schools	209
Total	5,257

Education authority schools (known as public schools) are financed by local government, partly through revenue support grants from central government and partly from local taxation. There is a small number of grant-aided schools, mainly in the special sector, which are supervised by boards of managers and receive grants direct from the Scottish Executive Education Department. Under the previous government a category of self-governing schools was created. Such schools opted to be managed entirely by a board of management but remained in the public sector and were funded by direct government grants, set to match the resources the school would have received under education authority management. Two schools were established, one of which has been returned to the education authority framework.

Independent schools charge fees and receive no direct grant, but are subject to inspection and registration.

THE STATE SYSTEM
PRE-SCHOOL EDUCATION

Pre-school education is for children from two to five years and is not compulsory, but the Scottish Executive has set a target of a nursery place for every three-year-old whose parents want it. It takes place in pre-school education centres, play groups, private nurseries or nursery schools (all of which may be provided either by or in partnership with the local authority, or by independent providers) or in nursery classes in primary schools.

Local authorities are responsible for the funding and management of services. All providers of pre-school education are subject to inspection.

LOCAL AUTHORITY PRE-SCHOOL CENTRES 1999–2000

No. of centres	1,343
No. of pupils	66,719
No. of teachers (full-time equivalent)	1,335
Staff to child ratio	7.3

PRIMARY EDUCATION

Primary education begins at five years and is almost always co-educational. The primary school course lasts for seven years (from primary 1 to 7) and pupils transfer to secondary courses at about the age of 12.

Primary schools consist mainly of infant schools for children aged five to seven, junior schools for those aged seven to 12, and combined junior and infant schools for both age groups. Many primary schools provide nursery classes for children under five (*see* above).

PRIMARY SCHOOLS 1999–2000

No. of schools	2,293
No. of pupils (000s)	429.3
No. of teachers (full-time 000s)	21.3
Pupil-teacher ratio	19.1

SECONDARY EDUCATION

Secondary schools are for children aged 11 to 16 and for those who choose to stay on to 18. Most secondary schools in Scotland are co-educational. All pupils in Scottish education authority secondary schools attend schools with a comprehensive intake. Most of these schools provide a full range of courses appropriate to all levels of ability from first to sixth year.

In an attempt to encourage young people from low income households to stay on post-16, the Education Maintenance Allowance Scheme is being piloted in certain areas, paying up to £40 per week to eligible students with bonuses of £75 and £50 for successful completion.

SECONDARY SCHOOLS 1999–2000

No. of schools	389
No. of pupils (000s)	316.4
No. of teachers (full-time 000s)	22.2
Pupil-teacher ratio	12.9

SPECIAL EDUCATIONAL NEEDS

Special education is provided for children with special educational needs, usually because they have a disability which either prevents or hinders them from making use of educational facilities of a kind generally provided for children of their age in schools within the area of the local authority concerned.

It is intended that pupils with special educational needs should have access to as much of the curriculum as possible, but there is provision for them to be exempt from it or for it to be modified to suit their capabilities. In such cases the authority is required to open a record of needs describing the special education appropriate. The number of full-time pupils with statements of special needs in 1999–2000 was (000s):

In publicly funded special schools	6.5
In public sector primary and secondary schools	8.7

The school placing of children with special educational needs is a matter of agreement between education authorities and parents. Parents have the right to say which school they want their child to attend, and a right of appeal where their wishes are not being met. Legislation places a duty on education authorities, whenever possible, to educate children with special educational needs in ordinary schools. However, for those who require a different environment or specialised facilities, there are special schools, both grant-aided by central government and independent, and special classes within ordinary schools. Education authorities are required to respond to reasonable requests for attendance to independent special schools and to send children with special educational needs to schools outwith Scotland if appropriate provision is not available within the country.

The Scottish Executive funds "Enquire", the national special educational needs information and advice service for parents and children on legislation, policy and provision.

SPECIAL SCHOOLS 1999–2000

Maintained schools	
No. of schools	185
No. of pupils (000s)	8.3
No. of teachers (full-time equivalent)	1,967
Pupil-teacher ratio	4.2
Non-maintained schools	
No. of schools	33
No. of pupils (000s)	1.0
No. of teachers (full-time equivalent)	334
Pupil-teacher ratio	3.1

ALTERNATIVE PROVISION

There is no legal obligation on parents anywhere in the United Kingdom to educate their children at school, provided that the local education authority is satisfied that the child is receiving full-time education suited to its age, abilities and aptitudes. The education authority need not be informed that a child is being educated at home unless the child is already registered at a state school, in which case the parents must arrange for the child's name to be removed from the school's register before education at home can begin. Parents educating their children at home are not required to be in possession of a teaching qualification.

Information and support on all aspects of home education can be obtained from Education Otherwise (*see* page 114).

INDEPENDENT SCHOOLS

Independent schools receive no grants from public funds. They charge fees, and are owned and managed under special trusts, with profits being used for the benefit of the schools concerned. There is a wide variety of provision, from kindergartens to large day and boarding schools, and from experimental schools to traditional institutions. A number of independent schools have been instituted by religious and ethnic minorities. In 1999, just under 3.9 per cent of pupils in Scotland attended independent schools, the same proportion as in 1998.

Most independent schools offer a similar range of courses to state schools and enter pupils for the same public examinations. Those in Scotland tend to follow the examination system which prevails in the rest of the United Kingdom, i.e. GCSE followed by A-levels, although some take the Scottish Education Certificate at Standard Grade followed by Highers or Advanced Highers.

Most Scottish independent schools in membership of the Headmasters' and Headmistresses' Conference, the Governing Bodies Association or the Governing Bodies of Girls' Schools Association are single-sex, but there are some mixed schools, and an increasing number of schools have mixed sixth forms.

Information on independent schools can be obtained from the Independent Schools Information Service.

INDEPENDENT SCHOOLS 1999–2000

No. of schools	134
No. of pupils (000s)	30.2
No. of teachers (full-time 000s)	2.5
Pupil-teacher ratio	10.3

THE CURRICULUM

The content and management of the curriculum in Scotland are not prescribed by statute but are the responsibility of education authorities and individual headteachers. Advice and guidance are provided by the Scottish Executive Education Department and Learning and Teaching Scotland, which also has a developmental role. The Scottish Executive Education Department and Learning and Teaching Scotland have produced guidelines on the structure and balance of the curriculum for the five to 14 age group as well as for each of the curriculum areas. There are also guidelines on assessment across the whole curriculum, on reporting to parents, and on standardised national tests for English language and mathematics at five levels. Testing is carried out on a voluntary basis when the teacher deems it appropriate; most pupils are expected to move from one level to the next at roughly two-year intervals. National testing is largely in place in most primary schools but secondary school participation rates are lower.

The curriculum for 14 to 16-year-olds includes study within each of eight modes: language and communication; mathematical studies; science; technology; social studies; creative activities; physical education; and religious and moral education. There is a recommended percentage of class time to be devoted to each area over the two years. Provision is made for teaching in Gaelic in Gaelic-speaking areas.

For 16 to 18-year-olds, National Qualifications (*see* below), an unified framework of courses and awards, brings together both academic and vocational courses. The Scottish Qualifications Authority awards the new certificates.

EXAMINATIONS AND QUALIFICATIONS

Scotland has its own system of public examinations, separate from that in England, Wales and Northern Ireland. At the end of the fourth year of secondary education, at about the age of 16, pupils take the Standard Grade of the Scottish Certificate of Education. Standard Grade courses and examinations have been designed to suit every level of ability, with assessment against nationally determined standards of performance.

For most courses there are three separate examination papers at the end of the two-year Standard Grade course. They are set at Credit (leading to awards at grade 1 or 2), General (leading to awards at grade 3 or 4) and Foundation (leading to awards at grade 5 or 6) levels. Grade 7 is available to those who, although they have completed the course, have not attained any of these levels. Normally pupils will take examinations covering two pairs of grades, either grades 1–4 or grades 3–6. Most candidates take seven or eight Standard Grade examinations.

For the post-16 age group a new system of courses and qualifications is being phased in under the 'Higher Still' reforms, bringing together academic and vocational qualifications. By 2004 National Qualifications will replace Highers (from 2000–1), the one-year Certificate of Sixth Year Studies (from 2001–2), National Certificate modules, and General Scottish Vocational Qualifications for everyone studying beyond Standard Grade in Scottish schools, and for non-advanced students in further education colleges. Standard Grade and Scottish Vocational Qualifications will remain. National Qualifications are available at five levels: Access, Intermediate 1, Intermediate 2, Higher and Advanced Higher. Courses are made up of internally assessed units, with external assessment of the full course determining the grade (A to C). The core skills of communication, numeracy, problem-solving, information technology and working with others are embedded in the 'Higher Still' qualifications, although the skills and levels covered vary between subjects; there are also separate core skill units.

All these qualifications are awarded by the Scottish Qualifications Authority.

At the end of the 1998–9 academic year, 29.4 per cent of all school leavers from publicly-funded schools left at the end of compulsory education (33.7 per cent of boys, 25 per cent of girls). The total number of school leavers was 58,722 and their achievement, by highest Scottish Certificate of Education qualification held, was (percentages):

Higher grades A—C	(%)
1—2	13.6
3—4	11.2
5—6	8.7

Standard grades	
1—2	19.1
3—4	29.0
5—6	2.7
None	3.8

THE INTERNATIONAL BACCALAUREATE

The International Baccalaureate is an internationally recognised two-year pre-university course and examination designed to facilitate the mobility of students and to promote international understanding. Candidates must offer one subject from each of six subject groups, at least three at higher level and the remainder at subsidiary level. Single subjects can be offered, for which a certificate is received. The International Baccalaureate diploma is offered by 43 schools and colleges in the United Kingdom, of which two are in Scotland.

RECORDS OF ACHIEVEMENT

The Scottish Qualification Certificate replaced the National Record of Achievement from the academic year 1999–2000. It is issued by the Scottish Qualifications Authority and records all qualifications achieved at all levels. The school report card gives parents information on their child's progress in school.

TEACHERS

All teachers in publicly maintained schools must be registered with the General Teaching Council for Scotland. They are registered provisionally for a two-year probationary period, which can be extended if necessary. Only graduates are accepted as entrants to the profession; primary school teachers undertake either a four-year vocational degree course or a one-year postgraduate course, while teachers of academic subjects in secondary schools undertake the latter. Most initial teacher training is classroom-based. Colleges of education provide both in-service and pre-service training for teachers which is subject to inspection by HM Inspectorate of Education. The colleges are funded by the Scottish Higher Education Funding Council, which also sets intake levels to teacher education courses.

The Scottish Qualification for Headship is aimed at aspiring headteachers and is both a development programme and a qualification.

The General Teaching Council advises Scottish Ministers on teacher supply and the professional suitability of all teacher training courses. It is also the body responsible for disciplinary procedures in cases of professional misconduct.

TEACHERS IN PUBLICLY MAINTAINED SCHOOLS 1999—2000
(full-time equivalent)

	Total	Male	Female
Primary			
Headteacher	2,262	501	1,761
Depute headteacher	968	81	887
Assistant headteacher	616	50	566
Senior teacher	3,246	220	3,026
Unpromoted teacher	15,548	701	14,847
Secondary			
Headteacher	392	347	45
Depute headteacher	391	303	88
Assistant headteacher	1,071	714	357
Principal teacher	7,089	4,181	2,907
Assistant principal teacher	3,021	1,302	1,719
Senior teacher	1,719	686	1,033
Unpromoted teacher	10,773	3,792	7,001

SALARIES

Teachers in Scotland are paid on a nine-point scale. The entry point depends on type of qualification, and additional allowances are payable under certain circumstances. Salaries for headteachers and depute headteachers vary depending on various factors including the type and size of school.

Salaries

	from 1 April 2001	from 1 April 2002
Head	£32,526–£60,252	£33,828–£62,661
Depute head	£32,526–£45,084	£33,828–£46,887
Principal teacher	£28,932–£33,750	£30,090–£35,100
Senior teacher	£26,424–£27,954	£27,480–£29,073
Teacher	£16,005–£25,644	£16,644–£25,670

FURTHER EDUCATION

Further education covers all provision to people aged over 16. Responsibility for further education lies with the Scottish Executive under the Minister for Enterprise and Lifelong Learning. The Executive also liaises with the Scottish Further Education Funding Council to administer further education funding and to ensure that colleges play a full part in carrying forward Scottish Ministers' policy objectives for further education.

There are 46 further education colleges, of which 42 are self-governing incorporated colleges run by their own boards of management. The boards include the principal, staff and student representatives among their members; at least half of whom must have experience of commerce, industry or professional practice. Two colleges, on Orkney and Shetland, are under Islands Council control, and two others, Sàbhal Mor Ostaig (the Gaelic college on Skye) and Newbattle Abbey College, are managed by trustees.

The Scottish Qualifications Authority (SQA) is the statutory awarding body for qualifications in the national education and training system in Scotland. It is both the main awarding body for qualifications for work including Scottish Vocational Qualifications (SVQs) and also their accrediting body. The SQA is by statute required to clearly separate its awarding and accrediting functions.

In further education in Scotland there are three main qualification families: National Qualifications; Higher National Qualifications (HNC and HND); and SVQs. In addition to Standard Grade qualifications, the new National Qualifications are available at five levels: Access, Intermediate 1, Intermediate 2, Higher and Advanced Higher.

Another feature of the new qualifications sytem is the Scottish Group Award (SGA). SGAs are built up unit by unit and are opportunities for credit transfer from other qualifications (such as Standard Grades or SVQs), providing an additional option for learners, especially adult returners.

Advanced-level courses offered by further education colleges and other institutions lead to the award of HNC and HND and, in some colleges, to degree level. HNCs and HNDs are long-established advanced level vocational qualifications covering a diverse and growing range of employment sectors.

SVQs are competence-based qualifications intended to guarantee a person's ability to do a particular job. They are suitable for workplace delivery since they are designed to national occupational standards of competence set by national training organisations. SVQs have mutual recognition with the National Vocational Qualifications available in the rest of the United Kingdom.

In the academic year 1999–2000 there were 38,176 full-time and sandwich-course students and 273,360 part-time students on non-advanced vocational courses of further education in further education colleges (excluding Newbattle Abbey College). In 1998–9 at the 42 incorporated

colleges there were 5,019 full-time and 8,546 part-time teaching staff. Salaries are determined at individual college level.

COURSE INFORMATION

Applications for further education courses are generally made directly to the colleges concerned. Information on further education courses in the UK and addresses of colleges can be found in the *Directory of Further Education* published annually by the Careers Research and Advisory Centre (*see* page 114).

HIGHER EDUCATION

The term 'higher education' is used to describe education above Higher and Advanced Higher grade, A-level and their equivalent, which is provided in universities, colleges of higher education and some further education colleges.

The Further and Higher Education (Scotland) Act 1992 removed the distinction between higher education provided by the universities and that provided by the former central institutions and other institutions, allowing all higher education institutions which satisfy the necessary criteria to award their own taught course and research degrees and to adopt the title of university. All the central institutions, the art colleges and some colleges of higher education have since adopted the title of university. The change of name does not affect the legal constitution of the institutions.

All higher education institutions are funded by the Scottish Higher Education Funding Council. The funding allocation planned for higher education in 2001–2 was £659.6 million (£609.4 million in 2000–1).

The number of students in higher education in Scotland in 1999–2000 was:

Full-time	161,941
postgraduate	18,028
first degree	104,661
sub-degree	39,252
Part-time	97,447
postgraduate	30,641
first degree	9,093
sub-degree	57,713
Total students	259,388
overseas	24,072
of which postgraduate	48,669
overseas	13,271

In the 1999–2000 academic year, there were 37,491 full-time undergraduate entrants to higher education institutions in Scotland (55.6% female); 34% were aged 21 or over. In 1999–2000, 47.6% of young Scots entered higher education either in

Scotland or elsewhere in the United Kingdom. In 1999-2000, there were 13,607 Scottish domiciled students registered with the Open University, 4,725 of whom were new entrants.

In 1999–2000, the 113,754 students on first degree courses were distributed among the subject groups as follows: business administration (14%); multi-disciplinary studies (12.3%); subjects allied to medicine (9.9%); social studies (9.7%); engineering and technology (8.3%); biological sciences (7.9%); mathematics and computing (5.%); physical sciences (4.8%); medicine and dentistry (4.4%); languages (4.4%); education and leisure (4.3%); creative arts (4.2%); architecture and building (3.8%); humanities (3.4%); mass communication (1.8%); and agriculture (1.5%).

UNIVERSITIES AND COLLEGES

The Scottish Higher Education Funding Council (SHEFC) funds 22 institutions of higher education, including 13 universities. Responsibility for universities in Scotland rests with Scottish Ministers. Advice to the Government on matters relating to the universities is provided by the SHEFC. The SHEFC receives a block grant from central government which it allocates to the universities and colleges.

The universities each have their own system of internal government, but most are run by two main bodies: the senate, which deals primarily with academic issues and consists of members elected from within the university; and the council, which is the supreme body and is responsible for all appointments and promotions, and bidding for and allocation of financial resources. At least half the members of the council are drawn from outwith the university. Joint committees of senate and council are common.

The institutions of higher education other than universities are managed by independent governing bodies which include representatives of industrial, commercial, professional and educational interests.

Each body appoints its own academic staff on its own conditions. The salary structure in the 'pre-1992' universities is in line with that in the rest of the United Kingdom.

SALARIES FOR NON-CLINICAL ACADEMIC STAFF IN UNIVERSITIES 2000–01

Professor	from £37,493
Senior lecturer	£32,510–£39,718
Lecturer grade B	£25,213–£30,967
Lecturer grade A	£18,731–£24,227

The salary scales for staff in the 'post-1992' universities and colleges of higher education in Scotland are as follows:

	1 September 2001
Head of Department	£45,697–£51,578
Senior lecturer	£28,999–£42,143
Lecturer	£17,616–£35,109

	1 March 2002
Head of Department	£46,154–£52,094
Senior lecturer	£29,289–£42,605
Lecturer	£17,792–£35,460

Although universities and colleges are expected to look to a wider range of funding sources than before, and to generate additional revenue in collaboration with industry, they are still largely financed, directly or indirectly, from government resources.

COURSES

In the United Kingdom all universities, including the Open University, and some colleges award their own degrees and other qualifications and can act as awarding and validating bodies for neighbouring colleges which are not yet accredited.

Higher education courses last full-time for at least four weeks or, if part-time, involve more than 60 hours of instruction. Facilities exist for full-time and part-time study, day release, sandwich or block release. Most of the courses outwith the universities have a vocational orientation and a substantial number are sandwich courses.

Higher education courses comprise:
- first degree and postgraduate (including research);
- Diploma in Higher Education (Dip.HE), a two-year diploma usually intended to serve as a stepping-stone to a degree course or other further study;
- Higher National Diploma (HND), awarded after two years of full-time or three years of sandwich-course or part-time study;
- Higher National Certificate (HNC), awarded after two years part-time study;
- preparation for professional examinations;
- in-service training of teachers.

In some Scottish universities the title of Master is sometimes used for a first degree in arts subjects; otherwise undergraduate courses lead to the title of Bachelor. Most undergraduate degree courses at universities and colleges of higher education take four years for Honours and three for the broad-based Ordinary degree, peculiar to the Scottish system. Professional courses in subjects such as medicine, dentistry and veterinary science take longer. Post-experience short courses are also forming an increasing part of higher education provision.

Details of courses on offer and of predicted entry requirements for the following year's intake are provided in *University and College Entrance: Official Guide*, published annually by the Universities and Colleges Admissions Service (UCAS). It includes degree, Dip.HE and HND courses at all universities (excluding the Open University) and most colleges of higher education.

Postgraduate studies vary in length, with taught courses which lead to certificates, diplomas or master's degrees usually taking less time than research degrees which lead to doctorates. Details of taught postgraduate courses and research degree opportunities can be found in the *Directory of Graduate Studies*, published annually for the Careers Research and Advisory Centre (CRAC).

ADMISSIONS

For admission to a degree, Dip.HE or HND, potential students apply through a central clearing house. All universities and most colleges providing higher education courses in the United Kingdom (except the Open University, which conducts its own admissions) are members of the Universities and Colleges Admission Service (UCAS).

Most applications for admission as a postgraduate student are made to individual institutions but there are two clearing houses of relevance. Applications for postgraduate teacher training courses are made through the Graduate Teacher Training Registry. For social work the Social Work Admissions System operates.

Details of initial teacher training courses in Scotland can be obtained from colleges of education and those universities offering such courses, and from the Committee of Scottish Higher Education Principals (COSHEP).

For contact details of the admissions bodies, etc., *see* page 114.

FEES

Since September 1998, new entrants to undergraduate courses at institutions in the United Kingdom have been liable for an annual contribution to their fees (up to £1,075 in 2001–2), depending on their own level of income and that of their spouse or parents. In autumn 2000 the student liability for tuition fees was abolished for all eligible Scottish-domiciled and EU students studying on full-time higher education courses at Scottish institutions. Those

from the rest of the United Kingdom in the fourth year of a four-year degree course at a Scottish institution may also be exempt from payment.

For postgraduate students on non loan-bearing courses, the maximum tuition fee to be reimbursed through the awards system in 2001—2 was £2,805.

STUDENT SUPPORT

Support for students on designated courses domiciled in Scotland is administered by the Student Awards Agency for Scotland (SAAS), an executive agency of the Department of Enterprise and Lifelong Learning. Designated courses are those full-time or sandwich courses leading to a degree, Dip.HE, HND, HNC, the initial teacher-training qualification, or other qualifications specifically designated as being comparable to a first degree. The schemes administered by SAAS include the Students' Allowances Scheme, the Postgraduate Students' Allowances Scheme, the Scottish Studentship Scheme, the Nursing and Midwifery Bursary Scheme and also the application process for student loans. SAAS also provides resources to the Student Loans Company, which pays student loans. Support for those students eligible for it includes the payment of tuition fees, loans, bursaries or grants. SAAS should be consulted for detailed information about eligibility for support and designated courses.

The support available for students who entered higher education between 1998/99 and 2000/01 and those who started in 2001/02 has certain elements in common. Depending on individual circumstances, they may be eligible for a student loan of up to £4,700 (the main support for living costs and partly means-tested); a loan for additional weeks (for unusually long courses); payment of tuition fees up to a maximum of £1,075, which is means-tested only for those studying outwith Scotland; and non-repayable supplementary grants for students who, for example, are disabled or have dependants. The student loan accrues interest linked to inflation and repayments begin from the April after graduation at 9% of income exceeding £10,000 a year. The changes made in the case of students starting their course in 2001-02 are the introduction of a non-repayable Young Students' Bursary of up to £2,000 a year for students from low-income families, recipients of which may also be entitled to an additional loan of £500, and the Mature Students' Bursary. From 2001-02 a Graduate Endowment is payable from 1 April after successful course completion by certain categories of students (£2,000 for students who entered higher education in 2001–2).

Students who started designated courses prior to September 1998 continue to be eligible for the mandatory means-tested maintenance grant, which then prevailed, from which a contribution is deductible on a sliding scale dependent on parental income (except for students who are over 25) or, in the case of married students, spouse's income. The maintenance grant, usually paid each term, covers periods of attendance during term as well as the Christmas and Easter vacations, but not the summer vacation. The basic grant rates for 2001–2 for domiciled students are:

Living in	Existing students
College/lodgings in London area	£2,310
College/lodgings outside London area	£1,870
Parental home	£1,430

Additional allowances are available if, for example, the course requires a period of study abroad. Students may also be eligible to apply for a student loan of up to £2,310. Repayment of the student loan, which is index-linked, normally begins the April after the course ends and comprises a fixed number of instalments unless income falls under 85% of the national average, in which case application may be made for deferment. Means-tested non-repayable supplementary grants are available to eligible students with dependants or who are disabled. Expenditure on student fees and maintenance in 1999–2000 was £193.3 million (provisional); 100,972 mandatory awards were made.

Hardship funds are distributed by SAAS to universities and colleges and administered by the further and higher education institutions themselves. They are available to students whose access to, or continued participation in, education might otherwise be inhibited by financial considerations or where real financial difficulties are faced. For the academic year 1999–2000, provision was £14 million (£8.7 million in 1998–9).

POSTGRADUATE AWARDS

Postgraduate students, with the exception of students on loan-bearing diploma courses such as teacher training, are not eligible to apply for student loans, but can apply for grants for postgraduate study. These are of two types, both discretionary: 30-week bursaries, which are means-tested and apply to certain vocational and diploma courses; and studentship awards, which depend on the class of first degree, especially for research degrees, are not means-tested, and cover students undertaking research degrees or taught master's degrees.

Postgraduate funding is provided by the Enterprise and Lifelong Learning Department through the Student Awards Agency for Scotland, the Scottish Executive Rural Affairs Department, and government research councils. An increasing number of scholarships are also available from research charities, endowments, and particular industries or companies.

The Scottish rates for 30-week bursaries for professional and vocational training in 2001–2 are:

Living in	
College/lodgings in London area	£3, 936
College/lodgings outside London area	£3,105
Parental home	£2,346

Studentship awards are payable at between £6,500 and £8,500 a year (2001–2).

ADULT AND CONTINUING EDUCATION

The term 'adult education' covers a broad spectrum of educational activities ranging from non-vocational courses of general interest, through the acquiring of special vocational skills needed in industry or commerce, to degree-level study at the Open University.

The Scottish Executive Enterprise and Lifelong Learning Department funds adult education, including that provided by the universities and the Workers' Educational Association, at vocational further education colleges (47 in 2001) and evening centres. In addition, it provides grants to a number of voluntary organisations.

Courses are provided by the education authorities, further and higher education colleges, universities, residential colleges, the BBC, independent television and local radio stations, and several voluntary bodies.

Although the lengths of courses vary, most courses are part-time. Newbattle Abbey College (see page 119), the only long-term residential adult education college in Scotland, offers one-year full-time diploma courses in European studies and Scottish studies which normally provide a university entrance qualification. Some colleges and centres offer short-term residential courses, lasting from a few days to a few weeks, in a wide range of subjects. Education authorities sponsor many of the colleges, while others are sponsored by universities or voluntary organisations.

Adult education bursaries for students at the long-term residential colleges of adult education are the responsibility of the colleges themselves. In Scotland the awards are funded by central government and administered by the education authorities. Information is available from the Scottish Executive Enterprise and Lifelong Learning Department.

The involvement of universities in adult education and continuing education has diversified considerably and is supported by a variety of administrative structures ranging from dedicated departments to a devolved approach. Membership of the Universities Association for Continuing Education is open to any university or university college in the United Kingdom. It promotes university continuing education, facilitates the interchange of information, and supports research and development work in continuing education.

Of the voluntary bodies, the biggest is the Workers' Educational Association (WEA), which operates throughout the UK, reaching about 150,000 adult students annually. As well as the Scottish Executive, LEAs make grants towards provision of adult education by WEA Scotland.

Advice on adult and community education, and promotion thereof, is provided by Community Learning Scotland (*see* page 114).

LOCAL EDUCATION AUTHORITY TERM DATES

(for session 2001-2)

The table below gives term dates for Local Education Authority schools in Scotland, along with Autumn, Spring and Summer mid-term holiday dates. In addition to the dates shown there may be in-service days or local holidays to be taken at the discretion of the local education authority and/or school. For further information on term dates, please contact your local education authority or visit www.scotland.gov.uk

AUTUMN TERM

Local Education Authority	From	Mid-term holiday inclusive	To
Aberdeen City	13/08/01	21/09/01 – 24/09/01	21/12/01
		08/10/01 – 19/10/01	
Aberdeenshire	14/08/01	08/10/01 – 19/10/01	21/12/01
Angus	14/08/01	01/10/01 – 12/10/01	21/12/01
		30/11/01 – 04/12/01	
Argyll & Bute	21/08/01	15/10/01 – 19/10/01	21/12/01
Clackmannanshire	21/08/01	01/10/01	21/12/01
		08/10/01 – 12/10/01	
Comhairle Nan Eilean Siar	16/08/01	15/10/01 – 24/10/01	21/12/01
(Western Isles)			
Dumfries and Galloway	21/08/01	15/10/01 – 19/10/01	21/12/01
		28/11/01 – 30/11/01	
Dundee City	14/08/01	01/10/01 – 12/10/01	21/12/01
		08/11/01 – 09/11/01	
East Ayrshire	20/08/01	21/09/01 – 25/09/01	21/12/01
		15/10/01 – 22/10/01	
East Dunbartonshire	20/08/01	21/09/00 – 24/09/01	21/12/01
		16/10/00 – 20/10/00	
East Lothian	21/08/01	17/09/01 – 18/09/01	21/12/01
		15/10/01 – 22/10/01	
East Renfrewshire	20/08/01	21/09/01 – 24/09/01	21/12/01
		15/10/01 – 19/10/01	
Edinburgh City	14/08/01	17/09/01 – 18/09/01	21/12/01
		15/10/01 – 22/10/01	
Falkirk	21/08/01	10/09/01	22/12/01
		08/10/01 – 12/10/01	
		19/11/01 – 20/11/01	
Fife	21/08/01	15/10/01 – 26/10/01	21/12/01
Glasgow City	20/08/01	21/09/01 – 24/09/01	21/12/01
		15/10/01 – 19/10/01	
Highland	21/08/01	15/10/01 – 29/10/01	21/12/01
Inverclyde	16/08/01	15/10/01 – 19/10/01	21/12/01
Midlothian	22/08/01	14/09/01 – 17/09/01	21/12/01
		15/10/01 – 19/10/01	
Moray	21/08/01	08/10/01 – 19/10/01	21/12/01
		12/11/01 – 13/11/01	
North Ayrshire (except Arran)	20/08/01	24/09/01	21/12/01
		15/10/01 – 19/10/01	
		15/11/01 – 19/11/01	
Arran	20/08/01	24/09/01	21/12/01
		08/10/01 – 19/10/01	
North Lanarkshire	20/08/01	21/09/01 – 24/09/01	21/12/01
Orkney Islands	21/08/01	12/10/01 – 24/10/01	21/12/01
Perth and Kinross	13/08/01	28/09/01 – 12/10/01	21/12/01

Local Education Authority	From	Mid-term holiday inclusive	To
Renfrewshire	21/08/01	21/09/01 – 24/09/01	21/12/01
Scottish Borders	21/08/01	08/10/01 – 12/10/01	21/12/01
Shetland Islands	22/08/01	12/10/01 – 20/10/01	20/12/01
South Ayrshire	21/08/01	21/09/01 – 24/09/01	21/12/01
		15/10/01 – 22/10/01	
South Lanarkshire	20/08/01	21/09/01 – 24/09/01	21/12/01
		15/10/01 – 19/10/01	
Stirling	21/08/01	08/10/01 – 12/10/01	21/12/01
West Dunbartonshire	21/08/01	21/09/01 – 24/09/01	21/12/01
		15/10/01 – 19/10/01	
West Lothian	21/08/01	17/09/01 – 18/09/01	21/12/01
		15/10/01 – 22/10/01	

SPRING TERM

Local Education Authority	From	Mid-term holiday inclusive	To
Aberdeen City	07/01/02	18/02/02	28/03/02
Aberdeenshire	07/01/02	18/02/02	28/03/02
Angus	07/01/02	15/02/02 – 18/02/02	29/03/02
Argyll & Bute	07/01/02	18/02/02 – 19/02/02	22/03/02
Clackmannanshire	07/01/02	14/02/02 – 18/02/02	28/03/02
Comhairle Nan Eilean Siar (Western Isles)	08/01/02		29/03/02
Dumfries and Galloway	07/01/02	15/02/02 – 20/02/02	28/03/02
Dundee City	07/01/02		28/03/02
East Ayrshire	07/01/02	15/02/02 – 19/02/02	22/03/02
East Dunbartonshire	07/01/02	18/02/02 – 19/02/02	22/03/02
East Lothian	07/01/02	22/02/02 – 26/02/02	28/03/02
East Renfrewshire	07/01/02	18/02/02 – 19/02/02	22/03/02
Edinburgh City	07/01/02	18/02/02 – 25/02/02	05/04/01
		29/03/02 – 01/04/02	
Falkirk	07/01/02	14/02/02 – 18/02/02	28/03/02
		06/03/02 – 07/03/02	
Fife	07/01/02	14/02/02 – 18/02/02	28/03/02
Glasgow City	07/01/02	18/02/02 – 19/02/02	22/03/02
Highland	07/01/02	07/02/02 – 11/02/02	28/03/02
Inverclyde	07/01/02	18/02/02	22/03/02
Midlothian	07/01/02	18/02/02 – 19/02/02	28/03/02
Moray	07/01/02	18/02/02	28/03/02
North Ayrshire (except Arran)	07/01/02	18/02/02 – 19/02/02	22/03/02
Arran	07/01/02	18/02/02	22/03/02
North Lanarkshire	07/01/02	15/02/02	22/03/02
Orkney Islands	07/01/02	11/02/02 – 13/02/02	28/03/02
Perth and Kinross	07/01/02		28/03/02
Renfrewshire	07/01/02	18/02/02 – 19/02/02	22/03/02
Scottish Borders	07/01/02		28/03/02
Shetland Islands	07/01/02		22/03/02
South Ayrshire	07/01/02	18/02/02 – 19/02/02	22/03/02
South Lanarkshire	07/01/02	18/02/02	22/03/02
Stirling	07/01/02		28/03/02
West Dunbartonshire	07/01/02	18/02/02 – 19/02/02	26/03/02
West Lothian	07/01/02	18/02/02 – 19/02/02	28/03/02

SUMMER TERM

Local Education Authority	From	Mid-term holiday inclusive	To
Aberdeen City	15/04/02	22/04/02 – 06/05/02	28/06/02
Aberdeenshire	15/04/02		28/06/02
Angus	15/04/02	06/05/02 24/05/02	27/06/02
Argyll & Bute	08/04/02	06/05/02	03/07/02
Clackmannanshire	15/04/02	06/05/02 – 07/05/02	28/06/02
Comhairle Nan Eilean Siar (Western Isles)	15/04/02		28/06/02
Dumfries and Galloway	15/04/02	06/05/02	28/06/02
Dundee City	15/04/02	06/05/02 24/05/02 – 27/05/02	27/06/02
East Ayrshire	09/04/02	06/05/02 24/05/02 – 27/05/02	28/06/02
East Dunbartonshire	08/04/02	24/05/02 – 27/05/02	28/06/02
East Lothian	15/04/02	06/05/02 – 07/05/02	28/06/02
East Renfrewshire	08/04/02	06/05/02 24/05/02 – 27/05/02	28/06/02
Edinburgh City	22/04/02	06/05/02 – 07/05/02 20/05/02 – 21/05/02	28/06/02
Falkirk	15/04/02		28/06/02
Fife	15/04/02	06/05/02 03/06/02	05/07/02
Glasgow City	08/04/02	06/05/02 24/05/02 – 27/05/02	04/07/02
Highland	15/04/02	06/05/02 – 07/05/02	04/07/02
Inverclyde	08/04/02	06/05/02	27/06/02
Midlothian	16/04/02	06/05/02 – 07/05/02	28/06/02
Moray	15/04/02	06/05/02 23/05/02 – 24/05/02	05/07/02
North Ayrshire (except Arran)	08/04/02	06/05/02 24/05/02 – 27/05/02	28/06/02
Arran	09/04/02	06/05/02	28/06/02
North Lanarkshire	08/04/02	06/05/02	28/06/02
Orkney Islands	15/04/02	06/05/02	28/06/02
Perth and Kinross	15/04/02	06/05/02	27/06/02
Renfrewshire	08/04/02	06/05/02 24/05/02 – 28/05/02	28/06/02
Scottish Borders	15/04/02	06/05/02	28/06/02
Shetland Islands	08/04/02		28/06/02
South Ayrshire	08/04/02	06/05/02 25/05/01 – 28/05/01	29/06/02
South Lanarkshire	08/04/02	06/05/02 24/05/02 – 27/05/02	28/06/02
Stirling	15/04/02		28/06/02
West Dunbartonshire	08/04/02	06/05/02 24/05/02 – 27/05/02	28/06/02
West Lothian	15/04/02	06/05/02 – 07/05/02 20/05/02 – 03/06/02 18/06/02	28/06/02

Source: Scottish Executive Education Department

ADMISSIONS AND COURSE INFORMATION

Careers Research and Advisory Centre
Sheraton House, Castle Park, Cambridge, CB3
0AX (Tel: 01223-460 277; Fax: 01223-311 708;
E-mail: enquiries@crac.org.uk;
Web: www.crac.org.uk).
Chief Executive: D. Thomas

Universities Scotland
53 Hanover Street, Edinburgh, EH2 2PJ
(Tel: 0131-226 1111; Fax: 0131-226 1100;
E-mail: d.caldwell@universities-scotland.ac.uk;
Web: www.universities-scotland.ac.uk).
Director: D. Caldwell

Graduate Teacher Training Registry
Rosehill, New Barn Lane, Cheltenham GL52
3LZ (Tel: 01242-544788; Fax: 01242-544962;
Web: www.gttr.ac.uk).
Registrar: Mrs J. Pearce

Social Work Admissions System
Rosehill, New Barn Lane, Cheltenham GL52
3LZ (Tel: 01242-544600; Fax: 01242-544962).
Admissions Officer: Mrs J. Pearce

Universities and Colleges Admissions Service
Rosehill, New Barn Lane, Cheltenham GL52
3LZ (Tel: 01242-222444; Fax: 01242-544960;
E-mail: info@ucas.ac.uk;
Web: www.ucas.com).
Chief Executive: M. A. Higgins

ADULT AND CONTINUING EDUCATION

Community Learning Scotland
Rosebery House, 9 Haymarket Terrace,
Edinburgh, EH12 5EZ (Tel: 0131-313 2488;
Fax: 0131-313 6800;
E-mail: info@cls.dircon.co.uk;
Web: www.communitylearning.org).
Chief Executive: C. McConnell

The Open University in Scotland
10 Drumsheugh Gardens, Edinburgh, EH3 7QJ
(Tel: 0131-225 2889; Fax: 0131-220 6730;
E-mail: R11@open.ac.uk;
Web: www.open.ac.uk).
Vice-Chancellor: Vacant

UNIVERSITIES ASSOCIATION FOR CONTINUING EDUCATION

University of Cambridge Board for Continuing Education
Madingley Hall, Madingley, Cambridge, CB3
8AQ (Tel: 01954-280279; Fax: 01954-280200;
E-mail: smi20@cam.ac.uk;
Web: www.uace.org.uk).
Chair: Prof. Sir Graeme Davies

WEA Scotland (Workers' Educational Assocation)
Riddle's Court, 322 Lawnmarket, Edinburgh,
EH1 2PG (Tel: 0131-226 3456; Fax: 0131-220
0306; E-mail: hq@weascotland.org.uk).
Scottish Secretary: Ms J. Connon

ADVISORY BODIES

Education Otherwise
PO Box 7420, London, N9 9SG (Tel: 0870-730
0074; Web: www.education-otherwise.org).

International Baccalaureate Organisation
Peterson House, Maithouse Avenue, Cardiff
State, Cardiff, CF23 8GL (Tel: 029-2054 7777;
Fax: 029-2054 7778; E-mail: ibca@ibo.org;
Web: www.ibo.org).
Director of Academic Affairs: Dr H. Drennan

Scottish Council of Independent Schools
21 Melville Street, Edinburgh, EH3 7PE
(Tel: 0131-220 2106; Fax: 0131-225 8594;
E-mail: information@scis.org.uk;
Web: www.scis.org.uk).
Director: Mrs J. Sischy

Scottish Studentship Advisory Group
c/o Student Awards Agency for Scotland
Gyleview House, 3 Redheughs Rigg, Edinburgh,
EH12 9HH (Tel: 0131-476 8228; Fax: 0131-244
5104; E-mail: SAS-8@scotland.gov.uk;
Web: www.student-support-saas.gov.uk).
Chairman: Prof. D. Harding

EXAMINING BODY

Scottish Qualifications Authority
Hanover House, 24 Douglas Street, Glasgow, G2
7NQ (Tel: 0845-279 100; Fax: 0141-242 2244;
E-mail: mail@sqa.org.uk;
Web: www.sqa.org.uk).
Chief Executive: B. Morton

FUNDING BODIES

Scottish Further Eduction Funding Council
Donaldson House, 97 Haymarket Terrace,
Edinburgh, EH12 5HD (Tel: 0131-313 6500;
Fax: 0131-313 6501; E-mail: info@sfc.ac.uk;
Web: www.sfefc.ac.uk).
Chief Executive: Prof. J. Sizer, CBE

Scottish Higher Education Funding Council
Donaldson House, 97 Haymarket Terrace,
Edinburgh, EH12 5HD (Tel: 0131-313 6500;
Fax: 0131-313 6501; E-mail: info@sfc.ac.uk;
Web: www.shefc.ac.uk).
Chief Executive: Prof. J. Sizer, CBE

Student Awards Agency for Scotland
Gyleview House, 3 Redheughs Rigg, Edinburgh,
EH12 9HH (Tel: 0131-476 8212; Fax: 0131-244
5717; E-mail: saas.geu@scotland.gov.uk;
Web: www.saas.gov.uk).
Chief Executive: D. Stephen

Student Loans Company Ltd
100 Bothwell Street, Glasgow, G2 7DJ
(Tel: 0141-306 2000; Fax: 0141-306 2006;
E-mail: colin–ward@slc.co.uk;
Web: www.slc.co.uk).
Chief Executive: C. Ward

LOCAL EDUCATION AUTHORITIES

Aberdeen
Summerhill Education Centre, Stronsay Drive,
Aberdeen, AB15 6JA (Tel: 01224-346060;
Fax: 01224-346061;
Web: www.aberdeen-education.org.uk).
Director of Education: J. Stodter

Aberdeenshire
Woodhill House Annexe, Westburn Road,
Aberdeen, AB16 5GJ (Tel: 01224-664630;
Fax: 01224-664615;
Web: www.aberdeenshire.gov.uk).
Director of Education and Recreation:
H. Vernal

Angus
County Buildings, Market Street, Forfar, DD8
3WE (Tel: 01307-461460; Fax: 01307-461848).
Director of Education: J. Anderson

Argyll and Bute
Argyll House, Alexandra Parade, Dunoon, PA23
8AJ (Tel: 01369-704000; Fax: 01639-708584;
Web: www.argyll-bute.gov.uk).
Director of Education: A. C. Morton

City of Edinburgh
Wellington Court, 10 Waterloo Place,
Edinburgh, EH1 3EG (Tel: 0131-469 3000;
Fax: 0131-469 3141;
E-mail: www.edinburgh.gov.uk).
Director of Education: R. Jobson

Clackmannanshire
Greenfield, Alloa, FK10 2AD
(Tel: 01259-452002; Fax: 01259-452230).
Chief Executive: K. Bloomer

Dumfries and Galloway
30 Edinburgh Road, Dumfries, DG1 1JG
(Tel: 01387-260427; Fax: 01387-260453;
Web: www.dumgal.gov.uk).
Director for Education: F. Sanderson

Dundee
Floor 8, Tayside House, Crichton Street, Dundee,
DD1 3RJ (Tel: 01382-434000; Fax: 01382-
433080; E-mail: education@dundeecity.gov.uk;
Web: www.dundeecity.gov.uk).
Director of Education: Mrs A. Wilson

East Ayrshire
Council Headquarters
London Road, Kilmarnock, KA3 7BU
(Tel: 01563-576000; Fax: 01563-576210;
E-mail: education@east-ayrshire.gov.uk;
Web: www.east-ayrshire.gov.uk).
Director of Educational and Social Services:
J. Mulgrew

East Dunbartonshire
Tom Johntson, Civic Way, Kirkintilloch,
Glasgow, G66 4TG (Tel: 0141-578 8000;
Fax: 0141-578 8653).
Director of Community Services: Ms S. Bruce

East Lothian
John Muir House, Haddington, EH41 3HA
(Tel: 01620-827562; Fax: 01620-827291;
E-mail: ablackie@eadtlothian.gov.uk).
**Director of Education and Community
Services:** A. Blackie

East Renfrewshire
Council Offices, Eastwood Park, Rouken Glen
Road, Giffnock, G46 6UG (Tel: 0141-577 3431;
Fax: 0141-577 3405;
Web: www.eastrenfrewshire.gov.uk).
Director of Education: Mrs E. J. Currie

Eilean Siar/Western Isles
Council Offices, Sandwick Road, Stornoway, Isle
of Lewis, HS1 2BW (Tel: 01851-703773;
Web: www.cne-siar.gov.uk).
Director of Education: M. Macleod

Falkirk
McLaren House, Marchmont Avenue, Polmont,
Falkirk, FK2 0NZ (Tel: 01324-506600; Fax:
01324-506601; Web: www.falkirk.gov.uk).
Director of Education: Dr G. Young

Fife
Fife House, North Street, Glenrothes, KY7 5LT
(Tel: 01592-413667; Fax: 01592-416744;
Head of Education: A. McKay

Glasgow
Nye Bevan House, 20 India Street, Glasgow, G2
4PF (Tel: 0141-287 6898; Fax: 0141-287 6892;
E-mail: education@glasgow.gov.uk;
Web: www.glasgow.gov.uk).
Director of Education Services: K. Corsar

Highland
Council Buildings, Glenurquhart Road,
Inverness, IV3 5NX (Tel: 01463-702802; Fax:
01463-702828;
E-mail: education@highland.gov.uk;
Web: www.highland.gov.uk).
Director of Education: B. Robertson

Inverclyde
105 Dalrymple Street, Greenock, PA15 1HT
(Tel: 01475-712824; Fax: 01475-712875;
Web: www.inverclyde.gov.uk).
Director of Education Services: B. McLeary

Midlothian
Fairfield House, 8 Lothian Road, Dalkeith, EH22
3ZG (Tel: 0131-270 7500; Fax: 0131-271 3751;
E-mail: education-services@midlothian.gov.uk).
Director of Education: D. MacKay

Moray
Council Offices, High Street, Elgin, IV30 1BX
(Tel: 01343-563097; Fax: 01343-563478).
Director of Educational Services:
D. M. Duncan

North Ayrshire
Cunninghame House, Irvine, KA12 8EE
(Tel: 01294-324400; Fax: 01294-324444;
E-mail: education@north-ayrshire.gov.uk;
Web: www.ers.north-ayrshire.gov.uk).
Corporate Director, Educational Services:
J. Travers

North Lanarkshire
Municipal Buildings, Kildonan Street, coatbridge,
ML5 3BT (Tel: 01236-812222; Fax: 01236-
812247; E-mail: education@northlan.gov.uk).
Director of Education: M. O'Neill

Orkney Islands
Council Offices, School Place, Kirkwall, Orkney,
KW15 1NY (Tel: 01856-873535; Fax: 01856-
870302; E-mail: education@orkney.gov.uk).
Director of Education: L. Manson

Perth and Kinross
Pullar House, 35 Kinnoull Street, Perth, PH1
5GD (Tel: 01738-476211; Fax: 01738-476210).
Director of Education and Children's Services:
B. Frew

Renfrewshire
Council Headquarters, South Building, Cotton
Street, Paisley, PA1 1LE (Tel: 0141-8425663;
Fax: 0141-8425699;
E-mail: education.leisure@renfrewshire.gov.uk;
Web: www.renfrewshire.gov.uk).
Director of Education and Leisure Services:
Ms S. Rae

Scottish Borders
Council Headquarters, Newtown St Boswells,
Melrose, Roxburghshire, TD6 0SA (Tel: 01835-
824000; Fax: 01835-825091).
Director of Education: J. Christie

Shetland
Hayfield House, Hayfield Lane, Lerwick, Shetland, ZE1 0QD (Tel: 01595-744000; Fax: 01595-692810; E-mail: education.services@sic.shetland.gov.uk; Web: www.shetland.gov.uk).
Head of Education Services: M. Payton

South Ayrshire
County Buildings, Wellington Square, Ayr, KA7 1DR (Tel: 01292-612000; Fax: 01292-612258).
Director of Education: M. McCabe

South Lanarkshire
Council Headquarters, Almada Street, Hamilton, ML3 0AE (Tel: 01698-454545; Fax: 01698-454465; E-mail: maggi.allan@southlanarkshire.gov.uk; Web: www.southlanarkshire.gov.uk).
Executive Director of Education Resources: Ms M. Allan

Stirling
Viewforth, Stirling, FK8 2ET (Tel: 01786-442678; Fax: 01786-442782; E-mail: jeyesg@stirling.gov.uk).
Director of Children's Services: G. Jeyes

West Dunbartonshire
Garshake Road, Dunbarton, G82 3PU (Tel: 01389-737301; Fax: 01389-737348; E-mail: ian.mcmurdo@west-dunbarton.gov.uk).
Director of Education and Cultural Services: I. McMurdo

West Lothian
Lindsay House, South Bridge Street, Bathgate, EH48 1TS (Tel: 01506-776000; Fax: 01506-776378; E-mail: education@westlothian.gov.uk).
Corporate Manager, Education Services: R. Stewart

UNIVERSITIES

Glasgow Caledonian University
Cowcaddens Road, Glasgow G4 0BA (Tel: 0141-331 3000; Web: www.gcal.ac.uk).
Full time students: 11,737
Chancellor: The Lord Nickson, KBE
Vice-Chancellor and Principal: Dr I. A. Johnston
Secretary: B. M. Murphy

Heriot-Watt University
Ricarton Campus, Edinburgh EH14 4AS (Tel: 0131-449 5111; Fax: 0131-451 3744; Web: www.hw.ac.uk).
Full-time students: 5,800
Chancellor: The Rt Hon. The Lord Mackay of Clashfern, PQ, QC, FRSE
Vice-Chancellor and Principal: Prof. J. S. Archer, FREng.
Secretary: P. L. Wilson
Academic-Registrar: Mrs R. J. Moir

Napier University
219 Colinton Road, Edinburgh EH14 1DJ (Tel: 0131-444 2266; Student enquiries: 0500-353570; Fax: 0131-455 6333; E-mail: info@napier.ac.uk; Web: www.napier.ac.uk).
Full-time students: 10,400
Chancellor: Lord Younger of Leckie, KT, KCVO, TD, PC, FRSE
Vice-Chancellor and Principal: Prof. J. Mavor
Secretary: Dr G. Webber
Academic Registrar: Ms L. Fraser

Robert Gordon University
Schoolhill, Aberdeen AB10 1FR (Tel: 01224-262000; Web: www.rgu.ac.uk).
Full-time students: 7,500
Chancellor: Sir Bob Reid
Vice-Chancellor and Principal: Prof. W. Stevely
Secretary: Dr A. Graves
Academic-Registrar: Mrs H. Douglas

University of Aberdeen
King's College, Aberdeen AB24 3FX (Tel: 01224-272000; Fax: 01224-272086; E-mail: pubrel@aboh.ac.uk; Web: www.abdn.ac.uk).
Full time students: 10,788
Chancellor: The Lord Wilson of Tillyorn, GCMG
Vice-Chancellor and Principal: Prof. C. D. Rice
Secretary: S. Cannon
Registrar: Dr T. Webb

University of Abertay Dundee
Bell Street, Dundee DD1 1HG (Tel: 01382-308000; Fax: 01382-308118; Web: www.abertay-dundee.ac.uk).
Full-time students: 4,436
Chancellor: The Earl of Airlie, KT, GCVO, PC
Vice-Chancellor and Principal: Prof. B. King
Vice Principal: Prof. J. McGoldrick
Secretary: Ms C. S. Lamb

University of Dundee
Dundee DD1 4HN (Tel: 01382-344000; Fax: 01382-201604; E-mail: secretary@dundee.ac.uk; Web: www.dundee.ac.uk).
Full-time students: 9,558
Chancellor: Sir James Black, FRCP, FRS
Vice-Chancellor and Principal: Sir Alan Langlands
Secretary: R. Seaton

University of Edinburgh
Old College, South Bridge, Edinburgh EH8 9YL (Tel: 0131-6501000; Web: www.ed.ac.uk).
Full-time students: 17,614
Chancellor: HRH The Prince Philip, Duke of Edinburgh, KG, KT, OM, GBE, PC, FRS
Vice-Chancellor and Principal: Prof. Sir Stewart Sutherland, FBA, FRSE
Secretary: M. J. B. Lowe, Ph.D
Director of Registry: Dr V. O'Halloran
Rector: R. Harper

University of Glasgow
University Avenue, Glasgow G12 8QQ (Tel: 0141-339 8855; Fax: 0141-330 4808; E-mail: postmaster@gla.ac.uk; Web: www.gla.ac.uk).
Full-time students: 19,900
Chancellor: Sir William Fraser, GCB, FRSE
Vice-Chancellor: Prof. Sir Graeme Davies, FREng, FRSE
Secretary of Court: D. Mackie, FRSA
Rector: G. Hemphill

University of Paisley
Paisley PA1 2BE (Tel: 0141-848 3000; Web: www.paisley.ac.uk).
Full-time students: 7,100
Chancellor: Sir Robert Easton, CBE
Vice-Chancellor: Prof. R. W. Shaw, CBE
Secretary: J. Fraser
Registrar: D. Rigg

University of St Andrews
College Gate, North Street, St Andrews, Fife KY16 9AJ (Tel: 01334-476 161; Web: www.st-and.ac.uk).
Chancellor: Sir Kenneth Dover, DLitt, FRSE, FBA
Vice-Chancellor: Dr. B. Lang
Secretary and Registrar: D. J. Corner
Rector: A. Neil

University of Stirling
Stirling FK9 4LA (Tel: 01786-473171; Fax: 01786-463000;
E-mail: pr-office@stir.ac.uk; Web: www.stir.ac.uk).
Full time students: 6,230
Chancellor: Dame Diana Rigg, DBE
Vice-Chancellor: Prof. A. Miller, CBE, FRSE
Secretary: K. J. Clarke
Academic Registrar: D. G. Wood

University of Strathclyde
John Anderson Campus, 16 Richmond Street, Glasgow, G1 1XQ (Tel: 0141-552 4400; Fax: 0141-552 0775; Web: www.strath.ac.uk).
Full time students: 12,833
Chancellor: The Rt Hon. Lord Hope of Craighead, PC
Vice-Chancellor and Principal: Prof. A. Hamnett, FRSE
Secretary: P. W. A. West
Academic Registrar: Dr S. Mellows

COLLEGES

Bell College of Technology
Crichton University Campus
Dudgeon House, Bankend Road, Dumfries, DG1 4SG (Tel: 01387-702100; Fax: 01387-702111).
Principal: Dr K. MacCallum

Bell College of Technology
Almada Street, Hamilton, Lanarkshire, ML3 0JB (Tel: 01698-283100; Fax: 01698-282131).
Principal: Dr K. MacCallum

Dumfries and Galloway College
Heathhall, Dumfries, DG1 3QZ (Tel: 01387-261261; Fax: 01387-250006; E-mail: info@dumgal.ac.uk; Web: www.dumgal.ac.uk).
Principal: T. Jakimciw

Fife College of Further and Higher Education
St Brycedale Avenue, Kirkcaldy, Fife, KY1 1EX (Tel: 01592-268591; Fax: 01592-640225; E-mail: enquiries@fife.ac.uk; Web: www.fife.ac.uk).
Principal: Mrs J. S. R. Johnston

Glasgow School of Art
167 Renfrew Street, Glasgow, G3 6RQ (Tel: 0141-353 4500; Fax: 0141-353 4528; Web: www.gsa.ac.uk).
Director: Prof. S. Reid

Inverness College
3 Longman Road, Longman South, Inverness, IV1 1SA (Tel: 01463-237000; Fax: 01463-711977;
E-mail: inverness.college@inverness.uhi.ac.uk;
Web: www.uhi.ac.uk).
Principal: Dr G. Clark

Lews Castle College
Stornoway, Isle of Lewis, HS2 0XR
(Tel: 01851-770000; Fax: 01851-770001;
Web: www.lews.uhi.ac.uk).
Principal: D. R. Green

Moray College
Moray Street, Elgin, Moray, IV30 1JJ
(Tel: 01343-576000; Fax: 01343-576001;
E-mail: greg.cooper@moray.uhi.ac.uk;
Web: www.moray.ac.uk).
Principal: Dr James Logan

Newbattle Abbey College
Dalkeith, Midlothian, EH22 3LL
(Tel: 0131-663 1921; Fax: 0131-654 0598;
E-mail: office@nac.sol.co.uk;
Web: www.newbattleabbeycollege.co.uk).
Principal: Ann Southwood

The North Highland College
Ormlie Road, Thurso, Caithness, KW14 7EE
(Tel: 01847-889000; Fax: 01847-889001;
E-mail: northhighlandcollege@groupwise.uhi.ac.uk;
Web: www.uhi.ac.uk/thurso).
Principal: H. Logan

Northern College
Dundee Campus, Gardyne Road, Dundee, DD5 1NY (Tel: 01382-464000;
Web: www.norcol.ac.uk).
Principal: D. Adams

Northern College
Hilton Place, Aberdeen, AB24 4FA (Tel: 01224-283500; Fax: 01224-283900;
Web: www.norcol.ac.uk).
Principal: D. Adams

Orkney College
Kirkwall, Orkney, KW15 1LX (Tel: 01856-569000; Fax: 01856-569001;
E-mail: orkney.college@orkney.uhi.ac.uk).
Principal: P. Scott

Queen Margaret University College
Leith Campus, Duke Street, Edinburgh, EH6 8HF (Tel: 0131-317 3000; Fax: 0131-317 3256;
E-mail: admissions@qmuc.ac.uk;
Web: www.qmuc.ac.uk).
Principal: Prof J. Stringer

Queen Margaret University College
Corstorphine Campus, Clerwood Terrace, Edinburgh, EH12 8TS (Tel: 0131-317 3000;
Fax: 0131-317 3256;
E-mail: admissions@qmuc.ac.uk;
Web: www.qmuc.ac.uk).
Principal: Prof J. Stringer

Queen Margaret University College
Scottish International Drama Centre
41 Elm Row, Edinburgh, EH7 4AH
(Tel: 0131-317 3900; Fax: 0131-317 3902;
E-mail: admissions@qmuc.ac.uk;
Web: www.qmuc.ac.uk).
Principal: Prof J. Stringer

Royal Scottish Academy of Music and Drama
100 Renfrew Street, Glasgow, G2 3DB
(Tel: 0141-332 4101; Fax: 0141-332 8901;
E-mail: registry@rsamd.ac.uk;
Web: www.rsamd.ac.uk).
Principal: Sir Philip Ledger, CBE, FRSE

Sàbhal Mor Ostaig
Sleat, Isle of Skye, IV44 8RQ
(Tel: 01471-888 000; Fax: 01471-888 001;
E-mail: oifis@smo.uhi.ac.uk;
Web: www.smo.uhi.ac.uk).
College Director: Dr. Norman N. Gillies

SAC (Scottish Agricultural College)
Central Office, Kings Buildings, West Mains Road, Edinburgh, EH9 3JG (Tel: 0131-535 4000; Fax: 0131-667 2601; Web: www.sac.ac.uk).
Principal and Chief Executive: Prof. K. Linklater

THE ENERGY INDUSTRIES

The main primary sources of energy in Britain are oil, natural gas, coal, nuclear power and water power. The main secondary sources (i.e. sources derived from the primary sources) are electricity, coke and smokeless fuels, and petroleum products.

Policy and legislation on the generation and supply of electricity from coal, oil and gas, and nuclear fuels, remains a matter reserved to the UK Government after devolution. The Department for the Environment, Food and Rural Affairs is responsible for promoting energy efficiency.

INDIGENOUS PRODUCTION OF PRIMARY FUELS (UK)

Million tonnes of oil equivalent

	1999	2000
Coal	25.4	21.5
Petroleum	150.2	138.3
Natural gas	99.3	108.5
Primary electricity		
Nuclear	22.22	19.64
Natural flow hydro	0.53	0.52
Total	297.7	288.5

INLAND ENERGY CONSUMPTION BY PRIMARY FUEL (UK)

Million tonnes of oil equivalent, seasonally adjusted and temperature corrected

	1999	2000
Coal	39.1	41.0
Petroleum	76.0	74.5
Natural gas	97.6	102.1
Primary electricity	24.05	21.44
Nuclear	22.28	19.70
Natural flow hydro	0.55	0.52
Net imports	1.22	1.22
Total	236.7	239.0

UK TRADE IN FUELS AND RELATED MATERIALS 2000p

	Quantity*	Value†
Imports		
Coal and other solid fuel	16.5	696
Crude petroleum	40.5	5,095
Petroleum products	20.8	3,430
Natural gas	2.0	135
Electricity	1.2	373
Total	80.9	9,729
Total (fob)‡	—	10,009
Exports		
Coal and other solid fuel	1.0	74
Crude petroleum	82.7	10,202
Petroleum products	32.3	4,872
Natural gas	8.3	577
Electricity	—	5
Total	124.4	15,729
Total (fob)‡	—	15,729

p provisional
* Million tonnes of oil equivalent
† £ million
‡ Adjusted to exclude estimated costs of insurance, freight, etc.
Source: Department of Trade and Industry

OIL AND GAS

The United Kingdom Continental Shelf (UKCS) is treated as a separate region in official economic statistics. Calculation of Scottish oil and gas outputs and revenue deriving from the UKCS is difficult and controversial. Recent research from Aberdeen University suggests that there is considerable variation from year to year in the Scottish proportion of UK tax revenue from oil and gas, depending on a number of factors, including division of the North Sea, relative expense of developing the North Sea fields, and oil price fluctuations. According to this analysis, Scotland's share of UK oil and gas revenue was 80 per cent in 1996–7, but the drop in oil prices reduced this to an estimated 75 per cent for 1997 and 66 per cent for 1998 (calendar years). The following table shows the total value of UKCS oil and gas production and investment in 1999–2000.

	1999	2000
	£m	£m
Total income	19,259	26,977
Operating costs	4,249	4,289
Exploration expenditure	457	377
Gross trading surplus	13,459	2,183
Contribution to GVA	1.9%	2.7%
Contribution to industrial investment	13%	12%

OIL

Until the 1960s Britain imported almost all its oil supplies. In 1969 oil was discovered in the Arbroath field of the UKCS. The first oilfield to be brought into production was the Argyll field in 1975, and since the mid-1970s Britain has been a major producer of crude oil.

There are estimated to be a maximum of 1,490 million tonnes of oil reserves in the UKCS. Royalties are payable on fields approved before April 1982 and petroleum revenue tax is levied on fields approved between 1975 and March 1993.

Licences for exploration and production are granted to companies by the Department of Trade and Industry; the leading British oil companies are British Petroleum (BP) and Shell Transport and Trading. At the end of 1999, 1,021 offshore licences and 396 onshore licences had been awarded of which 440 are still in existence, and there were 121 offshore oilfields in production in the UK.

There are four oil terminals and two refineries in Scotland.

OIL COMING ASHORE AT SCOTTISH TERMINALS 2000*

Million tonnes

Sullom Voe	28.4
Flotta, Orkney Islands	8.5
Forties (Landward)	34.7
Nigg Bay, Cromarty Firth	0.2
Total	71.8

* Figures do not reflect total oil production in Scotland, because some oil produced is exported directly by tanker from offshore fields

CAPACITY OF SCOTTISH REFINERIES 2000

Million tonnes p.a.

Grangemouth	10.1
Dundee	0.7
Total	10.8

GAS

In 1965 gas was discovered in the North Sea off the South Yorkshire coast, in the West Sole field, which became the first gasfield in production in 1967.

By the end of 2000 there were 90 offshore gasfields producing natural gas. There are estimated to be a maximum of 1,630 billion cubic metres of recoverable gas reserves in existing discoveries.

There are three gas terminals in Scotland, at St Fergus, Aberdeenshire.

GAS BROUGHT ASHORE AT SCOTTISH TERMINALS 2000*

Million cubic m

Far North Liquids and Associated Gas System (FLAGS) and Fulmar Line	10,300
Frigg and Miller Lines	10,600
Scottish Area Gas Evacuation (SAGE)	16,800
Total	37,700

* Figures do not reflect total Scottish gas production, because some gas produced is piped to terminals in England
Source: Department of Trade and Industry

Since 1986 the British gas industry, nationalised in 1949, has been progressively privatised. Competition was introduced into the industrial gas market from 1986, and supply of gas to the domestic market was opened to companies other than British Gas from April 1996 onwards. Gas companies can now also sell electricity to their customers. Similarly, electricity companies can also offer gas.

The Office of Gas and Electricity Markets is the regulatory body for the gas and electricity industries in Britain.

NATURAL GAS PRODUCTION AND SUPPLY (UK)

GWh

	1999	2000
Gross gas production	1,152,154	1,258,549
Exports	84,433	146,342
Imports	12,862	26,032
Gas available	1,011,157	1,061,953
Gas transmitted‡	1,011,284	1,043,911

‡ Figures differ from gas available mainly because of stock changes

NATURAL GAS CONSUMPTION
GWh

	1999	2000
Electricity generators	307,818	312,545
Iron and steel industry	21,838	21,331
Other industries	160,150	171,016
Domestic	355,895	358,066
Public administration, commerce and agriculture	118,227	119,897
Total	963,928	982,855

Source: Department of Trade and Industry

ELECTRICITY

There are currently 41 electricity generating companies in Britain. The structure of the electricity industry changed with the introduction in England and Wales of the New Electricity Trading Arrangements (NETA) on 27 March 2001. The new arrangements are based on bilateral trading between generators, suppliers, traders and customers and are designed to be more efficient and provide greater choice for market participants whilst maintaining the operation of a secure and reliable electricity system. The system includes forwards and futures markets — a balancing mechanism to enable the National Grid Company, as systems operator, to balance the system — and a settlement process. Competition was introduced into the domestic electricity market in 1998–9. Electricity companies can now also sell gas to their customers. Similarly, gas companies can also offer electricity. Generators sell the electricity they produce into an open commodity market (the Pool) from which buyers purchase.

In Scotland, three new companies were formed under the Electricity Act 1989: ScottishPower plc and Scottish Hydro-Electric plc (now Scottish and Southern Energy plc), which are responsible for generation, transmission, distribution and supply; and Scottish Nuclear Ltd. ScottishPower and Scottish Hydro-Electric were floated on the stock market in 1991 (the latter merged with Southern Electric plc to form Scottish and Southern Energy plc in December 1998). Scottish Nuclear was incorporated into British Energy in 1995.

ScottishPower operates six power stations in Scotland. Scottish and Southern Energy operates a large power station at Peterhead, 56 hydro stations in Scotland, and a diesel backup station in Lerwick, Shetland; it also operates a number of power stations in England and Wales.

The Electricity Association is the electricity industry's main trade association, providing representational and professional services for the electricity companies. EA Technology Ltd provides distribution and utilisation research, development and technology transfer. The Office of Gas and Electricity Markets (*see* page 53) is the regulatory body for the electricity industry.

ELECTRICITY PRODUCTION IN SCOTLAND 1998
GWh

	Electricity generated 1998	Amount exported to England	From renewable sources
ScottishPower	24,500	c.6,000	c.2%
Scottish and Southern Energy*	14,167	3,260	c.11%

* *Scottish and Southern Energy figures are for 1997–8 financial year*

NUCLEAR POWER

About half of Scotland's electricity is generated by nuclear power stations. British Energy plc owns two Advanced Gas-Cooled Reactors (AGRs) at Torness and Hunterston B. British Nuclear Fuels Ltd (BNFL) owns the Magnox nuclear reactor at Chapelcross.

BNFL, which is in public ownership, provides reprocessing, waste management and effluent treatment services. The UK Atomic Energy Authority is responsible for the decommissioning of nuclear reactors and other nuclear facilities used in research and development. UK Nirex, which is owned by the nuclear generating companies and the Government, is responsible for the disposal of intermediate and some low-level nuclear waste. The Nuclear Installations Inspectorate of the Health and Safety Executive is the nuclear industry's regulator.

In 1998 the closure was announced of the nuclear reactor at Dounreay, which started up in 1956.

NUCLEAR POWER GENERATION 2000-2001
Terawatt hours

Hunterston B	6.43
Torness	7.71
Total by British Energy	14.14
Chapelcross*	1.40

* *1998–9 figure*

BNFL
BNFL Risley, Warrington, Cheshire, WA3 6AS
(Tel: 01925-832000).
Chief Executive: J. Taylor

British Energy plc
3 Redwood Cresent, Peel Park, East Kilbride,
G74 5PR (Tel: 01355-262000; Fax: 01355-
265565; Web: www.britishenergy.com).
Chief Executive: P. Hollins (acting)

EA Technology Ltd
Capenhurst Technology Park, Capenhurst,
Chester, CH1 6ES (Tel: 0151-339 4181; Fax:
0151-347 2178; E-mail: marketing@eatl.co.uk;
Web: www.eatechnology.com).
Managing Director: Dr S. F. Exell

Electricity Association Ltd
30 Millbank, London, SW1P 4RD
(Tel: 020-7963 5700;
E-mail: enquiries@electricity.org.uk;
Web: www.electricity.org.uk).
Chief Executive: P. E. G. Daubeney

Scottish and Southern Energy plc
Inveralmond House, 200 Dunkeld Road, Perth,
PH1 3AQ (Tel: 01738-456000; Fax: 01738-
456005).
Chief Executive: J. Forbes

Scottish Renewables Forum
5 Leighton Avenue, Dunblane, Stirling, Scotland
FK15 0EB
Chief Executive: Robert Forrest

ScottishPower plc
1 Atlantic Quay, Glasgow, G2 8SP
(Tel: 0141-248 8200).
Chief Executive: Ian Russell

RENEWABLE ENERGY SOURCES

Renewable sources of energy principally include
biofuels, hydro, wind, waste and solar.

The UK Government intends to achieve 10 per
cent of the UK's electricity needs from renewables
by 2010 and to meet the UK's international
commitments to future reductions on greenhouse
gases. Following the establishment of the Scottish
Parliament, decisions on renewable sources of
energy have been devolved.

The Scottish Renewables Obligation Orders
(SROs) have been the Government's principal
mechanism for developing renewable energy
sources. They are similar to the Non-Fossil Fuel

Obligation Renewables Orders in England and
Wales. SRO Orders require ScottishPower and
Scottish and Southern Energy to buy specified
amounts of electricity from specified renewable
sources; the first order was made in 1994 and the
latest in March 1999.

Of the 109 projects awarded contracts so far (for
about 340 MW), 24 projects (72 MW capacity)
have been commissioned. Ten of these are wind
schemes (combined capacity $c.35.0$ MW), six are
hydro schemes (combined capacity $c.4.0$ MW),
and seven are waste-to-energy schemes (combined
capacity $c.22.7$ MW). Forty wind-farms are now
completed. The latest SRO Order included, for
the first time, three wave-power projects.

No specific mechanism to support the
development of solar energy projects exists, but
the Department of Trade and Industry currently
funds initiatives and channels European grant
funding. There are several small-scale (less than 1
MW) solar projects in operation in various places
around Scotland.

The Scottish Renewables Forum (SRF) works
to facilitate links between industry, the
Government and various non-government
organisations with a view to promoting the use of
sustainable energy sources in Scotland. The SRF
provides a unified representation of the interests of
its members, encompassing utilities, corporate
bodies as well as a range of smaller companies and
environmental organisations.

Scottish Renewables Forum
5 Leighton Avenue, Dunblane, Stirling, Scotland
FK15 0EB
(Tel: 01786 825839; Fax: 01786 821133;
E-mail: rob.forrest@scottishrenewables.com).

THE WATER INDUSTRY

Overall responsibility for national water policy in
Scotland rested with the Secretary of State for
Scotland until July 1999, when responsibility was
devolved to the Scottish Executive. Most aspects
of water policy are currently administered through
the Scottish Executive Rural Affairs Department.

Water supply and sewerage services were the
responsibility of the local authorities and the
Central Scotland Water Development Board until
1996. In April 1996 the provision of water and
sewerage services became the responsibility of
three public water authorities, covering the north,
east and west of Scotland, under the terms of the
Local Government etc. (Scotland) Act 1994.

The Act also provided for the Scottish Water and Sewerage Customers Council to be established to represent consumer interests. The Council is to be abolished under the provisions of the Water Industries Act 1999, whose provisions have been accepted by the Scottish Executive, and will be replaced in late 1999 by a Water Industry Commissioner, whose role is to promote customers' interests. The Commissioner will make longer-term recommendations about charging and efficiency to the Scottish Executive and will be advised by three water industry consultative committees, one for each water authority.

The Scottish Environment Protection Agency is responsible for promoting the cleanliness of rivers, lochs and coastal waters, and controlling pollution. Scotland has 60 designated bathing waters, and the Scottish Executive is committed to bringing these up to European standards and to improving the quality of rivers, lochs and coastal waters. A £1,800 million programme for modernising the infrastructure and activities of the water industry is planned, based on research carried out during 2000.

WATER: DEVELOPED RESOURCES IN SCOTLAND 1999-2000 (Extract[1])

1999 yield by Water Authority

	North	West	East	Total
Reservoirs and Lochs	346	1,372	1,380	3,099
River intakes	400	19	33	452
Boreholes	42	15	43	100
Springs	14	5	8	27
Total Supply Sources	802	1,412	1,464	3,678

1. Extract of table. For full table with explanatory notes please see the Scottish Executive website.
Source: The Scottish Executive Water Services Unit, Crown Copyright.

WATER CONSUMPTION 1997

Total (*Ml/day*)	2,336.3
Potable	2,320.3
Unmetered	1,781.7
Metered	538.5
Non-potable†	16.0
Total (*l/head/day*)	468.6
Unmetered	357.4
Metered and non-potable†	109.9

† 'Non-potable' supplied for industrial purposes. Metered supplies in general relate to commercial and industrial use and unmetered to domestic use
Source: The Scottish Office

METHODS OF CHARGING

The water authorities set charges for domestic and non-domestic water and sewerage provision through charges schemes which have to be approved by the Scottish Water and Sewerage Customers Council. The authorities are required to publish a summary of their charges schemes.

EAST OF SCOTLAND WATER AUTHORITY

Fairmilehead, 55 Buckstone Terrace, Edinburgh, EH10 6XH (Tel: 0131-445 4141; Fax: 0131-445 5040).
Chief Executive: Dr J. Hargreaves

NORTH OF SCOTLAND WATER AUTHORITY

Cairngorm House, Beechwood Park North, Inverness IV2 3ED (Tel: 0845 743 7437).
Chief Executive: Katherine Bryan

WEST OF SCOTLAND WATER

419 Balmore Road, Glasgow G22 6NU (Tel: 0808-100 5333; Fax: 0141-355 5146; Web: www.westscotlandwater.org.uk).
Chief Executive: C. Cornish

WATER INDUSTRY COMMISSIONER FOR SCOTLAND

Ochil House, Springkerse Business Park, Stirling FK7 7XE (Tel: 01786-430200; Fax: 01786-462018;
E-mail: enquiries@watercommissioner.co.uk;
Web: www.watercommissioner.co.uk).
Commissioner: A. Sutherland

WATER UK

1 Queen Anne's Gate, London, SW1H 9BT (Tel: 020-7344 1844; Fax: 020-7344 1866;
E-mail: info@water.org.uk;
Web: www.water.org.uk).
Water UK is the trade association for almost all the water service companies in the UK, including the three Scottish water authorities.
Chief Executive: Ms P. Taylor

THE FIRE SERVICE

The Scottish Executive Justice Department has overall responsibility for fire services, including the provision of training at the Scottish Fire Service Training School.

Each local council in Scotland is the fire authority for its area. There are six joint fire boards, comprising groups of council areas which have delegated their fire authority responsibilities to the boards. The remaining two councils, Dumfries and Galloway and Fife, each act as the fire authority for their whole council area. Membership of the joint boards comprises elected members of each of the constituent councils. The fire authorities are responsible for setting a budget, making an establishment scheme (which details fire brigade, fire stations and equipment), the 'mutual assistance' scheme for handling major incidents, and hearing disciplinary cases or appeals. Subject to the approval of the Scottish Ministers, fire authorities appoint a firemaster, who is responsible for brigade operations.

Fire brigades are financed by local government, with the exception of some central services (e.g. the Scottish Fire Service Training School) which are financed by the Scottish Executive. Joint fire boards set their budgets and requisition the necessary finance from their constituent councils. The two councils that directly administer their fire brigades set budgets as for their other services. The Scottish Executive pays an annual civil defence grant to each joint board for its role in emergency planning.

HM Inspectorate of Fire Services for Scotland carries out inspections of fire brigades in order to improve the efficiency, effectiveness and standards of the fire service. HM Chief Inspector of Fire Services publishes an annual report and other reports. The interests of fire authorities and members of the fire brigades are considered by the Scottish Central Fire Brigades Advisory Council, which advises Scottish Ministers on matters affecting the service.

The Dumfries and Galloway council area and the Fife council area do not have joint boards as a single authority covers the whole of the fire brigade area. The chairman/convenor of the authority for these two brigades is given with the brigade's details.

Central Scotland Fire Board
Municipal Buildings, Falkirk, FK1 5RS
(Tel: 01324-506070; Fax: 01324-506071;
E-mail: iain.tough@falkirk-lawadmin.demon.co.uk).
Convenor: T. Coll
Clerk to the Board: Ms E. Morton

Grampian Fire Board
Woodhill House, Westburn Road, Aberdeen, AB16 5GB (Tel: 01224-665430; Fax: 01224-665445).
Chairman: R. Stroud
Clerk to the Board: N. McDowall

Highland and Islands Fire Board
Council Headquarters, Glenurquhart Road, Inverness, IV3 5NX (Tel: 01463-702123; Fax: 01463-702182;
E-mail: rhona.moir@highland.gov.uk).
Convener of the Board: A. R. Macfarlane Slack
Clerk to the Board: J. F. P. Black

Lothian and Borders Fire Board
City Chambers, High Street, Edinburgh, EH1 1YJ (Tel: 0131-529 4237; Fax: 0131-529 7607;
E-mail: dougie.dolan@edinburgh.gov.uk).
Convenor: K. Harrold
Clerk to the Board: T. N. Aitchison

Strathclyde Fire Board
Council Offices, Almada Street, Hamilton, ML3 0AA (Tel: 01698-454872; Fax: 01698-454407;
E-mail: pach.exec@southlanarkshire.gov.uk).
Convener: J. Shaw
Clerk to the Board: W. Kirk

Tayside Fire Board
2 High Street, Perth, PH1 5PH
(Tel: 01738-475102; Fax: 01738-475110;
E-mail: j.angus@pkc.gov.uk).
Convener: F. Duncan, OBE
Clerk to the Board: J. Angus

FIRE BRIGADES

Central Scotland Fire Brigade
HQ, Main Street, Maddiston, Falkirk, FK2 0LG
(Tel: 01324-716996; Fax: 01324-715353;
E-mail: csfb@globalnet.co.uk;
Web: www.fire-org.co.uk).
Firemaster: vacant
Divisional Officer: Malcolm Wilson

Dumfries and Galloway Fire Brigade
Brigade HQ, Brooms Road, Dumfries, DG1
2DZ (Tel: 01387-252222; Fax: 01387-260995;
E-mail: fmr@dumgal.gov.uk).
Chairman: B. Conchie
Firemaster: L. Ibbotson

Fife Fire and Rescue Service
HQ, Strathore Road, Thornton, Kirkcaldy, KY1
4DF (Tel: 01592-774451; Fax: 01592-630105).
**Chairman - Public Protection and Regulation
Committee:** A. Keddie
Firemaster (acting): A. Wyse

Grampian Fire Brigade
HQ, 19 North Anderson Drive, Aberdeen, AB15
6DW (Tel: 01224-696666; Fax: 01224-692224;
E-mail: firemaster@grampianfirebrigade.co.uk;
Web: www.grampianfirebrigade.co.uk).
Firemaster: J. Williams

Highland and Islands Fire Brigade
HQ, 16 Harbour Road, Longman West,
Inverness, IV1 1TB (Tel: 01463-227000;
Fax: 01463-236979;
E-mail: firemaster@highland.fire-uk.org;
Web: www.hifb.org).
Firemaster: B. A. Murray

Lothian and Borders Fire Brigade
HQ, Lauriston Place, Edinburgh, EH3 9DE
(Tel: 0131-228 2401; Fax: 0131-228 6662;
E-mail: loth00@lothian.fire-uk.org;
Web: www.lothian.fire-uk.org).
Firemaster: C. Cranston

Strathclyde Fire Brigade
HQ, Bothwell Road, Hamilton, ML3 0EA
(Tel: 01698-300 999; Fax: 01698-338 444;
Web: www.strathclyde.fire-uk.org).
Convener: J. Shaw
Firemaster: J. Ord, O. St.J., QFSM

STAFF ASSOCIATIONS

**The Chief and Assistant Chief Fire Officers'
Association**
10–11 Pebble Close, Amington, Tamworth, B77
4RD (Tel: 01827-302300; Fax: 01827-302399;
E-mail: info@cacfoa.fire-uk.org;
Web: www.fire-uk.org).
President: R. Bull, QFSM
General Manager: A. S. Currey

**Scottish Central Fire Brigades Advisory
Council**
Scottish Executive Justice Department, Room
F1-9, Saughton House, Broomhouse Drive,
Edinburgh, EH11 3XD (Tel: 0131-244 2166;
Fax: 0131-244 2864;
E-mail: george.davidson@scotland.gov.uk).
Chairman: J. Hamill
Secretary: G. A. Davidson

BRIGADE STRENGTHS MARCH 1999

Wholetime uniformed personnel	4,506
Retained (uniformed on call)	2,547
Volunteer (no retainer fee)	1,215
Control room personnel	213
Non-uniformed personnel	789

SCOTLAND'S HEALTH

Public health policy is a devolved power and is now the responsibility of the Scottish Executive.

Health education in Scotland is the responsibility of the Health Education Board for Scotland. The role of the Board is to provide health information and advice to the public, health professionals, and other organisations, and to advise the Government on health education needs and strategies.

HEALTH TARGETS FOR SCOTLAND

A White Paper on public health in Scotland, *Towards a Healthier Scotland,* was published in February 1999. This announced initiatives to improve the health of people in Scotland, including prevention and early detection of cancer and coronary heart disease and redressing inequalities in health between richer and poorer communities in Scotland, and set targets to measure the impact of these measures by 2010. In certain fields, targets for 2000 already existed. Targets set for 2010 include:

- reducing by 20 per cent the death rate from all cancers of Scots under 75

- reducing by 50 per cent adult deaths from heart disease

- reducing by 50 per cent the death rate from cerebrovascular disease in Scots under 75

- eliminating dental disease in 60 per cent of five-year-olds

- reducing incidence of smoking by pregnant women from 29 to 20 per cent, and by young people by 20 per cent

- reducing the pregnancy rate among 13–15 year olds by 20 per cent

- reducing alcohol consumption exceeding recommended weekly limits from 33 to 29 per cent for men and from 13 to 11 per cent for women

- increasing the proportion of people taking 30 minutes of moderate exercise five or more times a week to 60 per cent of men and 50 per cent of women

Four 'demonstration projects' announced in the White Paper will concentrate on child health, sexual health, cancer and coronary heart disease.

A network of Healthy Living Centres promoting best practice in public health was announced in 1998, with £34.5 million funding over three years from the National Lottery's New Opportunities Fund.

DIET

Government plans to improve the Scottish diet were first outlined in 1991. The *Report on the Scottish Diet* (the James Report) was published in 1993 and, after further consultation, led to the announcement of the Scottish Diet Action Plan. This set targets for healthier eating among people in Scotland by 2005. These targets incorporated into the *Towards a Healthier Scotland* programme include:

- increasing average daily intake of non-sugar carbohydrates by 25 per cent through increased consumption of fruit, vegetables, bread (especially wholemeal and brown breads), breakfast cereals, rice, pasta and potato

- reducing average daily intake of fats to no more than 35 per cent, and of saturated fatty acids to no more than 11 per cent, of food energy

- reducing average daily sodium intake (from common salt and other sodium salts such as sodium glutamate) to 100 mmol

- reducing children's average daily intake of NME sugars by half to less than 10 per cent of total food energy

- doubling average weekly consumption of oil-rich fish

- increasing to over 50 per cent the proportion of mothers breastfeeding their babies for the first six weeks

SELECTED CAUSES OF DEATH, BY SEX 2000

	Males	Females
Certain infectious and parasitic diseases (inc. tuberculosis)	192	284
Tuberculosis	31	35
Neoplasms	7,609	7,646
Malignant neoplasms	7,480	7,478
Endocrine nutritional and metabolic diseases	384	444
Diseases of the blood and blood-forming organs and certain disorders involving the immune mechanism	41	73
Mental and behavioural disorders	900	1,409
Diseases of the nervous system and sense organs	596	719
Diseases of the skin and subcutaneous tissue	27	62
Diseases of the musculoskeletal system and connective tissue	103	302
Diseases of the circulatory system	11,058	12,599
Ischaemic heart disease	6,578	5,834
Other heart disease	697	1,010
Cerebrovascular disease	2,544	4,259
Diseases of the respiratory system	3,018	3,529
Diseases of the digestive system	1,435	1,487
Diseases of the genito-urinary system	360	484
Complications of pregnancy, childbirth and puerperium	—	8
Certain conditions originating in the perinatal period	96	74
Congential malformations, deformations and chromosomal abnormalities	90	64
Symptoms, signs and abnormal clinical and laboratory findings, otherwise unspecified	110	212
External causes of morbidity and mortality	1,492	892
Accidents, transport accidents and falls	1,199	1,162
Suicide and self-inflicted injury	512	136
Assault	68	25
All causes	27,511	30,288

Source: Registrar for Scotland Annual Report, Crown copyright 2001

TEN MOST FREQUENTLY DIAGNOSED CANCERS BY GENDER 1997

Type of Cancer	Males	Type of Cancer	Females
Lung	2,698	Breast	3,372
Prostate	1,807	Lung	1,881
Large Bowel	1,790	Large Bowel	1,586
Bladder	827	Ovary	654
Head and Neck	645	Corpus Uteri	454
Stomach	595	Stomach	421
Oesophagus	436	Non-Hodgkins lymphoma	419
Non-Hodgkin's lymphoma	391	Malignant Melanoma of skin	409
Kidney	318	Bladder	393
Leukemias	305	Cervix uteri	362

Source: ISD Scotland

SELECTED NOTIFIABLE INFECTIOUS DISEASES[1]

	1998	1999 (Jan-June)
Measels	700	252
Rubella	745	372
Chickenpox	30,181	15,083
Mumps	251	117
Scarlet fever	883	320
Whooping cough	225	101
Bacillary dysentry	103	32
Meningococcal infection	313	186
Viral hepititus	490	372
Poliomyelitis	—	—
Typhoid fever	3	1
Puerperal fever	2	3
Erysipelas	66	41
Paratyphiod fever	3	—
Legionellosis	42	8
Malaria	30	7
Lyme disease	11	3
Leptospirosis	4	—
Cholera	3	1
Diptheria	1	1

1. Figures for 1998 are confirmed notifications; figures for 1999 relate to January-June and are provisional notifications subject to amendment.
Source: Health in Scotland, 1999. (Crown Copyright)

AIDS REGISTRATIONS BY TRANSMISSION CATEGORY (Extract[1])

(Cumulative to 30 Sept. 2000)

Sexual intercourse between men	400
Sexual intercourse between men and women	179
Injecting drug use	368
Other	75
All transmission categories	1,031

1. Extract, for full table with explanatory notes please see source publication
Source: Scottish Health Statistics 2000 (Crown Copyright)

AIDS DEATHS BY TRANSMISSION CATEGORY (Extract[1])

(Cumulative to 30 Sept. 2000)

Sexual intercourse between men	*306*
Sexual intercourse between men and women	*101*
Injecting drug use	*305*
Other	*58*
All transmission categories	*770*

1. Extract, for full table with explanatory notes please see source publication
Source: Scottish Health Statistics 2000 (Crown Copyright)

HIV REPORTS BY TRANSMISSION CATEGORY (Extract[1])

(Cumulative to 30 Sept. 2000)

Sexual intercourse between men	*1,079*
Sexual intercourse between men and women	*635*
Injecting drug use	*1,204*
Other	*227*
All transmission categories	*3,145*

1. Extract, for full table with explanatory notes please see source publication
Source: Scottish Health Statistics 2000 (Crown Copyright)

NEW CASES OF SEXUALLY TRANSMITTED INFECTIONS (Extract*)

	1998-99	1999-2000
Males	10,604	11,272
Females	10,028	10,841

*Extract, for full table with explanatory notes please see source
Source: Scottish Health Statistics 2000 (Crown Copyright)

MENTAL ILLNESS HOSPITALS AND PSYCHIATRIC UNITS INPATIENT ADMISSIONS, BY SEX AND MAIN DIAGNOSIS (Extract[1])

	Males	Females
All Diagnoses	16,079	15,972
Dementia	2,285	3,079
Mental and Behavioural disorders due to alcohol	2,901	1,178
Mental and behavioural disorders due to drug misuse	734	280
Schizophrenia	2,517	1,269
Mood (affective) disorders	3,383	5,458
Bipolar affective disorder	607	1,025
Depressive episode	2,109	3,278
Recurrent depressive disorders	316	697
Other psychotic disorders	1,033	885
Disorders of childhood	26	12
Neurotic, stress-related and somatoform disorders	874	1,246
Personality disorders	312	482
Mental Handicap	174	135
Other conditions	1840	1,948

1. Extract: for full table with explanatory notes please see source
Source: Scottish Health Statistics 2000 (Crown Copyright)

SELF-REPORTED CIGARETTE SMOKING PREVALENCE, BY AGE AND GENDER, 1995 AND 1998

(Percentages)

Age Group	Men		Women	
	1995	1998	1995	1998
16-24	35	37	33	34
25-34	37	39	39	36
35-44	29	36	34	33
45-54	34	34	37	34
55-64	34	32	34	31
65-74	-	20	-	32
All ages	34	34	36	32

Source: 1998 Scottish Health Survey

PERCENTAGE OF PEOPLE WHO HAVE TAKEN ANY KIND OF DRUG AT SOME POINT IN THEIR LIVES BY AGE GROUP AND GENDER 1996 AND 2000 (Percentages)

Age Group	1996		2000	
	Males	Females	Males	Females
16-19	40.1	38.2	30.1	27.2
20-24	49.5	42.5	47.8	39.5
25-29	42.3	27.6	44.4	26.5
30-39	32.4	14.2	22.5	17.5
40-59	11.6	10.6	11.4	5.9

Source: 1996 and 2000 Scottish Crime Surveys (Crown Copyright)

CONSUMPTION OF SELECTED FOODS 1995

Men

Butter or hard margarine	24%
Soft margarine	24%
Reduced fat spread	16%
Low fat spread	31%
No spread used	5%
Whole milk	36%
Semi-skimmed milk	57%
Skimmed milk	6%
Other milk	0%
Wholemeal bread	16%
Brown, granary, wheatmeal bread	15%
White or softgrain bread	69%
Eats cereal	68%
Does not eat cereal	32%

Women

Butter or hard margarine	22%
Soft margarine	20%
Reduced fat spread	15%
Low fat spread	35%
No spread used	8%
Whole milk	29%
Semi-skimmed milk	59%
Skimmed milk	11%
Other milk	1%
Wholemeal bread	23%
Brown, granary, wheatmeal bread	19%
White or softgrain bread	58%
Eats cereal	71%
Does not eat cereal	29%

Source: Scottish Office, Scottish Health Survey 1995 (Crown copyright)

FREQUENCY OF CONSUMPTION OF SELECTED FOODS 1995

Men

Eats meat daily	6%
Eats fruit daily	39%
Eats cooked green vegetables daily	26%
Eats chips daily	5%

Women

Eats meat daily	3%
Eats fruit daily	52%
Eats cooked green vegetables daily	30%
Eats chips daily	2%

Source: Scottish Office, Scottish Health Survey 1995 (Crown copyright)

THE NATIONAL HEALTH SERVICE

The National Health Service (NHS) came into being on 5 July 1948. Its function is to provide a comprehensive health service designed to secure improvement in the physical and mental health of the population and to prevent, diagnose and treat illness. It was founded on the principle that treatment should be provided according to clinical need rather than ability to pay, and should be free at the point of delivery. However, prescription charges and charges for some dental and ophthalmic treatment have been introduced over the years.

The NHS covers a comprehensive range of hospital, specialist, family practitioner (medical, dental, ophthalmic and pharmaceutical), artificial limb and appliance, ambulance, and community health services. Everyone normally resident in the UK is entitled to use any of these services.

STRUCTURE

The structure of the NHS underwent a series of reorganisations in the 1970s and, especially, the 1990s. The National Health Service and Community Care Act 1990 introduced the concept of an 'internal market' in health care provision, whereby care was provided through NHS contracts, with health authorities or boards and GP fundholders (the purchasers) being responsible for buying health care from hospitals, non-fundholding GPs, community services and ambulance services (the providers). The Act provided for the establishment of NHS Trusts. These operate as self-governing health care providers independent of health authority control and responsible to the Minister for Health. They derive their income principally from contracts to provide services to health authorities and fund-holding GPs. The community care reforms, introduced in 1993, govern the way care is administered for elderly people, the mentally ill, the physically handicapped and people with learning disabilities.

The Scottish Executive Health Department is responsible for health policy and the administration of the NHS in Scotland. The NHS in Scotland is currently administered by health boards, which are responsible for health services in their areas and also for assessing the health care needs of the local population and developing integrated strategies for meeting these needs in partnership with GPs and in consultation with the public, hospitals and others. The health boards are overseen by the Management Executive at the

Scottish Executive Health Department. There are also local health councils, whose role is to represent the interests of the public to health authorities and boards.

PROPOSED REFORMS

In July 1999, responsibility for administering the NHS in Scotland was devolved from the Secretary of State for Scotland to the Scottish Executive. The White Paper *Designed to Care*, presented to Parliament by the then Secretary of State for Scotland, Donald Dewar, in 1997, lays the foundations for the work of the Scottish Parliament in developing Scotland's devolved health care service provision. The White Paper proposed several reforms, including the establishment of primary care trusts and the replacement of GP fundholding by networks of GPs organised in local health care co-operatives.

The primary health trusts will be responsible for the planning and provision of all primary health care, including mental health services and community hospitals. Their role will include support to general practice in delivering integrated primary health care services, strategic planning and policy development, and promoting improvements in the quality and standards of clinical care. The organisation of GPs into local health care co-operatives emphasises collective health care provision on a community basis. The co-operatives will have the option of holding budgets for providing primary and community services, and the present fundholding management allowance will be redirected towards their development.

Other reforms proposed in the White Paper include:

- a review of acute services, reduction and restructuring of the number of acute hospital trusts
- a single stream of funds to cover both hospital services and drugs
- development of health improvement programmes
- one-stop clinics that will provide tests, results and diagnosis on the same day
- use of new technology to support services, e.g. electronic links between all GP surgeries
- establishment of a Scottish health technology assessment centre
- establishment of a process of quality assurance for clinical services

FINANCE

The NHS is still funded mainly (81.5 per cent) through general taxation, although in recent years greater reliance has been placed on the NHS element of National Insurance contributions, patient charges and other sources of income. Total UK expenditure on the NHS in 1997–8 was £44,719 million, of which £42,787 million derived from public monies and £1,932 million from patient charges and other receipts. NHS expenditure represented 5.7 per cent of GDP.

The Government announced in July 1998 that an additional £21,000 million would be spent on the NHS between 1999 and 2002.

NET COSTS OF THE NATIONAL HEALTH SERVICE IN SCOTLAND: REVENUE AND EXPENDITURE 1998 AND 1999 (Extract[1])

Health board administration	84,237	78,415
Hospital and community health services, revenue	3,022,588	3,177,270
Hospital and community health services, capital	94,639	78,113
Family practitioner services	1,048,815	1,106,964
Central health services, revenue	130,923	120,482
Central health services, capital	2,547	5,271
State hospitals, revenue	16,666	17,904
State hospitals, capital	1,474	607
Training	3,449	3,464
Research	9,713	10,374
Disabled service	2,332	2,620
Welfare foods	12,936	12,211
Miscellaneous health services	18,995	18,776
Total NHS Cost	4,449,923	4,632,471

1. Extract: for complete table and explanatory notes see source
Source: Health in Scotland 1999 (Crown Copyright)

NET EXPENDITURE AND CAPITAL EXPENDITURE

(Year Ending 31 March 1999) (Extract[1])

Expenditure (£000s)	Revenue expenditure	Capital expenditure
Scotland	4,794,674	121,408
Argyll and Clyde	384,957	4,002
Ayrshire and Arran	328,748	6,084
Borders	100,516	1,319
Dumfries and Galloway	140,726	1,235
Fife	286,745	1,509
Forth Valley	233,936	3,825
Grampian	441,363	10,777
Greater Glasgow	875,474	27,443
Highland	195,759	4,840
Lanarkshire	456,241	16,011
Lothian	664,452	22,665
Orkney	22,089	1,438
Shetland	24,235	1,020
Tayside	389,993	8,788
Western Isles	36,952	943
State Hospital	17,708	851
CSA	107,989	5,229
Scottish Ambulance Service	86,791	3,429

1. Extract: for complete table and explanatory notes see source
Source: Health in Scotland 1999 (Crown Copyright)

EMPLOYEES

NHS WORKFORCE SUMMARY

(Extract[1])

Whole Time Equivalent	1998	1999
All staff and practitioners	111,986	112,894.7
Medical	11,539.6	11,539.6
Hospital	7,302.0	7,302.0
General practitioner	3,877.9	3,877.9
Community	359.6	359.6
Dental	2,495.4	2,495.4
Hospital	232.7	232.7
General practitioner	2,031.0	2,031.0
Community	231.7	231.7
Nursing and Midwifery (total)	51,353.0	51,353.0
Scientific and Professional (total)	1,668.0	1,668.0
Professions allied to medicine	6571.2	6,890.7
Technical (total)	5,381.9	5,550.1
Ambulance	2,357.6	2,357.6

1. Extract: for the complete table including explanatory notes see source
Source: Scottish Health Statistics 2000 (Crown Copyright)

SALARIES

General practitioners (GPs), dentists, optometrists and pharmacists are self-employed, and work for the NHS under contract. Average salaries as at 1 December 1998 were:

Consultant	£45,740—£59,040
Specialist Registrar	£22,510—£32,830
Registrar	£22,510—£27,310
Senior House Officer	£20,135—£26,910
House Officer	£16,145—£18,225
GP	*£49,030
Nursing Grades G—I (Senior Ward Sister)	£19,240—£26,965
Nursing Grade F (Ward Sister)	£16,310—£19,985
Nursing Grade E (Senior Staff Nurse)	£14,705—£17,030
Nursing Grades C—D (Staff/Enrolled Nurse)	£11,210—£14,705
Nursing Grades A—B (Nursing Auxiliary)	£8,315—£11,210

* Average intended net remuneration

HEALTH SERVICES

PRIMARY AND COMMUNITY HEALTH CARE SERVICES

Primary and community health care services comprise the family health services (i.e. the general medical, personal medical, pharmaceutical, dental, and ophthalmic services) and community services (including family planning and preventive activities such as cytology, vaccination, immunisation and fluoridation) commissioned by health boards and provided by NHS Trusts, health centres and clinics.

The primary and community nursing services include practice nurses based in general practice, district nurses and health visitors, community psychiatric nursing for mentally ill people living outside hospital, and ante- and post-natal care. Pre-school services at GP surgeries or child health clinics monitor children's physical, mental and emotional health and development, and provide advice to parents on their children's health and welfare.

The School Health Service provides for the health monitoring of schoolchildren of all ages, with a focus on prevention. The service includes medical and dental examination and advice to the local education authority, the school, the parents and the pupil of any health factors which may require special consideration during the pupil's school life.

FAMILY DOCTOR SERVICE

Any doctor may take part in the Family Doctor Service (provided the area in which he/she wishes to practise has not already an adequate number of doctors). GPs may also have private fee-paying patients.

GENERAL PRACTITIONER SERVICES 1997

Number of doctors	3,650
Average list size*	1,468
Percentage of patients with doctors in:	
single-handed practice	5.1
partnership	94.9

Excludes doctors with restricted lists, e.g. residents in homes, schools or other institutions.
Source: Scottish Office, Scottish Abstract of Statistics 1998 (Crown copyright)

PHARMACEUTICAL SERVICE

Patients may obtain medicines, appliances and oral contraceptives prescribed under the NHS from any pharmacy whose owner has entered into arrangements to provide this service, and from specialist suppliers of medical appliances. In rural areas, where access to a pharmacy may be difficult, patients may be able to obtain medicines and other prescribed health care products from their doctor.

Except for contraceptives (for which there is no charge), a charge of £5.90 is payable for each item supplied unless the patient is exempt and a declaration of exemption on the prescription form is completed; booklet HC11, available from main post offices and local social security offices, shows which categories of people are exempt.

GENERAL PHARMACEUTICAL SERVICES 1998-9 (Extract[1])

	1998	1999
Pharmacies open	1,143	1,145
Prescriptions dispensed	57,190,000	58,800,000
Average prescriptions per person	10.67	10.97
Gross cost of prescriptions	£599,670,000	£637,070,000
Average cost per person	£111.91	£118.90

1. Extract: for complete table with explanatory notes see source
Source: Health in Scotland 1999 (Crown Copyright)

DENTAL SERVICE

Dentists, like doctors, may take part in the NHS and also have private patients. They are responsible to the health boards in whose areas they provide services.

Patients may go to any dentist who is taking part in the NHS and is willing to accept them. Patients are required to pay 80 per cent of the cost of NHS dental treatment. Since 1 April 1998 the maximum charge for a course of treatment has been £340. As with pharmaceutical services, certain people are exempt from dental charges or have charges remitted; full details are given in booklet HC11.

GENERAL AND COMMUNITY DENTAL SERVICES 1998-99 (Extract[1])

	1998	1999
Adults: total registered	1,889,251	1,985,069
Adults: total treated	40,208	39,845

1. Extract: for complete table with explanatory notes see source
Source: Scottish Health Statistics 2000 (Crown Copyright)

GENERAL OPHTHALMIC SERVICES

General ophthalmic services are administered by health boards. Testing of sight may be carried out by any ophthalmic medical practitioner or ophthalmic optician (optometrist). The optician must give the prescription to the patient, who can take this to any supplier of glasses to have them dispensed. Only registered opticians can supply glasses to children and to people registered as blind or partially sighted.

Those on a low income may qualify for help with the cost of NHS sight testing. Certain categories of people qualify for sight testing free of charge or are automatically entitled to help with the purchase of glasses under an NHS voucher scheme; booklet HC11 gives details.

Diagnosis and specialist treatment of eye conditions, and the provision of special glasses, are available through the Hospital Eye Service.

GENERAL OPHTHALMIC SERVICES 1999-2000 (Extract[1])

	1999	2000
Ophthalmic medical practitioners	90	77
Ophthalmic opticians	1,253	1,252
NHS sight tests undertaken	657,000	850,000
Total gross costs	£29,595,000	32,694,000

1. Extract: for complete table and explanatory notes please see source
Source: Scottish Health Statistics 2000 (Crown Copyright)

HOSPITALS AND OTHER SERVICES

Hospital, medical, dental, nursing, ophthalmic and ambulance services are provided by the NHS to meet all reasonable requirements. Facilities for the care of expectant and nursing mothers and young children, and other services required for the diagnosis and treatment of illness, are also provided. Rehabilitation services (occupational therapy, physiotherapy and speech therapy) may also be provided, and surgical and medical appliances are supplied where appropriate.

Specialists and consultants who work in NHS hospitals can also engage in private practice, including the treatment of their private patients in NHS hospitals.

CHARGES

Certain hospitals have accommodation in single rooms or small wards which, if not required for patients who need privacy for medical reasons, may be made available to other patients for a small charge. These patients are still NHS patients and are treated as such.

In a number of hospitals, accommodation is available for the treatment of private in-patients who undertake to pay the full commercial-rate costs of hospital accommodation and services and (usually) separate medical fees to a specialist as well.

AMBULANCE SERVICE

The NHS provides emergency ambulance services free of charge via the 999 emergency telephone service. The Scottish Ambulance Service is responsible for all ambulance provision, including the air ambulance service. It controls a fleet of dedicated emergency air ambulance helicopters and two non-dedicated fixed-wing aircraft. In 1997–8, 2,412 missions were flown (917 emergency, 652 very urgent, 354 urgent, 489 pre-planned), compared to 2,156 missions in 1996–7.

The Patient's Charter in Scotland requires emergency ambulances to respond to 95 per cent of calls within 14 minutes in areas with a high population density (over 3 persons per acre), 18 minutes in areas of medium density (0.5–3 persons per acre), and 21 minutes in areas of low density (fewer than 0.5 persons per acre). In the year ending 31 March 1997, 104,075 responses were made in high-density areas, 105,955 in medium-density areas and 34,386 in low-density areas. The percentages of calls answered within the target times were 91, 96 and 92 per cent respectively.

NHS HOSPITAL ACTIVITY 1997–8[1]

Year ending 31 March

	1997	1998p
Bed complement	41,736	40,783
Average available staffed beds	38,427	36,619
In-patient discharges[2]	964,791	973,325
Mean stay (days)	11.7	11.0
Occupancy (% of beds)	80.3	80.2
In-patient true waiting list[3]	47,717	47,081
Day-case discharges	384,260	419,277
New out-patients[4]	2,675,025	2,708,811
Out-patient attendances	6,271,570	6,327,395

p provisional
1. Excludes NHS activity in joint-user and contractual hospitals
2. Comprises discharges, deaths, transfers out of hospitals and transfers between specialties within same hospital
3. Excludes day-case waiting lists and repeat and deferred waiting lists
4. At consultant clinics, including accident and emergency and genito-urinary medicine
Source: Scottish Office, Scottish Abstract of Statistics 1998 (Crown copyright)

AMBULANCE ACTIVITY
Year ending 31 March 1997

Health Board	Road Ambulance Service		Ambulance car service	
	Responses	Total mileage	Patient journeys	Mileage
Argyll and Clyde	225,727	1,599,498	16,112	218,903
Ayrshire and Arran	179,037	1,649,490	11,839	266,819
Borders	66,246	760,731	5,999	197,311
Dumfries and Galloway	71,313	1,053,711	5,420	273,841
Fife	174,454	1,347,668	23,686	422,619
Forth Valley	118,800	816,400	32,865	577,998
Grampian	193,614	1,854,597	22,222	283,498
Greater Glasgow	354,170	1,820,820	165,816	1,182,437
Highland	69,812	1,592,537	8,731	403,375
Lanarkshire	230,948	1,616,190	79,004	971,388
Lothian	296,804	1,907,680	55,300	663,926
Orkney	3,038	43,779	84	2,941
Shetland	8,197	60,361	—	—
Tayside	185,879	1,635,980	44,898	577,210
Western Isles	12,129	176,639	3,229	78,826
Scotland	2,190,168	17,936,081	475,205	6,121,092

HOSPICES

Hospice or palliative care for patients with life-threatening illnesses may be provided at the patient's home, in a voluntary or NHS hospice, or in hospital; it is intended to ensure the best possible quality of life for patients during their illness, and to provide help and support to both patients and their families. The Scottish Partnership Agency for Palliative and Cancer Care co-ordinates NHS and voluntary hospice services.

PATIENT'S CHARTERS

The Patient's Charter sets out the rights of patients in relation to the NHS (i.e. the standards of service which all patients will receive at all times) and patients' reasonable expectations (i.e. the standards of service that the NHS aims to provide, even if they cannot in exceptional circumstances be met). The Charter covers issues such as access to services, personal treatment of patients, the provision of information, registering with a doctor, hospital waiting times, care in hospitals, community services, ambulance waiting times, dental, optical and pharmaceutical services, and maternity services. Under the Charter, patients are guaranteed admission to a hospital within 18 months of being placed on a waiting list.

Health boards, NHS Trusts and GP practices may also have their own local charters setting out the standard of service they aim to provide.

COMPLAINTS

The Patient's Charter includes the right to have any complaint about the service provided by the NHS dealt with quickly, with a full written reply being provided by a relevant chief executive. There are two levels to the NHS complaints procedure: first, resolution of a complaint locally, following a direct approach to the relevant service provider; second, an independent review procedure if the complaint is not resolved locally. As a final resort, patients may approach the Health Service Commissioner if they are dissatisfied with the response of the NHS to a complaint.

NHS TRIBUNALS

The National Health Service Tribunal (Scotland) considers representations that the continued inclusion of a doctor, dentist, optician or pharmacist on the list of a health authority or health board would be prejudicial to the efficiency of the service concerned.

HEALTH BOARDS

Argyll and Clyde
Ross House, Hawkhead Road, Paisley, PA2 7BN
(Tel: 0141-842 7200; Fax: 0141-848 1414).
Chairman: M. D. Jones
General Manager: N. McConachie

Ayrshire and Arran
Boswell House, 10 Arthur Street, Ayr, KA7 1QJ
(Tel: 01292-611 040; Fax: 01292-885 906;
E-mail: mcmillanm@aapct.scot.nhs.uk;
Web: www.show.scot.nhs.uk/aahb).
Chairman: Dr J. Morrow
Chief Executive: Mrs W. Hatton

Borders
Newstead, Melrose, Roxburghshire, TD9 0SE
(Tel: 01896-825 500; Fax: 01896-823 401;
E-mail: bordershb@borders.scot.nhs.uk;
Web: www.show.scot.nhs.uk/bhb).
Chairman: D. A. C. Kilshaw, OBE
Chief Executive: Dr L. Burley

Dumfries and Galloway
Grierson House, The Crichton Hospital,
Bankend Road, Dumfries, DG1 4ZG
(Tel: 01387-272 700; Fax: 01387-252 375;
E-mail: lcallagh@dghb.scot.nhs.uk;
Web: www.show.scot.nhs.uk/dghb).
Chairman (acting): Dr R. Mack, CBE
Chief Executive: Malcolm Wright

Fife
Springfield House, Cupar, KY15 9UP
(Tel: 01334-656 200; Fax: 01334-652 210).
Chairman: Mrs Esther Roberton
Chief Executive: Mr. Tony Ranzetta

Forth Valley
33 Spittal Street, Stirling, FK8 1DX
(Tel: 01786-463 031; Fax: 01786-451 474;
E-mail: email@fuhb.scot.nhs.uk;
Web: www.show.scot.nhs.uk).
Chairman: E. Bell-Scott
General Manager: D. Hird Esq.

Grampian
Summerfield House, 2 Eday Road, Aberdeen,
AB15 6RE (Tel: 01224-558 565; Fax: 01224-
558 609).
Chairman: Dr C. MacLeod, CBE
Chief Executive: Mr Neil Campbell

Greater Glasgow
Dalian House, PO Box 15329, 350 St Vincent
Street, Glasgow, G3 8YZ (Tel: 0141-201 4444;
Fax: 0141-201 4601;
E-mail: webmaster@glasgow-hb.scot.nhs.uk;
Web: www.show.scot.nhs.uk/gghb).
Chairman: Prof. D. Hamblen
Chief Executive: C. J. Spry

Highland
Beechwood Park, Inverness, IV2 3HG
(Tel: 01463-717 123; Fax: 01463-235 189).
Chairman: Mrs C. Thomson
General Manager: Dr. Roger Gibbins

Lanarkshire
14 Beckford Street, Hamilton, Lanarkshire, ML3
0TA (Tel: 01698-281 313; Fax: 01698-423 134).
Chairman: I. Livingstone, CBE
Chief Executive: Prof. T. A. Divers

Lothian
148 Peasance, Edinburgh, EH8 9RS
(Tel: 0131-536 9000; Fax: 0131-536 9009;
Web: www.lothianhealth,scot.nhs.uk).
Chairman: David Cavanagh
Chief Executive: James Barbour

Orkney
Garden House, New Scapa Road, Kirkwall,
Orkney, KW15 1BQ (Tel: 01856-885 400; Fax:
01856-885 411;
E-mail: administration@orkney-hb.scot.nhs.uk).
Chairman: I. Leslie
Chief Executive: Mrs J. Wellden

Shetland
Brevik House, South Road, Lerwick, ZE1 0TG
(Tel: 01595-696 767; Fax: 01595-696 727).
Chairman: J. Telford
General Manager: Sandra Laurenson

Tayside
Gateway House, Luna Place, Technology Park,
Dundee, DD2 1TP (Tel: 01382-561 818; Fax:
01382-424 003; E-mail: www.show.scot.nhs.uk).
Chairman: Mr. P Bates
Chief Executive: T. Brett

Western Isles
37 South Beach Street, Stornoway, Isle of Lewis,
HS1 2BN (Tel: 01851-702 997; Fax: 01851-
706720).
Chairman: A. Matheson
General Manager: M. Maclennan

HEALTH PROMOTION

Health Education Board for Scotland
Woodburn House, Canaan Lane, Edinburgh,
EH10 4SG (Tel: 0131-536 5500; Fax: 0131-539
5501; Web: www.hebs.com).
Chairman: D. Campbell
Chief Executive: Prof. A. Tannahill

BLOOD TRANSFUSION SERVICE

Scottish National Blood Transfusion Service
21 Ellen's Glen Road, Edinburgh, EH17 7QT
(Tel: 0131-536 5700; Fax: 0131-536 5701).
National Director: A. McMillan-Douglas

PALLIATIVE CARE

Scottish Partnership Agency for Palliative and Cancer Care
1A Cambridge Street, Edinburgh, EH1 2DY
(Tel: 0131-229 0538; Fax: 0131-228 2967;
E-mail: office@spapcc.demon.co.uk;
Web: www.spapcc.demon.co.uk).
Director: Mrs M. Stevenson

NHS TRUSTS

Angus Local Healthcare Co-operative
Whitehills Hospital, Forfar, Angus, DD8 3DY
(Tel: 01307-464 551; Fax: 01307-465 129).

Argyll and Clyde Acute Hospitals NHS Trust
Vale of Leven District Hospital, Main Street,
Alexandria, Dunbartonshire, G83 0UA (Tel:
01389-754 121; Fax: 01389-755 948).
Chief Executive: D. A. Sillito

Argyll and Clyde Acute Hospital NHS Trust
Inverclyde Royal Hospital, Larkfield Road,
Greenock, PA16 0XN (Tel: 01475-633 777; Fax:
01475-656 155).
Chief Executive: D. Sillito

Argyll and Clyde Acute Hospitals NHS Trust
Lorn and Islands District General Hospital,
Glengallan Road, Oban, PA34 4HH (Tel: 01631-
567 500; Fax: 01631-567 134).
Hospital Manager: Melanie McColgan

Argyll and Clyde Acute Hospitals NHS Trust
Vale of Levan District General Hospital, Main
Street, Alexandria (Tel: 01389-754 121; Fax:
01389-755 948).
Chief Executive: D. Sillito

Ayrshire and Arran Primary Care NHS Trust
1A Hunter's Avenue, Ayr, KA8 9DW (Tel:
01292-281 821; Fax: 01292-513 655;
E-mail: enquiries@aapct.scot.nhs.uk;
Web: www.aapct.org.uk).
Chief Executive: Dr. Allan Gunning

Ayrshire Arran Acute Hospitals NHS Trust
Crosshouse Hospital, Kilmarnock, Ayrshire, KA2
0BE (Tel: 01563-521 133).

Borders Primary Care NHS Trust
Newstead, Melrose, Roxburghshire, TD6 9DB
(Tel: 01896-828 282; Fax: 01896-828 298;
Web: www.show.scot.nhs.uk).
Chief Executive: J. Turner

Borders General Hospital NHS Trust
Melrose, Roxburghshire, TD6 9BS (Tel: 01896-
826 000; Fax: 01896-823 476
Chief Executive: John Glennie

Dumfries and Galloway Acute and Maternity Hospitals NHS Trust
Bankend Road, Dumfries, DG1 4AP (Tel:
01387-246 246).
Chief Executive (acting): Mr. Jeff Ace

Dumfries and Galloway Primary Care NHS Trust
Mid- North, Crichton Hall, Bankend Road,
Dumfries, DG1 4TG (Tel: 01387-244 000; Fax:
01387-269 696; Web: www.show.scot.nhs.uk).
Chief Executive: David Fraser

Falkirk and District Royal Infirmary NHS Trust
Major's Loan, Falkirk, FK1 5QE (Tel: 01324-624
000; Fax: 01324-617 421).

Fife Acute Hospitals NHS Trust
Hayfield House, Hayfield Road, Kirkcaldy, Fife,
KY2 5AH (Tel: 01592-643 355; Fax: 01592-647
090; Web: www.faht.scot.nhs.uk).
Chief Executive: J. G. Connaghan

Fife Acute Hospitals NHS Trust
Queen Margaret Hospital, Whitefield Road,
Dumfermline, Fife, KY12 0SU (Tel: 01383-623
623; Fax: 01383-624 156;
E-mail: jane.macfarlane@faht.scot.nhs.uk;
Web: www.fajt.scot.nhs.uk).
Chief Executive: J. G. Connachan

Fife Primary Care NHS Trust
Cameron House, Cameron Bridge, Leven, Fife, KY8 5RG (Tel: 01592-712 812; Fax: 01592-712 762).
Chief Executive: G. J. Beechin
Manager, Corporate Affairs: W. A. Jamieson

Forth Valley Primary Care NHS Trust
Royal Scottish National Hospital
Old Denny Road, Larbert, Stirlingshire, FK5 4DS (Tel: 01324-570 700; Fax: 01324-562 367; Web: www.show.scot.nhs.uk).
Chief Executive: Mrs E. A. Hawkins

Grampian Healthcare NHS Trust
Primary Care NHS Trust
Bennachie, Royal Cornhill Hospital, Aberdeen, AB25 2ZH (Tel: 01224-557 313; Fax: 01224-557 607;
E-mail:
ewan.robertson@gpct.grampian.scot.nhs.uk).

Grampian University Hospitals NHS Trust
Aberdeen Royal Infirmary, Foresterhill House
Ashgrove Road West, Aberdeen, AB25 2ZN (Tel: 01224-681 818; Fax: 01224-550 597).
Chief Executive: A. Cumming

Highland Acute Hospital NHS Trust
Caithness General Hospital
Bankhead Road, Wick, Caithness, KW1 5NS (Tel: 01955-605 050; Fax: 01955-604 606).
Chief Executive: Mr. Richard Carey

Highland Primary Care NHS Trust
Royal Northern Infirmary, Inverness, IV3 5SF (Tel: 01463-242 860; Fax: 01463-713 844; Web: www.show.scot.nhs.uk).
Chief Executive: Miss F. Mackenzie

Inverclyde Royal Hospital
Larkfield Road, Greenock, Renfrewshire, PA16 0XN (Tel: 01475-656 040; Fax: 01475-636 753; E-mail: lesley.garrick@irh.scot.nhs.uk).
Hospital Manager: L. Garrick

Lanarkshire Acute Hospitals NHS Trust,
Bellshill Maternity Hospital
North Road, Bellshill, ML4 3JN (Tel: 01698-574 000; Fax: 01698-845 713).
Chief Executive: J. J. Owens

Lanarkshire Acute Hospitals NHS Trust
Hairmyres Hospital
Eaglesham Road, East Kilbride, South Lanarkshire, G75 8RG (Tel: 01355-220 292).
General Manager: D. Hume

Lanarkshire Acute Hospitals NHS Trust
Law Hospital, Carluke, ML8 5ER (Tel: 01698-361 100; Fax: 01698-376 671).
General Manager: G. Archibald

Lanarkshire Acute Hospitals NHS Trust
Trust Headquaters, Bellshill Maternity Hospital
North Road, Bellshill, Ml4 3JN (Tel: 01695-747 292; Fax: 01695-845 713).
General Manager: Ms R. Lyress

Lanarkshire Primary Care NHS Trust
Strathclyde Hospital, Airbles Road, Motherwell, ML1 3BW (Tel: 01698-245 000; Fax: 01698-245 009; Web: www.show.scot.nhs.uk).
Chief Executive: M. F. Hill

Lomond and Argyll Primary Care NHS Trust
Aros, Lochgilphead, Argyll, PA31 8LB (Tel: 01546-606 600; Fax: 01546-606 568; Web: www.abaros.demon.co.uk).
Chief Executive: M. J. Bews

Lothian Primary Care NHS Trust
Edenhall Hospital, Pinkieburn Road, Musselburgh, Midlothian, EH21 7TZ (Tel: 0131-536 8000; Fax: 0131-536 8152).

Lothian University Hospitals NHS Trust
1 Lauriston Place, Edinburgh, EH3 9YW (Tel: 0131-536 1000; Fax: 0131-536 1001).
Chief Executive: A. R. Stewart

Lothian University NHS Trust
c/o Royal Infirmary, Lauriston Place, Edinburgh, EH3 9YW (Tel: 0131-536 1000).
Chief Executive: A. Stewart

Lothian University Hospitals NHS Trust
Western General Hospital, Crewe Road South, Edinburgh, EH4 2XU (Tel: 0131-537 1000).
Chief Executive: A. Stewart

Renfrewshire and Inverclyde Primary Care NHS Trust
Merchiston Hospital, Brookfield, By Johnstone, PA5 8TY (Tel: 01505-384 000; Fax: 01505-384 001).
Chief Executive: G. Buchanan

Scottish Ambulance Service
National Headquarters, Tipperlinn Road, Edinburgh, EH10 5UU (Tel: 0131-446 7000; Fax: 0131-446 7001; Web: www.scottishambulance.com).

Stirling Royal Infirmary NHS Trust
Livilands, Stirling, FK8 2AU (Tel: 01786-434 000; Fax: 01786-450 588).
Chairman: Jim Currie

South Ayrshire Hospitals NHS Trusts
Ayr Hospital, Dalmellington Road, Ayr, KA6 6DX (Tel: 01292-610 555).

Southern General Hospital NHS Trust
1345 Govan Road, Glasgow, G51 4TF (Tel: 0141-201 1100; Fax: 0141-201 2999).
Chief Executive: Robert Calderwood.

South Glasgow University Hospitals NHS Trust
Management Office, 1345 Govan Road, Glasgow, G51 4TF (Tel: 0141-201 1100; Fax: 0141-201 2999).

Tayside Primary Care NHS Trust
Trust Offices, Ashludie Hospital, Monifieth, DD5 4HQ (Tel: 01382-627 802; Fax: 01382-527 899;
E-mail: hazel.mckenzie@tpct.scot.nhs.uk;
Web: www.show.scot.nhs.uk/tpct).
Chief Executive: W. J. Wells
Corporate Services Manager: Mrs M. E. Moulton

Tayside University Hospitals NHS Trust
Ninewells Hospital and Medical School, Dundee, DD1 9SY (Tel: 01382-660 111; Fax: 01382-632 422; E-mail:
bernadette.templeton@tuht.scot.nhs.uk).
Chief Executive: P. M. White

Tayside University Hospitals NHS Trust
Dundee Dental Hospital, Park Place, Dundee, DD1 4HR (Tel: 01382-660 111; Fax: 01382-204 427).
Chief Executive: P. M. White

Tayside University Hospital NHS Trust
Perth Royal Infirmary, Taympunt Terrace, Perth, PH1 1NX (Tel: 01738-623 311).
Chief Executive: P. M. White

Tayside University Hospitals NHS Trust
Kings Cross Hospital, Clepington Road, Dundee, DD3 8EA (Tel: 01382-660 111).
Chief Executive: P. M. White

Tayside University Hospitals NHS Trust
Stracathro Hospital, Brechin, Angus (Tel: 01356-665 001; Fax: 01356-665 100).
Chief Executive: P. M. White

Victoria Infirmary NHS Trust
Queens Park House, Langside Road, Glasgow, G42 9TY (Tel: 0141-201 6000).
Chief Executive: Robert Calderwood

West Glasgow Hospitals University NHS Trust
Western Infirmary, Dumbarton Road, Glasgow, G11 6NT (Tel: 0141-211 2000).
Chief Executive: Maggie Boil

West Lothian Healthcare NHS Trust
St John's Hospital at Howden
Howden Road West, Livingston, West Lothian, EH54 6PP (Tel: 01506-419 666; Fax: 01506-416 484; E-mail: admin@wlt.scot.nhs.uk).
Chief Executive: P. Gabbitas

Yorkhill NHS Trust
Royal Hospital for Sick Children, Dalnier Street, Yorkhill, Glasgow, G3 8SJ (Tel: 0141-201 0000; Fax: 0141-201 0836).

THE POLICE SERVICE

The Scottish Executive is responsible for the organisation, administration and operation of the police service. The Scottish Executive Justice Department works in partnership with chief constables and local police to implement this responsibility, which includes the making of regulations covering matters such as police ranks, discipline, hours of duty, and pay and allowances.

Police authorities are responsible for maintaining an effective and efficient police force in their areas. There are six joint police boards made up of local councillors; the other two police authorities are councils.

A review of the structure of police forces began in April 1998.

Police authorities are financed by central and local government grants and a precept on the council tax. They are responsible for setting a budget, providing the resources necessary to police the area adequately, appointing officers of the rank of Assistant Chief Constable and above, and determining the number of officers and civilian staff in the force.

All police forces in the UK are subject to inspection by HM Inspectors of Constabulary, who report to the Scottish Ministers.

COMPLAINTS

Chief constables are obliged to investigate a complaint against one of their officers; if there is a suggestion of criminal activity, the complaint is investigated by an independent public prosecutor.

THE SPECIAL CONSTABULARY

Each police force has its own special constabulary, made up of volunteers who work in their spare time. Special Constables have full police powers within their force and adjoining force areas, and assist regular officers with routine policing duties.

POLICE STRENGTHS

Officers	14,722
men	12,396
women	2,326
Special constables	1,528
Support staff	5132.5

Source: HMCICS Annual Report, 1999-2000

PAY

Basic rates of pay since 1 September 2000 have been:

Metropolitan Police
(Commander, Assistant Commissioner, Deputy Commissioner)

Fixed term	£66,435–£120,057
Not fixed term	£63,270–£114,195

RUC Chief Constable

Fixed term	£118,413–£126,263
Not fixed term	£112,617–£121,047

Chief Constables
(Greater Manchester, Strathclyde and West Midlands)

Fixed term	£104,412–£117,837
Not fixed term	£99,558–£112,353

*Chief Constables

Fixed term	£79,620–£113,718
Not fixed term	£75,825–£108,429

Designated Deputies

Fixed term	80% of the basic salary of their chief or £76,260, whichever is higher
Not fixed term	80% of the basic salary of their chief or £72,630, whichever is higher

Assistant Chief Constable

Fixed term	£66,435–76,200
Not fixed term	£63,270–£72,630
Superintendents (range 2)	£53,700–57,150
Superintendents (range 1)	£46,0380–£53,700
Inspectors and Chief	£33-849 (£35,397)
Inspectors	£39,393 (£40,944)
Sergeant	£26,169–£30,522
Constable	£17,133–£27,114

Figures in brackets are London Salaries
*Depending on the population of the police force area
Source: Home Office
Note: Salaries are due to be revised in September 2001.

SCOTTISH DRUG ENFORCEMENT AGENCY

The Scottish Drug Enforcement Agency is mandated to drive and co-ordinate a substantially enhanced multi-agency response to combat the threat from drug trafficking and other serious and organised crime in Scotland. *HQ*, Osprey House, Inchinnan Road, Paisley PA3 2RE
(Tel: 0141-302 1000; Fax: 0141-302 1099)
Director: James Orr Esq.

JOINT POLICE BOARDS

The Dumfries and Galloway council area and the Fife council area do not have joint boards as a single authority covers the whole of the police area. The chairman of the authority for these two forces is given with the force's details.

Central Scotland Joint Police Board
Municipal Buildings, Falkirk, FK1 5RS
(Tel: 01324-506070; Fax: 01324-506071;
E-mail: itough@falkirk.gov.uk).
Convener: I. Miller
Clerk to the Board: Ms E. Morton

Covers: Clackmannanshire, Falkirk and Stirling area

Grampian Joint Police Board
Town House, Aberdeen, AB10 1AQ
(Tel: 01224-523010; Fax: 01224-522965).
Convenor: G. Saluja
Clerk to the Board: C. Langley

Covers: Aberdeen City, Aberdeenshire and Moray areas

Lothian and Borders Police Board
City Chambers, High Street, Edinburgh, EH1 1YJ (Tel: 0131-529 4955; Fax: 0131-529 7607;
E-mail: mike.gray@edinburgh.gov.uk).
Convenor: Councillor L. Hinds
Clerk and Chief Executive to the Board: T. N. Aitchison

Covers: City of Edinburgh, East Lothian, Midlothian, Scottish Borders and West Lothian areas

Northern Joint Police Board
Council Offices, Glenurquhart Road, Inverness, IV3 5NX (Tel: 01463-702123; Fax: 01463-702182; E-mail: rhona.moir@highland.gov.uk).
Convener: Ms J. Home
Clerk to the Board: J. F. P. Black
Size of Force: 658

Covers: Highland, Orkney Islands, Shetland Islands and Western Isles areas

Strathclyde Joint Police Board
City Chambers, George Square, Glasgow, G2 1DU (Tel: 0141-287 4167; Fax: 0141-287 4173).
Chair: Councillor B. Maan
Clerk to the Board: J. Andrews
Size of Force: 7,000

Covers: Argyll and Bute, East Ayrshire, East Dunbartonshire, East Renfrewshire, Glasgow City, Inverclyde, North Ayrshire, North Lanarkshire, Renfrewshire, South Ayrshire, South Lanarkshire and West Dunbartonshire areas

Tayside Joint Police Board
St James House, St James Road, Forfar, DD8 2ZE (Tel: 01307-461460; Fax: 01307-464834; Web: www.taysidepolice.uk).
Chair: J. Corrigan
Clerk to the Board: Ms C. Coull
Size of Force: 16,500

Covers: Angus, Dundee City, Perth and Kinross areas

POLICE FORCES

Central Scotland Police HQ
Randolphfield, Stirling, FK8 2HD
(Tel: 01786-456000; Fax: 01786-451177;
Web: www.centralscotland.police.uk).
Chief Constable: A. Cameron
Size of Force: 732

Dumfries and Galloway Constabulary HQ
Cornwall Mount, Dumfries, DG1 1PZ
(Tel: 01387-252112; Fax: 01387-260501;
E-mail: police@dgpcis.demon.co.uk;
Web: www.dumfriesandgalloway.police.uk).
Chief Constable: D. Strang
Chair: B. Conchie
Size of Force: 448

Fife Constabulary HQ
Detroit Road, Glenrothes, Fife, KY6 2RJ
(Tel: 01592-418888; Fax: 01592-418444;
E-mail: fifepolice@fife.police.uk;
Web: www.fife.police.uk).
Chief Constable: P. Wilson, QPM
Chair: A. Keddie
Size of Force: 835

Grampian Police HQ
Queen Street, Aberdeen, AB10 1ZA
(Tel: 01224-386000; Fax: 01224-643366;
Web: www.grampian.police.uk).
Chief Constable: A. G. Brown, QPM
Clerk to the Board: C. J. Langley
Size of Force: 1,750

Lothian and Borders Police HQ
Fettes Avenue, Edinburgh, EH4 1RB
(Tel: 0131-311 3131; Fax: 0131-311 3038;
Web: www.lbp.police.uk).
Chief Constable: Sir Roy Cameron, QPM
Size of Force: 3,750

Northern Constabulary HQ
Old Perth Road, Inverness, IV2 3SY
(Tel: 01463-715555; Fax: 01463-720373;
Web: www.northern.police.uk).
Chief Constable: W. A. Robertson, QPM
Clerk: F. Black
Size of Force: 659

Strathclyde Police HQ
173 Pitt Street, Glasgow, G2 4JS
(Tel: 0141-532 2000; Fax: 0141-532 2409;
Web: www.strathclyde.police.uk).
Chief Constable: J. Orr, OBE, QPM
Size of Force: 7,352

Tayside Police HQ
PO Box 59, West Bell Street, Dundee, DD1 9JU
(Tel: 01382-223200; Fax: 01382-225772;
E-mail: forcedev@tayside.police.uk;
Web: www.tayside.police.uk).
Chief Constable: J. Vine, MCIPD
Director of Law and Administration: Ms C. Coull
Size of Force: 1,150

OTHER POLICE FORCES

British Transport Police Scottish Area HQ
90 Cowcaddens Road, Glasgow, G4 0LU
(Tel: 0141-332 3649; Fax: 0141-335 2155;
E-mail: elaine.russell.btpolice@ems.rail.co.uk;
Web: www.btp.police.uk).
Assistant Chief Constable, Scotland: S. Forrest
Size of Force: 2,200

Ministry of Defence Police
Operational Command Unit HQ Scotland
HMNB Clyde, Helensburgh, Dunbartonshire,
G84 8HL (Tel: 01436-674321 ext. 6441).
Operational Commander, Scotland:
Chief Supt. S. R. Mason
Size of Force: 857

UK Atomic Energy Authority Constabulary
UK HQ, Building E6 Culham Science Centre,
Abingdon, Oxon, OX14 3DB (Tel: 01235-463
760; Fax: 01235-463 764;
E-mail: constabulary@ukaea.org.uk).
Chief Constable: W. F. Pryke
Size of Force: 517

STAFF ASSOCIATIONS

Police officers are not permitted to join a trade
union or to take strike action. All ranks have their
own staff associations.

Association of Chief Police Officers in Scotland
Police Headquarters, Fettes Avenue, Edinburgh,
EH4 1RB (Tel: 0131-311 3051; Fax: 0131-311
3052; E-mail: acpos@ibp.police.uk).
Hon. Secretary: Sir Roy Cameron, QPM

Represents the Chief Constables, Deputy and
Assistant Chief Constables of the Scottish police
forces

The Association of Scottish Police Superintendents
Secretariat, 173 Pitt Street, Glasgow, G2 4JS
(Tel: 0141-221 5796; Fax: 0141-532 2489;
E-mail: policesupts@hotmail.com;
Web: www.scottishpolicesupers.co.uk).
General Secretary: J. Urquhart, QPM
President: F. J. McManus, LLB

Represents officers of the rank of Superintendent

The Scottish Police Federation
5 Woodside Place, Glasgow, G3 7QF
(Tel: 0141-332 5234; Fax: 0141-331 2436;
Web: www.spf.org.uk).
General Secretary: D. J. Keil, QPM

Represents officers up to and including the rank of
Chief Inspector

THE PRISON SERVICE

The Scottish Prison Service is an Agency of the Scottish Executive. The chief executive is responsible for operational matters and performance.

There are 16 prison establishments in Scotland, housing about 6,000 prisoners.

Convicted prisoners are classified according to their perceived security risk and are housed in establishments appropriate to that level of security. Female prisoners are housed in women's establishments or in separate wings of mixed prisons. Remand prisoners are, where possible, housed separately from convicted prisoners. Offenders under the age of 21 are usually detained in a young offenders' institution, which may be a separate establishment or part of a prison.

One prison, Kilmarnock, was built, financed and is being run by private contractors.

Her Majesty's Chief Inspector of Prisons is independent and reports annually to the Scottish Executive Justice Department on prison conditions and the treatment of prisoners. Every prison establishment also has an independent visiting committee made up of local volunteers appointed by the Justice Minister. Any prisoner whose complaint is not satisfied by the internal complaints procedures may complain to the Scottish Complaints Commissioner.

Women make up only 3 per cent of the Scottish prison population. Custody is less frequently used as a sanction against female offenders; in 1996, for example, only 4 per cent of women convicted of offences received a custodial sentence, whereas 11.1 per cent of all offenders received such a sentence.

AVERAGE DAILY POPULATION IN SCOTTISH PENAL ESTABLISHMENTS 1993–2000

1993–4	5,588
1994–5	5,630
1995–6	5,632
1996–7	5,992
1997–8	6,059
1998–9	6,029
1999–2000	5,974

Source: Scottish Prison Service, Annual Report and Accounts 1999-2000

AVERAGE DAILY PRISON POPULATION 1998-2000 (BY TYPE OF CUSTODY)

Type of Custody	1998-99	1999-2000
Remand	971	975
Persons under sentence		
Adult prisoners	4,348	4,320
Less than 4 years[1]	2,036	1,987
4 years or over (including life)[2]	2,312	2,333
Young offenders	710	679
Less than 4 years	518	502
4 years or over (including life)[3]	191	176
Persons under sentence: total[3]	5,057	4,999
Total[3]	6,029	5,974

1. Includes those prisoners sentenced by court martial, civil prisoners and others
2. Includes those persons recalled by supervision licence
3. Components may not add to totals due to rounding
Source: Scottish Prison Service, Annual Report and Accounts 1999-2000

MAIN CRIMES AND OFFENCES OF REMAND AND SENTENCED[1] PRISONERS IN CUSTODY ON 30 JUNE 1999 (Extract[2])

Main crime/offence	Remand total	Sentenced total
Total crimes and offences	981	5,060
Non-sexual crimes of violence	326	2,122
Crimes of indecency	30	400
Crimes of dishonesty	344	1,032
Fire-raising, vandalism	26	54
Other crimes	124	806
Miscellaneous offences	105	374
Motor vehicle offences	26	250
Unknown charge	—	5
Other jurisdiction charge	—	17

1. Civil prisoners are excluded from this table. However, on the 30th June 1999 there were no such prisoners in Scottish penal establishments
2. Extract: for complete table and explanatory notes see source
Source: Scottish Executive, Prison Statistics Scotland 1999 (Crown copyright)

OPERATING COSTS OF THE SCOTTISH PRISON SERVICE FOR THE YEAR ENDING 31 MARCH 2000

Total income	1,734,000
Total expenditure	219,975,000
Staff costs	127,724,000
Running costs	73,489,000
Other current expenditure	18,762,000
Operating cost	(218,241,000)
Cost of capital charges	(23,349,000)
Interest payable and similar charges	(15,000)
Interest receivable	93,000
Net cost of operations after interest	241,512,000
Lockerbie trial costs	3,387,000
Cost for financial year	244,899,000

Source: Scottish Prison Service, *Annual Report and Accounts 1999-2000*

SCOTTISH PRISON SERVICE

Calton House, 5 Redheughs Rigg, Edinburgh EH12 9HW (Tel: 0131-556 8400)

SALARIES

The following pay bands have applied since 1 October 2000–2001:

I	£37,375–£57,700
H	£31,150–£48,100
G	£26,050–£39,600

STAFF

The number of Scottish Prison Service staff (full-time and part-time) in post at 31 March 1998 was 4,856, of whom 4,069 were male and 787 female.

Chief Executive of Scottish Prison Service: Tony Cameron

Director of Custody: John Durno, OBE

Director, Human Resources: Peter Russell

Director, Finance and Information Systems: Willie Pretswell

Director, Strategy and Corporate Affairs: Ms Jinny Hutchison

Deputy Director, Regime Services and Supplies: John McNeill

Deputy Director, Estates and Buildings: David Bentley

Area Director, South and West: Mike Duffy

Area Director, North and East: Peter Withers

Head of Training, Scottish Prison Service College: Jack Matthews

Head of Communications: vacant

PRISON ESTABLISHMENTS

The figures given here refer to the average number of prisoners/young offenders in 2000–2001

*Aberdeen
Craiginches, Aberdeen AB9 2HN
Prisoners: 181
Governor: I. Gunn

Barlinnie
Barlinnie, Glasgow G33 2QX
Prisoners: 1,124
Governor: R. L. Houchin

Castle Huntly
Castle Huntly, Longforgan, nr Dundee DD2 5HL
Prisoners: 106
Governor: M. McAlpine

*‡Cornton Vale
Cornton Road, Stirling FK9 5NY
Prisoners and Young Offenders: 180
Governor: Mrs K. Donegan

*‡Dumfries
Terregles Street, Dumfries DG2 9AX
Young Offenders: 137
Governor: C. McGeever

Edinburgh
33 Stenhouse Road, Edinburgh EH1 3LN
Prisoners: 731
Governor: R. MacCowan

‡Glenochil
King O'Muir Road, Tullibody,
Clackmannanshire FK10 3AD
Prisoners and Young Offenders: 573
Governor: K. Donegan

Greenock
Gateside, Greenock PA16 9AH
Prisoners: 236
Governor: A. Park

*Inverness
Porterfield, Inverness IV2 3HH
Prisoners: 122
Governor: A. MacDonald

Kilmarnock (private prison)
Bowhouse, Mauchline Road, Kilmarnock
KA1 5JH
Prisoners: 500
Director: J. Bywalec

Low Moss
Low Moss, Bishopbriggs, Glasgow G64 2QB
Prisoners: 362
Governor: E. Murch

Noranside
Noranside, Fern, by Forfar, Angus DD8 3QY
Prisoners: 102
Governor: K. Rennie

Perth
3 Edinburgh Road, Perth PH2 8AT
Prisoners: 477
Governor: W. Millar

Peterhead
Salthouse Head, Peterhead, Aberdeenshire
AB4 6YY
Prisoners: 297
Governor: W. Rattray
Governor, Peterhead Unit: B. McConnell

‡Polmont
Brightons, Falkirk, Stirlingshire FK2 0AB
Young Offenders: 443
Governor: D. Gunn

Shotts
Shotts Ml7 4LF
Prisoners: 467
Governor: W. McKinlay
Governor, Shotts Unit: G. Storer

* Women's establishments or establishments with units for women
‡ Young Offender Institution or establishment with units for young offenders

SOCIAL SERVICES

Social work services became a devolved responsibility, for the Scottish Executive, on 1 July 1999. Services for vulnerable adults and children — and their families and carers — are provided or purchased by local authorities according to policies and standards set by the Scottish Executive. The regulation of social work services and the staff who work within them will be substantially enhanced by the introduction of the Scottish Commission for the Regulation of Care (from April 2002) and the Scottish Social Services Council (from October 2001).

Each authority has a Chief Social Work Officer, frequently known as the Director of Social Work. How each authority seeks to exercise its social work functions is a matter for the authority itself. The functions themselves cover 3 broad areas:

— Communiy Care (or adult) services;
— Children and family services;
— Criminal Justice social work services.

In the Scottish Executive, the oversight of Community Care functions is the responsibility of the Health Department. The oversight of children and family services' functions are with the Children and Young People Group of the Education Department. Oversight of the functions of criminal justice social work services is with the Justice Department. The Social Work Services Inspectorate undertakes inspection, policy advice and programme work.

FINANCE
Social work services are financed partly by central government, with decisions on expenditure allocations being made at local authority level.

NET EXPENDITURE ON SOCIAL WORK
(£000s)[1, 2]

	1999	2000[4]
Children	263,276	278,296
All community care client groups	257,915	246,863
Older people	269,999	302,662
Adults with mental health problems	30,780	29,462
Substance misuse	7,245	8,159
Adults with learning disabilities	118,419	137,809
Physically disabled adults	44,945	42,154
Services for HIV/AIDS	1,404	1,729
Total community care	**730,707**	**768,838**
Adult offenders	4,913	3,808
Non specific expenditure	162,423	149,436
Total Social Work	**1,161,319**	**1,200,378**

1. Extract: for the complete table please see source
2. Loan charges have been excluded for all years
3. Figures have been adjusted to reflect current prices using GDO deflators
4. 2000 figures are provisional and may change
Source: Scottish Executive, Scottish Community Care Statistics 2000 (Crown Copyright)

STAFF OF SCOTTISH SOCIAL WORK SERVICES[1]

Client Group	1999	2000
Children	4,959	5,384
Adults	21,241	21,300
Older people[2]	5,820	5,476
Physical disabilities[2]	727	484
Mental health problems[2]	378	300
Learning disabilities	2,999	3,077
Adults (not separately identified)[3]	11,317	11,963
Offenders	1,160	1,182
Generic provision	3,472	3,196
Management/ administration	2,996	3,101
Total	33,828	34,161

1. Staff numbers may fluctuate over time as a result of various factors, including changes in the way services are provided and changes in the number of vacancies
2. Staff in day centres, residential establishments and special locations providing services to specific client groups
3. Fieldwork staff providing services to adults and home care staff
Source: Scottish Executive, Staff of Scottish Local Authority Social Work Services (Crown Copyright)

OLDER PEOPLE

Services for older people are designed to enable them to remain living in their own homes for as long as possible and practical. Local authority services include advice, domestic help, meals in the home, alterations to the home to aid mobility, emergency alarm systems, day and/or night attendants, laundry services and the provision of day centres and recreational facilities. Charges

may be made for these services. Respite care may also be provided in order to allow carers temporary relief from their responsibilities.

Local authorities and the private sector also provide 'sheltered housing' for older people, sometimes with resident wardens.

If an older person is admitted to a care home, charges can be made according to a means test; if the person cannot afford to pay, the costs are met by the local authority.

RESIDENTIAL CARE HOMES FOR OLDER PEOPLE 2000

	Local Authority	Private	Voluntary	All homes
No. homes	219	268	157	631
No. beds	6,526	5,074	4,215	15,851
No. residents†	5,917	4,134	3,702	13,762

Source: Scottish Executive: Scottish Community Care Statistics 1999 (Crown Copyright)

PEOPLE WITH PHYSICAL DISABILITIES

Services for people with physical disabilities are designed to support them to lead ordinary independent lives in their own homes. Local authority services include advice, adaptations to the home, meals in the home, help with personal care, occupational therapy, educational facilities and recreational facilities. Respite care may also be provided in order to allow carers temporary relief from their responsibilities.

Special housing may be available for people with physical disabilities who can live independently, and care home accommodation for those who cannot.

RESIDENTIAL CARE HOMES FOR PEOPLE WITH PHYSICAL DISABILITIES 2000

Number of homes	44
Number of beds	868
Number of residents (including holiday/respite residents)	773

Source: Scottish Executive, Community Care Statistics 2000 (Crown Copyright)

FAMILIES AND CHILDREN

Local authorities are required to provide services aimed at safeguarding and promoting the welfare of children looked after or in need, wherever possible, allowing them to be brought up by their families. Services include advice, counselling, help in the home and the provision of family centres. Many authorities also provide short-term refuge accommodation for women and children.

DAY CARE

In allocating day-care places to children, local authorities can, where appropriate, give priority to children with special needs, whether in terms of their health, learning abilities or social needs.

The child care strategy for Scotland, under which day care and out-of-school child care facilities will be extended to match more closely the needs of working parents, was launched by Ministers in May 1988. The strategy is intended to ensure that quality, affordable childcare is available for children aged 0-14 in every neighbourhood.

Provisional results of a survey in 2001 of 4,328 facilities providing day-care and/or pre-school education for children in Scotland found that about 196,000 children attended facilities. Of the different facilities, 48 per cent were described as mainly being a nursery and 29 per cent as mainly being a playgroup. There were also playschemes, out-of-school care schemes, crèches and family centres. The largest age group attending centres was that of three-and four-year-olds.

In 1997 (the latest year for which there are published figures), there were also 8,243 childminders registered with local authorities, looking after 34,983 children under eight.

Source: Scottish Executive: Press Release—Provisional results of the 2001 pre-school and day-care census.

CHILD PROTECTION

Children considered to be at risk of physical injury, neglect or sexual abuse may be the subject of a child protection conference and placed on the local authority's child protection register after a decision has been made that an inter-agency agreement is needed to protect the child. Local authority social services staff, school nurses, health visitors and other agencies work together to prevent and detect cases of abuse. In Scotland in 1998-9 1,962 children were reported as having been registered following case conferences. Of these, 28.7 per cent were judged to be at risk of neglect, 42.6 per cent of physical injury, 17.6 per cent of sexual abuse and 10.71 per cent of emotional abuse. Of those initially referred for enquiries, 48 per cent were boys and 52 per cent girls.

Source: Scottish Executive—Child Protection Statistics for the year ended 31 March 1999.

LOCAL AUTHORITY CARE

The Children in Care (Scotland) Act 1995 governs the provision by local authorities of accommodation for children who have no parent or guardian or whose parents or guardians are unable or unwilling to care for them. A children's hearing may impose compulsory measures of suspension where a child is being neglected or abused, or is offending, or is misusing alcohol, drugs or volatile substances, or is not attending school. The hearing must be satisfied that doing something is better than doing nothing to minimise the state's involvement in the life of the child.

Children who are being looked after by local authorities may live at home, with friends or relatives, in other community accommodation, with foster carers who receive payments to cover the expenses of caring for the child or children, or in residential care. Children's homes may be run by the local authority or by the private or voluntary sectors.

CHILDREN IN CARE/LOOKED AFTER*

As at 31 March 2000

	1998	1999	2000
Boys	6,274 (58%)	6,529 (58%)	6,572 (58%)
Girls	4,530 (42%)	4,662 (42%)	4,737 (42%)
TOTAL	10,804	11,191	11,309

Source: Scottish Executive (Crown copyright)

At 31 March 1998 a total of 10,791 children (an average of 9.4 children per 1,000 members of the population aged 0–17 years) was being looked after. About 51 per cent of these were living at home; 25 per cent were with foster carers, 17 per cent were in residential care and 7 per cent were living with friends or relatives or in other community accommodation (*Source:* Scottish Office, *Statistical Bulletin* (Crown copyright)).

The number of children being looked after varies considerably from authority to authority, depending on factors such as the size of the authority, the size and age structure of the local population, and the authority's policy and resources.

The implementation of the Children in Care (Scotland) Act 1995 extended the powers and responsibilities of local authorities to look after children who would previously have left care at the age of 16. Also, a number of respite placements which were not hitherto considered as care now fall within the definition of being 'looked after'. Thus, although the number of children being looked after has been falling steadily for some years, the number of older teenagers in care increased between 1997 and 1998. The largest proportion of children being looked after is in the age band 12–16 years (45.7 per cent in 1998). Boys outnumber girls in all age bands.

ADOPTION

Local authorities are required to provide an adoption service, either directly or via approved voluntary societies. The number of adoption applications in Scotland has fallen steadily over the last decade, to only a little over half as many applications in 1998 as in 1988. Applications in 1998 were taken out for 469 children, 211 boys and 257 girls. The largest age group of children for whom adoption applications are made is 5–11 years, with the average age of children for whom applications are made being just under seven years. Less than 10 per cent of applications are made for children less than one year old.

PEOPLE WITH LEARNING DISABILITIES

Services for people with learning disabilities are designed to enable them to remain living in the community wherever possible. Local authority services include short-breaks and respite support in the home, the provision of day services, and help with other activities outside the home.

The review of services for people with learning disabilities, *The Same As You?* recommended that local authorities should develop alternatives to traditional day centres in order to support people in the community through employment, lifelong learning and social involvement. Residential care may be provided for people with disabilities generally in small or group homes, but a shift in the pattern of care is occurring with most people with learning disabilities living in various forms of supported accommodation including adult placements, small group homes and supported living arrangements.

RESIDENTIAL CARE HOMES FOR PEOPLE WITH LEARNING DISABILITIES, 1999–2000 (Extract[1])

	1999	2000
Number of homes	594	628
Number of beds	4,525	4,760
Number of residents (including holiday/ respite residents)	4,222	4,394

1. Extract: for complete table with explanatory notes see source
2. Source: Scottish Executive: Scottish Community Care Statistics 2000 (Crown Copyright)

PEOPLE WITH MENTAL HEALTH PROBLEMS

Under the Care Programme Approach, those with a mental illness are assessed by specialist services with the purpose of receiving a care plan reflecting their needs, and a key worker should be appointed for each patient. Regular reviews of the patient's progress should be conducted. Local authorities provide help and advice to those with a mental illness and their families, and places in day centres and social centres. In extreme cases social workers can apply for a mentally disordered person to be compulsorily detained in hospital. Where appropriate, hospital care or care in residential or nursing homes is provided.

A review of mental health legislation was published in January 2001 and a White Paper on mental health was to be published in 2001.

Mental Illness Specific Grants assist projects addressing care for people with mental health problems. In 2001–2, 398 such projects were supported by grants.

In 1998 there were 467 places in day centres and 815 people attending; an average of 27 places and 48 attendees per centre.

NUMBER OF DAY CENTRES[1] FOR PEOPLE WITH MENTAL HEALTH PROBLEMS, PLACES AND PEOPLE ATTENDING, 1997-1998 (Extract[2])

	1997	1998
Number of day centres	18	17
Number of places	572	467
Number attending	963	815

1. Includes centres with 4 places or less (which are usually residential homes).
2. Extract: for complete table please see source
Source: Scottish Executive: Scottish Community Care Statistics, (Crown Copyright).

TRANSPORT

UK airlines are operated entirely by the private sector. Scottish airports are served by several major British airlines, including British Airways, Air UK, Britannia Airways, British Midland, Monarch Airlines and EasyJet; by British Airways franchise Loganair (which operates several inter-island services) and franchised partner British Regional Airlines, and by other airlines such as Highland Airways, Gill-air and Business Air.

Among European airlines, SAS provides links to Scandinavia, KLM with the Netherlands and further afield, and RyanAir and Aer Lingus with Ireland. The Norwegian carrier Ugland Air provides oil industry charters from Sumburgh to Norwegian airports, and Wideroe, also Norwegian, operates scheduled flights in summer on the same route.

The Civil Aviation Authority (CAA) is responsible for the economic regulation of UK airlines and the larger airports, and for the safety regulation of the UK civil aviation industry. Through its subsidiary company National Air Traffic Services Ltd, the CAA is also responsible for the provision of air traffic control services over Britain and its surrounding seas and at most major British airports. It also runs the Air Travel Organiser's Licensing (ATOL) consumer protection scheme.

The CAA advises the Government on aviation issues, represents consumer interests, conducts economic and scientific research, produces statistical data. And provides specialist services and other training and consultancy services to clients world-wide.

AIRPORTS

Scottish Airports Ltd is a subsidiary of BAA plc, the world's leading commercial airport operator. It owns and operates Scotland's three principal airports at Glasgow, Edinburgh and Aberdeen which, together currently handle 14 million passengers annually. A total of 250,000 movements of aircraft and helicopters takes place each year and 29,300 metric tonnes of cargo and mail are carried through the airports.

Highlands and Islands Airports Ltd (HIAL) owns and operates ten Scottish airports and receives subsidies for providing links to remote areas of Scotland.

HIAL's airports are Barra, Benbecula, Campbeltown, Inverness, Islay, Kirkwall, Stornoway, Sumburgh, Tiree, and Wick.

A number of airports and small airfields are controlled by local authorities, including Dundee, Orkney and Shetland. Orkney Islands Council has airfields at Eday, North Ronaldsay, Papa Westray, Sanday, Stronsay and Westray. Shetland Islands Council runs Tingwall airport at Lerwick, and gives assistance to airstrips on Foula, Out Skerries and Papa Stour, which are run by local airstrip trusts. Fetlar and Whalsay have airstrips for emergency use, with only occasional other services according to need. Baltasound airstrip on Unst, currently owned by Shetland Islands Council, is maintained for emergency and ambulance use. It is available for emergency landings only. Fair Isle airfield is owned, like the whole island, by the National Trust for Scotland. Airports and airfields at Glenrothes, Cumbernauld and Perth (Scone) are privately owned. Scatsta in Shetland and Flotta in Orkney are also privately owned, principally serving the oil industry.

Airport operating hours at Barra are subject to tide variation, since aircraft land on and take off from the beach. Tiree's operating hours are also subject to the variations at Barra, as flights to and from Tiree are via Barra.

Operating hours vary seasonally at several smaller airports and airfields, including Campbeltown, Inverness, Islay and Wick.

PASSENGER JOURNEYS

Over 14 million passenger journeys were made through Scottish airports in 1997, including terminal, transit, scheduled and charter passengers. The following list covers BAA, HIAL and local authority controlled airports.

TERMINAL PASSENGERS 2000

	Scheduled	Charter
Aberdeen (BAA)	1,841,924	639,240
Barra (HIAL)	7,591	98
Benbecula (HIAL)	33,556	1,960
Campbeltown (HIAL)	7,468	526
Dundee	47,124	2,543
Edinburgh (BAA)	5,096,995	400,701
Glasgow (BAA)	4,817,687	2,106,529
Inverness (HIAL)	328,021	12,999
Islay (HIAL)	19,664	915
Kirkwall (HIAL)	84,786	2,004
Lerwick (Tingwall)	2,414	2,188
Prestwick (BAA)	810,228	94,630
Stornoway (HIAL)	85,799	4,290
Sumburgh (HIAL)	111,851	7,950
Tiree (HIAL)	4,826	102
Unst	1,407	22
Wick (HIAL)	18,869	1,615

Source: Civil Aviation Authority

BAA PLC

Scottish Airport Division, St Andrew's Drive, Glasgow Airport, Paisley KA9 4DG (Tel: 0141-887 1111; Fax: 0141-887 1699)

HIGHLANDS AND ISLANDS AIRPORTS LTD

Head Office, Inverness Airport, Inverness IV2 7JB (Tel: 01667-462445)

RAILWAYS

Responsibility for legislation on railways was not devolved to the Scottish Parliament but remains with the UK Government.

Since 1994, responsibility for managing Britain's nationalised railway infrastructure has rested with Railtrack, which was floated on the Stock Exchange in 1996. Railtrack owns all operational track and land pertaining to the railway system, manages the track and charges for access to it, and is responsible for signalling and timetabling. It also owns the stations, and leases most of them out to the train operating companies. Infrastructure support functions are provided by private-sector companies. Railtrack invests in infrastructure principally using finance raised by track charges, and takes investment decisions in consultation with rail operators. It is also responsible for overall safety on the railways.

Railtrack does not operate train services. Since 1994 all passenger services have been franchised to 25 private-sector train-operators, via a competitive tendering process overseen by the Director of the Office of Passenger Rail Franchising (now part of the Strategic Rail Authority). The Government continues to subsidise loss-making but socially necessary rail services. The Franchising Director is responsible for monitoring the performance of the franchisees and allocating and administering government subsidy payments.

The Office of the Rail Regulator was set up under the Railways Act 1993. It is headed by the Rail Regulator, who is independent of ministerial control. The regulater's principal function is to regulate Railtrack's stewardship of the national network, and to provide the economic regulation of the monopoly and dominant elements of the rail industry. The regulator also licenses operators of railway assets, approves agreements for access by operators to track, stations and light maintenance depots, and enforces domestic competition law. The International Rail Regulator licenses the operation of certain international rail services in the European Economic area, and access to railway infrastructure in Great Britain for the purpose of the operation of such services. The Office of the International Rail Regulator is co-located with the Office of the Rail Regulator, who fulfils both functions.

Rail Users' Consultative Committees monitor the policies and performance of train and station operators in their area. They are statutory bodies and have a legal right to make recommendations for changes.

OFFICE OF THE RAIL REGULATOR (ORR)

1 Waterhouse Square, 138–142 Holborn, London EC1N 2TQ (Tel: 020-7282 2000).
Rail Regulator: Tom Winsor

RAILTRACK

Scottish Office, Buchanan House, 58 Port Dundas Road, Glasgow G4 0LQ (Tel: 0141-335 2424).

SCOTRAIL

Caledonian Chambers, 87 Union Street, Glasgow G1 3TA (Tel: 0141-332 9811).

RAIL USERS' CONSULTATIVE COMMITTEE FOR SCOTLAND

5th Floor, Corunna House, 29 Cadogan Street, Glasgow G2 7AB (Tel: 0141-221 7760).

SERVICES

Scotland is served by Great North Eastern Railway, Scotrail Railways and Virgin Trains operating companies. There are 335 stations in passenger service. Railtrack owns all of these with the exception of the station at Prestwick Airport, which is privately owned. Figures from the Strategic Rail Authority show that passenger journeys within Scotland for the period 1999 to 2000 totalled 64.9 million. Total passenger journeys, including cross-border journeys originating in Scotland, totalled 67.5 million in the same year. The total revenue for internal and cross-border journeys originating in Scotland for 1999–2000 was £188.4 million. (These figures exclude cross-border passenger traffic originating outside of Scotland and journey on the Glasgow Underground.)

Railtrack publishes a national timetable which contains details of rail services operated over the Railtrack network, coastal shipping information and connections with Ireland, the Isle of Man, the Isle of Wight, the Channel Islands and some European destinations.

The national rail enquiries service offers telephone information about train times and fares for any part of the country:

NATIONAL RAIL ENQUIRIES
Tel: 0845-7484950

EUROSTAR
Tel: 08705186186

GLASGOW UNDERGROUND RAILWAY
The Glasgow Underground railway system opened in 1896, was electrified in 1935 and reopened following modernisation in 1980. It has 15 stations and 6.55 route miles of track. Strathclyde Passenger Transport is responsible for the Underground. In 2000–01 there were 14.4 million passenger journeys. Total ticket revenue in 2000–01 was £9.97 million, an increase of 3 per cent on the previous year.

STRATHCLYDE PASSENGER TRANSPORT
Consort House, 12 West George Street, Glasgow G2 1HN (Tel: 0141-332 6811).
Customer enquiries: 0870-608 2608

CHANNEL TUNNEL LINKS
Passenger services operated by Eurostar (UK) Ltd run from Waterloo station in London and Ashford, Kent, via the Channel Tunnel to Paris, Brussels and Lille. Connecting services from Edinburgh via London began in 1997.

ROADS

Responsibility for Scotland's road network and for policy on bus transport now rests with the Scottish Parliament and Ministers, operating through the Scottish Executive Development Department. The highway authority for non-trunk roads is, in general, the unitary authority in whose area the roads lie.

The costs of construction, improvement and maintenance are met by central government. Total expenditure on building and maintaining trunk roads in Scotland was estimated at £182 million in 2000–01.

ROAD LENGTHS
as at May 2001

	Miles	km
Total roads	33,484	53,886
Trunk roads (including motorways)	2,167	3,488
Motorways	334	537

MOTORWAYS

M8	Edinburgh to Newhouse, Baillieston to West Ferry Interchange
M9	Edinburgh to Dunblane
M73	Maryville to Mollinsburn
M74	Glasgow to Paddy's Rickle Bridge, Cleuchbrae to Gretna
M77	Ayr Road Route
M80	Stirling to Haggs/Glasgow (M8) to Stepps
M90	Inverkeithing to Perth
M876	Dennyloanhead (M80) to Kincardine Bridge

PRINCIPAL ROAD BRIDGES

Tay Road Bridge, over Firth of Tay
—2,245 m/7,365 ft
Forth Road Bridge, over Firth of Forth
—1,987 m/6,156 ft
Erskine Bridge, over River Clyde
—1,321 m/4,336 ft
Kessock Bridge, over Kessock Narrows
—1,052 m/3,453 ft
Skye Bridge, over Kyle of Lochalsh
—520 m/1,705 ft

ROAD PASSENGER SERVICES
There is an extensive network of bus and coach services in Scotland, particularly in rural areas. In 1999–2000 there were 431 million passenger bus journeys in Scotland: a fall of 30% compared to 1989–90.

Until 1988 most road passenger transport services in Great Britain were provided by the public sector; the Scottish Bus Group was the largest operator in Scotland. Since the late 1980s almost all bus and coach services in Great Britain have been privatised; the privatisation of the Scottish Bus Group was completed in 1991. However, local authorities can subsidise the provision of socially necessary services after competitive tendering.

One of the largest bus operators in Great Britain, Stagecoach Holdings, is based in Scotland, at Perth. National Express runs a national network of coach routes, mainly operating through franchises. There is also a large number of smaller private operators.

Information on local bus routes and timetables can be obtained from bus stations and tourist board offices; telephone numbers can be found in local telephone directories.

Highland Scottish Buses
Tel: 01463-233371

National Express Coach Services
Tel: 08705-808080/0990-808080

Scottish Citylink Express Coach Services
Tel: 08705-505050/0990-505050

Stagecoach Holdings
Tel: 01738-629339/442111 (administration)

POSTBUS SERVICES

Since 1968 the Royal Mail has operated a postbus service in Scotland, providing passenger transport in rural areas of the country. There are currently 119 postbuses covering 128 routes throughout Scotland, including the Western Isles, Orkney and Shetland and a similar network in England and Wales. Many of the services receive financial assistance from local councils. A wheelchair-accessible service in East Lothian was introduced in 1998.

The postbus service has its Scottish head office at the Royal Mail headquarters in Edinburgh but is largely administered from Inverness. Timetable information is available from the website, www.royalmail.com or from 08457-740 740.

ROYAL MAIL SCOTLAND AND NORTHERN IRELAND

HQ, 102 West Port, Edinburgh EH3 9HS

POST BUS SUPPORT

Royal Mail, 7 Strothers Lane, Inverness IV1 1AA (Tel: 01463-256228; customer services: 08457-740 740; Fax: 01463-256392)

DRIVING AND VEHICLE LICENCES

The Driver and Vehicle Licensing Agency (DVLA) is responsible for issuing driving licences, registering and licensing vehicles, and collecting excise duty in Great Britain. The Driving Standards Agency is responsible for carrying out driving tests and approving driving instructors.

A leaflet, *What You Need to Know About Driving Licences* (form D100), is available from post offices.

DRIVING LICENCE FEES

as at 1 April 2000

First provisional licence	£23.50
Changing a provisional to a full licence after passing a driving test	£8.50
Renewal of licence	£8.50
Renewal of licence including PCV or LGV entitlements	£28.50
Renewal after disqualification	£24.50
Renewal after drinking and driving disqualification	£33.50
Medical renewal	free
Duplicate Licence	£13.50
Exchange licence	£13.50
Removing endorsements	£13.50
Replacement (change of name or address)	free

DRIVING TEST FEES

(weekday rate/evening and Saturday rate)
as at 1 April 2000

For cars	£36.75/£46
For motor cycles*	£45/£55
For lorries, buses	£73.50/£92
For invalid carriages	free
For cars, after disqualification†	£73.50/£92.50
For motor cycles, after disqualification†	£90/110
Written theory test	£15.50

* Before riding on public roads, learner motor cyclists and learner moped riders are required to have completed Compulsory Basic Training, provided by DSA-approved training bodies. The CBT certificate currently costs £8.

†An extended driving test was introduced in 1992 for those convicted of dangerous driving.

All fees are subject to change.

MOTOR VEHICLE LICENCES

Registration and first licensing of vehicles is done through local Vehicle Registration Offices of the DVLA. Local facilities for relicensing are available at any post office which deals with vehicle licensing, or by postal application to the post offices shown on form V100, available at any post office. This form also provides guidance on registering and licensing vehicles.

Details of the present duties chargeable on motor vehicles are available at post offices and Vehicle Registration Offices.

VEHICLE EXCISE DUTY RATES

from 1 April 2001

	Twelve months £	Six months £
Motor Cars		
Light vans, cars, taxis, etc.		
Under 1200cc	105.00	57.75
Over 1200cc	160.00	88.00
Motor Cycles		
Not over 150 cc	15.00	—
150–250 cc	40.00	—
Others	60.00	35.75
Tricycles (not over 450 kg)		
Not over 150 cc	15.00	—
150–250cc	40.00	—
Others	65.00	35.75
Buses†		
Seating 9–16 persons	165.00	90.75
	(160)	(85.25)
Seating 17–35 persons	220.00	121.00
	(160)	(85.25)
Seating 36–60 persons	330.00	181.50
	(160)	(85.25)
Seating over 60 persons	500.00	275.00
	(160)	(85.25)

† *Figures in parentheses refer to reduced pollution vehicles*

MOT TESTING

Cars, motor cycles, motor caravans, light goods and dual-purpose vehicles more than three years old must be covered by a current MoT test certificate, which must be renewed annually. The MoT testing scheme is administered by the Vehicle Inspectorate.

A fee is payable to MoT testing stations, which must be authorised to carry out tests. The maximum fees, which are prescribed by regulations, are:

For cars and light vans	£34.00
For solo motor cycles	£13.70
For motor cycle combinations	£22.70
For three-wheeled vehicles	£26.60
Private passenger seats and ambulances	
9-12 seats	£35.90*
13-16 seats	£41.70*
over 16 seats	£54.15*
* including seat belt installation check	
For light goods vehicles between 3,000 and 3,500kg	£35.75

SHIPPING AND PORTS

Sea transport, both of passengers and freight, is important in Scotland, particularly between the many islands in the north and west and between the islands and the mainland. Major ferry operators include Stena Line (which runs a service between Stranraer and Belfast), P. & O. Scottish Ferries (serving Orkney and Shetland), and Caledonian MacBrayne (serving the Western Isles). P. & O. Scottish Ferries are also UK agents for Smyril, running services from Lerwick to Norway, Denmark, the Faröe Islands and Iceland. Shetland Islands Council operates an inter-island service in Shetland; inter-island services in Orkney are run by Orkney Ferries Ltd.

FERRY SERVICES

Passenger ferry services within Scotland include the following:

From	To
Aberdeen (P&O)	Lerwick (Shetland)
Aberdeen (P&O)	Stromness
Ardrossan (CM)	Brodick (Arran)
Claonaig (Kintyre) (CM)	Lochranza (Arran)*
Colintraive (Argyll) (CM)	Rhubodach (Bute)
Colonsay (CM)	Port Askaig (Islay)*
Fionnphort (Mull) (CM)	Iona
Gourock (CM)	Dunoon (Cowal)
Gourock (CM)	Kilcreggan, Helensburgh
Kennacraig (CM)	Port Ellen (Islay), Port Askaig
Largs (CM)	Cumbrae Slip (Cumbrae)
Lochaline (Lochaber) (CM)	Fishnish (Mull)
Mallaig (CM)	Armadale (Skye)*
Mallaig (CM)	Castlebay
Mallaig (CM)	Lochboisdale (S. Uist)
Mallaig small isles service (CM)	Eigg, Muck, Rum, Canna
Oban (CM)	Castlebay (Barra)
Oban (CM)	Colonsay
Oban (CM)	Craignure (Mull)
Oban (CM)	Lismore
Oban (CM)	Tobermory (Mull), Coll, Tiree
Otternish (N. Uist) (CM)	Leverburgh (Harris)
Sconser (Skye) (CM)	Raasay
Scrabster (P&O)	Stromness (Orkney)
Tarbert (Kintyre) (CM)	Portavadie (Cowal)*
Tayinloan (P&O)	Gigha
Tobermory (CM)	Kilchoan
Uig (Skye) (CM)	Tarbert (Harris)
Uig (CM)	Lochmaddy (N. Uist)
Ullapool (CM)	Stornoway (Lewis)
Wemyss Bay (CM)	Rothesay (Bute)

* *Summer only*
CM *Caledonian MacBrayne service*
P&O *P. & O. Scottish Ferries service*

Caledonian MacBrayne

Tel: 01475-650100 (general enquiries); 08705-650000 (car ferry reservations) Fax: 01475-637607

Hebridean Cruises

Services to Rum, Eigg, Muck and Canna
(Tel: 01687-450224; Fax: 01687-450224)

Orkney Ferries Ltd

Tel: 01856-872044/811397

P. & O. Scottish Ferries

Offices, PO Box 5, Jemieson Quay, Aberdeen, AB11 5NP (Tel: 01224-589 111 Fax: 01224-74 411; E-mail: passenger@poscotlandferries.co.uk Web: www.posf.co.uk)

Seacat

Tel: 0990-523523

Stena Line

Tel: 0990-707070 (passengers); 0845-0704000 (freight)

Viking Sea Taxis

Services to several small Shetland islands
Tel: 01595-692463/859431

PORTS

There are 57 ports of significant size in Scotland. Ports are owned and operated by private companies (including shipping lines), local authorities or trusts. The telephone number given for each port is the number of the port rather than of the port authority; wherever possible, a 24-hour number has been given.

RUN BY THE LOCAL AUTHORITY

Buckie Harbour	01542-831700
Burghead	01343-830371
Campbeltown	01586-552552
Cockenzie Harbour	01620-827282
Dunbar	01620-827282
Dunoon Pier	01369-702652
Flotta	01856-884000
Gairloch	01445-712140
Gigha	01546-602233
Girvan	01292-612302
Kinlochbervie	01971-521235
Kirkwall	01856-873636
Kyle of Lochalsh	01599-534167
Lochinver Harbour	01571-844247
Macduff	01261-832236
Oban (North Pier)	01631-568892
Perth	01738-624056
Rothesay	01700-503842
Scalloway	01806-242551
Stromness	01856-873636
Sullom Voe	01806-242551
Uig	01470-542381

RUN BY TRUSTS

Aberdeen	01224-597000
Fraserburgh	01346-515858
Invergordon	01349-852308
Inverness	01463-715715
Lerwick	01595-692991
Mallaig	01687-462154
Montrose	01674-672302
Peterhead	01779-474281
Scrabster	01847-892779
Stornoway	01851-702688
Tarbert (East Loch Tarbert)	01880-820344
Ullapool	01854-612091
Wick	01955-602030

RUN BY CALEDONIAN MACBRAYNE LTD

(Tel: 01475-650100):

Brodick	01770-302166
Gourock	01475-650100
Kennacraig	01880-730253
Largs	01475-674134
Lochboisdale	01878-700288
Oban (Ferry Terminal)	01631-562285
Port Ellen	01496-302047

RUN BY CLYDEPORT PLC
(Tel: 0141-221 8733)

Ardrossan	0141-221 8733
Glasgow	0141-221 8733
Greenock	0141-221 8733
Hunterston	0141-221 8733

RUN BY FORTH PORTS PLC
(Tel: 0131-554 6473)

Braefoot Bay	0131-555 8750
Burntisland	01592-873708
Dundee	01382-224121
Grangemouth	01324-777432
Granton	0131-554 4343
Leith	0131-554 4343
Methil	01333-426725

RUN BY OTHER OPERATORS

Ardrishaig (British Waterways)	01546-603210
Cairnryan (P.& O. European Ferries)	01581-200663
Stranraer (Stena Line)	01776-802121

MARINE SAFETY

By 1 October 2002 all roll-on, roll-off ferries operating to and from the UK will be required to meet the new international safety standards on stability established by the Stockholm Agreement.

The Maritime and Coastguard Agency was established in 1998 by the merger of the Coastguard Agency and the Marine Safety Agency, and is an executive agency of the Department of Transport, Local Government and the Regions. Its aims are to develop, promote and enforce high standards of marine safety, to minimise loss of life amongst seafarers and coastal users, and to minimise pollution of the sea and coastline from ships.

HM Coastguard in Scotland is divided into two search and rescue regions, one covering the north and east of Scotland and the other covering the west of Scotland and Northern Ireland.

Locations hazardous to shipping in coastal waters are marked by lighthouses and other lights and buoys. The lighthouse authority for Scotland (and the Isle of Man) is the Northern Lighthouse Board. The Board maintains 83 lighthouses, 117 minor lights and many buoys. No Scottish lighthouses are now manned; the last to convert to automated operation was Fair Isle in 1998.

Harbour authorities are responsible for pilotage within their harbour areas; and the Ports Act 1991 provides for the transfer of lights and buoys to harbour authorities where these are used for mainly local navigation.

LEGAL SCOTLAND

**INTRODUCTION TO THE SCOTTISH LEGAL SYSTEM
COURTS, JUDGES AND MAGISTRATES
LEGAL NOTES**

LEGAL SCOTLAND

THE SCOTTISH JUDICATURE

Scotland has a legal system separate from and differing greatly from the English legal system in enacted law, judicial procedure and the structure of courts.

The system of public prosecution is headed by the Lord Advocate and is independent of the police, who have no say in the decision to prosecute. The Lord Advocate, discharging his functions through the Crown Office in Edinburgh, is responsible for prosecutions in the High Court, sheriff courts and district courts. Prosecutions in the High Court are prepared by the Crown Office and conducted in court by one of the law officers, by an advocate-depute, or by a solicitor advocate. In the inferior courts the decision to prosecute is made and prosecution is preferred by procurators fiscal, who are lawyers and full-time civil servants subject to the directions of the Crown Office. A permanent, legally qualified civil servant known as the Crown Agent is responsible for the running of the Crown Office and the organisation of the Procurator Fiscal Service, of which he is the head.

Scotland is divided into six sheriffdoms, each with a full-time sheriff principal. The sheriffdoms are further divided into sheriff court districts, each of which has a legally qualified resident sheriff or sheriffs, who are the judges of the court.

CRIMINAL COURTS

In criminal cases sheriffs principal and sheriffs have the same powers; sitting with a jury of 15 members, they may try more serious cases on indictment, or, sitting alone, may try lesser cases under summary procedure. Minor summary offences are dealt with in district courts, which are administered by the local government authorities of the districts and the islands and presided over by lay justices of the peace (of whom there are about 4,000) and, in Glasgow only, by stipendiary magistrates. Juvenile offenders (children under 16) may be brought before an informal children's hearing comprising three local lay people.

The superior criminal court is the High Court of Justiciary, which is both a trial and an appeal court. Cases on indictment are tried by a High Court judge, sitting with a jury of 15, in Edinburgh and on circuit in other towns. Appeals from the lower courts against conviction or sentence are heard also by the High Court, which sits as an appeal court only in Edinburgh. There is no further appeal to the House of Lords in criminal cases.

CIVIL COURTS

In civil cases the jurisdiction of the sheriff court extends to most kinds of action. Appeals against decisions of the sheriff may be made to the sheriff principal and thence to the Court of Session, or direct to the Court of Session, which sits only in Edinburgh. The Court of Session is divided into the Inner and the Outer House. The Outer House is a court of first instance in which cases are heard by judges sitting singly, sometimes with a jury of 12. The Inner House, itself subdivided into two divisions of equal status, is mainly an appeal court. Appeals may be made to the Inner House from the Outer House as well as from the sheriff court. An appeal may be made from the Inner House to the House of Lords.

COURT OF SESSION JUDGES

The judges of the Court of Session are the same as those of the High Court of Justiciary, the Lord President of the Court of Session also holding the office of Lord Justice-General in the High Court. Senators of the College of Justice are Lords Commissioners of Justiciary as well as judges of the Court of Session. On appointment, a Senator takes a judicial title, which is retained for life. Although styled 'The Hon./Rt. Hon. Lord —', the Senator is not a peer.

SUDDEN DEATHS

The office of coroner does not exist in Scotland. The local procurator fiscal inquires privately into sudden or suspicious deaths and may report findings to the Crown Agent. In some cases a fatal accident inquiry may be held before the sheriff.

COURT OF SESSION AND HIGH COURT OF JUSTICIARY
The Lord President and Lord Justice-General
The Rt. Hon. the Lord Rodger of Earlsferry, *born* 1944, *apptd* 1996
Secretary: A. Maxwell

LORDS OF SESSION

FIRST DIVISION

The Lord President Rt. Hon. Lord Prosser (William Prosser), *born* 1934, *apptd* 1986
Rt. Hon. The Lord Cameron of Lochbroom (Cameron of Lochbroom), *born* 1931, *apptd* 1989
Hon. Lord Marnoch (Michael Bruce), *born* 1938 *apptd* 1990
Hon. Lord Penrose (George Penrose), *born* 1938, *apptd* 1990

SECOND DIVISION

Lord Justice Clerk, The Rt. Hon. Lord Cullen (William Cullen), *born* 1935, *apptd* 1997

LORDS OF SESSION

Hon. Lord Abernethy (Alistair Cameron), *born* 1938, *apptd* 1992
Hon. Lord Johnston (Alan Johnston), *born* 1942, *apptd* 1994
Hon. Lord Gill (Brian Gill), *born* 1942, *apptd* 1994
Hon. Lord Hamilton (Arthur Hamilton), *born* 1942, *apptd* 1995
Hon. Lord Dawson (Thomas Dawson), *born* 1948, *apptd* 1995
Hon. Lord Macfadyen (Donald Macfadyen), *born* 1945, *apptd* 1995
Hon. Lady Cosgrove (Hazel Aronson), *born* 1946, *apptd* 1996
Hon. Lord Nimmo Smith (William Nimmo Smith), *born* 1942, *apptd* 1996
Hon. Lord Philip (Alexander Philip), *born* 1942, *apptd* 1996
Hon. Lord Kingarth (Derek Emslie), *born* 1949, *apptd* 1997
Hon. Lord Bonomy (Iain Bonomy), *born* 1946, *apptd* 1997
Hon. Lord Eassie (Ronald Mackay), *born* 1945, *apptd* 1997
Hon. Lord Reed (Robert Reed), *born* 1956, *apptd* 1998
Hon. Lord Wheatley (John Wheatley), *born* 1941, *apptd* 1999
Hon. Lady Paton (Ann Paton), *apptd* 2000
Hon. Lord Carloway (Colin Sutherland), *born* 1954, *apptd* 2000
Hon. Lord Clarke (Matthew Clarke), *apptd* 2000

Rt. Hon. Lord Hardie (Andrew Hardie), *born* 1946, *apptd* 2000
Rt. Hon. Lord Mackay of Drumadoon (Donald Mackay), *born* 1946, *apptd* 2000
Hon. Lord McEwan (Robin McEwan), *born* 1943, *apptd* 2000

COURT OF SESSION AND HIGH COURT OF JUSTICIARY

Parliament House, Parliament Square, Edinburgh EH1 1RQ Tel: 0131-225 2595

Principal Clerk of Session and Justiciary (£33,391–£55,711): J. L. Anderson
Deputy Principal Clerk of Justiciary (£29,277–£45,365): vacant
Acting Deputy Principal Clerk of Justiciary: T. Higgins
Keeper of the Rolls, Deputy Principal Clerk of Session and Principal Extractor (£29,277–£45,365): D. Shand
Head of Administration (£23,500–£30,262): vacant
Depute Clerks of Session and Justiciary (£22,348–£29,380): M. Weir; N. J. Dowie; I. F. Smith; B. Watson; T. B. Cruickshank; Q. A. Oliver; F. Shannly; A. Finlayson; J. McLean; A. S. Moffat; G. G. Ellis; W. Dunn; C. C. Armstrong; R. M. Sinclair; D. W. Cullen; I. D. Martin; N. McGinley; J. Lynn; Mrs E. Dickson; K. O. Carter; Miss F. Petrie; Mrs P. McFarlane; R. MacPherson; G. Combe; D. Fraser; A. Johnston

SCOTTISH COURT SERVICE

Hayweight House, 23 Lauriston Street, Edinburgh EH3 9DQ Tel: 0131-229 9200

The Scottish Court Service is an executive agency within the Scottish Executive Justice Department. It is responsible to the Scottish Ministers for the provision of staff, court houses and associated services for the Supreme and Sheriff Courts.
Chief Executive: John Ewing

SHERIFF COURT OF CHANCERY

27 Chambers Street, Edinburgh EH1 1LB Tel: 0131-225 2525

The Court deals with service of heirs and completion of title in relation to heritable property.
Sheriff of Chancery: C. G. B. Nicholson, QC

HM COMMISSARY OFFICE

27 Chambers Street, Edinburgh EH1 1LB
Tel: 0131-225 2525

The Office is responsible for issuing confirmation, a legal document entitling a person to execute a deceased person's will, and other related matters.
Commissary Clerk: G. McIlwain

SCOTTISH LAND COURT

1 Grosvenor Crescent, Edinburgh EH12 5ER
Tel: 0131-225 3595; Fax: 0131-226 4812

The court deals with disputes relating to agricultural and crofting land in Scotland.
Chairman: The Hon. Lord McGhie (James McGhie), QC
Members: D. J. Houston; D. M. Macdonald; J. Kinloch (part-time)
Principal Clerk: K. H. R. Graham, WS

SHERIFFDOMS

GRAMPIAN, HIGHLAND AND ISLANDS

Sheriff Court House, Castle Street, Aberdeen AB10 1WP Tel: 01224-657200
Sheriff Principal: D. J. Risk, QC
Area Director North: J. R. Robertson

SHERIFFS AND SHERIFF CLERKS

Aberdeen and Stonehaven: D. Kelbie; A. Pollock; Mrs A. M. Cowan; C. J. Harris, QC; I. H. L. Miller; *G. K. Buchanan; *D. J. Cusine; *Sheriff Clerks:* Mrs E. Laing (*Aberdeen*); A. Hempseed (*Stonehaven*)
Peterhead and Banff: K. A. McLernan; *Sheriff Clerk:* B.J McBride (*Peterhead*); *Sheriff Clerk Depute:* David Altman (*Banff*)
Elgin: N. McPartlin; *Sheriff Clerk:* W. Cochrane
Inverness, Lochmaddy, Portree, Stornoway, Dingwall, Tain, Wick and Dornoch: W. J. Fulton; D. Booker-Milburn; J. O. A. Fraser; I. A. Cameron; *Sheriff Clerks:* Mrs A. Bayliss (*Inverness*); M. McBey (*Dingwall*); *Sheriff Clerks Depute:* Miss M. Campbell (*Lochmaddy and Portree*); Miss S. B. Armstrong (*Stornoway*); Iain Dunbar (*Tain*); Mrs J. McEwan (*Wick*); Len MacLachlan (*Dornoch*)
Kirkwall and Lerwick: C. S. Mackenzie; *Sheriff Clerks Depute:* Miss A. Moore (*Kirkwall*); M. Flanagan (*Lerwick*)

Fort William: C. G. McKay (also *Oban*); *Sheriff Clerk Depute:* Stephen McKenna

TAYSIDE, CENTRAL AND FIFE

Sheriff Court House, Tay Street, Perth PH2 8NL
Tel: 01738-620546
Sheriff Principal, R. Alastair Dunlop, QC
Area Director East: M. Bonar

SHERIFFS AND SHERIFF CLERKS

Arbroath: C. N. R. Stein; *Sheriff Clerk:* M. Herbertson
Dundee: R. A. Davidson; A. L. Stewart, QC; J. P. Scott; I. D. Dunbar; *Sheriff Clerk:* D. Nicoll
Perth: M. J. Fletcher; ; D. W. Pyle (floating); *Sheriff Clerk:* J. Murphy
Falkirk: A. V. Sheehan; A. J. Murphy; *C. Caldwell; *Sheriff Clerk:* R. McMillan
Forfar: K. A. Veal; *Sheriff Clerk:* S, Munro
Stirling: R. E. G. Younger; A. W. Robertson; *Sheriff Clerk:* Mrs G. McKeand
Alloa: W. M. Reid; *Sheriff Clerk:* Mrs G. McKeand
Cupar: G. J. Evans; *Sheriff Clerk:* A. Nicol
Dunfermline: J. S. Forbes; *Sheriff Clerk:* W. McCulloch
Kirkcaldy: F. J. Keane; Mrs L. G. Patrick; B. G. Donald; *Sheriff Clerk:* W. Jones

LOTHIAN AND BORDERS

Sheriff Court House, 27 Chambers Street, Edinburgh EH1 1LB
Tel: 0131-225 2525
Sheriff Principal: C. G. B. Nicholson, QC
Area Director East: M.G. Bonar

SHERIFFS AND SHERIFF CLERKS

Edinburgh: R. G. Craik, QC (*also Peebles*); R. J. D. Scott (*also Peebles*); Miss I. A. Poole; A. M. Bell; J. M. S. Horsburgh, QC; J. A. Farrell; *A. Lothian; I. D. Macphail, QC; C. N. Stoddart; N. M. P. Morrison, QC; *Miss M. M. Stephen; Mrs M. L. E. Jarvie, QC; N. J. Mackinnon (floater); Mrs K. E. C. Mackie (floater); *Sheriff Clerk:* J. M. Ross
Peebles: R. G. Craik, QC (*also Edinburgh*); R. J. D. Scott (*also Edinburgh*); *Sheriff Clerk Depute:* M. L. Kubeczka
Linlithgow: H. R. MacLean; G. R. Fleming, QC; P. Gillam (floater); *Sheriff Clerk:* R. D. Sinclair
Haddington: G. W. S. Presslie (*also Edinburgh*); *Sheriff Clerk:* J. O'Donnell
Jedburgh and Duns: T. A. K. Drummond, QC; *Sheriff Clerk:* I. W. Williamson

Selkirk: T. A. K. Drummond, QC; *Sheriff Clerk Depute*: L. McFarlane

NORTH STRATHCLYDE

Sheriff Court House, St James's Street, Paisley PA3 2HW Tel: 0141-887 5291
Sheriff Principal: B. A. Kerr, QC
Area Director West: I. Scott

SHERIFFS AND SHERIFF CLERKS

Oban: C. G. McKay (*also Fort William*); *Sheriff Clerk Depute*: J. G. Whitelaw
Dumbarton: J. T. Fitzsimons; T. Scott; S. W. H. Fraser; *Sheriff Clerk*: S. Bain
Paisley: J. Spy; C. K. Higgins; N. Douglas; D. J. Pender; *W. Dunlop (*also Campbeltown*); G. C. Kavanagh; *I. McDonald; *Sheriff Clerk*: Miss S. Hindes
Greenock: J. Herald (*also Rothesay*); Sir Stephen Young; *R. Swanney; *Sheriff Clerk*: J. Tannahill
Kilmarnock: T. M. Croan; D. B. Smith; T. F. Russell; *Sheriff Clerk*: G. Waddell
Dunoon, Mrs C. M. A. F. Gimblett; *Sheriff Clerk Depute*: Mrs C. Carson
Campbeltown: *W. Dunlop (*also Paisley*); *Sheriff Clerk Depute*: vacant
Rothesay: J. Herald (*also Greenock*); *Sheriff Clerk Depute*: Mrs C. K. McCormick

GLASGOW AND STRATHKELVIN

Sheriff Court House, PO Box 23, 1 Carlton Place, Glasgow G5 9DA Tel: 0141-429 8888
Sheriff Principal: E. F. Bowen, QC
Area Director West: I. Scott

SHERIFFS AND SHERIFF CLERKS

Glasgow: B. Kearney; B. A. Lockhart; Mrs A. L. A. Duncan; A. C. Henry; J. K. Mitchell; A. G. Johnston; Miss S. A. O. Raeburn, QC; D. Convery; I. A. S. Peebles, QC; C. W. McFarlane, QC; K. M. Maciver; H. Matthews, QC; J. A. Baird; Miss R. E. A. Rae, QC; Mrs P. M. M. Bowman; A. W. Noble; *J. D. Friel; *Mrs D. M. MacNeill, QC; J. A. Taylor; C. A. L. Scott; W. J. Totten; S. Cathcart; Miss L. M. Ruxton; *Sheriff Clerk*: R. Cockburn

SOUTH STRATHCLYDE, DUMFRIES AND GALLOWAY

Sheriff Court House, Graham Street, Airdrie ML6 6EE Tel: 01236-751121
Sheriff Principal: J. C. McInnes, QC
Area Director West: I. Scott

SHERIFFS AND SHERIFF CLERKS

Hamilton: L. Cameron; D. C. Russell; V. J. Canavan; W. E. Gibson; J. H. Stewart; H. S. Neilson; S. C. Pender; *Miss J. Pawrie; *T. Welsh; *A. Vannet; *Sheriff Clerk*: P. Feeney
Lanark: N. C Stewart; *Sheriff Clerk*: Mrs M. McLean
Ayr: N. Gow, QC; C. B. Miller, QC; *C. B. Miller; *Sheriff Clerk*: Miss C. D. Cockburn
Stranraer and Kirkcudbright: J. R. Smith (*also Dumfries*); *Sheriff Clerks*: W. McIntosh (*Stranraer*); B. Lindsay (*Kirkcudbright*)
Dumfries: K. G. Barr; K. Ross
Airdrie: R. H. Dickson; I. C. Simpson; J. C. Morris, QC; *Sheriff Clerk*: D. Forrester

STIPENDIARY MAGISTRATES

GLASGOW

R. Hamilton, *apptd* 1984; J. B. C. Nisbet, *apptd* 1984; R. B. Christie, *apptd* 1985; Mrs J. A. M. MacLean, *apptd* 1990

CROWN OFFICE AND PROCURATOR FISCAL SERVICE

CROWN OFFICE

25 Chambers Street, Edinburgh EH1 1LA
Tel 0131-226 2626
Crown Agent: A. C. Normand
Deputy Crown Agent: F. R. Crowe

PROCURATORS FISCAL

GRAMPIAN, HIGHLANDS AND ISLANDS REGION

Regional Procurator Fiscal: Mrs E. Angiolini (*Aberdeen*)
Procurators Fiscal: E. K. Barbour (*Stonehaven*); A. J. M. Colley (*Banff*); A.B. Hutchinson (*Peterhead*); D. J. Dickson (*Elgin*); J. Bamber (*Portree, Lochmaddy*); D. S. Teale (*Stornoway*); G. Napier (*Inverness*); R. W. Urquhart (*Kirkwall, Lerwick*); vacant (*Fort William*); A. N. MacDonald (*Dingwall, Tain*); G. Aitkin (*Wick*)

TAYSIDE, CENTRAL AND FIFE REGION

Regional Procurator Fiscal: B. K. Heywood (*Dundee*)

Procurators Fiscal: J. I. Craigen (*Forfar*); I. A. McLeod (*Perth*); W. J. Gallacher (*Falkirk*); C. Ritchie (*Stirling and Alloa*); E. B. Russell (*Cupar*); R. G. Stott (*Dunfermline*); Miss H. M. Clark (*Kirkcaldy*)

LOTHIAN AND BORDERS REGION

Regional Procurator Fiscal: N. McFadyen (*Edinburgh*)
Procurators Fiscal: Mrs C. P. Dyer (*Linlithgow*); A. J. P. Reith (*Haddington*); A. R. G. Fraser (*Duns, Jedburgh*); Mrs L. Thomson (*Selkirk*)

NORTH STRATHCLYDE REGION

Regional Procurator Fiscal: W. A. Gilchrist (*Paisley*)
Procurators Fiscal: F. Redman (*Campbeltown*); C. C. Donnelly (*Dumbarton*); W. S. Carnegie (*Greenock*); D. L. Webster (*Dunoon*); J. Watt (*Kilmarnock*); B. R. Maguire (*Oban*)

GLASGOW AND STRATHKELVIN REGION

Regional Procurator Fiscal: L. A. Higson (*Glasgow*)

SOUTH STRATHCLYDE, DUMFRIES AND GALLOWAY REGION

Regional Procurator Fiscal: D. A. Brown (*Hamilton*)
Procurators Fiscal: S. R. Houston (*Lanark*); J. T. O'Donnell (*Ayr*); A. S. Kennedy (*Stranraer*); D. J. Howdle (*Dumfries*); A. S. Kennedy (*Stranraer, Kirkcudbright*); D. Spiers (*Airdrie*)

LEGAL NOTES

These notes outline certain aspects of the law in Scotland as they might affect the average person. They focus principally on those aspects of Scots law which differ from the equivalent law in England and Wales. They are intended only as a broad guideline and are by no means definitive. The information is believed to be correct at the time of going to press, but the law is constantly changing, so expert advice should always be taken. In some cases, sources of further information are given in these notes.

Timely consultation with a solicitor is always advisable. Anyone in Scotland who does not have a solicitor can contact the Citizens' Advice Bureau (addresses in the telephone directory or at any post office or town hall) or the Law Society of Scotland (26 Drumsheugh Gardens, Edinburgh EH3 7YR) for assistance in finding one.

The legal aid and legal advice and assistance schemes exist to make the help of a lawyer available to those who would not otherwise be able to afford one. Entitlement depends upon an individual's means but a solicitor or Citizens' Advice Bureau will be able to advise about this.

ADOPTION OF CHILDREN

The adoption of children is mainly governed by the Adoption (Scotland) Act 1978 (as amended by the Children (Scotland) Act 1995).

Anyone over 21 who is domiciled in the United Kingdom, the Channel Islands or the Isle of Man or has been habitually resident in any of those places throughout the year immediately preceding the date of an application, whether married, single, widowed or divorced, can apply to adopt a child.

The only organisations allowed to arrange adoptions are the adoption agencies provided by local authorities (these agencies are known collectively as the Scottish Adoption Service) or voluntary agencies approved as adoption societies.

Once an adoption has been arranged, a court order is necessary to make it legal. Petitions for adoption are made to the Sheriff Court or the Court of Session.

Each of the child's natural parents (or guardians) must consent to the adoption, unless the court dispenses with the consent or the natural parent does not have parental responsibilities or parental rights. Once adopted, the child, for all practical purposes, has the same legal status as a child born to the adoptive parents and the natural parents cease to have any rights or responsibilities where the child is concerned. As a general rule, the adopted child ceases to have any rights to the estates of his/her natural parents.

Registration and Certificates
All adoptions in Scotland are registered by the General Register Office for Scotland. Certificates from the registers can be obtained in a similar way to birth certificates.

Further information on qualification to adopt a child, adoption procedures, and tracing natural parents or children who have been adopted can be obtained from:

British Agencies for Adoption and Fostering (BAAF)
Scottish Centre, 40 Shandwick Place, Edinburgh EH2 4RT
Tel: 0131-225 9285

Scottish Adoption Advice Service
16 Sandyford Place, Glasgow G3 7NB
Tel: 0141-339 0772

BIRTHS (REGISTRATION)

The birth of a child must be registered within 21 days at the registration office of either the district in which the baby was born or the district in which the mother was resident at the time of the birth.

If the child is born, either in or out of Scotland, on a ship, aircraft or land vehicle that ends its journey at any place in Scotland, the child, in most cases, will be registered as if born in that place.

Responsibility for registering the birth rests with the parents, except where the father of the child is not married to the mother and has not been married to her since the child's conception, in which case the mother is responsible for registration. Responsibility rests firstly with the parents, but if they fail particulars may be given to the registrar by:
– a relative of the mother or father (if he is married to the mother)
– the occupier of the house in which the baby was born
– a person present at the birth
– a person having charge of the child
Failure to register the birth within 21 days without reasonable cause may lead to a court decree being granted by a sheriff.

Further information is available from local registrars, whose addresses and telephone numbers can be found in local telephone directories.

CERTIFICATES OF BIRTHS, DEATHS OR MARRIAGES

Certificates of births, deaths or marriages that have taken place in Scotland since 1855 can be obtained from the General Register Office for Scotland or from the appropriate local registrar. The General Register Office for Scotland also keeps the Register of Divorces (including decrees of declaration of nullity of marriage), and holds parish registers dating from before 1855.

Fees for certificates (are:

Certificates (full or abbreviated) of birth, death, marriage or adoption, £8.00

Email application in course of Internet search, £10.00

General search in the indexes to the statutory registers and parochial registers, per day or part thereof:

Full day search (9 a.m. to 4.30 p.m.) £17.00
Afternoon (1 p.m. to 4.30 p.m.) search £10.00
Full day (9 a.m. to 4.30 p.m.) search with payment being made not less than 14 days in advance, £13.00 (only available for the period November 2001 to January 2002)
One week search, £65.00
Four week search, £220.00
One quarter search, £500.00
One year search, £1,500.00

Further information can be obtained from:
The General Register Office for Scotland
New Register House, Edinburgh EH1 3YT
Tel: 0131-334 0380; Fax: 0131-314 4400
Certificate Ordering line: 0131 314 4411

CONSUMER LAW

UK legislation governing the sale and supply of goods applies to Scotland as follows:
– the Sale of Goods Act 1979 applies with some modifications and has been amended by the Sale and Supply of Goods Act 1994
– the Supply of Goods (Implied Terms) Act 1973 applies
– the Supply of Goods and Services Act 1982 does not extend to Scotland but some of its provisions were introduced by the Sale and Supply of Goods Act 1994
– only Parts II and III of the Unfair Contract Terms Act 1977 apply
– the Trade Descriptions Act 1968 applies with minor modifications
– the Consumer Credit Act 1974 applies

DEATHS

If the death was expected, the doctor who attended the deceased during their final illness should be contacted. If the death was sudden or unexpected, the family doctor (if known) and police should be contacted immediately.

If the cause of death is quite clear the doctor will either:

– issue a certificate of cause of death needed by the registrar, provided that there are no unusual circumstances. If the body is to be cremated, the doctor will arrange for the signature of the second doctor needed to complete the cremation certificate; or

– if the doctor is uncertain as to the cause of death he will report the death to the local procurator fiscal who will make enquiries.

A fatal accident inquiry will be held before a sheriff where the death has resulted from an accident during the course of the employment of the person who has died, or where the person who has died was in legal custody, or where the Lord Advocate deems it in the public interest that an inquiry be held.

A death may be registered in any registration district in which the deceased was ordinarily resident immediately before his/her death or, if different, in the registration district in which the death took place. The death must normally be registered within eight days. If the death has been referred to the local procurator fiscal it cannot be registered until the registrar has received authority from the procurator fiscal to do so. Failure to register a death may lead to a court decree being granted by a sheriff.

Whereas in most circumstances in England and Wales a certificate for burial or cremation must be obtained from the registrar before the burial or cremation can take place, in Scotland a body may be buried (but normally not cremated) before the death is registered.

Further information can be obtained from the General Register Office for Scotland (*see* above for contact details).

DIVORCE AND RELATED MATTERS

There are two main types of matrimonial action: those seeking the annulment of a marriage, and those seeking a judicial separation or divorce.

An action for 'declarator of nullity' can be brought only in the Court of Session.

An action for judicial separation or divorce may be raised in the Court of Session. It may also be raised in the Sheriff Court if either party was resident in the sheriffdom for 40 days immediately before the date of the action or for 40 days ending not more than 40 days before the date of the action. The fee for starting a divorce petition in the Sheriff Court is £74.

Nullity of Marriage

A marriage is void (i.e. invalid) from the beginning if:

– the parties were within the prohibited degrees of consanguinity, affinity or adoption

– the parties were not male and female

– either of the parties was already married

– either of the parties was under the age of 16

– either of the parties did not truly consent to marry, e.g. in consequence of mental illness, intoxication, force or fear, or in a sham marriage where the intention was to avoid deportation

– the formalities of the marriage were defective, e.g. each of the parties did not submit a notice of intention to marry (a marriage notice) to the district registrar for the registration district in which the marriage was to be solemnized

A marriage may be voidable (i.e. a decree of nullity may be obtained but in the meantime the marriage remains valid) if either party was unable to consummate the marriage.

Where a spouse is capable of sexual intercourse but refuses to consummate the marriage, this is not a ground of nullity in Scots law, though it could be a ground for divorce.

When a marriage is void, it generally has no legal effect at all, and there is therefore no specific need to seek a declarator of nullity in the Court of Session (although it may be wise to do so, e.g. if one of the parties wishes to marry again). Nevertheless, a child conceived during a valid marriage is presumed to be the child of the 'husband'. A child's mother has parental responsibilities and parental rights in relation to the child whether or not she is or has been married to his father. A child's father has such responsibilities and rights in relation to the child only if married to the mother at the time of the child's conception or subsequently. A father is regarded as having been married to the mother at any time when he was a party to a purported marriage with her which was:

– voidable; or

– void but believed by them in good faith at that time to be valid.

When a marriage has been annulled, both parties are free to marry again.

Divorce

Divorce dissolves the marriage and leaves both parties at liberty to marry again. The sole ground for divorce is the irretrievable breakdown of the marriage; this must be proved on one or more of the following grounds:

- the defender has committed adultery; however the pursuer cannot rely on an act of adultery by the other party if, after discovery of the act of adultery, he or she has continued or resumed living together with the defender at any time after the end of a period of three months on which cohabitation has been continued or resumed
- the defender has behaved in such a way that the pursuer cannot reasonably be expected to continue living with him/her
- desertion, which is established by the defender having left the pursuer for a period of two years immediately preceding the action. Irretrievable breakdown is not established if, after the two year desertion period has expired, the parties resume living together at any time after the end of three months from the date when they first resume living together
- the defender and the pursuer have lived separately for two years immediately before the raising of the action and the defender consents to the decree
- the defender and the pursuer have lived separately for five years immediately before the raising of the action

Where a divorce action has been raised, it may be sisted or put on hold for a variety of reasons, including, though rarely, enabling the parties to seek to effect a reconciliation if the court feels that there may be a reasonable prospect of such reconciliation. If the parties do cohabit during such postponement, no account is taken of the cohabitation if the action later proceeds.

A simplified procedure for 'do-it-yourself' divorce was introduced in 1983 for certain divorces. If the action is based on two or five years' separation and will not be opposed, and if there are no children under 16, no financial claims and there is no sign that the applicant's spouse is unable to manage his or her affairs because of mental illness or handicap, the applicant can write directly to the local sheriff court or to the Court of Session for the appropriate forms to enable him or her to proceed. The fee is £57, unless the applicant receives income support, family credit or legal advice and assistance, in which case there is no fee.

The extract decree will be made available fourteen days after the divorce has been granted. The extract decree dissolves or annuls the marriage.

Further information can be obtained from any sheriff court, solicitor, Citizens' Advice Bureau, the Lord Advocate's Office, or the following:

The Court of Session

Parliament House, Parliament Square, Edinburgh EH1 1RQ
Tel: 0131-225 2595

EMPLOYMENT LAW

Pay and Conditions

Responsibility for employment legislation rests with the UK Parliament and the legislation applies to all parts of Great Britain, with the exception of some separate anti-discrimination legislation for Northern Ireland.

The Employment Rights Act 1996 consolidates the statutory provisions relating to employees' rights. It covers matters such as pay and conditions (including authorized deductions from pay, trade union membership, disputes, and the rights of part-time employees (and termination of employment (including redundancy and unfair dismissal). The Working Time Regulations 1998, National Minimum Wage Act 1998 and Part-time Employees (Prevention of Less Favourable Treatment) Regulations 2000 now supplement the 1996 Act. Procedure at Employment Tribunals is governed by separate Scottish regulations.

A number of laws protect employees from discrimination in employment on the grounds of sex, race or disability:

- The Equal Pay Act 1970 (as amended)
- The Sex Discrimination Act 1975 (as amended by the Sex Discrimination Act 1986)
- The Race Relations Act 1976
- The Disability Discrimination Act 1995

The Equal Opportunities Commission and the Commission for Racial Equality have the function of eliminating such discriminations in the workplace and can provide further information and assistance. The Disability Rights Commission has been in operation since April 2000 and aims to encourage good practice in the treatment of disabled people and can provide information and assistance.

Equal Opportunities Commission

Stock Exchange House, 7 Nelson Mandela Place, Glasgow G2 1QW
Tel: 0141-248 5833; Fax: 0141-248 5834

Commission for Racial Equality

45 Hanover Street, Edinburgh EH2 2PJ
Tel: 0131-226 5186; Fax: 0131-226 5243

Disability Rights Commission

1st Floor, Riverside House, Gorgie Road, Edinburgh EH11 3AF

Tel: 08457 622 633; Fax: 08457 622 688

HUMAN RIGHTS

The Human Rights Act came into force on 2 October 2000. It incorporates into domestic UK law certain rights and freedoms set out in the articles of the European Convention on Human Rights. Rights such as Article 2 (right to life), Article 3 (prohibition of torture, an inhuman or degrading treatment), Article 4 (prohibition of slavery or forced labour), Article 6 (right to fair trial), Article 8 (right to respect for private and family life), Article 9 (freedom of thought, conscience and religion), Article 10 (freedom of expression), Article 11 (the right to freedom of association, including joining a trade union), Article 14 (freedom from discrimination in respect of convention rights).

Both the UK Parliament and the Scottish Parliament are required to Legislate in a way compatible with the convention. Section 3 of the Act provides that so far as is possible to do so, Primary Legislation and Subordinate Legislation must be read and given effect to in a way which is compatible with convention rights. Section 4 provides that certain Courts may make Declarations of Incompatibility, which may then trigger remedial action.

HOUSE PURCHASE

A contract for the sale of a house in Scotland rarely takes the form of a single document. The purchaser's solicitor issues a formal written offer to purchase. This is usually issued once a survey of the property has been carried out, but can more unusually be issued 'subject to survey'. The seller's solicitor will issue a qualified acceptance of the offer. This is then adjusted between the parties' solicitors until a final concluding letter is issued. At this point the contract is formed and both parties are contractually bound. The letters passing between the solicitors are known as 'missives'.

Some conditions contained within the missives may require the seller to provide information so that the purchaser may be satisfied that the property is unaffected by any statutory notices for repairs or by any planning proposals. Property enquiry reports are obtained by the seller's solicitor from either the local authority or private companies who provide this information. These reports disclose whether the property is adversely affected, if it is served by public water and sewage services, and whether the roads adjoining the property are maintained by the local authority.

The purchaser will also examine the title deeds for the property to make sure that there are no flaws in the title to be granted to the purchaser. Searches in the appropriate property register are made. A search is also carried out against both the purchaser and the seller to ensure there is no reason why either party cannot proceed with the transaction.

On the day of settlement the purchaser's solicitor will pass the purchase price to the seller's solicitor who in turn passes over the disposition, title deeds, an obligation to deliver a clear search brought down to disclose the recording of the purchaser's title, and keys. The disposition is the deed which transfers ownership of the property from the seller to the purchaser. This deed has to be registered in the appropriate property register in order for the purchaser to have a right to the property – either the Register of Sasines or the newer Land Register which is being phased in by county to replace the old Register of Sasines.

ILLEGITIMACY AND LEGITIMATION

Under the Legitimation (Scotland) Act 1968, which came into operation on 8 June 1968, an illegitimate person automatically becomes legitimate when his/her parents marry, even where one of the parents was married to a third person at the time of the birth.

Illegitimate and legitimate people are given, for all practical purposes, equal status under the Law Reform (Parent and Child) Scotland Act 1986.

The Children (Scotland) Act 1995 gives the mother parental responsibility for her child when she is not married to the child's father. The father has no automatic parental rights when unmarried to the mother, but can acquire parental responsibility by applying to the court. The father of any child, regardless of parental rights, has a duty to aliment that child until he/she is 18 or has completed full-time education, whichever date is later. The Child Support Agency are entitled to make an assessment if this is not done, and the mother of the child can apply to the Child Support Agency for this to be done.

JURY SERVICE

A person charged with any serious crime is tried before a jury. Jury trials in Scottish civil cases in the Court of Session are becoming more common. In Scotland there are 12 members of a jury in a civil case in the Court of Session (the civil jury trial is confined to the Court of Session and a restricted number of actions) and 15 in a criminal trial. Jurors are expected to sit for the duration of the trial.

Every parliamentary or local government elector between the ages of 18 and 65 who has lived in the UK, the Channel Islands or the Isle of Man for any period of at least five years since reaching the age of 13 is qualified to serve on a jury in Scotland, unless ineligible or disqualified.

Those disqualified from jury service include:

- those who have at any time been sentenced by a court in the UK, the Channel Islands and the Isle of Man to a term of imprisonment or custody of five years or more
- those who have within the previous ten years served any part of a sentence of three months or more of imprisonment or detention

Members of the judiciary are ineligible for ten years after ceasing to hold their post, and others concerned with the administration of justice become eligible again only five years after ceasing to hold office. Members and officers of the Houses of Parliament, the Scottish Parliament and members of the Scottish Executive, full time serving members of the armed forces, registered and practising members of the medical, dental, nursing, veterinary and pharmaceutical professions, ministers of religion, persons in holy orders and those who have served on a jury in the previous five years are excusable as of right.

The maximum fine for a person serving on a jury knowing himself/herself to be ineligible is £1,000. The maximum fine for failing to attend without good cause is also £1,000.

Further information can obtained from:

The Clerk of Justiciary
High Court of Justiciary, Lawnmarket, Edinburgh EH1 2NS; Tel: 0131-225 2595

LANDLORD AND TENANT

When a property is rented to a tenant, the rights and responsibilities of the landlord and the tenant are determined largely by the tenancy agreement but also the general law of Scotland. The main provisions are mentioned below, but it is advisable to contact the Citizens' Advice Bureau or the local authority housing department for detailed information.

Assured and short assured tenancies exist for lettings after 2 January 1989; the relevant legislation is the Housing (Scotland) Act 1988.

If a tenancy was granted on or after 2 January 1989, the tenant may have an assured tenancy giving that tenant greater rights. The tenant could, for example, stay in possession of the dwelling for as long as the tenant observed the terms of the tenancy. The landlord cannot obtain possession from such a tenant unless the landlord can establish a specific ground for possession (the grounds are set out in the 1988 Act) and obtains a court order. The rent payable continues throughout the period of the lease unless the rent has been fixed by the Rent Assessment Committee of the local authority. The Committee also has powers to determine other terms of the lease.

The 1988 Act also introduced short assured tenancies, which are tenancies of not less than six months where a notice has been served to the effect that the tenancy is a short assured tenancy. A landlord in a short assured tenancy has all the rights of a landlord in an ordinary assured tenancy to recover possession and also the right to regain possession on timeously giving notice to quit to the tenant, whether or not the tenant has observed the terms of the tenancy.

Most tenancies created before 2 January 1989 were regulated tenancies and the Rent (Scotland) Act 1984 still applies where these exist. The Act defines, among other things, the circumstances in which a landlord can increase the rent when improvements are made to the property. The provisions of the 1984 Act do not apply to tenancies where the landlord is the Crown, a local authority, the development corporation of a new town or a housing corporation.

The Housing (Scotland) Act 1987 and its provisions relate to local authority responsibilities for housing, the right to buy, and local authority secured tenancies.

Tenancies in agricultural properties are governed by the Agricultural Holdings (Scotland) Act 1991.

Business premises in Scotland are not controlled by statute to the same extent as in England and Wales, although the Shops (Scotland) Act 1949 gives some security to tenants of shops. Tenants of shops can apply to the sheriff for a renewal of tenancy if threatened with eviction. This application may be dismissed on various grounds, including where the landlord has offered to sell the property to the tenant at an agreed price or, in the absence of agreement as to price, at a price fixed by a single arbiter appointed by the parties or the sheriff. The Act extends to properties where the Crown or government departments are the landlords or the tenants.

Under the Leases Act 1449 the landlord's successors (either purchasers or creditors) are bound by the agreement made with any tenants so long as the following conditions are met:

– the lease, if for more than one year, must be in writing
– there must be a rent
– there must be a term of expiry, and
– the tenant must have entered into possession

Many leases contain references to term and quarter days.

LEGAL AID

Under the Legal Aid (Scotland) Act 1986 and subsequent Regulations, people on low or moderate incomes may qualify for help with the costs of legal advice or representation. The scheme is administered by the Scottish Legal Aid Board.

There are three types of legal aid: civil legal aid, legal advice and assistance, and criminal legal aid.

Civil Legal Aid

Applications for legal aid are made through a solicitor; the Citizens' Advice Bureau will have addresses for local solicitors.

Civil legal aid is available for proceedings in the following:
– the House of Lords
– the Court of Session
– the Lands Valuation Appeal Court
– the Scottish Land Court
– sheriff courts
– the Lands Tribunal for Scotland
– the Employment Appeal Tribunals
– the Restrictive Practices Court

Civil legal aid is not available for defamation actions, small claims or simplified divorce procedures.

Eligibility for civil legal aid is assessed and a civil legal aid certificate granted provided that:
– the applicant qualifies financially, and
– the applicant has reasonable grounds for taking or defending the action, and
– it is reasonable to grant legal aid in the circumstances of the case (for example, civil legal aid will not be granted where it appears that the applicant will gain only trivial advantage from the proceedings).

The financial criteria for eligibility are:
– a person is eligible if disposable income is £9,034 or less and disposable capital is £8,560 or less
– if disposable income is between £2,767 and £9,034, contributions are payable
– if disposable capital exceeds £3,000, contributions are payable
– those receiving income support or income related job seeker's allowance will qualify automatically

Emergency legal aid cover may be granted before a full application has been made and a means test has been carried out. In such cases means testing is carried out later and the applicant is required to meet the cost of any aid received which exceeded their entitlement.

A statutory charge is made if a person is awarded money or property in a case for which they have received legal aid.

Legal Advice and Assistance

The legal advice and assistance scheme covers the costs of getting advice and help from a solicitor and, in some cases, representation in court under the 'assistance by way of representation' scheme (*see* below).

A person is eligible:
– if disposable income does not exceed £186 a week. If disposable income is between £79 and £186 a week, contributions are payable
– if disposable capital does not exceed £1,000 (£1,335 if the person has one dependant, £1,535 if two dependants, with an additional £100 for every other dependant). There are no contributions from capital

If a person is eligible, an initial amount of authorized expenditure can be incurred without the prior authority of the Scottish Legal Aid Board. The initial limit is £80 in most cases, but a higher initial limit of £150 applies in some circumstances, for example where a civil matter is only likely to be resolved in court, legal aid will be available to the client and the initial work is reasonable. Any increase in authorized expenditure must first be applied for to and granted by the Scottish Legal Aid Board.

Legal advice and assistance covers giving advice, writing letters, making an application for civil/criminal legal aid and seeking the advice of an advocate. Advice and assistance does not, in general, cover appearance before a court or tribunal other than advice by way of representation.

Assistance by way of representation is available in certain cases such as certain less serious criminal cases, some mental health proceedings and civil proceedings for fine default or breach of a court order.

Criminal Legal Aid

The procedure for application for criminal legal aid depends on the circumstances of each case. In solemn cases (more serious cases, such as homicide) heard before a jury, a person is automatically entitled to criminal legal aid until they are given bail or placed in custody. Thereafter, it is for the court to decide whether to grant legal aid. The court will do this if the person accused cannot meet the expenses of the case without 'undue hardship' on him or his dependants. In summary (less serious) cases the procedure depends on whether the person is in custody:

- anyone taken into custody has the right to free legal aid from the duty solicitor up to and including the first court appearance. Thereafter, if the person has decided to plead guilty, the duty solicitor will continue to act for him/her until the case is finished. If the person pleads not guilty to any charge, they must apply to the Scottish Legal Aid Board so that their solicitor can prepare their defence and represent them at the trial. The duty solicitor may be willing to act for the accused, or they can choose their own solicitor.
- if the person is not in custody and wishes to plead guilty, they are not entitled to criminal legal aid but may be entitled to legal advice and assistance, including assistance by way of representation. The court will not assign the person a solicitor, and they must therefore choose their own if they wish one.
- if the person is not in custody and wishes to plead not guilty, they can apply for criminal legal aid. This must be done within 14 days of the first court appearance at which they made the plea. Again, the person must choose their own solicitor.

The Scottish Legal Aid Board will grant criminal legal aid if satisfied that the applicant or their family would suffer undue hardship if they had to pay for their own defence and that it is in the interests of justice to grant legal aid (the Board will consider, for example, whether there are difficult legal points to be decided, whether the applicant's job or liberty is at risk, and whether the applicant has a realistic defence).

If criminal legal aid is awarded, no contribution from the person will be required.

Further information may be obtained from:

Scottish Legal Aid Board
44 Drumsheugh Gardens, Edinburgh EH3 7SW
Tel: 0131-226 7061; Fax: 0131-220 4878

MARRIAGE

Regular Marriages

A regular marriage is one which is celebrated by a minister of religion or authorised registrar or other celebrant. Each of the parties must complete a marriage notice form and return it to the district registrar for the area in which they are to be married, irrespective of where they live, at least 15 days before the ceremony is due to take place. The district registrar must then enter the date of receipt and certain details in a marriage book kept for this purpose, and must also enter the names of the parties and the proposed date of the marriage in a list which is displayed in a conspicuous place at the registration office. This entry remains displayed until the date of the marriage has passed. All persons wishing to enter into a regular marriage in Scotland must follow the same preliminary procedure regardless of whether they intend to have a civil or a religious ceremony.

A marriage schedule, which is prepared by the registrar, will be issued to one or both of the parties in person up to seven days before a religious marriage; for a civil marriage the schedule will be available at the ceremony. The schedule must be handed to the celebrant before the ceremony starts; it must be signed immediately after the wedding and the marriage must be registered within three days.

Civil (as opposed to religious) marriage ceremonies are normally conducted by the district registrar in his office. However, if one of the parties cannot attend the registrar's office because of serious illness or serious bodily injury, the registrar may, on application by either party, solemnize the marriage anywhere in his registration district if delay of the wedding is undesirable.

In the case of a religious marriage, the authority to conduct a marriage is deemed to be vested in the authorized celebrant (a minister, priest or other such religious person) conducting the ceremony rather than the building in which it takes place; open-air religious ceremonies are therefore permissible in Scotland.

Marriage by Cohabitation with Habit and Repute

If two people live together constantly as husband and wife and are generally held to be such by the neighbourhood and among their friends and relations, there may arise a presumption from which marriage can be inferred. Before such a marriage can be registered, however, a decree of declarator of marriage must be obtained from the Court of Session.

Civil Fees

The basic statutory fee is £79, comprising a £13 per person fee for a statutory notice of intention to marry, a £45 fee for solemnization of the marriage in a registry office, and an £8.00 fee for a copy of the marriage certificate.

Further information can be obtained from the General Register Office for Scotland (*see* p. 164 for contact details).

TOWN AND COUNTRY PLANNING

The principal legislation governing the development of land and buildings is the Town and Country Planning (Scotland) Act 1997. The uses of buildings are classified by the Town and Country Planning (Use Classes) (Scotland) Order 1997. It is advisable in all cases to contact the planning department of the local authority to check whether planning or other permission is needed.

VOTERS' QUALIFICATIONS

All persons registered in the electoral registers (which are compiled on a local basis) and over the age of 18 are entitled to vote in Scottish Parliament, UK Parliament, European Parliament and local government elections. To qualify for registration, a person must be:

- resident in the relevant constituency or ward on 10 October in the year before the electoral register comes into effect
- over 18 years old or will attain the age of 18 during the 12 months following the publication of the annual register on 16 February
- a UK, European Union, Commonwealth or Republic of Ireland citizen

Peers registered in Scotland are entitled to vote in Scottish Parliament, European Parliament and local government elections.

Overseas electors (namely British citizens not resident in the UK on the qualifying date for the electoral register but who were registered as parliamentary electors at some point in the preceding 20 years) are only entitled to vote in UK Parliament and European Parliament elections. Similar provisions apply to enable those who were too young to be registered during the previous 20 years to register provided a parent or guardian was registered.

Peers and European Union citizens are not eligible to vote in UK Parliament elections.

Voters must be entered on an electoral register, which runs from 16 February each year to the following 15 February. Supplementary lists of electors are published throughout the duration of the register.

Further information can be obtained from the local authority's electoral registration officer (details in local telephone directories).

WILLS AND INTESTACY

Wills

In Scotland any person over 12 and of sound mind can make a will. The person making the will can only freely dispose of the heritage and what is known as the 'dead's part' of the estate because:

- the spouse has the right to inherit one-third of the moveable estate if there are children or other descendants, and one-half of it if there are not
- children are entitled to one-third of the moveable estate if there is a surviving spouse, and one-half of it if there is not

The remaining portion is the dead's part, and legacies and bequests are payable from this. Debts are payable out of the whole estate before any division.

From August 1995, wills no longer needed to be 'holographed' and it is now only necessary to have one witness. The person making the will still needs to sign each page. It is better that the will is not witnessed by a beneficiary although the attestation would still be sound and the beneficiary would not have to relinquish the gift.

Subsequent marriage does not revoke a will but the birth of a child who is not provided for may do so. A will may be revoked by a subsequent will, either expressly or by implication, but in so far as the two can be read together both have effect. If a subsequent will is revoked, the earlier will is revived.

Wills may be registered in the sheriff court books of the Sheriffdom in which the deceased lived or in the Books of Council and Session at the Registers of Scotland. If the will has been registered in the Books of Council and Session, the original will can be inspected and a copy obtained for a small fee. On the other hand, if the will has been registered in the sheriff court books, the original would have been returned to the ingiver; however, copies may still be obtained for a small fee from the photographed copy kept in the register.

Confirmation

Confirmation (the Scottish equivalent of English probate) is obtained in the sheriff court of the sheriffdom in which the deceased was resident at the time of death. Executors are either 'nominate' (named by the deceased in the will) or 'dative' (appointed by the court in cases where no executor is named in a will or in cases of intestacy). Applicants for confirmation must first provide an inventory of the deceased's estate and a schedule of debts, with an affidavit. In estates under £25,000 gross, confirmation can be obtained under a simplified procedure at reduced fees with no need for a solicitor. The local sheriff clerk's office can provide assistance.

Further information can be obtained from:

Registers of Scotland

Meadowbank House, 153 London Road, Edinburgh, EH8 7AU
Tel: 0131-659 6111

Intestacy

Intestacy occurs when someone dies without leaving a will or leaves a will which is invalid or which does not take effect for some reason. In such cases the person's estate (property, possessions, other assets following the payment of debts) passes to certain members of the family.

Under the Succession (Scotland) Act 1964, no distinction is made between 'moveable' and 'heritable' property in intestacy cases.

A surviving spouse is entitled to 'prior rights'. This means that the spouse has the right to inherit:
- the matrimonial home up to a value of £130,000, or one matrimonial home if there is more than one, or, in certain circumstances, the value of the matrimonial home
- the furnishings and contents of that home, up to the value of £22,000
- a cash sum of £35,000 if the deceased left children or other descendants, or £58,000 if not

These figures are increased from time to time by regulations.

Once prior rights have been satisfied, what remains of the estate is generally divided between the surviving spouse and children (legitimate and illegitimate) according to 'legal' rights. Legal rights are:

Jus relicti(ae) – the right of a surviving spouse to one-half of the net moveable estate, after satisfaction of prior rights, if there are no surviving children; if there are surviving children, the spouse is entitled to one-third of the net moveable estate;

Legitim – the right of surviving children to one-half of the net moveable estate if there is no surviving spouse; if there is a surviving spouse, the children are entitled to one-third of the net moveable estate after the satisfaction of prior rights.

Where there are no surviving spouse or children, half of the estate is taken by the parents and half by the brothers and sisters. Failing that, the lines of succession, in general, are:
- to descendants
- if no descendants, then to collaterals (i.e. brothers and sisters) and parents
- surviving spouse
- if no collaterals or parents or spouse, then to ascendants collaterals (i.e. aunts and uncles), and so on in an ascending scale

If all lines of succession fail, then the estate passes to the Crown.

Relatives of the whole blood are preferred to relatives of the half blood. The right of representation, i.e. the right of the issue of a person who would have succeeded if he/she had survived the intestate, also applies.

BUSINESS

SCOTLAND

BUSINESS SCOTLAND

THE SCOTTISH ECONOMY

The economy of Scotland is small in relation to that of the UK as a whole (under 10% on most measures), which in turn is small compared to the EU and World economies. The 'openness' is reflected in Scotland's large trade flows with the rest of the UK, Europe and also with the rest of the World. It is also apparent in the importance of foreign direct investment to the Scottish economy. The regional dimension is evident in the degree of integration of the Scottish labour market with that of the rest of the UK as reflected, for example, in the historically large net out-migration flows from Scotland. The regional dimension is also reflected in the fact that key policy influences on the national economy, notably monetary and fiscal policies, are reserved to the Westminster Parliament. None of this implies that the economic powers devolved to the Scottish Parliament, established in May 1999, are incapable of significantly influencing the Scottish economy. However, it is undoubtedly true that many of the major influences on the performance of the Scottish economy remain outwith the control of the Scottish (and indeed even the Westminster) Parliaments. The Scottish economy remains heavily dependent on the fortunes of the rest of the UK, the EU and World economies. Furthermore, in line with other developed economies, including that of the UK, Scotland has over the longer-term become a predominantly service-based economy, where some 75% of employment is accounted for by the service sectors, although aspects of manufacturing activity continue (notably that associated with computers) to exhibit success.

As in any economy total output produced in Scotland can be thought of as reflecting both the scale (or capacity) of the economy, and the rate of utilisation of that capacity. For a given size of labour force, for example, Scottish output is likely to be lower when the unemployment rate is high since the labour force is unlikely to be fully utilised in these circumstances. This article considers: the scale of the Scottish economy as a whole; the openness of the economy; its regional nature and the implications for public finances; capacity utilisation; the sectoral structure of the Scottish economy; and other salient features.

This is necessarily a brief overview; additional discussion of the topis here can be found in a recent review of the Scottish Economy (Jeremy Peat and Stephen Boyle, *An Illustrated Guide to the Scottish Economy*, Duckworth, London, 1999). The Scottish Executive's twice-yearly *Scottish Economic Report* is a valuable source of information and commentary on the Scottish Economy. Further analysis is available in the Fraser of Allander Institute's *Quarterly Economic Commentary*. The principal source for the statistical information presented here is the Scottish Executive, and the Office of National Statistics (ONS), as published in the Scottish Executive's new annual *Scottish Economic Statistics*. In particular, *Scottish Economic Statistics (2000, 2001)* and various issues of the publication that preceded this, *Scottish Economic Bulletin (nos. 54, 56 and 58)* together with recent issues of *Regional Trends* are the main data sources employed here. Trade figures are due in part to the Scottish Council Development and Industry. Earnings data are from the *New Earnings Survey*. Data on household spending and consumption come from the ONS Family Spending survey.

The Scale of the Scottish Economy

Many aspects of economies are thought to depend on their scale or size. The most commonly employed indicator of an economy's scale is its Gross Domestic Product (GDP), which measures the value of the goods and services produced in an economy over a particular period (usually a single year). Scotland's GDP in 1998 was £61,052 million (at 1998 prices) or 8.2% of UK GDP. These data, however, exclude the oil and gas output from the UK Continental Shelf, which is treated as a separate region in the national accounts. If, say, 80% of this output were attributed to Scotland, estimated GDP would have been increased by over 20%. Other measures of scale include population and labour force. Table 1 indicates that Scotland's share of U.K population and labour force were 8.6% and 8.7% respectively in 1998. Scotland is therefore a comparatively small region of the UK, except where scale is measured in terms of land area. Scotland accounts for over 32% of the UK's land area and has the lowest population density (average population per square kilometre) of all eleven standard regions of the UK (and just over a tenth of the density of the South East).

TABLE 1.   THE SCALE OF THE SCOTTISH REGION IN 1998

Region	Scotland	UK	Scotland per cent of UK
Area (sq km)	77,097	240,883	32.0
Population (000's)	5,120	59,237	8.6
Population Density (person/sq metre)	66.4	245.9	27.0
Labour Force (000's, 1998)	2,439	28,097	8.7
GDP (1998 basic prices, £ million)	61,052	747,544	8.2
GDP per head	11,902	12,455	95.6

Although it is not a measure of scale, the final row of Table 1 shows GDP per head of population. This is the most commonly employed measure of the economic prosperity of regions and nations. Scottish GDP per head, at £11,902 in 1998 is 95.6% of the UK average. Attribution of 20% of the output of oil and gas would increase GDP per head significantly, and raise Scotland from 5th to 3rd position in the ranking of UK regions (after South East England and East Anglia). These most recent estimates of GDP, which are based on the European System of Accounts 1995, have cast doubt on the validity of the earlier view that Scottish GDP per head had effectively converged on that of the UK. These new estimates suggest that while Scottish GDP per head rose to 98.9% of the corresponding UK estimate in 1995, it fell to 96.8% in 1996, fell again to only 95.5% of UK GDP per head in 1997 and then rose slightly to 95.6% in 1998.

Table 2 indicates that there is considerable variation in GDP per head among the sub-regions of Scotland. In 1996, for example, GDP per head in North Eastern Scotland was 35% higher than in Scotland as a whole, whereas in Highlands and Islands it was over 20% below the Scottish average. The dominance of South Western Scotland is also apparent, since it accounts for some 42% of Scottish GDP. Smaller regions naturally show even greater variations in GDP per head, ranging from only 56% of the Scottish figure in East Lothian and Midlothian to 148% in the city of Edinburgh.

TABLE 2.   GROSS DOMESTIC PRODUCT AT FACTOR COST (Current Prices) FOR NUTS 1, 2 AND 3 AREAS IN SCOTLAND, 1996 (Revised)

	£ million	£ per head population	£ per head pop. (Scotland = 100)
Scotland	54,430	10,614	100
North Eastern Scotland (Aberdeen City, Aberdeenshire and North East Moray)	7,347	14,453	135
Eastern Scotland	21,026	11,116	104
Angus and Dundee City	2,642	10,123	95
Clackmannanshire and Fife	3,465	8,704	81
East Lothian and Midlothian	1,009	5,999	56
Scottish Borders	1,000	9,422	88
Edinburgh, City of	7,131	15,888	148
Falkirk	1,580	11,046	103
Perth and Kinross and Stirling	2,168	10,068	95
West Lothian	2,030	13,466	126
South Western Scotland	22,964	9,747	91
East and West Dunbartonshire, Helensburgh and Lomond	1,690	7,211	67
Dumfries and Galloway	1,469	9,955	93
East Ayrshire and North Ayrshire Mainland	1,954	7,637	71
Glasgow City	7,895	12,808	120
Inverclyde, East Renfrewshire and Renfrewshire	3,472	9,814	92
North Lanarkshire	2,594	7,959	74
South Ayrshire	1,294	11,286	105

South Lanarkshire	2,596	8,445	79
Highlands and Islands	3,093	8,308	78
Caithness and Sutherland and Ross and Cromarty	733	8,157	76
Inverness and Nairn and Moray, Badenoch and Strathspey	897	8,152	77
Lochaber, Skye and Lochalsh and Argyll and the Islands	759	7,540	70
Eilean Siar (Western Isles)	233	8,072	75
Orkney Islands	177	8,949	84
Shetland Islands	293	12,748	119

THE OPENNESS OF THE SCOTTISH ECONOMY

Smaller economies tend to be more open than their larger counterparts, often in a number of respects. Scotland has, like many other economies, been affected by increasing 'globalisation', with openness to international trade and capital flows growing through time. A number of dimensions of openness are briefly considered.

Trade

One important feature of the scale of an economy is that smaller economies tend, in general, to be more open to trade. Both exports and imports tend to be relatively more important for small economies. The Scottish input-output tables for 1996 imply that Scotland's exports amounted to £43,014 million in total. The export to GDP ratio implied is nearly 80%, whereas for the UK as a whole the export to GDP ratio was around 30% in 1997. Admittedly, however, a great deal of Scotland's trade consisted of exports to the other regions of the UK. Scotland's exports to the rest of the World accounted for some 38% of Scottish GDP. Scotland appears to be significantly more open than the UK as a whole (which itself is open relative to the OECD). However, Scotland also imports more, relatively, than the UK as a whole. In 1996 its imports from RUK, at £22,103 million, exceeded its exports to this region, implying a trade deficit. However, Scotland's imports from ROW were only £16,793 million, implying a trade surplus with the rest of the World.

Manufacturing exports are estimated to account for some 75% of total exports to the rest of the world, and 75% of these were, in turn, attributable in 1996 to only three subsectors: office machinery (including computers, 37.1%), radio, television and communications (16.3%) and whisky (12.4%). Caution is required in interpreting these figures as contributions to the nation's balance of trade, however, since office machinery, for example, also imports a much larger proportion of its inputs than the Whisky industry.

According to the Scottish Council Development and Industry's survey of manufactured exports for 1998, Scotland's main export markets outside of the UK remain the EU (63%) and North America (11.2%). The UK as a whole is less dependent on the EU (56.1%) and more on North America (15.3%) than Scotland. When, as has happened since the launch of European Monetary Union, sterling increases in value against the euro, the implication is that Scottish exporters may be more adversely affected than those in the UK as a whole.

Foreign Ownership

In recent years, foreign ownership has grown more rapidly than international trade, partly as a result of reduced restrictions on international capital flows and the more global perspective of multinational companies. The aggregate stock of foreign owned companies in the world is estimated to have doubled between 1975 and 1994. This important aspect of increasing openness is also a feature of the Scottish economy. Foreign direct investment/ inward investment has been an increasingly important feature of the manufacturing sector, with the number of plants rising from 65 in 1950 to 357 in 1994, by which time foreign-owned plants accounted for over a quarter of manufacturing employment and a third of total sales. The service sector too is increasingly affected. These trends are in part a consequence of a regional policy stance that has sought to encourage inward investment. Inward investors tended to be concentrated in the fastest growing "high tech" sectors such as electronics, producing computers and workstations or semiconductors. Foreign-owned components of manufacturing tend to have higher productivity, export a higher proportion of their output (but import a larger proportion of input) and pay higher wages. There is also the suggestion that they improve efficiency in supplier and customer firms.

Migration and population change

A further feature of the openness of the Scottish economy is the degree of integration of the Scottish and rest of the UK labour markets. Perhaps the most distinctive manifestation of this in Scotland, as in most regional economies, is the existence of significant migration flows. While in any single year net migration flows have been of a fairly modest scale, these have cumulatively resulted in significant flows of population out of Scotland and into the rest of the UK and overseas, resulting in a lower population than otherwise would have been the case. In 1861, for example, Scotland's share of UK population stood at 12.5%, while by 1998 it had fallen to 8.6%. The population of the UK as a whole increased by around 20% in the 1951-99 period, whereas in Scotland population was broadly static. Over the last thirty years the population of Scotland has in fact fallen by around 1%. During the 1960s net out-migration averaged around 32,000, though this declined in the 1970s, and fell to around half that level in the 1980s. Throughout the 1990s population was fairly stable, with net in-migration in a number of years.

This cumulative net out-migration has reduced the population of working age in Scotland below what it otherwise would have been (to around 3.2 million currently). Of these around 70% actually participate actively in the labour market. Historically male participation rates were much higher than those for females, but these have virtually converged. (In the 1960s male rates were in the high 90% range, and females in the mid 40% range.) Net out-migration therefore reduces the available supply of labour (for a given participation rate), and there is some suggestion too that it is selective in terms of age and skill. However, migration flows are an important means by which regional labour markets function and, with no additional growth in employment, lower net out-migration would have implied much higher unemployment rates here.

Significant net out-migration flows can create even greater problems for smaller sub-regions. For example, loss of population from the City of Glasgow has reduced the numbers of households paying taxes to the City, thus creating funding problems.

THE REGIONAL CONTEXT AND PUBLIC SECTOR FINANCES

The scale of a regional economy, particularly in terms of its geographical size and population density, is important in understanding the level of regions' public expenditure per head of population. In particular, where the population of a region is geographically dispersed the provision of a given level of public services becomes more expensive, and this is part of the explanation of the public sector deficit in Scotland.

The devolution debate has tended to focus considerable attention on regional public finances, especially in Scotland. Many elements of government revenues and some elements of government expenditure are not directly measured at the regional level and so have to be estimated somehow. This has given rise to some controversy, although most commentators take the view that Scotland receives more than its population's share of public expenditures while contributing roughly its population's share to tax revenues. Accordingly, many believe that there is a public sector deficit in Scotland, with public sector expenditures exceeding revenues (even when the unemployment rate in Scotland, and so expenditure on benefits, is low).

Public expenditure in Scotland is divided into three elements: identifiable (Scottish Office spending plus Social Security); non-identifiable (largely public goods such as defence, foreign affairs etc); other spending (servicing of debt etc). Only the identifiable component is entirely reliably estimated, with Scotland's share of the other expenditures being determined in some more or less mechanical way, normally using population shares. Total expenditure was estimated to be £32.3 billion in 1997/8, of which £24.4 billion was identifiable. This amounted to 10.2% of UK government expenditure, well in excess of Scotland's population share of 8.6%. This could conceivably be justifiable in terms of a greater need for public expenditure given the greater cost of providing comparable public services in Scotland. However, the last "needs assessment" exercise was conducted in 1976 and suggested that Scottish identified expenditure should be 116% of the corresponding English level, whereas this is currently around 130%. Since there is also some evidence that Scotland has become more affluent relative to the UK as a whole, there is some pressure to reduce Scotland's share of expenditures. The data for 1998/9 are presented in Table 3. (Figures and percentages may not add up to totals due to rounding).

TABLE 3.   GOVERNMENT EXPENDITURE IN SCOTLAND AND THE UK, 1998/9

	Scotland		UK		Scotland as a share of UK
	£ billion	% Exp.	£ billion	% Exp.	
Identifiable of which:	25.7	77.7	253.2	76.5	10.2
Scottish Executive[1]	15.6	—	—	—	—
Social Security	9.2	—	—	—	—
Non-identifiable	3.2	9.8	37.8	11.4	8.6
Other (estimated)[2]	4.3	13.1	40.9	12.4	10.6
of which:					
Debt interest	2.5	—	29.5	—	—
Reconciliation	0.1	0.2	−0.9	−0.3	—
Aggregate Expenditure (before EU adjustment)	33.4	—	331	—	10.1
EU adjustment	−0.3	−0.8	—	—	—
Aggregate Expenditure[3] (after EU adjustment)	33.1	100	331	100	10
Population (1997)	—	—	—	—	8.6
GDP (1997)	—	—	—	—	8.3

[1] Scottish Executive 1998/99 includes associated Departments such as the General Register Office for Scotland, the Scottish Record Office, the Register of Scotland, and the Scottish Courts Administration. It also includes the Scotland Office.
[2] Includes ESA95 treatment of contributions to the EU in respect of VAT, customs duties, and agricultural and sugar levies.
[3] After EU Adjustment, treating main EU programme expenditure as transfers to non-government sectors.

In fact, the Barnett formula, which governs the allocation of expenditures to the Scottish 'block' (or assigned budget under devolution), implies that Scotland receives a fixed share of any change in comparable expenditures in England and Wales. Without any modifications to this formula it would eventually imply a movement towards equal public expenditure per head across all the regions of the UK. This would appear to conflict with the 'principle of equalisation' according to which public expenditures should be such as to provide comparable public services in all parts of the UK. (This would imply higher expenditures where service delivery is more expensive.)

Total public sector revenues in 1997/8 were estimated to be £26.7 billion excluding oil and gas, amounting to 8.6% of total UK revenues, precisely Scotland's population share. (Table 4 presents the data for 1998/9.) This implies a public sector deficit (excess of expenditure over revenues) of £5.6 billion. There is considerable controversy surrounding Scotland's share of oil and gas revenues. If no adjustment at all were made for this, the deficit would amount to nearly 10% of GDP. While this is considerably in excess of the Maastricht requirement of 3% of GDP as indicating a sustainable fiscal deficit, and suitability for membership of the common European currency, this implies that none of the revenues from North Sea oil accrue to Scotland. There are, too, doubts concerning some aspects of the calculations (as well as the rigour with which such criteria are in fact applied), and the controversy will no doubt continue. Fluctuations in the oil price imply similar fluctuations in the scale of any measured deficit/ surplus that includes revenues from this source.

TABLE 4. ESTIMATED GOVERNMENT REVENUES FOR SCOTLAND 1998/9			
	UK £ billion	Scottish estimate £ billion[3]	Estimated % share of UK
Income tax (after tax credits)	86.4	6.4	7.4
Social security contributions	55.1	4.7	8.6
Value added tax	52.3	4.3	8.2
Local authority revenues	27.5	2.5	9.2
All other revenues[1,4]	112.3	10.3	9.1
Total receipts[2]	333.5	28.2	8.4

[1] *The figures for the individual items in the table are on a cash basis; an accruals adjustment is included in all other revenues. Includes estimates of all other taxes and duties, other receipts and accounting adjustments.*

[2] *Excluding North Sea revenues.*

[3] *Percentages are based on unrounded figures.*

[4] *All other revenues include the ESA95 change relating to certain UK contributions to the EU; this deducts contributions in respect of VAT, customs duties and agricultural and sugar levies from total receipts. Amounts for the windfall tax are also included*

CHANGES IN THE SCALE OF THE SCOTTISH ECONOMY OVER TIME

While an appreciation of the absolute and relative scale of the Scottish economy at a particular point in time is useful, it provides only a snapshot of performance. It is also very important to understand the evolution of the Scottish economy through time. While it has already been noted that significant reductions in the Scottish population have occurred most attention tends to be focused on the rate of economic growth (though these are linked).

An economy's rate of economic growth is often measured in terms of its average percentage rate of change of GDP over time. Table 8 shows the rate of growth for Scotland. Perhaps the most striking feature of the data is the volatility apparent in growth rates measured as rates of change of actual GDP. This reflects the fact that actual output tends to vary in a cyclical manner, with the level of GDP actually falling in recessions and so generating negative growth rates. The cycles in activity in Scotland and the rest of the UK (RUK) are broadly in phase, although Scotland did not experience the late 1980s boom, and the last recession was exceptional in that the RUK was more adversely affected than Scotland, a reversal of the historical pattern. However, the trend rate of growth over the period is positive in both regions. In the RUK region the simple average of growth rates over the period was 2.4%, whereas for Scotland it was 1.5%. While the difference may not seem substantial, if such a growth rate differential were to be sustained, the cumulative effect on levels of GDP would be dramatic. Naturally, however, estimates of differential growth depend critically on the period over which they are measured. Over the 1990s, for example,

the average annual growth rate in Scotland was, at 1.7%, again less than that in RUK (2.0%), but from 1991 to 1995 Scotland's growth rate exceeded that of RUK largely as a consequence of the differential impact of the last recession. Over the long-run, Scotland's average growth rate has been higher, at just over 2%.

Nonetheless, Scottish GDP per head had, at least until recently, been thought to have caught up with that in the UK. This would be possible in a regional economy like Scotland, even with slower GDP growth, since in every decade of this century Scotland has lost population through net out-migration. The factors governing regional and national growth remain little understood, though recently considerable emphasis has been placed on public investment in infrastructure, investment in human resources (through education and training) and research and development activity, as well as population and physical capital growth.

Data on total employment from the Labour Force Survey are available from 1984. These indicate that employment grew by around 12% in both Scotland and the UK over the period to 1998. Employment grew through most of the 1980s, peaking at around 2.3 million in 1992, before contracting substantially and then gradually recovering to the 1992 level. Growth in employees in employment was slightly less (10% over the period), with growth in self-employment accounting for the remainder. Most of the growth in employment over the period, however, is accounted for by an expansion in part-time female employment (which rose by some 87,000 or 17% over the period to 610,000 in 1998). Around 2.3 million people were in work in Scotland in 1999, of whom 2 million (nearly 90%) were employees. There were 213,000 self-employed and 21,000 on training schemes.

REGIONAL UTILISATION OF RESOURCES

The most obvious measure of the regional utilisation of resources is the regional unemployment rate, although at best this measures the utilisation of the labour force. Traditionally, attention has focused on an unemployment rate measured in terms of claimants of the relevant benefit. Since the benefits system has changed considerably through time, so too will this rate of unemployment quite independently of any change in labour utilisation. Some of the difficulties of interpretation are overcome by adoption of the government's new "headline" rate of unemployment, which is measured through a household survey using the International Labour Organisation (ILO) definition. Recent unemployment rates for Scotland and the UK are presented in Table 5. Unemployment rates tend to fluctuate with the cycle in GDP: as activity increases, so too does employment, although typically with a lag, and this tends to push unemployment rates down. The unemployment rates peaked in the mid-1980s, and then fell until the beginning of the 1990s when economic activity slowed and unemployment rose. From 1993 unemployment has tended to fall. In the UK context, it has often been argued that there exists a North-South divide, with Northern regions (including Scotland) typically experiencing lower growth and higher unemployment. The unemployment differentials did appear to be fairly stable until recently when the Scottish unemployment rate fell below that of the UK. However, the signs are that this disruption to the historical pattern may prove to be a short-lived reflection of the especially severe impact of the last recession on the South.

TABLE 5.	REGIONAL UNEMPLOYMENT RATES (SPRING, ILO DEFINITION)	
	Scotland	UK
1986	13.9	11.2
1987	14.9	10.8
1988	12	8.8
1989	9.7	7.2
1990	9.3	6.8
1991	9.3	8.4
1992	9.5	9.7
1993	10.2	10.3
1994	10	9.6
1995	8.3	8.6
1996	8.7	8.3
1997	8.5	7.3
1998	7.7	6.8
1999	7.4	5.9
2000	7.6	5.6

Unemployment rates vary significantly among the sub-regions of Scotland, as is apparent from Table 6. In December 2000 claimant counts (typically less than the corresponding ILO measure) varied from 1.8% in Aberdeen city to 11.0% in East Ayrshire. Unemployment rates are also systematically higher for men than for women. In the first quarter of 1999, for example, the overall headline rate of unemployment (ILO) was 7.6% (as against 6.3% for the UK). The unemployment rate for men was 8.5%, however, as against 6.4% for women. (The differential is more substantial on the claimant count measure. In October 1999, for example, the claimant count measure of the male unemployment rate was 7.5% and that for females was 2.5%.) The duration of unemployment spells has been tending to fall with the overall unemployment rate, however, men also tend to suffer disproportionately from long spells of unemployment (on a claimant basis).

TABLE 6. CLAIMANT COUNT UNEMPLOYMENT RATE (% EMPLOYEE JOBS AND CLAIMANTS): BY SCOTTISH SUB-REGION, December 2000

Aberdeen City	1.8
Aberdeenshire	3.2
Angus	5.9
Argyll and Bute	6.4
Clackmannanshire	8.5
Dumfries and Galloway	5.8
Dundee City	7.3
East Ayrshire	11.0
East Dunbartonshire	6.8
East Lothian	3.9
East Renfrewshire	6.4
Edinburgh, City of	2.6
Eilean Siar (Western Isles)	8.4
Falkirk	5.9
Fife	6.6
Glasgow City	5.4
Highland	6.3
Inverclyde	4.6
Midlothian	4.6
Moray	4.9
North Ayrshire	9.1
North Lanarkshire	6.4
Orkney Islands	4.0
Perth and Kinross	3.3
Renfrewshire	4.5
Scottish Borders, The	3.7
Shetland Islands	2.4
South Aryshire	5.8
South Lanarkshire	5.5
Stirling	3.8
West Dunbartonshire	8.8
West Lothian	4.4

THE SECTORAL STRUCTURE OF THE SCOTTISH ECONOMY

Gross Domestic Product by Industry Groups

Table 7 presents estimates of Gross Domestic Product by Industry groups in 1996. The traditional notion of Scotland as being characterised by specialisation in heavy industries with shipbuilding as a key activity, as reflected in the proud "Clyde built" label, was true of the first half of the century, but is now outdated. Services now account for over 63% of output (68% in the UK). In employment terms services are even more dominant, accounting for 75% of total employment in Scotland.

TABLE 7 GROSS DOMESTIC PRODUCT BY INDUSTRY GROUPS, 1996

	Scotland	per cent Scot.	UK	per cent UK
Agriculture etc	1,642	3.0	11,790	1.9
Mining & Quar.	1,220	2.2	4,398	0.7
Manufacturing	12,103	22.2	137,006	21.8
Elect. Gas etc.	1,828	3.4	13,606	2.2
Construction	3,282	6.0	33,746	5.4
Distribution, Hotels etc	7,237	13.3	93,091	14.8
Transport etc.	4,181	7.7	54,056	8.6
Financial & Bus. Serv.	10,780	19.8	164,282	26.1
Public admin etc.	3,709	6.8	38,244	6.1
Education, Health etc.	8,250	15.2	81,876	13.0
Other Services	2,160	4.0	24,713	3.9
Adjustment for Fin. Serv.	− 1962	− 3.6	− 26,968	− 4.3

There is a broad similarity between the industrial structure of Scotland's economy and that of the UK as a whole. Both have come to be dominated by services, although there are, of course, some differences in detail. The most noticeable relative specialisation in Scotland is in mining and quarrying where Scotland accounts for nearly 28% of UK GDP. agriculture, hunting forestry and fishing accounts for 13.9% of the UK total, whereas Scotland as a whole recall contributes 8.6% of UK GDP. There is also comparative specialisation in electricity, gas etc. contributes 13.4% of UK GDP. However, each of these sectors is really rather small in terms of their percentage contribution to GDP in each region. Financial and business services is the most important contributor to UK GDP (26.1%), but is second most important in Scotland (accounting for 19.8% of GDP). In Scotland the manufacturing sector is most important (22.2%), but is only slightly more important relatively than in the UK as a whole (21.8%). The rankings of the third and fourth most important sectors in the UK as a whole, distribution, hotels and catering etc (14.8%) and education, social work and health services (13.0%), are again reversed for Scotland. Scotland has historically enjoyed a higher than average share of education and health expenditures, partly reflecting a perceived greater need here. Transport, public administration and construction feature as the next most important sectors in terms of contribution to GDP, with Scotland comparatively specialised in the latter two sectors. However, the differences in structure are comparatively slight, or concentrated in comparatively small sectors: the predominant impression is of the similarity of the industrial structures of Scotland and the UK.

Of course, a single year's data on industry groups output shares gives no indication of the extent of re-structuring that has occurred over time. In fact the Scottish economy has undergone significant structural change even over the last few decades. The decline in manufacturing reflects the contraction in the heavier industries like steel and shipbuilding, but conceals rapid growth in the electronics sector where substantial inward investment has stimulated the creation of 'Silicon Glen'. The growth in the financial sector has been one of Scotland's recent success stories. It is truly international in scope, manages over £200 billion of funds, and is characterised by over 30 major financial institutions, many of which are household names (such as the Bank of Scotland and the Royal Bank of Scotland). The life and general assurance sector contains a number of world leaders, such as Standard Life. While some part of the apparent shift to services may reflect a shedding of formerly 'in-house' services (reducing measured output in manufacturing and increasing it in services), there is no doubt that a substantial genuine re-structuring has occurred in the Scottish economy over the latter part of the century.

Less dramatic, but nonetheless substantial, changes have occurred in the outputs of other sectors. Thus agriculture's share has fallen from 5% to 3% and construction's from 8% to 6%. The 1990s have proved to be a very mixed decade for Scottish Agriculture, with total income for farming initially rising more than threefold in the first half of the decade to a peak of £737 million, in part due to changes in EU support mechanisms. However, farm incomes then fell by almost 66% in the period to 1998, due in part to the impact of BSE. It is as yet too early to assess the likely economic impact of the recent Foot and Mouth disease on Scottish Agriculture, though it clearly will be significant.

These general comments on structural change are reinforced by inspection of the indices of sectoral Gross Value Added that are reported in Table 5. Thus, for example, manufacturing output grew by only 9% between 1973 and 1995 (in which year all indices are set to equal 100), whereas in total industries averaged around 27% growth. Over this period construction fared worst, with growth of less than 4% over the 26-year period. Business, financial and other services grew by some 40%. Since 1995, agriculture etc. has fared particularly badly, followed by construction. Electricity, gas and water supply has registered the greatest growth, followed by the service industries.

TABLE 8. INDICES FOR GROSS VALUE ADDED FOR SCOTLAND 1973 TO 1999

1995 = 100

	Total	Agriculture Forestry & Fishing	Mining & Quarrying	Electricity Gas & Water Supply	Manufac- turing	Construc- tion	Distribu- tion, Hotels & Catering	Transport, Storage & Communi- cation	Business, Financial, Public & Other Services
GDP 1995 weights[3]	72.9	30	16	31	226	64	134	76	447
1973	72.9	67.8	52.1	66.3	91.7	96.3	63.5	73.3	59.5
1974	72.8	72.8	52.9	64	91.2	86.5	64	73.9	61.2
1975	71.8	67.9	63.6	64.5	86.8	90.3	61.3	72.9	61.6
1976	73	60.1	62.8	66.6	87	87.8	62.9	75.5	65.1
1977	74.3	62.7	60.3	69.6	86.6	91.4	63.2	77.6	67
1978	76.1	64.5	71.5	71.3	86.7	91.1	67.6	79.5	68.9
1979	76.9	62.2	78.7	75.8	86.4	86.4	69.9	81.9	70.6
1980	75.4	67.1	85.6	72.1	80.5	81.6	66.5	79.9	73
1981	74.4	70.5	88.3	74.3	78.3	71.1	65.9	80.8	73.8
1982	75.5	72	94.6	70.9	79	73.2	67.9	79.7	75.3
1983	76.5	70.6	98.2	70.3	78.6	74.9	69	81.6	77.3
1984	79.4	77.8	89.6	79.5	81.9	74.6	72.2	84.4	80
1985	81.7	76.6	102.8	80.7	83.7	75.9	74.8	87.1	82.4
1986	82	81.7	96.8	77.1	81.2	77.2	76.2	87.7	84.4
1987	83.6	81	91.7	79.2	81.1	75.8	79.2	92.9	86.9
1988	87	79.4	94.5	83	86.3	79.6	86	93.5	89
1989	89.3	84.9	98	80.6	88.6	82.4	90.5	95.7	90.6
1990	91.3	87.7	104	86.6	90.2	89	90.2	94.6	92.6
1991	91.4	86.5	110.3	91.1	87.8	91.2	88.7	93.8	94.6
1992	92.7	88	112.9	92	88	97.1	90.8	94.2	95.6
1993	95	84.5	110.1	93.2	91.2	100	95.6	95.5	97.2
1994	96.9	93.7	108.3	94.7	95.7	92.3	97.2	99	97.2
1995	100	100	100	100	100	100	100	100	100
1996	102.8	103.6	104.4	103.2	102.9	100.4	106.8	102.1	104.3
1997	105.6	99.6	105.7	111.2	108.7	101.1	108	109.5	108.1
1998	107.3	98.3	108.1	113.2	111.5	98.3	111.6	113.5	112
1999	109.9	98.8	114.1	120.3	113.9	101.7	117.5	114.9	117.3

There has been little comment so far on the discovery and exploitation of North Sea Oil, which now has a history spanning over two decades. The special treatment of North Sea oil production in the national accounts has already been noted, as has the fact that the that attribution of a share of this to the Scottish economy could substantially increase Scottish GDP (though the precise share that can be deemed "Scottish" remains controversial). Naturally, the offshore activity generated much associated onshore activity. In 1994 some 21 thousand people were employed directly by the Oil and Gas industry, but over 60,000 jobs were attributed to the sector in total, through jobs in supporting activities.

While a prolonged period of low oil prices cast a shadow over the likelihood of further development of the less accessible fields, the impact of this has been mitigated to some degree by technological change. The industry is expected to continue to make a significant contribution to the Scottish economy, although the revenues from oil and gas production are in decline. The real oil price (oil prices divided by an index of retail prices) fell by around 80% between the peak of 1980 and the trough of 1998. While oil prices have more than doubled since the OPEC meeting in early 1999, this has little immediate impact on current activity in the oil and gas industry: investment and subsequent activity depends on the (real) oil price expected to prevail in the medium to longer term. However, the continued strengthening of the oil price is likely to generate increased activity.

Another omission from the discussion of structural changes up to this point is the tourism industry. The reason for this is that official statistics do not recognise the existence of a tourism 'industry' as such. Many industries are particularly sensitive to tourist expenditures, such as hotels and catering, but they are typically not exclusively devoted to satisfying tourist needs. Accordingly, the importance of tourism is estimated in a variety of ways, stemming from data collected on the numbers of visits, average duration of visits and average daily tourist expenditures. Spending by tourists is estimated to be in excess of £2 billion per year and estimates of the employment impact range up to 75 thousand.

Sectoral employment patterns

The sectoral pattern of employment, summarised in Table 9, tells a similar story of a shift to a service economy. The primary industries are here defined as: agriculture, hunting, forestry and fishing; mining and quarrying and electricity, gas and water supply. Inspection of Table 9 reveals that they account for 3.5% of Scottish employee jobs, and only 2.1% of total UK employee jobs, so Scotland is more specialised in these industries than is the U.K. as a whole. The tertiary industries cover all services and dominate the Scottish economy, accounting for 74% of employment, rather less than their 76% share in the UK. The major part of the production and construction industries make up the secondary sector. Scotland is slightly more specialised in these industries, with 22.1% of its employment concentrated here as against just over 21.4% for the UK as a whole.

The longer-term picture is one of a significant contraction in the secondary sector, concentrated in Scotland's traditional heavy industries, combined with a substantial expansion in the tertiary sector. In 1970, for example, the production industries accounted for over 900 thousand employees or 44% of total employees in employment in Scotland, with the tertiary sector accounting for 1,049 employees or just under 51% of the total.

Table 9 also presents data on the sex composition of employee jobs in Scotland and the UK. In terms simply of numbers of employee jobs the workforce in both regions is now fairly evenly divided between males and females. Indeed in Scotland slightly over half of all employees' jobs are now held by females. In fact this reflects the outcome of a sustained increase in female employment and steady contraction in male employment. In 1970, for example, female employment accounted for 38.4% of total employment. However, some 45% of female employment is part-time whereas only 11% of male employment is part-time. If part-time employment is taken to be 'third time', then female full-time-equivalent employment is only 42% of the total of such employment. The trends in female employment in part reflect changes in Scotland's industrial structure, in particular the shift to services from heavy manufacturing.

Table 10 provides a more detailed picture of the current sectoral composition of employment in Scotland. The largest concentration of employment is in the wholesale, retail trade and repairs sector which accounts for 16.3% of total employees in Scotland and 17.4% in the UK as a whole. Manufacturing is the second biggest employer with 15.5% of employees in Scotland and 17.0% in the UK. The third most important employer in Scotland is health and social work with 13.1% of employees, and the fourth is real estate, renting and business activities with 11.1%. The positions of these two sectors are reversed in the UK, accounting for 10.7% and 14.2% respectively of total employment there.

TABLE 9 EMPLOYEE JOBS BY SEX AND BROAD INDUSTRY GROUP (December 1998, not seasonally adjusted)

| | Male | | Female | | Total | Primary | Secondary | Tertiary |
	Full-time	Part-time	Full-time	Part-time				
Scotland	898	114	556	462	2030	72	448	1,510
U.K.	10,646	1,570	6,344	5,448	24,008	513	5,211	18,284

TABLE 10 EMPLOYEE JOBS BY INDUSTRY (December 1998, not seasonally adjusted, 000s)

	Scotland	% Scot.	UK	% UK
Agriculture etc (A, B)	32	1.6	296	1.2
Mining & Quar. (C)	24	1.2	74	0.3
Manufacturing (D)	315	15.5	4,077	17.0
Elect. Gas etc (E)	16	0.8	143	0.6
Construction (F)	133	6.5	1,133	4.7
Wholesale etc (G)	332	16.3	4,174	17.4
Hotels & rest. (H)	113	5.6	1,300	5.4
Transport etc (I)	110	5.4	1,416	5.9
Financial Inter. (J)	89	4.4	1,029	4.3
Real Estate etc (K)	225	11.1	3,405	14.2
Public admin etc (L)	125	6.2	1,328	5.5
Education (M)	152	7.5	1,931	8.0
Health & Social Work (N)	266	13.1	2,571	10.7
Other Services (O,Q)	99	4.9	1,128	4.7

The biggest difference in relative specialisation occurs in mining and quarrying, wherein Scotland employs over 32% of total UK employees, as compared to its overall employment share of 8.5%, although the sector accounts for only 1.3% of total Scottish employment. The next biggest specialisation in Scotland relative to the UK are in construction (11.7% of total UK employment in this sector), electricity, gas and water supply (11.1%), agriculture, hunting, forestry and fishing (10.8%), and health and social work (10.3%). The most under-represented sectors relative to the UK are: real estate, renting and business activities (with 6.6% of total UK employment in this sector); manufacturing (7.7%), education (7.8%) and wholesale, retail trade and repairs (7.9%). The current position, therefore, does not offer a clear cut support for the view that Scotland is over-represented in the contracting sectors and under-represented in the expanding sectors, although the data used here remains quite highly aggregated.

It is worth noting that there are some marked differences in sectors relative importance as a source of employment and as a contributor to GDP. These reflect differences in labour productivity, which are considered below.

The historical situation with respect to the sectoral distribution was somewhat different, however, with Scotland specialised in heavy manufacturing. The precise changes are difficult to establish given the various changes in sectoral definitions and other sources of discontinuities in the data, but some orders of magnitude can be established. In 1970, for example, employment in manufacturing industries was 708 thousand, so it has fallen by 55% of that total to reach its current level. In contrast employment in Services has risen by over 44% since that date.

The Structure of Scottish Manufacturing

The regional distribution of gross value added by manufacturing sub-sector for 1993 is shown in Table 11. It is interesting to note that Scotland was comparatively specialised in: wood and wood products (13.5% of total UK employment in this sub-sector); Food, products, beverages and tobacco (including whisky, 12.2%); electrical and optical equipment (10.9%). Scotland was comparatively under-represented in: leather and leather products (3.4%); manufactures not elsewhere specified (3.8%); chemicals etc (4.7%).

TABLE 11.	SCOTTISH SHARE OF UK MANUFACTURING GVA AT FACTOR COST BY SECTOR IN 1993	
	Scotland	*UK*
Food Products, bev., tob.	12.2	87.8
Textiles and textile products	12	88
Leather and leather products	3.4	96.6
Wood and wood products	13.5	86.5
Pulp, paper, publishing & print.	7.5	92.5
Chemicals, chemical products	4.7	95.3
Rubber and plastic products	6.8	93.2
Other non-metallic mineral products	7.2	92.8
Metals & fabricated metal products	6.7	93.3
Machinery and equipment	8	92
Electrical and optical equipment	10.9	89.1
Transport equipment	4.8	95.2
Manufactures n.e.s.	3.8	96.2
Total	**7.8**	**92.2**

TABLE 12.	DISTRIBUTION OF MANUFACTURING BY BROAD SECTOR IN 1993	
	Scotland	*UK*
Food, Drink and Tobacco	21.4	14
Modern	67	75.6
Traditional	11.6	10.4
Total	**100**	**100**

Modern	**Traditional**
Pulp, paper, publishing & print.	Textiles and textile products
Chemicals, chemical products	Leather and leather products
Rubber and plastic products	Wood and wood products
Other non-metallic mineral products	Manufactures n.e.s.
Metals & fabricated metal products	
Machinery and equipment n.e.s.	
Electrical and optical equipment	
Transport equipment	

* n.e.s: not elsewhere specified

Further detail on the structure of manufacturing in Scotland is presented in Table 12, where total manufacturing has been subdivided into three sub-sectors: food, drink and tobacco; a modern sector and a traditional sector. Naturally, these latter two distinctions are subjective and open to potential objections. A striking feature of this table is Scotland's relative dependence on the Food, Drink and Tobacco sub-sector, and a slightly greater concentration in the more traditional manufacturing activities. Food, Drink and Tobacco primarily services the domestic economy. While Whisky is, as we have seen, a very notable exception to this general rule, it accounts for only 20% of the sub-sector's employment.

A longer term perspective on the structure of Scottish manufacturing is provided by Table 13, which presents indices of Gross Value Added by manufacturing sub-sectors for the period 1973-1999. Note that the output of four manufacturing sectors actually contracted over the 26 year period. In the case of metals and metal products, this decline was particularly dramatic, with output falling by nearly two thirds. However, food, drink and tobacco experienced a contraction of over 20% of output and textiles output fell by nearly 30%. The only comparative success story is in engineering and allied industries, though note that output here fluctuated around a fairly static trend until the late 1980s. This reflects, in part, the experience of electronics.

TABLE 13. GVA INDEX BY DETAILED MANUFACTURING SECTOR, SCOTLAND 1974 TO 1999

1995 = 100

	Manufacturing	Refined Petroleum	Chemicals and	Metals and Metaling	Engineering and	Food and Drink	Textiles, Footwear	Total Other
GDP 1995 weight	226	4	20	19	88	35	16	44
1974	91	85	102	273	54	127	120	97
1975	87	71	89	248	54	123	112	86
1976	87	82	103	225	52	124	117	88
1977	87	92	100	216	51	124	122	88
1978	87	97	98	205	49	129	121	91
1979	86	89	95	198	51	129	114	92
1980	81	74	87	161	49	125	102	83
1981	78	70	84	174	50	117	95	77
1982	79	76	85	167	53	114	88	76
1983	79	98	92	148	51	112	89	79
1984	82	81	93	167	55	111	99	80
1985	84	85	96	160	57	108	110	82
1986	81	86	97	125	56	106	106	84
1987	81	62	98	128	54	106	112	88
1988	86	70	94	137	61	108	115	95
1989	89	87	94	132	65	104	110	102
1990	90	94	97	133	66	107	111	103
1991	88	94	93	142	64	102	104	98
1992	88	96	92	130	67	101	104	98
1993	91	95	93	112	78	104	100	96
1994	96	99	97	97	92	99	102	98
1995	100	100	100	100	100	100	100	100
1996	103	100	113	100	106	98	103	97
1997	109	100	126	105	117	97	105	98
1998	112	102	124	119	126	92	94	96
1999	114	101	127	111	136	93	86	94

Although it is not apparent from the aggregate data presented above, in recent years the experience of manufacturing in Scotland is essentially a tale of two distinct sub-sectors: electronics and the rest of manufacturing. Between the first quarters of 1990 and 1998 electronics grew by 200% as compared to growth of about 29% in the UK. Over the same period manufacturing as a whole grew by some 26% in Scotland but only by around 4% in the UK as a whole. However, the manufacturing sector excluding electronics actually contracted by some 13% in Scotland while remaining fairly constant in the UK as a whole. Silicon Glen has been the major success story of Scottish manufacturing. The recent past (specifically the year 2000) has, however, seen a reversal of the fortunes of UK and Scottish electronics with the former growing more rapidly. It is too early to say whether this is due to cyclical factors or the 'maturing' of the industry through, for example, saturation of the PC market. It is apparent, however, that the uncertain future of the industry, exacerbated by the downturn in the US economy is currently having a differential impact on the Scottish economy.

ADDITIONAL FEATURES OF THE SCOTTISH ECONOMY

The Department of Trade and Industry now produces regular reviews of regional competitiveness. Considerable emphasis is attached to this concept since it is defined as the ability of regions to generate high income and employment levels while remaining exposed to domestic and international competition. Some indicators, such as GDP per head and unemployment rates discussed above are primarily regarded as the outcome of the competitiveness process. Other indicators, such as labour productivity and the rate of new firm formation are reported as sources of differential competitiveness. Finally, other indicators such as average earnings have a less clear cut status: lower earnings reduce costs and increase competitiveness, but higher earnings also make it easier to sustain higher income levels.

There are two features of regional competitiveness: price competitiveness and non-price competitiveness. Scotland's ability to compete on price depends on the costs of its inputs and the productivity of those inputs. While attention should really focus on all inputs, data on labour is more readily available than on land and capital. In April 1999, the average gross weekly earnings of male employees in Scotland amounted to £378 or about £19,000 per year. Real earnings increased for both males and females over the period from 1986, by some 17% for males and 22% for females. Real wages rose by more in Great Britain, however, by 22% for males and 34% in Great Britain. By April 1999, average male earnings had risen to £406 per week. The average for all employees was £365 about £35 (9%) less than the Great Britain average. Data for April 2000 for a range of occupations is presented in Table 14.

Scottish earnings as a percentage of the corresponding Great Britain figure vary between just less than 90% for associate professional and technical occupations to 98.4% for craft and related occupations. Perhaps surprisingly, given their lower geographic mobility, manual occupations are closer to Great Britain earnings levels than non-manual. However, this may reflect greater homogeneity among manual workers and/ or the effects of national bargaining. Female earnings are only 74.7% of male earnings in Scotland on average. There is considerable variation across occupations, from 63.4% in craft and related occupations to 88.8% in clerical and secretarial. Naturally, these averages reflect, to a degree the distribution of employment by sex across industries and considerable caution should be exercised in deducing anything about possible 'discrimination'.

The general rise in real earnings does not necessarily imply that competitiveness declined in Scotland relative to elsewhere, nor does it imply that Scottish competitiveness improved relative to Great Britain as a whole, as increases in wage costs can be offset by increases in labour productivity. However, aggregate labour productivity (as reflected in GDP per employee) was, until recently, thought to have converged on the national average, though doubt has now been cast on this. Evidence on this is mixed. Recent Scottish Executive estimates suggest that aggregate Scottish output per employee is some 5% to 8% below that of the UK, and over 40% below that of the USA. However, data for Gross Value-Added per employee (from the Scottish Production Database) suggest that labour in the production industries as a whole is approximately 12% more productive in Scotland than in England. There were substantial variations in output per head across sectors, however, ranging from a low of

TABLE 14. AVERAGE WEEKLY WAGE OF FULL-TIME EMPLOYEES, SCOTLAND AND GREAT BRITAIN, April 2000

Occupational Group	Scotland Males	Scotland Females	Scotland All	GB All	Scotland as % GB	Scotland Female % Male
Managers and administrators	619.4	426.5	561.8	608.1	92.4	68.9
Professional occupations	593	491.4	546.8	559.6	97.7	82.9
Associate professional and technical occupations	464.2	382	420.1	469	89.6	82.3
Clerical and secretarial occupations	286.9	254.8	264.1	282	93.7	88.8
Craft and related occupations	373.4	236.9	362.4	368.2	98.4	63.4
Personal and protective service occupations	351.2	233.9	298.1	306	97.4	66.6
Sales occupations	335.6	214.3	277.5	305.6	90.8	63.9
Plant and machine operatives	337.1	238	319.8	328.7	97.3	70.6
Other occupations	285.9	187	264	280.9	94	65.4
All Non-Manual Occupations	496.4	335.3	414.2	452.4	91.6	67.5
All Manual Occupations	335.4	217.3	312.4	323.6	96.5	64.8
All Occupations	423	316.1	379.8	410.6	92.5	74.7

£23,876 in food to a high of £111,560 in coke, oil and nuclear processing. This highlights the need for caution in interpreting productivity differentials, since these are clearly heavily influenced by the capital intensity of the industry, among other things.

Firms do not, however, compete on price alone, and rates of new firm formation, expenditures on research and development and innovation rates have all been postulated to contribute to regional competitiveness. However, on these criteria Scotland tends to perform poorly, with the South East tending to dominate. (Ashcroft *et al,* 1994). Scotland is not favoured either by its 'peripherality'. Although single indices of peripherality are problematic, it may be worth noting that Scotland has been ranked as the second most peripheral economy of the standard regions of the UK, with Northern Ireland the only economy to fare worse in this respect.

BANKING

Deposit-taking institutions may be broadly divided into two sectors: the monetary sector, which is predominantly banks, and those institutions outside the monetary sector, of which the most important are the building societies and National Savings. Both sectors are supervised by the Financial Services Authority. As a result of the conversion of several building societies into banks in recent years, the size of the banking sector, which was already substantially greater than the non-bank deposit-taking sector, has increased further.

The main institutions within the British banking system are the Bank of England (the central bank), the retail banks, the merchant banks and the overseas banks. In its role as the central bank, the Bank of England acts as banker to the Government and as a note-issuing authority; it also oversees the efficient functioning of payment and settlement systems.

Since May 1997, the Bank of England has had operational responsibility for monetary policy. At monthly meetings of its monetary policy committee the Bank sets the interest rate at which it will lend to the money markets.

Financial Services Regulation

In May 1997 the Government announced plans to establish a new statutory single financial regulator responsible for the supervision of banks, building societies, insurance companies, investment firms and markets. It will replace the current framework, established under a number of different statutes. The new regulator is the Financial Services Authority (FSA).

The FSA is acquiring its full range of responsibilities in two stages. The first stage was completed on 1 June 1998 when the FSA acquired responsibility, under the Bank of England Act 1998, for supervising banks, listed money market institutions and related clearing houses; the Bank of England had previously exercised this responsibility. The second stage will follow on the implementation of the Financial Services and Markets Act 2000, which is expected by the end of November 2001. At that stage the FSA will acquire its full range of powers and will take on responsibility for the regulation and registration functions of the following regulators and supervisors:

Self-Regulating Organisations
Investment Management Regulatory Organisation (IMRO)

Personal Investment Authority (PIA)
Securities and Futures Authority Ltd (SFA)

Others
Building Societies Commission
Friendly Societies Commission
Registry of Friendly Societies

All the above organisations are based at the FSA's offices in Canary Wharf.

The FSA also supervises the recognised professional bodies and recognised investment exchanges and clearing houses, ensuring that they continue to fulfil their regulatory responsibilities.

The new legislation gives the FSA four statutory objectives: to maintain confidence in the UK financial system; to promote public understanding of the financial system; to secure an appropriate degree of protection for consumers; to contribute to the reduction of financial crime.

The new legislation requires the FSA to pursue its objectives in a way that is efficient and economic in the use of its resources; takes account of the responsibilities of firms' own management; facilitates innovation in financial services; balances restrictions on firms with the benefits of regulation; takes account of the international nature of financial services business and the value of competition between firms; seeks to minimise any adverse effects on competition.

The FSA is currently finalising the details of the new regulatory regime. To help it consult the regulated industry and consumers it has established a Practitioner Forum and Consumer Panel.

Central Register/Public Enquiries

The FSA maintains the Central Register of all firms which are authorised to carry on investment business and authorised deposit takers. The entry for each firm gives its name, address and telephone number; a reference number; its authorisation status; and states which organisation regulates it; and whether it can handle client money. The FSA has issued a series of booklets aimed at providing generic advice to consumers and providing contact points for help and further information. These are also available on the FSA website. The FSA has also established a Consumer Helpline: 0845 606 1234 and Website: www.fsa.gov.uk/consume.

Authorised Institutions

Banking in the UK is regulated by the Banking Act 1987, as amended by the European Community's Second Banking Co-ordination directive, which came into effect on 1st January 1993, now itself part of the Banking Consolidation Directive 2000. The Banking Act 1987 established a single category of banks eligible to take deposits from the public; these are known as authorised institutions. Authorisations under the Act has, since June 1998, been granted by the Financial Services Authority; it is an offence for anyone not on its list of authorised institutions to conduct deposit-taking business, unless they are exempted from the requirements of the Act (e.g. building societies) and certain international development bodies. The FSA is also responsible for supervision of banks and the supervision of clearing and settlement systems.

The implementation of the Second Banking Co-ordination Directive banks permits banks incorporated and authorised in one EU member state to carry on certain banking activities in other member state without the need for authorisation by that state. Consequently, the FSA no longer authorises banks incorporated in other EU states with branches in the UK; the authorisation of their home state supervisor is sufficient provided that certain notification requirements are met. UK banks, in turn, benefit form these so-called "passporting" arrangements.

Financial Services Compensation Scheme (FSCS)

A new single compensation scheme is to be established by FSA, under the Financial Services and Markets act, to replace the six existing compensation schemes. The current schemes are the Deposit Protection Scheme, the Building Societies Investor Protection Scheme, the Policyholders Protections Scheme, the Investors Compensation Scheme, the Friendly Societies Protection Scheme and the Section 43 Scheme. FSCA will apply different provisions for claims in respect of insurance, deposits and investment business. FSCS will be operationally independent from FSA but accountable to it.

FSCS
Lloyds Chambers, 1 Portsoken Street, London E1

Financial Services Authority
25 The North Colonnade, Canary Wharf, London E14 5HS (Tel: 020-7676 1000; Email: publicenquiries@fsa.gov.uk; Web: www.fsa.gov.uk)
Chairman: Sir Howard Davies

OFFICIAL INTEREST RATES 2000-2001	
8 February 2001	5.75%
5 April 2001	5.50%
10 May 2001	5.25%
2 August 2001	5.00%

Retail Banks
The major retail banks are Abbey National, Alliance and Leicester, Bank of Scotland, Barclays, Clydesdale, Halifax, HSBC (formerly Midland), Lloyds/TSB, National Westminster, Northern Rock, Royal Bank of Scotland and the Woolwich. The Clydesdale Bank is also a major retail bank in Scotland.

Retail banks offer a wide variety of financial services to companies and individuals, including current and deposit accounts, loan and overdraft facilities, automated teller (cash dispenser) machines, cheque guarantee cards, credit cards and debit cards.

The Banking Ombudsman scheme provides independent and impartial arbitration in disputes between a bank and its customer.

Banking hours differ throughout the UK. Many banks now open longer hours and some at weekends, and hours vary from branch to branch. Current core opening hours in Scotland are Monday to Friday 9 a.m. to 5 p.m.

Payment Clearings
The Association for Payment Clearing Services (APACS) is an umbrella organisation for payment clearings in the UK. It operates three clearing companies: BACS Ltd, the Cheque and Credit Clearing Company Ltd, and CHAPS Clearing Company Ltd.

ASSOCIATION FOR PAYMENT CLEARING SERVICES (APACS)

Mercury House, Triton Court, 14 Finsbury Square, London EC2A 1LQ (Tel: 020-7711 6200).

BACS LTD

De Havilland Road, Edgware, Middx HA8 5QA (Tel: 0870-165 0019).
Bulk clearing of electronic debits and credits (e.g. direct debits and salary credits)

CHEQUE AND CREDIT CLEARING COMPANY LTD

Mercury House, Triton Court, 14 Finsbury Square, London EC2A 1LQ (Tel: 020-7711 6200).
Bulk clearing systems for inter-bank cheques and paper credit items in Great Britain

CHAPS CLEARING COMPANY LTD

Mercury House, Triton Court, 14 Finsbury Square, London EC2A 1LQ (Tel: 020-7711 6200).
Same-day clearing for electronic funds transfers throughout the UK in sterling and globally in euro

MAJOR RETAIL BANKS: FINANCIAL RESULTS 1999

Bank Group	Profit before taxation £m	Profit after taxation £m	Total assets £m	Number of UK branches
Abbey National	1,783	1,261	180,744	750
Alliance and Leicester	455.2	317.9	27,579	316
Bank of Scotland	1,011.9	580.6	59,796	325
Barclays	1,918	1,380	219,494	1,950
Clydesdale	146.2	99.4	7,861	274
Halifax	1,705	1,171	145,000	814
HSBC*	1,724	1,201	106,468	1,670
Lloyds/TSB Group	3,621	2,520	176,091	2,309
NatWest Group	2,142	1,641	185,993	1,727
Northern Rock	202.6	136.6	18,157	107
Royal Bank of Scotland Group	1,001.0	637.0	79,676	664
Woolwich	495.9	331.3	33,239	406

* Formerly known as Midland Bank

CURRENCY

The unit of currency is the pound sterling (£) of 100 pence. The decimal system was introduced on 15 February 1971.

Since 1 January 1999, trade within the European Union has been conducted in the single European currency, the euro; euro notes and coins will not enter circulation until 2002.

COIN

	Metal	Standard Weight (g)	Standard diameter (cm)
Penny	bronze	3.564	2.032
Penny	copper-plated steel	3.564	2.032
2 pence	bronze	7.128	2.591
2 pence	copper-plated steel	7.128	2.591
5p	cupro-nickel	3.25	1.80
10p	cupro-nickel	6.5	2.45
20p	cupro-nickel	5.0	2.14
25p Crown	cupro-nickel	28.28	3.861
50p	cupro-nickel	13.5	3.0
*50p	cupro-nickel	8.00	2.73
£1	nickel-brass	9.5	2.25
†£2	nickel-brass	15.98	2.84
£2	cupro-nickel, nickel-brass	12.00	2.84
£5 Crown	cupro-nickel	28.28	3.861

* New 50p coin introduced on 1 September 1997
† Commemorative coins; not intended for general circulation

LEGAL TENDER

Gold (dated 1838 onwards, if not below least current weight)	to any amount
£5 (Crown since 1990)	to any amount
£2	to any amount
£1	to any amount
50p	up to £10
25p (Crown pre-1990)	up to £10
20p	up to £10
10p	up to £5
5p	up to £5
2p	up to 20p
1p	up to 20p

BANKNOTES

Bank of England notes are currently issued in denominations of £5, £10, £20 and £50 for the amount of the fiduciary note issue, and are legal tender in England and Wales. No £1 notes have been issued since 1984 and in 1998 the outstanding notes were written off.

The current E series of notes was introduced from June 1990. The predominant identifying feature of each note is the portrayal on the back of a prominent British historical figure. The figures portrayed in the current series are:

£5 June 1990—	George Stephenson
£10 November 2000—	Charles Darwin*
£20 June 1991—February 2001	Michael Faraday
£20 June 1999—	Sir Edward Elgar
£50 April 1994—	Sir John Houblon

Although the Bank of England stopped issuing a £1 note in 1983, the Scottish £1 note continues to be issued.

The version of the Bank of England £10 banknote issued in April 1992, bearing a portrait of Charles Dickens, remains legal tender. No plans have been announced to remove it from circulation. The old £20 note bearing a portrait of Michael Faraday has been taken out of circulation but is still accepted by banks.

Legal Tender

Bank of England banknotes which are no longer legal tender are payable when presented at the head office of the Bank of England in London.

Scottish banknotes are not legal tender but they are an authorised currency and enjoy a status comparable to that of Bank of England notes. They are generally accepted by banks irrespective of their place of issue.

Scottish Banknotes

The banks of issue in Scotland are the Bank of Scotland, the Clydesdale Bank and the Royal Bank of Scotland.

BANK OF SCOTLAND

The Mound, Edinburgh EH1 1YZ
(Tel: 0131-442 7777).
Chief Executive: Peter Burt
Denominations of notes issued: £5, £10, £20, £50, £100

£5	HM The Queen
£10, £20, £50 and £100	Sir Walter Scott

CLYDESDALE BANK

30 St Vincent Place, Glasgow G1 2HL
(Tel: 0141-248 7070).
Chairman: Lord Sanderson of Bowden
Chief Executive: John R. Wright
Denominations of notes issued: £5, £10, £20, £50, £100

£5	Robert Burns
£10	Mary Slessor
£20	Robert the Bruce
£50	Adam Smith
£100	Lord Kelvin

ROYAL BANK OF SCOTLAND

PO Box 31, 42 St Andrew Square, Edinburgh
EH2 2YE (Tel: 0131-556 8555).

Chairman: Rt. Hon. Viscount Younger of Leckie,
KT, KCVO
Chief Executive: Frederick Goodwin

Denominations of notes issued: £1, £5, £10,
£20, £100

£1	Edinburgh Castle
£5	Culzean Castle
£10	Glamis Castle
£20	Brodick Castle
£100	Balmoral Castle

Earlier Royal Bank of Scotland Banknotes feature
a portrait of Lord Ilay, its first governor

NOTE CIRCULATION IN SCOTLAND
in the four weeks ending 21 July 2001

	Circulation authorised by certificate £	Average circulation £	Average amount of Bank of England notes and coin held* £
Bank of Scotland	1,289,222	635,000,000	646,700,000
Clydesdale Bank	498,773	481,376,699	486,733,109
Royal Bank of Scotland	888,355	1,066,493,397	1,072,235,392

*Includes Bank of England notes deposited at the Bank of England which, by virtue of the
Currency and Bank Note Act 1928, are to be treated as gold coin by the Bank

LOCAL ENTERPRISE COMPANIES

Local enterprise companies operate under the aegis of either Highlands and Islands Enterprise (HIE) or Scottish Enterprise (SE). These two statutory bodies were set up in 1991 to further the development of the Scottish economy, working with the private and public sectors. Many of their functions are delegated to the local enterprise companies.

Argyll and the Islands Enterprise (HIE)
The Enterprise Centre, Kilmory Industrial Estate, Lochgilphead, Argyll, PA31 8SH (Tel: 01546-602281/602563; Fax: 01546-603964; E-mail: info@aie.co.uk; Web: www.aie.co.uk).
Chief Executive: K. Abernethy

Caithness and Sutherland Enterprise
Tollemache House, High Street, Thurso, Caithness, KW14 8AZ (Tel: 01847-896115; Fax: 01847-893383; E-mail: case@hient.co.uk; Web: www.case-lec.co.uk).
Chief Executive: N. Money

Forth Valley Enterprise (SE)
Laurel House, Laurelhill Business Park, Stirling, FK7 9JQ (Tel: 01786-451919; Fax: 01786-478123; E-mail: forthvalleyinfo@scotent.co.uk; Web: www.scottish-enterprise.com).
Chief Executive: Lorna Jack

Glasgow Development Agency (SE)
Atrium Court, 50 Waterloo Street, Glasgow, G2 6HQ (Tel: 0141-204 1111).
Chief Executive: Ron Culley

Inverness and Nairn Enterprise
The Green House, Beechwood Business Park North, Inverness, IV2 3BL (Tel: 01463-713504; Fax: 01463-712002; E-mail: ine.general@hient.co.uk; Web: www.ine.co.uk).
Chief Executive: W. Sylvester

Lochaber Enterprise (HIE)
St Mary's House, Gordon Square, Fort William, PH33 6DY (Tel: 01397-704326; Fax: 01397-705309; E-mail: lochaber@hient.co.uk; Web: www.lochaberenterprise.co.uk).
Chief Executive: Ms J. Wright

Moray, Badenoch and Strathspey Enterprise (HIE/SE)
Unit 8, Elgin Business Centre, Maisondieu Road, Elgin, Morayshire, IV30 1RH (Tel: 01343-550567; Fax: 01343-550678; E-mail: mbse@hient.co.uk).
Chief Executive: R. Ruane

Orkney Enterprise
14 Queen Street, Kirkwall, Orkney, KW15 1JE (Tel: 01856-874638; Fax: 01856-872915; E-mail: orkney@bis.uk.com).
Chief Executive: K. Grant

Ross and Cromarty Enterprise (HIE)
69–71 High Street, Invergordon, Ross and Cromarty, IV18 0AA (Tel: 01349-853666; Fax: 01349-853833; E-mail: info@race.co.uk; Web: www.race.co.uk).
Chief Executive: G. Cox

Scottish Enterprise Ayrshire (SE)
17–19 Hill Street, Kilmarnock, KA3 1HA (Tel: 01563-526623; Fax: 01563-543636; E-mail: ayrshire@scotent.co.uk; Web: www.scottish-enterprises.co.uk).
Chief Executive: Mrs E. McCann

Scottish Enterprise Borders
Bridge Street, Galashiels, TD1 1SW (Tel: 01896-758991; Fax: 01896-758625; Web: www.scottish-enterprise.com/borders).
Chief Executive: J. McFarlane

Scottish Enterprise Dumfries and Galloway
Solway House, Dumfries Business Park, Tinwald Downs Road, Heathhall, Dumfries, DG1 3SJ (Tel: 01387-245000; Fax: 01387-246224; Web: www.scottish-enterprise.com/dumfriesandgalloway).
Chief Executive: Mrs I. Walker

Scottish Enterprise Dunbartonshire
2nd Floor, Spectrum House, Clydebank Business Park, Clydebank, Glasgow, G81 2DR (Tel: 0141-951 2121; Web: www.scottish-enterprise.com/dunbartonshire).
Chief Executive: D. Anderson

Scottish Enterprise Edinburgh and Lothian
Apex House, 99 Haymarket Terrace, Edinburgh, EH12 5HD (Tel: 0131-3134000; Fax: 0131-3134231; Web: www.scottish-enterprise.com/edinburghandlothian).
Chief Executive: D. Crichton

Scottish Enterprise Fife
Kingdom House, Saltire Centre, Glenrothes, Fife, KY6 2AQ (Tel: 01592-623000; Fax: 01592-623149; E-mail: esfife@scotnt.co.uk; Web: www.scotttish-enterprise.com).
Chief Executive: D. Waring

Scottish Enterprise Grampian
27 Albyn Place, Aberdeen, AB10 1DB
(Tel: 01224-252000; Fax: 01224-213417; E-mail: segrampianenquiries@scotent.co.uk; Web: www.scottish-enterprise.com).
Chief Executive: E. Gillespie

Scottish Enterprise Lanarkshire
New Lanarkshire House, Strathclyde Business Park, Bellshill, ML4 3AD (Tel: 01698-745454; Fax: 01698-842211; E-mail: selenquiry@scotent.co.uk; Web: www.scottish-enterprise.com/lanarkshire).
Chief Executive: Liz Connelly

Scottish Enterprise Renfrewshire (SE)
27 Causeyside Street, Paisley, PA1 1UL
(Tel: 0141-848 0101; Fax: 0141-848 6930; Web: www.scottish-enterprise.com/renfrewshire).
Chief Executive: Mrs L. McMillan

Scottish Enterprise Tayside (SE)
45 North Lindsay Street, Dundee, DD1 1HT
(Tel: 01382-223100; Fax: 01382-322988; E-mail: set.reception@scotent.co.uk; Web: www.scottish-enterprise.com).
Chief Executive: G. McKee

Shetland Enterprise (HIE)
Toll Clock Shopping Centre, 26 North Road, Lerwick, Shetland ZE1 0DE (Tel: 01595-693177; Fax: 01595-693208; E-mail: shet@hie.co.uk; Web: www.shetland.hie.co.uk).
Chief Executive: D. Finch

Skye and Lochalsh Enterprise (HIE)
Kings House, The Green, Portree, Isle of Skye, IV51 9BS (Tel: 01478-612841; Fax: 01478-612164; E-mail: sale@hient.co.uk; Web: www.sale.hie.co.uk).
Chief Executive: R. Muir

Western Isles Enterprise (WIE)
James Square, 9 James Street, Stornoway, Isle of Lewis, HS1 2QN (Tel: 01851-703703; Fax: 01851-704130; E-mail: wie@hient.co.uk; Web: www.wie.co.uk).
Chief Executive: D. MacAulay

PROFESSIONAL AND TRADE BODIES

The Certification Officer is responsible for receiving and scrutinising annual returns from employers' associations. Many employers' associations are members of the Confederation of British Industry (CBI).

CONFEDERATION OF BRITISH INDUSTRY, SCOTLAND

Beresford House, 5 Claremont Terrace, Glasgow G3 7XT (Tel: 0141-332 8661; Fax: 0141-333 9135; Email: allan.hogarth@cbi.org.uk; Web: www.cbi.org.uk).

CBI Scotland is part of the Confederation of British Industry, which was founded in 1965. CBI Scotland is an independent non-party political body financed by industry and commerce. It exists primarily to ensure that the Government and Scottish Executive understands the intentions, needs and problems of business in Scotland. It is the recognised voice of business in Scotland and is consulted as such by the Government and Scottish Executive.

CBI Scotland represents the interests of some 26,500 businesses in Scotland of all sizes and across all sectors.

The governing body of CBI Scotland is its elected Council, which meets four times a year in various parts of Scotland. The Council is assisted by eight expert Committees which advise on the main aspects of policy. The Council and the Committees establish policy in respect of matters devolved to Scotland and contribute their views to the policy formation process of the CBI as a whole on matters reserved to Westminster and in Europe. CBI Scotland has a sister office in Brussels.
Chairman: H. Currie
Director: I. McMillan

PROFESSIONAL AND TRADE BODIES

The following list includes the main professional institutions, employers' associations and trade associations in Scotland, and the Scottish offices of UK institutions.

Aberdeen Fish Curers and Merchants Association
South Esplanade West, Aberdeen, AB11 9FJ
(Tel: 01224-897744; Fax: 01224-871405).
Managing Director: R. H. Milne

Advanced Concrete and Masonry Centre
Faculty of Communication, Engineering and
Science, University of Paisley, Paisley, PA1 2BE
(Tel: 0141-848 3267; Fax: 0141-848 3275;
E-mail: peter.bartos@paisley.ac.uk;
Web: www.civing.paisley.ac.uk/acm).
Director: Prof. P. J. M. Bartos

**Association of Chartered Certified
Accountants**
1 Woodside Place, Glasgow, G3 7QF (Tel: 0141-
309 4050; Fax: 0141-309 4090;
E-mail: members@accaglobal.com;
Web: www.accaglobal.com).
Head of ACCA Scotland: S. Riddle

Association of Scottish Colleges
Argyll Court, Castle Business Park, Stirling, FK9
4TY (Tel: 01786-892100; Fax: 01786-892109;
E-mail: enquiries@ascol.org.uk;
Web: www.ascol.org.uk).
Chief Officer: T. Kelly

Association of Scottish Shellfish Growers
Mountview, Ardvasar, Isle of Skye, IV45 8RU
(Tel: 01471-844 324; Fax: 01471-844 324;
E-mail: douglasmacleod@cs.com).
Chairman: D. McLeod

Boiler and Radiator Manufacturers Association
Savoy Tower 77 Renfrew Street, Glasgow, G2
3BZ
(Tel: 0141-3320826; Fax: 0141-3325788;
E-mail: barma@metcom.org.uk).
Secretary: J. Carruthers

Booksellers' Association
Milngavie Bookshop, 37 Douglas Street,
Milngavie, Glasgow, G62 6PE (Tel: 0141-956
4752; Fax: 0141-956 4819;
E-mail: enquiries@scotlandsbooks.co.uk;
Web: www.scotlandsbooks.co.uk).
Hon. Secretary: R. Lane

**Brewers' and Licensed Retailers' Association
of Scotland**
6 St Colme Street, Edinburgh, EH3 6AD
(Tel: 0131-225 4681; Fax: 0131-220 1132;
Web: www.scottishhubs.co.uk).
Secretary: G. Miller

British Box and Packaging Association
64 High Street, Kirkintilloch, Glasgow, G66 1PR
(Tel: 0141-777 7272; Fax: 0141-777 7747;
E-mail: npcorg@aol.com;
Web: www.boxpackaging.org.uk).
President: A. Glen

British Christmas Tree Growers Association
18 Cluny Place, Edinburgh, EH10 4RL
(Tel: 0131-447 0499; Fax: 0131-447 6443;
E-mail: 100553.2161@compuserve.com;
Web: www.christmastree.org.uk).
Secretary: R. M. Hay, CBE

British Disposable Products Association
64 High Street, Kirkintilloch, Glasgow, G66 1PR
(Tel: 0141-777 7272; Fax: 0141-777 7747;
E-mail: npcorg@aol.com;
Web: www.bdpa.co.uk).
Chairman: B. Clarke

**British Hospitality Association – Scottish
Office**
Saltire Court, 20 Castle Terrace, Edinburgh,
EH1 2EN (Tel: 0131-200 7484; Fax: 0131-228
8888; E-mail: john.a.loudon@dundas.wilson.com).
Secretary: J. Loudon

**British Marine Industries Federation -
Scotland**
Westgate, Toward, Dunoon, Artyll, PA23 7VA
(Tel: 01369-870251; Fax: 01369-870251;
E-mail: bmif-s@clydemarinepress.co.uk).
President: D. Wilkie

British Medical Association – Scottish Office
14 Queen Street, Edinburgh, EH2 1LL
(Tel: 0131-247 3000; Fax: 0131-247 3001;
E-mail: info.edinbirgh@bma.org.uk;
Web: www.bma.org.uk).
Scottish Secretary: Dr W. O'Neill

British Polyolefin Textiles Association
Priestoun, Edzell, Angus, DD9 7UD
(Tel: 01356-648521; Fax: 01356-648521).
Secretary: R. H. B. Learoyd

**British Veterinary Association – Scottish
Branch**
SAC Veterinary Science Division, Mill of
Crabstone, Aberdeen, AB21 9TB
(Tel: 01224-711177; Fax: 01224-711184).
Hon. Secretary: D. Gray

Business Enterprise Scotland
18 Forth Street, Edinburgh, EH1 3LH
(Tel: 0131-550 3839; Fax: 0131-550 3839;
E-mail: bes@bes.org.uk;
Web: www.bes.org.uk/bes).
Chief Executive: R. Miller

CBS Network
Society Place, West Calder, W. Lothian, EH55
8EA (Tel: 01506-871 370; Fax: 01506-873 079;

E-mail: info@cbs-network.org.uk;
Web: www.cbs-network.org.uk).
Company Secretary: J. Pearce

Central Council for Education and Training in Social Work
James Craig Walk, Edinburgh, EH1 3BA
(Tel: 0131-244 1949; Fax: 0131-220 6717).
Head: Ms K. Peart (acting)

Chartered Institutes of Arbitrators (Arbiters) – Scottish Branch
Whittinghame House, 1099 Great Western Road, Glasgow, G12 0AA (Tel: 0141-334 7222; Fax: 0141-334 7700;
E-mail: scottish-arbitrator@blsa.co.uk;
Web: www.scottish-arbitrators.org).
Hon. Secretary and Treasurer: B. L. Smith

Chartered Institute of Bankers in Scotland
Drumsheugh House, 38B Drumsheugh Gardens, Edinburgh, EH3 7SW (Tel: 0131-473 7777; Fax: 0131-473 7788; E-mail: info@ciobs.org.uk;
Web: www.ciobs.org.uk).
Chief Executive: C. W. Munn

Chartered Institute of Housing in Scotland
6 Palmerston Place, Edinburgh, EH12 5AA
(Tel: 0131-255 4544; Fax: 0131-225 4566;
Web: www.cin.org).
Director: A. Ferguson

Chartered Institute of Marketing
3rd Floor, 100 Wellington Street, Glasgow, G2 6DH (Tel: 0141-221 7700; Fax: 0141-221 7766;
E-mail: glasgow@cim.co.uk;
Web: www.cim.co.uk).
Director, Scotland: C. Gardiner

Chartered Institute of Public Finance and Accountancy
CIPFA Scotland, 8 North West Circus Place, Edinburgh, EH3 6ST (Tel: 0131-220 4316; Fax: 0131-220 4305; E-mail: cipfa.scotland@cipfa.org).
Director: I. P. Doig

Chartered Institution of Water and Environmental Management – Scottish Branch
Scottish Environment Protection Agency
Erskine Court, Castle Business Park, Stirling, FK9 4TR (Tel: 01786-457700; Fax: 01786-446885; E-mail: bob.sargent@sepa.org.uk;
Web: www.ciwem.org.uk).
Chief Executive: B. Sargent

CML Scotland
Savile Row, London, W1X 1AF
(Tel: 020-74402227; Fax: 01475-551880).
Chairman: K. Foster

Committee of Scottish Clearing Bankers
The Drumsheugh House, 38 Drumsheugh Gardens, Edinburgh, EH3 7SW (Tel: 0131-473 7770; Fax: 0131-473 7799;
E-mail: info@scotbanks.co.uk;
Web: www.scotbanks.co.uk).
Chairman: S. Grimshaw

Confederation of Passenger Transport UK - Scotland
41 Laigh Road, Newton Mearns, Glasgow, G77 5EX (Tel: 0141-577 6455; Fax: 0141-616 0866;
E-mail: pthompson@cptscotland.fsnet.co.uk).
Regional Secretary: P. Thompson

COSLA (Convention of Scottish Local Authorities)
Rosebery House, 9 Haymarket Terrace, Edinburgh, EH12 5XZ (Tel: 0131-474 9200; Fax: 0131-474 9292; E-mail: carol@cosla.gov.uk; Web: www.cosla.gov.uk).
Chief Executive: Ms O. Aitken

Dietitians Scotland
BDA Scottish Forum, Charles House,
148–9 Great Charles Street, Queensway, Birmingham, B3 3HT (Tel: 0121-200 8021; Fax: 0121-200 8081; E-mail: j.grigg@bda.uk.com; Web: www.qmuc.ac.uk/dietweb).
Senior Lecturer: Dr F. Pender

Direct Marketing Association (UK) Ltd
41 Comely Bank, Edinburgh, EH4 1AF
(Tel: 0131-315 4422; Fax: 0131-315 4433;
Web: www.dma.org.uk).
Manager: J. Scobie

Edinburgh Chamber of Commerce and Enterprise
27 Melville Street, Edinburgh, EH3 7JF
(Tel: 0131-477 7000; Fax: 0131-477 7002;
E-mail: info@ecce.org; Web: www.ecce.org).
Chief Executive: W. Furness

Faculty of Actuaries in Scotland
18 Dublin Street, Edinburgh, EH1 3PP
(Tel: 0131-240 1300; Fax: 0131-240 1313;
E-mail: faculty@actuaries.org.uk;
Web: www.actuaries.org.uk).
Secretary: W. Mair

Faculty of Advocates
Advocates Library, Parliament House,
Edinburgh, EH1 1RF (Tel: 0131-226 5071).
Dean: G. N. H. Emslie, QC

Federation of Civil Engineering Contractors
105 West George Street, Glasgow, G2 1QL
(Tel: 0141-221 3181; Fax: 0141-204 1202).
Chief Executive: P. T. Hughes

Federation of Master Builders
11 Mentone Gardens, Edinburgh, EH9 2DJ
(Tel: 0131-667 5888; Fax: 0131-667 5548;
E-mail: ian@fmb.org.uk; Web: www.fmb.org.uk).
Director-General: I. Davis

Federation of Small Businesses – Scottish Office
74 Berkeley Street, Glasgow, G3 7DS
(Tel: 0141-221 0775; Fax: 0141-221 5954;
E-mail: scotland.policy@fsb.org.uk;
Web: www.fsb.org.uk).
Scottish Policy Convener: J. Torrance

Forestry Contracting Association
Dalfling, Blairdaff, Inverurie, Aberdeenshire,
AB51 5LA (Tel: 01467-651368; Fax: 01467-
651595; E-mail: members@fcauk.com
Chief Executive: B. Hudson

Forest Industries Development Council
53 George Street, Edinburgh, EH2 2HT
(Tel: 0131-220 9290; Fax: 0131-220 9291;
E-mail: mail@fide.org.uk).
Executive Director: P. Wilson

Freight Transport Association Ltd
Hermes House, Melville Terrace, Stirling, FK8
2ND (Tel: 01786-457500; Fax: 01786-450412;
E-mail: stirling@fta.co.uk; Web: www.fta.co.uk).
Executive Director: R.M. Armstrong

General Teaching Council for Scotland
Clerwood House, 96 Clermiston Road,
Edinburgh, EH12 6UT (Tel: 0131-314 6000;
Fax: 0131-314 6001; E-mail: gtcs@gtcs.org.uk;
Web: www.gtcs.org.uk).
Chief Executive: M. McIver

Glasgow Chamber of Commerce and Manufacturers
30 George Square, Glasgow, G2 1EQ
(Tel: 0141-204 2121; Fax: 0141-221 2336;
E-mail: chamber@glasgowchamber.org;
Web: www.glasgowchamber.org).
Chief Executive: D. Tannahill

Harris Tweed Authority
6 Garden Road, Stornoway, Isle of Lewis, HS1
2QJ (Tel: 01851-702269; Fax: 01851-702600;
E-mail: enquiries@harristweed.org;
Web: www.harristweed.org).
Chief Executive and Secretary: I. A. Mackenzie

Headteachers' Association of Scotland
Jordanhill Campus, University of Strathclyde,
Southbrae Drive, Glasgow, G13 1PP
(Tel: 0141-950 3298; Fax: 0141-950 3434;
E-mail: head.teachers@strath.ac.uk).
General Secretary: G. S. Ross

Heating and Ventilating Contractors Association
Bush House, Bush Estate, Midlothian, EH26
0SB (Tel: 0131-445 5580; Fax: 0131-445 2502;
E-mail: hvca.bushhouse@lineone.net;
Web: www.hvca.org.uk).
Executive Officer: B. Dyer

ICFM Scotland (Institute of Charity Fundraising Managers)
c/o Bank of Scotland, 12 Bankhead Crossway
South, Edinburgh, EH11 4EN
(Tel: 0131-453 6517;
E-mail: annemorrison@icfmscotland.freeserve.co.uk;
Web: www.icfm.org.uk).
Development Officer: Ms A. Morrison

Independent Federation of Nursing in Scotland
Office 5, 18 Crowhill Road, Bishopbriggs, G64
1QY (Tel: 0141-772 9222; Fax: 0141-762 3776;
E-mail: ifoninscotland@cs.com).
General Secretary: Ms I. F. O'Neill

Institute of Auctioneers and Appraisers in Scotland
The Rural Centre, West Mains, Ingliston,
Newbridge, Midlothian, EH28 8NZ
(Tel: 0131-472 4067; Fax: 0131-472 4067).
Secretary: W. Blair

Institute of Chartered Accountants of Scotland
CA House, 21 Haymarket Yards, Edinburgh,
EH12 5BH (Tel: 0131-347 0100; Fax: 0131-347
0105; E-mail: enquiries@icas.org.uk;
Web: www.icas.org.uk).
Chief Executive: D. A. Brew

Institute of Chartered Foresters
7A St Colme Street, Edinburgh, EH3 6AA
(Tel: 0131-225 2705; Fax: 0131-220 6125;
E-mail: icf@charteredforesters.org;
Web: www.charteredforesters.org).
Executive Director: Ms M. Dick, OBE

Institute of Energy (Scotland)
Merchiston Campus – School of the Built
Environment, Napier University, 10 Colinton
Road, Edinburgh, EH10 5DT (Tel: 0131-455
2253).
Chairman: J. Currie

**Institute of Environmental Management and
Assessment**
St Nicholas House, 70 New Port, Lincoln, LN1
3DP (Tel: 01522-540069; Fax: 01522-540090;
E-mail: info@iema.net; Web: www.iema.net).
Chief Executive Officer: R. Foster

Institute of Food Science and Technology
Caledonian University, City Campus, Glasgow,
G4 0BA (Tel: 0141-331 8514; Fax: 0141-331
3208; E-mail: k.aidoo@gcal.ac.uk).
Hon. Secretary: Dr K. Aidoo

**Scottish IPA (Institute of Practitioners in
Advertising)**
c/o 25 Rutland Square, Edinburgh, EH1 2BW
(Tel: 0777-578 7253; Fax: 0131-473 1577;
Web: www.scottishipa.co.uk).
Chairman: G. Brooksbank

**Institution of Engineers and Shipbuilders in
Scotland**
Clydeport Building, 16 Robertson Street,
Glasgow, G2 8DS (Tel: 0141-248 3721; Fax:
0141-221 2698; E-mail: secretary@iesis.org).
President: Prof. D. Kirkwood

Institute of Healthcare Management
Mews Cottage, Bellevue Lane, Ayr, KA7 2DS
(Tel: 01292-280814; Fax: 01292-280814;
E-mail: d.mcneill@ihmscotland@ihmscotland.co.uk;
Web: www.ihmscotland.co.uk).
Secretary: D. McNeill

**International Association of Drilling
Contractors (North Sea Chapter)**
Wood International Centre, Craigshaw Drive,
West Tullos, Aberdeen, AB12 3AG
(Tel: 01224-874 800; Fax: 01224-875 600;
E-mail: dennis.krahn@iadc.org;
Web: www.iadc.org).
Director of European Offshore Affairs:
D. Krahn

Law Society of Scotland
26 Drumsheugh Gardens, Edinburgh, EH3 7YR
(Tel: 0131-226 7411; Fax: 0131-225 2934;
E-mail: lawscot@lawscot.org.uk;
Web: www.lawscot.org.uk).
Chief Executive: D. R. Mill

The Malt Distillers Association of Scotland
1 North Street, Elgin, IV30 1UA (Tel: 01343-544
077; Fax: 01343-548523;
E-mail: mdas@grigor-young.co.uk).
Secretary: Grigor and Young Solicitors

Mining Institute of Scotland
1/3 Russell Gardens, Edinburgh, EH12 5PG
(Tel: 0131-346 0653; Fax: 0131-346 0667;
E-mail: d.seath@btinternet.com).
Branch Secretary: D. Seath

**National Board for Nursing, Midwifery and
Health Visiting for Scotland**
22 Queen Street, Edinburgh, EH2 1NT
(Tel: 0131-226 7371; Fax: 0131-225 9970;
Web: www.nbs.org.uk).
Chief Executive: D. C. Benton

National Farmers' Union of Scotland
Rural Centre, West Mains, Ingliston, Newbridge,
Midlothian, EH28 8LT (Tel: 0131-472 4000;
Fax: 0131-472 4010; Web: www.nfus.org.uk).
Chief Executive: E. Rainy Brown

National Federation of Retail Newsagents
6A Weir Street, Falkirk, FK1 1RA (Tel: 01324-
625293; Fax: 01324-613128; Web: www.nfn.org.uk).
Chief Executive: R. Clarke

National Federation of Roofing Contractors
PO Box 28011, Edinburgh, EH16 6WN
(Tel: 0131-448 0266; Fax: 0131-440 4032;
E-mail: amckinney@support-services.fsbusiness.co.uk).
Secretary: A. McKinney

National Specialist Contractors Council
PO Box 28011, Edinburgh, EH16 6WN
(Tel: 0131-448 0266; Fax: 0131-440 4032;
Web: www.scottish-trades.co.uk).
Secretary: A. McKinney

Offshore Contractors' Association
58 Queens Road, Aberdeen, AB15 4YE
(Tel: 01224-326070; Fax: 01224-326071;
E-mail: admin@oca-online.co.uk;
Web: www.oca-online.co.uk).
Chief Executive: I. M. Bell

Procurator Fiscals' Society
Stuart House, 181 High Street, Linlithgow,
EH49 7EN (Tel: 01506-844556; Fax: 01506-
670102).
Procurator Fiscal: Mrs C. Dyer

Producers Alliance for Cinema and Television (PACT) Scotland
249 West George Street, Glasgow, G2 4QE
(Tel: 0141-302 1720; Fax: 0141-302 1721;
Web: www.pact.co.uk).
Manager: Ms M. Scott

Professional Association of Teachers
4–6 Oak Lane, Edinburgh, EH12 6XH
(Tel: 0131-317 8282; Fax: 0131-317 8111;
E-mail: patalba@dial.pipex.com;
Web: www.pat.org.uk).
Secretary for Scotland: R. J. S. Christie

Professional Golfers' Association
Glenbervie Golf Club, Stirling Road, Larbet, Falkirk, FK5 4SJ (Tel: 01324-562451;
Fax: 01324-562190).
Scottish Region Secretary: P. Lloyd

Property Managers Association Scotland Ltd
2 Blythswood Square, Glasgow, G2 4AD
(Tel: 0141-248 4672; Fax: 0141-221 9270).
Secretary: J. Millar

Quality Meat, Scotland
Rural Centre, Ingliston, Newbridge, Midlothian, EH28 8NZ (Tel: 0131-472 4040; Fax: 0131-472 4038; E-mail: info@gmscotland.co.uk;
Web: www.qualitymeatscotland.com).
Managing Director: A. Muir

Road Haulage Association Ltd
Roadway House, 17 Royal Terrace, Glasgow, G3 7NY (Tel: 0141-332 9201; Fax: 0141-331 2077;
E-mail: scotland-northernireland@rha.net;
Web: www.rha.net).
Regional Director: P. Flanders

Royal College of General Practitioners Scotland
25 Queen Street, Edinburgh, EH2 1JX
(Tel: 0131-260 6800; Fax: 0131-260 6836;
E-mail: scottish@rcgp.org.uk;
Web: www.rcgp-scotland.org.uk).
Chairman: Dr W. Reith

Royal College of Nursing of the United Kingdom
42 South Oswald Road, Edinburgh, EH9 2HH
(Tel: 0131-662 1010; Fax: 0131-662 1032).
Scottish Board Secretary: J. Kennedy

Royal College of Physicians and Surgeons of Glasgow
232-242 St Vincent Street, Glasgow, G2 5RJ
(Tel: 0141-221 6072; Fax: 0141-221 1804;

E-mail: registra@rcpsglasg.ac.uk;
Web: www.rcpsglasg.ac.uk).
Registrar: Mr R.K Littlejohn

Royal College of Physicians of Edinburgh
9 Queen Street, Edinburgh, EH2 1JQ
(Tel: 0131-225 7324; Fax: 0131-220 3939;
E-mail: e.tait@rcpe.ac.uk;
Web: www.rcpe.ac.uk).
Secretary: Dr A. C. Parker

Royal College of Surgeons of Edinburgh
Nicolson Street, Edinburgh, EH8 9DW
(Tel: 0131-527 1600; Fax: 0131-557 6406;
E-mail: info@rcsed.ac.uk;
Web: www.rcsed.ac.uk).
Chief Executive: J. R. C. Foster

The Royal Environmental Health Institute of Scotland
3 Manor Place, Edinburgh, EH3 7DH
(Tel: 0131-225 6999; Fax: 0131-225 3993;
E-mail: rehis@rehis.org.uk;
Web: www.rehis.org).
Chief Executive: J. Frater

Royal Incorporation of Architects in Scotland
15 Rutland Square, Edinburgh, EH1 2BE
(Tel: 0131-229 7545; Fax: 0131-228 2188;
E-mail: stombs@rias.org.uk;
Web: www.rias.org.uk).
Secretary: S. Tombs

Royal Institution of Chartered Surveyors
9 Manor Place, Edinburgh, EH3 7DN
(Tel: 0131-225 7078; Fax: 0131-226 3599;
E-mail: emasterman@rics.org.uk;
Web: www.rics.org.uk).
Director: Ms E. Masterman

Royal Pharmaceutical Society of Great Britain
36 York Place, Edinburgh, EH1 3HU
(Tel: 0131-556 4386; Fax: 0131-558 8850;
E-mail: info@rpsis.com;
Web: www.rpsgb.org.uk).
Secretary: Dr S. Stevens

Royal Scottish Forestry Society
Hagg-on-Esk, Canonbie, Dumfriesshire, DG14 0XE (Tel: 01387-371518; Fax: 01387-371418;
E-mail: rsfs@ednet.co.uk; Web: www.rsfs.org).
Administrative Director: A. G. Little

Royal Town Planning Institute
57 Melville Street, Edinburgh, EH3 7HL
(Tel: 0131-226 1959; Fax: 0131-226 1909;
E-mail: scotland@rtpi.org.uk).
Director: G. U'ren

Scottish and Northern Ireland Plumbing Employers' Federation
2 Walker Street, Edinburgh, EH3 7LB
(Tel: 0131-225 2255; Fax: 0131-226 7638;
E-mail: info@snipef.org;
Web: www.snipef.org).
Director and Secretary: R. D. Burgon

The Scottish Assessors' Association
Chesser House, 500 Gorgie Road, Edinburgh, EH11 3YJ (Tel: 0131-469 5589; Fax: 0131-469 5599; E-mail: lvjb@callnetuk;
Web: www.lothian-vjb.gov.uk).
President: J. A. Cardwell

Scottish Federation of Housing Associations
38 York Place, Edinburgh, EH1 3HU
(Tel: 0131-556 5777; Fax: 0131-557 6028;
E-mail: sfha@sfha.co.uk; Web: www.sfha.co.uk).
Director: David Orr

Scottish Association of Master Bakers
4 Torphichen Street, Edinburgh, EH3 8JQ (Tel: 0131-229 1401; Fax: 0131-229 8239;
E-mail: master.bakers@samb.co.uk;
Web: www.samb.co.uk).
Chief Executive: I. Hay

Scottish Association of Sign Language Interpreters (SASLI)
54 Queen Street, Edinburgh, EH2 3NS
(Tel: 0131-225 9995; Fax: 0131-225 9932;
E-mail: mail@sasli.org.uk;
Web: www.sasli.org.uk).
Director: Mrs D. Mair

Scottish Building Contractors Association
4 Woodside Place, Glasgow, G3 7QF
(Tel: 0141-353 5050; Fax: 0141-332 2928;
E-mail: smith@sbca.freeserve.co.uk).
Association Secretary: N. J. Smith

Scottish Building
Carron Grange, Carrongrange Avenue, Stenhousemuir, FK5 3BQ (Tel: 01324-555550;
Fax: 01324-555551;
E-mail: info@scottish-building.co.uk;
Web: www.scottish-building.co.uk).
Chief Executive: S. C. Patten, FRSA

Scottish Chambers of Commerce
12 Broughton Place, Edinburgh, EH1 3RX
(Tel: 0131-557 9500; Fax: 0131-558 3257;
E-mail: mail@scottishchambers.org.uk;
Web: www.scottishchambers.org.uk).
Director: L. Gold, CBE

Scottish Chiropractic Association
St Boswells Chiropractic Clinic, 16 Jenny Moores Road, St Boswells, Melrose, TD6 0AL
(Tel: 01835-824026; Fax: 01835-824046;
E-mail: sca@scottishborders.co.uk;
Web: www.sca-chiropractic.org.uk).
President: Dr J.G. Wight

The Scottish Committee of Optometrists
7 Queens Buildings, Queensferry Road, Rosyth, Fife, KY11 2RA (Tel: 01383-419444; Fax: 01383-416778; E-mail: scoptom@aol.com;
Web: www.scottishoptometrists.co.uk).
Chairman: F. A. Munro

The Timber Frame Industry Association
TRADA Offices, Office 30, Stirling Business Centre, Wellgreen Place, Stirling, FK8 2DZ
(Tel: 01786-445075; Fax: 01786-474412;
E-mail: office@timber-frame.org;
Web: www.timber-frame.org).
Chairman: R. Macfarlane

Scottish Conveyancing and Executry Services Board
1 John's Place, Leith, Edinburgh, EH6 7EL
(Tel: 0131-555 6521; Fax: 0131-553 5011;
E-mail: info@scesb.co.uk; Web: www.scesb.co.uk).
Secretary: E. B. Simmons

Scottish Council for Development and Industry
23 Chester Street, Edinburgh, EH3 7ET
(Tel: 0131-225 7911; Fax: 0131-220 2116;
E-mail: enquiries@scdi.org.uk;
Web: www.scdi.org.uk).
Chief Executive: A. Wilson

Scottish Crofters Union
Old Mill, Broadford, Isle of Skye, IV49 9AQ
(Tel: 01471-822529; Fax: 01471-822799;
E-mail: crofters.union@talk21.com;
Web: www.scu.co.uk).
Director: R. Dutton

Scottish Daily Newspaper Society
48 Palmerston Place, Edinburgh, EH12 5DE
(Tel: 0131-220 4353; Fax: 0131-220 4344;
E-mail: info@sdns.org.uk).
Director: J. B. Raeburn

Scottish Dairy Association
4A Torphichen Street, Edinburgh, EH3 8JQ
(Tel: 0131-221 0109; Fax: 0131-221 0220;
E-mail: admin@scotdairy.org.uk).
Company Secretary: K. Hunter

Scottish Dance Teachers' Alliance
101 Park Road, Glasgow, G4 9JE
(Tel: 0141-339 8944; Fax: 0141-357 4994;
E-mail: alliance@mcmail.com).
President: Ms S. McDonald

Scottish Decorators Federation
222 Queensferry Road, Edinburgh, EH4 2BN
(Tel: 0131-343 3300; Fax: 0131-315 2289).
Director: I. Rogers

Scottish Employers' Council for the Clay Industries
Caradale Brick, Etna Works, Lower Bathville, Armadale, W. Lothian., EH48 2LZ
(Tel: 01501-730671; Fax: 01501-732991).
Managing Director: V. J. Burgoyne

Scottish Engineering
105 West George Street, Glasgow, G2 1QL
(Tel: 0141-221 3181; Fax: 0141-204 1202;
E-mail: consult@scottishengineering.org.uk).
Chief Executive: P. Hughes, OBE, FREng.

Scottish Financial Enterprise
91 George Street, Edinburgh, EH2 3ES
(Tel: 0131-247 7700; Fax: 0131-247 7709;
E-mail: info@sfe.org.uk; Web: www.sfe.org.uk).
Chief Executive: R. Perman

Scottish Grocers Federation
222–224 Queensferry Road, Edinburgh, EH4 2BN (Tel: 0131-343 3300; Fax: 0131-343 6147).
Chief Executive: D.S. Landsburgh

Scottish House-Builders Association
Carron Grange, Carrongrange Avenue, Stenhousemuir, FK5 3BQ (Tel: 01324-555550; Fax: 01324-555551;
E-mail: info@scottish-building.co.uk).
Manager: B. Black

Scottish Institute for Wood Technology
University of Abertay Dundee, Bell Street, Dundee, DD1 1HG
(Tel: 01382-308930; Fax: 01382-308663;
E-mail: mltdcrs@tay.ac.uk;
Web: www.scieng.tay.ac.uk/siwt/index.htm).
Technical Director: Dr D. Sinclair

Scottish Law Librarians Group
c/o Shepherd and Wedderburn, Saltire Court, 20 Castle Terrace, Edinburgh, EH1 2ET
(Tel: 0131-228 9900; Fax: 0131-228 1222).
Librarian: Ms F. McLaren

Scottish Library and Information Council
1 John Street, Hamilton, ML3 7EU
(Tel: 01698-458888; Fax: 01698-458899;
E-mail: slic@slainte.org.uk).
Director: R. Craig

Scottish Library Association
1 John Street, Hamilton, ML3 7EU
(Tel: 01698-458888; Fax: 01698-458899;
E-mail: sla@slainte.org.uk;
Web: www.slainte.org.uk).
Director: R. Craig

Scottish Local Government Information Unit
Room 507, Baltic Chambers, 50 Wellington Street, Glasgow, G2 6HJ (Tel: 0141-226 4636; Fax: 0141-221 8786; Web: www.slgiu.gov.uk).
Director: P. Vestri

Scottish Master Wrights' and Builders' Association
98 West George Street, Glasgow, G2 1PJ
(Tel: 0141-333 1679; Fax: 0141-333 1675).
General Secretary: J. F. Lindsay

Scottish Motor Trade Association
3 Palmerston Place, Edinburgh, EH12 5AF
(Tel: 0131-225 3643; Fax: 0131-220 0446;
E-mail: info@smta.co.uk;
Web: www.smta.co.uk).
Director: D. R. W. Robertson

Scottish Museums Council
County House, 20–22 Torphichen Street, Edinburgh, EH3 8JB (Tel: 0131-229 7465; Fax: 0131-229 2728;
E-mail: inform@scottishmuseums.org.uk;
Web: www.scottishmuseums.org.uk).
Director: Ms J. Ryder

Scottish Newspapers Publishers' Association
48 Palmerston Place, Edinburgh, EH12 5DE
(Tel: 0131-220 4353; Fax: 0131-220 4344;
E-mail: info@snpa.org.uk;
Web: www.snpa.org.uk).
Director: J. B. Raeburn

Scottish Pharmaceutical Federation
135 Wellington Street, Glasgow, G2 2XD
(Tel: 0141-221 1235; Fax: 0141-248 5892;
E-mail: spf@npanet.co.uk).
Secretary: F. E. J. McCrossin

Scottish Pelagic Fishermen's Association Ltd
1 Frithside Street, Fraserburgh, Aberdeenshire, AB43 9AR (Tel: 01346-510714; Fax: 01346-510614; E-mail: spfaltd@btinternet.com).
Secretary: D. Duthie

Scottish Plastering and Drylining Association
PO Box 28011, Edinburgh, EH16 6WN
(Tel: 0131-448 0266; Fax: 0131-440 4032;
E-mail: amckinney@support-services.fsbusiness.co.uk).
Secretary: A. McKinney

Scottish Print Employers' Federation
48 Palmerston Place, Edinburgh, EH12 5DE
(Tel: 0131-220 4353; Fax: 0131-220 4344;
E-mail: info@spef.org.uk;
Web: www.spef.org.uk).
Director: J. B. Raeburn

Scottish Publishers' Association
Scottish Book Centre, 137 Dundee Street, Edinburgh, EH11 1BG (Tel: 0131-228 6866;
Fax: 0131-228 3220;
E-mail: info@scottishbooks.org;
Web: www.scottishbooks.org).
Director: Ms L. Fannin

Quality Meat, Scotland
Rural Centre, Ingliston, Newbridge, Midlothian, EH28 8NZ (Tel: 0131-472 4040; Fax: 0131-472 4038; E-mail: info@gmscotland.co.uk;
Web: www.qualitymeatscotland.com).
Managing Director: A. Muir

Scottish Quality Trout
Motherwell Food Park, Bellshill, Lanarkshire, ML4 3JA (Tel: 01698-742666; Fax: 01698-742666; E-mail: info@sqt.org; Web: www.sqt.org).
Chief Executive: G. Russell

Scottish Quality Salmon Ltd
Durn Isla Road, Perth, PH2 7HG
(Tel: 01738-587000; Fax: 01738-621454;
E-mail: enquiries@scottishsalmon.co.uk;
Web: www.scottishsalmon.co.uk).
Chief Executive: B. M. Simpson

Scottish Retail Consortium
222–224 Queensferry Road, Edinburgh, EH4 2BN (Tel: 0131-332 6619/9298; Fax: 0131-332 6597).
Director: P. Browne

Scottish IS
Innovation Centre, 1 Michaelson Square, Kirkton Campus, Livingston, EH54 7DP (Tel: 01506-472200; Fax: 01506-472209;
E-mail: info@scotlandis.com;
Web: www.scotlandis.com).
Chief Executive: Frank Binnie

Scottish Timber Trade Association
Office 14, John Player Building, Stirling Enterprise Park, Springbank Road, Stirling, FK7 7RP (Tel: 01786-451623; Fax: 01786-473112;
Web: www.stta.org.uk).
Secretary: D. J. Sulman

The Scotch Whisky Association
20 Atholl Crescent, Edinburgh, EH3 8HF
(Tel: 0131-222 9200; Fax: 0131-222 9248;
E-mail: enquiries@swa.org.uk;
Web: www.scotch-whisky.org.uk).
Chief Executive: H. Morison

SELECT
Bush House, Bush Estate, Midlothian, EH26 0SB (Tel: 0131-445 5577; Fax: 0131-445 5548;
E-mail: admin@select.org.uk;
Web: www.select.org.uk).
Managing Director: M. D. Goodwin, OBE

Skin, Hide and Leather Traders Association Ltd
Douglas House, Douglas Road, Melrose, Roxburghshire, TD6 9QT (Tel: 01896-822233;
Fax: 01896-823344; E-mail: offices@andaco.com;
Web: www.shalta.org).
Secretary-General: A. D. Cox, MBE

Society of Indexers – Scottish Group
Bentfield, 3 Marine Terrace, Gullane, E. Lothian, EH31 2AY (Tel: 01620-842247; Fax: 01620-842247; E-mail: annemccarthy@btinternet.com;
Web: www.socind.demon.co.uk).
Group Organizer: Mrs A. McCarthy

Society of Local Authority Chief Executives and Senior Managers
Angus Council, The Cross, Forfar, Angus, DD8 1BX (Tel: 01307-473020; Fax: 01307-461874;
E-mail: chiefexec@angus.gov.uk;
Web: www.angus.gov.uk).
Hon. Secretary: A. B. Watson

Society of Scottish Artists
4 Barony Street, Edinburgh, EH3 6PE
(Tel: 0131-557 2354; Web: www.s-s-a.org).
Secretary: Mrs S. Cornish

SPEED
P.O. Box 013718, North Berwick, EH39 5YR
(Tel: 0131-654 1500; Fax: 0131-654 1510;
E-mail: speed@speed.org.uk;
Web: www.speed.org.uk).
Secretary: I. Rodgers

Stone Federation Great Britain - Scottish Section
PO Box 28011, Edinburgh, EH16 6WN
(Tel: 0131-448 0266; Fax: 0131-440 4032).
Secretary: A. McKinney

Timber Growers Association Ltd
5 Dublin Street Lane South, Edinburgh, EH1 3PX (Tel: 0131-538 7111; Fax: 0131-538 7222;
E-mail: tga@timber-growers.co.uk;
Web: www.timber-growers.co.uk).
Chief Executive: J. Gunn

UK Forest Products Association
John Player Building, Stirling Enterprise Park, Springbank Road, Stirling, FK7 7RP
(Tel: 01786-449029; Fax: 01786-473112;
E-mail: dsulman@ukfpa.co.uk;
Web: www.ukfpa.co.uk).
Executive Director: D. J. Sulman

UK Offshore Operators Association Ltd
9 Albyn Terrace, Aberdeen, AB10 1YP
(Tel: 01224-626652; Fax: 01224-626503;
E-mail: info@ukooa.co.uk;
Web: www.oilandgas.org.uk).
Director-General: J. May

TRADE UNIONS

The Certification Officer is responsible for certifying the independence of trade unions, receiving and scrutinising annual returns from trade unions, dealing with complaints about trade union elections and ensuring compliance with statutory requirements governing political funds and union mergers.

The Central Arbitration Committee determines claims for statutory recognition under the Employment Relations Act 1999 and certain issues relating to the implementation of the European Works Council Directive, the Committee also arbitrates trade disputes and adjudicates on disclosure of information complaints.

CERTIFICATION OFFICE FOR TRADE UNIONS AND EMPLOYERS' ASSOCIATIONS, SCOTLAND

58 Frederick Street, Edinburgh EH2 1LN
(Tel: 0131-226 3224).
Assistant Certification Officer for Scotland:
J. L. J. Craig

CENTRAL ARBITRATION COMMITTEE

3rd Floor, Discovery House, 28—42 Banner Street, London EC1Y 8QE
(Tel: 020-7251 9747; Fax: 020-7251 3114).
Chairman: Sir Michael Burton
Secretary: C. Johnston

SCOTTISH TRADES UNION CONGRESS

333 Woodlands Road, Glasgow G3 6NG
(Tel: 0141-337 8100; Fax: 0141-337 8101;
Email: info@stuc.org.uk).

The Congress was formed in 1897 and acts as a national centre for the trade union movement in Scotland. The STUC promotes the rights and welfare of those in work and helps the unemployed. It helps its member unions to promote membership in new areas and industries, and campaigns for rights at work for all employees, including part-time and temporary workers, whether union members or not. It makes representations to government and employers. The Annual Congress in April elects a 38-member General Council on the basis of six industrial sections.

In 2001 the STUC consisted of 46 unions with a membership of 628,159 and 34 directly affiliated Trade Councils.
Chairperson: D. Bleiman
General Secretary: B. Speirs

UNIONS AFFILIATED TO THE SCOTTISH TRADES UNION CONGRESS

Certification Officer for Trade Unions and Employers' Associations, Scotland
58 Frederick Street, Edinburgh, EH2 1LN (Tel: 0131-226 3224; Fax: 0131-200 1300).
Assistant Certification Officer for Scotland: J. L. J. Craig

Amalgamated Engineering and Electrical Union (AEEU)
145–165 West Regent Street, Glasgow, G2 4RZ (Tel: 0141-248 7131; Fax: 0141-221 3898; E-mail: glasgow@aeeu.org.uk; Web: www.aeeu.org.uk).
Scottish Regional Secretary: D. Carrigan

Associated Society of Locomotive Engineers and Firemen (ASLEF)
9 Arkwright Road, Hamstead, London, NW3 6AB (Tel: 020-7317 8600; Fax: 020-7794 6406; E-mail: info@aslef.org.uk).
General Secretary: M. Rix

Association of First Division Civil Servants
2 Caxton Street, London, SW1H 0QH (Tel: 020-7343 1111; Fax: 020-7343 1105; E-mail: head-office@fda.org.uk; Web: www.fda.org.uk).
General Secretary: J. Baume

Association of University Teachers
6 Castle Street, Edinburgh, EH2 3AT (Tel: 0131-226 6694; Fax: 0131-226 2066; E-mail: scotland&ne@aut.org.uk; Web: www.aut.org.uk/auts.html).
Assistant General Secretary: D. Bleiman

British Actors' Equity Association
114 Union Street, Glasgow, G1 3QQ (Tel: 0141-248 2472; Fax: 0141-248 2473; E-mail: lboswell@glasgow.equity.org.uk).
Scottish Organiser and Northern Ireland Secretaries: L. Boswell; D. McFarlane

British Air Line Pilots Association (BALPA)
81 New Road, Harlington, Hayes, Middx, UB3 5BG (Tel: 020-8476 4000; Fax: 020-8476 4077; E-mail: balpa@balpa.org; Web: www.balpa.org).
General Secretary: C. Darke

British Dietetic Association
Department of Nutrition and Dietetics, Raigmore Hospital, Old Perth Road, Inverness, IV2 3UJ (Tel: 01463-704000).
Scottish Officer: J. Grigg

British Orthoptic Society
Orthoptic Department, Royal Alexandra Hospital, Corsebar Road, Paisley, PA2 2PN (Tel: 0141-580 4347; Fax: 0141-580 4135).
Chairman: J. Carpenter
Scottish Representative (Head Orthoptist): Mrs. Diane Russell

British Orthoptic Society
Orthoptic Department, Perth Royal Infirmary, Taymount Terrace, Perth, PH1 1NX (Tel: 01738-623311; Fax: 01738-473306).
Chairman: J. Carpenter
Scottish Representative (Head Orthoptist): Mrs. Diane Russell

Broadcasting, Entertainment, Cinematograph and Theatre Union (BECTU)
114 Union Street, Glasgow, G1 3QQ (Tel: 0141-248 9558; Fax: 0141-248 9588; Web: www.bectu.org.uk).
Scottish Organiser: P. McManus

Communication Workers Union
Granthouse Inn, Duns, Berwickshire, TD11 3RW; E-mail: dundee@cwu106.freeserve.co.uk; Web: www.cwu.org).
Regional Secretary Scotland:
George E. Robertson

Communication Workers Union
Dundee (E) Branch, Room 201, Telephone Exchange, 8 Willisdon Street, Dundee, DD1 1DB (Tel: 01382-223612/302385; Fax: 01382-202094; E-mail: dundee@cwu106.freeserve.co.uk; Web: www.cwu.org).
Regional Secretary Scotland:
George E. Robertson

Connect
22A Caroline Street, St Paul's Square, Birmingham, B3 1UE (Tel: 0121-236 2637; Fax: 0121-236 2616; E-mail: birmingham@connectuk.com; Web: www.connectuk.com).
Chief Executive: S. Petch

The Educational Institute of Scotland
46 Moray Place, Edinburgh, EH3 6BH
(Tel: 0131-225 6244; Fax: 0131-220 3151;
E-mail: membership@eis.org.uk;
Web: www.eis.org.uk).
General Secretary: R. A. Smith

Engineers' and Managers' Association
30 New Street, Musselburgh, E. Lothian, EH21
6JP (Tel: 0131-665 4487; Fax: 0131-665 7513;
E-mail: scot@ema.org.uk;
Web: www.ema.org.uk).
National Officer: Ms A. Douglas

Fire Brigades Union, The
4th Floor, 52 St Enoch Square, Glasgow, G1 4AA
(Tel: 0141-221 2309; Fax: 0141-204 4575;
E-mail: office@fbu-ho.org.uk;
Web: www.fbu-ho.org.uk).
Scottish Regional Secretary: T. Tierney

GMB
Fountain House, 1–3 Woodside Crescent,
Glasgow, G3 7UJ (Tel: 0141-332 8641;
Fax: 0141-332 4491;
E-mail: robert.parker@gmb.org.uk).
Regional Secretary: R. Parker

Independent Union of Halifax Staff
Simmons House, 46 Old Bath Road, Charvil,
Reading, RG10 9QR (Tel: 0118-934 1808;
Fax: 0118-932 0208).
General Secretary: G. Nichols

Institution of Professionals, Managers and Specialists
18 Melville Terrace, Stirling, FK8 2NQ
(Tel: 01786-465999; Fax: 01786-465516;
E-mail: denneya@ipms.org.uk;
Web: www.ipms.org.uk).
National Officer: A. Denney

Manufacturing, Science and Finance Union (MSF)
1 Woodlands Terrace, Glasgow, G3 6DD
(Tel: 0141-331 1216; Fax: 0141-331 1835;
E-mail: glasgow@msf.org.uk;
Web: www.msf.org.uk).
National Secretary: J. Wall

Musicians' Union
11 Sandyford Place, Sauchiehall Street, Glasgow,
G3 7NB (Tel: 0141-248 3723; Fax: 0141-204
3510; E-mail: info@musiciansunion.org.uk;
Web: www.musiciansunion.org.uk).
Scottish District Organizer: I. Smith

NASUWT (National Association of Schoolmasters/Union of Women Teachers)
6 Waterloo Place, Edinburgh, EH1 3DG
(Tel: 0131-523 1110; Fax: 0131-523 1119;
E-mail: rc-scotland@mail.nasuwt.org.uk;
Web: www.nasuwt-scotland.org).
Scottish Official: P. O'Donnell

National League of the Blind and Disabled
43 Byron Avenue, Northfield, Aberdeen, AB16
7LD (Tel: 01224-693966).
Scottish Secretary: George Reid

National Union of Journalists (NUJ)
114 Union Street, Glasgow, G1 3QQ
(Tel: 0141-248 6648; Fax: 0141-248 2473;
E-mail: paul.h@nuj.org.uk).
Scottish Organiser: P. Holleran

National Union of Knitwear, Footwear and Apparel Trades
Orwell, 6 London Road, Kilmarnock, KA3 7AD
(Tel: 01563-527476; Fax: 01563-537851;
E-mail: john-steele@kfat-scot.freeserve.co.uk;
Web: www.kfat.org.uk).
District Secretary: J. Steele

National Union of Marine, Aviation and Shipping Transport Officers
Oceanair House, 750–760 High Road, London,
E11 3BB (Tel: 020-8989 6677; Fax: 020-8530
1015; E-mail: info@numust.org;
Web: www.numast.org).
General Secretary: B. D. Orrell
Deputy General Secretary: P. McEwen

National Union of Mineworkers (NUM)
30 New Street, Musselburgh, EH21 6JP
(Tel: 0131-665 4111; Fax: 0131-665 4104).
Scottish Area Secretary: N. Wilson

National Union of Rail, Maritime and Transport Workers (RMT)
180 Hope Street, Glasgow, G2 2UE
(Tel: 0141-332 1117; Fax: 0141-333 9583;
E-mail: p.mcgarry@rmt.org.uk).
Regional Organizer: P. McGarry

Public and Commercial Services Union (PCS)
6 Hillside Crescent, Edinburgh, EH7 5DY
(Tel: 0131-556 0407; Fax: 0131-557 5613;
E-mail: pauld@pcs.org.uk;
Web: www.pcs.org.uk).
Scottish Secretary: E. Reilly

Scottish Carpet Workers' Union
Viewfield Business Centre, 62 Viewfield Road, Ayr, KA8 8HH (Tel: 01292-261676; Fax: 01292-261676).
Secretary: R. Smillie
Chairperson: P. Bell

Scottish Further and Higher Education Association
Suite 2C, Ingram House, 227 Ingram Street, Glasgow, G1 1DA (Tel: 0141-221 0118; Fax: 0141-221 2583; E-mail: sfhea@easynet.co.uk; Web: www.sfhea.org.uk).
General Secretary: E. H. Smith

Scottish Prison Officers' Association
21 Calder Road, Edinburgh, EH11 3PF (Tel: 0131-443 8105; Fax: 0131-444 0657).
General Secretary: D. Turner

Scottish Secondary Teachers' Association
15 Dundas Street, Edinburgh, EH3 6QG (Tel: 0131-556 5919; Fax: 0131-556 1419; E-mail: info@ssta.org; Web: www.ssta.org.uk).
General Secretary: D. H. Eaglesham

The Society of Chiropodists and Podiatrists
1 Fellmongers Path, Tower Bridge Road, London, SE1 (Tel: 020-7234 8620; Fax: 020-7234 8621; E-mail: enq@scpod.org.uk; Web: www.feetforlife.org).
Chief Executive: Ms H. B. De Lyon

The Society of Radiographers
6 Victoria Road, Brookfield, Johnstone, Renfrewshire, PA5 8TZ (Tel: 01505-382039; Fax: 01505-382039; E-mail: elizabeths@sor.org; Web: www.sor-scotland.org).
Scotland Officer: Ms E. Stow

Transport and General Workers' Union (TGWU)
290 Bath Street, Glasgow, G2 4LD (Tel: 0141-332 7321; Fax: 0141-332 6157).
Regional Secretary: A. Baird

Transport Salaried Staffs' Association
180 Hope Street, Glasgow, G2 2UE (Tel: 0141-332 4698; Fax: 0141-332 9879; E-mail: glasgow@tssa.org.uk; Web: www.tssa.org.uk).
Development Manager: R. S. King

UNiFI
146 Argyle Street, Glasgow, G2 8BL (Tel: 0141-221 6475/6; Fax: 0141-204 3315; E-mail: info@unifi.org.uk; Web: www.unifi.org.uk).
Deputy General Secretary: S. Boyle

UNISON
UNISON House, 14 West Campbell Street, Glasgow, G2 6RX (Tel: 0141-332 0006; Fax: 0141-331 1203; Web: www.unison.org.uk).
Scottish Secretary: M. Smith

Union of Construction, Allied Trades and Technicians (UCATT)
53 Morrison Street, Glasgow, G5 8LB (Tel: 0141-420 2880; Fax: 0141-420 2881).
Scottish Secretary: A. S. Ritchie

Union of Shop, Distributive and Allied Workers (USDAW)
Muirfield, 342 Albert Drive, Glasgow, G41 5PG (Tel: 0141-427 6561; Fax: 0141-427 3155).
Scottish Divisional Officer: F. Whitelaw

THE VOLUNTARY SECTOR IN SCOTLAND

There are around 44,000 voluntary or non-profit organisations in Scotland, of which more than half are registered as charities. It is estimated that four new charities are created in Scotland every working day. Income from public donations is about £500 million a year. Recent research carried out by the Scottish Council for Voluntary Organisations (SCVO) into the size and characteristics of the voluntary workforce found that registered charities in Scotland in 1998/99 employed 59,806 paid staff (equivalent to 49,000 full-time posts), an increase of nearly 9,000 over the 1996 figure. The wider non-profit sector, including Scottish branches of English-registered UK-level charities and voluntary organisations without charity status, employs 100,000 people and generates an annual turnover of as much as £2 billion. Among paid voluntary-sector workers, 68 per cent are women. About 700,000 Scots work on a voluntary basis for non-profit organisations; again, a majority are women.

Voluntary-sector organisations are defined by their independence from the state and by the fact that they are run by unpaid volunteers (although they may employ paid workers), as well as by their non-profit status. However, the sector is increasingly involved in meeting needs and providing services in key areas of government policy such as social inclusion and health, housing and homelessness, and environmental protection. Other fields covered by voluntary organisations include community development; residential care, including care of elderly people; playschemes and other services for children and youth; human rights; peace issues; gender equality and women's rights; racial equality; labour and professional relations; religious interests; mental health; disabilities; racial equality and minorities issues; drugs/alcohol abuse; animal care and wildlife protection; international development and humanitarian aid; and consumers' interests. There are also a great many voluntary organisations promoting arts and culture, sports and outdoor activities, and informal education. The sector is very diverse, including organisations of all sizes and ranging from single-issue groups and campaigns to service provision and advocacy. Voluntary groups and organisations play a key role in the economy at the local level and in community well-being.

The fastest growth in the non-profit sector is occurring in the largest charities, those with annual incomes of over £500,000 a year. Many of these are now delivering a range of social care and

health services which were previously carried out by central and local government. At the same time, however, smaller charities have experienced a sharp drop in resources owing to reductions both in local authority funding and public donations. Nearly 90 per cent of small non-profit organisations (those with annual incomes of less than £25,000) have no paid staff at all but rely entirely on volunteers.

The significant role played by the voluntary sector in policy development and service provision, at the community level, and its weight as an economic sector complementary to the public and private sectors, are recognised in the Scottish Compact. Launched in 1998, the Compact sets out the principles underlying the relationship of co-operation between the Scottish government and the voluntary sector, and was drawn up by a joint working group consisting of representatives of the Scottish Office (before devolution) and the voluntary sector. As well as promoting good practice and encouraging volunteering as an expression of active citizenship, the Compact enables the voluntary sector to have a voice in policy-making through dialogue with government.

The Scottish Executive is committed to supporting the voluntary sector by creating a more stable funding environment for it, including providing core funding to national voluntary organisations and other funding packages where appropriate.

In June 2000 estimated Scottish Executive expenditure on the voluntary sector for the next two years was reported to be as follows:

ESTIMATED SCOTTISH EXECUTIVE EXPENDITURE ON THE VOLUNTARY SECTOR FOR 2000/01 AND 2001/02

	2000/01 £ million	2001/02 £ million
Annual Expenditure Report	6.0	5.9
Infrastructure bodies– Scottish Council for Voluntary Organisations, Volunteer Development Scotland	0.6	0.6
Councils for Voluntary Services	1.3	1.3
Local Volunteer Development Agencies	1.0	1.0
Active Communities Initiative	0.6	0.8
Millennium Volunteers	0.7	0.7
Unemployed Voluntary Action Fund	0.9	0.9
Ethnic Minority Grant Scheme Unallocated	0.3	0.3

Source: Scottish Parliament, Written Answers for the week 12–16 June 2000.

RECENT ISSUES

On 29 March 2000, Scottish justice minister Jim Wallace announced the membership and remit of an independent commission to revise charity law in Scotland. The main provisions are in Part I of the Law Reform (Miscellaneous Provisions) (Scotland) Act 1990. Public charitable collections are regulated under section 119 of the Civic Government (Scotland) Act 1982, and educational endowments are governed by the Education (Scotland) Act 1980.

Voluntary organisations which have pressed for such a review for several years welcomed the move, pointing out that charity law in Scotland is in serious need of updating and systematising. Much of it rests on an obsolete definition of charity itself. The current definition of a charitable organisation is unclear, resulting in anomalies; for instance, at present private schools qualify for charity status but self-help groups, credit unions and groups campaigning for equal rights do not. There is no register of charities in Scotland. Also, there is little co-ordination between the existing regulatory bodies: the Inland Revenue grants charitable status, the Scottish Charity Office investigates allegations, and the Scottish Executive funds and works with charities.

Because of its major focus on work with disadvantaged communities and groups, and especially on social inclusion and on training and employment opportunities for unemployed people, the voluntary sector also has an interest in the review of Scotland's two Enterprise Networks (Scottish Enterprise and Highlands and Islands Enterprise), announced by Henry McLeish, Minister for Enterprise and Lifelong Learning, late in 1999. The Enterprise Networks provide a range of training and economic development services in various areas of Scotland.

THE EUROPEAN DIMENSION

Many voluntary organisations in Scotland are involved in activities and projects implementing the European Union's national and regional Structural Fund programmes, which give financial support to measures addressing the needs of less well-off or geographically isolated regions and societal groups in Europe. The European Social Fund (ESF) is the most important Structural Fund for the voluntary sector. In 1999, Scottish voluntary organisations accounted for £60 million in Structural Fund projects. Approximately £14 million of this came through the 1999 ESF Objective 3 programme, which targets long-term unemployment and the integration of young people and others into working life and supports projects in the areas of training and retraining,

capacity-building, advice and counselling. The new ESF Objective 3 programme for the period 2000—6 makes over £320 million available for raising employability and addressing social exclusion, including promoting lifelong learning and equal opportunities, much of which will be channelled through the voluntary sector.

SCOTTISH COUNCIL FOR VOLUNTARY ORGANISATIONS

The Scottish Council for Voluntary Organisations (SCVO), established in 1936, is the umbrella body for voluntary organisations in Scotland and aims to promote and advocate the independence, interests and value of the voluntary sector among the major players in Scottish life and the wider community. The SCVO has over 2,000 member organisations which it serves from offices in Edinburgh, Glasgow and Inverness. Its services to the voluntary sector include training, seminars and conferences, advice on funding, legislation and management of voluntary organisations, and research on voluntary sector issues. It has a database of sources of charitable funding, and its European Unit provides an initial point of contact for charities seeking access to European funds. It publishes a weekly newspaper, *Third Force News*, and a variety of other publications addressing practical issues of voluntary organisation management and analysing government policy and other issues affecting the sector. There is also a Parliamentary Information and Advice Service, which has published a *Guide to the Scottish Parliament* and a *Guide to Parliamentary Lobbying in Scotland* as tools for voluntary organisations with a policy advocacy role.

SCVO has a Racial Equality Unit, which promotes racial equality in Scottish voluntary organisations, gives advice and training on racial equality issues in the sector, and provides support services to the black and minority ethnic sector. The SCVO also has a Scottish Voluntary HIV and AIDS Forum, which is the co-ordinating body for the voluntary sector's response to HIV and AIDS in Scotland, and includes both organisations concerned specifically with HIV and others which include HIV within a broader remit.

COUNCILS FOR VOLUNTARY SERVICE

Councils for Voluntary Service (CVS) are a network of 55 local community development agencies across Scotland. They are co-ordinated by CVS Scotland, which operates within the SCVO and provides training, information, publications and advice to member CVS. The membership of each CVS is drawn from local voluntary and community groups, numbering on average up to 100, and each CVS plans its activities to meet needs identified by the local voluntary-sector community. CVS develop partnerships with other local organisations (councils, health authorities, enterprise companies, etc.) and act as channels by which local groups can express their views on local decision- and policy-making.

The addresses of CVS and further information on them may be obtained from the Development Officer, CVS Scotland, at the SCVO office in Edinburgh, or from the SCVO website.

ORGANISATIONS

It would be impossible to include here a full list of voluntary-sector organisations in Scotland. SCVO has a database containing details of all its members, which can be consulted on its website.

SCVO (REGISTERED OFFICE)

18/19 Claremont Crescent, Edinburgh EH7 4QD (Tel: 0131-556 3882; Fax: 0131-566 0279; E-mail: enquiries@scvo.org.uk; Web: www.scvo.org.uk).

SCVO WEST OF SCOTLAND (ALSO RACIAL AND EUROPEAN UNITS)

9th Floor, Fleming House, 134 Renfrew Street, Glasgow G3 6ST (Tel: 0141-332 5660, 0141-332 5667; Fax: 0141-3324225).

SCVO NORTH OF SCOTLAND

9 Ardross Terrace, Inverness IV3 5NQ (Tel: 01463 235633; Fax: 01463 716003).

VOLUNTEER DEVELOPMENT SCOTLAND

72 Murray Place, Stirling FK8 2BX (Tel: 01786 479593).

IDEAS

34—36 Rose Street North Lane, Edinburgh EH2 2NP (Tel: 0131-225 5949; Fax: 0131-225 7618; E-mail: scotdec@aol.com).

SCOTTISH COUNCIL FOR CIVIL LIBERTIES

146 Holland Street, Glasgow G2 4NG

SCOTTISH COUNCIL FOR RACIAL EQUALITY

18 Belvedere Park, Edinburgh EH6 4LR

SCOTTISH PENSIONERS' FORUM

333 Woodlands Road, Glasgow G3 6NG (Tel: 0141-337 8100; Fax 0141-337 8101).

WOMEN'S FORUM SCOTLAND

102 Earlbank Avenue, Scotstoun, Glasgow G14 9DY (Tel: 0141-579 7355).

MEDIA

SCOTLAND

TELEVISION
RADIO
THE PRESS
BOOK PUBLISHERS

C

MEDIA SCOTLAND

CROSS-MEDIA OWNERSHIP

There are rules on cross-media ownership to prevent undue concentration of ownership. These were amended by the Broadcasting Act 1996. Radio companies are now permitted to own one AM, one FM and one other (AM or FM) service; ownership of the third licence is subject to a public interest test. Local newspapers with a circulation under 20 per cent in an area are also allowed to own one AM, one FM and one other service, and may control a regional Channel 3 television service subject to a public interest test. Local newspapers with a circulation between 20 and 50 per cent in an area may own one AM and one FM service, subject to a public interest test, but may not control a regional Channel 3 service. Those with a circulation over 50 per cent may own one radio service in the area (provided that more than one independent local radio service serves the area) subject to a public interest test.

Ownership controls on the number of television or radio licences have been removed; holdings are now restricted to 15 per cent of the total television audience or 15 per cent of the total points available in the radio points scheme. Ownership controls on cable operators have also been removed. National newspapers with less than 20 per cent of national circulation may apply to control any broadcasting licences, subject to a public interest test. National newspapers with more than 20 per cent of national circulation may not have more than a 20 per cent interest in a licence to provide a Channel 3 service, Channel 5 or national and local analogue radio services.

BROADCASTING

The British Broadcasting Corporation (BBC) is responsible for public service broadcasting in the UK. Its constitution and finances are governed by royal charter and agreement. On 1 May 1996 a new royal charter came into force, establishing the framework for the BBC's activities until 2006.

The Independent Television Commission and the Radio Authority were set up under the terms of the Broadcasting Act 1990. The ITC is the regulator and licensing authority for all commercially-funded television services, including cable and satellite services. The Radio Authority is the regulator and licensing authority for all independent radio services.

Complaints

The Broadcasting Standards Commission was set up in April 1997 under the Broadcasting Act 1996 and was formed from the merger of the Broadcasting Complaints Commission and the Broadcasting Standards Council. The Commisson is the statutory body for standards and fairness in broadcasting. It is the only organisation in broadcasting to cover all television and radio. This includes BBC and commercial broadcasters as well as text, cable, satellite and digital services. The Commission has three main tasks, set out in the 1996 Broadcasting Act:
— produce codes of practice relating to standards and fairness
— consider and adjudicate on complaints
— monitor, research and report on standards and fairness in broadcasting.

BROADCASTING STANDARDS COMMISSION

7 The Sanctuary, London SW1P 3JS (Tel: 020-7808 1000; Fax: 020-7233 0397; E-mail: bsc@bsc.org.uk; Web: www.bsc.org.uk).

Chairman: Lord Dubs of Battersea
Director: Stephen Whittle

TELEVISION

All channels are broadcast in colour on 625 lines UHF from a network of transmitting stations. Transmissions are available to more than 99 per cent of the population.

The BBC broadcasts two UK-wide television services, BBC 1 and BBC 2; in Scotland these services are designated BBC Scotland on 1 and BBC Scotland on 2. News 24 is a 24-hour BBC television news service broadcast by cable during the day and on BBC 1 at night.

The ITV Network Centre is wholly owned by the ITV companies and undertakes the commissioning and scheduling of those television programmes which are shown across the ITV network. Through its sister organisation, the ITV Association, it also provides a range of services to the ITV companies where a common approach is required.

The total number of receiving television licences in the UK at the end of March 2001 was 22,814,000, of which 98.8 per cent were for colour televisions. Annual television licence fees are: black and white £36.50; colour £109.00.

British Sky Broadcasting is the UK's broadband entertainment company, distributing sports, movies, entertainment and news to 9.5 million households throughout the UK (5.5m via digital and analogue satellite, 2.7m via cable and 1.1m via digital terrestrial television). The launch of the UK's first digital television service, Sky digital on 1 October 1998 has been the fastest, most successful digital roll-out in Europe, attracting more than 5m viewers to date. Sky also embraces alternative platforms including interactive TV, WAP telephones, ADSL and the web. British Sky Broadcasting is one of the largest private sector employers in Scotland with more than 6000 individuals, the majority being employed at call centres in Livingston and Dunfermline. Digital television multiplex licences have been awarded, including one to SDN Ltd which guarantees space for Gaelic programmes in Scotland.

BBC TELEVISION

BBC Scotland
BBC Broadcasting House, Queen Margaret Drive, Glasgow G12 8DG (Tel: 0141-339 8844).
Controller: J. McCormick

BBC Broadcasting House, Beechgrove Terrace, Aberdeen AB15 5ZT (Tel: 01224-625233).

BBC Broadcasting House, 5 Queen Street, Edinburgh EH2 1JF (Tel: 0131-225 3131).

INDEPENDENT TELEVISION

INDEPENDENT TELEVISION NETWORK COMPANIES IN SCOTLAND

Border Television Ltd
The Television Centre, Carlisle, CA1 3NT (Tel: 01228-525 101).
Managing Director: Nick Cusick
Chairman: J. Graham
Area covered: the Borders

Grampian Television plc
Queen's Cross, Aberdeen, AB15 4XJ (Tel: 01224-846 846; Fax: 01224-846 800; E-mail: gtv@grampiantv.co.uk; Web: www.grampiantv.co.uk).
Area covered: northern Scotland

Scottish TV Ltd
Cowcaddens, Glasgow, G2 3PR (Tel: 0141-300 3000; Fax: 0141-300 8030; Web: www.scottishtv.co.uk).
Chief Executive: D. Emslie
Controller, Regional Programming: S. Ross
Area covered: Central Scotland

OTHER INDEPENDENT TELEVISION COMPANIES

Channel 5 Broadcasting Ltd
22 Long Acre, London, WC2E 9LY (Tel: 020-7550 5555; Fax: 020-7550 5554; Web: www.channel5.co.uk).

Channel Four (Nations and Regions)
227 West George Street, Glasgow, G2 2ND (Tel: 0141-568 7100; Fax: 0141-568 7103; Web: www.channel4.com).
Head of Programmes, Nations and Regions: S. Cosgrove

GMTV Ltd (Breakfast Television)
London Television Centre, Upper Ground, London, SE1 9TT (Tel: 020-7827 7000; Fax: 020-7827 7249; Web: www.gmtv.co.uk).
Managing Director: Paul Corley
Director of Programmes: P. McHugh

Independent Television News Ltd
200 Gray's Inn Road, London, WC1X 8XZ (Tel: 020-7833 3000; E-mail: contact@itn.co.uk; Web: www.itn.co.uk).

ITN Scottish Bureau
c/o STV, Cowcaddens, Glasgow, G2 3PR (Tel: 0141-332 1093; Fax: 0141-332 1083).

Teletext Ltd (Scottish Editor)
c/o Newstel Information Ltd, Pentagon Centre,
36 Washington Street, Glasgow, G3 8AZ
(Tel: 0141-221 4457; Fax: 0141-204 0522;
E-mail: scoteditor@teletext.co.uk;
Web: www.teletext.co.uk).
Scottish Editor: Hugh MacDiarmid

DIRECT BROADCASTING BY SATELLITE TELEVISION

British Sky Broadcasting Ltd
Grant Way, Isleworth, Middx, TW7 5QD
(Tel: 020-7705 3000).
Chief Executive: Tony Ball

RADIO

UK domestic radio services are broadcast across three wavebands: FM (or VHF), medium wave (also referred to as AM) and long wave (used by BBC Radio 4). In the UK the FM waveband extends in frequency from 87.5 MHz to 108 MHz and the medium wave band extends from 531 kHz to 1602 kHz. Some radios are still calibrated in wavelengths rather than frequency. To convert frequency to wavelength, divide 300,000 by the frequency in kHz.

The frequencies allocated for terrestrial digital radio in the UK are 217.5 to 230 MHz. It is necessary to have a radio set with a digital decoder in order to receive digital radio broadcasts.

BBC RADIO

BBC Radio broadcasts five network services to the UK, Isle of Man and the Channel Islands. There is also a tier of national regional services, including Scotland. The BBC World Service broadcasts over 1,000 hours of programmes a week in 43 languages including English.

BBC NETWORK SERVICES

BBC Radio
Broadcasting House, Portland Place, London, W1A 1AA (Tel: 020-7580 4468).
Director General: Greg Dyke

BBC World Service
Bush House, Strand, London, WC2B 4PH
(Tel: 020-7240 3456; Fax: 020-7557 1258;
E-mail: worldservice.letters@bbc.co.uk;
Web: www.bbc.co.uk).

BBC RADIO SCOTLAND

BBC Scotland
Queen Margaret Drive, Glasgow, G12 8DG
(Tel: 0141-339 8844).
Controller: J. McCormick

INDEPENDENT RADIO

INDEPENDENT NATIONAL RADIO STATIONS

Classic FM
Classic FM House, 7 Swallow Place, London, W1B 2AG (Tel: 020-7343 9000; Fax: 020-7344 2700; Web: www.classicfm.com).
Chief Executive: P. Taylor
Managing Director: R. Lewis
Frequencies: 99.9–101.9 FM

talkSPORT
18 Hatfields, London, SE1 8DJ
(Tel: 020-7959 7800; Fax: 020-7959 7805;
E-mail: swoodward@talksport.co.uk;
Web: www.talksport.net).
Chief Executive: K. McKenzie
Frequencies: 1053/1089 AM

Virgin Radio
1 Golden Square, London, W1R 4DJ
(Tel: 020-7434 1215; Web: www.virginradio.co.uk).
Chief Executive: John Pearson
Frequencies: 1215/1197/1233/1242/1260 AM

INDEPENDENT LOCAL RADIO STATIONS

96.3 QFM
26 Lady Lane, Paisley, PA1 2LG
(Tel: 0141-887 9630).
Managing Director: Gus McKenzie
Frequency: 96.3 FM

Argyll FM
27–29 Longrow, Cambeltown, Argyll, PA28 6ER
(Tel: 01586-551800; Fax: 01586-551888).
Chairman: C. Middleton
Frequencies: 106.5, 107.1, 107.5 FM

Beat 106
The Four Winds Pavilion
Pacific Quay, Glasgow, G51 1EB
(Tel: 0141-566 6106; Fax: 0141-566 6110;
E-mail: info@beat106.com;
Web: www.beat106.com).
Managing Director: Hugh Murray
Frequencies: 105.7/106.1 FM

Central FM
201 High Street, Falkirk, FK1 1DU
(Tel: 01324-611164).
Managing Director: Evelyn Queen
Frequency: 103.1 FM

Clan FM
Radio House, Rowantree Avenue, Newhouse Industrial Estate, Newhouse, Lanarkshire, ML1 5RX (Tel: 01698-733107; Fax: 01698-733318; E-mail: studio@clan-fm.co.uk; Web: www.clan-fm.co.uk).
Managing Director: Ms C. Johnston
Frequencies: 107.5 and 107.9 FM

Clyde 1 (FM) and 2 (AM)
Clydebank Business Park, Clydebank, Glasgow, G81 2RX (Tel: 0141-565 2200; Fax: 0141-565 2265; E-mail: info@radioclyde.com; Web: www.clydeonline.co.uk).
Managing Director: P. Cooney
Frequencies: 102.5 FM; 103.3 FM (Firth of Clyde); 97.0 FM (Vale of Leven); 1152 AM

Forth AM and FM
Forth House, Forth Street, Edinburgh, EH1 3LF (Tel: 0131-556 9255; Fax: 0131-558 3277; E-mail: fortham@srh.co.uk or forthfm@srh.co.uk; Web: www.forthonline.co.uk).
Managing Director: S. Wilkie
Frequencies: 1548 AM, 97.3/97.6/102.2 FM

Heartland FM
Atholl Curling Ring, Lower Oakfield, Pitlochry, Perthshire, PH16 5HQ (Tel: 01796-474040; Fax: 01796-474007;
E-mail: mailbox@heartlandfm.co.uk).
Chairman: M. Dobson
Programme Controller: Ms M. Hobson
Frequency: 97.5 FM

Isles FM
PO Box 333, Stornoway, Isle of Lewis, HS1 2PU (Tel: 01851-703333; Fax: 01851-703322;
E-mail: isles—fm@radiolink.net;
Web: www.islesfm.co.uk).
Managing Director: Ann Moqbel
Programme Controller: G. Afrin
Frequency: 103.0 FM

Kingdom FM
Haig House, Haig Business Park, Markinch, Fife, KY7 6AQ (Tel: 01592-753753; Fax: 01592-757788; E-mail: kingdomfm@aol.com).
Chief Executive: I. Sewell
Programme Controller: K. Brady
Frequencies: 95.2/96.1 FM

Lochbroom FM
Radio House, Mill Street, Ullapool, Wester Ross, IV26 2UN (Tel: 01854-613131; Fax: 01854-613132; E-mail: radio@lochbroomfm.co.uk; Web: www.lochbroomfm.co.uk).
Chairman: K. Guy
Station Manager: Ms S. Guy
Frequency: 102.2 FM

Moray Firth Radio
Scorguie Place, Inverness, IV3 8UJ (Tel: 01463-224433; Fax: 01463-243224; E-mail: mfr@mfr.co.uk; Web: www.morayfirth.co.uk).
Managing Director: Gary Robinson
Frequencies: 97.4 FM, 1107 AM, Local opt-outs: 96.6 FM (MFR Speysound); 102.8 FM (MFR Keith Community Radio); 96.7 FM (MFR Kinnaird Radio); 102.5 FM (MFR Caithness)

NECR (North-East Community Radio)
The Shed, School Road, Inverurie, Aberdeenshire, AB51 0UX (Tel: 01467-632909).
Frequencies: 97.1 FM (Braemaar); 102.1 FM (Meldrum and Inverurie); 102.6 FM (Kildrummy); 103.2 FM (Colpy)

Nevis Radio
Inverlochy, Fort William, Inverness-shire, PH33 6LU (Tel: 01397-700007;
E-mail: studio@nevisradio.co.uk;
Web: www.nevisradio.co.uk).
Station Manager: G. Wright
Frequencies: 96.6 FM (Fort William); 97.0 FM (Glencoe); 102.3 FM (Skye); 102.4 FM (Loch Leven)

Northsound One (FM) and Two (AM)
45 Kings Gate, Aberdeen, AB15 4EL (Tel: 01224-337000; Fax: 01224-400003).
Managing Director: R. Webster
Frequencies: 1035 AM, 96.9/97.6/103.9 FM

Oban FM
132 George Street, Oban, Argyll, PA34 5NT (Tel: 01631-570057; Fax: 01631-570530;
E-mail: us@oban-fm.freeserve.co.uk).
Managing Director: J. G. S. Mackay
Studio Manager: I. Mackay
Frequency: 103.3 FM

Radio Borders
Tweedside Park, Galashiels, TD1 3TD (Tel: 01896-759444).
Managing Director: Danny Gallagher
Frequencies: 96.8/97.5/103.1/103.4 FM

Radio Tay AM and Tay FM
6 North Isla Street, Dundee, DD3 7JQ (Tel: 01382-200800; Fax: 01382-423252;
E-mail: taynews@srh.co.uk).
Managing Director: A. Ballingall
Frequencies: 1161 AM, 102.8 FM (Dundee); 1584 AM, 96.4 FM (Perth)

RNA FM
Arbroath Infirmary, Rosemount Road, Arbroath, Angus, DD11 2AT (Tel: 01241-879660; Fax: 01241-439664).
Hon. Secretary: M. J. B. Finlayson
Frequency: 96.6 FM

Scot FM
1 Albert Quay, Leith, EH6 7DN (Tel: 0131-625 8400; Fax: 0131-625 8401).
Managing Director: M. Hall
Programme Director: J. Crawford
Frequencies: 100.3/101.1 FM
Area covered: central Scotland

SIBC
Market Street, Lerwick, Shetland, ZE1 0JN (Tel: 01595-695299; Fax: 01595-695696;
E-mail: info@sibc.co.uk;
Web: www.sibc.co.uk).
Managing Director: Ms I. Walterson
Frequencies: 96.2/102.2 FM

South West Sound
Unit 40, The Loreburne Centre
High Street, Dumfries, DG1 2BD
 (Tel: 01387-250999; Fax: 01387-265629;
E-mail: xwestsoundfm@netscapeonline.co.uk;
Web: www.west.sound.co.uk).
Station Director: Ms F. Blackwood
Frequencies: 96.5/97.0/103.0 FM

Wave 102
8 South Tay Street, Dundee, DD1 1PA (Tel: 01382-901000; Fax: 01382-900999;
E-mail: info@wave102.co.uk;
Web: www.wave102.co.uk).
Managing Director: G. Mackenzie
Head of News and Features: Ms G. Lawrie
Frequency: 102.0 FM

Waves Radio Peterhead
Unit 2, Blackhouse Industrial Estate, Peterhead, AB42 1BW (Tel: 01779-491012; Fax: 01779-490802;
E-mail: waves@radiophd.freeserve.co.uk;
Web: www.wavesfm.com).
Directors: N Spence
Frequency: 101.2 FM

West Sound AM and West FM
Radio House, 54A Holmston Road, Ayr, KA7
3BE (Tel: 01292-283662; Fax: 01292-283665;
E-mail: westsound@srh.co.uk;
Web: www.west-sound.co.uk).
Chief Executive: R. Findlay
Managing Director: Ms S. Borthwick
Frequencies: 1035 AM, 96.7 FM (Ayr); 97.5
FM (Girvan)

THE PRESS

The press is subject to the laws on publication and the Press Complaints Commission was set up by the industry as a means of self-regulation. It is not state-subsidised and receives few tax concessions. The income of most newspapers and periodicals is derived largely from sales and from advertising; the press is the largest advertising medium in Britain.

COMPLAINTS

The Press Complaints Commission was founded by the newspaper and magazine industry in January 1991 to replace the Press Council (established in 1953). It is a voluntary, non-statutory body set up to operate the press's self-regulation system following the Calcutt report in 1990 on privacy and related matters, when the industry feared that a failure to regulate itself might lead to statutory regulation of the press. The Commission is funded by the industry through the Press Standards Board of Finance.

The Commission's objects are to consider, adjudicate, conciliate, and resolve complaints of unfair treatment by the press; and to ensure that the press maintains the highest professional standards with respect for generally recognised freedoms, including freedom of expression, the public's right to know, and the right of the press to operate free from improper pressure. The Commission judges newspaper and magazine conduct by a code of practice drafted by editors, agreed by the industry and ratified by the Commission.

Seven of the Commission's members are editors of national, regional and local newspapers (including one from Scotland) and magazines, and nine, including the chairman, are drawn from other fields. One member has been appointed Privacy Commissioner with special powers to investigate complaints about invasion of privacy.

PRESS COMPLAINTS COMMISSION

1 Salisbury Square, London EC4Y 8JB
(Tel: 020-7353 1248;
E-mail: complaints@pcc.org.uk).
Chairman: Lord Wakeham, pc
Director: G. Black

NEWSPAPERS

Newspapers are usually financially independent of any political party, though most adopt a political stance in their editorial comments, usually reflecting proprietorial influence. Ownership of the national and regional daily newspapers is concentrated in the hands of large corporations whose interests cover publishing and communications. The rules on cross-media ownership, as amended by the Broadcasting Act 1996, limit the extent to which newspaper organisations may become involved in broadcasting.

Scotland has a number of daily and Sunday newspapers (including Scottish editions of some of the UK national newspapers), as well as local daily and weekly newspapers. The following list shows the main editorial offices of the major newspapers in Scotland, including the Scottish editorial offices of UK national newspapers.

NATIONAL DAILY NEWSPAPERS

Daily Telegraph
5 Coates Crescent, Edinburgh, EH3 7AL
(Tel: 0131-225 3313; Fax: 0131-225 4877).

The Herald
200 Renfield Street, Glasgow, G2 3PR
(Tel: 0141-302 7000; Fax: 0141-302 7070;
Web: www.theherald.co.uk).
Editor: H. Reid

Scottish Daily Mail
200 Renfield Street, Glasgow, G2 3PZ
(Tel: 0141-331 4700; Fax: 0141-331 4707).

Scottish Mirror
One Central Quay, Glasgow, G3 8DA
(Tel: 0141-221 2121; Fax: 0141-309 3351;
E-mail: reporters@mirror.co.uk).
Editor: M. Foote

REGIONAL DAILY NEWSPAPERS

Daily Record
One Central Quay, Glasgow, G3 8DA
(Tel: 0141-309 3000; Fax: 0141-309 3340;
E-mail: editors@daily.record.co.uk;
Web: www.record-mail.co.uk).

Edinburgh Evening News
108 Holyrood Road, Edinburgh, EH8 8AS
(Tel: 0131-620 8620; Fax: 0131-620 8696;
Web: www.edinburghnews.com).

Evening Express
PO Box 43, Lang Stracht, Mastrick, Aberdeen, AB15 6DF (Tel: 01224-690222; Fax: 01224-699575; E-mail: ee.editor@ajl.co.uk;
Web: thisisnorthscotland.co.uk).

Greenock Telegraph
Pitreavie Business Park, Dunfermline, KY11 8QS
(Tel: 01383-728201; Fax: 01383-737040;
E-mail: dromanes@dunfermlinepress.co.uk).

Paisley Daily Express
14 New Street, Paisley, PA1 1YA (Tel: 0141-887
7911; Fax: 0141-887 6254;
E-mail: pde@s-un.co.uk;
Web: www.inside-scotland.co.uk/renfrewshire).

The Press and Journal
PO Box 43, Lang Stracht, Mastrick, Aberdeen,
AB15 6DF (Tel: 01224-690222; Fax: 01224-
344114; E-mail: pj.editor@ajil.co.uk;
Web: thisisnorthscotland.co.uk).
Editor: D. Tucker

WEEKLY NEWSPAPERS

Mail on Sunday in Scotland
200 Renfield Street, Glasgow, G2 3PZ
(Tel: 0141-331 4700; Fax: 0141-353 2461).

Scotland on Sunday
108 Holyrood Road, Edinburgh, EH8 8AS
(Tel: 0131-620 8620; Fax: 0131-620 8491;
E-mail: spectrum—sos@scotlandonsunday.com;
Web: www.scotlandonsunday.com).
Editor: J. McGurk

Scottish Sunday Express
Park House, Park Circus Place, Glasgow, G3 6AF
(Tel: 0141-352 2519; Fax: 0141-332 8538;
E-mail: scotsunday@express.co.uk).
Editor: T. McDonald

Sunday Mail
One Central Quay, Glasgow, G3 8DA
(Tel: 0141-309 3000; Fax: 0141-309 3587).
Editor: P. Cox

Sunday Post
Courier Place, Dundee, DD1 9QJ
(Tel: 01382-223131; Fax: 01382-201064;
E-mail: mail@sundaypost.com;
Web: www.sundaypost.com).

Weekly News
Courier Place, Dundee, DD1 9QJ (Tel: 01382-
223131; Fax: 01382-201390;
E-mail: weeklynews@dcthomson.co.uk).
Editor: D. Hishmurgh

CONSUMER PERIODICALS

ArtWork
Mill Business Centre, PO Box 3, Ellon,
Aberdeenshire, AB41 9EA (Tel: 01651-842429;
Fax: 01651-842180; E-mail: editorial@artwork.co.uk;
Web: www.artwork.co.uk).
Editor: B. Williams

British Philatelic Bulletin
Tallents House, 21 South Gyle Cresent,
Edinburgh, EH12 9PB (Tel: 08475-641641; Fax:
0131-316 7337; Web: www.royalmail.com).
Editor: J. Holman

Caledonia
4 Heriot Row, Edinburgh, EH3 6HU
(Tel: 0131-557 5600; Fax: 0131-557 8665;
E-mail: editor@scotthouse.co.uk;
Web: www.caledonia-magazine.com).
Editor: I. Gale

Childminding
Suite 3, 7 Melville Terrace, Stirling, FK8 2ND
(Tel: 01786-445377; Fax: 01786-449062;
E-mail: information@childminding.org;
Web: www.childminding.org).
Editor: Miss A. McGrath

Classic Stitches
80 Kingsway East, Dundee, DD4 8SL
(Tel: 01382-223131; Fax: 01382-452491;
E-mail: editorial@classicstitches.com;
Web: www.classicstitches.com).
Editor: Ms B. Neilson

East Lothian Life
1 Beveridge Row, Belhaven, Dunbar, EH42 1TP
(Tel: 01368-863593; Fax: 01368-863593;
E-mail: info@east-lothian-life.co.uk;
Web: www.east-lothian-life.co.uk).
Editor: Ms P. Jaffray

The Forth Naturalist & Historian
University of Stirling, Stirling, Stirlingshire, FK9
4LA (Tel: 01259-215091; Fax: 01756-464994;
E-mail: lindsay.corbett@stir.ac.uk;
Web: www.stir.ac.uk/department/
naturalsciences/earth).
Hon. Secretary: L. Corbett

Gairm (The Gaelic Magazine)
29 Waterloo Street, Glasgow, G2 6BZ
(Tel: 0141-221 1971; Fax: 0141-221 1971).
Editor: Prof. D. S. Thomson

Heritage Scotland
28 Charlotte Square, Edinburgh, EH2 4ET
(Tel: 0131-243 9300; Fax: 0131-243 9301;
E-mail: information@nts.org.uk;
Web: www.nts.org.uk).
Editor: I. Gardner

History & Computing
22 George Square, Edinburgh, EH8 9LF
(Tel: 0131-650 4220; Fax: 0131-662 0053;
E-mail: journals@eup.ed.ac.uk;
Web: www.eup.ed.ac.uk).

I Do
One Central Quay, Glasgow, G3 8DA
(Tel: 0141-309 1444; Fax: 0141-309 1430;
E-mail: ido@dailyrecord.co.uk).
Editor: Ms A. Dewar

Journal of the Royal College of Surgeons of Edinburgh
22 George Square, Edinburgh, EH8 9LF
(Tel: 0131-650 4220; Fax: 0131-662 0053;
E-mail: journals@eup.ed.ac.uk;
Web: www.eup.ed.ac.uk).

The List
14 High Street, Edinburgh, EH1 1TE
(Tel: 0131-558 1191; Fax: 0131-557 8500;
E-mail: editor@list.co.uk;
Web: www.list.co.uk).
Editor: M. Fisher

Lothian at Leisure
PO Box 6, Haddington, East Lothian, EH41
3NQ (Tel: 01620-822578; Fax: 01620-825079;
E-mail: 101324.2142@compuserve.com).
Editor: R. Brown

Paragraph
22 George Square, Edinburgh, EH8 9LF
(Tel: 0131-650 4220; Fax: 0131-662 0053;
E-mail: journals@eup.ed.ac.uk;
Web: www.eup.ed.ac.uk).

Parliamentary History
22 George Square, Edinburgh, EH8 9LF
(Tel: 0131-650 4220; Fax: 0131-662 0053;
E-mail: journals@eup.ed.ac.uk;
Web: www.eup.ed.ac.uk).
Editor: Dr C. Jones

People's Friend
80 Kingsway East, Dundee, DD4 8SL
(Tel: 01382-223131; Fax: 01382-452491;
E-mail: peoplesfriend@dcthompson.co.uk).
Editor: S. Matheson

Romanticism
22 George Square, Edinburgh EH8 9LF
(Tel: 0131-650 4220; Fax: 0131-662 0053;
E-mail: journals@eup.ed.ac.uk;
Web: www.eup.ed.ac.uk).
Editor: N. Roe

Scenes (Scottish Environment News)
Wester Lairgs, Inverarnie, Farr, Inverness IV2
6XH (Tel: 01808-521368; Fax: 01808-521368;
E-mail: enquiries@scenes.org.uk;
Web: www.scenes.org.uk).
Editor: Sue Fenton

The Scots Magazine
2 Albert Square, Dundee, DD1 9QJ
(Tel: 01382-223131; Fax: 01382-322214;
E-mail: scotsmagazine@dcthompson.co.uk;
Web: www.scotsmagazine.com).

Scottish Field
Royston House, Caroline Park, Edinburgh, EH5
1QJ (Tel: 0131-551 2942; Fax: 0131-551 2938;
E-mail: editor@scottishfield.co.uk).
Editor: A. MacKenzie

Scottish Historical Review
22 George Square, Edinburgh, EH8 9LF
(Tel: 0131-650 4220; Fax: 0131-662 0053;
E-mail: journals@eup.ed.ac.uk;
Web: www.eup.ed.ac.uk).

Scottish Transport
PO Box 78, Glasgow, G3 6ER
(Tel: 0141-334 6161; Fax: 0141-357 1993

Scottish Wildlife
Cramond House, Kirk Cramond, Cramond
Glebe Road, Edinburgh, EH4 6NS (Tel: 0131-
312 7765; Fax: 0131-312 8705;
E-mail: enquiries@swt.org.uk;
Web: www.swt.org.uk).
Editor: A. Reynolds

Shetland Life
Prince Alfred Street, Lerwick, ZE1 0EP
(Tel: 01595-693622; Fax: 01595-694637;
E-mail: info@shetland-times.co.uk;
Web: www.shetland-times.co.uk).
Editor: J. R. Nicolson

Shout
2 Albert Square, Dundee, DD1 9QJ
(Tel: 01382-223131; Fax: 01382-200880;
E-mail: shout@dcthomson.co.uk).
Editor: Ms J. Brown

Spectrum
Craigmillar Park, Edinburgh, EH16 5NB
(Tel: 0131-662 4445; Fax: 0131-662 1968;
E-mail: scot.braille@dial.pipex.com;
Web: www.scottish-braille-press.org).

Translation and Literature
22 George Square, Edinburgh, EH8 9LF
(Tel: 0131-650 4220; Fax: 0131-662 0053;
E-mail: journals@eup.ed.ac.uk;
Web: www.eup.ed.ac.uk).
Editor: S. Gillespie

Young Scot
Rosebery House, 9 Haymarket Terrace,
Edinburgh, EH12 5EZ (Tel: 0131-313 2488; Fax:
0131-313 6800; E-mail: info@youngscot.org;
Web: www.youngscot.org).

TRADE PERIODICALS

ACCA Student Accountant
1 Woodside Place, Glasgow, G3 7QF
(Tel: 0141-309 4195; Fax: 0141-331 2448;
E-mail: info@accaglobal.com;
Web: www.accaglobal.com).

Allscot News
PO Box 6, Haddington, East Lothian, EH41
3NQ (Tel: 01620-822578; Fax: 01620-825079).

Ayrshire Dairyman Newsletter
Ayrshire Cattle Society of Great Britain and
Ireland, 1 Racecourse Road, Ayr, KA7 2DE
(Tel: 01292-267123; Fax: 01292-611973;
E-mail: society@ayrshires.org;
Web: www.ayrshires.org).

Multex.com
10–12 Young Street, Edinburgh, EH2 4JB
(Tel: 0131-473 7070; Fax: 0131-473 7080;
E-mail: estimates@multex-uk.com;
Web: www.global-estimates.com).

**The Blue Book: The Directory of the Law
Society of Scotland**
4 Hill Street, Edinburgh, EH2 3JZ
(Tel: 0131-225 7828; Fax: 0131-220 1833;
E-mail: order.line@butterworths.com;
Web: www.butterworthsscotland.com).

Botanical Journal of Scotland
22 George Square, Edinburgh, EH8 9LF
(Tel: 0131-650 4220; Fax: 0131-662 0053;
E-mail: journals@eup.ed.ac.uk;
Web: eup.ed.ac.uk).

Braille Science Journal
Craigmillar Park, Edinburgh, EH16 5NB
(Tel: 0131-662 4445; Fax: 0131-662 1968;
E-mail: scot.braille@dial.pipex.com;
Web: scottish-braille-press.org).

British Journal of Oral & Maxillofacial Surgery
Robert Stevenson House, Baxters Place, Leith
Walk, Edinburgh, EH1 3AF (Tel: 0131-556
2424; Fax: 0131-558 1278;
E-mail: journals@harcourt.com;
Web: www.harcourt-international.com).

The Business
Chamber of Commerce Buildings, Panmure
Street, Dundee, DD1 1ED (Tel: 01382-201122;
Fax: 01382-229544;
E-mail: admin@dundeechamber.co.uk;
Web: www.dundeechamber.co.uk).

Business Bulletin
27 Albyn Place, Aberdeen, AB10 1DB
(Tel: 01224-575100; Fax: 01224-213221;
E-mail: lora.graham@agcc.co.uk;
Web: www.agcc.co.uk).

Business Power Scotland
PO Box 6, Haddington, East Lothian, EH41
3NQ (Tel: 01620-822578; Fax: 01620-825079).

Peebles Media Group Ltd
Bergius House, 20 Clifton Street, Glasgow, G3
7LA (Tel: 0141-567 6000; Fax: 0141-331 1395;
E-mail: info@peeblesmedia.com;
Web: www.peeblesmedia.com).

**CA Magazine - Journal of the Institute of
Chartered Accountants in Scotland**
1A St Bernard's Row, Edinburgh, EH4 1LA
(Tel: 0131-343 7500; Fax: 0131-343 7505;
E-mail: camagazine-editorial@icas.org.uk;
Web: www.icas.org.uk).

Cartographic Journal
Centre for Remote Sensing and Mapping Science
Department of Geography, University of
Aberdeen, Aberdeen, AB24 3UF (Tel: 01224-
272324; Fax: 01224-272331;
E-mail: d.r.green@abdn.ac.uk;
Web: www.cartography.org.uk).

Current Orthopaedics
Robert Stevenson House, Baxters Place, Leith
Walk, Edinburgh, EH1 3AF (Tel: 0131-556
2424; Fax: 0131-558 1278;
E-mail: journals@harcourt.com;
Web: www.harcourt-interantional.com).

Current Paediatrics
Robert Stevenson House, Baxters Place, Leith Walk, Edinburgh, EH1 3AF (Tel: 0131-556 2424; Fax: 0131-558 1278;
E-mail: journals@harcourt.com;
Web: www.harcourt-interantional.com).

Dance Research
22 George Square, Edinburgh, EH8 9LF (Tel: 0131-650 4220; Fax: 0131-662 0053;
E-mail: journals@eup.ed.ac.uk;
Web: www.eup.ed.ac.uk).

The Drum
3 Park Street South, Glasgow, G3 6BG (Tel: 0141-332 3255; Fax: 0141-332 2012;
E-mail: info@thedrum.co.uk;
Web: www.thedrum.co.uk).

Edinburgh Gazette
21 South Gyle Crescent, Edinburgh, EH12 9EB (Tel: 0131-479 3143; Fax: 0131-479 3311).

ENT News
9 Gayfield Square, Edinburgh, EH1 3NT (Tel: 0131-557 4184; Fax: 0131-557 4701;
E-mail: patricia@pinpoint-scotland.com;
Web: www.ent-news.com).

Eye News
9 Gayfield Square, Edinburgh, EH1 3NT (Tel: 0131-557 4184; Fax: 0131-557 4701;
E-mail: eyenews@pinpoint-scotland.com;
Web: www.eye-news.com).

Geogscot
RSGS, Graham Hills Building, 40 George Street, Glasgow, G1 1QL (Tel: 0141-552 3330; Fax: 0141-552 3331; E-mail: rsgs@strath.ac.uk;
Web: www.geo.ed.ac.uk/rsgs).

Glasgow Chamber of Commerce Journal
30 George Square, Glasgow, G2 1EQ (Tel: 0141-204 2121; Fax: 0141-221 2336;
E-mail: marketing@glasgowchamber.org).

Health Bulletin
St Andrew's House, Regent Road, Edinburgh, EH1 3DG (Tel: 0131-244 2292; Fax: 0131-244 2835).

The Independent Community Pharmacist
23A Normandy Street, Alton, Hampshire, GU34 1DD (Tel: 01420-543203; Fax: 01420-549884;
E-mail: icpeditorial@calmags.co.uk).

The Journal of Hand Surgery (British Volume)
Robert Stevenson House, Baxters Place, Leith Walk, Edinburgh, EH1 3AF (Tel: 0131-556 2424; Fax: 0131-459 1177;
E-mail: journals@harcourt.com;
Web: www.harcourt-international.com).

Lothian Leader
PO Box 6, Haddington, East Lothian, EH41 3NQ (Tel: 01620-822578; Fax: 01620-825079).

Media Education Journal
Scottish Screen, 249 West George Street, Glasgow, G2 4QE (Tel: 01224-481976;
E-mail: d@murphy47.freeserve.co.uk;
Web: www.ames.org.uk).

Medical Hypotheses
Robert Stevenson House, Baxters Place, Leith Walk, Edinburgh, EH1 3AF (Tel: 0131-556 2424; Fax: 0131-558 1278;
Web: www.harcourt-international.com).

Nautical Magazine
4–10 Darnley Street, Glasgow, G41 2SD (Tel: 0141-429 1234; Fax: 0141-420 1694;
E-mail: info@skipper.co.uk;
Web: www.skipper.co.uk).

Oilnews and Gas International
PO Box 6, Haddington, East Lothian, EH41 3NQ (Tel: 01620-822578; Fax: 01620-825079).

Packaging Scotland
Bergius House, Clifton Street, Glasgow, G3 7LA (Tel: 0141-567 6000; Fax: 0141-331 1395;
E-mail: packagingscotland@peeblesmedia.com;
Web: www.peeblesmedia.com).

Portfolio - The Catalogue of Contemporary Photography in Britain
43 Candlemaker Row, Edinburgh, EH1 2QB (Tel: 0131-220 1911; Fax: 0131-226 4287;
E-mail: info@portfoliocatalogue.com;
Web: www.portfoliocatalogue.com).

Royal College of Physicians of Edinburgh
9 Queen Street, Edinburgh, EH2 1JQ (Tel: 0131-225 7324; Fax: 0131-220 3939;
E-mail: editorial@rcpe.ac.uk;
Web: www.rcpe.ac.uk).

Roustabout Magazine
Suite 5, International Base, Greenwell Road, East Tullos, Aberdeen, AB12 3AX (Tel: 01224-876582; Fax: 01224-879757;
E-mail: info@rousaboutmagazine.co.uk).

Scottish Beekeeper - Journal of the Scottish Beekeepers Association
Brothock printing works, Burnside Drive, Arbroath, Angus, DD11 1NS (Tel: 01241-872000; Fax: 01241-870707;
E-mail: printing@thehearldpress.fsnet.co.uk).

Scottish Business Insider
7 Castle Street, Edinburgh, EH2 3AH (Tel: 0131-535 5555; Fax: 0131-220 1203;
E-mail: customerservices@insider.co.uk;
Web: www.insider.co.uk).

Scottish Caterer
Bergius House, Clifton Street, Glasgow, G3 7LA (Tel: 0141-331 1022; Fax: 0141-331 1395;
Web: www.peeblesmedia.com).

Scottish Educational Journal
46 Moray Place, Edinburgh, EH3 6BH (Tel: 0131-225 6244; Fax: 0131-220 3151;
E-mail: kblackwell@eis.org.uk;
Web: www.eis.org.uk).

Scottish Law Directory & Fees Supplement
4 Hill Street, Edinburgh, EH2 3JZ (Tel: 0131-225 4703; Fax: 0131-220 4260;
E-mail: susan.lawrie@butterworths.com;
Web: www.butterworthsscotland.com).

Scottish Law Gazette
24 Easter Cornton Road, Stirling, FK9 5ES (Tel: 01786-472125).

Scottish Planning & Environmental Law
Tontine House, 8 Gordon Street, Glasgow, G1 3PL (Tel: 0141-248 8541; Fax: 0141-248 8277;
E-mail: publications@planex.co.uk;
Web: www.planex.co.uk).

The Times Educational Supplement Scotland
Scott House, 10 South St Andrew Street, Edinburgh, EH2 2AZ (Tel: 0131-557 1133; Fax: 0131-558 1155; E-mail: scoted@tes.co.uk;
Web: www.tes.co.uk/scotland).

The Times Law Reports
4 Hill Street, Edinburgh, EH2 3JZ
(Tel: 0131-225 4703; Fax: 0131-220 4260;
E-mail: eric.ypung@butterworths.com;
Web: www.butterworthsscotland.com).

Transport News
Wheatsheaf House, Montgomery Street, East Kilbride, Glasgow, G74 7JS (Tel: 01355-279077; Fax: 01355-279088;
E-mail: readersletters@transportnews.co.uk;
Web: www.transportnews.co.uk).

Urology News
9 Gayfield Square, Edinburgh, EH1 3NT (Tel: 0131-478 8404; Fax: 0131-557 4701;
E-mail: rona@pinpoint-scotland.com).

Utilitas
22 George Square, Edinburgh, EH8 9LF (Tel: 0131-650 4220; Fax: 0131-662 0053;
E-mail: journals@eup.ed.ac.uk;
Web: www.eup.ed.ac.uk).

Yachting Life
Wheatsheaf House, Montgomery Street, East Kilbride, Glasgow, G74 4JS (Tel: 01355-279077; Fax: 01355-279088;
E-mail: readersletters@yachtinglife.co.uk;
Web: www.yachtinglife.co.uk).

BOOK PUBLISHERS

The following list comprises details for a number of publishing companies in Scotland.

SCOTTISH PUBLISHERS ASSOCIATION
Scottish Book Centre, 137 Dundee Street, Edinburgh, EH11 1BG (Tel: 0131-228 6866).

AA Enterprises
7 Mount Road, Berwick-upon-Tweed (Tel: 01289-304489).

Acair Ltd
7 James Street, Stornoway, Isle of Lewis, HS1 2QN (Tel: 01851-703020; Fax: 01851-703294; E-mail: acair@sol.co.uk; Web: www.acairbooks.com).

Argyll Publishing
Glendaruel, Argyll, PA22 3AE (Tel: 01369-820229; Fax: 01369-820372; E-mail: argyll.publishing@virgin.net; Web: www.deliberatelythirsty.com).

Association for Scottish Literary Studies
Department of Scottish History, University of Glasgow, 9 University Gardens, Glasgow, G12 8QH (Tel: 0141-330 5309; Fax: 0141-330 5309; E-mail: d.jones@scothist.arts.gla.ac.uk; Web: www.asls.org.uk).

Atelier Books
6 Dundas Street, Edinburgh, EH3 6HZ (Tel: 0131-557 4050; Fax: 0131-557 8382).

Black & White Publishing
99 Giles Street, Edinburgh, EH6 6BZ (Tel: 0131-625 4500; Fax: 0131-625 4501).

Barrington Stoke Ltd
10 Belford Terrace, Edinburgh, EH4 3DQ (Tel: 0131-315 4933; Fax: 0131-315 4934; Web: www.barringtonstoke.co.uk).

Birlinn Ltd
Unit 8, Canongate Venture, 5 New Street, Edinburgh, EH8 8BH (Tel: 0131-556 6660; Fax: 0131-557 6250; E-mail: info@birlinn.co.uk; Web: www.birlinn.co.uk).

Black Ace Books
PO Box 6557, Forfar, DD8 2YS (Web: www.blackacebooks.com).

Brown, Son & Ferguson, Ltd
4–10 Darnley Street, Glasgow, G41 2SD (Tel: 0141-429 1234; Fax: 0141-420 1694; E-mail: info@skipper.co.uk; Web: www.skipper.co.uk).

Canongate Books
14 High Street, Edinburgh, EH1 1TE (Tel: 0131-557 5111; Fax: 0131-557 5211; E-mail: info@canongate.co.uk; Web: www.canongate.net).

Chambers Harrap Publishers Ltd
7 Hopetoun Crescent, Edinburgh, EH7 4AY (Tel: 0131-556 5929; Fax: 0131-556 5313; E-mail: enquiries@chambersharrap.co.uk; Web: www.chambersharrap.com).

Chapman
4 Broughton Place, Edinburgh, EH1 3RX (Tel: 0131-557 2207; Fax: 0131-556 9565; E-mail: editor@chapman-pub.co.uk; Web: www.chapman.pub.co.uk).

Harcourt Health Sciences
Robert Stevenson House
1–3 Baxter's Place, Edinburgh, EH1 3AF (Tel: 0131-556 2424; Fax: 0131-556 1278; Web: www.harcourt.international.com).

Citizens Advice Scotland
26 George Square, Edinburgh, EH8 9LD (Tel: 0131-667 0156; Fax: 0131-668 4359; Web: www.cas.org.uk).

Dionysia Press
20A Montgomery Street, Edinburgh, EH7 5JS (Tel: 0131-478 7247; Fax: 0131-477 0754).

Edinburgh University Press
22 George Square, Edinburgh, EH8 9LF (Tel: 0131-650 4218; Fax: 0131-662 0053; E-mail: timothy.wright@eup.ed.ac.uk; Web: www.eup.ed.ac.uk).

EPER
University of Edinburgh, 21 Hill Place, Edinburgh, EH8 9DP (Tel: 0131-650 6200; Fax: 0131-667 5927; Web: www.ials.ed.ac.uk).

Floris Books
15 Harrison Gardens, Edinburgh, EH11 1SH (Tel: 0131-337 2372; Fax: 0131-346 7516; E-mail: floris@floris.demon.co.uk).

Forth Naturalist and Historian
The University of Stirling, Stirling, FK9 4LA
(Tel: 01259-215091; Fax: 01786-464994;
E-mail: lindsay.corbett@stir.ac.uk;
Web: www.stir.ac.uk/departments/
naturalsciences/Forth–naturalist/index.htm).

Glasgow City Libraries Publications Board
The Mitchell Library, North Street, Glasgow, G3
7DN (Tel: 0141-287 2846).

The Gleneil Press
Whittingehame, Haddington, E. Lothian, EH41
4QA (Tel: 01620-860292; Fax: 01620-860292;
Web: www.gleneil.com).

Glowworm Books Ltd
Unit 7, Greendykes Industrial Estate, Greendykes
Road, Broxburn, W. Lothian, EH52 6PG
(Tel: 01506-857570; Fax: 01506-858100;
E-mail: admin@glowwormbooks.co.uk;
Web: www.glowwormbooks.co.uk).

Goblinshead
130B Inveresk Road, Musselburgh, Midlothian,
EH21 7AY (Tel: 0131-665 2894; Fax: 0131-653
6566; E-mail: goblinshead@sol.co.uk).

W. Green
The Scottish Law Publisher, 21 Alva Street,
Edinburgh, EH2 4PS (Tel: 0131-225 4879;
Fax: 0131-225 2104;
E-mail: enquiries@wgreen.co.uk;
Web: www.wgreen.co.uk).

Johnstone Media
55 Melville Street, Edinburgh, EH3 7HL
(Tel: 0131-220 5380; Fax: 0131-225 5524;
E-mail: info@johnstonemedia.com;
Web: www.johnstonemedia.com).

Keppel Publishing
The Grey House, Kenbridge Road, New
Galloway, Kirkcudbrightshire, DG7 3RP
(Tel: 01644-420272; Fax: 01644-420277;
E-mail: keppel@greyhouse.sol.co.uk).

Lomond Books
36 West Shore Road, Granton, Edinburgh, EH5
1QD (Tel: 0131-551 2261; Fax: 0131-552 1703).

Luath Press Ltd
543/2 Castlehill, The Royal Mile, Edinburgh,
EH1 2ND (Tel: 0131-225 4326; Fax: 0131-225
4324; E-mail: gavin.macdougall@luath.co.uk;
Web: www.luath.co.uk).

Mainstream Publishing Co
7 Albany Street, Edinburgh, EH1 3UG
(Tel: 0131-557 2959; Fax: 0131-556 8720;
Web: www.mainstreampublishing.com).

Mercat Press
53–59 South Bridge, Edinburgh, EH1 1YS
(Tel: 0131-622 8252; Fax: 0131-557 9742;
E-mail: orders@mercatpress.com;
Web: www.mercatpress.com).

The National Archives of Scotland
HM General Register House, Edinburgh, EH1
3YY (Tel: 0131-535 1314; Fax: 0131-535 1360;
E-mail: research@nas.gov.uk;
Web: www.nas.gov.uk).

National Galleries of Scotland
Belford Road, Edinburgh, EH4 3DS
(Tel: 0131-624 6257/6261; Fax: 0131-315 2963;
E-mail: publications@natgalscot.ac.uk;
Web: www.natgalscot.ac.uk).

National Museums of Scotland Publishing Limited
Chambers Street, Edinburgh, EH1 1JF
(Tel: 0131-247 4026; Fax: 0131-247 4012;
Web: www.nms.ac.uk).

Neil Wilson Publishing Ltd
Suite 303A, The Pentagon Centre, 36
Washington Street, Glasgow, G3 8AZ
(Tel: 0141-221 1117; Fax: 0141-221 5363;
E-mail: info@nwp.sol.co.uk;
Web: www.nwp.co.uk).

The New Iona Press
7 Drynie Terrace, Inverness, IV2 4UP
(Tel: 01463-242384; Fax: 01463-242384;
E-mail: mairi@ionapress.demon.co.uk).

The Orcadian Ltd
PO Box 18, Hell's Half Acre, Hatston, Kirkwall,
Orkney, KW15 1DW (Tel: 01856-879000; Fax:
01856-879001; Web: www.orcadian.co.uk).

Parish Education
21 Young Street, Edinburgh, EH2 4HU
(Tel: 0131-332 0343;
Web: www.churchofscotland.org.uk/boards/
parisheducation).

Polygon
22 George Square, Edinburgh, EH8 9LF
(Tel: 0131-650 4213; Fax: 0131-662 0053;
E-mail: polygon.press@eup.ed.ac.uk;
Web: www.eup.ed.ac.uk).

RCAHMS
John Sinclair House, 16 Bernard Terrace, Edinburgh, EH8 9NX (Tel: 0131-662 1456; Fax: 0131-662 1477; E-mail: postmaster@rcahms.gov.uk; Web: www.rcahms.gov.uk).

Rutland Press
15 Rutland Square, Edinburgh, EH1 2BE (Tel: 0131-229 7545; Fax: 0131-228 2188; E-mail: rutland@rias.org.uk).

St Andrew Press
121 George Street, Edinburgh, EH2 4YN (Tel: 0131-225 5722; E-mail: coss.saintandrew@dial.pipex.com).

The Saltire Society
9 Fountain Close, 22 High Street, Edinburgh, EH1 1TF (Tel: 0131-556 1836; Fax: 0131-557 1675; E-mail: saltire@saltire.org.uk; Web: www.saltire-society.demon.co.uk).

Scottish Book Trust
Scottish Book Centre, 137 Dundee Street, Edinburgh, EH11 1BG (Tel: 0131-229 3663; Fax: 0131-228 4293; E-mail: scottish.book.trust@dial.pipex.com; Web: www.scottishbooktrust.com).

Scottish Cultural Press and Scottish Children's Press
Unit 14, Leith Walk Business Centre, 130 Leith Walk, Edinburgh, EH6 5DT (Tel: 0131-555 5950; E-mail: scp@spl.co.uk).

Scottish Natural Heritage
Publications Section, Battleby, Redgorton, Perth, PH1 3EW (Tel: 01738-444177; Fax: 01738-827411; Web: www.snh.org.uk).

Scottish Text Society
27 George Square, Edinburgh, EH8 9LD; Web: www.scan.org.uk/scottishtextsociety.html).

The Shetland Times Ltd
Prince Alfred Street, Lerwick, Shetland, ZE1 0EP (Tel: 01595-693622; Fax: 01595-694637; E-mail: cblack@shetland-times.co.uk; Web: www.shetland-books.co.uk).

Sportscotland
Caledonia House, Redheughs Rigg, South Gyle, Edinburgh, EH12 9DQ (Tel: 0131-317 7200; Fax: 0131-317 7202; Web: www.sportscotland.org.uk).

Stenlake Publishing
Ochiltree Sawmill, The Lade, Ochiltree, Ayrshire, KA18 2NX (Tel: 01290-423114; Fax: 01290-423114; E-mail: stenlake@yahoo.com; Web: www.stenlake.co.uk).

Straightline Publishing Ltd
29 Main Street, Bothwell, Glasgow, G71 8RD (Tel: 01698-853000; Fax: 01698-854208; E-mail: admin@straightline.demon.co.uk).

Tuckwell Press Ltd
The Mill House, Phantassie, East Linton, E. Lothian, EH40 3DG (Tel: 01620-860164; Fax: 01620-860164; Web: www.tuckwellpress.co.uk).

West Dunbartonshire Libraries
Levenford House, Helenslee Road, Dumbarton, G82 4AH (Tel: 01389-608039; Fax: 01389-608044).

Whittles Publishing
Roseleigh House, Harbour Road, Latheronwheel, Caithness, KW5 6DW (Tel: 01593-741240; Fax: 01593-741360; E-mail: whittl@globalnet.co.uk).

Wild Goose Publications
Unit 16, 6 Harmony Row, Govan, Glasgow, G51 3BA (Tel: 0141-440 0985; Fax: 0141-440 2338; E-mail: admin@wgp.iona.org.uk; Web: www.iona.org.uk).

ADVERTISING

ADVERTISING AGENCIES

Adpartners Ltd
280 St Vincent Street, Glasgow, G2 5RL
(Tel: 0141-226 3711; Fax: 0141-221 0070;
Web: www.adpartners.com).
Managing Director: W. Muir

Contact Corporate Merchandise
Suite 427, Baltic Chambers, 50 Wellington
Street, Glasgow, G2 6HJ (Tel: 0141-221 3480;
Fax: 0141-221 3477).

Creative Direct Ltd
126 Calton Road, Edinburgh, EH8 8JQ
(Tel: 0131-558 1111; Fax: 0131-557 8282;
E-mail: creative.direct@easynet.co.uk;
Web: www.creative-dir.co.uk).

Davidson Advertising
1 Houston Street, Glasgow, G5 8RS
(Tel: 0141-429 4206; Fax: 0141-429 4207;
E-mail: info@davidsonadvertising.co.uk;
Web: www.davidsonadvertising.co.uk).

Direct Media Advertising
Beckford Street Business Centre, 28 Beckford
Street, Hamilton, Lanarkshire, ML3 0BT
(Tel: 01698-283203; Fax: 01698-283204;
E-mail: pat@media4.demon.co.uk).
Managing Director: P. Craig

Drummond Advertising
Drummond House, 281 Clepington Road,
Dundee, Angus, DD3 8BD (Tel: 01382-889995;
Fax: 01382-813187).

Edmonds Advertising
23 Mitchell Street, Edinburgh, EH6 7BD
(Tel: 0131-467 8333; Fax: 0131-555 2660;
E-mail: mail@edmonds.co.uk;
Web: www.edmonds.co.uk).

Ernie Nicholls Media
8A Castle Terrace, Edinburgh, EH1 2DP
(Tel: 0131-229 3398; Fax: 0131-229 2858;
E-mail: enmedia.co.uk).
Managing Director: E. Nicholls

Feather Brooksbank
The Old Assembly Hall, 37 Constitution Street,
Leith, Edinburgh, EH6 7BG (Tel: 0131-555
2554; Fax: 0131-555 2556).
Director: G. Brooksbank

Frame Cunningham Holden Edy (Scotland) Ltd
58 West Regent Street, Glasgow, G2 2QZ
(Tel: 0141-353 4380; Fax: 0141-353 4381;
E-mail: info@framecunningham.co.uk).

Hay Smith Advertising Ltd
15 Mentone Gardens, Edinburgh, EH9 2DJ
(Tel: 0131-623 3200; Fax: 0131-623 3203;
E-mail: haysmithadv@cableinet.co.uk;
Web: haysmith.co.uk).

Holt Marketing Communications Ltd
3 Cluny Gardens, Edinburgh, EH10 6BE
(Tel: 0131-446 9991;
E-mail: info@holt-marketing.com;
Web: www.holt-marketing.com).

The Leith Advertising Agency Ltd
The Canon Mill, Canon Street, Edinburgh, EH3
5HE (Tel: 0131-557 5840; Fax: 0131-557 5837;
Web: www.leith.co.uk).
Managing Director: P. Adams

The Levy McCallum Advertising Agency
203 St Vincent Street, Glasgow, G2 5NH
(Tel: 0141-248 7977; Fax: 0141-221 5803;
E-mail: ads@levymccallum.co.uk;
Web: www.levymccallum.co.uk).
Managing Director: O. Thomson

The Levy McCallum Advertising Agency
29 Stafford Street, Edinburgh, EH3 7BJ (Tel:
0131-225 9733; Fax: 0131-220 0248;
E-mail: ads@levymccallum.co.uk;
Web: www.levymaccallum.co.uk).

Marketing Concepts Ltd
172 Leith Walk, Edinburgh, EH6 5EB
(Tel: 0131-555 5678).

McKinstrie Wilde Millhouse
62 Newhaven Road, Edinburgh, EH6 5QB
(Tel: 0131-554 4441; Fax: 0131-554 9496;
E-mail: info@mckinstriewilde.co.uk;
Web: www.mckinstriewilde.co.uk).
Managing Director: A. McKinstrie

Mearns & Gill Advertising Ltd
7 Carden Place, Aberdeen, AB10 1PP
(Tel: 01224-646311; Fax: 01224-631882;
E-mail: info@mearns-gill.com;
Web: www.mearns-gill.com).
Managing Director: A. Mearns

Navigator Responsive Advertising Ltd
Bupa House, 116 Dundas Street, Edinburgh,
EH3 5EE (Tel: 0131-556 8002; Fax: 0131-557
8413; Web: www.navigator-ra.co.uk).
Managing Director: A. Carolan

Oneagency
14 Links Place, Edinburgh, EH6 7EZ
(Tel: 0131-625 0100; Fax: 0121-625 0101;
E-mail: info@oneagency.uk.com).

Osprey Scotland
Great   Michael   House,   14   Links   Place,
Edinburgh, EH6 7EZ (Tel: 0131-553 9200; Fax:
0131-553 9201;
E-mail: info@osprey-scotland.co.uk).
Managing Director: V. Meiklejohn

CULTURAL

SCOTLAND

CULTURAL, HISTORICAL AND RECREATIONAL SCOTLAND

HISTORY

7th–5th millennia BC – The earliest evidence of human settlement in Scotland was by Middle Stone Age hunter-gatherers and fishermen. Radiocarbon dating of large shell mounds on the island of Oronsay suggests that occupation was under way by the middle of the millennium.

4th–3rd millennia BC – New Stone Age farmers began around 4000 BC to cultivate crops and rear livestock on the western and northern coasts and islands and in Orkney. Forests began to be cleared and the making of pottery began. Apart from the Neolithic settlements at Skara Brae in Orkney and Jarlshof in Shetland, however, the principal monuments from this period, most of which date from c. 3000 BC, are religious. Communal burial took place in massive chambered cairns, such as those at Maeshowe and Isbister (Orkney) and Nether Largie South (Kilmartin, Argyll); while stone circles and other monuments, e.g. the Calanais (Callanish) standing stones (Lewis) and the Ring of Brodgar (Orkney), served ritual purposes.

c.2000 BC onwards – Metalworking and use of bronze artefacts began. Settlement by the Early Bronze Age 'Beaker people', so called from the distinctive style of their drinking vessels, was mainly in eastern Scotland, although quantities of Beaker ware has also been found in the west, dating back perhaps to the mid-third millennium. There is evidence that the largest of the hilltop forts previously attributed to the Iron Age, such as Traprain Law (East Lothian) and Eildon Hill (Roxburghshire), may belong to the Bronze Age. Similar types of artefact found in widely separated locations are evidence of networks of exchange across Europe, in which Scotland participated.

From about 1300 BC the climate became colder and wetter, a trend which was possibly exacerbated by the effect of intense volcanic activity in Iceland (1159). Bronze Age communities gradually retreated from the uplands and marginal farming areas.

c.700 BC– AD 200 – Further settlement as tribes were displaced from further south by new incursions from the Continent. This movement was accompanied by the development of Iron Age tools and weapons such as the sword and the rotary quern for grinding grain. In this period, communities became more self-contained and competition and conflict between them increased. The building efforts previously put into ritual and mortuary structures was diverted into strong and imposing fortified dwellings and settlements.

Many hillforts of different types were built throughout Scotland during the first millennium BC. The huge drystone broch towers, such as those of Mousa (Shetland), Midhowe (Orkney) and Dun Carloway (Lewis), were at their peak in the latter half of the millennium and the first century AD, and other forms, such as wheelhouses, roundhouses and crannogs, were common, with regional variations. It is possible that these large buildings also reflected growing material prosperity and served a political purpose as symbols of the power of local and tribal leaders.

AD 43 onwards – Julius Agricola, the Roman governor of Britain AD 77–84, advanced deep into Caledonia, culminating with a victory at Mons Graupius in the north-east, probably in AD 84; however, Agricola was recalled to Rome shortly afterwards and his forward policy was not pursued.

AD 122–410: Hadrian set the northern boundary of the Roman empire in Britain and ordered the construction of a wall to defend it. Hadrian's Wall marked the frontier until the Roman troops withdrew, except AD c.144–190, when the frontier moved north to the Forth – Clyde isthmus and a turf-built curtain wall, the Antonine Wall, was manned and policed. Tolls and the surrender of weapons were demanded of anyone wishing to cross it. There were frequent invasions and counter-invasions by Romans and Picts in the following centuries, though the last major Roman campaign north of the Forth, carried out under Emperor Severus in 210, was a muted success and after Severus's death in 211 the Roman legions fell back to merely defending the border. The Picts, on the other hand, became much bolder in the fourth century, uniting against Rome with other peoples not only in Scotland but Ireland and the continent and at one point (AD 367) reaching as far south as London.

Although the Roman hold on the territory north of Hadrian's Wall was never more than tenuous, some Roman influence in parts of Scotland persisted until the fourth century, the legions finally being withdrawn from Britain altogether around 407–410.

2nd–9th centuries – This period is marked by the gradual coalescing of the many small tribes existing in the Roman period into larger and more definable kingdoms, and continual warfare between them. The Picts, a loose confederation of a dozen or so tribes occupying the territory north of the Forth, appear to have dominated the north and east by the fifth century. The Scots, a Gaelic-speaking people of northern Ireland, colonised the area of Argyll and Bute from about AD 500, establishing the kingdom of Dalriada centred on Dunadd, and then expanded eastwards and northwards. The Britons, speaking a Brythonic Celtic language, colonised Scotland from the south from the first century BC; they lost control of south-eastern Scotland (incorporated into the kingdom of Northumbria) to the Angles in the early seventh century but retained south-western Scotland and Cumbria.

However, it was the arrival of the Vikings in the eighth century that constituted the next major influence on Scotland. Viking raids from the late eighth century were consolidated into a permanent Norse presence by settlement on the mainland and islands of the north and west from the early ninth century onwards.

397 – First Christian church in Scotland established by St Ninian at Whithorn.

c.563 – St Columba (d. 597) arrived from Ireland with twelve companions and established a monastery and a missionary base on Iona. Columba and his monks accomplished the conversion to Christianity of the Picts as far afield as Fife. The island became a place of pilgrimage and a centre of Christian scholarship: the eighth-century Book of Kells, now in the library of Trinity College, Dublin, was probably largely produced at the abbey of Iona and was moved to Ireland, with Columba's remains, by monks fleeing Viking raids aound 800.

612 – Death of St Kentigern (also known as St Mungo), reputedly founder and first bishop of the city of Glasgow.

685 – Northward incursions by the Northumbrian Angles were halted by Picts at Battle of Nechtansmere, near Forfar. This defeat for the Northumbrians effectively checked their northward expansion into Scotland.

Scotland's First Law?

In 697 St Adomnán, an abbot of Iona and biographer of St Columba, drew up a Law of the Innocents, which aimed to protect non-combatants – women, children and members of religious communities – from violence in war. Written on Iona, the law was promulgated and enforced in Ireland, Scotland and Pictland.

---

c.736 – King Aengus of the Picts captured Dunadd, royal centre of Dalriada, thus acquiring overlordship of the Scots. In 756, in league with the Northumbrians, he defeated the north Britons at Dumbarton.

c.794 onwards – Viking raids took place and Norse settlements were established in Argyll, Caithness and Sutherland, Orkney, Shetland, and the Western Isles. By 890 Orkney, Shetland, the Hebrides and Caithness had become part of the kingdom of Norway under Harald Fairhair and in 987 Earl Sigurd of Orkney annexed Sutherland, Ross and Moray.

843 – Unification of the areas which now comprise Scotland began, when Kenneth mac Alpin, King of the Scots from c.834, became also King of the Picts, joining the two lands to form the kingdom of Alba (comprising Scotland north of a line between the Forth and Clyde rivers). Kenneth mac Alpin was helped in this enterprise by the severe defeat inflicted on the mainland Picts by the Danes in 839, weakening their resistance.

890 – Orkney, Shetland, Caithness and the Hebrides became part of the Norwegian kingdom of Harald Fairhair.

903 – St Andrews became the religious capital of Scotland after Kenneth mac Alpin's new religious centre at Dunkeld was destroyed by the Vikings.

c.973–4 – Lothian, the eastern part of the area between the Forth and the Tweed was ceded or leased to Kenneth II of Alba by Edgar of England.

1010 – Malcolm II defeated a Norse army at Dufftown and further secured his northern border by the marriage of his daughter to the Earl of Orkney.

c.1018 – Malcolm II's victory over a Northumbrian army at Carham restored Scottish possession of Lothian, lost earlier in his reign. At about this time Malcolm placed his grandson Duncan on the throne of the British kingdom of Strathclyde, bringing under Scots rule virtually all of what is now Scotland. The hybrid name 'Scotland' began to supplant the Gaelic name 'Alba' (still the name of the country in Gaelic).

1040 – Duncan I was slain in battle by Macbeth, who ruled until 1057. Macbeth fell at the battle of Lumphanan to Malcolm Canmore, who was aided by Earl Siward of Northumbria and Edward the Confessor of England.

1098 – Magnus III of Norway devastated the Western Isles; but an uprising in the mid twelfth century drove the Norse from most of mainland Argyll. From then on, the Norse possessions were gradually incorporated into the kingdom of Scotland.

Late 11th century onwards – Frequent conflict continued between Scotland and England over territory and the extent of England's political influence, and between the Scottish crown and rebellious Highland leaders such as Somerled, who became Lord of the Isles in 1156. At the same time Scotland was developing as a fully-fledged medieval society. Towns and burghs developed, encouraged by contact with the Normans, who brought trade and the marketplace, and by the court's increasing sophistication. David I granted the status of burgh, with special trading privileges, to numerous towns. Many had become royal burghs by the end of the 12th century. In return they paid rents and customs. As well as centres of trade and craftsmanship, royal burghs were centres of justice where the king's sheriffs held courts.

In the same period (roughly 1113–78) many of the great Scottish abbeys were founded under Alexander I, David I and William I (who founded Arbroath Abbey in 1178).

The number of burghs increased sharply during the reign of Alexander III. By 1283 most of the towns in Scotland, with exception of a few in the West Highlands and the Hebrides, had acquired the status of either royal or baronial burghs.

1237 – The Treaty of York established Scotland's border with England.

1266 – The Treaty of Perth, by which Magnus IV of Norway ceded the Hebrides and the Isle of Man to Scotland after an unsuccessful Norwegian expedition in 1263 by Haakon IV was settled.

1296–1328 – Wars of Independence. The failure of the Scottish royal line with the death of Margaret of Norway in 1290 led to disputes over the throne which were resolved by the adjudication of Edward I of England. He awarded the throne to John Balliol in 1292, but Balliol's refusal to be a puppet King led to war.

A Parliament held in Stirling in 1295 overturned Balliol's government and appointed a ruling Council, which made an alliance with Philip IV of France against England, formalising a relationship which had already existed for 200 years. (The treaty has become known as 'the Auld Alliance', and was the basis for Scottish military support for France in the following centuries. Scots fought in the army of Joan of Arc).

Balliol surrendered to Edward I and Edward attempted to rule Scotland himself. Resistance was led by William Wallace, who defeated the English under Hugh de Cressingham, Edward's Lord High Treasurer, at Stirling Bridge in 1297 but Wallace was later defeated by a large force under Edward himself at Falkirk the following year, and Robert Bruce, who seized the throne in 1306. Bruce had regained most of Scotland by 1311 and, famously, routed Edward II's army at Bannockburn in 1314, following up the victory by incursions deep into northern England and even into Ireland in the succeeding years.

Edward did not renounce his claim to Scotland, however, and when Bruce rejected a papal truce in 1317, Pope John XXII excommunicated him and placed Scotland under interdict. The bishops' reply, in a letter dated 6 April 1320 and probably written by Bernard Linton, Abbot of Arbroath and Chancellor of Scotland, passionately defended Scotland's independence, and has become known as the Declaration of Arbroath.

England finally recognised Scotland's independence in the Treaty of Northampton in 1328. However, this was not the end of the story. By 1336 the forces of Edward III had penetrated Scotland again as far as Elgin; and although David II imposed a degree of stability and order in the 1360s, the conflict between Scotland and England was by no means settled when he died.

The Journeying Stone of Destiny

Reputedly brought to Scotland from Ireland by King Fergus in the sixth century, Scotland's ancient symbol of kingship graced the coronation ceremonies of generations of Scottish monarchs. The Dalriadic Kings were enthroned upon it at Iona, Dunadd and finally Scone, which became its supposedly permanent home c. 840. However, in 1296, the English King Edward I sealed his defeat of John Balliol by removing the Stone to London and placing it in Westminster Abbey, where – although the Treaty of Northampton granted its return to the Scots – it stayed for the next six-and-a-half centuries, being incorporated into the coronation ceremonies of English and then British monarchs.

In 1950 the Stone nearly succeeded in going home when a group of Nationalist students took it from Westminster Abbey early on Christmas morning; but it stayed in Scotland for only a few months, being placed symbolically in Arbroath Abbey, and was back in London for the coronation of Queen Elizabeth II. It was not until 1996, the 700th anniversary of its first removal, that the Stone was finally formally returned to Scotland.

1349 – Bubonic plague, the 'Black Death' which had swept through England in 1347, reached Scotland and spread throughout the country.

1371 onwards – The first Stewart kings, Robert II and Robert III, were weak administrators, and the power of the barons and rivalries between them resulted in vendettas and lawlessness on which parliamentary attempts at legislation had little practical effect. In particular, the throne had little control of the Highlands or the Western Isles. Although David II had subdued the Lord of the Isles in 1369, the Western Isles were for practical purposes independent

The Highlands and Lowlands were in many respects becoming two nations. Predating and underlying the basically Norman feudal system which functioned in the lowlands, was the clan system, based on attachment to the land and loyalty to the clan chieftain. This continued to exist in the Highlands in an undiluted form and to pose continual challenges to the King's power in the north and west.

1390 – The burning of Elgin cathedral and town by the 'Wolf of Badenoch' – Alexander Stewart, Earl of Buchan and youngest brother of Robert III took place. Though in part an act of reprisal for

opposition from the Bishop of Moray, this was also part of a wider campaign of terror waged by the Wolf to maintain Stewart control in the north – and to enrich himself.

1407 – The city of Bruges gave Scots trading rights, opening the way for trade with the Continent; these were later suspended (1412–15) by the Hanseatic League because of Scottish piracy.

1414 – Scotland's first university was founded at St Andrews. Teaching had begun in 1410 and the papal bull giving formal recognition was issued in 1414. The foundation of the universities of Glasgow and Aberdeen followed later in the century, in 1451 and 1495 respectively. Edinburgh University, founded in 1583, is Britain's oldest secular university foundation.

1411 – The outbreak of open war in the Highlands began. Donald, Lord of the Isles, was defeated at the Battle of Harlaw near Inverurie by the Earl of Mar (the Wolf's son) and a local army including burgesses of Aberdeen. Donald retreated to the west, but with his local power intact.

1424 – James I set in motion a series of legislative reforms aimed at controlling the nobles, creating a fair and efficient judiciary, and raising national revenue. In 1426 parliament abolished all laws other than the King's. James backed this up by force in 1428 by arresting and in some cases executing about 50 Highland chiefs. Their resentment was instrumental in his death.

1468–9 – Orkney and Shetland ceded to Scotland as a pledge for the unpaid dowry of Margaret of Denmark, wife of James III, though Danish claims of suzerainty persisted, to be relinquished only in 1590 with the marriage of Anne of Denmark to James VI.

1493 – After continual strife in the reign of James III, James IV annexed the lands and titles of John, Lord of the Isles, to the crown, and made a series of expeditions to the west between 1493 and 1498. However, he was soon (1504–7) faced with rebellion from John's son Donald Dubh. The integration of the west into the kingdom remained fragile, and James's granting of governorships to the Earls of Argyll and Huntly in 1500–1 bolstered the power of the Campbells and Gordons and provoked long-standing resentment from other clans.

1507 – Scotland's first printing press was licensed to Andrew Myllar and Walter Chepman by James IV, whose court promoted literature, learning and music. Their first book contained poems by William Dunbar.

1511–13 – In 1511, reviving the Auld Alliance, James signed a new treaty with Louis XII of France in which Scotland pledged to make war on England if France did so. He found himself almost at once drawn into a war of little direct relevance to Scotland, supporting the French against the Holy League of Pope Julius II, of which England, under Henry VIII, was a member. In 1513 James took on an English army at Flodden; although it was the largest and best-armed Scottish force ever to have entered England, the result was a disastrous defeat for the Scots, in which James IV, many of his nobles, and thousands of soldiers died.

1532 – The creation of the Court of Session by an Act of Parliament established a permanent 15-man College of Justice. A central criminal court, and the High Court of Justiciary was later founded. The present-day court system is based on these institutions.

1544–50 – Hostilities were renewed with England. The 'Rough Wooing' was a savage campaign waged by Henry VIII on the Catholic, pro-French Scottish monarchy in retaliation for the breaking of a treaty by which Mary (later Queen of Scots) was to marry his son Edward. The whole of the south-east was ravaged and the great Border abbeys sacked.

1555–60 – The doctrines of Luther and Calvin, introduced into Scotland by John Knox, a priest disaffected by the growing secularity and wealth of the Catholic church, quickly became popular among the local clergy and the lesser nobility. The outlawing of Knox and his followers in 1559 provoked riots by Protestants which flared briefly into war. The 'Reformation Parliament', held on 1 August 1560 in the name of Queen Mary but without a royal presence, abolished the Latin Mass and rejected the jurisdiction of the Pope. Only a month earlier, the Treaty of Leith effectively ended the Auld Alliance and French troops withdrew from Scotland. The Protestant majority in government was established, and was sufficiently secure to force Mary's abdication in 1567.

1603 – James VI of Scotland succeeded Elizabeth I on the throne of England (his mother, Mary Queen of Scots, was the great-granddaughter of Henry VII), his successors reigning as sovereigns of Great Britain. James became an absentee monarch, and England and Scotland remained distinct in important ways, each retaining its own parliament and legal system.

The Union improved the physical links between Scotland and England and reduced much of the cross-border bickering and raiding. However, Scotland was in many respects not treated as England's equal: it could not trade with England or the colonies England later acquired without paying duties.

1608 – The emigration of thousands of Border families to the province of Ulster, which James VI was colonising escalated.

1614 – The logarithmic tables of Edinburgh scholar and inventor John Napier were published.

1618 – James VI attempted to bring the Church in Scotland into line with English practice in the Five Articles of Perth, passed by a General Assembly of the Church in August.

1632–40 – Building of Parliament House in Edinburgh, confirming its status as capital city of Scotland. Glasgow, meanwhile, was growing rapidly as a centre of industry, commerce and foreign trade. The building of a deep-water harbour at Port Glasgow began in 1667.

1638 – The National Covenant was signed, overturning the Five Articles and reasserting the people's right to keep the reformed church. The Covenant overturned the Articles, sacked the Scottish bishops and proscribed the use of the Book of Common Prayer.

1666 – The Pentland Rising, a popular revolt began. Unsupported by landowners it opposed the repression of Covenanters which followed the Restoration, and in particular the prohibition of conventicles (outdoor religious meetings). It failed when a poorly armed force of a few thousand Covenanters was defeated by government troops at Rullion Green.

1681 *Viscount of Stair (1619–95)* by James Dalrymple was published, detailing the Institutions of the Law of Scotland and establishing Scots law as an independent and coherent system distinct from English law.

1688–9 – After the abdication (by flight) in 1688 of James VII and II, the crown devolved upon William III (grandson of Charles I) and Mary II (elder daughter of James VII and II). In April 1689 the Convention of the Estates issued the Claim of Right and the Articles of Grievances, which asserted the independence of the Scottish Parliament and Presbyterianism as the established Church. William and Mary were offered the Scottish crown on condition that they accepted these proposals.

From April 1689, Graham of Claverhouse roused the Highlands on behalf of James, but died after a military success at Killiecrankie in July.

1692 – The Massacre of Glencoe. The clan chiefs who had opposed William were offered pardon if they took an oath of allegiance before 1 January 1692 and threatened with persecution if they did not. The small clan of MacDonald of Glencoe missed the deadline by a few days. News that the chief had taken the oath was kept from the Privy Council, and a detachment of Campbell soldiers was sent to Glencoe and billeted with the MacDonalds with secret orders to destroy them. Thirty-eight people were killed. The violation of the tradition of hospitality and the Government's implication in the massacre turned Glencoe into a Jacobite rallying banner.

1695 – Establishment of the Bank of Scotland in Edinburgh, Scotland's first bank. It had a monopoly until around the time of the Act of Union, when the financial settlement required by the Union and the losses sustained by the collapse of the Darien scheme led to the foundation, also in Edinburgh, of the Royal Bank of Scotland in 1727. The Clydesdale Bank, Scotland's third major bank today, was founded in Glasgow in 1838, around the same time as three other Glasgow-based banks (the Union Bank of Scotland, the Western Bank of Scotland, and the City of Glasgow Bank), in a bid to challenge the financial power of Edinburgh and service the ever-growing industrial and commercial needs of Glasgow.

1698–1700 – The Darien Venture. In 1695, an Act of Parliament was passed establishing the Company of Scotland Trading to Africa and the Indies, modelled on the London East India Company and intended to revive Scotland's depressed overseas trade. Darien, in Panama, was chosen as the site for a Scottish colony which would be a crossroads for world trade. Large amounts of money were invested in the scheme, but three successive attempts at settling in Darien and trading, between 1698 and 1700, failed miserably through inability to cope with the tropical climate, attacks from the Spanish, and a complete absence of trade. About 2,000 people died and the disaster not only crippled individual investors financially but dealt further blows to the already weak Scottish economy.

1707 – The Act of Union was passed, joining Scotland and England politically under one Parliament in London, in which Scotland would have 45 seats (in both Houses).

Recognition of Scottish law was an integral part of the settlement, and, although certain laws have been superseded or nullified subsequently, the Scottish legal system today remains based on that in force at the time of the Union.

1714–15 – After the death of Anne (younger daughter of James VII and II), the throne devolved upon George I (great-grandson of James VI and I). In 1715, armed risings on behalf of James Stuart (the Old Pretender, son of James VII and II) led to the indecisive battle of Sheriffmuir, and the Jacobite movement died down until 1745.

1723 – The Society for Improvement in the Knowledge of Agriculture formed in Edinburgh. In 1727 the Commissioners and Trustees for Improving Manufactures and Fisheries were established. New ideas and technology were being developed by Scots farmers and manufacturers. Some heads of clans became increasingly concerned with making profit from their lands, either by selling land or by adopting the methods of improvement, which often involved turning large areas over to cattle and sheep at the expense of small tenants. The depopulation of the Highlands began.

From 1723 to 1725 there were outbreaks of protest by the Galloway Levellers, dispossessed tenants who had been evicted by lairds in Galloway in order to enclose pastures for fattening cattle.

The Clans and the Land

While political and social relations in lowland Scotland gradually became largely formalised and institutionalised during the Middle Ages, Highland society, isolated by geography and language, continued to be organised in the clan system, which originated in – and still retained many features of – the tribal organisation of early Gaelic society, based on strong but informal bonds of loyalty and trust and occupation of land. Clan members were those people, including non-relatives, living on the lands owned by the chieftain, and for whom chieftains assumed a patriarchal responsibility in return, particularly, for the loyal support of fighting men. Clan territory boundaries were broadly established by the 16th century.

Chiefs leased tracts (or 'tacks') of land to clan members (originally relatives) or allies to guarantee their security and also their allegiance. The traditional tack carried with it the requirement to provide military service. The tacksmen, in turn, sublet their land to tenants who worked for them on the land in return. Highland cattle were the principal source of wealth, and the tacksmen's power over the poorer tenants was potentially almost absolute.

Over time, the clan chiefs became members of the national aristocracy; they spent time in England and abroad and became part of European society. This was not the case with ordinary Highlanders, who at the beginning of the eighteenth century still spoke only Gaelic and were largely illiterate. By this time, however, some heads of clans were beginning to see themselves as landowners (and landlords) rather than chiefs. The leading chiefs were largely absentees. The bonds of responsibility to their tenants began to loosen as land began to signify money rather than ancestral tradition. This shift was an important facilitator of the Highland Clearances.

1745 – Charles Stuart (the Young Pretender) defeated the Royalist troops at Prestonpans and advanced as far as Derby (1746). From Derby, the adherents of 'James VIII and III' (the title claimed for his father by Charles Stuart) fell back on the defensive. The Highland army of 5,000, exhausted and outnumbered by the Duke of Cumberland's 9,000-strong force, was finally crushed catastrophically at Culloden on 16 April 1746. Prince Charles fled the country, and retaliation against the Jacobites by the victorious army was extremely savage.

1747–8 – Anxious to prevent the rise of any form of social and cultural organisation which could become a rallying point for further rebellion, the Government passed legislation intended to annihilate the clan system. The Abolition of Heritable Jurisdictions Act of 1747 confiscated the lands of those chiefs who had rebelled (the forfeited estates were later returned, in 1784), and the Disarming Act of 1748 proscribed the bearing of weapons and the playing of the Great Pipes. The wearing of Highland dress was also outlawed from 1746—82, although it made a comeback, in a somewhat romanticised form, in the early 19th century.

c.1750 onwards – Imports of tobacco and cotton were established as mainstays of the non-agrarian economy. Revenue from the processing and re-export of these commodities financed the development of Scottish merchant banking and further industry.

1754 – The 'Royal and Ancient Golf Club' was founded at St Andrews.

1759 – Birth of Robert Burns at Alloway, Ayrshire (d. 1796).

1767 – Building of Edinburgh New Town (designed by James Craig) began, with the draining and clearing of land to the north of the Castle and the laying out of Princes Street, George Street and Queen Street. Building continued in phases until 1840.

Elsewhere, from the 1770s onward, a new model of village planning, stone-built and based on a central market square or high street, was applied by landowners, businessmen and government bodies in over a hundred villages, with the specific aim of economic development.

1770 – An Act of Parliament created the Clyde Trust, authorising plans to deepen the Clyde. This initiated a process of development which led to the building of the great shipyards and docks in Glasgow in the following century.

Other technological and industrial developments around this time (e.g. the opening of the Carron Ironworks in 1759; James Watt's patenting of an improved steam engine in 1769; the introduction of large water-powered spinning mills from 1779) laid the basis for Scotland's industrial economy in the 19th and 20th centuries.

1771 – Birth of Sir Walter Scott, Edinburgh (d. 1832).

1776 – Adam Smith (1723–90) published *The Wealth of Nations*. David Hume (b. 1711) died. The suspension of tobacco imports caused by the American War of Independence caused financial crisis in Glasgow, but the Glasgow merchants had other commodities, including exports of their own – coal, linen and ale, for instance – which ensured their survival.

1785–1820 – The first period of the Highland Clearances. As the majority of Highland estates were reorganised for sheep-farming, thousands of tenants were evicted or 'cleared' from land they had farmed for generations with no security of tenure other than the unwritten contract of clan loyalty. Clearances took place across Sutherland in 1785–6, 1800, 1807, 1809, 1812–14 and 1819–20, one of the harshest being the clearance of Strathnaver on the northern coast in 1814. Some of the evicted tenants were encouraged to emigrate to the Lowlands and overseas, and a great many did so; others were moved forcibly to the coast where they were expected to survive as fishermen. The Clearances were the principal impetus for the mass diaspora of Scots to North America and the Antipodes.

New Lanark, A Model Community

In 1785, David Dale, a Glasgow merchant, built a new industrial village near the old market town of Lanark. Built in a valley near the Falls of Clyde and using the river as a power source for its cotton mills, New Lanark became one of the largest cotton-manufacturing centres in Scotland, and continued in operation until 1968.

New Lanark was most renowned, however, as the place where the pioneering and enlightened ideas of Robert Owen were put into practice. Between 1800 and 1825 Owen ploughed much of the profits from the industry into improving life for the workers and their families, outlawing child labour, founding schools whose curriculum and disciplinary regime were far ahead of their time, and providing free medical care for workers and subsidised food at the village shop.

1790 – The Forth–Clyde Canal, Britain's first sea-to-sea canal was opened. The 250 miles of military road-building by General Wade in the early 18th century had improved communications in the Highlands, and from 1802 onwards Thomas Telford, engineer to the Commission for Highland Roads and Bridges, oversaw the construction of nearly 1,000 miles of roads. The Caledonian Canal was built between 1804 and 1822.

1793 – Beginning of war with France and formation of Highland regiments (e.g. Cameron Highlanders, Argyll Highlanders, Gordon Highlanders). Lairds recruited energetically in the Highlands, and the Scottish regiments played a significant part in the creation and defence of the British Empire, and in all Britain's wars of the 19th and 20th centuries.

1799 – The emancipation of coal-miners and salt workers from serfdom took place. An Act of Parliament in 1606 had allowed for serfdom of these workers on the grounds that they were 'necessary servants'.

1820 – Following years of economic depression and discontent among workers, exacerbated by rising grain prices after the Corn Laws of 1815, a series of riots and a widespread strike in the west culminated in a march from Glasgow to Falkirk and an attempt by a small band of radicals to seize the Carron ironworks. Both actions were crushed by government forces and the leaders executed or transported. The incidents became known as the 'Radical War'.

1830 onwards – New smelting processes enabled the development of the iron industry and related industries, such as coal-mining, also flourished. In the 1830s Scotland boasted the largest chemical works in the world.

1832 – The First Reform Bill increased Scotland's representation at Westminster to 53 seats and extended the franchise to over 60,000 voters. The population of Scotland at the time was 2,364,000 (1831 census).

1838–9 – The Scottish Chartists' Organisation was formed in the wake of the Reform Bill. By 1839 there were 80 local Chartist Associations. Although their aims were modest and limited exclusively to electoral reform, they were viewed with alarm by the authorities. In 1848, 10,000 Chartists demonstrated on Calton Hill in Edinburgh and caused riots in Glasgow; but the movement became overshadowed by trade unionism.

1840–54 – The second wave of Highland Clearances, from Ross-shire and the Isles began. The Highland and Island Emigration Society was formed in 1853 under the patronage of Prince Albert, offering ships and assistance to emigrants. Large-scale emigration was increased by severe famine in 1846–7.

1841 – Govan shipyard was founded by Robert Napier. Aided by a fast-growing local steel industry, by the 1870s and 1880s Scotland had become the world leader in shipbuilding, particularly with the introduction of the large steel-hulled steamships that supplanted the tea clippers.

1842 – First visit to Scotland by Queen Victoria and Prince Albert. The royal family bought Balmoral Castle in 1853.

Opening of Edinburgh–Glasgow railway.

1850s onward – Development of the herring fishing industry on the east coast. New rail technology and later the use of steamboats increased catches vastly, and the development of the railways enabled efficient transport of the processed fish.

1855 – The United Coal and Iron Miners' Association, Scotland's first effective labour organisation was founded.

1867 – The voting franchise was extended to all males and Scottish Women's Suffrage Society was formed. In 1869 women gained the right to vote in municipal elections, but they were not to win the right to vote in parliamentary elections on the same terms as men until 1928.

1872 – The Education (Scotland) Act, bringing burgh and parish schools under state control was introduced; but education was not provided free until 1892. The Scottish Leaving Certificate was introduced in 1888.

1873 – The Scottish Football Association and Glasgow Rangers football club were founded. Celtic was founded in 1887.

1882 – The Highland Land Leagues were formed, and 'Battle of the Braes' in Skye, when crofters defied police and landlords in defence of their grazing rights began. Continuing trouble with crofters forced the government to set up a Royal Commission of enquiry, leading to the adoption of the Crofters' (Holdings) Act in 1886, which gave crofters security of tenure, fixed rents and other rights.

1882 – The Scottish Labour Party was formed, with James Keir Hardie as a founder member. However, Labour did not win the largest share of either votes or parliamentary seats in Scotland until 1922.

1885 – The Scottish Office in Whitehall was established, and post of Secretary for Scotland. In 1928 the post was upgraded to Secretary of State for Scotland, thus reinstating a post which had been abolished in 1745.

1886 – The Scottish Home Rule Association was founded, with both Labour and Liberal support. The concept of Home Rule was limited to Scotland's management of Scottish affairs, leaving wider areas such as foreign policy to Westminster, which would retain Scottish MPs.

1897 – The Scottish Trades Union Congress was formed, at least partly in opposition to the British TUC, which was felt to represent the smaller Scottish unions inadequately. Organised labour was to achieve considerable strength during the Great War and its aftermath (for instance in the 1919 strike for a 40-hour working week) and was particularly militant during the inter-war period.

1909 – Construction of the naval dockyard at Rosyth began.

1910 – Twenty Liberal MPs set up a Scottish National Committee to promote self-government, but the issue was shelved until after World War I, when the Scottish Home Rule Association was refounded (1918) and the Scots National League, with its roots in radical politics, was formed in (1921). This was renamed the National Party of Scotland in 1927.

1924 – James Ramsay MacDonald was elected Prime Minister and Secretary of State for Foreign Affairs in Britain's first Labour government. He returned as Prime Minister in 1929–31 and 1931–35 (in a coalition government with the Conservatives).

Successive draft Home Rule Bills presented to Parliament in 1924, 1926, 1927 and 1928 failed.

1934 – The Scottish National Party was formed through a merger of the National Party of Scotland and the Scottish Party (formed 1932). The diverse nature of its components and their points of view, added to indifferent or unfavourable attitudes towards Home Rule on the part of government and large sections of the public, which meant that the party was slow to cohere. In 1946 it produced its statement of aims and policy, and in 1967 it won its first seat in Parliament when Winifred Ewing won the Hamilton by-election.

1930s – Scottish literary renaissance.

1937 – Scottish Gaelic Text Society established.

1939–45 – Industrial decline, which had already begun to worsen with the Depression (1929–31), was temporarily reversed by the need for production in the war effort. There was full employment and women workers were particularly active both in industry and on the land, as they had been in the Great War.

1948 – East Kilbride and Glenrothes become Scotland's first New Towns.

1959 onwards – Large oil and gas reserves discovered were in North Sea. In 1974 Highland One, the world's largest oil platform, was launched from Nigg on the Cromarty Firth. The first oil was pumped ashore in 1975. The oil industry has become an important, if insecure, source of revenue and employment particularly for the north-east. In particular, the installation of the large Sullom Voe terminal in Shetland, based on agreements between the oil companies and the Island Council, has brought economic benefits to the islands.

1971 onwards – By the beginning of the 1970s the once industrially vibrant Upper Clyde was reduced to five shipyards, linked in the Upper Clyde Shipbuilders consortium. Under Edward Heath's Conservative government there was a series of sell-offs and liquidations of part of the consortium. The workers responded by organising a 'work-in' by 300 men. In February 1972 the government agreed to allow three shipyards to continue.

Nonetheless, the long, slow attrition of Scotland's industrial base was only momentarily halted, and in the next two decades mines, shipyards, iron and steel works and factories continued to be closed down and dismantled, a process accelerated with the emergence of the globalised economy. The fishing industry also contracted severely.

To some extent the heavy industries have been replaced by energy supply (oil and gas, hydroelectric power), manufacturing (computers, office machinery, television, radio and communications equipment), chemicals, tourism and related industries, and whisky. Membership of the European Union has also benefited agriculture, urban regeneration and small-scale industry in the Highlands and Islands.

1975 – Major changes in local government introduced by the Local Government (Scotland) Act 1973 took place. The structure was reorganised again in 1994.

1976 – The Crofting Reform Act enabled crofters to buy their land.

1979 – A referendum on the Scotland and Wales Act took place, which was introduced by the Labour government of James Callaghan to give some degree of devolution to Scotland and Wales. The referendum failed to reach the requisite 40 per cent of affirmative votes, partly because of a high level of abstention, and the Act was abandoned.

1988 – 166 people killed were in a fire on the Piper Alpha oil rig on the 6 July. On 21 December a bomb placed by Libyan terrorists caused a PanAm jumbo jet to explode over Lockerbie, killing 259 passengers and 11 townspeople.

1990 – Glasgow held the title of European City of Culture.

1994 onwards – Contamination of British cattle herds by BSE (bovine spongiform encephalitis) depressed the Scottish beef industry. Confidence in British beef was not fully restored until early 2000.

1997 – A referendum on the reinstatement of a separate Scottish Parliament took place. This time the people voted Yes, by a considerable majority, for a Scottish Parliament with powers to raise or lower taxes.

1999 – The elections for Scottish Parliament took place on 6 May, carried out using a partial proportional representation system of voting for the first time in Britain. On 12 May the Parliament met for the first time since 1709. The official date of devolution was 1 July 1999.

A lost parliamentary manuscript found
In 1999, the year in which the Scottish Parliament was restored, a lost 17th-century manuscript, recording activities of the pre-Union Scottish government which has been missing since the council was abolished in 1708, was rediscovered. The book contains notes taken from the records of the Scottish Parliament, 1424–1621, and the Scottish privy council, 1561–1633. Written by an Edinburgh lawyer, Sir George Mackenzie of Rosehaugh, who was Lord Advocate 1677–86, the book is believed to have been lost some time after the national historian Cosmo Innes, put in a request to consult it to its owner, the Marquess of Bute, in 1842. The manuscript has been returned to the archives of Bute House, now the official residence of the First Minister.

Reign

c.834–860	**Kenneth MacAlpin,** king of Scots, and also of Picts from 843; Kenneth I of Alba
860–63	**Donald I**
863–77	**Constantine I**
877–78	**Aed**
878–89	**Giric**
889–900	**Donald II**
900–43	**Constantine II** (abdicated)
944–54	**Malcolm I**
954–63	**Indulf**
963–67	**Dubh (Duff)**
967–71	**Culain**
971–95	**Kenneth II**
995–97	**Constantine III**
997	**Kenneth III**
997–1005	**Grig**
1005–34	**Malcolm II** (c.954–1034)

THE HOUSE OF ATHOLL

1034–40	**Duncan I**
1040–57	**Macbeth** (c.1005–57)
1057–58	**Lulach** (c.1032–58)
1058–93	**Malcolm III (Canmore)** (c.1031–93)
1093–97	**Donald III Ban** (c.1033–1100) Deposed May 1094, restored November 1094
1094	**Duncan II** (c.1060–94)
1097–1107	**Edgar** (c.1074–1107)
1107–24	**Alexander I (The Fierce)** (c.1077–1124)
1124–53	**David I (The Saint)** (c.1085–1153)
1153–65	**Malcolm IV (The Maiden)** (c.1141–65)
1165–1214	**William I (The Lion)** (c.1142–1214)
1214–49	**Alexander II** (1198–1249)
1249–86	**Alexander III** (1241–86)
1286–90	**Margaret (The Maid of Norway)** (1283–90) First Interregnum 1290–92 Throne disputed by 13 competitors. Crown awarded to John Balliol by adjudication of Edward I of England

THE HOUSE OF BALLIOL

1292–96	**John (Balliol)** (c.1250–1313) Second Interregnum 1296–1306 Edward I of England declared John Balliol to have forfeited the throne for contumacy in 1296 and took the government of Scotland into his own hands

THE HOUSE OF BRUCE

1306–29	**Robert I (Bruce)** (1274–1329)
1329–718	**David II** (1324–71)
1332	**Edward Balliol** son of John Balliol, crowned King of Scots September, expelled December
1333–36	**Edward Balliol** restored as king of Scots

THE HOUSE OF STEWART

1371–90	**Robert II (Stewart)** (1316–90)
1390–1406	**Robert III** (c.1337–1406)
1406–37	**James I** (1394–1437)
1437–60	**James II** (1430–60)
1460–88	**James III** (1452–88)
1488–1513	**James IV** (1473–1513)
1513–42	**James V** (1512–42)
1542–67	**Mary** (1542–87)
1567–1625	**James VI (and I of England)** (1566–1625) Succeeded 1603 to the English throne, so joining the English and Scottish crowns

THE HOUSE OF STUART
Reign
1603–25	**James I (and VI of Scotland)** (1566–1625)
1625–49	**Charles I** (1600–49) Commonwealth declared 19 May 1649 1649–53 Government by a council of state
1653–58	**Oliver Cromwell,** Lord Protector
1658–59	**Richard Cromwell,** Lord Protector
1660–85	**Charles II** (1630–85)
1685–88	**James II (and VII)** (1633–1701) Interregnum 11 December 1688 to 12 February 1689
1689–1702	**William III** (1650–1702)
1689–94	**Mary II** (1662–94)
1702–14	**Anne** (1665–1714)

THE HOUSE OF HANOVER
1714–27	**George I (Elector of Hanover)** (1660–1727)
1727–60	**George II** **(1683–1760)**
1760–1820	**George III** (1738–1820) Regency 1811–20 Prince of Wales regent owing to the insanity of George III
1820–30	**George IV** (1762–1830)
1830–37	**William IV** **(1765–1837)**
1837–1901	**Victoria** (1819–1901)

THE HOUSE OF SAXE-COBURG AND GOTHA
1901–10	**Edward VII** (1841–1910)

THE HOUSE OF WINDSOR
1910–36	**George V** (1865–1936)
1936	**Edward VIII** (1894–1972)
1936–52	**George VI** (1895–1952)
1952–	**Elizabeth II** (1926–)

EDINBURGH

Edinburgh is the capital of and seat of government in Scotland. The city is built on a group of hills and contains in Princes Street one of the most beautiful thoroughfares in the world. In 1995 UNESCO designated Edinburgh Old and New Towns a World Heritage Site. There are three universities: Edinburgh (1583), Heriot-Watt (1966), and Napier (1992). The Edinburgh International Festival, held in August each year, has become one of the world's principal festivals of the performing arts.

The principal buildings include: the Castle, which now houses the Stone of Scone and also contains St Margaret's Chapel (12th century), the oldest building in Edinburgh, and the Scottish National War Memorial (1923); the Palace of Holyroodhouse (begun 1501 by James IV, rebuilding completed 1679); Parliament House (1632–40), the present seat of the judicature; St Giles' Cathedral (15th century, but the site of a church since ad 854); St Mary's (Scottish Episcopal) Cathedral (Sir George Gilbert Scott); the General Register House (Robert Adam, 1774); the National and the Signet Libraries (founded 1682 and 1722); the National Gallery (1859); the Royal Scottish Academy; the National Portrait Gallery (1889); the Royal Museum of Scotland (1861); the New Royal Observatory (1896); St Cecilia's Hall (1762), the first purpose-built concert hall in Scotland; the Usher Hall; and the Edinburgh International Conference Centre, opened in 1995. The Museum of Scotland opened 1998. The new Scottish Parliament building is due to open in 2003.

Other places of interest include Arthur's Seat (a volcanic hill 251 m/823 ft high overlooking the city), Calton Hill, the Royal Botanic Garden Edinburgh, the Physic Garden (1676), and the Firth of Forth road bridge (1964) and rail bridge (1890).

OTHER PRINCIPAL CITIES

ABERDEEN
Aberdeen, 130 miles north-east of Edinburgh, received its charter as a royal burgh in 1179. Scotland's third largest city, Aberdeen is the second largest Scottish fishing port and the main centre for offshore oil exploration and production. It is also an ancient university town (Aberdeen University, founded 1495; Robert Gordon University, 1992) and a distinguished research

centre. Other industries include engineering, food processing, textiles, paper manufacturing and chemicals.

Places of interest include: King's College (from 1500); St Machar's Cathedral (1370–1424); Brig o' Balgownie (1314–18), Duthie Park (1881) and Winter Gardens (1972); Hazlehead Park; the Kirk of St Nicholas (from 12th century); the Mercat Cross (1686); Marischal College (founded 1593, present building 1891), the second largest granite building in Europe, and Marischal Museum; Provost Skene's House (from 1545); the Art Gallery (1884); Robert Gordon's College (begun by William Adam, 1731) and Robert Gordon University; the Gordon Highlanders Museum; the Satrosphere Hands-On Discovery Centre, and the Aberdeen Maritime Museum, which incorporates Provost Ross's House (1593) and the former Trinity Church.

DUNDEE

Dundee, which received its charter as a royal burgh in 1327, is situated on the north bank of the Tay estuary. The city's port and dock installations are important to the offshore oil industry and the airport also provides servicing facilities. Principal industries include textiles, computers and other electronic industries, lasers, printing, tyre manufacture, food processing, carpets, engineering, clothing manufacture and tourism. There are two universities, Dundee (1967) and Abertay Dundee (1994).

The unique City Churches — three churches under one roof, together with the 15th-century St Mary's Tower — are the city's most prominent architectural feature. Dundee has two historic ships: the Dundee-built RRS Discovery (built 1901), which took Captain Scott to the Antarctic, lies alongside Discovery Quay, and the frigate Unicorn (built 1825), the only British-built wooden warship still afloat, is moored in Victoria Dock. Places of interest include Mills Public Observatory, the Tay road and rail bridges, the Dundee Museum and Art Gallery (1872), McManus Galleries, the new Contemporary Arts Centre, Barrack Street Museum, Claypotts Castle (a town house built 1569–88), Broughty Castle (1454), Caledon Shipyard (1874), and Verdant Works (Textile Heritage Centre).

GLASGOW

Glasgow, a royal burgh (1611), is Scotland's principal commercial and industrial centre. The city occupies the north and south banks of the river Clyde, formerly one of the chief commercial estuaries in the world. The main industries include engineering, electronics, finance, chemicals and printing. The city has also developed recently as a cultural, tourism and conference centre. It was designated European City of Culture in 1990 and City of Architecture and Design in 1999. There are two universities: Glasgow (1451) and Strathclyde (1964). The city was raised to an archdiocese in 1492.

Among the chief buildings are the 13th-century Gothic Cathedral, the only mainland Scottish cathedral to have survived the Reformation intact; the University (Sir George Gilbert Scott); the City Chambers; the Royal Exchange (1829); the Royal Concert Hall; St Mungo Museum of Religious Life and Art, Pollok House; the Hunterian Museum (1805); the People's Palace (1898); the New Glasgow School of Art (Charles Rennie Mackintosh, 1896); Glasgow Art Gallery and Museum, Kelvingrove (1893); the Gallery of Modern Art; the Burrell Collection museum and the Mitchell Library (1911). The city is home to the Scottish National Orchestra (founded 1950), Scottish Opera (founded 1962) and Scottish Ballet.

INVERNESS

Inverness, a royal burgh, is the largest town in the Highlands and their administrative centre. It is situated at the northern end of the Great Glen, where the River Ness flows into the Beauly Firth, now spanned by the Kessock Bridge across to the Black Isle. Originally built on the axis between the medieval castle and the Old High Church, the town now has a population of 50,000. Inverness Castle was occupied and then destroyed by the Jacobites in 1746 and in the 19th century replaced by a courthouse and prison. The battlefield at Culloden, where the Jacobites were finally defeated on 16 April 1746, lies to the east of the town.

Other important buildings include the late Victorian Town House (1882), the Highland Council Buildings (1876), the episcopal St Andrew's Cathedral (1869), and the modern Eden Court Theatre (1976). Industries include light engineering, biotechnology, electronics, service industries and tourism. Nearby is the oil platform construction yard at Ardersier.

PERTH

Perth is situated in north-central Scotland, on the right bank of the Tay. It became a burgh in 1106 and a royal burgh in 1210, and was one of the cities which fulfilled the function of Scottish capital until the mid-15th century, a number of Parliaments and Council meetings being held there in the medieval period. The Blackfriars monastery was a favoured residence of James I, who founded Charterhouse, the last monastery to be established in Scotland, in Perth in 1425.

Little now remains to indicate Perth's former position as one of the chief towns of medieval Scotland, the ancient monasteries and castles having fallen victim to floods and conflict. The main buildings are St John's Kirk (founded by David I c.1125; Perth was also known as St John's Town until the 16th century); Perth Bridge; the King James VI Hospital; the Old Academy; the Sheriff Court buildings; Huntingtower Castle (16th century); Scone Palace (built 1802–13 on the site of the medieval palace); and Balhousie Castle (present building, 1862).

The city lies between two large areas of open parkland and has a wealth of fine Georgian buildings. The principal industries are now tourism, agriculture, insurance, whisky and transport.

STIRLING

Stirling, a royal burgh since c.1124, lies on the River Forth in the centre of Scotland. It was one of the chief cities to serve as the Scottish capital between the 13th and the 16th centuries, and the castle was a royal residence from c.1226. Stirling was the site of the Parliament which took over the government from John Balliol in 1295, the birthplace of James IV and the site of the coronations of Mary and of James VI.

Stirling's strategic situation led to its being the site of several battles. English armies were defeated at the Battle of Stirling Bridge in 1297 by Scots led by William Wallace, and at Bannockburn in 1314 by forces led by Robert Bruce.

The local economy comprises mainly service industries with some manufacturing. The city houses the headquarters of Scottish Amicable, the Bank of Bermuda and Scottish Natural Heritage. Stirling is also an important tourist centre.

Places of interest include Stirling Castle; Argyll's Lodgings; the National Wallace Monument (1887); the Bannockburn Heritage Centre; Rob Roy Centre; Old Town Jail; Inchmahome Priory (1238); Cambuskenneth Abbey (1147); the Church of the Holy Rood (16th and 17th centuries); the Smith Art Gallery and Museum; and the Changing Room contemporary art gallery.

LANGUAGES

The main language of Scotland is English. Gaelic and Lowland Scots are recognised minority languages and the various Scots dialects are widely spoken. Language is one of the aspects in which Orkney and Shetland are distinct from the rest of Scotland. Having been under Norse and Nordic influence and actual dominion until the fifteenth century, much longer than any other part of the country, they manifest a strong Norse influence in their place-names and dialect. Norn, an old Norse language, was commonly spoken in many of the islands until the eighteenth century, long after English had become the official language. Norse colonisation also influenced language and place-names in the Hebrides, but to a lesser extent.

GAELIC

The Gaelic language was introduced into Scotland from Ireland in the fifth century or before, and was at its strongest from the ninth to the 12th centuries. Despite the steady advance of English from the Middle Ages onwards, Gaelic remained the main language in much of rural Scotland until the early 17th century. However, in 1616 James VI and I passed an Act proscribing Gaelic, and with the suppression of Highland culture following the Jacobite rising of 1745 and the depopulation of Gaelic-speaking areas by the Highland clearances in the 19th century, the language declined.

The movement for the revival of Gaelic grew in the late 19th and early 20th centuries. A clause was inserted in the Education Act 1918 allowing Gaelic to be taught in Gaelic-speaking areas, although it was not until 1958 that a local education authority (Inverness-shire) first adopted a bilingual policy, teaching Gaelic in primary schools in Gaelic-speaking areas.

At the time of the 1991 census, 1.4 per cent of the population of Scotland, mainly in the Highlands and the Western Isles, were able to speak Gaelic. This represents a fall of 0.2 per cent since the 1981 census. The percentage of Gaelic speakers was highest among people aged 65 and over (2.2 per cent), and lowest among people aged three to 15 (0.9 per cent). Geographically, by far the highest proportion of Gaelic speakers to total population occurred in the Western Isles area, where over 68 per cent of people speak Gaelic.

The following table shows the total number of persons aged three and over who speak Gaelic, by region and as a percentage of the total population, at the 1991 census.

Region	Total persons	% of population
Borders	103,881	0.5
Central	267,492	0.6
Dumfries and Galloway	147,805	0.4
Fife	341,199	0.5
Grampian	503,888	0.5
Highland	204,004	7.5
Lothian	726,010	0.6
Strathclyde	2,248,706	0.8
Tayside	383,848	0.7
Orkney Islands	19,612	0.5
Shetland Islands	22,522	0.5
Western Isles	29,600	68.4
Total	4,998,567	1.4

The following table shows Gaelic speakers as a percentage of the total population, by age group, at the 1981 and 1991 censuses.

Age	1981	1991
3—15	1.0	0.9
16—44	1.4	1.1
45—64	2.0	1.6
65 +	2.7	2.2
Total	1.6	1.4

Source: General Register Office (Scotland), 1991 Census Monitor for Scotland (Crown copyright)

PROMOTION OF GAELIC

In recent years, more official measures have been taken to promote the revival of Gaelic, and the Scottish Executive includes a junior minister for Gaelic.

Gaelic is taught as an academic subject at universities including Aberdeen, Edinburgh and Glasgow, at numerous colleges of education, and in some schools, principally in Gaelic-speaking areas. Fifty-nine primary schools in Scotland offer Gaelic-medium education, and the Scottish Executive is committed to increasing the supply of Gaelic-medium teachers and locating training for them in the Highlands. Sàbhal Mor Ostaig is the Gaelic-medium further and higher education college.

BBC programmes in Gaelic are broadcast throughout the country. BBC Scotland delivered 116 hours of Gaelic television programmes in 1997–8 and an average of 45 hours of Gaelic radio programmes per week. The Scottish and Grampian independent stations also broadcast regular Gaelic television programmes. The Gaelic-language radio station BBC Radio nan Gaidheal is now available to 90 per cent of the audience in Scotland. There are local community radio stations in Stornoway, Ullapool, Portree and Fort William.

In 1992, the Gaelic Television Committee/ Comataidh Telebhisein Gàidhlig (now the Gaelic Broadcasting Committee/Comataidh Craolaidh Gàidhlig) was established to fund up to 200 additional hours of Gaelic-medium television. The committee's remit was extended to radio programmes by the Broadcasting Act 1996. The Scottish Executive provides £8.5 million a year to the Committee, which is based in Stornaway.

A number of institutions for the promotion of the Gaelic language and culture exist. Comunn na Gàidhlig is the national development agency for Scottish Gaelic. It promotes the use of the Gaelic language, the continuance of Gaelic culture in education and the arts, and the integration of Gaelic into social and economic development, including the promotion of Gaelic businesses. An Comunn Gaidhealach promotes Gaelic culture through everyday use of the language and encourages the traditions of music, literature and folklore.

Fèisean nan Gàidheal, the National Association of Gaelic Arts Youth Tuition Festivals, is the independent umbrella association of the Fèis movement, which has existed since 1981, when a group on the island of Barra organised a tuition festival to begin to reverse the decline of traditional Gaelic music and dance. There are now 31 Fèisean, not only in the areas where Gaelic is still commonly spoken, but also in Edinburgh, Glasgow and Aberdeen.

LOWLAND SCOTTISH

Several dialects, known collectively as Lowland Scots, Lallans or Doric, are widely spoken in the south, east and extreme north of the country. 'Scots' is the term commonly used in Scotland itself and in the European Charter for Minority and Regional Languages, which recognises Scots as a minority language. In the last 20 years the term 'Doric' has come to be used locally in the north-east to refer exclusively to the group of dialects in that area.

Although the UK government ratified the European Charter in 1998, no official recognition or encouragement has yet been given to Scots. The General Register Office (Scotland) has estimated that 1.5 million, or 30 per cent of the population, are Scots speakers. Scots is vividly alive as a literary language too, appearing particularly in new drama.

PROMOTION OF SCOTS

Courses in Scots language and literature are taught at several universities, further and higher education colleges and community colleges. The Scots Language Resource Centre is the lead agency for the promotion of Scots and supports other bodies engaged in the promotion and study of Scots language and culture, including the Scottish National Dictionary Association, the Scots Language Society, the Scots Leid Associe, the Scots Speakers' Curn and Scots Tung.

The Scottish Executive's National Cultural Strategy, launched in August 2000, contains a specific section on 'promoting Scotland's languages as cultural expressions and as means of accessing Scotland's culture' and proposes a variety of actions to promote and preserve Scotland's linguistic diversity.

CLANS AND CLAN CHIEFS

The word 'clan', derived from the Gaelic 'clann', meaning children, originally referred to an extended family or tribe occupying a certain area of land. This was the early form of Gaelic society. After the Jacobean rebellion in 1745-6, the clan system was suppressed by the Government in order to forestall further rebellion, and gradually declined as an organising force in Scottish society. However, the clans continue to be one of the strongest social and emotional links between Scots in Scotland and abroad and a potent symbol of what it means to be Scottish. Their links with the land are not entirely severed either: many clan chiefs still live on the land, and in the buildings, which have been the clan seat for centuries.

The title of chief is usually hereditary, passing to the nearest heir. However, a chief may nominate a successor, subject to the confirmation of the Lord Lyon King of Arms. If a title is dormant, the Lord Lyon can award it to a person bearing the clan name, although this decision may be revoked if a proven heir is found within 20 years.

The style 'of that Ilk' began to be used by some chiefs in the late 16th-century. More recently, chiefs who do not have an estate have been recognised as 'of that Ilk.' Certain chiefs use the prefix 'The'. The duplication of surnames by chiefs (e.g. Macdonald of Macdonald) is a feature that became common after the Act of Union 1707.

Only chiefs of whole names or clans are included here, except certain special instances (marked *) who, though not chiefs of a whole name, were or are for some reason (e.g. the Macdonald forfeiture) independent. Under decision (Campbell-Gray, 1950) that a bearer of a 'double- or triple-barrelled' surname cannot be held chief of a part of such, several others cannot be included in the list at present.

STANDING COUNCIL OF SCOTTISH CHIEFS

52 Leith Walk, Edinburgh, EH6 5HW
Tel: 0131-554 6321

STYLES

There are a number of different styles for chiefs of clans and names; the appropriate use depends on the title and designation of the person, and for exact guidance a specialist source should be consulted. The following examples show the more common styles:

F— represents forename
S— represents surname
D— represents designation

Examples:
The S—
The S— of D—
F— S— of D—
Sir F— S— of D—, Bt.
F— S— of that Ilk
Madam/Mrs/Miss S— of D— (according to preference)
Dame F— S— of D—, DBE

CLAN CHIEFS

THE QUEEN'S HOUSEHOLD
Court of the Lord Lyon
HM New Register House, Edinburgh, EH1 3YT
(Tel: 0131-556 7255; Fax: 0131-557 2148;
Web: www.royal.gov.uk)

AGNEW
Sir Crispin Agnew of Lochnaw, Bt, QC
6 Palmerston Road, Edinburgh, EH9 1TN
(Tel: 0131-668 3792; Fax: 0131-668 4357;
E-mail: aofl@sol.co.uk)

ANSTRUTHER
Sir Ralph Anstruther of that Ilk, Bt, GCVO, MC
Balcaskie Estate Office, Balcaskie, Pittenweem, Fife, KY10 2RD

ARBUTHNOTT
The Viscount of Arbuthnott, KT, CBE, DSC
Arbuthnott House, Laurencekirk,
Kincardineshire, AB30 1PA

BARCLAY
Peter C. Barclay of Towie Barclay and of that Ilk
69 Oakwood Court, Abbotsbury Road, London,
W14 8JF (Tel: 020-7603 0552)

BORTHWICK
The Lord Borthwick
Crookston, Heriot, Midlothian, EH38 5YS
(Tel: 01875-835 236; Fax: 01875-835 236)

BOYD
The Lord Kilmarnock
194 Regent's Park Road, London, NW1 8XP

BOYLE
The Earl of Glasgow
Kelburn, Fairlie, Ayrshire, KA29 0BE
(Tel: 01475-568 685; Fax: 01475-568 121;
Web: www.kelburncastle.com)

BRODIE
Ninian Brodie of Brodie
Brodie Castle, Forres, Morayshire, IV36 2TE
(Fax: 01309-641 600)

BRUCE
The Earl of Elgin and Kincardine, KT,
Broomhall, Dunfermline, Fife, KY11 3DU
(Fax: 01383-872 904;
E-mail: lord.elgin@virgin.net)

BURNETT
J. C. A. Burnett of Leys
St Nicholas House, 68 Station Road, Banchory,
Kincardineshire (Tel: 01330-823 749;
E-mail: burnette@leysestate.demon.co.uk)

CAMERON
Sir Donald Cameron of Lochiel, KT, CVO
Achnacarry, Spean Bridge, Inverness-shire
(Tel: 01397-712 768)

CAMPBELL
The Duke of Argyll
Inverary, Argyll, PA32 8XF

CARNEGIE
His Grace The Duke of Fife
Elsick House, Stonehaven, Kincardineshire,
AB39 3NT (Fax: 0167-4810 208)

CATHCART
Maj-Gen. The Earl Cathcart
14 Smith Terrace, London, SW8 4DL
(Tel: 01328-829 258)

CHARTERIS
The Earl of Wemyss and March, KT
Gosford House, Longniddry, East Lothian,
EH32 0PX

CHISHOLM
Hamish Chisholm of Chisholm (The Chisholm)
Elmpine, Beck Row, Bury St Edmunds, Suffolk

CLAN BUCHAN
David S. Buchan of Auchmacoy
Auchmacoy House, Ellon, Aberdeenshire
(Tel: 01358-720 291)

CLAN CARMICHAEL
Richard J. Carmichael of Carmichael
Carmichael, Biggar, South Lanarkshire, ML12
6PG (Tel: 01899-308 336; Fax: 01899-308 481;
E-mail: chiefcarm@aol.com;
Web: www.carmichael-scottland.com)

CLAN CHATTAN
M. K. Mackintosh of Clan Chattan
Maxwell Park, Gwelo, Zimbabwe

CLAN MacTHOMAS SOCIETY
Andrew P. C. MacThomas of Finegand
29 Bennan Gardens, Broughty Ferry, Dundee,
DD5 3EJ

CLAN MAITLAND SOCIETY
The Rt. Hon Earl of Lauderdale
12 St Vincent Street, Edinburgh, EH3 6SH
(E-mail: maitland@lauderdale.u-net.com;
Web: www.lauderdale.u-net.com)

COCHRANE
The Earl of Dundonald
Lochnell Castle, Ledaig, Argyllshire
(Web: www.clancocrane.org)

COLQUHOUN
Sir Ivar Colquhoun of Luss, Bt
Camstraddan, Luss, Dunbartonshire, G83 8NX

CRANSTOUN
David A. S. Cranstoun of that Ilk and Corehouse,
TD, MA, MSc, PhD, DL
Corehouse, Lanark, ML11 5TQ
(Tel: 0131-667 1514)

CUMMING
Sir William Cumming of Altyre, Bt
Altyre, Forres, Moray

DARROCH OF GOUROCK
Capt. Duncan Darroch of Gourock
The Red House, Branksome Park Road,
Camberley, Surrey (Tel: 01276-23053)

DAVIDSON
Alister G. Davidson of Davidson
21 Winscombe Street, Takapuna, Auckland,
New Zealand

DEWAR
Kenneth Dewar of that Ilk and Vogrie
The Dower House, Grayshott, nr Hindhead,
Surrey

DRUMMOND
The Rt Hon Earl of Perth, PC
62 Hutington Place, Edinburgh, EH7 4AT

DUNBAR
Sir James Dunbar of Mochrum, Bt
211 Gardenville Drive, Yorktown, Virginia,
23693

DUNDAS
David D. Dundas of Dundas
8 Derna Road, Kenwyn, 7700

DURIE
Andrew Durie of Durie
Finnich Malise, Croftamie, Stirlingshire, G63
0HA (Tel: 01360-660 257; Fax: 01360-660 101;
E-mail: finnichmalise@talk21.com)

ELIOTT CLAN SOCIETY
Mrs Margaret Eliott of Redheugh
Redheugh, Newcastleton, Roxburghshire
(Web: www.elliotclan.com)

ERSKINE
The Earl of Mar and Kellie, Jamie Erskime
Hilton Farm, Alloa, FK10 3PS (Tel: 01259-212
438; Fax: 01259-212 020)

FARQUHARSON
Capt. A. Farquharson of Invercauld, MC,
Invercauld, Braemar, Aberdeenshire, AB35 5TT

FERGUSSON
Sir Charles Fergusson of Kilkerran, Bt
Kilkerran, Maybole, Ayrshire

FORBES
The Lord Forbes, KBE
Balforbes, Alford, Aberdeenshire, AB33 8DR

FORSYTH
Alistair Forsyth of that Ilk
Ethie Castle, by Arbroath, Angus, DD11 5SP

FRASER
The Lady Saltoun
Inverey House, Aberdeenshire, AB35 5YB

FRASER (OF LOVAT)
The Lord Lovat
Beaufort Lodge, Beauly, Inverness-shire, IV4
7AZ

GAYRE
R. Gayre of Gayre and Nigg
Minard Castle, Minard, Inverary, Argyll, PA32
8YB

GORDON
The Marquess of Huntly
Aboyne Castle, Aberdeenshire, AB34 5JP

GRAHAM
The Duke of Montrose
Buchanan Auld House, Drymen, Stirlingshire
(Tel: 01360-660 307)

GRANT
The Lord Strathspey
The House of Lords, London, SW1A 0PW

GRIERSON
Sir Michael Grierson of Lag, Bt
40C Palace Road, London, SW2 3NJ

HAIG
The Earl Haig, OBE
Bemersyde, Melrose, Roxburghshire, TD6 9DP
(Tel: 01835-822 762)

HALDANE
Martin Haldane of Gleneagles
Gleneagles, Auchterarder, Perthshire
(Tel: 01764-682 388;
E-mail: haldane@gleneagles.org;
Web: www.gleneagles.org)

HANNAY
Ramsey Hannay of Kirkdale and of that Ilk
Cardoness House, Gatehouse-of-Fleet,
Kirkcudbrightshire

HAY
The Earl of Erroll
99 Harford Street, London, SW6 6PN
(Tel: 01767-650 251; Fax: 01767-651 553;
E-mail: secretary@hay.org;
Web: www.clanhay.org)

HENDERSON
Dr. John Henderson of Fordell
7 Owen Street, Toowoomba 4350, Queensland
(Tel: +61 7463 26352; Fax: +61 7463 26352;
E-mail: johnhenderson@enten.net.au)

HUNTER
Madam Pauline Hunter of Hunterston
and that Ilk
Plovers Ridge, Lon Cecrist, Treaddur Bay,
Holyhead, Gwynedd (Tel: 01407-860 500; Fax:
01407-860 792; Web: www.clanhunter.com)

IRVINE OF DRUM
David C. Irvine of Drum
Holy Leaf Cottage, Inchmarlo, Banchory,
Aberdeenshire, AB31 4BR (Tel: 01330-823 702;
E-mail: drum26@btinternet.com)

JARDINE
Sir Alexander Jardine of Applegirth, Bt
Ash House, Thwaites, Millom, Cumbria, LA18
5HY

JOHNSTONE
The Earl of Annandale and Hartfell
Annandale Estates Office, St Anns, Lockerbie,
Dumfriesshire, DG11 1HQ (Tel: 01576-470 317;
Fax: 01576-470 455)

KEITH
The Earl of Kintore
The Stables, Keith Hall, Inverurie,
Aberdeenshire, AB51 0LD

KENNEDY
The Marquess of Ailsa
Cassillis House, Maybole, Ayrshire
(Tel: 01655-882 103; Fax: 01655-882 101)

KERR
The Marquess of Lothian, KCVO
Ferniehurst Castle, Jedburgh, Roxburghshire,
TN8 6NX (Tel: 01835-864 023; Fax: 01835-
864 156)

KINCAID
Madam Arabella Kincaid of Kincaid
Stoneyeld, Downton, Nr Ludlow, Shropshire,
SY8 2HX

LAMONT
Peter N. Lamont of that Ilk
St Patrick's College, Manley, NSW, 2095

LEASK
Madam Leask of Leask
1 Vincent Road, Sheringham, Norfolk

LENNOX
Edward J. H. Lennox of that Ilk
Pools Farm, Downton on the Rock, Ludlow,
Shropshire

LESLIE
The Earl of Rothes
Tanglewood, West Tytherley, Salisbury, Wilts,
SP5 1LX
(Web: www.clanlesliesociety.org)

LINDSAY
The Earl of Crawford and Balcarres, KT, PC
Balcarres, Colinsburgh, Fife

LOCKHART
Angus H. Lockhart of the Lee
Newholm, Dunsyre, Lanark, ML11 8NQ
(Tel: 01555-840 273; Fax: 01555-840 044)

LUMSDEN
Gillem Lumsden of that Ilk and Blanerne
Stapeley House, Hoe Benham, Newbury, Berks,
RG20 8PX (Tel: 01488-657 441; Fax: 01488-
657 908;
E-mail: gillem@btinternet.com)

MACALESTER
William St J. S. McAlester of Loup and Kennox
2 Avon Road East, Christchurch, Dorset)

MACDONALD
The Lord Macdonald (The Macdonald of
Macdonald)
Kinloch Lodge, Sleat, Isle of Skye

MACDONALD OF SLEAT (CLAN VISDEIN)
Sir Ian Macdonald of Sleat, Bt
Thorpe Hall, Rudston, Driffield, East Yorkshire,
YO25 4JE (Tel: 01262-420 239; Fax: 01262-420
588; E-mail: ian@macdonaldofsleat.co.uk)

MACDONELL OF GLENGARRY
Ranald MacDonell of Glengarry
74 Haverhill Road, London, SW12 0HB
(Tel: 020-8675 3545)

MACGREGOR
Brig. Sir Gregor MacGregor of MacGregor, Bt
Bannatyne, Newtyle, Blairgowrie, Perthshire,
PH12 8TR

MACINTYRE
James W. MacIntyre of Glencoe
Apartment 3H, 15301 Pine Orchard Drive, Silver
Spring, Maryland

MACKAY
The Lord Reay
House of Lords, London, SW1

MACKENZIE
The Earl of Cromartie
Castle Leod, Strathpeffer, Ross-shire, IV14 9AA

MACKINNON
Madam Anne Mackinnon of Mackinnon
16 Purleigh Road, Bridgwater, Somerset

MACKINTOSH
The Mackintosh, John L Mackintosh
Moy Hall, Inverness, IV13 7YQ (Tel: 01808-511
211; Web: www.clanchattan.org.uk)

MACLAREN
Donald MacLaren of MacLaren and Achleskine
Achleskine, Kirkton, Balquhidder, Lochearnhead

MACLEAN
The Hon. Sir Lachlan Maclean of Duart, Bt
Arngask House, glenfarg, Perthshire, PH2 9QA

MACLEOD
John MacLeod of MacLeod
MacLeod Estate, Dunvegan Castle, Isle of Skye
(Tel: 01470-521 206; Fax: 01470-521 205;
E-mail: info@dunvegancastle.com;
Web: www.dunvegancastle.com)

MACMILLAN
George MacMillan of MacMillan
Finlaystone, Langbank, Renfrewshire

MACNAB
J. C. Macnab of Macnab (The Macnab)
Leuchars Castle Farmhouse, Leuchars, Fife,
KY16 0EY (Tel: 01334-838 777; Fax: 01334-
838 283)

MACNAGHTEN
Sir Patrick Macnaghten of Macnaghten and
Dundarave, Bt
Dundarave, Bushmills, Co. Antrim

MACNEACAIL
Iain Macneacail of Macneacail of Scorrybreac
12 Fox Street, Ballina, NSW

MACNEIL OF BARRA
Ian R. Macneil of Barra (The Macneil of Barra)
95/6 Grange Loan, Edinburgh

MACPHERSON
The Hon. Sir William Macpherson of Cluny, TD
Newton Castle, Blairgowrie, Perthshire, PH10
6SV

MAKGILL
The Viscount of Oxfuird
Kemback, Stoke, Andover, Hants, SP11 0NP
(Tel: 01264-738 302; Fax: 01264-738 088)

MALCOLM (MACCALLUM)
Robin N. L. Malcolm of Poltalloch
Duntrune Castle, Lochgilphead, Argyll
(Tel: 01546-510 283;
Web: www.duntrune.com)

MATHESON
Maj. Sir Fergus Matheson of Matheson, Bt
Old Rectory, Hedenham, Bungay, Suffolk,
NR35 2LD

McBAIN
J. H. McBain of McBain
7025 North Finger Rock Place, Tucson, Arizona

MENZIES
David R. Menzies of Menzies
Wester Auchnagallin Farmhouse, Braes of Castle
Grant, Grantown on Spey, PH26 3PL

MOFFAT
Madam Moffat of that Ilk
St Jasual, Bullocks Farm Lane, Wheeler End
Common, High Wycombe, HP14 3NH (Tel:
01494-881 089)

MONCREIFFE
Peregine Moncreiffe of that Ilk
Easter Monceiffe, Bride of Earn, Perthshire

MONTGOMERIE
The Earl of Eglinton and Winton
Balhomie, Cargill, Perth, PH2 6DS

MORRISON
Dr Iain M. Morrison of Ruchdi
Magnolia Cottage, The Street, Walberton, Sussex

MUNRO
Hector W. Munro of Foulis
Foulis Castle, Evanton, Ross-shire, IV16 9UX

MURRAY
The Duke of Atholl
Blair Castle, Blair Atholl, Perthshire

NESBITT (or NISBET)
Mark Andrew Nesbitt of that Ilk
1 Pier Head, Wapping High Street, London,
E12 1PN

NICOLSON
The Lord Carnock
90 Whitehall Court, London, SW1A 2EL

OGILVY
The Earl of Airlie, KT, GCVO, PC
Cortachy Castle, Kirriemuir, Angus

RAMSAY
The Earl of Dalhousie
Brechin Castle, Brechin, Angus, DD7 6SH

RATTRAY
James S. Rattray of Rattray
Craighall, Rattray, Perthshire

ROBERTSON
Alexander G. H. Robertson of Struan
(Struan-Robertson)
The Breach Farm, Goudhurst Road, Cranbrook,
Kent

ROLLO
The Lord Rollo
Pitcairns, Dunning, Perthshire

ROSE
Miss Elizabeth Rose of Kilravock
Kilravock Castle. Croy, Inverness

ROSS
David C. Ross of that Ilk
Shandwick, Perth Road, Stanley, Perthshire

RUTHVEN
The Earl of Gowrie, PC
34 King Street, London, WC2

SCOTT
The Duke of Buccleuch and Queensberry, KT,
VRD
Bowhill, Selkirk

SCRYMGEOUR
The Earl of Dundee
Birkhill, Cupar, Fife

SEMPILL
The Lord Sempill
3 Vanburgh Place, Edinburgh, EH6 8AE

SHAW
John Shaw of Tordarroch
Newhall, Balblair, by Conon Bridge, Ross-shire

SINCLAIR
The Earl of Caithness
137 Claxton Grove, London, W6 8HB

SKENE
Danus Skene of Skene
Nether Pitlour, Straathmiglo, Fife

STIRLING
Fraser J. Stirling of Cader
44A Oakley Street, London, SW3 5HA

STRANGE
Maj. Timothy Strange of Balcaskie
Little Holme, Porton Road, Amesbury, Wilts

SUTHERLAND
The Countess of Sutherland
House of Tongue, Brora, Sutherland

SWINTON
John Swinton of that Ilk
123 Superior Avenue SW, Calgary, Alberta

THE MACDOWALLS OF GALLOWAY
Prof. Fergus D. H. Macdowall of Garthland
9170 Ardmore Drive, North Saanich, B.C.
(Tel: 250-656-0500; Fax: 250-656-0500)

THE MARJORIBANKS FAMILY
Andrew Marjoribanks of that Ilk
10 Newark Street, Greenock
(E-mail: john@marjoribanks.com)

TROTTER
Alexander Trotter of Mortonhall
Charterhall, Duns, Berwickshire

URQUHART
Kenneth T. Urquhart of Urquhart
507 Jefferson Park Avenue, Jefferson, New
Orleans, Louisiana, 70121

WALLACE
Ian F. Wallace of that Ilk
5 Lennox Street, Edinburgh, EH4 1QB

WEDDERBURN OF THAT ILK
The Master of Dundee
Birkhill, Cupar, Fife

WEMYSS
David Wemyss of that Ilk
Invermay, Forteviot, Perthshire

THE NATIONAL FLAGS

THE SCOTTISH FLAG

The flag of Scotland is known as the Saltire. It is a white diagonal cross on a blue field (saltire argent in a field azure) and symbolises St Andrew, the patron saint of Scotland.

A traditional explanation for the adoption of the St Andrew's cross as the symbol of Scotland is that the Saltire appeared in the sky to the Pictish king Hungus as an omen of victory over the Anglo-Saxons at the battle of Aethelstaneford. The Saltire was adopted as a national symbol at about the same time as St Andrew was adopted as Scotland's patron saint, and by the mid 14th century it was being used on coins. From about that time also, it has been used as a symbol of the struggle for independence.

In Scotland, HM The Queen and her representatives (The First Minister, The Lord Lyon, The Lord High Commissioner to the General Assembly and the Lord Lieutenants) use a flag called the Royal Lion Rampant (Scotland). The flag features a red lion rampant on a yellow field. George V granted permission for Scots to use the flag as a sign of loyalty.

THE NATIONAL FLAG

The national flag of the United Kingdom is the Union Flag, generally known as the Union Jack.

The Union Flag is a combination of the cross of St George, patron saint of England, the cross of St Andrew, patron saint of Scotland, and a cross similar to that of St Patrick, patron saint of Ireland.

The Union Flag was first introduced in 1606 after the union of the kingdoms of England and Scotland under one sovereign. The cross of St Patrick was added in 1801 after the union of Great Britain and Ireland.

DAYS FOR FLYING FLAGS

It is the practice to fly the Union Flag daily on some customs houses. In all other cases, flags are flown on government buildings by command of The Queen.

Days for hoisting the Union Flag are notified to the Department for Culture, Media and Sport by The Queen's command and communicated by the department to other government departments. On the days appointed, the Union Flag is flown on government buildings in the UK from 8 a.m. to sunset.

Both the Union Flag and the Saltire are flown in Scotland. The Saltire is flown from government buildings alongside, but not superior to, the Union Flag on the flag-flying days, which are the same days as those announced by the Department for Culture, Media and Sport. On Europe Day only, the EU flag flies alongside the Union Flag and the Saltire.

The Queen's Accession	6 February
Birthday of The Duke of York	19 February
Birthday of The Earl of Wessex	10 March
Commonwealth Day (2001)	12 March
Birthday of The Queen	21 April
*Europe Day	9 May
Coronation Day	2 June
The Queen's Official Birthday (2001)	16 June
Birthday of The Duke of Edinburgh	10 June
Birthday of Queen Elizabeth the Queen Mother	4 August
Birthday of The Princess Royal	15 August
Birthday of The Princess Margaret	21 August
Remembrance Sunday (2001)	11 November
Birthday of The Prince Charles, Duke of Rothesay	14 November
The Queen's Wedding Day	20 November
St Andrew's Day	30 November

* The Union Flag should fly alongside the EU flag. On government buildings that have only one flagpole, the Union Flag should take precedence

FLAGS AT HALF-MAST

Flags are flown at half-mast (e.g. two-thirds up between the top and bottom of the flagstaff) on the following occasions:

(a) From the announcement of the death up to the funeral of the Sovereign, except on Proclamation Day, when flags are hoisted right up from 11a.m. to sunset

(b) The funerals of members of the royal family, subject to special commands from The Queen in each case

(c) The funerals of foreign rulers, subject to special commands from The Queen in each case

(d) The funerals of prime ministers and ex-prime ministers of the UK, subject to special commands from The Queen in each case

(e) Other occasions by special command of The Queen

On occasions when days for flying flags coincide with days for flying flags at half-mast, the following rules are observed. Flags are flown:

(a) although a member of the royal family, or a near relative of the royal family, may be lying dead, unless special commands are received from The Queen to the contrary
(b) although it may be the day of the funeral of a foreign ruler

If the body of a very distinguished subject is lying at a government office, the flag may fly at half-mast on that office until the body has left (provided it is a day on which the flag would fly) and then the flag is to be hoisted right up. On all other government buildings the flag will fly as usual.

THE ROYAL STANDARD
The Royal Standard is hoisted only when the Queen is actually present in the building, and never when Her Majesty is passing in procession.

NATIONAL ANTHEM
The official national anthem throughout the UK is God Save The Queen.

At national events and international competitions (primarily sporting), Scottish songs are sometimes used, including Scotland the Brave at the Commonwealth Games and Flower of Scotland for international rugby matches.

In 1998 the Herald newspaper ran a competition for a new Scottish anthem and the winner, announced in January 1999, was William Jackson's Land of Light.

NATIONAL DAY
The national day is 30 November, the festival of St Andrew, the patron saint of Scotland.

St Andrew, one of the apostles and brother of Simon Peter, was born at Bethsaida on the Sea of Galilee and lived at Capernaum. He preached the gospel in Asia Minor and in Scythia along the shores of the Black Sea and became the patron saint of Russia. It is believed that he suffered crucifixion at Patras in Achaea, on a crux decussata (now known as St Andrew's Cross) and that his relics were removed from Patras to Constantinople and thence to Scotland, probably in the eighth century, since which time he has been the patron saint of Scotland. The church and settlement founded at the place where the relics were brought ashore became the town of St Andrews.

THE HEAD OF STATE

ELIZABETH II, by the Grace of God, of the United Kingdom of Great Britain and Northern Ireland and of her other Realms and Territories Queen, Head of the Commonwealth, Defender of the Faith

Her Majesty Elizabeth Alexandra Mary of Windsor, elder daughter of King George VI and of HM Queen Elizabeth the Queen Mother
Born 21 April 1926, at 17 Bruton Street, London W1
Ascended the throne 6 February 1952
Crowned 2 June 1953, at Westminster Abbey
Married 20 November 1947, in Westminster Abbey, HRH The Prince Philip, Duke of Edinburgh, KG, KT, OM, GBE, AC, QSO, PC (born 10 June 1921, son of Prince and Princess Andrew of Greece and Denmark, naturalised a British subject 1947, created Duke of Edinburgh, Earl of Merioneth and Baron Greenwich 1947)
Official residences: Buckingham Palace, London SW1A 1AA; Palace of Holyroodhouse, Edinburgh; Windsor Castle, Berks
Private residences: Balmoral Castle, Aberdeenshire; Sandringham, Norfolk

THE HEIR TO THE THRONE

HRH THE PRINCE CHARLES, DUKE OF ROTHESAY (Prince Charles Philip Arthur George), KG, KT, GCB and Great Master of the Order of the Bath, AK, QSO, PC, ADC(P)
Born 14 November 1948, created Prince of Wales and Earl of Chester 1958, succeeded as Duke of Cornwall, Duke of Rothesay, Earl of Carrick and Baron Renfrew, Lord of the Isles and Prince and Great Steward of Scotland 1952
Married 29 July 1981 Lady Diana Frances Spencer (Diana, Princess of Wales (1961–97), youngest daughter of the 8th Earl Spencer and the Hon. Mrs Shand Kydd), marriage dissolved 1996
Issue:
HRH Prince William of Wales (Prince William Arthur Philip Louis), born 21 June 1982
HRH Prince Henry of Wales (Prince Henry Charles Albert David), born 15 September 1984
Residences:
St James's Palace, London SW1A 1BS; Highgrove, Doughton, Tetbury, Glos GL8 8TN
Office:
St James's Palace, London SW1A 1BS. Tel: 020-7930 4832

ORDER OF SUCCESSION TO THE THRONE

1 HRH The Prince Charles, Duke of Rothesay
2 HRH Prince William of Wales
3 HRH Prince Henry of Wales
4 HRH The Duke of York
5 HRH Princess Beatrice of York
6 HRH Princess Eugenie of York
7 HRH The Earl of Wessex
8 HRH The Princess Royal
9 Peter Phillips
10 Zara Phillips
11 HRH The Princess Margaret, Countess of Snowdon
12 Viscount Linley
13 Hon. Charles Linley
14 Lady Sarah Chatto
15 Samuel Chatto
16 Arthur Chatto
17 HRH The Duke of Gloucester
18 Earl of Ulster
19 Lady Davina Windsor
20 Lady Rose Windsor
21 HRH The Duke of Kent
22 Baron Downpatrick
23 Lady Marina Charlotte Windsor
24 Lady Amelia Windsor
25 Lord Nicholas Windsor
26 Lady Helen Taylor
27 Columbus Taylor
28 Cassius Taylor
29 Lord Frederick Windsor
30 Lady Gabriella Windsor
31 HRH Princess Alexandra, the Hon. Lady Ogilvy
32 James Ogilvy
33 Alexander Ogilvy
34 Flora Ogilvy
35 Marina, Mrs Paul Mowatt
36 Christian Mowatt
37 Zenouska Mowatt
38 The Earl of Harewood

The Earl of St Andrews and HRH Prince Michael of Kent lost the right of succession to the throne through marriage to a Roman Catholic. Their children remain in succession provided that they are in communion with the Church of England.

THE QUEEN'S HOUSEHOLD

Office: Buckingham Palace, London SW1A 1AA
(Tel: 020-7930 4832; Web: www.royal.gov.uk)

The Lord Chamberlain is the most senior member of The Queen's Household and under him come the heads of the six departments: the Private Secretary, the Keeper of the Privy Purse, the Comptroller of the Lord Chamberlain's Office, the Master of the Household, the Crown Equerry, and the Director of the Royal Collection. Positions in these departments are full-time salaried posts.

There are also a number of honorary or now largely ceremonial appointments which carry no remuneration or a small honorarium.

THE QUEEN'S HOUSEHOLD IN SCOTLAND

*Hereditary Lord High Constable of Scotland, The Earl of Erroll
*Hereditary Master of the Household in Scotland, The Duke of Argyll
Lord Lyon King of Arms, Sir Malcolm Innes of Edingight, KCVO, WS
*Hereditary Banner-Bearer for Scotland, The Earl of Dundee
*Hereditary Bearer of the National Flag of Scotland, The Earl of Lauderdale
*Hereditary Keeper of the Palace of Holyroodhouse, The Duke of Hamilton and Brandon
*Governor of Edinburgh Castle, Maj.-Gen. R. D. S. Gordon, CBE
*Historiographer, Prof. T. C. Smout, CBE, FBA, FRSE, FSA Scot.
*Botanist, Prof. D. Henderson, CBE, FRSE
*Painter and Limner, vacant
*Sculptor in Ordinary, Prof. Sir Eduardo Paolozzi, CBE, RA
*Astronomer, Prof. J. Brown, Ph.D., FRSE
*Heralds and Pursuivants

ECCLESIASTICAL HOUSEHOLD

*Dean of the Chapel Royal, Very Revd J. Harkness, CB, OBE
*Dean of the Order of the Thistle, Very Revd G. I. Macmillan, CVO
*Chaplains in Ordinary: 10
Domestic Chaplain, Balmoral, Revd R. P. Sloan

MEDICAL HOUSEHOLD

*Physicians in Scotland, P. Brunt, OBE, MD, FRCP; A. Toft, CBE, FRCPE
*Surgeons in Scotland, J. Engeset, FRCS; I. Macintyre
Apothecary to the Household at Balmoral, D. J. A. Glass
Apothecary to the Household at the Palace of Holyroodhouse, Dr J. Cormack, MD, FRCPE, FRCGP

*ROYAL COMPANY OF ARCHERS (QUEEN'S BODYGUARD FOR SCOTLAND)

Captain-General and Gold Stick for Scotland, Maj. Sir Hew Hamilton-Dalrymple, Bt., KCVO
President of the Council and Silver Stick for Scotland, The Duke of Buccleuch and Queensberry, KT, VRD
Adjutant, Maj. the Hon. Sir Lachlan Maclean, Bt., CVO
Secretary, Capt. J. D. B. Younger
Treasurer, J. M. Haldane of Gleneagles
Members on the active list: c.400

OTHER HONORARY APPOINTMENTS

Poet Laureate (1999–2009), A. Motion

ROYAL SALUTES

Royal salutes are authorised at Edinburgh Castle and Stirling Castle, although in practice Edinburgh Castle is the only operating saluting station in Scotland.

A salute of 21 guns is fired on the following occasions:
(a) the anniversaries of the birth, accession and coronation of The Queen
(b) the anniversary of the birth of HM Queen Elizabeth the Queen Mother
(c) the anniversary of the birth of HRH Prince Philip, Duke of Edinburgh
 A salute of 21 guns is fired in Edinburgh on the occasion of the opening of the General Assembly of the Church of Scotland.
 A salute of 21 guns may also be fired in Edinburgh on the arrival of HM The Queen, HM Queen Elizabeth the Queen Mother, or a member of the royal family who is a Royal Highness on an official visit.

THE ROYAL ARMS

SHIELD

1st and 4th quarters (representing Scotland) — Or, a lion rampant within a double tressure flory counterflory Gules
2nd quarter (representing England) — Gules, three lions passant guardant in pale Or
3rd quarter (representing Ireland) — Azure, a harp Or, stringed Argent
The whole shield is encircled with the Thistle

SUPPORTERS

Dexter (right) — a unicorn Argent, armed, crined, imperially crowned and unguled Or, gorged with a coronet composed of crosses patées and fleurs-de-lis, a chain affixed, passing between the forelegs, and reflexed over the back
Sinister (left) — a lion rampant guardant Or, imperially crowned

CREST

Upon an imperial crown Proper a lion sejant affrontée Gules imperially crowned Or, holding in the dexter paw a sword and in the sinister a sceptre erect, also Proper

BADGE

A thistle, slipped and leaved proper

Flags bearing an earlier version of the royal arms of Scotland — Or, a lion rampant Gules, armed and langued Azure, within a double tressure flory counter-flory of fleur-de-lis of the second — are often flourished by supporters of the Scottish team at football and rugby matches.

THE MOST ANCIENT AND MOST NOBLE ORDER OF THE THISTLE

Postnominal initials, KT (Knights); LT (Ladies)
Ribbon, Green
Motto, Nemo me impune lacessit (No one provokes me with impunity)

The Order of the Thistle is an exclusively Scottish order of knighthood. There is evidence of an order of chivalry in Scotland from at least the Middle Ages; James II created an order of knighthood in 1452, and James III (1460–88) may also have created an order and certainly used the thistle as the royal emblem. However, the present Order of the Thistle was founded by James VII and II in 1687, comprising the sovereign and eight knights. Following James's exile, the Order fell into abeyance until 1703 when it was revived by Queen Anne, who increased the number of knights to 12; since 1827 the maximum number of knights has been 16. Conferment of the Order also confers a knighthood on the recipient.

The Order's motto, Nemo me impune lacessit, is the motto of all Scottish regiments; it is usually translated into Scots as 'Wha daur meddle wi' me?'.

SOVEREIGN OF THE ORDER

The Queen

ROYAL KNIGHTS AND LADIES

HM Queen Elizabeth the Queen Mother, 1937
HRH The Prince Philip, Duke of Edinburgh, 1952
HRH The Prince Charles, Duke of Rothesay, 1977
HRH The Princess Royal, 2000

KNIGHTS BRETHREN AND LADIES

The Earl of Wemyss and March, 1966
Sir Donald Cameron of Lochiel, 1973
The Duke of Buccleuch and Queensberry, 1978
The Earl of Elgin and Kincardine, 1981
The Lord Thomson of Monifieth, 1981
The Earl of Airlie, 1985
Capt. Sir Iain Tennant, 1986
The Viscount Younger of Leckie, 1995
The Viscount of Arbuthnott, 1996
The Earl of Crawford and Balcarres, 1996
Lady Marion Fraser, 1996
The Lord Macfarlane of Bearsden, 1996
The Lord Mackay of Clashfern, 1997
The Lord Wilson of Tillyorn, 2000

Chancellor, The Duke of Buccleuch and Queensberry, KT, VRD
Dean, The Very Revd G. I. Macmillan, CVO
Secretary and Lord Lyon King of Arms, R. O. Blair, LVO, WS
Usher of the Green Rod, Rear-Adm. C. H. Layman, CB, DSO, LVO
Chapel, The Thistle Chapel, St Giles's Cathedral, Edinburgh

PRECEDENCE IN SCOTLAND

The Sovereign
The Prince Philip, Duke of Edinburgh
The Lord High Commissioner to the General Assembly of the Church of Scotland (while the Assembly is sitting)
The Duke of Rothesay (eldest son of the Sovereign)
The Sovereign's younger sons
The Sovereign's cousins
Lord-Lieutenants*
Lord Provosts of cities being ex officio Lord-Lieutenants of those cities*
Sheriffs Principal*
Lord Chancellor of Great Britain
Moderator of the General Assembly of the Church of Scotland
Keeper of the Great Seal (The First Minister)
Presiding Officer of the Scottish Parliament
Secretary of State for Scotland
Hereditary High Constable of Scotland
Hereditary Master of the Household
Dukes, according to their patent of creation:
   (1) of England
   (2) of Scotland
   (3) of Great Britain
   (4) of the United Kingdom
   (5) those of Ireland created since the Union
       between Great Britain and Ireland

Eldest sons of Dukes of the Blood Royal
Marquesses, according to their patent of creation:
  (1) of England
  (2) of Scotland
  (3) of Great Britain
  (4) of the United Kingdom
  (5) those of Ireland created since the Union
      between Great Britain and Ireland
Dukes' eldest sons
Earls, according to their patent of creation:
  (1) of England
  (2) of Scotland
  (3) of Great Britain
  (4) of the United Kingdom
  (5) those of Ireland created since the Union
      between Great Britain and Ireland
Younger sons of Dukes of Blood Royal
Marquesses' eldest sons
Dukes' younger sons
Lord Justice-General
Lord Clerk Register
Lord Advocate
Advocate-General
Lord Justice-Clerk
Viscounts, according to their patent of creation
  (1) of England
  (2) of Scotland
  (3) of Great Britain
  (4) of the United Kingdom
  (5) those of Ireland created since the Union
      between Great Britain and Ireland
Earls' eldest sons
Marquesses' younger sons
Lord-Barons, according to their patent of
creation:
  (1) of England
  (2) of Scotland
  (3) of Great Britain
  (4) of the United Kingdom
  (5) those of Ireland created since the Union
      between Great Britain and Ireland
Viscounts' eldest sons
Earls' younger sons
Lord-Barons' eldest sons
Knights of the Garter
Knights of the Thistle
Privy Counsellors
Senators of College of Justice (Lords of Session)
Viscounts' younger sons
Lord-Barons' younger sons
Sons of Life Peers
Baronets
Knights Grand Cross of the Order of the Bath
Knights Grand Commanders of the Order of the
Star of India
Knights Grand Cross of the Order of St Michael
and St George

Knights Grand Commanders of the Order of the
Indian Empire
Knights Grand Cross of the Royal Victorian
Order
Knights Commanders of the Order of the Bath
Knights Commanders of the Order of the Star
of India
Knights Commanders of the Order of St Michael
and St George
Knights Commanders of the Order of the
Indian Empire
Knights Commanders of the Royal Victorian
Order
Solicitor-General for Scotland
Lyon King of Arms
Sheriffs Principal, except as shown above
Knights Bachelor
Sheriffs
Commanders of the Royal Victorian Order
Companions of the Order of the Bath
Companions of the Order of the Star of India
Companions of the Order of St Michael and St
George
Companions of the Order of the Indian Empire
Lieutenants of the Royal Victorian Order
Companions of the Distinguished Service Order
Eldest sons of younger sons of Peers
Baronets' eldest sons
Knights' eldest sons, in the same order as their
fathers
Members of the Royal Victorian Order
Baronets' younger sons
Knights' younger sons, in the same order as their
fathers
Queen's Counsel
Esquires
Gentlemen
* During term of office and within their own counties/
cities/sheriffdoms

FORMS OF ADDRESS

It is only possible to cover here the forms of
address for peers, baronets and knights, their wife
and children, Privy Counsellors, and holders of
certain political, legal and civic posts; for chiefs of
clans, see pages 250-255. Greater detail should be
sought in one of the publications devoted to the
subject.

Both formal and social forms of address are
given where usage differs; nowadays, the social
form is generally preferred to the formal, which
increasingly is used only for official documents and
on very formal occasions.

The form of address for a woman holding office is given if different from that of a man holding the same position, but only where a woman holds or has held that particular office, as new styles tend to be adopted only when circumstances require it.

F— represents forename
S— represents surname
D— represents a designation, e.g. a title (peer) or city (convenor)

BARON
see Lord of Parliament

BARON'S WIFE
see Lord of Parliament's wife

BARON'S CHILDREN
see Lord of Parliament's children

BARONESS IN OWN RIGHT
see Lady of Parliament in own right

BARONESS (WOMAN LIFE PEER)
Envelope, may be addressed in same way as for a Lord of Parliament's wife, or, if she prefers (formal), The Right Hon. the Baroness D—; (social), The Baroness D—
Letter (formal), My Lady; (social), Dear Lady D—
Spoken, Lady D—

BARONET
Envelope, Sir F— S—, Bt.
Letter (formal), Dear Sir; (social), Dear Sir F—
Spoken, Sir F—

BARONET'S WIFE
Envelope, Lady S—
Letter (formal), Dear Madam; (social), Dear Lady S—
Spoken, Lady S—

CHAIRMAN OF SCOTTISH LAND COURT
As for Lords of Session

CONVENER OF COUNCIL
Envelope, The Convener of D—
Letter, Dear Convener
Spoken, Convener

COUNTESS IN OWN RIGHT
As for an Earl's wife

COURTESY TITLES
The heir apparent to a Duke, Marquess or Earl uses the highest of his father's other titles as a courtesy title. The holder of a courtesy title is not styled The Most Hon. or The Right Hon., and in correspondence 'The' is omitted before the title. The heir apparent to a Scottish title may use the title 'Master'.

DAME
Envelope, Dame F— S—, followed by appropriate post-nominal letters
Letter (formal), Dear Madam; (social), Dear Dame F—
Spoken, Dame F—

DUKE
Envelope (formal), His Grace the Duke of D—; (social), The Duke of D—
Letter (formal), My Lord Duke; (social), Dear Duke
Spoken (formal), Your Grace; (social), Duke

DUKE'S WIFE
Envelope (formal), Her Grace the Duchess of D—; (social), The Duchess of D—
Letter (formal), Dear Madam; (social), Dear Duchess
Spoken, Duchess

DUKE'S ELDEST SON
see Courtesy titles

DUKE'S YOUNGER SONS
Envelope, Lord F— S—
Letter (formal), My Lord; (social), Dear Lord F—
Spoken (formal), My Lord; (social), Lord F—

DUKE'S DAUGHTER
Envelope, Lady F—S
Letter (formal), Dear Madam; (social), Dear Lady F—
Spoken, Lady F—

EARL
Envelope (formal), The Right Hon. the Earl (of) D—; (social), The Earl (of) D—
Letter (formal), My Lord; (social), Dear Lord D—
Spoken (formal), My Lord; (social), Lord D—

EARL'S WIFE
Envelope (formal), The Right Hon. the Countess (of) D—; (social), The Countess (of) D—
Letter (formal), Madam; (social), Lady D—
Spoken (formal), Madam; (social), Lady D—

EARL'S CHILDREN

Eldest son, *see* Courtesy titles

Younger sons, The Hon. F— S—(for forms of address, *see* Lord of Parliament's children)

Daughters, Lady F— S—(for forms of address, *see* Duke's daughter)

KNIGHT (BACHELOR)

Envelope, Sir F— S—

Letter (formal), Dear Sir; (social), Dear Sir F—

Spoken, Sir F—

KNIGHT (ORDERS OF CHIVALRY)

Envelope, Sir F— S—, followed by appropriate post-nominal letters. Otherwise as for Knight Bachelor

KNIGHT'S WIFE

As for Baronet's wife

LADY OF PARLIAMENT IN OWN RIGHT

As for Lord of Parliament's wife

LIFE PEER

As for Lord of Parliament/Baroness in own right

LIFE PEER'S WIFE

As for Lord of Parliament's wife

LIFE PEER'S CHILDREN

As for Lord of Parliament's children

LORD ADVOCATE

Usually admitted a member of the Privy Council on appointment.

Envelope, The Right (Rt.) Hon. the Lord Advocate, or The Right (Rt.) Hon. F— S—

Letter (formal), My Lord (if a peer), or Dear Sir; (social), Dear Lord Advocate, or Dear Lord D—/ Mr S—

Spoken, Lord D—/Mr S—

LORD HIGH COMMISSIONER TO THE GENERAL ASSEMBLY

Envelope, His/Her Grace the Lord High Commissioner

Letter, Your Grace

Spoken, Your Grace

LORD JUSTICE-CLERK

Envelope, The Hon. the Lord Justice-Clerk; if a Privy Counsellor, The Right (Rt.) Hon. the Lord Justice-Clerk

Letter (formal), My Lord; (social), Dear Lord Justice-Clerk

Spoken (formal), My Lord; (social), Lord Justice-Clerk

LORD JUSTICE-GENERAL

Usually admitted a member of the Privy Council on appointment

Envelope, The Right (Rt.) Hon. the Lord Justice-General

Letter (formal), My Lord; (social), Dear Lord Justice-General

Spoken (formal), My Lord; (social), Lord Justice-General

LORD OF PARLIAMENT

Envelope (formal), The Right Hon. Lord D—; (social), The Lord D

Letter (formal), My Lord; (social), Dear Lord D—

Spoken, Lord D—

LORD OF PARLIAMENT'S WIFE

Envelope (formal), The Right Hon. Lady D—; (social), The Lady D—

Letter (formal), My Lady; (social), Dear Lady D—

Spoken, Lady D—

LORD OF PARLIAMENT'S CHILDREN

Envelope, The Hon. F— S—

Letter, Dear Mr/Miss/Mrs S—

Spoken, Mr/Miss/Mrs S

LORD/LADY OF SESSION

Envelope, The Hon. Lord/Lady D—; if a Privy Counsellor, The Right (Rt.) Hon. Lord/Lady D—

Letter (formal), My Lord/Lady; (social), Dear Lord/Lady D—

Spoken (formal), My Lord/Lady; (social), Lord/ Lady D—

LORD OF SESSION'S WIFE

As for the wife of a Lord of Parliament, except that there is no prefix before 'Lady'

LORD PROVOSTS — ABERDEEN AND DUNDEE

Envelope, The Lord Provost of Aberdeen/Dundee

Letter (formal), My Lord Provost; (social), Dear Lord Provost

Spoken, My Lord Provost

LORD PROVOSTS — EDINBURGH AND GLASGOW

Envelope, The Right (Rt.) Hon. the Lord Provost of Edinburgh/Glasgow; or (Edinburgh only) The Right (Rt.) Hon. F— S—, Lord Provost of Edinburgh

Letter (formal), My Lord Provost; (social), Dear Lord Provost

Spoken, My Lord Provost

LORD PROVOST'S WIFE/CONSORT

Envelope, The Lady Provost of D— (may be followed by her name)

Letter (formal), My Lady Provost; (social), Dear Lady Provost

Spoken, My Lady Provost/ Lady Provost

MARQUESS

Envelope (formal), The Most Hon. the Marquess of D—; (social), The Marquess of D—

Letter (formal), My Lord; (social), Dear Lord D—

Spoken (formal), My Lord; (social), Lord D—

MARQUESS'S WIFE

Envelope (formal), The Most Hon. the Marchioness of D—; (social), The Marchioness of D—

Letter (formal), Madam; (social), Dear Lady D

Spoken, Lady D—

MARQUESS'S CHILDREN

Eldest son, *see* Courtesy titles

Younger sons, Lord F— S—(for forms of address, *see* Duke's younger sons)

Daughters, Lady F— S—(for forms of address, *see* Duke's daughter)

MARQUIS

see Marquess; 'Marquis' is sometimes used for titles predating the Union

MASTER

The title is used by the heir apparent to a Scottish peerage, though usually the heir apparent to a Duke, Marquess or Earl uses his courtesy title rather than 'Master'.

Envelope, The Master of D—

Letter (formal), Dear Sir; (social), Dear Master of D—

Spoken (formal), Master, or Sir; (social), Master, or Mr S—

MASTER'S WIFE

Addressed as for the wife of the appropriate peerage style, otherwise as Mrs S—

MEMBER OF SCOTTISH PARLIAMENT

Envelope, Mr/Miss/Mrs S—, MSP

Letter, Dear Mr/Miss/Mrs S—

Spoken, Mr/Miss/Mrs S—

MODERATOR OF THE GENERAL ASSEMBLY

Envelope, The Rt. Revd the Moderator of the General Assembly of the Church of Scotland

Letter (formal), Dear Moderator/Dear Sir; (social), Dear Dr/Mr S—/Dear Moderator

Spoken, Moderator

After their year in office, former Moderators are styled The Very Reverend

PRESIDING OFFICER

Style/title used before the Scottish Parliament elections, e.g. if a minister is a privy counsellor, he is styled Rt. Hon.

Envelope (ministerial business), addressed by his appointment; (personal), Sir F—/Mr/ Miss/Mrs S—, The Presiding Officer

Letter, Dear Sir F—/Mr/Miss/Mrs S—

Spoken, addressed by his appointment or name

PRIVY COUNSELLOR

Envelope, The Right (or Rt.) Hon. F— S—

Letter, Dear Mr/Miss/Mrs S—

Spoken, Mr/Miss/Mrs S

It is incorrect to use the letters pc after the name in conjunction with the prefix The Right Hon., unless the Privy Counsellor is a peer below the rank of Marquess and so is styled The Right Hon. because of his rank. In this case only, the postnominal letters may be used in conjunction with the prefix The Right Hon.

PROVOST

Envelope, The Provost of D—, or F— S—, Esq., Provost of D—/Mrs F— S—, Provost of D

Letter, Dear Provost

Spoken, Provost

SCOTTISH MINISTER

Style/title used before the Scottish Parliament elections, e.g. if a minister is a privy counsellor, he/she is styled Rt. Hon.

Envelope (ministerial business), minister addressed by his/her appointment; (personal), Mr/Miss/Mrs S—, followed by the minister's appointment

Letter, Dear Mr/Miss/Mrs S—

Spoken, addressed by his/her appointment or name

SHERIFF PRINCIPAL AND SHERIFF

Envelope, Sheriff F— S—

Letter, Dear Sheriff S—

Spoken (formal), My Lord/Lady (in court); (social), Sheriff S—

VISCOUNT

Envelope (formal), The Right Hon. the Viscount D—; (social), The Viscount D—

Letter (formal), My Lord; (social), Dear Lord D—

Spoken, Lord D—

VISCOUNT'S WIFE

Envelope (formal), The Right Hon. the Viscountess D—; (social), The Viscountess D

Letter (formal), Madam; (social), Dear Lady D—

Spoken, Lady D—

VISCOUNT'S CHILDREN

As for Lord of Parliament's children

Chiefs of Clans and Names

As there are a number of different styles for chiefs of clans and names, forms of address vary widely. Male chiefs are styled by their designation or estate rather than their surname; 'Esquire' is not added. A female chief is styled Madam or Mrs/Miss (according to her preference) in addition to her estate. For a list of examples, see also Chiefs of Clans and Names, page 250.

Envelope, chief's designation

Letter (formal), Dear Chief (if writer is a member of the clan or name); Dear Sir/Madam; (social), 'Dear' followed by chief's designation

CHIEF'S WIFE

As for her husband, with the addition of 'Mrs'.

CHIEF'S HEIR APPARENT

As for the chief, with the addition of 'younger' (yr), e.g.

F— S— of D— , yr

F— S— , yr. of D—

CLUBS

Ayr County Club
Savoy Park Hotel, Racecourse Road, Ayr, KA7 2UT (Tel: 01292-266112).

Caledonian Club
32 Abercromby Place, Edinburgh, EH3 6QE (Tel: 0131-557 2675; Fax: 0131-556 5744).

Glasgow Art Club
185 Bath Street, Glasgow, G2 4HU (Tel: 0141-248 5210).

New Club
86 Princes Street, Edinburgh, EH2 2BB (Tel: 0131-226 4481; Fax: 0131-225 9649; E-mail: info@newclub.co.uk; Web: www.newclub.co.uk).

Royal Forth Yacht Club
Middle Pier, Granton Harbour, Edinburgh, EH5 1HF (Tel: 0131-552 8560; Fax: 0131-552 8560; E-mail: info@royalforth.mariner.co.uk; Web: www.royalforth.org).

Royal Highland Yacht Club
Raslie House, Slockavullin, Argyll, PA31 8QG (Tel: 01546-510261; Fax: 01546-510261; E-mail: rhyctr@rhyc.org.uk; Web: www.rhyc.org.uk).

Royal Northern and Clyde Yacht Club
Rhu, Helensburgh, Argyll and Bute, G84 8NG (Tel: 01436-820 322; Fax: 01439-821 296).

Royal Northern and University Club
9 Albyn Place, Aberdeen, AB10 1YE (Tel: 01224-583292; Fax: 01224-571082; E-mail: secretary@rnuc.org.uk; Web: www.rnuc.org.uk).

Royal Scottish Automobile Club
11 Blythswood Square, Glasgow, G2 4AG (Tel: 0141-221 3850; Fax: 0141-221 3805; E-mail: club@rsac.co.uk; Web: www.rsac.co.uk).

Royal Tay Yacht Club
34 Dundee Road, West Ferry, Dundee, DD5 1LX (Tel: 01382-477516; E-mail: rtayyc@Rya.online.net; Web: www.rtyc@i12.com).

Royal Western Yacht Club
Braidhurst Cottage, Shandon, Helensburgh, Argyll and Bute, G84 8NP (Tel: 01436-820256; Fax: 01436-820256).

Western Club
32 Royal Exchange Square, Glasgow, G1 3AB (Tel: 0141-221 2016; Fax: 0141-248 6630; E-mail: secretary@westernclub.co.uk; Web: www.westernclub.co.uk).

HISTORIC BUILDINGS AND MONUMENTS

Scotland is rich in buildings of historical and architectural value. They date from all periods from the Middle Ages to the 20th-century, and include castles, strongholds and keeps, palaces, tower houses, historic houses and mansions, churches, cathedrals, chapels, abbeys and priories, formal gardens, industrial buildings and military installations.

There are about 2,000 castles and towers in Scotland. Among the oldest castles still visible are Castle Sween, in Knapdale, Argyll, whose oldest parts may date from the 11th-century, and Cubbie Roo's Castle, built in 1145 by the Norseman Kolbein Hruga on the island of Wyre, Orkney, where there is also a later twelfth-century chapel. Dunvegan Castle in Skye is the oldest continuously inhabited castle in Scotland, having been occupied by the MacLeods for 700 years, although its present appearance is the result of massive 19th-century remodelling. Many castles were subject to frequent rebuilding over the centuries, and new castles were still being built as late as the nineteenth century, the most famous example being Balmoral, built in 1855 for Prince Albert. The north-east of Scotland is particularly rich in castles, and the Aberdeen and Grampian Tourist Board together with the Scottish Tourist Board promote exploration of this heritage by sign-posting a Castle Trail in the region.

Tower houses, which became popular from the 15th century and were the major form of secular building in the sixteenth, were a peculiarly (though not exclusively) Scottish type of fortified dwelling for the local nobility. Good examples are Claypotts Castle, near Dundee, and Craigievar and Crathes Castles, Aberdeenshire.

Ecclesiastical buildings have an equally long and chequered history and many of the oldest buildings, such as St Ninian's Chapel, Isle of Whithorn, and the abbey buildings on the island of Iona, replace even earlier structures. The ruined Orphir church near Kirkwall, Orkney, is Scotland's only surviving round church, probably dating from before 1122. The monastery foundations of King Alexander I (reigned 1107–24) and his brother David I (1124–53) resulted in the building of St Margaret's Chapel in Edinburgh Castle, Inchcolm Abbey, on a small island in the Firth of Forth, and a string of great abbeys in the Borders (Dryburgh, Jedburgh, Melrose, Kelso, Sweetheart, Glenluce, etc.) in the twelfth and thirteenth centuries. The Border abbeys suffered severely in the conflicts of the 14th century, however, and much of what is visible today reflects 15th-century rebuilding.

Scotland's built heritage from later centuries spans a wide variety of structures. From the late seventeenth and eighteenth centuries there are great houses such as Hopetoun House, Edinburgh, Duff House, Banff, and other buildings by William and Robert Adam, and the military bridges built by General Wade in the Highlands. The Industrial Revolution produced mills, factories, built harbours and shipyards, and the unique industrial village of New Lanark, purpose-built in 1785 as a cotton-manufacturing centre and made famous by the social ideas of Robert Owen in the 1820s. From the early 20th-century, the Hill House, Helensburgh, is a fine example of the work of Charles Rennie Mackintosh, Scotland's best-known architect. Coming almost up to the present day, the state of military structures around the Scottish coasts from both world wars is the subject of a recent review by Historic Scotland.

Under the Planning (Listed Buildings and Conservation Areas) (Scotland) Act 1997 and the Ancient Monuments and Archaeological Areas Act 1979, the Scottish Executive is responsible for listing buildings and scheduling monuments in Scotland on the advice of Historic Scotland, the Historic Buildings Council for Scotland and the Ancient Monuments Board for Scotland.

Listed buildings are classified into Grade A, Grade B and Grade C. All buildings of interest erected before 1840 which are in use and are still largely in their original condition, are listed. More recent buildings are selected according to their individual character and quality. The main purpose of listing is to ensure that care is taken in deciding the future of a building. No changes which affect the architectural or historic character of a listed building can be made without listed building consent (in addition to planning permission where relevant). It is a criminal offence to demolish a listed building, or alter it in such a way as to affect its character, without consent. There are currently about 44,462 listed buildings in Scotland.

All monuments proposed for scheduling are considered to be of national importance. Where buildings are both scheduled and listed, ancient monuments legislation takes precedence. The main purpose of scheduling a monument is to preserve it for the future and to protect it from damage, destruction or any unnecessary interference. Once a monument has been scheduled, scheduled monument consent is required before any works are carried out. The scope of the control is more extensive and more detailed than that applied to listed buildings, but certain minor works may be carried out without consent. It is a criminal offence to carry out unauthorised work to scheduled monuments. There are currently about 7,035 scheduled monuments in Scotland, but the full number of buildings which meet scheduling standards is probably twice this. Both scheduling and listing are ongoing processes.

Whereas most listed buildings are currently in use or could be returned to use (even if it is not their original use), monuments that are scheduled have usually fallen into disuse and are unlikely to be used again in anything like their original form. In fact, a structure used as a dwelling house or in ecclesiastical use cannot be scheduled. Thus houses, bridges, factories, public buildings, war memorials and so on are more likely to be listed than scheduled, and terms of public access differ from those of access to scheduled monuments. The Forth Bridge, for instance, is a listed building – the largest in Scotland – and so are some traditional blue police boxes and red telephone boxes.

Historic Scotland, the government agency responsible for scheduling and listing, has around 330 monuments in its care. It provides financial assistance to financial assistance to private owners towards the costs of conserving and repairing important monuments and buildings. It also undertakes research into building conservation and publishes educational material on Scotland's built heritage.

The National Trust for Scotland, an independent trust, also cares for many castles, historic buildings and sites. A number of councils also care for historic buildings, while others are privately owned or cared for by independent conservation trusts.

OPEN TO THE PUBLIC

The following is a selection of the many historic buildings and monuments open to the public. Opening hours vary. Many properties are closed in winter and some are also closed in the mornings. Most properties are closed on Christmas Eve, Christmas Day, Boxing Day and New Year's Day, and many are closed on Good Friday. Information about a specific property should be checked by telephone.

Closed in winter (usually October to March)

†*Closed in winter, and in mornings in summer*

HS   *Historic Scotland property*

NTS   *National Trust for Scotland property*

Abbot House, Dunfermline. Tel: 01383-733266. Dates from 16th-century. Owners have included Anne of Denmark, wife of James VI

*Abbotsford House, Melrose, Borders. Tel: 01896-752043. Sir Walter Scott's house

Aberdour Castle (HS), Aberdour, Burntisland, Fife. Tel: 01383-860519. Closed Sun. mornings, Thurs. afternoons, and Fri. in winter. 14th-century castle built by the Douglas family

Abernethy Round Tower (HS), nr Perth. Site of a Culdee Celtic Christian establishment. Built by the Culdees in 9th-or 10th-century, one of only two examples in Scotland

†Aikwood Tower, nr Selkirk, Borders. Tel: 01750-52253. Open Apr.–Sep., only Tues., Thurs. and Sun. afternoons. A 16th-century fortified tower house. Home of Sir David Steel

*Alloa Tower (NTS), Alloa. Tel: 01259-211701. Closed mornings. Ancestral home of Earls of Mar for 400 years

Arbroath Abbey (HS), Arbroath, Angus. Tel: 01241-878756. Site of Declaration of Arbroath 1320. Founded 1178, completed 1233, granted abbey status 1285

Ardchattan Priory (HS), Loch Etive, nr Oban. Ruins of a Valliscaulian priory founded 1231 by Duncan MacDougall. Burnt by Cromwell's troops in 1654

Argyll's Lodging (HS), Stirling. Tel: 01786-461146. Fine example of a 17th-century town residence. Built by Sir William Alexander of Menstrie, first Earl of Stirling

*Armadale Castle, Ardvasar, Skye. Tel: 01471-844227. The seat of the Macdonalds since 1790

†Arniston House, Gorebridge. Tel: 01875-830515. Open Jul.–Sep. on Sun., Tues. and Thurs. afternoons only. Designed by William Adam for Robert Dundas, judge who dented the Campbell monopoly of Scottish patronage

†Ayton Castle, Eyemouth, Berwickshire. Tel: 01890-781212. Neo-baronial red sandstone castle built 1845–8

†Balfour Castle, Shapinsay, Orkney. Tel: 01865-711282. Completed 1848 by the Balfour family of Westray

Balgonie Castle, nr Glenrothes. Tel: 01592-750119. A 14th-century keep and courtyard. Occupied by Rob Roy and 200 clansmen in 1716

Balhousie Castle, Perth. Tel: 01738-621281. Neo-baronial mansion of 1862, built for the Earl of Kinnoull

Ballindalloch Castle, Bridge of Avon, Aberlour. Tel: 01807-500206. Begun 1546, historically a Grant seat

Balmerino Abbey (NTS), Balmerino, nr Leuchars. Remains of a Cistercian abbey founded 1229 by Alexander II and built by the religious house of Melrose

Balmoral Castle, nr Braemar. Tel: 013397-42334. Open mid-April to end July. Baronial-style castle built for Victoria and Albert. The Queen's private residence

Balvaird Castle (HS), Balvaird, Abernethy. Tel: 0131-668 8800. Tower house on the Ochil Hills. Built 1500 by Sir Andrew Murray

*****Balvenie Castle (HS),** Dufftown, Keith, Banffshire. Tel: 01340-820121. A 13th-century castle owned by the Comyns

*****Barcaldine Castle,** Peninsula of Benderloch. Tel: 01631-720598. Early 17th century Campbell tower house

*****Barrie's Birthplace (NTS),** Kirriemuir. Birthplace of author of Peter Pan, J. M. Barrie

Beauly Priory (HS), Beauly. Ruins of priory founded 1230 by the Bisset family for the Valliscaulian order, later Cistercian

*****The Binns (NTS),** nr Linlithgow. Closed Fridays. Castellated mansion built between 1612 and 1630. Originally property of the Livingstones of Kilsyth but sold to the Dalziels

*****Bishop's and Earl's Palaces (HS),** Kirkwall, Orkney. Tel: 01856-871918. A 12th-century hall-house and an early 17th-century palace

Black House, Arnol (HS), Lewis, Western Isles. Tel: 01851-710395. Closed Sun., also Fri. in winter. Traditional Lewis thatched house

Blackness Castle (HS), nr Linlithgow, W. Lothian. Tel: 01506-834807. Following the Treaty of Union 1707, one of only four castles in Scotland to be garrisoned

*****Blair Castle,** Blair Atholl. Tel: 01796-481207. Mid 18th-century mansion with 13th-century tower; seat of the Dukes of Atholl

*****Bod of Germista,** Lerwick, Shetland. Closed Mon. and Tues. Birthplace of Arthur Anderson, first MP of Shetland

*****Bonawe Iron Furnace (HS),** Argyll and Bute. Tel: 01866-822432. Charcoal-fuelled ironworks founded in 1753

Bothwell Castle (HS), Uddingston, Glasgow. Tel: 01698-816894. Closed Sun. mornings, Thurs. afternoons, and Fri. in winter. Largest 13th-century castle in Scotland. Built by Moray family as protection against Edward I of England

†**Bowhill,** Selkirk. Tel: 01750-22204. House open July only; grounds open April—June, Aug. except Fri., daily in July. Seat of the Dukes of Buccleuch and Queensberry; fine collection of paintings, including portrait miniatures. Includes Newark Castle, a ruined 15th-century keep and courtyard within grounds of Bowhill

*****Braemar Castle,** Braemar. Tel: 01339-741219. Closed Fridays. Built 1628 by John Erskine, Earl of Mar. Used as a garrison following Jacobite rising

Brechin Cathedral, Brechin. Religious building here since 900 AD. Current building restored 1900–2. Adjacent 11th-century round tower, one of only two which survive in Scotland

*****Brodick Castle (NTS),** Isle of Arran. Tel: 01770-302202. Gardens open all year. Site of the ancient seat of the Dukes of Hamilton

*****Brodie Castle (NTS),** Forres, Moray. Tel: 01309-641371. Grounds open all year. A 16th-century castle with later additions

Brough of Birsay (HS), Orkney. Remains of Norse church and village on the tidal island of Birsay

†**Broughton House (NTS),** Kirkcudbright, Galloway. Tel: 01557-330437. Home of Edward Hornel, member of late 19th-century Scottish art establishment. Japanese garden

Broughty Castle (HS), Broughty Ferry, Dundee. Tel: 01382-76121. Tower house built around 1454 to guard the Firth of Tay

Burleigh Castle (HS), Milnathort. Tel: 0131-668 8800. Red-sandstone tower built around 1500. Home of the Balfours of Burleigh

Burns Cottage and Museum, Alloway, Ayrshire. Tel: 01292-441215. Birthplace of Robert Burns

Caerlaverock Castle (HS), nr Dumfries. Tel: 01387-770244. Fine early classical Renaissance building. Built c.1270

Callendar House, Falkirk. Tel: 01324-503770. Closed Sun. mornings. Large ornate mansion of 1870s incorporating towers and turrets of a 14th–15th century castle

*****Cambuskenneth Abbey, (HS)** Stirling. Grounds open all year. Ruins of 12th-century abbey founded by David I on site of an Augustinian settlement

*****Cardoness Castle (HS),** Gatehouse of Fleet. Tel: 01557-814427. Closed Sun. mornings. Late 15th-century stronghold

*****Carlyle's Birthplace (NTS),** Ecclefechan, Lockerbie, Dumfriesshire. Tel: 01576-300666. Closed Oct.–April and Sat. mornings. Birthplace of Thomas Carlyle

Carnasserie Castle (HS), nr Kilmartin. Tel: 0131-668 8800. Built by John Corsewell in 1560s, who published first ever book in Gaelic, Knox's Liturgy, 1567

Carrick House, Eday, Orkney. Tel: 01857-622260. Built by Laird of Eday, 1633. Associated with pirate John Gow, on whom Sir Walter Scott's *The Pirate* is based

Carsluith Castle (HS), Carsluith, Creetown. Tel: 0131-668 8800. A 16th-century tower house built by Richard Brown. Abandoned 1748

Castle Campbell (HS) (NTS), Dollar Glen, nr Stirling. Tel: 01259-742408. Closed Sun. mornings, Thurs. afternoons, and Fri. in winter. 15th-century castle with parapet walk. John Knox preached here in 1556

*Castle Fraser (NTS), Sauchen, Inverurie, Aberdeenshire. Tel: 01330-833463. Garden and grounds open all year. Castle built between 1575 and 1636

Castle Menzies, nr Aberfeldy. Tel: 01887-820982. Closed Sun. mornings. A 16th-century tower house. Occupied by Oliver Cromwell's force in 1650s

Castle of Old Wick (HS), Wick. Tel: 0131-668 8800. Ruins of one of oldest castles in Scotland. Built 12th-century, when this part of Scotland was ruled from Orkney by the Norsemen

*Castle Stalker, nr Port Appin. Tel: 01631-730234. Open by appointment. Built on tiny rock island by the Stewarts of Appin in 16th-century and gifted to King James IV

*Castle Stuart, Petty. Tel: 01463-790745. Built between 1621–5 by James Stuart, 3rd Earl of Moray. Visited by Bonny Prince Charlie prior to Culloden

Castle Sween, (HS) Kilmichael. Tel: 0131-668 8800. Ruins of 11th-century castle. Earliest stone castle in Scotland

*Cawdor Castle, Inverness. Tel: 01667-404615. A 14th-century keep with 15th and 17th century additions. Setting of Shakespeare's Macbeth

*Claypotts Castle, (HS) Broughty Ferry. Tel: 01786-450000. Open only Sat and Sun., July–Sept. Z-shaped tower house built 1569—88 for the Strachans, then the Grahams

Corgarff Castle (HS), Strathdon, Aberdeenshire. Tel: 01975-651460. Closed weekdays in winter. Former 16th-century tower house converted into barracks

†Craigievar Castle (NTS), nr Alford. Tel: 01339-883635. Built by a Baltic trader, 'Willy the Merchant', in 1626

Craigmillar Castle (HS), Edinburgh. Tel: 0131-661 4445. Closed Sun. mornings, Thurs. afternoons, and Fri. in winter. Where the murder of Lord Darnley, second husband of Mary Queen of Scots, was plotted

*Craignethan Castle (HS), nr Lanark. Tel: 01555-860364. Castle dating from the 16th-century, with Britain's only stone vaulted artillery chamber. Last major castle built in Scotland

*Crathes Castle (NTS), nr Banchory. Tel: 01330-844525. Garden and grounds open all year. A 16th-century baronial castle in woodland, fields and gardens

*Crichton Castle (HS), nr Pathhead, Midlothian. Tel: 01875-320017. Castle with Italian-style faceted stonework facade

Crookston Castle (NTS), Pollok, Glasgow. Tel: 0141-226 4826. Built 12th century by Robert de Croc. Visited by Mary, Queen of Scots. Became first property of NTS, in 1931.

Cross Kirk (HS), Peebles. Ruins of Trinitarian Friary founded 1474, dedicated to St Nicholas

*Crossraguel Abbey (HS), nr Maybole, Ayrshire. Tel: 01655-883113. Remains of 13th-century abbey

Culross Abbey (HS), Culross. Remains of Cistercian abbey founded 1217 by Malcolm, Earl of Fife

*Culross Palace (NTS), Town House and Study, Culross, Dunfermline. Tel: 01383-880359. Town House and Study closed mornings. Refurbished 16th- and 17th-century buildings

*Culzean Castle (NTS), S. Ayrshire. Tel: 01655-760274. Country park open all year. An 18th-century Adam castle with oval staircase and circular saloon

†Dalmeny House, South Queensferry, Edinburgh. Tel: 0131-331 1888. Open only July–August, Mon., Tue. and Sun. afternoons. Seat of the Earls of Rosebery

*Darnaway Castle, Darnaway, Forres. Tel: 01309-641469. Open only July–Aug. Now a gothic mansion of 1802-12. Original castle acquired by the Stuarts in 1562

Dean Castle, Kilmarnock. Tel: 01563-522702. Keep dates from 1350. Castle burnt 1735, now restored. Originally owned by the Boyd family

*Delgatie Castle, Delgatie, Turriff. Tel: 01888-562750. Original castle dates to 1030, current building 1570. Taken from Earl of Buchan 1314 and granted to the Hays

Dirleton Castle (HS), Dirleton, North Berwick, E. Lothian. Tel: 01620-850330. 12th-century castle with 16th-century gardens

Dornoch Cathedral, Dornoch. Founded 1224. Cathedral of Bishops of Caithness. Restored 19th century

Doune Castle (HS), Doune, Perthshire. Tel: 01786-841742. Closed Sun. mornings, Thurs. afternoons, and Fri. in winter. 14th-century castle built for the Regent Albany

†Drum Castle (NTS), Drumoak, by Banchory, Aberdeenshire. Tel: 01330-811204. Grounds open all year. Late 13th-century tower house

Drumcoltran Tower (HS), Tel: 0131-668 8800. Built around 1550 for the Maxwell family. Still inhabited in 1890s

***Drumlanrig Castle,** nr Thornhill, Dumfriesshire. Tel: 01848-330248. Open May–August only. A 17th-century courtyard mansion. Home of Duke of Buccleuch and Queensberry

***Drumlanrig's Tower,** Hawick, Borders. Tel: 01450-372457. Closed Sun. mornings. Only building left unburnt after burning of Hawick by English in 1570

Dryburgh Abbey (HS), Scottish Borders. Tel: 01835-822381. Closed Sun. mornings in winter. A 12th-century abbey containing tomb of Sir Walter Scott

***Duart Castle,** nr Craignure, Mull. Tel: 01680-812309. Headquarters of MacLean Clan from 13th-century

Duff House (HS), Banff. Tel: 01261-818181. Closed Mon.–Wed. in winter. Georgian mansion housing part of National Galleries of Scotland collection. Built by William Adam

Duffus Castle (HS), Old Duffus, Elgin. Tel: 0131-668 8800. Dates in part to 1151. Originally a royal stronghold. Abandoned in late 17th century

Dumbarton Castle (HS), Dumbarton. Tel: 01389-732167. Closed Sun. mornings, Thurs. afternoons, and Fri. in winter. Castle overlooking River Clyde. A royal seat from where Mary, Queen of Scots sailed for France in 1548

Dunblane Cathedral (HS), Dunblane. Tel: 01786-823338. Closed Sun. mornings. Dates from 13th-century, in Gothic style

***Dundonald Castle (HS),** Dundonald, Kilmarnock, Ayrshire. Tel: 01563-851489. Castle built by the Stewart royal dynasty

Dundrennan Abbey (HS), nr Kirkcudbright. Tel: 01557-500262. Closed weekdays in winter. Remote 12th-century abbey. Where Mary, Queen of Scots spent her last night on Scottish soil

Dunfermline Palace and Abbey (HS), Dunfermline, Fife. Tel: 01383-739026. Closed Sun. mornings, Thurs. afternoons, and Fri. in winter. Remains of palace and Benedictine abbey

Dunnottar Castle, Stonehaven. Tel: 01569-762173. Closed Sun. mornings and weekends Nov.–Easter. A 12–17th century fortress on a sheer cliff jutting into the sea. One of Scotland's finest ruined castles

***Dunrobin Castle,** Golspie, Sutherland. Tel: 01408-633177. Closed Sun. mornings. The most northerly of Scotland's great castles, seat of the Earls of Sutherland

Dunstaffnage Castle and Chapel (HS), nr Oban. Tel: 01631-562465. Closed Sun. mornings, Thurs. afternoons, and Fri. in winter. Fine 13th century castle, briefly the prison of Flora Macdonald

***Dunvegan Castle,** Skye. Tel: 01470-521206. A 13th-century castle with later additions; home of the chiefs of the Clan MacLeod; trips to seal colony

Earl's Palace (HS), Birsay, Orkney. Ruins of 16th century courtyard castle, started by Robert Stewart, Earl of Orkney

***Earl's Palace (HS),** Kirkwall, Orkney. Tel: 01856-875461. Ruins of 17th century palace, built by Patrick Stewart, Earl of Orkney, illegitimate half-brother of Mary Queen of Scots

Edinburgh Castle (HS). Tel: 0131-225 9846. Includes the Scottish National War Memorial, Scottish United Services Museum and historic apartments

Edzell Castle (HS), nr Brechin. Tel: 01356-648631. Closed Sun. mornings, Thurs. afternoons and Fri. in winter. Medieval tower house; unique walled garden. Gardens by Sir David Lindsay in 1604

***Eilean Donan Castle,** Wester Ross. Tel: 01599-555202. A 13th-century castle with Jacobite relics. Established by Alexander II to protect the area from the vikings

***Elcho Castle (HS),** nr Perth. Tel: 01738-639998. 16th century fortified mansion

Elgin Cathedral (HS), Moray. Tel: 01343-547171. Closed Sun. mornings, Thurs. afternoons and Fri. in winter. A 13th-century cathedral with fine chapterhouse

***Falkland Palace (NTS),** Falkland, Cupar, Fife. Tel: 01337-857397. Country residence of the Stewart kings and queens, built between 1502 and 1541

***Fasque House,** nr Fettercairn. Tel: 01561-340202. Family home of Prime Minister William Gladstone 1789–1809

***Fearn Abbey,** Fearn. Open May–Sept., Sat. and Sun. only. A 14th century church, one of the oldest pre-Reformation Scottish churches still used for worship

†**Finlaystone House,** nr Port Glasgow. Tel: 01475-540285. Only open Sun. afternoons April–Aug. Mansion dating from 1760, incorporating 15th century castle of the Cunningham Earls of Glencairn, where John Knox preached in 1556

***Floors Castle,** Kelso. Tel: 01573-223333. Largest inhabited castle in Scotland; seat of the Dukes of Roxburghe

Fort Charlotte, Lerwick, Shetland. Begun by Charles II in 1665 during war against Dutch. Named in honour of George III's queen in 1780s

Fort George (HS), Highland. Tel: 01667-462800. Closed Sunday mornings in winter. An 18th century fort

*Fyvie Castle (NTS), nr Turriff, Grampian. Tel: 01651-891266. Closed mornings May–June and Sept, grounds open all year. Fifteenth century castle with finest wheel stair in Scotland

*Georgian House (NTS), Edinburgh. Tel: 0131-226 3318. Closed Sun. mornings. Fine example of 18th century New Town architecture

*Gladstone's Land (NTS), Edinburgh. Tel: 0131-226 5856. Closed Sun. mornings. Typical 17th century Old Town tenement building with remarkable painted ceilings

*Glamis Castle, Angus. Tel: 01307-840393. Seat of the Lyon family (later Earls of Strathmore and Kinghorne) since 1372. Scene of the murder of Duncan in Shakespeare's Macbeth

Glasgow Cathedral (HS). Tel: 0141-552 6891. Closed Sun. mornings. Medieval cathedral with elaborately vaulted crypt

Glenbuchat Castle (HS), Glenbuchat, Strathdon. Tel: 0131-668 8800. Ruins of tower house built 1590 by John Gordon and Helen Carnegie. Owned by Gordons until 1738

Glenfinnan Monument (NTS), Glenfinnan, Highland. Tel: 01397-722250. Visitor centre closed in winter. Monument erected by Alexander Macdonald of Glenaladale in 1815 in tribute to the clansmen who fought and died in the cause of Prince Charles Edward Stuart

†Glenluce Abbey (HS), Glenluce, Dumfries and Galloway. Tel: 01581-300541. Ruins of Cistercian abbey of the Blessed Virgin Mary, dating from 1192

Greenknowe Tower (HS), Gordon. Tel: 0131-668 8800. Built 1581 by James Seton of Touch and Janet Edmonstone. Owned late 17th century by Walter Pringle of Stichel, writer and Covenanter

†Haddo House (NTS), nr Tarves, Ellon, Aberdeenshire. Tel: 01651-851440. Garden and country park open all year. Georgian mansion house, home to Earls of Gordon and Marquesses of Aberdeen

Hailes Castle (HS), East Linton. Tel: 0131-668 8800. Oldest parts date from 13th century. Built by the Dunbars, Earls of the March. Destroyed in 1650 by Cromwell's troops

*Hermitage Castle (HS), nr Newcastleton, Roxburghshire. Tel: 01387-376222. Closed on Sun. mornings. Now open through winter. Fortress in the Scottish Borders

*The Hill House (NTS), Helensburgh. Tel: 01436-673900. Designed by Charles Rennie Mackintosh

*Hill of Tarvit Mansionhouse (NTS), nr Cupar, Fife. Tel: 01334-653127. Mansionhouse closed mornings; grounds open all year. Rebuilt in 1906, with collection of paintings, furniture and Chinese porcelain. Former home of geographer and cartographer Sir John Scott

*Holmwood House (NTS), Glasgow. Tel: 0141-637 2129. Closed mornings. House designed by Alexander 'Greek' Thomson

Holyroodhouse and Holyrood Abbey (HS) Edinburgh. Tel: 0131-556 1096. Open all year except when monarch in residence. Official residence of monarch of Scotland. Range of buildings dating from 16th century. Remodelled and extended for Charles II 1671–8

*Hopetoun House, nr Edinburgh. Tel: 0131-331 2451. House designed by Sir William Bruce, enlarged by William Adam

*House of Dun (NTS), nr Montrose. Tel: 01674-810264. Closed mornings; grounds open all year. Georgian house with walled garden. Built in 1730 for David Erskine, Laird of Dun

*House of the Binns (NTS), nr Edinburgh. Tel: 01506-834255. Closed Fri.; parkland open daily. Home of Dalyell family since 1612

Huntingtower Castle (HS), nr Perth. Tel: 01738-627231. Closed Sun. mornings, Thurs. afternoons, and Fri. in winter. Castle with painted ceilings. James VI held captive here

Huntly Castle (HS). Tel: 01466-793191. Closed Sun. mornings, Thurs. afternoons and Fri. in winter. Ruin of a 16th- and 17th-century house. Centre of the Gordon family. Sheltered Robert the Bruce

*Inchcolm Abbey (HS), Firth of Forth. Tel: 01383-823332. Abbey founded in 1192 on island in Firth of Forth

*Inchmahome Priory (HS), nr Aberfoyle. Tel: 01877-385294. A 13th-century Augustinian priory on an island in the Lake of Menteith. Mary, Queen of Scots, as a 5-year old, was hidden here before being taken to France

Innerpeffray Chapel and Library (HS), nr Crieff. Closed Dec.–Jan. Thurs. and Sun. mornings. Chapel founded by Lord Drummond 1508, although site of a church since 1342. Adjoining building houses the oldest library in Scotland, founded 1691

*Inveraray Castle, Argyll. Tel: 01499-302203. Gothic-style 18th-century castle; seat of the Dukes of Argyll

*Inverness Castle, Inverness. Closed Sunday. A 19th-century red-sandstone edifice on site of earlier castles. Currently houses the Sheriff Court

Iona Abbey, Inner Hebrides. Tel: 01828-640411. Monastery founded by St Columba in AD 563

Italian Chapel, Lamb Holm, Orkney. Tel: 01856-781268. Two Nissan huts painted in the style of an Italian chapel

Jedburgh Abbey (HS), Scottish Borders. Tel: 01835-863925. Romanesque and early Gothic church founded c.1138

*****Kelburn Castle,** Fairlie, Largs. Tel: 01475-568685. Open only July and Aug. Tower house built 1581. Home of the Boyle family, the Earls of Glasgow from 1703

*****Kellie Castle (NTS),** nr Pittenweem, Anstruther. Tel: 01333-720271. Closed mornings; grounds open all year. Restored 14th-century castle

Kelso Abbey (HS), Scottish Borders. Remains of great abbey church founded 1128

Kilchurn Castle (HS), nr Dalmally. Closed Oct–Mar. Ruins of 15th-century castle on a rocky spit. Campbell stronghold

Kildalton Chapel (HS), nr Port Ellen, Islay. Ruined 12th- or 13th-century chapel dedicated to St John the Beloved. Grounds have the finest surviving intact High Cross in Scotland, dating from 8th-century

*****Kildrummy Castle (HS),** nr Alford, Aberdeenshire. Tel: 01975-571331. 13th century castle, from where the 1715 Jacobite Rising was organised

†**Kilravock Castle,** nr Nairn. Tel: 01667-493258. Open only Wed afternoons April–Oct. Stately home dating from 15th-century. Bonnie Prince Charlie was entertained here on eve of Culloden, 1745

Kings College Chapel, Aberdeen. Closed Sat and Sun. College building completed 1495 in honour of James IV

Kinloch Castle, Rum. Open Tues. and Thurs. afternoons only. Built 1900 as a base for a few weeks each autumn for Sir George Bullough who brought the island as a sporting estate 1888

Kinnaird Head Castle Lighthouse and Museum (HS), Fraserburgh, Aberdeenshire. Tel: 01346-511022. Northern Lighthouse Company's first lighthouse, still in working order

†**Kisimul Castle,** Castlebay, Barra. Tel: 01871-310336. Open May–Sept, Mon., Wed. and Sat. afternoons. Islet fortress of the MacNeil clan. Original castle dates from 1120

Lauriston Castle, Edinburgh. Tel: 0131-336 1921. Closed Fri., and weekdays in winter. A 1590s tower house set in 30 acres of parkland

*****Leighton Library,** Dunblane. Closed weekends in summer. Oldest private library in Scotland, housing 4,500 books in 90 languages, printed 1500 to 1840

*****Leith Hall (NTS),** nr Kennethmont, Huntly. Tel: 01464-831216. Closed mornings; grounds open all year. Mansion house with semicircular stables, in 286-acre estate. Home of the Leith family since 1650

*****Lennoxlove House,** Haddington. Tel: 01620-823720. Closed Mon., Tues. and Thurs. Art collection belonging to Duke of Hamilton

Lincluden Collegiate Church (HS), Dumfries. Nunnery founded here by Uchtred, son of Fergus, Lord of Galloway. Present ruins date from 15th-century

Linlithgow Palace (HS). Tel: 01506-842896. Closed Sun. mornings Oct–Mar. Ruin of royal palace in park setting. Birthplace of Mary, Queen of Scots

Loch Doon Castle (HS), Craigmalloch, Loch Doon. Tel: 0131-668 8800. Ruins of 13th-century castle built by Earls of Carrick

*****Lochleven Castle (HS),** on an island in Loch Leven. Tel: 01388-040483. Closed Sun. mornings, Thurs. afternoons, and Fri. in winter. Scene of Mary, Queen of Scots' imprisonment

Lochmaben Castle (HS), Castle Mains, Lochmaben. Tel: 0131-668 8800. Extensive ruins. Originally the seat of the Bruces. Mary Queen of Scots visited in 1656 with Darnley

*****Lochranza Castle (HS),** Isle of Arran. Tel: 0131-668 8800. Acquired by the Montgomeries in 1452, lost to the Hamiltons 1705

MacLellan's Castle (HS), Kirkcudbright, Galloway. Tel: 01557-331856. Closed Sun. mornings Oct–Mar. Built 1577 for Sir Thoam Maclellan of Bombie

*****Manderston House,** nr Duns, Berwickshire. Tel: 01361-883450. Open Thurs. and Sun. afternoons. Edwardian country house of Miller family

*****Maxwelton House,** nr Moniaive, Dumfriesshire. Tel: 01848-200385. Closed Saturdays. A 17th-century tower house. Home of the Laurie family

†**Mellerstain House,** nr Earlston, Borders. Tel: 01573-410225. Work of William and Robert Adam dating from 1725. Formal Edwardian gardens

Melrose Abbey (HS), Scottish Borders. Tel: 01896-822562. Ruin of Cistercian abbey founded c.1136. Founded by David I

†**Menstrie Castle,** Menstrie. Tel: 01259-213131. Open only Sat. and Sun. afternoons May–Sept. Restored 16th-century mansion, birthplace of Sir William Alexander, first Earl of Stirling

*****Miller's Birthplace (NTS),** Cromarty. Closed Sun. mornings. Birthplace of author, geologist and folklorist Hugh Miller (1802–56)

Morton Castle (HS), Morton Mains, Carronbridge. Tel: 0131-668 8800. Ruins of late 13th-century castle at foot of Lowther Hills. Principal seat of the Douglas Earls of Morton

*Mount Stuart House, Isle of Bute. Tel: 01700-503877. Closed Tues. and Thurs. Spectacular Victorian Gothic house with stained glass and marble.

Muness Castle (HS), Unst, Shetland. Tel: 0131-668 8800. Ruins of 16th-century tower house built by Lawrence Bruce of Cultmolindie, Chamberlain of the Lordship of Shetland

*Neidpath Castle, nr Peebles. Tel: 01721-720333. Closed Sun. mornings. Wall hangings depicting life of Mary Queen of Scots

New Abbey Corn Mill (HS), nr Dumfries. Tel: 01387-850260. Closed Sun. mornings, Thurs. afternoons and Fri. in winter. Water-powered mill

New Lanark, nr Lanark. Tel: 01555-661345. Open all year. Industrial village built in 1785 by David Dale for the manufacture of cotton; became famous under enlightened management (1800–25) of Robert Owen.

*Newark Castle (HS), Port Glasgow, Renfrewshire. Tel: 01475-741858. Virtually intact 15th-century castle

Noltland Castle (HS), Westray, Orkney. Tel: 0131-668 8800. Ruined 16th-century tower house. Built by Gilbert Balfour, Master of the Household of Mary Queen of Scots

Orchardton Tower (HS), Old Orchardton, Palnackie. Tel: 0131-668 8800. Only cylindrical tower house in Scotland. Built for John Carnys around 1456

Orphir Church (HS), nr Kirkwall, Orkney. Ruined remains of only surviving round church in Scotland, dating from 12th-century

Paisley Abbey, Paisley. Tel: 0141-889 7654. Closed Sun. Built on site of town's original settlement, 1163 by Walter, son of Alan, Steward of Scotland. Became an abbey in 1219

Palace of Holyroodhouse, Edinburgh. Tel: 0131-556 7371. Closed when the Queen is in residence. The Queen's official Scottish residence. Main part of the palace built 1671–9

Parliament House, Edinburgh. Closed Sat and Sun. Stronghold of the independent Scots Parliament 1639 until Treaty of Union 1707

*Paxton House, near Berwick upon Tweed, Borders. Tel: 01289-386291. A Palladian country house built in 1758

*Pitmedden Great Garden (NTS), Pitmedden, Aberdeenshire. Tel: 01651-842352. Formal 17th-century garden

Pittencrieff House, Dunfermline. Estate house, 1610. Exhibits of local history. A 76-acre park

Pluscarden Abbey, nr Elgin. Founded by Alexander II in 1230. One of only two abbeys in Scotland with permanent community of monks

Pollok House (NTS), Glasgow. Tel: 0141-649 7151. Eighteenth-century house with collection of paintings, porcelain and furnishings, set in Pollok Country Park

Preston Tower, Prestonpans. Tel: 0131-226 5922. A 15th-century tower house, enlarged in 17th century. Residence of the Hamiltons of Preston. Burned by Cromwell in 1650

Provost Skene's House, Aberdeen. Tel: 01224-641086. Closed Sun. mornings. A 16th-century house with period room settings. Aberdeen's oldest surviving private house, dating from 1545

*Queen Mary's House, Jedburgh. Tel: 01835-863331. Closed Dec–Feb. Altered 16th-century tower house. Belonged to Scotts of Ancrum. Mary Queen of Scots lay very ill here for many days in 1566

Ravenscraig Castle (HS), Kirkcaldy. Ruins of 15th-century castle and courtyard. Nearby steps inspiration for John Buchan's novel 'The 39 Steps'

Restenneth Priory, nr Forfar. Site of 8th-century priory built by King Nechtan of the Picts; adapted as Augustinian priory in 12th century. Remains 12th–15th centuries

Rothesay Castle (HS), Isle of Bute. Tel: 01700-502691. Closed Sun. mornings, Thurs. afternoons, and Fri. in winter. A 13th-century circular castle

Ruthven Barracks (HS), Kingussie. Garrison built after the 1715 rebellion, taken by Jacobites 1744. Blown up following battle of Culloden

Scalloway Castle (HS), Scalloway, Shetland. Tel: 0131-668 8800. Ruins of 17th-century tower house built by Patrick Stewart, Earl of Orkney, 1600

*Scone Palace, Perth. Tel: 01738-552300. House built 1802–13 on the site of a medieval palace. Once the site of the Stone of Destiny

*Scotstarvit Tower (NTS), Craigrothie, Cupar. Tel: 01334-653127. Closed November–Easter and Mon–Fri. in Oct. Erected between 1550 and 1579 for the Inglis family

Scott Monument, Edinburgh. Tel: 0131-529 4068. Monument affording fine views of the city

Seton Collegiate Church (HS), nr Tranent, East Lothian. Founded 1492 by the 4th Lord Seton. Monuments survive within church

Skipness Castle, (HS) Tarbert, Argyll. Tel: 0131-668 8800. Ruins of 13th-century castle and chapel overlooking Kilbrannon Sound, probably built by the Macdonald Lord of the Isles

*Smailholm Tower (HS), Scottish Borders. Tel: 01573-460365. Well-preserved tower-house

Spynie Palace (HS), Elgin, Moray. Tel: 01343-546358. Closed weekdays in winter. Residence of Bishops of Moray from 14th to 17th centuries

St Giles Cathedral, Edinburgh. Church on site since 854, existing building dates from 15th century following sacking by the English in 1385

St Andrews Castle and Cathedral (HS), Fife. Tel: 01334-477196 (castle); 01334-472563 (cathedral). Ruins of 13th-century castle and remains of the largest cathedral in Scotland

St Blane's Church (HS) Kingarth, Bute. Site of Celtic community of 6th century. In centre of site is a 12th-century chapel

St Clement's Church (HS) Rodel, Harris. A 16th-century cruciform-plan church. Built by Alasdair Crotach MacLeod

St John's Kirk, Perth. Founded by David I, 1126. Present building dates from 15th century. John Knox preached here

St Machar's Cathedral, Aberdeen. Medieval cathedral of Bishops of Aberdeen. Reputedly founded 580 by Machar, follower of Columba

St Magnus Cathedral, Kirkwall, Orkney. Closed Sun. mornings. Founded 1137 by Orkney Earl Rognvald. Dedicated to St Magnus the Martyr. Completed 1500 and one of finest in Scotland

St Ninian's Chapel (HS), Isle of Whithorn, Galloway. Ruins of 13th-century chapel on site associated with St Ninian

Stirling Castle and Argyll's Lodging (HS). Tel: 01786-450000. A 17th-century town house, seat of the Campbell Earls of Argyll

*Stranraer Castle, Stranraer. Tel: 01776-705088. Closed Sun. Also known as Castle of St John. Built c.1511. Exhibitions trace history of castle

Strome Castle (NTS), Stromemore, Lochcarron. Ruins of 15th-century castle built for Alan Macdonald Dubh, 12th chief of the Camerons. Destroyed 1602 by Colin McKenzie of Kintail

Sweetheart Abbey (HS), New Abbey Village, Dumfries. Tel: 01387-850397. Closed Sun. mornings, Thurs. afternoons, and Fri. in winter. Remains of 13th/early 14th-century abbey; burial site of John Balliol's heart

Tantallon Castle (HS), E. Lothian. Tel: 01620-892727. Closed Sun. mornings, Thurs. afternoons and Fri. in winter. Fortification with earthwork defences and a 14th-century curtain wall with towers

*Thirlstane Castle, Lauder, Berwickshire. Closed Sat. Tel: 01578-722430. One of finest castles in Scotland owned by Maitland family since 16th century

*Threave Castle (HS), Dumfries and Galloway. Late 14th-century tower on an island; reached by boat, long walk to castle

Tolquhon Castle (HS), nr Aberdeen. Tel: 01651-851286. Closed weekdays in winter. Mansion house with 15th-century tower

Torosay Castle, Craignure, Mull. Tel: 01680-812421. Castellated mansion of 1858 built for the Campbells of Possel. A 18th-century Venetian statues and Japanese garden

*Traquair House, Innerleithen, Peeblesshire. Tel: 01896-830323. Scotland's oldest inhabited house. Bonnie Prince Charlie stayed here in 1745. Working 18th century brewery. Gardens and maze

Tullibardine Chapel (HS), nr Crieff. Medieval church founded 1446, rebuilt 1500. One of most complete small collegiate churches in Scotland

Urquhart Castle (HS), Loch Ness. Tel: 01456-450551. Ruins of 13th-17th-century castle built as a base to guard the Great Glen. Taken by Edward I of England

Wallace Monument, Stirling. Tel: 01786-472140. Closed Jan. and Feb. Exhibitions about Sir William Wallace and others, and a diorama showing the view from the top of the monument

*Whithorn Priory (HS), nr Newton Stewart, Dumfries and Galloway. Tel: 01988-500700. Site of first Christian church in Scotland, dedicated to St Ninian in 5th-century. Popular place of pilgrimage in medieval times

ARCHAEOLOGICAL SITES

Many visible traces remain throughout Scotland of prehistoric and early historic (to end of first millennium AD) settlement. Mesolithic sites well over 6,000 years old have been found in many parts of Scotland, generally in coastal areas and along rivers. Stone, Bronze and Iron Age settlement and the Pictish period of the early Christian era are extensively represented. Archaeological sites can be found and visited in all parts of Scotland, but the north and west and the islands are particularly rich in them, partly because the stone that was used in construction there is more durable than the wood and turf commonly used for building in the south of Scotland, and partly also because the disturbance due to modern agriculture has been less intensive in the Highlands and Islands. However, the north-east also has a good number of ancient sites.

THE NEOLITHIC PERIOD

The Neolithic period, c. 4000–2000 BC, was characterised by communal monuments serving both the living and the dead, such as stone circles, henges and domestic settlements as well as chambered cairns and other massive communal burial places. Among the best-preserved chambered cairns are the 'Tomb of the Eagles' at Isbister, South Ronaldsay, and Maes Howe on Mainland, both in Orkney. Neolithic communities include Skara Brae on Orkney and the first layers of the large Jarlshof site in Shetland. The Neolithic period also produced many of the best-known standing stones and stone circles, which had ritual and perhaps astronomical functions. Examples are the standing stone circle at Callanish (Calanais) on Lewis, the Twelve Apostles in Dumfries, Scotland's largest stone circle, and the Ring of Brodgar (Brogar) on Orkney. However, standing stones continued to be erected right through to the early Middle Ages, and can be found throughout Scotland, often in spectacular settings.

THE BRONZE AGE

During the Bronze Age, c.2000–700 BC, burial took place in individual cairns and tombs, sometimes arranged in 'cemeteries' and sometimes located within existing stone monuments, as at Cairnpapple, West Lothian. Although they are not as numerous as Iron Age settlements, traces of Bronze Age domestic settlements exist, for instance, on the island of Whalsay, Shetland, and at Lairg, Sutherland.

Towards the end of the Bronze Age the building of enclosed and fortified settlements increased. Some of the largest hillforts in the south of Scotland show evidence of having been built in the later Bronze Age (e.g. Traprain Law, East Lothian, and Eildon Hill, Borders), and they appear to have continued in occupation for many centuries, as the important hoard of Roman silver found at Traprain Law suggests.

THE IRON AGE

The different forms of Iron Age dwelling vary widely with time and place, and include several different kinds of roundhouse of timber or stone, massive hilltop forts or enclosures sheltering a number of small roundhouses, drystone broch towers and broch villages, and crannogs – artificial islet dwellings built in lochs and joined to the shore by defended causeways. The wide regional variations are partly – but not entirely – accounted for by the geography of the country, which posed different defensive problems in different places: small dispersed settlements grew up in the broken landscapes of the north and west, where arable land was interrupted and access made difficult by deep sea-lochs and high, steep mountains, while large hillforts were more characteristic of the more open, rolling country of the east and the lowlands with its broad, flat upland summits.

Probably the best known of these structures, being the best preserved, are the brochs. These are concentrated particularly in the north and west and in Orkney and Shetland, although a group of lowland brochs was built in Angus, Perthshire and the Borders, most probably in the first century AD. Stone hut circles and roundhouses predominate in the north and east; traces of similar timber buildings are found in the lowlands; crannogs belong particularly to the Highlands and the south-west (and to Ireland). A group of Iron Age wheelhouses comprises one of the many layers of settlement at Jarlshof in Shetland.

THE ROMANS AND AFTER

While traces of the first Roman invasion of Scotland under Agricola (AD 81–83) can be seen in the remains of a string of forts thrown up to block the Forth-Clyde isthmus, and later forts, signal stations and roads built to consolidate the Roman gains, the most visible sign of the troubled Roman presence in what is now Scotland is the Antonine Wall.

From the seventh to ninth centuries – the so-called Dark Ages – symbol stones and cross-slabs were erected by the Picts, who by the seventh century had mostly been converted to Christianity. These stones occur throughout Scotland, with concentrations in the Pictish territory along the east coast and the Moray Firth and in the far north. While there are some Pictish stones in the West Highlands, the great carved crosses characteristic of the area ruled by the Lords of the Isles until the end of the 15th-century illustrate a later artistic tradition dating from the middle ages and centred upon Iona.

The Pictish symbol stones from the seventh and early eighth centuries, usually carved only on one face and most often with the figures of animals, are probably gravestones. Examples are at Aberlemno, Forfar (Angus), Papil (Shetland), and a collection of most of the Pictish stones found in Sutherland is now in the grounds of Dunrobin Castle Museum, near Golspie.

A slightly later introduction in the eighth and ninth centuries was the more intricately carved and more obviously Christian cross-slab, in which ornamented crosses on one face are often combined with Pictish symbols on the other. The decoration of these slabs shows the influence of the Dalriadic (originally Irish) style that also produced Book of Kells on Iona. Some of them may have served as landmarks where people might gather for worship or private prayer, or as the focus of religious processions. A battle scene on one of the stones at Aberlemno may depict the victory of the Picts over the Northumbrians at

Nechtansmere (685). Other excellent examples are at Shandwick, Rosemarkie and Nigg (Ross and Cromarty); but many of the slabs are no longer in their original positions and have been re-erected (or even incorporated) inside churches and other buildings.

Aberlemno Sculptured Stones (HS), nr Forfar, Angus. cross-slab with Pictish symbols and four other sculptured Pictish stones

Achavanich Stone Setting, nr Latheron, Caithness. Thirty-six small standing stones arranged in shape of a horseshoe. Nearby cairn dates to Neolithic period

Achnabreck Cup and Ring Marks (HS), nr Lochgilphead, Kilmartin Glen, Argyll. Among the most impressive and largest ring marks in Scotland, dating over a long period of time

Aiky Brae Recumbent Stone Circle, Old Deer, Aberdeenshire. Hilltop circle dating from third or second millennium BC

Antonine Wall (HS), between the Clyde and the Forth. Adm. free. Built c. AD 142, consists of ditch, turf rampart and road, with forts every two miles

Arbory Hill Fort, Abington, Lanarkshire. Stone fort with earlier ditches and ramparts. Includes hut circles

Ardestie, Carlungie and Tealing Souterrains (HS), nr Monifieth, Angus. Iron age food cellars, the first two 80 feet and 150 feet in length respectively. Probably in use between AD 150 and AD 450. Nearby stone huts. Sites approximately 1 mile apart

Auchagallon Cairn (HS), nr Blackwaterfoot, Arran. Stone cairn surrounded by stone circle

Balfarg Henge, nr Glenrothes, Fife. Timber circle built around 3000 BC. Stone circle – only two stones remain. Possible ritual site in fourth millennium bc

Ballinaby Standing Stones, nr Bruichladdich, Islay. Originally three standing stones of second millennium BC, two remain. The tallest at 5 metres is one of the tallest standing stones in western Scotland

Ballochmyle Cup and Ring Marks, nr Mauchline, Ayrshire. As well as cup and rings, motifs include geometric shapes. Discovered 1986. One of the largest in Britain

Ballymeanoch Standing Stones, nr Kilmartin, Kilmartin Glen, Argyll. Four stones lying parallel to two others. Nearby fallen stone has a hole through it. Possibly used to seal marriage vows, hands would be joined through the hole in the stone

Barnhouse Settlement, nr Stromness, Orkney. Reconstructed foundations of a Neolithic village. With fifteen houses, similar to those found at Skara Brae

Barpa Langass Chambered Cairn, nr Lochmaddy, North Uist. Chambered burial cairn, 25 metres in diameter and 4 metres in height. Chamber has collapsed and is too dangerous to enter but can be viewed from outside

Ben Freiceadain, nr Dorrery, Caithness. Extensive fort of first millennium BC, known as Buaile Oscar. Occupies the summit of the hill. Within the fort is the remains of a Neolithic chambered cairn. Close-by are Neolithic and Bronze Age cairns

Benie Hoose, Whalsay, Shetland. Bronze Age house, over 1,800 tools discovered here. Nearby chambered tomb

Blackhammer Chambered Cairn (HS), Rousay, Orkney. Chambered tomb with seven burial compartments

Brough of Birsay (HS), Mainland, Orkney. Pictish settlement on a small tidal island. Remains of Norse church and village

Burghead Fort and Well (HS), Burghead, Moray. Promontory fort dating from first millennium AD, one of the main centres of Pictish power

Burgi Geos (HS), Yell, Shetland. Iron Age Fort and field system

Cairn of Get (HS), nr Ulbster, Caithness. Chambered cairn dating from fourth or third millennium BC. Excavations in 1866 revealed bones of at least seven people along with animal bone, flint and pottery fragments. Nearby cairn maybe a Bronze Age cairn or a Pictish grave of first millennium AD

Cairnholy Chambered Cairns (HS), nr Creetown, Dumfries and Galloway. Remains of two chambered cairns overlooking Wigtown Bay. Traces of fires and pottery suggest possible sites for ceremonies connected with burials

Cairnbaan Cup and Ring Marks (HS), nr Lochgilphead, Argyll. Two rock outcrops carved with cups and rings

Cairnpapple Hill (HS), nr Bathgate, West Lothian. Tel: 01506-634622. Closed Oct.-Mar. Burial site dating from 3000 BC to 1400 BC. Three standing stones in centre surrounded by a henge. Used for burials and held sacred into the Iron Age

Caisteal Grugaig Broch, Totaig, Inverness-shire. Late first-millennium broch on hillside overlooking the junction of Loch Alsh, Loch Duich and Loch Long

Calanais (Callanish) Standing Stones (HS). Callanish, Lewis. Tel: 01851-621422. Visitor centred closed Sundays. Slabs of gneiss up to 4.7 metres in height, arranged in a the shape of a Celtic Cross. Transported here between 3000 BC and 1500 BC. Many stones aligned with the sun and stars; possible lunar observatory

Capo Long Barrow, nr Brechin, Kincardine and Deeside. Situated in clearing in Inglislmaldie Forest. Neolithic earthen long mound measuring 80 metres in length and 28 metres in width. Probable burials and mortuary structures

Carn Liath (HS), nr Golspie, Sutherland. Iron Age broch. Excavations in late 19th century uncovered beads, rings and bangles

Castle Haven, nr Borgue, Dumfries and Galloway. Galleried dun. Restored early 20th-century

Castlelaw Hill Fort (HS), nr Glencorse, Midlothian. Iron Age fort in Pentland Hills. Includes fenced enclosure dating to first millennium BC and 20-metre long souterrain dug into silted-up ditch of fort, probably of Roman origin

Caterthuns Forts (HS), nr Menmuir, Angus. Iron Age fort and settlements sat on top of neighbouring hills, Brown Caterthun and White Caterthun. Excavations suggest dates 700 BC to 300 BC for stoneworks

Catpund Quarries, nr Cunningsburgh, Shetland. In Norse times, the biggest soapstone quarry in the world

Chesters Hill Fort (HS), nr Drem, East Lothian. Oval Iron Age fort. Within hill fort are at least 20 hut circles

Clach a' Charridh, nr Shandwick, Ross and Cromarty. Late 8th or early 9th century cross-slab and one of the most impressive of all Pictish monuments standing in original position on hill overlooking Shandwick. Covered by glass for protection

Clach an Trushal Standing Stone, nr Barvas, Lewis. At over 6 metres in height, is one of the tallest in Scotland

Clava Cairns (NTS), nr Inverness, Highlands. Also known as Balnuaran of Clava. Burial chambers clustered on bank of River Nairn, near site of Culloden. Erected some time around 2000 BC and encircled by standing stones. Cremated remains have been found

Cleaven Dyke, nr Blairgowrie, Perthshire. Long bank over 2 km in length and flanked by ditches. Probably the route along which communal ritual of funerary ceremonies would have passed

Clickhimin Broch (HS), nr Lerwick, Shetland. Broch tower and Iron Age outbuildings on what was once a small island in Clickhimin Loch. Settlement began around 700 BC

Cnoc Freiceadain Chambered Cairns (HS), nr Thurso, Caithness. Two long cairns now covered in grass. One which measures 78 metres in length, is one of the largest in Scotland

Corrimony Chambered Cairn (HS), nr Drumnadrochit, Glen Urquhart, Highlands. Circular cairn similar to the Clava Cairns near Inverness dating to third millennium BC. Excavations have found that the chamber contained a crouched body

Craig Phadrig Fort, nr Inverness. Dates from millennium BC with additions 6th–7th centuries AD. Occupies summit of wooded hill owned by Forestry Commission

Cullerlie Stone Circle (HS), nr Westhill, Aberdeenshire. Circle of eight boulders surrounding eight cairns dating to second millennium BC. Excavations revealed circular pit containing cremated human bone

Culsh Souterrain (HS), nr Tarland, Aberdeenshire. Iron age underground passage and food-cellar, 12 metres long and 2 metres wide and high

Cuween Hill Chambered Cairn (HS), nr Finstown, Orkney. Chambered tomb which contained the skulls of 24 dogs and the skeletal remains of eight humans

Dreva Craig Fort, nr Biggar, Borders. Fort, hut circles and field systems dating to the late Iron Age. Round houses inside the fort

Dun-Da-Lamh Fort, nr Laggan, Inverness-shire. Dating to first millennium AD, built on ridge known as the Black Craig

Dun Ardtreck, nr Corbost, Ardtreck Point, Skye. Dun or fort. Ruins lie on stack of rock 20 metres above the shore. Walls up to 3 metres thick with traces of a gallery

Dun Beag Broch (HS), nr Dunvegan, Struanmore, Skye. One of the best preserved brochs on Skye. Excavations have found a variety of artefacts including pottery, beads, rings, numerous tools and bone and horn objects

Dun Bharpa Chambered Cairn, nr Castlebay, Barra. Impressive chambered cairn measuring 25 metres in diameter and 5 metres in height. No longer possible to enter cairn

Dun Charlabhaig (Carloway) Broch (HS), Carloway, Lewis. One of the best preserved brochs on Scotland's Atlantic coast. Measures up to 9 metres at its tallest point. Nearby Doune Broch Centre. Tel: 01851-643338. Closed Nov.–Mar, and Sundays.

Dun Dornaigil Broch (HS), nr south end of Loch Hope, Caithness. Also known as Dun Dornadilla. One section almost 7 metres high. Interior full of rubble. Broch tower which may have housed local nobility

Dun Fiadhairt Broch, nr Dunvegan, Skye. Also known as Dun of Iardhard. On shores of Camalig Bay. Excavated in 1914. Objects found include pottery, an amber necklace and a terracotta model of a bale of goods of Roman origin

Dun Gerashader Fort, Portree, Skye. A once-powerful fort with walls 4 metres thick. Most of the dun has gone to make dry walls on nearby farms, but traces of walls still recognisable

Dun Lagaidh, Loch Broom, Ross and Cromarty. Three successive fortifications built on a ridge on western shore of Loch Broom. Vitrified fort dates to first millennium BC, the dun to the early centuries AD; also medieval castle, probably built 12th-century AD

Dun Mor Broch, Vaul, nr Scarinish, Tiree. Constructed first century BC, continued in use until the Norse period. Broch survives up to 2 metres in height

Dun Ringill, Kilmarie, Skye. Galleried dun. Foundations of two medieval buildings inside the dun

Dun Telve Broch (HS), nr Glenelg, Lochalsh. One of the best preserved Iron Age broch towers in Scotland, although much of the wall is missing. Built around 2000 years ago to protect surrounding settlements from raiders. Excavations have found pottery and stone cups which may have been used as lamps

Dun Troddan Broch (HS), nr Glenelg, Lochalsh. Lies less than 1 mile from Dun Telve. A section of the wall and staircase survive. Together the two are also known as Glenelg Broch

Dun an Sticar Broch, nr Lochmaddy, North Uist. One of best preserved brochs in the Western Isles, surviving to a height of 3 metres. Medieval rectangular house inside dun. Nearby causeway is also medieval in date. Can only be viewed from the outside

Dunfallandy Stone (HS), nr Pitlochry, Perthshire. Pictish sculptured cross-slab, dating from 9th-century

Dwarfie Stane Rock (HS), Hoy, Orkney. Chambered tomb cut from a solid block of sandstone, dating to 3000 BC. Named "Dvergasteinn" by the Norse settlers who believed it to be the home of dwarfs

Easter Aquorthies Stone Circle (HS), nr Inverurie, Aberdeenshire. Dating from third millennium BC. Circle measures almost 20 metres

in diameter. Raised in centre, indicative of a burial cairn. Different stone types include pink porphyry, red and grey granite and red jasper

Edin's Hall Broch (HS), nr Preston, Borders. Oval Iron Age fort with ditches and a broch built in a corner of the fort. Internal diameter of 17 metres and walls 5 metres thick

Eildon Hill Fort, nr Melrose, Borders. Summit of Eildon Hill North. Occupied since Bronze Age. Included some 300 houses dating to Bronze and Iron Ages. Also traces of a Roman signal station

Eileach an Naoimh (HS), island in Garvellach group, north of Jura. Ruins of beehive cells from an early Christian community. Small underground cell. Supposedly traditional burial place of Eithne, Columba's mother.

Embo Chambered Cairn, Embo, Sutherland. Dating to between fourth and second millennium BC. Remains of stone cairn containing two Neolithic burial chambers and also Bronze Age graves

Finavon Fort, nr Forfar, Angus. Pictish or Roman fort on the ridge of Finavon Hill. Destroyed by fire and vitrified by the heat

Glassel Stone Setting, nr Banchory, Aberdeenshire. Oval setting of five granite pillars dating to second millennium BC

Grain Souterrain (HS), Kirkwall, Orkney. Now in centre of an industrial site. Iron Age food cellar almost 2 metres below the ground dating to the first millennium BC. Excavations have found a hearth, animal bones and shells

Grey Cairns of Camster (HS), nr Lybster, Caithness. Burial chambers built 4000–5000 years ago. Includes a massive round cairn 18 metres in diameter and a long cairn 70 metres in length covered with two separate round cairns

Gurness Broch (HS), nr Evie, Orkney. Closed Oct.–Mar. Best preserved broch in the area, surrounded by a complex of later buildings. Some houses date to late Iron Age. Iron Age house has been reconstructed next to the visitors' centre

High Banks Cup and Ring Marks, nr Kirkcudbright, Dumfries and Galloway. Over 350 cup and cup and ring marks, some of the most impressive of south-west Scotland

Hill o' Many Stanes (HS), nr Lybster, Caithness. Also known as the Mid Clyth stone rows. Consists of 200 boulders forming 22 parallel rows down the side of the hill. Purpose unknown but possibly an astronomical observatory

Holm of Papa Westray Chambered Cairns (HS), Island and Holm of Papa Westray, Orkney. Two chambered tombs, one at either end of the island, the one to the north being part of an earlier tomb

Holyrood Park Settlements (HS), Edinburgh. Natural wilderness in heart of Edinburgh containing four forts and several settlements dating from late Bronze Age and Iron Age. Forts on Arthur's Seat, above Samson's Rib and beside Dunsapie Loch. Hut circles near Hunter's Bog

Ibister Chambered Cairn, nr St Margaret's Hope, South Ronaldsay, Orkney. Tel: 01856-831339. Closed afternoons Nov.–Mar. Also known as 'Tomb of the Eagles', as bones and talons from white-tailed sea eagles were uncovered here. Ancient chambered burial cairn. Remains of 340 people recovered during excavations in 1970s

Jarlshof Settlement (HS), Sumburgh Head, Shetland. Tel: 01950-460112. Closed Oct.–Mar. Largest and most impressive archaeological site in Scotland. Covers three acres, with more than 4000 years of continuous occupation. Earliest buildings date to Neolithic period. Iron Age buildings include a broch, roundhouses and wheelhouses. Norse farmhouses. Latest building dates to the 17th-century laird's house

Kemp's Walk Fort, nr Stranraer, Dumfries and Galloway. The largest of Galloway's promontory forts, overlooking Broadsea Bay and measuring 83 metres by 44 metres

Kildonan Dun, nr Campbeltown, Kintyre. Drystone-walled dun dating to first or second century AD. Re-occupied 9th–12th-centuries. Occupied into medieval times

Kilphedir Broch and Hut Circles, Kilphedir, Sutherland. Broch and hut circles dating to the late Bronze Age. Pottery, stone and flint tools have been unearthed during excavations

Kintraw Cairns and Standing Stone, nr Kilmartin, Argyll. Cairns excavated 1956–60 and unearthed cremated bone, shells and jet beads. Site possibly marks the sunset at mid-winter solstice as the sun set through notch in Paps of Jura

Knap of Howe (HS), Papa Westray, Orkney. The island's prime prehistoric site dating from 3500 BC. Neolithic farm-building lays claims to be the oldest standing house in Europe. Bone and stone implements have been uncovered during excavations in the 1930s and 1970s

Knock Farril Fort, nr Dingwall, Ross and Cromarty. Date from late second or first millennium BC. Occupies summit of ridge overlooking Strath Peffer

Knowe of Yarsar, Rousay, Orkney. Chambered cairn dating to 3500 BC. Remains of 29 humans discovered here along with deer bones

Liddle Burnt Mound, nr St Margaret's Hope, Orkney. Probably Bronze Age in date. One of very few to have been excavated. Consists of a central stone-built trough, surrounded by paving and a stone wall, possibly a windbreak. Served as a cooking area or sauna

Loanhead of Daviot Stone Circle (HS), nr Inverurie, Aberdeenshire. Dated to third or second millennia BC. Recumbent stone circle over 20 metres in diameter consisting of eight standing stones, the recumbent and flankers. Ring cairn later constructed within circle. Beside circle is a Bronze Age cremation cemetery. Excavations uncovered remains of 30 humans in urns and pits

Lochbuie Stone Circle, Lochbuie, Mull. Circle containing nine stones, one replaced by a boulder, and three outliers. Possibly used for astronomical observations

Lundin Links Standing Stones, Lundin Links golf course, Fife. Three standing stones remaining of a stone circle, the tallest 5 metres in height. According to legend the gravestones of three Danish warriors defeated by Macbeth

Machrie Moor Stone Circles (HS), nr Blackwaterfoot, Arran. The area of Machrie Moor contains hut circles, chambered cairns, round cairns and six Bronze Age stone circles, the most impressive has three sandstone pillars over 5 metres in height

Maes Howe Chambered Cairn (HS), West Mainland, Orkney. Tel: 01856-76106. Closed Thurs. afternoons, Fri. and Sun. mornings Nov.–Mar. Probably the most impressive Neolithic burial chamber in Europe dating from around 3000 BC. Original capping destroyed in 12th-century

Maiden Stone (HS), Chapel of Garioch, Aberdeenshire. One of the finest Pictish stones in Grampian dating from 9th-century

Meigle Sculptured Stones (HS), Meigle, Angus. Tel: 01828-640612. Exhibition in museum, closed Oct.–Mar. Collection of 25 sculptured stones. Early Christian and Dark Age sculpture

Memsie Round Cairn (HS), Rathen, Aberdeenshire. Dating to Bronze Age, great cairn of bare stones, 24 metres in diameter and over 4 metres in height. Only survivor of a cemetery of three large cairns on the low ridge of Cairn Muir

Midhowe Broch (HS), Rousay, Orkney. Originally built as fortified family house. Continuously occupied until second century AD. A number of houses surround the broch

Midhowe Chambered Cairn (HS), Rousay, Orkney. 100 foot communal burial chamber dating to 3500 BC. Chamber divided into 12 compartments where remains of 25 people were found in a crouched position

Mither Tap o' Bennachie, nr Inverurie, Aberdeenshire. Granite tor, the summit of which is flanked by stone-walled hillfort dating to first millennium AD. Excavations in 1870s revealed ten hut foundations. Area north of Bennachie may be site of battle of Mons Graupius in AD 84

Mousa Broch (HS), Mousa, Shetland. The best preserved prehistoric broch in Scotland standing over 13 metres in height. Thought to be around 2000 years old. In the courtyard are remains of a wheelhouse, built around third century AD

Mutiny Stones Long Cairn, nr Longformacus, Borders. About 80 metres long and 20 metres wide, one of very few long cairns in the Borders

Na Fir Bhreige, nr Lochmaddy, North Uist. Also known as 'the Three False Men'. Three standing stones which according to legend represent three spies buried alive or three men who deserted their wives and were turned to stone by a witch

Ness of Burgi Fort (HS), nr Sumburgh, Shetland. Blockhouse positioned across the neck of the Scatness Peninsula. Access difficult and dangerous in bad weather

Nether Largie Cairns (HS), Kilmartin, Kilmartin Glen, Argyll. Bronze Age and Neolithic cairns. Three cairns forming part of a large complex of stones and tombs in the Kilmartin Glen. Nether Largie South is a chambered cairn. Carved with cupmarks

New and Old Kinord Settlement, nr Ballater, Kincardine and Deeside. Probably dates from latter part of first millennium BC. Hut circles in an enclosure, the largest 19 metres in diameter. Settlement also contains a souterrain

Ord Archaeological Trail, The Ord, Lairg, Sutherland. Tel: 01549-402638. Hill overlooking Loch Shin containing a number of structures dating from Neolithic to post-Medieval period. Two chambered cairns near summit. Hut circles date from 1500 BC

Pobull Fhinn Stone Circle, nr Lochmaddy, North Uist. Originally 48 stones of which 30 remain. Occupies amphitheatre cut into hillside

Quoyness Chambered Cairn (HS), nr Kettletoft, Sanday, Orkney. Megalithic tomb dating from around 2000 BC. Partially re-constructed. Human bones found during excavations in 1860s

Raedykes Ring Cairns, nr Stonehaven, Aberdeenshire. Strung out along the crest of Campstone Hill, an important group of early ritual sites dating to the third or second millennium BC

Rennibister Souterrain (HS), nr Kirkwall, Orkney. Iron Age semi-underground structure used to store grain and produce dating to first millennium BC. Excavations uncovered remains of 18 people—rare to fine human bones in an earth-house, so possibly converted to a burial vault

Ring of Brodgar Circle and Henge (HS), nr Stromness, Orkney. Neolithic circle and one of the largest stone circles in Scotland. originally 60 stones of which just 36 remain. Only the ditch remains of the henge. Possibly part of a ritual complex which included Maes Howe and the Stones of Stenness

Rubh' an Dunain Cairn and Dun, nr Glenbrittle, Skye. When cairn was excavated in 1930s pottery and flints artefacts were uncovered as well as bones of several people. Near the cairn are the remains of an Iron Age fort, one of best preserved galleried duns in Skye

Scatness Broch and Settlement, Sumburgh, Shetland. Tel: 01595-694688. Accessible July and Aug. Excavations currently taking place west of the airport. Ancient broch and Iron Age village which may include Norse occupation. One of the buildings was reused by the Vikings as a smithy

St Vigeans Sculptured Stones (HS), nr Arbroath, Angus. Exhibition closed Oct.–Mar. Early Christian and Pictish stones housed in cottages

Scord of Brouster Settlement, nr Bridge of Walls, Shetland. Ruined houses and field boundaries occupied between 3000 and 1500 BC

Skara Brae Settlement (HS), nr Stromness, Orkney. Tel: 01856-841815. Closed Sun. morning Oct.–Mar. One of the best preserved Stone Age settlements in Europe, dating back to 3000 BC. Excavated by V.G. Childe in 1920s. Reconstructed house next to visitor centre. Visitor centre displays stone and bone artefacts as well as pottery discovered during excavations

Staneydale Settlement (HS), nr Bridge of Walls, Shetland. Shattered Neolithic structure. Surrounding oval-shaped houses in ruins. Probably once an important community meeting-place

Stone of Settar, Eday, Orkney. Orkney's most distinctive standing stone

Stones of Stenness and Henge (HS), nr Stromness, Orkney. Originally a circle of 12 rock slabs, just four remain. Dates back to the same time as the nearby Neolithic village, the Barnhouse Settlement

Strathpeffer Symbol Stone, Strathpeffer, Ross and Cromarty. Pictish symbol stone dating from 7th-or-8th century AD. Often called The Eagle Stone

Strontoiller Cairn and Standing Stones, nr Oban, Argyll. Standing stone stands 4 metres high. According to legend it is said to mark the grave of Diarmid, a mythical hero of Ireland. Excavations of the cairn have found cremated bone along with quartz chips and pebbles

Sueno's Stone (HS), Forres, Moray. Probably the most remarkable sculptured stone in Scotland. Dating from 9th-century and over 22 feet in height. Protected by glass enclosure

Sunhoney Stone Circle, nr Banchory, Aberdeenshire. Consists of 11 standing stones of red granite and a recumbent stone of grey granite carved with cupmarks. Within the circle is a ring cairn

Tap o' Noth Fort, nr Rhynie, Aberdeenshire. Timber-laced stone rampart, originally 8 metres thick, on top of a high hill. Up to 150 hut platforms within fort

Taversoe Tuick Chambered Cairn (HS), Rousay, Orkney. Two-storey chambered cairn dating to 3500 BC. Piles of bones found in lower chamber, cremated remains in upper chamber. Pottery bowls also recovered

Temple Wood Stone Circles (HS), nr Kilmartin, Kilmartin Glen, Argyll. Stone circle 12 metres in diameter. One stone is decorated with two concentric circles and another with a double spiral. Excavations have revealed an earlier timber and stone circles

Tinto Hill Cairn, nr Biggar, Lanarkshire. One of largest Bronze Age round cairns in Scotland, situated on top of Tinto Hill. Measures 45 metres in diameter and 6 metres in height

Tirefour Broch, nr Achnacroish, Lismore. Iron Age broch. Stands up to 5 metres in height on one side

Tomnaverie Stone Circle (HS), nr Aboyne, Aberdeenshire. Dating from third or second millennium bc. Red granite circle, 18 metres in diameter. Four uprights and the recumbent remain in place. Ring of smaller stones within the circle

Torhouse Stone Circle (HS), nr Wigtown, Dumfries and Galloway. Circle of 19 granite boulders. Three stones in middle of the circle

Torwoodlee Fort and Broch, nr Galashiels, Borders. Ruins of broch now less than 1 metre in height. Built on site of an earlier fort. Probably demolished by the Romans

Traprain Law Fort, nr East Linton, East Lothian. Two ramparts on summit of Traprain Law. Artefacts dating back to the Neolithic period have been unearthed. Collection of late Roman silver found under floor of one of the many houses around the summit

Tullos Hill Round Cairns, Loirston, nr Aberdeen. Four cairns, the remains of an important cairn cemetery of the Bronze Age

Twelve Apostles Stone Circle, nr Dumfries, Dumfries and Galloway. The largest stone circle in Scotland and one of the largest in Britain, measuring 87 metres at widest point. 11 stones remain. Originally thought to have consisted of 18 stones

Tynron Doon, nr Moniaive, Achengibbert Hill, Dumfries and Galloway. Iron Age fort on summit of the hill. Used until relatively recently with tower house built in late 16th-century. Outlines of hut circles

Unival Chambered Cairn, nr Claddach Illeray, North Uist. Square cairn now robbed of much of its stone

Unstan Chambered Cairn (HS), nr Stromness, Orkney. Situated on promontory in the Loch of Stenness. Concentric rings of drystone walling. Skeletal remains found in chambers along with animal and bird bones and shards of pottery known as Unstan Ware

Vinquay Chambered Cairn, Eday, Orkney. Neolithic burial chamber dating from around 3000 BC

Wag of Forse Broch and Settlement, nr Latheron, Caithness. Turf-walled enclosure and remains of a number of houses including roundhouses and brochs. Also rectangular buildings known as 'wags'. Best preserved dwelling is 12 metres long with two rows of stone pillars

Wideford Hill Chambered Cairn, nr Kirkwall, Orkney. Neolithic burial chamber, similar to chambered cairn at Maes Howe

Yoxie Biggins, Whalsay, Shetland. Bronze Age house. Also known as The Standing Stones of Yoxie as the megaliths were used to form the walls, many still standing. Excavations have unearthed stone tools and pottery

MUSEUMS AND GALLERIES

There are almost 300 museums and galleries in Scotland, of which 288 are fully or provisionally registered with the Museums and Galleries Commission. Registration indicates that they have an appropriate constitution, are soundly financed, have satisfactory collection management standards and public services, and have access to professional curatorial advice. Museums should achieve full or provisional registration status in order to be eligible for grants from the Museums and Galleries Commission and from the Scottish Museums Council. Of the registered museums in Scotland, 136 are run by a local authority and 111 are independently run.

The national collections in Scotland are the National Galleries of Scotland and the National Museums of Scotland, which are funded by direct government grant-in-aid. In line with the National Cultural Strategy, launched in August

2000, the National Museums of Scotland removed admission charges at the Royal Museum and the National Museum of Scotland, both in Edinburgh, from 1 April 2001. An online art museum (www.24hourmuseum.org.uk) has also been awarded national collection status.

Local authority museums are funded by the local authority and may also receive grants from the Museums and Galleries Commission. Independent museums and galleries mainly rely on their own resources but are also eligible for grants from the Museums and Galleries Commission.

The Scottish Museums Council is one of ten area museum councils in the UK. It is an independent charity that receives an annual grant from the Scottish Executive, and gives advice and support to museums in Scotland. It may offer improvement grants and also assists with training and marketing.

OPEN TO THE PUBLIC

The following is a selection of the museums and art galleries in Scotland. Opening hours vary. Most museums are closed on Christmas Eve, Christmas Day, Boxing Day and New Year's Day; some are closed on Good Friday or the May Day Bank Holiday. Most small museums, especially in rural areas, are closed during the winter (this can be defined as any period from October to May). Some smaller museums close at lunchtimes, on Saturday and/or Sunday mornings, or all day Sunday; others may open only on a few days each week. Information about a specific museum or gallery should be checked by telephone with the museum itself, where telephone numbers are given, or with the local tourist office.

Local authority museum/gallery

ABERDEEN

*Aberdeen Art Gallery
Schoolhill. Tel: 01224-523700. Mornings. Art from the 18th to 20th-century

*Aberdeen Maritime Museum
Shiprow. Tel: 01224-337700. Maritime history, including shipbuilding and North Sea oil

*Arts Centre Gallery
King Street. Tel: 01224-635208. Exhibitions of contemporary art

Gordon Highlanders Museum
St Luke's, Viewfield Road. Tel: 01224-311200

Marischal Museum
University of Aberdeen, Broad Street. Tel: 01224-274301. Foreign ethnography, local history and archaeology

*Tolbooth Museum of Civic History
Castle Street. Tel: 01224-621167. The history of Aberdeen, housed in what was originally the city's prison

ALFORD

Grampian Transport Museum
Main Street. Tel: 01975-562292. Large collection of road transport vehicles

ANSTRUTHER

Scottish Fisheries Museum
St Ayles, Harbourhead. Tel: 01333-310628. Marine aquarium, fishing boats, period interior and other fishing artefacts

ARBROATH

St Vigean's Museum
St Vigean's. Pictish and earlier remains, including the Drosten Stone, a memorial

*Signal House Museum
Ladyloan. Tel: 01241-875598. Local history museum

ARBUTHNOTT

Grassic Gibbon Centre
Life of locally born author Lewis Grassic Gibbon

ARRAN

Brodick. Arran Heritage Museum.
Tel: 01770-302636. Collection of old tools and furniture in converted 18th-century crofter's farm

BANFF

Duff House (HS)
Tel: 01261-818181. Restored William Adam mansion, housing part of National Galleries of Scotland collection.

BARRA

Baile na Creige (Craigston). Black House Museum.
Thatched crofthouse museum

Castlebay. Barra Heritage Centre.
Tel: 01871-810413. History of Barra and postal system of Western Isles

BETTYHILL

Strathnaver Museum
The old church. Tel: 01641-521418. Local artefacts. Story of the Strathnaver Clearances

BIGGAR

Gladstone Court Museum
North Back Road. Aspects of 19th-century life

Greenhill Covenanters' Museum
Biggar Burn. History of Covenanting Movement

Moat Park Heritage Centre
Kirkstyle. 6,000 year history of Clydesdale

Puppet Museum
Broughton Road. Tel: 01899-220631.
Marionettes from around the world

BIRNAM

Perthshire Visitor Centre
Bankfoot. 'The Macbeth Experience', the true
story of Macbeth

BLANTYRE

David Livingstone Centre
Station Road. Tel: 01698-823140. Museum
relating the life of David Livingstone

BRECHIN

Brechin Museum and Library
St Ninian Square. Tel: 01356-622687. History,
civic memorabilia, geology and painting

BROUGHTON

John Buchan Centre.
Housed in old Free Church. Museum dedicated to
the life and work of novelist John Buchan

BUTE

Rothesay. Bute Museum.
Stuart Street. Tel: 01700-505067. Archaeological
and antiquarian collection. Natural history and
geological exhibits

CAMPBELTOWN

Campbeltown Museum and Library
Hall Street. Tel: 01586-552281. Local history of
Kintyre

CLATTERINGSHAWS LOCH

Galloway Deer Museum
Galloway Forest Park. Wildlife, geology and
history of the area

CLYDEBANK

Clydebank Museum
Dumbarton Road. Social and industrial history,
shipbuilding

COLDSTREAM

Coldstream Museum
Market Square. History of the Coldstream
Guards

CORPACH, nr FORT WILLIAM

Treasures of the Earth. Exhibition of rocks,
crystals, gemstones and fossils. Re-created mine

CRAIL

Crail Museum and Heritage Centre
Marketgate. Local history

CREETOWN

Creetown Gem Rock Museum and Gallery
Chain Road. Tel: 01671-820357. Minerals,
crystals and gemstones from around the world

CROMARTY

Cromarty Museum
The Old Courthouse, Church Street. Tel: 01381-
600418. Local history

CUPAR

Fife Folk Museum
Village Green, Ceres. Tel: 01334-828380.
Historical farming and agricultural exhibits

DOUNE, nr STIRLING

Doune Motor Museum.
Legendary cars including Bentley, Jaguar, Aston
Martin and Rolls Royce

DUMFRIES

*Burns House
Burns Street. Tel: 01387-255297. The house
where Robert Burns died

*Dumfries Museum and Camera Obscura
The Observatory. Tel: 01387-253374. Occupies
18th century windmill. Natural history,
archaeology and folk collections

Robert Burns Centre
Mill Road. Tel: 01387-264808. Displays and
exhibitions relating to Robert Burns and to
Dumfries during his lifetime

DUNBAR

Dunbar Town House Museum
High Street. Tel: 01368 863734. Housed in
former prison. Archaeology and local history

John Muir House
High Street. Birthplace of explorer and naturalist Museum dedicated to his life and work

DUNBEATH

Laidhay Croft Museum
The Highlands before the Clearances

DUNDEE

*Broughty Castle Museum
Broughty Ferry. Tel: 01382-436916. A former estuary fort housing a museum of local history, arms and armour, seashore life and whaling

Discovery Point
Riverside. Tel: 01382-201245. Visitor centre telling the story of Scott's voyage to Antarctica; incorporates the Discovery

Dundee Contemporary Arts
Nethergate. Tel: 01382-432000. Galleries and exhibitions

*McManus Galleries
Albert Square. Tel: 01382-432084. Local history museum and gallery showing temporary art exhibitions. Permanent collection contains seascapes by William McTaggart

DUNFERMLINE

Dunfermline Museum
Viewfield Terrace. Tel: 01383-313838. Local history and social life. Linen and coalmining industries

DUNOON

Dunoon Museum
Castle Hill. History of the Clyde steamers

EDINBURGH

Bank of Scotland Museum
The Mound.Tel: 0131-243 5467. The story of 300 years of banking in Scotland from 1695. Scottish banknotes and coins

Britannia, Leith docks
Tel: 0131-555 5566. Former royal yacht with royal barge and royal family picture gallery. Tickets must be pre-booked

*City Art Centre
Market Street. Tel: 0131-529 3993. Late 19th and 20th-century art and temporary exhibitions

Dean Gallery
Belford Road. Tel: 0131-624 6200. Contemporary works, including sculpture by Sir Eduardo Paolozzi

*Fruit Market Gallery
Market Street. Tel: 0131-225 2383. Contemporary art gallery

*Huntly House Museum
Canongate. Tel: 0131-529 4143. Local history, silver, glass and Scottish pottery

*Museum of Childhood
High Street. Tel: 0131-529 4142. Toys, games, clothes and exhibits relating to the social history of childhood

Museum of Fire
Lauriston Place. Tel: 0131-228 2401. Story of Lothian and Borders fire brigade, the oldest fire brigade in the United Kingdom, founded 1824

Museum of Flight
East Fortune Airfield, nr North Berwick. Tel: 01620-880308. Display of aircraft

National Gallery of Scotland
The Mound. Tel: 0131-624 6200. Paintings, drawings and prints from the 16th to 20th-century, and the national collection of Scottish art

National Museum of Scotland
Chambers Street. Tel: 0131-247 4422. Scottish history from prehistoric times to the present

*The People's Story
Canongate. Tel: 0131-529 4057. Edinburgh life since the 18th century

Royal Museum of Scotland
Chambers Street. Tel: 0131-225 7534. Scottish and international collections from prehistoric times to the present

Royal Scots Regimental Museum
Edinburgh Castle. Tel: 0131-310 5016

Scottish Agricultural Museum
Ingliston. Tel: 0131-333 2674. History of agriculture in Scotland

Scottish National Gallery of Modern Art
Belford Road. Tel: 0131-624 6200. Twentieth-century painting, sculpture and graphic art

Scottish National Portrait Gallery
Queen Street. Tel: 0131-624 6200. Portraits of eminent people in Scottish history, and the national collection of photography

Scottish United Services Museum
Edinburgh Castle. Tel: 0131-225 7534. Collections connected to the Scottish armed forces since the 17th century

Talbot Rice Art Gallery
University of Edinburgh, Old College, South Bridge. Tel: 0131-650 2211. Permanent collection contains 17th-century works from Low Countries, bronzes. Temporary exhibitons of contemporary art

*The Writers' Museum
Lawnmarket. Tel: 0131-529 4901. Robert Louis Stevenson, Walter Scott and Robert Burns exhibits

ELGIN

Elgin Museum
High Street. Tel: 01343-543675. One of United Kingdom's oldest museums. Anthropological collection, fossils, natural history and Pictish relics

EYEMOUTH

Eyemouth Museum
Market Place. Tapestry commemorating east coast fishing disaster of 1881

FORFAR

Meffen Institute Museum and Art Gallery
High Street. Tel: 01307-464123. Exhibits of Neolithic, Pictish and Celtic remains. Re-created historical street scenes

FORRES

Falconer Museum
Tolbooth Street. Tel: 01309-673701. Photographic collection of Moray. Archives of Hugh Falconer, palaeontologist

FORT AUGUSTUS

The Clansmen Centre
Traditional Highland culture

FORT WILLIAM

West Highland Museum
Cameron Square. Tel: 01397-702169. Includes tartan collections, exhibits relating to 1745 uprising, archaeological material

FRASERBURGH

*Museum of Scottish Lighthouses
Kinnaird Head. Tel: 01346-511022. Lighthouse artefacts, including the original Kinnaird Head lighthouse

GAIRLOCH

Gairloch Heritage Museum
Tel: 01445-712287. Geology, archaeology, fishing and farming

GATEHOUSE OF FLEET

Mill on the Fleet Museum
High Street. History of Galloway from inside an old bobbin mill

GLAMIS

Angus Folk Museum (NTS)
Tel: 01307-840288. Local artefacts and section on local bothies

GLASGOW

*Burrell Collection
Pollokshaws Road. Tel: 0141-649 7151. Paintings, textiles, furniture, ceramics, stained glass and silver from classical times to the 19th century

Centre for Contemporary Arts
350 Sauchiehall Street. Tel (temporary): 0141-332 7521. Exhibitions covering broad range of contemporary arts, including visual and performance arts

Collins Gallery
University of Strathclyde, Richmond Street. Tel: 0141-552 4400 ext. 2558. Touring exhibitions of contemporary work by Scottish artists

*Gallery of Modern Art
Queen Street. Tel: 0141-229 1996. Collection of contemporary Scottish and world art

*Glasgow Art Gallery and Museum
Kelvingrove. Tel: 0141-287 2699. Includes Old Masters, 19th-century French paintings and armour collection. Celebrates its centenary in 2001. Glasgow School of Art, Renfrew Street. Tel: 0141-353 4500. Exhibitions, mainly of contemporary art, in Rennie Mackintosh building

*House for an Art Lover
Bellahouston Park, Dumbreck Road. Tel: 0141-353 4449. Based on Rennie Mackintosh designs

Hunterian Art Gallery
Hillhead Street. Tel: 0141-330 5431. Rennie Mackintosh and Whistler collections; Old Masters, Scottish paintings and modern paintings, sculpture and prints

Hunterian Museum
University Avenue. Tel: 0141-330 4221. Scotland's oldest public museum, dating back to 1807. Exhibitions include Scotland's only dinosaur and Romans in Scotland

Lighthouse
Mitchell Lane. Converted Mackintosh building of 1895. Legacy of City of Architecture and Design 1999. Temporary exhibitions on design and architecture

*McLellan Galleries
Sauchiehall Street. Tel: 0141-332 7521.
Temporary exhibitions.

*Museum of Transport
Bunhouse Road. Tel: 0141-287 2720. Includes a
reproduction of a 1938 Glasgow street, cars since
the 1930s, trams and a Glasgow subway station

*People's Palace Museum
Glasgow Green. Tel: 0141-554 0223. History of
Glasgow since 1175

Piping Centre
McPhater Street. Collection of instruments and
artefacts from 14th century to present day

*Pollok House (NTS)
Pollokshaws Road. Tel: 0141-616 6410. Palladian
house containing the Stirling Maxwell art
collection

*Provand's Lordship
Castle Street. Tel: 0141-553 2557. Exhibition of
period displays housed in medieval buildings.
Oldest extant house in city (1471)

Royal Highland Fusiliers Museum
Sauchiehall Street. Tel: 0141-332 5639

*St Mungo Museum of Religious Life and Art
Castle Street. Tel: 0141-553 2557. Explores
universal themes through objects of all the main
world religions

*Scotland Street School Museum of Education
Scotland Street. Tel: 0141-429 1202. The history
of education in Scotland, in a building designed by
Rennie Mackintosh

Springburn Museum
Atlas Square, Ayr Street. Tel: 0141-557 1405.
Social history. Railway companies of Springburn

Tenement House
Renfrew Street. History of tenements in Scotland.

GLENCOE

Glencoe and North Lorn Folk Museum
Glencoe. Closed in winter. Restored cottage with
local and natural history exhibits

GLEN ESK

Glenesk Folk Museum
Costumes, photographs, maps and tools from the
Angus glens

GLENFINNAN

Glenfinnan Station Museum
Located in old station booking office. History of
the West Highland Railway line

GOLSPIE

Dunrobin Castle Museum
Castle and formal gardens. Heads and horns
bagged by the 5th Duke and Duchess of
Sutherland, Chinese opium pipes and
ethnographic artefacts acquired by the
Sutherlands

GRANGEMOUTH

Grangemouth Museum
Bo'Ness Road. History of Grangemouth as one of
Scotland's first planned industrial towns

GREENOCK

Custom House
Dockside. Displays featuring work of Customs
and Excise and illicit whisky distilleries

*McLean Museum and Art Gallery
Kelly Street. Tel: 01475-715624. Local and
natural history museum and temporary art
exhibitions

GULLANE

Myreton Motor Museum
Vintage cars, motorcycles, military vehicles and
motoring memorabilia

HAMILTON

Hamilton Transport Museum
Housed in a 17th-century coaching inn. Bygone
methods of transport

HAWICK

Hawick Museum and Scott Gallery
Wilton Lodge Park. Tel: 01450-373457. 19th and
20th-century Scottish art

HELMSDALE

Timespan Heritage Centre
Story of Viking raids, witch-burning, Clearances,
fishing, gold-prospecting

INNERLEITHEN NR GALASHIELS

Robert Smail's Printing Works (NTS)
Working museum with original 19th-century
machinery

INVERARAY

Auchindrain Folk Museum
Old township portraying life before the
Clearances

Combined Operations Museum
Housed in old stables. Wartime role of Inveraray as training centre for D-Day landings

Inveraray Jail
Church Square. Tel: 01499-302381. A 19th-century courthouse with two prisons

Inveraray Maritime Museum and schooner *Arctic Penguin*
Maritime Heritage Centre, Inveraray Pier. Tel: 01499-302213. Museum of Clyde ships and shipyards

INVERNESS

Balmain House
Huntly Street. Museum portraying development of Highland music

*Inverness Museum and Art Gallery
Castle Wynd. Tel: 01463-237114. The history, geology and geography of the Highlands

Queen's Own Highlanders Regimental Museum
Fort George, nr Inverness. Tel: 01463-224380

INVERURIE

Archaeolink Prehistory Park, Oyne
Pictish heritage of Aberdeenshire including reconstructed Iron Age farm and a hillside archaeological site

IONA

Infirmary Museum
Iona Abbey. History of the abbey. Contains stone pillow allegedly used by Columba

Iona Heritage Centre
Displays on social history of the island over last 200 years, including the Clearances

IRVINE

Scottish Maritime Museum
Laird Forge, Gottries Road. Tel: 01294-278283. Full-size ships, an exhibition gallery, an educational centre and a restored tenement flat

ISLAY

Port Charlotte. Museum of Islay Life
Tel: 01496-850358. History of the island and of 18th-century illegal whisky distillers

ISLE OF EASDALE

Easdale Folk Museum
Tel: 01852-300370. History of the island.

JEDBURGH

Jedburgh Castle Jail and Museum
Castlegate. Prison life throughout the ages

JOHN O'GROATS

Last House Museum
Tel: 01955-611250. Local history museum in a restored 18th-century house

KENMORE

Scottish Crannog Centre
Loch Tay. Authentic reconstruction of Bronze Age house in loch.

KILLIN

Breadalbane Folklore Centre
Contains 1,300-year-old 'healing stones' of St Fillian

KILMARTIN

Kilmartin House Museum
Tel: 01546-510278. Landscape and archaeology of Argyll

KINGUSSIE

*Highland Folk Museum
Duke Street. Tel: 01540-661307. Highland artefacts

KIRKCALDY

*Kirkcaldy Museum and Art Gallery
War Memorial Gardens. Tel: 01592-412860. Historical displays and collection of paintings including works by the Scottish Colourists and Camden Town group

McDouall Stuart Museum (NTS)
Rectory Lane, Dysart. Birthplace of John McDouall Stuart and account of his emigration to Australia in 1838

KIRKCUDBRIGHT

Harbour Cottage Gallery
Variety of temporary art exhibitions

Stewartry Museum
St Mary Street. Tel: 01557-331643. Life and times of the Solway coast

Tolbooth Art Centre
High Street. Work by Hornel and his associates

KIRKINTILLOCH

Auld Kirk Museum
The Cross. Tel: 0141-578 0144. Records and photographs of local industries

KIRRIEMUIR

Aviation Museum
Lifetime collection of Richard Moss. Military uniforms, photographs, World War II memorabilia and airfix models

LANARK

Lanark Museum
West Port. Tel: 01555-666680. Local history

LEWIS

Arnol. Black House Museum (HS).
Restored blackhouse. Exhibits dating from 1870s. Inhabited until 1964

Barabhas (Barvas). Morven Art Gallery.
Exhibitions

Bernera (Bearnaraigh). Bernera Museum
Tel: 01851-612331. Exhibition of lobster fishing. St Kilda mailboat

Bostadh (Bosta). Iron Age House
Replica Iron Age house

Bru (Brue). Oiseval Gallery
Photographic gallery

Carlabhagh (Carloway). Doune Broch Centre.
Reconstruction of broch

Siabost (Shawbost). Shawbost Crofting Museum
Created by local schoolchildren in 1970. Local artefacts relating to crofting, fishing and weaving

*Stornoway. An Lanntair Gallery
Town Hall, South Beach. Tel: 01851-703307. Contemporary art exhibitions; work of local artists

Stornoway. Museum nan Eilean
Francis St. Island's history until the Mackenzie takeover. Archaeological exhibits

Tabost (Habost). Comunn Eachdriadh Nis (Ness Historical Society)
Photographs. 6th/7th-century cross from Isle of Rona

Uig. Uig Heritage Centre
Tel: 01851-672456. Replica of Lewis Chessmen. History of blackhouses. Temporary exhibitions

LINLITHGOW

Linlithgow Story
High Street. Tel: 01506-670677. Local history and 15th-century coins

LOSSIEMOUTH

Lossiemouth Fisheries and Community Museum
Pitgaveny Quay. Tel: 01343-813772. History of fishing in the area, scale models

LYBSTER

Clan Gunn Heritage Centre and Museum
Between Latheron and Lybster. History of Clan Gunn and its septs

MALLAIG

Mallaig Heritage Centre
Photographic display of town and crofting and fishing life of Morar, Knoydart and the Small Isles

MEIGLE

Meigle Museum (HS)
Glen Isla. Collection of early Christian and Pictish inscribed stones

MELROSE

Trimontium Exhibition
Market Square. Celtic tools and weapons from Eildon Hills. Roman archaeological finds

MINTLAW

Aberdeenshire Farming Museum
Aden Country Park. Exhibits recalling traditional farming life

MOFFAT

Moffat Museum
Church Gate. Tel: 01638-220868. Local history, geology, farming and local crafts

MONTROSE

Montrose Museum and Art Gallery
Panmure Place. Tel: 01674-673232. One of Scotland's oldest museums, dating from 1842. Pictish relics including the Samson Stone dating from 900

William Lamb Memorial Studio
Market Street Work of local sculptor William Lamb (1893–1951)

MOTHERWELL

*Motherwell Heritage Centre
High Road. Tel: 01698-251000. Includes
Technopolis, a multi-media local history
exhibition

MULL

Dervaig. Old Byre Heritage Centre
Glen Bellart. Crofting life on Mull

Fionnphort, Ross of Mull. Columba Centre
Opened 1997 on 1400th anniversary of the saint's
death. Exhibits portraying life of Columba

Tobermory. Mull Museum
Main Street. Artefacts include objects from the
San Juan, a Spanish galleon which sank in the area

NAIRN

Fishertown Museum
Old Fishertown. Exhibits on life of the fishing
families

NEW ABBEY, nr DUMFRIES

**Shambellie House. National Museum of
Scotland's museum of costume.**
Costume and dress late 18th to early 20th-
centuries

NEWBURGH

Laing Museum
Collection donated by banker and historian Dr
Alexander Laing, 1892. Includes antiques and
geological finds of the area

NEWHAVEN nr LEITH

Newhaven Heritage Museum
Variety of costumes and memorabilia of the
fishing local industry

NEWTONGRANGE

Scottish Mining Museum
Lady Victoria Colliery. Tel: 0131-663 7519.
Museum of mining history. Houses Scotland's
largest steam engine

NEWTONMORE

Highland Folk Park
and Sat. Living history museum, reconstructions
of a working croft and a village of blackhouses

NEWTON STEWART

Newton Stewart Museum
York Road. Many exhibits depicting local history

NITHSDALE nr DUMFRIES

Ellisland Farm
Built by Robert Burns, housing many of his
personal effects

NORTH UIST

Lochmaddy
Taigh Chearsabhagh. Tel: 01876-500293.
Converted 18th-century merchant's house. Local
history museum and arts centre

ORKNEY

Burray. Orkney Fossil and Vintage Centre
Local fossils of fish and other sea creatures

Kirkwall, Mainland. Orkney Wireless Museum
Junction Road. Radio equipment through the
ages, especially from the two world wars.

*Kirkwall. Tankerness House Museum
Broad Street. Tel: 01856-873191. Two restored
farmsteads

**Mainland. Kirbuster and Corrigall Farm
Museums**
Life of an Orkney farmstead mid-19th century

**St Margaret's Hope, South Ronaldsay.
Smiddy Museum**
Cromarty Square. Village smithy museum, old
tools, drills and bellows

St Mary's, Mainland. Norwood Museum
Tel: 01856-781217. Antiques collected by local
stonemason Norrie Wood

Stromness, Mainland. Piers Art Centre
Temporary exhibitions, painting and sculpture by
local artists

Stromness. Stromness Museum
Natural history. Artefacts from shipwrecks and
expeditions

PAISLEY

Coats Observatory
Oakshaw Street. Records of astronomical and
meteorological data since 1884. Exhibitions of
telescopes and seismic recorders

*Paisley Museum and Art Galleries
High Street. Tel: 0141-889 3151. Local and
natural history and a collection of Paisley shawls

Sma' Shot Cottages
George Place. Re-creations of 18th- and 19th-
century daily life

PEEBLES

*Tweeddale Museum and Picture Gallery
Chambers Institute, High Street. Tel: 01721-724820. Local history museum and contemporary art gallery

PERTH

Black Watch Regimental Museum
Balhousie Castle, Hay Street. Tel: 01738-621281 ext. 8530

Fergusson Gallery
Marshall Place. Tel: 01738-441944. Paintings and sculpture by J. D. Fergusson, Scottish Colourist

*Perth Museum and Art Gallery
George Street. Tel: 01738-632488. Local history museum and art exhibitions

PETERHEAD

Arbuthnot Museum
St Peter Street. Tel: 01779-477778. Photographs of NE Scotland, Peterhead Harbour shipping records, history of whaling

Peterhead Maritime Heritage Museum
South Road. History of Fishing industry in Peterhead

PITLOCHRY

Clan Donnachaidh Museum
Bruar. Tel: 01796-483264. History of the clan

PITMEDDEN

Museum of Farming Life
Pitmedden Gardens. Tools, farm machinery, cottage life and bothy

ROSEMARKIE

Groam House Museum
Pictish culture including the Rosemarkie Cross Slab

RUTHWELL

Savings Bank Museum
Tel: 01387-870640. Work and times of Henry Duncan (1774-1846), founder of the Savings Bank Movement

ST ANDREWS

British Golf Museum
Bruce Embankment. Tel: 01334-478880. Museum of the history and development of golf

*St Andrews Museum
Kinburn Park, Double Dykes Road. Tel: 01334-412690. Local history and temporary exhibitions

SALTCOATS

North Ayrshire Museum
Manse Street. Tel: 01294-464174. Local history including the Ardrossan area

SELKIRK

Halliwell's House Museum
High Street. Tel: 01750–20054. History on industrialisation of Tweed Valley

SHETLAND

Boddam, Mainland. Shetland Crofthouse Museum
Housed in thatched croft of 1870. 19th-century crofting life

Burravoe, Yell. Old Haa Museum
Local artefacts, history of local herring and whaling industry.

Esha Ness, Mainland. Tangwick Haa Museum
History of remote areas of Scotland, shells and sand. The Gunnister Man found in 1951 preserved in peat

*Lerwick. Shetland Museum
Lower Hillhead. Tel: 01595-695057. Museum depicting all aspects of island life

Scalloway, Mainland
Scalloway Museum, Main Street. Local relics. Story of the Shetland Bus

Tingwall, Mainland.
Tingwall Agricultural Museum. Equipment from Shetlands crofts and farms

Walls, Mainland. Walls Museum
Knitwear, crofting life

Weisdale, Mainland. Bonhoga Gallery
Weisdale Mill. Former mill built 1855, now a converted arts centre. Touring and local exhibitions of painting and sculpture

Weisdale. Shetland Textile Working Museum
Temporary exhibitions, knitted patterns of Shetland and Fair Isle

SKYE

Armadale. Clan Donald Visitor Centre
Tel: 01471-844398. History of the Gaels and of the MacDonalds, Lords of the Isles. Housed in neo-Gothic Armadale Castle

Boreraig. MacCrimmon Piping Heritage Centre
Museum and ancestral holdings of MacCrimmons, hereditary pipers to the MacLeod chiefs

Dunvegan. Colbost Croft Museum
Restored blackhouse and illegal whisky still Boreraig. Boreraig Park. Open-air museum of traditional horse-drawn farm machinery

Dunvegan. Giant Angus MacAskill Museum
Restored thatched smithy. Named after hero toured with Tom Thumb

Glendale. Toy Museum
Holmisdale House. Toys and games from last 200 years

Kilmuir. Skye Museum of Island Life
Way of life on Skye 100 years ago. Local history

Luib. Luib Folk Museum
Restored blackhouse

Portree. An Tuireann Arts Centre
Struan Road. Housed in converted fever hospital. Temporary exhibitions

Staffin. Staffin Museum
Fossil finds from the area, including dinosaur bone discovered 1994

SOUTH QUEENSFERRY

Queensferry Museum
High Street. Tel: 0131-331 5545. Local history from 16th-century. History of Forth Road and Forth Rail bridges

SOUTH UIST

Tobha Mor. Kildonan Museum
Local history. Hebridean kitchens through the ages. Crofting life last 200 years

SPEAN BRIDGE

Clan Cameron Museum
Achnacarry. Tel: 01397-712480. History on the Clan Cameron

STIRLING

Argyll and Sutherland Highlanders Museum
Stirling Castle. Tel: 01786-475165

Smith Art Gallery and Museum
Dumbarton Road. Tel: 01786-471917. Scottish paintings and artefacts

STONEHAVEN

Tolbooth, The Harbour
Museum of local history and fishing.

STRANRAER

*Stranraer Museum
George Street. Tel: 01776-705088. Exhibition on farming, archaeology and polar explorers

STRATHDON

Lost Gallery
Tel: 01975-651287. Work of some of Scotland's leading modern artists

STRATHPEFFER

Highland Museum of Childhood
Railway Station. Growing up in the Highlands, folklore and festivals

TAIN

Tain Museum
Castle Brae. Tain silver, archaeology, clan memorabilia

TARBERT, KINTYRE.

An Tairbeart Heritage Centre
Campbeltown Road. Temporary exhibitions on local history and 19th-century crofthouse

THURSO

Thurso Heritage Museum
High Street. Artefacts including the Pictish Skinnet Stone. Exhibits on coastal transport and fishing

TIREE

Sandaig. Thatched Hose Museum
Local life in 19th-century

Scarinish. An Iodhlann
Temporary exhibitions

TOMINTOUL

Tomintoul Museum
Central Square. Tel: 01807-580285. Reconstructions of old farm kitchen and smithy

ULLAPOOL

Ullapool Museum
West Argyll Street. Tel: 01854-612987. Crofting, fishing, local religion and emigration

WANLOCKHEAD, VIA BIGGAR

Scottish Leadmining Museum
Tel: 01659-74387. The history of leadmining in Scotland

WESTER KITTOCHSIDE, nr EAST KILBRIDE

Museum of Scottish Country Life (National Museums of Scotland/NTS)
Tel: 01355-224181. Georgian farmhouse and steadings, with new building housing rural life collections of National Museums of Scotland. Galleries on environment, rural technologies and people; education centre, film house, picture gallery, and other amenities. Historic farm in operation all year, demonstrating traditional and modern methods of period around 1950. Opened 2001.

WICK

Wick Heritage Centre
Bank Row, Pultneytown. Artefacts from old fishing days, including fully-rigged boats

GARDENS

Scotland's varied climate allows for a very wide range of plants to be grown. Particularly on the west coast and in the islands of the west and south-west, mild weather caused by the Gulf Stream makes it possible to grow palms, tender perennials, and plants from the southern hemisphere; while acid, peaty soil and the frequency of rain and low cloud provide a suitable climate for plants usually thought of as typically Scottish, such as rhododendrons and heathers. Several national collections of plants are housed in Scotland.

The National Trust for Scotland is the country's largest garden owner, with just over 700 acres under intensive cultivation supporting over 13,500 different sorts of plants. The Trust acquired its first garden in 1945 when it accepted Culzean Castle. Several years later Inverewe, Brodik, Falkland Palace and Pitmedden Gardens were added. The Trust now has in its care 34 major gardens and designed landscapes and another 30 smaller gardens. It plays an important role in promoting the conservation of the art and craft of horticulture, through its School of Practical Gardening at Threave.

Each year some 400 Scottish gardens, most privately owned, open their gates to the public for one or more weekends under the banner of Scotland's Gardens Scheme. Founded in 1931, the Scheme is an independent charity and the money raised from garden visitors supports the Queen's Nursing Institute (Scotland) and the gardens fund of the National Trust for Scotland. In addition garden owners may donate up to 40 per cent of their takings to a charity of their choice. The National Scotland's Gardens Scheme Handbook is available from any National Trust for Scotland shop or by post from the Trust's headquarters.

Historic Scotland and Scottish Natural Heritage jointly maintain an Inventory of Gardens and Designed Landscapes in Scotland. The Inventory provides a representative sample of historic gardens and landscapes of special interest, and includes botanic gardens, parks, private gardens and policies in country estates. The Inventory is currently being extended.

The following is a list of gardens in Scotland which are regularly open to the public, including botanic gardens and historical gardens. Also included are gardens in the grounds of castles and houses which are open to public, and in some cases gardens which are open to the public although the buildings are not.

* Closed in winter (usually October or November to March)

† Also appears in Historic Buildings and Monuments list

NTS National Trust for Scotland property

HS Historic Scotland property

Achamore
Isle of Gigha, Argyll and Bute. Tel: 01583-505267. Established by Sir James Horlick of the hot drink fame. Rhododendrons and azaleas

*Achnacloich, Connel
Oban, Argyll and Bute. Tel: 01631-710221. Spring bulbs, azaleas, Japanese maples

*An Cala
Easdale, Isle of Seil, Argyll. Tel: 01852-300237. Created in 1930s. Water features

Arbuthnott House
Laurencekirk, Kincardineshire. Tel: 01561-361226. Late 17th-century herbaceous borders, roses, rhododendrons, hostas

*Ardencraig Rothesay
Isle of Bute. Closed Sat. and Sun. mornings. Victorian hothouses

Ardkinglas Woodland Garden
Cairndow, Loch Fyne. Rhododendrons, azaleas, conifers

*Ardtornish
Lochaline, Morvern, Oban, Highland. Tel: 01967-421288. Shrubs, deciduous trees, conifers, rhododendrons

Arduaine (NTS)
Oban, Argyll and Bute. Tel: 01852-200366. Originally planted early 1900s. Restored after 1971. 20 acres. Lawns, lily ponds, mature woods, rhododendrons and magnolias

†Armadale Castle and Museum of the Isles
Armadale, Sleat, Isle of Skye. Tel: 01471-844305. Pond gardens, herbaceous border, lawns and ornamental trees

*Ascog Fernery and Garden
nr Rothesay, Bute. Closed Mons., Tues. Victorian fernery. Boasts a fern reputed to be 1,000 years old

*Attadale
Strathcarron, Highland. Tel: 01520-722217. Water features, rhododendron walk, herb plot

†Ballindalloch Castle
Grantown-on-Spey, Highland. Tel: 01807-500205. A 1937 rock garden, rose and fountain garden

*†Balmoral Castle
Ballater, Aberdeenshire. Tel: 013397-42334. A 3-acre garden; rare coniferous forest trees, sunken rose garden, water garden

*Bell's Cherrybank Gardens
Cherrybank, Perth. Tel: 01738-621111. Two 18-acre gardens; includes 830 varieties of heather, largest collection of heathers in Britain

*Bolfracks
Aberfeldy, Perth and Kinross. Tel: 01887-820207. A 3-acre garden. Spring bulbs, shrub roses, gentians

*Branklyn (NTS)
116 Dundee Road, Perth. Tel: 01738-625535. Alpine plants and rhododendrons on 2-acre hillside

†Brodick Castle (NTS)
Isle of Arran, North Ayrshire. Tel: 01770-302202. Plants from Himalayas, China and South America, bog garden

*†Broughton House (NTS)
12 High Street, Kirkcudbright, Dunfries and Galloway. Tel: 01557-330437. Open afternoons only April 9–Oct. Created by artist E. A. Hornel. Sunken courtyard, Japanese garden, rose parterre

*Broughton Place
Broughton, Biggar, Scottish Borders. Tel: 01899-830234. Closed Wed. An 18th-century beech avenue. National collections of thalictrums and tropaeolums

Cambo
Kingsbarns, St. Andrews, Fife. Tel: 01333-450054. Walled garden. Ornamental garden, lilac walk

*Candacraig
Dinnet, Aberdeenshire. Tel: 01975-651226. Closed Sat. and Sun. mornings. An 1820s garden, cottage-garden flowers, mecanopsis, primulas

†Castle Fraser (NTS)
Sauchen, Inverurie, Aberdeenshire. Tel: 01330-833463. A 17th–18th-century designed landscape, herbaceous border, walled garden

*Castle Kennedy
Stranraer, Wigtownshire, Dumfries and Galloway. Tel: 01776-702024. Laid out 1730. A 75-acre garden noted for monkey-puzzle trees, magnolias, rhododendrons, spring bulbs

*†Cawdor Castle
Cawdor, Nairn, Highland. Tel: 01667-404615. Herbaceous borders, peony border, rose tunnel, thistle garden, holly maze

*Cluny House
Aberfeldy, Perth and Kinross. Tel: 01887-820795. Wild garden. National Collection of Asiatic primulas; meconopsis, rhododendrons

Crarae
Minard, Inveraray, Argyll and Bute. Tel: 01546-886614. Laid out early 20th-century as a 'Himalayan ravine' with 400 rhododendrons, azaleas, eucalyptus and conifers

†Crathes Castle (NTS)
Banchory, Aberdeenshire. Tel: 01330-844525. Eight themed gardens, rare shrubs, herbaceous borders. National Collection of Malmaison carnations

Cruickshank Botanic Garden
University of Aberdeen, St. Machar Drive, Aberdeen. Tel: 01224-272704. Closed weekends Oct.–April. Eleven acres; arboretum, rose garden, water gardens. Essentially for research

*†Culzean Castle (NTS)
Maybole, South Ayrshire. Tel: 01655-884400. Camelia house and orangery, 563-acre country park, 30-acre garden, walled garden, herbaceous borders

*Dawyck Botanic
Stobo, Peebleshire, Scottish Borders. Tel: 01721-760254. Branch of Royal Botanic Garden Edinburgh. 300 years of tree-planting. Fine arboretum, beech walk, azalea terrace

*†Drum Castle (NTS)
Drumoak, by Banchory, Aberdeenshire. Tel: 01330-811204. Closed weekdays in Oct. Garden of historic roses. Herbaceous borders, plants from 17th to 20th centuries

*†Drummond Castle
Muthill, Crieff, Perth and Kinross. Tel: 01764-681257. Open afternoons only May–Oct. Laid out by John Drummond, 2nd Earl of Perth, 1630. French and Italian influence. A 17th-century Scottish garden

*†Dunrobin Castle
Golspie, Sutherland, Highlands. Tel: 01408-633177. Closed Sun. mornings. Victorian formal gardens in French style, laid out 1850. Water features, roses, clematis, sweet peas

†Dunvegan Castle
Isle of Skye. Tel: 01470-521206. Closed weekends Nov.-Feb. Box-wood parterre, mixed borders, fern houses, woodland waterfall dell, walled garden

†Edzell Castle (HS)
Edzell, Brechin, Angus. Tel: 01356-648631. Closed Sun. mornings Oct.–Mar. Walled garden dating from 1930s but laid out as it may have looked in early 1600s

*†Falkland Palace (NTS)
Falkland, Fife. Tel: 01337 857397. Closed Sun. mornings. Shrub island borders, herbaceous borders, delphiniums, orchard

Finlaystone
Langbank, Renfrewshire. Tel: 01475-540285. A ten-acre garden and 70-acre woodland laid out 1900. Herbaceous borders, copper beeches, Celtic paving maze, bog garden

*†Floors Castle
Kelso, Roxburghshire. Tel: 01573-223333. Herbaceous borders, walled kitchen garden

*†Glamis Castle
Glamis, Forfar, Angus. Tel: 01307-840393. Landscaped 1790s by designer influenced by 'Capability' Brown. Two-acre Italian garden, herbaceous borders, gazebos

Glasgow Botanic Gardens
730 Great Western Road, Glasgow. Tel: 0141-334 2422 Glasshouses contain orchids, cacti and ferns. Paths alongside wooded banks of River Kelvin

*Glenarn
Rhu, Dunbartonshire. Tel: 01436-820493. Woodland garden established 1920s. Rhododendrons, magnolias, olearias, pieris

*Glenwhan
Dunragit, Stranraer, Dumfries and Galloway. Tel: 01581-400222. A twelve-acre hillside garden laid out 1979. Exotic plants, trees and shrubs, lakes and bog gardens, rhododendrons, primula

Greenbank (NTS)
Flenders Road, Clarkston, Glasgow. Tel: 0141-639 3281. Walled garden, water features, woodland walks, herb garden

†Haddo House (NTS)
nr Tarves, Ellon, Aberdeenshire. Tel: 01651-851440. With 177 acres of woodland, lakes and ponds, home to otters, red squirrel, pheasants and deer

†Hill of Tarvit (NTS)
Cupar, Fife. Tel: 01334-653127. Rose garden, perennials and annuals, ornamental trees

Hirsel
Coldstream, Berwickshire. Tel: 01890-882834. Spring bulbs, rhododendrons, rose beds, herbaceous borders

*House of Pitmuies
Guthrie, by Forfar, Angus. Tel: 01241-828245. Walled gardens, rhododendrons, semi-formal gardens with old fashioned roses and delphiniums

Inveresk Lodge (NTS)
Musselburgh, East Lothian. Tel: 0131-665 1855. Closed Sat. Oct.–Mar. and Sat. and Sun. mornings April–Sept. Semi-formal gardens, shrub roses, conservatory

Inverewe (NTS)
Poolewe, Highlands 2LG. Tel: 01445-781200. Brainchild of Osgood Mackenzie; created from 1865 covering the Am Ploc Ard peninsula. Wild garden, rock gardens, rhododendrons, vegetable garden and orchard. Species from around the world. National collections of olearias and ourisias. Hydroponicum

Jura House
Ardfin, Isle of Jura, Argyll and Bute. Tel: 01496-820315. Walled garden. Fuchsias, ferns and lichens. Antipodean plants. Organic walled garden

Kailzie
Peebles, Peebleshire, Scottish Borders. Tel: 01721-720007. A 17-acre walled-garden. Spring bulbs, secret gardens, laburnum, rhododendrons, azaleas, mecanopsis, primulas. Trout pond

†Kellie Castle (NTS)
Pittenweem, Fife. Tel: 01333-720271. Lawn edged with box-hedges and borders, roses, vegetable garden, woodland walks

*†Kildrummy Castle (HS)
Alford, Aberdeenshire. Tel: 01975-571203. Rock garden, water garden, Japanese garden, maples, rhododendrons, acers, mecanopsis

Kilmory Woodland Park
nr Lochgilphead. Gardens laid out in 1830 around Kilmory Castle

*Kinross House
Kinross, Perth and Kinross. A four-acre formal walled garden designed 1680s. Herbaceous borders, rose borders, ornamental yew hedges

*Leckmelm Shrubbery and Arboretum
Little Leckmelm House, Lochbroom, Ullapool, Highland. A ten-acre arboretum

†Leith Hall (NTS)
Huntly, Aberdeenshire. Tel: 01464-831216. Rock garden, perennial borders, catmint border, water features

*Logan Botanic Garden
Port Logan, Stranraer, Dumfries and Galloway. Tel: 01776-860231. Outpost of Edinburgh's Royal Botanic Garden. Exotic plants from around the world. Excellent collection of Scottish tender perennials. A one hundred year old walled garden. Water garden, palms and ferns. Eucalyptus, magnolias

Malleny (NTS)
Balerno, Edinburgh. Tel: 0131-449 2283. Three-acre walled garden with Deodar cedar. With 17th-century clipped yews. Herbaceous borders, herb and ornamental vegetable garden. National Collection of 19th-century shrub roses

*†Manderston
Duns, Scottish Borders. Tel: 01361-883450. Open May–Sept., Thurs. and Sun. afternoons only. With 56 acres including formal terraces, woodland garden, formal walled garden, water features

*Megginch Castle
Errol, Perthshire. Tel: 01821-642222. Gardens and Gothic courtyard of 1806. Yew and holly topiary, 1000 year old yews, 18th-century walled garden and annual border

*†Mellerstain House
nr Earlston, Borders. Tel: 01573-410225. Parkland and formal Edwardian gardens, rose garden laid out by Sarah, 12th Countess of Haddington

*Mertoun
St Boswell's, Roxburghshire, Scottish Borders. Open April–Sept. weekends, public holidays and Mon. afternoons. A 26-acre flower garden beside the Tweed. Azaleas, herbaceous border, ornamental pond. 3-acre walled garden

*Monteviot
Jedburgh, Scottish Borders. Open afternoons only, April–Oct. River garden with herbaceous perennials and shrubs. Rose gardens, water garden

*†Mount Stuart House
Rothesay, Isle of Bute. Closed Tues. and Thurs. With 300-acres of designed landscape. A mature pinetum, lime tree avenue, conifers, rock gardens, kitchen and herb garden, exotic southern hemisphere plants

*Pitmedden (NTS)
Pitmedden, Ellon, Aberdeenshire. Tel: 01651-842352. A 17th-century patterned garden, box hedging and annuals. Herbaceous borders

Priorwood Garden (NTS)
Melrose. Closed Jan.–Mar. and Sun. morning. Orchard; flowers suitable for drying

Royal Botanic Garden
Edinburgh. Inverleith Row, Edinburgh. Tel: 0131-552 7171. Established 17th century, now a 75-acre site. Noted for rhododendrons and azaleas. Rock garden, peat and woodland gardens, herbaceous borders. Arboretum. Glasshouses display orchids, giant water-lilies and 200-year-old West Indian palm tree. Chinese Garden

St Andrews Botanic Garden
Canongate, St Andrews. Tel: 01334-477178. Peat, rock and water gardens

*Sea View
Durnamuck, Dundonnell, Highland. Tel: 01854-633317. Began 1990 on shores of Little Loch Broom. Heather bed, rock garden, orchard, bog garden

*Teviot Water Garden
Kirkbank House, Eckford, Kelso, Scottish Borders. Tel: 01835-850734. Waterfalls, aquatic plants, perennials, grasses, ferns, bamboos

Threave (NTS)
Stewartry, Castle Douglas, Dumfries and Galloway. Tel: 01556-502575. A 65-acre garden used as a school of horticulture since 1960. Perennials and annuals.Walled garden, vegetable garden and orchard. Woodland and rock gardens. Specialty rose garden and rhododendrons. Arboretum

†Torosay Castle
Craignure, Isle of Mull, Argyll and Bute. Tel: 01680-812421. Formal Italian garden with Italian rococo statues. Water garden, Japanese garden, rhododendrons, azaleas. Australian and New Zealand trees and shrubs

University of Dundee Botanic Garden
Riverside Drive, Dundee. Tel: 01382-566939. A 23-acre garden, glasshouses

*Younger Botanic Gardens
Dunoon, Argyll and Bute. Tel: 01369-706261. Offshoot of Edinburgh's Royal Botanic Gardens. Flowering trees and shrubs. With 250 species of rhododendrons and Great Redwoods planted in 1863; magnolias; arboretum

THE ARTS IN SCOTLAND

The distinctive character of the arts in Scotland is recognised worldwide. While the country is perhaps most widely known for the works of certain writers (Scott, Burns, MacGonagall) and for its traditional music and dance, and the popular concepts of 'Scottishness', Scotland has produced, and continues to produce, internationally important works of art, architecture, literature, classical music, and cinema. Scotland has 152 art galleries and 180 performing arts venues. In the performing arts, Scottish musicians and actors are outstanding in many fields.

Crafts, too, are thriving. A significant percentage (14 per cent) of the total population involved in crafts in Britain works in Scotland, a proportion which rose sharply during the 1980s, possibly under the influence of rapidly expanding tourism.

Around 50,000 people in Scotland work in the cultural sector, and the creative industries (including architecture, arts and cultural industries, advertising, design, film, interactive leisure software, music, new media, publishing, radio and television) are worth an estimated £5 billion to the Scottish economy annually. Glasgow's designation as European City of Culture in 1990 is widely held to have given a big stimulus to its wider regeneration in the 1990s, and this was boosted by it being City of Architecture and Design in 1999.

NATIONAL CULTURAL STRATEGY

In August 2000 the Scottish Executive released its National Cultural Strategy for Scotland, a new policy framework to guide the work of national government, local government and cultural bodies in planning, promoting and resourcing cultural activity. The Strategy sets out the Scottish Executive's objectives regarding promoting creativity, celebrating Scotland's diverse cultural heritage, realising the potential contribution of culture to education at all stages, and ensuring an effective national framework of support to all aspects of culture in national life. It calls for a holistic approach to the arts within the departments of the Scottish Executive itself, especially those concerned with education,

tourism and the creative industries. The Scottish Executive announced the allocation of an additional £7.25 million to kick-start the Strategy.

The Strategy's priorities include:
- developing a political and economic climate supportive to people working in the arts
- enhancing Scotland's creative industries
- celebrating excellence in the arts, including recognising the importance of Scottish traditional arts
- supporting companies with national scope beyond the existing companies generally thought of as 'national companies' (Scottish Opera, Scottish Ballet, the Royal Scottish National Orchestra and the Scottish Chamber Orchestra)
- promoting all the languages of Scotland, including non-European languages spoken as well as Gaelic and Scots
- conserving, presenting and promoting Scotland's cultural heritage
- promoting international cultural exchange
- promoting and enhancing the arts in education and lifelong learning, with an emphasis on the importance of equal access to learning and tuition, especially for schoolchildren
- developing wider opportunities for cultural access, overcoming perceptions of the arts as a preserve of the elite
- maximising the social benefits of culture to both individuals and communities

Among the activities under way or contemplated are the development of a national architecture strategy, the development of a policy on contemporary popular music, and the formation of a ministerial task force to carry forward the work of promoting the arts as an important strand of cultural tourism. Delivering the priorities outlined in the Strategy is a commitment of the Scottish Executive's budget spending in financial year 2002–2003.

Annual planned Scottish Executive budget expenditure on sports and culture (£m)

2000–01	2001–02	2002–03	2003–04
127.3	145.8	151.2	156

Source: Scottish Executive, *The Scottish Budget annual expenditure report of the Scottish Executive*, chapter 11

ARTS FESTIVALS IN SCOTLAND

Founded in 1947, the Edinburgh International Festival (EIF) was the first major festival of the arts to be established in Europe as it recovered from the cataclysm of World War II. It was the initiative of Rudolph Byng, director of the Glyndebourne Festival Opera. Ironically, London, Oxford and Cambridge all turned down Byng's proposals for a festival in the style of Salzburg or Bayreuth, and the Edinburgh Festival quickly expanded to become one of the world's major festivals of the arts, attracting world-class performers in music, opera and drama each August, surrounded by a flotilla of other events. In 1999 an estimated 400,000 people attended Festival events. Simultaneously with the EIF, the Festival Fringe and the Edinburgh International Film, Jazz and Book Festivals are held. The Fringe in particular has grown exponentially in recent years and now features thousands of events at hundreds of venues. In 1998 it decided to shift its dates to a week before the opening of the EIF; the decision proved controversial but has been sustained. In 2000 the Edinburgh Military Tattoo which always accompanies the Festival celebrated its 50th anniversary.

Edinburgh is the largest but by no means the only arts festival held regularly in Scotland. The annual St Magnus Festival in Orkney (June) is an important event, particularly for classical music, with a strong focus on new music and on involving the local community. There are big festivals at Glasgow (Celtic Connections, January; Glasgow International Jazz Festival, July; World Pipe Band Championship, August); Aberdeen (Aberdeen International Youth Festival, July; Aberdeen Alternative Festival, October; Bon Accord Festival, June), Perth (Perth Festival of the Arts, May), Dundee (Dundee City Festival, June), Caithness (Northlands Festival, September, an annual celebration of Scottish and Nordic cultures in the north of Scotland), and many other places. There is even an annual Mendelssohn festival on the Isle of Mull.

Scotland's Voice is a new traditional music festival in Edinburgh, held for the first time in July 2000. Festivals focusing chiefly on traditional music and jazz are held in many towns and regions throughout the country. A large pop music festival, 'T in the Park', is held annually in Perth in July.

Detailed information on festivals can be obtained from the Scottish Arts Council, tourist boards, and the Scottish Music Information Centre.

THE SCOTTISH ARTS COUNCIL

The Scottish Arts Council (SAC) is the principal channel for government funding of the contemporary arts and crafts in Scotland and a key actor in the development of Scotland's arts and cultural policy. It receives an annual grant from the Scottish Executive, most of which is distributed to arts organisations and individual artists and craftspeople across Scotland, and is the channel for distributing National Lottery funds to the arts in Scotland. It also does important work in the promotion of arts education in schools.

However, despite the support of the SAC, arts funding is a perennial problem, particularly for many of the larger institutions. Because Scotland has a small population relative to its size, expected audiences outwith the Edinburgh–Glasgow 'central belt' and the major arts festivals are inevitably lower than in, for instance, the south-east of England, and it is not always easy to attract funding or sponsorship, particularly for permanent entities such as galleries and performance spaces or the national performing companies. Scottish Opera, for instance, has suffered periodic funding crises almost since its foundation, and a lively debate surrounds its current funding and the balance between its roles of promoting and commissioning new indigenous opera (such as James MacMillan's *Inés de Castro*, premièred in 1996) and presenting high-quality and high-profile productions of well-known works (such as the current productions of Wagner's *Ring* cycle).

ARTS COUNCIL GRANTS

Annual grant to SAC from Scottish Executive:

2000–1:   £27.772 million
2001–2:   £35.9 million
2002–3:   £35.6 million
2003–4:   £36.6 million

SUMMARY OF SAC BUDGET, 2000/01 AND 2001/02: GRANT ALLOCATION, LOTTERY AND GENERAL FUND COMBINED

Budget item	2001/02 £	2000/01 £
Operating costs	4,600,000	4,447,417
Artform and programme budgets:		
Visual Arts	2,502,558	2,240,531
Crafts	431,531	363,363
Combined Arts	3,267,974	2,986,999
Dance	3,564,677	3,169,416
Drama	6,221,406	5,706,331
Literature	1,432,093	1,247,169
Music	13,060,319	11,402,455
Central Funds	670,477	656,319
Policy Development Schemes	850,000	
National Cultural Strategy	500,000	850,000
Contingency–General Fund	247,540	270,000
Access and Participation	1,400,000	1,500,000
Advancement	1,350,000	1,795,000
Arts Activities Reserve		500,000
Audience and Sales Development	500,000	500,000
Awards for All	1,000,000	1,000,000
Capital Programme	10,000,000	9,000,000
Children and Young People	1,000,000	1,000,000
Contingency–Lottery Fund	100,000	105,000
Creative Scotland Awards	400,000	400,000
Creative Skills and Development	500,000	500,000
Creative Industries	150,000	
Cross Border Touring	150,000	120,000
Cross Sectoral Partnerships		150,000
Local Authority Partnerships	400,000	400,000
Social Inclusion Partnerships	400,000	300,000
Year of Cultural Diversity	250,000	
Total Programme costs	50,348,575	46,162,583
TOTAL EXPENDITURE	54,948,575	50,610,000

Source: Scottish Arts Council

LOTTERY FUNDING TO THE ARTS

The SAC has distributed well over £100 million in National Lottery funds to Scottish artists and arts organisations since 1994. As elsewhere in Britain, the bulk of Lottery funding tends to go to building projects, and some of these have been impressive, e.g. The Hub, Edinburgh (an all-year-round base for the Edinburgh Festival, opened in June 1999, containing an auditorium, rehearsal space, café-bar, and ticket office); Dundee Contemporary Arts Centre (opened in March 1999, containing two art cinema screens, galleries, a printmaking studio, and a café-bar); An Tuireann Arts Centre in Portree, Skye; and refurbishment of the Tron Theatre, Glasgow. However, funding is also available for creative activities; for instance, between 1995 and 2000 the SAC lottery fund provided over £1 million in finance for the production of films in Scotland. (Since 2000 Scottish Screen has taken over responsibility for managing lottery funding for film.)

On 14 May 2001, the SAC announced the latest round of lottery awards, totalling a little over £2 million. Fifty-nine grants of sums between £3,700 and £100,000 were made, with most regions of Scotland and most disciplines represented. A strong emphasis was placed on access to the arts for children and young people.

RESEARCH AND POLICY DEVELOPMENT

As part of an ongoing research programme, the SAC has initiated several pieces of research on the impact of the arts in Scotland, including a two-year study of the impact of lottery-funded arts buildings. The Scottish Executive has taken up the SAC's recommendation, made in a recent study on cultural statistics, that it play a central co-ordinating role in gathering and disseminating statistics on cultural activity, as an aid to planning.

The SAC has followed the National Cultural Strategy process closely and has published a comprehensive response to the strategy. It is the principal channel for additional or specific funding to initiatives under the strategy.

AWARDS

The SAC issues a number of awards for excellence in the different arts. A new set of awards, started in 2000 are the Creative Scotland Awards, 14 of which, each worth £25,000, are awarded annually to established artists living in Scotland and working in architecture, crafts, dance, design, digital media, drama/theatre, film/video, literature, music, photography, visual arts, and other art forms. The substantial size of the awards reflects their purpose in enabling artists to undertake new projects of significant scope. The 2001 awards were made on Burns Night (25 January) 2001. The award winners are:

Visual arts: Roderick Doyle, Nathan Coley, Elizabeth Ogilvie;
Music: Lyell Cresswell, Savourna Stevenson, Kevin MacKenzie;
Drama: Graham Etough, Tom McGrath;
Dance: Marissa Zanotti;
Literature, film and new media: John Burnside, Kathleen Jamie, Angus Peter Campbell, Matt Hulse, Amy Hardie.

COUNCIL MEETINGS
All SAC Council meetings are public and are held at different venues around the country.

Information on the Scottish Arts Council, its funding policies, and the arts in Scotland can be obtained from the SAC Helpdesk Tel: 0131-240 2443/4.

LITERATURE
It is impossible here to survey the whole wealth of Scottish literature; but we can mention a few of the best-known authors, beginning with William Dunbar and Robert Henryson, two of the 'Scottish Chaucerians' of the 15th and 16th centuries. These poets were all clearly influenced by Chaucer, but were by no means imitators of him. Writing in Scots, Dunbar, court poet to James IV, wrote celebratory poetry for the king but also mordant satire with equal virtuosity. Henryson returned several times to classical themes such as the tales of Orpheus and Eurydice, Troilus and Cressida (his most overt reference to Chaucer, but with an alternative ending), and his *Morall Fabillis*, which look back to Aesop. Sir David Lindsay's great morality play, *Ane Satyre of the Thrie Estaitis*, is the first surviving play in Scottish literature.

The 18th and early 19th centuries produced the two most famous figures in Scottish literature: Robert Burns and Sir Walter Scott. The immense popularity of both authors has turned them into icons of 'Scottishness', though from very different perspectives. Both were immensely prolific, and both confronted the enormous changes taking place in Scottish society and governance after the suppression of Jacobitisim. But whereas Burns, the son of an Ayrshire tenant farmer, is loved for his celebration of ordinary people and democratic values and for his ability to express personal feelings, particularly love, in vivid and apparently simple verse and song, the novels and poems of Scott (who came from a more prosperous farming family in the Borders and had a successful career as a lawyer) reflect a vision of history that, while romantic and mythologising, also helped to revive and sustain an idea of Scottish identity and nation.

From the late Victorian era and the turn of the 20th century come several well-known authors such as Robert Louis Stevenson, J. M. Barrie, and John Buchan. Then, from the 1920s onward, there was a fresh flowering of Scottish literature which has become known as the 'Scottish Renaissance'. One of its instigators, and its main poet, was Hugh McDiarmid, possibly most famous for *A drunk man looks at the thistle* (1926). The novels of Neil M. Gunn, Sir Compton Mackenzie, Lewis Grassic Gibbon, Jessie Kesson and others deal in different ways with social change and social conditions of the time – and, in the case of Gunn in particular, of other times in Scotland's history. The poems and novels of George Mackay Brown are also steeped in history, landscape and lore; that of his native Orkney.

The last two decades have seen a new generation of Scottish novelists and a shift of attention towards often uncompromising realism and urban themes. These writers include James Kelman, Janice Galloway, Candia McWilliam and Irvine Welsh. Since early 2000 the Edinburgh-based children's author J. K. Rowling has achieved great celebrity – and become one of the world's most highly-paid authors – through the runaway success of her series of *Harry Potter* novels.

Lewis Grassic Gibbon
February 2001 marked the centenary of the birth of Lewis Grassic Gibbon (pseudonym of James Leslie Mitchell, 1901–35), novelist, short-story writer, and journalist. Born near Kirktown of Auchterless, Aberdeenshire, Gibbon lived and worked as a journalist in Aberdeen, Glasgow and London before moving to Welwyn Garden City, Hertfordshire. Here he wrote his best-known work, the novel trilogy *A Scots Quair* (for which he adopted his mother's name as a pseudonym), set in the rural society of the Mearns where he spent his formative years. An extremely prolific writer considering his short life, he wrote 17 books in seven years, including, as well as the *Quair* (1932–4), *Stained Radiance* (1930), *The Thirteenth Disciple* (1931) *Three Go Back* (1932), and *Gay Hunter* (1934). He was of socialist opinions and wide-ranging interests; his short stories appeared in *Scottish Scene*, a miscellany co-written with Hugh MacDiarmid, and he also wrote on the great explorers, human prehistory and history, and Mesoamerican archaeology. His last, unfinished novel, *The Speak of the Mearns*, was posthumously published in 1982.

Nigel Tranter
Nigel Tranter (1909–2000), novelist and historian was born in Glasgow. He published over 140 books, including the many historical novels for which he is best known, children's fiction, and non-fiction works chiefly on the history, lore and landscape of Scotland. Under the pseudonym Nye Tredgold, he also published a series of novels set in the American West. His novels on Scottish themes include: *Trespass* (1937), *Margaret the Queen* (1979), *Columba* (1987), *Highness in Hiding* (1995), and the quadrilogy *Sword of State*, the last volume of which was published in 2000. Non-fiction includes: *The fortified house in Scotland* (6 vols, 1962–6).

GAELIC LITERATURE

Alongside literature in English and Scots stands a strong tradition of poetry and prose in Gaelic reaching back to at least the early Middle Ages and encompassing heroic ballads narrating the deeds of legendary figures; an oral tradition of prose sagas; poems of praise written by professional bards in the services of clan chiefs and the nobility; songs and love poems, many of them anonymous, from the 16th and 17th centuries; poems of satire and nostalgia expressing a specifically Gaelic consciousness in response to the slow disintegration of Highland culture after the Jacobite rebellion and, later, the Clearances; and religious prose works. Much of the oral tradition in both prose and poetry was collected and written down in the 18th and 19th centuries. An Comunn Gaidhealach, founded in 1891 to promote Gaelic language and culture, increased interest in Gaelic writing in Gaelic-language periodicals which published stories and essays. Contemporary issues began to be written about in Gaelic.

Iain Crichton Smith (1928–98) was among those instrumental in maintaining and enriching the tradition of Gaelic prose writing after World War II, with novels and collections of stories. Sorley Maclean (1911–96) is a seminal figure in 20th century Gaelic poetry; and he has been followed by a generation of young writers, particularly poets, carrying writing in Gaelic strongly into the new millennium.

CURRENT INSTITUTIONS

Several organisations of different kinds exist for the promotion of Scottish literature. The Association for Scottish Literary Studies, based at the University of Glasgow, promotes the study, teaching and writing of Scotland's literature and languages. Founded in 1970, it is now an international organisation with members in over 20 countries. It publishes a variety of periodicals (e.g. *Scottish Studies Review*), and in addition publishes each year an edition of a Scottish work which has either gone out of print or needs to be reintroduced to a contemporary readership, and an anthology of new writing.

The Scottish Poetry Library is a reference and lending library promoting Scottish and other poetry. Among other services, it has a computerised index to its collection called INSPIRE (International and Scottish Poetry Information Resource). The Society of Authors in Scotland is an independent trade union representing writers' interests in all areas of the profession.

The literary journal and magazine scene in Scotland is also lively, with old and new periodicals including the *Edinburgh Review*, *Cencrastus* (Edinburgh), *Cutting Teeth* (Glasgow), *Dark Horse* (Glasgow), *Inscotland* (Edinburgh, formerly *Books in Scotland*), *Markings* (Kirkcudbright), *Northwords* (Inverness), *Poetry Scotland* (Edinburgh), and *Scottish Studies* (Edinburgh). *Gairm*, the only all-Gaelic quarterly in existence, has been published since 1952; *Lallans*, the journal of the Scots Language Society, publishes work in Scots.

In addition, many of the major Scottish publishers specialise in Scottish literature, e.g. Canongate, Polygon, Chapman, and a number of small and locally focused presses.

In February 2001 the first Literature Forum for Scotland was inaugurated, bringing together representatives of literature organisations, writers, publishers, and the Literature Department and Literature Committee of the SAC. It was established in response to an audit of Scottish literature organisations commissioned in 2000 by the SAC, and will examine the formulation of a national policy for literature and publishing in Scotland.

EVENTS AND AWARDS

Coinciding with the Edinburgh International Festival, the annual Edinburgh International Book Festival holds readings, meetings and interviews with writers and publishers, and sells a wide range of modern and antiquarian books.

The Scottish Arts Council issues Spring and Autumn Book Awards and has recently instituted annual Children's Book Awards. Other awards include the Dundee Book Prize (University of Dundee), the Fidler Award for children's literature (c/o Scottish Book Trust), the James Tait Black Memorial Prize (Department of English Literature at the University of Edinburgh), the Macallan/*Scotland on Sunday* Short Story Competition, the RLS Memorial Award (National Library of Scotland), the Scottish International Open Poetry Competition, the Saltire Society Scottish Literary Awards, and the Scottish Writer of the Year (c/o Scottish Book Trust).

In 2001–2 the SAC has instituted a pilot New Writers' Bursaries Scheme, offering eight bursaries to writers with few or no previous publications.

SAC SPRING BOOK AWARD WINNERS 2001

The following five writers won prizes of £1,000 each in the SAC's annual Spring Book Awards, announced on 18 April 2001:

Alasdair Campbell, *The Nessman* (novel)
Douglas Dunn, *The Year's Afternoon* (collection of poems)
Margaret Elphinstone, *The Sea Road* (historical novel)
Alan Spence, *Seasons of the Heart* (collection of haiku)
Christopher Whyte, *The Cloud Machinery* (novel)

SAC CHILDREN'S BOOK AWARD WINNERS 2001

The 2001 SAC Children's Book Awards, totalling £6,000, were presented on 30 May. The winners were:

Diana Hendry, *Harvey Angell Beats Time*
Julie Lacome, *Ruthie's Big Old Coat*
Lindsay McRae, *How to Avoid Kissing Your Parents in Public*
Tom Pow, illustrated by Robert Ingpen, *Who Is the World For?*
Alison Prince, *Second Chance*
JK Rowling, *Harry Potter and the Goblet of Fire*
Lindsey Fraser, ed., *Points North* (short story collection, highly commended).

THEATRE

The development of a Scottish theatre tradition can be effectively dated only to the late 19th century. In the early 16th century, mystery and morality plays such as Sir David Lindsay's *Ane Satyre of the Thrie Estaitis*, were performed in a theatrical context very similar to that of England at the time. However, theatre then virtually disappeared in Scotland under pressure from the Reformation, the removal of the court and with it artistic patronage to London in 1603, and, later, the censorship of the Licensing Act of 1737, directed chiefly against political satire. When theatrical performance did surface again it was often in the form of music hall, which began in the early 19th century, nurtured performers such as Harry Lauder, Harry Gordon and, later, comedy actors such as Jimmy Logan and Stanley Baxter, and declined in popularity only in the 1950s and 1960s.

The 20th century saw the development of a distinct Scottish voice in the theatre and at the same time the establishment of many theatres and theatre companies presenting a broader repertoire. Several of the existing repertory companies were founded between 1935 and 1965. Companies concentrating on plays by Scottish authors, such as the Scottish National Players, were founded in the early 20th century but have disappeared. However, the promotion of indigenous talent has been taken up by others, often by touring companies, for instance 7:84 Scotland, formed in 1973. In the late 1990s, the Traverse Theatre, an important arena for new work, has increasingly featured work by Scottish playwrights, both established dramatists such as Liz Lochhead and Edwin Morgan and a new generation including Mike Cullen, David Greig, Stephen Greenhorn, Zinnie Harris, and Nicola McCartney. The Traverse in Edinburgh and the Tron Theatre in Glasgow both have annual showcase festivals of new writing.

In the National Cultural Strategy (August 2000) the Scottish Executive expressed the view that the time is right to begin working towards the establishment of a national theatre for Scotland, and proposed a feasibility study for a company with a national remit. However, while the Scottish Arts Council has welcomed this proposal, the debate about whether Scotland should have a national theatre analogous to existing national companies such as Scottish Opera or Scottish Ballet is long-running and unresolved. The Federation of Scottish Theatre proposed a Scottish national theatre which would be a commissioning institution, without a specific building or a permanent company, under which existing companies and artists would present new work as national theatre productions. But the potential constraints on artistic freedom implied in a high degree of public funding are of concern to many practitioners in the Scottish theatre.

Sir James (Jimmy) Shand (1908–2000), musician. Born East Wemyss, Fife. One of Scotland's best-known country dance musicians and band leaders, as popular in the countries of the Scottish diaspora as in Scotland itself, particularly in the 1950s and 1960s. He made many appearances on television, for instance in Andy's Stewart's *White Heather Club*. Awarded MBE 1962; knighted 1999.

Jimmy Logan (James Short, 1928–2001), actor and entertainer. Born Glasgow. Awarded OBE 1996 and elected a Fellow of the RSAMD in 1998. He began working in the theatre at 14 and by 1944 was in pantomime, in which he acted for many years. His 'straight' acting debut was in 1949, in a film, *Floodtide*. He had dramatic roles in many plays, including *The Mating Game* (1973), *The Entertainer* (1984), *The Comedians* (1991), and *Death of a Salesman* (1992), and is also remembered for his show based on the life of Scottish music-hall entertainer Sir Harry Lauder (1870–1950). In 1964 he bought and refurbished the Glasgow Metropole Theatre, but the Glasgow authorities blocked any further development of it.

CURRENT INSTITUTIONS

While Scotland may not yet have a single 'national' company, it has a large number of theatre companies and venues great and small. While the Edinburgh Festival Theatre boasts the largest stage in Britain; the Mull Theatre at Dervaig, Isle of Mull, one of the smallest professional theatres in the world. The Perth Theatre is the oldest continuously producing rep in Scotland and in 2000 celebrated its 100th birthday and its 65th year as a repertory theatre. The Traverse, formed in 1963, was Scotland's first studio theatre company and has always focused on new productions from within and outside of Scotland. In the early 1990s it moved into new premises next to the Usher Hall in Edinburgh. In Glasgow, the Citizens' Theatre is known for productions of European drama. Other important repertory theatres are the Dundee Rep, the Pitlochry Festival Theatre, and Byre (St Andrews), whose new theatre was officially opened on 5 June 2001. Other major theatre buildings range from the Edwardian splendour of His Majesty's Theatre at Aberdeen (1904–6) and the spare lines of the Traverse in Edinburgh (1992) to imaginative conversions of other buildings, such as the Byre Theatre at St

Andrews, a former cowshed which opened as a theatre in 1933 and reopened in June 2001 after rebuilding.

Several touring companies are active, some attached to larger institutions. Touring theatre, dance and opera companies are extremely important in Scotland given the low population density and widely-spaced communities outside the central belt.

A number of projects also recognise the social benefits of participation in theatre for communities and individuals. Dundee Rep's Theatre Community Department includes a community drama outreach team, a specialist drama therapy service, and an arts advocacy project. Citizens' Theatre, located in the Gorbals in Glasgow – still one of Scotland's poorest areas – has long been committed to work involving the local community, and its Community Performance project, held for the third time in 2000, follows up a number of previous initiatives in community involvement in drama. At Theatre Workshop Edinburgh disabled performers work alongside able-bodied.

Educational institutions for theatre include the Royal Scottish Academy of Music and Drama, to which the drama school was added in 1945, and Scottish Youth Theatre. The Federation of Scottish Theatre is a professional association of Scottish theatre companies, the voice of Scottish theatre to funding bodies and the public, and the umbrella organisation for anyone professionally involved in theatre in Scotland.

THEATRE HIGHLIGHTS 2000–2001

NEW PLAYS:

Peter Arnott, *A Little Rain*, last play in a trilogy commissioned by 7:84.

Liz Lochhead, *Medea*, a new version in Scots, staged by Theatre Babel

Henry Adam, *Among unbroken hearts*, the Traverse Theatre's annual Writers' Project play for 2000

Zinnie Harris, *Further than the Furthest Thing*, joint production by Tron Theatre, Glasgow, and National Theatre, London

Iain Heggie, *The King of Scotland*, premiered at the Edinburgh Festival 2000

Douglas Maxwell, *Decky Does a Bronco*, premiered at the Edinburgh Festival 2000

Douglas Maxwell, *James II*, a historical comedy, previewing at Traverse March 2001.

Nicola McCartney, *Heritage*.

MAJOR PRODUCTIONS:

Molière's *Hypochondriak* at Royal Lyceum, Edinburgh, new production of Hector MacMillan's 1987 translation of *Le Malade Imaginaire*

Theatre Babel's production of J M Barrie's *Peter Pan*

Two productions of Québécois plays: Michel Tremblay's *Solemn Mass for a Full Moon in Summer* (Traverse Theatre/Barbican) and Jeanne-Mance Delisle's *The Reel of the Hanged Man* (Stellar Quines)

Productions of Edwin Morgan's *Phaedra* and *AD: A Trilogy of Plays on the Life of Jesus*, celebrating the dramatist's 80th birthday

Samuel Beckett festival in Glasgow 2000, various productions as part of an international Beckett festival.

MUSIC

CLASSICAL MUSIC

There is archaeological evidence of music-making in Scotland as far back as the eighth century BC, in finds such as a fragment of a bronze horn of that date, a carnyx (a long bronze war trumpet) from about 200 BC–AD 200, and representations of musical instruments on Pictish stone carvings of the eighth to tenth centuries AD.

The first music manuscripts containing Scottish music date from the 13th century, although some of the music in them, such as the chants for St Columba, may be older. They bear witness to a highly developed tradition of church music in Scotland, which seems to have reached its peak in the early 16th century with the work of Robert Carver, Scotland's greatest pre-Reformation composer and one of its greatest of any period. The manuscript containing all his extant work is one of the few music books to have survived the destruction wrought by the Reformation. Choral music from the late 16th century shows how radically the style of music permitted in church changed from the complex polyphony of Carver to unornamented hymn tunes and psalm settings, in Scots rather than Latin. Instrumental music, such as the keyboard works of William Kinloche, dating from *c.*1610, shows a continuing secular tradition with some distinct echoes of contemporary French styles. However, the Union of the Crowns in 1603 and the removal of the court to London and its patronage of the arts was a severe blow to classical musicians.

From the late 17th century a flow of composers and performers between Scotland and Italy began, stimulated in part by the fast-growing popularity of the violin in Scotland. One of the first to travel was John Clerk of Penicuik, who studied with Corelli. Among his many cantatas was one celebrating the ill-fated Darien venture of 1689; like its subject, it was abandoned unfinished. William McGibbon (1695–1756) was a leading Scottish composer of the late Baroque period, writing sonatas for violin and flute, trio sonatas and variations on Scottish folk tunes.

In the late 18th and the 19th centuries, political and social turbulence and a shortage of resources limited the production of composed music. Sir Alexander Campbell Mackenzie (1947–1935), although based chiefly in London and Germany, produced several works on Scottish themes; his *Scottish Concerto* was made famous by the pianist Paderewski.

In the late 20th century, after the foundation of the Edinburgh International Festival and the establishment of the major orchestras and Scottish Opera and Ballet, a new wave of outstanding composers based in Scotland arose. These include Sally Beamish, James MacMillan, Sir Peter Maxwell Davies, Thea Musgrave, Ronald Stevenson, William Sweeney and Judith Weir. The new generation currently active includes Stuart Macrae, Magnus Robb, and Marc Yeats.

WORLD PREMIÈRES OF WORKS BY SCOTTISH COMPOSERS, 2000–2001

The period January 2000–June 2001 saw 112 world premières of new works by Scottish composers, and at least 18 Scottish premières. Many of these took place in Scotland or at major Scottish festivals such as the St Magnus Festival, but many other works had their first performance in London, other towns in England, or further afield – in Brussels, New York or Auckland, for instance. Works premièred include:

Janet Beat, *Dynamism* (piano quartet)

Rory Boyle, *All Blether* (piano quartet)

Tommy Fowler, 7 works including *A White Fan Spreading Out and Lasting Forever* (violin/clarinet);

Edward McGuire, 11 works including Concertos for violin and double bass; *Memory* (a cappella voices); *Harbour of Harmonies* (piano);

John McLeod, 5 works including *Symphonies of Stone and Water* (piano/chamber orchestra);

James MacMillan, 5 works including *Exsultet* (percussion/orchestra); *Magnificat* (choir/orchestra); *Parthenogenesis* (music theatre);

Stuart Macrae, Piano Quintet; *Portrait II* (orchestra); *Sinfonia* (orchestra);

Peter Maxwell Davies, 7 works including Symphony no.8 ('Antarctic');

Thea Musgrave, *Aurora* (orchestra);

Magnus Robb, *Luscinian Blue* (orchestra);
William Sweeney, *Seeking Wise Salmon* (version for large chamber ensemble);
Judith Weir, Piano Quartet.

Source: Scottish Music Information Centre

TRADITIONAL MUSIC

Alongside – and intertwined with – the history of composed classical music runs a strong double strand of Gaelic and Scots traditional music, unbroken for centuries. It is an oral tradition, and although many of the old songs and tunes have been written down since the 17th century and have been the subject for much scholarship, the tradition is passionately alive today and continually developing. The Gaelic tradition is the oldest of all, and was probably brought to Scotland with the early settlers from Ireland. Its characteristic instrument is the clàrsach, or Celtic harp. A well-known form of Gaelic song is the *waulking song*, a strongly rhythmic work song which accompanied the hand-treatment of linen or tweed cloth. The tradition of Scots-language songs and ballads began later, in about the 13th century, and included epic narrative ballads as well as work songs and dance forms. The industrial revolution, the Clearances, and emigration were later ballad themes.

The 17th century, while something of a fallow period for large-scale classical compositions, was one of the richest times for the ballad tradition and especially for Gaelic music. In was in this period that the music of the pipes and the uniquely Scottish *piobaireachd* or *pibroch* form were developed. Similarly, in the 19th century, perhaps the strongest area of musical activity, in part inspired by romantic views of Scottish history, was the collection, notation and arrangement of folksongs, ballads and fiddle tunes. In fact, people had been writing ballads down since the 16th century, and Robert Burns was an avid collector and writer of songs (many of which were recorded by the traditional singer Jean Redpath in the 1970s). The National Mod, an annual, competitive festival of performing arts in Gaelic, was instituted in 1892 and remains an important instrument for the promotion of Gaelic culture.

The last 20 years have seen a big upsurge in traditional music and popular music with strong folk elements, building upon the pioneering work of Ewan McColl and his recordings of Scottish popular ballads in the 1950s and 1960s. A few key figures of the many musicians in this movement are the Boys of the Lough with the Shetland fiddle player Aly Bain, the Whistlebinkies, fiddler Alasdair Fraser, singers Cathy-Ann McPhee and Sheena Wellington, and bands singing in Gaelic such as Runrig and Capercaillie.

A POLICY FOR CONTEMPORARY POPULAR MUSIC

In March 2001, the SAC issued a policy statement on support for contemporary popular music, in line with its response to the National Cultural Strategy and after a two-year consultation process. This is the first time a British arts council has proposed a policy on pop music. The policy statement covers a wide range of current music styles and recommends actions including encouragement for the development of a national showcase event for new talent, support for training young promoters, agents and managers, and support for pilot touring projects. An additional allocation of £150,000 has been made by the Scottish Executive to the SAC to implement this policy.

CURRENT MUSICAL INSTITUTIONS

Scotland's contemporary musical life is underpinned by several national performing companies: the Royal Scottish National Orchestra (RNSO; founded 1890), Scottish Opera (founded 1962 under Alexander Gibson), and the Scottish Chamber Orchestra (SCO; founded 1974). Each of these has an associated chorus, and there is also an Edinburgh Festival Chorus which performs specifically for the Festival. The BBC Scottish Symphony Orchestra is based in Glasgow. There are also a number of smaller professional orchestras and vocal groups of international status, such as the BT Scottish Ensemble, the Paragon Ensemble and Cappella Nova.

The National Youth Orchestras of Scotland (NYOS), formed in 1979, comprises four orchestras: the National Youth Orchestra of Scotland (symphony orchestra), Camerata Scotland (a pre-professional chamber orchestra), the National Children's Orchestra of Scotland, and the National Youth Jazz Orchestra of Scotland. Together, they aim to provide a continuous sequence of practical music education and playing experience from nursery-school age to the professional level.

The Royal Scottish Academy of Music and Drama, in Glasgow, is the chief higher education institution for music, theatre and opera. It began in 1928 as the Scottish National Academy of Music, becoming the Royal Scottish Academy of Music in 1944 and adding the drama school the following year.

For traditional music, the Traditional Music and Song Association of Scotland, founded in 1966, is a valuable resource centre. Also in Glasgow, the Piping Centre is a national centre for the promotion of the bagpipes and their music.

DANCE

CLASSICAL DANCE

Scottish Ballet is Scotland's national classical dance company. Originally formed in Bristol in 1957 as Western Theatre Ballet, it moved to Glasgow in 1969, and on 3 May that year had a famous debut together with Scottish Opera in Berlioz's *The Trojans*. The company's arrival to take on the role of Scotland's national ballet company followed a series of unsuccessful attempts to establish such a company from about 1940 onwards, one candidate for which had been the Glasgow-based Celtic Ballet Company run by Margaret Morris, wife of the Colourist painter J. D. Fergusson.

Scottish Ballet performs both large-scale classics with a full dance company and orchestra in major theatres such as the Edinburgh Festival Theatre and chamber works for much smaller forces in spaces as small as a village hall or school gym. Its Education Unit carries out an extensive programme of education and outreach work in schools from nursery to secondary level (both mainstream and special education), universities and colleges of further education, community groups and hospitals, and with senior citizens' groups and sight- and hearing-impaired adults. It organises summer schools and courses, and can tailor projects to meet the needs of specific groups.

In recent years Dundee has become a focus for dance and dance education, with its own full-time professional dance company, Scottish Dance Theatre, based at the Dundee Repertory Theatre, and Scotland's only contemporary dance school, Scottish School of Contemporary Dance, which was founded in 1999 and is based at Dundee College. An aim of the school was to enable students to pursue their training for the profession in Scotland rather than having to travel elsewhere. A new multi-purpose venue, The Space, is being built to accommodate dance and drama classes, workshops and master classes for the local community and college students, and other facilities for the community and business.

The Dance School of Scotland, at Knightswood Secondary School in Glasgow, is Scotland's first full-time dance course for secondary-level students offering dance, singing and drama training within the state comprehensive school system

TRADITIONAL DANCE

Traditional Scottish dance encompasses various forms: sets or dances for groups of four of more people, dances for couples, and solo dances. Strictly speaking, 'Highland dancing' refers to the dancing which has its roots in the creation of the Highland regiments in the 18th and 19th centuries and the development of Highland Games, which always included dancing. The solo Sword Dance, for instance, is certainly as old as the 18th century and possibly older. In that context the pipes would have provided the music, but as Highland dancing became fashionable with Queen Victoria's patronage of Highland Games, other instruments, especially the violin, became associated with dancing. Dances for couples became popular in the 19th century under the influence of dances from England and further afield. Scottish country dancing seems always to have been a democratic affair; much the same dances were performed at balls and at village gatherings. No doubt the steps were familiar to most people; in the 19th century dances would often be taught by dancing masters at village schools.

Modern Scottish country dancing or 'ceilidh dancing' generally means set dancing. The term 'country dance' is a corruption of the French 'contredanse', referring to the fact that in these dances two lines of dancers typically stand facing ('opposite') each other. Ceilidhs (literally, the Gaelic word *céilidh* means 'visit') were an essential feature of social life in the Highlands, accompanying most celebrations, particularly weddings, and dancing is still a standard ingredient of weddings today, as well as Christmas and other celebrations. However, ceilidh dancing nowadays is most often performed by non-experts. As dancing became more popular among people who were not necessarily skilled at it, the practice of having a caller to call out the steps was adopted, and this still occurs sometimes. Formal Scottish country dances are also still held, where the dancers are expected to know the steps.

From quite early in the 20th century a movement to record and preserve traditional dances arose. The Scottish Country Dance Society was formed in 1923 (later adding 'Royal' to its title); it has published a large amount of dance music. Thirty years later, the Scottish Official Board of Highland Dancing was founded to preserve the traditional forms. Also concerned with researching and conserving Scotland's dance traditions is the Scottish Traditions of Dance Trust.

Traditional dance has a competitive as well as a social side, and several Highland dancing competitions are held each year. Dunoon hosts the World Highland Dancing championships, attracting competitors from not only Scotland but also around the world.

FILM

Until the 1990s, the film industry in Scotland was small. Scottish directors and actors tended to migrate to London or Hollywood and few feature directors derived their thematic material from their own country and culture before the 1980s, when Bill Douglas and Bill Forsyth began to make feature films showing a picture of Scotland that reached beyond the folkloric to address issues such as city life, poverty, or growing up . Yet Scots have been involved in moving pictures for many decades, ever since Queen Victoria was filmed at Balmoral in 1895. Among the most notable figures is John Grierson, founding father of the British documentary.

Scotland's rollcall of well-known and highly regarded film actors is long. Current stars such as Ewan McGregor, Robert Carlyle, John Hannah, Peter Mullan, Alan Cumming, Douglas Henshall, and others are just the latest in a long line – many of them also well known for their stage work – including Dame Flora Robson (1902–84), James Robertson Justice (1905–75), Deborah Kerr CBE (1921–), Gordon Jackson (1923–90), Ian Bannen (1928–99), Sir Sean Connery (1930–), Phyllida Law (1932–), Tom Conti (1941–), Bill Paterson (1946–), Billy Connolly (1942–), and Phyllis Logan (1956–).

But it is since 1994, the year in which Danny Boyle's *Shallow Grave* appeared, that the film industry in Scotland has been experiencing a boom. The unexpected success of that film, the immense popularity of Mel Gibson's *Braveheart* (1995), and particularly the runaway success in 1996 of Boyle's next film, *Trainspotting* (the most profitable British film ever, making £45 million in global box-office earnings), made the mid-1990s a watershed for Scottish film. Since then a stream of successful and well-received Scottish features has appeared, including *Small Faces* (Gillies MacKinnon, 1996), *Mrs Brown* (John Madden, 1997), *Carla's Song* and *My Name is Joe* (Ken Loach, 1995 and 1998), *Orphans* (Peter Mullan,

1999), *Ratcatcher* (Lynne Ramsay, 1999), *Women Talking Dirty* (Coky Giedroyc, 1999), and *Complicity* (Gavin Millar, 2000).

On the small screen, whereas representations of Scotland once tended to be synonymous with *Dr Finlay's Casebook*, Scottish themes as well as Scottish locations, from the gritty (*Roughnecks*, *Rebus*) to the light-hearted (*Monarch of the Glen*, *Hamish McBeth*), are now more and more frequently seen on British television. Scottish actors known for their television work include Siobhan Redmond (also a renowned theatre actor, especially through her collaboration with Liz Lochhead), Richard Wilson, Annette Crosbie, Daniela Nardini, Gregor Fisher, Elaine C. Smith, and Stanley Baxter. The Edinburgh Television Festival, held each year immediately after the Edinburgh International Film Festival, has become an important fixture for television professionals throughout the UK. Conceived as a Scottish millennium project, the *Castaway* television series, filmed on the Hebridean island of Taransay, was the first real-life drama of its type to be made in the UK.

Much of this growth in the film and television industry is due to the development of an institutional infrastructure and the increased availability of funding from the SAC (particularly via the National Lottery), Scottish Screen, Channel 4, the BBC, and the Glasgow Film Fund.

At the 2001 Cannes Film Festival, Scotland's only entry, *Daddy's Girl* by Irvine Allan, won a special jury prize for a short film.

SCOTLAND THE PHOTOGENIC

Interest in Scotland's potential as a source of film locations has dramatically increased. Over 40 feature films were shot entirely or partly in Scotland in the 1990s by directors as varied as Franco Zeffirelli, Brian de Palma, Ken Loach, Lars von Trier and Mel Gibson, as well as by Scottish directors. Even 'Bollywood', the Indian commercial film industry, seeking ever more exotic locations for its popular spectaculars, has used Scottish castles as a backdrop. In 2001, as well as a number of television series, six films had begun production using Scottish locations by the end of May, including *Morven Callar* (Lynne Ramsay), *The Last Great Wilderness* (Alistair Mackenzie), and *Rocket Post* (David Kellaway).

The connection between more Scottish locations appearing on screen and more tourists appearing in Scotland has not passed unnoticed, either. In April 2000 Scottish Screen joined forces with the Scottish Tourist Board, Scottish Trade

International and Historic Scotland to publish a brochure promoting Scottish film locations to the industry.

FILM EXHIBITION

Developments in commercial distribution and exhibition in Scotland parallel those elsewhere in Britain, with a trend towards big-chain multiplexes and a corresponding reduction in other cinemas. The principal chains operating in Scotland are UCI, Odeon, Virgin, ABC, Warner Village and Showcase. There are still some cinemas in smaller communities run by the Scottish chain Caledonian Cinemas, and a few family-run enterprises such the Pavilion, Galashiels, and the Dominion in Edinburgh.

Outside the major conurbations, however, permanent commercial cinemas are rare. The SAC has identified a cinema shortage, and National Lottery funding has recently been awarded to cinema development projects in Newton Stewart, Thurso, Portree, Stornoway, and Stranraer, and to Britain's first mobile cinema. The Screen Machine, a lorry trailer which converts to a 110-seat cinema, tours the Highlands and Islands showing mainstream and other films. It is administratively based in Inverness.

The Edinburgh International Film Festival is Scotland's largest annual film event and is now a world-class festival, premiering both British and international films. In 2000 it showed the world première of Terence Davies' *House of Mirth*, which uses Glasgow as a location (standing in for turn-of-the-century New York!), and UK premières of Lars von Trier's *Dancer in the Dark* and Wong Kar-Wai's *In the Mood for Love*. Scotland also hosts annual French and Italian film festivals with showings in Glasgow, Edinburgh and Aberdeen, often showing British premieres of French and Italian films.

A Pioneer of Television

The inventor John Logie Baird (1888–1946), a pioneer of television and radio, was a native of Helensburgh. His achievements in sending images by telephone wire from London to Glasgow and then across the Atlantic enabled the BBC to show its first television picture in 1929. However, his technological innovations were overtaken by those of IBM in the mid-1930s, although he continued to experiment with colour, 3-D and other developments, and radar.

SCOTTISH SCREEN

Scottish Screen is the public body responsible for promoting and developing all aspects of film, television and multimedia in Scotland, through the support of industrial and cultural initiatives. It took over the Scottish Film Production Fund in 1996 and is a major financer of films in Scotland. In 2000 it took over from the Scottish Arts Council the role of distributing body for National Lottery funding for film. For the financial year 2001–2 it has received £2.2 million from the Scottish Executive and £2.6 million in lottery funding. Scottish Screen supports and facilitates the production of films by Scottish film-makers, the use of Scottish locations by national and international film-makers, the preservation of Scotland's film heritage, and increased cinema-going and understanding of film in Scotland. Its large information service, which houses the Shiach Library of film scripts and other materials and holds a wide range of trade directories and periodicals related to film and television, is a free public reference facility. It runs a variety of long and short training courses, industry-related initiatives and educational activities, and is a first port of call for both Scottish film-makers developing a project and foreign film-makers looking for locations and facilities. It is a member of the Cinema Exhibitors' Association, the trade association for the cinema industry, and works with the commercial sector where appropriate.

The Scottish Film and Television Archive, set up in 1976, preserves Scotland's heritage of films from the past, both professional and amateur. It holds some 20,000 reels of film from 1897 onwards, largely on 16 and 35 mm with some acquisitions of 9.5mm and 8mm film and videotape. The collection is mostly non-fiction, including thousands of old feature films, home movies, newsreels, government information films and early advertisements for local businesses, unearthed and donated by members of the public. The television archive includes Gaelic broadcast material from 1993 onwards. The archive can be browsed online through the website of the Performing Arts Data Service (PADS).

Scottish Screen provides support to seven art cinemas, which in 1998–9 recorded 400,000 admissions. They are:

- Eden Court Theatre, Inverness
- Dundee Contemporary Arts, Dundee
- MacRobert Arts Centre, Stirling
- Adam Smith Theatre, Kirkcaldy
- Filmhouse, Edinburgh
- Glasgow Film Theatre, Glasgow
- Robert Burns Centre, Dumfries

Oscar-Winning Short Films
Seawards the Great Ships was made for Films of Scotland and the Clyde Shipbuilders Association in 1960. An evocative testimony to the achievements of the shipbuilders on the Clyde and to the men of the 'black squads', it was directed by Hilary Harris from a treatment by John Grierson. It won an Oscar for best live-action short film 1961.

Thirty-five years later, the 1995 Oscar for best live-action short film went to Peter Capaldi's Franz Kafka's *It's a Wonderful Life*.

BAFTA SCOTLAND
The Scottish branch of BAFTA, the British Film and Television Awards, held its first awards ceremony in 1991 and has been an annual event since then, alternating awards in the 'mainstream' film and television industry with New Talent awards until November 2000, when New Talent Awards were presented. From 2001, however, BAFTA Scotland plans to establish an annual mainstream Scottish awards event, to be held in November, with the New Talent awards, also held annually, moving to a different date, possibly 2002.

BAFTA SCOTLAND NEW TALENT AWARDS 2000
- Best Television Production: *Coming soon* (episode 1), written and directed by Annie Griffin, produced by Anna Campeau
- Best Writer: May Miles Thomas for *One life stand*
- Best Animation: *How the sea was salt*, by Campbell McAllister
- Best Director, television: Caroline Paterson for *Tinsel town* (episode 5)
- Best New Media: *Timewalk Village*, by Eolas Media Ltd
- Best Director, film: May Miles Thomas for *One life stand*
- Best Documentary: *Body and soul*, by Kara Johnston
- Best Film performance: Maureen Carr for *One life stand*
- Outstanding Craft Award: Simon Dennis for *Sex and death*
- Best Producer: Robbie Allen for *Tinsel town*
- Best Composer and Original Sound Design: Paul Leonard-Morgan for *Reflections upon the origins of the pineapple*
- Best Short Film: *What do busy people do all day?*, directed by Martin Morison, produced by Becky Lloyd, written by Mark Jenkins and Martin Morrison

- Best Television Performance: Stuart Wilkinson for *Kings of the wild frontier*
- Best Drama: *One life stand*, by May Miles Thomas
- Scottish Screen Award for Outstanding Achievement: *One life stand*, by May Miles Thomas

Glasgow Film Office Production Award Winners:
- Art Department: Andy Harris
- Camera: Alick Fraser
- Costume: Kate Carin
- Editing: John Gow
- Floor: David Gilchrist
- Make-up: Irene Napier
- Locations: Janet Riddoch
- Sounds: Louis Kramer AMPS
- Production: Willy Wands

VISUAL ARTS

ART IN EARLY SCOTLAND
Evidence of artistic skill in Scotland from the earliest times survives in finely wrought gold jewellery and bronze weapons; in the bronze boar's head from the Deskford carnyx (*see* Classical Music); in the early Christian stones and slabs which combine Pictish spirals and stylised animal motifs with ornamented crosses and other motifs of Irish origin, visible also in the great illuminated books such as that of Kells. The seventh to ninth centuries were a high point for Celtic art.

Though the arrival of the Vikings is often thought of merely as a time of destruction, their long occupation of parts of Scotland did make a cultural contribution, reflected most strongly in the 12th-century Lewis chess pieces, whether these were locally made or imported from Norway.

REFORMATION AND RECOVERY
Far more thoroughgoing destruction was inflicted by the Reformation. The double blow of the Reformation and the departure of the court to London in 1603 was devastating. Only a few tantalising fragments – remnants of wall paintings (Dunkeld cathedral), textile fragments, maps – give clues to the flourishing visual culture under James IV and James V that was lost in this period and the mid-17th century Bishops' Wars.

It was not until the 1640s that Scottish artists appeared again in their own country. The portraits painted by George Jameson of Aberdeen, including his self-portrait against a background of other paintings, establish him as the first Scottish painter in the modern sense. The Scottish School of Portraiture was to find its highest expression in the works of Allan Ramsay and Henry Raeburn in the following century. But before them came a series of painters including John Michael Wright, Jameson's most distinguished pupil. Wright's portrait of Lord Mungo Murray in Highland dress, echoed both in costume and pose by Raeburn's famous picture of Alasdair Macdonell of Glengarry over a century later, created an image of 'Scottishness' that was to become persistent.

THE SCOTTISH ENLIGHTENMENT

The neoclassicism of the 18th century was mainly expressed through architecture, but as the century progressed landscape paintings began to be produced which show the influence of Continental neoclassicists such as Claude Lorrain. A circle of intellectuals and artists grew up in Edinburgh, and Scotland's first art school, the Academy of St Luke, was established in 1729. Portraitists like William Aikman (1682–1731) found it easier to get commissions in London than in Scotland, though some, such as Aberdonians John Alexander (1686–c.1766) and William Mosman (1700–71), spent most of their careers in Scotland after studying in Rome.

The second half of the 18th century was marked by the interaction of art and philosophy – Allan Ramsay, together with his friends the philosopher David Hume and the economist Adam Smith, formed the Select Society – and further development of art training institutions, such as the Foulis Academy in Glasgow (1754) and the Trustees' Academy in Edinburgh (1766). Ramsay is the outstanding figure of this period. His genius lay in his empathetic interpretation of the sitter in either formal or intimate portraits, and in his delicate luminosity of style.

Alongside the classical themes favoured by several painters of this period (e.g. the six huge canvases by Gavin Hamilton (1723–98)) depicting scenes from Homer's *Iliad*, there grew up a romantic interest in the Celtic past, a pioneer in this respect being Alexander Runciman (1736–85), who chose the harper Ossian and other themes from Celtic legend for his etchings and some sketches for a set of murals (now lost) for the house of Sir James Clerk of Penicuik. This began a process of Celtic revival and reclamation of the Scottish past which is some respects is still going on, and a duality between classicism and Celticism that was to continue throughout the century.

Henry Raeburn was the second great portraitist of the Scottish Enlightenment, and probably the best-known painter of the century, not least because of his famous *Rev. Robert Walker Skating* in Edinburgh's National Gallery. His major portraits date from the early 1790s and are works of great humanity and perception as well as masterly essays in the study of light.

After its zenith with Raeburn, portraiture became less central to Scottish painting (although an active school of portrait sculpture developed in the early 19th century), and landscape and genre painting came to the fore. Alexander Nasmyth was the seminal figure in landscape painting. To the usual art education in London and Rome he added an acquaintance with northern European – particularly Dutch – landscape painting and an interest in the relationship between human beings and landscape, nature and culture; this can be seen in his two canvases of Edinburgh, which juxtapose the wild natural forms of Calton Hill and Arthur's Seat with the perspectives of human construction. Nasmyth was also an influential teacher.

In genre painting, David Wilkie became the master of paintings depicting daily life. His paintings 'tell a story' and assert the dignity of ordinary people; some of them implicitly comment on the social and economic reality of the time.

WILDERNESS AND DISPOSSESSION

In 1826 a group of 11 artists formed themselves into the Scottish Academy as a representative body for Scottish artists. The academy was modelled loosely on the Royal Academy in London. It obtained its royal charter in 1837, and its members were instrumental in founding the National Gallery of Scotland, which opened in 1859.

As the 19th century progressed, a school of painting emerged which could lay claim to be distinctively Scottish. Many of its members had studied at the Trustees' Academy, which became the principal art school in the country under Robert Scott Lauder (1803–61). Lauder painted scenes from Scott's Waverley novels, among other subjects, and was one of a diverse circle including David Octavius Hill (1802–70), also a pioneering photographer, Horatio McCulloch (1805–67), Thomas Faed (1826–1900) and William Dyce (1806–64). These artists painted the Highlands as uninhabited wilderness and spectacle, while at the same time depicting themes of emigration and exile from the land, for instance in Faed's *Highland Mary* (1857) and his famous *The Last of the Clan* (1865), or McCulloch's *The Emigrant's Dream of his Highland Home* (1860).

At this time there was a vogue for large public sculptures of important Scottish and British figures. Outstanding here is John Steell

(1804–91), whose figure of Sir Walter Scott forms the central element of the Scott Memorial in East Princes Street Garden, Edinburgh.

THE RISE OF GLASGOW AS AN ART CENTRE

Toward the end of the century, a new approach to landscape painting was introduced by William McTaggart, who used an almost impressionist technique, particularly noticeable in his coastal scenes and seascapes. He too took up the theme of the Highland Clearances and emigration in a series of 'Emigrant Ship' canvases of the 1890s.

In the 1880s Glasgow took over from Edinburgh as the epicentre of Scottish painting. The Glasgow Institute of the Fine Arts had been set up in 1861 as a counterpart – and in part a challenge – to Edinburgh's Royal Scottish Academy, and a sizeable group of artists, nicknamed the 'Glasgow Boys' (although one at least was a woman) coalesced around a reaction to the Victorian concept of landscape and a tendency to look to France for inspiration. Following McTaggart's lead, this as the first group of Scottish painters who regularly painted in the open air, and this led to a change in landscape subject matter from mountain and moor to rivers, coasts and villages. The 'Boys' also returned to subjects from ordinary life, such as John Lavery's *Tennis party* of 1885 or James Guthrie's more down-to-earth *A Hind's Daughter* (1883), with hints of Cézanne in its brushwork. It is possible to discern a line of descent from these works, via the jewel-like watercolours of Arthur Melville (1855–1904), to the treatment of colour and paint characteristic of the Colourists a few decades later.

Also in the early 1890s, Charles Rennie Mackintosh was at the centre of a group of artists, fellow-students at the Glasgow School of Art: Margaret Macdonald (1863-1933), who became Mackintosh's wife, her sister Frances (1874–1921), and Herbert MacNair (1868–1955). The decorative style they developed, close to Art Nouveau but identifiably their own, has become very famous, and inspired the work of a wider circle of graphic and applied artists. Mackintosh's own landscape paintings, however, overshadowed by the popularity of his design, have not fully received the appreciation they deserve. In Edinburgh, the clear thematic and stylistic links between the Arts and Crafts movement and the Celtic Revival are illustrated in the work of Phoebe Anna Traquair (1852–1936), which encompasses a vast range of crafts from metalwork to murals. Her murals for the Catholic Apostolic Church are an impressive example.

THE 20TH CENTURY

The four Colourists – Samuel Peploe, J. D. Fergusson, F. C. B. Cadell and G. L. Hunter – are distinguished by their freshness and spontaneity and the brilliance of light and colour in their paintings. All four spent considerable time in France and it is likely the Fauves were an influence on them and, later, Matisse.

By the 1930s, Modernism was firmly established in Scottish painting in the works of William Crozier (1897–1930), Anne Redpath (1895–1965), William Johnstone (1897–1981), James Cowie (1880–1956) and others. The continental influence (Matisse, Klee, Cubism) remained strong, but landscape continued to be a principal source of subject matter. The influence of the Colourists continued to be felt after World War II and to show up in Scottish interpretations of newer styles. But great diversity characterises artists of the 1950s and after, such as Robert MacBryde (1913–66), Robert Colquhoun (1914–62), Joan Eardley (1921–63), and the sculptors Eduardo Paolozzi (1924–) and Ian Hamilton Finlay. Among yet more recent work are large projects working in the landscape by George Wyllie, Kate Whiteford and Will Maclean; Maclean's three large works on Lewis (1996), commemorating the struggle between landlords and tenants at the turn of the 20th century, raise again questions of national history and identity. Calum Colvin, a winner of one of the SAC's Creative Scotland Awards, is taking up the Celtic thread with an exhibition of digital and analog photographic works based on James Macpherson's *The Poems of Ossian and Related Works*. A resurgence of figurative art has informed the work of the new generation of Glasgow painters such as Alexander Moffat; and the opening of the Glasgow Gallery of Modern Art in 1996 has made a new space available for the work of Scotland's new generation of artists.

CURRENT INSTITUTIONS

Most of the art institutions set up in the last century continue in existence, though they have all undergone changes and sometimes crisis over the years. Bodies existing today include the following.

The Royal Scottish Academy (RSA) is the main exhibiting body promoting the works of living Scottish professional artists. It has about 40 full members and 50 associate members, elected from the disciplines of architecture, painting, printmaking and sculpture, and holds a large annual exhibition.

The Royal Glasgow Institute of the Fine Arts, established in 1861 also has a gallery and exhibition space, and holds lectures.

Royal Society of Painters in Watercolours promotes the status of watercolour as a major art. It holds an annual exhibition at the RSA galleries, and also issues financial awards.

The principal remit of the Royal Fine Art Commission for Scotland is to advise government on the visual impact of new constructions.

Among institutions for art education and training, many are part of universities. Glasgow School of Art is one of the very few remaining independent art schools in the United Kingdom. It was founded in 1845 as a Government School of Design and added the study and practice of the fine arts and architecture to its curriculum in the late 19th century. The present building, commissioned in 1896, is one of Charles Rennie Mackintosh's masterpieces. The School's degrees are accredited by the University of Glasgow.

At Aberdeen, Gray's School of Art, which is part of the Robert Gordon University, has almost as long a history as the Glasgow School of Art. It was founded in 1850, gifted to Robert Gordon's College by John Gray, an engineer and philanthropist. A new Gray's School was built at its current location in 1966.

Other art schools include the Edinburgh College of Art and the Duncan of Jordanstone College of Art in Dundee.

ARCHITECTURE

A HERITAGE IN STONE

Stone has always been a characteristic material of Scottish architecture, and this has ensured a very large and varied built heritage from all periods, with buildings more likely to have been destroyed by conflict than just to have fallen into decay. The prevailing styles of the Middle Ages, except in the Highlands and Islands, were very similar to those found in England and France, since it was to these countries that the kings responsible for the upsurge in building from the 12th century onwards looked. Norman-style churches such as Dalmeny church, near South Queensferry, and Dunfermline Abbey date from the early part of this period. The Gothic style which followed can be seen at its best in what survives of the Border abbeys, of which Melrose is both one of the latest (having been completely destroyed in the 14th century and rebuilt in the 15th) and most elaborate.

Over the medieval period, the typical form of the castle settled into that of a keep with a courtyard defended by a heavy curtain wall. Many castles dating from the 14th and 15th centuries survive: some well-known examples are Glamis,

Dunvegan and the much-photographed Eilean Donan. Smaller castles of the period, such as Smailholm (Borders), show the features that were to evolve into the tower house, the typical dwelling of the Scottish lairds from the 15th to the 17th centuries. Here the jewel in the crown is widely held to be Craigievar Castle (Aberdeenshire), largely because its elegant original lines escaped Victorian remodelling. Meanwhile, beauty as much as strength was the principle governing the creation of the great palaces of the Stewart kings, such as Linlithgow, Falkland and Stirling, which show strong French Renaissance influences; while in the crowded city of Edinburgh (now the Old Town), confined within the city wall, a jigsaw of closes and wynds with six- and seven-storey tenements proliferated, becoming ever more cramped and jumbled.

CLASSICISM AND ROMANTICISM

The first Scottish buildings whose architects are known date from the early 17th century. The names of William Wallace, William Ayton, and John and Robert Mylne are associated with the building of George Heriot's Hospital (now a school) in Edinburgh, begun in 1628, while the palace of Holyroodhouse was rebuilt, after a fire in 1650, to a design by Sir William Bruce, assisted by Robert Mylne (1633–1710). Mylne was one of a dynasty of master masons and architects, spanning 200 years from the late 16th century and based in Dundee.

In the late 18th century, a more flourishing economy fuelled a boom in building and a flowering of the English Classical style, which is best illustrated by Edinburgh's New Town, designed by James Craig in 1767 and with later contributions by Robert Adam (Charlotte Square, 1791). Robert and his father William Adam, probably Scotland's greatest classicists, designed Mellerstain House (Borders), and were responsible for both the interior and exterior of a large extension to Hopetoun House (South Queensferry), originally built by William Bruce. This was also the period of construction of new towns and villages, part of the policy of Improvement.

Victorian architecture was heavily influenced by retrospection and a romantic idea of Scotland, but innovative in its eclectic borrowing from any and every style of the past. In a revival of the Scottish baronial style, the turrets and crenellations of 16th century tower houses reappeared not only on country mansions but suburban villas. As the cities mushroomed, the tenement, at varying levels of luxury, became the typical urban dwelling. Church-building took off again and neo-Gothic churches are to be seen in every Scottish town. Gilbert Scott's Glasgow University Building of 1867 is a fine example of this style, as is St John's Tolbooth on the High Street, Edinburgh, originally built as General Assembly Rooms by James Gillespie Graham in 1842, later transformed by Augustus Pugin, and converted in 1999 to a new administrative and social centre for the Edinburgh Festival, the Hub.

Looking even further back to classical models, but also forward in his use of them, was Alexander 'Greek' Thomson in Glasgow. His churches at St Vincent Street (1859), and Caledonian Road (1856) are particularly important examples of neoclassical architecture; while in his use of Egyptian-inspired decoration and severely horizontal composition, for instance in the Egyptian Halls, Union Street (1871–3), he was well ahead of his time. A major exhibition of his work as part of Glasgow's year as City of Architecture and Design (1999) has contributed to a revaluation of Thomson.

MACKINTOSH AND AFTER

Glasgow's other major architect, and probably Scotland's best known architect and designer ever, is, of course, Charles Rennie Mackintosh, whose greatest work was carried out at the turn of the 20th century. One of the greatest exponents of the British Arts and Crafts movement, Mackintosh was also a designer of furniture and textiles and a painter, and his elegant Art Nouveau decoration, which has been overly imitated in recent years, has perhaps distracted attention from architecture such as the Glasgow School of Art (1897), his most famous building, the Willow Tea Rooms in Sauchiehall Street, and Hill House (Helensburgh, 1902), a Scottish tower house for the 20th century with an exquisitely detailed interior.

Glasgow continues to produce innovative buildings at the end of the 20th century, such as Sir Norman Foster's Clyde Auditorium, nicknamed 'the Armadillo' because of its use of overlapping shells reminiscent of the Sydney Opera House. In Dundee, Richard Murphy's Contemporary Arts Centre, converted from a former garage and car showroom, combines a spacious, clean-lined interior with a sweeping, curvilinear frontage.

Meanwhile, in Edinburgh, the new National Museum of Scotland (1996–8), built mostly of sandstone, has been widely acclaimed. At the time of writing, the most controversial architectural project in Scotland must be the new Scottish Parliament Building in Edinburgh. An architectural competition in 1997 awarded the design contract to the Catalan architect Enric Miralles, who submitted an imaginative and elegant design; but progress has been dogged by budget problems and the project has been dealt a further blow by Miralles' untimely death, at the age of 45, in July 2000.

SOME KEY FIGURES IN THE ARTS

WRITERS

Ballantyne, R.M. (1825–94), children's writer, born Edinburgh. After working for Hudson's Bay Company in Canada, 1841–47, published *Hudson's Bay, Everyday Life in the Wilds of North America* (1848). Wrote over 90 books, mainly children's adventure stories, the best-known being *The Coral Island* (1857). Autobiography: *Personal Reminiscences in Book-making* (1893).

Barrie, Sir James M. (1860–1937), playwright and novelist, born Kirriemuir, Angus. Beginning his career with magazine articles and novels (e.g. *The Little Minister*, 1891, later dramatised), he became a successful playwright. Best known for *Peter Pan* (1904); other work includes *Quality Street* (1902), *The Admirable Crichton* (1902), *The Boy David* (1936).

Boswell, James (1740–95), biographer and travel writer, born Edinburgh. With Samuel Johnson, undertook extensive tour of Scotland in 1773. Account of journey written by Johnson but Boswell published *Journal of a Tour to the Hebrides* (1785). Contributed over 40 articles to *London Magazine* (1777–83). Published biography of Johnson in 1791. Other work includes *An Account of Corsica* (1768).

Brown, George Mackay (1921–1996), poet, novelist and short-story writer, born Stromness. Orkney forms the subject and backdrop of most of his work. Work includes: poetry: *Loaves and Fishes* (1959), *Fishermen with Ploughs* (1971), *Stone: Poems* (1987); novels: *Greenvoe* (1972), *Magnus* (1973), *Beside the Ocean of Time* (1994; Scottish Book of the Year); short stories: *A Calendar of Love* (1967), *The Masked Fisherman and Other Stories* (1989). Collaborated with or inspired Peter Maxwell Davies in several works.

Buchan, John (1875–1940), novelist, biographer, historian, essayist, journalist, editor, poet and publisher, born Perth. As well as pursuing a varied career as diplomat (from 1901), war correspondent (c. 1915) and MP (1927–35), he wrote 100 books, including *The Thirty-Nine Steps* (1915), *Greenmantle* (1916), *Witch Wood* (1927), *Castle Gay* (1930), and biographies of Montrose, Cromwell, and Scott.

Burns, Robert (1759–96), poet and songwriter, born Alloway, Ayrshire. Regarded as Scotland's national poet, and its chief writer and collector of ballads and songs. Inspired by his travels round Scotland, from 1788 onwards he contributed hundreds of songs to collections edited by James Johnson and George Thomson. Published his first collection of poems, *Poems Chiefly in the Scottish Dialect*, in 1786; Among his most famous poems are 'Auld lang syne', 'O my luve is like a red, red rose', 'Ae fond kiss', 'Tam O'Shanter' (1790), 'Is there for honest poverty' (1793).

Carlyle, Thomas (1795–1881), essayist, historian and critic, born Ecclefechan, Dumfriesshire. Very highly regarded during his own day, his works are idiosyncratic and difficult to classify today. They include *Sartor Resartus* (1835), *The French Revolution* (1837), *On Heroes, Hero-worship and the Heroic in History* (1841), *Past and Present* (1843), *Oliver Cromwell's Letters and Speeches* (1845), *The History of Frederick the Great* (1858–65)

Cronin, A.J. (1896–1981), novelist, born Cardross, Dunbartonshire. His works, based on his own experiences as a doctor, include *Hatter's Castle* (1931), *The Keys of the Kingdom* (1942) and *The Green Years* (1945); the latter two were filmed. *The Citadel* (1937), based on the practices of Harley Street doctors, led indirectly to creation of National Health Service. The 1960s television and radio series *Dr Finlay's Casebook* were based on Cronin's experiences.

Doyle, Sir Arthur Conan (1859–1930), author, born Edinburgh. The novella *A Study in Scarlet* (1887) introduced his most famous characters, Sherlock Holmes and Dr Watson. Published two series of Sherlock Holmes tales in the *Strand Magazine* (1891–93 and from 1903), and a novel, *The Hound of the Baskervilles* (1902). Other works include adventure novels *The Lost World* (1912) and *The Poison Belt* (1913), historical romances, and two propagandist works justifying Britain's involvement in the Boer War in South Africa.

Dunbar, William (1460–*c*.1513), poet. Court poet to James IV, writing both eulogism and works of social and moral criticism. Works include *Lament for the Makaris* (maker, is the old Scots word Dunbar used to describe his contemporary poets), *The Thrissil and the Rois* (nuptial song for marriage of James IV and Margaret Tudor in 1503), *The Flyting of Dunbar and Kennedie, Dance of the Sevin Deidly Synnes*.

Galloway, Janice (1956–), novelist and short-story writer, born Ayrshire. Work includes several prizewinning novels: *The Trick is to Keep Breathing*

(1989), *Blood* (1992), *Foreign Parts* (1994). Has also written a play, *Fall* (1997–98), collaborated with Sally Beamish and Alasdair Nicolson on three song cycles, and is working with Beamish on an opera libretto, *Monster*, scheduled for production 2002.

Gibbon, Lewis Grassic (James Leslie Mitchell, 1901–35), novelist, journalist, and historian, born Aberdeenshire. Works include: *A Scots Quair* (trilogy, 1932–4), *Stained Radiance* (1930), *Scots Scene: or, The Intelligent Man's Guide to Albyn* (1934, with Hugh MacDiarmid); *Speak of the Mearns* (unfinished, published 1982).

Gray, Alasdair (1934–), novelist, playwright, painter and book designer, born Glasgow. His first and largest novel, *Lanark*, was begun in the 1950s but not published until 1981. Other works include: *Janine* (1982), *Poor Things* (1992), *Printer's Devil* (1995), *The Book of Prefaces* (2000). *Why Scots Should Rule Scotland* (1992, 2nd edn 1997) argues for Scottish independence.

Gunn, Neil M. (1891–1973), novelist, born Dunbeath, Caithness. After meeting Hugh MacDiarmid in the 1920s, became involved both in political nationalism and the literary renaissance. His novels are imbued with a deep sense of history and place. Works include: *The Grey Coast* (1926), *Morning Tide* (1930), *Highland River* (1937), *The Silver Darlings* (1941), *The Serpent* (1943).

Henryson, Robert (*c*.1420–*c*.1490), poet. Probably a schoolmaster at Dunfermline Abbey school. One of the Scottish 'Chaucerians'. Extant works include: *The Testament of Cresseid*, *The Morall Fabillis of Esope the Phrygian*, *Robene and Makyne*.

Hogg, James (1770–1835), poet and novelist, born Ettrick, Borders. Known as 'The Ettrick Shepherd'. His first published work was a volume of ballads, *The Mountain Bard* (1807). *The Queen's Wake* (1813) made him famous, relating a poetic contest at the court of Queen Mary. Other works include: *The Poetic Mirror* (1816), *The Three Perils of Man* (1822), *The Three Perils of Women* (1823), *Tales of the Wars of Montrose* (1835), and *The Shepherd's Calendar* (1829), written for *Blackwood's Magazine*.

Kelman, James (1946–), novelist and short-story writer, born Glasgow. The social realism and social analysis of his work has influenced the younger generation of Scottish writers. Works include: *Greyhound for Breakfast* (1987), *A Disaffection* (1989), *How Late It Was, How Late* (1994, Booker Prize); short stories, *The Good Times* (1998).

Lochhead, Liz (1947–), poet and playwright, born Motherwell. Poetry includes: *Memo for Spring* (1972), *The Grimm Sisters* (1981), *True Confessions and New Clichés* (1985); plays include: *Blood and Ice* (1982), *Mary Queen of Scots Got Her Head Chopped Off* (1989), *Perfect Days* (1998), *Medea* (2000).

MacDiarmid, Hugh (Christopher Murray Grieve, 1892–1978), born Langholm, Dumfriesshire. Poet, critic and journalist. Key figure of Scottish 20th-century literary renaissance, writing chiefly in Scots. Works include: *Sangschaw* (1925), *A Drunk Man Looks at the Thistle* (1926), *In Memoriam James Joyce* (1954), *'On a raised beach'* (1934).

MacGonagall, William (1825/1830–1902), affectionately hailed as 'the world's worst poet'. Born Edinburgh. A weaver by trade, he became an amateur actor in Dundee and later published verse in broadsheet and book forms. Works include *'Railway bridge of the silv'ry Tay'* (1877), *'The Tay Bridge Disaster', 'The death of Lord and Lady Dalhousie'*; a selection was published as *Poetic Gems* (1890).

Mackenzie, Sir Compton (1883–1972), novelist, playwright, journalist and broadcaster, born West Hartlepool of Scottish ancestry. Works include *Sinister Street* (1918); Gallipoli Memories (1929), based on his experiences in the fist world war; *The Four Winds of Love* (6 vols., 1937–45); and *Whisky Galore* (1947), made famous as a film. Awarded OBE 1919, knighted 1952.

Maclean, Alistair (1982–1987), novelist, born Glasgow. Wrote 30 popular novels of which 28 sold over a million copies in the UK, including *HMS Ulysses* (1955), based on his own wartime experiences, and *The Guns of Navarone* (1957).

McWilliam, Candia (1955–), novelist and short-story writer, born Edinburgh. Works include: *A Case of Knives* (1988), *A Little Stranger* (1989), *Debatable Land* (1994; Guardian Fiction Prize); short stories, *Wait Till I Tell You* (1997); editor, *Shorts II: The Macallan/Scotland on Sunday Short Story Collection*.

Munro, Neil (1864–1930), novelist, journalist and poet, born Inverary, Argyll. Editor of *Glasgow Evening News* 1918–27. Early works include *The Last Pibroch* (1896), a collection of Celtic tales and *Gilean the Dreamer* (1899), a story of 19th century Scottish life. Best known today for collections of stories of 'Para Handy', beginning with *The Vital Spark* (1906). He also wrote a number of historical novels and some poetry.

Oliphant, Margaret (1828–1897), novelist, born Wallyford, near Edinburgh. Wrote over 100 novels as well as non-fiction and articles for *Blackwood's Magazine*. Novels include: *Passages in the Life of Mrs Margaret Maitland* (1849); *Caleb Field* (1851); *Katie Stewart* (1853, serialised in *Blackwood's*); *A Quiet Heart* (1854). Between 1861 and 1876, wrote a seven-volume series of novels on English country life, 'The Chronicles of Carlingford'.

Ramsay, Allan (1684–1758), poet and editor, born Leadhills, Lanarkshire. Wrote collections of verse in Scots and English, 1721, 1728; editor of *The Ever Green* (anthology of Middle Scots poetry) and *Tea-Table Miscellany* (traditional songs and ballads plus some compositions of his own). His pastoral *The Gentle Shepherd* (1725) was later made into a ballad opera. Father of the painter Allan Ramsay.

Scott, Sir Walter (1771–1832), novelist, poet, editor and critic, born Edinburgh. Regarded as a great author even in his own lifetime, he produced over 25 novels as well as poetry, *Lives and Works of Dryden* (18 vols, 1808) and *Swift* (19 vols, 1814), and contemporary history, such as a nine-volume life of Napoleon Bonaparte. Poetry includes: *The Lay of the Last Minstrel* (1805), *The Lady of the Lake* (1810), and a ballad collection, *Minstrelsy of the Scottish Border* (1802–3); novels include: *Waverley* (1814), *Rob Roy* (1817), *The Heart of Midlothian* (1818), *Ivanhoe* (1819), *Kenilworth* (1821), and *St Ronan's Well* (1823).

Smollett, Tobias (1721–71), novelist, historian and travel writer. Born Dumbarton. First publication, *The Tears of Scotland* (1746) centred on the Jacobite Rising of 1745. Novels include: *The Adventures of Roderick Random* (1748), *The Adventures of Peregrine Pickle* (1751), and *The Adventures of Ferdinand Count Fathom* (1753); travel writing includes: *A Compendium of Authentic and Entertaining Voyages* (7 vols, 1756). His final work, *The Expedition of Humphrey Clinker* (1771), was considered his finest.

Spark, Dame Muriel (1918–), novelist, short-story writer, biographer and poet. Born Edinburgh. Her 1961 novel *The Prime of Miss Jean Brodie*, has become her best-known work through its adaptation as a play and film. Other works include *The Comforters* (1957, her first novel), *The Ballad of Peckham Rye* (1960), *Loitering with Intent* (1995), *Curriculum Vitae: A Volume of Autobiography* (1993), and *Aiding and Abetting* (2000), her most recent novel. Awarded OBE in 1967, Dame of British Empire 1993.

Stevenson, Robert Louis (1850–94), novelist, poet, playwright, essayist, travel writer. Born Edinburgh. Despite suffering from tuberculosis for most of his life, he travelled widely, gathering material for books such as *Travels with a Donkey in the Cevennes* (1879), and, much later, *In the South Seas*. Novels include *Treasure Island* (1883), *The Strange Case of Dr Jekyll and Mr Hyde* (1886), *Kidnapped* (1886); *The Master of Ballantrae* (1889). Short stories include *'Thrawn Janet'* and *'The beach at Falesa'*. Poetry includes *A Child's Garden of Verses* (1885), recalling his own childhood.

Welsh, Irvine (1961–), novelist and short-story writer, born Edinburgh. His stories, rooted in young urban working-class life, are characterised by *noir* humour and first-person narratives. Works include: short stories: *The Acid House* (1994); novels: *Trainspotting* (1994), *Marabou Stork Nightmares* (1996), *Filth* (1998), *Glue* (2001).

COMPOSERS

Carver, Robert (1487–1566), Scotland's greatest 16th-century composer. Studied at the Flemish University of Leuven 1503–4 and was a canon of the Augustinian abbey of Scone from 1508. His 19 surviving works include: motets *O bone Jesu* (19 parts), *Gaude flore virginali*; 5 masses including the 10- part *Missa Dum sacrum mysterium* (1506), which was sung at the coronation of James V in 1513.

Clarke (or Clerk), Sir John of Penicuik (1676–1755), Studied at Glasgow and Leiden. Works include: cantatas: *Leo Scotiae irritatus, Dic mihi, saeve puer* (1690s); violin sonata (*c*.1705). Also an architect.

Davies, Sir Peter Maxwell (1934–), born Manchester. Has lived and worked in Orkney since 1970. Founder of St Magnus festival in 1977. His over 200 published works include: *Job*; *The Doctor of Myddfai*; *The martyrdom of St Magnus*; *Eight songs for a mad king*; *Orkney Wedding with Sunrise*; 10 Strathclyde Concertos, 8 symphonies. Awarded CBE 1981, knighted 1987

MacMillan, James (1959–), born Kilwinning, Ayrshire. Works include: *The Tryst* (1984), setting of text by William Soutar; *The confession of Isabel Gowdie* (1990), *Veni, veni Emmanuel* (1992), percussion concerto for Evelyn Glennie and SCO; *Seven last words from the Cross* (1993); cello concerto for Mstislav Rostropovich; *Inés de Castro* (opera, 1996); *Parthenogenesis* (2001).

McGuire, Edward (1948–), born Glasgow. Works include: operas *Calgacus* (1997) and *The Loving of Etain* (1990); *A Glasgow Symphony* (1990); *Celtic Epic* (1997), orchestra and traditional musicians; several new works 2000–01. Also a performer and composer of traditional music associated since the early 1970s with the traditional music group the Whistlebinkies.

Macrae, Stuart (1976–), born Inverness. His first major work, *Boreraig* (1996), was performed by the BBC Philharmonia, who also performed *The Witch's Kiss* (1997). Other works include: *Landscape and the Mind: Distance, Refuge* (1997); *Elemental* (1999); *Sinfonia* for chamber orchestra (2000).

Musgrave, Thea (1928–), born Edinburgh. Works include: *Journey through a Japanese landscape* (marimba and wind orchestra, 1994); *Helios* (oboe concerto, 1995); *Autumn Sonata (A concerto for bass clarinet and orchestra)*; *Simón Bolívar* (opera, 1995)

Peebles, David (*c*.1510–79), a canon at the Augustinian prioriy of St Andrews whose four-part harmonisations of metrical psalm tunes from *The Scottish Psalter*, produced under the supervision of Thomas Wode, vicar of St Andrews, were collected in the *Wode Part-Books*. Other extant works include: *Si quis diligit me*; *Quam multi, Domine*.

Stevenson, Ronald (1928–), born Lancashire, now based in the Borders. Best known for his piano works, especially *Passacaglia on DSCH* (1963), based on the composer Shostakovich's musical initials, and *Barra Flyting Toccata*. Other works include: violin concerto 1992; cello concerto *In memoriam Jacqueline du Pré*; song cycles *A Child's Garden of Verses, Nine Haiku, Border Boyhood*; over 200 songs.

Sweeney, William (1950–), born Glasgow. Strongly influenced by traditional Gaelic music and jazz; has made several settings of work by Scottish poets in Gaelic and Scots. Works include: *An Turus* (1997), collaboration with poet Aonghas MacNeacail; *Salm an fhearainn/Psalm of the land* (1987), also to Gaelic text by MacNeacail; *An rathad ur/The new road* (1988), *Coilltean Ratharsair/The woods of Raasay* (1993), setting of poem by Sorley Maclean.

Weir, Judith (1954–), born Cambridge of Scottish parents. Has worked at Glasgow University (1979–82) and RSAMD (1988–91). Artistic director of Spitalfields Festival, London, 1995–2000. Works include: operas *A night at the Chinese opera* (1987), *The vanishing bridegroom* (1990); *Blond Eckbert* (1994); *Moon and star* (chorus/orchestra, 1995), written for the 1995 Proms.

DANCERS

Clark, Michael (1962–), dancer and choreographer, born Aberdeen. Formed his own company at the age of 22. Works include: *I Am Curious, Orange* (1988), *Mmm* (1993), *O* (1994). Also appeared as Caliban in Peter Greenaway's film *Prospero's Books*.

Kemp, Lindsay (1939–), dancer, choreographer and mime artist. Formed Lindsay Kemp Company 1973. Works include *Flowers, Salomé, Duende, Alice, Onnagata, Dreamdances* (1998). Has appeared in films, including *Sebastiane* (Derek Jarman, 1975) and *Savage Messiah* (Ken Russell, 1972).

MacMillan, Sir Kenneth (1929–92), choreographer., born Dunfermline. In 1946 became a founder memer of Sadlers Wells Theatre Ballet. Principal choreographer, Royal Ballet, 1977–92. A leading figure in contemporary ballet. Works include: *Danses Concertantes* (1955), *The Invitation* (1960), *Romeo and Juliet, Anastasia, The Prince of the Pagodas, The Judas Tree* (Olivier Award,1992). Knighted 1983.

Morris, Margaret (1891–1980), dancer and dance teacher. Developed a dance method and notation system and a system of movement therapy which have influenced many later dance teachers. Founder of Celtic Ballet Company and Celtic Ballet Theatre, Glasgow, in 1940.

FILM-MAKERS

Boyle, Danny (1956–), born Manchester. Began his career in theatre, and has also directed many television features, including *Mr Wroe's Virgins* and episodes of *Inspector Morse*. Films include: *Shallow Grave* (1994), *Trainspotting* (1996), *The Beach* (2000)

Douglas, Bill (1937–91), film-maker, born Newcraighall. His autobiographical trilogy – *My Childhood* (1972), *My Ain Folk* (1973), *My Way Home* (1978) – describes growing up in a Scottish mining community.

Forsyth, Bill (1946–), director, writer and producer, born Glasgow. Known for small-scale, quiet comedies. Works include: *That Sinking Feeling* (1979), *Gregory's Girl* (1981), *Local Hero* (1983), *Being Human* (1993), *Gregory's Two Girls* (1999).

Grierson, John (1898–1972), pioneer documentary film-maker and producer, born Deanston. He produced a vast number of documentaries but directed relatively few. They include: *Drifters* (1929), made for theEmpire Marketing Board Film Unit, which he founded in 1928; *Industrial Britain* (1933), *Song of Ceylon* (1934), *Night Mail* (1936). Founder of the National Film Board of Canada in 1939. Coined the word 'documentary' in 1925.

Hardy, Forsyth (1910–94), writer and producer. Founded Edinburgh Film Guild, Scottish Film Council and the Edinburgh International Film Festival.

Kissling, Werner (1885–1988), photographer, born Germany. His film *Eriskay, a Poem of Remote Lives* (1935) was the first ever film in which the Gaelic language was spoken.

Mackendrick, Alexander (1912–93), animator, screenwriter, and director, born Boston of Scottish parents. Works include: *Whisky Galore* (1949), *The Maggie* (1954), *The Ladykillers* (1955), *The Man in the White Suit* (1951)

MacKinnon, Gillies (1948–), director and writer, born Glasgow. Works include: *Small Faces* (1996), *Regeneration* (1997), *Hideous Kinky* (1998)

Mullan, Peter, director/writer and actor, born Glasgow. Works include: *Good Day for the Bad Guys* (1995), *Fridge* (1996), *Orphans* (1997). Acting credits include: *My Name is Joe* (Ken Loach, 1998), *The Claim* (Michael Winterbottom, 2000)

Ramsay, Lynne (1969–), director/writer, born Glasgow. Her first feature-length film, *Ratcatcher* (1999), set in a Glasgow tenement in the 1970s, won many awards, including a BAFTA award for best newcomer in British Film (2000), the Guardian New Director Award at the 1999 Edinburgh Film Festival, the Sutherland Award for first feature films at the 1999 London Film Festival, and the Grand Prix at the Bratislava Film Festival 1999. Two of her short films, *Small Deaths* (1995) and *Gasman* (1998), won Grand Jury prizes at Cannes.

VISUAL ARTISTS

Bellany, John, CBE (1942–), painter and printmaker, born Port Seton. Works inspired by religion and by the sea and the life of east-coast fishing communities. Works include: *Allegory* (1964), *Homage to John Knox* (1969), *The Old Man and the Sea, Celtic Sacrifice, The Sea People, Odyssey: Elegy for Alexander Kasser* (1998).

Blackadder, Elizabeth, OBE (1931–), born Falkirk. Early works were landscapes, inspired by travels in Mediterranean Europe (e.g. *Church in Salonika*, 1954; *Façade, Mistra*, 1963) and Scotland (*Wall Town*, 1961; *Beach, Elgol*, 1965); more recently she has concentrated on still life and images of flowers and cats, in oils, watercolour and prints (e.g. *Chinese Still-Life with Fan*, 1982; *Still-Life with Cats*, 1991–4; *Shop Window, Kyoto*, 1998). First Scottish woman painter to become an academician of both the Royal Scottish Academy and the Royal Academy. Awarded OBE in 1982. Large retrospective exhibition held 2000.

Cowie, James (1880–1956), born Monquhitter, Aberdeenshire. Art master at Bellshill Academy from 1914, painted several pictures of schoolgirls. Works include: *Two Schoolgirls* (c. 1937), *Falling Leaves* (1934), *Self-portrait: The Blue Shirt* (1945–50).

Crozier, William (1897–1930), landscape painter, born Edinburgh. A member of the Edinburgh School; not widely known today, he was once thought the most original of the group. Works include: *Buildings, Trees and River* (1920), *Red Roofs, Pennan* (1924), *Edinburgh from Salisbury Crags* (1927), *Tuscan Landscape* (1927).

Davie, Alan (1920–), born Grangemouth. Abstract expressionist painter, with an interest also in ancient Scotland. Works include: *Playing card adventure no. 4* (1964), *Jingling space* (1950).

Dyce, William (1806–1864), born Aberdeen. Influenced by Italian Renaissance painting and later Pre-Raphaelitism. Advised on murals for new House of Lords building. Works include: *Titian's first essay in colour* (1857), *Christ as the Man of Sorrows* (1860), *Pegwell Bay, Kent – a Recollection of October 5th, 1858*.

Finlay, Ian Hamilton (1925–), poet, sculptor and landscape artist. A trademark is the inclusion of printed or incised words in his work. Since the 1960s he has created a garden with sculpture and installations called 'Little Sparta', at his home, Stonypath, in Dunsyre, Lanarkshire.

Harvey, Jake (1948–), sculptor, born Langholm, Borders. Works include: Hugh MacDiarmid memorial near Langholm (1984), *Cup Stones* (1993), inspired by prehistoric Scottish art.

Jameson, George (c.1589–1644), born Aberdeen. Influenced by contemporary painters of the Low Countries, he is considered the founder of Scottish portraiture. Works include: portraits of Mary Erskine, Countess Marischal (1626), self-portrait (c. 1637–40).

Johnstone, William (1897–1981). Studied in Paris and the USA; his works reflect Cubist and Surrealist influences and inner landscapes of the unconscious. Works include: *A point in time* (1929–38), *Ode to the North Wind*, *Celebration of Earth, Air, Fire and Water* (1974).

McTaggart, William (1835—1910), landscape painter, born Macrihanish, Kintyre. His land and seascapes are grounded in the social reality of rural and coastal Scotland. Works include: *A Ground Swell, Carradale* (1883), *Sailing of the Emigrant Ship* (1895), *The Coming of St Columba* (1895).

Nasmyth, Alexander (1758–1840), painter, builder and architect. Known as 'the father of Scottish landscape'. Works include: *Edinburgh from Calton Hill* (1825), *Princes Street with the Commencement of the Building of the Royal Institution* (1825); portrait of his friend Robert Burns (1787).

Paolozzi, Sir Eduardo (1924–), sculptor, born Leith. Pioneer of Pop Art in Europe, interested in surrealism and in the iconography of machines. Has created much public sculpture. Works include: *Icarus* (1957), *Master of the Universe* (1989), *Newton After Blake* (1997, for the new British Library), *London–Paris* (2000). Designed mosaics for Tottenham Court Road underground station, London. Also made collages such as *Bunk* (1947). In 1986, appointed Her Majesty's Sculptor-in-Ordinary for Scotland by the Queen. Awarded CBE 1968; knighted 1988.

Raeburn, Henry (1756–1823), born Edinburgh. Foremost portrait painter of his day, he painted many of his contemporary politicians, scientists and philosophers, including Scott, Hume, Boswell, the fiddler Niel Gow (1793), Colonel Alasdair Macdonell of Glengarry (1811); Sir John and Lady Clerk of Penicuik (1792); *The Rev. Robert Walker Skating*. Admired for the confidence and ease of his style and for his sense of his sitters' personalities.

Ramsay, Allan (1713–84), born Edinburgh. Son of the poet. After studies in Italy, settled in London, becoming portrait painter to George III (e.g. portraits of George III as Prince of Wales, 1737, Queen Charlotte, 1763). Also painted eminent Scots (e.g. John Stuart, 3rd Earl of Bute, Flora Macdonald), philosophers Hume and Rousseau (1766), and his two wives Anne Bayne (1740) and Margaret Lindsay (early 1760s).

Read, Catherine (1723–78), portraitist and pastellist. One of the earliest Scottish women artists, but based for much of her life in London, she specialised in portraits of women. Works include portrait of Frances Moore Brooke (d. 1789), who emigrated from England Canada's first novelist.

Redpath, Anne (1895–1965), painter, born Galashiels. A member of the Edinburgh School, strongly influenced by French painting, in particular Matisse. Still-lifes and interiors include *The Indian rug* (*c.* 1942), *The white cyclamen*, *The mantelpiece*. Elected to RSA 1951.

Steell, Sir John (1804–91), sculptor, born Aberdeen. Was Queen Victoria's Sculptor in Scotland. Works include most of Edinburgh's major public statues, e.g. Scott (1845), Queen Victoria, Prince Albert, Wellington, and Burns (in Thanes Embankment Gardens); and a bust of Florence Nightingale (1862).

Traquair, Phoebe Anna (1852–1936), muralist, embroiderer, bookbinder, illuminator and illustrator, jeweller. A key figure in the late Arts and Crafts movement in Edinburgh. Painted murals for a mortuary for the Royal Hospital for Sick Children (1885), the Song School of St Mary's Cathedral, Edinburgh (1888-92) and the Catholic Apostolic Church, Mansfield Place, Edinburgh. In 1920, elected first honorary woman member of RSA.

Wilkie, David (1785–1841), born Fife. Founder of Scottish 19th-century school of genre painting, influencing many painters of his own and succeeding generations. His scenes of village life and Scottish history contain not only social commentary but a philosophical Enlightenment interpretation of Scottish history. Works include: *The village politicians* (1806), *The Blind Fiddler* (1806), *Distraining for Rent* (1815); *The Cottars' Saturday Night* (1837).

Wright, John Michael (1617–94), born London of Scottish parentage, returned to Scotland in 1630s to become pupil of George Jameson, and spent much of 1640s in Rome. As a Jacobite, lost favour after the accession of William of Orange. Works include portraits of the architect Sir William Bruce (1664), Lord Mungo Murray (*c.*1680).

THE SCOTTISH COLOURISTS

The group of four painters known as the Scottish Colourists can be seen as the heirs to the Glasgow Boys. All four studied in Paris, were clearly influenced by developments in French art at the turn of the 20th century, from Cézanne and Gauguin to Matisse and Derain, and found thematic inspiration equally in Scotland and France. However, they never formally constituted a group and exhibited jointly only three times in their lifetimes. Fergusson moved to France permanently in 1909, while the other three remained based in Scotland.

A major exhibition of the Colourists' work, organised by the Scottish National Gallery of Modern Art, was held in 2000 in Scotland and at the Royal Academy, London, and revived a keen interest in the work of this evocative and influential group of Scottish painters.

Cadell, Francis Campbell Boileau (1883–1937), born Edinburgh. Works include: *Afternoon* (1913), *Lunga from Iona*, *Still Life (The Grey Fan)* (*c.*1920-5), *The Blue Jug* (*c.*1922), *The Black Hat* (1914), *The Orange Blind* (c. 1927).

Fergusson, John Duncan (1874–1961), born Perthshire. Works include: *Rhythm* (1911), *Les Eus* (*c.*1910–13), *In the Sunlight*. Fergusson was also an influential sculptor.

Hunter, G. Leslie (1877–1931), born Rothesay. Works include: *Houseboats, Balloch* (*c.*1924), *Provençal Landscape* (1929), *Reflections, Balloch* (c. 1930). *Village in Fife*

Peploe, Samuel John (1871–1935), born Edinburgh. Works include: *Ben More from Iona* (1925), *Palm Trees, Antibes* (1928), *Portrait of Peggy MacRae*; *Still Life with Roses* is one of many still lifes.

ARCHITECTS

Adam, Robert (1728–1792), born Kirkcaldy. Led Classical revival in England in both architecture and decoration, using and adapting Greco-Roman (e.g. Etruscan vase decoration), Italian and French Renaissance elements. Works in Scotland include: Register House, Charlotte Square (Edinburgh, 1791), Culzean Castle (Ayrshire, from 1777)

Adam, William (1684–1748), father of Robert and James, both also architects. A signatory of the 1729 charter establishing the Academy of St Luke in Edinburgh, Scotland's first art school. Designed the Roman Baroque front of Hopetoun House (South Queensferry, Edinburgh, from 1721); Duff House (Banff, 1735); Robert Gordon's College, Aberdeen (1739).

Bruce, Sir William (*c.*1630–1710), born Blairhall, West Fife. As Surveyor and Master of Works to Charles II from 1671, rebuilt and extended the Palace of Holyroodhouse, Edinburgh, in the Palladian style (1671–9). Also responsible for original design of Hopetoun House (1699–1702), Kinross House (1685–93), and other great houses for Scottish lairds.

Graham, James Gillespie (1776–1855), born Dunblane. Designed churches and large country houses in the Neo-Gothic style. Works include: St John's Tolbooth (Edinburgh, 1842), St Mary's Roman Catholic Cathedral (Edinburgh, 1813–14), Armadale Castle, Isle of Skye (1815), extensions to Brodick Castle, Arran (1844). Also designed interiors, such as the State Dining Room at Hopetoun House.

Mackintosh, Charles Rennie (1868–1928), born Glasgow. With his wife, Margaret Macdonald, her sister Frances, and Herbert MacNair, a principal figure of the Scottish Arts and Crafts movement, and creator of the 'Glasgow Style'. As famed for his furniture and textile designs as for his buildings, he also produced landscape and flower paintings. His architecture is anti-Classical and often (e.g. in the Hill House) looks back to the Scottish baronial style of late medieval tower-houses. Works include: Glasgow School of Art (1897–99, 1907–09), Hill House, Helensburgh (1902), Willow Tea Rooms, Glasgow (1904). He designed few religious buildings.

Thomson, Alexander 'Greek' (1817–75), born Balfron, Stirlingshire, but identified with Glasgow, where most of his work is to be found. Designed churches, warehouses, tenements, villas, and (in the 1850s) several mansion houses in the fashionable village of Cove on the Rosneath peninsula. Despite his nickname, Italian, Scottish Baronial, Gothic and even Egyptian elements are found in his style. His use of glass and iron in buildings was revolutionary. Works include: Moray Place, Strathbungo (1859); United Presbyterian Churches at Caledonian Road (1856) and St Vincent Street (1857–59); Egyptian Halls, Union Street (1871–73).

ARTS ORGANISATIONS

The following list of arts organisations includes those organisations and institutions which are in receipt of revenue grants or three-year funding from the Scottish Arts Council.

7:84 Theatre Company
333 Woodlands Road, Glasgow, G3 6NG
(Tel: 0141-334 6686; Fax: 0141-334 3369;
E-mail: 7.84-theatre@btinternet.com).
Artistic Director: G. Laird

An Lanntair
Town Hall, South Beach, Stornoway, Isle of Lewis, HS1 2BX (Tel: 01851-703307;
E-mail: lanntair@sol.co.uk;
Web: www.lantair.com).
Director: R. Murray

An Tuireann
Arts Centre, Struan Road, Portree, Isle of Skye, IV51 9EG (Tel: 01478-613306;
Fax: 01478-613156;
E-mail: exhibitions@anttuireann.org.uk;
Web: www.antuireann.org.uk).
Director: Ms N. Campbell

Arches Theatre Company
30 Midland Street, Glasgow, G1 4PR
(Tel: 0141 221 4001; Web: www.thearches.co.uk)

art.tm (Highland Printmakers Workshop)
20 Bank Street, Inverness, IV1 1QU
(Tel: 01463-712240; Fax: 01463-239991;
E-mail: info@arttm.org.uk;
Web: www.arttm.org.uk).
Director: G. Rogers

Artlink (Edinburgh and the Lothians)
13a Spittal Street, Edinburgh, EH3 9DY
(Tel: 0131-229 3555; Fax: 0131-228 5257;
E-mail: artlink@easynet.co.uk;
Web: easyweb.easynet.co.uk/artlink).
Director: J-B van den Berg

Art in Partnership
233 Cowgate, Edinburgh, EH1 IJQ
(Tel: 0131-225 4463; Fax: 0131-225 6879;
E-mail: info@art-in-partnership.org.uk;
Web: www.art-in-partnership.org.uk/aip/).
Executive Director: R. Breen

Association for Scottish Literary Studies
Department of Scottish History, University of Glasgow, 9 University Gardens, Glasgow, G12 8QH (Tel: 0141-330 5309; Fax: 0141-330 5309;
E-mail: d.jones@scothist.arts.gla.ac.uk;
Web: www.asls.org.uk).
General Manager: D. Jones

Awarehaus Theatre
Aberdeen Arts Centre, 33 King Steet, Aberdeen, AB24 5AA; E-mail: tina@ahaus.freeserve.co.uk

Benchtours
Bonnington Mill, 72 Newhaven Road, Edinburgh, EH6 5QG (Tel: 0131 555 3585; Fax: 0131 2555 595; E-mail: info@benchtours.com; Web: benchtours.com).

Borderline Theatre Company
North Harbour Street, Ayr, KA8 8AA
(Tel: 01292-281010; Fax: 01292-263825;
E-mail: enquiries@borderlinetheatre.co.uk;
Web: www.borderlinetheatre.co.uk).
Chief Executive: E. Jackson

Brunton Theatre Company
High Street, Musselburgh, Edinburgh, EH21 6AA (Tel: 0131 665 9900).

BT Scottish Ensemble
5 Newton Terrace Lane, Glasgow, G3 7PB
(Tel: 0141-221 2222; Fax: 0141-221 4444;
E-mail: scottishensemble@yahoo.com).
General Manager: Ms H. Duncan

Cappella Nova
172 Hyndland Road, Glasgow, G12 9HZ
(Tel: 0141-552 0634; Fax: 0141-552 4053;
E-mail: rebecca@cappella-nova.com;
Web: www.cappella-nova.com).
Chief Executive: Ms R. Tavener

Collective Gallery
22-28 Cockburn Street, Edinburgh, EH1 1NY
(Tel: 0131-220 1260; Fax: 0131-220 5585;
E-mail: collgall@aol.com).

Crawford Arts Centre
93 North Street, St Andrews, KY16 9AD
(Tel: 01334-474610; Fax: 01334-479880;
E-mail: crawfordarts@crawfordarts.free-online.co.uk;
Web: www.crawfordarts.free-online.co.uk).
Director: D. Sykes

Cutting Edge Theatre Company
Bernard Street, Edinburgh (Tel: 0131-554 5701;
E-mail: 106340.512@compuserve.com).

Dumfries and Galloway Arts Association
28 Edinburgh Road, Dumfries, DG1 1JQ
(Tel: 01387-253383; Fax: 01387-253303).
Director: Ms J. Wilson

Dundee Contemporary Arts
152 Nethergate, Dundee, DD1 4DY
(Tel: 01382-606220; Fax: 01382-606221;
E-mail: dca@dundeecity.gov.uk;
Web: www.dca.org.uk).
Head of Communication: Jeni Iannetta

Eden Court Theatre
Bishop's Road, Inverness, IV3 5SA
(Tel: 01463-234234; Fax: 01463-713810;
E-mail: admin@eden-court.co.uk;
Web: www.eden-court.co.uk).
Director: C. Marr

Edinburgh International Book Festival
Scottish Book Centre, 137 Dundee Street,
Edinburgh, EH11 1BG (Tel: 0131-228 5444;
Fax: 0131-228 4333;
E-mail: admin@edbookfest.co.uk;
Web: www.edbookfest.co.uk).
Director: Ms C. Lockerbie

Edinburgh Festival Fringe Society
The Fringe Office, 180 High Office, Edinburgh,
EH1 1QS (Tel: 0131-226 5257; Fax: 0131-220
4205; E-mail: admin@edfringe.com;
Web: www.edfringe.com).
Director: P. Gudgin

Edinburgh Printmakers
23 Union Street, Edinburgh, EH1 3LR
(Tel: 0131-557 2479; Fax: 0131-558 8418;
E-mail: printmakers@ednet.co.uk;
Web: www.edinburgh-printmakers.co.uk).
Director: D. Watt

Edinburgh Sculpture Workshop
25 Hawthornvale, Edinburgh, EH6 4JT
(Tel: 0131-551 4490; Fax: 0131-551 4491;
E-mail: admin@edinburgh-sculpture.org.uk;
Web: www.edinburgh-sculpture.org.uk).
Chairman: Prof. Bill Scott

Fablevision
7 Water Row, Glasgow, G51 3UW
(Tel: 0141 425 2020; Fax: 0141 425 2020;
E-mail: fablevision.org.uk;
Web: fablevisn.org.uk).

Factional Theatre
10 Dalcross Street, Glasgow, G11 5RF (Tel: 0141
586 7564; E-mail: info@factional.co.uk).

Federation of Scottish Theatre
25 Ainslie Place, Edinburgh, EH3 6AJ
(Tel: 0131 467 2525; E-mail: fst@cableinet.co.uk;
Web: www.scottishtheatre.org).

The Gaelic Books Council (Comhairle nan Leabhraichean)
22 Mansfield Street, Glasgow, G11 5QP
(Tel: 0141-337 6211; Fax: 0141-341 0515;
E-mail: fios@gaelicbooks.net;
Web: www.gaelicbooks.net).
Director: I. MacDonald

Grey Coast Theatre Comapany
Scapa House, Castlegreen Road, Thurso, KW14
7LS (Tel: 01847 8903 840; Fax: 01847 8903 840;
E-mail: admin@greycoast.demon.co.uk;
Web: www.greyacoast.demon.co.uk/).

Glasgow Print Studio
22 King Street, Glasgow, G1 5QP
(Tel: 0141-552 0704; Fax: 0141-552 2919;
E-mail: gallery@gpsart.co.uk;
Web: www.gpsart.co.uk).
Chief Executive: J. McKechnie

Greenock Arst Guild
Campbell Street, Greenock, PA16 8AP
(Tel: 01475 723 038; Fax: 01475 721 811;
Web: www.geocities.com/broadway/orchestra/9054/).

Grid Iron
85 East Claremont Street, Edinburgh, EH7 4HU
(Tel: 0131 558 1879; Fax: 0131 558 8048;
E-mail: jude@gridiron.org.uk).

Hebrides Ensemble
11 Palmerston Place, Edinburgh, EH12 5AF
(Tel: 0131-225 2006; Fax: 0131-225 2006).
Chief Executive: F. J. Carroll

The Lemon Tree Trust
5 West North Street, Aberdeen, AB24 5AT
(Tel: 01224-647999; Fax: 01224-630888;
E-mail: info@lemontree.org;
Web: www.lemontree.org).
Director: Ms S. Powell

Lung Ha's Theatre Company
Central Hall, West Tolcross, Edinburgh, EH3
9BP (Tel: 0131 228 8998; Fax: 0131 229 8965;
E-mail: lungha@ednet.co.uk).

MacRobert Arts Centre
University of Stirling, Stirling, FK9 4LA
(Tel: 01786-467155; Fax: 01748-451369;
E-mail: macrobert-art@stirling.ac.uk;
Web: www.stirling.ac.uk/macrobert
and macrobert/stir.ac.uk/wow).
Director: Liz Moran

Magnectic North Theatre Productions Ltd
18 Brandon Terrace, Edinburgh, EH3 5DZ
(Tel: 0131 556 3299).

Moniack Mhor
Teavarran, Kiltarlity, Beauly, Inverness-shire, IV4
7HT (Tel: 01463-741675; Fax: 01463-741733;
E-mail: m-mhor@arvonfoundation.org;
Web: www.arvonfoundation.org).
Director: Chris Aldridge

Morpheus Theatre
1st Left, 3 Downside Road, Glasgow, G12 9YB
(Tel: 0141 334 6236;
E-mail: morpheus–98@hotmail.com).

Mull Little Theatre/Taigh-Cluiche Beag Mhuile
Dervaig, Isle of Mull, Argyll, PA75 6QW
(Tel: 01688 400245;
E-mail: mulltheatre@tesco.net;
Web: www.holidaymull.org/theatre).

Making Music Scotland (The National Federation of Music Societies)
63 Threestanes Road, Strathaven, Lanarkshire,
ML10 6EB (Tel: 01357-522138; Fax: 01357-
522138; E-mail: l.young@makingmusic.org.uk;
Web: www.makingmusic.org.uk/scotland).
Secretary: Ms L. Young

New Stage Theatre
C/O Steve Brown, 42 Herriot St, Glasgow, G12
9YB (Tel: 0141 423 9024; Fax: 0141 423 9648;
E-mail: steve.brown@easynet.co.uk).

Out of the Darkness Theatre Company
The Flat, Elgin Town Hall, 1 Trinty Place, Elgin,
IV30 1UD (Tel: 01343 543 500).

Peacock Visual Arts
21 Castle Street, Aberdeen, AB11 5BQ
(Tel: 01224-639539; Fax: 01224-627094;
E-mail: info@peacockvisualarts.co.uk;
Web: www.peacockvisualarts.co.uk).
Chief Executive: L. Gordon

Perth Theatre
185 High Street, Perth, PH1 5UW
(Tel: 01738-472700; Fax: 01738-624576;
E-mail: theatre@perth.org.uk;

Web: www.perth.org.uk/perth/theatre.htm).
General Manager: P. Hackett

Pitlochry Festival Theatre
Pitlochry, PH16 5DR (Tel: 01796-484600;
Fax: 01796-484616;
E-mail: admin@pitlochty.org.uk;
Web: www.pitlochry.org.uk).
General Manager: Nikki Axford

Proiseact nan Ealan/National Gaelic Arts Agency
10 Shell Street, Stornoway, HS1 2BS
(Tel: 01851-704493; Fax: 01851-704734;
E-mail: pne@gaelic-arts.com;
Web: www.gaelic-arts.com).
Director: M. MacLean

Project Ability
Centre for Developmental Arts
18 Albion Street, Glasgow, G1 1LH
(Tel: 0141-552 2822; Fax: 0141-552 3490;
E-mail: info@project-ability.co.uk;
Web: www.project-ability.co.uk).
General Manager: Ms A. Knowles

Raindog
Strathclyde Arts Centre, 12 Washington Street,
Glasgow, G3 8AZ (Tel: 0141 204 3122/3;
Fax: 0141 204 3368;
E-mail: raindog.tc@dial.pipex.com).

Royal Lyceum Theatre Company
Grindlay Street, Edinburgh, EH3 9AX
(Tel: 0131-248-4800; Fax: 0131-228 3955;
E-mail: royallyceumtheatre@cableinet.co.uk;
Web: www.lyceum.org.uk).
Artistic Director: K. Ireland

Royal Scottish National Orchestra
73 Claremont Street, Glasgow, G3 7JB
(Tel: 0141-226 3868; Fax: 0141-221 4317;
E-mail: admin@rsno.org.uk;
Web: www.rsno.org.uk).
Chief Executive: Simon Crookall

St Magnus Festival
60 Victoria Street, Kirkwall, Orkney, KW15 1DN
(Tel: 01856-871445; Fax: 01856-871170;
E-mail: info@stmagnusfestival.com;
Web: www.stmagnusfestival.com).
Director: Glenys Hughes

Scottish Academy of Asian Arts
Govanhill Neighbourhood Centre, 6-8 Dairy
Street, Govanhill, Glasgow, G42 8JL (Tel: 0141
423 2210; Fax: 0141 204 3368;
E-mail: saasianarts@etscapeonline.co.uk).

Scottish Ballet
261 West Princes Street, Glasgow, G4 9EE
(Tel: 0141-331 2931; Fax: 0141-331 2629;
E-mail: scotballet@colloquium.co.uk;

Web: www.scottishballet.co.uk).
Director: N. L. Quirk

Scottish Chamber Orchestra
4 Royal Terrace, Edinburgh, EH7 5AB
(Tel: 0131-557 6800; Fax: 0131-557 6933;
E-mail: info@sco.org.uk;
Web: www.sco.org.uk).
Managing Director: R. McEwan

Scottish Dance Theatre
Dundee Repertory Theatre
Tay Square, Dundee, DD1 1PB
(Tel: 01382-342600; Fax: 01382-228609;
E-mail: aroberts@dundeereptheatre.co.uk;
Web: www.dundeereptheatre.co.uk/
scottishdancetheatre).
Senior Administrator: Ms A. Chinn

Scottish International Children's Festival
45A George Street, Edinburgh, EH2 2HT
(Tel: 0131-225 8050; Fax: 0131-225 6440;
E-mail: info@imaginate.org.uk;
Web: www.imaginate.org.uk).
Communications Director: Ms A. Carney

Scottish Music Information Centre
1 Bowmont Gardens, Glasgow, G12 9LR
(Tel: 0141-334 6393; Fax: 0141-337 1161;
E-mail: info@smic.org.uk;
Web: www.smic.org.uk).
Chief Executive: Andrew Logan

Scottish Opera
39 Elmbank Crescent, Glasgow, G2 4PT
(Tel: 0141-248 4567; Fax: 0141-221 8812;
E-mail: scotopera@hotmail.com;
Web: www.scottishopera.org.uk).
Chief Executive: C. Barron

The Scottish Poetry Library
5 Crichton's Close, Edinburgh, EH8 8DT
(Tel: 0131-557 2876; Fax: 0131-557 8393;
E-mail: inquiries@spl.org.uk;
Web: www.spl.org.uk).
Chief Executive: Dr R. Marsack

Scottish Publishers Association
Scottish Book Centre, 137 Dundee Street,
Edinburgh, EH11 1BG (Tel: 0131-228 6866;
Fax: 0131-228 3220;
E-mail: enquiries@scottishbooks.org;
Web: www.scottishbooks.org).
Director: L. Fannin

Scottish Sculpture Workshop
1 Main Street, Lumsden, Huntly, Aberdeenshire,
AB54 4JN (Tel: 01464-861372; Fax: 01464-
861550; E-mail: admin@ssw.org.uk;
Web: www.ssw.org.uk).
Director: Chris Freemantle

Scottish Storytelling Centre
The Netherbow Arts Centre, 43-45 High Street,
Edinburgh, EH1 1SR (Tel: 0131-556 9579; Fax:
0131-557 5224;
E-mail: netherbow-storytelling@dial.pipex.com;
Web: www.storytellingcentre.org.uk).
Co-ordinator: J. Bremner

Scottish Community Drama Association
5 York Place, Edinburgh, EH13EB (Tel: 0131
557 5552; E-mail: headquarters@scda.org.uk;
Web: www.scda.org.uk).

Scottish Youth Theatre
6th Floor, Gordon Chambers, 90 Mitchell Street,
Glasgow, G1 3NQ (Tel: 0141 221 5127;
Fax: 0141 221 9123;
E-mail: info@scottishyoutheatre.org;
Web: www.scot-artorg/syt).

Scottish Youth Dance
69 Dublin Street, Edinburgh, EH3 6NS
(Tel: 0131-556 8844; Fax: 0131-556 7766;
E-mail: info@scottishyouthdance.org;
Web: www.scottishyouthdance.org).
Director: Mrs J. Savin

Sound of Progress
3rd Floor, 18 Albion Street, Glasgow, G1 1LH
(Tel: 0141-552 3575).

Shetland Arts Trust
Pitt Lane, Lerwick, Shetland, ZE1 0DW
(Tel: 01595-694001; Fax: 01595-692941;
E-mail: admin@shetland-arts-trust.co.uk;
Web: www.shetland-music.com).
General Manager: A. Watt

StellaR Quines
c/o Teldford College, Fourth Campus,
Muirhouse Avenue, Edinburgh, EH4 4AE
(Tel: 0131 343 3146).

Street Level
26 King Street, Glasgow, G1 5QP
(Tel: 0141-552 2151; Fax: 0141-552 2323;
E-mail: info@sl-photoworks.demon.co.uk;
Web: www.sl-photworks.demon.co.uk).
Director: M. Dickson

Suspect Culture
128 Elderslie Street, Glasgow, G3 7AW
(Tel: 0141-248 8052; Fax: 0141-221 4470;
E-mail: suspectculture@btinternet.com).
Artistic Director: G. Eatough

Talbot Rice Gallery
Old College, South Bridge, Edinburgh, EH8
9YL (Tel: 0131-650 2211; Fax: 0131-650 2211;
E-mail: valeriefiddes@ed.ac.uk;
Web: www.trg.ed.ac.uk).
Curator: Prof. D. Macmillan

Theatre Cryptic
The Arthouse, 752-756 Argyle Street, Glasgow, G3 8UJ (Tel: 0141-221 6363; Fax: 0141 221 5121).

Theatre Babel
11 Sandyford Place, Sauchiehall Street, Glasgow, G3 7NB (Tel: 0141-226 8806;
E-mail: enquiries@theatrebabel.co.uk;
Web: www.scot-art.org/babel).

Theatre Alba
52c Mansfield Avenue, Musselburgh, EH4 4AE
(Tel: 0131-343 3146;
E-mail: alba@benhar.demon.co.uk).

Theatre Workshop
34 Hamilton Place, Edinburgh, EH3 5AX
(Tel: 0131-225 7942; Fax: 0131-220 0112;
E-mail: info@live.co.uk).
Director: R. Rae

Tosg Theatre Company
Sabhal Mor Ostaig, Sleat, Isle of Skye, IV44 8RQ
(Tel: 01471-888542; Fax: 01471-888541;
E-mail: tosg@tosg.org; Web: www.tosg.org).
Artistic Director: S. Mackenzie

The Traditional Music and Song Association of Scotland
95–97 St Leonard's Street, Edinburgh, EH8 9QY
(Tel: 0131-667 5587; Fax: 0131-662 9153;
E-mail: tmsa@tmsa.demon.co.uk
National Organiser: E. Cowie

Traverse Theatre
Cambridge Street, Edinburgh, EH1 2ED
(Tel: 0131-228 3223; Fax: 0131-229 8443;
Web: www.traverse.co.uk).
Chief Executive: P. Howard

Travelling Gallery
City Arts Centre, 2 Market Street, Edinburgh, EH1 1DE (Tel: 0131-529 3930; Fax: 0131-529 8977;
E-mail: travel@city-art-centre.demon.co.uk).
Chief Executive: Alison Chisholm

Tron Theatre
63 Trongate, Glasgow, G1 5HB
(Tel: 0141-552 6748; Fax: 0141-552 6657;
E-mail: boxoffice@tron.co.uk;
Web: www.tron.co.uk).
General Manager: N. Murray

Theatre Replico
3/2 255 Langside Road, Glasgow, G42 8XX
(Tel: 0141-424 0954; E-mail: replico@hotmail.com;
Web: www.replico.co.uk).

Theatre Workshop
34 Hamilton Place, Edinburgh, EH3 5AX
(Tel: 0131-225 7942).

Visible Fictions
c/o Paisley Arts Centre, New Street, Paisley, PA1 1EZ (Tel: 0141-887 1010).

WASPS
256 Alexandra Parade, Glasgow, G31 3AJ
(Tel: 0141-554 2499; Fax: 0141-556 5340;
E-mail: info@waspsstudios.org.uk;
Web: www.waspsstudios.org.uk).
Director: D. Cook

FAIRS

HISTORY OF FAIRS IN SCOTLAND

Many of the agricultural shows that are now a regular feature of Scottish life can be traced back to mediaeval and later fairs. Originally licensed under royal charter, and later under the jurisdiction of the local laird or trades guilds, fairs of different kinds were important centres for buying and selling goods and hiring agricultural and domestic labour, as well as for social interaction and entertainment. There was considerable specialisation in the products traded at different fairs, and taxes were levied on every item sold at a fair, often by the local laird, at some places until quite late in the 19th century.

Fairs usually took place in market squares or on moors, links or other open ground close to towns, and could last for up to two weeks. They were the occasion for large movements of people and livestock about the country; for tradesmen such as packmen or pedlars, travelling from town to town and fair to fair with their horse-drawn carts or caravans laden with goods was their whole livelihood. In the west, boats would bring traders from the Western Isles to fairs such as that at Greenock. Some fairs even attracted merchants from the Continent.

Many of the traditional dates of fairs correspond with key dates in the religious calendar. Fairs were often held on the quarter days – Candlemas (2 February), Whitsun (25 May), Lammas (1 August) and Martinmas (11 November) – or on the feast day of the saint to which the local church was dedicated. Important saints' days were also popular dates, and fairs held on these days reflected the names of the saints celebrated: for instance Andermas Fairs, held on St Andrew's Day, 30 November, and Marymas Fairs, those held on 15 August, the feast of the Assumption of the Virgin Mary. These fairs had a more overt religious aspect and included the saying of Mass; but there was also generally plenty of drinking, dancing and sports, including horse-races. Fortune-telling was common, although it was strictly speaking illegal. The Church of

Scotland considered fairs immoral, and James VI abolished the holding of fairs and feasts on saints' days. In contrast, Holy Fairs were sacramental occasions, days of worship, fasting and no work. Usually held during the spring and autumn, these survive today in the annual spring and autumn holiday weekends, which are still held on different in dates in different parts of Scotland.

Lammas Fairs were held in many towns across Scotland, but the biggest and most famous was that at St Andrews. It is still held in the streets in early August and is Scotland's oldest surviving market fair. Originally a feeing fair, it was established in 1620 by Charter from James VI. Another popular Lammas Fair was held in Kirkwall on the first Tuesday after 11 August. Hallowmas Fairs were held in autumn to celebrate the feast of All Saints Day, 1st November. The most famous, at its peak during the 18th century, was held in Edinburgh.

FAIRS AS LABOUR MARKETS

Feeing fairs were held every six months, usually at the Whitsun and Martinmas terms, which were the times of year when farm workers would be paid their wages and would either renew their hire or move to a different farm. Other feeing fairs were held at Candlemas and Lammas, the latter being a labour market for shearers and reapers for the harvest season. In Aberdeen, Feeing Day was known as Muckle Friday. Foys were feasts and entertainments given to bid farewell to departing workers and welcome new workers to a farm. Anster Fair, held at Anstruther in Fife, was a foy held for those leaving for Great Yarmouth to work in the gutting and packing of herring. The Johnmas Foy held each June at Lerwick celebrated the arrival in Shetland of the Dutch herring fleet.

LIVESTOCK TRADING

Many fairs became renowned for the trade of livestock. Following the Union of the Crowns in 1603, cattle fairs and cross-border trade between England and Scotland grew in importance, and the Crieff Tryst became an important cattle fair to which both English and Scottish drovers would bring their cattle. The main centre moved to Falkirk in 1777, which became the site of the largest livestock tryst in Scotland. During the mid 19th century about 300,000 cattle were sold at the three great cattle fairs held in August, September and October. Other centres included Brechin, Pennymuir, the Gorgie Market in Edinburgh, which remained a major meeting for livestock owners up to the mid 19th century, and the Ellon

Fair, near Aberdeen, which was an important north-eastern cattle trading centre before the advent of the railway.

Other fairs, particularly in the Borders, specialised in sheep and lambs. These included Stirling, and Ettrick in the former county of Selkirkshire. Langholm in Dumfriesshire, just eight miles from the English border, became a major centre of cross-border trade; while Lockerbie's Lammas fair became the largest Scottish centre of all and was renowned for its August lamb sale, held on Lamb Hill.

Pigs were sold at Dunfermline's Pudding Fairs, held in November and December and named after the white puddings made from the slaughtered animals. Horse fairs such as the Keltonhill Fair, held at Rhonehouse in Galloway on St John's Day, 24 June, developed from gypsy gatherings. At Whitesands in Dumfriesshire there was an annual fair devoted to the sale of hare-skins; while the Cardross Whelk Fair was held on the shores of the Clyde from 1822 onward. At the Kipper Fair, which marked the end of the salmon fishing season at Ayr until the 1830s, smoked salmon was distributed free to all the public houses.

THE ROYAL HIGHLAND SHOW

The Royal Highland Show is organised each June by the Royal Highland and Agricultural Society of Scotland (RHASS). This four-day event, held at Ingliston, near Edinburgh airport, is Scotland's national showcase for the land-based and allied industries, and is attended by an annual average of 150,000 people. As well as its famous livestock parade and show, it includes sheepdog trials, show jumping, exhibitions on forestry, the countryside, Scottish food, around 1,0000 trade stands, craft and flower pavilions, and a variety of entertainments. It is also the largest trade exhibition of agricultural machinery in Britain. Around 4,000 livestock competed in the 2000 show in 400 categories. The 2001 event, scheduled to take place 21–24 June, had to be cancelled due to the foot and mouth outbreak.

The RHASS has promoted agriculture in Scotland since its foundation in 1784, when it was established with the aim of improvement of the Highlands and Islands and the conditions of their people. The Chair of Agriculture at the University of Edinburgh was established on the Society's initiative in 1790. It supports education in agriculture-related subjects, giving financial support to courses in agriculture, veterinary science and forestry at universities and colleges, and issues awards in recognition of excellence in various aspects of agriculture such as technical innovation, food, and forest management.

CLOTH AND SEED FAIRS

A number of fairs specialised in the trade of certain items. During the spring many towns held Seed Fairs, where flax, corn, oats, wheat and seed potatoes were sold. In Edinburgh, Grassmarket was the corn and livestock market of the city. In 1560 the market was moved to the foot of the West Bow and in 1587 to a site behind St Giles' but in 1716 it returned to Grassmarket, where the Corn Exchange was erected in 1849.

Amongst the more famous of the cloth fairs were the Links Market at Linkstown in Fife and the Lawnmarket in Edinburgh. The cloth market at Edinburgh's Lawnmarket was established by James III in 1477. At Linkstown, two fairs a year took place, the spring fair specialising in lintseed and linen goods. Although the original form of the fair has declined, the Links Market is still held each year along the promenade of Kirkcaldy, a burgh formed from Linkstown and nearby Abbotshall. Other towns also dealt in cloth: at Kirkintilloch, Dunbartonshire, there were Lintseed Saturdays in spring for the sale of this commodity. Kirkmadrine in Galloway had an annual Sooty Poke Fair, named after the weavers' custom of carrying their wares in bags stained with soot. Other fairs included St Conan's Fair, Glenorchy, and Shott's Yarn Fair, Lanarkshire, held each August until the early 19th century. Wool was also traded at a number of towns, and linen and sheets at Aberdeen's Muckle Paise Market.

Yet other fairs were places for trade in domestic and agricultural implements, such as wrought iron goods, dairy utensils, spinning wheels and cooper's barrels, knives and weapons, certain towns being renowned for each commodity. One fair, the Old Cumnock Scythe Fair, even specialised in sand, sold as a sharpening agent for knife and weapon blades.

By the 20th century most Scottish fairs were degenerating into funfairs. The Industrial Revolution had brought about a fundamental change in their role as centres of rural trade and social contact, as towns grew rapidly and became more accessible and shops became the main theatre of local commerce. However, many towns and villages across Scotland now hold an annual agricultural show, and these events have taken over from the fairs as meeting places for farmers and livestock traders.

THE GLASGOW FAIR

Of all the summer fairs held across Scotland, that of Glasgow is the largest and most famous. Originating in 1190, when King William I granted the Bishop of Glasgow the right to hold an annual fair beginning on 7th July, the fair was held at a variety of locations around the city. By the end of the 18th century it had moved to the Saltmarket, around Jail Square; but the development of the retail trade led to the decline of the fair as a market and its transformation into a place of popular entertainment. In the mid 19th century it began to sprawl into the neighbouring Glasgow Green, and, following protest from the local residents, a new site for the Fair was found in 1871 at Vinegar Hill near Camlachie. However, the Fair returned to Glasgow Green in the 20th century.

In the 19th century the Glasgow Fair marked the closure of most industries for an annual trade holiday, which became known as the Fair Week and later Fair Fortnight, beginning the second Friday in July. At one time huge spectacles were displayed in annual competition, including such things as waterfalls and re-enactments of the battles of the Boer War. Today the Fair is an extremely popular annual festival of entertainment, but it now consists of standard fairground attractions, although in 1990, when Glasgow held the title of European City of Culture, there were attempts to revive more traditional fair entertainments such as juggling, dancing, music and theatre.

SPORT AND PHYSICAL RECREATION

AMERICAN FOOTBALL

Britain's only professional American Football team is the Scottish Claymores, a team established in 1995 and named after the two-edged sword formerly used by warriors of the Scottish clans. They play their games at Murrayfield and Hampden Park.

The team competes in a six-team NFL Europe League against during an annual 11-week season from April to June. Each NFL Europe League season culminates in the World Bowl. The NFL Europe League is allied to the National Football League, America's biggest sports league and is a joint venture between NFL and Fox Sports, a division of News Corporation. All six NFL League teams (Scotland, Amsterdam, Barcelona, Berlin, Dusseldorf and Frankfurt) are owned by the joint venture partners.

The Scottish Claymores hosted the World Bowl in 1996, defeating Frankfurt Galaxy 32 — 27 in front of a large crowd of 38,982 at Murrayfield. The Claymores have won through to the finals of the World Bowl 2000, held in Frankfurt.

ANGLING

Fishing as a sport can be dated to the early 17th century. Rod fishing for food probably existed in the Highlands much earlier, but most of the clan chiefs and tacksmen (leaseholders or tenants) would have had ghillies to provide them with fish. By the latter half of the 18th century the Duke of Gordon was letting salmon fishing for sport on the Spey; and with the arrival of railways and the building of new roads and bridges, parts of Scotland hitherto practically inaccessible were opened up for field sports. By then, much of Scotland, especially the Highlands, had already become a playground for the rich; sporting estates and hunting and fishing lodges sprang up across the country (see also Deerstalking, p. 329; Environmental Protection and Conservation, p. 374).

Scotland's oldest angling club is the Ellem Fishing Club, founded in 1829 by gentlemen from Edinburgh and Berwickshire. The influential sporting writer William Scrope, who also popularised deerstalking, helped to boost interest in fly-fishing in the late 1800s. Victorian anglers fished with huge 18-foot rods of split cane and green heart wood imported from the colonies.

The protection of salmon was the subject of legislation probably before the eleventh century and was first recorded by the Scottish Parliament in 1318. In 1862 Scotland was divided into 101 salmon fishery districts, each with a catchment area consisting of a river or a system of rivers. District Salmon Fishery Boards were created by the owners of the salmon rivers fishings, and they form the basis of the present-day organisation of the sport. Almost all river fishings are in private ownership and the fishing policy is determined by the owner.

Today, salmon and trout fishing in Scotland is enormously popular. Arrangements for fishing by time-share even developed in the 1980s. Thousands of anglers compete in annual events such as the Worldwide Trout Open fly-fishing competition. However, the industry, estimated at a value of £140 million a year, is now threatened by shrinking numbers of salmon and sea trout in the rivers and increased danger of disease spread by fish escaping from salmon farms.

The largest authenticated salmon ever caught by rod and line in Scotland was a huge fish weighing 29kg fish (64lbs) caught on the Tay by Miss G.W. Ballantine in 1922. The sea trout record was set in 1989 by Mr S. Burgoyne's catch of a 10kg (22½ lb) fish on the River Leven, which flows out of Loch Lomond.

Central Scotland Anglers' Association
53 Fernieside Crescent, Edinburgh
(Tel: 0131-664 4685).

BOXING

The rules of boxing were first drawn up by Sir John Sholto Douglas, 8th Marquess of Queensberry (1844–1900). In 1866 he published a code of 12 rules, the first being that gloves had to be worn. There has been a gradual modification of the rules over the years, but the Queensberry Rules laid the foundations of modern boxing.

Amateur boxing in Scotland is administered by the Scottish Amateur Boxing Association, founded in 1909. There are 86 directly affiliated clubs. Tournaments are regularly held with England, Wales and Ireland and the Commonwealth Games and Olympics are contested every four years. The best Scottish performance was by Dick McTaggart, gold medallist at the 1956 Melbourne Olympic Games.

Scotland has produced six world champions at the professional level: four at flyweight, Benny Lynch (1935), Jackie Paterson (1943), Walter McGowan (1966) and Clinton, and two at lightweight, Kenny Buchanan (1970) and Jim Watt (1979).

The record attendance for a Scottish boxing match was 32,000, for the fight between Tommy Milligan and Frank Moody at the Carntyne Stadium in 1928. Milligan was the welterweight champion of Great Britain and Europe in 1924.

CRICKET

Cricket was introduced to Scotland by English soldiers garrisoned in the country in the years following the Jacobite rising of 1745 and by immigrant English workers in the paper, textile and iron industries. But it was developed and codified by Richard Nairn, a Jacobite who had settled in Hampshire after the '45. Nairn also introduced the middle stump. Records exist of Scottish immigrants playing cricket at Savannah, Georgia, in the United States, in the 1730s. A match involving English officers is believed to have been played at Perth as early as 1750, but the first cricket match in Scotland for which records are extant was played in September 1785 at Shaw Park, Alloa, between the Duke of Atholl's XI and a Colonel Talbot's team.

The oldest known cricket club in Scotland is that of Kelso, in the Borders, dating back to 1820, when Kelso was a garrison town; but the Perthshire club claims the longest continuous existence from 1826. Teams representing Scotland have played matches since 1865. The governing body for cricket in Scotland is the Scottish Cricket Union (SCU). It was originally set up in 1879 but then disbanded in 1883. Grange Club in Edinburgh acted as the Scottish equivalent of the MCC until the SCU was re-formed in 1908. The Western Division Union and Border Leagues date from the 1890s and the county championship from 1902. Scotland's only victory over a Test-playing nation took place on 29 July 1882, when Australia were defeated in a one-day match at Raeburn Place, Edinburgh.

Scottish players have often appeared in English county teams, but more rarely at test-match level. Douglas Jardine, born of Scottish parents in India, captained England during the famous 'Bodyline' tour of Australia in 1932–33. J. D. F. Larter, born in Inverness, played 10 tests for England between 1962 and 1965. Mike Denness, born in Bellshill, Lanarkshire, captained England from 1973 to 1975.

Since 1980, Scotland have taken part, by invitation, in England's Benson and Hedges Cup and NatWest Trophy one-day competitions. There are annual three-day matches against Ireland and the MCC with regular games against overseas touring sides. The Triple Crown Tournament, inaugurated in 1993 and involving the England Amateur XI, Wales, Ireland and

Scotland, was won by Scotland in 1994 and 1995. In 1992 Scotland resigned from the UK Cricket Council and in 1994 it was elected to associate membership of the International Cricket Council (ICC). This gave Scotland autonomy in world cricket, and the Scottish team competed for the first time in the ICC Trophy in Kuala Lumpur in March/April 1997, reaching the semi-finals. The national side also won through to the final stages of the 1999 Cricket World Cup. Although they reached only the first stage, top scorer Gavin Hamilton has since represented England in a test match.

As of 2000, 150 local cricket clubs are affiliated to the SCU, but there are estimated to be well over 200 clubs existing in Scotland. The most famous win at this level by a Scottish club was by Freuchie over Rowledge at Lords in the final of the national Village Cup competition in 1985.

Scottish Cricket Union

Caledonia House, South Gyle, Edinburgh EH12 9DQ (Tel No. 0131-317 7247; Website: www.scu.org.uk).

CURLING

Curling is a traditional winter sport which has been played in Scotland for over 450 years. Often described as a sort of 'bowls on ice', it is still occasionally played on a frozen outdoor rink, but is usually played on an indoor ice-rink. The game involves sliding smooth-bottomed 18kg discs of granite, called 'stones', across the ice towards a target circle, known as the 'house'. Each team consists of four players, and the 'skip', or captain, standing behind the house, nominates the shot required. Once the shot has been made, two players accompany the stone along the ice with brooms, sweeping the ice in front of the stone according to instructions from the skip. Sweeping, originally intended to remove twigs and leaves from the path of the stone when the game was played on a frozen loch, pond or river, influences the speed and distance which the stone travels across the ice.

Rival claims to the origins of curling have been made by Scotland and the Netherlands. The Dutch claim that 16th-century paintings by Pieter Bruegel the elder (1530–69) show a game similar to curling being played on frozen canals. Claims by Scotland are based on a varied collection of old stones which have been salvaged from lochs and ponds over the centuries. While the controversy about origins goes on, what is certain is that the Scots have nurtured the game, provided the rules of play and exported it throughout the world.

The early curling stones were called 'loofies' (*lof* being the old Scots world for the palm of the hand) because they resembled this shape. They had grooves for fingers and thumb and were thrown with a quoiting action. Over 300 years ago strong-arm curling was introduced. 'Channel' stones were used: they were given this name because they were taken from the channels of rivers and had been worn smooth by the water. The stones had rough handles inserted in them, and over time bigger and bigger stones became used. The object was to hurl them into the house where it would be difficult to dislodge them.

Spherical stones replaced rough and irregularly shaped stones towards the end of the 18th century, and with the introduction of these stones came a whole new aspect to curling. Skill and accuracy took over from brute strength, and with the turning of the hand on delivery, the round stones 'curled' consistently on the ice. Solid iron crampits were used as footholds during delivery, thus replacing the old 'cramps' and 'tramps' (iron or steel pads) with prongs underneath, which were attached to the boots with straps. Nowadays the modern hack is used throughout the curling world.

The earliest curling club was probably formed at Muthill, Tayside in 1739. The famous Duddingston Club in Edinburgh, founded in 1795, formulated the first curling rules in 1804 and 12 of the Duddingston regulations for play for the basis of the much-enlarged modern rulebook.

The Grand Caledonian Curling Club was established in Edinburgh in 1838 and became the Royal Caledonian Curling Club (RCCC) in 1843 after a visit by Queen Victoria to Scone Palace, where the Earl of Mansfield demonstrated the game to her on a polished ballroom floor. The Club's first president was the sports greatest innovator, John Cairnie of Largs.

The Scots made their first tour to Canada in 1902–3 with a team of 28 members, who toured the country for three months. The first indoor game to be held in Scotland was at Glasgow in 1907. In 1909 the Canadians first toured in Scotland and 500 curlers attended a welcoming banquet in Edinburgh. As a result of these tours came the Strathcona Cup (first presented by RCCC president Lord Strathcona and Mount Royal), which is played every five years on a home-and-away basis.

The only Olympic Gold Medal to be awarded in the sport to date was won by a British team in Chamonix in 1924. All the members of the team were Scots.

Scottish women began touring with the men in the 1950s on exchange tours to Canada and the USA and play against European countries was arranged on a regular basis.

The most prestigious tournament is the World Championship (known as the Scotch Cup from 1959 to 1967 and the Silver Broom from 1968 to 1985), which was launched in Scotland in 1959, and is sponsored by the Scotch Whisky Association. It was originally played between the champion teams from Scotland and Canada, but the competition quickly grew into the men's World Championship.

The formation of the International Curling Federation (ICF) was initiated by the RCCC in 1965 during the World Championship for the Scotch Cup. A meeting was attended by office-bearers and representatives from Scotland, Canada, the USA, Norway, Sweden and Switzerland to consider setting up an international committee. The following year the Scotch Cup was held in Canada, at Vancouver, and the six countries that attended the previous meeting met again, along with a representative from France. The International Curling Federation was officially established on 1 April 1966. Major Allan Cameron, President of the RCCC was its first president. The Federation became independent in 1973 and in 1982 was recognised as the governing body of world curling. In 1991 the ICF became the World Curling Federation (WCF).

The Ladies World Championship was established in Scotland in 1979 and sponsored by the Royal Bank of Scotland. For the first three years this tournament was played in Scotland, but it is now played in a different country each year. Scotland were the winners of the World Junior Curling Championships in 1991. In February/March 2000 the world championships were held at Glasgow, with the Canadian men and women both receiving top honours.

The outdoor game has now all but disappeared. The greatest outdoor curling match, the 'Bonspiel', now only takes place in exceptionally severe winters and has occurred just 33 times in the last 150 years or so. It is traditionally held on the Lake of Menteith, Perthshire, between teams representing the North and the South of Scotland. The match is announced only when the ice on the lake is 10 inches (253mm) thick. This depth was increased from the previous limit of 8 inches (203mm) after the last Bonspiel, held on 7 February 1979, when the rarity of the occasion attracted a crowd of 10,000 onto the ice, threatening the safety of all concerned.

Royal Caledonian Curling Club
Cairnie House, Ingliston Showground,
Newbridge, Midlothian EH28 2NB
(Tel 0131-333 3003).

World Curling Federation
81 King Street, Edinburgh EH3 6RN
(Tel: 0131-333 3003; Fax: 0131-333 3323).

DEERSTALKING

Deerstalking became established in the Highlands during the 19th century, and marked a change in practice from earlier methods of hunting deer, in which deer were driven into an enclosed space, either a natural pass or a built enclosure, and shot by waiting riflemen. The new sport was based on approaching the deer as closely as possible, and killing it with a single shot. In the early days deerhounds were used as a back-up to the rifle, which often wounded the deer without killing it outright. The introduction of telescopic sights in the 1880s was at first considered unsporting, as it gave the stalker an unfair advantage.

The 19th-century fashion for deerstalking, fuelled by the creation of deer forests, lodges, bothies and improved access into the hills, was even further promoted when Queen Victoria and Prince Albert took a long lease on the Balmoral estate in 1848. Deerstalking inspired the work of Sir Edwin Landseer, painter of the famous *Monarch of the Glen* and himself a keen stalker. The growth of the sport gave rise to the professional stalker, or gamekeeper. The gamekeeper looked after the sporting estate all year round and acted as a guide to stalkers in the open season.

Paradoxically, the organised pursuit of deer helped to increase their chances of survival, by reducing poaching, and the numbers of deer steadily increased through the 19th century. By the end of the century over seven million acres were given over to deer forest.

Today deer face competition from many sources — hikers, climbers, skiers and tourists, as well as foresters. New forestry plantations deny the deer low ground. Poaching has made a comeback. Nonetheless, deer and the sport of deerstalking continue to flourish.

EQUESTRIAN SPORTS

In the 12th century, William the Lion organised a horse race, known as the Lanark Silver Bell, on Lanark Moor, making Scotland the birthplace of British horse racing. Scotland once boasted 15 racecourses. Lanark, the oldest, closed in 1977, and today just five survive: Ayr, Edinburgh, Hamilton Park, Kelso and Perth.

The Scottish Grand National is held at Ayr. It moved from Belleisle, where racing had taken place since 1576, to today's site in 1907. The largest crowd for a race meeting in Scotland was 20,000, on Scottish Grand National Day 1969. Ayr is also the home of the September Gold Cup. Edinburgh racecourse was founded in 1816 as Musselburgh Race Course, and the current course opened in 1978. Evening race meetings were first held in Scotland at Hamilton Park, near Glasgow, which was also the first course to install plastic safety racing barriers comprehensively. Crowds exceeding 7,000 regularly attend the 'Saints and Sinners' evening meeting, a charity fundraising event.

Scotland has produced a number of racing celebrities over the years. Matt Dawson was a trainer who won the Derby in 1860 and on five subsequent occasions, as well as 23 other major classics. Charlie Cunningham rode and trained his own horses at Wooden, Kelso, with great success between 1865 and 1891 Despite his great height (6 feet 3 inches), he was champion amateur jockey in 1852. In the 1950s George Boyd produced 700 winners from his east coast stables. Willie Carson is the most successful Scottish jockey, being five times champion jockey and having ridden almost 4,000 winners in Great Britain during his career.

Scotland's most famous horse, Peaty Sandy, was the first Scottish horse to win the Coral Welsh National, which he did in 1981. He won 20 of his 74 jumping races, never falling until the last fence of his last race, and earning £100,000 in total.

Pony trekking as an organised leisure activity originated in Scotland. It was introduced to encourage people to explore the country via its old drove roads, by the late Lieutenant Commander Jock Kerr Hunter, who opened Scotland's first riding school in the 1940s. Since then, riding centres have increased to around 60 across Scotland. All are approved by either the Trekking & Riding Society of Scotland (TRSS) or the British Horse Society (BHS).

FOOTBALL

Association football (also, but less commonly, known as 'soccer' in Scotland) shares its early history with rugby, both having a common origin in early ball games of the Roman era.

Rapid growth and regulation of the game began in the second half of the 19th century, as the cities grew more populous and the introduction of Saturday afternoons a leisure created a demand for public entertainment. The Queen's Park Football Club was founded in Glasgow in 1867 and the first recognised match took place in 1868. However, as most of Scotland's population became centred on

Glasgow, Edinburgh and one or two smaller cities, football clubs in more isolated and less populous areas found it hard to arrange fixtures with other clubs. With no formal structure, matches were often irregular and organised in a casual manner. It was not unusual to find, when a fixture had been arranged between clubs, that the two teams were playing to different sets of rules.

The Scottish Football Association (SFA) is the second oldest football association in the world. It came into being after a meeting in Glasgow on 13 March 1873 to establish an annual cup competition, proposed by Queen's Park FC and attended by the teams that played Scottish Club Association rules. The original eight clubs belonging to the SFA were Queen's Park, Clydesdale, Vale of Leven, Dumbreck, Third Lanarkshire Rifle Volunteers, Eastern, Granville and Rovers. Queens Park were the first winners, in 1873–74, of the cup competition which later became the Scottish FA Cup. However, Queens Park's amateur status, which it still maintains to this day, contributed to its decline as the trend towards professionalism grew. The Glasgow clubs, Rangers (founded 1873) and Celtic (1888), went on to dominate Scottish football. It was the Scottish Cup that produced what is still regarded as the world's highest ever football score, the 36–0 victory of Arbroath over Bon Accord of Aberdeen in 1885. Bon Accord were in fact a cricket club and had been mistakenly sent an invitation to play in the Cup. The SFA continues to be the governing body of football in Scotland and has ultimate responsibility for the regulation and development of the game. A total of 79 clubs are affiliated to the SFA for the season 2001–2002. The SFL was increased to 42 members for the season 2000-2001 with the addition of Elgin City and Peterhead, both from the Highland League.

Junior football is administered by the Scottish Junior Football Association, founded in Glasgow in 1886.

The Scottish Football League (SFL) was founded in 1890 of which only a handful of the original member clubs are still in existence, namely Celtic, Dumbarton, Hearts, Partick Thistle, Rangers and St Mirren. The inaugural championship of 1890-91 was shared by Dumbarton and Rangers. Regional associations include The Highland Football League, founded 1893 and The East of Scotland League, founded in 1930. All these leagues are administered by the SFA

The Scottish Women's Football Association was founded in 1972. It now has over 4,000 registered players and is the fastest growing sport for women in the country. Scottish women's

football was given a boost in 2000 with the news that the national squad was to receive £66,000 of National Lottery funding. This would allow 22 members of the team, through the Talented Athlete programme, to develop their sporting skills and also compete in tournaments such as the Pacific Cup in Australia.

The national stadium for Scotland games is Hampden Park. It officially opened in 1903 and recent development has made it into one of the finest stadiums in the world, capable of holding 52,000 spectators. A British record crowd of 149,547 watched a Scotland v England international at Hampden Park in 1937 and just eight days later a crowd of 147,365 watched Celtic v Aberdeen there in the Scottish Cup Final. The highest attendance at a league match in Britain was 118,567 for Rangers v Celtic match at Ibrox in 1939. These attendance levels are no longer attainable because of safety regulations limiting crowd numbers, among other factors.

Scotland's worst sporting disaster occurred at Ibrox Stadium, home of Rangers, where 66 spectators lost their lives on 2 January 1971 when some spectators lost their footing on a stairway while leaving the stadium at the end of the traditional New Year match between Rangers and Celtic.

The first ever live TV coverage of league football in Scotland was for an Aberdeen v Hearts match in 1986.

THE INTERNATIONAL DIMENSION
The first official international football match in history was played on 30 November 1872 at the West of Scotland cricket ground in Partick, Glasgow, between England and Scotland, in front of about 4,000 spectators.

In 1886 the football associations from Scotland, England, Wales and Ireland set up the International Football Association Board to control the rules of the game. The SFA joined the Fédération Internationale de Football Association (FIFA), football's world governing body, in 1910 and was a founding member of the Union des Associations Européennes de Football (UEFA) in 1954.

The first official international match against a continental team was in 1929, when Scotland beat Norway 7–3 in Oslo. Scotland's international teams lost only 3 of their first 43 international matches and first participated in the World Cup in 1954, having previously turned down a chance to appear in 1950. Scotland have reached the World Cup final stages on seven other occasions, namely 1958, 1974, 1978, 1982, 1986, 1990 and 1998. The five consecutive appearances

1974–1990 constitute a record for the competition for a team qualifying solely through its efforts on the field and not through special circumstances such as automatic qualification as hosts or cup holders. The current manager, Craig Brown, is the 13th manager of the national team.

PREMIER DIVISION TEAMS FOR SEASON 2001–2002

Aberdeen Football Club (founded 1903; entered League 1904)
Pittodrie Stadium, Pittodrie Street, Aberdeen AB24 5QH (Tel: 01224 650400; Fax: 01224 644173;
Ticket Office: 01224 632328;
Email: address: feedback@afc.co.uk;
Web: www.afc.co.uk)
Manager: Ebbe Skovdahl

Celtic Football Club (founded 1888; entered League 1890)
Celtic Park, 95 Kerrydale Street, Glasgow G40 3RE (Tel: 0141-556 2611; Fax: 0141-551 8106;
Ticket Office: 0141-551 8653;
Email: celtic.view@celticfc.btinternet.com;
Web: www.celticfc.co.uk).
Manager: Martin O'Neil

Dundee Football Club (founded 1893; entered League 1893)
Dens Park stadium, Sandeman Street, Dundee DD3 7JY (Tel: 01382-889966; Fax: 01382-832284;
Ticket Office: 01382-204777;
Email: dundeefc@dfc.co.uk;
Web: www.dundeefc.co.uk).
Manager: Ivano Bonetti

Dundee United Football Club (founded 1909; entered League 1910)
Tannadice Park, Tannadice Street, Dundee DD3 7JW (Tel: 01382-833166; Fax: 01382-889398;
Ticket Office: 01382-833166;
Email: dundee.united.fc@cableinet.co.uk;
Web: www.dundeeunitedfc.co.uk).
Manager: Alex Smith

Dunfermline Athletic Football Club (founded 1885; entered League 1921)
East End Park, Halbeath Road, Dunfermline KY12 7RB
(Tel: 01383 724295; Fax: 01383 723468;
Ticket Office: 01383 724295;
Web: www.dunfermline-athletic.com).
Manager: Jimmy Calderwood

Heart of Midlothian Football Club (founded 1874; entered League 1890)
Tynecastle Stadium, Gorgie Road, Edinburgh EH11 2NL (Tel: 0131-200 7200; Fax: 0131-200 7222;
Ticket Office: 0131-200 7201/9;
Web-site: www.heartsfc.co.uk)
Manager: Craig Levein

Hibernian Football Club (founded 1875; entered League 1893)
Easter Road Stadium, Albion Road, Edinburgh EH7 5QG (Tel: 0131-661 2159; Fax: 0131-659 6488;
Ticket Office: 0131-661 1875
Email club@hibernianfc.co.uk;
Web: www.hibernianfc.co.uk).
Manager: Alex McLeish

Kilmarnock Football Club (founded 1869; entered League 1896)
Rugby Park, Rugby Road, Kilmarnock KA1 2DP (Tel: 01563-525184; Fax: 01563-522181;
Ticket Office: 01563-545300
Email: kfc@sol.co.uk/kilmarnockfc@sol.co.uk;
Web: www.kilmarnockfc.co.uk).
Manager: Bobby Williamson

Livingston Football Club (founded 1943; entered League 1974)
Almondvale Stadium, Alderstone Road, Livingston EH54 7DN (Tel: 01506-417000; Fax: 01506 418888;
Ticket Office: 01506-417000;
Web: www.livingstonfc.co.uk).
Manager: Jim Leishman

Motherwell Football Club (founded 1886; entered League 1893)
Fir Park, Fir Park Street, Motherwell ML1 2QN (Tel: 01698 333333; Fax: 01698 338001;
Ticket Office: 01698 333030;
Email: mfc@motherwellfc.co.uk;
Web: www.motherwellfc.co.uk).
Manager: Billy Davies

Rangers Football Club (founded 1873; entered League 1890)
Ibrox Stadium, 150 Edmiston Drive, Glasgow G51 2XD (Tel: 0870 600-1972;
Fax: 0870 600-1978;
Ticket Office: 0870 600-1993;
Web: www.rangers.co.uk).
Manager: Dick Advocaat

St Johnstone Football Club (founded 1884; entered League 1911)
McDiarmid Park, Crieff Road, Perth PH1 2SJ
(Tel: 01738-459090; Fax: 01738-625771;
Ticket Office: 01738-455000;
Email: paul.fraser@huntingtower.sol.co.uk;
Web: www.stjohnstonefc.co.uk).
Manager: Sandy Clark

FOOTBALL ASSOCIATIONS

Scottish Football Association
6 Park Gardens, Glasgow G3 7YF
(Tel: 0141-332 6372).

Scottish Football League
188 West Regent Street, Glasgow G2 4RY
(Tel: 0141-248 3844).

Highland Football League
35 Hamilton Drive, Elgin IV30 2NN
(Tel 01343-544995).

East of Scotland League
2 Baberton Mains Court, Edinburgh EH14 3ER
(Tel: 0131-442 1402).

GOLF

Golf is commonly regarded as the quintessentially Scottish game, but there is some evidence that it may have originated in Holland. The most likely derivation, however, is the Scots verb 'gowf', meaning to cuff or strike hard.

In 1457 a Scottish Act of Parliament by James II banned both golf and football because they interfered with his subjects' archery practice. James III in 1471 and James IV in 1491 also adopted this Act. It was not until 1502 that Scots were able to indulge in their national pastime. During the Stewart era, the links of Leith and St. Andrews were the chief centres of golf. When James VI acquired the English throne, he introduced golf south of the border. At this time it was the local bowmakers who were called upon to manufacture clubs and balls.

The modern history of golf began with the formation of clubs in the 18th century. The Gentlemen Golfers of Edinburgh (now the Honourable Company of Edinburgh Golfers) was founded in 1744 and is generally considered to be the first golf club, with Edinburgh Town Council granting a Silver Cup to the 'Gentlemen', which became the first golf trophy. The first competition for the Silver Cup was played on the Links of Leith on 7 March 1744 and from this event sprang the first known rules of golf.

The club played at Musselburgh from 1836 to 1891, and their present home is Muirfield. Musselburgh Golf Club came into being in 1744, although golf had probably already been played there for as many as 300 years. In the mid 19th century Musselburgh became the focus of Scottish golf, not only as the home of the Gentlemen Golfers of Edinburgh but also the home of the Edinburgh Burgess Golfing Society, founded 1773 and the Bruntsfield Links Golf Club, founded 1761. The first women's golf tournament, for the town's fishwives, was held at the Musselburgh Golf Club in 1811. The town was also the centre of golf ball and club manufacturing and it was here that a tool to cut the standard $4\frac{1}{4}$-inch hole was introduced in 1829.

The Society of St Andrews Golfers was formed 14 May 1754 and drew up a set of 13 rules for their annual golfing competition. In 1834 the name was changed to The Royal & Ancient Golf Club of St Andrews (R & A) after the society received royal patronage from William IV. Although the R & A has the function of lawgiver in golf, the parchment on which the original 13 rules of golf were drafted is in the possession of the Honourable Company of Edinburgh Golfers and a copy hangs in the Muirfield clubhouse. The standard round of golf at St Andrews was 22 holes (11 holes to the shoreline and 11 back), but in 1764 this was reduced to 18 holes, bringing St Andrews into line with other clubs.

The first known professional tournament was played at St Andrews in 1819. In 1821 James Cheape, Laird of Strathtyrum, purchased the St Andrews Links to preserve it for the game of golf. The Links were re-purchased by St Andrews Town Council in 1894 for £5,000 and were run by the Green Committee of St Andrews Link. The first clubhouse at St Andrews was built in 1835 by the Union Club offering facilities to sportsmen. By 1854 a new clubhouse was opened behind the first tee on the Old Course.

At Prestwick Golf Club, founded in 1851, the first Open Championship was held in 1860. The winner, Willie Park Snr, received the Challenge Belt, and the runner-up was the local favourite, 'Old Tom' Morris from St Andrews. In 1870 the Challenge Belt would become the property of the player who won the Open three years in succession. This was achieved by 'Young Tom' Morris, whose father had become keeper of the green at St Andrews in 1864.

The first 12 Open Championships, 1860–72, were played at Prestwick over three rounds of the 12-hole links. There was no championship in 1871. The R & A and the Honourable Company of Edinburgh Golfers then joined with Prestwick in contributing towards the Silver Claret Jug, which became the permanent trophy for the Open. The competition was played in rotation at Prestwick, St Andrews and Musselburgh, and this began a tradition of rotating the venue for the Open among several courses which has been maintained up to the present. The last Open to be played at Prestwick was in 1925. The R & A removed it from the rota after the crowd engulfed the Scottish American Macdonald Smith of Carnoustie in that year. Musselburgh hosted the Open on six occasions between 1874 and 1889, the Scot Willie Auchterlonie winning the 1883 tournament, but when the Honourable Company moved to Muirfield in 1891, they took the competition with them. Muirfield have since staged the competition 14 times between 1892 and 1992.

The Open was first played at St Andrews in 1873 and was won by the local Tom Kidd. In 1919 the R & A took over responsibility for organising the Open. The holding of the 129th Open there in July 2000 brought St Andrews' total of Opens to 26, one more than that of Prestwick, the original venue.

Spectators were charged gate money for the first time at the 1926 Open, and as the popularity of the championship grew, the ability to accommodate spectators influenced the selection of venues, which by then included places both north and south of the border. Other British Open Championship courses in Scotland include Troon, where more golf is probably played than in any other town in Scotland, and where the Open was first played in 1923. It has been played there several times between 1950 and 1997. Turnberry, founded 1902, has hosted three Open Championships, in 1977, 1986 and 1994, replacing Carnoustie on the rota.

Golf is first recorded at Carnoustie as long ago as 1650, but a club was not formed until 1842. The first Open to be played there was in 1931 and was won by Edinburgh-born Tommy Armour, who had emigrated to the United States in the 1920s. The competition has been held at Carnoustie at irregular intervals but returned to a revamped course in 1999 following a 24-year absence. It was won in a dramatic play-off by Paul Lawrie of Aberdeen. The only other modern Scottish winner of the Open is Sandy Lyle, who won in 1985.

The Scottish PGA Championship is staged at the Monarch's Course, Gleneagles, during August. The most successful Scottish golfer of the modern era is Colin Montgomerie, who in May 2000 won the Benson & Hedges Tournament at Wentworth for a record-breaking third consecutive year, thus maintaining his position at the top of the European order of merit.

In 1897 Britain's leading golf clubs asked the R & A to take charge of setting up and administering a universal code of rules for golf, and since then every new golfing nation with connections to the R & A has agreed to abide by them. The rules set up by the R & A were freely available to all by 1908 and a sponsorship deal was struck with Royal Insurance for the publication of all English-language copies. The United States, however, set their own rules, and these were used until 1952 for contests inside that country. In at least one case the United States led the way: in 1938 the United States Golf Association (USGA) limited the number of clubs a golfer can carry to 14, and in the following year the R & A followed suit.

The R & A and USGA have worked together since 1952 to create a common international set of rules. These supreme authorities of the game meet every four years to agree any revisions that are required.

Several Scots have won tournaments outside of Britain. Gordon Brand Jnr has won the Scandinavian Open, Bernard Gallacher both the Spanish and French Opens, Sam Torrance the Zambian Open in 1975 and the Spanish Open in 1982, Sandy Lyle the US Masters in 1988. Scotswomen have won their share of UK and overseas tournaments as well: Jessie Valentine won the New Zealand Ladies in 1935 and the French Ladies in 1936, Cathy Panton the British Ladies Open in 1976, Gillian Stewart the European Open in 1984, and Dale Reid the European Open in 1988.

Television coverage of golf was provided live from St Andrews for the first time in 1955.

The Amateur Championships were played at Royal Dornoch, Sutherland, for the first time in 1985. The British Golf Museum opened at St Andrews in 1990.

There are currently over 400 golf courses in Scotland, and Scotland boasts the highest course in Britain, Leadhills in Strathclyde, which is 1,500 feet (457 metres) above sea level.

Championship courses:
- St Andrews – Tel 01334-475757.
- Carnoustie – Tel 01241-853789.
- Gleneagles – Tel 01764-663543.
- Turnberry – Tel 01655-331000.
- Muirfield – Tel 01620-842255.
- Royal Dornoch – Tel 01862-810219.

British Golf Museum, Bruce Embankment, St Andrews, Fife KY16 9AB
(Tel: 01334-478880; Fax: 01334-473306;
Web: www.britishgolfmuseum.co.uk).

HIGHLAND AND BORDER GAMES

The origins of Highland and Border games lie in competitions arranged by ancient kings and clan chiefs to help them select the strongest men as their champions, the fastest cross-country runners as their couriers, and the best pipers and dancers to entertain both themselves and their guests. The earliest organised games probably date back to the eleventh century, when Malcolm Canmore held contests to find the best soldiers for the struggles against the Normans. Games took place in Ceres, Fife, in 1314, when victorious soldiers returning from the Battle of Bannockburn discovered an outlet for their high spirits by taking part in athletic competitions. However, the holding of games was prohibited following the suppression of the Jacobite Rising in 1746, when large gatherings, the wearing of the kilt and the playing of the bagpipes – in fact any expression of Scottish culture – were forbidden.

Highland games began to be formally organised again in the 1820s as part of a romantic revival of Highland culture and traditions, encouraged by Sir Walter Scott and King George IV, and became an annual occurrence across Scotland. The first 'modern' Highland games took place in 1819 at St Fillians, Perthshire, organised by the Highland Society. Events at the Invergarry games in the 1820s included twisting the four legs from a cow, for which a fat sheep was offered as the prize. Queen Victoria's love for Scottish things and her patronage of the Braemar Gathering from 1848 contributed to this revival of interest and involvement in the games.

HIGHLAND GAMES TODAY

Highland games today are organised and run by their own committees under the rules of the Scottish Games Association (SGA), which was established in 1946. The objectives of the SGA are to encourage and foster the highest standards of ethics and performance, lay down and enforce rules and regulations covering all aspects of traditional Highland Games activities and to assist committees in the improvement of their events. All competitors must register with the SGA prior to participating in any events.

Highland and Border games are held annually between May and September. In spite of their name, they are held all over Scotland. The events cover a full range of running and cycle track events, light field and heavy field events, along with Highland dancing and piping. The Border Games have more emphasis on track competitions.

The most distinctive events are known as the 'heavies'. Weights of 28lbs and 56lbs are thrown for distance, with that of 56lbs thrown for height over a bar. The famous Scottish caber events have athletes running while carrying an entire tree trunk, some over 20ft in length, and then tossing it end over end.

All competitors in heavy field events must wear a kilt. Some Games use stones in the putting events and the Scottish hammer has a rigid wooden or bamboo handle, with the throwers wearing special boots with an extended sole beyond the toe so that they can 'dig in' and throw without turning their whole body.

Tug-of-war takes place at the more traditional Highland Games and involves teams of five or eight men plus a coach. Draws take place before the competition starts, the judge tossing a coin to decide the direction of the pull. The length of the pull is 12 feet and the team with the best of three pulls is declared the winner.

Just as important as the sporting events are the piping competitions for both individuals and bands, as well as the dancing competitions, where girls, some as young as three years old, perform the intricate steps of dances such as the Highland Fling, the Sword Dance and the *Seann Triubhas*.

The most famous Highland games are the Braemar Gathering, which have been attended regularly by successive generations of the Royal Family since the days of Queen Victoria, and the Cowal Highland Gathering, the largest of its kind in the world, which ends with the massed pipes and drums of over 150 bands marching through the streets of Dunoon, Argyll.

As Scots have moved and settled throughout the world they have taken with them their love of the Games, and today there are events in Europe, America, Asia and to Australia. Many of the overseas venues have attracted large numbers of exiled Scots, their descendants and friends.

For more information about the Highland Games, contact the local Tourist Board (*see* p. 464) in the area concerned.

Scottish Games Association, 24 Florence Place, Perth PH1 5BH (Tel: 01738 627782).

MOTOR RALLYING AND RACING

Scotland's terrain has made it a favourite location for motor rallying ever since a Glasgow-built car finished in second place in a 500-mile trial organised by the Automobile Club of Britain in 1901. Scotland's principal annual motor sports event, the international RSAC Scottish Rally, was established in 1932 but was born out of a series of reliability trials begun in 1903 by the Scottish Automobile Club, formed in 1899 and the forerunner of the Royal Scottish Automobile Club (RSAC). The rally is held in June and covers 700 miles. At the UK level, the RAC Lombard Rally includes some Scottish stages. The first Scot to win the RAC Rally was Colin MacRae in 1994. He also won in the three years following, and was the first Briton to become World Rally Champion in 1995.

Scots have made a major contribution to motor-racing since the 1950s. Ecurie Ecosse was formed in 1952 as a non-profit-making syndicate of Scottish racing enthusiasts. In 1956 and 1957 the team won the Le Mans 24-hour race. One of Scotland's famous Grand Prix drivers, Jim Clark, began his career with the Border Reivers, a Berwickshire team formed in the 1950s. In 1961, Innes Ireland became the first Scot to win a major Grand Prix, in the USA, and in his wake Jim Clark won 25 Grand Prix races and twice became World Champion, in 1963 and 1965. Jackie Stewart topped this by winning three World Championships (1969, 1971 and 1973). In the late 1990s Stewart attempted to boost Scottish interest in motor-racing by forming a Grand Prix team under his own name, but met with little success. David Coulthard won several Grand Prix races during the latter part of the 1990s but has yet to be crowned World Champion. At the mid-point of the 2001 Formula 1 season he currently lies in second place.

RUGBY

A game similar to rugby, called *harpastum*, was played in Scotland during the time of the Romans. It involved two teams running, passing and throwing a small round ball, the aim being to cross the opponents' line at the far end of a rectangular field. This game still lives on in certain street games in Hawick and Jedburgh.

During the 15th and 16th centuries, football (which bore more resemblance to rugby in these days) was banned by royal edict on the grounds that it interfered with archery practice. The first recorded match between teams representing Scotland and England took place in 1599. The venue was Bewcastle in Cumbria, and the result, a number of English taken prisoner and one man disembowelled. Could this have been the first recorded incidence of football hooliganism?

By the mid nineteenth century some private schools, colleges and universities in Scotland played a game that involved kicking and handling of the ball. H. H. Almond of Merchiston School,

Edinburgh, is generally credited with popularising rugby among schools. In 1846 rules were formally introduced, which brought some consistency to this new sport. However, the first senior game in Scotland took place in 1858 and was played between Edinburgh Academicals and a University team. It was spread out over four successive Saturdays and involved around 50 players. As a result, in 1868, a number of Scottish clubs formulated a book of rules called the 'Green Book'.

Captains from five Scottish rugby clubs got together in 1870 and discussed challenging English clubs to represent their respective countries to the first international rugby match. The game took place on 27 March 1871 at Raeburn Place (a cricket field) at Edinburgh Academy, with Scotland winning. This gave Scotland the distinction of being both the first hosts and first winners ever in an international rugby match. The match initiated the fixture which has since become a highlight of the rugby calendar and which since 1879 has been known as the Calcutta Cup. Scotland has won the cup 41 times compared to England's 58, and there have been 17 drawn matches. Scotland's win on 2 April 2000 was their first since 1990 and prevented England from securing a grand slam (beating all nations) in the first Six-Nations tournament.

The Scottish Football Union (SFU) was formed on 3 March 1873, comprising eight clubs, soon to be joined by six others from the Borders. One of its main objectives was to find a pitch for international matches. The first few international fixtures had been played at Old Hampden Park in Glasgow, Powderhall in Edinburgh and the West of Scotland Cricket Club's ground in Hamilton. The SFU purchased a ground at Inverleith in Edinburgh, thus becoming the first Home Union to own and run its own rugby ground. The first international match at the new location was in 1899 against Ireland.

On 25 April 1883 the first seven-a-side tournament took place at The Greenyards after Ned Haig, a butcher by trade, suggested a tournament in order to raise cash for his club, Melrose. Melrose defeated their close neighbours and rivals, Gala, in the final. Most clubs now organize sevens tournaments at the end of the season, but the Melrose Sevens continues to be the top tournament of its class.

Rugby's popularity continued to grow after World War I, but Inverleith could no longer hold the large crowds that flocked to see Scottish games. In 1922 the SFU purchased 19 acres of land at Murrayfield, which had previously been the home of the Edinburgh Polo Club. Funds were raised for the new stadium by an issue of debentures and on 21 March 1925 it officially opened with an international match against England and 70,000 spectators cheering throughout the immensely exciting game. Scotland once again defeated England by a score of 14–11.

The year 1925 saw changes at the administration level with the SFU becoming the Scottish Rugby Union (SRU). Most of the rugby club grounds were used to grow potatoes during World War II and the armed forces arranged a game between England and Scotland Services Internationals, which took place at Inverleith, as Murrayfield was being used as a supply depot.

In 1955 Scotland's defeat of Wales at Murrayfield ended a 17-game winless streak, which started when the Fourth Springboks from South Africa visited the UK in 1950–1. In 1960 Scotland became the first of the home unions to tour foreign countries when they went to South Africa – a tradition that continues to this day. The highest attendance for a rugby match in Scotland is 104,000 for Scotland's 12–10 win over Wales at Murrayfield in 1975.

In 1986 HRH the Princess Royal accepted an invitation to become patron of the SRU. A year later Scotland reached the quarter-finals of the first Rugby World Cup in New Zealand, but lost to the mighty All Blacks, who became the eventual winners.

In 1990 Scotland won their third Grand Slam (the first one was in 1925 and the second in 1984) by defeating Wales, Ireland and France, finally beating England at Murrayfield 13-7.

The 125th anniversary of the first international rugby match was celebrated n 1996, followed by the 125th anniversary of the SFU (SRU) in 1998 and Murrayfield celebrated its 75th birthday in March 2000.

Approximately 300 clubs belong to the SRU and there are 200 affiliated schools. Member clubs account for some 13,500 people currently playing the game and around 32,000 are non-playing members of clubs. From the 1975–76 season onwards club rugby was standardised as seven divisions, with district divisions beneath.

RUGBY CLUBS FORMING DIVISION 1 FOR THE 2001-2002 SEASON ARE:

Aberdeen GSFP RFC (club founded 1893)

Rubislaw Playing Fields, 86 Queens Road, Aberdeen AB10 6XA (Tel: 01224-316827
E-mail: derek@derekyounger.freeserve.co.uk).

Boroughmuir RFC (club founded 1919)

Meggetland, Colinton Road, Edinburgh EH14 1AS (Tel: 0131-443 7571;
Email: admin@boroughmuirfc.co.uk;
Web: www.boroughmuirfc.co.uk).

Currie RFC (club founded 1970)

5 Malleny, Malleny Park, Balerno, Midlothian EH14 7AF (Tel: 0131-449 2432; Fax: 0131-449 7688; Web: www.currierfc.freeserve.co.uk).

Gala RFC

Lindisfarne, 12 Glendinning Terrace, Galashiels TD1 2JW (Tel: 01896-755145;
Fax: 01896-755270;
Web: www.bordernet.co.uk/rugby).

Glasgow Hawks RFC (club founded 1997 on merger of Glasgow Accies & GHK)

The Pavilion, Old Anniesland, 689 Crow Road, Glasgow G13 1LQ (Tel: 0141-950 1222:
Fax: 0141-959 9972;
E-mail:hugh.barrow@ntlworld.com;
Web: www.glasgowhawks.com).

Hawick Rugby Football Club (club founded 1873)

Mansfield Park, Hawick TD9 8AL (Tel: 01450-370687 or 374216; Fax 01450-373619;
Emails: enquiries@hawickrfc.co.uk/
ellistrin@compuserve.com;
Web: www.hawickrfc.co.uk).

Heriots FP RFC (club founded 1890)

52 Netherbank, Edinburgh EH16 6YR
(Tel: 0131-552 5925; Fax: 0131-551 4519;
Email: Douglas–bruce@talk21.com;
Web: www.george-heriots.com).

Kirkcaldy RFC (club founded 1873)

The Pavillion, Beveridge Park, Balwearie Road, Kirkcaldy KY2 5LZ (Tel: 01592-263470;
Web: www.kirkcaldyrfc.co.uk/intro/intro.htm).

Melrose RFC (club founded 1877)

The Greenyards, Melrose TD6 9SA
(Tel: 01896-822993;
Email: mrfc@melrose.bordernet.co.uk;
Web: www.melroserugby.bordernet.co.uk).

Stirling County (club founded 1904)

Bridgehaugh Park, Causewayhead Road, Stirling FK9 5AP (Tel: 01786-478866;
Fax: 01786-447767;
Web: www.stirlingcountyrfc.co.uk).

SHINTY

The Gaelic name for shinty, *camanachd*, identifies the sport as possibly the oldest organised team game in western Europe. Many of the ancient Irish heroes were said to have played shinty. Cu Chulainn, the hero of the Ulster cycle of tales, is said to have attended an ancient training school for young heroes, where *camanachd* was part of the curriculum. In 563 Columba left Ireland for Scotland because of a quarrel that had supposedly broken out during a game of *camanachd*, so tradition says the game was brought to Scotland in that year, if not before. Its roots were shared with Irish hurling until the mid 14th century.

The first written records mentioning shinty date from the 14th and 15th centuries. A 15th-century memorial stone on the island of Iona depicts not only the owner's broadsword beneath his name in the old Lombard script, but also a caman (stick) with a ball beside it. The following description of the game is from Jamieson's *Dictionary of the Scottish Language* (1821): "A game in which bats, somewhat resembling a golf-club, are used. At every fair or meeting of the country people, there were contests at racing, wrestling, putting the stone, etc., and on holidays all the males of the district, young and old, met to play at football, but oftener at shinty. Shinty is a game played with sticks, crooked at the end, and balls of wood".

Shinty has remained popular in the Highlands, although Lowland law against it and the enforced observation of the Sabbath in many places affected the game, as it was customarily played on Sundays. The custom of playing on Sundays eventually faded away, but the game survived Culloden, the Highland Clearances, and later waves of migration out of the Highlands, and is still played according to virtually the same rules as it was centuries ago.

By the mid 19th century the popularity of the game had declined until it was played only in the glens of Lochaber, Strathglass and Badenoch. Captain Chisholm of Glassburn published a code of rules for the Strathglass Club in 1880 and in February 1887 Strathglass (led by Chisholm) played against Glen-Urquhart in a 15-a-side game at Inverness. Strathglass won the game, but the following year they were defeated. Following the loss, Chisholm revised the rules he had published earlier.

Celtic Club rules drawn up in Glasgow were played in the south of the country. The lack of set rules prompted a meeting of representatives from all the leading clubs on 10 October 1893 at Kingussie, which led to the formation of the Camanachd Association. This became the governing body of the game and drew up rules to control play and competitions which are still followed today.

The Challenge Trophy was set up in 1895 and Kingussie defeated Glasgow Cowal 2-0 at Inverness in 1896 in the first final. The trophy has been contested annually, except during the two world wars. Shinty's premier competition is now known as the Glenmorangie Camanachd Cup and is played each year at one of five regular venues – An Aird, Fort William; Bught Park, Inverness; Mossfield Park, Oban; The Dell, Kingussie; and a venue in Glasgow. The cup final attracts shinty's biggest crowd of the season, usually 3000 to 5000, and is normally played on the first Saturday in June. The biggest crowd ever to watch a shinty match is believed to have been at Murrayfield in Edinburgh, now home of Scotland's rugby team. The occasion was the 1948 Edinburgh Highland Games. The teams were Newtonmore and Ballachulish and instead of a trophy the prize for this game were sets of pots and pans! The Sutherland Cup began in 1918 to provide a competition for junior clubs.

THE MODERN GAME

Shinty is played by teams of 12, each player armed with a curved stick known as a *caman*. The caman used to be made from a piece of ash or hickory cut from a tree with a natural bend in it; modern shinty sticks are manufactured using strips of wood glued together or from fibre-glass and aluminium. The ball is more or less the same size as a tennis ball, but the interior is made of cork and woollen fabric and the ball is covered in leather. The game is similar to hockey but there are significant differences. In shinty, the feet can be used to stop the ball and the ball may be carried on the caman, which can be swung above shoulder level.

There are currently 38 shinty clubs in Scotland competing in leagues and a variety of cup competitions, often dominated by Speyside rivals Kingussie and Newtonmore. Although, in the past it was usual in the Highlands to hold the principal games at New Year (1 January) or Old New Year (12 or 13 January), shinty is nowadays played virtually all year round. In the old contests, there was no limit to the numbers taking part. Players arrived and departed at will, and often play continued from the morning until darkness fell. New Year matches are still held in Skye, Lewis, Fort William and Inverness.

There are no international matches apart from play against Irish hurling teams, which has happened sporadically since 1897. The first of these meetings took place in Glasgow, where

Scotland won 11–2, and was followed by a return match in Dublin, also won by Scotland 2–0. Subsequent matches were played in the 1920s and 1932. The series resumed in the 1970s, when the Irish had the better of the exchanges, and again in the late 1980s. The challenges have been held annually since 1993 and are played alternately in Scotland and Ireland, usually in October.

On 3 October 1993, the Camanachd Association began a year-long series of special events marking its centenary as shinty's ruling body. In a reconstruction of the 1893 match between Kingussie and Cowal at The Dell, the players and spectators were led to the field in procession, with pipers at the head.

The Camanachd Association,

Algarve, Badabrie, Banavie, Fort William, Invernesshire, PH33 7LX (Tel: 01397-772772).

SKIING

Compared with other sports, skiing in Scotland is a relatively recent introduction. It dates back to 1890, when W. W. Naismith, founder of the Scottish Mountaineering Club, ventured into the hills on wooden Nordic-style skis to test the efficacy of skis as a form of cross-country transport. However, Nordic skiing did not catch on in Scotland because snow conditions were — as they remain — too unpredictable, there were few dependable routes, and the equipment was heavy and cumbersome.

Scotland offered more potential for the development of Alpine, or downhill, skiing, and the Scottish Ski Club was founded in 1907, shortly after the Ski Club of Great Britain (founded 1903). The founder members of the Club were all mountaineers and included Naismith.

Alpine skiing was just becoming popular in Scotland when World War I broke out. The Scottish Ski Club did not reconvene until 1929. By that time equipment had improved, and this, plus easier access to the hills and a string of cold, snowy winters, all generated a surge in popularity of skiing in the 1930s and 1940s. Powered ski-tows were introduced on Ben Lawers, Glen Clunie and Glenshee in the late 1940s, and the first permanent ski-lift in Scotland was installed at Glencoe in 1956. The development of Aviemore as Scotland's first snow sports centre began in the early 1960s and it is still Scotland's principal centre for snow sports.

Skiing and snowboarding now take place at five major resorts: Glenshee, The Lecht and Cairngorm (near Aviemore) and Glencoe and Aonach Mor in the Nevis range. National and international events are staged, weather permitting. The uncertainty of weather conditions is the greatest obstacle faced by snow sports and the resort facilities that depend on them. A succession of mild winters in the 1990s, for instance, has seriously threatened the viability of the companies who run the resorts.

However, there are artificial slopes at some of the major resorts and elsewhere in Scotland. The biggest dry ski slope in Europe is at Edinburgh's Hillend Park.

The Scottish National Ski Council (SNSC) was formed in 1963. It was renamed Snowsport Scotland in 1998 and is the national governing body for all sports that take place on snow and artificial slopes in Scotland. In January 2000 33 clubs were affiliated to Snowsport Scotland; many of them were involved in setting up the SNSC in 1963 and are still actively involved in running its successor.

Snowsport Scotland

Caledonia House, South Gyle, Edinburgh EH12 9DQ (Tel 0131-317-7280; Web: www.snsc.demon.co.uk).

Cairngorm Ski Area

Cairngorm, Aviemore PH22 1RR (Tel: 01479-861261; Fax: 01479-861207; Ski report Tel: 01479-861261; Email: cairngorm@sol.co.uk; Web: www.aviemore.co.uk/ www.ski.scotland.net).

Glencoe Ski Centre

Kingshouse, Glencoe, Argyll PA39 4HZ (Tel: 01855-851226; Fax: 01855-851233; Ski report: 01855-851232; Email: glencoe @sol.co.uk; Web: www.ski.scotland.net).

Glenshee Ski Centre

Cairnwell, Braemar, Aberdeenshire AB35 5XU (Tel: 01339-741320; Fax: 01339-741665; Ski report: 01339-741628. Email: glenshee @sol.co.uk; Web: www.ski.scotland.net).

Lecht Ski Centre

Strathdon, Aberdeenshire AB3 8YB (Tel: 01975-651440; Fax: 01975-651426; Ski Report: 01975-651440; Email: thelecht@sol.co.uk Web-site: www.ski.scotland.net).

Nevis Range

Torlundy, Fort William PH33 6SW (Tel: 01397-705825: Fax no: 01397 705854; Ski Report: 01397 705825; Email: nevisrange@sol.co.uk Web: www.ski.scotland.net).

WALKING AND MOUNTAINEERING

Scotland is a walker's paradise. It has thousands of walks and climbs on coastal footpaths, nature trails, woodland trails, long-distance footpaths and hundreds of mountain peaks. It is known worldwide for its rock climbs.

The earliest recorded rock climb in the UK took place in 1698, on Stac na Biorrach, St Kilda, by Sir Robert Murray. The first recorded ascent of Ben Nevis was that of James Robertson in 1771; Ben MacDui and Braeriach were both climbed in 1810 by the Revd George Keith .

Scotland has 284 mountains over 3,000 feet (914 metres) high, and these have become known as Munros, after Sir Hugh Munro, who first listed them in 1891. Sir Hugh's list has undergone several revisions over the years, most recently in 1998, when the number of peaks increased from 277 to 284. Munro himself died in 1909 just before climbing the last of the 238 summits he had identified; however, they had already been conquered by the Reverend A. E. Robertson in 1901, who achieved the feat over a period of 10 years. In 1974, Hamish Brown completed the challenge of 277 Munros, covering 1639 miles and 449,000 feet (136,855 metres) of ascent in just 112 days. Kathy Murgatroyd repeated this feat for the women in 1982. George Keeping was the first to complete the entire round on foot in 1984. Hugh Symonds climbed all the Munros in 66 days and 22 hours in 1990. Munro-bagging, as it has become known, is a popular pastime, especially since most of the Munros are reasonably accessible and within easy reach of public roads.

Peaks between 2,500 and 3,000 feet (762–914 metres) in height, with a drop of at least 500 feet (152.4 metres) between each listed hill and any adjacent higher one, are called Corbetts. They are named after J. Rooke Corbett, who listed them in 1930. Currently 222 mountains are classed as Corbetts. The current record for completing all the Munros and Corbetts was set by Craig Caldwell in 1985–86 when he achieved the feat in 377 days. A further list of hills in the Lowlands of 2,000–2,500 feet (609-762 metres) was produced by Percy Donald, giving these hills the nickname of Donalds. In 1992, the popular walking magazine *The Great Outdoors* published a list of 244 hills compiled by Fiona Graham. The list included every hill between 2,000 feet and 2,500 feet in the Highlands. A Graham must have a descent all round of 150 metres, or be the highest point for two miles all round.

The principal hill-walking and climbing areas are in the Highlands, include Glencoe, Lochaber, the Cairngorms, the Monadhliath, Kintail, Wester Ross, Torridon, and Skye. The accepted freedom to roam allows extensive walking and climbing, although access may be restricted during the lambing season (April and May) and the deerstalking season (mid-August to around 20 October).

Scotland has several long-distance footpaths (LDFs). By far the longest is the Southern Upland Way, which crosses the country from coast to coast, is 212 miles. The best known is the West Highland Way, which runs for 95 miles from Milngavie on the outskirts of Glasgow to Fort William at the southern end of the Great Glen. This is eventually expected to link up with the Great Glen Way which, when completed, will run from Fort William to Inverness. The final section of the Speyside Way, Ballindalloch to Aviemore, was officially opened on 8 April 2000. The route now stretches for some 65 to 80 miles, including all the spurs, from Buckie on the Moray coast to Aviemore. St Cuthbert's Way spans the border, stretching 60 miles from Melrose to Lindisfarne in Northumberland. Many other cross-country routes include drove roads, the long-established paths through the hills along which clansmen once led their cattle to or from markets held in the larger settlements.

Scottish Rights of Way Society

John Cotton Business Centre, 10-12 Sunnyside, Edinburgh EH7 5RA (Tel: 0131-652-2937).

The hillphones service has been organised by the Mountaineering Council of Scotland and Scottish Natural Heritage with aims of improving communications between deerstalking and hillwalking. Weather information for walkers and climbers is provided by the Met. Office.

Hillphones: Grey Corries and Mamore

including Sgurr Eilde Mor and Stob Coire Easain (Tel: 01855-831511).

Glen Dochart and Glen Lochay

including Meall Glas and Sgiath Chuil (Tel: 01567-820886).

North Arran Hills

covering the northern half of the island (Tel: 01770-302363).

South Glen Shiel

including The Saddle and the South Cluanie Ridge (Tel: 01599-511425).

Drumochter

including Geal Charn and A'Bhuidheanach Bheag (Tel: 01528-522200).

Glenshee
including Carn a'Gheoidh and Creag, Leacach (Tel: 01250-885288).

Callater and Clunie
including Carn an t-Sagairt Mor and Carn an Tuirc (Tel: 01339-741997).

Invercauld
including Ben Avon and Beinn a'Bhuird (Tel: 01339-741911).

Balmoral and Lochnagar
including White Mounth (Tel: 01339-755532).

Glen Clova
including Driesh and Tom Buidhe (Tel: 01575-550335).

WRESTLING

Scottish wrestling is known as 'backhold' and has a style and rules which are different from those of standard wrestling. The Scottish Amateur Wrestling Association organises and registers wrestlers. The sport is still quite widespread in Scotland, and is most commonly practised at Highland Games. In backhold, the wrestlers take hold of each other's waist with the right hand under the left arm. Both men then close their hands and when the referee shouts 'Hold', the bout commences. If any part of a wrestler's body, except the soles of his feet, touches the ground, he loses the bout. The wrestlers are not permitted to break their grip until the opponent is on the ground. Bouts are normally the best of three or five.

The earliest depiction of wrestling in Scotland is to be found on two carved Pictish stones dating from the 6th and 7th centuries, which are housed in the National Museum of Antiquities in Edinburgh.

In the Western Isles, wrestling was made popular by the men of a Highland regiment known as the Lovat Scouts, formed in 1900. The Highlanders practised two forms of wrestling, one using the same rules as the rest of Scotland and an alternative form which did not allow tripping of opponents, which developed in Europe into the 'classical' style of wrestling. An ancient Norse style of wrestling known as *Hryggspenna* is still practised in the Hebrides.

Scottish Amateur Wrestling Association
Kelvin Hall, Argyll Street, Glasgow G3 8AW (Tel: 0141-334 3843).

YACHTING

Pioneered in the Netherlands during the 17th century, boats offered practical ways and means of travelling along the waterways throughout the country. Modern yachting was introduced to Britain by Charles II, who was given a Dutch pleasure boat named *Mary* shortly after his return from exile in the Low Countries in 1660 and went on to build a fleet of pleasure craft. The word 'yacht' comes from the Dutch word *jaght*, which means a small cargo or passenger carrier. In the early 18th century yachting was considered a rather eccentric occupation because of the discomforts associated with it.

However, sailing off the west coast of Scotland and among the western and northern islands is now a very popular pastime and sport, although the weather and currents can be tricky. Several yachting events take place each year, generally during the summer. Yacht races of the famous Scottish Series off the west coast and the Round Mull Three-Day Yacht Race, held in June, are the largest events. During May there is also an annual race between Bergen in Norway and Shetland. The Scottish Hebridean Islands Peak Race is the biggest combined sailing and fell-running competition in the world.

Royal Yachting Association (Scotland)
Caledonia House, South Gyle, Edinburgh EH12 9DQ (Tel: 0131-317-7388; Web: www.rya.org.uk).

North of Scotland Yachting Association, 18 Crown Avenue, Inverness IV2 3NF.

OTHER SPORTS IN BRIEF

- The first **skating** club in Britain was the Edinburgh Ice Skating Society, formed in 1778.
- The first **lacrosse** club in Britain was the Glasgow Lacrosse Club founded in 1867.
- **Orienteering** in the UK was inaugurated by the Scottish Council of Physical Recreation at the 1962 Championships held at Dunkeld in Perthshire.
- The oldest **rowing** club in Scotland is the St Andrews Boat Club, Edinburgh, formed in 1850.
- The oldest **archery** club is the Society of Kilwinning Archers. They have contested the Papingo Shoot since 1488.
- The oldest surviving **Royal (Real) tennis** court in Britain and still in use is at Falkland Palace, built for James V in 1539.

SCOTLAND'S OLYMPIC MEDALLISTS, SYDNEY 2000

In the Olympic games held in Sydney in September 2000, Scotland's athletes won a total of nine medals (three gold and six silver), a number not equalled since the 1912 Stockholm Games, when Scottish athletes carried off seven gold, one silver and one bronze medals. The 2000 games also gave Scotland's participants their first gold medals since the 1988 Seoul games, and represented a huge improvement on the 1996 Atlanta Games, where Scottish competitors, participating as always as part of the UK team, won a solitary bronze medal.

Stephanie Cook OBE (1972–). Athlete, born Irvine. Gold, women's modern pentathlon. This was the first time the event had been included in the Olympics. She received an OBE in 2001.

Mark Covell (1967–). Yachtsman, born Glasgow. Covell was the crewman and Ian Walker at the helm when they won silver in the two-man star yachting event. They teamed up in 1999 after two tragedies: Walker had lost his partner in a car crash in 1997 and Covell's helm Glynn Charles perished in the storm-ravaged 1999 Sydney–Hobart race. Covell also won gold at the 1997 and 1998 world championships, in the 5.5 metre class.

Katherine Grainger (1975–). Rower, born Glasgow. Silver, quadruple sculls, with fellow Scot Gillian Lindsay and Guin and Miriam Batten; they were the first British women ever to win an Olympic medal for rowing. Grainger also won gold at the 1996 Henley Regatta coxless pairs, the 1997 world junior championships coxless pairs, and the 1998 British championships single sculls.

Chris Hoy (1976–). Cyclist, born Edinburgh. Silver, as member of Olympic sprint cycle team. Also won gold at 1998 British championships Olympic sprint and 1999 European championships Olympic sprint, and silver at 1999 and 2000 world championships Olympic sprint. Represented Scotland at the 1987 BMX world championships.

Andrew Lindsay (1977–). Rower, born in Portree, Skye. Gold, men's eight. Lindsay rowed in the key position of bow to help Great Britain win in this blue riband event – the first time Britain had won the men's eight since the 1912

Olympics in Stockholm, which had also included two Scots, Philip Fleming and Angus Gillan. Lindsay also won gold at the 2000 World Cup overall eights and bronze at the 1994 World Junior Championship eights.

Gillian Lindsay (1973–). Rower, born Paisley. Silver, quadruple sculls, with Katherine Grainger, Guin and Miriam Batten. Together with Miriam Batten, she won the scull pairs at the World Championships in 1998, the pair becoming the first British women to win a World Rowing Championship gold.

Craig MacLean (1971–). Cyclist, born Grantown-on-Spey. Silver, as member of Olympic sprint cycle team. Also won gold at 1998 British championships (1 km and sprint) and 1999 European Championships (Olympic sprint), and silver at 1999 and 2000 world championships (Olympic sprint). Represented Scotland at 1986 BMX world championships.

Shirley Robertson OBE (1968–). Sailor, born Dundee. Gold, Europe class dinghy sailing; this made her the first Scottish woman to win an Olympic gold medal since 1912 and also Britain's first female Olympic sailing medallist. Won 4th place in 1996 Atlanta Olympics in this class. Awarded OBE in 2001.

Ian Stark (1954–). Badminton; born Galashiels. Became Scotland's most prolific Olympian by winning his fourth silver medal in the three-day team event at the Sydney 2000 Olympics. He also won silver medals for the same discipline in 1984 and 1988 Olympics, and silver for the three-day individual event in 1988. Also won gold medals at the 1991 European championships (team and individual events), the 1997 European championships (team), and the 1999 Badminton International three-day event.

SCOTLAND'S PARALYMPIC MEDALLISTS, SYDNEY 2000

Great Britain finished second in the medal table with 41 gold, 43 silver and 47 bronze medals. The Scots in the British team won 8 gold, 14 silver and 10 bronze medals. At the 1996 Paralympic games in Atlanta, Scots won 9 gold, 11 silver and 7 bronze medals. The success of British athletes at the Sydney Paralympics was recognised with MBEs for Caroline Innes, who won two gold medals in the 200 and 400m, Kenny Cairns, who won silver in the 200m freestyle swimming, and Isabel Newstead, who won gold in the 10m air pistol and has amassed 14 medals in competition since the 1980 games, in a variety of disciplines including swimming, discus, shot, javelin and air pistol.

James Anderson (1963–) Swimming. 50m freestyle silver; 100m freestyle silver; 200m freestyle silver. Broke world records in all four of his events at the 1999 European championships. Won two gold medals at 1996 Paralympics and three silvers in 1992 Paralympics.

Kenneth Cairns MBE (1957–) Swimming. 100m freestyle gold; 50m freestyle silver; 200 metre freestyle silver (Paralympic Games record); 4 x 50m freestyle relay bronze. Gold winner European championships 1997, 1999), world championship 1998, Nordic Open 2000. Awarded MBE 2000.

Lara Ferguson (1980–) Swimming. 4 x 100m medley relay silver; 100m breaststroke bronze. Two golds in 1997 European championships.

Kay Gebbie (1955–) Equestrianism. Freestyle gold; Team gold; set test bronze. Won gold medals at British championships 2000 and 1998.

Caroline Innes MBE (1974–) Athletics. 400m gold; 200m gold; 100m silver. Also won gold for 100m in 1996 Paralympics, and six gold medals in British and World championships 1996–99. Awarded MBE 2000.

Paul Johnston (1974–) Swimming. 4 x 50m freestyle relay bronze. Won five golds in 1997 world championships.

Pauline Latto (1975–) Athletics. Javelin silver. At 1998 British championships, won four golds and was British record-holder in her class in 100m, 200m, 400m and javelin.

Janice Lawton (1948–) Athletics. Discus silver. Won gold at 1994 world championships in javelin, and has garnered many silvers in javelin, discus and shot in various paralympic championships since 1994.

Andrew Lindsay (1979–) Swimming. 100m backstroke gold. Has also won gold in European championships 1995, 1997, 1998, 1999 and 2000, and silver in 1996 Paralympics and 1997 European championships.

Margaret McEleny MBE (1965–) Swimming. 50m breaststroke gold; 150m individual medley bronze; 4 x 50m medley bronze. Also won two gold medals at European championships 1999, two at world championships 1998, and one at 1996 Paralympics. Awarded MBE 2000.

Isabel Newstead MBE (1955–) Air pistol. 10m gold. Since 1988 has won paralympic gold medals in three sports – swimming (1980, 1984), shooting (2000), and discus (1988) – and many bronze and silver medals in other paralympic championships. Finished 6th overall in 1996 Paralympics. Awarded MBE 2000.

Paul Noble (1965–) Swimming. 4 x 100m medley relay silver. Golds at 1997 European championships, 1992 and 1988 Paralympic Games.

Stephen Payton (1977–) Athletics. 400m silver; 4 x 100m relay silver; 100m bronze; 200m bronze. Has many golds to his credit: 2000 Australian Open, 2000 French Indoor Open, 1999 European championships, 1998 world championships (4), 1996 and 1994 Paralympic Games (3 each).

Allan Stuart (1981–) Athletics. 400m silver. Won gold at 2000 Cyprus Junior International, 2000 West of Scotland championship – both able-bodied competitions. First athlete with a disability to represent a Scotland able-bodied team.

Tracy Wiscombe (1979–) Swimming. 200m freestyle silver; 50m freestyle bronze; 100m freestyle bronze. Won six golds in European championships 1999, two in 1998 world championship, and two at 1996 Paralympic Games.

SCOTTISH SPORTING
PERSONALITIES

ALL-ROUNDERS

Sir Thomas Lipton (1850–1931). Grocer and entrepreneur, born in Glasgow, who became a millionaire through his tea plantations in Sri Lanka. Started the World Cup in football in 1910. He also unsuccessfully challenged for the Americas Cup in yachting several times.

Leslie Balfour Melville (1854–1937). Possibly Scotland's greatest ever sportsman. His sports included golf, cricket, rugby union and tennis. He won the Scottish Lawn Tennis Championships in 1879 and the British Amateur Golf Championship in 1895. At one time he was captain of the Royal and Ancient Golf Club. He represented his country in rugby union against England in 1872. He is best remembered as a cricketer representing Scotland 1876–1910; in 1882, as captain, opening batsman and wicket-keeper, he led Scotland to victory over Australia.

ATHLETICS

Walter Menzies Campbell CBE (1941–). Now a Liberal Democrat politician, and MP for North East Fife since 1987, he was formerly a successful athlete and competed in the 1964 Olympic games in Tokyo and the 1966 Commonwealth Games in Jamaica. He held the British 100m record 1967–1974. He was awarded the CBE in 1987.

Eric Henry Liddell (1902-45). Born in Tientsin, China. At the 1924 Paris Olympics, owing to his religious principles, he refused to run in the 100-metre heats because they were held on a Sunday. However, he went on to win two medals at the Games, a bronze in the 200m and a gold in the 400m. His achievements are remembered in the 1981 film *Chariots of Fire*.

Liz McColgan (1964–). Long-distance runner, born in Dundee. She won the gold medal for the 10,000m at the 1986 and 1990 Commonwealth Games, silver for the same distance at the 1988 Olympic Games (Seoul) and bronze for the 3,000m in the 1990 Commonwealth Games. She was the 1990 world 10,000 metre champion and gained the UK women's record for the 10,000m in 1991. She had the fastest marathon debut, 2 hours 27.32 minutes, in the New York marathon and also won the London Marathon in 1996.

Tom McKean (1963–). Born in Bellshill. In his specialist distance, 800m, he won the European Cup in 1985, 1987 and 1989, the World Cup in 1989, and the European championships in 1990. He also won silver medals in the 1986 Commonwealth Games (Edinburgh) for the 800m and the 4 x 100 metre relay.

Duncan McLean (1884–1980). Had the longest career in the world in athletics. Having broken the record for the 100 yards sprint in 9.9 seconds in 1904, he set another world record for men of his age group, of 21.7 seconds for the same event 73 years later, in 1977, at the age of 92.

Yvonne Murray MBE (1964–). Born in Edinburgh. Her specialist distance was 3,000m, in which she won bronze medals at the 1986 Commonwealth Games and the 1988 Olympics and silver at the 1986 European Championship and the 1990 Commonwealth Games. Gold medals, 3,000m, European Championships, 1990; 10,000m, Commonwealth Games, 1994. At various times during her career she held the Scottish women's record for 1,500m, 1 mile, 2,000m, 3,000m and 5,000m. Awarded the MBE in 1990.

Cameron Sharp (1960–). Gold medal, 4 x 100m relay, Commonwealth Games, Edmonton, 1978. Silver medal, 200m, European Championship, 1982. Bronze medals, 100m, 200m, and 4 x 100m relay, Commonwealth Games, Brisbane, 1982; 4 x 100m relay, Commonwealth Games, Edinburgh, 1986. He was involved in a serious car accident in 1991 which left him physically and mentally disabled.

Dougie Walker (1973–). Born in Inverness. Represented Scotland in the 1994 Commonwealth Games. Became the Commonwealth and European 300m record holder and won gold medals for the 200m and 4 x 100m relay in the 1998 European Championships.

Alan Wells (1952–). Born in Edinburgh. He won a gold medal in the 100m and a silver medal at the 200m at the 1978 Commonwealth Games. At the 1980 Olympics he won gold for the 100m and silver for the 200m, becoming the oldest-ever winner in the history of the Olympic 100m. He also won gold medals for the 100m and 200m at the 1982 Commonwealth Games in Brisbane.

BOXING

Ken Buchanan (1945–). Born in Edinburgh. Probably Scotland's greatest ever boxer. Became world lightweight champion in 1970 and successfully defended the title before being beaten in 1972. In 1970 a New York journalists' poll declared him the best in the world, relegating Muhammad Ali to third place. He won back the European lightweight championship in 1972.

Sir John Sholto Douglas (1844–1900). Succeeded to the Queensberry title in 1858, becoming the 8th Marquis of Queensberry and Viscount Drumlanrig. Best known for devising the *Queensberry Rules* for boxing in 1867, and for his instrumental part in the trial and imprisonment of the playwright Oscar Wilde.

Benny Lynch (1913–1946). Born in Glasgow. As the first world flyweight champion, he also became the first Scot to hold a world boxing title, capturing both the world title in 1935, defending it successfully for three years, and then winning the American title in 1937. Also won the British and European flyweight titles. However, he died in poverty aged only 33.

Walter McGowan (1942–). Born in Burnbank, near Hamilton. He won the world flyweight championship in 1966, but lost that title in 1968, after fighting at bantamweight.

Jackie Paterson (1920–1966). Born in Springside, Ayrshire. Came to prominence by winning the world flyweight championship at Hampden in 1943. However, it was a title he was unable to defend, owing to the war and ill health, and he lost the title in 1948.

Alex 'Bud' Watson (1914–). Born in Leith. Has held the most titles in a boxing career, 10 in all, including the Scottish heavyweight title in 1938, and 1942–43, the lightweight championship 1937–39, 1943–45 and 1947, and the ABA (Amateur Boxing Association) light-heavyweight title in 1945 and 1947.

Jim Watt MBE (1948–). Born in Glasgow. Became a professional boxer in 1968. British lightweight champion on two occasions; European lightweight champion 1977–79; world lightweight champion 1979–81, successfully defending his title on four occasions. Awarded the MBE in 1980.

CLIMBING & MOUNTAINEERING

James Robertson. Appointed by the Commissioners of the Forfeited Estates to carry out a botanical and mineralogical survey of the Highlands in the years after the 1745 rebellion, he made the first recorded ascents of several mountains over 3,000 feet, including Ben Hope, Ben Wyvis and Ben Kilbreck in 1767 and Ben Nevis in 1771.

Alexander Nicolson (1827–1893), born Huabost, Skye. Scotland's first mountaineer in the modern sense. At different times in his life a journalist, academic and sheriff-substitute, in 1865 he began exploring the Cuillin peaks, then still largely unknown to mountaineers. His four ascents of Sgurr nan Gillean are commemorated in the naming of a steep cleft leading to the summit as Nicolson's Chimney. He also made the first recorded ascents of Sgurr Alasdair (named after him, in the Gaelic form of his name) and Sgurr Dubh.

W. W. Naismith. A pioneer of Scottish mountaineering and a founder of the Scottish Mountaineering Club, 1889. Accomplished first recorded ascent of Crowberry Ridge in 1895/6 and a solo ascent of the Eiger in the 1880s. Also made first recorded use of skis in Scotland, 1890. In 1892 he developed a formula for estimating route times in the Scottish Highlands.

Dougal Haston (1940–1977). Born in Currie. Among other achievements, he was a member of the British team which conquered the south face of Annapurna in 1970, and later (1975) took part in the first ascent of the south-west face Mount Everest and the first ascent of Mt McKinley in Alaska. He was also the first British mountaineer to climb the north face of the Eiger. Died in an avalanche in the Alps.

Hamish Brown MBE (1934–). Born in Colombo. Has climbed and travelled widely in Scotland, the Alps, the Himalayas, the Andes, and the Atlas Mountains in Morocco, and has published over 20 books specialising in mountaineering and travel subjects. Completed all the Munros in a single 112-day trip (involving 449,000 feet of ascent), and has also trekked the Atlas Mountains from end to end. Awarded the MBE in 2000.

Tom Patey (1934–1970). Rock-climber. Achieved unprecedented output of new rock- and ice-climbing routes in the 1950s and 1960s, among them winter routes on Lochnagar and Creag Meagaidh and a number of summer routes in the Northern Highlands. Together with Hamish MacInnes and Graeme Nicol, made first winter ascent of Zero Gully on Ben Nevis. In February 1965 he participated in the first winter traverse of the Cuillin Ridge by two ropes. Died in a fall from the Maiden seastack.

Hamish McInnes OBE (1930–) Mountaineer and innovator in climbing and mountain rescue equipment. Has climbed Everest, many Alpine peaks, and the peak of Roraima in Brazil. Leader of Glencoe Mountain Rescue team and an international authority on mountain rescue. In 1957 he participated, with Tom Patey and Graeme Nicol, in the first winter ascent of Zero Gully on Ben Nevis. His designs for winter climbing tools culminated in the development, in 1970, together with Yvon Chouinard, of a curved ice axe pick which enabled standards in ice climbing to rise rapidly.

David Cuthbertson. A key member of a group of Scottish climbers who have pushed standards of rock and ice climbing forward from the late 1970s. He made new routes of extreme technical difficulty on outcrops and mountains in various Scottish locations, including the north peak of the Cobbler, in 1979 (with R. Kerr), Sron na Ciche in Skye (with Gary Latter), and Dumbarton Rock.

CRICKET

Mike Denness (1940–). Born in Bellshill, Lanarkshire. Scorer of 25,886 first-class runs between 1959 and 1980. Represented Scotland before captaining England 1973–1975. He was also a successful captain of Kent and Essex CCCs.

Gavin Hamilton (1974–). Born in Broxburn. An all-rounder who has represented both Scotland and England at international level. Since 1994 he has played his county cricket for Yorkshire. In the 1999 World Cup, playing for Scotland, he scored two fifties against strong opposition. Selected to tour South Africa with the England team in 1999–2000.

Brian Hardie (1950–). Born in Stenhousemuir. An all-rounder who has represented Scotland as well as Essex, for whom he won four championship medals in a 17-year career in English county cricket.

Douglas Jardine (1900–1958). Born in Bombay, of Scottish parents. He followed his father into the Oxford University team and made his debut with Surrey in 1923, becoming became captain of Surrey in 1932 and, shortly after, of England. A controversial figure, he is mostly remembered as the captain of England in the 'bodyline' series of 1932–33 against Australia, where he directed his bowlers to aim short-pitched deliveries at the batsmen, a tactic used successfully against Don Bradman. Jardine left cricket after 1934.

Richard Nairn (Nyren) (c1734-1797). A Jacobite who settled in Hampshire after the 1745 Rising. He introduced certain laws to the game of cricket, including the use of the middle stump.

CYCLING

Robert Millar. The only Scot to have won a stage in the Tour de France, capturing the 'King of the Mountains' stage in 1984 and finishing overall fourth in the tournament.

Graeme Obree (1965–). The most influential figure in bicycle dynamics for most of the 1990s. Developed the 'Superman' position in cycling, which has since been banned. Pursuit Olympic champion 1992. Won the 4000m individual pursuit world title 1993–96. Also in 1993, he won the 1-hour cycling record with a distance of 51.6km, on a bicycle costing just £100 and incorporating a part from a washing-machine.

DARTS

Jocky Wilson (1951–). Born in Kirkcaldy. Scotland's most successful darts player. While unemployed he won the Butlin's Grand Masters competition in 1979. By 1980 he had become one of the world's top eight darts players. In 1982 he won the Embassy World Professional Championship trophy, the first Scot to gain the title. He became World Champion again in 1989.

FOOTBALL

Jim Baxter (1939–2001). Born in Hill o' Beath. Known as 'Slim Jim', he played for Raith Rovers before moving to Rangers. A midfielder, he scored 24 goals in 254 games for Rangers between 1960 and 1970. He was a member of the 1961 Rangers team which was the first Scottish side to reach the final of a European tournament. He won three championships, 1960–61, 1962–63 and 1963–64, as well as three Scottish Cups, 1963, 1964 and 1965, and 34 full international caps for Scotland.

Billy Bremner (1942–1997). Born in Glasgow, spent most of his playing career at Leeds United, where he was possibly the most revered of all Leeds United players, as a half-back, 1959–76. He won 54 full international caps for Scotland, and captained the national team at the 1974 World Cup Finals.

Sir Matt Busby CBE (1909–1994). Son of a Scottish miner. Played half-back with Manchester City and Liverpool before World War II. Won only one full cap for Scotland but captained his country in several wartime internationals. Manchester United manager 1945–69 and briefly 1970–71. Rebuilt the team to win the FA Cup in 1963, the League Championship in 1965 and 1967, and the European Cup 1967. He was knighted after this last triumph, and was elected a vice-president of the Football League in 1982.

Kenny Dalglish MBE (1951–). Born in Glasgow, he played for Celtic 1968–77 before signing for Liverpool. Became player-manager of Liverpool in 1985 and managed Blackburn Rovers 1991–95, before returning briefly to Celtic. Won a total of 102 full international caps for Scotland, which remains a record for any player, scoring 30 international goals. Awarded an MBE in 1985.

Tommy Docherty (1928–). One of the most controversial characters in football. Won 25 caps for Scotland. Began his playing career for Celtic, before making 324 appearances for Preston North End. He also played for Arsenal and Chelsea and has managed a host of clubs in England, Scotland and Australia, including Queens Park Rangers. Under his guidance Scotland qualified for the 1974 World Cup Finals.

Sir Alex Ferguson CBE (1941–). Began playing career in 1957 for Stranraer. Went on to play for Queens Park, St Johnstone, Dunfermline, Rangers, Falkirk and finally Ayr United in 1973. His career as manager began at East Stirling in 1974, followed by St Mirren. He became the most successful manager for Aberdeen, 1978–86, where he won three league titles, four Scottish Cups and the European Cup Winners Cup. Briefly took over as manager of the Scottish national team in 1986 following the death of Jock Stein. Since November 1986 he has been at Manchester United, which has become the top English team under his guidance. Awarded CBE in 1995, knighted 1999.

Archie Gemmill (1947–). Born in Paisley and began playing career for St Mirren. He went on to play for a number of English clubs, including Preston North End, Derby County and Nottingham Forest. Capped by Scotland 43 times, scoring eight goals, which included the most memorable goal scored in the World Cup Finals of 1978, when Scotland beat Holland.

Denis Law (1940–). Born in Aberdeen but spent more than half of his playing career at Man United, 1962–73. Also played for Huddersfield, Man City and Turin. Played inside forward, winning 55 full international caps for Scotland.

Jim Leighton (1958–). The most-capped Scottish goalkeeper, with 91 appearances for Scotland. Played in four World Cups. Apart from a few seasons in the 1990s with Hibernian, much of his career has been with Aberdeen, where he has made over 900 appearances since 1978.

Ally McCoist (1962–). Born in Glasgow. Played for St Johnstone and Sunderland before joining Rangers in 1983. In 15 years he scored more than 300 goals in over 500 appearances in all competitions, and he remains the top scorer in Rangers' history. Won 59 full international caps for Scotland. In 1998 he left Rangers for Kilmarnock. He is better known nowadays for his appearances on television.

Jimmy McCrory. One of the greatest Celtic players. During his career with Celtic 1922–38 he scored 550 goals, once scoring eight goals in a single game against Dunfermline. He is the only British player to have averaged a goal a game during his career. However, despite this record he won only seven international caps for Scotland. Manager of Celtic 1945–65

Bobby Murdoch (1944–2001). Joined Celtic in 1959 aged 15. In 1967 he played a major part in the goal that helped Celtic become the first to lift the European Cup. Scottish Football Writers' player of the year 1969; scored a memorable goal for Scotland in a 1-1 World Cup qualifier against West Germany. Won 12 international caps for Scotland. In 1973 left Celtic for Middlesbrough.

Rose Reilly (1960–). The first Scot to captain an Italian first division women's team, where she has won eight championships and five cup-winners' medals. In 1987 she was the first Scot to win the Women's World Cup, playing for Italy.

Bill Shankly (1913–1981). Born in Glenbuck, Ayrshire. He became a professional footballer in 1932, signing first for Carlisle and then Preston North End. During his playing career he won seven caps for Scotland. After World War II he turned to management, managing several English teams and becoming Liverpool's most revered manager (1959–74). He won eight league titles and number of FA Cup successes and in 1973 the UEFA Cup.

Jock Stein CBE (1922–1985). The most successful football manager ever in Scotland. His playing career began at Albion Rovers, and he was signed up by Celtic in 1951. After managing Dunfermline Athletic and Hibernian, he became Celtic's most successful manager, 1965–78. During this time Celtic won nine consecutive League Championships, seven Scottish Cups and, in 1967, the European Cup. After managing Leeds United for a short while, he took over the Scottish national team. He died on 10 September 1985, just as Scotland qualified for the 1986 World Cup Finals.

GOLF

Tommy Armour (1895–1968). Born in Edinburgh. Successful amateur golfer, although partially losing his sight in World War I. Turned professional 1924 and became one of the many Scottish golfers who emigrated to the USA to capitalise on the early American golfing boom. He won the US PGA title in 1924 and 1930 and won three of the four Grand Slams but never the US Masters. Won the first British Open to be played at Carnoustie, in 1931.

James Braid (1870–1950). Born in Elie but moved to England in 1893, becoming a golf-club maker. He became a professional golfer and was a founder member of the Professional Golfers' Association (PGA). Won five British Open Championships over a 10 year period between 1901–10, including Muirfield (1901), Prestwick (1908) and St Andrews (1910).

Paul Lawrie MBE (1969–). Winner of 1992 UAP Under-25s Championship, 6th in 1993 British Open Championship. Trailing by 10 strokes he came from behind to win the 1999 British Open Championship at Carnoustie following a play-off against Frenchman Jean Van de Velde and American Justin Leonard. Awarded MBE in 2000.

Sandy Lyle (1958–). Made his international amateur debut at 14 and was a prolific winner before turning professional in 1977. Has won a total of 17 European Tour events, including the 1985 British Open Championship (becoming the first Briton since 1969 to win this trophy). First British golfer to win the US Masters (1988).

Catriona Matthew (1969–). Born in Edinburgh. She enjoyed a successful amateur career and was the 1986 Scottish Girls champion and the 1988 and 1989 Scottish Under-21 Stroke Play champion. Won the Scottish amateur title 1991, 1993 and 1994. She won the 1993 British Amateur title and was a member of the 1990, 1992 & 1994 Curtis Cup teams. When she turned professional she made her Solheim Cup debut as a member of the 1998 European team. She became WPGA champion for 1998.

Colin Montgomerie MBE (1963–). Scotland's top golfer. Won seven successive titles on the European Circuit, an unprecedented track record, finally lost his place as top player on that circuit in 2000. Runner-up in US Open in 1994 and 1997 and US PGA in 1997. Winner of the PGA title in 1998 and World Match Play title in 1999. Awarded MBE in 1998.

Tom Morris ('Old Tom') (1821–1908). Born in St Andrews. He competed in every Open championship up to and including 1896. He won the Open four times, including 1867, when he was 46, and remains the oldest ever winner. In 1851 he created the first purpose-built golf course in Scotland, at Prestwick. He is commemorated in the name of the final hole at the Royal and Ancient at St Andrews.

Tom Morris ('Young Tom') (1851–1875). Born in St Andrews. Along with his father he has passed into the folklore of golf. In 1868, at the age of 17, he became the youngest ever Open champion. He recorded his first championship hole-in-one at Prestwick, where he registered the first of four consecutive Open titles, a feat still unequalled. He died in his sleep on Christmas Day 1875, aged just 24.

Andrew Oldcorn (1960–). Born in Bolton, Lancashire but raised in Edinburgh. Won the English Amateur Championship but after many years living in Scotland was eventually given status as a Scot. Won all four of his matches in the 1983 Walker Cup. Produced his best ever golf to win the 2001 Volvo PGA Championship.

Willie Park Snr (1834–1903). Born in Musselburgh. Winner of the first professional golf tournament, the Open, held at Prestwick in 1860. He went on to win three more Opens, in 1863, 1866 and 1875. His brother Mungo Park won in 1874 and his son Willie Jnr won in 1887 and 1889.

Dale Reid (1959–). Born in Ladybank. As an amateur she represented Scotland internationally in 1978. She turned professional in 1979 and has achieved 24 victories, including the European Open in 1988. She finished first on the Women's Professional Order of Merit in 1984 and 1987, and represented Europe in the 1990, 1992, 1994 and 1996 Solheim Cup matches.

Isabella Robertson (1936–). Winner of the British Ladies' Open Amateur Golf Championship at the age of 45 in 1981.

Sam Torrance MBE (1953–). Became a professional golfer at the age of 16 and has won several events over the last 30 years including the 1982 Spanish Open. The most recent of his 21 titles is the Peugeot Open de France in 1998. He holed the winning putt where Europe beat the Americans in the Ryder Cup for the first time in 28 years. He was the European Ryder Cup team captain in 2001. He was an early pioneer of the broom handle putter. Awarded MBE in 1996.

HORSE-RACING

Willie Carson (1942–). Born in Stirling, he became one of Britain's most successful jockeys. He was champion jockey on five occasions and the first 'Jockey to the Queen' in 1977. He retired in 1997 with 3,838 winners during his career, which included a record 14 British classics, among them the Derby at Epsom, which he won on four occasions, 1979, 1980, 1989 and 1994.

MOTOR SPORTS

Jim Clark OBE (1936–1968). Formula 1 racing driver; launched his racing career, which included 25 Grand Prix wins, by driving for the Ecurie Ecosse team. Formula 1 world champion 1963 and 1965, driving for Lotus. Won the Indy 500 at Indianapolis in 1965. Awarded an OBE in 1964. Killed in a Formula 2 race at Hockenheim, Germany, in 1968.

David Coulthard (1971–). Formula 1 racing driver. Began his career in Scottish Junior Karting; champion 1983, 1984 and 1985. Scottish open cart champion 1986, 1987 and 1988; British Super Kart 1 champion 1986 and 1987. Moved to Formula Ford racing 1989, winning the Dunlop/Autosport Championship, the P&O Ferries Junior Championship, and the McLaren/Autosport Young Driver of the Year award. In 1992, won the Le Mans 24 hours (GT class). Switched to Formula 1 racing in 1994. His first Grand Prix win was in Portugal in 1995, and he has had several more wins, the most recent being the Brazilian Grand Prix 2001. He has finished third in the championship 1995, 1997 and 1998.

Bob McGregor McIntyre (1928–1962). Born in Glasgow. Motorcycle racer, known as 'The Flying Scotsman'. He began off-road racing in 1948 but soon turned to track racing. He won his very first competition at Balado Airfield, Kinross. He made his name with the Isle of Man TT race, where he recorded the first-ever 100mph lap. He was killed while competing at Alton Park in 1962.

Colin McRae (1968–) Rally driver; made his debut in 1986, winning his first world rally the following year. British Rally Champion 1991, 1992 and 1998. In 1994 he became the first Scot to win an RAC rally. Between 1991 and 1998 he drove for the 555 Subaru World Rally Team. Has won many individual rallies, becoming overall World Rally Champion in 1995. In 1999 switched to the Ford Martini World Rally Team.

Sir Jackie Stewart OBE (1939–). Formula 1 racing driver; launched his racing career in 1961, switching to Formula 1 racing in 1965 and winning his first race that year for BRM at Monza. In 1968 he joined the Tyrell team. Formula 1 world champion 1969, 1971 and 1973. Won 27 Grand Prix races in his career. In 1996, together with his son Paul, he formed the Stewart Grand Prix team. In 1999, having achieved fourth place in the constructors championship, he sold the company to Ford. Awarded OBE 1972; knighted 16 June 2001.

Richard Noble (1946–). Born in Edinburgh. He broke the land speed record in 1983, clocking up 1,012 km/hour (633 mph) in the Nevada Desert, USA. He regained the title in 1997 with the Thrust SSC team, which broke the sound barrier, reaching 1,220 km/hour (763 mph).

RUGBY

Gordon Lamont Brown (1947–2001). Born in Troon. Scotland's greatest rugby forward. Capped 30 times for Scotland, touring Argentina in 1969 and Australia in 1970. Played nine times for the British Lions. Following a brawl, he stopped playing for Scotland, but continued to play for the victorious Lions in New Zealand in 1971 and South Africa in 1974. He holds the world record of eight tries scored by a forward on an international tour.

Gavin Hastings (1962–). Born in Edinburgh. Capped for Scotland 61 times, 20 times as captain of his country. He also played in three World Cups for Scotland between 1987 and 1995. He holds records for the most points scored for Scotland in a rugby international (44 against Ivory Coast in 1995) and the most points scored for Scotland in an international career, 676 in total.

Scott Hastings (1964–). Born in Edinburgh. With 66 internationals to his name, he remains Scotland's most capped rugby international.

SAILING, YACHTING, CANOEING

Sir Chay Blyth CBE BEM (1940–). Born in Hawick. In 1966, with John Ridgeway, rowed across the Atlantic from Cape Cod to the Aran isles on a 20-foot dory. They completed the crossing in 90 days setting the record for the fastest modern-day double-handed crossing. In 1971, on the ketch *British Steel*, he became the first person to sail non-stop westwards around the world against prevailing winds and currents, completing the journey in 292 days. He has accumulated a long list of racing successes and in 1986 co-skippered the successful Blue Riband transatlantic attempt on *Virgin Atlantic Challenger III*.

Peter Haining. World sculling champion for 1993, 1994 and 1995. He was also Scottish champion and along with George P. Parsonage held the double-scull record for rowing the length of Loch Ness. George Parsonage also held the single-scull record for rowing the length of Loch Ness.

Rodney Pattison (1943–). Born in Campbeltown. At the 1968 Olympics in Mexico, on *Super'docious*, he and Iain Macdonald Smith won five first places and a second, with three penalty points, the lowest ever penalty score in an Olympic regatta, winning the gold in the Flying Dutchman class. In 1972 Munich Olympics, his yacht was called *Superdoso* and again he won gold in the Flying Dutchman class. Four years later at the 1976 Montreal games he won silver for the same event.

Jock Wishart (1955–). Born in Dumfries. International adventurer and yachtsman. Captain of the *Cable & Wireless Adventurer* on the record-breaking fastest circumnavigation of the globe (26,000 miles) in 1998. He raised money for this by rowing across the Atlantic Ocean in a 3,000-mile race in 1997. He was project leader of the team that broke the 1989 Round Britain Powerboat record. He was also a member of the first team to walk unsupported to the geomagnetic North Pole in 1992 and organized the first ever televised trek to the magnetic North Pole in 1996.

SNOOKER

Stephen Hendry MBE (1969–). Born in Edinburgh. Turned professional in1985 at 16 and dominated the game during the 1990s. Has won the World Snooker Championship seven times between 1990, when he became the youngest world champion, and 1999. He holds the record for the most titles won in a single season, nine in 1991–92, and has gathered a total of 72 major titles worldwide. Awarded MBE in 1999.

John Higgins (1975–). Turned professional in 1992 but came to prominence in 1994-95. His most successful year was 1999, when he rose to no.1 in the world rankings having won German and British Opens as well as the Embassy World Championship in 1998.

SQUASH

Peter Nicol MBE (1973–). Born in Inverurie, son of the Scottish national squash team coach. First came to prominence at the British Open Junior Championships, and by 1992 had entered the world rankings. He won the British National title in 1996 and became world no.2 in 1997. By 1998 he was world no.1, the first Briton for 25 years to win the British Open. He took the gold medal for Scotland at the 1998 Commonwealth Games in Kuala Lumpur. Awarded MBE in 1999.

SWIMMING

Isabella Moore. Until the 2,000 Sydney Olympics she was the only Scottish woman to have won an Olympic gold medal, which she achieved as a member of the 100m freestyle swimming team at the 1912 Olympic games held in Stockholm.

David Wilkie (1954–). Born in Edinburgh. Won silver medal in the 200m breaststroke at the 1972 Olympics in Munich. He went on to win a gold medal for the same event at the 1974 Commonwealth Games and the 1976 Olympics in Montreal, winning with a world-record time. he also won a silver medal for the 100 metre breaststroke at the Montreal Olympics.

WRESTLING

George Kidd (1925–1998). Born in Dundee. Scotland's top wrestler. By 1947 he was Scottish lightweight champion, by 1948 British champion, by 1949 European champion and by 1950 world champion. Over the next 20 years he successfully defended his world lightweight title 49 times. When he retired undefeated as world lightweight champion in 1976, he had lost only 19 of the 1,800 bouts in his 30-year career.

SPORTSCOTLAND (FORMERLY THE SCOTTISH SPORTS COUNCIL

Caledonia House, South Gyle, Edinburgh EH12 9DQ (Tel: 0131-317 7200)
Chief Executive: F. A. L. Alstead, CBE

SPORTSCOTLAND NATIONAL CENTRES

Cumbrae, Millport, Isle of Cumbrae KA28 0HQ (Tel: 01475-530757; Fax: 01475-674720; Web: www.nationalcentrecumbrae.org.uk)
Principal: R. Smith

Glenmore Lodge, Aviemore, Inverness-shire PH22 1QU (Tel: 01479-861256; Fax: 01479-861212; Web: www.glenmorelodge.org.uk)
Principal: T. Walker

Inverclyde, Burnside Road, Largs, Ayrshire KA30 8RW (Tel: 01475-674666; Fax: 01475-674720; Web: www.nationalcentreinverclyde.org.uk)
Principal: J. Kent

SPORTS BODIES

The following list includes the main organisations concerned with sports and physical recreation in Scotland.

SPORTSCOTLAND NATIONAL CENTRES

Inverclyde, Burnside Road, Ayrshire, KA30 8RW (Tel: 01475-674666;
E-mail: bob.smith@sportscotland.org.uk;
Web: www.sportscotland.org.uk).
Office Manager: Carol Benson

SPORTSCOTLAND NATIONAL CENTRES

Glenmore Lodge, Aviemore, Inverness-shire, PH22 1QU (Tel: 01479-861256;
E-mail: bob.smith@sportscotland.org.uk;
Web: www.sportscotland.org.uk).
Office Manager: Carol Benson

SPORTSCOTLAND NATIONAL CENTRES

Cumbrae, Millport, Isle of Cumbrae, KA28 0HQ (Tel: 01475-530013;
E-mail: bob.smith@sportscotland.org.uk;
Web: www.sportscotland.org.uk).
Office Manager: Carol Benson

ANGLING

SCOTTISH ANGLERS NATIONAL ASSOCIATION

Caledonia House, South Gyle, Edinburgh, EH12 9DQ (Tel: 0131-339 8808; Fax: 0131-317 7202;
E-mail: admin@sana.org.uk;
Web: www.sana.org.uk).
Administrator: Mr A. Wallace

SCOTTISH FEDERATION FOR COARSE ANGLING

8 Longbraes Gardens, Kirkcaldy, Fife, KY2 5YJ (Tel: 01592-642242;
E-mail: stephen.clerkin@btinternet.com;
Web: www.sfca.co.uk).
Secretary: S. Clerkin

ARCHERY

SCOTTISH FIELD ARCHERY ASSOCIATION

c/o 65 Napier Avenue, Bathcate, W. Lothian, EH48 1DF (Tel: 01506-656524; Fax: 01506-656524; E-mail: sfaa-archery@hotmail.com;
Web: www.staa-archery.com).
Liaison Officer: P.A. Sutherland

ASSOCIATION FOOTBALL

SCOTTISH AMATEUR FOOTBALL ASSOCIATION

Hampden Park, Glasgow, G42 9DB
(Tel: 0141-620 4550).
Secretary: H. Knapp

SCOTTISH FOOTBALL ASSOCIATION

Hampden Park, Glasgow, G42 9AY
(Tel: 0141-616 6000; Fax: 0141-616 6001;
E-mail: info@scottishfa.co.uk;
Web: www.scottishfa.co.uk).
Chief Executive: D. Taylor

SCOTTISH FOOTBALL LEAGUE

Hampden Park, Glasgow, G42 9EB
(Tel: 0141-620 4160; Fax: 0141-620 4161;
E-mail: info@sfl.scottishfootball.com;
Web: www.scottishfootball.com).
Secretary: P. Donald

SCOTTISH SCHOOLS FOOTBALL ASSOCIATION

Hampden Park, Glasgow, G42 9AZ
(Tel: 0141-620 4570; Fax: 0141-620 4571).
General Secretary: J. C. Watson

SCOTTISH WOMEN'S FOOTBALL ASSOCIATION

Hampden Park, Glasgow, G42 9DF
(Tel: 0141-620 4580; Fax: 0141-620 4581;
E-mail: swfa@supanet.com).
Executive Administrator: Mrs M. McGonigle

ATHLETICS

SCOTTISH ATHLETICS FEDERATION

Caledonia House, South Gyle, Edinburgh, EH12
9DQ (Tel: 0131-317 7320; Fax: 0131-317 7321;
Web: www.saf.org.uk).
Chief Executive: David Joy

BADMINTON

SCOTTISH BADMINTON UNION

Cockburn Centre, 40 Bogmoor Place, Glasgow,
G51 4TQ (Tel: 0141-445 1218; Fax: 0141-425
1218;
E-mail: enquiries@scotbadminton.demon.co.uk;
Web: www.scotbadminton.demon.co.uk).
Chief Executive: Miss Anne Smillie

SCOTTISH SCHOOLS BADMINTON UNION

The Sheiling, Browsburn Road, Airdrie, ML6
9QG (Tel: 01236-760943; Fax: 01236-621320;
E-mail: h.ainsley@cableinet.co.uk).
Secretary: H. Ainsley

BASKETBALL

BASKETBALL SCOTLAND

Caledonia House, South Gyle, Edinburgh, EH12
9DQ (Tel: 0131-317 7260; Fax: 0131-317 7489;
E-mail: sba@basketball-scotland.com;
Web: www.basketball-scotland.com).
Chief Executive Officer: Mr R.J. Thompson

SCOTTISH SCHOOLS BASKETBALL ASSOCIATION

Caledonia House, South Gyle, Edinburgh, EH12
9DQ (Tel: 0131-317 7260; Fax: 0131-317 7489).
Chairman: A. Turner

BILLIARDS

SCOTTISH BILLIARDS AND SNOOKER ASSOCIATION

PO Box 147, Dunfermline, KY12 8ZB
(Tel: 01383-625373; Fax: 01383-626373).
Secretary: A. T. Craig

BOWLS

SCOTTISH BOWLING ASSOCIATION

50 Wellington Street, Glasgow, G2 6EF
(Tel: 0141-221 8999/2004; Fax: 0141-221 8999;
E-mail: scottishbowling@aol.com).
Secretary: R. Black

SCOTTISH INDOOR BOWLING ASSOCIATION

41 Montfode Court, Ardrossan, Ayrshire, KA22
7NJ (Tel: 01294-468372; Fax: 01294-605937).
Secretary: J. Barclay

SCOTTISH WOMEN'S BOWLING ASSOCIATION

Kingston House, 3 Jamaica Street, Greenock,
PA15 1XX (Tel: 01475-724676; Fax: 01475-
724676).
Secretary: Mrs E. Allan

SCOTTISH WOMEN'S INDOOR BOWLING ASSOCIATION

39/7 Murray Burn Park, Edinburgh, EH14 2PQ
(Tel: 0131-453 2305; Fax: 0131-453 2305).
Hon. Secretary: Mrs M. Old

BOXING

SCOTTISH AMATEUR BOXING ASSOCIATION

96 High Street, Lochee, Dundee, DD2 3AY
(Tel: 01382-508261; Fax: 01382-611412).
Executive Director: F. Hendry

CANOEING

SCOTTISH CANOE ASSOCIATION

Caledonia House, South Gyle, Edinburgh, EH12
9DQ (Tel: 0131-317 7314; Fax: 0131-317 7319;
E-mail: enquiry@scot-canoe.org;
Web: www.scot-canoe.org).
Chief Executive: Mrs Ruth Crone

CAVING

GRAMPIAN SPELEOLOGICAL GROUP

8 Scone Gardens, Edinburgh, EH8 7DQ
(Tel: 0131-661 1123; Fax: 0131-661 1123;
E-mail: goon90@hotmail.com;
Web: www.sat.dundee.ac.uk/~arb/gsg).
Recorder: A. Jeffreys

CRICKET

SCOTTISH CRICKET UNION

National Cricket Academy, MES Sports Centre,
Ravelston, Edinburgh, EH4 3NT (Tel: 0131-313
7420; Fax: 0131-313 7430;
E-mail: admin.scu@btinternet.com;
Web: www.scu.org.uk

CROQUET

SCOTTISH CROQUET ASSOCIATION

14 Greenbank Crescent, Edinburgh, EH10 5SG
(Tel: 0131-665 8822;
E-mail: sca@tonyfoster.co.uk;
Web: www.grue.demon.co.uk/sca).
Treasurer: T. Foster

CYCLING

CTC SCOTLAND

10 Woodhall Terrace, Edinburgh, EH14 5BR
(Tel: 0131-453 3366).
Secretary: P. Hawkins

SCOTTISH CYCLISTS UNION

The Velodrome, Meadowbank Stadium, London
Road, Edinburgh, EH7 6AD (Tel: 0131-652
0187; Fax: 0131-661 0474;
E-mail: scottish.cycling@btinternet.com;
Web: www.btinternet.com/~scottish.cycling).
Executive Development Officer: J. Riach
Administrator: Ms L. Dickson

DANCE AND KEEP FIT

THE BRITISH ASSOCIATION OF TEACHERS OF DANCING

23 Marywood Square, Glasgow, G41 2BP
(Tel: 0141-423 4029; Fax: 0141-423 0677;
E-mail: enquiries@batd.co.uk;
Web: www.batd.co.uk).
Secretary: Mrs K. Allan

ROYAL SCOTTISH COUNTRY DANCE SOCIETY

12 Coates Crescent, Edinburgh, EH3 7AF
(Tel: 0131-225 3854; Fax: 0131-225 7783;
E-mail: info@rscdshq.freeserve.co.uk;
Web: www.rscds.org).
Secretary: Ms E. Gray

SCOTTISH DANCESPORT

93 Hillfoot Drive, Bearsden, Glasgow, G61 3QG
(Tel: 0141-563 2001; Fax: 0141-563 2001).
General Secretary and Administrator: Mrs M.
Fraser

SCOTTISH OFFICIAL BOARD OF HIGHLAND DANCING

32 Grange Loan, Edinburgh, EH9 2NR
(Tel: 0131-668 3965; Fax: 0131-662 0404).
Director of Administration: Miss M. Rowan

EQUESTRIANISM

THE TREKKING AND RIDING SOCIETY OF SCOTLAND

Steadingfield, Wolfhill, by Perth, PH2 6DA
(Tel: 01821-650210; Fax: 01821-650210).
Secretary: Mrs M. Graham

FENCING

SCOTTISH FENCING

Cockburn Centre, 40 Bogmoor Place, Glasgow, G51 4TQ (Tel: 0141-445 1602; Fax: 0141-445 1602; E-mail: scottishfencing@aol.com; Web: www.scottish-fencing.com).
Executive Administrator: Mrs L. Rose

FIELD SPORTS

SCOTTISH COUNTRYSIDE ALLIANCE

East Gate, Royal Highland Showground, Ingliston, Edinburgh, EH28 8NF (Tel: 0131-335 0200; Fax: 0131-335 0201;
E-mail: info@scottishcountrysidealliance.org).
Director: A. Murray

GLIDING

SCOTTISH GLIDING ASSOCIATION

48 McIntosh Drive, Elgin, Moray, IV30 6AW (Tel: 01343-547701; Fax: 01343-547701;
E-mail: ray@dalfaber.globalnet.co.uk;
Web: www.gliding.org).
Secretary: vacant
Chairman: G. Douglas

GOLF

THE GOLF FOUNDATION

Foundation House, The Spinney, Hoddesdon Road, Stanstead Abbotts, Ware, Herts, SG12 8GF (Tel: 01920-876200; Fax: 01920-876211; E-mail: info@golf-foundation.org;
Web: www.golf-foundation.org).
Executive Director: M. Round

THE ROYAL AND ANCIENT GOLF CLUB OF ST ANDREWS

St Andrews, Fife, KY16 9JD (Tel: 01334-472112; Fax: 01334-477580;
E-mail: thesecretary@randagc.org;
Web: www.randa.org).
Secretary: P. Dawson

SCOTTISH GOLF UNION

Scottish National Golf Centre, Drumoig, Leuchars, St Andrews, KY16 0DW (Tel: 01382-549500; Fax: 01382-459510;
E-mail: sgu@scottishgolf.com;
Web: www.scottishgolf.com).
Chief Executive: H. Grey

SCOTTISH LADIES GOLFING ASSOCIATION

Scottish National Golf Centre, Drumoig, Leuchars, St Andrews, Fife, KY16 0DW (Tel: 01382-549502;
Web: www.scottishgolf.com).
Secretary: Mrs S. Simpson

SCOTTISH SCHOOLS GOLF ASSOCIATION

The Waid Academy, St Andrews Road, Anstruther, Fife, KY10 3HD (Tel: 01333-592000; Fax: 01334-592049).
Secretary: Mrs D. Scott

GYMNASTICS

SCOTTISH GYMNASTICS

Woodhall Mill, Lanark Road, Edinburgh, EH14 5DL (Tel: 0131-458 5657; Fax: 0131-458 5659; E-mail: info@scottishgymnastics.com;
Web: www.scottishgymnastics.com).
President: Mrs L. Milne

HIGHLAND AND BORDER GAMES

SCOTTISH GAMES ASSOCIATION

24 Florence Place, Perth, PH1 5BH (Tel: 01738-627782; Fax: 01738-639622; E-mail: andrew@highlandgames.org.uk; Web: www.highlandgames-sga.com).
Secretary: A. Rettie

HOCKEY

SCOTTISH HOCKEY UNION

589 Lanarck Road, Edinburgh, EH14 (Tel: 0131-453 9070; Fax: 0131-653 9070; E-mail: info@scottish-hockey.org.uk; Web: www.scottish-hockey.org.uk).
Chairman: G. Ralph
General Manager: C. Grahamslaw

ICE SKATING

SCOTTISH ICE SKATING ASSOCIATION

c/o The Ice Sports Centre, Riversdale Crescent, Edinburgh, EH12 5XN (Tel: 0131-337 3976; Fax: 0131-337 9239).
Administrator: J. Macdonald

JU-JITSU

SCOTTISH JU-JITSU ASSOCIATION

3 Dens Street, Dundee, DD4 6BU
(Tel: 01382-458262; Fax: 01382-458262;
E-mail: scottishjujitsu@aol.com;
Web: www.scottish-jujitsu.com).
General Secretary: R. G. Ross

JUDO

SCOTTISH JUDO FEDERATION

Caledonia House, South Gyle, Edinburgh, EH12
9DQ (Tel: 0131-317 7270; Fax: 0131-317 7050;
E-mail: info@scotjudo.org;
Web: www.scotjudo.org).
Chief Executive: C. McIver
Hon. Secretary: G. Campbell

LACROSSE

SCOTTISH LACROSSE ASSOCIATION

Scottish Lacrosse Administration Office
St Leonards School, St Andrews, Fife, KY16 9QJ
(Tel: 01334-472126; Fax: 01334-476152;
E-mail: stleonards@fife.org).
Secretary: Mrs J. Caithness

LAWN TENNIS

TENNIS SCOTLAND LTD

Craiglockhart Tennis and Sports Centre, 177
Colinton Road, Edinburgh, EH14 1BZ
(Tel: 0131-444 1984; Fax: 0131-444 1973;
E-mail: gduncan@slta.org.uk).
Secretary and Director of Administration: Mrs
G. Duncan
Director of Tennis: M. Hulbert

MODERN PENTATHLON

SCOTTISH MODERN PENTATHLON ASSOCIATION

16 Plewlands Terrace, Edinburgh, EH10 5JZ
(Tel: 0131-447 7427; Fax: 0131-229 2088).
Chairman: R. Reekie

MOTOR SPORT

SCOTTISH AUTO CYCLE UNION LTD

28 West Main Street, Uphall, W. Lothian, EH52
5DW (Tel: 01506-858354; Fax: 01506-855792).
Office Manager: E. W. Jones
Administrator: Ms Y. Kelly

ROYAL SCOTTISH AUTOMOBILE CLUB (MOTOR SPORT) LTD

11 Blythswood Square, Glasgow, G2 4AG
(Tel: 0141-204 4999; Fax: 0141-204 4949;
E-mail: rsac—motorsport@compuserve.com;
Web: www. Rsacmotorsport.co.uk).
Secretary: J. C. Lord

MOUNTAINEERING

MOUNTAIN RESCUE COMMITTEE OF SCOTLAND

31 Craigfern Drive, Blanefield, Glasgow, G63
9DP (Tel: 01360-770431; Fax: 0141-950 3132;
E-mail: lomondbob@talk21.com;
Web: www.mrc-scotland.org.uk).
Secretary: Dr R. H. Sharp

MOUNTAINEERING COUNCIL OF SCOTLAND

Ground Floor, The Old Granary, West Mill
Street, Perth, PH1 5QP (Tel: 01738-638227;
Fax: 01738-442095;
Web: www.mountaineering-scotland.org.uk).
National Officer: K. Howett

SCOTTISH MOUNTAIN LEADER TRAINING BOARD

Glenmore, Aviemore, Inverness-shire, PH22
1QU (Tel: 01479-861248; Fax: 01479-861249;
E-mail: smltb@aol.com).
Secretary: A. Fyffe

NETBALL

NETBALL SCOTLAND

Hillington Business Park, 24 Ainslie Road,
Hillington, Glasgow, G52 4RU (Tel: 0141-570
4016; Fax: 0141-570 4017;
E-mail: netballscotland@btinternet.com;
Web: www.netballscotland.freeserve.co.uk).
Administrator: D. McLaughlaMargaret Martin

ORIENTEERING

SCOTTISH ORIENTEERING ASSOCIATION

10 Neuk Crescent, Houston, Johnstone, PA6
7DW (Tel: 01505-613094;
E-mail: donald@soa.almac.co.uk;
Web: www.scottish-orienteering.org).
Development Officer: D. Petrie

PARACHUTING

SCOTTISH SPORT PARACHUTE ASSOCIATION

Strathallan Airfield, Nr Auchterarder, Perthshire, PH3 1LA (Tel: 01764-662572; E-mail: info@sspa.co.uk; Web: www.sspa.co.uk).
Chairman: Ms A. Johnson

POLO

SCOTTISH BICYCLE POLO ASSOCIATION

16 Edmiston Drive, Linwood, Paisley, PA3 3TD (Tel: 01505-328105).
Secretary: Mr Andrew McGee

SCOTTISH POLO ASSOCIATION

Iona Designs, 4 High Street, Auchterarder (Tel: 01382-330234; Fax: 01382-223135).
Chairman: David Gemmell

POOL

SCOTTISH POOL ASSOCIATION

3 Strath Gardens, Dores, Inverness, IV2 6TT (Tel: 01463-751282; Fax: 01463-751396).
Hon. General Secretary: N. A. Donald

ROWING

SCOTTISH AMATEUR ROWING ASSOCIATION

71 Gillbrae Crescent, Georgetown, Dumfries, DG1 4DJ (Tel: 01387-264233).
Secretary: G. West

SCOTTISH SCHOOLS ROWING COUNCIL

1 Kirkhill Gardens, Edinburgh, EH16 5DF (Tel: 0131-667 5389; Fax: 0131-229 6363).
Secretary: R. H. C. Neill

RUGBY UNION

SCOTTISH RUGBY UNION

Murrayfield, Roseburn Street, Edinburgh, EH12 5PJ (Tel: 0131-346 5000; Fax: 0131-346 5001; E-mail: bill.hogg@sru.org.uk; Web: www.sru.org.uk).
Chief Executive: W. S. Watson
Secretary: I. A. L. Hogg

SCOTTISH SCHOOLS RUGBY UNION

59 Lochinver Crescent, Dundee, DD2 4TY (Tel: 01382-660907; Fax: 01382-435701; E-mail: headteacher@harris-academy.dundeecity.sch.uk).
Hon. Secretary: D. C. M. Stibbles

SHINTY

THE CAMANACHD ASSOCIATION

Algarve, Badabrie, Banavie, Fort William, Inverness-shire, PH33 7LX (Tel: 01397-772772; Fax: 01397-772255; E-mail: executive@camanachd.freeserve.co.uk; Web: www.shinty.com).
Executive Officer: A. MacIntyre

SHOOTING

SCOTTISH AIR RIFLE AND PISTOL ASSOCIATION

45 Glenartney Court, Glenrothes, Fife, KY7 6YF (Tel: 01592-743929).
Secretary: E. B. Wallace

SCOTTISH ASSOCIATION FOR COUNTRY SPORTS

River Lodge, Trochry, Dunkeld, PH8 0DY (Tel: 01350-723259; Fax: 01350-723259; Web: www.sacs.org.uk).
Director: D. Cant

SCOTTISH PISTOL ASSOCIATION

Cumbrae House, Powmill, By Dollar, Clackmannanshire, FK14 7NW (Tel: 01499-500640; Fax: 01499-500640).
Joint Secretaries: Mrs N. Credland

SCOTTISH SMALL-BORE RIFLE ASSOCIATION

128 Easton Drive, Shieldhill, Falkirk, FK1 2DW (Tel: 01324-720440; E-mail: secretary@ssra.co.uk; Web: www.ssra.co.uk).
Secretary: S. J. McIntosh, MBE

SCOTTISH TARGET SHOOTING FEDERATION

77 Malbet Park, Edinburgh, EH16 6WB (Tel: 0131-664 9674; Fax: 0131-664 9674).
Hon. Secretary: C. R. Aitken

SKIING

BRITISH SKI AND SNOWBOARD FEDERATION

Hillend, Biggar Road, Midlothian, EH10 7EF
(Tel: 0131-445 7676; Fax: 0131-445 7722;
E-mail: britski@easynet.co.uk;
Web: www.ifyouski.com).
Operations Director: Mrs F. McNeilly

SCOTTISH SCHOOL SKI ASSOCIATION

Dollar Academy, Dollar, FK14 7DU
(Tel: 01259-742 511; Fax: 01259-742 867).
Chairman: Mrs L. Hutchison

SKIING AND SNOWBOARDING

SNOWSPORT SCOTLAND

Hillend, Biggar Road, Midlothian, EH10 7EF
(Tel: 0131-445 4151; Fax: 0131-445 4949;
E-mail: admin@snsc.demon.co.uk;
Web: www.snsc.demon.co.uk).
Development Manager: B. Crawford

SPORTS COUNCILS

SPORTSCOTLAND

Caledonia House, South Gyle, Edinburgh, EH12
9DQ (Tel: 0131-317 7200; Fax: 0131-317 7202;
E-mail: library@sportscotland.org.uk;
Web: www.sportscotland.org.uk).
Chief Executive: I. Robson
Chairman: A. Dempster

SQUASH RACKETS

SCOTTISH SQUASH LIMITED

Caledonia House, South Gyle, Edinburgh, EH12
9DQ (Tel: 0131-317 7343; Fax: 0131-317 7734;
E-mail: scottishsquash@aol.com;
Web: www.scottishsquash.com).
Administration Manager: Derek Welch
President: A. McCue

SUB AQUA

SCOTTISH SUB AQUA CLUB

Cockburn Centre, 40 Bogmoor place, Glasgow,
G51 4TQ (Tel: 0141-425 1021; Fax: 0141-425
1021; E-mail: ab@hqssac.demon.co.uk;
Web: www.scotsac.com).
Administrative Secretary: Mrs A. Bannon
General Secretary: Ms M. Galloway

SWIMMING

SCOTTISH AMATEUR SWIMMING ASSOCIATION

Holmhills Farm, Greenlees Road, Cambuslang,
Glasgow, G72 8DT (Tel: 0141-641 8818; Fax:
0141-641 4443; E-mail: scotswim@aol.com).
Chief Executive: P. Bush

SCOTTISH SCHOOLS SWIMMING ASSOCIATION

55 Dalgety Gardens, Dalgety Bay, Dunfermline,
KY11 9LF (Tel: 01383-825428).
Hon. Secretary: Mrs C. Rees

SCOTTISH SWIMMING AWARDS OFFICE

Holmhills Farm, Greenlees Road, Cambuslang,
G72 8DT (Tel: 0141-646 0490; Fax: 0141-646
0491; E-mail: swimawards@aol.com).
Administration Officer: Marilyn Sweet

TABLE TENNIS

SCOTTISH TABLE TENNIS ASSOCIATION

Caledonia House, South Gyle, Edinburgh, EH12
9DQ (Tel: 0131-317 8077; Fax: 0131-317 8224;
E-mail: ralph@stta.freeserve.co.uk;
Web: www.sol.co.uk/t/tabletennis/).
Chairman: D. Clifford
Administration Secretary: R. Knowles

TRIATHLON

SCOTTISH TRIATHLON ASSOCIATION

Glenearn Cottage, Edinburgh Road, Port Seton,
E. Lothian, EH32 0HQ (Tel: 01875-811344;
Fax: 01875-811344;
E-mail: Jacqui.Dunlop@btinternet.com;
Web: www.tri-scotland.org).
Secretary: Ms J. Dunlop

TUG-OF-WAR

SCOTTISH TUG OF WAR ASSOCIATION

47 Finlay Avenue, East Calder, W. Lothian,
EH53 0RP (Tel: 01506-881650;
Fax: 01506-881650;
E-mail: garygillespie@STOWA47.freeserve.co.uk).
Secretary: G. Gillespie

VOLLEYBALL

SCOTTISH VOLLEYBALL ASSOCIATION
48 The Pleasance, Edinburgh, EH8 9TJ
(Tel: 0131-556 4633; Fax: 0131-557 4314;
E-mail: sva@callnetuk.com;
Web: www.scottishvolleyball.org).
Director: N. S. Moody
Executive Officer: Ms K. Benney

WALKING

RAMBLERS' ASSOCIATION SCOTLAND
Kingfisher House, Auld Mart Business Park,
Milnathort, Kinross, KY13 9DA (Tel: 01577-
861222; Fax: 01577-861333;
E-mail: enquiries@scotland.ramblers.org.uk;
Web: www.ramblers.org.uk).
Director: D. Morris

WRESTLING

SCOTTISH AMATEUR WRESTLING ASSOCIATION
Kelvin Hall International Sports Arena, Argyle
Street, Glasgow, G3 8AW (Tel: 0141-334 3843;
Fax: 0141-334 3843;
Web: www.britishwrestling.org).
Administrator: Rhonda Polak

YACHTING

ROYAL YACHTING ASSOCIATION SCOTLAND
Caledonia House, South Gyle, Edinburgh, EH12
9DQ (Tel: 0131-317 7388; Fax: 0131-317 8566;
Web: www.scotsport.co.uk/sail/).
Hon. Secretary: S. Boyd

ENVIRONMENTAL
SCOTLAND

— ENVIRONMENTAL SCOTLAND —

THE LAND

AREA

	Scotland		UK	
	sq. miles	sq. km	sq. miles	sq. km
Land	29,767	77,097	93,006	240,883
Inland water*	653	1,692	1,242	3,218
Total	30,420	78,789	94,248	244,101

*Excluding tidal water

Source: The Stationery Office, Annual Abstract of Statistics 1999 (Crown Copyright)

GEOGRAPHY

Scotland occupies the northern portion of the main island of Great Britain and includes the Inner and Outer Hebrides, and the Orkney, Shetland, and many other islands. It lies between 60° 51; 30; and 54° 38; N. latitude and between 1° 45; 32 and 6° 14; W. longitude, with England to the south, the Atlantic Ocean on the north and west, and the North Sea on the east.

The greatest length of the mainland (Cape Wrath to the Mull of Galloway) is 274 miles, and the greatest breadth (Buchan Ness to Applecross) is 154 miles. The customary measurement of the island of Great Britain is from the site of John o' Groats house, near Duncansby Head, Caithness, to Land's End, Cornwall, a total distance of 603 miles (965 km) in a straight line and approximately 900 miles (1,440 km) by road.

RELIEF

The highest parts of the United Kingdom lie in Scotland. As part of Highland Britain, 65 per cent of Scottish landscape lies above 120m (400ft), of which 6 per cent is above 600m (2,000ft), while 20 per cent lies below 60m (200ft).

There are three natural orographic divisions of mainland Scotland. The southern uplands have their highest points in Merrick (2,764 ft/814 m), Rhinns of Kells (2,669 ft/814 m), and Cairnsmuir of Carsphairn (2,614 ft/796 m), in the west; and the Tweedsmuir Hills in the east (Broad Law 2,756 ft/830 m, Dollar Law 2,682 ft/817 m, Hartfell 2,651 ft/808 m).

The central lowlands, formed by the valleys of the Clyde, Forth and Tay, divide the southern uplands from the northern Highlands, which extend almost from the extreme north of the mainland to the central lowlands, and are divided into a northern and a southern system by the Great Glen.

The Grampian Mountains, which entirely cover the southern Highland area, include in the west Ben Nevis (4,406 ft/1,343 m), the highest point in the British Isles, and in the east Cairngorm Mountains (Ben Macdui 4,296 ft/1,309 m, Braeriach 4,248 ft/1,295 m, Cairn Gorm 4,084 ft/1,246 m). The north-western Highland area contains the mountains of Wester and Easter Ross (Carn Eighe 3,880 ft/1,183 m, Sgurr na Lapaich 3,775 ft/1,150 m).

Created, like the central lowlands, by a major geological fault, the Great Glen (60 miles/96 km long) runs between Inverness and Fort William, and contains Loch Ness, Loch Oich and Loch Lochy. These are linked to each other and to the north-east and south-west coasts of Scotland by the Caledonian Canal, the River Lochy and the long sea-loch Loch Linnhe, providing a navigable passage between the Moray Firth and the Inner Hebrides.

HYDROGRAPHY

The western coast is fragmented by peninsulas and islands and deeply indented by sea-lochs (fjords), the longest of which is Loch Fyne (42 miles long) in Argyll. Although the east coast tends to be less fractured and lower, there are several great drowned inlets (firths), for instance the Firth of Forth, the Firth of Tay and the Moray Firth. The Firth of Clyde is the chief example of this feature in the west.

The lochs are the principal hydrographic feature. The largest in Scotland and in Britain is Loch Lomond (27.46 sq. miles/71.12 sq. km), in the Grampian valleys; the longest and deepest is Loch Ness (24 miles/38 km long and 800 ft/244 m deep), in the Great Glen. Loch Shin (20 miles/32 km long) and Loch Maree in the Highlands are the longest lochs in the north-west Highlands.

The longest river is the Tay (117 miles/188 km), noted for its salmon. It flows into the North Sea, with Dundee on the estuary, which is spanned by the Tay Bridge (10,289 ft/3,137 m), opened in 1887, and the Tay Road Bridge (7,365 ft/2,245 m), opened in 1966. The present Tay rail bridge is the second to have been built; the original collapsed in 1879, only a year after completion, with the loss of 150 lives.

Other noted salmon rivers are the Dee (90 miles/144 km) which flows into the North Sea at Aberdeen, and the Spey (110 miles/172 km), the swiftest flowing river in the British Isles, which flows into the Moray Firth. The Tweed, which gave its name to the woollen cloth produced along its banks, marks in the lower stretches of its 96-mile (155 km) course the border between Scotland and England.

The most important river commercially is the Clyde (106 miles/171m), formed by the junction of the Daer and Portrail water, which flows through the city of Glasgow to the Firth of Clyde. During its course it passes over the picturesque Falls of Clyde, Bonnington Linn (30ft/9m), Corra Linn (84ft/26m), Dundaff Linn (10ft/3m) and Stonebyres Linn (80ft/24m), above and below Lanark. The Forth (66 miles/106km), upon which stands Edinburgh, is spanned by the Forth (Railway) Bridge (1890), which is 5,330 feet (1,625m) long, and the Forth (Road) Bridge (1964), which has a total length of 6,156 feet (1,987m) (over water) and a single span of 3,300 feet (1,006m).

On 26 May 2001 the Forth and Clyde canal, linking the North Sea and the Atlantic via the firths of Forth and Clyde, was reopened after decades of closure.

The highest waterfall in Scotland, and the British Isles, is Eas a'Chùal Aluinn with a total height of 658 feet (200m), which falls from Glas Bheinn in Sutherland. The Falls of Glomach, on a head-stream of the Elchaig in Wester Ross, have a drop of 370 feet (113m).

THE ISLANDS

Scotland's northern and western coasts are fringed by 790 islands and islets, products of the same geological forces that have shaped its deeply indented coastlines. They fall into four main groups: Orkney, Shetland, and the Inner and Outer Hebrides. There are also some offshore islands, which lie in the North Atlantic well outwith the main Outer Hebrides group but are still part of the Outer Hebrides. Rockall, 184 miles west of St Kilda, was annexed in 1955 and added to the territories of the UK by an Act of Parliament in 1972.

Only 130 of the islands are inhabited today, although some of them became uninhabited only in the last century or so, some after many centuries of habitation, such as Mousa, site of one of the major Iron Age brochs but uninhabited since the mid 19th century. The last families to leave the St Kilda group were evacuated in 1930 (a military base and missile-tracking station were installed on Hirta in 1957, but the island is not permanently occupied). A number of the uninhabited islands are, or contain, nature reserves, principally for the protection of birds.

ORKNEY

The Orkney Islands lie about six miles north of the mainland, separated from it by the Pentland Firth. Of the 90 islands and islets (holms and skerries) in the group, about one-third are inhabited.

The principal islands and their areas are:

Mainland (with Burray, South Ronaldsay, and Hunda)	58,308 ha/144,079 acres
Hoy	14,381 ha/35,380 acres
Graemsay	409 ha/1,011 acres
Flotta	876 ha/2,165 acres
Rousay	4,860 ha/12,009 acres
Shapinsay	2,948 ha/7,285 acres
Stronsay	3,275 ha/8,093 acres
Eday	2,745 ha/6,783 acres
Sanday	5,043 ha/12,461 acres
Westray	4,713 ha/11,646 acres
Papa Westray	918 ha/2,268 acres
North Ronaldsay	690 ha/1,705 acres

Most of the inhabited islands are low-lying and fertile owing to the geological underlay of Old Red Sandstone, and farming, principally of beef cattle, is the main economic activity. Flotta is the site of a large oil terminal.

Hoy is the highest of the islands (highest point Ward Hill, 479 m/1,571ft) and has the most dramatic landscape. Although most of the Orkney Islands are low-lying, St John's Head on Hoy (350m/1,148ft) is one of the highest sea-cliffs in the British Isles.

Several of the islands contain rare flora – e.g. Hoy, where rare alpine plants are to be found – and several contain nature reserves specialising in birds. Mainland boasts over 600 species of flowering plant, some of which are extremely rare.

North Ronaldsay, the northernmost island, is very isolated but also sufficiently fertile to support a small farming population. It has been cotinuously populated since prehistoric times. A species of small sheep, descendants of the original Orkney sheep, is unique to the island.

SHETLAND

The Shetland Islands lie about 50 miles north of Orkney, with Fair Isle about half-way between the two groups. Out Stack, off Muckle Flugga, one mile north of Unst, is the most northerly point in the British Isles (60° 51′ 30″ N. lat.). Lerwick, the capital, is in fact almost equidistant from

Aberdeen and Bergen in Norway. Foula, the most westerly of the Shetland Islands, is the most isolated inhabited island in the British Isles. The group contains over 100 islands, of which 16 are populated.

The principal islands and their areas are:

Mainland (with Muckle Roe, West and East Burra, and Trondra)	100,230 ha/247,668 acres
Bressay	2,805 ha/6,932 acres
Fair Isle	768 ha/1,898 acres
Fetlar	4,078 ha/10,077 acres
Foula	1,265 ha/3,126 acres
Housay (with Bruray and Grunay)	218 ha/539 acres
Unst	12,068 ha/29,820 acres
Whalsay	1,970 ha/4,868 acres
Yell	21,211 ha/52,412 acres

Shetland's geology is different from that of Orkney, resulting in a harsher, more dramatic landscape, with impressive sea cliffs (e.g. the Kame of Foula, 376m/1,233ft) and also in poorer soil, which has made fishing traditionally more important than agriculture as a livelihood. The islands are largely treeless, and peat bog, grass and heather moorland are characteristic. The North Atlantic Drift, an extension of the Gulf Stream, keeps Shetland's climate milder than its northern latitude would suggest.

THE HEBRIDES

The Inner and Outer Hebrides, stretching from Lewis, the most northerly island, to Ailsa Craig, the most southerly, comprise over 500 islands and islets, of which about 100 are inhabited, although mountainous terrain and extensive peat bogs and heather mean that only a fraction of the total land area is under cultivation.

THE INNER HEBRIDES

The Inner Hebrides lie off the west coast of Scotland, relatively close to the mainland. The largest and best known of the islands is Skye (1,648 sq. km/ 643 sq. m), which contains the spectacular Cuillin Hills (highest peak Sgurr Alasdair 993m/3,257ft), the more smoothly shaped Red Cuillin (highest peak Beinn na Caillich, 732m/2,403ft), Bla Bheinn (928m/3,046ft), and, in the north if the island, the strange formations of the Quiraing and the Storr (719m/2,358ft). Skye is itself surrounded by several small islands, and not far to the south-west are the Small Isles, Rum, Eigg, Muck, and Canna. Muck is low-lying and is the most fertile of the Small Isles; Eigg and Rum are craggier. Some of the rock

formations on Rum are geologically unique. Further north, off the north-west coast, lie a few small islands of which the principal group is the Summer Isles, about a dozen islands lying off the Coigach peninsula. Tanera Mór, the largest of the group, has tourist facilities. Still further north, Handa is famous for its rich bird life.

Major islands in the southern Inner Hebridean islands include:

- Arran – area 43.201 ha/106,750 acres; highest points Goat Fell (874m/2,868ft) Caisteal Abhail (834m/2,735ft); geologically very complex, it was described by Scottish geologist Sir Archibald Geikie (1835–1924) as 'a complete synopsis of Scottish geology';
- Bute – area 12,217 ha/30,188 acres; undulating and relatively fertile, hence much of its land is cultivated, with some woodland, although it is today chiefly geared up for tourism;
- Colonsay and Oronsay – area 4,617 ha/11,409 acres; a wide stretch of shell sand between them may be crossed on foot at low tide;
- Islay – 61,956 ha/151,093 acres; its large peat deposits colour the water used in its famous whiskies;
- Jura – 36,692 ha/90,666 acres; highest points the picturesque Paps of Jura (Beinn an Oir, 785m/2,575ft, Beinn Shiantaidh, 755m/2,476ft, and Beinn a' Chaolais, 734m/2,408ft); poor soils mean that much of the land is now used only for deerstalking;
- Mull – area 941 sq. km/367 sq. m; highest point Ben More, 966m/3,168ft, the highest example of volcanic Tertiary basalt in Britain; some natural woodland remains and there is relatively little heather; sea lochs cut deeply into the coastline;
- Iona – area 877 ha/2,167 acres; best known for its religious aspects, it attracts visitors from all over the world;
- Coll and Tiree – areas 7,685 ha/18,989 acres and 7,834 ha/19,358 acres respectively; a single island until relatively recently in geological time, they are flattish in profile; their rock contains quartz and marble (which was briefly mined at Tiree in the late eighteenth century); the coasts are fringed with dunes and machair, and on Tiree are favourable for surfing and windsurfing. Tiree is also much more fertile than Coll and supports crofting.

THE OUTER HEBRIDES

The Outer Hebrides are separated from the mainland by the Minch.

The main islands are:

- Lewis and Harris with Great Bernera – total area 220,020 ha/5,389,369 acres; highest point Clisham, 799m/2,621ft; Great Bernera is joined to Lewis by a bridge; much of Lewis is ancient, deep peat bog, while its south-western end and Harris are more mountainous;
- Barra with Vatersay – area 6,385 ha/16,889 acres; highest point Heaval (383m/ 1,256ft); the two islands are linked by a causeway completed in 1990;
- North and South Uist with Benbecula, Baleshare, Grimsay, Vallay, Kirkibost, and Oronsay – total area 72,827 ha/179,956 acres; highest point Beinn Mhór (620m/2,034 ft), on South Uist; North Uist is very low-lying, with half its total area under water; all one long island until the Ice Age; Vallay, Kirkibost and Oronsay are now uninhabited;
- Berneray – located in the Sound of Harris, this island is now joined to North Uist by a causeway built in 1999;
- Eriskay – area 703 ha/1,737 acres; famed as the spot where, in 1745, Bonnie Prince Charlie first set foot in Scotland, and for its traditional music; however, the island itself is rather barren;
- Scalpay – now part of Lewis and Harris, joined to Harria by a bridge completed in 1998.

THE OFFSHORE ISLANDS

The offshore Hebridean islands are:

- Flannan Isles (seven islands known as the Seven Hunters), 21 miles west of Butt of Lewis;
- Sula Sgeir, 41 miles north of Butt of Lewis;
- Rona, 10 miles east of Sula Sgeir;
- St Kilda archipelago, 100 miles WSW of Butt of Lewis, consisting of Hirta (main island), Soay, Boreray and Dun.

GEOLOGY

The geology of Scotland is extremely complex. Its rugged mountains, hundreds of rocky islands, fjord-like lochs, moorlands and glens are the result of a gradual modification by weather, erosion, the work of ice and water and, most recently, human intervention. The British Geological Survey (BGS) is the nation's laboratory concerned with understanding onshire and offshire geology, geochemistry and groundwater. Its activities cover geological resources such as minerals and oil, environmental pollution and hazards from abandoned mines, waste, landslips, earthquakes and magnetic storms. There is a strong environmental interface where the ecosystem meets the ground and the landscape and where geochemistry impacts on human and animal health.

British Geological Survey (Scotland), Murchison House, West Mains Road, Edinburgh EH9 3LA (Tel: 0131-667 1000; Fax: 0131-667 1877; Email: c.browitt@bgs.ac.uk; Web: www.bgs.ac.uk).

Director, BGS Scotland: Dr Chris Browitt
Onshore Geology: Dr Martin Smith
Offshore Geology: Dr Nigel Fannin
Earthquakes and Geomagnetism: Dr David Kerridge

Years BP	Event
c. 2,500–3,000 million	Metamorphic Lewisian gneiss, found in north-western Scotland and the Outer Hebrides, is formed.
c. 1,000 million	These rocks uplifted to form the mountain ranges of north-west Scotland, at the time linked to what are now Greenland and Canada. In the Inner Hebrides, Coll and Tiree form part of the Lewisian landform of the far north-west.
c. 900 million	Torridonian sandstone, the oldest sedimentary rock in Britain, is deposited by rivers from Greenland in north-west Scotland, forming Torridonian mountains, e.g. Liathach (1054m/3,436ft) and An Teallach (1,062m/3,484ft), once over 10,000 feet high. Further north, sand fills an old valley in Assynt, leaving relict mountains, e.g. Suilven (731m/2,399ft), rising abruptly from barren moorland.
from c. 800 million	The formation of the rocks that make up most of the Highlands we now see begins, when the area is an ocean trough. River deposits pour into this trough for some 400–500 million years.
c. 670 million	Scotland (at the time 30° south of the Equator) is covered by huge ice-sheet, resulting in glacial deposits which form Inner Hebrides south if Coll and Tiree.
c. 500 million	Caledonian Mountains are thrust up and folded as the American and European tectonic plates start to converge. Subsequent glaciation and weathering mould the rocks into what are now the Grampians and Cairngorms. These rocks, mostly

granites, lavas and schists, make up the largest outcrop of granite in the United Kingdom, covering 410 sq. km (160 sq. miles) and its most extensive area above 3,000 feet, including Britain's highest mountain, Ben Nevis (1,343m / 4,406ft).

c. 400 million Scotland lies 20° south of the Equator. Collisions of the crustal plates cause cracks or fault lines (e.g. the Great Glen). Highland Boundary Fault (Firth of Clyde to Stonehaven) and Southern Upland Fault (Stranraer to Dunbar) form boundaries of a great central rift valley into which Old Red Sandstone, debris from Caledonian Mountains to the north, pours for 50 million years. Widespread volcanic activity, especially in what is now Central Lowlands, producing Ochil Hills, Pentland Hills, also Glencoe.

340 million Arthur's Seat (251m/833ft), in Edinburgh, Scotland's best preserved extinct volcano, active. The igneous rocks of this area, a mixture of lavas and granite, extend to the Cheviot Hills on the English border.

350–300 million Carboniferous period: Scotland lies at Equator. Volcanic activity ceases; warm seawater floods central rift valley. Tropical swamps and deltas result, laying down rock types which give rise to limestone, coal, oil-shale and ironstone. East and north of the Caledonian Mountains, sedimentary Old Red Sandstone, deposited in shallow seas, is eventually uplifted, producing the sandstone lowlands of the Moray Firth area, Caithness and Orkney. Erosion after this uplift can now be seen in cliffs and sea stacks, e.g. the Old Man of Hoy.

300–200 million Permian and Triassic periods: New Red Sandstone formed. Much of this is now under water, notably under the North Sea, providing the basis for North Sea oil reserves.

70–50 million Jurassic period: American and European continents begin to pull apart; faults develop, forming the North Atlantic. Major volcanic upheaval affects Inner Hebrides, parts of Argyll and Arran. Extensive lava flows from massive volcanoes bury the older rocks; there is further faulting and uplift. Ben More (966m/ 3,169ft), the highest mountain on Mull, consists entirely of lava. Lava flows result in the contorted landscape of northern Skye. Erosion of these volcanic rocks produces the gabbro of the Cuillin ridge, Skye. Small Isles also a product of volcanic activity.

from 50 million Scotland gradually attains its present shape.

from 3 million Three periods of glaciation occur, each lasting thousands of years. Scotland's ice-cap is centred in the Grampians. Intense glaciation produces the characteristic U-shaped valleys, some filled with water (e.g. Loch Lomond). Glacial erosion can also be seen in the mountain areas as corries and troughs, and in the lowlands and plateaux. Large areas of Lewis and Sutherland are moulded down into the characteristic knob and lochan terrain. Lowland areas accumulate layers of glacial deposits, such as those on which Glasgow is built.

c. 10,000 End of the Ice Age: glacial deposits result in the white sands found on Barra, the Uists and parts of the west coast. As the ice recedes, the sea-level rises, leading to formation of the fjord-like coastline of western Scotland; post-glacial drowning in Shetland produces a similar effect.

8,000 to present Human activity, e.g. deforestation, mining, quarrying, dumping, is the greatest cause of change in the shape and structure of the land.

CLIMATE

Scotland's temperate climate owes much to the warm ocean current known as the Gulf Stream. In the same latitude in the northern hemisphere, only the west coast of Canada, close to the border of Alaska, enjoys a similar climate. Pressure systems rolling in off the Atlantic control Scotland's climate, especially on the west coast, which is significantly wetter than the rest of the country, but milder in winter, due to the influence of the Gulf Stream. The climate of some of the Western Isles is sufficiently mild to allow introduced subtropical plant species to grow.

RAINFALL

Rainfall varies markedly from west to east across Scotland. The rugged scenic areas are very wet: the Western Highlands, especially around Loch Quoich, average 4000mm (157 inches) a year, falling on average over 250 days per annum. By contrast the east coast averages less than 800mm (31 inches) falling on an average of 175 days per annum, with Dunbar, at 555mm (22 inches), being the driest. It is the heavy rainfall which provides the natural resource for the generation of hydro-electricity. There is a marked seasonal variation in average monthly rainfall in the west of Scotland, the wettest months being September to January; this seasonal variation is less marked in the east. There is a much greater chance of enjoying dry, settled weather in spring and early summer.

The wettest day on record was 17 January 1974, when 238.4mm (9.39 inches) fell at Sloy Main Adit on Loch Lomond. A local storm produced 254mm (10 inches) in just over 24 hours at Cruadach on Loch Quoich in December 1954.

The most damaging floods in the last 200 years include the Moray floods of August 1829, when record levels were reached on the Spey and Dee. Massive floods occurred on 5-6 February 1989 in widespread storms from Loch Shin to Loch Lomond. Kinlochhourn registered 306mm (12.05 inches), the highest two-day total ever recorded in Britain. The floods of April 2000 caused millions of pounds of damage to parts of eastern Scotland, and more so to central Scotland and Edinburgh.

SUNSHINE

Monthly averages of mean daily sunshine show a strong bias in favour of late spring and early summer, especially on the west coast and the Western Isles, where May is the sunniest month of the year, closely followed by June. April on the west coast is often more sunny than July or August. The sunniest parts of Scotland are in Angus, Fife, the Lothians, Ayrshire, Dumfries and Galloway, and the western coastal fringes from the Uists to the Firth of Clyde and the Solway Firth. In any given year, Dunbar, on average, is the sunniest place in Scotland with 1,523 hours. The dullest parts of Scotland are the mountain regions of the Highlands, with an average of less than 1,100 hours of sunshine a year. The sunniest months on record were May 1946 and May 1975, when 329 hours of bright sunshine were registered at Tiree. Conversely, the dullest month on record was January 1983 with just 0.6 hours (36 minutes) recorded at Cape Wrath.

Scotland's relatively high latitude means that winter days are very short, but in compensation, summer days are long with extended twilight. Around the longest day of the year darkness is never complete in the north of Scotland. In Shetland this is called the 'simmer dim'. Lerwick has about four hours more daylight, including twilight, at mid-summer than London. The least sunshine in Britain is at Lochhranza on the Isle of Arran, where the south-east end of the village is in continuous shadow from 18 November to 8 February each year.

TEMPERATURE

In winter the temperature in Scotland is influenced by the surface temperature of the surrounding sea. The North Sea is cooler than the waters off the west coast, thus the temperature decrease across the country is from west to east. The average winter daytime maximum varies from 6.5 to 7.5 Celsius on the west coast to 5.5 to 6.0 Celsius on the east coast. At night, the average minimum temperature ranges from 1.5 to 2.5 Celsius on the west coast to a little below 0 Celsius over low ground in Central Scotland. The coldest nights occur when skies are clear, winds are light and there is a covering of snow on the ground. The lowest temperature reading recorded in Britain was −27.2 Celsius at Braemar in upper Deeside on 11 February 1895, repeated on 10 January 1982.

In spring, summer and autumn the effect of latitude on the heat received from the sun is a dominant factor; hence Scotland is cooler than England, with the greatest difference in the summer. The mid-summer daily maximum varies from 16 to 18 Celsius on the west coast to 19 Celsius in the east central highlands. The night minimum averages out at around 10-10.5 Celsius across the bulk of Scotland. The extreme south-west, Arran, southern Kintyre peninsula, and Mull and Islay, as well as the Berwick-on-Tweed area, are all about a degree warmer. There are few excessively hot days or nights. The hottest day in Scotland was at Dumfries on 2 July 1908, when the temperature soared to 32.8 Celsius. This temperature was equalled on a few other occasions between 1868 and 1908, namely at Selkirk, Swinton in Berwickshire and Stenton near Dunbar.

Warm or even hot weather can occur in inland Scotland, but it is often accompanied by a large daily range of temperature in the glens, especially in spring and early summer. Occasionally the temperature will fall below freezing at night and rise to the mid-twenties during the day. The greatest range of temperature in one day occurred at Tummel Bridge, Tayside on 9 May 1978. At night the temperature dipped to −7 Celsius, the following afternoon soaring to 22 Celsius giving a range of 29 degrees.

WIND

Many of the major Atlantic depressions pass close to or over Scotland, making strong winds and gales frequent. The windiest areas are the Western Isles, the north-west coast, Orkney and Shetland. Even in these extreme western and northern parts of Scotland the highest frequency of gales occurs during the winter months and prolonged spells of strong winds are unusual between May and August. An exceptional storm occurring during the second week of June 2000 gave the strongest summer winds for more than 30 years over much of the country.

A day with a gale is defined as one on which the mean wind speed at the standard measuring height of 10 metres above ground reaches a value of 34 knots (39 mph) or more over any period of 10 minutes during the 24 hours. The frequency of gales in a year varies from 4 at Glasgow to 47 in Lerwick. The gale of January 1968 was probably the most destructive, causing extensive damage especially to forestry plantations in west and central Scotland. The strongest gust recorded at a low-level site is 123 knots (142 mph) at Fraserburgh, Grampian on 13 February 1989. The strongest gust recorded at high-level is 150 knots (173 mph) at Cairngorm Automatic Weather Station on 20 March 1986.

The frequency of winds from different directions also varies with the seasons. Winds from an easterly component are much more frequent from April through early June than they are during the autumn and winter, when westerlies are predominant. The lowest barometric pressure measured in Britain is 925.5 millibars (27.33 inches) at Ochtertyre on 26 January 1884.

SNOW

The frequency of snow cover varies considerably from place to place and year to year. On low ground in the Western Isles and in most coastal areas of Scotland, snow lies on average for less than 10 days in a year. This increases to around 20 days in the north and north-east and up to 70 days inland at Braemar. Temperature generally falls with height, and rain which reaches the ground at low levels may fall as snow over high ground. As a result there is a marked increase with height in the number of days with snow falling and lying. Snow cover can exceed 100 days in the Cairngorm mountains.

The windiness of Scotland's winter months determines the pattern of snow cover. When snowfall is accompanied by strong winds the snow is mostly deposited on leeward slopes, exposed areas often being left bare. Natural hollows become filled to a considerable depth. It is the existence of these high-level corries which has enabled the development of the skiing industry in Scotland. It is rare for complete snow cover to persist for long except near the summits of the highest mountains. On average snow lies for six to seven months on the tops of Ben Nevis and Ben Macdui, but snow bed are even more persistent and many survive well into the summer, some semi-permanent and only disappear in very occasional summers. The oldest snow bed in Britain has persisted for 50 years, and is on Braeriach, the third highest mountain in Scotland.

VISIBILITY

In contrast to popular clichés about Scotland's mistiness, the general visibility over Scotland is very good. The greater part of the country is remote from the industrial and populous areas of Britain and continental Europe. Smoke fogs are now rare even in industrial areas of central Scotland, and the growing obsolescence of open fires for domestic heating has greatly reduced pollution.

Inland fogs on calm, clear nights usually clear quickly the following morning except possibly in the glens. When poor visibility occurs on or near the east coast or in the Northern Isles the cause is, more often than not, a sea fog from the North Sea known locally as haar. Haar occurs from time to time, mainly from April to September, often accompanied by glorious sunshine just a few miles inland. It is caused by warmer air flowing over colder sea, which causes evaporation from the sea surface.

Moist south-west winds can result in very low cloud which can be quite dense and reduce visibility to under 100 metres. The west is more prone to this type of fog, which tends to shroud all high ground in cloud and is a potential hazard to hillwalkers. One of the longest-lasting fogs in the world is at the summit of Ben Nevis, which is cloaked in low cloud for around 300 days a year.

THE HISTORICAL PERSPECTIVE

At a time when global warming is high on climatologists' agendas, there is ample historical and archaeological evidence that the changes in Scotland's climate observable today are not unique. Scotland has undergone, and is still undergoing, considerable climate change and variability.

There was a significant increase in warmth, for instance, from c. ad 800 to 1300, when the treeline and limits of cultivation were higher compared to today. Climatic upheavals towards the end of this period, including severe storms, flooding along low coasts, and droughts, affected vegetation and animals, and therefore also the lives of the people of Scotland. A protracted run of wet summers between 1313 and 1320 resulted in crop failure, starvation and disease.

A period of gradual cooling set in from the fourteenth century onward. The 1430s especially were noted for a series of extremely severe winters. The history of clan raids and cattle stealing from the Lowlands shows the impact of a deteriorating climate. During the 'Little Ice Age' of the 16th to 18th centuries, sea temperatures off the north and east coasts of Scotland were some 5°C cooler than today, and snow was permanent on the Cairngorms. Frosts, a short growing season and low summer temperatures resulted repeatedly in famine and loss of livestock, occurring with increasing frequency and severity. The 1740s witnessed probably the most severe winter weather on record.

The 19th and 20th-centuries have seen a gradual improvement in Scotland's climate, although with occasional regressions. The last decade of the 20th century witnessed a significant rise in average temperature and weather events, especially storms and flooding, have become more extreme.

THE FUTURE

What will be the impact and consequences of global warming on the climate of Scotland? In short, the climate is likely to become warmer, wetter and windier. An overall increase in world temperature would mean more moisture. Storms thrive on available moisture, hence Atlantic storms would become even more frequent and destructive. Increased storminess is likely to be accompanied by increased rainfall and the melting of the polar ice-cap will result in a rise in sea-level. As a result, flooding, including flooding of coastal areas, has been identified as one of the main impacts of climate change for Scotland. This has implications for the design standards of existing river flood prevention schemes.

LAND USE		

USES OF LAND

Percentage of total area

	Scotland	UK
Agricultural Land		
Crops and bare fallow	8	20
Grasses and rough grazing[1]	65	51
Other[2]	2	3
Forest and Woodland[3]	15	10
Urban land not otherwise specified[4]	11	15

1 Includes grasses over and under five years old, and sole right and common grazing
2 Set-aside and other land on agricultural holdings. Excludes woodland on agricultural holdings
3 Forestry Commission data; covers both private and state-owned land. Includes woodland on agricultural holdings
4 Land used for urban and other purposes, e.g. transport and recreation, and for non-agricultural, semi-natural environments, e.g. grouse moors, sand dunes, inland waters.
Source: The Stationery Office, Digest of Environmental Statistics 20, 1998 (Crown Copyright)

Much of Scotland is open hill and moorland; less than 30 per cent is developed farmland or woodland and only 11 per cent is urban land (1998 figures). The Caithness and Sutherland peatlands constitute Europe's largest area of blanket bog, extending over about 400,000 hectares. The following table gives the distribution of different kinds of land cover at the end of the 1980s.

SCOTLAND'S LAND COVER IN THE 1980s

Land cover	Area covered (%)
Grassland	28
Mire	23
Heather moorland	15
Arable land	11
Woodland	14
Fresh water	3
Built and bare ground	4
Bracken	2

Source: Adapted from E.C. Mackey, M.C. Shewry and G.J. Taylor, Land cover change in Scotland from the 1940s to the 1980s. TSO/SNH.

FORESTS AND FORESTRY

Forests and woodlands cover about 16 per cent of Scotland, and nearly half of these are less than 30 years old. While very little remains of Scotland's old broad-leaved woodland, large tracts of land have been taken over by productive and commercial forestry. One of the most visible, and most debated, current features of the Scottish landscape, particularly — but not exclusively — in the Highlands, is the presence of large swathes of non-native species of conifer. Although the practice of planting exotic conifer species had been pioneered in the nineteenth century by some landowners, much of this planting was introduced after the second world war. In particular the Dedication Scheme, aimed at restoring what was seen as the Highlands' lost fertility and at bringing employment to the region, allowed private landowners tax exemptions for timber production. More recently, in the 1980s, individual buyers from business and media circles acquired big tracts of northern Scotland and began planting conifers there, the choice of tree depending more on quick returns on investment than on use of native tree species. This loophole was closed by the 1988 Finance Act, and although quite a number of individuals and companies still invest heavily in forestry in Scotland, production-oriented forestry is now balanced by a concept and a policy driven by the twin concerns of conservation and access, the result of a recognition of the poor economic return to the community from the forest industry and pressure from environmentalists from the 1980s onward.

Scotland's state-owned forests are managed by the Forestry Commission, which is responsible for their production and amenities and also acts as an advisory and implementing body for UK government forestry policy towards both public and private sectors. Although its remit is UK-wide, the Commission is based in Edinburgh in recognition of the fact that Scotland accounts for about half the nation's publicly-owned forestry. Since 1992 the Commission has been reorganised into two units: Forest Enterprise, which is responsible for the management of state-owned forests, and the Forest Authority, which implements government policy on privately-owned woodland and carries out research. Privately-owned forestry also owes much to Forestry Commission expertise and financial assistance in the form of grants and tax incentives. Forestry is a major source of rural employment.

The Scottish Executive intends to restore or create a further 15,000 hectares (c. 37,000 acres) of native woodland by 2003.

LAND OWNERSHIP

In 1998 there were 1,500 private landowners in Scotland. Three per cent of Scotland's land area was covered by cities and towns; 12 per cent was owned by public bodies, such as the Forestry Commission. Among the institutional and individual private owners who account for the rest, the National Trust for Scotland is one of the

largest. The pattern of private ownership is dominated by fewer and larger landowners. In 1996:

50% of the 19 million acres in private ownership was owned by 608 people;
40% was owned by 283 people
30% was owned by 136 people
20% was owned by 58 people
10% was owned by 18 people.[1]

[1]Robin Callander, *How Scotland is owned.* Edinburgh: Canongate, 1997

THE TOP FIVE NON–PUBLIC LANDOWNERS IN SCOTLAND
- Buccleuch Estates Ltd
- National Trust for Scotland
- Blair Trust and Sarah Broughton
- Invercauld and Torloisk Trusts
- Alcan Highland Estates Ltd

Land changes hands faster in the Highlands than elsewhere in Scotland. Research carried out in 1983 showed that about 6 per cent of Highland estates changed hands every year compared with 2 per cent for the rest of Scotland, and only four estates had remained in the same hands for over a century. Estates are owned by individuals and entities other than individuals — joint owners, trusts, non-governmental organisations (NGOs) and companies, including investment forestry companies. Some owners are resident all year round and make a living from their estates; some use them as holiday homes; others, particularly owners of land under forestry, exploit them commercially but live elsewhere. Recent figures produced by Highland Council show that foreign owners now control 365,000 hectares (about 900,000 acres) in the Highlands, while other research suggests that overseas buyers now control as much as 18 per cent of all land in Scotland.

The agility of turnover has also been beneficial for the non-profit sector, whose holdings in Scotland have doubled in size since 1980 and are expected to double again by 2010. About 30 non-profit organisations, including 'green charities' such as the National Trust for Scotland (NTS), the John Muir Trust (JMT), the Royal Society for the Protection of Birds (RSPB) and the Scottish Wildlife Trust, own or lease about 21,800 hectares (about 540,000) acres in the Highlands. The RSPB now holds 30,358 hectares (75,015 acres) in the Highlands and Islands, compared to 16,000 hectares (nearly 40,000 acres) 10 years ago; while the John Muir Trust is now one of the biggest landowners on Skye. In spring 2000 JMT purchased 1,694 hectares (4,185 acres) including Ben Nevis, together with two neighbouring mountains and the upper Glen Nevis nature reserve, from the Fairfax-Lucy family, who had owned the land for the past 150 years.

At the same time, some crofting communities are acquiring the land on which they live and work. In 1993 the Assynt Crofters' Trust accomplished the first ever community buy-out of estate land in Scotland, and are now developing projects there to strengthen the local economy and conserve the environment. Following this pioneering example, Eigg, one of the small isles south of Skye, was sold in 1997 for £1.5 million to the Isle of Eigg Heritage Trust, which is jointly controlled by the island's 75 residents, Highland Council and Scottish Wildlife Trust. (Two other islands of the group, Rum and Canna, already belong to national conservation agencies.) In Knoydart, one of Scotland's most isolated inhabited peninsulas, crofters won control over the land they lived on in a community buy-out in 1998. Several other land takeovers or buy-outs by crofters or local trusts have occurred in the last few years. Scottish land reform legislation currently under way will be accompanied by the establishment of an £11 million Scottish Land Fund to aid local buy-outs.

ACCESS

With the growth in large-scale and mechanised agriculture and forestry, tourism, and the popularity of outdoor pursuits, public access to the countryside has become an increasingly urgent question, especially in the Highlands and other areas of great natural beauty. Changes in the pattern of land ownership are also generating more challenges to the long-standing but contested 'right to roam'.

A total of 9,315 miles (14,904 km) of known public rights of way in Scotland has been mapped by the Scottish Rights of Way Society (see below). However, only 3 per cent of this total has legally secure status as a public right of way. The status of much of the rest is open to challenge, and while many of these rights of way are well used and not at risk, many others are blocked, not in regular use, or not known about by the public. Little information is available about these routes, or about the extent of the network of other paths and tracks which are used by the public but which cannot be claimed as rights of way.

The government's commitment to access legislation followed publication in November 1998 of recommendations by the Access Forum and their endorsement by Scottish Natural Heritage. The January 1999 conclusions of the Land Reform Policy Group recognised the importance of public access to the countryside as part of the wider land reform agenda and the need for change in the current access arrangements in Scotland and for a law which would cover a right of responsible access to land for purposes of informal recreation and passage, on enclosed land as well as open ground and hills. Legislation for a right of access for informal recreation on all land and water in Scotland is therefore included in the forthcoming Land Reform Bill.

THE ACCESS FORUM

The creation of a multisectoral Access Forum was among the results of a review of access to the countryside carried out by SNH in 1994. The Forum brings together representative bodies for land management and public and private agencies with a role in facilitating open-air recreation and enjoyment in landscape and the countryside in Scotland. It aims to promote greater understanding of countryside access issues and improved arrangements for access, while minimising the impact of greater access on land management and conservation. The Forum does not attempt to resolve specific local access issues: its role is to foster debate and work towards solutions to the main problems at a general level. An early achievement was the agreement of a Concordat on Access to Scotland's Hills and Mountains. A separate group has been established to review arrangements for access over water.

The Scottish Rights of Way Society
Members of the Access Forum

Association of Deer Management Groups (L*)
Convention of Scottish Local Authorities (L & W)
Forestry Commission (L)
Mountaineering Council of Scotland (L)
National Farmers' Union of Scotland (L & W)
Ramblers' Association Scotland (L)
Scottish Countryside Activities Council (L)
Scottish Crofters' Union (L)
Scottish Landowners' Federation (L & W)
Scottish Natural Heritage (L & W)
Scottish Rights of Way Society (L)
Scottish Sports Association (L & W)
Sport Scotland (L & W)
Scottish Tourist Board (L & W)
Association of District Salmon Fisheries Board (W)
Royal Yachting Association Scotland (W)
Scottish Anglers' National Association (W)
Scottish Canoe Association (W)
Water Authorities (represented by East of Scotland Water Authority) (W)

* L = concerned with access over land; W = concerned with access over water

The Scottish Rights of Way Society is the successor to the Scottish Rights of Way and Recreation Society Ltd, formed in 1845 for the preservation, maintenance and defence of public rights of way in Scotland. It gives advice on matters relating to rights of way and, where practicable, seeks to secure the recognition of rights of way by agreement. It also signposts the major rights of way in Scotland and maintains a national Catalogue of Rights of Way.

LAND REFORM

Land reform in Scotland has been regarded as a high priority for the Scottish government since well before devolution. In preparation for the advent of the Scottish Parliament, a Land Reform Policy Group was set up in October 1997 to identify and assess proposals for reform in rural Scotland. The Group issued two consultation papers in 1998 and published its final recommendations in January 1999, setting out a comprehensive Land Reform Action Plan, covering ownership, tenure and access, which has been adopted by the Scottish Executive. This was followed by a White Paper in July 1999.

The Action Plan is an integrated package of legislative and non-legislative measures, which include:

(a) Legislation to reform and modernise existing property laws, including legislation to abolish the feudal system and to replace it with a system of outright ownership of land;

(b) Legislation on land reform, including legislation to allow time to assess the public interest when major properties change hands, giving a community the right to buy such land when it changes hands, and increasing powers of compulsory purchase in the public interest;

(c) Legislation on the countryside and natural heritage, including reform of access arrangements and creation of National Parks;

(d) Legislation on agricultural holdings, including provisions for more flexible tenancy arrangements, extension of the role of the Scottish Land Court and greater protection for tenants against eviction, legislation to permit wider diversification and part-time farming by farm tenants;

(e) Legislation on crofting, including legislation to give all crofting communities the right to buy their croft land, to allow the creation of new crofts and the extension of crofting to new areas, to devolve regulatory decisions to local bodies, to remove the link between crofting grants and agricultural production, and to clarify the law on crofter forestry;

(f) Non-legislative changes, e.g. increasing the involvement of local communities in the management of publicly-owned land, developing codes of good practice for rural land ownership and land use, and setting up a substantially enhanced lottery-funded Scottish Land Fund.

On 24 November 1999 it was announced that crofting 'right-to-buy' legislation (section E) would be brought forward and included in the Land Reform Bill (section B), instead of in a later Bill specifically on crofting.

The Scottish Executive produces periodic Progress Reports on the Action Plan.

• Key Progress on Legislation Since July 2000. The Abolition of Feudal Tenure (Scotland) Act (section A) was passed on 3 May 2000 (Royal Assent 9 June 2000) and is due to be enacted early in 2002.

• Consultation on the Draft Title Conditions (Scotland) Bill, which follows the Abolition of Feudal Tenure (Scotland) Act 2000, was launched on 1 May 2001. This Bill is intended to reform, modernise and simply the law relating to all conditions and burdens on land contained in title deeds.

• The Bill to reform leasehold casualties, introduced to Parliament on 11 May 2000; passed its second stage on 14 February 2001.

• The National Parks (Scotland) Act was passed by the Scottish Parliament on 5 July 2000 (Royal Assent 9 August 2000). The boundaries of the first National Park, Loch Lomond and Trossachs, were formally defined in June 2001 (see National Parks, p. 375).

• Consultation on the White Paper on agricultural holdings legislation (section D) was complete by February, and issuing of a draft Bill is planned for autumn 2001.

• The Draft Land Reform (Scotland) Bill (section B) was launched for consultation on 22 February 2001, with the intention of introducing the Bill to Parliament in September. The consultation period for the Bill was extended to 30 June 2001, owing in part to the difficulties created by the foot and mouth disease outbreak which began in late February. The Bill has three aims:

1. to establish the principle of a rights of responsible access to the countryside (land and inland water) for recreation and passage;

2. to support community ownership of sectors of the countryside;

3. to support crofting community ownership of sectors of the countryside (referring to Action Plan section E).

• Simultaneously with the Draft Land Reform Bill, the Draft Scottish Outdoor Access Code – Public access to the outdoors: rights and responsibilities, drawn up by Scottish Natural Heritage in consultation with the Access Forum, was published for consultation in parallel with the Bill.

Progress on Non-legislative Measures

A number of the non-legislative measures included in section F have now been achieved. Among them is the setting up of the Scottish New Opportunities Land Fund of £10.78 million to assist communities' right to buy. Community Land Units of Scottish Enterprise and Highlands & Islands Enterprise will administer this in 2001–2. The Fund was formally launched on 26 February 2001.

The Scottish Executive's codes of practice relating to land ownership and management were due to be published by 31 May 2001. It is expected that compliance with these codes will be made a precondition for agricultural subsidies and grant funding to forestry.

Commitments have also been forthcoming from a number of public bodies with landholdings to increasing local community involvement in the management of their land, and guidance on the use of existing compulsory purchase powers has been issued.

THE ENVIRONMENT

The UK government is committed to sustainable development under the terms of the 1992 Rio Declaration, and to meeting internationally agreed targets with regard to the reduction of greenhouse gases, improving air and water quality, protecting the sea, increasing and protecting forest and woodland areas, making energy savings, reducing and recycling waste, reducing empty housing, and so on. While these targets apply to Scotland as part of the UK, policy on sustainable development and the environment has been devolved to the Scottish Parliament and Executive, which is free to adopt a separate approach to sustainable development in accordance with Scottish circumstances and priorities.

SUSTAINABLE DEVELOPMENT

A series of policy documents dating from before devolution outline the Scottish government's approach to sustainable development. Down to earth: A Scottish perspective on sustainable development (February 1999) covers planning for sustainability in energy, industry, waste management, housing, transport, and other areas. Two strategic documents under the general title Scotland the sustainable?, published by the Secretary of State for Scotland's Advisory Group on Sustainable Development (March 1999) recommended the setting of objectives, activities, targets, and timescales, the establishment of a Sustainable Development Commission, and support for innovation in sustainable development initiatives, and laid out an action plan for the Scottish Parliament and Executive.

Since devolution, the Scottish Parliament and Executive have frequently reiterated this commitment to sustainable development. Rural Scotland is a particular priority. The rural areas of the country constitute 89 per cent of its landmass and 29 per cent of the population, and, despite a low population density of 0.21 persons per hectare, 29 per cent of employment. Twelve per cent of all rural Scottish employees are engaged in agriculture.

AVERAGE POPULATION DENSITY IN RURAL SCOTLAND, SCOTLAND AND THE EUROPEAN UNION

Rural Scotland	All Scotland	EU
0.21	0.66	1.1

Source: Scottish Executive, Rural Scotland: A new approach' appendix 1: A profile of rural Scotland. www.scotland.gov.uk/library2/doc15/rsna-07.asp

Rural Scotland: A new approach (May 2000) sets out the Scottish Executive's commitments as regards support for rural life and the natural environment and promotion of their sustainability. The Rural Stewardship Scheme, to be launched later in 2000, aims to promote a viable and environmentally friendly farming industry and support farmers' management of natural resources.

RESOURCES TO BE DEVOTED BY SE TO AGRI-ENVIRONMENT SCHEMES, 1999–2002

1999–2000	2000–2001	2001–2002
£18.9m	£20.2m	£21.5m

Source: Scottish Executive, Rural Scotland: A new approach', chap.5,'Sustaining and making the most of its natural and cultural heritage'.

Scottish Natural Heritage (SNH) and the Scottish Environment Protection Agency (SEPA) have a statutory duty to take sustainable development into account in all their overall environmental functions. SNH's budget has been increased from £39 million in 1999–2000 to £46.5 million in 2001–2002.

More generally, the Executive established in February 2000 a Ministerial Group on Sustainable Scotland, chaired by Sarah Boyack, the then Environment Minister, which would work with representatives of the business and environment sectors to identify practical ways of integrating sustainability considerations into areas such as waste, energy and transport.

In the European context, the Scottish Executive is committed, like the UK as a whole, to sustainable development as a principle underpinning its overall policies and programmes in the environmental, social and economic areas. A long-term strategic view is seen as vital, and sustainability is defined as being not only about the environment but also about social and economic progress. In line with the definition of sustainable development in the Treaty of Amsterdam (1997), the Scottish Executive's approach links the promotion of environmental sustainability firmly with its existing commitments to economic growth with social cohesion and inclusion. Environmental sustainability is being included together with economic growth and social cohesion in the ambit of European Structural Funds programmes for the period 2000–2006.

As elsewhere in the world, local government and organisations seek to promote sustainable development through the Local Agenda 21 programme, under which local authorities draw up a sustainable development strategy for their area, to protect and enhance the local environment while meeting social needs and promoting economic success. The programme is managed by the Local Agenda 21 Steering Group, made up of representatives from the Local Government Association, the Convention of Scottish Local Authorities, the Association of Local Authorities of Northern Ireland, the TUC, the Advisory Committee on Business and the Environment, the World-Wide Fund for Nature, and other organisations.

Although local authorities are under no statutory obligation to take part in Local Agenda 21, most local authorities are engaged in or committed to the programme, and have a Local Agenda 21 officer or responsible staff member. They can contribute to a wide variety of activities related to planning, transport, waste management and pollution control, an so on, depending on local circumstances and needs. There is also LA21 involvement in Local Biodiversity Action Plans, which aim to contribute to local public awareness of biodiversity issues and the contribution local action can make to preserving biodiversity at the national and global levels.

For Local Agenda 21 officers and contacts at each council, see Council Directory. The government web-site about sustainable development in Scotland is at Web: www.sustainable.scotland.gov.uk

Advisory Committee on Business and the Environment

Floor 6/E8, Ashdown House, 123 Victoria Street, London, SW1E 6DE (Tel: 020-7944 6278; Fax: 020-7944 6559;

E-mail: peter.brunt@defra.gsi.gov.uk;

Web: www.environment.detr.gov.uk/acbe/index.htm).

Chairman: C. Fay

Association of Salmon Fishery Boards

5A Lennox Street, Edinburgh, EH4 1QB (Tel: 0131-343 2433; Fax: 0131-332 2556;

E-mail: a.r.wallace@btinternet.com).

Director: A. Wallace

Improvement and Development Agency (Local Agenda 21)
Layden House, 76–78 Turnmill Street, London, EC1M 5LG (Tel: 020-7296 6599; Fax: 020-7296 6666; Web: www.ida.gov.uk).
Chief Executive: Mr. Mel Usher

Inspector of Salmon and Freshwater Fisheries
Pentland House, 47 Robb's Loan, Edinburgh, EH14 1TY (Tel: 0131-244 6227; Fax: 0131-244 6313; E-mail: david.dunkley@scotland.gsi.gov.uk; Web: www.scotland.gov.uk).
Inspector: D. A. Dunkley

Scottish Executive Sustainable Development Team
1-H Bridge, Victoria Quay, Edinburgh, EH6 6QQ (Tel: 0131-244 7311; Fax: 0131-244 0195; E-mail: sustainable@scotland.gov.uk; Web: www.sustainable.scotland.gov.uk).
Team Leader: G. Pearson

UK Biodiversity Group
DETR, First Floor, Temple Quay House, 2 The Square, Temple Quay, Bristol, BS1 6EB (Tel: 0117-372 8974; Web: www.ukbap.org.uk).
Secretariat: J. Robbins

ENVIRONMENTAL PROTECTION AND CONSERVATION

THE CHANGING COUNTRYSIDE

Particularly in the Highlands, changes in land ownership and use over the past 50 years have been far-reaching. Among the factors involved are grazing pressure from greatly increased numbers of sheep and deer, the loss of land around lochs and rivers to hydro-electric schemes, the rapid expansion of commercial forestry, and a growing tendency for land to be purchased by new owners who are not experienced in the sustainable management of rural and forested estates.

The process of change on the land in Scotland is practically as old as its human habitation. There is evidence that much forest was cleared in prehistoric times as the first farming communities became established. Up to the early 18th century, agricultural life was dominated by seasonal farming cycles. Change accelerated sharply particularly after the suppression of the Jacobite rebellion of 1745, with the disintegration of the old clan society, a marked growth in population (not fully offset at first by emigration), and most of all by agricultural improvement and the introduction of sheep farming into the Highlands, aimed at pacifying the Highlands and exploiting them economically. Also, throughout the late eighteenth, nineteenth, and early twentieth centuries, much of the Highlands was developed and managed by large landowners as productive forests and sporting estates, including deer forests,[1] grouse moors, and angling reaches.

Later, the development of hydro-electric schemes from the 1930s required the damming of rivers, resulting in increases in the area of lochs and reducing the grazing land available to both domestic animals and deer.

The Hill Farming Act of 1946 and subsequent legislation on agriculture ensured subsidies that underpinned the hill farming sector until the UK joined the European Economic Community (now the European Union) in 1973 and British agriculture of all kinds became subject to the European Common Agricultural Policy. These developments have further shaped patterns of land use across Scotland. The new legislation currently in progress will constitute the next landmark in the shaping of Scotland's countryside.

[1] Since the Middle Ages, the word 'forest' has been used in Scotland to describe a hunting reserve, especially of deer. A deer forest does not necessarily contain trees.

SCOTTISH NATURAL HERITAGE

Scottish Natural Heritage (SNH) is the government's statutory adviser on the conservation and enhancement of Scotland's natural heritage and on its enjoyment and understanding by the public. It was formed in 1992 under the Natural Heritage (Scotland) Act of 1991, through a merger of the Countryside Commission for Scotland with the Nature Conservancy Council for Scotland. As well as its advisory function to government and others, it carries out certain executive tasks on behalf of government, working in partnership with a range of other bodies in conservation and sustainable management projects in environmentally fragile areas of Scotland, particularly focusing on Sites of Special Scientific Interest. It is involved in managing the Natura 2000 programme. SNH also engages extensively in environmental education activities.

NATURAL HERITAGE DESIGNATIONS

Natural heritage designations are given to areas of land or water which it is considered important to preserve or manage sensitively in the interests of scientific knowledge, preservation of flora or fauna, or enhancement of the natural landscape. There is no strict definition of a designation, and they cover a very wide variety of landscape and conservation scenarios. Designated areas can be of many different sizes, again according to the situation they address. Nowadays designated land is being managed more frequently in the context of a working countryside, laying emphasis on sustainability and a harmonious interaction between human intervention and natural processes rather than on preservation for its own sake.

The system of designations has evolved over about 50 years according to perceived need. Some, but by no means all, are supported by Acts of Parliament: this will be the case, for instance, with Scottish National Parks. Since designation also tends to respond to particular conservation needs, such as the protection of a specific kind of landscape or of particular flora or fauna, a single area of land or water may have more than one designation. National designations can also overlap with European designations or those emanating from international conventions.

Scottish Natural Heritage is the principal body responsible for implementing the provisions of different natural heritage designations, but several other public and non-governmental bodies, including local authorities, the Forestry Commission/Forest Enterprise, the National Trust for Scotland, Historic Scotland, the Royal Society for the Protection of Birds and other wildlife protection organisations, and the John Muir Trust, also own, lease or manage extensive areas in the interests of conserving and promoting Scotland's natural or cultural heritage.

NATIONAL PARKS

Legislation setting the framework for National Parks in Scotland was introduced to the Scottish Parliament on 27 March 2000. The National Parks (Scotland) Act was passed by the Scottish Parliament on 5 July 2000 and received Royal assent on 9 August 2000. It sets out the framework for all future National Parks in Scotland. It identifies the aims of National Parks to:

* conserve and enhance the natural and cultural heritage of the area;
* promote sustainable use of the natural resources of the area;
* promote understanding and enjoyment (including enjoyment in the form of recreation) of the special qualities of the area by the public;
* promote sustainable economic and social development of the area's communities.

On 19 September 2000 Scottish ministers made a formal proposal under the National Parks (Scotland) Act 2000 to establish parks in the Loch Lomond and Trossachs area and the Cairngorms. The initial consultation on the proposed Loch Lomond and Trossachs National Park closed on 9 February 2001 and a series of public meetings followed. To aid the process a consultation document was produced which outlined the whole process as well as offering options for the development of the park. On 11 June 2001 the extent of the park and its management were announced. The park will extend as far south as Balloch and Dunoon, west to just beyond Lochgoilhead, north to Tyndrum, and east to Callander, including the Cowal Peninsula and the Argyll Forest Park. It is expected to be up and running in 2002.

Public consultation concerning the proposed Cairngorms National Park took place until 30th April 2001. Scottish Natural Heritage (SNH), as reporter to Government, then embarked on a consultation exercise designed to discover the public's views on key issues including the area the designation should cover, the make-up of the governing board, its powers and the Park's name. This is expected to be completed autumn 2001. After receiving SNH's advice, ministers will prepare a draft Designation Order and consult further. The Scottish Parliament will then consider the draft Designation Order, expected around March 2002. If all this runs smoothly a

Park Authority could be established and the Cairngorms National Park could become operational in 2003.

SITES OF SPECIAL SCIENTIFIC INTEREST (SSSIs)

Sites of Special Scientific Interest (SSSI) is a legal notification applied to land which Scottish Natural Heritage (SNH) identifies as being of special interest because of its flora, fauna, geological or physiographical features. As well as land they can include rivers, freshwater areas, and inter-tidal areas, including mudflats, as far as the mean low water of spring tides. In some cases, SSSIs are managed as nature reserves.

SNH must notify the designation of a SSSI to the local planning authority, every owner/occupier of the land, and the Scottish Executive. Forestry and agricultural departments and a number of other bodies are also informed of this notification.

Objections to the notification of a SSSI are delat with by the appropriate regional board or the main board of SNH, depending on the nature of the objection. Unresolved objections on scientific grounds must be referred to the Advisory Committee for SSSI. The protection of these sites depends on the co-operation of individual landowners and occupiers. Owner/occupiers must consult SNH and gain written consent before they can undertake certain listed activities on the site. Funds are available through management agreements and grants to assist owners and occupiers in conserving sites' interests. As a last resort a site can be purchased.

At 31 March 1999 there were 1,448 SSSIs in Scotland with an area of 919,597 ha/2,272,324 acres, almost 12 per cent of the country. Many large sites are in the north and west of the country; the largest complex, in the Flow Country of Caithness and Sutherland, totalling over 150,000 hectares (370,650 acres).

The forthcoming Land Reform Bill includes legislation to revise the SSSI system; part of the aim of this is to make the arrangements for SSSIs more user-friendly and involve local communities more in their management. SNH is already increasingly entering into agreements with landowners to manage SSSIs on their land positively in addition to their normal practices.

In early March 2001, the Scottish Executive published its proposals to improve the protection of SSSIs and combat 'wildlife crime'. The Wildlife and Countryside Act 2001 had already introduced tougher wildlife protection laws in England and Wales, and the environment minister, Sam Galbraith, launched a range of proposed measures under the title The Nature of Scotland. These include giving Scottish police the power of arrest in cases of suspected wildlife crime and allowing courts the discretion to impose jail sentences in such cases. Other proposals are aimed at encouraging farmers and other land managers to enter into conservation contracts based on payments for positive action to care for SSSIs. The proposals have been welcomed by the Royal Society for the Protection of Birds and also, cautiously, by the National Farmers' Union of Scotland.

NATIONAL NATURE RESERVES (NNRs)

National Nature Reserves are defined in the National Parks and Access to the Countryside Act 1949 and the Wildlife and Countryside Act 1981 as land designated for the study and preservation of flora and fauna, or of geological or physiographical features. They have four main functions:

- habitat management, such as fencing, controlled grazing by sheep, and tree-planting;
- research;
- historical and other interpretation of the landscape;
- access and amenity.

SNH allows access to all reserves provided this is compatible with the wildlife conservation interests of the area. In practice this means that there is open public access to most NNRs.

SNH can designate as a NNR land which is being managed as a nature reserve under an agreement with one of the statutory nature conservation agencies. This arrangement applies to 67 per cent of the current NNRs. NNRs may also be designated on land already held and managed by SNH 30 per cent or land held and managed as a nature reserve by another approved body. SNH can make by-laws to protect reserves from undesirable activities, subject to confirmation by the SE.

There are 71 NNRs in Scotland, occupying 114,277 hectares/282,378 acres, about 1.4 per cent of the country. All NNRs are also SSSIs. They cover a wide range of habitats:

Habitat	Percentage of total NNRs
Uplands	68
Coastlands	12
Woodlands	10
Peatlands	6
Open water	3
Lowlands	1

Scotland was the first part of Britain to acquire an NNR, with the designation of Beinn Eighe (4,758 ha/11,757 acres) in Wester Ross in 1951. The largest NNR in Scotland and indeed the whole of Britain is the Cairngorms National Nature Reserve (25,949ha/64,120 acres). Other well-known NNRs are Ben Lawers, Isle of Rum, Creag Meagaidh, Spey Valley, Loch Lomond, Inverpolly (north of Ullapool), and Sands of Forvie (north of Aberdeen).

NATIONAL NATURE RESERVES

National Nature Reserve	SSSI within which the Nature Reserve lies	Local Authority	Area (ha)
Abernethy Forest	Abernethy (inc. Dell Woods)	Highland	2,296
Achanarras Quarry	Achanarras Quarry	Highland	43
Allt Nan Carnan	Allt Nan Carnan	Highland	7
Ariundle Oakwood	Ariundle	Highland	70
Beinn Eighe	Beinn Eighe	Highland	4,758
Ben Lawers	Ben Lawers	Perthshire and Kinross	4,035
Ben Lui	Ben Lui	Argyll and Bute/Stirling	2,104
Ben Wyvis	Ben Wyvis	Highland	5,673
Blar Nam Faoileag	Blar Nam Faoileag	Highland	2,126
Blawhorn Moss	Blawhorn Moss	West Lothian	69
Braehead Moss	Braehead Moss	South Lanarkshire	87
Caenlochan	Caenlochan	Angus	1,680
Caerlaverock	Upper Solway Flats & Marshes	Dumfries and Galloway	7,706
Cairngorms	Cairngorms	Highland/Aberdeenshire/Moray	25,949
Cairnsmore of Fleet	Cairnsmore of Fleet	Dumfries and Galloway	1,922
Claish Moss	Claish Moss	Highland	563
Clyde Valley Woodlands	Cartland Craigs	South Lanarkshire	51
	Cleghorn Glen	South Lanarkshire	
Corrieshalloch Gorge	Corrieshalloch Gorge	Highland	5
Cragbank Wood	Cragbank & Wolfhopelee Woods	Scottish Borders	9
Craigellachie	Craigellachie	Highland	257
Creag Meagaidh	Creag Meagaidh	Highland	3,948
Den of Airlie	Den of Airlie	Angus/Perthshire and Kinross	87
Dinnet Oakwood	Dinnet Oakwood	Aberdeenshire	13
Dunnet Links	Dunnet Links	Highland	465
Eilean Na Muice Duibhe	Eilean Na Muice Duibhe	Argyll and Bute	360
Flanders Moss	Flanders Moss	Stirling	210
Forvie	Sands of Forvie & Ythan Estuary	Aberdeenshire	973
Glasdrum Wood	Glasdrum	Argyll and Bute	169
Glen Diomhan	Arran Northern Mountains	North Ayrshire	10
Glen Nant	Glen Nant	Argyll and Bute	59
Glen Roy	Parallel Roads of Lochaber	Highland	1,168
Glen Tanar	Glen Tanar	Aberdeenshire	4,185
Glencripesdale	Glencripesdale	Highland	609
Gualin	Foinaven	Highland	2,522
Hermaness	Hermaness	Shetland Isles Council	964
Inchnadamph	Ben More Assynt	Highland	1,295
Invernaver	Invernaver	Highland	552
Inverpolly	Inverpolly	Highland	10,857
Isle of May	Isle of May	Fife	57
Keen of Hamar	Keen of Hamar	Shetland Isles Council	30
Kirkconnell Flow	Kirkconnell Flow	Dumfries and Galloway	142
Loch a'Mhuilinn	Loch a'Mhuilinn	Highland	67
Loch Druidibeg	Loch Druidibeg	Western Isles	1,677
Loch Fleet	Loch Fleet	Highland	1,058
Loch Leven	Loch Leven	Perthshire and Kinross	1,597

National Nature Reserve	SSSI within which the Nature Reserve lies	Local Authority	Area (ha)
Loch Lomond	Aber Bog, Gartocharn Bog & Bell Moss Endrick Mouth & Islands	WestDumbarton/Stirling WestDumbarton	428
Loch Maree Islands	Loch Maree	Highland	200
Mealdarroch	Tarbert to Skipness Coast	Argyll and Bute	205
Milton Wood	Milton Wood	Perthshire and Kinross	24
Moine Mhor	Moine Mhor	Argyll and Bute	493
Monach Isles	Monach Isles	Western Isles	577
Morrone Birkwood	Morrone Birkwood	Aberdeenshire	225
Morton Lochs	Morton Lochs	Fife	24
Mound Alderwoods	Mound Alderwoods	Highland	267
Muir of Dinnet	Muir of Dinnet	Aberdeenshire	1,415
Nigg and Udale Bays	Cromarty Firth	Highland	640
North Rona and Sula Sgeir	North Rona and Sula Sgeir	Western Isles	130
Noss	Noss	Shetland Isles Council	313
Rannoch Moor	Rannoch Moor	Perthshire and Kinross	1,499
Rassal Ashwood	Rassal	Highland	85
Rum	Rum	Highland	10,684
St Abb's Head	St Abb's Head to Fast Castle Head	Scottish Borders	77
St Cyrus	St Cyrus & Kinnaber Links	Aberdeenshire	92
St Kilda	St Kilda	Western Isles	853
Silver Flowe	Merrick Kells	Dumfries and Galloway	191
Strathfarrar	Glen Strathfarrar	Highland	2,189
Strathy Bogs	Strathy Bogs	Highland	281
Taynish	Taynish Woods	Argyll and Bute	362
Tentsmuir Point	Tayport Tentsmuir Coast	Fife	515
Tynron Juniper Wood	Tynron Juniper Wood	Dumfries and Galloway	5
Whitlaw Mosses	Whitlaw Mosses	Scottish Borders	19
		TOTAL:	**114,277**

NATIONAL SCENIC AREAS (NSAs)

National Scenic Areas have a broadly equivalent status to the Areas of Outstanding Natural Beauty in England and Wales. They were identified by the Countryside Commission for Scotland (now part of SNH) and introduced by the government under town and country planning legislation in 1980. The NSA is the main landscape designation in Scotland and is unique to Scotland. At mid-1999 there were 40 of these, covering a total area of 1,001,800 hectares (2,475,448 acres).

National Scenic Areas would continue to exist after the designation of National Parks. A review is in progress to determine whether any areas should be added to or removed from the current list.

Development within National Scenic Areas is dealt with by the local planning authority, which is required to consult Scottish Natural Heritage concerning certain categories of development. Land management uses can also be modified in the interest of scenic conservation.

Assynt-Coigach (Highland), 90,200 ha/222,884 acres

Ben Nevis and Glen Coe (Highland/Argyll and Bute/Perth and Kinross), 101,600 ha/251,053 acres

Cairngorm Mountains (Highland/ Aberdeenshire/Moray), 67,200 ha/166,051 acres

Cuillin Hills (Highland), 21,900 ha/54,115 acres

Deeside and Lochnagar (Aberdeenshire/Angus), 40,000 ha/98,840 acres

Dornoch Firth (Highland), 7,500 ha/18,532 acres

East Stewartry Coast (Dumfries and Galloway), 4,500 ha/11,119 acres

Eildon and Leaderfoot (Scottish Borders), 3,600 ha/8,896 acres

Fleet Valley (Dumfries and Galloway), 5,300 ha/ 13,096 acres

Glen Affric (Highland), 19,300 ha/47,690 acres

Glen Strathfarrar (Highland), 3,800 ha/9,390 acres

Hoy and West Mainland (Orkney Islands), 14,800 ha/36,571 acres

Jura (Argyll and Bute), 21,800 ha/53,868 acres

Kintail (Highland), 15,500 ha/38,300 acres

Knapdale (Argyll and Bute), 19,800 ha/48,926 acres

Knoydart (Highland), 39,500 ha/97,604 acres

Kyle of Tongue (Highland), 18,500 ha/45,713 acres

Kyles of Bute (Argyll and Bute), 4,400 ha/ 10,872 acres

Loch na Keal, Mull (Argyll and Bute), 12,700 ha/ 31,382 acres

Loch Lomond (Argyll and Bute/Stirling/West Dunbartonshire), 27,400 ha/67,705 acres

Loch Rannoch and Glen Lyon (Perth and Kinross/Stirling), 48,400 ha/119,596 acres

Loch Shiel (Highland), 13,400 ha/33,111 acres

Loch Tummel (Perth and Kinross), 9,200 ha/ 22,733 acres

Lynn of Lorn (Argyll and Bute), 4,800 ha/ 11,861 acres

Morar, Moidart and Ardnamurchan (Highland), 13,500 ha/33,358 acres

North-west Sutherland (Highland), 20,500 ha/ 50,655 acres

Nith Estuary (Dumfries and Galloway), 9,300 ha/ 22,980 acres

North Arran (North Ayrshire), 23,800 ha/ 58,810 acres

River Earn (Perth and Kinross), 3,000 ha/7,413 acres

River Tay (Perth and Kinross), 5,600 ha/13,838 acres

St Kilda (Western Isles), 900 ha/2,224 acres

Scarba, Lunga and the Garvellachs (Argyll and Bute), 1,900 ha/4,695 acres

Shetland (Shetland Islands), 11,600 ha/28,664 acres

Small Isles (Highland), 15,500 ha/38,300 acres

South Lewis, Harris and North Uist (Western Isles), 109,600 ha/270,822 acres

South Uist Machair (Western Isles), 6,100 ha/ 15,073 acres

The Trossachs (Stirling), 4,600 ha/11,367 acres

Trotternish (Highland), 5,000 ha/12,355 acres

Upper Tweeddale (Scottish Borders), 10,500 ha/ 25,945 acres

Wester Ross (Highland), 145,300 ha/359,036 acres

LOCAL NATURE RESERVES (LNRs)

The 1949 National Parks and Access to the Countryside Act gives local authorities the power to designate local nature reserves, where they own or lease the land and have an agreement with the landowner. They are managed in consultation with SNH. Conservation trusts can also own and manage non-statutory LNRs. LNRs have an educational as well as a conservation purpose and should have facilities to enable people both to enjoy and to understand them.

The acquisition in June 2000 of two new LNRs in Dundee brings the total number of LNRs in Scotland to 33, covering a total of about 9,343 hectares (23,086 acres). Many LNRs are located in or on the edge of cities, for instance Kincorth Hill, Aberdeen, and Corstorphine Hill, Edinburgh; but large areas of countryside such as Findhorn Bay in Moray, Wigtown Bay, Dumfries and Galloway, and Montrose Basin, Angus, are also LNRs.

Other designations which local authorities can make are:

• Regional Parks: large areas, principally in private ownership and not dedicated exclusively to conservation, landscape or heritage purposes, but where initatives can be taken by local authorities to increase informal recreation land uses. There are four Regional Parks in Scotland, of between 6,500 and 44,000 hectares: Clyde–Muirsheil, Fife, the Pentland Hills, and Loch Lomond;

• Country Parks: also in multiple use, though here recreation is the main use of the land. Close to, or within, urban areas and smaller than Regional Parks (40–600 hectares), they are mostly owned and managed by local authorities. There are 36 in Scotland.

LOCAL NATURE RESERVES		
Local Nature Reserve	Unitary Authority	Area (ha)
Aberlady Bay	East Lothian	582.0
Arnhall Moss	Aberdeenshire	9.6
Balquidderock Wood	Stirling	6.0
Birnie and Gaddon Lochs, Collessie	Fife	28.2
Bishop Loch	Glasgow City	24.3
Broughty Ferry	Dundee City	3.9

Local Nature Reserve	Unitary Authority	Area (ha)
Castle & Hightae Lochs	Dumfries & Galloway	109.4
Corstophine Hill	Edinburgh	67.3
Coul Den, Glenrothes	Fife	10.7
Coves Community Park	Inverclyde	44.0
Den of Maidencraig	Aberdeen City	15.0
Donmouth	Aberdeen City	36.0
Duchess Wood	Argyll & Bute	22.0
Dumbreck Marsh	North Lanarkshire	18.6
Eden Estuary	Fife	891.0
Findhorn Bay	Moray	1,200.0
Gartmorn Dam	Clackmannan	44.0
Hermitage of Braid/ Blackford Hill	Edinburgh	59.4
Hogganfield Park	Glasgow City	46.0
Inner Tay	Dundee City	1,176.0
Jennys Well	Renfrewshire	6.0
Kincorth Hill	Aberdeen City	41.0
Langlands Moss	South Lanarkshire	20.0
Montrose Basin	Angus	1,024.0
Mull Head	Orkney	243.5
Paisley Moss	Renfrewshire	4.0
Perchy Pond	North Lanarkshire	40.7
Scotstown Moor	Aberdeen City	34.0
Straiton Pond	Midlothian	5.2
Torry Bay	Fife	683.0
Trottick Mill Ponds	Dundee City	3.0
Waters of Philorth	Aberdeenshire	0.3
Wigtown Bay	Dumfries & Galloway	2,844.7
TOTAL		9,342.8

FOREST NATURE RESERVES (FNRs)

Forest Enterprise (an executive agency of the Forestry Commission) is responsible for the management of the Commission's forests. It has created 46 Forest Nature Reserves with the aim of protecting and conserving special forms of natural habitat, flora and fauna. There are about 300 SSSIs on the estates, some of which are also Nature Reserves.

Forest Nature Reserves extend in size from under 50 hectares (124 acres) to over 500 hectares (1,236 acres). Several of the largest are in Scotland, including the Black Wood of Rannoch, by Loch Rannoch; Culbin Forest, near Forres; Glen Affric, near Fort Augustus; Kylerhea, Isle of Skye; and Starr Forest, in Galloway Forest Park.

Other forest areas managed by the Forestry Commission are:

- Forest Parks: large tracts of Forestry Commission land, often containing areas of scenic importance, and managed by Forestry Enterrpise as multi-purpose forestry. The first Forest Park in Britain was in Scotland, Argyll Forest Park, established 1935;
- Caledonian Forest Reserves: like FNRs, established by Forestry Enterprise as representing the best of the Forestry Commission's conservation areas. There are 18 of these, covering 16,000 hectares of native oak and pine woods in the Highlands;
- Woodland Parks: smaller versions of Forest Parks, usually located nearer to population centres.

FOREST NATURE RESERVES

The following list of Forest Nature reserves described as being the very best of their kind has been supplied by the Forestry Commission and derives from a much bigger list, space for which is precluded here.

Black Burn – nr Hawick. Wetlands. Scottish small reed, fibrous tussock sedge

Black Wood of Rannoch – Loch Rannoch. Native pinewood. Insects, fungi, lichens, otter, pine marten

Culbin Forest – near Forres. Pine forest on sand dunes. Red squirrel; capercaillie; osprey

Eilean Ruairidh Mor – Loch Awe. Semi-natural oakwood, 42 lichens, 67 plants, butterflies

Glenan – nr Tighnabruaich. Range of habitats – coastal, woodland, moorland. Nightjar, bryophytes

Glen Affric – nr Fort Augustus. Native pinewood. Pine marten, diver, dragonflies

Glen Nant – nr Taynuilt. Native deciduous woodland. 151 mosses, lichens, 175 moths and butterflies

Knockman Wood – nr Newton Stewart. Semi-natural oakwood. Fallow deer, butterflies, barn owl; 126 lichens

Kylerhea – Skye. Ancient birchwood, ashwood, oakwood. Otter, seal, golden eagle

Leiterfearn – nr Fort Augustus. Ashwood, hazel coppice. Loch flora, butterflies

Lochaber Loch – nr Dumfries. Ancient oak coppice. Loch flora, butterflies

Loch Lomond Oakwood – Loch Lomond. Ancient broadleaved woods. Wood warbler, pied flycatcher

Redmyre – nr Auchtermuchty. Loch with rich flora including slender sedge; bats

Retreat Wood – nr Castle Douglas. Oald oaks, epiphyte flora, redstart

Ryovan Pass – nr Aviemore. Caledonian pine; red deer, roe deer, wildcat

Starr Forest – Galloway Forest Park. Forest lochs. Black-throated diver, peregrine falcon, golden eagle

MARINE RESERVES

There is statutory provision for Marine Nature Reserves analogous to NNRs, covering the management of marine sites in British waters, but it has never been used in Scotland.

However, SNH has published a list of possible marine Special Areas for Conservation under the EC Habitats Directive, which identifies certain marine species found in Scottish waters as rare, endangered or vulnerable. Consultation on these possible sites is in progress.

ENVIRONMENTALLY SENSITIVE AREAS (ESAs)

Ten large areas of Scotland, totalling 1.4 million hectares in area, are designated under the Agriculture Act 1986 as Environmentally Sensitive Areas. These are areas where traditional farming practices have been important in maintaining the conservation, landscape or heritage aspects of the land. Farmers and crofters living in these areas can qualify for agricultural support payments, which enable them to manage their land in environmentally sensitive ways and contribute to maintaining features of natural of cultural heritage, including improving public access. The scheme is managed by the Scottish Executive.

EUROPEAN UNION NATURAL HERITAGE DESIGNATIONS

Two pieces of EU legislation in particular apply to the conservation of the natural environment in Scotland:

- Council Directive 92/43/EEC on the conservation of natural habitats and of wild fauna and flora, commonly known as the EC Habitats Directive (1992);
- Council Directive 79/409/EEC on the conservation of wild birds, commonly known as the EC Birds Directive (1979).

The implementation of these two Directives was brought into UK law by the Conservation (Natural Habitats, & c.) Regulations (1994).

SPECIAL AREAS OF CONSERVATION (SACs)

SACs are areas designated to safeguard rare or endangered fauna and flora under the terms of the EC Habitats Directive. SACs on land are normally also SSSIs.

In June 2000 the then Scottish Environment Minister, Sarah Boyack, announced that 90 possible candidate SACs (CSACs) had been identified, including Cape Wrath, Fair Isle, the Monadhliath mountains, and the Sound of Barra. Following consultation and the selection of a definitive list, these will be proposed to the European Commission for SAC status.

In January 2001, the list of CSACs to be submitted to the European Commission was extended to include the Cairngorms. The Cairngorm CSAC covers seven SSSIs: Abernethy Forest, Cairngorms, Eastern Cairngorms, Glenmore Forest, Inchrory, North Rothiemurchas Pinewood and the Northern Corries. The area contains a high diversity of habits and species of European importance, including high-altitude plant communities, bog woodland, alpine and boreal heaths and native Scots pine forests. The area is also important to the Scottish otter population. The area of the CSAC is likely to coincide to a considerable extent with that of the proposed Cairngorms National Park.

SPECIAL PROTECTION AREAS (SPAs)

SPAs are land and marine sites devoted to the protection of birds under the terms of the EC Wild Birds Directive. Following the publication in July 1999 of selection guidelines for SPAs by the Joint Nature Conservation Committees, the Scottish Executive has developed a programme to classify appropriate sites as SPAs. SPAs on land are normally also SSSIs.

In May 2000 SPA status was announced for three areas providing habitat for some of Scotland's most important birds: an extension to Glenmore Forest in the existing Cairngorms SPA (Scottish crossbill, capercaillie); Fiacaill a' Choire

Chais, to the west of the Cairn Gorm summit (dotterel and various raptors); and Loch Urigill and six other lochs around Inverpolly NNR in south-west Sutherland (black-throated diver). These new sites bring the total number of Scottish SPAs to 117.

NATURA 2000

The Habitats Directive introduced the idea of 'Natura 2000', symbolising the conservation of precious natural resources into the new millennium; and this name has been given to a European network consisting of SACs and SPAs, aiming to maintain rare, endangered or vulnerable species and conserve their habitats throughout Europe.

INTERNATIONAL CONVENTIONS

The UK is party to a number of international conventions protecting wildlife and its habitats including:
- the Ramsar Convention on Wetlands of International Importance (ratified 1976)
- the Bonn Convention on the Conservation of Migratory Species of Wild Animals (ratified 1979)
- the Bern Convention on the Conservation of European Wildlife and Natural Habitats (ratified 1972)
- the Convention on Trade in Endangered Species of Wild Fauna and Flora (CITES) (ratified 1975)

WORLD HERITAGE SITES

These are areas of outstanding natural or cultural value identified and listed by the World Heritage Committee of UNESCO under the Convention on World Cultural and Natural Heritage (1972). They may be urban or rural.

St Kilda is listed as a World Heritage Site. It was the first such site awarded in Scotland and the first for a wildlife area in Britain.

Edinburgh Old and New Towns were accorded World Heritage Site status in 1995. The Heart of Neolithic Orkney is also a World Heritage Site.

WILDLIFE CONSERVATION

The Wildlife and Countryside Act 1981 gives legal protection to a wide range of wild animals and plants. Subject to parliamentary approval, the Secretary of State for the Environment, Transport and the Regions may vary the animals and plants given legal protection. The most recent variation of Schedules 5 and 8 came into effect in March and April 1998.

Under Section 9 and Schedule 5 of the Act it is illegal without a licence to kill, injure, take, possess or sell any of the listed animals (whether alive or dead) and to disturb its place of shelter and protection or to destroy that place.

Under Section 13 and Schedule 8 of the Act it is illegal without a licence to pick, uproot, sell or destroy any of the listed plants and, unless authorised, to uproot any wild plant.

The Act lays down a close season for wild birds (other than game birds) from 1 February to 31 August inclusive, each year. Exceptions to these dates are made for:

Capercaillie – 1 February to 30 September

Snipe – 1 February to 11 August

Wild Duck and Wild Goose (below high water mark) – 21 February to 31 August

Birds which may be killed or taken in Scotland outside the close season (except on Sundays and on Christmas Day) are the above-named, plus coot, certain wild duck (gadwall, goldeneye, mallard, pintail, pochard, shoveler, teal, tufted duck, wigeon), certain wild geese (Canada, greylag, pink-footed), moorhen, golden plover and woodcock.

Certain wild birds may be killed or taken subject to the conditions of a general licence at any time by authorised persons: crow, collared dove, gull (great and lesser black-backed or herring), jackdaw, jay, magpie, pigeon (feral or wood), rook, sparrow (house) and starling. Conditions usually apply where the birds pose a threat to agriculture, public health, air safety, other bird species, and to prevent the spread of disease.

All other British birds are fully protected by law throughout the year.

A Private Member's Bill on the protection of wild mammals, seeking to ban hunting of wild mammals with dogs, has been introduced to the Scottish Parliament. An independent report commissioned by the Scottish Executive, assessing the possible economic impacts of this

Bill on fox hunting with hounds and on gamekeepers employed on Scottish sporting estates, was published on 26 June 2000.

PROTECTED SPECIES

The lists below contain details of protected species of bird, animal and plant in the UK. Degrees of protection for certain species are determined statutorily. For further information please contact Scottish Natural Heritage.

BIRDS

(At All Times)

Common name	Scientific name
Avocet	*Recurvirostra avosetta*
Bee-eater	*Merops apiaster*
Bittern	*Botaurus stellaris*
Bittern, Little	*Ixobrychus minutus*
Bluethroat	*Luscinia svecica*
Brambling	*Fringilla montifringilla*
Bunting, Cirl	*Emberisa cirlus*
Bunting, Lapland	*Calcarius lapponicus*
Bunting, Snow	*Plectrophenax nivalis*
Buzzard, Honey	*Pernis apivorus*
Chough	*Pyrrhocorax pyrrhocorax*
Corncrake	*Crex crex*
Crake, Spotted	*Porzana porzana*
Crossbills (all species)	*Loxia*
Curlew, Stone	*Burhinus oedicnemus*
Divers (all species)	*Gavia*
Dotterel	*Charadrius morinellus*
Duck, Long-tailed	*Clangula hyemalis*
Eagle, Golden	*Aquila chrysaetos*
Eagle, White-tailed	*Haliaetus albicilla*
Falcon, Gyr	*Falco rusticolus*
Fieldfare	*Turdus pilaris*
Firecrest	*Regulus ignicapillus*
Garganey	*Anas querquedula*
Godwit, Black-tailed	*Limosa limosa*
Goshawk	*Accipiter gentilis*
Grebe, Black-necked	*Podiceps nigricollis*
Grebe, Slavonian	*Podiceps auritus*
Greenshank	*Tringa nebularia*
Gull, Little	*Larus minutus*
Gull, Mediterranean	*Larus melanocephalus*
Harriers (all species)	*Circus*
Heron, Purple	*Ardea purpurea*
Hobby	*Falco subbuteo*
Hoopoe	*Upupa epops*
Kingfisher	*Alcedo atthis*
Kite, Red	*Milvus milvus*
Merlin	*Falco columbarius*
Oriole, Golden	*Oriolus oriolus*
Osprey	*Pandion haliaetus*
Owl, Barn	*Tyto alba*
Owl, Snowy	*Nyctea scandiaca*
Peregrine	*Falco peregrinus*
Petrel, Leach's	*Oceanodroma leucorhoa*
Phalarope, Red-necked	*Phalaropus lobatus*
Plover, Kentish	*Charadrius alexandrinus*
Plover, Little Ringed	*Charadrius dubius*
Quail, Common	*Coturnix coturnix*
Redstart, Black	*Phoenicurus ochruros*
Redwing	*Turdus iliacus*
Rosefinch, Scarlet	*Carpodacus erythrinus*
Ruff	*Philomachus pugnax*
Sandpiper, Green	*Tringa ochropus*
Sandpiper, Purple	*Calidris maritima*
Sandpiper, Wood	*Tringa glareola*
Scaup	*Aythya marila*
Scoter, Common	*Melanitta nigra*
Scoter, Velvet	*Melanitta fusca*
Serin	*Serinus serinus*
Shorelark	*Eremophila alpestris*
Shrike, Red-backed	*Lanius collurio*
Spoonbill	*Platalea leucorodia*
Stilt, Black-winged	*Himantopus himantopus*
Stint, Temminck's	*Calidris temminckii*
Swan, Bewick's	*Cygnus bewickii*
Swan, Whooper	*Cygnus cygnus*
Tern, Black	*Chlidonias niger*
Tern, Little	*Sterna albifrons*
Tern, Roseate	*Sterna dougallii*
Tit, Bearded	*Panurus biarmicus*
Tit, Crested	*Parus cristatus*
Treecreeper, Short-toed	*Certhia brachydactyla*
Warbler, Cetti's	*Cettia cetti*
Warbler, Dartford	*Sylvia undata*
Warbler, Marsh	*Acrocephalus palustris*
Warbler, Savi's	*Locustella luscinioides*
Whimbrel	*Numenius phaeopus*
Woodlark	*Lullula arborea*
Wryneck	*Jynx torquilla*

(During the Close Season)

Common name	Scientific name
Goldeneye	*Bucephala clangula*
Goose, Greylag (in Outer Hebrides, Caithness, Sutherland and Wester Ross only)	*Anser anser*
Pintail	*Anas acuta*

ANIMALS

Common name	Scientific name
Adder	*Vipera berus*
Anemone, Ivell's Sea	*Edwardsia ivelli*
Anemone, Startlet Sea	*Nematosella vectensis*
Apus	*Triops cancriformis*

Bats, Horseshoe (all species)	*Rhinolophidae*
Bats, Typical (all species)	*Vespertilionidae*
Beetle	*Graphoderus zonatus*
Beetle	*Hypebaeus flavipes*
Beetle	*Paracymus aeneus*
Beetle, Lesser Silver Water	*Hydrochara caraboides*
Beetle, Mire Pill	*Curimopsis nigrita*
Beetle, Rainbow Leaf	*Chrysolina cerealis*
Beetle, Stag	*Lucanus cervus*
Beetle, Violet Click	*Limoniscus violaceus*
Burbot	*Lota lota*
Butterfly, Northern Brown Argus	*Aricia artaxerxes*
Butterfly, Adonis Blue	*Lysandra bellargus*
Butterfly, Chalkhill Blue	*Lysandra coridon*
Butterfly, Large Blue	*Maculinea arion*
Butterfly, Silver-studded Blue	*Plebejus argus*
Butterfly, Small Blue	*Cupido minimus*
Butterfly, Large Copper	*Lycaena dispar*
Butterfly, Purple Emperor	*Apatura iris*
Butterfly, Duke of Burgundy Fritillary	*Hamearis lucina*
Butterfly, Glanville Fritillary	*Melitaea cinxia*
Butterfly, Heath Fritillary	*Mellicta athalia* (otherwise known as *Melitaea athalia)*
Butterfly, High Brown Fritillary	*Argynnis adippe*
Butterfly, Marsh Fritillary	*Eurodryas aurinia*
Butterfly, Pearl-bordered Fritillary	*Boloria euphrosyne*
Butterfly, Black Hairstreak	*Strymonidia pruni*
Butterfly, Brown Hairstreak	*Thecla betulae*
Butterfly, White Letter Hairstreak	*Stymonida w-album*
Butterfly, Large Heath	*Coenonympha tullia*
Butterfly, Mountain Ringlet	*Erebia epiphron*
Butterfly, Chequered Skipper	*Carterocephalus palaemon*
Butterfly, Lulworth Skipper	*Thymelicus acteon*
Butterfly, Silver Spotted Skipper	*Hesperia comma*
Butterfly, Swallowtail	*Papilio machaon*
Butterfly, Large Tortoiseshell	*Nymphalis polychloros*

Butterfly, Wood White	*Leptidea sinapis*
Cat, Wild	*Felis silvestris*
Cicada, New Forest	*Cicadetta montana*
Crayfish, Atlantic Stream	*Austropotamobius pallipes*
Cricket, Field	*Gryllus campestris*
Cricket, Mole	*Gryllotalpa gryllotalpa*
Damselfly, Southern	*Coenagrion mercuriale*
Dolphin (all species)	*Cetacea*
Dormouse	*Muscardinus avellanarius*
Dragonfly, Norfolk Aeshna	*Aeshna isosceles*
Frog, Common	*Rana temporaria*
Goby, Couch's	*Gobius couchii*
Goby, Giant	Gobius cobitis
Grasshopper, Wart-biter	*Decticus verrucivorus*
Hatchet Shell, Northern	*Thyasira gouldi*
Hydroid, Marine	*Clavopsella navis*
Lagoon Snail	*Paludinella littorina*
Lagoon Snail, De Folin's	*Caecum armoricum*
Lagoon Worm, Tentacled	*Alkmaria romijni*
Leech, Medicinal	*Hirudo medicinalis*
Lisard, Sand	*Lacerta agilis*
Lisard, Viviparous	*Lacerta vivipara*
Marten, Pine	*Martes martes*
Moth, Barberry Carpet	*Pareulype berberata*
Moth, Black-veined	*Siona lineata* (otherwise known as *Idaea lineata)*
Moth, Essex Emerald	*Thetidia smaragdaria*
Moth, Fiery Clearwing	*Bembecia chrysidiformis*
Moth, Fisher's Estuarine	*Gortyna borelii*
Moth, New Forest Burnet	*Zygaena viciae*
Moth, Reddish Buff	*Acosmetia caliginosa*
Moth, Sussex Emerald	*Thalera fimbrialis*
Mussell, Fan	*Atrina fragilis*
Mussell, Freshwater Pearl	*Margaritifera margaritifera*
Newt, Great Crested (otherwise known as Warty newt)	*Triturus cristatus*
Newt, Palmate	*Triturus helveticus*
Newt, Smooth	*Triturus vulgaris*
Otter, Common	*Lutra lutra*
Porpoise (all species)	*Cetacea*
Sandworm, Lagoon	*Armandia cirrhosa*
Sea Fan, Pink	*Eunicella verrucosa*
Sea Mat, Trembling	*Victorella pavida*
Sea Slug, Lagoon	*Tenellia adspersa*
Shad, Allis	*Alosa alosa*
Shad, Twaite	*Alosa fallax*
Shark, Basking	*Cetorhinus maximus*
Shrimp, Fairy	*Chirocephalus diaphanus*
Shrimp, Lagoon Sand	*Gammarus insensibilis*

Slow-worm	*Anguis fragilis*
Snail, Glutinous	*Myxas glutinosa*
Snail, Sandbowl	*Catinella arenaria*
Snake, Grass	*Natrix helvetica (otherrwise known as Natrix natrix)*
Snake, Smooth	*Coronella austriaca*
Spider, Fen Raft	*Dolomedes plantarius*
Spider, Ladybird	*Eresus niger*
Squirrel, Red	*Sciurus vulgaris*
Sturgeon	*Acipenser sturio*
Toad, Common	*Bufo bufo*
Toad, Natterjack	*Bufo calamita*
Turtles, Marine (all species)	*Dermochelyidae and Cheloniidae*
Vendace	*Coregonus albula*
Vole, Water	*Arvicola terrestris*
Walrus	*Odobenus rosmarus*
Whale (all species)	*Cetacea*
Whitefish	*Coregonus lavaretus*

PLANTS

Common name	**Scientific name**
Adder's-tongue, Least	*Ophioglossum lusitanicum*
Alison, Small	*Alyssum alyssoides*
Anomodon, Long-leaved	*Anomodon longifolius*
Beech-lichen, New Forest	*Enterographa elaborata*
Blackwort	*Southbya nigrella*
Bluebell	*Hyacinthoides non-scripta*
Bolete, Royal	*Boletus regius*
Broomrape, Bedstraw	*Orobanche caryophyllacea*
Broomrape, Oxtongue	*Orobanche loricata*
Broomrape, Thistle	*Orobanche reticulata*
Cabbage, Lundy	*Rhynchosinapis wrightii*
Calamint, Wood	*Calamintha sylvatica*
Caloplaca, Snow	*Caloplaca nivalis*
Catapyrenium, Tree	*Catapyrenium psoromoides*
Catchfly, Alpine	*Lychnis alpina*
Catillaria, Laurer's	*Catellaria laureri*
Centaury, Slender	*Centaurium tenuiflorum*
Cinquefoil, Rock	*Potentilla rupestris*
Cladonia, Convoluted	*Cladonia convoluta*
Cladonia, Upright Mountain	*Cladonia stricta*
Clary, Meadow	*Salvia pratensis*
Club-rush, Triangular	*Scirpus triquetrus*
Colt's-foot, Purple	*Homogyne alpina*
Cotoneaster, Wild	*Cotoneaster integerrimus*
Cottongrass, Slender	*Eriophorum gracile*
Cow-wheat, Field	*Melampyrum arvense*
Crocus, Sand	*Romulea columnae*
Crystalwort, Lisard	*Riccia bifurca*

Cudweed, Broad-leaved	*Filago pyramidata*
Cudweed, Jersey	*Gnaphalium luteoalbum*
Cudweed, Red-tipped	*Filago lutescens*
Cut-grass	*Leersia oryzoides*
Deptford Pink (in respect of England and Wales only)	*Dianthus armeria*
Diapensia	*Diapensia lapponica*
Dock, Shore	*Rumex rupestris*
Earwort, Marsh	*Jamesoniella undulifolia*
Eryngo, Field	*Eryngium campestre*
Feather-moss, Polar	*Hygrohypnum polare*
Fern, Dickie's Bladder	*Cystopteris dickieana*
Fern, Killarney	*Trichomanes speciosum*
Flapwort, Norfolk	*Lieocolea rutheana*
Fleabane, Alpine	*Erigeron borealis*
Fleabane, Small	*Pulicaria vulgaris*
Fleawort, South Stack	*Tephroseris integrifolia (ssp maritima)*
Frostwort, Pointed	*Gymnomitrion apiculatum*
Fungus, Hedgehog	*Hericium erinaceum*
Galingale, Brown	*Cyperus fuscus*
Gentian, Alpine	*Gentiana nivalis*
Gentian, Dune	*Gentianella uliginosa*
Gentian, Early	*Gentianella anglica*
Gentian, Fringed	*Gentianella ciliata*
Gentian, Spring	*Gentiana verna*
Germander, Cut-leaved	*Teucrium botrys*
Germander, Water	*Teucrium scordium*
Gladiolus, Wild	*Gladiolus illyricus*
Goblin Lights	*Catolechia wahlenbergii*
Goosefoot, Stinking	*Chenopodium vulvaria*
Grass-poly	*Lythrum hyssopifolia*
Grimmia, Blunt-leaved	*Grimmia unicolor*
Gyalecta, Elm	*Gyalecta ulmi*
Hare's-ear, Sickle-leaved	*Bupleurum falcatum*
Hare's-ear, Small	*Bupleurum baldense*
Hawk's-beard, Stinking	*Crepis foetida*
Hawkweed, Northroe	*Hieracium northroense*
Hawkweed, Shetland	*Hieracium zetlandicum*
Hawkweed, Weak-leaved	*Hieracium attenuatifolium*
Heath, Blue	*Phyllodoce caerulea*
Helleborine, Red	*Cephalanthera rubra*
Helleborine, Young's	*Epipactis youngiana*
Horsetail, Branched	*Equisetum ramosissimum*
Hound's-tongue, Green	*Cynoglossum germanicum*
Knawel, Perennial	*Scleranthus perennis*
Knotgrass, Sea	*Polygonum maritimum*
Lady's-slipper	*Cypripedium calceolus*
Lecanactis, Churchyard	*Lecanactis hemisphaerica*
Lecanora, Tarn	*Lecanora archariana*

Lecidea, Copper — *Lecidea inops*
Leek, Round-headed — *Allium sphaerocephalon*
Lettuce, Least — *Lactuca saligna*
Lichen, Arctic Kidney — *Nephroma arcticum*
Lichen, Ciliate Strap — *Heterodermia leucomelos*
Lichen, Coralloid Rosette — *Heterodermia propagulifera*
Lichen, Ear-lobed Dog — *Peltigera lepidophora*
Lichen, Forked Hair — *Bryoria furcellata*
Lichen, Golden Hair — *Teloschistes flavicans*
Lichen, Orange Fruited Elm — *Caloplaca luteoalba*
Lichen, River Jelly — *Collema dichotomum*
Lichen, Scaly Breck — *Squamarina lentigera*
Lichen, Stary Breck — *Buellia asterella*
Lily, Snowden — *Lloydia serotina*
Liverwort — *Petallophyllum ralfsi*
Liverwort, Lindenberg's Leafy — *Adelanthus lindenbergianus*
Marsh-mallow, Rough — *Althaea hirsuta*
Marshwort, Creeping — *Apium repens*
Milk-Parsley, Cambridge — *Selinum carvifolia*
Moss — *Drepanocladius vernicosus*
Moss, Alpine Copper — *Mielichoferia mielichoferi*
Moss, Baltic Bog — *Sphagnum balticum*
Moss, Blue Dew — *Saelania glaucescens*
Moss, Blunt-leaved Bristle — *Orthotrichum obtusifolium*
Moss, Bright Green Cave — *Cyclodictyon laetevirens*
Moss, Cordate Beard — *Barbula cordata*
Moss, Cornish Path — *Ditrichum cornubicum*
Moss, Derbyshire Feather — *Thamnobryum angustifolium*
Moss, Dune Thread — *Bryum mamillatum*
Moss, Flamingo — *Desmatodon cernuus*
Moss, Glaucous Beard — *Barbula glauca*
Moss, Green Shield — *Buxbaumia viridis*
Moss, Hair Silk — *Plagiothecium piliferum*
Moss, Knothole — *Zygodon forsteri*
Moss, Large Yellow Feather — *Scorpidium turgescens*
Moss, Millimetre — *Micromitrium tenerum*
Moss, Multifruited River — *Cryphaea lamyana*
Moss, Nowell's Limestone — *Zygodon gracilis*
Moss, Rigid Apple — *Bartramia stricta*
Moss, Round-leaved Feather — *Rhyncostegium rotundifolium*
Moss, Schleicher's Thread — *Bryum schleicheri*
Moss, Triangular Pygmy — *Acaulon triquetrum*

Moss, Vaucher's Feather — *Hypnum vaucheri*
Mudwort, Welsh — *Limosella australis*
Naiad, Holly-leaved — *Najas marina*
Naiad, Slender — *Najas flexilis*
Orache, Stalked — *Halimione pedunculata*
Orchid, Early Spider — *Ophrys sphegodes*
Orchid, Fen — *Liparis loeselii*
Orchid, Ghost — *Epipogium aphyllum*
Orchid, Lapland Marsh — *Dactylorhisa lapponica*
Orchid, Late Spider — *Ophrys fuciflora*
Orchid, Lisard — *Himantoglossum hircinum*
Orchid, Military — *Orchis militaris*
Orchid, Monkey — *Orchis simia*
Pannaria, Caledonia — *Pannaria ignobilis*
Parmelia, New Forest — *Parmelia minarum*
Parmentaria, Oil Stain — *Parmentaria chilensis*
Pear, Plymouth — *Pyrus cordata*
Penny-cress, Perfoliate — *Thlaspi perfoliatum*
Pennyroyal — *Mentha pulegium*
Pertusaria, Alpine Moss — *Pertusaria bryontha*
Physcia, Southern Grey — *Physcia tribacioides*
Pigmyweed — *Crassula aquatica*
Pine, Ground — *Ajuga chamaepitys*
Pink, Cheddar — *Dianthus gratianopolitanus*
Pink, Childling — *Petroraghia nanteuilii*
Plantain, Floating Water — *Luronium natans*
Polypore, Oak — *Buglossoporus pulvinus*
Pseudocyphellaria, Ragged — *Pseudocyphellaria lacerata*
Psora, Rusty Alpine — *Psora rubiformis*
Puffball, Sandy Stilt — *Battarraea phalloides*
Ragwort, Fen — *Senecio paludosus*
Ramping-fumitory, Martin's — *Fumaria martinii*
Rampion, Spiked — *Phyteuma spicatum*
Restharrow, Small — *Ononis reclinata*
Rock-cress, Alpine — *Arabis alpina*
Rock-cress, Bristol — *Arabis stricta*
Rustworth, Western — *Marsupella profunda*
Sandwort, Norwegian — *Arenaria norvegica*
Sandwort, Teesdale — *Minuartia stricta*
Saxifrage, Drooping — *Saxifraga cernua*
Saxifrage, Marsh — *Saxifraga hirculus*
Saxifrage, Tufted — *Saxifraga cespitosa*
Solenopsora, Serpentine — *Solenopsora liparina*
Solomon's-seal, Whorled — *Polygonatum verticillatum*
Sow-thistle, Alpine — *Cicerbita alpina*
Spearwort, Adder's-tongue — *Ranunculus ophioglossifolius*
Speedwell, Fingered — *Veronica triphyllos*
Speedwell, Spiked — *Veronica spicata*

Spike-rush, Dwarf	*Eleocharis parvula*
Stack Fleawort, South: (see above under Fleawort, South Stack)	
Star-of-Bethlehem, Early	*Gagea bohemica*
Starfruit	*Damasonium alisma*
Stonewort, Bearded	*Chara canescens*
Stonewort, Foxtail	*Lamprothamnium papulosum*
Strapwort	*Corrigiola litoralis*
Sulphur-tresses, Alpine	*Alectoria ochroleuca*
Threadmoss, Long-leaved	*Bryum neodamense*
Turpswort	*Geocalyx graveolens*
Violet, Fen	*Viola persicifolia*
Viper's-grass	*Scorzonera humilis*
Water-plantain, Ribbon leaved	*Alisma gramineum*
Wood-sedge, Starved	*Carex depauperata*
Woodsia, Alpine	*Woodsia alpina*
Woodsia, Oblong	*Woodsia ilvensis*
Wormwood, Field	*Artemisia campestris*
Woundwort, Downy	*Stachys germanica*
Woundwort, Limestone	*Stachys alpina*
Yellow-rattle, Greater	*Rhinanthus serotinus*

CLOSE SEASONS AND RESTRICTIONS ON GAME

Shooting game or hares at night is prohibited, with certain exceptions. Although there are no legal restrictions, it is not customary to kill game on a Sunday or Christmas Day. If shooting is to take place on a Sunday, it should begin after noon.

All dates are inclusive.

GAME BIRDS

Black game (heathfowl)	11 December to 19 August
Grouse (muirfowl)	11 December to 11 August
Partridge	2 February to 31 August
Pheasant	2 February to 30 September
Ptarmigan	11 December to 11 August

HUNTING AND GROUND GAME

There is no statutory close time for fox-hunting or rabbit-shooting, nor for hares. However, under the Hares Preservation Act 1892 the sale of hares (except imported ones) or leverets in Great Britain is prohibited from 1 March to 31 July inclusive. The recognised date for the opening of the fox-hunting season is 1 November, and it continues until the following April.

DEER

The statutory close seasons for deer are:

Fallow deer

Male	1 May to 31 July
Female	16 February to 20 October

Red deer

Male	21 October to 30 June
Female	16 February to 20 October

Roe deer

Male	21 October to 31 March
Female	1 April to 20 October

Sika Deer

Male	21 October to 30 June
Female	16 February to 20 October

Red/Sika Hybrids

Male	21 October to 20 June
Female	16 February to 20 October

ANGLING

Brown Trout

The statutory close time for fishing for brown trout is from 7 October to 14 March inclusive.

Salmon

The Scottish Parliament is responsible for the regulation of salmon fishing, through the Scottish Executive Rural Affairs Department. Local management is devolved to district salmon and fishery boards. The annual close time for salmon fishing in each salmon fishery is set by law. District salmon fishery boards may apply to change the annual close time for their district. Weekly close time for nets is 6 p.m. on Friday to 6 a.m. on Monday. Weekly close time for salmon angling is Sunday. Details of regulations may be obtained from the Inspector of Salmon and Freshwater Fisheries.

Inspector of Salmon and Freshwater Fisheries

Pentland House, 47 Robb's Loan, Edinburgh EH14 1TY (Tel: 0131-244 6227; Fax: 0131-244 6313)

Association of District Salmon Fishery Boards

5A Lennox Street, Edinburgh EH4 1QB
(Tel: 0131-343 2433)

Sea Trout

The regulations on fishing for sea trout are the same as those on fishing for salmon.

Coarse Fishing

The Scottish Parliament is responsible for the regulation of coarse fishing, through the Scottish Executive Rural Affairs Department.Information may be obtained from the Inspector of Salmon and Freshwater Fisheries.

Licences

No licence is required to fish in Scotland. In the case of salmon fishing, a person must have a legal right to fish or written permission from a person having such right. To fish for freshwater fish, including trout, permission should be obtained from the riparian owner. Where a protection order is in force, it is an offence to fish for freshwater fish in inland waters without a permit.

THE PEOPLE

POPULATION

The first official census of population in Great Britain was taken in 1801 and a census has been taken every ten years since, except in 1941 when there was no census because of war. The last official census took place in April 2001 but its results were not available at the time of going to press. In 1999, the population of Scotland was just over 5 million: this is compared to around 4.4 million in 1900.

CENSUS RESULTS (SCOTLAND) 1801–1991

	Total	Male	Female
1801	1,608,000	739,000	869,000
1811	1,806,000	826,000	980,000
1821	2,092,000	983,000	1,109,000
1831	2,364,000	1,114,000	1,250,000
1841	2,620,000	1,242,000	1,378,000
1851	2,889,000	1,376,000	1,513,000
1861	3,062,000	1,450,000	1,612,000
1871	3,360,000	1,603,000	1,757,000
1881	3,736,000	1,799,000	1,936,000
1891	4,026,000	1,943,000	2,083,000
1901	4,472,000	2,174,000	2,298,000
1911	4,761,000	2,309,000	2,452,000
1921	4,882,000	2,348,000	2,535,000
1931	4,843,000	2,326,000	2,517,000
1951	5,096,000	2,434,000	2,662,000
1961	5,179,000	2,483,000	2,697,000
1971	5,229,000	2,515,000	2,714,000
1981	5,131,000	2,466,000	2,664,000
1991	4,998,567	2,391,961	2,606,606

ESTIMATED POPULATION BY SEX AND AGE, SCOTLAND, 1999

Age	Persons	Males	Females
All ages	5,119,200	2,485,648	2,633,522
0-14	946,010	484,272	461,738
15-29	1,000,401	509,469	490,932
30-44	1,187,063	591,535	595,528
45-59	942,136	462,371	479,765
60-74	698,823	318,838	379,985
75 and over	344,767	119,163	225,604

General Register Office for Scotland, Crown Copyright 2000

POPULATION SUMMARY, SCOTLAND AND OTHER COUNTRIES, 1998

	Population (millions)	Male life expectancy at birth (years)	Female life expectancy at birth (years)	Persons aged under 15 as % of total population	Persons aged 65-79 as % of total population	Numbers and rates
Scotland	5.1	72.6	78.1	19	12	39
EU	376.4	74.1	80.5	17	12	24
Austria	8.1	74.2	80.5	17	12	29
Belgium	10.2	73.8	80.5	18	13	15
Denmark	5.3	73.1	78.2	18	11	46
Eire	3.8	73.3	78.7	23	9	27
Finland	5.2	73.3	80.3	19	11	37
France	59.2	74.2	82.1	19	11	37
Germany	82.2	73.7	80.0	16	12	39
Greece	10.5	75.1	81.4	16	13	3
Italy	57.7	74.9	81.3	15	13	8
Luxembourg	0.4	73.5	79.6	19	11	17
Netherlands	15.9	74.7	80.3	18	10	19
Portugal	10.0	71.4	78.7	17	12	20
Spain	39.4	74.4	81.6	16	13	11
Sweden	8.9	76.7	81.8	19	13	54
UK	59.6	74.3	79.5	19	12	37
US	278.4	72.8	79.5	22[1]	10[1]	32
Japan	126.7	76.8	83.2	15[1]	12[1]	n/a

Source: General Register Office for Scotland, Eurostat, United Nations
[1] 1997 Figures

PROJECTED POPULATION 2001–21 (MID-YEAR)

Age	2001	2011	2021
0-14	924,000	837,000	801,000
15-29	975,000	959,000	877,000
30-44	1,195,000	1,008,000	905,000
45-59	967,000	1,100,000	1,085,000
60-74	695,000	778,000	902,000
75+	351,000	375,000	423,000
Total	5,107,000	5,057,000	4,993,000

Source: The Stationery Office, Annual Report of the Registrar-General for Scotland 1997 (Crown copyright)

POPULATION OF ETHNIC MINORITIES IN SCOTLAND 1999

Known ethnic group	LFS data 1999, Percentage (excluding unknowns)
White	98.4
Non-white	1.6
Black	0.2
Indian	0.2
Pakistani/Bangladeshi	0.6
Chinese	0.3
Other ethnic minorities	0.3
All	100

Source: Labour Force Survey, 1999 data

AVERAGE POPULATION DENSITY

The average density of population at the 1991 census was 0.65 persons per hectare. For population density by council area, see Council Directory.

BIRTHS

During the 20th century, there has been an overall reduction in the size of families, with fewer large families with many children. In 2000, there were just over 53 thousand births in Scotland, the lowest level since civil registration began in 1855. In 1999, 46.7 per cent of live births were to mothers aged over 30 and 15 per cent to mothers aged over 35, compared to 29 per cent in 1990.

LIVE BIRTHS, SCOTLAND 1989-2000

Year	All Live Births
1989	63,480
1990	65,973
1991	67,024
1992	65,789
1993	63,337
1994	61,656
1995	60,051
1996	59,296
1997	59,440
1998	57,319
1999	55,147
2000	53,076

Source: Registrar General for Scotland Annual Report, Crown Copyright 2001

ABORTIONS

A total of 12,080 legal pregnancy terminations were performed in Scotland in 1997 (an increase of about 9 per cent since 1990), of which women aged between 20 and 34 accounted for over half. The number of girls under 16 undergoing aboryions in 1997 was 289, 2.4 per cent of the total; but the percentage of under-16s undergoing abortions rose by 16 per cent between 1990 and 1997.

LEGAL ABORTIONS 1999
By age of mother, provisional

Under 16	251
16–19	2,630
20–34	7,704
35–44	1,536
45 and over	23
Total	12,144

p provisional
Source: The Stationery Office, Annual Abstract of Statistics 2001 (Crown copyright)

DEATHS

DEATH RATES (EXTRACT OF POPULATION AND MIGRATION)
Deaths per thousand population

	1988	1997	1998	UK
Males	12.3	11.4	11.4	10.3
Females	12.1	11.8	11.4	10.9

Sources: General Register Office for Scotland, Scottish Statistics 2000, Office of National Statistics

MARRIAGE AND DIVORCE

Year	Marriages		Divorces	
	No.	Rate*	No.	Rate*
1987	35,813	14.0	12,133	10.2
1988	35,599	14.0	11,472	9.8
1989	35,326	13.9	11,659	10.0
1990	34,672	13.6	12,272	10.5
1991	33,762	13.2	12,399	10.6
1992	35,057	13.7	12,479	10.8
1993	33,366	13.0	12,787	11.1
1994	31,480	12.3	13,133	11.5
1995	30,663	11.9	12,249	10.8
1996	30,242	11.8	12,308	10.9
1997	29,811	11.6	12,222	11.0
1998	29,668	11.6	12,384	11.2
1999	29,940	11.7	11,864	10.8

* Per 1,000 members of population.
Source: The Stationery Office, Annual Abstract of Statistics 2001 (Crown copyright)

RELIGIOUS

SCOTLAND

INTRODUCTION TO RELIGION IN SCOTLAND
INTER CHURCH AND FAITH CO-OPERATION
CHRISTIAN CHURCHES
NON-CHRISTIAN FAITHS
THE CHURCH OF SCOTLAND
THE SCOTTISH EPISCOPAL CHURCH
THE ROMAN CATHOLIC CHURCH
PRESBYTERIAN CHURCHES
OTHER CHURCHES

RELIGIOUS SCOTLAND

About 24 per cent of the population of Scotland (about 1.2 million people) professes active membership of a religious faith. Of this number, the overwhelming majority (92.9 per cent) is Christian (in the Trinitarian sense); 65 per cent of Christians (725,494 people) adhere to the Church of Scotland and other Presbyterian churches, 22 per cent (249,180) to the Roman Catholic Church, just under 5 per cent (54,382) to the Scottish Episcopal Church, 2 per cent (23,732) to Orthodox churches, and 6 per cent (71,550) to other Christian churches, including Methodists, Baptists, Pentecostal churches, Congregational churches, assemblies of Brethren, the Religious Society of Friends (Quakers) and the Salvation Army. About 14 per cent of the adult population regularly attends a Christian church.

About 0.75 per cent of the population (37,271 people) is affiliated to non-Trinitarian churches, e.g. Jehovah's Witnesses, the Church of Jesus Christ of Latter-Day Saints (Mormons), the Church of Christ, Scientist and the Unitarian churches.

Just under 1 per cent of the population (47,971 people) are adherents of other faiths, including Buddhism, Hinduism, Islam, Judaism, Sikhism and a number of new religious movements. There are sizeable Islamic communities in Glasgow and Edinburgh, and a significant Jewish community, particularly in Glasgow. The Samye Ling Tibetan Buddhist Centre, based in Eskdalemuir, Dumfriesshire, is building a Buddhist retreat centre on Holy Island, a small island off the Isle of Arran.

Over the past decade adherence to religion has been falling overall, but a steady decline in membership of the Trinitarian Christian churches and Judaism has been offset by a growth in non-Trinitarian churches, Islam and other faiths. By the first years of the new century a projected 22 per cent of Scotland's population will be adherents of a religion, of whom 91 per cent will be members of Christian churches.

ADHERENTS TO RELIGIONS IN SCOTLAND

	1990	1995	2000 (projected estimate)
Christianity (Trinitarian)	1,255,268	1,125,092	1,032,013
Non-Trinitarian churches	34,704	37,271	42,258
Buddhism	1,370	1,950	2,270
Hinduism	3,550*	3,950*	4,275
Judaism	3,274	2,341†	1,700
Islam	21,000	24,600*	30,275
Sikhism	8,400*	12,000*	13,650
Other	3,092	3,888	3,967
Total	1,330,658	1,211,092	1,130,408

* Estimate
† Heads of households, male or female, affiliated to synagogues. The figures represent about one-third of the Jewish community
Source: Based on tables from UK Christian Handbook Religious Trends No. 1 1998-9 (Christian Research/Paternoster Publishing, 1998); figures in text are for 1995

ADULT CHURCH ATTENDANCE IN SCOTLAND

	1990	1995	2000 (projected estimate)	2005
Church of Scotland	236,200	216,300	196,200	177,600
Other Presbyterian	21,100	17,900	15,000	12,000
Baptist	19,900	18,300	16,900	15,600
Episcopal	16,100	16,600	17,100	17,900
Roman Catholic	283,600	248,900	233,300	198,200
Independent	31,700	35,100	37,000	39,500
Other churches	20,500	22,600	24,300	26,000
Total	629,100	575,700	539,800	486,800
% of adult population	15.2	13.8	13.3	12.0%

Source: UK Christian Handbook Religious Trends No. 1 1998-9

INTER-CHURCH AND INTER-FAITH CO-OPERATION

The main umbrella body for the Christian churches in the UK is the Council of Churches for Britain and Ireland (formerly the British Council of Churches). Ecumenical bodies in Scotland are

Action of Churches Together in Scotland (ACTS) and the Churches Agency for Inter-Faith Relations in Scotland. The Church of Scotland, the Methodist Church, the Religious Society of Friends (Quakers), the Roman Catholic Church, the Salvation Army, the Scottish Episcopal Church and the United Reformed Church belong to both. ACTS also includes the Congregational Federation, the Scottish Congregational Church and the United Free Church; the Eastern Orthodox Church has associate membership. The Evangelical Alliance, representing evangelical Christians, has an office in Scotland.

The Scottish Inter-Faith Council is composed of Christians, Buddhists, Hindus, Jews, Muslims, Sikhs and representatives from other inter-faith groups. Churches Together in Britain and Ireland also has a Commission on Inter-Faith Relations.

Several of the UK-wide inter-church and inter-faith bodies do not have offices in Scotland; in these cases the contact details for the UK office are given.

Action of Churches Together in Scotland
Scottish Churches House, Kirk Street, Dunblane, Perthshire FK15 0AJ (Tel: 01786-823588; Fax: 01786 825844; E-mail: acts.ecum@dial.pipex.com Web: www.acts.dial.pipex.com).
General Secretary: Dr K. Franz

Churches Agency for Inter-Faith Relations in Scotland
Flat 1/1, 326 West Princes Street, Glasgow G4 9HA (Tel: 0141-339 8174;
E-mail: ismyth@bigfoot.com).
Secretary: Sr I. Smyth

Council of Christians and Jews
5th Floor, Camelford House, 87-89 Albert Embankment, London SE1 (Tel: 020-7820 0090; Fax: 020-7820 0504;
E-mail: cjrelations@ccj.org.uk
Web: www.ccj.org.uk).
Director: Sr M. Shepherd

Churches Together in Britain and Ireland
Inter-Church House, 35-41 Lower Marsh, London SE1 7SA (Tel: 020-7523 2121; Fax: 020-7928 0010; E-mail: info@ctbi.org.uk
Web: www.ctbi.org.uk).
General Secretary: Dr D. Goodbourn

Evangelical Alliance Scotland
Challenge House, 29 Canal Street, Glasgow G4 0AD (Tel: 0141-332 8700; Fax: 0141-332 8704; E-mail: scotland@eauk.org Web: www.eauk.org).
General Secretary: Revd D. Anderson

Free Churches' Council
27 Tavistock Square, London WC1H 9HH (Tel: 020-7387 8413; Fax: 020-7329 3925; E-mail: mail@freechurches.org).
General Secretary: Revd G. H. Roper

Inter Faith Network for the United Kingdom
5-7 Tavistock Place, London WC1H 9SN (Tel: 020-7388 0008; Fax: 020-7387 7968; E-mail: ifnet@interfaith.org.uk
Web: www.interfaith.org.uk).
Director: B. Pearce

Scottish Inter-Faith Council
St Mungo's Museum of Religious Life and Art, 2 Castle Street, Glasgow G4 0RH (Tel: 0141-5532557; Fax: 0141-5524744; E-mail: sifc@freeuk.com).
Secretary: Sr I. Smyth

NON-CHRISTIAN FAITHS

Several non-Christian religions with significant membership in Scotland do not have representative bodies specific to Scotland. In the following list, contact details for the UK body, or bodies, are given where no Scottish representative body has been identified.

BAHÁ'Í FAITH
The Bahá'í faith was founded by Mirza Husayn-'Ali, known as Bahá'u'lláh (Glory of God), who was born in Iran in 1817.

The Bahá'í faith recognises the unity and relativity of religious truth and teaches that there is only one God, whose will has been revealed to mankind by a series of messengers, such as Zoroaster, Abraham, Moses, Buddha, Krishna, Christ, Muhammad, the Báb and Bahá'u'lláh, whose common purpose was to bring God's message to mankind. It teaches that all races and both sexes are equal and deserving of equal opportunities and treatment, that education is a fundamental right and encourages a fair distribution of wealth.

The Bahá'í Information Office
27 Rutland Gate, London SW7 1PD (Tel: 020-7584 2566; Fax: 020-7584 9402; Email: nsa.bahai.org.uk
Web: www.bahai.org.uk).
Secretary General: The Hon. Barnabas Leith

BUDDHISM
Buddhism originated in northern India in the teachings of Siddhartha Gautama, known to his followers as the Buddha ('the one who knows'). It

is most generally accepted that he lived in the sixth/fifth centuries BC. Although Buddhism died out in its country of origin, it spread widely through Asia developing into a number of forms which are superficially very different. This diversity makes it difficult to summarise Buddhist doctrines in a form which would be accepted by all Buddhists, but the following points would likely be accepted by the majority: Buddhists do not believe in one kind of supreme deity central to religions more familiar in the West. Instead, the course of the universe is determined by the law of karma, a form of moral causation. According to this, the good and bad volitions of beings tend to produce pleasant or painful consequences in present and future lives. Karma generally operates to maintain beings in the familiar cycle of rebirth and death (samsara) which is inevitably a state of suffering (dukkha) in the long run notwithstanding the possibility of interludes of happiness and fulfilment. Buddhism teaches that escape from this cycle requires the threefold development of morality (including the practice of qualities such as generosity and patience), concentration (development of the powers of the mind, including loving-kindness and compassion for all beings) and wisdom (insight into the real nature of things, including out own mind and body). The methods of achieving this development vary from one school of Buddhism to another. The Buddhist Society seeks to raise awareness of Buddhist teachings and practice without favouring one school above another. It runs courses, gives lectures and publishes books about Buddhism.

The Buddhist society

58 Eccleston Square, London SW1V 1PH
(Tel: 020-7834 5858; Fax: 020-7976 5238;
Email: info@thebuddhistsociety.org.uk.
Web: www.thebuddhistsociety.org.uk).
Registrar: Margaret Connan

Kagyu Samye Ling Monastery and Tibetan Centre

Eskdalemuir, Langholm, Dumfriesshire DG13 0QL (Tel: 01387-373232; Fax: 01387-373223; E-mail: *scotland@samyeling.org*
Web: www.samyeling.org).
Abbot: Lama Yeshe Losal

HINDUISM

Hinduism has no historical founder but had become highly developed in India by about 1200 bc. Most Hindus hold that satya (truthfulness), ahimsa (non-violence), honesty, physical labour and tolerance of other faiths are essential for good living. They believe in one supreme spirit (Brahman), and in the transmigration of atman (the soul). Most Hindus accept the doctrine of karma (consequences of actions), the concept of samsara (successive lives) and the possibility of all atmans achieving moksha (liberation from samsara) through jnana (knowledge), yoga (meditation), karma (work or action) and bhakti (devotion).

Most Hindus recognise the authority of the Vedas, the oldest holy books, and accept the philosophical teachings of the Upanishads, the Vedanta Sutras and the Bhagavad-Gita.

Brahman is formless, limitless and all-pervading, and is represented in worship by murtis (images or statues). Brahma, Vishnu and Shiva are the most important gods worshipped by Hindus; their respective consorts are Saraswati, Lakshmi and Durga or Parvati, also known as Shakti. There are believed to have been ten avatars (incarnations) of Vishnu, of whom the most important are Rama and Krishna. Other popular gods are Ganesha, Hanuman and Subrahmanyam. All gods are seen as aspects of the supreme God, not as competing deities.

The commonest form of worship is a puja, in which offerings of red and yellow powders, rice grains, water, flowers, food, fruit, incense and light are made to the murti (image) of a deity.

Arya Pratinidhi Sabha (UK) and Arya Samaj London

69a Argyle Road, London W13 0LY
(Tel: 020-8991 1732).
President: Prof. S. N. Bharadwaj

International Society for Krishna Consciousness (ISKCON)

Karuna Bhavan, Bankhouse Road, Lesmahagow, Lanarkshire ML11 0ES (Tel: 0155-894790; Fax 0155-894 526; E-mail: scotland@iskon.org.uk).

National Council of Hindu Temples (UK)

Bhaktivedanta Manor, Dharam Marg, Hilfield Lane, Aldenham, Watford WD2 8EZ
(Tel: 01923-856269; Fax: 01923-856269;
E-mail: bimal.krnsa.bcs@pamtio.net).
President: Mr O. P. Sherma

Swaminarayan Hindu Mission
105–119 Brentfield Road, London NW10 8JB
(Tel: 020-8-965 2651; Fax: 020-8965 6313;
E-mail: shm@swaminarayan-baps.org.uk
Web: www.swaminarayn-baps.org.uk).
Secretaru: A. Patel

Vishwa Hindu Parishad (UK)
48 Wharfedale Gardens, Thornton Heath, Surrey
CR7 6LB (Tel: 020-8684 9716).
General Secretary: K. Ruparelia

ISLAM
Islam (which means 'peace arising from submission to the will of Allah' in Arabic) is a monotheistic religion which was taught by the Prophet Muhammad, who was born in Mecca (Makkah) in ad 570.

For Muslims (adherents of Islam), there is one God (Allah), who holds absolute power. His commands were revealed to mankind through the prophets, who include Abraham, Moses and Jesus, but his message was gradually corrupted until revealed finally and in perfect form to Muhammad through the angel Jibril (Gabriel) over a period of 23 years. This last, incorruptible message has been recorded in the Qur'an (Koran), and is held to be the essence of all previous scriptures. The Ahadith are the records of the Prophet Muhammad's deeds and sayings (the Sunnah) as recounted by his immediate followers. The Shari'ah is the sacred law of Islam based upon prescriptions derived from the Qur'an and the Sunnah of the Prophet.

There is no central organisation, but the Islamic Cultural Centre, which is the London Central Mosque, and the Imams and Mosques Council are influential bodies; there are many other Muslim organisations in Britain.

Islamic Council of Scotland
30 Clyde Place, Glasgow G5 8AA
Director: B. Man

Imams and Mosques Council
20—22 Creffield Road, London W5 3RP
(Tel: 020-8992 6636; Fax: 020-8993 3946).
Director: M.S. Raza

Muslim World League
46 Goodge Street, London W1P 1FJ
(Tel: 020-7636 7568; Fax: 020-7637 5034;
E-mail: mwl@webstar.co.uk
Web: www.mwl@aol.com).
Secretary: G. Rahman

Union of Muslim Organisations of the UK and Eire
109 Campden Hill Road, London W8 7TL
(Tel: 020-7221 6608; Fax: 020-7792 2130).
General Secretary: Dr S. A. Pasha

JAINISM
Jainism was founded in the sixth century BC by Vardhamana Jnatiputra, known as Mahavira (The Great Hero), but it traces its roots to a succession of 24 Jinas (those who overcome), of which Mahavira is considered the last.

Jains believe that the universe is eternal and exists as a series of layers, including heaven, the earth and hell. Karma, the fruit of past actions, determines the place of every person and creature within the universe. Moksha (liberation from an endless succession of reincarnations) is achieved by enlightenment, which can be attained only through asceticism.

Institute of Jainology
Unit 18, Silicon Business Centre, 26/28 Wadsworth Road, Greenford, Middx UB6 7JZ (Tel: 020-8997 2300; Fax: 020-8997 4964).

Jain Centre
Oxford Street, Leicester LE1 5XU
(Tel: 0116-254 3091).

JUDAISM
The primary authority of Judaism is the Hebrew Bible or Tanakh. The first section (Torah) records how the descendants of Abraham were led by Moses out of their slavery in Egypt to Mount Sinai where God's law was revealed to them as the chosen people. The often two sections are Nevi'im (Prophets) and Ketuvim (Sacred Writings). The Talmud, which consists of commentaries on the Mishnah (the first text of rabbinical Judaism), is also held to be authoritative. Orthodox Jews regard Jewish law as derived from God and therefore unalterable; Reform and Liberal Jews seek to interpret it in the light of contemporary considerations; and Conservative Jews aim to maintain most of the traditional rituals but to allow changes in accordance with tradition.

The Chief Rabbi of the United Hebrew Congregations of the Commonwealth is the rabbinical authority of the Orthodox sector of the Ashkenazi Jewish community. His authority is not recognised by the Reform Synagogues of Great Britain (the largest progressive group), the Union of Liberal and Progressive Synagogues, the Union of Orthodox Hebrew Congregations, the Federation of Synagogues, the Sephardi community, or the Assembly of Masorti

Synàgogues. He is, however, generally recognised outside the Jewish community as the public religious representative of the totality of British Jewry. The Chief Rabbi is President of the Beth Din (Court of Judgment) of the United Synagogue. The Board of Deputies of British Jews is the representative body of British Jewry.

Chief Rabbinate
735 High Road, London N12 0US
(Tel: 020-8343 6301).
Chief Rabbi: Prof. Jonathan Sacks
Executive Director: Mrs S. Weinberg

Beth Din (Court of the Chief Rabbi)
735 High Road, London N12 0US
(Tel: 020-8343 6280; Fax: 020-8343 6257;
E-mail: info@londonbethdin.fsnet.co.uk.).
Registrar: Mr D. Frei
Dayanim: Rabbi C. Ehrentreu; Rabbi I. Binstock; Rabbi C. D. Kaplin; Rabbi M. Gelley

Board of Deputies of British Jews
Commonwealth House, 1-19 New Oxford Street, London WC1A 1NU (Tel: 020-7543 5400; Fax: 020-7543 0010; E-mail: info@bod.org.uk Web: www.bod.org.uk).
Director External Issues: Mr J. Sacker

Assembly of Masorti Synagogues
1097 Finchley Road, London NW11 0PU
(Tel: 020-8201 8772).
Director: H. Freedman

Federation of Synagogues
65 Watford Way, London NW4 3AQ
(Tel: 020-8202 22263; Fax: 020-8201 8917;
E-mail: office@masorti.org.uk
Web: www.masorti.org.uk).
Director: H. Freedman

Reform Synagogues of Great Britain
The Sternberg Centre for Judaism, 80 East End Road, London N3 2SY (Tel: 020-8349 5640 Fax: 020-8349 5699;
E-mail: admin@reformjudaism.org.uk
Web: www.reformjudiasm.org.uk).
Chief Executive: Rabbi A. Bayfield

Spanish and Portuguese Jews' Congregation
2 Ashworth Road, London W9 1JY
(Tel: 020-7289 2573; Fax: 020 7289 2709).
Chief Administrator and Secretary: H. Miller

Union of liberal and Progressive Synagogues
The Montagu Centre, 21 Maple Street, London W1T 4BE (Tel: 020-7580 1663; Fax: 020-7436 4184; E-mail: montaguculps.org
Web: www.ULPS.org).
Executive Director: Rabbi Dr C. H. Middleburgh

Union of Orthodox Hebrew Congregations
140 Stamford Hill, London N16 6QT
(Tel: 020-8802 6226; Fax: 020-8809 7092).
Administator: A. Klein

United Synagogue
Adler House, 735 High Road, London N12 0US
(Tel: 020-8343 8989; Fax: 020-8343 6262;
E-mail: infogeneral@unitedsynagogue.org.uk
Web: www.unitedsynagogue.org.uk
Senior Administrator: Jackie Stanley

SIKHISM

The Sikh religion dates from the birth of Guru Nanak in the Punjab in 1469, who taught that there is one God and that different religions are like different roads leading to the same destination. He condemned religious conflict, ritualism and caste prejudices. 'Guru' means teacher but in Sikh tradition has come to represent the divine presence of God giving inner spiritual guidance. Nanak's role as the human vessel of the divine guru was passed on to nine successors, the last of whom (Guru Gobind Singh) died in 1708. The immortal guru is now held to reside in the sacred scripture, Guru Granth Sahib, and so to be present in all Sikh gatherings.

Every gurdwara (temple) manages its own affairs and there is no central body in the UK. The Sikh Missionary Society provides an information service.

Sikh Missionary Society UK
10 Featherstone Road, Southall, Middx UB2 5AA (Tel: 020-8574 1902; Fax: 020-85741912).
Hon. General Secretary: Mr Kirpal Singh Rai

World Sikh Foundation
33 Wargrave Road, South Harrow, Middx HA2 8LL (Tel: 020-8864 9228; Fax: 020-8864 9228).
Circulation Manager: Mrs H. Bharara

ZOROASTRIANISM

Zoroastrianism was founded by Zarathushtra in Persia around 1500 BC. Zarathushtra's words are recorded in five poems called the Gathas, which, together with other scriptures, forms the Avesta.

Zoroastrianism teaches that there is one God, Ahura Mazda (the Wise Lord), and that all creation stems ultimately from God; the Gathas teach that human beings have free will, are responsible for their own actions and can choose between good and evil: Zoroastrians believe that after death, the immortal soul is judged by God, and is then sent to paradise or hell.

In Zoroastrian places of worship, an urn containing fire is the central feature; the fire symbolises the presence of Ahura Mazda in every human being.

World Zoroastrian Organisation
135 Tennison Road, London SE25 5NF

THE CHRISTIAN CHURCHES

Christianity is believed to have reached the Roman province of Britain from Gaul in the third century or slightly earlier, but spread no further northwards than the limits of Roman rule, leaving the northern part of Britain to be evangelised by Celtic missionaries. The first Christian church in Scotland, at Whithorn, was established by St Ninian in ad 397. But it was with the arrival *c.* ad 563 of St Columba from Ireland on the island of Iona, and his creation there of an abbey and missionary centre, that Christianity in Scotland took firm root. It was slow to spread, however, despite the work of missionaries such as St Kentigern (also known as St Mungo), the patron saint of Glasgow. Iona remained the religious centre until the time of the Viking raids, in the early ninth century.

After the Synod of Whitby (AD 663) asserted the practices of the Roman Church over those of the Celtic, the Roman Church gradually became dominant throughout Scotland. In *c.* AD 850 the Pictish king Kenneth mac Alpin established a new religious centre at Dunkeld, but this too was destroyed by the Vikings and the religious centre shifted to St Andrews, where the cult of that saint was growing.

Malcolm III (1058–93) introduced a number of reforms in the Church, including the banning of Gaelic from use in church services. His wife Margaret encouraged monastic foundations and revived the monastery at Iona. In the reign of David I (1124–53), a full episcopal structure with nine bishoprics was established, with St Andrews as the leading see.

THE REFORMATION

By the late 15th-century the church was the largest and richest institution in the country, with revenues far exceeding those of the state. However, the widening gap between the higher clergy, who often combined religious and secular functions, and the underpaid parish priests provided fertile ground for dissent among the lower clergy when the new Reform doctrines of Luther and Calvin were introduced in the mid-16th-century from the continent by John Knox, a disaffected priest.

The Reformers' ideas quickly became popular, particularly in the east and among the lesser nobility. In 1555 nobles who favoured the Protestant cause were organised, with the help of Knox, into the Lords of the Congregation; in 1557, these reforming nobles signed the 'First Bond', in which they declared their intention to overthrow the Roman church. The regent, Mary of Guise, outlawed Knox and his followers, provoking riots by Protestants and a brief war in 1559.

A Parliament (the 'Reformation Parliament') called on 1 August 1560 in the name of Queen Mary but without a royal presence, abolished the Latin Mass and rejected the jurisdiction of the Pope; the first assembly of the Church of Scotland ratified the Confession of Faith, drawn up by a committee including John Knox.

In 1578, the Second Book of Discipline provided for the establishment of the kirk session as the governing body for each church and set out the overall organisation of the Kirk into presbyteries, provinces and a general assembly.

THE BISHOPS' WARS

In 1592 Parliament passed an Act guaranteeing the liberties of the Kirk and its Presbyterian government, although James VI and I and later Stewart monarchs made several attempts to restore episcopacy. Scottish fears that Charles I would reinstate Roman Catholicism led to the signing in 1638 of the National Covenant, which reasserted the right of the people to keep the reformed church. At the end of 1638 the General Assembly abolished the episcopacy and proscribed the use of the Book of Common Prayer. In the ensuing Bishops' Wars of 1639–40, an army of Covenanters took Durham and Newcastle before peace was restored in 1641. When the civil war broke out in 1644, the Scottish Covenanters sided with Cromwell's army, concluding the Solemn League and Covenant with the English Parliament on condition that England would adopt a Presbyterian church.

The restoration of Charles II in 1660 brought a reinstatement of episcopacy and intolerance of Presbyterianism. Covenanters were persecuted and the Covenant declared illegal. Several waves of protest and repression followed. James VII and II issued decrees in 1687–8 allowing Catholics and Quakers, and later Presbyterians, to hold meetings in private houses; the various Presbyterian factions reunited, fearing a return to Catholicism. A Presbyterian church was restored in 1690 and secured by the Act of Settlement 1690 and the Act of Union 1707.

The 18th, 19th and early 20th centuries saw a series of divergent and convergent movements in the Kirk and the formation of successive splinter groups, which subsequently regrouped. Five smaller Presbyterian churches exist today.

MEMBERSHIP OF INSTITUTIONAL CHURCHES IN SCOTLAND 1995

	Membership	Churches	Ministers/ priests
Total membership of institutional churches	1,053,542	2,757	2,573
Presbyterian*	725,494	1,958	1,382
Roman Catholic (mass attendance)	249,180	464	936
Anglican	55,136	320	244
of which			
Scottish Episcopal	54,382	316	230
Orthodox	23,732	15	11

* Including Church of Scotland and other Presbyterian churches

MEMBERSHIP OF FREE CHURCHES IN SCOTLAND 1995

	Membership	Churches	Ministers/ priests
Total free church membership	71,550	1,087	593
Baptist	18,083	208	180
Independent[1]	27,572	470	146
of which			
Scottish Congregational	8,673	62	38
Brethren assemblies	12,826	323	50
Methodist	6,312	76	31
New Churches	3,460	40	29
Pentecostal[2]	6,681	112	89
Other[3]	9,442	200	269
of which			
Quakers	705	31	—
Lutherans	775	7	4
Salvation Army	5,187	112	178

1. Total of Brethren, Congregational and other independent churches
2. Total of mainstream Afro-Caribbean and Overseas Apostolic
3. Total of Central, Holiness, Lutheran and overseas nationals churches and denominations
Source: UK Christian Handbook Religious Trends No. 1 1998-9

THE CHURCH OF SCOTLAND

The Church of Scotland is the established (e.g. national) church of Scotland. It was established in 1567, and its contractual relation with the state is expressed in a series of statutes from that year onward, concluding with an Act of 1921 setting out the constitution of the new Church and one of 1925 handing over the state endowments to the Church.

The Church is Reformed and Evangelical in doctrine, and Presbyterian in constitution, e.g. based on a hierarchy of councils of ministers and elders and, since 1990, of members of a diaconate. At local level the kirk session consists of the parish minister and ruling elders. At district level the presbyteries, of which there are 47, consist of all the ministers in the district, one ruling elder from each congregation, and those members of the diaconate who qualify for membership. The General Assembly is the supreme authority, and is presided over by a Moderator chosen annually by the Assembly. The Sovereign, if not present in person, is represented by a Lord High Commissioner who is appointed each year by the Crown.

The Church of Scotland has about 700,000 members, 1,200 ministers and 1,600 churches. There are about 100 ministers and other personnel working overseas.

Lord High Commissioner (2001): Rt. Hon The Viscount Younger of Leckie
Moderator of the General Assembly (2001): The Rt. Revd John D. Miller
Principal Clerk: Revd F. A. J. Macdonald
Depute Clerk: Revd Marjory MacLean
Procurator: P. S. Hodge, QC
Law Agent and Solicitor of the Church: Mrs J. S. Wilson
Parliamentary Agent: Revd G. Blount
General Treasurer: D. F. Ross

CHURCH OFFICE

121 George Street, Edinburgh EH2 4YN (Tel: 0131-225 5722).

PRESBYTERIES AND CLERKS

Edinburgh: Revd W. P. Graham
West Lothian: Revd D. Shaw
Lothian: J. D. McCulloch
Melrose and Peebles: Revd J. H. Brown
Duns: Revd James Cutler
Jedburgh: Revd A. D. Reid
Annandale and Eskdale: Revd C. B. Haston
Dumfries and Kirkcudbright: Revd G. M. A. Savage
Wigtown and Stranraer: Revd D. Dutton
Ayr: Revd J. Crichton
Irvine and Kilmarnock: Revd C. G. F. Brockie
Ardrossan: Revd D. Broster
Lanark: Revd I. D. Cunningham
Paisley: Revd D. Kay
Greenock: Revd D. Mill
Glasgow: Revd A. Cunningham

Hamilton: Revd J. H. Wilson
Dumbarton: Revd D. P. Munro
South Argyll: Revd M. A. J. Gossip
Dunoon: Revd R. Samuel
Lorn and Mull: Revd J. A. McCormick
Falkirk: Revd Ian W. Black
Stirling: Revd G. G. Cringles
Dunfermline: Revd W. E. Farquhar
Kirkcaldy: Revd B. L. Tomlinson
St Andrews: Revd P. Meager
Dunkeld and Meigle: Revd B. Dempsey
Perth: Revd D. G. Lawson
Dundee: Revd J. A. Roy
Angus: Revd M. I. G. Rooney
Aberdeen: Revd A. Douglas
Kincardine and Deeside: Revd J. W. S. Brown
Gordon: Revd E. Glen
Buchan: Revd R. Neilson
Moray: Revd G. Melvyn Wood
Abernethy: Revd J. A. I. MacEwan
Inverness: Revd A. S. Younger
Lochaber: Revd A. Ramsay
Ross: Revd T. M. McWilliam
Sutherland: Revd J. L. Goskirk
Caithness: Mrs M. Gillies
Lochcarron/Skye: Revd A. I. Macarthur
Uist: Revd M. Smith
Lewis: Revd T. S. Sinclair
Orkney (Finstown): Revd T. Hunt
Shetland (Lerwick): Revd C. Greig
England (London): Revd W. A. Cairns
Europe (Geneva):

The minimum stipend of a minister in the Church of Scotland in 1999 was £16,737.

THE SCOTTISH EPISCOPAL CHURCH

The Scottish Episcopal Church was founded after the Act of Settlement (1690) established the presbyterian nature of the Church of Scotland. The Scottish Episcopal Church is in full communion with the Church of England but is autonomous. The governing authority is the General Synod, an elected body of approximately 170 members which meets once a year. The diocesan bishop who convenes and presides at meetings of the General Synod is called the Primus and is elected by his fellow bishops.

There are 48,385 members of the Scottish Episcopal Church, of whom 30,988 are communicants. There are seven bishops, 457 serving clergy, and 327 churches and places of worship.

The General Synod of the Scottish Episcopal Church

21 Grosvenor Crescent, Edinburgh EH12 5EE
(Tel: 0131-225 6357; Fax: 0131-346 7247;
E-mail: office@scotland.anglican.org
Web: www.scotland.anglican.org).
Secretary General: J. F. Stuart

Primus of the Scottish Episcopal Church

Most Revd A. Bruce Cameron (Bishop of
Aberdeen and Orkney), elected 2000

DIOCESES

Aberdeen and Orkney
Bishop, Rt. Revd A. Bruce Cameron, b. 1941,
cons. 1992, elected 1992
Clergy: 53

Argyll and the Isles
Bishop, Rt. Revd Douglas M. Cameron, b. 1935,
cons. 1993, elected 1992
Clergy: 24

Brechin
Bishop, Rt. Revd Neville Chamberlain, b. 1939,
cons. 1997, elected 1997
Clergy: 30

Edinburgh
Bishop-elect, Rt. Revd Brian A. Smith, b. 1943,
elected 2001
Clergy: 143

Glasgow and Galloway
Bishop, Rt. Revd Idris Jones, b. 1943, cons. 1998,
elected 1998
Clergy: 105

Moray, Ross and Caithness
Bishop, Rt. Revd John Crook, b. 1940, cons.
1999, elected 1999
Clergy: 32

St Andrews, Dunkeld and Dunblane
Bishop, Rt. Revd Michael H. G. Henley, b. 1938,
cons. 1995, elected 1995
Clergy: 70

The minimum stipend of a diocesan bishop of the
Scottish Episcopal Church is £24,354 in 2000 (i.e.
1.5 x the minimum clergy stipend of £16,236).

THE ROMAN CATHOLIC CHURCH

The Roman Catholic Church is one worldwide
Christian church, with an estimated 890.9 million
adherents, acknowledging as its head the Bishop
of Rome, known as the Pope (Father). The Pope
is held to be the successor of St Peter and a direct
line of succession is therefore claimed from the
earliest Christian communities. The Pope
exercises spiritual authority over the Church with
the advice and assistance of the Sacred College of
Cardinals, the supreme council of the Church. He
is also advised about the concerns of the Church
locally by his ambassadors, who liaise with the
Bishops' Conference in each country.

The Roman Catholic Church universally and
the Vatican City State are run by the Curia, which
is made up of the Secretariat of State, the Sacred
Council for the Public Affairs of the Church, and
various congregations, secretariats and tribunals
assisted by commissions and offices. The Vatican
State has its own diplomatic service, with
representatives known as nuncios and apostolic
delegates.

The Bishops' Conference
The Bishops' Conference of Scotland is the
permanently constituted assembly of the Bishops
of Scotland. To promote its work, the Conference
establishes various agencies which have an
advisory function in relation to the Conference.
The more important of these agencies are called
Commissions and each one has a Bishop President
who, with the other members of the
Commissions, is appointed by the Conference.

The Roman Catholic Church in Scotland has
around 705,650 baptised members, 2 archbishops,
6 bishops, 907 priests and 464 parishes.

Secretariat of the Bishops' Conference of Scotland
64 Aitken Street, Airdrie, ML6 6LT
(Tel: 01236 764061; Fax: 01236-762489).
President: HE Cardinal Thomas J. Winning
General Secretary: Very Revd Mgr Henry
Docherty
Episcopal Secretary: Rt. Revd Maurice Taylor

ARCHDIOCESES

St Andrews and Edinburgh
Archbishop: Most Revd Keith Patrick O'Brien,
Con. 1985
Clergy: 192
Diocesan Curia: 113 Whitehouse Loan,
Edinburgh EH9 1BD. Tel: 0131-452 8244

Glasgow
Archbishop: HE Cardinal Thomas J. Winning, cons. 1971, apptd. 1974
Clergy: 253
Diocesan Curia: 196 Clyde Street, Glasgow G1 4JY (Tel: 0141-226 5898).

DIOCESES

Aberdeen
Bishop: Rt. Revd Mario Conti, cons. 1977
Clergy: 58
Bishop's Residence: 3 Queen's Cross, Aberdeen AB2 6BR (Tel: 01224-319154).

Argyll and the Isles
Bishop: Rt. Revd Ian Murray, con. 1999
Clergy: 33
Diocesan Curia: St Columba's Cathedral, Esplanade, Oban PA34 5AB (Tel: 01631-571003).

Dunkeld
Bishop: Rt. Revd Vincent Logan, cons. 1981
Clergy: 51
Diocesan Curia: 29 Roseangle, Dundee DD1 4LR (Tel: 01382-25453).

Galloway
Bishop: Rt. Revd Maurice Taylor, cons. 1981
Clergy: 66
Diocesan Curia: 8 Corsehill Road, Ayr KA7 2ST (Tel: 01292-266750).

Motherwell
Bishop: Rt. Revd Joseph Devine, cons. 1977, apptd.1983
Clergy: 168
Diocesan Curia: Coursington Road, Motherwell ML1 1PW (Tel: 01698-269114).

Paisley
Bishop: Rt. Revd John A. Mone, cons. 1984, apptd. 1988
Clergy: 86
Diocesan Curia: c/o St Lawrence's, 6 Kilmacolm Road, Greenock PA16 7UH (Tel: 01475-892143).
Bishop Emeritus: Rt. Revd. Stephen McGill, cons. 1960, apptd. 1968
13 Newmarket Street, Greenock PA16 7UH (Tel: 01475-783696)

PRESBYTERIAN CHURCHES

THE FREE CHURCH OF SCOTLAND

The Free Church of Scotland was formed in 1843, when over 400 ministers withdrew from the Church of Scotland as a result of interference in the internal affairs of the church by the civil authorities. In 1900, all but 26 ministers joined with others to form the United Free Church (most of which rejoined the Church of Scotland in 1929). In 1904 the remaining 26 ministers were recognised by the House of Lords as continuing the Free Church of Scotland. This Church is also known as the'Wee Frees'.

The Church maintains strict adherence to the Westminster Confession of Faith of 1648 and accepts the Bible as the sole rule of faith and conduct. Its General Assembly meets annually. It also has links with Reformed Churches overseas. The Free Church of Scotland has 6,000 members, 90 ministers and 140 churches.
General Treasurer: I. D. Gill, The Mound, Edinburgh EH1 2LS (Tel: 0131-226 5286).

UNITED FREE CHURCH OF SCOTLAND

The United Free Church of Scotland has existed in its present form since 1929, but has its origins in divisions in the Church of Scotland in the 18th century. The Secession Church broke away from the Church of Scotland in 1733, and the Relief Church in 1761. In 1847 the Secession and Relief Churches united, becoming the United Presbyterian Church of Scotland. In 1900 this church united with a majority of the Free Church of Scotland to become the United Free Church of Scotland. The majority of members rejoined the Church of Scotland in 1929, with the minority continuing as the United Free Church.

The Church accepts the Bible as the supreme standard of faith and conduct and adheres to the Westminster Confession of Faith. It is opposed to the state establishment of religion. The system of government is presbyterian. It has approximately 6,000 members, 41 ministers and 70 churches.
Moderator: Revd A. D. Scrimgeour
General Secretary: Revd J. O. Fulton, 11 Newton Place, Glasgow G3 7PR (Tel: 0141-332 3435).

THE FREE PRESBYTERIAN CHURCH OF SCOTLAND

The Free Presbyterian Church of Scotland was formed in 1893 by two ministers of the Free Church of Scotland who refused to accept a Declaratory Act passed by the Free Church General Assembly in 1892. The Free Presbyterian

Church of Scotland is Calvinistic in doctrine and emphasises observance of the Sabbath. It adheres strictly to the Westminster Confession of Faith.

The Church has about 3,000 members in Scotland and about 4,000 in overseas congregations. It has 23 ministers and 50 churches.

Moderator: Rev K.D Macleod, FP House, Ferry Road, Leverburgh, Isle of Harris, HS5 3UA (Tel: 01859-520 271).

Clerk of Synod: Revd J. MacLeod, 16 Matheson Road, Stornoway, Isle of Lewis HS1 2LA (Tel: 01851-702755).

ASSOCIATED PRESBYTERIAN CHURCHES OF SCOTLAND

The Associated Presbyterian Churches came into being in 1989 as a result of a division within the Free Presbyterian Church of Scotland. Following two controversial disciplinary cases, the culmination of deepening differences within the Church, a presbytery was formed calling itself the Associated Presbyterian Churches (APC). The APC has about 1,000 members, 15 ministers and 20 churches.

Clerk of the Scottish Presbytery: Revd A. MacPhail, Fernhill, Polvinster Road, Oban, PA34 5TN (Tel: 01631-567076).

REFORMED PRESBYTERIAN CHURCH OF SCOTLAND

The Reformed Presbyterian Church of Scotland has its origins in the Covenanter movement. After the 'Glorious Revolution' of 1688, a minority of Presbyterians in southern Scotland did not accept the religious settlement and remained outside the Church of Scotland. Known as 'Cameronians', they met in 'Societies' and formed the Reformed Presbyterian Church of Scotland in 1743. In 1872 the majority of the church joined the Free Church of Scotland.

The Church regards the Bible as its sole standard and adheres strictly to the Westminster Confession of Faith. The Church is Presbyterian in structure, with the Synod the supreme court. At present there are four congregations and approximately 150 members and adherents.

Clerk of Synod (pro tem): Revd A. Sinclair Horne, 17 George IV Bridge, Edinburgh EH1 1EE (Tel: 0131-220 1450).

OTHER CHURCHES

Afro-West Indian United Council of Churches
c/o New Testament Church of God, Arcadian Gardens, High Road, London, N22 5AA (Tel: 020-8888 9427).
Secretary: Bishop E. Brown

Council of African and Afro-Caribbean Churches UK
31 Norton House, Sidney Road, London, SW9 0UJ (Tel: 020-7274 5589; Fax: 020-7274 4726; E-mail: olu–abiola@lineone.net).
Chairman: His Grace The Most Revd Father Olu A. Abiola

Baptist Union of Scotland
14 Aytoun Road, Glasgow, G41 5RT (Tel: 0141-423 6169; Fax: 0141-424 1422; E-mail: admin@scottishbaptist.org.uk; Web: www.scottishbaptist.org.uk).
General Secretary: Rev William Sleck

Eastern Orthodox Church (Patriarchate of Constantinople)
5 Craven Hill, London, W2 3EN (Tel: 020-7723 4787; Fax: 020-7224 9301).
Representative in Great Britain: Archbishop Gregorios of Thyateira and Great Britain

Lutheran Church
Lutheran Council of Great Britain, 30 Thanet Street, London, WC1H 9QH (Tel: 020-7554 2900; Fax: 020-7383 3081; E-mail: enquiries@lutheran.org.uk; Web: www.lutheran.org.uk).
General Secretary: Revd T. Bruch

Methodist Church
20 Inglewood Crescent, East Kilbride, Glasgow, G75 8QD (Tel: 01355-237 411).

Assemblies of God
3 Cypress Grove, Aberdeen, AB23 8LB (Tel: 01224-828 379; Fax: 01224-828 379; E-mail: johnstrachan@compuserve.com).
Minister: John S. Strachan

The Religious Society of Friends (Quakers)
Friends House, Euston Road, London, NW1 2BJ (Tel: 020-7663 1000; Fax: 020-7663 1001; E-mail: qcomms@quaker.org.uk; Web: www.quaker.org.uk).
Recording Clerk: Elsa Dicks

The Salvation Army
Scotland Secretariat, 30 Rutland Square, Edinburgh, EH1 2BW (Tel: 0131-221 9699; Fax: 0131-221 1482;
E-mail: scotland@salvationarmy.org.uk).
General: J. Gowans
UK Territorial Commander: A. Hughes

United Reformed Church
PO Box 189, Glasgow, G1 2BX
(Tel: 0141-332 7667).
Moderator: Revd J. Arthur

The Seventh-Day Adventist Church
Stanborough Park, Watford, WD25 9JZ
(Tel: 01923-672 251; Fax: 01923-893 212;
E-mail: buc@adventist.org.uk;
Web: www.adventist.org.uk).
President of the British Union Conference: Pastor C. R. Perry

NON-TRINITARIAN CHURCHES

The Church of Christ Scientist
2 Elysium Gate, 126 New Kings Road, London, SW6 4LZ (Tel: 020-7371 0600).
District Manager for Great Britain and Ireland: H. Joynes

The Church of Jesus Christ of Latter-Day Saints
751 Warwick Road, Solihull, W. Midlands, B91 3DQ (Tel: 0121-712 1202).
President of the Europe North Area: Elder S. J. Condie

Jehovah's Witnesses
Watch Tower House, The Ridgeway, London, NW7 1RN (Tel: 020-8906 2211; Fax: 020-8371 0051; E-mail: pr@wtbts.org.uk;
Web: www.watchtower.org/ www.jw-media.org).

General Assembly of Unitarian and Free Christian Churches
Essex Hall, 1–6 Essex Street, Strand, London, WC2R 3HY (Tel: 020-7240 2384; Fax: 020-7240 3089 E-mail: ga@unitarian.org.uk;
Web: www.unitarian.org.uk).
General Secretary: J. J. Teagle

SCOTLAND AND
THE WORLD

TIME ZONES
INTERNATIONAL DIRECT DIALLING
CONSULATES

— SCOTLAND AND THE WORLD —

Time Zones

Standard time differences from the Greenwich meridian

+ hours ahead of GMT
− hours behind GMT
* may vary from standard time at some part of the year (Summer Time or Daylight Saving Time)
‡ some areas may keep another time zone

h hours
m minutes

	h	m
Afghanistan	+ 4	30
*Albania	+ 1	
Algeria	+ 1	
*Andorra	+ 1	
Angola	+ 1	
Anguilla	− 4	
Antigua and Barbuda	− 4	
Argentina	− 3	
*Armenia	+ 4	
Aruba	− 4	
Ascension Island	0	
*Australia	+ 10	
ACT, NSW (except Broken Hill area) Qld, Tas., Vic, Whitsunday Islands		
*Broken Hill area (NSW)	+ 9	30
*Lord Howe Island	+ 10	30
Northern Territory	+ 9	30
*South Australia	+ 9	30
Western Australia	+ 8	
*Austria	+ 1	
*Azerbaijan	+ 4	
*Bahamas	− 5	
Bahrain	+ 3	
Bangladesh	+ 6	
Barbados	− 4	
*Belarus	+ 2	
*Belgium	+ 1	
Belize	− 6	
Benin	+ 1	
*Bermuda	− 4	
Bhutan	+ 6	
Bolivia	− 4	
*Bosnia-Hercegovina	+ 1	
Botswana	+ 2	
Brazil		
western states	− 5	
central states	− 4	
N. and NE coastal states	− 3	
*S. and E. coastal states, including Brasilia	− 3	

	h	m
Fernando de Noronha Island	− 2	
British Antarctic Territory	− 3	
British Indian OceanTerritory	+ 5	
Diego Garcia	+ 6	
British Virgin Islands	− 4	
Brunei	+ 8	
*Bulgaria	+ 2	
Burkina Faso	0	
Burundi	+ 2	
Cambodia	+ 7	
Cameroon	+ 1	
Canada		
*Alberta	− 7	
*‡British Columbia	− 8	
*‡Labrador	− 4	
*Manitoba	− 6	
*New Brunswick	− 4	
*Newfoundland	− 3	30
*Northwest Territories		
east of 85° W.	− 5	
85° W. − 102° W.	− 6	
*Nunavut	− 7	
*Nova Scotia	− 4	
Ontario		
*east of 90° W.	− 5	
west of 90° W.	− 5	
*Prince Edward Island	− 4	
Québec		
east of 63° W.	− 4	
*west of 63° W.	− 5	
‡Saskatchewan	− 6	
*Yukon	− 8	
Cape Verde	− 1	
Cayman Islands	− 5	
Central African Republic	+ 1	
Chad	+ 1	
*Chatham Islands	+ 12	45
*Chile	− 4	
China (inc. Hong Kong and Macao)	+ 8	
Christmas Island (Indian Ocean)	+ 7	
Cocos (Keeling) Islands	+ 6	30
Colombia	− 5	
Comoros	+ 3	
Congo (Dem. Rep.)		
Haut-Zaïre, Kasai, Kivu, Shaba	+ 2	
Kinshasa, Mbandaka	+ 1	
Congo-Brazzaville	+ 1	
Costa Rica	− 6	
Côte d'Ivoire	0	
*Croatia	+ 1	
*Cuba	− 5	
*Cyprus	+ 2	

	h	m		h	m
*Czech Republic	+1		*Iraq	+3	
*Denmark	+1		*Ireland, Republic of	0	
*Færøe Islands	0		*Israel	+2	
*Greenland	−3		*Italy	+1	
Danmarkshavn, Mesters Vig	0		Jamaica	−5	
*Scoresby Sound	−1		Japan	+9	
*Thule area	−4		*Jordan	+2	
Djibouti	+3		*Kazakhstan		
Dominica	−4		western	+4	
Dominican Republic	−5		central	+5	
East Timor	+9		eastern	+6	
Ecuador	−5		Kenya	+3	
Galápagos Islands	−6		Kiribati	+12	
*Egypt	+2		Line Islands	+14	
El Salvador	-6		Phoenix Islands	+13	
Equatorial Guinea	+1		Korea, North	+9	
Eritrea	+3		Korea, South	+9	
Estonia	+2		Kuwait	+3	
Ethiopia	+3		*Kyrgyzstan	+5	
*Falkland Islands	−4		Laos	+7	
Fiji	+12		Latvia	+2	
*Finland	+2		*Lebanon	+2	
*France	+1		Lesotho	+2	
French Guiana	−3		Liberia	0	
French Polynesia	-10		Libya	+2	
Guadeloupe	−4		*Liechtenstein	+1	
Martinique	−4		Line Islands not part of Kiribati	-10	
Réunion	+4		Lithuania	+1	
Marquesas Islands	−9	30	*Luxembourg	+1	
Gabon	+1		*Macedonia	+1	
The Gambia	0		Madagascar	+3	
*Georgia	+3		Malawi	+2	
*Germany	+1		Malaysia	+8	
Ghana	0		Maldives		
*Gibraltar	+1		Mali	0	
*Greece	+2		*Malta	+1	
Grenada	−4		Marshall Islands	+12	
Guam	+10		Ebon Atoll	−12	
Guatemala	−6		Mauritania	0	
Guinea	0		Mauritius	+4	
Guinea-Bissau	0		*Mexico	−6	
Guyana	−4		*Nayarit, Sinaloa, S. Baja California	−7	
Haiti	−5		Sonora	−7	
Honduras	−6		N. Baja California	−8	
*Hungary	+1		Micronesia		
Iceland	0		Caroline Islands	+10	
India	+5	30	Kosrae, Pingelap, Pohnpei	+11	
Indonesia			*Moldova	+2	
Java, Kalimantan (west and	+7		*Monaco	+1	
central), Madura, Sumatra			Mongolia	+8	
Bali, Flores, Kalimantan	+8		Montserrat	−4	
(south and east), Lombok,			Morocco	0	
Sulawesi, Sumbawa, West Timor			Mozambique	+2	
Irian Jaya, Maluku,	+9		Myanmar	+6	30
*Iran	+3	30	*Namibia	+1	

	h m		h m
Nauru	+12	Sierra Leone	0
Nepal	+5 45	Singapore	+8
*Netherlands	+1	*Slovakia	+1
Netherlands Antilles	-4	*Slovenia	+1
New Caledonia	+11	Solomon Islands	+11
*New Zealand	+12	Somalia	+3
*Cook Islands	-10	South Africa	+2
Nicaragua	-6	South Georgia	-2
Niger	+1	*Spain	+1
Nigeria	+1	*Canary Islands	0
Niue	-11	Sri Lanka	+6
Norfolk Island	+11 30	Sudan	+3
Northern Mariana Islands	+10	Suriname	-3
*Norway	+1	Swaziland	+2
Oman	+4	*Sweden	+1
Pakistan	+5	*Switzerland	+1
Palau	+9	*Syria	+2
Panama	-5	Taiwan	+8
Papua New Guinea	+10	Tajikistan	+5
*Paraguay	-4	Tanzania	+3
Peru	-5	Thailand	+7
Philippines	+8	Togo	0
*Poland	+1	*Tonga	+13
*Portugal	0	Trinidad and Tobago	-4
*Azores	-1	Tristan da Cunha	0
*Madeira	0	Tunisia	+1
Puerto Rico	-4	*Turkey	+2
Qatar	+3	Turkmenistan	+5
Réunion	+4	*Turks and Caicos Islands	-5
*Romania	+2	Tuvalu	+12
*Russia		Uganda	+3
Zone 1	+2	*Ukraine	+2
Zone 2	+3	United Arab Emirates	+4
Zone 3	+4	*United Kingdom	0
Zone 4	+5	*United States of America	
Zone 5	+6	Alaska	-9
Zone 6	+7	Aleutian Islands, east of 169° 30W.	-9
Zone 7	+8	Aleutian Islands, west of 169° 30W.	-10
Zone 8	+9	eastern time	-5
Zone 9	+10	central time	-6
Zone 10	+11	Hawaii	-10
Zone 11	+12	mountain time	-7
Rwanda	+2	Pacific time	-8
St Helena	0	Uruguay	-3
St Christopher and Nevis	-4	Uzbekistan	+5
St Lucia	-4	Vanuatu	+11
*St Pierre and Miquelon	-3	*Vatican City State	+1
St Vincent and the Grenadines	-4	Venezuela	-4
Samoa	-11	Vietnam	+7
Samoa, American	-11	Virgin Islands (US)	-4
*San Marino	+1	Yemen	+3
São Tomé and Princípe	0	*Yugoslavia (Fed. Rep. of)	+1
Saudi Arabia	+3	Zambia	+2
Senegal	0	Zimbabwe	+2
Seychelles	+4		

Source: reproduced with permission from data produced by
HM Nautical Almanac Office

INTERNATIONAL DIRECT DIALLING (IDD)

International dialling codes are composed of four elements which are dialled in sequence:

(i) the international code
(ii) the country code (*see* below)
(iii) the area code
(iv) the customer's telephone number

Calls to some countries must be made via the international operator. (*Source:* BT)

† Connection is currently unavailable
‡ Calls must be made via the international operator
p A pause in dialling is necessary whilst waiting for a second tone
* Varies in some areas
** Varies depending on carrier

Country	IDD from UK	IDD to UK
Afghanistan	†	†
Albania	00 355	00 44
Algeria	00 213	00*p*44
Andorra	00 376	00 44
Angola	00 244	00 44
Anguilla	00 1 264	011 44
Antigua and Barbuda	00 1 268	011 44
Argentina	00 54	00 44
Armenia	00 374	810 44
Aruba	00 297	00 44
Ascension Island	00 247	00 44
Australia	00 61	00 11 44
Austria	00 43	00 44
Azerbaijan	00 994	810 44
Azores	00 351	00 44
Bahamas	00 1 242	011 44
Bahrain	00 973	0 44
Bangladesh	00 880	00 44
Barbados	00 1 246	011 44
Belarus	00 375	810 44
Belgium	00 32	00 44
Belize	00 501	00 44
Benin	00 229	00*p*44
Bermuda	00 1 441	011 44
Bhutan	00 975	00 44
Bolivia	00 591	00 44
Bosnia-Hercegovina	00 387	00 44
Botswana	00 267	00 44
Brazil	00 55	00 44
British Virgin Islands	00 1 284	011 44
Brunei	00 673	00 44
Bulgaria	00 359	00 44
Burkina Faso	00 226	00 44
Burundi	00 257	90 44
Cambodia	00 855	00 44
Cameroon	00 237	00 44
Canada	00 1	011 44
Canary Islands	00 34	00 44
Cape Verde	00 238	0 44
Cayman Islands	00 1 345	011 44
Central African Republic	00 236	19 44
Chad	00 235	15 44
Chile	00 56	00 44
China	00 86	00 44
Hong Kong	00 852	001 44
Colombia	00 57	009 44
Comoros	00 269	00 44
Congo, Dem. Rep. of	00 243	00 44
Congo, Republic of	00 242	00 44
Cook Islands	00 682	00 44
Costa Rica	00 506	00 44
Côte d'Ivoire	00 225	00 44
Croatia	00 385	00 44
Cuba	00 53	119 44
Cyprus	00 357	00 44
Czech Republic	00 420	00 44
Denmark	00 45	00 44
Djibouti	00 253	00 44
Dominica	00 1 767	011 44
Dominican Republic	00 1 809	011 44
Ecuador	00 593	00 44
Egypt	00 20	00 44
El Salvador	00 503	0 44
Equatorial Guinea	00 240	00 44
Eritrea	00 291	00 44
Estonia	00 372	800 44
Ethiopia	00 251	00 44
Falkland Islands	00 500	0 44
Faroe Islands	00 298	009 44
Fiji	00 679	05 44
Finland	00 358	00 44**
France	00 33	00 44
French Guiana	00 594	00 44
French Polynesia	00 689	00 44
Gabon	00 241	00 44
The Gambia	00 220	00 44
Georgia	00 995	810 44
Germany	00 49	00 44
Ghana	00 233	00 44
Gibraltar	00 350	00 44
Greece	00 30	00 44

Greenland	00 299	009 44	Martinique	00 596	00 44
Grenada	00 1 473	011 44	Mauritania	00 222	00 44
Guadeloupe	00 590	00 44	Mauritius	00 230	00 44
Guam	00 1 671	001 44	Mayotte	00 269	10 44
Guatemala	00 502	00 44	Mexico	00 52	98 44
Guinea	00 224	00 44	Micronesia,	00 691	011 44
Guinea-Bissau	00 245	099 44	Federated States		
Guyana	00 592	001 44	of		
Haiti	00 509	00 44	Moldova	00 373	810 44
Honduras	00 504	00 44	Monaco	00 377	00 44
Hungary	00 36	00 44	Mongolia	00 976	00 44
Iceland	00 354	00 44	Montenegro	00 381	99 44
India	00 91	00 44	Montserrat	00 1 664	011 44
Indonesia	00 62	001 44**	Morocco	00 212	00p44
		00844**	Mozambique	00 258	00 44
Iran	00 98	00 44	Myanmar	00 95	00 44
Iraq	00 964	00 44	Namibia	00 264	00 44
Ireland,	00 353	00 44	Nauru	00 674	00 44
Republic of			Nepal	00 977	00 44
Israel	00 972	00 44**	Netherlands	00 31	00 44
Italy	00 39	00 44	Netherlands Antilles	00 599	00 44
Jamaica	00 1 876	011 44	New Caledonia	00 687	00 44
Japan	00 81	001 44**	New Zealand	00 64	00 44
		004144**	Nicaragua	00 505	00 44
		006144**	Niger	00 227	00 44
Jordan	00 962	00 44*	Nigeria	00 234	009 44
Kazakhstan	00 7	810 44	Niue	00 683	00 44
Kenya	00 254	00 44	Norfolk Island	00 672	0101 44
Kiribati	00 686	00 44	Norway	00 47	00 44
Korea, North	00 850	00 44	Oman	00 968	00 44
Korea, South	00 82	001 44**	Pakistan	00 92	00 44
		00244**	Palau	00 680	011 44
Kuwait	00 965	00 44	Panama	00 507	00 44
Kyrgystan	00 996	00 44	Papua New Guinea	00 675	05 44
Laos	00 856	00 44	Paraguay	00 595	00 44**
Latvia	00 371	00 44			003 44**
Lebanon	00 961	00 44	Peru	00 51	00 44
Lesotho	00 266	00 44	Philippines	00 63	00 44
Liberia	00 231	00 44	Poland	00 48	00 44
Libya	00 218	00 44	Portugal	00 351	00 44
Liechtenstein	00 423	00 44	Puerto Rico	00 1 787	011 44
Lithuania	00 370	810 44	Qatar	00 974	00 44
Luxembourg	00 352	00 44	Réunion	00 262	00 44
Macao	00 853	00 44	Romania	00 40	00 44
Macedonia	00 389	99 44	Russia	00 7	810 44
Madagascar	00 261	00 44	Rwanda	00 250	00 44
Madeira	00 351 91	00 44*	St Christopher and	00 1 869	011 44
Malawi	00 265	101 44	Nevis		
Malaysia	00 60	00 44	St Helena	00 290	0 44
Maldives	00 960	00 44	St Lucia	00 1 758	011 44
Mali	00 223	00 44	St Pierre	00 508	00 44
Malta	00 356	00 44	and Miquelon		
Mariana Islands,	00 1 670	011 44	St Vincent and the	00 1 784	001 44
Northern			Grenadines		
Marshall Islands	00 692	011 44	Samoa	00 685	0 44

Samoa, American	00 684	00 44
San Marino	00 378	00 44
São Tomé and Princípe	00 239	00 44
Saudi Arabia	00 966	00 44
Senegal	00 221	00*p*44
Serbia	00 381	99 44
Seychelles	00 248	00 44
Sierra Leone	00 232	00 44
Singapore	00 65	001 44
Slovak Republic	00 421	00 44
Slovenia	00 386	00 44
Solomon Islands	00 677	00 44
Somalia	00 252	16 44
South Africa	00 27	09 44
Spain	00 34	00 44
Sri Lanka	00 94	00 44
Sudan	00 249	00 44
Suriname	00 597	00 44
Swaziland	00 268	00 44
Sweden	00 46	007 44**
		00944**
		008744**
Switzerland	00 41	00 44
Syria	00 963	00 44
Taiwan	00 886	002 44
Tajikistan	00 7	810 44
Tanzania	00 255	00 44
Thailand	00 66	001 44
Tibet	00 86	00 44
Togo	00 228	00 44
Tonga	00 676	00 44
Trinidad and Tobago	00 1 868	011 44
Tristan da Cunha	00 2 897	‡
Tunisia	00 216	00 44
Turkey	00 90	00 44
Turkmenistan	00 993	810 44
Turks and Caicos Islands	00 1 649	0 44
Tuvalu	00 688	00 44
Uganda	00 256	00 44
Ukraine	00 380	810 44
United Arab Emirates	00 971	00 44
Uruguay	00 598	00 44
USA	00 1	011 44
Uzbekistan	00 998	810 44
Vanuatu	00 678	00 44
Vatican City State	00 390 66982	00 44
Venezuela	00 58	00 44
Vietnam	00 84	00 44
Virgin Islands (US)	00 1 340	011 44
Yemen	00 967	00 44
Yugoslav Fed. Rep.	00 381	99 44
Zambia	00 260	00 44
Zimbabwe	00 263	00 44

CONSULATES

The list below is of Consulates based in Scotland.

American Consulate General
3 Regent Terrace, Edinburgh, EH7 5BW
(Tel: 0131-556 8315).

Austrian Consulate
Alderwood, 49 Craigcrook Road, Edinburgh, EH4 3PH (Tel: 0131-332 3344; Fax: 0131-332 1777).

Consulate of Canada
Standard Life House
30 Lothian Road, Edinburgh, EH1 2DH
(Tel: 0131-220 4333).
3 George Street, Edinburgh, EH2 2XZ
(Tel: 0131-220 4333).

The Danish Consulate
215 Balgreen Road, Edinburgh, EH11 2RZ
(Tel: 0131-337 6352; Fax: 0131346 8737).
Eadie House, 74 Kirkintilloch Road,
Bishopbriggs, Glasgow, G64 2AH
(Tel: 0141-762 2288; Fax: 0141-772 3854).

Faroese Commercial Attache
150 Market Street, Aberdeen, Aberdeenshire, AB11 5PP (Tel: 01224-592 777).

Finnish Consulate
Broomage Avenue, Larbert, Stirlingshire, FK5 4NQ (Tel: 01324-562 241).
22 Hanover Street, Edinburgh, EH2 2EN
(Tel: 0131-225 1295).

French Consulate General
11 Randolph Crescent, Edinburgh, EH3 7TT
(Tel: 0131-225 7954; Fax: 0131-225 8975;
Web: www.consulfrance-edimbourg.org).

Honorary Consul of The Federal Republic of Germany
16 Eglinton Crescent, Edinburgh, Midlothian, EH12 5DG (Tel: 0131-337 2323; Fax: 0131-346 1578;
E-mail: 106071.2110@compuserve.com).
Pentagon Centre, 36 Washington Street, Glasgow, G3 8AZ (Tel: 0141-226 8443; Fax: 0141-226 8441;
E-mail: 106071.2110@compuserve.com).
12 Albert Street, Aberdeen, Aberdeenshire, AB25 1XQ (Tel: 01330-844414;
E-mail: 106071.2110@compuserve.com).

Greek Consulate
19 Walker Street, Edinburgh, EH3 7HX
(Tel: 0131-226 1309; Fax: 0131-220 4281).

Icelandic Consulate
24 Jane Street, Edinburgh, EH6 5HD (Tel: 0131-555 3532; Fax: 0131-555 3606).

Consulate General of India
17 Rutland Square, Edinburgh, EH1 2BB
(Tel: 0131-229 2144; Fax: 0131-229 2155;
E-mail: indian@consulate.fsnet.co.uk).

Irish Consulate General
16 Randolph Crescent, Edinburgh, EH3 7TT
(Tel: 0131-226 7711; Fax: 0131-226 7704;
E-mail: info@congenirl.totalserve.co.uk).

Italian Consulate
Italian Vice-Consulate
Brebner Court, Castle Street, Aberdeen, AB11 5BQ (Tel: 01224-647135; Fax: 01224-627406).
32 Melville Street, Edinburgh, EH3 7PG
(Tel: 0131-226 3631; Fax: 01224-627406).

Japanese Consulate General
2 Melville Crescent, Edinburgh, EH3 7HW
(Tel: 0131-225 4777; Fax: 0131-225 4828).

The Netherlands Consulate
3 Annandale Terrace, Dalnottar Avenue, Old Kilpatrick, Glasgow, G60 5DJ
(Tel: 01389-875744; Fax: 01839-875744;
Web: www.netherlands-emabassy.org.uk).
100 Union Street, Aberdeen, AB10 1QR
(Tel: 01224-561 616; Fax: 01224-561 616;
Web: www.netherlands-emabassy.org.uk).
53 George Street, Edinburgh, EH2 2HT
(Tel: 0131-220 3226;
Web: www.netherlands-embassy.org.uk).

The Royal Norwegian Consulate General
86 George Street, Edinburgh, EH2 3BU
(Tel: 0131-226 5701; Fax: 0131-220 4976;
E-mail: cons.gen.edinburgh@mfa.no;
Web: www.norway.org.uk).
18 Woodside Cresent, Glasgow, G3 7UL
(Tel: 0141-333 0618; Fax: 0141-353 2190;
E-mail: cons.gen.glasgow@mfa.no;
Web: www.norway.org.uk).

Philippines Consulate
1 Bankhead Medway, Edinburgh, EH11 4BY
(Tel: 0131-453 3222; Fax: 0131-453 6444;
E-mail: ian@shapesfurniture.co.uk).

The Polish Consulate
2 Kinnear Road, Edinburgh, EH3 5PE
(Tel: 0131-552 0301).

Spanish Consulate General
63 North Castle Street, Edinburgh, EH2 3LJ
(Tel: 0131-220 1843; Fax: 0131-226 4568).

Swedish Consulate General
22 Hanover Street, Edinburgh, EH2 2EP
(Tel: 0131-220 6050; Fax: 0131-220 6006).

Swiss Consular Agency

66 Hanover Street, Edinburgh, EH2 1HH
(Tel: 0131-226 5660; Fax: 0131-226 5332).

Taipei Respresentative Office in the UK

1 Melville Street, Edinburgh, EH3 7PE
(Tel: 0131-220 6886; Fax: 0131-226 6884;

E-mail: troed@dial.pipex.com).

SOCIETIES AND INSTITUTIONS

— SOCIETIES AND INSTITUTIONS —

The listing below includes major charities, think tanks, special interest groups and recreational groups in Scotland, and the Scottish offices of UK organisations.

Scottish Adoption Advice Service
16 Sandyford Place, Glasgow, G3 7NB
(Tel: 0141-339 0772; Fax: 0141-248 8032).
Project Leader: Mrs J. Atherton; Mrs R. McMillan

Adoption Association
2 Commercial Street, Leith, Edinburgh, EH6 6JA (Tel: 0131-553 5060; Fax: 0131-553 6422).
Director: Ms A. Sutton

Advocates for Animals
Queensferry Chambers, 10 Queensferry Street, Edinburgh, EH2 4PG (Tel: 0131-225 6039; Fax: 0131-220 6377;
E-mail: advocates.animals@virgin.net;
Web: www.advocatesforanimals.org.uk).
Director: L. Ward

Age Concern Scotland
113 Rose Street, Edinburgh, EH2 3DT
(Tel: 0131-220 3345; Fax: 0131-220 2779;
E-mail: enquiries@acsinfo3.freeserve.co.uk).
Director: Ms M. O'Neill

Alcoholics Anonymous
Baltic Chambers, 50 Wellington Street, Glasgow, G2 (Tel: 0141-226 2214;
Web: www.alcoholics-anonymous.org.uk).

Alzheimer Scotland - Action on Dementia
22 Drumsheugh Gardens, Edinburgh, EH3 7RN
(Tel: 0131-243 1453; Fax: 0131-243 1450;
E-mail: alzscot@alzscot.org;
Web: www.alzscot.org).
Chief Executive: J. Jackson

Amnesty International Scotland
11 Jeffrey Street, Edinburgh, EH1 1DR
(Tel: 0131-557 2957; Fax: 0131-557 8501).
Fundraising Manager: G. Pope
Development Manager: R. Burnett

An Comunn Gàidhealach
109 Church Street, Inverness, IV1 1EY
(Tel: 01463-231 226; Fax: 01463-715 557).
Chief Executive: D. J. MacSween

Apex Trust Scotland
9 Great Stuart Street, Edinburgh, EH3 7TP
(Tel: 0131-220 0130; Fax: 0131-220 6796;
E-mail: apex-hq@sol.co.uk;
Web: www.apexscotland.org.uk).
Director: Ms J. Hewitt
Depute Director: P. Dunion

Army Benevolent Fund Scotland
The Castle, Edinurgh, EH1 2YT
(Tel: 0131-310 5132; Fax: 0131-310 5075).
Director - Scotland: Lt.-Col. I. Shepherd

Arthritis Care in Scotland
Phoenix House, 7 South Avenue, Clydebank, G61 7LG (Tel: 0141952 5433; Fax: 0141-952 5433; Web: www.athritiscare.org.uk).
Director - Scotland: Ms P. Wallace
Administrator - Scotland: Ms K. Green

Arts and Business Scotland
13 Abercromby Place, Edinburgh, EH3 6LB
(Tel: 0131-558 1277; Fax: 0131-558 3370;
E-mail: scotland@AandB.org.uk;
Web: www.AandB.org.uk).
Chief Executive: C. Tweedy
Director: Ms A. Hogg

Association for Mental Health
Cumbrae House, 15 Carlton Court, Glasgow, G5 9JP (Tel: 0141-568 7000; Fax: 0141-568 7001;
E-mail: enquire@samh.org.uk;
Web: www.samh.org.uk).
Chief Executive: Ms S. M. Barcus

Association for the Protection of Rural Scotland
3rd Floor, Gladstone's Land
483 Lawnmarket, Edinburgh, EH1 2NT
(Tel: 0131-225 7012/3; Fax: 0131-225 6592;
E-mail: aprs@aprs.org.uk;
Web: www.aprs.org.uk).
Director: Mrs J. Geddes

Association of Deer Management Groups
Dalhousie Estate Office, Brechin, Angus, DD9 6SG (Tel: 01356-624 566; Fax: 01356-623 725;
E-mail: dalhousieestates@btinternet.com).
Chairman: S. C. Gibbs
Secretary: R. M. J. Cooke

Association of Head Teachers in Scotland
Room B34, Northern College of Education
Gardyne Road, Dundee, DD5 1NY (Tel: 01382-458 802; Fax: 01382-455 622).
General Secretary: J. C. Smith

Association of Registrars of Scotland
77 Bank Street, Alexandria, G83 0LE
(Tel: 01389-608 980; Fax: 01389-608 982).
Hon. Secretary: A. P. P. Gallagher

Association of Scotland's Self-Caterers
Dalreoch, Dunning, Perth, PH2 0QJ
(Tel: 01764-684 100; Fax: 01764-684 633;
E-mail: secretary@assc.co.uk;
Web: www.assc.co.uk).
Chairman: D. M. A. Smythe
Secretary: Mrs W. W. Marshall

Association of Scottish Community Councils
21 Grosvenor Street, Edinburgh, EH12 5ED
(Tel: 0131-225 4033; Fax: 0131-225 4033;
E-mail: ascc@compuserve.com;
Web: www.ascc.org.uk).
Chairman: Ian Jarvie
Secretary: D. Murray

Association of Speakers Clubs
Beanlands Chase, 20 Rivermead Drive, Garstang,
Preston, Lancashire, PR3 1JJ (Tel: 01995-602 560; Fax: 01995-602 560;
E-mail: natsecasc@lineone.net).
National Secretary: Ms D. M. Dickinson

The Automobile Association
Fanum House, Erskine Harbour, Erskine,
Renfrewshire, PA8 6AT (Tel: 0141-848 8622;
Fax: 0141-848 8623;
E-mail: neil.greig@theaa.com;
Web: www.theaa.com).
Head of Motoring Policy: N. Greig

Ayrshire Archaeological and Natural History Society
10 Longlands Park, Ayr, KA7 4RJ
(Tel: 01292-441915).
Hon. Secretary: Dr T. Mathews
President: W. Layhe

Ayrshire Cattle Society of Great Britain and Ireland
1 Racecourse Road, Ayr, KA7 2DE
(Tel: 01292-267 123; Fax: 01292-611 973;
E-mail: society@ayrshires.org;
Web: www.ayrshires.org).
General Manager: David Sayce

BAFTA Scotland
249 West George Street, Glasgow, G2 4QE
(Tel: 0141-302 1770; Fax: 0141-302 1771;
E-mail: info@baftascotland.co.uk;
Web: www.baftascotland.co.uk).
Director: Ms A. Forsyth

Barnardo's Scotland
235 Corstorphine Road, Edinburgh, EH12 7AR
(Tel: 0131-334 9893; Fax: 0131-316 4008;
E-mail: martin.crewe@barnardos.org.uk;
Web: www.barnardos.org.uk).
Director: H.R. Mackintosh

The Big Issue Foundation Scotland
29 College Street, Glasgow, G1 1QH
(Tel: 0141-559 5555; Fax: 0141-552 4940).
Chief Executive: J. Cropper

Birth Resource Centre
40 Leamington Terrace, Edinburgh, EH10 4JL
(Tel: 0131-229 3667; Fax: 0131-229 6259;
E-mail: NadineEdw@aol.com).
Co-ordinators: Ms N. Edwards; Ms A.
McLaughlin; Ms D. Purdue; Ms E. Mollan

Botanical Society of Scotland
c/o Royal Botanic Garden, Inverleith Row,
Edinburgh, EH3 5LR (Tel: 0131-552 7171; Fax:
0131-248 2901).
Hon. General Secretary: R. Galt

Boys' and Girls' Clubs of Scotland
88 Giles Street, Edinburgh, EH6 6BZ
(Tel: 0131-555 1729; Fax: 0131-555 5921;
E-mail: bgcf@freezone.co.uk;
Web: www.freezone.co.uk/bqcscotland).
Chief Executive: T. Leishman

The Boys' Brigade – Scottish Headquarters
Carronvale House, Carronvale Road, Larbert,
FK5 3LH (Tel: 01324-562 008; Fax: 01324-552 323; E-mail: carronvale@boys-brigade.org.uk;
Web: www.boys-brigade.org.uk).
Director for Scotland: Tom Boyle

British Agencies for Adoption and Fostering
40 Shandwick Place, Edinburgh, EH2 4RT
(Tel: 0131-225 9285; Fax: 0131-226 3778;
E-mail: scotland@baaf.org.uk;
Web: www.baaf.org.uk).
Director - Scotland: Ms B. Hudson
Chief Executive: Mrs F. Collier

British Association of Social Workers
28 North Bridge, Edinburgh, EH1 1QG
(Tel: 0131-225 4549; Fax: 0131-220 0636;

E-mail: r.stark@scotland.basw.co.uk;
Web: www.basw.co.uk).
Professional Officer: Mrs R. Stark

British Deaf Association Scotland
3rd Floor, Princes House, 5 Shandwick Place,
Edinburgh, EH2 4RG (Tel: 0131-221 1137; Fax:
0131-221 7960; Web: www.bda.org.uk).
Development Manager, Scotland:
Ms L. Mitchell

British Deer Society (Scottish Office)
Trian House, Comrie, Perthshire, PH6 2HZ
(Tel: 01764-670 062; Fax: 01764-670 062;
E-mail: scottishsecretary@bds.org.uk;
Web: www.bds.org.uk).
Secretary: H. Rose

British Limbless Ex-Servicemen's Association
24 Dundas Street, Edinburgh, EH3 6JN
(Tel: 0131-538 6966).
President: A. Delworth, MBE

British Lung Foundation
Royal College of Physicians and Surgeons
232–242 St Vincent Street, Glasgow, G2 5RJ
(Tel: 0141-204 4110; Fax: 0141-204 4110;
E-mail: redballoon@blfscotland.org.uk;
Web: www.lunguk.org).
Manager: Jim Gardner

British Red Cross
Alexandra House, 204 Bath Street, Glasgow, G2
4HL (Tel: 0141-332 9591; Fax: 0141-332 8493;
Web: www.redcross.org.uk).
Director: G. McLoughlin

Business for Scotland
29 Montrose Avenue, Hillington Park, Glasgow,
G52 4LA (Tel: 0141-882 4151; Fax: 0141-810
5547; E-mail: sbarber@busforscot.co.uk;
Web: www.businessforscotland.org).
Chairman: T. Hamilton

CancerBACUP
2-Feb, 30 Bell Street, Glasgow, G1 1LG
(Tel: 0141-553 1553; Fax: 0141-553 2686;
E-mail: jennyw@cancerbacup.org;
Web: www.cancerbacup.org.uk).
Chief Executive: Ms J. Rule

Capability Scotland
22 Corstorphine Road, Edinburgh, EH12 6HP
(Tel: 0131-337 9876; Fax: 0131-346 7864;
E-mail: capability@capability-scotland.org.uk;
Web: www.capability-scotland.org.uk).
Chief Executive: A. Dickson

Carers National Association
3rd Floor, 91 Mitchell Street, Glasgow, G1 3LN
(Tel: 0141-221 9141; Fax: 0141-221 9140;
E-mail: info@carerscotland.demon.co.uk).
Chief Executive: Ms D. Whitworth
Director - Scotland: J. Wilkes

Carnegie Dunfermline Trust
Abbey Park House, Dunfermline, Fife, KY12
7PB (Tel: 01383-723638; Fax: 01383-721862;
E-mail: admin@carnegietrust.com).
Secretary and Treasurer: W. C. Runciman

Carnegie Hero Fund Trust
Abbey Park House, Dunfermline, Fife, KY12
7PB (Tel: 01383-723 638; Fax: 01383-721 862).
Secretary: W. C. Runciman

Carnegie United Kingdom Trust
Comely Park House, Dunfermline, Fife, KY12
7EJ (Tel: 01383-721 445; Fax: 01383-620 682;
Web: www.carnegieuktrust.org.uk).
Secretary: C. J. Naylor, OBE

Centre for Scottish Cultural Studies
University of Strathclyde, Livingstone Tower, 26
Richmond Street, Glasgow, G1 1XH
(Tel: 0141-548 3518; Fax: 0141-552 3493;
E-mail: ken.simpson@strath.ac.uk).
Director: Dr K. G. Simpson

Centre for Scottish Public Policy
16 Forth Street, Edinburgh, EH1 3LH
(Tel: 0131-477 8219; Fax: 0131-477 8220;
E-mail: mail@jwcentre.demon.co.uk).
Conference Officer: P. Herd

Chartered Institute of Bankers in Scotland
Drumsheugh House, 38B Drumsheugh Gardens,
Edinburgh, EH3 7SW (Tel: 0131-473 7777; Fax:
0131-473 7788; E-mail: info@ciobs.org.uk;
Web: www.ciobs.org.uk).
Chief Executive: C. W. Munn

Chest, Heart and Stroke Scotland
65 North Castle Street, Edinburgh, EH2 3LT
(Tel: 0131-225 6963; Fax: 0131-220 6313;
E-mail: admin@chss.org.uk;
Web: www.chss.org.uk).
Chief Executive: D. H. Clark

ChildLine Scotland
18 Albion Street, Glasgow, G1 1LH (Tel: 0141-
552 1123. Helpline: 0800-1111; Fax: 0141-552
3089; E-mail: scotland@childline.org.uk;
Web: www.childline.org.uk).
Director: Ms A. Houston

Children 1st (Royal Scottish Society for Prevention of Cruelty to Children)
Melville House, 41 Polwarth Terrace, Edinburgh, EH11 1NU (Tel: 0131-337 8539; Fax: 0131-346 8284; E-mail: info@children1st.org.uk; Web: www.children1st.org.uk).
Chief Executive: Mrs M. McKay
Director of Children and Family Services: Ms C. Dewar

Children in Scotland
Princes House, 5 Shandwick Place, Edinburgh, EH2 4RG (Tel: 0131-228 8484; Fax: 0131-228 8585; E-mail: info@childreninscotland.org.uk; Web: www.childreninscotland.org.uk).
Chief Executive: Dr B. Cohen

Christian Aid Scotland
41 George IV Bridge, Edinburgh, EH1 1EL (Tel: 0131-220 1254; Fax: 0131-225 8861; E-mail: edinburgh@christian-aid.org; Web: www.christian-aid.org.uk).
National Secretary: Revd J. Wylie

The Church of Scotland Guild
121 George Street, Edinburgh, EH2 4YN (Tel: 0131-225 5722; Fax: 0131-220 3113; E-mail: guild@cofscotland.org.uk; Web: www.churchofscotland.org.uk).
General Secretary: Mrs A. M. Twaddle
Information Officer: Mrs F. J. Lange

Citizens Advice Scotland
26 George Square, Edinburgh, EH8 9LD (Tel: 0131-667 0156; Fax: 0131-668 4359).
Chief Executive Officer: Mrs K. Lyle

Clyde Area Biological Records Centre
Foremount House, Kilbarchan, Renfrewshire, PA10 2EZ (Tel: 01505-702419).
Chairman: Dr J. A. Gibson

College of Homeopathy
17 Queens Crescent, Glasgow, G4 9BL (Tel: 0141-332 3917).
Principal: Ms M. Roy

Comunn Na Gàidhlig
5 Mitchell's Lane, Inverness, IV2 3HQ (Tel: 01463-234 138; Fax: 01463-237 470; E-mail: oifis@cnag.org.uk; Web: www.cnag.org.uk).
Chief Executive: A. Campbell

Community Care Forum
c/o 18–19 Claremont Crescent, Edinburgh, EH7 4QD (Tel: 0131-557 2711; Fax: 0131-557 2711;

E-mail: karen.jackson@scvo.org.uk).
National Development Officer: Ms K. Jackson

Community Service Volunteers Scotland
Wellgate House, 200 Cowgate, Edinburgh, EH1 1NQ (Tel: 0131-622 7766; Fax: 0131-622 7755; E-mail: edinburgh@csvscotland.u-net.com; Web: www.csv.org.uk).
Director, Scotland: Ms C. Stevens

Scottish Cot Death Trust
Royal Hospital for Sick Children, Yorkhill, Glasgow, G3 8SJ (Tel: 0141-357 3946; Fax: 0141-334 1376; E-mail: hb1w@clinmed.gla.ac.uk; Web: www.gla.ac.uk/Acad/ChildHealth/SCDT).
Executive Director: Ms H. Brooke

Council for Arbitration
Exel House, 30 Semple Street, Edinburgh, EH3 8BL (Tel: 0131-226 2552; Fax: 0131-226 2501; E-mail: jim.arnott@macroberts.co.uk).
Chief Executive: J. Arnott

Council for Scottish Archaeology
c/o National Museums of Scotland, Chambers Street, Edinburgh, EH1 1JF (Tel: 0131-247 4119; Fax: 0131-247 4126; E-mail: csa@nms.ac.uk; Web: www.britarch.ac.uk/csa).
Director: D. Lynn

Alcohol Focus Scotland
2nd Floor, 166 Buchanan Street, Glasgow, G1 2LW (Tel: 0141-572 6700; Fax: 0141-333 1606; E-mail: enquiries@alcohol-focus-scotland.org.uk; Web: www.alcohol-focus-scotland.org.uk).
Chief Executive: J. Law

Cystic Fibrosis Trust
Princes House, 5 Shandwick Place, Edinburgh, EH2 4RG (Tel: 0131-211 1110; Fax: 0131-221 1110; E-mail: hmacfarlane@cftrust.org.uk; Web: www.cftrust.org.uk).
Chief Executive: Ms R. Barnes
Regional Support Co-ordinator: Mrs H. MacFarlane

Diabetes UK
Savoy House, 140 Sauchiehall Street, Glasgow, G2 3DH (Tel: 0141-332 2700; Fax: 0141-332 4880; E-mail: scotland@diabetes.org.uk; Web: www.diabetes.org.uk).
National Manager: Mrs D. Henry

The Duke of Edinburgh's Award
69 Dublin Street, Edinburgh, EH3 6NS
(Tel: 0131-556 9097; Fax: 0131-557 8044;
E-mail: scotland@theaward.org;
Web: www.theaward.org).
Secreteray for Scotland: Miss J. Shepherd

Scottish Dyslexia Association Scotland
Stirling Business Centre, Wellgreen, Stirling,
FK8 2DZ (Tel: 01786-446 650; Fax: 01786-471
235; E-mail: dyslexia.scotland@dial.pipex.com;
Web: www.dyslexia.scotland.dial.pipex.com).
Chairman: Mrs E. Reilly

Dyslexia Institute Scotland
74 Victoria Crescent Road, Dowanhill, Glasgow,
G12 9JN (Tel: 0141-334 4549; Fax: 0141-339
8879; E-mail: glasgow@dyslexia-inst.org.uk;
Web: www.dyslexia-inst.org.uk).
Principal: Mrs E. Mackenzie

Earl Haig Fund Scotland
New Haig House, Logie Green Road, Edinburgh,
EH7 4HR (Tel: 0131-557 2782; Fax: 0131-557
5819; E-mail: earlhaigfund@hotmail.com).
Chief Executive: Maj.-Gen. J. D. MacDonald,
CB, CBE

Edinburgh Bibliographical Society
c/o National Library of Scotland, George IV
Bridge, Edinburgh, EH1 1EW (Tel: 0131-226
4531; Fax: 0131-220 6662).
President: Miss B. E. Moon
Hon. Editor of the Transactions: K. Dunn

**Employment Opportunities for People with
Disabilities**
Unit 26, Adelphi Centre, 12 Commercial Road,
Glasgow, G5 0PQ (Tel: 0141-429 8429; Fax:
0141-429 4023;
E-mail: eopps.glasgow@connectfree.co.uk;
Web: www.opportunities.org.uk).
 Director: G. Young

**ENABLE (Scottish Society for the Mentally
Handicapped)**
7 Buchanan Street, Glasgow, G1 3HL
(Tel: 0141-226 4541; Fax: 0141-204 4398;
E-mail: enable@enable.org.uk).
Director: N. Dunning

Engender
13 Gayfield Square, Edinburgh, EH1 3NX
(Tel: 0131-558 9596;
E-mail: engender@engender.org.uk;
Web: www.engender.org.uk).
Convenor: Ms S. Robertson

Epilepsy Action of Scotland
48 Govan Road, Glasgow, G51 1JL
(Tel: 0141-427 4911; Helpline 0141-427 5225;
Fax: 0141-419 1709;
E-mail: enquiries@epilepsyscotland.org.uk;
Web: www.epilepsyscotland.org.uk).
Chief Executive: Ms H. Mounfield

Erskine Hospital
Bishopton, Renfrewshire, PA7 5PU
(Tel: 0141-812 1100; Fax: 0141-812 3733;
Web: www.erskine.org/welcome.htm).
Chief Executive: Col. M. F. Gibson, OBE

The European Movement
13A Melville Street, Edinburgh, EH3 7PE
(Tel: 0131-220 0377; Fax: 0131-220 0377;
E-mail: scotland@euromove.org.uk;
Web: www.euromove.org.uk).
National Organiser: Ms B. MacLeod

Ex-Services Mental Welfare Society
Hollybush House, Hollybush, by Ayr, KA6 7EA
(Tel: 01292-560 214; Fax: 01292-560 871;
E-mail: rdsi@combatstress.org.uk;
Web: www.combatstress.com).
Regional Director, Scotland and Ireland: Wg
Cdr. D. Devine

Fair Isle Bird Observatory Trust
Fair Isle Bird Observatory, Fair Isle, Shetland,
ZE2 9JU (Tel: 01595-760 258; Fax: 01595-760
258; E-mail: fairisle.birdobs@zetnet.co.uk;
Web: www.fairislebirdobs.co.uk).
Administrator: Mrs H. Shaw

Family History Society
164 King Street, Aberdeen, AB24 5BD
(Tel: 01224-646 323; Fax: 01224-639 096;
E-mail: enquiries@anesfhs.org.uk;
Web: www.anesfhs.org.uk).
Chairperson: Mrs G. Murton

Family Planning Association Scotland
Unit 10, Firhill Business Centre
76 Firhill Road, Glasgow, G20 7BA
(Tel: 0141-576 5088; Fax: 0141-576 5006;
E-mail: fpascotland@dial.pipex.com;
Web: www.fpa.org.uk).
Director: Susan Stewart
Information Officer: Ms J. Nicholson

Fèisean Nan Gàidheal
Meall House, Portree, Isle of Skye (Tel: 01478-
613 355; Fax: 01478-613 399; E-mail: fios@feisen.org;
Web: www.feisean.org).
Director: A. Cormack
Development Officer: D. Boag

Findhorn Foundation
The Park, Findhorn, Forres, Moray, IV36 3TZ
(Tel: 01309-690 311; Fax: 01309-691 301;
E-mail: reception@findhorn.org;
Web: www.findhorn.org).
Co-Chairpersons: Ms M. Hollander

Fishmongers' Company
Fala Acre, Fala Village, Pathhead, Midlothian,
EH37 5SY (Tel: 01875-833 246; Fax: 01875-
833 246).
Salmon Fisheries Inspector: W. F. Beattie,
MBE

**Fraser of Allander Institute for Research on the
Scottish Economy**
University of Strathclyde, Curran Building, 100
Cathedral Street, Glasgow, G4 0LN
(Tel: 0141-548 3958; Fax: 0141-552 8340;
E-mail: fraser@strath.ac.uk;
Web: www.fraser.strath.ac.uk).
Director: J. Ireland
Policy Director: B. Ashcroft

Friends of the Earth Scotland
72 Newhaven Road, Edinburgh, EH6 5QG
(Tel: 0131-554 9977; Fax: 0131-554 8656;
E-mail: info@foe-scotland.org.uk;
Web: www.foe-scotland.org.uk).
Director: K. Dunion, OBE

The Game Conservancy Trust
Scottish Headquarters, Couston, Newtyle,
Perthshire, PH12 8UT (Tel: 01828-650 543; Fax:
01828-650 560; E-mail: imccall@gct.org.uk;
Web: www.gct.org.uk).
Director: I. McCall

The Girls' Brigade in Scotland
Boys' Brigade House, 168 Bath Street, Glasgow,
G2 4TQ (Tel: 0141-332 1765; Fax: 0141-331
2681; E-mail: hq@girls-brigade-scotland.org.uk;
Web: www.girls-brigade-scotland.org.uk).
National Director: Mrs A. Webster

Guide Association Scotland
16 Coates Crescent, Edinburgh, EH3 7AH
(Tel: 0131-226 4511; Fax: 0131-220 4828;
E-mail: administrator@scottishguides.org.uk).
Executive Director: Miss S. Pitches

Guide Dogs for the Blind Association
Princess Alexandra House, Dundee Road, Forfar,
DD8 1JA (Tel: 01307-463 531; Fax: 01307-465
233; Web: www.gdba.org.uk).
Operations Director: Ms J. Patmore

Hawick Archaeological Society
Orrock House, Stirches Road, Hawick,
Roxburghshire, TD9 7HF (Tel: 01450-375 546).
Hon. Secretary: I. W. Landles

Hearing Dogs for Deaf People
29 Craighiehall Crescent, West Freelands,
Erskine, Renfrewshire, PA8 7DD
(Tel: 0141-812 6542).
**Community Fund-raiser and Scottish
Representative:** Ms M. Arthur

Hebridean Wale and Dolphin Trust
28 Main Street, Tobermory, Isle of Mull, Argyll,
PA75 6NU (Tel: 01688-302 620; Fax: 01688-302
728; E-mail: hwdt@sol.co.uk;
Web: www.hwdt.org).
Executive Director: Ms C. Fleming
Scientific Director: Dr C. Parsons

Help the Aged
Heriot House, Heriothill Terrace, Edinburgh,
EH7 4DY (Tel: 0131-556 4666; Fax: 0131-557
5115; Web: www.helptheaged.co.uk).
Scottish Executive: Ms E. Duncan

Highland Cattle Society
59 Drumlanrig Street, Thornhill, Dunfries, DG3
5LY (Tel: 01848-331 866; Fax: 01848-331 183;
E-mail: info@highlandcattlesociety.com;
Web: www.highlandcattlesociety.com).
Secretary: A. H. G. Wilson

Housing Association Ombudsman for Scotland
2 Belford Road, Edinburgh, EH4 3BL
(Tel: 0131-220 0599; Fax: 0131-220 0577).
Ombudsman: Barney Crockett

Scottish Human Rights Centre
146 Holland Street, Glasgow, G2 4NG
(Tel: 0141-332 5960; Fax: 0141-332 5309;
E-mail: shrc@dial.pipex.com;
Web: www.shrc.pipex.com).
Director: Prof. A. Miller

Immigration Advisory Service
115 Bath Street, Glasgow, G2 2SZ
(Tel: 0141-248 2956; Fax: 0141-221 5388;
E-mail: glasgow@iasuk.org;
Web: www.iasuk.org).
Chief Executive: K. Best

Imperial Cancer Research Fund
Scottish Fundraising Centre
Wallace House, Maxwell Place, Stirling, FK8 1JU
(Tel: 01786-446 689; Fax: 01786-446 691;
E-mail: appealsscot@icrf.icnet.uk;

Web: www.imperialcancer.co.uk).
Fundraising Director: J. Brady

Institute of Chartered Accountants of Scotland
CA House, 21 Haymarket Yards, Edinburgh, EH12 5BH (Tel: 0131-347 0100; Fax: 0131-347 0105; E-mail: enquiries@icas.org.uk; Web: www.icas.org.uk).
Chief Executive: D. A. Brew

Inverness Field Club
Swallowhill House, Lentran, Inverness, IV3 8RJ (Tel: 01463-831 057;
E-mail: invernessfieldclub@btinternet.com; Web: www.btinternet/invernessfieldclub).
Hon. Secretary: Mrs G. Cameron

John Muir Trust
41 Commercial Street, Edinburgh, EH6 6JD (Tel: 0131-554 0114/ 1324; Fax: 0131-555 2112; E-mail: admin@jmt.org; Web: www.jmt.org).
Director: N. Hawkins

Jubilee 2000 Scottish Coalition
121 George Street, Edinburgh, EH2 4YN (Tel: 0131-225 4321; Fax: 0131-226 4293; E-mail: jubileescot@freeuk.com; Web: www.jubileescot.freeuk.com).
Co-ordinator: Mr D. Anthoney

Keep Scotland Beautiful
7 Melville Terrace, Stirling, FK8 2ND (Tel: 01786-471 333; Fax: 01786-464 611; E-mail: ksb@tidybritain.org.uk).
Director: J. P. Summers

King George's Fund for Sailors
HMS Caledonia, Rosyth, Dunfermline, KY11 2XH (Tel: 01383-419 969; Fax: 01383-419 969; E-mail: scotland@kgfs.org.uk; Web: www.kgfs.org.uk).
Area Organiser: Lt. Cdr. R. Nurick, RN
Assistant Area Organiser: Mrs M. White

Leonard Cheshire Scotland
161 Lower Granton Road, Edinburgh, EH5 1EY (Tel: 0131-538 5544; Fax: 0131-538 5566; E-mail: info@scot.leonard-cheshire.org.uk; Web: www.leonard-cheshire.org).
Director of Scottish Services: Mr Stephen Neale
Fundraising Manager: Ms J. Pike

Leukaemia Research Fund
43 Westbourne Gardens, Glasgow, G12 9XQ (Tel: 0141-339 0690; Fax: 0141-339 0690).
Executive Director: D. L. Osborne
Scottish Secretary: Mrs M. Naddell

Macmillan Cancer Relief
9 Castle Terrace, Edinburgh, EH1 2DP (Tel: 0131-229 3276; Fax: 0131-228 6710; Web: www.macmillan.org.uk).
Director for Scotland and Northern Ireland: I. R. L. Gibson

Mental Health Foundation Scotland
5th Floor, Merchants House, 30 George Square, Glasgow, G2 1EG (Tel: 0141-572 0125; Fax: 0141-572 0246; E-mail: scotland@mhf.org.uk; Web: www.mentalhealth.org.uk).
Director, Scotland: Ms M. Halliday

The Mission to Seafarers Scotland
Containerbase, Gartsherrie Road, Coatbridge, Lanarkshire, ML5 2DS (Tel: 01236-440 132).
Adminstration Manager
Secretary: Mrs Lesley Hutton

The National Association for Gifted Children in Scotland
PO Box 2024, Glasgow, G32 9YD (Tel: 0141-639 4797; Fax: 0141-778 0556; E-mail: nagcs.org@talk21.com).
Chairman: D. M. Henderson
Counsellor: Mrs S. Divecha

National Asthma Campaign Scotland
2A North Charlotte Street, Edinburgh, EH2 4HR (Tel: 0131-226 2544; Fax: 0131-226 2401; E-mail: enquiries@asthma5.demon.co.uk; Web: www.asthma.org.uk).
Chief Executive: Ms A. Bradley
Director: Marjory O'Donnell

National Blood Transfusion Association
c/o Scottish National Blood Transfusion Service 21 Ellen's Glen Road, Edinburgh, EH17 7QT (Tel: 0131-536 5700; Fax: 0131-536 5301).
SecretaryDirector: Dr Bob Perry

National Childbirth Trust
Stockbridge Health Centre, 1 India Place, Edinburgh, EH3 6EH (Tel: 0131-260 9201).
Administrator: Ms K. McGlew

Fostering Network
2nd Floor, Ingram House, 227 Ingram Street, Glasgow, G1 1DA (Tel: 0141-204 1400; Fax: 0141-204 6588; E-mail: linda.curran@fostercare-scotland.org.uk; Web: www.fostercare.scotland.org.uk).
Administrator: Ms L. Curran
Manager: B. Ritchie

National House-Building Council (NHBC)
42 Colinton Road, Edinburgh, EH10 5BT
(Tel: 0131-313 1001; Fax: 0131-313 1211;
Web: www.nhbc.co.uk).
Director: M. MacLeod

The National Trust for Scotland
28 Charlotte Square, Edinburgh, EH2 4ET
(Tel: 0131-243 9300; Fax: 0131-243 9301;
E-mail: information@nts.org.uk;
Web: www.nts.org.uk).
Director: T. Croft

National Union of Students Scotland
29 Forth Street, Edinburgh, EH1 3LE
(Tel: 0131-556 6598; Fax: 0131-557 5679;
E-mail: nus.scot@dircon.co.uk;
Web: www.nusonline.co.uk).
President: M. Telford
Director: L. Jarnecki

The Scottish National War Memorial
The Castle, Edinburgh, EH1 2YT
(Tel: 0131-226 7393; Fax: 0131-225 8920;
Web: www.snwm.org.uk).
Secretary to the Trustees: Lt.-Col. I. Shepherd

NCH Action for Children Scotland
17 Newton Place, Glasgow, G3 7PY
(Tel: 0141-332 4041; Fax: 0141-332 7002;
Web: www.ncha.org.uk).
Director (acting): J. Connelly

One Parent Families Scotland
13 Gayfield Square, Edinburgh, EH1 3NX
(Tel: 0131-556 3899/ 4563; Fax: 0131-557 9650;
E-mail: opfs@gn.apc.org;
Web: www.opfs.org.uk).
Director: Ms S. Robertson

Ornithologists' Club
21 Regent Terrace, Edinburgh, EH7 5BT
(Tel: 0131-556 6042; Fax: 0131-558 9947;
E-mail: mail@the.soc.org.uk;
Web: www.the.soc.org.uk).
Secretary: Miss S. Laing

Outward Bound Scotland
Loch Eil Centre, Achdalieu, Corpach, Fort
William, PH33 7NN (Tel: 01397-772 866; Fax:
01397-773 905;
Web: www.outwardbound-uk.org).
Director: Sir Michael Hobbs, KCVO, CBE
General Manager: T. Shepherd

Oxfam in Scotland
5th Floor, Fleming House, 134 Renfrew Street,
Glasgow, G3 6ST (Tel: 0141-331 1455; Fax:
0141-331 2264; Web: www.oxfam.org.uk).
Head of Oxfam Scotland: Mrs M. Hearle

PA News Ltd
124 Portman Street, Kinning Park, Glasgow, G41
1EJ (Tel: 0141-429 0037; Fax: 0141-429 1596;
Web: www.pressassociation.press.net).
Editor, PA Scotland: Melanie Harvey

**Parkinson's Disease Society - Scottish
Resource**
10 Claremont Terrace, Glasgow, G3 7XR
(Tel: 0141-332 3343; Fax: 0141-353 2701;
E-mail: pds.scotland@community-care.net).
Regional Manager: D. R. McNiven

PDSA (People's Dispensary for Sick Animals)
Community Activities Office, Veterinary Centre
Muiryfauld Drive, Tollcross, Glasgow, G31 5RT
(Tel: 0141-778 9229; Fax: 0141-778 9229;
E-mail: crawford.lynn@pdsa.org.uk).
Regional Fundraising Manager:
Ms L. Crawford

PHAB Scotland
Norton Park, 57 Albion Road, Edinburgh, EH7
5QY (Tel: 0131-475 2313; Fax: 0131-475 2685;
E-mail: info@phab.org.uk;
Web: www.phab.org.uk).
Chief Executive: Miss F. Hird

Post Office Users' Council for Scotland
Queen Margaret University College, Clerwood
Terrace, Edinburgh, EH12 8TS (Tel: 0845-601
3265; Fax: 0131-334 3972;
E-mail: scotland@postwatch.co.uk;
Web: www.postwatch.co.uk).
Chairman: Dr. Tom Begg
Director: Tricia Dow

The Poverty Alliance
162 Buchanan Street, Glasgow, G1 2LL
(Tel: 0141-353 0440; Fax: 0141-353 0686;
E-mail: admin@povertyalliance.org;
Web: www.povertyalliance.org).
Director: D. Killeen

Prince's Scottish Youth Business Trust
6th Floor, Mercantile Chambers
53 Bothwell Street, Glasgow, G2 6TS (Tel: 0141-
248 4999; E-mail: team@psybt.org.uk;
Web: www.psybt.org.uk).
Director: Mark Strudwick, CBE
Director of Operations: Ann Scott

Prince's Trust Scotland
The Guildhall (1st Floor), 57 Queen Street, Glasgow, G1 3EW (Tel: 0141-204 4409; Fax: 0141-221 8221;
E-mail: volscot@princes-trust.org.uk;
Web: www.princes-trust.org.uk).
Office Manager: Mrs Y. Murphy-Beggs

The Princess Royal Trust for Carers
Campbell House, 215 West Campbell Street, Glasgow, G2 4TT (Tel: 0141-221 5066; Fax: 0141-221 4623;
E-mail: infoscotland@carers.org;
Web: www.carers.org).
Chief Executive: Ms A. Ryan

Quarriers
Head Office, Quarriers Village, Bridge of Weir, Renfrewshire, PA11 3SX (Tel: 01505-612 224; Fax: 01505-613 906;
E-mail: enquiries@quarriers.org.uk;
Web: www.quarriers.org.uk).
Chief Executive: P. Robinson

Queen Victoria School
Dunblane, Perthshire, FK15 0JY (Tel: 01786-822 288; Fax: 0131-310 2955/ 2926;
E-mail: enquiries@qvs.org.uk;
Web: www.qvs.org.uk).
Headmaster: B. Raine

Queen's Nursing Institute
31 Castle Terrace, Edinburgh, EH1 2EL (Tel: 0131-229 2333; Fax: 0131-228 9066;
E-mail: qnis@aol.com;
Web: www.qnis.co.uk).
Finance Director: Michael S. Chambers

Scottish Record Society
Department of History, University of Glasgow, Glasgow, G12 8QH (Tel: 0141-339 8855 ext. 5682).
Hon. Secretary: Prof. J. Kirk

Robert Burns World Federation Ltd
Dean Castle Country Park, Dower House, Kilmarnock, KA3 1XB
(Tel: 01563-572 469; Fax: 01563-572 469;
E-mail: robertburnsfederation@kilmarnock.26.freeserve.co.uk).
Chief Executive: Mrs S. Bell

Royal Academy of Engineering
Department of Petroleum Engineering, Heriot-Watt University, Riccarton, Edinburgh, EH14 4AS (Tel: 0131-451 3128; Fax: 0131-451 3127;
E-mail: brian.smart@pet.hw.ac.uk;

Web: www.pet.hw.ac.uk).
Head of Department: Prof. B. G. D. Smart

Royal British Legion Scotland
New Haig House, Logie Green Road, Edinburgh, EH7 4HR; Fax: 0131-557 5819;
E-mail: rblshq@care4free.net).
General Secretary

Royal Caledonian Horticultural Society
6 Kirkliston Road, South Queensferry, EH30 9LT (Tel: 0131-331 1011;
E-mail: tom.mabbott@edinburgh.almac.co.uk;
Web: www.rchs.fsnet.co.uk).
Secretary: T. Mabbott

Royal Celtic Society
23 Rutland Street, Edinburgh, EH1 2RN (Tel: 0131-228 6449; Fax: 0131-229 6987;
E-mail: gcameron@stuartandstuart.co.uk).
Secretary: J. G. Cameron

Royal Faculty of Procurators in Glasgow
12 Nelson Mandela Place, Glasgow, G2 1BT (Tel: 0141-331 0533; Fax: 0141-332 9401;
E-mail: i.c.pearson@btinternet.com;
Web: www.rfpg.org).
General Manager: I. C. Pearson

Royal Highland and Agricultural Society of Scotland
Royal Highland Centre, Ingliston, Edinburgh, EH28 8NF (Tel: 0131-335 6200; Fax: 0131-333 5236; E-mail: info@rhass.org.uk;
Web: www.rhass.org.uk).
Chief Executive: R. Jones

Royal National Institute for Deaf People
Crowngate Business Centre, Brook Street, Glasgow, G40 3AP (Tel: 0141-564 0053. Textphone: 0141-550 5750; Fax: 0141-550 8215;
Web: www.rnid.org.uk).
Director: Ms L. Lawson

Royal National Institute for the Blind Scotland
Dunedin House, 25 Ravelston Terrace, Edinburgh, EH4 3TP (Tel: 0131-311 8500; Fax: 0131-311 8529; Web: www.rnib.org.uk).
Director: Mike Cairns

Royal National Lifeboat Institution Scotland
Bellevue House, Hopetoun Street, Edinburgh, EH7 4ND (Tel: 0131-557 9171; Fax: 0131-557 6943; E-mail: ro/scot@rnli.org.uk;
Web: www.rnli.org.uk).
National Organiser, Scotland: Mrs M. Caldwell

Royal National Mission to Deep Sea Fishermen
Scottish Regional Office, Melita House, Station Road, Polmont, Stirlingshire, FK2 0UD
(Tel: 01324-716 857; Fax: 01324-716 423;
E-mail: ian.rnmdsf@talk21.com).
Director - Scotland: I. Baillie

Royal Naval and Royal Marine Association
Heriot Hill House, 1 Broughton Road, Edinburgh, EH7 4EW (Tel: 0131-556 2973).
Hon. Secretary: W. Tovey

Royal Scottish Academy
17 Waterloo Palce, Edinburgh, EN1 3BG
(Tel: 0131-558 7097; Fax: 0131-557 6417;
E-mail: info@royalscottishacademy.org.uk;
Web: www.royalscottishacademy.org.uk).
Administrative Secretary: B. Laidlaw
Assistant Administrative Secretary: Ms M. Wilson

Royal Scottish Agricultural Benevolent Institution
Ingliston, Edinburgh, EH28 8NB
(Tel: 0131-333 1023/1027; Fax: 0131-333 1027;
E-mail: rsabi@charity.vfree.com;
Web: www.rsabi.org.uk).
Director: I. C. Purves-Hume
Welfare Secretary: Ms E. Brath

Royal Scottish Geographical Society
Graham Hills Building, 40 George Street, Glasgow, G1 1QE (Tel: 0141-552 3330; Fax: 0141-522 3331; E-mail: rsgs@strath.ac.uk;
Web: www.geo.ed.ac.uk/~RSGS/).
Director: Dr D. M. Munro

Royal Scottish Pipe Band Association
45 Washington Street, Glasgow, G3 8AZ
(Tel: 0141-221 5414; Fax: 0141-221 1561).
Executive Officer: Mr. Iain Embelton

Royal Society for the Prevention of Accidents (RoSPA)
Slateford House, 53 Lanark Road, Edinburgh, EH14 1TL (Tel: 0131-455 7657; Fax: 0131-443 9442; E-mail: mmcdonnell@rospa.com;
Web: www.rospa.co.uk).
Road Safety Manager (Scotland): M. A. McDonnell

The Royal Society for the Protection of Birds
Dunedin House, 25 Ravelston Terrace, Edinburgh, EH4 3TP (Tel: 0131-311 6500; Fax: 0131-311 6569; E-mail: rspb.scotland@rspb.org.uk;
Web: www.rspb.org.uk).
Director: Stuart Housden

Royal Society of Edinburgh
22–26 George Street, Edinburgh, EH2 2PQ
(Tel: 0131-240 5000; Fax: 0131-240 5024;
E-mail: rse@rse.org.uk;
Web: www.royalsoced.org.uk).
Executive Secretary: Dr W. Duncan

Royal United Kingdom Beneficent Association
PO Box 16058, Gargunnock, nr Stirling, FK8 3YN (Tel: 01786-860 446; Fax: 01786-860 446).
Representative: Mrs M. Graham

Royal Zoological Society of Scotland
National Zoological Park, Edinburgh Zoo, 134 Corstorphine Road, Edinburgh, EH12 6TS
(Tel: 0131-334 9171; Fax: 0131-316 4050;
E-mail: marketing@rzss.org.uk;
Web: www.edinburghzoo.org.uk).
Director: Prof. D. Waugh, Ph.D.

SACRO, Safeguarding Communities Reducing Offending
1 Broughton Market, Edinburgh, EH3 6NU
(Tel: 0131-624 7270; Fax: 0131-624 7269;
E-mail: info@national.sacro.org.uk;
Web: www.sacro.org.uk).
Chief Executive: Ms S. Matheson
Publicity Officer: Ms L. Connelly

St Andrew Animal Fund
Queensferry Chambers, 10 Queensferry Street, Edinburgh, EH2 4PG (Tel: 0131-225 2116; Fax: 0131-220 6377;
E-mail: advocates.animals@virgin.net;
Web: advocatesforanimals.org.uk).
Secretary: L. Ward

St Andrew's Children's Society Ltd
Gillis Centre, 113 Whitehouse Loan, Edinburgh, EH9 1BB (Tel: 0131-452 8248; Fax: 0131-452 8248; E-mail: info@standrews-children.org.uk).
Director: S. J. Small
Chairperson: Ms M. McEvoy

Saltire Society
9 Fountain Close, 22 High Street, Edinburgh, EH1 1TF (Tel: 0131-556 1836; Fax: 0131-557 1675; E-mail: saltire@saltire.org.uk;
Web: www.saltire-society.demon.co.uk).
Adminstrator: Mrs K. Munro

Save the Children in Scotland
2nd Floor, Haymarket House
8 Clifton Terrace, Edinburgh, EH12 5DR
(Tel: 0131-527 8200; Fax: 0131-527 8201;
E-mail: scotland@scfuk.org.uk;
Web: www.savethechildrenscot.org.uk).

Programme Director: Mrs A. Davies

Scots Language Resource Centre Association
A. K. Bell Library, 2–8 York Place, Perth, PH2 8EP (Tel: 01738-440 199; Fax: 01738-477 010; E-mail: slrc@sol.co.uk; Web: www.pkc.gov.uk/slrc/index/html).
National Information Officer: S.A. Robertson
Convener: Prof. R. Johnstone

Scots Language Society
c/o Scots Language Resource Centre
A. K. Bell Library, York Place, Perth, PH2 8EP (Tel: 01738-440 199; Fax: 01738-646 505; E-mail: D.Brown1@tesco.net).
Membership Secretary: D. H. Brown

Scots Leid Associe
The A.K. Bell Library, York Place, Perth, PH2 8EP (Tel: 01738-440 199;
E-mail: d.brown1@tesco.net;
Web: www.geocities.com/Athens/sparta/2933/).
Lallans Editor: J. Law

Scots Tung
27 Stoneyhill Avenue, Musselburgh, Midlothian, EH21 6SB (Tel: 0131-665 5440/9351;
E-mail: rfairnie@btinternet.com;
Web: www.mlove.free-online.co.uk/
(sharedwiScotsSpeikersCurn-Glesca)).
Convener: R. Heinsar
Secretar: F. Fairnie

Scottish Association of Law Centres
c/o Paisley Law Centre, 65 George Street, Paisley, PA1 2JY (Tel: 0141-561 7266; Fax: 0141-561 7164; E-mail: LW@PaisleyLawCentre.co.uk).
Secretary: Ms L. Welsh

Scottish Business in the Community
PO Box 408, Bankhead Avenue, Edinurgh, EH11 4HE (Tel: 0131-442 2020; Fax: 0131-442 3555; E-mail: info@sbscot.com;
Web: www.sbcscot.com).
Chief Executive: Ms S. Barber

Scottish Campaign for Nuclear Disarmament
15 Barrland Street, Glasgow, G41 1QH (Tel: 0141-423 1222; Fax: 0141-243 1231;
E-mail: cndscot@dial.pipex.com;
Web: www.cndscot.dial.pipex.com).
Administrator: J. Ainslie

Scottish Child Law Centre
1st Floor, Old College, South Bridge, Edinburgh, EH8 9YL (Tel: 0131-667 6333; Fax: 0131-662 1713; Web: www.sclc.org.uk).

Scottish Childminding Association
Suite 3, 7 Melville Terrace, Stirling, FK8 2ND (Tel: 01786-445 377; Fax: 01786-449 062;
E-mail: information@childminding.org;
Web: www.childminding.org).
Director: Mrs A. McNellan, MBE

Scottish Church History Society
Crown Manse, 39 Southside Road, Inverness, IV2 4XA (Tel: 01463-231 140; Fax: 01463-230 537).
Hon. Secretary: Revd Dr P. H. Donald

Scottish Civic Trust
The Tobacco Merchants House, 42 Miller Streeet, Glasgow, G1 1DT (Tel: 0141-221 1466; Fax: 0141-248 6952; E-mail: sct@scotnet.co.uk; Web: www.scotnet.co.uk/sct).
Director: J. N. P. Ford

Scottish Council for National Parks
15 Park Terrace, Stirling, FK8 2JT (Tel: 01786-465 714).
Hon. Secretary: B. Parnell

Scottish College of Complementary Medicine
c/o The Complementary Medicine Centre, 11 Park Circus, Glasgow, G3 6AX (Tel: 0141-332 4924; Fax: 0141-353 3783; E-mail: complementary medicinecentre@compuserve.com;
Web: complementarymedicinecentre.co.uk).
Clinic Directors: B. Fleming; Ms R. Chappell

Scottish Conservation Bureau
Historic Scotland, Longmore House, Salisbury Place, Edinburgh, EH9 1SH (Tel: 0131-668 8668; Fax: 0131-668 8669;
E-mail: hs.conservation.bureau@scotland.gov.uk;
Web: www.historic-scotland.gov.uk).
Conservation Bureau Manager: C. E. Brown

Scottish Council for Voluntary Organisations (SCVO)
18–19 Claremont Crescent, Edinburgh, EH7 4QD (Tel: 0131-556 3882; Fax: 0131-556 0279;
E-mail: enquiries@scvo.org.uk;
Web: www.scvo.org.uk).
Chief Executive: M. Sime
Deputy Director: H. Campbell

The Scottish Council of Deafness
Clerwood House, 96 Clermiston Road, Edinburgh, EH12 6UT (Tel: 0131-314 6075; Fax: 0131-314 6077;
E-mail: admin@scod.org.uk;
Web: www.scod.org.uk).
Director: Ms L. Lawson

Scottish Council of Physical Education
Department of Sports Studies, Gannochy Sports
Centre, University of Stirling, Stirling, FK9 4LA
(Tel: 01786-466 906; Fax: 01786-466 919; E-
mail: r.n.gowrie@stir.ac.uk).
Sports Development Co-ordinator: R. Gowrie

Scottish Crofters Union
Old Mill, Broadford, Isle of Skye, IV49 9AQ
(Tel: 01471-822 529; Fax: 01471-822 799;
E-mail: crofters.union@talk21.com;
Web: www.scc.co.uk).
Director: vacant
Crofting Adviser: vacant

Scottish Downs Syndrome Association
158–160 Balgreen Road, Edinburgh, EH11 3AU
(Tel: 0131-313 4225; Fax: 0131-313 4285;
E-mail: info@sdsa.org.uk;
Web: www.sdsa.org.uk).
Director: Ms K. Watchman
Office Manager: Ms P. Hernandez

Scottish Drugs Forum
Shaftesbury House, 5 Waterloo Street, Glasgow,
G2 6AY (Tel: 0141-221 1175; Fax: 0141-248
6414; E-mail: enquiries@sdf.org.uk;
Web: www.sdf.org.uk).
Information Officer: Ms I. Hendry

The Scottish Genealogy Society
Library and Family History Centre, 15 Victoria
Terrace, Edinburgh, EH1 2JL (Tel: 0131-220
3677; Fax: 0131-220 3677;
E-mail: info@scotsgenealogy.com;
Web: www.scotsgenealogy.com).
Hon. Secretary: Miss J. P. S. Ferguson
Hon. Librarian: Mrs H. Rose; J Cranstoun

Scottish Kennel Club
Eskmills Park, Station Road, Musselburgh,
EH21 7PQ (Tel: 0131-665 3920; Fax: 0131-653
6937; E-mail: info@scottishkennelclub.org;
Web: www.scottishkennelclub.org).
Secretary-General: I. A. Sim
Assistant Secretary: Mrs A. W. Fox

Scottish Law Agents' Society
11 Parliament Square, Edinburgh, EH1 1RF
(Tel: 0131-225 5051; Fax: 0131-225 5051;
E-mail: secretary@slas.co.uk;
Web: www.slas.co.uk/INDEX–1.html).
Secretary: Mrs J. H. Webster, WS

Scottish Motor Neurone Disease Association
76 Firhill Road, Glasgow, G20 7BA
(Tel: 0141-945 1077; Fax: 0141-945 2578;

E-mail: info@scotmnd.sol.co.uk;
Web: www.scotmnd.org.uk).
Chief Executive: C. Stockton

Scottish National Dictionary Association
27 George Square, Edinburgh, EH8 9LD
(Tel: 0131-650 4149; Fax: 0131-650 4149;
E-mail: mail@snda.org.uk;
Web: www.snda.org.uk).
Editorial Director: Ms I. Macleod

The Scottish Natural History Library
Foremount House, Kilbarchan, Renfrewshire,
PA10 2EZ (Tel: 01505-702 419).
Editor: Dr J. A. Gibson

**Scottish National Federation for the Welfare of
the Blind**
5 Balmashanner Rise, Forfar, Angus, DD8 1PD
(Tel: 01307-463 099;
E-mail: snfwb@care4free.net).
Hon. Secretary and Treasurer: J. Duncan

**The Scottish National Institution for the War
Blinded**
PO Box 500, Gillespie Crescent, Edinburgh,
EH10 4HZ (Tel: 0131-229 1456; Fax: 0131-229
4060; E-mail: enquiries@rbas.org.uk).
Secretary and Treasurer: J. B. M. Munro

Scottish Parent Teacher Council
63–65 Shandwick Place, Edinburgh, EH2 4SD
(Tel: 0131-228 5320/1; Fax: 0131-228 5320;
E-mail: sptc@sol.co.uk;
Web: www.sol.co.uk/s/sptc).
Administrator: Mrs L. Grant
Development Manager: Mrs J. Gillespie

Scottish Refugee Council
1st Floor, Wellgate House, 200 Cowgate,
Edinburgh, EH1 1NQ
(Tel: 0131-225 9994; Fax: 0131-225 9997;
E-mail: info@scottishrefugeecouncil.org.uk;
Web: www.scottishrefugeecouncil.org.uk
Informationa and Press Officer: Sophia
Marriage

Scottish Rights of Way and Access Society
24 Annandale Street, Edinburgh, EH7 4AN
(Tel: 0131-558 1222; Fax: 0131-558 1222;
E-mail: info@scotways.com;
Web: www.scotways.com).
Secretary: A. C. H. Valentine

Scottish Spina Bifida Association (SSBA)
190 Queensferry Road, Edinburgh, EH4 2BW
(Tel: 0131-332 0743; E-mail: mail@ssba.org.uk).

Chief Executive: A. H. D. Wynd
Association Administrator: G.M. Jones

Scottish Wildlife Trust
Cramond House, Kirk Cramond, Cramond
Glebe Road, Edinburgh, EH4 6NS
(Tel: 0131-312 7765; Fax: 0131 312 8705;
E-mail: enquiries@swt.org.uk;
Web: www.swt.org.uk).
Chief Executive: S. Sankey

Scottish Youth Hostels Association
7 Glebe Crescent, Stirling, FK8 2JA
(Tel: 01786-891 400; Fax: 01786-891 333;
E-mail: enquiries@syha.org.uk;
Web: www.syha.org.uk).
General Secretary: W. B. S. Forsyth

Scottish Women's Aid
Norton Park, 57 Albion Road, Edinburgh, EH7
5QY (Tel: 0131-475 2372; Fax: 0131-475 2384;
E-mail: swa@swa-l.demon.co.uk

Scottish Youth Theatre
3rd Floor, Forsyth House, 111 Union Street,
Glasgow, G1 3TA (Tel: 0141-221 5127; Fax:
0141-221 9123; E-mail: admin@scottishyouth
theatre.freeserve.co.uk;
Web: www.scottishyouththeatre.freeserve.co.uk).
Chief Executive: Ms M. McCluskey
Marketing Officer: Ms P. Luti

Scout Association Scottish Council
Fordell Firs, Hillend, Dunfermline, KY11 7HQ
(Tel: 01383-419 073; Fax: 01383-414 892;
E-mail: shq@scouts-scotland.org.uk;
Web: www.scouts-scotland.org.uk).
Chief Executive: J. A. Duffy

The Sea Cadets
Northern Area HQ, HMS Caledonia, Rosyth,
Fife, FK11 2XH (Tel: 01383-416 300; Fax:
01383-419 772;
E-mail: ao@seacadetsnorthern.org.uk;
Web: www.seacadetsnorthern.org.uk).
Area Office Manager: A. E. Parr

Shelter Scotland
4th Floor, Scotia Bank House, 6 South Charlotte
Street, Edinburgh, EH2 4AW (Tel: 0131-473
7170; Fax: 0131-473 7199;
E-mail: liz@shelter.org.uk;
Web: www.shelter.org.uk).
Director: Ms E. Nicholson

Society for Autistic Children
Hilton House, Alloa Business Park, Whins Road,
Alloa, FK10 3SA (Tel: 01259-720 044; Fax:
01259-720 051).
Director of Fundraising: Mr. B. Tait

Society of Antiquaries of Scotland
Royal Museum, Chambers Street, Edinburgh,
EH1 1JF (Tel: 0131-247 4115/4133; Fax: 0131-
247 4163).
Director: Mrs F. Ashmore, FSA

**Society of Solicitors in the Supreme Court of
Scotland**
SSC Library, Parliament House, 11 Parliament
Square, Edinburgh, EH1 1RF (Tel: 0131-225
6268; Fax: 0131-225 2270;
E-mail: ssc.library@dial.pipex.com).
Secretary: I. L. S. Balfour
Librarian: C. A. Wilcox

Society of Writers to HM Signet
Signet Library, Parliament Square, Edinburgh,
EH1 1RF (Tel: 0131-220 3426; Fax: 0131-220
4016; E-mail: wssoc@dial.pipex.com;
Web: www.signetlibrary.co.uk).
General Manager: M. R. McVittie
Librarian: Miss A. Walker

Sports Aid Foundation
76 Constitution Street, Leith, Edinburgh, EH6
6RP (Tel: 0131-555 4584; Fax: 0131-555 4584).
Director: Mr G. Bowmaker

SSAFA Forces Help
New Haig House, Logie Green Road, Edinburgh,
EH7 4HR (Tel: 0131-557 1697; Fax: 0131-557
5819).
Branch Secretary: Ms J. Spence

The Standing Council of Scottish Chiefs
Hope Chambers, 52 Leith Walk, Edinburgh,
EH6 5HW (Tel: 0131-554 6321; Fax: 0131-553
5319; E-mail: bevkel@btinternet.com).
General Secretary: George Way of Plean

Sue Ryder Foundation Scotland
General Office, Unit 23, Thistle Business Park,
Broxburn, West Lothian, EH52 5AS
(Tel: 01506-852 183).
Regional Manager: Tom Watt

Sustrans Scotland
163 Fountainbridge, Edinburgh, EH3 9RX;
E-mail: sustrans@sustrans-scot.freeserve.co.uk;
Web: www.sustrans.org.uk).
Manager in Scotland: Tony Grant

Chief Executive: J. Grimshaw

The Thistle Foundation
Niddrie Mains Road, Edinburgh, EH16 4EA
(Tel: 0131-661 3366; Fax: 0131-661 4879;
E-mail: jfisher@thistle.org.uk;
Web: www.thistle.org.uk).
Director: Ms J. Fisher

Turning Point Scotland
121 West Street, Glasgow, G5 8BA
(Tel: 0141-418 0882; Fax: 0141-420 6170;
E-mail: tps—scotland@dial.pipex.com).
Chief Executive: Ms N. Maciver
Fundraising Co-ordinator: K. Blackie

Unit for the Study of Government in Scotland
Governace of Scotland Forum, Chisholm House,
High School Yards, Edinburgh, EH1 1LZ
(Tel: 0131-650 2456; Fax: 0131-650 6345;
E-mail: ladams@ed.ac.uk).
Administrative Secretary: Mrs L. Adams
Chief Executive: Prof. D. McCrone

United Nations Association
40 Grosvenor Lane, Glasgow, G12 9AA
(Tel: 0141-339 5408; Fax: 0141-339 5408;
E-mail: frances.mildmay@btinternet.com).
National Officer: Ms F. Mildmay

Variety Club of Scotland
437 Crow Road, Glasgow, G11 7DZ
(Tel: 0141-357 4411; Fax: 0141-334 4796;
E-mail: kandy@varietyclub.org.uk;
Web: www.varietyclub.org.uk).
Executive Secretary: Mrs P. A. Jenkins
Fundraiser: Kandy Dundas

Victim Support Scotland
15–23 Hardwell Close, Edinburgh, EH8 9RX
(Tel: 0131-668 4486; Fax: 0131-662 5400;
E-mail: info@victimsupportsco.demon.co.uk;
Web: www.victimsupportsco.demon.co.uk).
Director: Mr D. McKenna

Wildfowl and Wetlands Trust - Caerlaverock
Eastpark Farm, Caerlaverock, Dumfriesshire,
DG1 4RS (Tel: 01387-770 200; Fax: 01387-770
539; E-mail: caerlaverock@wwt.org.uk;
Web: www.wwt.org.uk).
Centre Manager: J. B. Doherty

Women's Royal Voluntary Service
Clerwood House, 96 Clermiston Road,
Edinburgh, EH12 6UT (Tel: 0131-314 0600;
Fax: 0131-334 6813; Web: www.wrvs.org.uk).
Administration Manager: Margaret Marshall

Women's Rural Institutes
42 Heriot Row, Edinburgh, EH3 6ES
(Tel: 0131-225 1724; Fax: 0131-225 8129;
E-mail: uwri@swri.demon.co.uk;
Web: www.swri.demon.co.uk).
General Secretary: Mrs A. Peacock

Woodland Trust Scotland
Glenruthven Mill, Abbey Road, Auchterarder,
Perthshire, PH3 1DP
(Tel: 01764-662 554; Fax: 01764-662 553;
E-mail: angeladouglas@woodland-trust.org.uk;
Web: www.woodland-trust.org.uk).
Chief Executive: M. J. Townsend
Operations Director - Scotland: Ms A. Douglas

WWF Scotland (World Wide Fund for Nature)
8 The Square, Aberfeldy, Perthshire, PH15 2DD
(Tel: 01887-820 449; Fax: 01887-829 453).
Head: S. Pepper

YMCA Scotland
James Love House, 11 Rutland Street,
Edinburgh, EH1 2AE (Tel: 0131-228 1464; Fax:
0131-228 5462;
E-mail: info@ymcascotland.org.uk;
Web: www.ymcascotland.org).
National Secretary: J. Knox

Youth Clubs Scotland
Balfour House, 19 Bonnington Grove,
Edinburgh, EH6 4BL (Tel: 0131-554 2561; Fax:
0131-555 5223; E-mail: office@ycs.org.uk).
Chief Executive: Ms C. Downie

Youthlink Scotland
Central Hall, West Tollcross, Edinburgh, EH3
9BP (Tel: 0131-229 0339; Fax: 0131-229 0339;
E-mail: info@youthlink.co.uk;
Web: www.youthlink.co.uk).
Chief Executive: G. Johnston
Information Officer: R. Brewster

YWCA (Young Women's Christian Association of Great Britain)
7B Randolph Crescent, Edinburgh, EH3 7TH
(Tel: 0131-225 7592; Fax: 0131-467 7008;
E-mail: ywca—scotland@compuserve.com).
Chief Executive: E. Samson
Operations Director: Candice Tait

SCOTLAND EVENTS

OF THE YEAR

EVENTS OF THE YEAR
FORTHCOMING EVENTS
SPORTS EVENTS
GAMES AND GATHERINGS
TOURIST BOARDS

EVENTS OF THE YEAR

July 2000

1. A government report criticised Tayside University Hospitals Trust for a lack of effective financial controls after finding a shortfall of £11.2 million in its budget. Plans were revealed to reduce the size of some committees in the Scottish Parliament from 11 members to seven. A Lottery grant of £500,000 was pledged to build a sports centre to serve the areas of Dumbiedykes, St. Leonards and the Pleasance in Edinburgh. **2.** The Scottish Tourist Board revealed plans to employ an independent watchdog to grade food in tourist destinations. **3.** The Government conservation agency Scottish National Heritage made awards totalling £130,000 to seven of the country's richest landowners, including £26,000 to the Queen to repair foot paths around Balmoral. **4.** The Holyrood Parliament building project received a set back due to the sudden death of its architect, Enric Miralles. **6.** The Scottish Tourist Board reported that the number of foreign tourists visiting Scotland had fallen by 10% resulting in a £123 million loss of income. The Scottish Executive reaffirmed its commitment to creating a new university in the Highlands by amalgamating 13 colleges in a £100 million project. **8.** The Queen registered the name 'Balmoral' in preparation for its use as a brand name. A report by the Rail Passengers Council stated that Scottish Passengers get the worst compensation deals in the UK. **10.** A report by the Scottish Health Advisory Service was critical of security and organisation at Carstairs State Hospital, after a patient attacked and sexually assaulted a female nurse. Figures released by the Scottish Executive revealed a dramatic increase in the number of homes being repossessed in Scotland's major cities; repossessions in Glasgow increased from 479 in 1994 to 1,190 in 1999 and from 245 to 625 in Edinburgh over the same period. This was compared with a 17% reduction throughout the rest of the UK. **11.** Women's groups accused the Scottish Executive of failing victims of domestic violence when Jack Straw, the Home Secretary, revealed a £7 million package to tackle abuse in England and Wales. **12.** John Spellar, the Junior Defence Minister, announced that because of a public enquiry and organised protests a £25 million military training centre on the England-Scotland border would not be completed until at least 2004. **13.** A report revealed that almost

35,000 pupils were expelled or suspended from school in Scotland in 1999. **17.** 120,000 local government employees prepared to strike after pay negotiations with the Convention of Scottish Local Authorities broke down. **18.** Firstgroup buses launched a high-frequency 'Overground' network to compete with Lothian Buses in the capital, Edinburgh. **20.** Scottish Borders Council offered financial assistance to St Andrews nursing home in Drygrange after it came to light that staff had worked on less than half pay rather than let the home close. **21.** John Prescott, the Deputy Prime Minister, revealed a plan to spend £180 billion over 10 years to improve transport links between England and Scotland. Historic Scotland announced properties to be preserved in Edinburgh including the Tollcross Clock, a 19th century railway tunnel at East Trinity Road and 2 police boxes at the Grassmarket on the Royal Mile. **22.** Young Scots for Independence, the youth wing of the Scottish National Party, called for an investigation into the party's finances. **23.** An ancient battleground, traditionally believed to be where Scots King Kenneth McAlpin defeated the Picts to unite the two races in 843 AD, was granted protection by Historic Scotland thwarting plans by Stirling University to build two rugby pitches on the site. **29.** 1,000 demonstrators marched from George Square to Kelvingrove in Glasgow to call for the legalisation of cannabis. **30.** A survey of Scotland's NHS Trusts revealed they paid a total of £4.1 million compensation for medical negligence in 1999. Plans were revealed to reduce the number of Members of the Scottish Parliament from 129 to 99.

August 2000

1. Historic Scotland revealed its intention to make the Forth Road Bridge a structure of national importance. **2.** Fife Council apologised for overspending by £1.8 million on its education budget. **4.** The Queen Mother's 100th birthday was celebrated at Glamis Castle in Angus, where she spent her childhood. **8.** Mark Larcarowicz, Edinburgh council's chief executive for transport, revealed plans to extend the pedestrianisation of the Scottish capital's streets during the festival period. **9.** The Scottish Executive released figures revealing that 64% of 16-21 year-olds went into higher or further education in 1998/9; in 1988/9 the figure was 42%. **10.** Universities around the UK were sent the wrong results for 35,000 students who sat Scottish Higher examinations.

11. 2,000 students failed to receive the results of their Higher examinations and 1,400 more received partial or incorrect results. The Scottish Qualifications Authority (SQA) blamed the mix up on a computer error. 12. The SQA called into question the validity and accuracy of the grades presented to all 147,000 pupils who sat Higher, Intermediate and Standard exams. A massive programme of re-marking was undertaken. 15. The Royal College of Nursing in Scotland threatened the Scottish Executive with industrial action if it did not agree to re-evaluate reductions made on nurses' paid leave. 21. A report showed that deaths from drug use in Scotland had increased from 276 in 1998 to 340 in 1999. 25. Statistics published in the Health Statistics Quarterly revealed that Glasgow has the highest death rate in the UK with 1,420 deaths per 100,000 males.

September 2000

1. The Scottish Qualifications Authority (SQA) admitted that key computer checks were not carried out on many exam results before they were issued. The revelation meant that some grades may have been lower than they should have been and that some pupils may have failed when they should have passed. The SQA insisted that its appeal procedure would compensate for the missing checks. The Prime Minister (Tony Blair) dismissed calls for the resignation of Scottish Education Minister Sam Galbraith. Glasgow City Council formally launched a £220 million project to modernise 29 schools in many of the poorer inner city parts of the city, making it the largest Private Finance Investment project in the UK. 2. Many updated results of the Higher Examinations were sent to the wrong schools, causing further delays in the publication of results. 4. Following a two year review of the way in which the health service in Scotland allocated its funds, a revised system to be phased in over the next five years was announced. Cash will be allocated to deprived and rural areas where there is a greater need, rather than on a 'per capita' basis. 6. Figures showed that the number of 'urgent' appeals from pupils needing the result of their appeals for University entrance had risen from 400 in 1999 to 6,250 in 2000 following breakdowns in the SQA's systems. 9. Protesters, demonstrating about the high cost of tax on fuel, set up barricades at oil refineries around England and Scotland, causing widespread panic-buying of fuel. 11. Following reports showing that a quarter of all British petrol stations were dry the Prime Minister declared that he would not cave in to protesters. A meeting of

the Privy Council, attended by the Queen, sanctioned the use, if necessary, of contingency powers to require oil companies to ensure the even distribution of fuel across the country. 12. A limited number of tankers were released from the blockades around the country, including Grangemouth, in order to meet the needs of the emergency services and other essential industries. Demonstrators brought traffic to a standstill in Edinburgh, Aberdeen and Perth. 13. Troops were put on standby to intervene in the fuel crisis as the health service went on emergency alert, schools and businesses closed, and supermarkets started rationing. 14. Protesters lifted the blockades at refineries around the country but threatened that the blockades would return if tax on fuel was not cut within 60 days. 15. The SQA admitted that the backlog of appeals on Highers and Standard Grade Exams (sat in May) might not be resolved until Christmas. A statement reported that the Authority was aiming to have the 6,250 urgent appeals dealt with by 20 September and the Higher exams by the end of October however, the Standard Grades could not be guaranteed by the end of the year. 18. The Scottish Executive Finance Minister, Jack McConnell, announced a huge increase in public spending. He predicted that overall expenditure would rise by an additional £4 billion over the next three years. 19. The SQA revealed that more than 2,500 candidates had had their appeals upheld. This represented 40% of the 6,400 urgent appeals. 20. Libraries, rubbish collection, museums and schools were affected when 60,000 local council employees went on strike as part of their campaign to force the authorities to improve a wage offer above the rate of inflation.

October 2000

1. Susan Deacon, the Health Minister, announced a £100 million care package for the elderly in Scotland. The plans will take place over the next three years and will mean more elderly people can be looked after at home. Under the scheme, there will be free nursing care and greater protection for the homes of the elderly if they need residential care. 8. An Edinburgh University study into the suicide rate in Scotland found that the number of males aged 25 to 34 who had taken their own lives had risen by 245% in almost 30 years. 9. Doubts were raised by the BBC's Frontline Scotland programme, about the seaworthiness of the Solway Harvester which sank off the coast of the Isle of Man on 11 January 2000 killing its five crew. The programme found that four of the operating company's boats had been lost in the last

15 years, with the loss of 15 lives. **10.** Donald Dewar, Scotland's First Minister, died after suffering a brain haemorrhage following a fall. The latest Government figures showed that in-patients and day care waiting lists in Scottish hospitals grew by 4,215 to 86,549 between March and June 2000 and the number of patients waiting more than 12 months increased by 81 to 553. **11.** Latest figures showed a 15% drop in the number of applications for places at Scottish Universities from students living in England. Despite a ruling by the European Court of Justice which overturned a European Union directive to ban tobacco advertising and sponsorship from 2001, the Scottish Parliament announced plans to go ahead with the ban in Scotland. **12.** A new visitor centre, using interactive exhibits and touch-screen displays, was opened beside the construction work for the new Scottish Parliament building in Holyrood. It aims to provide visitors with a flavour of what the new building will look like when it is completed in 2003. **13.** The Scottish Parliament reconvened briefly as a tribute to the late Donald Dewar. A minute silence was held as a mark of respect and tributes were heard from a number of leading politicians. A new hi-tech system was introduced in Perth in which city centre buses were fitted with transponders which trigger a change in traffic lights in favour of approaching buses. The Scottish Labour party announced that the election for an interim leader would take place in Stirling on 21 October. **14.** Bill Morton, the Interim head of Scotland's exam body revealed plans for a middle management shake-up in response to the exam fiasco earlier in the year. The 21 section heads within middle management are to be replaced by a smaller number of general managers. **16.** The charity, National Children's Homes (NCH) estimated that 100,000 Scottish children live in families that have suffered violence or abuse. The report also showed that 80 children become homeless every day and that 11,000 are looked after by councils because of problems in their family. **17.** The Revd John D. Miller was appointed as the Moderator of the General Assembly of the Church of Scotland. **18.** The funeral of Donald Dewar took place at Glasgow Cathedral. **20.** It was announced that the Edinburgh Hogmany Party was to be renamed The Royal Bank of Scotland Street Party after the Royal Bank of Scotland agreed a three-year sponsorship deal worth more than £300,000. **24.** French company, Framatome, won two contracts worth £4 million as part of the decommissioning of the Dounreay nuclear plant. **25.** Thousands of rail users faced days of disruption and delays after Railtrack closed the West Coast main line for

safety checks. The date of the by-elections for the Scottish Parliament and Westminster seats, due to the death of Donald Dewar was scheduled for 23 November. **26.** The West Coast main line reopened ahead of schedule but Railtrack warned that temporary speed restrictions would remain in place, affecting both passenger and freight services. The official BSE inquiry report found that Ministers and Whitehall were guilty of repeatedly misleading the public about the threat to human health posed by mad cow disease, but there was no deliberate attempt to lie or protect farming interests at the expense of the consumer. UK Energy Minister Helen Liddell launched an investigation into the environmental impact of oil and gas exploration between Shetland and the Faroe Islands. Residents of Burrelton, near Coupar Angus, occupied a planned mobile phone mast site next to a primary school amid fears that microwave radiation could affect the health of the children at the 78 pupil school. **27.** An offer of a 6.1% pay increase for local council staff was rejected by the workforce and further strikes throughout Scotland were threatened. **29.** Rail travel chaos in Scotland was made worse by a landslip, caused by flood water, on the Glasgow to Edinburgh line. The new First Minister Henry McLeish unveiled full details of his cabinet reshuffle. **30.** The Labour Party announced that Bill Butler was to defend the late Donald Dewar's Glasgow Anniesland seat in the Scottish Parliament.

November 2000

1. More than 600 local government staff began indefinite strike action over a long-running wages dispute. The Scottish Qualifications Authority failed to meet its target of 31 October to complete all non-urgent Higher appeals from students. **2.** Abbey National confirmed that it was in talks with the Bank of Scotland that might lead to a takeover offer. Liberal Democrat candidate Matthew Duncan, 22, became Aberdeen City Council's youngest councillor after winning the by-election for the Murtle ward. Postal workers in Paisley began an unofficial strike after a postman was suspended for allegedly failing to deliver an agreed amount of mail. **3.** Alasdair Morrison, Minister for Enterprise and Lifelong Learning, opened the new £13 million Lews College campus on Stornoway. **4.** The Word of Life (International) Church in Aberdeen had its assets frozen after accumulating debts of £160,000. **5.** Sarah Boyak, the Transport Minister, announced that the government would increase its contribution to the completion of the M74 motorway by £63 million bringing Government funding for the project to £203 million. **6.** Hundreds of homes throughout Lothian, Fife and the Borders were put on flood alert after two days of constant rain. The Scottish National Party announced its candidates for the two by-elections arising from the death of Donald Dewar. Tom Chalmers would contest the Scottish Parliament seat and Grant Thomas would run to represent Anniesland in Westminster. **7.** Defence Minister Lewis Moonie, announced that all British ex-serviceman who were imprisoned by the Japanese during World War II, including over 300 Scots, were each to receive a one off compensation payment of £10,000. Scottish Secretary Dr John Reid, was made to attend a private meeting of a Westminster Committee looking into allegations that he used public money to fund Labour's Scottish election campaign. **8.** The Scottish Parliament announced that they were to hold an inquiry into the treatment of asylum seekers in Scotland. Postal workers in Paisley ended their unofficial strike action. **9.** Transport Minister Sarah Boyack announced £33 million of funding for 19 new projects to improve transport across Scotland. Social Justice Minister Jackie Ballie announced £12 million of investment to replace Glasgow's old style homeless shelters with supported accommodation which would better meet the needs of homeless people. Education Minster Jack McConnell announced the appointments to the interim board at the Scottish Qualifications Authority. **12.** Scotland's only inshore oilfield, the Beatrice Field in the inner Moray Firth, was shut down after a leak was found in a pipeline. It was expected to be shut for approximately six months. **13.** A dozen lorries left John O'Groats as part of the slow moving Scottish fuel protest convoy which travelled to the Scottish Parliament in Edinburgh. Wendy Alexander, Minister for Enterprise and Lifelong Learning, announced changes to the higher education means-test to help thousands of lower and middle-income families. First Minister Henry McLeish announced a new £70 million Children's Change Fund to help the most disadvantaged and vulnerable children in Scotland. **14.** A convoy of Scotland's fuel protesters left Stirling to hand a petition demanding a cut in the tax on fuel into the Scottish Parliament in Edinburgh. **15.** Aberdeen based anti-paedophile campaigners working under the banner of Freedom for Children announced that they were to set up a website which names and shames sex offenders. The convoy of fuel protesters arrived in Edinburgh to hand over their petition to the Scottish Parliament. It was announced that Aberdeen City Council was to get £413,000 from the Scottish

Executive to help it tackle health and community care problems caused by winter. Scottish Forestry Minister Rhona Brankin announced the doubling of the freight-facilities grant to £36 million in an attempt to take timber transport off Scotland's roads and on to rail and sea services. A public health report to Tayside Health Board revealed that Tayside teenagers have the highest pregnancy rate in Scotland. **16.** Public service union Unison held a third one day strike when 70,000 local government workers walked out in pursuit of a higher pay rise offer. Thousands of postal workers in Scotland took part in a strike ballot over allegations of bullying tactics by management. Pensioner Rita Gillooly died after developing Guillain Barre Syndrome following a flu injection. **17.** The UGC multi-screen cinema in Glagow, due to open in 2001, was voted Scotland's ugliest building in a competition run by architectural magazine Prospect. Airdrie was the winner of Prospect's Carbuncle Award for Scotland's most dismal town. **20.** The Royal Bank of Scotland announced that they were to fund a £1.7 million fund to help students from poorer backgrounds secure places at Scottish universities. The Scottish Executive unveiled a £4.25 million plan to fortify the Fife coastline. **21.** Research by the British Heart Foundation found that people living in Glasgow are the most likely in the world to die from heart disease. **22.** The Scottish Institute of Sport, aiming to promote Scots at the top sporting levels, was opened by Craig Brown in Stirling. **23.** Labour won both by-elections arising from the death of Donald Dewar. The Food Standards Agency declared a 'national outbreak' of salmonella food poisoning in Scotland after 85 people were struck down with the illness. **24.** It was announced that universities were to be paid a premium of £750 a year for students whose parents earn less than £10,000 a year. The money is to be made available from October 2001. **27.** The 112 ft high Ferris wheel which had been constructed in Edinburgh's Princes Street Gardens as a centrepiece of Edinburgh's Festive Season celebrations had to be dismantled because of safety fears. **28.** Defence Minister John Spellar confirmed that 819 squadron, which provides anti-nuclear submarine defences for the Clyde area, was to be disbanded with the loss of more than 300 jobs at HMS Gannet, at Prestwick. It was confirmed that two more people had been affected by the outbreak of Salmonella in Scotland. **29.** A Commons Committee failed to reach a decision on claims that Scottish Secretary John Reid used public money to fund Labour's Scottish election campaign. Work began on the £6.4 million national swimming academy at the

University of Stirling. **30.** Defence Secretary Geoff Hoon rejected calls for a review of the Ministry of Defence investigation into the 1994 Chinook helicopter crash on the Mull of Kintyre which killed 29 people. Nuclear Submarine HMS Triumph suffered superficial damage after hitting the seabed during exercises off the west coast of Scotland. The Princess Royal was made 'Lady of the Order of the Thistle' in recognition of her work and close ties with Scotland. A Scottish insurer, Royal Scottish Assurance (RSA) was handed a record fine of £2 million by the Financial Services Authority for miscalculating endowment mortgages in the early 1990s. First Minister Henry McLeish unveiled an £18 million package to fund prevention, protection and provision plans for those who suffer domestic violence. More than 300 people from Perth and Kinross descended on the Scottish Parliament to voice their fears about the future of the Perth Royal Infirmary which was included in an on-going review in Tayside.

December 2000

1. The £200,000 temporary ice rink in George Square in Glasgow was officially opened by the Lord Provost. Figures released by the Health Education Board for Scotland estimated that 200 Scots had contracted the HIV virus over the past year. The figures also showed that heterosexual sex had overtaken homosexual sex as the main route for the spread of the infection in Scotland. Fort Augustus Abbey on the shores of Loch Ness, one of the largest buildings in the highlands, was sold to former wildlife TV presenter Terry Nutkins. **3.** Dounreay nuclear plant in Caithness was hit by a power cut. It's recently revamped emergency back-up system failed to operate after the loss of the mains supply. An immediate investigation was started. Figures released by the homeless charity Shelter showed that the number of homeless people in Scotland was at an all time high. Plans to centralise emergency calls to Scotland's ambulance service were approved. Under the plan Scotland's current eight centres will be reorganised into three larger centres at Paisley, Edinburgh and Inverness with a further non-emergency base at Dundee. Bank of Scotland announced that it was to buy ICC, a state owned Irish bank, for more than £200 million. Scottish Health Minister Susan Deacon announced that a further nine nurse consultants were to be created in the NHS in Scotland, bringing the total up to twelve. The Scottish Conservatives announced that Craig Stevenson was their candidate for the Falkirk West by-election. The Ministry of Defence agreed to a four year delay in job cuts at RAF Buchan. More than

200 higher education workers attended a rally at Aberdeen University as part of a nationwide protest against low pay and deteriorating union relations. **4.** A radioactive particle was discovered near Dounreay Castle, an area previously thought to be clear from contamination. **6.** Education Minister Jack McConnell announced that every state primary and secondary school in Scotland would receive a share of a £17 million investment to carry out vital repairs and maintenance. MSPs voted to abolish poindings and warrant sales in Scotland. However, they also agreed to delay implementation of the bill until 2002 so that alternative means of debt recovery could be devised. **8.** Figures released by Age Concern Scotland claimed that 2,000 elderly people a year were dying unnecessarily because of poverty. **9.** First Minister Henry McLeish was formally confirmed as the leader of the Scottish Labour Party. **10.** A flood warning was issued for the Water of Leith and the River Almond in Edinburgh. **11.** Scotland's late first minister was remembered at a special thanksgiving service in Brussels. **12.** A committee of MSPs agreed to investigate why the blood transfusion service failed to introduce a test for hepatitis C earlier than 1987. An official enquiry into the method of electing the speaker of the House of Commons got underway. Henry McLeish confirmed Higher Education Institution status for the University of the Highlands and Islands (UHI) and also announced a £2 million cash injection for the project. **13.** It was announced that a new NHS 24 hour helpline was to be set up which would allow NHS patients in Scotland to seek guidance, health information and advice by qualified NHS nurses over the phone. Former education minister, Sam Galbraith came under attack as the Scottish Executive debated its first ever no confidence motion. **14.** Health Minister Susan Deacon unveiled a plan whereby over £100 million would be spent in the next three years to reduce waiting lists and streamline health trust management. The Health Minister also announced that a new flu drug, Relenza, will be prescribed by the NHS to high-risk groups in Scotland. **15.** Motherwell and Wishaw MP Frank Roy was officially censured by a cross-party committee of MPs for placing a bet on the outcome of the recent election for the House of Commons speaker. **16.** Stirling University announced that Professor Colin Bell, vice-chancellor and principal of Bradford University will succeed Professor Andrew Mill as principal when he retires in September 2001. **18.** Inverness was declared one of Britain's new millennium cities. **22.** Labour MP Eric Joyce, won

the by-election for the Westminster seat of Falkirk West. **23.** Sir Jimmy Shand, one of Scotland's most famous accordianists, died aged 92.

January 2001

2. Thousands of homes around Scotland were left without mains water supplies as problems were caused by the sudden thaw and undetected burst pipes. **8.** Jim Petrie, the man who drew the Minnie the Minx cartoon for the Beano for 40 years announced his retirement. Official figures revealed that Inverclyde had the highest proportion of heroin users in the country. **9.** It was announced that William Rae would replace Sir David Orr as chief constable of Strathclyde Police in July 2001. **10.** The first total eclipse of the moon of the 21st century was visible to the naked eye. One of the best places to view it from was in Western Scotland. **11.** Health Minister Susan Deacon announced a £7 million strategy to combat the spread of HIV in Scotland. **15.** Alex Salmond was chosen to stand as the Scottish National Party's general election candidate for the Banff and Buchan seat. **17.** A £16 million University, Learndirect Scotland, dedicated to the skills of industry was launched by First Minister Henry McLeish. **24.** Following the resignation of Peter Mandelson, the Scottish Secretary Dr John Reid, was immediately appointed to replace him as Northern Ireland Secretary. Helen Liddell was then appointed Scottish Secretary.

February 2001

5. Most of Scotland was badly disrupted due to severe snow and strong winds. Nearly 100 schools closed, 3,000 people were without electricity and travel around much of the country was hazardous. **8.** Plans to close a number of Scotland's infamous jails including Peterhead and Barlinnie were abandoned. **9.** The lighthouse at Port Appin, on the west coast of Scotland, was painted entirely pink with yellow spots, in the style of TV's Mr Blobby, by demonstrators campaigning against its proposed closure. **12.** Members of Scotland's teaching unions voted overwhelmingly to accept a 21.5% pay rise. **14.** Health Secretary Alan Milburn announced that families of the victims of the brain disease vCJD would receive £25,000 as an interim compensation payment. **15.** Scottish Transport Minister Sarah Boyack survived a vote of no confidence following her announcement that road maintenance contracts worth £350 million, previously held by councils, had been awarded to private companies. **21.** Former Conservative minister Lord Mackay of Ardbrecknich died at the age of 62 after a

suspected heart attack. **22.** The European Commission banned all exports of British livestock, meat and dairy products in the wake of the discovery of foot and mouth disease. **23.** The first tests for foot and mouth disease began in some Scottish farms. **26.** Scotland again suffered extensive disruption and school closures following another bout of severe snow. Almost 100,000 homes were without electricity and 70 passengers were stranded on a train for 14 hours after leaving London for Scotland. A £10 million Scottish Land Fund, backed by the National Lottery, designed to help Scotland's rural communities buy and manage the land they live on was launched. Edinburgh Zoo closed to the public as a result of the foot and mouth outbreak.

March 2001

1. Scotland's first cases of foot and mouth disease were confirmed following two positive tests, both in Dumfries and Galloway. **2.** A third case of foot and mouth was confirmed. **6.** A fleet of 160 fishing boats sailed across the River Forth as fishermen demonstrated about the lack of support for the Scottish fishing industry. **7.** Chancellor Gordon Brown presented the Budget to the House of Commons. The number of cases of foot and mouth in Scotland rose to eleven. **9.** The number of cases of foot and mouth in Scotland rose to sixteen. **12.** Restricted movements of livestock on Scottish farms began in an attempt to ease the suffering of animals in areas unaffected by foot and mouth. The number of reported incidents of the disease in Scotland rose to 23. Archaeologists completed an operation to remove an Iron Age chariot which had been discovered on an Edinburgh building site near Newbridge. **13.** The Strategic Rail Authority (SRA) announced that the East and West Coast main lines, which link Scotland to London would receive a major upgrade as part of a 10-year investment plan. The package also set aside cash for the redevelopment of Edinburgh Waverley station and several other stations throughout Scotland. **15.** Agriculture Minister Nick Brown announced that all animals 'at risk' of foot and mouth must be slaughtered including all sheep and pigs within a two mile radius of infected farms. **19.** Inverness officially became a city when the Letters Patent, confirming its new status, were formally handed over by Lord Gray of Contin, the Lord Lieutenant for the area. **20.** The slaughter of approximately 1,800 animals believed to be at risk of contracting foot and mouth began in Scotland. Scotland's Environment Minister Sam Galbraith announced his resignation due to health problems. Following the announcement, First Minister Henry McLeish confirmed that most of the environment portfolio would be incorporated into the Rural Affairs Department, water and energy would be dealt with by Enterprise Minister Wendy Alexander and planning by Transport Minister Sarah Boyack. **23.** Troops were sent into one of the area worst affected by foot and mouth, Dumfries and Galloway, to help with the transportation and burning of carcasses. **27.** NHS figures showed that the number of nurses working in Scotland had fallen by more than 1,000 since 1996. **30.** Peers voted in favour of a House of Lords inquiry into the 1994 Chinook helicopter crash on the Mull of Kintyre.

April 2001

1. More than 12,000 people took part in a march against drugs organised by the Daily Record in Glasgow. Prime Minister, Tony Blair, ruled out the possibility of a general election on 3 May 2001 due to the foot and mouth crisis and delayed the English council elections until 7 June. **4.** Edinburgh Zoo was reopened to the public after a five week closure as a precaution against foot and mouth disease. It was announced that a joint initiative by the Scottish and Executive would see £6.3 million being spent to encourage people to visit Scotland despite the foot and mouth crisis. **5.** Scottish First Minister, Henry McLeish, had a 25 minute meeting with American President George Bush whilst on a trip to the USA to try to boost Scotland's tourist industry. **11.** The Fife-based company Deep Water Recovery and Exploration claimed to have found the Royal Mail steamship which was sunk by a German torpedo in 1916. On board was a cargo of precious gems and gold, worth tens of millions of pounds belonging to an Indian maharajah. **15.** Rod Lynch was appointed the new chief executive of visitscotland, the former Scottish Tourist Board, and immediately caused controversy by holidaying in the USA. **17.** Health Minister Susan Deacon announced the creation of two mobile intensive care units to give critically ill children immediate treatment anywhere in Scotland. **19.** Newly appointed chief executive of visitscotland, Rod Lynch, was sacked after revealing his involvement with an Essex-based firm that ministers felt was inappropriate. **22.** Education Minister Jack McConnell appointed Colin MacLean as a national exam co-ordinator to ensure there would not be a repeat of the 2000 SQA exam crisis. **23.** Thousands of Scottish prison officers staged an unofficial strike in various prisons throughout the country following the implementation of unpopular new shift patterns.

May 2001

9. Scotland's political parties began their first full day of campaigning for the general election following the announcement of a 7 June poll. **12.** Fuel protestors calling for lower duty on petrol paraded through the streets of Aberdeen and Inverness. **15.** In a ceremony dating back almost 300 years, news of the dissolution of the UK Parliament was proclaimed to the public in the centre of Edinburgh. **18.** NHS figures showed that the number of doctors in training in Scotland has dropped in the past year. **21.** The Forth and Clyde Canal, which links the east and west coasts of Scotland, was reconnected after 40 years. **22.** Pupils at Aberdeen Grammar School were screened for tuberculosis after a 14-year-old boy was identified as possibly suffering from the disease. **28.** Submarines from around the world began to arrive at the Faslane Naval Base on the Clyde, for the largest ever gathering of submarines and their crews, as part of celebrations to mark 100 years of the Royal Navy's Submarine Service.

June 2001

1. Figures from the Universities and College Admissions Service (UCAS) showed the past year had seen a 13.5% drop in the number of Scottish applications to study in English institutions and the number of people applying to study at institutions in Scotland had increased by 3.4%. **4.** The Scottish Executive announced plans to set up a register of adults who could pose a threat to children. **5.** Edinburgh Castle suffered minor damage when a fire broke out in a roof space. Scotland's oldest person, Agnes Kinnear, died aged 109 at Ashludie Hospital in Monifeith in Angus. **7.** The first general election since devolution was held. **11.** Three girl guides were hospitalised after becoming infected with the potentially fatal E-coli bug while on a camping trip in Bettieburn, in Inverclyde. **13.** South African President Thabo Mbeki addressed MSPs in the Scottish Parliament on the second day of his state visit to Britain. **14.** The Scottish Executive announced that a section of the A1 route between eastern Scotland and England was to be upgraded, with part of the stretch turned to dual carridgeway. In addition, the Glasgow Southern Orbital route, to join the proposed M77 extension between Fenwick and Malletsheugh, was also authorised. **17.** Cardinal Thomas Winning, 76, died following a heart attack. Government agencies admitted that bones were secretly removed from the bodies of hundreds of babies in Scotland in the 1960s for testing to the dangers of nuclear weapons trials. **18.** Dundee's Lord Provost Helen

Wright was removed from office by a majority vote of the city council following allegations regarding her expenses. **19.** Alan Ezzi, director of the controversial new Scottish Parliament building project resigned after only seven months in the post after 'mutual expectations were not realised'. **20.** Derek and Sheila Wilson, of Thornton, Fife, won £11.1 million in Scotland's biggest ever individual lottery win. **21.** The Prince of Wales was one of twelve dignitaries to receive an honorary degree in celebration of the University of Glasgow's 550th anniversary. The Scottish Executive announced that almost one third of all quangos would be abolished following an extensive review of public bodies. The Scottish Executive approved an increase in the funding available to complete its new building at Holyrood. **27.** Plaid Cymru and the Scottish National Party announced a new joint parliamentary group at Westminster made up from four Plaid Cymru members and five SNP, making it the third biggest opposition group in the Commons. **27.** Thousands of homes in north-east Scotland were left without power following severe storms. **28.** The children of the late First Minister of Scotland Donald Dewar donated his collection of literature to the Scottish Parliament to be the main feature of a reading room dedicated to Mr Dewar in the new Holyrood building. Angus Mackay, Scotland's Finance Minister, pledged £200 million to fund free personal care for the elderly from April 2002. **29.** Demonstrators against the closure of Govanhill Pool in Glasgow, reached the 100th day of their sit-in protest.

ACCIDENTS AND DISASTERS

July 2000

4. Three people from Kiveton were killed when their Toyota Land Cruiser hit an oncoming car on the A57 near Sheffield. **12.** Investigators revealed that an emergency on a shuttle flight from London to Edinburgh in July 1999 was caused when fluid from a leaking toilet interfered with the plane's autopilot. **13.** The Prime Minister announced he would initiate a new investigation into the 1994 crash of a Chinook helicopter on the Mull of Kintyre, which killed two pilots, only if new evidence came to light. **17.** 170 people were evacuated from Greenock's G1 night-club when a fire broke out. **18.** 15-year-old Steven Doyle was shot in the back of the head by his step-brother when they were hunting vermin on a country estate near Dunbar. He died several days later in hospital. **22.** James Graham, 65, a builder from Edinburgh, was trapped by masonry when a

building façade collapsed on him. He escaped without serious injury. **27.** Flash floods were reported at Morningside and Stretton in Edinburgh after a 30 minute downpour. **29.** Two children were struck and killed by a train on the Cambrian coast railway. **30.** Vanessa McCulloch and her 7 month old daughter escaped without injury when her car careered off the A9 near Perth and plunged 150 feet down a wooded hillside.

August 2000

6. Three people were killed when their car collided with a lorry on the A83 in Argyle. **7.** The Road Safety Association called for caution on Scotland's roads after six people were killed in accidents over the previous weekend. **8.** A coach crashed in the town of Vieron in France killing Craig Norsworthy, 15, and injuring 11 other members of the Edinburgh Boys' Brigade. **10.** 1-month-old Anna Broad was killed when a car hit her pram, outside her home in Granton, Edinburgh. A farmer was found dead, entangled in an electric fence used to contain his cattle, on his farm near Dalkeith. **22.** Stuart Haldie, 43, and Dorothy Morris, 49, went missing while diving near Oban. Authorities assumed they had drowned but had yet to recover any bodies. **23.** Stuart Flannigan, 26, who was orphaned by the Lockerby disaster, was struck and killed by a train near his home in Heywood, near Westbury. **25.** Aileen Woods, a Scottish business woman, was killed when a Gulf Air Airbus crashed into the sea off the coast of Bahrain.

September 2000

1. An electrical fault caused a fire in the central carriage of a train as it arrived at Blantyre Station, Lanarkshire. Nobody was injured but one person was treated for shock.

October 2000

3. Two men died in a two vehicle crash near Banchory. **5.** Catherine Crowe, 18, from Wick, was killed in a car crash near Thurso. **6.** The body of 23-year-old David Gallagher was found in a field in Cathkin Braes, Glasgow. Police immediately began a murder hunt. **8.** A car containing three people plunged into the Caledonian Canal in Inverness. All three were saved by a passing American tourist. **10.** Nine-month old Natalie Burns, died in a house fire in Lanarkshire. Her mother and two brothers were taken to hospital for treatment. **11.** A Ministry of Defence report suggested that a combination of bad weather and pilot error was responsible for a Tornado crash which killed two airmen. The

Tornado, from RAF Lossiemouth, crashed a mile and a half south east of Kirkeaton in Cumbria in October 1999. **14.** Three-year-old Cameron Munro went missing while walking with his parents in a densely wooded area of Sunderland known as the Falls of Shin. A massive search operation was launched. **15.** Cameron Munro, was found safe and well by a search and rescue dog handler under the roots of a fallen tree where he had taken refuge and gone to sleep. One woman died and a man was in critical condition in Perth Royal Infirmary after apparently using very dangerous drugs stolen from a chemist's shop in Dundee. Police issued a warning to all drug users in Dundee of the potential fatal effects of the drugs. Fifteen people were rescued by helicopter when a ferry ran aground on the remote island of St Kilda, 50 miles west of the Outer Hebrides. Nobody was injured. A fishing boat with four fisherman aboard sank off Shetland after it hit an object in the water. All crew were safely rescued by the Shetland Coastguard. **22.** Two people died and one was seriously injured after being trapped by rubble following a gas explosion at a house in Dundee. A fire broke out at the Sullom Voe oil terminal in Shetland. Firefighters spent more than five hours tackling the blaze in the terminals gas plant but nobody was injured. **24.** An investigation into an explosion in Dundee which killed two people revealed a gas main failure as the likely cause. **28.** Two men from Aberdeen had to be rescued by the mountain rescue team after going missing overnight in the Cairngorms. A 52-year-old woman died and two people were injured after an accident involving a car and a lorry on the A77 south of Ballantrae.

November 2000

4. Five teenagers were injured, two seriously, when the car they were travelling in left the road and flipped into a field on the A947 Turriff-Aberdeen road. A Rangers fan was killed and three others seriously injured when their minibus overturned on the M6 between Carlisle and Penrith as they travelled home from a game. **11.** An elderly woman was killed and two people were injured after a two-vehicle crash on the A82 Fort William – Inverness road. A Scots couple, along with four other people were killed in a multiple car pile-up on the A1 motorway in North Yorkshire. **13.** Three fishermen were injured when their vessel sank within 15 minutes of striking a mysterious object near Lochinver Harbour. **14.** A man died and another was injured when the stolen car they were in crashed and burst into flames in Drum

Brae, Edinburgh. **15.** A report from the Marine Accident Investigation Branch blamed the crewman on watch for the loss of the fishing boat Betty James, off Rum, in July 2000. It concluded that the watchman fell asleep and failed to alter course, allowing the vessel to run aground. Defence Secretary Geoff Hoon announced that he would not reopen the inquiry into the Chinook helicopter crash which killed 29 people when it crashed on the Mull of Kintyre in 1994. **16.** The owners of Donside Paper Mill in Aberdeen were fined £40,000 after admitting a safety breach. This breach resulted in the death of worker Lee England in October 1999 when he was crushed by rollers. Three people escaped with minor injuries after their car plunged into Peterhead Harbour. **19.** Three Japanese students had to be airlifted to safety from Ben Nevis after becoming disorientated on the UK's highest peak. **26.** A Virgin London to Glasgow train derailed at Mossend South Junction, near Motherwell. No-one was seriously injured, although a few people were treated for minor injuries. **29.** Two fishermen were rescued from a sinking fishing boat in gale force winds on the Kintyre Peninsula in Loch Fyne. **30.** A pilot was killed when his light aircraft crashed near Fortingal in Perthshire. An investigation was immediately launched.

December 2000

3. Margaret Kent, from Dumfries, was killed and five others injured, including a baby, in a collision on the A702 near Carlops. **4.** A 21-year-old driver died when her car left the A96 two miles south of Huntly. **13.** A plane carrying pilot Ewan Spalding and passenger Robert Maclean, both from Muir of Ord in Ross-shire, disappeared after taking off from Inverness Airport to attend a business meeting in Benbecula, in the Western Isles. A massive search and rescue operation was launched. Craig Stewart, 20 drowned in the River Ness after being swept from Ness Bridge during a night out in Inverness. **14.** Roger Wild, a mountain guide, was cleared of blame for the deaths of four venture scouts in an avalanche accident on Aonarch Mor, near Ben Nevis, in December 1998. **16.** A man died after falling 80 ft from North Bridge in Edinburgh, through the glass roof of Waverley Railway Station and onto a railway line. **17.** The RAF and mountain rescue teams called off their search for the two airmen who disappeared while flying the Scottish Highlands. No clues had been found as to what happened to the light aircraft carrying Ewan Spalding and Robert Maclean after it took off from Inverness Airport. **22.** One man died and a second was left seriously injured after being hit by a train whilst walking on the line near Bargeddie Railway Station in Lanarkshire.

January 2001

2. A five coach train, travelling from Inverness to Glasgow ran into landslide debris on the track. None of the 111 passengers were injured. **22.** The bodies of two experienced hillwalkers were recovered after going missing overnight in Glen Doll. **24.** Mark Peacock and Judy Laider survived a violent landing and freezing temperatures when their small plane crashed in Lochnager, near Braemar. **29.** Eleven people were injured in an explosion at a ceramics factory in Clydebank.

February 2001

6. Two people were injured in a train derailment caused by poor weather conditions on the Inverness to Edinburgh line. **25.** The bodies of Robert MacLean and Ewan Spalding, the two Scottish businessmen who went missing whilst on a private flight to Benbecula on 13 December 2000, were recovered at Liatach in Torridon. **27.** Two men were killed when their Royal Mail plane crashed into the Firth of Forth, minutes after taking off from Edinburgh Airport.

March 2001

5. The Government approved the setting up of a new inquiry into the 1994 Mull of Kintyre crash, which led to the deaths of all 29 people on board. Six fishermen drowned when their vessel sank 180 miles off the west coast of Scotland. **21.** Fire virtually destroyed Morgan Academy in Dundee. **22.** An underground train in Glasgow derailed on the inner circle. Nobody was injured. **26.** Two US airmen went missing in the Cairgorms after crashing during low level exercises over the Scottish mountain range. **28.** Searchers recovered the body of one of the US airmen missing in the Cairngorms. **30.** The body of the second US airman was recovered in the Cairngorms.

April 2001

1. A 35-year-old woman from Scotland died and four other Britons survived more than 23 hours in shark-infested waters after their yacht capsized off the coast of Australia. **3.** Four people were killed and one seriously injured when a lorry and a car collided on the A9 Inverness-Perth road. **12.** Scotrail announced that they were to introduce airline-style announcements on all their trains to inform passengers about emergency evacuation procedures and safety rules.

May 2001

7. A cargo vessel, Lys Foss, carrying hazardous chemicals ran aground near the Island of Mull. **11.** 31-year-old Naval officer, Alistair Stewart died after falling 700ft during a climb in the Lost Valley in Glencoe. **13.** James Harris from Dunbar and Rochard Smith from Edinburgh died whilst investigating a Second World War shipwreck off the east coast of Scotland. **14.** Four children were rescued in Ayrshire after being swept out to sea in two separate incidents. **18.** A road accident involving a total of 17 people, four of whom died, occurred on the A9 motorway to the Highlands. **24.** Four crewmen were winched to safety from a Buckie-registered fishing boat, off the west coast of Scotland after an engine fire. **26.** Brian Gordon from Edinburgh died whilst on a diving expedition with the Strathclyde University Diving Club to a shipwreck off Dunoon.

June 2001

5. A man was killed and 38 people injured when a tour coach crashed on the Isle of Skye. **14.** Provisional figures for 2000 showed that the number of people killed on Scotland's roads increased from 1999. **15.** A passenger plane carrying 36 people on the Glasgow to Leeds-Bradford Airport flight was forced to make an emergency landing after being struck by lightning. Nobody was injured although several passengers were treated for shock.

ARTS AND MEDIA EVENTS

July 2000

1. The Scottish Ballet was denied a £100,000 grant by the Arts Council of England forcing the company to abandon its proposed tour of England in the autumn. **2.** Ray Bowyer, who quit the reality TV show 'Castaway', was banned from returning to the remote Scottish Island of Taransay where the show was filmed. **5.** The 54th Edinburgh International Film Festival announced it would honour Sean Connery. **8.** The two day 'T In The Park' music festival began in Kinross, Perthshire. **10.** Ron Copsey, from Middlesex, became the second contestant to quit the BBC show 'Castaway'. **14.** The Glasgow based Herald newspaper announced cut backs that would lead to the dismissal of at least twenty of its senior writers. **18.** The chest that contained the funds of the ill-fated Darien expedition from Scotland to Panama in 1690 was put on display in the National Museum of Scotland in Edinburgh. **22.** Scottish Opera revealed plans to perform Wagner's ring cycle over the next four years. **26.** The Scottish Arts Council revealed it had spent £137,559,890 on projects since 1995. **30.** It was revealed that a Scottish National Theatre Company was to be formed with the publication of a cultural strategy document in August. Funding for the £2.8 million project was not confirmed. Edinburgh's annual Jazz and Blues festival began. **31.** Carlton Communications revealed its intention to buy Scotland's two major TV stations, Scottish and Grampion.

August 2000

4. 8,500 people attended the first night of the 50th Edinburgh Military Tattoo. **5.** Castle FM, a commercial radio station broadcasting to Edinburgh and the surrounding area, was launched. **6.** 100,000 people watched the cavalcade that marked the beginning of the 2000 Edinburgh Fringe festival. It was revealed that an art film featuring a Princess Diana look-alike gesturing obscenely, which was banned from Leicester Square in London, was to be shown as part of the Fringe festival. **12.** The National Galleries of Scotland celebrated their 150th anniversary by offering free entry. **13.** The Edinburgh Film festival began. **26.** The American comedian Rich Hall was awarded the Perrier Comedy Award at the Edinburgh Fringe.

September 2000

2. 'Global Village 2000' saw 600 students from 85 countries gathered in the central square of Glasgow to promote peace and understanding between nations. **28.** The £3 million plans for a new Royal Art Gallery at Holyrood in Edinburgh were unveiled. The Queen's Gallery will be created from two converted buildings, close to the Palace of Holyroodhouse and the site of the new Scottish Parliament. It is scheduled to open in August 2002 to mark the Queen's Golden Jubilee.

October 2000

9. Officials from the National Gallery in Scotland were offered the chance to buy a rare pen and ink drawing by Michelangelo. The artwork of the woman in mourning is said to be highly significant and was discovered at Castle Howard stately home in Yorkshire. **26.** It was announced that The World Rose Convention is to be held in Glasgow in 2004 and in anticipation of the event the City Council is to spend £400,000 creating two new rose gardens in the city. **30.** A review of the Burrell Collection in Glasgow began amid fears that it could contain art looted by the Nazis.

November 2000

2. The Minister for Environment, Sport and Culture announced an extra £27 million of funding for the arts in Scotland. More than half the money will go to the Scottish Arts Council with some of the extra money earmarked for a Scottish National Theatre. **3.** Glasgow's Burrell Collection of art had to be closely examined after suggestions that some of it may have been stolen from Jewish families in Europe during the war. **12.** A Bristol Beaufighter, one of the world's rarest aeroplanes was bought for nearly £200,000 by the Museum of Flight at East Fortune in East Lothian. **18.** The BBC Scottish Symphony Orchestra became the first Scots orchestra to tour the Republic of China when they played their opening concert at the Shanghai Festival. **21.** Alford's Grampian Transport Museum was awarded a £16,500 Heritage Lottery Grant towards the cost of buying the only known surviving example of a Scottish-built Sentinel steam wagon.

December 2000

1. Ronald Frome won Scotland's highest literary prize, the Saltire Society Book of the Year Award, for his novel The Lantern Bearers. **2.** The location of Edinburgh's ferris wheel was criticised by the Scottish Civic Trust because of its proximity to the Scott Monument. **3.** More than 20,000 people attended the parade marking the start of Edinburgh's Christmas festival. **5.** Plans were revealed to find private investors to fund the Kings Theatre in Glasgow and save it from an annual deficit of £150,000. **11.** The £13 million Lighthouse building in Glasgow, Scotland's centre for architecture and design, was revealed to be operating at a deficit of £320,000. **13.** Six bronze figures worth £10,000, including a 19th century bust of Dr David Livingstone, were stolen from the Malcolm Innes Gallery in Edinburgh. **20.** The Fruitmarket Gallery in Edinburgh revealed that it used a £162,225 lottery grant to create a light display to be turned on during Hogmany. **21.** Scottish Ballet performed the first night of Aladdin, its new show. **22.** Pop star Madonna and the film director Guy Richie married in a private ceremony at Skibo Castle near Dornoch.

January 2001

1. The 29 participants of the BBC Castaway programme that completed the challenge left the island of Taransay, where they had lived in isolation for the past year. **5.** The Amsterdam Gallery in Edinburgh launched a scheme which allowed people to rent works of art for their homes for £10 a month. **29.** In an Orange British Academy Film Award poll, Scottish actors Sir Sean Connery and Julie Walters were voted the greatest British movie actors of all time. **30.** One of the most respected authors of books on Scottish history, John Prebble, died at the age of 85.

February 2001

1. Jack Milroy, who was one half of the Scottish comedy duo Francie and Josie, died. **28.** A poll commissioned to mark World Book Day found that Scots were the most avid readers compared to the rest of Britain. They spend approximately 5.8 hours a week reading, compared to a national average of 4.6 hours.

March 2001

2. Harry Potter creator, J. K. Rowling, from Edinburgh, received her OBE from the Prince of Wales at Buckingham Palace for her services to children's literature. **14.** A tapestry worth £40,000 was stolen from Glasgow's Burrell Collection. **29.** A mystery benefactor donated more than £1 million to the National Museums of Scotland. **31.** A lock of hair believed to be from the head of Mary Queen of Scots was bought by the Scottish Borders Council Museum for £1,800.

April 2001

1. The Royal Museum and Museum of Scotland stopped charging for entrance after receiving a grant from the Scottish Executive. **17.** Following a ten-day investigation into reported sightings of ghosts in the vaults and tunnels of Edinburgh Castle, scientists claimed to have results that may prove that some of the chambers under the castle are haunted.

May 2001

7. A poll conducted by MORI revealed that the majority of Scottish internet users were discouraged from shopping on-line because of fears over security; only 7% of users occasionally bought something on-line and only 2% were regular shoppers. **16.** Tayside Police were forced to cancel the promotion of a drug education website targeting school children after it was loaded with pornographic images. **22.** Three of Scotland's best known writers Alasdair Gray, James Kelman and Tom Leonard were appointed professors of creative writing by Glasgow University. **29.** J. K. Rowling, author of the Harry Potter books, was awarded the annual Scottish Arts Council Children's Book Award at a

ceremony in Glasgow. **30.** Glasgow City Council confirmed that 232 of its works of art, including work by Picasso, Cezanne, Whistler and Degas, were on a list of treasures suspected to have been looted by the Nazis.

June 2001

6. The line up of the annual Edinburgh Fringe festival was announced. 1,462 shows were planned to be staged by 666 groups from 50 different countries. **7.** The National Gallery of Scotland in Edinburgh opened an exhibition of the works of Rembrandt, the 17th century Dutch master. The exhibition was the most expensive ever staged in Scotland and included Rembrandt's 'The Golden Juno' worth £20 million. **9.** Inverness received support from the Scottish Department of Sport and Culture for its attempt to be named European City of Culture in 2008. A 15th century tradition was resurrected when the annual meeting of the High Council of the Clan Donald was held in Glencoe. **14.** A painting by Gavin Hamilton, titled Douglas was bought by the Scottish National Portrait Gallery in Edinburgh for more than £1 million with help from the National Lottery. **25.** 600 people attended the funeral of Cardinal Thomas Winning at St. Andrews Cathedral in Glasgow and hundreds more watched the service on screens in churches in the area. **30.** 1,000 people attended a multicultural festival at Sighthill in Glasgow to promote relations between local people and the 3,500 asylum seekers who live in the city.

CRIMES AND LEGAL AFFAIRS

July 2000

1. Tommy Dingwall, former Lord Provost of Glasgow, was cited to appear in court over an alleged assault. Former Scottish international footballer Frank McAvennie pleaded not guilty to charges of conspiring to supply Ecstasy and Amphetamines in a night-club in March. **2.** A report revealed that the number of trains hit by projectiles had increased from 178 to 240 in the previous year. **3.** Police launched a crackdown on the illegal fishing of Scotland's endangered freshwater pearl mussels. It was announced that a squad of police dedicated to patrolling the centre of Edinburgh would be operational by Christmas. **4.** Dr James Carrier, 52, a lecturer in Social Anthropology at Edinburgh University was sacked after he sexually harassed three female students. The trial of William Varey, a former Scots Guardsman accused of involvement in a £500,000 cannabis ring, was mistakenly abandoned because it was erroneously believed that a judge and jury were unavailable. The 12 month deadline to bring his case to court passed on 31 June. Taxi drivers raised court action against the City of Edinburgh Council to press for more cab licences at Edinburgh Airport. **5.** A government crackdown on football hooligans travelling abroad was undermined when it was revealed that English trouble-makers would be able to avoid restrictions by leaving from Scotland. Steven Reid, 34, a psychology lecturer from Edinburgh, was found guilty of manslaughter on grounds of diminished responsibility after beating 24-year-old Elizabeth Stay to death with a rolling pin in November 1999. Darryl Walker, a male nurse who was filmed taking part in the May Day Riots in London, was granted bail by an English magistrate on the condition that he didn't travel south of the border until his next court hearing. **7.** Lieutenant-Colonel Andrew Buxton, from Glasgow, was relieved of his duties with the peace keeping forces in Kosovo after being discovered in a brothel in the capital, Pristina. **9.** Ellen Milner, widow of the founder of Milner Laboratories, launched legal action against Kevin Leech, owner of the John O'Groats Hotel, for mismanagement of funds. Mr Leech had reportedly borrowed £57 million in 1997 to renovate the hotel but no work had yet been carried out. **10.** A senior Scottish Prison Officer voiced fears that low morale and poor organisation were undermining the service. Police blamed a 68% increase in alcohol related crime in Edinburgh on the low price of beer in some of the city's bars. **11.** James McNab, 37, from Fife appeared in court charged with seven counts of assault at the 'T in the Park' music festival near Kinross. He was one of 28 people charged over the weekend. **12.** A 12-year-old boy mugged two children at knifepoint in Fairfield, Perth. **13.** Stuart Clumps, promoter of the 'T in the Park' festival, was robbed at his home in Stirlingshire by a gang of armed men. Thomas Stevenson pleaded guilty to recklessly concealing a reptile, resisting arrest and shameless indecency after a policeman who was questioning him over allegations of indecent exposure was bitten by a 4 foot boa-constrictor concealed in Mr Stevenson's trousers. Two men were arrested after attempting to petrol bomb a village police station in Moray. **14.** A gang of five female eastern European asylum-seekers were being hunted by Police in the Borders region following a raid on a jewellery shop in Hawick. **15.** Police conducted nearly 100 DNA tests in connection with the rape of a 19-year-old girl in Kirkaldy, Fife in April. **20.** The Court of Session in Edinburgh granted Phillip King, an oil worker, the right to sue Bristow Helicopters for the

psychological distress he suffered as a result of an emergency on one of their flights. **22.** Sandra Gregory, a Scottish teacher sentenced to 25 years in a Thai prison for smuggling heroin, was released after receiving a pardon from the King of Thailand. **26.** The first two weeks of a police crackdown on criminals who target tourists resulted in 51 arrests and the recovery of £3,000 of stolen property. **30.** A 23-year-old man appeared in court after police seized £150,000 worth of cocaine and cannabis from his home in Aberdeen.

August 2000

1. Gene Drozdza, 67, from Craigie in Ayr, was called to give evidence against a retired US army reserve Colonel Georg Trofimoff, the highest ranking US officer to be charged with espionage. **3.** Four men from Glasgow, convicted for a total of 25 years for forging banknotes worth nearly £1 million were set free after a court of appeal found technical errors with the prosecution's case. Isabel Blyth, a tour guide at Edinburgh Castle, brought sexual discrimination charges against her employers. **4.** A 19-year-old man appeared in court charged with assaulting Billy Thompson, 33, son of Arthur Thompson, a key figure in organised crime in Glasgow. James Montgomery, 33, who was being held on remand at Bowhouse Prison in Kilmarnock while awaiting trial, was released by mistake and absconded. Alison Campbell, 26, was jailed for 5 years for throwing her 6-year-old son to his death from the 14th floor of a tower block. **6.** Government guidelines for Scottish Police stated that the public should not be told the identity of sex offenders in their area. Scott McCallum and Kevin Black from Newburgh, Fife, were arrested in Sweden after £30,000 worth of cannabis was found in their luggage. **23.** David Asbury, 24, was released on bail after serving 3 years of a sentence for the murder of Marion Ross. Emergence of new evidence facilitated a re-trial. **25.** The Association of Chief Police Officers in Scotland announced plans to cement a closer relationship between Scotland's 8 regional forces with the possibility of creating a single national force in the future. **26.** It was revealed that sexual offenders could apply for a Taxi Driver's License within 3 years of being convicted. **31.** Scotland's Police Forces revealed that 26,000 cases of domestic violence were reported in 1999. The figures were dismissed as "The tip of the iceberg" by Scottish Women's Aid who claimed that as many as 1 in 5 Scottish women were victims of abuse.

September 2000

1. The Lockerbie trial was adjourned for three weeks after judges were told that no more evidence could be heard until the issue of CIA documents was resolved. The CIA was asked by the Crown to search for more classified documents relating to dealings with key Crown witness, Abdul Majid Giaka, a former Libyan spy. **3.** Calls for a public enquiry into the removal of dead children's organs at Yorkhill Hospital in Glasgow were rejected. Health Minister, Susan Deacon said a further examination of the situation was needed. **12.** The former Scottish international striker, Frank McAvennie appeared in court charged with being part of a four-man conspiracy planning to deal in £110,000 worth of ecstasy and amphetamines. **20.** A Roman Catholic nun, Marie Docherty, also known as Sister Alphonso, was convicted of four counts of repeatedly abusing, humiliating and cruelly treating young girls at former children's homes run by the Church of Scotland in Aberdeen. **21.** Judges at the Lockerbie trial ruled that Abdul Majid Giaka, a Libyan double agent working for the CIA should enter the witness box without further delays. **22.** The Scottish Executive announced that an independent review group was to be set up in Scotland to decide whether hospitals should seek consent before retaining the organs of dead patients. **26.** The former Libyan spy, Abdul Majid Giaka, a key prosecution witness, told the Lockerbie trial that he saw the accused with a suitcase similar to the one alleged to have contained the bomb. **28.** The Libyan spy giving evidence in the Lockerbie trial denied that he was offered $4 million if the two men accused of the bombing were convicted. **30.** Former Scottish international striker, Frank McAvennie was cleared of conspiring to deal amphetamines and ecstasy worth £110,000.

October 2000

2. The Lockerbie trial began hearing arguments to ascertain whether the diary of one of the accused would be admissible in court. Defence lawyers argued that a notebook belonging to Al Amin Khalifa Fhimah was seized by Scottish police officers without a search warrant. **3.** A legal battle for custody of three-month-old Ellie Campbell commenced in Edinburgh. The baby's mother died four days after giving birth, sparking a battle for custody between Ellie's French father and her Scottish relatives. A judge at the Court of Session in Edinburgh delayed a ruling on who should care for the baby, pending an independent assessment of the relatives. Louise and Alan Maserton from Angus, began proceedings to use the European

Human Rights laws in a bid to choose the sex of their next child. The couple who already have four sons, lost their daughter Nicole in an accident and wanted to use IVF treatment to have a girl. Nightclub owner Charles Geddes of Elgin was found guilty of shameless indecency after encouraging male and female customers at his club to flash in exchange for ten minutes worth of free drinks. **4.** Lockerbie trial judges ruled that a diary belonging to one of the accused men could be used in evidence against him. A 'nationwide offensive' against crime was launched at Scotland's National Stadium at Hampden following a significant rise in violent crime in Scotland in 1999. The three months campaign aimed to reduce the number of violent attacks, murders, attempted murders, serious assaults and weapon carrying. **5.** Parents of dead children whose organs were removed without their families' consent, staged a demonstration outside Yorkhill Hospital in Glasgow in order to highlight their renewed calls for a public enquiry. **7.** A Scotland-wide crackdown on serious crime, part of the Safer Scotland Campaign, was launched. **8.** Dr Frank Smith, a radiologist at Woodend Hospital Aberdeen, was cleared of blame for misreading x-rays of cancer patients. The Lockerbie trial was adjourned until 17 October pending further enquiries into 'sensitive' information given to the prosecution by the Government. **11.** The Strathclyde Police Force launched a new helpline, aimed at establishing an accurate picture of crimes against homosexuals in Scotland. It has been designed to allow gays, lesbians, bi-sexuals and transgendered people to report crimes against them in confidence. **12.** New figures showed that Scotland's largest police force area, Strathclyde, achieved its lowest crime levels in 25 years. Overall there were 6.5% fewer crimes committed in the first half of 2000 in the Strathclyde area. **14.** Police pledged to investigate details of a possible new suspect in their 30 year old hunt for the serial killer Bible John. Bible John was a serial killer who murdered Patricia Docker, Jemima McDonald and Helen Puttock in Glasgow in 1969 and who was never caught. **15.** It was announced that, following the conviction in September of Sister Marie Docherty, fifty nuns were named in more than 400 compensation claims from former residents of Nazareth House homes in Aberdeen and Midlothian. **16.** Mark and Stephen Johnston were jailed for two years nine months and fifteen months respectively for mounting a failed petrol-bomb attack on Elgin police station. **17.** Isabella Dougan began proceedings against Law Hospital in Lanarkshire, claiming that she was left disabled after doctors failed to spot that she had suffered a brain haemorrhage. The Lockerbie Trial was once again adjourned (until October 23) to allow the prosecution team to make further investigations into information received. **18.** Strathclyde Police, who cover Glasgow and the West of Scotland, became the first police force in Britain to be fitted with light-weight body armour which can be worn under shirts and uniforms. **20.** Seventeen-year-old Leroy Sheridan was found with serious injuries on a piece of wasteland in Glasgow. He died a short time after arriving at hospital. A 17-year-old man was arrested in connection with the murder. **23.** Sebastian Borges, a gynaecologist from Caithness, appeared before a professional conduct committee accused of indecent behaviour towards three women. Two men robbed a petrol station in Edinburgh of £10,000. Nine-year-old Katrina McKenzie was stabbed at the Fountain Bridge Leisure Park in Edinburgh. An 11-year-old boy was arrested shortly afterwards. A couple, travelling from Helensburgh to Luss, were pulled from their car and robbed in a lay-by after thieves tricked them into pulling off the road. **24.** Sixty eight-year-old Ian Hay Gordon, originally from Scotland, began an appeal against his conviction of the 1952 murder of Patricia Curran. An enquiry cleared the Scottish National Blood Transfusion Service of blame for more than 300 haemophiliacs contracting Hepatitis C from blood products in the 1980s. **25.** The Scottish Executive announced a £250,000 package to tackle anti-social behaviour. **26.** A Scottish prison warden, John Duncan was fined £700 after attacking an Englishman who asked him for directions. Duncan claimed he thought he was making fun of his accent. 36-year-old John Davidson was found murdered in a flat in Edinburgh. Paul Hodge, who threw coins at the old firm game in which the referee Hugh Dallas suffered a head wound, was jailed for three months. **27.** Two laptop computers containing potentially life-saving data on heart patients were stolen from Glasgow Royal Infirmary. **28.** A 14-year-old boy was arrested after stealing a bus from a garage in Aberdeen. **29.** Lizanne McPherson, 30, appeared at Edinburgh Sheriff Court accused of murdering John Davidson. **30.** Samantha Brown was jailed for six years after torturing and robbing Lindsay McKinnon at her flat in Glasgow in March 2000. **31.** Scotland's first city centre policing unit was launched in Edinburgh.

November 2000

1. Colin Tierney was jailed for life for murdering his ex-girlfriend with a hammer in Winchburgh, West Lothian, on 27 June 2000. Wendy Ironside, the wife of Aberdeen Council convenor Len Ironside, admitted stealing more than £2,000 in cash and cheques from the garage where she works. Sentencing was deferred for six months. **2.** Fife Police Sergeant Colin Hay was convicted of assaulting two sailors in cells at Dunfermline Police Station in January 1999. **3.** Nicole Lavelle, 16, from Stirlingshire, took her father to court to force him to pay £700 in school fees. **4.** An 11-year-old girl was sexually attacked in the Newington area of Edinburgh. **5.** An inmate in Edinburgh's Saughton Prison took a fellow inmate hostage. Nobody was injured in the incident. **6.** An investigation was launched after teenager Leigh Shields alleged that he was ordered to scuttle the sister vessel of the ill-fated Solway Harvester which went down in high winds and heavy seas off the Isle of Man in January. David Scott, a former principle of the Donaldson's College for the Deaf in Edinburgh, was convicted of assaulting a pupil. Justice Minister Jim Wallace announced that a review of Scotland's eight police forces had ruled out the possibility of mergers although some functions would be centralised. **7.** Substantial amounts of heroin and cannabis and hundreds of tablets were seized when police raided six addresses in Aberdeen and took 13 people into custody. The Lockerbie trial resumed following an adjournment and the defence team immediately applied for more time to investigate new evidence. **8.** A formal request was sent to Syria for an undisclosed document which could affect the trial of the two Libyans accused of the Lockerbie trial. **9.** Five laptops containing vital statistical data on clinical trials involving heart and cancer patients were stolen from Monklands General Hospital in Airdrie. **10.** Mohammed Abu Talb, a Palestinian convicted in Sweden for bombing offences, began giving evidence at the Lockerbie trial. Ewan McGillvray, father-in-law of the Rangers footballer Billy Dodds, was jailed for nine years for sexually abusing young girls. **12.** Tommy Sheridan, the only Scottish Socialist Member of the Scottish Parliament was found guilty of a breach of the peace during a protest against nuclear weapons at Faslane naval base on the Clyde. **13.** Inmates at Peterhead Prison near Aberdeen began legal action through the European Court of Human Rights against the Scottish Prison Service. Their main complaints included having to slop out their own toilets, not having televisions in their cells and not having enough natural light inside the jail. Offshore contractor Solt Offshore, was fined £60,000 at Aberdeen Sheriff Court for failing to provide a safe working environment following the death of one of its divers, Christopher Hill, in August

1999. Andrew Bell was jailed for 3 months and David Kerr for 60 days for refusing to turn off their mobile phones whilst in Edinburgh Royal Infirmary, despite warnings that their phones may affect life-saving machinery. Scott McAusland from Glasgow, was jailed for five years for slashing two Celtic fans as they celebrated a 5-0 win over Dundee in April 1999. **14.** Defence lawyers at the Lockerbie trial began to question Mohammed Abu Talb, the man accused of the bombing. **15.** The Lockerbie trial was adjourned to allow the judges to consider a claim by defence lawyers that Mohammed Abu Talb should be charged with contempt for refusing to answer questions. Dutch Justice Minister Benk Korthals upheld a decision by the Netherland's supreme court to extradite William Begg, the man accused of murdering and dismembering Barry Wallace in December 1999, to Scotland. **16.** Mansour Omran Ammar Saber, a Libyan secret service agent appeared at the Lockerbie trial and denied any involvement in the bombing. **19.** Darren Aggasild, 25, was arrested after trying to murder two women in a nightclub in Aberdeen. **20.** Pierre Sallinger, a senior American journalist, told the Lockerbie trial that he knew who carried out the bombing and it wasn't either of the men accused. The special court in the Netherlands, however, would not allow him to name who he believed to be involved. John Vine was sworn in as Chief Constable of Tayside Police. A lorry driver in West Lothian was abducted at knife-point and made to hand over his vehicle containing £100,000 worth of computer equipment and designer clothing. **21.** Brian Meighan, David Pugh and Kevin Kane were jailed for a total of 18 years after being found guilty of gang raping a young mother in an Edinburgh tower block in November 1999. The Lockerbie trial was adjourned for a week to allow the defence teams to prepare their cases. **22.** A man attempted to snatch a nine-year-old girl as she made her way to school in Aberdeen. **23.** Maurice Beckitt, who ran the Peffermill Dental Centre where 10-year-old Darren Denhom died following a tooth extraction, was struck off the dentists register. **26.** Celtic fan Michael Cusick was brutally attacked in his home following an old firm football match. The police treated the incident as attempted murder. **27.** More than 60 people were arrested after 81 addresses were raided by drug squads in the Lothians. Crack cocaine, heroine, ecstasy and cannabis were amongst the drugs seized, together with £17,000 in cash. **28.** The judges in the Lockerbie trial were told that there was insufficient evidence to sustain the case against one of the accused, Al Amin Khalifa Fhimah. The two men accused of fatally stabbing Asian waiter

Surjit Singh Chhoker in Lanarkshire in 1998, were found not guilty at Glasgow Crown Court. A pre-Christmas raid on Paddy's Market in Glasgow's Briggait area netted £100,000 of counterfeit goods including 50,000 duty free cigarettes, 30 kilos of hand-rolling tobacco and 30 litres of spirits. Aliyah Sataar, 16, was abducted by two men as she walked along a street in Glasgow. **29.** Judges in the Lockerbie trial rejected an appeal by one of those accused, Al Amin Khalifa Fhimah, to throw out the case against him. The Lord Advocate, Colin Boyd QC, rejected demands for a public enquiry into the prosecution of three men cleared of murdering Asian waiter Surjit Chhokar but agreed to hold two private inquiries into the police investigation. Michael Butler, the head teacher of a school in Inverness was fined £1,000 after being found guilty of assaulting four children with learning difficulties. **30.** Colin Swanson was jailed for life after murdering his girlfriend Karen Collins on 19 July 2000 and burying her body in a shallow grave in an Inverness cemetery.

December 2000

5. Lawyers for one of the two Libyans accused of the Lockerbie bombing began presenting his defence at the Scottish court in the Netherlands. **6.** Police in Lockerbie seized 750,000 cigarettes found in a van carrying roofing felt during an anti-smuggling operation. Robert Jones was jailed for four years for Scotland's biggest ever VAT fraud which saw him netting more than £4.6 million in less than three months. Figures released by the Scottish Executive revealed that the number of killings in Scotland had risen to the highest level since 1995. **8.** Drugs with a street value of £400,000 were seized in Glasgow following a joint operation involving approximately 60 police and customs officers. **17.** Scottish Socialist MSP Tommy Sheridan was jailed for 14 days after refusing to pay a £250 fine for a blockade outside Faslane nuclear base. **19.** It was announced that William Beggs, the man suspected of killing Scottish teenager Barry Wallace and dumping his severed limbs in Loch Lomond, is to appeal against extradition from the Netherlands. **20.** The third Scottish Crime Survey showed that violent crime in Scotland had soared by a third over the last four years. Iain Hay Gordon, 68, from Glasgow, was cleared of the murder of Patricia Curran, 38 years after he was found guilty of the crime but insane and committed to an asylum. **24.** Ministry of Defence police revealed that 74 workers at the Faslane nuclear submarine base on the Clyde, were being investigated for theft. **31.** A 28-year-old woman was sexually assaulted during

Edinburgh's Hogmanay celebrations by four men who grabbed her at random, dragged her down a side street and fled only when disturbed by other revellers.

January 2001

5. The Court of Justice in The Hague refused an application for an injunction to block the extradition of William Begg from Kilmarnock, the man accused of murdering and dismembering 18-year-old Barry Wallace in December 1999. **8.** The Lockerbie bombing trial resumed in the Netherlands after a month long break to give the defence lawyers more time to gather information to continue their case. The defence teams revealed that they would offer no further evidence. **9.** Police figures showed an increase in the number of drink-drivers over the Christmas period. Two of the three charges faced by the men charged with the Lockerbie bombing were dropped. The two men faced one charge of murdering the 259 people on board. The prosecutors closed their case in the Lockerbie trial. **10.** The stepdaughter of an Inverness businessman was kidnapped in the Phillippines and held for ransom. She was released in February. **23.** Niall McDonald from Aberdeen was found guilty of murdering his wife in January 2000.

February 2001

1. The judges in the Lockerbie trial announced their verdict. Abdelbaset Ali Mohmed al-Megrahi was found guilty but his co-accused, Al-Amin Khalifa Fhimah was released as the judges considered there was insufficient evidence to convict him. **2.** Abdelbaset Ali Mohmed al-Megrahi was sentenced to life imprisonment, with a minimum of twenty years. **3.** Three Western men, one of whom was from Glasgow, appeared on Saudi television and confessed to being involved in a bombing campaign in the Saudi capital in November 2000. The authorities announced that they were to be tried under Saudi law which could result in their execution. **5.** The father of one of the victims of the bombing campaign in Saudi Arabia called for the death penalty of the men accused if they are convicted. **7.** A 39-year-old man was stabbed during an argument with rival fans following the CIS Insurance Cup semi-final between Celtic and Rangers. Abdelbaset Ali Mohmed al-Megrahi, the man convicted of the Lockerbie bombing, lodged an appeal against his conviction. **12.** Labour MP George Halloway, Socialist MSP Tommy Sheridan and Green Party MEP Caroline Lucas were amongst 60 protesters arrested by police during a demonstration at the Trident nuclear base, Faslane. Police seized drugs with an estimated street value of several hundred pounds during a four-day operation in Tayside. **14.** Latest figures from Strathclyde Police, Scotland's largest police area, showed that murders and attempted murders had fallen to their lowest levels for five years. **21.** Deputy Justice Minister Iain Gray announced that Glasgow Sheriff Court had been chosen as the location for Scotland's first US and Canadian-style drugs court. This court will deal with drug-using petty offenders separately. **22.** William Duff, a dentist from Glasgow who admitted defrauding the National Health Service and using dirty needles on patients was jailed for three years. **23.** Stephen Kelly from Glasgow, was found guilty of recklessly infecting his former girlfriend with HIV, despite knowing of his condition, in a landmark Scottish legal case. He was later jailed for five years.

March 2001

5. World darts champion Phil Taylor was found guilty of indecently assaulting two 23-year-old women after a darts exhibition in Fife. **11.** Seven female anti-war protesters were arrested after chaining themselves to a French Frigate near Faslane Naval Base. **10.** Four-year-old Luke Gragan disappeared from his house in Ayrshire in the early hours of the morning. His body was later found in a nearby nature reserve. John Gourlay was later charged with Luke's abduction and murder. **11.** The charred body of a baby boy was discovered on a footpath in Edinburgh's Craigmillar area. **19.** Lawyers acting for Adbeldaset Ali Mohmed al-Megrahi, the Libyan convicted of the Lockerbie bombing, were granted an extra six weeks to work on his appeal. **27.** Bill Condie, from Clackmannanshire was among nine expatriate workers kidnapped by gunmen in Somalia. **29.** The Lithuanian Government formally submitted a request for the extradition of Anton Grecas, a war crime suspect living in Edinburgh. Edinburgh Sheriff Court ruled that two men from the city, accused by the Estonian Government of organising a scheme to smuggle opium out of the country, could be extradited. **30.** Three Scottish High Court judges ruled that Britain's Trident nuclear weapons were not illegal under international law, after a group of anti-nuclear campaigners argued that the International Court of Justice in the Hague, had expressed the view that nuclear weapons were illegal.

April 2001

1. A prisoner and three policemen were hospitalised after a fire broke out in a cell at Hamilton police station. **2.** 15,000 campaigners, including the Chancellor of the Exchequer Gordon Brown, marched through Glasgow in an anti-drugs protest. **3.** Kenneth Bagnall, a former judge, was acquitted of embezzling funds from his law publishing company. **6.** Police in Edinburgh charged 70 teenagers following an operation to reduce the number of attacks on the city's buses by stone-throwing youths. **7.** Women's groups criticised plans proposed by Scotland's police force to give rape victims a lie-detector test to ascertain whether their allegations were true. Four boys aged between 11 and 14 confessed to committing more than 150 crimes in and around Edinburgh in the previous three months. **8.** Statistics released by the Scottish Executive revealed that sentences handed out in rural courts were on average twice as long as those given in urban areas. **9.** Nadeem Ramzan, a police officer in the Shetland Isles, was reinstated after allegations that he had indecently assaulted a woman were disproved. **11.** Kenny Richey from Edinburgh, who had been held on death row in the United States for 10 years, was denied an appeal against his conviction for murdering a 2-year-old girl in a house fire in 1986. Mark Burke, 25, from Balnorock in Glasgow was jailed for 7 years for an apparently motiveless attack on his mother and her partner. **18.** Lothian and Borders police began an investigation into allegations that three detectives had undertaken a campaign to discredit Deputy Chief Constable Tom Wood, their senior officer. Michael Shevan, a prisoner at Aberdeen's Craiginches Prison, was recaptured 5 hours after he absconded while cleaning the prison's gatehouse. **20.** Susan McLeod, 24, was charged with murder after the bodies of three dead babies were found in her Glasgow flat. **23.** Crime statistics released from the Scottish Executive showed a drop in most areas of recorded crime during 2000 with the overall figure down 3% to 423,000. Plans were revealed by the Scottish Parliament to require members of the judiciary to declare any connection with the freemasons.

May 2001

6. The head and skeleton of a man, later identified as 42-year-old Michael Munro, was discovered in the garden of house in Buckie. **16.** Inspector Adam Carruthers, an officer with Dumfries and Galloway Police was found guilty of raping two women and indecently assaulting two others. **18.**

It was announced that an £8.3 million state-of-the-art communications centre is to be built for Lothian and Borders Police. **19.** Teacher Grant Dunn, originally from Oban, shot 19-year-old Emanuela Ferro outside her school in Pinerolo, Italy. Dunn, who then shot himself, was thought to have been infatuated with the girl. **20.** Police launched an investigation after the body of a 15-year-old boy was discovered in a house in Dundee. **28.** John Dean, originally from Essex, was charged with the murder of Michael Munro, whose skeleton was discovered in a garden in Buckie earlier in the month. **29.** Angus Sinclair, 56, went on trial for the rape and murder of 17-year-old Mary Gallacher in Glasgow in 1978. **31.** Four British men, including David Mornin from Greenock, were jailed for two years and sentenced to 500 lashes in Saudi Arabia for illegal alcohol trading.

June 2001

1. The Scottish Executive announced tougher regulations governing the movement of registered sex offenders. Under the reforms offenders must register in person with local police within four days, rather than in person or by post in 14 days. **5.** A siege at Craiginches Prison, when a prison officer was held hostage, was resolved after 12 hours of negotiations. A ScotRail employee was stabbed whilst on duty in Glasgow's Queen Street station after leading two men to move from a stairway in the station's lower level. **6.** Five people were arrested following a two hour blockade by protesters at the Ministry of Defence's Coulport Arms Depot on Loch Long. **6.** Adam Curruthers, a 38-year-old inspector with Dumfries and Galloway Police, was found guilty of raping two women and jailed for 12 years. **11.** Eight pupils were suspended from Kinguisie High School after being caught with live ammunition. **14.** Police launched a murder enquiry after a fire in an Edinburgh flat claimed the life of an 18-year-old man. A siege at Sughton Prison in Edinburgh in which two nursing officers were taken hostage, ended peacefully after 12 hours. **15.** Senior UN officials met ELN leaders in Columbia in an attempt to secure the release of Ally Taylor from Inverurie who was taken prisoner by rebels in the Colombian jungle in August 1999. **18.** A fire, which was treated as suspicious, caused the closure of the Sacred Heart Primary School in Bellshill, near Glasgow. Police investigating the disappearance of Elgin woman Arlene Fraser in 1998 resumed a search of her home. **19.** A 29-year-old man was arrested following the seizure of heroin with a street value of approximately £9 million during a vehicle search outside Lockerbie. **20.** Two men were charged with conspiracy to murder in connection with the inquiry into the disappearance of Arlene Fraser. **25.** Police announced that they were investigating possible financial irregularities at Borders Council in connection with a £4 million deficit in the authority's education budget.

July 2000

1. It was revealed that 400 dock-workers were to be made redundant in a restructuring of the former naval dockyards at Rosyth. **2.** Stagecoach, the Perth based transport company, spent $12 million on 30 new buses from the US. **3.** Textiles manufacturers in the Borders put a £1.5 million investment programme on hold until the threat of increased US import tariffs on cashmere products was resolved. **4.** It was revealed that Glasgow's £27 million celebration of architecture and design may have created as few as 10 design jobs for the city. The Borders' Council rejected proposals by the fast food chain McDonalds to build a franchise at Wilderhaugh, ignoring two petitions from local people bearing almost 10,000 signatures. The Bank of Scotland struck its fifth major outsourcing deal since 1998, agreeing to transfer 40 staff and responsibility for its tax and trustee services to the accountancy firm Mazars Neville Russell. **7.** The Royal Bank of Scotland and Scottish Power unveiled their first joint Internet venture, Work24.Co.UK. **11.** Forth Ports confirmed that Bill Thomson, its former chairman, was asked to resign after engineering a £357 million take-over bid with Duke Street Capital, a private equity firm, without the board's knowledge or consent. **12.** Duncan Whyte, head of Weir Group, the Glasgow based pumps and valves maker, was sacked after 13 months with a £500,000 pay off. **15.** Figures released by the Edinburgh Solicitors' Property Centre showed that house prices in the Scottish capital had risen by 12.3% in the same period last year. The average price of a property was £99,433. **17.** Campsie Spring, a Scottish firm specialising in bottled mineral water, lobbied MPs to renew its contract to supply the House of Commons. A report by Lloyds TSB Commercial Scotland revealed that 43% of Scottish businesses reported increased orders in the first 6 months of 2000, the UK average was 41%. **18.** Scottish Power sold its Contracting Services division to ALSTROM, the energy and transport infrastructure specialist, for £20 million. **22.** The creation of nearly 1,000 telecommunications jobs

in Fife and Perth was announced by Henry McLeish, the Enterprise Minister. ADC, a network equipment supplier was to recruit 600 people, a further 300 will be employed at a call centre for Perth-based CGNU. **31.** Statistics revealed that home ownership in Scotland had increased from 49.1% of the population in 1989 to 62.4% in 1999.

August 2000

1. A nation-wide protest against high fuel prices resulted in a 10% drop in petrol sales in Scotland. **3.** Glasgow based Scottish Power sold Powercor, its Australian utility, for £890 million. **8.** British Energy sold its Swalec electricity supply arm to Scottish and Southern energy for £257 million. **18.** The Ailsa-Troon boat yard revealed it would close when it completed its existing contracts, costing 91 workers their jobs. **21.** Lloyds TSB Scotland revealed an 11% rise in housing prices over the previous 3 months. **23.** 123 jobs were lost when Colour Box, the Scottish manufacturer of ceramic animals, liquidated after announcing debts of £1 million.

September 2000

4. The mobile phone company One 2 One announced that it was to set up a new call centre in Dundee, bringing the total number of people employed by call centres in Scotland to around 40,000. **5.** Shell announced that it was to increase its planned investment in capital projects in the North Sea by 50% in 2001 to a total of $1.2 billion. **7.** BP announced that it was to increase expenditure in the oil and gas fields in Scottish waters to $4 billion over the next four years. **8.** Motorola, Scotland's biggest manufacturing employer, announced that they were setting up a research and development centre for the semiconductor industry which will create another 550 new jobs over the next few years. **11.** A Government report showed that the number of people out of work and claiming benefit had fallen to a 24 year low of 111,300. However, Scotland still had the highest unemployment rate of all the UK regions. **20.** Scottish tourist industry chiefs revealed that there had been a 13% decline in visitor numbers in the past year. Scottish Enterprise Minister, Henry McLeish launched a tourism skills group to ensure that all managers connected with the tourist industry get the correct training.

October 2000

3. Henry McLeish, Scottish Enterpise Minister, ordered a review of the Scottish Tourist Board structure, by PricewaterhouseCoopers. **4.** An announcement was released that 90 new jobs were to be created at Ferguson Shipbuilders in Glasgow after it clinched a £17 million contract. **8.** Scottish medical imaging company, Voxar, secured new investment worth £5.4 million which would allow them to double in size by employing 150 new staff at their new Edinburgh base. **9.** The Scottish Enterprise International Benchmark Report 2000 showed that 29% of businesses in Scotland use e-commerce compared to 27% of business from the UK as a whole. **11.** Industry regulators discovered that only nine of the 143 safety improvements ordered at the Dounreay nuclear plant two years ago, had been carried out. **19.** Japanese company Oki, which makes printers and faxes, confirmed that it was to lay off 240 full-time staff and 100 temporary workers at its Cumbernauld plant. **23.** A report by the Industry Leadership Team (ILT), a group of key representatives from the offshore oil and gas industries, predicted that increased investment in these industries would create about 250,000 jobs, the majority of which will be in Scotland. **26.** The Govan shipyard in Glasgow lost out on a major ferry contract but won an order to build two Ministry of Defence vessels worth more than £150 million. The work safeguarded more than 1,000 jobs. **28.** Politicians and union leaders took to the streets of Glasgow to thank those who supported the campaign to safeguard the Govan shipyard. **31.** Ferguson Shipbuilders in Glasgow won a £2 million contract to build one of three new ferries for Orkney and Shetland.

November 2000

2. Burton's Biscuits, which employs 800 people at its Sighthill plant, was bought by American investment company Hicks, Muse, Tate and Furst. **7.** Clackmannanshire Council announced the creation of 150 jobs, with plans to construct better play areas for children, landscaped gardens and better car parking facilities. **4.** The Environment Minister, Sam Galbraith, rejected the planning application to create a superquarry on the coast of Harris at Lingerbay. **8.** Mobil was given the go-ahead to build a new boilerhouse at the St Fergus terminal, near Peterhead. The expansion, due to get under way by the end of 2000, created 50 new construction jobs. **13.** A work transfer, involving the construction of eight landing craft for the Ministry of Defence being switched to Govan from the Ailsa Troon yard in Ayrshire, safeguarded up to 150 shipbuilding jobs

in the Clyde yard. **14.** It was revealed that the ExxonMobil oil giant had uncovered a huge natural oil field, 100 miles north-west of Shetland. **15.** The European Commission cleared a £100 million aid package for the UK's coal industry, which helped to safeguard 650 jobs at the Longannet mine in Fife. **16.** Halliburton Subsea Systems in Caithness were awarded a £65 million order with Kerr McGee to supply subsea pipeline bundles for its Leadon Field development in the North Sea. The contract safeguarded 200 jobs at the base. It was announced that Kvaerner Energy in Clydebank was to close with the loss of 200 jobs after the collapse of a buy-out plan. **20.** Pelikan Hardcopy Scotland, one of the North-east's largest employers, announced that it was to axe up to 40 jobs at its Turriff plant after transferring part of its operation to China. **22.** A £2 million Heritage Lottery Fund grant was awarded to Oban-based charity The Nadair Trust, which represents a partnership of 34 statutory, private and voluntary organisations in Argyll. The grant will help to create 40 jobs in the Argyll islands. **23.** The supermarket chain Asda announced a £70 million investment plan which will create 550 jobs throughout Scotland. Safeways announced that it was to spend half a billion pounds expanding and refurbishing its UK stores. **27.** US computer component manufacturer Seagate announced plans to close its only remaining plant in Scotland which employed 85 people. The centre in Irvine was shut in March 2001. Two Scottish Banks, The Bank of Scotland and the Clydesdale Bank were rated to have the worst quality of service in a UK-wide survey carried out by the Forum of Private Businesses.

December 2000

4. It was announced that Swankie Food Products in Arbroath had been bought by a consortium of two fish processors who will move production to their Aberdeen facilities with the loss of 30 jobs. **13.** It was announced that more than 250 jobs would be created with the expansion of One 2 One's call centre in Forres at the beginning of 2001. The European Commission approved a £17.5 million funding package to secure the future of Longannet coal mine in Fife, which employs 650 people. **14.** Sixteen Landmark Home Furnishings stores across Scotland closed suddenly, leaving thousands of disappointed customers and hundreds of jobs in jeopardy. **15.** It was announced that North Sea cod fishing quotas would be cut by nearly 50% in 2001 and the quotas for other species would also face big reductions. Bus building company, Alexander, based in

Falkirk, secured Britain's biggest ever bus building order, worth £35 million. The contract secured the jobs of its 1,000 workers until October 2001 and created 30 new jobs for local workers. **19.** Almost thirty jobs were lost when North-East fish transport company Chillspeed R7M announced they were going into liquidation. **21.** National Australia Group, which owns the Clydesdale and Yorkshire banks announced that they were to open an £80 million telephone banking centre in Kilmarnock, Ayrshire by the summer of 2001, with the creation of approximately 500 jobs. The contract to provide the £500,000 worth of granite for the outside of the new Parliament building was awarded to Fyfe Glenrock and Aggregate Industries in Kemnay. **22.** Kvaerner Energy in Clydebank closed down with the loss of 200 jobs after a buy-out plan by former managers collapsed.

January 2001

3. A £600 million contract to service and repair engines for British Airways which will last 20 years, was won by the Rolls Royce plant in East Kilbride. **9.** Textiles company Daks Simpson announced plans to lose over 250 jobs at its plant in Lanarkshire. **15.** Research by management consultants Ernst and Young found that Scottish firms had, on average, the lowest turnover and the lowest number of employees in the UK. **16.** BT Scotland announced the creation of 200 jobs at a new £1 million technical helpdesk to be set up in Fort William. **17.** Brewers Scottish and Newcastle announced that they would be shedding 1,300 jobs over the next four years at its Scottish Courage Beer Unit. **22.** Prestwick Airport was sold by transport group Stagecoach to a consortium of local businessmen for £33.4 million. **23.** The European Union announced the closure to fishermen of large areas of the spawning grounds in the North Sea between mid-February and the end of April, in an attempt to preserve the stock of fish. **26.** Scottish Coal announced that they were creating 130 new jobs at their Longannet mine in Clackmannanshire. **30.** Lloyds TSB bid £19.8 billion for Abbey National.

February 2001

4. Figures released by financial and business advice firm Grant and Thornton suggested that the overall failure rate of Scottish businesses rose by over 70% in 2000. **12.** More than 100 maintenance technicians at the Dounreay nuclear plant began a two-day strike in protest at pay and conditions. **13.** Insurance giant Prudential, the parent company of Scottish Amicable announced that it would shed 2,000 jobs in the next year. The European

Agriculture Commissioner Franz Fischler announced plans to limit subsidies for beef cattle farmers. The proposals meant that only herds of less than 90 cattle would continue to qualify for the special beef premium. Emergency measures designed to protect North Sea cod stocks by making many areas off limits to fishermen until the end of April 2001, came into force. **14.** Employment agency Manpower announced plans to create 200 new jobs at a new call centre in Selkirk. **21.** Brewing and pub group Scottish Courage announced that it was to cut 170 jobs in its Fountainbridge plant in Edinburgh. **23.** The Trade and Industry Secretary Stephen Byers referred the £19 billion takeover bid by Lloyds TSB for Abbey National to the UK's Competition Commission. Polaroid announced plans to cut more than 230 jobs at its Vale of Levan plant in Dunbartonshire. **27.** A study by the Equal Opportunities Commission Equal Pay Task Force concluded that the gap between women's and men's pay in Scotland is wider than in the rest of Britain. **28.** Abbey National announced that it had terminated merger talks with the Bank of Scotland, over complications presented by the counter bid from Lloyds TSB.

March 2001

1. The Royal Bank of Scotland announced that its pre-tax profits had risen by a quarter to £3.3 billion in 2000, following the takeover of the Natwest. **5.** Almost 100 vessels from Scottish ports sailed to the Firth of Forth to demonstrate for government aid to help safeguard the future of their industry. **6.** Scottish Enterprise announced that it was to shed 350 jobs as part of an efficiency drive. **14.** Official figures showed that unemployment in Scotland had fallen to its lowest level in 25 years. **15.** Computer manufacturers Compaq announced that they were to cut 5,000 jobs, 700 of which would be at their plant in Erskine. **22.** Figures showed that over 200 jobs had been lost in Dumfries and Galloway as a result of the foot and mouth crisis. **27.** Almost 2,000 postal staff in the West of Scotland began an unofficial strike at disciplinary action being taken against a colleague, which they said was too lenient. **28.** Enterprise Minister Wendy Alexander unveiled details of emergency measures worth £13.5 million to assist the Scottish tourism industry. **30.** A £75 million refit contract for the Rosyth naval dockyard, which was expected to secure employment at the yard for the next 4 years, was announced by the Ministry of Defence.

April 2001

2. The Edinburgh-based Drambuie Liquer Company announced that it was to shut its plant at Kirkliston in West Lothian over the next six months to launch a joint venture was the whisky firm Glenmorangie. **12.** Scots food giant Baxters, which has operated in Fochabers for 133 years, announced that it was to move its entire marketing division to Glasgow as part of a move to push the brand on the international market place. **24.** The Motorola plant at Bathgate announced that it was to close with the loss of 3,000 jobs. **25.** The Halifax and the Bank of Scotland announced that they were in talks over a £26 billion merger. **26.** The clothing company Jaegar announced that it was to close its factory in Campbeltown, with the loss of more than 160 jobs.

May 2001

4. Chiefs at the Bank of Scotland and Halifax agreed terms over their £28 billion merger to establish a new bank called HBOS which will have its headquarters in Edinburgh. **8.** Mobile phone company One2One announced that it was to delay plans to create 1,000 jobs at a call centre in Dundee. **14.** Motorola announced that it would cease production at its Bathgate Factory at the end of June 2001. **16.** The Halifax Bank's internet insurance firm e-sure announced that it was bringing 400 new jobs to Glasgow. Supermarket chain Safeway announced the creation of 640 jobs in Edinburgh in new convenience style stores. **29.** A delegation from the Scottish Borders presented an economic recovery plan to First Minister Henry McLeish in the wake of the foot and mouth crisis. **31.** Scottish Life policyholders voted in favour of shedding the insurer's mutual status and selling the company to Royal London for £1.1 billion.

June 2001

6. Rosyth dockyard secured a contract to refit Royal Navy aircraft HMS Illustrious which would provide up to 1,000 jobs at the yard until 2006. In spite of the news, the owner of the yard Babdock Rosyth said it would still go ahead with redundancies in the summer of 2001. **10.** Radio station Scot FM was bought by the Guardian Media Group for £25.5 million. **13.** The European Commission proposed that fishing catches be cut by up to 50 per cent in an effort to safeguard threatened stocks of cod and hake. **14.** GlaxoSmithKline announced that they were to cut more than 2,000 jobs in streamlining following the merger in 2000 of Glaxo Wellcome and Smithkline Beecham. The move included

cutbacks at its factory in Montrose. **18.** Scottish Power announced that it would close half its 160 High Street stores and sell the other half to rival chain Powerhouse Retail, incurring large job losses. **27.** Scotland's tourist board VisitScotland announced a management restructure involving the axing of six senior posts.

ENVIRONMENT AND SCIENCE

July 2000

1. A study into lung cancer by the Beaston Oncology Centre in Glasgow revealed that only 6% of Scottish patients suffering from the disease survive for 5 years after diagnosis, compared to 10% on the continent and 14% in the US. **6.** Scottish Farmers received £1.13 million compensation from Advanta, a Canadian firm that wrongly supplied them with GM (Genetically Modified) grain. **10.** Scotland's only farm-scale trial of GM crops at New Craig Farm in Daviot was vandalised when protesters trampled and uprooted a half acre plot of GM oil seed rape. The Cetacean Research and Rescue Unit from Gardenstown in Aberdeenshire received a £13,000 grant to buy equipment to save stranded whales. **16.** A report claimed that the number of cases of the sexually transmitted disease chlamydia, increased in Scotland by 50% over the last 5 years. **19.** The Crown Estate Commission revealed it would not challenge clan chief John McLeod of McLeod over his plan to sell the Black Cuillin Hills in Skye for £10 million. **21.** New Craig Farm sowed a second batch of GM rape seed. **27.** It was revealed that the 5,800 acre Eilean Darach estate, which contains the mountain An Teallach, was to be sold for an undisclosed figure. **28.** Customs officials at Edinburgh Airport launched a new initiative to clamp down on smugglers of rare and exotic animals. **29.** Nine of Scotland's beaches, those at Irvine, New Town, Ayr South, Ettrick Bay, St. Andrews, East Sands, Stonehaven, Turnberry and Eyemouth, were listed among 47 British beaches that failed to satisfy basic European safety laws.

August 2000

4. £157 million was pledged to aid the development of agriculture in a 6 year plan unveiled by Scottish Agriculture. **7.** Anglers in the Highlands reported record catches of salmon in July despite a 90% drop in salmon numbers over the last 25 years. **24.** The Scottish Executive approved plans for three farms in Aberdeenshire and one in Monlochy to grow test samples of genetically modified oil seed rape.

September 2000

1. A report by the Director of the Arts Medical Centre at Thomas Jefferson University Hospital in Philadelphia claimed that the seasoning of the sheepskin bag which is used to make bagpipes, is a potential health risk. The skin is treated with a mixture of honey and glycerine which, it was claimed, acts as a perfect culture for fungus such as aspertillus and cyrptococcus. **18.** Scottish Natural Heritage announced that they were to trial a re-introduction of beavers into Scotland in a forest area on the Kintyre Peninsula in Argyll. **30.** An investigation carried out by the Scottish Environmental Protection Agency, revealed that workers at Dounreay Nuclear Plant had been contaminating their own homes with radioactive particles from their clothing.

October 2000

3. Six reported sightings of a 'large black cat' in different parts of West Lothian in a fortnight, sparked speculation that a family of runaway panthers were breeding in the hills. The SSPCA said the animals were likely to be descendants of big cats released into the Scottish wilds 25 years ago. **5.** A project to re-home hedgehogs to parts of the UK where they are declining was set up in North and South Uist after the number of hedgehogs grew to 5,000. They are believed to be the cause of a dramatic drop in the number of birds such as dunlin, redshank and snipe on the island. **6.** Six dolphins became stuck in a coastal outlet in the Dornoch Firth, north of Cromarty. A major rescue operation was launched but only one survived. **9.** The UK Atomic Energy Authority disclosed that the £4 billion programme to decommission Dounreay Nuclear Plant in Cromarty, which is due to close in 2004, will take 60 years to complete. The report also stated that it could be a further 300 years before the site would be completely free of radioactivity. **10.** The Royal Society for the Protection of Birds (RSPB) reported that a 'totally unacceptable' number of birds of prey are still being killed in Scotland every year. The organisation called for tougher punishments, including jail terms for habitual offenders. **13.** The Marine Conservation Society's latest figures showed that nine of Scotland's 60 identified bathing beaches failed to meet minimum water quality standards in 2000, compared to seven in 1999. There was also a decrease in the number of beaches reaching the highest standards. **17.** Scientists at the Univeristy of Glasgow discovered that it may be possible to identify some patients at risk of heart disease by monitoring the levels of the enzyme phospholipase A2, carried in their blood. **27.** A baby minke whale which became stranded on the shores of Loch Dunvegan in Skye, was rescued by volunteers who used a floating pontoon to move the two ton animal.

November 2000

2. Scientists received consent from the Scottish Executive to build the world's largest experimental artificial reef in Loch Linnhe near the island of Lismore. **3.** A team from Aberdeen University developed the first remotely operated camera in the world that can create three-dimensional photographic records of deep-sea life. **13.** Wildlife volunteers in Shetland failed to save a giant turtle which had become tangled in netting. Fishermen from the European Union's North Sea countries held talks with scientists and EU advisers in Brussels on the conservation of fish stocks. **15.** A new cancer research centre, headed by two world leaders in the field Sir David Lane and Sir Alfred Cuschieri, was opened at Ninewells Hospital in Dundee. **16.** The University of Aberdeen was awarded the Queen's Anniversary Prize for higher and further education, in recognition of the achievements of the department of biomedical physics and bioengineering in developing new techniques for medical imaging. **20.** The world's first commercial wave-power station, on Islay, began operating. **22.** An extensive underwater survey of previously unexplored seabed around St Kilda revealed a clear picture of a shoreline dating back at least 180,000 years. The study showed that, instead of a group of islands, St Kilda was one large, mountainous island. It was announced that four Scottish hospitals, Raigmore Hospital, Aberdeen Royal Infirmary, Monklands Hospital and Ninewells Hospital were to pilot a new cervical screening technique called 'liquid based cytology', which could halve the number of borderline smear tests. **27.** Researchers at Aberdeen University announced that they had established a link between having a low IQ and developing dementia in later life. **30.** Environment Minister Sam Galbraith set out a 10-year plan to increase the amount of Scotland's energy produced from renewable sources. It aims to have 18% of the country's energy produced in this way by 2010.

December 2000

5. Researchers from the Roslin Institute near Edinburgh announced that they had discovered a way of creating chickens which lay eggs that can be used to fight cancer. The whites of their eggs will form the basis of new medication that could be commercially available within two years. **6.** A survey co-ordinated by the RSPB found that Strathspey is the top mainland site in Britain and Ireland for nesting waders. **10.** Scientists at Aberdeen University discovered a method of making cannabis soluble meaning that cannabis could be used in sprays, aerosols or injections. **21.** A research team at Edinburgh University discovered a test which could help improve the treatment of Alzheimer's disease sufferers.

January 2001

4. Research revealed that farmed salmon contain up to ten times the amount of pesticides and chemicals found in wild salmon. **6.** A study revealed 13% of Scottish children were overweight and 3% obese. **7.** Scientists from Strathclyde University published a study suggesting that certain types of mushroom can help cancer patients recover following surgery, radiotherapy and chemotherapy. **12.** Edinburgh City Council revealed plans to cull seagulls in the city by destroying their eggs. **19.** The Royal Bank of Scotland reneged on a £22 million loan to Huntington Life Sciences, Britain's biggest animal testing company, following protests outside the company's headquarters. **20.** Pitliver Estate, the home of the Duke of Kent during the second world war, was put on the market for £1.5 million. **24.** Parliament agreed to allow stem cell research using cells from human embryos up to 14-days-old. **26.** The Parent Truth group launched a £75,000 poster campaign in an attempt to get the Scottish Parliament to ban the sale of the morning-after pill to schoolgirls.

February 2001

12. A study commissioned by the Scottish Executive found that Scotland is to get wetter but warmer and face more extreme weather conditions as a result of climate change. **21.** A UK-wide survey by the Marine Conservation Society (MCS) found that Scotland's beaches have the highest level of sewage debris in Britain.

March 2001

1. The first cases of foot and mouth disease in Scotland for 40 years were confirmed in the Dumfries and Galloway borderland. **2.** A report found that a quarter of British butterfly species, including many in Scotland, had declined by 50 per cent over the last 200 years due to changes in climate and agricultural practices. **3.** The first 4,200 animals in Scotland diagnosed with foot and mouth were destroyed. Three farms in Dumfriesshire and Kirkcudbrightshire were confirmed to have the disease and 50 more were

under observation because of possible infection. A train carrying nuclear fuel flasks from Sellafield derailed at Skateraw near Dunbar. **4.** A £1.8 million government initiative to fight tuberculosis was unveiled. 200,000 school children were to be vaccinated as part of the scheme. **5.** 69 cases of foot and mouth were confirmed throughout the UK, with 6 in Scotland. **7.** 160 fishing boats sailed down the Firth of Forth in protest against the government's mismanagement of cod and haddock stocks. **12.** The total number of confirmed cases of foot and mouth in Scotland reached 23, with 164 in the UK as a whole. **15.** It was announced that nicotine patches would be made available on prescription in Scotland to help smokers quit the habit. **16.** The Scottish Executive announced plans to halt the foot and mouth epidemic by slaughtering 200,000 apparently healthy sheep at more than 500 farms in Dumfries and Galloway. **17.** Scottish Ministers rejected plans to fund a tie-up project to protect immature fish stocks. **22.** The number of foot and mouth outbreaks in Scotland rose to 61. **26.** A government enquiry was launched following allegations that the BP refinery in Grangemouth was responsible for spreading poisonous particles over a 40-mile radius. **27.** A team from Oxford University concluded that the Scottish Wildcat, or a species very like it, still survives in the highlands. **31.** The number of confirmed cases of foot and mouth in Scotland passed 100.

April 2001

1. Nine Greenpeace protesters chained themselves to the Drill Star rig in the Cromarty Firth to prevent it from leaving to begin operations in the North Sea. They were attempting to get the oil company Jet to adopt green fuels. **6.** Six Greenpeace demonstrators attached themselves to the Santa Fe 135 oil rig 75 miles north of Aberdeen. They were protesting at the oil industry's contribution to global warming. **11.** PPL Therapeutics, the Scottish-based company that created Dolly the Sheep produced a litter of five transgenetic cloned pigs. **23.** Deputy Health Minister Malcom Chisolm announced that the tuberculosis immunisation programme was to be re-launched in Scottish secondary schools. **24.** A multi-million pound project using high-tech sonar equipment to try to find 'Nessie' began at Loch Ness. **28.** The Scottish Executive announced that trials of genetically modified crops were to go ahead at five farms in the north of Scotland.

May 2001

4. Of the 111 beaches in Scotland surveyed by the Marine Conservation Society, only 20 were recommended due to falling hygiene standards. **13.** A report by the Moray Firth Partnership warned that rising pollution and over-fishing the Moray Firth is threatening the survival of Scotland's only resident colony of bottle-nosed dolphins. An earthquake measuring 2.9 on the Richter scale shook Dumfries. **22.** Anti-nuclear campaigners presented a petition with more than 10,000 signatures to the Scottish Parliament calling for MSPs to investigate health risks to people living near the nuclear base at Faslane on the Clyde. Carol Davidson, a care worker at Aberdeen's Royal Cornhill Hospital died from the flesh-eating condition necrotising fascilitis. **28.** The world's first eaglet produced through the insemination of frozen sperm was born at a farm in South Lanarkshire. **30.** The Westfield Biomass Plant at Cardenden in Fife, which aims to use ground-breaking technology to convert tonnes of poultry litter into electricity for thousands of homes, was officially opened by Scotland's Environment Minister Rhonda Brankin.

June 2001

3. Government funds were granted to Robert Gordon University in Aberdeen to conduct research into the use of underwater turbines to generate electricity from the currents of the Pentland Firth between Orkney and the Scottish mainland. **12.** A study of the seven wrecks of the German High Seas fleet, which was scuttled in the Scapa Flow, Orkney, in 1919, was begun by Heriot-Watt University. **18.** A scheme to reintroduce golden eagles into Northern Ireland began with the transfer of 70 golden eagle chicks from Scotland to County Donegal. **22.** Much of the Scottish Borders region was reopened in the aftermath of the foot and mouth epidemic. The Scottish Department for Rural Development revealed plans to designate 81 areas from Galloway to Shetland as protected shellfish waters in an attempt to increase the quality of Scottish shellfish. **23.** The UK's Energy Minister, Brian Wilson, revealed a £4 billion scheme to decommission the nuclear reactor at Dounreay in Caithness. **24.** Highland Light and Power revealed it faced further delays in the construction of 4 hydro-electric dams in the Flowerdale and Sheildaig Forest areas of Wester Ross, following objections from conservation groups. **25.** Ross Finnie, Scotland's Rural Development Minister, revealed a new strategic report on the future of Scottish farming, proposing a system of EU support and land-management contracts to reward multi-purpose farms. **27.** The HMS Exmouth, second world war destroyer sunk in 1940 with the loss of 189 crew, was discovered off the coast of Scotland by Navy Divers. Glasgow's £75 million Science Centre was denied a public entertainment licence due to design flaws creating possible hazards for children. **28.** Dr Luigi Piccardi, from the Centre for the Study of Geology in Florence, published a report claiming that the Loch Ness monster was the result of seismic activity beneath the Loch which releases bubbles of gas. **29.** The Scottish Fisherman's Federation criticised European conservation proposals to increase the mesh size of nets used in the North Sea. **30.** The Glasgow Science Centre opened its doors to the public.

SPORT

July 2000

1. Martin O'Neill, the new manager of Celtic, denied being involved in the sacking of the team's former manager Kenny Dalglish. **2.** Scottish football chiefs revealed their bid to host the Euro 2008 football championship. David Millar became the first Scot to win the Yellow Jersey in the Tour de France after winning the time trial around the Futurescope theme-park. **3.** Scotland lost 48-14 against New Zealand at Eden Park in Auckland during their Rugby tour. **4.** The Scottish Rugby Union squad cancelled the Fiji leg of their New Zealand tour and returned home. **5.** David Millar lost the Yellow Jersey to Laurent Jalabert of France. **7.** Rhona Brankin, the Deputy Sports Minister, announced Scotland's aim to host the 2009 Ryder Cup. **9.** Executives from Rangers Football club bought a 51% stake in the Australian Northern Spirit Football Team. **12.** The Standard Life Loch Lomond Invitational golf tournament began. **15.** The South African Ernie Els won the Loch Lomond golf tournament. **19.** The Scottish Open Golf Tournament began in St Andrews. Police pledged to prosecute any streakers who disrupt play. **23.** Tiger Woods won the 129th Scottish Open Golf Tournament. **26.** Alison Sheppherd of Glasgow opened her British Olympic Swimming Trials programme in Sheffield by setting a new Commonwealth record in the 50m freestyle, in a time of 25.12 seconds.

August 2000

4. England and Wales took the top two places in the European Women's Lacrosse Championship in Glasgow; Scotland claimed bronze after defeating the Czech Republic. **22.** The International Amateur Athletics federation upheld a 2-year ban on the Scottish sprinter Dougie Walker for his alleged use of steroids in 1998. **24.** The Scottish PGA golf championship began in Gleneagles, at the Monarch's course. **27.** The 159th Lonarch Highland Games gathering was held. It was attended by stars including Billy Connolly, Robin Williams, Steve Martin and Judy Dench. **28.** Pierre Fulke from Sweden won the Scottish PGA Golf Tournament.

September 2000

3. Celtic Football Club achieved their highest scoring victory in the Glasgow derby since 1957 with a 6-2 win. The win meant an end to Celtic's losing run of seven games against Rangers. **10.** Scottish racing driver David Coulthard narrowly missed being struck by another car as it flew past his head in a major pile-up shortly after the beginning of the Italian Grand Prix. **18.** Former Director of Celtic Football Club, Kenny Dalglish, announced that he planned to sue the club after he was pushed out of his job following the arrival of the new manager, Martin O'Neill.

October 2000

1. Scotland's most capped goal-keeper, Jim Leighton, was told to leave the Scotland training camp in Italy after it was revealed that he had written a book critical of Scotland manager Craig Brown and coach Alan Hodgkinson. **3.** The Olympic team returned to Britain with their highest medal total at the Olympics since 1924. Medals won by Scottish competitors amounted to 3 gold and 6 silver. **5.** Colin Macrae, the former World Rally Champion, was injured in a crash during a race in Corsica. He was knocked unconscious and suffered a broken cheek bone and a bruised lung. **7.** Scotland won their first World Cup Qualifier with a 2-0 win over San Marino. **11.** Scotland drew 1-1 in their World Cup Qualifier against Croatia. The goal was Kevin Gallagher's first international goal in three years. **15.** Police announced that they were to investigate the altercation between Dundee United boss, Jim McLean and BBC reporter, John Barnes. **17.** FIFA announced that Scotland manager, Craig Brown, would be banned from the touch-line at the next World Cup Qualifier following an outburst in the dug-out during the Scotland v Croatia match. **19.** Former Dundee United chairman Jim McLean was charged with assaulting BBC reporter John Barnes. **20.** The former Celtic and West Ham striker, Frank McAvennie, avoided a jail sentence for his second offence of possessing cocaine, when he was given a two year conditional discharge and ordered to pay £150 costs at Newcastle Crown Court. **26.** The bid to attract the Ryder Cup to Scotland in 2009 was formally launched by the government and the private sector. **27.** The procurator fiscal at Dundee decided not to press charges against former Dundee United chairman Jim McLean over an altercation with BBC sports reporter John Barnes. **31.** The Princess Royal officially opened the new multi-million pound facilities at Musselburgh Racecourse near Edinburgh.

November 2000

7. Rangers were knocked out of the Champions League following a 2-2 draw with Monaco. **9.** Celtic were knocked out of the UEFA cup following a 2-1 defeat by Girondins de Bordeaux. **10.** Mechanical failure forced Colin McRae out of the Australian rally – effectively ending his world championship hopes. **14.** It was revealed that Aberdeen Football Club made a £3.3 million loss during the 1999 season, despite two cup finals and a £2.1 million share rights issue. **19.** Airdrie won the Bell's Scottish League Challenge Cup after beating Livingstone 3-2 in a penalty shoot out after the game ended 2-2 at the end of extra time. **23.** Rangers signed Norwegian striker Tore Andre Flo from Chelsea, making him the most expensive player signed by a Scottish club. **25.** Dumbarton Football Club opened its new ground located near Dumbarton Castle rock. **26.** Rangers beat Celtic 6-1 at Ibrox, moving Rangers up from mid-table to third in the Scottish Premier League. **28.** Hearts Football Club announced that poor financial results in the last financial year had led to a loss of £3.7 million. **30.** Rangers enjoyed a 1-0 win against Kaiserslautern in the UEFA Cup first leg tie.

December 2000

7. Rangers were knocked out of the UEFA Cup by Kaiserslautern who defeated them 3-0. **15.** Kenny Dalglish was awarded more than £600,000 from Celtic following his sacking as director of football. The future of Greenock club Morton was uncertain after the club called in an administrator. Scotland's male curling team failed to qualify for curling's world championships for the first time. Former Scotland international footballer Peter Cormack was sacked after only 10 days as manager of Cowdenbeath. **20.** Hearts Football Club announced plans to leave Tynecastle and move to a new home on the west side of Edinburgh. Judy Murray was awarded the new post of full-time High Performance National Coach for Scottish tennis. **21.** Arbroath were ordered to replay their Scottish Cup first round tie with Montrose after it was discovered that the club had fielded two suspended players in their team.

January 2001

2. Thousands of people attended Ibrox Stadium where a memorial service was held for the 66 Rangers fans who died in a crushing incident there on 2 January 1971 following the Rangers-Celtic New Year derby. **21.** Stephen Hendry, John Higgins and Alan McManus beat the Republic of Ireland 6-2 in the final of the Coalite Nations Cup snooker in Reading. Scot Paul Foster defeated Richard Corsie to win the World Indoor Singles Bowls Championship for the second time.

February 2001

13. Receivers locked the players and management team of Airdrie football club out of the grounds for running up many thousands of pounds of unpaid running fees and the club was thrown out of the Scottish Cup for failing to fulfil their fixtures. **14.** Ebbe Skovdahl, the Danish manager of Aberdeen Football Club, agreed a one year extension to his contract. **20.** An agreement was reached to form a Celtic Rugby Union League consisting of Welsh teams, Irish districts and Scottish districts. **23.** Scottish sprinter John Skeete tested positive for the banned steroid stanozolol but claimed that his dietary supplement had been tampered with. It was announced that Strathclyde Police constable Sir John Orr was to become Kilmarnock's new chairman. Earlston Golf Club, which has been without a course of its own for more than 50 years, bought land on the moon for £101 through an internet company with a view to developing a course.

March 2001

8. Rangers signed Jamaican international Marcus Gayle from Wimbledon in a £1 million deal. **11.** Rangers were knocked out of the Scottish Cup by Dundee United who progressed to the semi-finals. **17.** Scotland recorded their first victory in the Six Nations championships with a 23-19 victory over Italy at Murrayfield. **18.** Celtic defeated Kilmarnock 3-0 in the CIS Cup final at Hampden. **19.** Norwich City completed the signing of Scotland midfielder Gary Holt from Kilmarnock. Former Scotland and British Lions legend Gordon Brown died of cancer at the age of 53. **22.** Former Scottish international Andy Goram joined Manchester United in a £100,000 loan deal. Gordon Petric's three-year contract with Hearts was ended two years prematurely by

mutual agreement. A management deal between the interim liquidators of Airdronians Football Club and hotelier Jim Innes allowed the club to stay in business until the end of the season at least. Jim Innes announced that he hoped to raise enough money to conclude a full takeover which would guarantee the club's future. Scotland drew 2-2 with Belgium at Hampden during their World Cup Qualifier. **26.** Scottish golfer Janice Moodie finished joint second at the LPGA Nibisco Championship at Rancho Mirage in California. **28.** Scotland defeated San Marino 4-0 in their World Cup Qualifying match. Colin Hendry was later investigated by Fifa over an elbowing incident in the closing minutes of the match. **29.** An independent disciplinary committee ruled that sprinter John Skeete had his dietary supplements spiked with banned steroids. **30.** Hearts signed Andy Webster from Arbroath for £70,000 and Gary Bollan from St Johnstone.

April 2001

1. Ronnie O'Sullivan beat Stephen Hendry 9-8 in the final of the Irish Masters in Dublin. David Coulthard won the Brazilian Grand Prix. **4.** Former Scotland forward Darren Jackson was released from his contract at Hearts. **9.** The Scottish Women's Curling team finished fourth at the World Curling Championships in Lausanne. **11.** Dave Mill from Perthshire, set out on his expedition to be the first man to walk solo and unaided to the North Pole from the treacherous Canadian side. **22.** Celtic were presented with the Premier League trophy after their 1-0 win over Hearts at Parkhead. **24.** East Fife appointed Dave Clarke as manager following the departure of Rab Shannon. **26.** Fifa imposed a six-match ban on Scotland captain Colin Hendry after reviewing footage of his conduct during a World Cup qualifying match at Hampden in March.

May 2001

1. World darts champion Phil Taylor was fined £2,000 for indecently assaulting two women fans after a darts competition in Fife in 1999. **8.** Royal Troon was awarded the 2004 Open Championship. **13.** McLaren driver David Coulthard won the Austrian Grand Prix. **14.** Russell Latapy was sacked by Hibs after missing training ahead of an Edinburgh derby and spending the evening socialising with his international team mate Dwight Yorke. **15.** Celtic football legend Boby Murdoch, aged 56, died in hospital two days after suffering a stroke. **16.** Melrose back-row forward Tom Weir was disciplined with a 26-week ban for stamping following an incident during a match against Boroughmuir in April. **17.** Scotland captain Colin Hendry had his ban from international football halved to three games following an appeal to the Fifa disciplinary panel. **20.** Kilmarnock Football Club secured a place in the 2002 UEFA Cup when they defeated Celtic 1-0. **31.** Morton Football Club sacked their entire playing staff following financial collapse.

June 2001

13. Scottish Rugby Union announced it had made record payments of £2 million to local Rugby Clubs in 2000 and reduced its debt by £2.7 million. **23.** 23-year-old Ian Edmond from Edinburgh beat the Scottish record for the 200 metre breaststroke, set by David Wilkie in the 1976 Olympics, with a time of 2.12.70. **29.** Scotland's Cricket team beat Fiji by six wickets on the opening day of the ICC Trophy tournament in Toronto.

— FORTHCOMING EVENTS —

For the Year 2002

January

11-12 January Scalloway Fire Festival

19 October-13 January The Fine Art of Photography, Scottish National Portrait Gallery

16-3 February Celtic Connections, Glasgow

29 January Lerwick Up Helly Aa

February

2 February Caledonian Canine Show, Edinburgh

3 November-24 February Japan Festival, Royal Museum of Scotland

8-9 February Nesting and Girlsta Up Helly Aa

9-10 February Edinburgh Antiques Fair
† Perth Bull Sales

March

23-31 March The World Irish Dancing Championships

23-31 March Altogether a Delightful Country, Royal Museum of Scotland

30 March–1 April Great North of Scotland Model Railway Show

April

6-16 April Edinburgh International Science festival

*25-29 April Shetland Folk Festival

May

2-6 May Isle of Bute Jazz Festival

June

26 June Royal Northern Crop Event, Oldmedrum

29 -7 July Stockbridge Festival

July

*6-7 July T in the Park Festival, Balado Kinross

6-8 July Educational Institute of Scotland, Caird Hall

*7-13 July Hebredean Celtic Festival

*7-13 July Ceolas Music Summer School

13-16 July World Flower Show, Glasgow

13-14 July Glamis – Scottish transport Extravaganza

19-28 July Auchterarder Festival

26-4 August Edinburgh International Jazz and Blues Festival
†Game Conservancy Scottish Fair, Scone Palace, Perth (01620 850577)
† St Magnus Festival, Orkney

August

*1st week August Hebridean Maritime Festival

2-24 Edinburgh Military Tattoo

4-26 Edinburgh Festival Fringe

*9-24 Edinburgh International Book Festival

11-15 Edinburgh International Film Festival

13-2 September Edinburgh International Festival

30-2 September Walk Shetland 2002

† Turriff Show, Turriff Showground, Turriff, nr Aberdeen (www.turriffshow.org)
† Perth Show, South Inch Perth (01738 623780)
† Moy Game Fair, same days as Perth Show.

September

7-14 Scottish Borders Festival of Walking

12-16 Haddington Music Festival

26-29 Auld Rock Legends Storytelling Festival

October

10-20 Shetland Accordion and Fiddle Festival
† Perth Bull Sales

November

*23-25 Fiddle 2002

December

31 Hogmanay

* provisional
† dates unavailable at the time of publication

SPORTS EVENTS

January
Scottish Cross-Country Ski Championships
Eric Liddell Memorial New Year Sprint

February
Aviemore Nordic Skiing Festival
North of Scotland Cross-Country Ski Championships
Scottish Curling Championship (different venue each year)

April
Gala Rugby Sevens, Galashiels

May
Bergen to Shetland Yacht Race
Bruichladdich Islands Peaks Race (Sailing Oban to Troon with 3 stops for runs of Ben More, 3 Paps of Jura and Goat Fell on Arran)
Comrie to Crieff Raft Race
Goatfell Hill Race
Scottish Hebridean Islands Peak Race (The biggest combined sailing & fell-running competition in the world)
Bell Lawrie Scottish Series (sailing), Tarbert, Kintyre. (Last week in May).

June
Highland Balloon Festival
Highland Cross Biathlon (50 mile course from Kintail to Beauly; 20 miles of hill track & forestry trails on foot to Glen Affric, then 30 miles cycle to Beauly)
North of Scotland Inflatable Boats Race (545 mile marathon)
Scottish Hang-Gliding Championships
Scottish Horse Driving Trials
Round Mull three-day yacht race
Shinty Camanachd Cup Final
Royal Highland Show – Show-Jumping
RSAC Scottish Rally (Scotland's biggest annual motorsport event)
Scottish Open Full-Bore Championships

July
Clan Donald Archery Tournaments, Armadale, Skye
Loch Lomond Invitational golf tournament
Aberdeen International Football Festival
West Highland Yachting Week (continues into August)
RYA Scottish Single-Handed Championships (Sailing)
RSAC Scottish Hillrally

Iron Man Triathlon, Aberfeldy: swim 2.4 miles, cycle 112 miles, run full marathon of 26.2 miles. (Contact number 01887-820922)

August
Edinburgh Croquet Tournament
Glen Nevis River Race
Highland Field Sports Fair
Inverleith Petanque Club Open Triples Tournament
Scottish Alternative Games, Parton, nr Castle Douglas
Scottish Championship Horse Trials, Lauder
Scottish Six-Day Festival of Orienteering
Scottish PGA Championship, Gleneagles (golf)
West Highland Yachting Week (begins late July)
International Horse Trials and Country Fair, Blair Castle (01796-481543)

September
Ben Nevis Race (For amateurs: race to the top of the highest mountain in Scotland and back again)
Clydesdale Horseshoeing Competition, Closeburn (golf)
Aberfeldy half-marathon (Contact number 01887-820922)

October
Tiree Wave Classic, Tiree (Surfing)
International Windsurfing Championships, Tiree
Alfred Dunhill Cup, St Andrews
Kinlochewe Mountain Heritage

November
Scottish League Cup Final
Scottish International Badminton Championships

GAMES AND GATHERINGS

Highland games and gatherings are held in most towns and districts in the Highlands, and also in other parts of Scotland, in the summer, including Aberlour, Aboyne, Alva, Argyllshire, Ballater, Beauly, Blair Atholl, Blairgowrie, Blairmore, Braemar, City of Aberdeen, Cowal, Crieff, Drumtochty, Dufftown, Forfar, Forres, Glenisla, Glen Moray and Elgin, Helmsdale and District, Lochearnhead, Balquhidder and Strathyre, Lonach, Oldmeldrum, Stirling, Stonehaven, Tomintoul and Strathavon. Annual agricultural shows are also held in many places. Further details can be obtained from the Scottish Games Association (tel: 01738-627782) and the various local tourist boards (*see* list below).

RIDINGS

Ridings of the Marches and Common Ridings are held in the Borders region between June and August in: Annan, Biggar, Galashiels, Hawick, Linlithgow, Lockerbie, Selkirk, Lauder, Langholm, Sanquhar, and other places. Of some antiquity, they symbolise the people's patrolling of the disputed borderlands, or Marches, between England and Scotland, and the laying of claim to common lands.

Festivals of arts and music are organised in a large number of places. The larger festivals are included in the list below, but there are many others, for instance those of: Banchory, Kirkcudbright, Inverclyde and Renfrew, Gatehouse of Fleet, Harris, Islay, Langholm and Eskdale, Peebles, Mallaig (Feis Na Mara).

Folk festivals include: Inverness, Islay, Isle of Arran, Isle of Skye, Penicuik, Stonehaven, Stromness, and Shetland.

The dates on which these events will be held in 2001/2, and other information about them, can be obtained from the Scottish Tourist Board, regional/local tourist boards, or the relevant local authorities.

Many events, particularly local ones, are not planned very far in advance or may be subject to alteration. For up-to-date information, contact the local tourist board (for list of these, *see* below).

TRADITIONAL/FOLKLORIC EVENTS

Fèisean (festivals), as outlined below, are held at different times and various locations throughout the year. All are tuition based, and in most cases prior notification has to be given if you are considering taking part. Many of the fèisean are exclusively for children, although some accommodate a wider participation. The fèis organiser will be able to tell you what is on offer

eg. dancing, learning an instrument, singing, etc. Each fèis culminates in a concert or cèilidh on the final night. This is open to all.

Fèis Obar Dheathain (Aberdeen)
Tel 01224-846846

Fèis Dhun Eideann (Edinburgh)
Tel 0131-447 1252

Fèis Oigridh Ile (Isle of Islay)
Tel 01496-302059

Fèis an Earraich (Portree)
Tel 01478-612386

Fèis Rois Oigridh (Ullapool)
Tel 01349-862600

Fèis Asainte (Lochinver)
Tel 01571-844262

Fèis Lochabair Bheò (Fort William)
Tel 01397-702090

Fèis Latharna (Oban)
Tel 01631-566135

Fèis Rois Inbhich (Dingwall)
Tel 01349-862600

Fèis Tìr an Eòrna (North Uist)
Tel 01876-580630

Fèis Eige (Isle of Eigg)
Tel 01687-482410

Fèis Chataibh (Golspie)
Tel 01408-621924

Fèis Bharraigh (Isle of Barra)
Tel 01871-810562

Fèis Tìr a' Mhurain (South Uist)
Tel 01878-710341

Fèis Thiriodh (Isle of Tiree)
Tel 01879-220323

Fèis Eilean na Hearadh (Isle of Harris)
Tel 01859-502050

Fèis nan Garbh Chriochan (Acharachle)
Tel 01687-470261

Fèis Eilean an Fhraoich (Isle of Lewis)
Tel 01851-870264

Fèis Srath Fharragaig (Gorthleck)
Tel 01456-486641

Fèis na h-Oige (Inverness)
Tel 01463-223860

Fèis a' Bhaile (Inverness)
Tel 01463-230141

Fèis Rois nan Deugairean (Gairloch)
Tel 01349-862600

Fèis Spè (Nethybridge)
Tel 01540-661141

Fèis Mhuile (Isle of Mull)
Tel 01681-700431

464 Forthcoming Events

Aberdeen and Grampian
27 Albyn Place, Aberdeen AB10 1YL
(Tel: 01224-632727; Fax: 01224-581367;
Email: info@agtb.org; Web: www.agtb.org).

Angus and Dundee
21 Castle Street, Dundee DD1 3AA (Tel: 01382-
527527; Fax: 01382-527551;
Email: enquiries@angusanddundee.co.uk
Web: www.angusanddundee.co.uk).

Ayrshire and Arran
Unit 2, 15 Skye Road, Prestwick, Ayrshire KA9
2TA (Tel: 01292-288688; Fax: 01292-288686;
Email: ayr@ayrshire-arran.com;
Web: www.ayrshire-arran.com).

Dumfries and Galloway
64 Whitesands, Dumfries DG1 2RS
(Tel: 01387-253862; Fax: 01387-245551;
Email: info@dgtb.ossian.net;
Web: www.dumfriesandgalloway.co.uk).

Edinburgh and Lothians
4 Rothesay Terrace, Edinburgh EH3 7RY
(Tel: 0131-473 3800; Fax: 0131-473 3881;
Email: esic@eltb.org; Web: www.edinburgh.org).

Fife
Haig House, Balgonie Road, Markinch KY7
6AQ (Tel: 01592-750066; Fax: 01592-611180;
Email: fife.tourism@kftb.ossian.net;
Web: www.standrews.co.uk).

Greater Glasgow and Clyde Valley
11 George Square, Glasgow G2 1DY
(Tel: 0141-204 4480; Fax: 0141-204 4772;
Email: inquiries@seeglasgow.com;
Web: www.seeglasgow.com).

Orkney
6 Broad Street, Kirkwell, Orkwell KW15 1NX
(Tel: 01856-872856; Fax: 01856-875056;
Email: info@otb.ossian.net; Web: www.visitorkney.com).

Perthshire
Lower City Mills, West Mill Street, Perth PH1
5QP (Tel: 01738-627958; Fax: 01738-630416;
Email: info@ptb.ossian.net;
Web: www.perthshire.co.uk).

Scottish Borders
Shepherds Mill, Whinfield Road, Selkirk TD7
5DT (Tel: 01750-20555; Fax: 01750-21886;
Email: sbtb@scot-borders.co.uk;
Web: www.scot-borders.co.uk).

Shetland Islands
Market Cross, Lerwick, Shetland ZE1 0LU
(Tel: 01595-693434; Fax: 01595-695807;
Email: shetland.tourism@zetnet.co.uk;
Web: www.shetland-tourism.co.uk).

Stirling
Castle Esplanade, Stirling FK8 1EH
(Tel: 01786-479901; Fax: 01786-451881;
Email: info@scottish.heartlands.org;
Web: www.scottish.heartlands.org).

Western Isles
South Beach, Stornoway, Isle of Lewis HS1 2XY
(Tel: 01851-703088; Fax: 01851-705244;
Email: stornowaytic@witb.ossian.net
Web: www.witb.co.uk).

ASTRONOMY

AND TIDES

ASTRONOMICAL DATA
TIDAL DATA

─── ASTRONOMY AND TIDES ───

Lighting-up Time

The legal importance of sunrise and sunset is that the Road Vehicles Lighting Regulations 1989 (SI 1989 No. 1796) make use of the front and rear position lamps on vehicles compulsory during the period between sunset and sunrise. Headlamps on vehicles are required to be used during the hours of darkness on unlit roads or whenever visibility is seriously reduced. The hours of darkness are defined in these regulations as the period between half an hour after sunset and half an hour before sunrise.

In all laws and regulations, sunset refers to the local sunset, e.g. the time at which the Sun sets at the place in question. This common-sense interpretation has been upheld by legal tribunals. Thus the necessity for providing for different latitudes and longitudes is evident.

Sunrise and Sunset

The times of sunrise and sunset are those when the Sun's upper limb, as affected by refraction, is on the true horizon of an observer at sea-level. Assuming the mean refraction to be 34', and the Sun's semi-diameter to be 16', the time given is that when the true zenith distance of the Sun's centre is $90° + 34' + 16'$ or $90° 50'$, or, in other words, when the depression of the Sun's centre below the true horizon is 50'. The upper limb is then 34' below the true horizon, but is brought there by refraction. An observer on a ship might see the Sun for a minute or so longer, because of the dip of the horizon, while another viewing the sunset over hills or mountains would record an earlier time. Nevertheless, the moment when the true zenith distance of the Sun's centre is 90° 50' is a precise time dependent only on the latitude and longitude of the place, and independent of its altitude above sea-level, the contour of its horizon, the vagaries of refraction or the small seasonal change in the Sun's semi-diameter; this moment is suitable in every way as a definition of sunset or sunrise for all statutory purposes.

Twilight

Light reaches us before sunrise and continues to reach us for some time after sunset. The interval between darkness and sunrise or sunset and darkness is called twilight. Astronomically speaking, twilight is considered to begin or end when the Sun's centre is 18° below the horizon, as no light from the Sun can then reach the observer.

As thus defined, twilight may last several hours; in high latitudes at the summer solstice the depression of 18° is not reached, and twilight lasts from sunset to sunrise. The need for some sub-division of twilight is met by dividing the gathering darkness into four stages.

(1) *Sunrise or Sunset,* as defined above

(2) *Civil twilight,* which begins or ends when the Sun's centre is 6° below the horizon. This marks the time when operations requiring daylight may commence or must cease. The interval of time between (1) and (2) varies considerably throughout the year and also varies according to latitude. The shortest interval, about 35 minutes, occurs in southern Scotland at the equinoxes. The longest interval on the Scottish Mainland occurs in the far north, at the summer solstice, where it is over 80 minutes.

(3) *Nautical twilight,* which begins or ends when the Sun's centre is 12° below the horizon. This marks the time when it is, to all intents and purposes, completely dark

(4) *Astronomical twilight,* which begins or ends when the Sun's centre is 18° below the horizon. This marks theoretical perfect darkness. It is of little practical importance, especially if nautical twilight is tabulated

To assist observers the durations of civil, nautical and astronomical twilights are given at intervals of ten days. The beginning of a particular twilight is found by subtracting the duration from the time of sunrise, while the end is found by adding the duration to the time of sunset.

JANUARY 2002

SUNRISE AND SUNSET (GMT)

	Edinburgh		Glasgow		Inverness	
	3° 11′ 55° 56′		4° 14′ 55° 52′		4° 12′ 57° 28′	
	h m	h m	h m	h m	h m	h m
1	8 44	15 49	8 47	15 54	8 58	15 43
2	8 43	15 50	8 47	15 55	8 58	15 44
3	8 43	15 52	8 47	15 56	8 57	15 45
4	8 43	15 53	8 46	15 58	8 57	15 47
5	8 42	15 54	8 46	15 59	8 56	15 48
6	8 42	15 56	8 45	16 00	8 56	15 50
7	8 41	15 57	8 45	16 02	8 55	15 51
8	8 40	15 59	8 44	16 04	8 54	15 53
9	8 39	16 01	8 43	16 05	8 53	15 55
10	8 39	16 02	8 42	16 07	8 53	15 56
11	8 38	16 04	8 42	16 08	8 52	15 58
12	8 37	16 06	8 41	16 10	8 51	16 00
13	8 36	16 07	8 40	16 12	8 49	16 02
14	8 35	16 09	8 39	16 14	8 48	16 04
15	8 34	16 11	8 38	16 16	8 47	16 06
16	8 33	16 13	8 36	16 17	8 46	16 08
17	8 31	16 15	8 35	16 19	8 44	16 10
18	8 30	16 17	8 34	16 21	8 43	16 12
19	8 29	16 19	8 33	16 23	8 42	16 14
20	8 28	16 21	8 31	16 25	8 40	16 16
21	8 26	16 23	8 30	16 27	8 38	16 18
22	8 25	16 25	8 28	16 29	8 37	16 20
23	8 23	16 27	8 27	16 31	8 35	16 23
24	8 22	16 29	8 25	16 33	8 34	16 25
25	8 20	16 31	8 24	16 35	8 32	16 27
26	8 18	16 33	8 22	16 37	8 30	16 29
27	8 17	16 35	8 21	16 39	8 28	16 32
28	8 15	16 37	8 19	16 42	8 26	16 34
29	8 13	16 39	8 17	16 44	8 24	16 36
30	8 11	16 41	8 15	16 46	8 22	16 38
31	8 10	16 43	8 13	16 48	8 20	16 41

DURATION OF TWILIGHT AT 56° N. (IN MINUTES)

January	1st	11th	21st	31st
Civil	47	45	43	41
Nautical	96	93	90	87
Astronomical	141	138	134	130

MOON PHASES

January		d	h	m
Last Quarter		6	03	55
New Moon		13	13	29
First Quarter		21	17	46
Full Moon		28	22	50

FEBRUARY 2002

SUNRISE AND SUNSET (GMT)

	Edinburgh		Glasgow		Inverness	
	3° 11′ 55° 56′		4° 14′ 55° 52′		4° 12′ 57° 28′	
	h m	h m	h m	h m	h m	h m
1	8 08	16 46	8 12	16 50	8 18	16 43
2	8 06	16 48	8 10	16 52	8 16	16 45
3	8 04	16 50	8 08	16 54	8 14	16 48
4	8 02	16 52	8 06	16 57	8 12	16 50
5	8 00	16 54	8 04	16 59	8 10	16 52
6	7 58	16 57	8 02	17 01	8 08	16 55
7	7 56	16 59	8 00	17 03	8 06	16 57
8	7 54	17 01	7 58	17 05	8 03	16 59
9	7 52	17 03	7 56	17 08	8 01	17 02
10	7 49	17 05	7 53	17 10	7 59	17 04
11	7 47	17 08	7 51	17 12	7 56	17 06
12	7 45	17 10	7 49	17 14	7 54	17 09
13	7 43	17 12	7 47	17 16	7 52	17 11
14	7 41	17 14	7 45	17 19	7 49	17 14
15	7 38	17 16	7 42	17 21	7 47	17 16
16	7 36	17 18	7 40	17 23	7 45	17 18
17	7 34	17 21	7 38	17 25	7 42	17 21
18	7 31	17 23	7 35	17 27	7 40	17 23
19	7 29	17 25	7 33	17 29	7 37	17 25
20	7 27	17 27	7 31	17 32	7 35	17 28
21	7 24	17 29	7 28	17 34	7 32	17 30
22	7 22	17 32	7 26	17 36	7 29	17 32
23	7 19	17 34	7 24	17 38	7 27	17 34
24	7 17	17 36	7 21	17 40	7 24	17 37
25	7 15	17 38	7 19	17 42	7 22	17 39
26	7 12	17 40	7 16	17 44	7 19	17 41
27	7 10	17 42	7 14	17 47	7 17	17 44
28	7 07	17 44	7 11	17 49	7 14	17 46

DURATION OF TWILIGHT AT 56° N. (IN MINUTES)

February	1st	11th	21st	31st
Civil	41	39	38	37
Nautical	86	83	81	80
Astronomical	130	126	124	124

MOON PHASES

February		d	h	m
Last Quarter		4	13	33
New Moon		12	07	41
First Quarter		20	12	02
Full Moon		27	09	17

| MARCH 2002 | APRIL 2002 |

SUNRISE AND SUNSET (GMT)

	Edinburgh 3° 11′ 55° 56′		Glasgow 4° 14′ 55° 52′		Inverness 4° 12′ 57° 28′	
	h m	h m	h m	h m	h m	h m
1	7 05	17 47	7 09	17 51	7 11	17 48
2	7 02	17 49	7 06	17 53	7 09	17 50
3	7 00	17 51	7 04	17 55	7 06	17 53
4	6 57	17 53	7 01	17 57	7 03	17 55
5	6 55	17 55	6 59	17 59	7 01	17 57
6	6 52	17 57	6 56	18 01	6 58	17 59
7	6 49	17 59	6 54	18 03	6 55	18 02
8	6 47	18 01	6 51	18 06	6 52	18 04
9	6 44	18 03	6 48	18 08	6 50	18 06
10	6 42	18 05	6 46	18 10	6 47	18 08
11	6 39	18 07	6 43	18 12	6 44	18 11
12	6 37	18 10	6 41	18 14	6 42	18 13
13	6 34	18 12	6 38	18 16	6 39	18 15
14	6 31	18 14	6 36	18 18	6 36	18 17
15	6 29	18 16	6 33	18 20	6 33	18 19
16	6 26	18 18	6 30	18 22	6 31	18 22
17	6 24	18 20	6 28	18 24	6 28	18 24
18	6 21	18 22	6 25	18 26	6 25	18 26
19	6 18	18 24	6 22	18 28	6 22	18 28
20	6 16	18 26	6 20	18 30	6 20	18 30
21	6 13	18 28	6 17	18 32	6 17	18 33
22	6 10	18 30	6 15	18 34	6 14	18 35
23	6 08	18 32	6 12	18 36	6 11	18 37
24	6 05	18 34	6 09	18 38	6 08	18 39
25	6 02	18 36	6 07	18 40	6 06	18 41
26	6 00	18 38	6 04	18 42	6 03	18 43
27	5 57	18 40	6 01	18 44	6 00	18 46
28	5 55	18 42	5 59	18 46	5 57	18 48
29	5 52	18 44	5 56	18 48	5 55	18 50
30	5 49	18 46	5 54	18 51	5 52	18 52
31	5 47	18 48	5 51	18 53	5 49	18 54

SUNRISE AND SUNSET (GMT)

	Edinburgh 3° 11′ 55° 56′		Glasgow 4° 14′ 55° 52′		Inverness 4° 12′ 57° 28′	
	h m	h m	h m	h m	h m	h m
1	5 44	18 50	5 48	18 55	5 46	18 56
2	5 41	18 52	5 46	18 57	5 44	18 59
3	5 39	18 54	5 43	18 59	5 41	19 01
4	5 36	18 57	5 41	19 01	5 38	19 03
5	5 34	18 59	5 38	19 03	5 35	19 05
6	5 31	19 01	5 35	19 05	5 33	19 07
7	5 28	19 03	5 33	19 07	5 30	19 09
8	5 26	19 05	5 30	19 09	5 27	19 12
9	5 23	19 07	5 28	19 11	5 24	19 14
10	5 21	19 09	5 25	19 13	5 22	19 16
11	5 18	19 11	5 23	19 15	5 19	19 18
12	5 16	19 13	5 20	19 17	5 16	19 20
13	5 13	19 15	5 17	19 19	5 14	19 23
14	5 11	19 17	5 15	19 21	5 11	19 25
15	5 08	19 19	5 12	19 23	5 08	19 27
16	5 06	19 21	5 10	19 25	5 06	19 29
17	5 03	19 23	5 07	19 27	5 03	19 31
18	5 01	19 25	5 05	19 29	5 00	19 34
19	4 58	19 27	5 02	19 31	4 58	19 36
20	4 56	19 29	5 00	19 33	4 55	19 38
21	4 53	19 31	4 58	19 35	4 52	19 40
22	4 51	19 33	4 55	19 37	4 50	19 42
23	4 48	19 35	4 53	19 39	4 47	19 44
24	4 46	19 37	4 50	19 41	4 45	19 47
25	4 44	19 39	4 48	19 43	4 42	19 49
26	4 41	19 41	4 46	19 45	4 40	19 51
27	4 39	19 43	4 43	19 47	4 37	19 53
28	4 36	19 45	4 41	19 49	4 35	19 55
29	4 34	19 47	4 39	19 51	4 32	19 58
30	4 32	19 49	4 36	19 53	4 30	20 00

DURATION OF TWILIGHT AT 56° N. (IN MINUTES)

March	1st	11th	21st	31st
Civil	37	37	37	38
Nautical	80	80	81	84
Astronomical	124	125	128	135

DURATION OF TWILIGHT AT 56° N. (IN MINUTES)

April	1st	11th	21st	31st
Civil	38	39	42	44
Nautical	84	89	96	106
Astronomical	136	147	165	204

MOON PHASES

March	d	h	m
Last Quarter	6	01	24
New Moon	14	02	02
First Quarter	22	02	28
Full Moon	28	18	25

MOON PHASES

April	d	h	m
Last Quarter	4	15	29
New Moon	12	19	21
First Quarter	20	12	48
Full Moon	27	03	00

MAY 2002

SUNRISE AND SUNSET (GMT)

	Edinburgh 3° 11' 55° 56'		Glasgow 4° 14' 55° 52'		Inverness 4° 12' 57° 28'	
	h m	h m	h m	h m	h m	h m
1	4 30	19 51	4 34	19 55	4 27	20 02
2	4 27	19 53	4 32	19 57	4 25	20 04
3	4 25	19 55	4 30	19 59	4 23	20 06
4	4 23	19 57	4 27	20 01	4 20	20 08
5	4 21	19 59	4 25	20 03	4 18	20 11
6	4 19	20 01	4 23	20 05	4 16	20 13
7	4 17	20 03	4 21	20 07	4 13	20 15
8	4 14	20 05	4 19	20 09	4 11	20 17
9	4 12	20 07	4 17	20 11	4 09	20 19
10	4 10	20 09	4 15	20 13	4 07	20 21
11	4 08	20 11	4 13	20 15	4 04	20 23
12	4 06	20 13	4 11	20 17	4 02	20 25
13	4 04	20 15	4 09	20 19	4 00	20 27
14	4 03	20 17	4 07	20 21	3 58	20 29
15	4 01	20 19	4 05	20 22	3 56	20 31
16	3 59	20 21	4 03	20 24	3 54	20 33
17	3 57	20 22	4 02	20 26	3 52	20 35
18	3 55	20 24	4 00	20 28	3 50	20 37
19	3 54	20 26	3 58	20 30	3 48	20 39
20	3 52	20 28	3 56	20 32	3 47	20 41
21	3 50	20 29	3 55	20 33	3 45	20 43
22	3 49	20 31	3 53	20 35	3 43	20 45
23	3 47	20 33	3 52	20 37	3 41	20 47
24	3 46	20 34	3 50	20 38	3 40	20 49
25	3 44	20 36	3 49	20 40	3 38	20 50
26	3 43	20 38	3 47	20 41	3 37	20 52
27	3 41	20 39	3 46	20 43	3 35	20 54
28	3 40	20 41	3 45	20 45	3 34	20 56
29	3 39	20 42	3 43	20 46	3 32	20 57
30	3 38	20 44	3 42	20 47	3 31	20 59
31	3 36	20 45	3 41	20 49	3 30	21 00

DURATION OF TWILIGHT AT 56° N. (IN MINUTES)

May	1st	11th	21st	31st
Civil	44	48	53	57
Nautical	106	120	141	187
Astronomical	204	TAN	TAN	TAN

MOON PHASES

May	d	h	m
Last Quarter	4	07	16
New Moon	12	10	45
First Quarter	19	19	42
Full Moon	26	11	51

JUNE 2002

SUNRISE AND SUNSET (GMT)

	Edinburgh 3° 11' 55° 56'		Glasgow 4° 14' 55° 52'		Inverness 4° 12' 57° 28'	
	h m	h m	h m	h m	h m	h m
1	3 35	20 46	3 40	20 50	3 28	21 02
2	3 34	20 48	3 39	20 52	3 27	21 03
3	3 33	20 49	3 38	20 53	3 26	21 05
4	3 32	20 50	3 37	20 54	3 25	21 06
5	3 32	20 51	3 36	20 55	3 24	21 07
6	3 31	20 53	3 35	20 56	3 23	21 08
7	3 30	20 54	3 35	20 57	3 22	21 10
8	3 29	20 55	3 34	20 58	3 21	21 11
9	3 29	20 56	3 33	20 59	3 21	21 12
10	3 28	20 57	3 33	21 00	3 20	21 13
11	3 28	20 57	3 32	21 01	3 20	21 14
12	3 27	20 58	3 32	21 02	3 19	21 15
13	3 27	20 59	3 32	21 03	3 19	21 15
14	3 27	21 00	3 31	21 03	3 18	21 16
15	3 26	21 00	3 31	21 04	3 18	21 17
16	3 26	21 01	3 31	21 05	3 18	21 17
17	3 26	21 01	3 31	21 05	3 18	21 18
18	3 26	21 02	3 31	21 05	3 18	21 18
19	3 26	21 02	3 31	21 06	3 18	21 19
20	3 26	21 02	3 31	21 06	3 18	21 19
21	3 26	21 03	3 31	21 06	3 18	21 19
22	3 26	21 03	3 31	21 06	3 18	21 19
23	3 27	21 03	3 32	21 07	3 18	21 19
24	3 27	21 03	3 32	21 07	3 19	21 19
25	3 28	21 03	3 32	21 07	3 19	21 19
26	3 28	21 03	3 33	21 06	3 20	21 19
27	3 29	21 03	3 33	21 06	3 20	21 19
28	3 29	21 02	3 34	21 06	3 21	21 19
29	3 30	21 02	3 35	21 06	3 22	21 18
30	3 31	21 02	3 35	21 05	3 22	21 18

DURATION OF TWILIGHT AT 56° N. (IN MINUTES)

June	1st	11th	21st	31st
Civil	58	61	63	61
Nautical	TAN	TAN	TAN	TAN
Astronomical	TAN	TAN	TAN	TAN

MOON PHASES

June	d	h	m
Last Quarter	3	00	05
New Moon	10	23	46
First Quarter	18	00	29
Full Moon	24	21	42

JULY 2002

SUNRISE AND SUNSET (GMT)

	Edinburgh 3° 11′ 55° 56′		Glasgow 4° 14′ 55° 52′		Inverness 4° 12′ 57° 28′	
	h m	h m	h m	h m	h m	h m
1	3 31	21 01	3 36	21 05	3 23	21 17
2	3 32	21 01	3 37	21 04	3 24	21 17
3	3 33	21 00	3 38	21 04	3 25	21 16
4	3 34	21 00	3 39	21 03	3 26	21 16
5	3 35	20 59	3 40	21 03	3 27	21 15
6	3 36	20 58	3 41	21 02	3 28	21 14
7	3 37	20 57	3 42	21 01	3 30	21 13
8	3 38	20 56	3 43	21 00	3 31	21 12
9	3 40	20 56	3 44	20 59	3 32	21 11
10	3 41	20 55	3 45	20 58	3 33	21 10
11	3 42	20 53	3 47	20 57	3 35	21 09
12	3 43	20 52	3 48	20 56	3 36	21 07
13	3 45	20 51	3 49	20 55	3 38	21 06
14	3 46	20 50	3 51	20 54	3 39	21 05
15	3 48	20 49	3 52	20 53	3 41	21 03
16	3 49	20 47	3 54	20 51	3 43	21 02
17	3 51	20 46	3 55	20 50	3 44	21 00
18	3 52	20 45	3 57	20 48	3 46	20 59
19	3 54	20 43	3 58	20 47	3 48	20 57
20	3 55	20 42	4 00	20 45	3 49	20 56
21	3 57	20 40	4 02	20 44	3 51	20 54
22	3 59	20 39	4 03	20 42	3 53	20 52
23	4 00	20 37	4 05	20 41	3 55	20 50
24	4 02	20 35	4 07	20 39	3 57	20 48
25	4 04	20 33	4 08	20 37	3 59	20 47
26	4 06	20 32	4 10	20 36	4 01	20 45
27	4 07	20 30	4 12	20 34	4 02	20 43
28	4 09	20 28	4 14	20 32	4 04	20 41
29	4 11	20 26	4 16	20 30	4 06	20 39
30	4 13	20 24	4 17	20 28	4 08	20 37
31	4 15	20 22	4 19	20 26	4 10	20 35

DURATION OF TWILIGHT AT 56° N. (IN MINUTES)

July	1st	11th	21st	31st
Civil	61	58	53	49
Nautical	TAN	TAN	146	123
Astronomical	TAN	TAN	TAN	TAN

MOON PHASES

July	d	h	m
Last Quarter	2	17	19
New Moon	10	10	26
First Quarter	17	04	47
Full Moon	24	09	07

AUGUST 2002

SUNRISE AND SUNSET (GMT)

	Edinburgh 3° 11′ 55° 56′		Glasgow 4° 14′ 55° 52′		Inverness 4° 12′ 57° 28′	
	h m	h m	h m	h m	h m	h m
1	4 16	20 20	4 21	20 24	4 12	20 32
2	4 18	20 18	4 23	20 22	4 14	20 30
3	4 20	20 16	4 25	20 20	4 16	20 28
4	4 22	20 14	4 27	20 18	4 19	20 26
5	4 24	20 12	4 29	20 16	4 21	20 24
6	4 26	20 10	4 30	20 14	4 23	20 21
7	4 28	20 08	4 32	20 12	4 25	20 19
8	4 30	20 06	4 34	20 10	4 27	20 17
9	4 32	20 03	4 36	20 07	4 29	20 14
10	4 34	20 01	4 38	20 05	4 31	20 12
11	4 36	19 59	4 40	20 03	4 33	20 09
12	4 38	19 57	4 42	20 01	4 35	20 07
13	4 39	19 54	4 44	19 58	4 37	20 05
14	4 41	19 52	4 46	19 56	4 39	20 02
15	4 43	19 50	4 48	19 54	4 42	20 00
16	4 45	19 47	4 50	19 51	4 44	19 57
17	4 47	19 45	4 52	19 49	4 46	19 55
18	4 49	19 43	4 54	19 47	4 48	19 52
19	4 51	19 40	4 56	19 44	4 50	19 49
20	4 53	19 38	4 58	19 42	4 52	19 47
21	4 55	19 35	4 59	19 39	4 54	19 44
22	4 57	19 33	5 01	19 37	4 56	19 42
23	4 59	19 30	5 03	19 34	4 58	19 39
24	5 01	19 28	5 05	19 32	5 01	19 36
25	5 03	19 25	5 07	19 29	5 03	19 34
26	5 05	19 23	5 09	19 27	5 05	19 31
27	5 07	19 20	5 11	19 24	5 07	19 28
28	5 09	19 18	5 13	19 22	5 09	19 26
29	5 11	19 15	5 15	19 19	5 11	19 23
30	5 13	19 13	5 17	19 17	5 13	19 20
31	5 15	19 10	5 19	19 14	5 15	19 18

DURATION OF TWILIGHT AT 56° N. (IN MINUTES)

August	1st	11th	21st	31st
Civil	49	45	42	40
Nautical	121	107	97	90
Astronomical	TAN	210	168	148

MOON PHASES

August	d	h	m
Last Quarter	1	10	22
New Moon	8	19	15
First Quarter	15	10	12
Full Moon	22	22	29
Last Quarter	31	02	31

SEPTEMBER 2002	OCTOBER 2002

SUNRISE AND SUNSET (GMT)

	Edinburgh		Glasgow		Inverness	
	3° 11′ 55° 56′		4° 14′ 55° 52′		4° 12′ 57° 28′	
	h m	h m	h m	h m	h m	h m
1	5 17	19 08	5 21	19 12	5 17	19 15
2	5 19	19 05	5 23	19 09	5 19	19 12
3	5 20	19 02	5 25	19 07	5 21	19 09
4	5 22	19 00	5 27	19 04	5 24	19 07
5	5 24	18 57	5 29	19 01	5 26	19 04
6	5 26	18 55	5 31	18 59	5 28	19 01
7	5 28	18 52	5 33	18 56	5 30	18 59
8	5 30	18 49	5 35	18 54	5 32	18 56
9	5 32	18 47	5 36	18 51	5 34	18 53
10	5 34	18 44	5 38	18 48	5 36	18 50
11	5 36	18 42	5 40	18 46	5 38	18 47
12	5 38	18 39	5 42	18 43	5 40	18 45
13	5 40	18 36	5 44	18 40	5 42	18 42
14	5 42	18 34	5 46	18 38	5 44	18 39
15	5 44	18 31	5 48	18 35	5 47	18 36
16	5 46	18 28	5 50	18 32	5 49	18 33
17	5 48	18 26	5 52	18 30	5 51	18 31
18	5 50	18 23	5 54	18 27	5 53	18 28
19	5 52	18 20	5 56	18 25	5 55	18 25
20	5 54	18 18	5 58	18 22	5 57	18 22
21	5 55	18 15	6 00	18 19	5 59	18 20
22	5 57	18 12	6 02	18 17	6 01	18 17
23	5 59	18 10	6 04	18 14	6 03	18 14
24	6 01	18 07	6 06	18 11	6 05	18 11
25	6 03	18 04	6 07	18 09	6 07	18 08
26	6 05	18 02	6 09	18 06	6 10	18 06
27	6 07	17 59	6 11	18 03	6 12	18 03
28	6 09	17 57	6 13	18 01	6 14	18 00
29	6 11	17 54	6 15	17 58	6 16	17 57
30	6 13	17 51	6 17	17 55	6 18	17 55

SUNRISE AND SUNSET (GMT)

	Edinburgh		Glasgow		Inverness	
	3° 11′ 55° 56′		4° 14′ 55° 52′		4° 12′ 57° 28′	
	h m	h m	h m	h m	h m	h m
1	6 15	17 49	6 19	17 53	6 20	17 52
2	6 17	17 46	6 21	17 50	6 22	17 49
3	6 19	17 43	6 23	17 48	6 24	17 46
4	6 21	17 41	6 25	17 45	6 26	17 44
5	6 23	17 38	6 27	17 42	6 29	17 41
6	6 25	17 36	6 29	17 40	6 31	17 38
7	6 27	17 33	6 31	17 37	6 33	17 35
8	6 29	17 30	6 33	17 35	6 35	17 33
9	6 31	17 28	6 35	17 32	6 37	17 30
10	6 33	17 25	6 37	17 30	6 39	17 27
11	6 35	17 23	6 39	17 27	6 42	17 25
12	6 37	17 20	6 41	17 25	6 44	17 22
13	6 39	17 18	6 43	17 22	6 46	17 19
14	6 41	17 15	6 45	17 20	6 48	17 17
15	6 43	17 13	6 47	17 17	6 50	17 14
16	6 45	17 10	6 49	17 15	6 52	17 11
17	6 47	17 08	6 52	17 12	6 55	17 09
18	6 50	17 05	6 54	17 10	6 57	17 06
19	6 52	17 03	6 56	17 07	6 59	17 03
20	6 54	17 00	6 58	17 05	7 01	17 01
21	6 56	16 58	7 00	17 02	7 04	16 58
22	6 58	16 56	7 02	17 00	7 06	16 56
23	7 00	16 53	7 04	16 58	7 08	16 53
24	7 02	16 51	7 06	16 55	7 10	16 51
25	7 04	16 49	7 08	16 53	7 13	16 48
26	7 06	16 46	7 10	16 51	7 15	16 46
27	7 08	16 44	7 12	16 48	7 17	16 43
28	7 10	16 42	7 14	16 46	7 19	16 41
29	7 13	16 39	7 17	16 44	7 22	16 39
30	7 15	16 37	7 19	16 42	7 24	16 36
31	7 17	16 35	7 21	16 39	7 26	16 34

DURATION OF TWILIGHT AT 56° N. (IN MINUTES)

September	1st	11th	21st	31st
Civil	39	38	37	37
Nautical	89	85	82	80
Astronomical	147	136	129	125

DURATION OF TWILIGHT AT 56° N. (IN MINUTES)

October	1st	11th	21st	31st
Civil	37	37	38	39
Nautical	80	80	81	83
Astronomical	125	124	124	126

MOON PHASES

September	d	h	m
New Moon	7	03	10
First Quarter	13	18	08
Full Moon	21	13	59
Last Quarter	29	17	03

MOON PHASES

October	d	h	m
New Moon	6	11	18
First Quarter	13	05	33
Full Moon	21	07	20
Last Quarter	29	05	28

NOVEMBER 2002

SUNRISE AND SUNSET (GMT)

	Edinburgh		Glasgow		Inverness	
	3° 11′ 55° 56′		4° 14′ 55° 52′		4° 12′ 57° 28′	
	h m	h m	h m	h m	h m	h m
1	7 19	16 33	7 23	16 37	7 28	16 32
2	7 21	16 31	7 25	16 35	7 31	16 29
3	7 23	16 29	7 27	16 33	7 33	16 27
4	7 25	16 26	7 29	16 31	7 35	16 25
5	7 27	16 24	7 31	16 29	7 38	16 22
6	7 30	16 22	7 34	16 27	7 40	16 20
7	7 32	16 20	7 36	16 25	7 42	16 18
8	7 34	16 18	7 38	16 23	7 44	16 16
9	7 36	16 16	7 40	16 21	7 47	16 14
10	7 38	16 15	7 42	16 19	7 49	16 12
11	7 40	16 13	7 44	16 17	7 51	16 10
12	7 42	16 11	7 46	16 15	7 53	16 08
13	7 44	16 09	7 48	16 13	7 56	16 06
14	7 46	16 07	7 50	16 12	7 58	16 04
15	7 48	16 05	7 52	16 10	8 00	16 02
16	7 51	16 04	7 54	16 08	8 02	16 00
17	7 53	16 02	7 56	16 07	8 04	15 58
18	7 55	16 01	7 58	16 05	8 07	15 57
19	7 57	15 59	8 00	16 04	8 09	15 55
20	7 59	15 57	8 02	16 02	8 11	15 53
21	8 01	15 56	8 04	16 01	8 13	15 52
22	8 02	15 55	8 06	15 59	8 15	15 50
23	8 04	15 53	8 08	15 58	8 17	15 49
24	8 06	15 52	8 10	15 56	8 19	15 47
25	8 08	15 51	8 12	15 55	8 21	15 46
26	8 10	15 49	8 14	15 54	8 23	15 44
27	8 12	15 48	8 16	15 53	8 25	15 43
28	8 14	15 47	8 17	15 52	8 27	15 42
29	8 15	15 46	8 19	15 51	8 29	15 41
30	8 17	15 45	8 21	15 50	8 31	15 40

DURATION OF TWILIGHT AT 56° N. (IN MINUTES)

November	1st	11th	21st	31st
Civil	40	41	43	45
Nautical	84	87	90	93
Astronomical	127	130	134	138

MOON PHASES

November	d	h	m
New Moon	4	20	34
First Quarter	11	20	52
Full Moon	20	01	34
Last Quarter	27	15	46

DECEMBER 2002

SUNRISE AND SUNSET (GMT)

	Edinburgh		Glasgow		Inverness	
	3° 11′ 55° 56′		4° 14′ 55° 52′		4° 12′ 57° 28′	
	h m	h m	h m	h m	h m	h m
1	8 19	15 44	8 23	15 49	8 33	15 39
2	8 20	15 43	8 24	15 48	8 34	15 38
3	8 22	15 43	8 26	15 47	8 36	15 37
4	8 24	15 42	8 27	15 46	8 38	15 36
5	8 25	15 41	8 29	15 46	8 39	15 35
6	8 27	15 41	8 30	15 45	8 41	15 34
7	8 28	15 40	8 32	15 45	8 42	15 34
8	8 29	15 40	8 33	15 44	8 44	15 33
9	8 31	15 39	8 34	15 44	8 45	15 33
10	8 32	15 39	8 36	15 43	8 47	15 32
11	8 33	15 38	8 37	15 43	8 48	15 32
12	8 34	15 38	8 38	15 43	8 49	15 32
13	8 35	15 38	8 39	15 43	8 50	15 31
14	8 36	15 38	8 40	15 43	8 51	15 31
15	8 37	15 38	8 41	15 43	8 52	15 31
16	8 38	15 38	8 42	15 43	8 53	15 31
17	8 39	15 38	8 43	15 43	8 54	15 31
18	8 40	15 39	8 44	15 43	8 55	15 32
19	8 41	15 39	8 44	15 43	8 56	15 32
20	8 41	15 39	8 45	15 44	8 56	15 32
21	8 42	15 40	8 46	15 44	8 57	15 33
22	8 42	15 40	8 46	15 45	8 57	15 33
23	8 43	15 41	8 47	15 45	8 58	15 34
24	8 43	15 41	8 47	15 46	8 58	15 34
25	8 43	15 42	8 47	15 47	8 59	15 35
26	8 44	15 43	8 47	15 47	8 59	15 36
27	8 44	15 44	8 48	15 48	8 59	15 37
28	8 44	15 45	8 48	15 49	8 59	15 38
29	8 44	15 46	8 48	15 50	8 59	15 39
30	8 44	15 47	8 48	15 51	8 59	15 40
31	8 44	15 48	8 48	15 52	8 59	15 41

DURATION OF TWILIGHT AT 56° N. (IN MINUTES)

December	1st	11th	21st	31st
Civil	45	47	47	47
Nautical	93	96	97	96
Astronomical	138	141	142	141

MOON PHASES

December	d	h	m
New Moon	4	07	34
First Quarter	11	15	49
Full Moon	19	19	10
Last Quarter	27	00	31

—————— TIDAL DATA ——————

Constants

The constant tidal difference may be used in conjunction with the time of high water at a standard port shown in the predictions data to find the time of high water at the places listed below.

These tidal differences are very approximate and should be used only as a guide to the time of high water at the places below. More precise local data should be obtained for navigational and other nautical purposes.

All data allow high water time to be found in Greenwich Mean Time; this applies also to data for the months when British Summer Time is in operation and the hour's time difference should be allowed for.

Example

To find the time of high water at Stranraer at 2 January 2002:

Appropriate time of high water at Greenock

Afternoon tide 2 January	1720 hrs
Tidal difference	− 0020 hrs
High water at Stranraer	1700 hrs

The columns headed 'Springs' and 'Neaps' show the height, in metres, of the tide above datum for mean high water springs and mean high water neaps respectively.

Tidal Predictions

The following tidal data are daily predictions of the time and height of high water at Greenock and Leith. The time of the data is Greenwich Mean Time; this applies also to data for the months when British Summer Time is in operation and the hour's time difference should be allowed for. The datum of predictions for each port shows the difference of height, in metres from Ordnance data (Newlyn).

The tidal information for Greenock and Leith is reproduced with the permission of the UK Hydrographic Office and the Controller of HMSO. Crown copyright reserved.

Port	Diff.	h	m	Springs	Neaps
Aberdeen	Leith	−1	19	4.3	3.4
Ardrossan	Greenock	−0	15	3.2	2.6
Ayr	Greenock	−0	25	3.0	2.5
Glasgow	Greenock	+0	26	4.7	4.0
Lerwick	Leith	−3	48	2.2	1.6
Oban	Greenock	+5	43	4.0	2.9
Rosyth	Leith	+0	09	5.8	4.7
Scrabster	Leith	−6	06	5.0	4.0
Stranraer	Greenock	−0	20	3.0	2.4
Stromness	Leith	−5	26	3.6	2.7
Ullapool	Leith	−7	40	5.2	3.9
Wick	Leith	−3	26	3.5	2.8

JANUARY 2002 *high water* GMT

LEITH — Year 2002 Zone Time UT (GMT) | **GREENOCK** — Year 2002 Zone Time UT (GMT)

Day		Leith hr	ht m	hr	ht m	Greenock hr	ht m	hr	ht m
1	Tu	03 35	5.6	15 54	5.6	01 34	3.3	13 41	3.7
2	We	04 20	5.7	16 37	5.6	02 22	3.3	14 23	3.8
3	Th	05 08	5.6	17 24	5.5	03 10	3.3	15 06	3.8
4	Fr	05 58	5.4	18 15	5.4	03 59	3.2	15 52	3.7
5	Sa	06 51	5.2	19 11	5.2	04 51	3.2	16 41	3.6
6	Su	07 52	4.9	20 18	5.1	05 47	3.1	17 35	3.5
7	Mo	08 59	4.8	21 28	5.0	06 48	3.0	18 37	3.3
8	Tu	10 06	4.7	22 35	4.9	07 59	3.0	19 50	3.2
9	We	11 12	4.8	23 40	5.0	09 14	3.0	21 15	3.2
10	Th			12 13	4.9	10 15	3.2	22 23	3.2
11	Fr	00 40	5.1	13 07	5.0	11 06	3.3	23 19	3.2
12	Sa	01 34	5.2	13 54	5.2	11 51	3.4		
13	Su	02 22	5.2	14 35	5.3	00 08	3.2	12 33	3.5
14	Mo	03 04	5.2	15 14	5.3	00 53	3.2	13 11	3.6
15	Tu	03 44	5.2	15 50	5.3	01 34	3.2	13 48	3.6
16	We	04 21	5.1	16 25	5.3	02 11	3.2	14 23	3.6
17	Th	04 57	5.0	16 59	5.2	02 47	3.2	14 57	3.6
18	Fr	05 33	4.9	17 35	5.1	03 23	3.2	15 32	3.5
19	Sa	06 11	4.8	18 15	4.9	04 00	3.2	16 07	3.4
20	Su	06 53	4.6	18 58	4.7	04 38	3.1	16 46	3.3
21	Mo	07 39	4.5	19 46	4.6	05 20	3.0	17 28	3.1
22	Tu	08 31	4.4	20 42	4.4	06 06	2.9	18 18	3.0
23	We	09 31	4.3	21 48	4.4	06 58	2.9	19 16	2.9
24	Th	10 35	4.4	22 57	4.5	08 00	2.8	20 30	2.8
25	Fr	11 39	4.6			09 15	2.9	21 49	2.9
26	Sa	00 03	4.7	12 39	4.8	10 22	3.1	22 54	3.0
27	Su	01 02	5.0	13 30	5.1	11 14	3.3	23 47	3.1
28	Mo	01 53	5.3	14 15	5.4	12 00	3.4		
29	Tu	02 38	5.6	14 57	5.6	00 38	3.2	12 45	3.6
30	We	03 22	5.8	15 39	5.7	01 28	3.3	13 30	3.7
31	Th	04 06	5.8	16 22	5.8	02 16	3.3	14 13	3.8

FEBRUARY 2002 *high water* GMT

LEITH — Year 2002 Zone Time UT (GMT) | **GREENOCK** — Year 2002 Zone Time UT (GMT)

Day		Leith hr	ht m	hr	ht m	Greenock hr	ht m	hr	ht m
1	Fr	04 52	5.8	17 08	5.8	03 01	3.3	14 57	3.9
2	Sa	05 39	5.6	17 55	5.6	03 44	3.3	15 40	3.9
3	Su	06 28	5.3	18 47	5.4	04 27	3.3	16 24	3.7
4	Mo	07 22	5.0	19 48	5.1	05 11	3.2	17 10	3.6
5	Tu	08 24	4.7	20 58	4.8	05 58	3.0	18 00	3.3
6	We	09 32	4.5	22 10	4.7	06 54	2.9	18 59	3.1
7	Th	10 43	4.5	23 24	4.6	08 23	2.9	20 35	2.9
8	Fr	11 55	4.6			09 52	3.0	22 16	2.9
9	Sa	00 34	4.7	12 58	4.8	10 49	3.1	23 16	3.0
10	Su	01 31	4.9	13 47	5.0	11 36	3.3		
11	Mo	02 16	5.0	14 27	5.1	00 04	3.0	12 19	3.4
12	Tu	02 54	5.1	15 02	5.3	00 47	3.1	12 58	3.5
13	We	03 28	5.2	15 34	5.3	01 24	3.1	13 34	3.5
14	Th	03 59	5.1	16 04	5.3	01 57	3.1	14 07	3.5
15	Fr	04 30	5.1	16 35	5.3	02 27	3.1	14 37	3.4
16	Sa	05 03	5.0	17 07	5.2	02 56	3.1	15 07	3.4
17	Su	05 37	4.9	17 42	5.0	03 27	3.2	15 39	3.4
18	Mo	06 14	4.8	18 19	4.9	04 00	3.1	16 13	3.3
19	Tu	06 55	4.6	19 01	4.7	04 36	3.1	16 51	3.1
20	We	07 41	4.4	19 50	4.5	05 17	3.0	17 34	2.9
21	Th	08 38	4.3	20 56	4.3	06 04	2.8	18 29	2.8
22	Fr	09 48	4.2	22 16	4.3	07 03	2.7	19 43	2.7
23	Sa	11 03	4.4	23 36	4.5	08 25	2.7	21 21	2.7
24	Su			12 12	4.7	09 51	2.9	22 40	2.9
25	Mo	00 42	4.9	13 09	5.0	10 52	3.1	23 37	3.1
26	Tu	01 36	5.3	13 55	5.4	11 42	3.4		
27	We	02 21	5.6	14 38	5.7	00 27	3.2	12 29	3.6
28	Th	03 04	5.9	15 19	5.9	01 16	3.3	13 14	3.7

MARCH 2002 high water GMT

LEITH — Year 2002 Zone Time UT (GMT)
GREENOCK — Year 2002 Zone Time UT (GMT)

		LEITH hr	ht m	hr	ht m	GREENOCK hr	ht m	hr	ht m
1	Fr	03 47	5.9	16 02	6.0	02 00	3.3	13 58	3.8
2	Sa	04 31	5.8	16 47	6.0	02 41	3.4	14 41	3.9
3	Su	05 16	5.6	17 34	5.8	03 19	3.4	15 22	3.9
4	Mo	06 03	5.3	18 25	5.4	03 55	3.4	16 03	3.8
5	Tu	06 52	4.9	19 23	5.0	04 33	3.3	16 45	3.5
6	We	07 50	4.6	20 32	4.7	05 15	3.1	17 30	3.2
7	Th	08 59	4.4	21 47	4.4	06 05	2.9	18 24	2.9
8	Fr	10 14	4.3	23 08	4.4	07 11	2.8	19 38	2.7
9	Sa	11 35	4.4			09 28	2.8	22 12	2.7
10	Su	00 25	4.6	12 43	4.6	10 30	3.0	23 06	2.9
11	Mo	01 20	4.8	13 32	4.9	11 18	3.2	23 50	3.0
12	Tu	02 02	5.0	14 11	5.1	12 00	3.3		
13	We	02 36	5.1	14 43	5.2	00 28	3.0	12 39	3.4
14	Th	03 06	5.1	15 12	5.3	01 03	3.0	13 14	3.3
15	Fr	03 34	5.2	15 40	5.3	01 33	3.0	13 44	3.3
16	Sa	04 02	5.2	16 09	5.3	01 59	3.1	14 11	3.3
17	Su	04 33	5.1	16 40	5.2	02 25	3.1	14 39	3.3
18	Mo	05 06	5.0	17 14	5.1	02 53	3.2	15 11	3.3
19	Tu	05 41	4.9	17 50	4.9	03 25	3.2	15 45	3.2
20	We	06 19	4.7	18 31	4.7	03 58	3.1	16 21	3.1
21	Th	07 02	4.5	19 21	4.5	04 34	3.0	17 02	2.9
22	Fr	07 56	4.3	20 25	4.3	05 17	2.8	17 55	2.7
23	Sa	09 08	4.2	21 48	4.3	06 15	2.7	19 14	2.6
24	Su	10 32	4.3	23 12	4.6	07 42	2.7	21 04	2.6
25	Mo	11 46	4.6			09 22	2.8	22 27	2.8
26	Tu	00 21	5.0	12 44	5.1	10 29	3.1	23 22	3.0
27	We	01 14	5.4	13 31	5.5	11 20	3.4		
28	Th	01 59	5.7	14 14	5.8	00 10	3.2	12 08	3.6
29	Fr	02 42	5.9	14 57	6.0	00 55	3.3	12 54	3.7
30	Sa	03 24	5.9	15 41	6.1	01 37	3.4	13 39	3.8
31	Su	04 07	5.8	16 26	6.0	02 15	3.4	14 21	3.8

APRIL 2002 high water GMT

LEITH — Year 2002 Zone Time UT (GMT)
GREENOCK — Year 2002 Zone Time UT (GMT)

		LEITH hr	ht m	hr	ht m	GREENOCK hr	ht m	hr	ht m
1	Mo	04 51	5.6	17 14	5.7	02 50	3.5	15 02	3.8
2	Tu	05 37	5.3	18 06	5.3	03 25	3.4	15 41	3.7
3	We	06 25	4.9	19 04	4.9	04 02	3.3	16 23	3.4
4	Th	07 21	4.6	20 10	4.5	04 43	3.2	17 08	3.1
5	Fr	08 28	4.3	21 22	4.3	05 32	3.0	18 02	2.8
6	Sa	09 43	4.2	22 42	4.3	06 35	2.8	19 15	2.6
7	Su	11 04	4.3			08 48	2.7	21 50	2.6
8	Mo	00 00	4.5	12 14	4.5	10 02	2.9	22 41	2.8
9	Tu	00 55	4.7	13 04	4.8	10 50	3.1	23 22	2.9
10	We	01 35	4.9	13 43	5.0	11 32	3.2	23 59	3.0
11	Th	02 08	5.0	14 15	5.1	11 32	3.2	12 10	3.2
12	Fr	02 37	5.1	14 44	5.2	00 32	3.0	12 45	3.2
13	Sa	03 04	5.2	15 12	5.3	01 02	3.0	13 14	3.2
14	Su	03 33	5.2	15 43	5.3	01 27	3.1	13 41	3.2
15	Mo	04 04	5.2	16 15	5.2	01 53	3.2	14 12	3.2
16	Tu	04 38	5.1	16 51	5.1	02 22	3.2	14 45	3.2
17	We	05 13	5.0	17 29	5.0	02 54	3.3	15 21	3.1
18	Th	05 51	4.8	18 13	4.8	03 28	3.2	15 59	3.0
19	Fr	06 35	4.6	19 05	4.6	04 03	3.1	16 43	2.8
20	Sa	07 29	4.4	20 08	4.5	04 46	2.9	17 42	2.6
21	Su	08 42	4.3	21 29	4.5	05 46	2.8	19 08	2.6
22	Mo	10 06	4.4	22 49	4.7	07 14	2.7	20 50	2.6
23	Tu	11 18	4.7	23 55	5.0	08 54	2.9	22 06	2.8
24	We			12 16	5.1	10 02	3.1	23 00	3.0
25	Th	00 48	5.4	13 05	5.5	10 56	3.4	23 46	3.2
26	Fr	01 34	5.6	13 50	5.8	11 44	3.5		
27	Sa	02 17	5.8	14 34	6.0	00 30	3.3	12 31	3.6
28	Su	03 00	5.8	15 20	6.0	01 11	3.4	13 17	3.7
29	Mo	03 44	5.7	16 08	5.8	01 48	3.4	14 00	3.7
30	Tu	04 28	5.5	16 57	5.6	02 24	3.5	14 42	3.6

MAY 2002 *high water* GMT

LEITH
Year 2002 Zone Time UT (GMT)

		hr		ht m	hr		ht m
1	We	05	13	5.3	17	49	5.2
2	Th	06	01	5.0	18	45	4.8
3	Fr	06	55	4.7	19	45	4.5
4	Sa	07	58	4.4	20	50	4.3
5	Su	09	07	4.3	22	00	4.2
6	Mo	10	18	4.3	23	13	4.3
7	Tu	11	27	4.4			
8	We	00	12	4.6	12	22	4.7
9	Th	00	56	4.8	13	03	4.9
10	Fr	01	30	4.9	13	39	5.0
11	Sa	02	02	5.1	14	11	5.1
12	Su	02	33	5.2	14	44	5.2
13	Mo	03	05	5.2	15	18	5.2
14	Tu	03	38	5.2	15	54	5.2
15	We	04	13	5.2	16	32	5.2
16	Th	04	50	5.1	17	14	5.1
17	Fr	05	31	4.9	18	00	4.9
18	Sa	06	18	4.8	18	53	4.8
19	Su	07	13	4.6	19	56	4.7
20	Mo	08	23	4.6	21	09	4.7
21	Tu	09	40	4.7	22	22	4.8
22	We	10	49	4.9	23	27	5.0
23	Th	11	47	5.2			
24	Fr	00	21	5.3	12	39	5.4
25	Sa	01	10	5.4	13	28	5.6
26	Su	01	55	5.6	14	16	5.7
27	Mo	02	39	5.6	15	04	5.7
28	Tu	03	23	5.6	15	53	5.6
29	We	04	08	5.4	16	42	5.4
30	Th	04	53	5.2	17	32	5.1
31	Fr	05	39	5.0	18	22	4.8

GREENOCK
Year 2002 Zone Time UT (GMT)

hr		ht m	hr		ht m
03	00	3.5	15	23	3.5
03	38	3.4	16	06	3.3
04	19	3.2	16	53	3.0
05	08	3.0	17	49	2.8
06	08	2.8	18	57	2.6
07	34	2.7	20	49	2.6
09	16	2.8	21	56	2.7
10	12	3.0	22	42	2.9
10	56	3.1	23	21	2.9
11	34	3.1	23	56	3.0
			12	08	3.1
00	26	3.1	12	40	3.1
00	55	3.1	13	11	3.1
01	24	3.2	13	47	3.1
01	57	3.3	14	25	3.1
02	32	3.3	15	05	3.0
03	07	3.3	15	48	2.9
03	46	3.2	16	39	2.8
04	32	3.1	17	45	2.7
05	34	2.9	19	04	2.6
06	56	2.9	20	25	2.7
08	24	3.0	21	36	2.9
09	34	3.2	22	32	3.0
10	30	3.3	23	20	3.1
11	20	3.4			
00	04	3.3	12	09	3.5
00	46	3.3	12	56	3.5
01	25	3.4	13	41	3.4
02	03	3.5	14	25	3.4
02	41	3.5	15	08	3.3
03	20	3.4	15	53	3.1

JUNE 2002 *high water* GMT

LEITH
Year 2002 Zone Time UT (GMT)

		hr		ht m	hr		ht m
1	Sa	06	28	4.8	19	15	4.6
2	Su	07	23	4.6	20	09	4.4
3	Mo	08	22	4.4	21	06	4.3
4	Tu	09	23	4.4	22	06	4.3
5	We	10	24	4.4	23	05	4.4
6	Th	11	21	4.5	23	59	4.6
7	Fr				12	13	4.7
8	Sa	00	44	4.8	12	58	4.8
9	Su	01	24	5.0	13	39	5.0
10	Mo	02	02	5.1	14	18	5.1
11	Tu	02	39	5.2	14	57	5.2
12	We	03	16	5.2	15	36	5.3
13	Th	03	54	5.3	16	17	5.3
14	Fr	04	34	5.2	17	01	5.3
15	Sa	05	17	5.2	17	49	5.2
16	Su	06	04	5.1	18	41	5.0
17	Mo	06	58	4.9	19	39	4.9
18	Tu	08	01	4.9	20	45	4.8
19	We	09	12	4.9	21	53	4.8
20	Th	10	19	5.0	22	57	4.9
21	Fr	11	21	5.1	23	56	5.0
22	Sa				12	19	5.2
23	Su	00	48	5.2	13	14	5.4
24	Mo	01	37	5.3	14	05	5.4
25	Tu	02	23	5.4	14	54	5.4
26	We	03	08	5.4	15	41	5.4
27	Th	03	52	5.4	16	27	5.2
28	Fr	04	34	5.2	17	11	5.1
29	Sa	05	16	5.1	17	54	4.9
30	Su	05	58	4.9	18	38	4.7

GREENOCK
Year 2002 Zone Time UT (GMT)

hr		ht m	hr		ht m
04	01	3.3	16	40	3.0
04	47	3.1	17	33	2.8
05	41	3.0	18	29	2.7
06	44	2.8	19	29	2.7
07	58	2.8	20	36	2.7
09	13	2.8	21	42	2.8
10	09	2.9	22	34	2.9
10	52	2.9	23	15	3.0
11	30	3.0	23	52	3.1
			12	07	3.0
00	26	3.2	12	46	3.0
01	01	3.3	13	28	3.0
01	38	3.3	14	12	3.0
02	16	3.4	14	57	3.0
02	56	3.4	15	46	2.9
03	38	3.4	16	40	2.9
04	26	3.3	17	41	2.8
05	24	3.1	18	45	2.8
06	32	3.1	19	52	2.8
07	49	3.1	21	01	2.9
09	04	3.1	22	03	3.0
10	07	3.2	22	56	3.1
11	02	3.2	23	44	3.2
11	53	3.3			
00	27	3.3	12	42	3.2
01	09	3.4	13	29	3.2
01	48	3.4	14	14	3.1
02	26	3.5	14	57	3.1
03	04	3.4	15	39	3.0
03	43	3.3	16	22	3.0

JULY 2002 *high water* GMT

LEITH
Year 2002 Zone Time UT (GMT)

		hr		ht m	hr		ht m
1	Mo	06	43	4.8	19	23	4.5
2	Tu	07	32	4.6	20	12	4.4
3	We	08	25	4.5	21	05	4.3
4	Th	09	22	4.4	22	00	4.3
5	Fr	10	20	4.4	22	58	4.4
6	Sa	11	20	4.5	23	56	4.6
7	Su	12	18	4.6			
8	Mo	00	49	4.8	13	10	4.8
9	Tu	01	36	5.0	13	56	5.0
10	We	02	18	5.2	14	39	5.3
11	Th	02	58	5.3	15	21	5.4
12	Fr	03	38	5.4	16	03	5.5
13	Sa	04	19	5.5	16	47	5.5
14	Su	05	02	5.5	17	34	5.4
15	Mo	05	49	5.4	18	23	5.3
16	Tu	06	39	5.3	19	17	5.1
17	We	07	36	5.1	20	17	4.9
18	Th	08	43	5.0	21	23	4.7
19	Fr	09	53	4.9	22	29	4.7
20	Sa	11	01	4.9	23	34	4.8
21	Su				12	08	5.0
22	Mo	00	35	4.9	13	08	5.1
23	Tu	01	29	5.1	14	01	5.2
24	We	02	15	5.2	14	47	5.3
25	Th	02	57	5.3	15	29	5.3
26	Fr	03	37	5.3	16	09	5.2
27	Sa	04	14	5.3	16	46	5.1
28	Su	04	50	5.2	17	22	5.0
29	Mo	05	26	5.1	17	59	4.8
30	Tu	06	04	5.0	18	39	4.7
31	We	06	45	4.8	19	23	4.5

GREENOCK
Year 2002 Zone Time UT (GMT)

hr		ht m	hr		ht m
04	24	3.2	17	06	2.9
05	08	3.1	17	52	2.9
05	57	2.9	18	40	2.8
06	51	2.8	19	30	2.8
07	53	2.7	20	28	2.8
09	03	2.8	21	35	2.8
10	06	2.8	22	34	2.9
10	57	2.9	23	20	3.0
11	43	3.0			
00	02	3.2	12	29	3.0
00	43	3.3	13	16	3.0
01	23	3.4	14	05	3.0
02	05	3.5	14	53	3.0
02	47	3.5	15	41	3.0
03	30	3.5	16	30	3.0
04	16	3.5	17	20	3.0
05	06	3.4	18	12	2.9
06	03	3.2	19	09	2.9
07	08	3.1	20	20	2.8
08	31	3.0	21	37	2.9
09	51	3.0	22	38	3.0
10	54	3.0	23	29	3.2
11	48	3.1			
00	14	3.3	12	38	3.1
00	56	3.4	13	23	3.1
01	35	3.4	14	04	3.0
02	12	3.4	14	41	3.0
02	47	3.4	15	17	3.0
03	21	3.4	15	53	3.0
03	55	3.3	16	30	3.0
04	32	3.2	17	09	3.0

AUGUST 2002 *high water* GMT

LEITH
Year 2002 Zone Time UT (GMT)

		hr		ht m	hr		ht m
1	Th	07	31	4.6	20	12	4.4
2	Fr	08	25	4.4	21	08	4.3
3	Sa	09	27	4.3	22	09	4.3
4	Su	10	34	4.3	23	14	4.4
5	Mo	11	43	4.5			
6	Tu	00	17	4.7	12	45	4.8
7	We	01	12	4.9	13	37	5.1
8	Th	01	58	5.2	14	21	5.4
9	Fr	02	39	5.5	15	04	5.6
10	Sa	03	19	5.7	15	45	5.8
11	Su	04	00	5.8	16	29	5.8
12	Mo	04	43	5.8	17	13	5.7
13	Tu	05	28	5.7	18	00	5.4
14	We	06	17	5.5	18	51	5.2
15	Th	07	12	5.3	19	48	4.9
16	Fr	08	18	5.0	20	54	4.6
17	Sa	09	33	4.7	22	05	4.5
18	Su	10	49	4.7	23	19	4.6
19	Mo				12	04	4.8
20	Tu	00	27	4.8	13	08	4.9
21	We	01	23	5.0	13	57	5.1
22	Th	02	07	5.2	14	37	5.2
23	Fr	02	44	5.3	15	13	5.2
24	Sa	03	19	5.4	15	46	5.2
25	Su	03	50	5.4	16	17	5.2
26	Mo	04	21	5.3	16	49	5.1
27	Tu	04	53	5.2	17	23	5.0
28	We	05	28	5.1	17	59	4.8
29	Th	06	06	4.9	18	39	4.7
30	Fr	06	48	4.7	19	25	4.5
31	Sa	07	37	4.4	20	19	4.3

GREENOCK
Year 2002 Zone Time UT (GMT)

hr		ht m	hr		ht m
05	12	3.0	17	51	2.9
05	59	2.9	18	38	2.8
06	56	2.7	19	32	2.8
08	07	2.7	20	40	2.8
09	27	2.7	21	54	2.9
10	36	2.9	22	53	3.0
11	30	3.0	23	41	3.2
			12	19	3.1
00	25	3.4	13	08	3.1
01	08	3.5	13	56	3.2
01	51	3.6	14	41	3.2
02	34	3.7	15	24	3.2
03	16	3.7	16	05	3.2
03	58	3.7	16	46	3.2
04	43	3.5	17	30	3.1
05	31	3.3	18	20	2.9
06	28	3.0	19	25	2.8
07	52	2.8	21	15	2.8
09	52	2.8	22	24	3.0
10	56	3.0	23	16	3.2
11	47	3.0			
00	01	3.3	12	32	3.1
00	42	3.4	13	11	3.1
01	20	3.4	13	47	3.1
01	54	3.4	14	18	3.1
02	25	3.4	14	47	3.1
02	54	3.4	15	17	3.2
03	25	3.3	15	49	3.2
03	57	3.2	16	24	3.1
04	34	3.1	17	03	3.0
05	16	2.9	17	48	2.9

SEPTEMBER 2002 *high water* GMT

LEITH
Year 2002 Zone Time UT (GMT)

		hr		ht m	hr		ht m
1	Su	08	40	4.3	21	25	4.3
2	Mo	09	55	4.3	22	38	4.4
3	Tu	11	13	4.5	23	49	4.6
4	We	12	22	4.8			
5	Th	00	47	5.0	13	16	5.2
6	Fr	01	34	5.3	14	00	5.6
7	Sa	02	16	5.7	14	42	5.9
8	Su	02	56	5.9	15	23	6.0
9	Mo	03	37	6.1	16	05	6.0
10	Tu	04	20	6.1	16	49	5.8
11	We	05	06	5.9	17	35	5.5
12	Th	05	55	5.6	18	24	5.2
13	Fr	06	51	5.2	19	20	4.8
14	Sa	07	59	4.8	20	28	4.6
15	Su	09	17	4.6	21	44	4.5
16	Mo	10	38	4.5	23	03	4.5
17	Tu	11	58	4.7			
18	We	00	15	4.8	12	58	4.9
19	Th	01	08	5.0	13	43	5.1
20	Fr	01	50	5.2	14	19	5.2
21	Sa	02	24	5.4	14	50	5.3
22	Su	02	54	5.4	15	18	5.3
23	Mo	03	23	5.4	15	47	5.3
24	Tu	03	52	5.4	16	17	5.2
25	We	04	23	5.3	16	49	5.1
26	Th	04	57	5.2	17	24	5.0
27	Fr	05	34	5.0	18	02	4.8
28	Sa	06	16	4.7	18	45	4.6
29	Su	07	05	4.5	19	37	4.4
30	Mo	08	06	4.3	20	46	4.3

GREENOCK
Year 2002 Zone Time UT (GMT)

hr		ht m	hr		ht m
06	12	2.7	18	44	2.8
07	26	2.6	19	55	2.8
09	01	2.7	21	20	2.9
10	24	2.9	22	28	3.1
11	19	3.1	23	19	3.3
			12	07	3.2
00	05	3.5	12	53	3.3
00	50	3.7	13	37	3.3
01	33	3.8	14	18	3.4
02	16	3.9	14	56	3.4
02	57	3.9	15	33	3.4
03	37	3.8	16	10	3.4
04	18	3.6	16	51	3.2
05	04	3.3	17	39	3.1
05	57	3.0	18	39	2.9
07	19	2.7	20	53	2.9
09	55	2.8	22	07	3.1
10	50	3.0	22	57	3.3
11	34	3.1	23	40	3.4
			12	13	3.2
00	20	3.5	12	48	3.2
00	57	3.5	13	19	3.2
01	29	3.4	13	47	3.2
01	58	3.4	14	13	3.3
02	25	3.4	14	41	3.3
02	55	3.3	15	11	3.3
03	27	3.3	15	45	3.3
04	02	3.1	16	21	3.2
04	42	2.9	17	03	3.0
05	36	2.7	17	58	2.9

OCTOBER 2002 *high water* GMT

LEITH
Year 2002 Zone Time UT (GMT)

		hr		ht m	hr		ht m
1	Tu	09	25	4.3	22	06	4.4
2	We	10	46	4.5	23	20	4.7
3	Th	11	56	4.9			
4	Fr	00	19	5.1	12	50	5.4
5	Sa	01	07	5.5	13	35	5.7
6	Su	01	49	5.8	14	17	6.0
7	Mo	02	30	6.1	14	58	6.1
8	Tu	03	13	6.2	15	40	6.0
9	We	03	58	6.2	16	24	5.8
10	Th	04	46	5.9	17	10	5.5
11	Fr	05	37	5.6	17	59	5.2
12	Sa	06	35	5.1	18	55	4.9
13	Su	07	44	4.8	20	04	4.6
14	Mo	08	59	4.5	21	21	4.5
15	Tu	10	18	4.5	22	38	4.5
16	We	11	36	4.6	23	48	4.8
17	Th				12	34	4.9
18	Fr	00	41	5.0	13	17	5.1
19	Sa	01	22	5.2	13	51	5.2
20	Su	01	56	5.3	14	21	5.3
21	Mo	02	26	5.4	14	48	5.3
22	Tu	02	54	5.4	15	16	5.3
23	We	03	24	5.4	15	47	5.3
24	Th	03	57	5.3	16	20	5.2
25	Fr	04	33	5.2	16	54	5.1
26	Sa	05	11	5.0	17	32	4.9
27	Su	05	54	4.8	18	14	4.7
28	Mo	06	44	4.6	19	06	4.5
29	Tu	07	44	4.5	20	14	4.4
30	We	08	59	4.5	21	35	4.5
31	Th	10	18	4.7	22	48	4.8

GREENOCK
Year 2002 Zone Time UT (GMT)

hr		ht m	hr		ht m
06	59	2.6	19	16	2.8
08	44	2.7	20	48	2.9
10	10	2.9	22	01	3.2
11	02	3.2	22	54	3.4
11	47	3.3	23	41	3.6
			12	30	3.4
00	27	3.8	13	11	3.5
01	12	3.9	13	50	3.6
01	55	3.9	14	27	3.6
02	36	3.9	15	02	3.6
03	16	3.8	15	40	3.6
03	57	3.6	16	21	3.4
04	43	3.3	17	09	3.2
05	39	2.9	18	10	3.0
07	08	2.7	20	08	3.0
09	37	2.9	21	37	3.1
10	27	3.0	22	29	3.3
11	07	3.2	23	13	3.4
11	43	3.3	23	52	3.5
			12	16	3.3
00	28	3.4	12	47	3.3
01	00	3.4	13	14	3.4
01	28	3.3	13	40	3.4
01	56	3.3	14	08	3.5
02	28	3.3	14	40	3.5
03	03	3.3	15	14	3.5
03	40	3.1	15	49	3.4
04	21	3.0	16	30	3.2
05	17	2.8	17	24	3.1
06	43	2.7	18	42	3.0
08	22	2.8	20	14	3.1

NOVEMBER 2002 *high water* GMT

LEITH
Year 2002 Zone Time UT (GMT)

GREENOCK
Year 2002 Zone Time UT (GMT)

		hr	ht m	hr	ht m		hr	ht m	hr	ht m
1	Fr	11 26	5.0	23 47	5.2	09 42	3.0	21 30	3.3
2	Sa			12 21	5.4	10 35	3.2	22 27	3.5
3	Su	00 37	5.6	13 08	5.7	11 21	3.4	23 16	3.7
4	Mo	01 22	5.9	13 51	5.9			12 03	3.5
5	Tu	02 06	6.1	14 33	6.0	00 03	3.8	12 44	3.6
6	We	02 52	6.1	15 17	5.9	00 50	3.9	13 23	3.7
7	Th	03 40	6.0	16 01	5.8	01 34	3.9	14 01	3.7
8	Fr	04 30	5.8	16 48	5.5	02 17	3.8	14 39	3.8
9	Sa	05 23	5.5	17 37	5.2	02 59	3.7	15 17	3.7
10	Su	06 20	5.1	18 32	4.9	03 43	3.5	16 00	3.6
11	Mo	07 24	4.7	19 38	4.7	04 31	3.2	16 48	3.4
12	Tu	08 31	4.5	20 49	4.5	05 29	3.0	17 47	3.2
13	We	09 41	4.4	22 00	4.5	06 44	2.8	19 07	3.1
14	Th	10 52	4.5	23 06	4.7	08 42	2.9	20 48	3.1
15	Fr	11 53	4.7			09 43	3.0	21 50	3.3
16	Sa	00 01	4.8	12 39	4.9	10 27	3.2	22 38	3.3
17	Su	00 46	5.0	13 16	5.0	11 05	3.3	23 19	3.4
18	Mo	01 23	5.1	13 48	5.2	11 41	3.3	23 56	3.3
19	Tu	01 56	5.2	14 18	5.3			12 13	3.4
20	We	02 28	5.3	14 49	5.3	00 29	3.3	12 43	3.5
21	Th	03 02	5.3	15 22	5.3	01 00	3.3	13 11	3.5
22	Fr	03 37	5.3	15 56	5.3	01 32	3.3	13 43	3.6
23	Sa	04 14	5.2	16 31	5.2	02 08	3.3	14 17	3.6
24	Su	04 54	5.1	17 10	5.0	02 46	3.2	14 52	3.6
25	Mo	05 38	5.0	17 53	4.9	03 27	3.1	15 30	3.5
26	Tu	06 28	4.8	18 44	4.8	04 13	3.0	16 13	3.4
27	We	07 25	4.7	19 46	4.7	05 12	2.9	17 06	3.2
28	Th	08 33	4.7	21 01	4.7	06 27	2.8	18 16	3.2
29	Fr	09 45	4.8	22 13	4.9	07 48	2.9	19 36	3.2
30	Sa	10 52	5.0	23 14	5.2	09 04	3.0	20 54	3.3

DECEMBER 2002 *high water* GMT

LEITH
Year 2002 Zone Time UT (GMT)

GREENOCK
Year 2002 Zone Time UT (GMT)

		hr	ht m	hr	ht m		hr	ht m	hr	ht m
1	Su	11 50	5.2			10 03	3.2	21 58	3.5
2	Mo	00 08	5.5	12 41	5.5	10 53	3.4	22 52	3.6
3	Tu	00 59	5.7	13 28	5.6	11 38	3.5	23 42	3.7
4	We	01 48	5.8	14 12	5.7			12 21	3.6
5	Th	02 37	5.9	14 57	5.7	00 31	3.7	13 02	3.7
6	Fr	03 27	5.8	15 43	5.6	01 18	3.7	13 42	3.8
7	Sa	04 17	5.6	16 30	5.5	02 04	3.6	14 22	3.8
8	Su	05 09	5.3	17 18	5.3	02 48	3.5	15 02	3.8
9	Mo	06 01	5.1	18 09	5.0	03 33	3.4	15 45	3.7
10	Tu	06 55	4.8	19 04	4.8	04 21	3.2	16 30	3.5
11	We	07 51	4.5	20 05	4.6	05 13	3.1	17 22	3.3
12	Th	08 49	4.4	21 06	4.5	06 10	3.0	18 21	3.2
13	Fr	09 48	4.4	22 06	4.5	07 10	2.9	19 28	3.1
14	Sa	10 47	4.4	23 04	4.6	08 18	2.9	20 46	3.1
15	Su	11 43	4.6	23 57	4.7	09 27	3.0	21 52	3.1
16	Mo			12 31	4.8	10 20	3.1	22 42	3.1
17	Tu	00 44	4.9	13 13	5.0	11 04	3.3	23 24	3.2
18	We	01 27	5.0	13 50	5.1	11 41	3.4		
19	Th	02 06	5.1	14 27	5.2	00 01	3.2	12 15	3.4
20	Fr	02 44	5.2	15 02	5.3	00 37	3.2	12 48	3.5
21	Sa	03 21	5.3	15 38	5.3	01 15	3.2	13 23	3.6
22	Su	04 00	5.3	16 15	5.3	01 55	3.2	14 00	3.6
23	Mo	04 41	5.3	16 54	5.2	02 37	3.2	14 39	3.6
24	Tu	05 24	5.2	17 37	5.2	03 21	3.1	15 19	3.6
25	We	06 12	5.1	18 25	5.1	04 08	3.1	16 03	3.5
26	Th	07 04	5.0	19 20	5.0	05 00	3.0	16 52	3.4
27	Fr	08 03	4.8	20 24	4.9	05 59	2.9	17 49	3.3
28	Sa	09 10	4.8	21 35	4.9	07 03	2.9	18 54	3.3
29	Su	10 17	4.8	22 43	5.0	08 16	3.0	20 11	3.2
30	Mo	11 20	5.0	23 46	5.2	09 28	3.1	21 28	3.3
31	Tu			12 18	5.1	10 28	3.2	22 33	3.4

INDEX